ha は ハ	ba ば バ								わ ワ	n̄ ん ン
hi ひ ヒ	bi び ビ	pi						▲i ゐ ヰ		
fu *hu ふ フ	bu ぶ ブ	pu	mu む ム	yu ゆ ユ	ru る ル					
he へ ヘ	be べ ベ	pe ぺ ペ	me め メ		re れ レ	▲e ゑ ヱ				
ho ほ ホ	bo ぼ ボ	po ぽ ポ	mo も モ	yo よ ヨ	ro ろ ロ	o を ヲ				
hya ひゃ ヒャ	bya びゃ ビャ	pya ぴゃ ピャ	mya みゃ ミャ		rya りゃ リャ					
hyu ひゅ ヒュ	byu びゅ ビュ	pyu ぴゅ ピュ	myu みゅ ミュ		ryu りゅ リュ					
hyo ひょ ヒョ	byo びょ ビョ	pyo ぴょ ピョ	myo みょ ミョ		ryo りょ リョ					

▲ Not used in modern Japanese.

aa	ii	uu	ee	oo
ああ あー	いい いー	うう うー	ええ えい えー	おお おう おー
アア アー	イイ イー	ウウ ウー	エエ エイ エー	オオ オウ オー

Long vowels as described in this dictionary.

fa	fi	fo
ファ	フィ	フォ
di	dii	tii
ディ	ディー	ティー

Used for words of foreign origin.

THE KENKYUSHA

ENGLISH-JAPANESE LEARNER'S POCKET DICTIONARY

Editor in Chief SHIGERU TAKEBAYASHI

研究社
英日ポケット辞典

編集代表 竹林 滋

KENKYUSHA

THE KENKYUSHA
ENGLISH-JAPANESE LEARNER'S POCKET DICTIONARY

研究社 英日ポケット辞典

© Copyright 1996 in Japan
by Kenkyusha Limited

Published by
Kenkyusha Limited
11-3, Fujimi 2-chome, Chiyoda-ku
Tokyo 102, Japan

First published 1996
Printed in Japan
ISBN 4-7674-2310-4 C0582

Contents

Inside front cover
A Table of Japanese Sounds

Inside back cover
Map of Japan

Editor in Chief
Shigeru Takebayashi
Professor Emeritus at Tokyo University of Foreign Studies

Managing Editor
Kazuhiko Nagai

Senior Editors
Christopher Barnard
Atsuko S. Kondoh

Lexicographers
Kenneth Jones
Yo Kitamura
Yoko Nishino
Chieko Shimazu
Shigeru Yamada

Publishing Administration
Josuke Okada
Hiroshi Hiruma
Osamu Hijikata
Shigeki Sasaki

Keyboarders
Susumu Enomoto
Ichiro Hashimoto
Noriko Shimada

Printing Administration
Eiichiro Kosakai
Takashi Suzuki

Editorial Assistance
Kikue Suzuki

Preface

This dictionary is the companion volume to *The Kenkyusha Japanese-English Learner's Pocket Dictionary*. This dictionary is intended for those people who seek to express themselves in Japanese in everyday situations. Thus all entries have been selected to meet daily needs, paying particular attention to the frequency of occurrence of words and phrases.

The Japanese translation equivalent of each English entry is given first in romanized form, with the pitch accent marked; this is then followed by the translation in Japanese orthography. The particular attention given to recording verb entries should be of great convenience to users of this dictionary. The verb class of all verbs (consonant-stem, vowel-stem, irregular) is recorded, and appropriate examples are given to show how the verbs are conjugated. In entries of transitive verbs the particle which occurs with a particular verb is listed. This is a feature of *The Kenkyusha English-Japanese Learner's Pocket Dictionary* which conventional romanized English-Japanese dictionaries do not have.

This dictionary gives copious illustrative examples of complete Japanese sentences. These are recorded in such a way as to present common and useful Japanese word combinations (such as frequently occurring noun/verb collocations), whilst at the same time making the grammatical structure of Japanese as clear as possible. Also, the dictionary lists very many practical expressions which occur in daily conversation. Such expressions are immediately useful to those users of the dictionary who as yet have little knowledge of Japanese grammar. When necessary, short explanatory notes are included to further clarify meanings or to point out cultural connotations of certain words and expressions.

We hope this small dictionary proves useful and helpful to learners of the Japanese language.

The Editors

Guide to the Use of the Dictionary

1. Romanization

The romanization used in this dictionary is based on the standard Hepburn system with the following modifications:

1. 1 Long vowels are indicated by doubled vowel letters, 'aa, ii, uu, ee, oo,' instead of the conventional transcription which, depending on the particular vowel, either uses macrons or doubles the vowel letter.

> aˈachi (arch) アーチ
> suˈpiido (speed) スピード
> yuˈubiñ (mail) ゆうびん(郵便)
> keˈezai (economy) けいざい(経済)
> koˈoeñ (park) こうえん(公園)

1. 2 When the vowel sequence 'ei' is pronounced as a long 'e,' it is written as 'ee.'

> seˈeto (pupil) せいと(生徒)
> seˈtsumee (explanation) せつめい(説明)

But a word like けいと (knitting wool) is written as 'keito' in order to show that it is composed of two separate word elements 'ke (wool)' and 'ito (thread)'.

1. 3 When there is a sequence of three or more identical vowel letters, a hyphen is used to clarify the word elements.

> keˈe-ee (management) けいえい(経営)
> soˈo-oñ (noise) そうおん(騒音)

1. 4 'ñ' is used to transcribe the syllabic 'n' (ん/ン).

> shiˈñbuñ (newspaper) しんぶん(新聞)
> keˈñkoo (health) けんこう(健康)

1. 5 When the small 'っ/ッ' precedes a consonant, the sequence is transcribed as a double consonant, except in the case of 'ch,' which is written 'tch.'

> aˈppaku (pressure) あっぱく(圧迫)
> fuˈtoˈtta (fat) ふとった(太った)
> piˈtchaa (pitcher) ピッチャー

1. 6 The small 'っ' in interjections is transcribed with an apostrophe. This sign represents a glottal stop after the preceding vowel.

> a' あっ (Oh!)   e' えっ (Eh!)

2. Accentuation

Japanese has a pitch accent system. The accent of standard Japanese is explained in terms of two significant levels of pitch: high and low, and the accent nucleus. In this dictionary accent nucleus is marked with ⌐, and the syllable which follows the nucleus is pronounced low. The automatic rise on the second syllable is marked with ⌐.

2. 1 Words with an accent nucleus on the first syllable.

> hi⌐ (fire) ひ(火)
> ne⌐ko (cat) ねこ(猫)

2. 2 Words with a nucleus on the second syllable.

> i⌐nu⌐ (dog) いぬ(犬)
> ko⌐ko⌐ro (mind) こころ(心)

2. 3 Words with a nucleus on the third syllable.

> o⌐toko⌐ (man) おとこ(男)
> ko⌐ojo⌐o (factory) こうじょう (工場)

2. 4 Words with a nucleus on the fourth syllable.

> o⌐tooto⌐ (younger brother) おとうと(弟)
> wa⌐tashibu⌐ne (ferry) わたしぶね(渡し船)

2. 5 Words without an accent nucleus are automatically pronounced with the first syllable low and all succeeding syllables are kept high.

> ke (hair) 毛
> ka⌐tachi (shape) かたち(形)
> to⌐modachi (friend) ともだち(友達)

3. Kinds of verbs

Verbs are classified into three groups: consonant-stem verbs, vowel-stem verbs and irregular verbs.

3. 1 Consonant-stem verbs, which are marked Ⓒ, have a consonant preceding final 'u' in the dictionary form: **kaku** (write), yomu (read). Note that all verbs ending in vowel plus 'u' in their dictionary form are also consonant-stem verbs; the original 'w' in these verbs has simply been lost in the modern language: kawu>kau (buy), hirowu>hirou (pick up).

3.2 Vowel-stem verbs, which are marked $\boxed{V}$, have a final 'ru' preceded by 'i' or 'e' in the dictionary form: miru (see), taberu (eat).

3.3 Irregular verbs, which are marked $\boxed{I}$, are 'suru' (do) and 'kuru' (come).

4. Conjugations of verbs

4.1 Dictionary form
All Japanese verbs end in 'u.'

4.2 Continuative form (masu-form)
  $\boxed{C}$ = replace the final 'u' with 'i'
    kaku (write) > kaki-masu, yomu (read) > yomi-masu
  $\boxed{V}$ = drop the final 'ru'
    miru (see) > mi-masu, taberu (eat) > tabe-masu
  $\boxed{I}$ suru (do) > shi-masu, kuru (come) > ki-masu

4.3 Negative form (nai-form)
  $\boxed{C}$ = replace the final 'u' with 'a'
    kaku (write) > kaka-nai, yomu (read) > yoma-nai

  Verbs which end in vowel plus 'u': replace the final 'u' with 'wa.'

  kau (buy) > kawa-nai, hirou (pick up) > hirowa-nai

  $\boxed{V}$ = drop the final 'ru'
    miru (see) > mi-nai, taberu (eat) > tabe-nai
  $\boxed{I}$ suru (do) > shi-nai, kuru (come) > ko-nai

4.4 Gerund (te-form)
  $\boxed{C}$ = change sounds according to the final consonant of the stem
    to-bu (jump) > toñ-de
    oyo-gu (swim) > oyoi-de
    no-mu (drink) > noñ-de
    shi-nu (die)   > shiñ-de
    ma-ku (sow)   > mai-te

no-ru (ride) > not-te
hana-su (tell) > hanashi-te
ma-tsu (wait) > mat-te
ka-u (buy) > kat-te
[V] = drop the final 'ru'
     miru (see) > mi-te, taberu (eat) > tabe-te
[I] suru (do) > shi-te, kuru (come) > ki-te

4.5 Provisional form (ba-form)
    [C] = replace the final 'u' with 'e'
        kaku (write) > kake-ba, yomu (read) > yome-ba
    [V] = replace the final 'u' with 'e'
        miru (see) > mire-ba, taberu (eat) > tabere-ba
    [I] suru (do) > sure-ba, kuru (come) > kure-ba

4.6 Tentative form
    [C] = replace the final 'u' with 'oo'
        kaku (write) > kak-oo, yomu (read) > yom-oo
    [V] = replace the final 'ru' with 'yoo'
        miru (see) > mi-yoo, taberu (eat) > tabe-yoo
    [I] suru (do) > shi-yoo, kuru (come) > ko-yoo

4.7 Imperative form
    [C] = replace the final 'u' with 'e'
        kaku (write) > kak-e, yomu (read) > yom-e
    [V] = replace the final 'ru' with 'ro'
        miru (see) > mi-ro, taberu (eat) > tabe-ro
    [I] suru (do) > shi-ro, kuru (come) > ko-i

5. Particles

The translation of transitive verbs is given with the particle(s) which usually precede these verbs, such as '... o' and '... ni.' When a word has more than two meanings, the particles of the second and the following translation are omitted.

6. Brackets in illustrative examples

    Round brackets (   ) indicate that omission is possible.
    Square brackets [   ] indicate alternative possibilities.

7. Abbreviations

adj.	adjective
adv.	adverb
art.	article

aux.	auxiliary verb
conj.	conjunction
def. art.	definite article
indef. art.	indefinite article
int.	interjection
n.	noun
pref.	prefix
prep.	preposition
rel. adj.	relative adjective
rel. adv.	relative adverb
rel. pron.	relative pronoun
v.	verb
vi.	intransitive verb
vt.	transitive verb

A

a *indef. art.* ★ In Japanese, there are no words corresponding to the English articles, and 'a' is not translated: read a book (*hoñ o yomu*) 本を読む.

1 (one) hiˈtoˈtsu 一つ; iˈchiˈ 1: an apple (*riñgo hitotsu*) りんご一つ / a sheet of paper (*ichi-mai no kami*) 1枚の紙 / an hour (*ichi-jikañ*) 1時間.

2 (a certain) aˈru ある: in a sense (*aru imi de*) ある意味で.

3 (any) ... to iˈu monoˈ ...というもの: A dog is a faithful animal. (*Inu (to iu mono) wa chuujitsu na doobutsu desu.*) 犬(というもの)は忠実な動物です.

4 (per) ... ni (tsuˈ)ki ...に(つき): I work seven hours a day. (*Watashi wa ichi-nichi ni (tsuki) nana-jikañ hataraku.*) 私は1日に(つき)7時間働く.

abandon *vt.* **1** (give up) ... o yaˈmeru ...をやめる Ⅴ; suˈteru 捨てる Ⅴ: abandon a plan (*keekaku o yameru*) 計画をやめる / abandon hope (*kiboo o suteru*) 希望を捨てる.

2 (leave) ... o miˈsuteru ...を見捨てる Ⅴ: He abandoned his wife and children. (*Kare wa tsuma to kodomo o misuteta.*) 彼は妻と子どもを見捨てた.

abbreviate *vt.* ... o shoˈoryaku suru ...を省略する Ⅰ; ryaˈkuˈsu 略す Ⅽ: 'January' is abbreviated to 'Jan.' (*'January' wa 'Jan.' to ryakusareru.*) January は Jan. と略される.

abbreviation *n.* shoˈoryaku 省略; ryaˈkugo 略語: 'TV' is an abbreviation for 'television.' (*'TV' wa 'television' no ryakugo desu.*) TV は television の略語です.

ability *n.* **1** (competence) noˈoryoku 能力: He has the ability to pay. (*Kare wa shiharau nooryoku ga aru.*) 彼は支払う能力がある.

2 (talent) saˈinoo 才能: He is a man of great ability. (*Kare wa sainoo no aru hito desu.*) 彼は才能のある人です.

able *adj.* **1** (capable) ... koˈtoˈ ga deˈkiˈru ...ことができる: She is able to play the piano. (*Kanojo wa piano o hiku koto ga dekiru.*) 彼女はピアノを弾くことができる.

2 (skillful) yuˈunoo na 有能な: an able manager (*yuunoo na keeeesha*) 有能な経営者.

aboard *prep.* ... ni noˈtte ...に乗って: He is now aboard a ship. (*Kare wa ima fune ni notte imasu.*) 彼は今船に乗っています.
— *adv.* ... ni noˈtte ...に乗って: go aboard (*norikomu*) 乗り込む.

abolish *vt.* ... o haˈishi suru ...を廃止する Ⅰ: abolish capital punishment (*shikee o haishi suru*) 死刑を廃止する.

about *prep., adv.* **1** (nearly) yaˈku 約; oˈyoso およそ: We walked about five kilometers. (*Watashi-tachi wa yaku go-kiro aruita.*) 私たちは約5キロ歩いた.

2 (concerning) ... ni tsuˈite ...について: This is a book about dogs. (*Kore wa inu ni tsuite no hoñ desu.*) これは犬についての本です.

3 (around) aˈchiˈ-kochi あちこち: The children ran about the park. (*Kodomo-tachi wa kooeñ o achikochi kakemawatta.*) 子どもたちは公園をあちこち駆け回った.

be about to do ⟨verb⟩–(y)oo to suru ...(よ)うとする Ⅰ: He was about to leave the room. (*Kare wa heya o deyoo to shita.*) 彼は部屋を出ようとした.

above *prep.* **1** (over) ... no uˈeˈ ni ...の上に: The moon rose above the hill. (*Tsuki ga oka no ue ni nobotta.*) 月が丘の上に昇った.

2 (more than) iʲjoo 以上: The height of the tree is above five meters. (*Sono ki no takasa wa go-meetoru ijoo aru.*) その木の高さは5メートル以上ある.

abroad *adv.* gaˈikoku e [ni] 外国へ[に]: I would like to go abroad. (*Watashi wa gaikoku e ikitai.*) 私は外国へ行きたい. / She is living abroad. (*Kanojo wa gaikoku ni sunde iru.*) 彼女は外国に住んでいる.

absence *n.* (from school) keˈsseki 欠席; (from work) keˈkkin 欠勤; (lack) keˈtsuboo 欠乏: absence of vitamin C (*bitamin C no ketsuboo*) ビタミンCの欠乏.

absent *adj.* yaˈsuˈnde (iru) 休んで(いる); fuˈzai no 不在の; keˈsseki shite 欠席して: He has been absent from school for the past two days. (*Kare wa kono futsuka-kan gakkoo o yasunde iru.*) 彼はこの二日間学校を休んでいる.

absolute *adj.* **1** zeˈttai no 絶対の: I have absolute trust in him. (*Watashi wa kare ni zettai no shinrai o oite imasu.*) 私は彼に絶対の信頼をおいています.
2 maˈttaku no まったくの: You are an absolute fool. (*Kimi wa mattaku no baka da.*) 君はまったくのばかだ.

absolutely *adv.* maˈttaku まったく: It's absolutely impossible to do so. (*Soo suru koto wa mattaku fukanoo da.*) そうすることはまったく不可能だ.

absorb *vt.* ... o kyuˈushuu suru ...を吸収する Ⓣ; suˈikoˈmu 吸い込む Ⓒ: This cloth absorbs water well. (*Kono nuno wa mizu o yoku kyuushuu suru.*) この布は水をよく吸収する.

abstain *vi.* (... o) yaˈmeru (...を)やめる Ⓥ; tsuˈtsushiˈmu 慎む Ⓒ: abstain from smoking (*tabako o yameru*) たばこをやめる.

abstract *adj.* chuˈushoo-teki na 抽象的な: an abstract idea (*chuushoo-teki na kangae*) 抽象的な考え / an abstract painting (*chuushoo-ga*) 抽象画.

absurd *adj.* fuˈgoˈori na 不合理な;

baˈkaˈgeta ばかげた: make an absurd mistake (*bakageta machigai o suru*) ばかげた間違いをする.

abundant *adj.* hoˈofu na 豊富な; yuˈtaka na 豊かな: The country is abundant in natural resources. (*Sono kuni wa tennen shigen ga hoofu da.*) その国は天然資源が豊富だ.

abuse *vt.* (use wrongly) ... o raˈnˈyoo suru ...を乱用する Ⓣ; aˈkuyoo suru 悪用する Ⓣ: abuse one's authority (*shokken o ranyoo suru*) 職権を乱用する.
— n. (wrong use) raˈnyoo 乱用; (cruel treatment) gyaˈkutai 虐待: child abuse (*jidoo gyakutai*) 児童虐待.

academy *n.* seˈnmon-gaˈkkoo 専門学校: an academy of music (*ongaku-gakkoo*) 音楽学校.

accent *n.* **1** naˈmari なまり: a Northeastern accent (*toohoku namari*) 東北なまり.
2 (pitch accent) aˈkusento アクセント: the accent in a word (*tango no akusento*) 単語のアクセント.

accept *vt.* **1** (take) ... o uˈketoru ...を受け取る Ⓣ: He accepted her gift. (*Kare wa kanojo no okurimono o uketotta.*) 彼は彼女の贈り物を受け取った.
2 (agree to) ... o miˈtomeru ...を認める Ⓥ: I don't accept what he says. (*Watashi wa kare no iu koto wa mitomemasen.*) 私は彼のいうことは認めません.
3 (undertake) ... o toˈru ...をとる Ⓒ; hiˈkiukeˈru 引き受ける Ⓥ: I'll accept responsibility for the accident. (*Watashi ga sono jiko no sekinin o torimasu.*) 私がその事故の責任をとります.

acceptable *adj.* **1** (satisfactory) maˈnzoku na 満足な; uˈkeirerareru 受け入れられる: Such an offer is not acceptable to me. (*Sonna mooshide wa ukeireraremasen.*) そんな申し出は受け入れられません.
2 (pleasing) yoˈrokobareˈru 喜ばれる: an acceptable gift (*yoroko-*

bareru okurimono) 喜ばれる贈り物.

acceptance *n.* (accepting) u⌈ke-ire 受け入れ; (approval) sho⌈odaku 承諾: find general acceptance (*ippañ ni ukeirerareru*) 一般に受け入れられる.

accident *n.* ji⌈ko 事故: cause an accident (*jiko o okosu*) 事故を起こす / meet with an accident (*jiko ni au*) 事故にあう / prevent an accident (*jiko o fusegu*) 事故を防ぐ / a traffic accident (*kootsuu jiko*) 交通事故.

by accident *adv.* gu⌈uzeñ 偶然: I met her by accident. (*Watashi wa guuzeñ kanojo ni atta.*) 私は偶然彼女に会った.

accidental *adj.* gu⌈uzeñ no 偶然の; o⌈moigakena⌉i 思いがけない: an accidental meeting (*guuzeñ no deai*) 偶然の出会い.

accommodate *vt.* 1 (of a vehicle) ... o no⌈seru ...を乗せる V; (hold) shu⌈uyoo suru 収容する I: This car can accommodate four passengers. (*Kono kuruma wa yo-niñ noseru koto ga dekimasu.*) この車は4人乗せることができます. / This hall can accommodate three hundred people. (*Kono hooru wa sañ-byaku-niñ o shuuyoo dekimasu.*) このホールは300人を収容できます.

2 (adjust) ... ni na⌈re⌉ru ...に慣れる V: He soon accommodated himself to his new circumstances. (*Kare wa atarashii kañkyoo ni sugu nareta.*) 彼は新しい環境にすぐ慣れた.

3 (help) ... ni (... o) ka⌈su ...に(...を)貸す C: I accommodated him with some money. (*Watashi wa kare ni o-kane o kashite yatta.*) 私は彼にお金を貸してやった.

accommodation *n.* shu⌈kuhaku-shi⌉setsu 宿泊施設: We need accommodations for five. (*Go-niñ buñ no shukuhaku-shisetsu ga hoshii.*) 5人分の宿泊施設が欲しい.

accompany *vt.* 1 (go with) ... ni tsu⌈ite iku ...について行く C: I accompanied him on his walk. (*Watashi wa kare no sañpo ni*

tsuite itta.) 私は彼の散歩について行った.

2 (play) ... no ba⌈ñsoo o suru ...の伴奏をする I: accompany a song on the piano (*piano de uta no bañsoo o suru*) ピアノで歌の伴奏をする.

3 ... o to⌈mona⌉u ...を伴う C: A cold is often accompanied by fever. (*Kaze wa shibashiba netsu o tomonau.*) かぜはしばしば熱を伴う.

accomplish *vt.* ... o ta⌈s⌉see suru ...を達成する I; ka⌈ñsee suru 完成する I: He accomplished the task in a week. (*Kare wa sono shigoto o isshuu-kañ de kañsee shita.*) 彼はその仕事を1週間で完成した.

accord *n.* i⌈tchi 一致: We came to an accord with them regarding that matter. (*Watashi-tachi wa sono moñdai ni tsuite kare-ra to ikeñ ga itchi shita.*) 私たちはその問題について彼らと意見が一致した.

accordingly *adv.* 1 so⌈re ni ooji⌉te それに応じて; shi⌈tagatte 従って: He understood the danger and acted accordingly. (*Kare wa kikeñ o shitte sore ni oojite koodoo shita.*) 彼は危険を知っていてそれに応じて行動した.

2 da⌈kara だから; so⌈re de それで: She had fever; accordingly we sent her home. (*Kanojo wa netsu ga atta. Da kara uchi made okutta.*) 彼女は熱があった. だから家まで送った.

according to *prep.* ... ni yo⌈re⌉ba ...によれば; ... ni shi⌈tagatte ...に従って: According to this book, what you say is wrong. (*Kono hoñ ni yoreba, anata no iu koto wa machi-gatte imasu.*) この本によれば, あなたの言うことは間違っています.

account *n.* 1 (explanation) se⌈tsu-mee 説明: demand an account (*setsumee o motomeru*) 説明を求める / give an account (*setsumee suru*) 説明する.

2 (of a bank) ko⌈oza 口座: open [close] a bank account (*kooza o hiraku [tojiru]*) 口座を開く[閉じる].

3 (of money) ka⌈ñjo⌉o 勘定: We

paid our account of 5,000 yen. (*Goseñ-eñ no kañjoo o haratta.*) 5 千円の勘定を払った.

account for *vt.* ... no se⌐tsumee ga tsu⌐ku ...の説明がつく C: That accounts for his conduct. (*Sore de kare no koodoo no setsumee ga tsuku.*) それで彼の行動の説明がつく.

accuracy *n.* se⌐ekakusa 正確さ: He took the measurement with accuracy. (*Kare wa suñpoo o seekaku ni hakatta.*) 彼は寸法を正確に測った.

accurate *adj.* se⌐ekaku na 正確な; me⌐ñmitsu na 綿密な: an accurate calculation (*seekaku na keesañ*) 正確な計算 / He is accurate in his work. (*Kare wa shigoto ga meñmitsu da.*) 彼は仕事が綿密だ.

accuse *vt.* ... o u⌐t'tae'ru ...を訴える V; hi⌐nañ suru 非難する I: She accused him of stealing her money. (*Kanojo wa kare ga kanojo no o-kane o nusuñda to itte kare o uttaeta.*) 彼女は彼が彼女のお金を盗んだと言って彼を訴えた.

accustom *vt.* ... o na⌐ra'su ...を慣らす C: accustom a dog to the cold (*inu o samusa ni narasu*) 犬を寒さに慣らす.

be accustomed to ... *vt.* ... ni na⌐rete iru ...に慣れている V: I am accustomed to getting up early. (*Watashi wa hayaku okiru koto ni narete iru.*) 私は早く起きることに慣れている.

ache *vi.* ... ga i⌐ta'i ...が痛い; u⌐zu'ku うずく C: My tooth aches. (*Ha ga itai.*) 歯が痛い.
— *n.* i⌐tami' 痛み: The ache in my leg has gone. (*Ashi no itami ga kieta.*) 足の痛みが消えた.

achieve *vt.* ... o ta⌐ssee suru 達成する I; na⌐shitoge'ru 成し遂げる V: achieve one's purpose (*mokuteki o tassee suru*) 目的を達成する.

achievement *n.* **1** ta⌐ssee 達成: the achievement of one's aims (*mokuteki no tassee*) 目的の達成.
2 gyo⌐oseki 業績: His achieve-

ments as a scientist are outstanding. (*Kare no kagakusha to shite no gyooseki wa subarashii.*) 彼の科学者としての業績はすばらしい.

acid *adj.* su⌐ppa'i 酸性の; sa⌐ñsee no 酸性の: sour fruit (*suppai kudamono*) 酸っぱい果物 / acid rain (*sañseeu*) 酸性雨.
— *n.* sa⌐ñ 酸.

acknowledge *vt.* **1** (admit) ... o mi⌐tomeru ...を認める I: He acknowledged his mistakes. (*Kare wa jibuñ no machigai o mitometa.*) 彼は自分の間違いを認めた.
2 (express thanks) ... no re⌐e o iu ...の礼を言う C: I forgot to acknowledge the gift. (*Okurimono no ree o iu no o wasureta.*) 贈り物の礼を言うのを忘れた.

acknowledgment *n.* **1** (legal admission) ji⌐niñ 自認: acknowledgment of guilt (*yuuzai no jiniñ*) 有罪の自認.
2 (confirmation of receipt) u⌐ketori no tsuuchi 受取の通知; u⌐ketori-shoo 受取証: an acknowledgment of a letter (*tegami o uketotta to iu tsuuchi*) 手紙を受け取ったという通知.
3 (thanks) ka⌐ñsha 感謝.

acquaint *vt.* (let know) ... ni (... o) shi⌐raseru ...に(...を)知らせる V: I acquainted him with the fact. (*Watashi wa kare ni sono jijitsu o shiraseta.*) 私は彼にその事実を知らせた.

be acquainted with ... *vt.* ... to shi⌐riai da ...と知り合いだ: He and I have been acquainted for ten years. (*Kare to wa juu-neñ-rai no shiriai desu.*) 彼とは10年来の知り合いです.

acquaintance *n.* chi⌐jiñ 知人; shi⌐riai 知り合い: He's not a friend, only an acquaintance. (*Kare wa yuujiñ de wa naku, tañ-naru shiriai desu.*) 彼は友人ではなく、単なる知り合いです.

acquire *vt.* **1** (gain) ... o e⌐ru ...を得る V; te⌐ ni i⌐reru 手に入れる V: acquire land (*tochi o te ni ireru*) 土地を手に入れる.

2 (of a skill, habit) ... o mi `ni tsu-
ke`ru …を身に付ける Ⓥ; o`boe`ru 覚
える Ⓥ: acquire a bad habit (*warui
kuse o oboeru*) 悪い癖を覚える.

acre *n.* e`ekaa エーカー. ★ 1 acre =
about 4,050 square meters.

across *prep.* ★ 'Across' does not
have exact equivalents, but can
often be translated with the particle 'o' and an appropriate verb.
1 (from one side to the other side)
... o yo`kogi`tte …を横切って: run
across the road (*michi o hashitte
yokogiru*) 道を走って横切る / John
swam across the river. (*Joñ wa
kawa o oyoide watatta.*) ジョンは川
を泳いで渡った.
2 (the other side) ... no mu`koo-
gawa ni …の向こう側に: He lives
across the street. (*Kare wa michi
no mukoogawa ni suñde imasu.*)
彼は道の向こう側に住んでいます.
— *adv.* **1** (width) ha`ba ga ... 幅が
…: This river is 50 meters across.
(*Kono kawa wa haba ga gojuu-
meetoru aru.*) この川は幅が 50 メート
ルある.
2 (the other side) mu`koo e [ni] 向
こうへ[に]: go across (*mukoo e iku*)
向こうへ行く.

act *vi.* **1** (do, behave) ko`odoo suru
行動する Ⓘ; fu`ruma`u 振る舞う Ⓒ:
She acted like a queen. (*Kanojo wa
jo-oo no yoo ni furumatta.*) 彼女は
女王のように振る舞った.
2 (perform on the stage) (... ni) shu-
`tsueñ suru …に)出演する Ⓘ: act in
a play (*geki ni shutsueñ suru*) 劇に
出演する.
3 (have an effect) ki`ku 効く Ⓒ:
This drug acts quickly. (*Kono
kusuri wa sugu kiku.*) この薬はすぐ
効く.
— *vt.* **1** (do a play) ... o e`ñjiru …
を演じる Ⓥ: He acted the part of
Hamlet. (*Kare wa Hamuretto no
yaku o eñjita.*) 彼はハムレットの役を演
じた.
2 (behave) ... ko`to o suru …ことを
する Ⓘ: act the fool (*baka na koto o*

suru) ばかなことをする.
— *n.* **1** (deed) o`konai 行い; ko`oi
行為: do an act of kindness (*shiñsetsu na okonai o suru*) 親切な行いを
する.
2 (law) ho`oree 法令; jo`oree 条令.
3 (division of a play) ma`ku` 幕: a
comedy in three acts (*sañ maku no
kigeki*) 3 幕の喜劇.

action *n.* **1** (doing something)
ka`tsudoo 活動; ji`kkoo 実行: I put
my plan into action. (*Watashi wa
jibuñ no keekaku o jikkoo ni utsushita.*) 私は自分の計画を実行に移した.
2 (behavior) ko`oi 行為; ko`odoo
行動: a kind action (*shiñsetsu na
kooi*) 親切な行為.
3 (effect) sa`yoo 作用; ha`taraki 働
き: the action of the heart (*shiñzoo
no hataraki*) 心臓の働き.

active *adj.* **1** (lively) ka`ppatsu na
活発な; ka`tsudoo-teki na 活動的な:
He is not as active as he used to be.
(*Kare wa izeñ hodo kappatsu de
wa nai.*) 彼は以前ほど活発ではない.
2 (working) ka`tsudoo shite iru 活
動している: an active volcano (*kak-
kazañ*) 活火山.

activity *n.* **1** (doings) ka`tsudoo
活動; ka`tsuyaku 活躍: artistic ac-
tivities (*geejutsu katsudoo*) 芸術活
動.
2 (being active) ka`ppatsu 活発;
ka`kki 活気: The street was bus-
tling with activity. (*Toori wa kakki ni afurete ita.*) 通りは活気にあふれ
ていた.

actor *n.* ha`iyuu 俳優; da`ñyuu 男
優: a film actor (*eega haiyuu*) 映画
俳優.

actress *n.* jo`yuu 女優: a stage
actress (*butai joyuu*) 舞台女優.

actual *adj.* **1** (real) ji`ssai no 実際
の; ge`ñjitsu no 現実の: an actual
incident (*jissai no jikeñ*) 実際の事
件.
2 (present) ge`ñzai no 現在の: the
actual state of affairs (*geñjoo*) 現状.

actually *adv.* **1** (really) ji`ssai ni
実際に; ho`ñtoo ni 本当に: Did he

actually do it? (*Kare wa jissai ni soo shita ñ desu ka?*) 彼は実際にそうしたんですか.

2 (as a matter of fact) ji「tsu」wa 実は; ho「ñtoo wa 本当は: Actually, I failed in the exam. (*Jitsu wa, watashi wa shikeñ ni shippai shita ñ desu.*) 実は, 私は試験に失敗したんです.

acute *adj.* **1** (keen) su「rudo」i 鋭い; e「ebiñ na 鋭敏な: an acute sense of smell (*surudoi shuukaku*) 鋭い臭覚.
2 (of pains and diseases) ha「geshi」i 激しい; kyu「usee no 急性の: an acute pain in the stomach (*i no hageshii itami*) 胃の激しい痛み / acute pneumonia (*kyuusee haieñ*) 急性肺炎.
3 (of a situation) shi「ñkoku na 深刻な; ju「udai na 重大な: an acute shortage of food (*shiñkoku na shokuryoo-busoku*) 深刻な食料不足.

adapt *vt.* **1** (make suitable) ... ni ka「izoo suru ...に改造する ▯; ka「isaku suru 改作する ▯: adapt a book for children (*hoñ o kodomo muki ni kakikaeru*) 本を子ども向きに書きかえる.
2 (adjust) ... o (... ni) a「wase」ru ...を(...に)合わせる ▯; te「kigoo saseru 適合させる ▯: adapt a plan to a new situation (*keekaku o atarashii jitai ni awaseru*) 計画を新しい事態に合わせる.

add *vt.* **1** (join) ... o ku「waeru ...を加える ▯; ta「su 足す ▯: add cream to tea (*koocha ni kuriimu o kuwaeru*) 紅茶にクリームを加える / add five and six (*go to roku o tasu*) 5と6を足す.
2 (say in addition) ... to tsu「kekuwaete iu ...とつけ加えて言う ▯: "I wish you good luck," he added. (*"Koouñ o inorimasu" to kare wa tsukekuwaeta.*) 「幸運を祈ります」と彼は付け加えた.
　add to ... *vt.* ... o ma「su ...を増す ▯; ... ga fu「e」ru ...が増える ▯: I am adding to my weight. (*Watashi wa taijuu ga fuete iru.*) 私は体重が増えている.

add up *vt.* ... o go「okee suru ...を合計する ▯: add up the figures (*suuji o gookee suru*) 数字を合計する.

addition *n.* **1** (adding) tsu「ika 追加.
2 (calculating) ta「shi」zañ 足し算: be quick at addition (*tashizañ ga hayai*) 足し算が速い.
3 (of a house) ta「temashi 建て増し: an addition to a house (*ie no tatemashi*) 家の建て増し.

additional *adj.* tsu「ika no 追加の: an additional charge (*tsuika ryookiñ*) 追加料金.

address *n.* **1** (place) ju「usho 住所; a「tena あて名: Give me your address, please. (*Anata no juusho o oshiete kudasai.*) あなたの住所を教えてください.
2 (speech) e「ñzetsu 演説: make an address (*eñzetsu o suru*) 演説をする.
── *vt.* **1** (write) ... ni a「tena o ka」ku ...にあて名を書く ▯: I addressed the envelopes for the invitation. (*Watashi wa shootaijoo no fuutoo ni atena o kaita.*) 私は招待状の封筒に宛名を書いた.
2 (speak) ... ni ha「nashikake」ru ...に話しかける ▯; ha「nashi」o suru 話をする ▯: I was addressed by a girl. (*Watashi wa oñna-no-ko ni hanashikakerareta.*) 私は女の子に話しかけられた. / address an audience (*chooshuu ni hanashi o suru*) 聴衆に話をする.

adequate *adj.* **1** (enough) ju「ubu」ñ na 十分な: My salary is not adequate. (*Watashi no kyuuryoo wa juubuñ de wa nai.*) 私の給料は十分ではない.
2 (suitable) (... ni) te「ki」shita (...に)適した; fu「sawashi」i ふさわしい: an adequate person for the job (*sono shigoto ni tekishita hito*) その仕事に適した人.

adjective *n.* ke「eyo」oshi 形容詞.

adjoin *vt.* ... ni ri「ñsetsu suru ...に隣接する ▯: My house adjoins the park. (*Watashi no ie wa kooeñ ni* *riñsetsu shite imasu.*) 私の家は公園に隣接しています。

adjust *vt.* **1** (fit) ... o (... ni) cho「o-setsu suru ...を(...に)調節する ①; a 「wase「ru 合わせる ⑤: adjust the stool to the height of the piano (*isu o piano no takasa ni awasete choo-setsu suru*) いすをピアノの高さに合わせて調節する。
2 (settle) ... o se「esañ suru ...を清算する ①: adjust one's fare (*uñchiñ o seesañ suru*) 運賃を清算する。
—— *vi.* (... ni) ju「ñnoo suru (...に)順応する ①: adjust to one's new surroundings (*atarashii kañkyoo ni juñnoo suru*) 新しい環境に順応する。

adjustment *n.* cho「osee 調整; cho「otee 調停; se「esañ 清算: make some adjustments to the plan (*kee-kaku o ikura-ka choosee suru*) 計画をいくらか調整する / fare adjustment (*uñchiñ no seesañ*) 運賃の清算。

administer *vt.* **1** (manage) ... o ka「ñri suru ...を管理する ①; o「same「ru 治める ①: administer a company (*kaisha o kañri suru*) 会社を管理する。
2 (give) ... o a「taeru ...を与える ⑤: administer punishment (*batsu o ataeru*) 罰を与える。

administration *n.* **1** (government) se「efu 政府; gyo「osee 行政.
2 (management) ka「ñri 管理; u「ñee 運営: the administration of a library (*toshokañ no uñee*) 図書館の運営。

administrator *n.* ka「ñri「sha 管理者.

admiration *n.* **1** (admiring) ka「ñtañ 感嘆; sho「osañ 称賛: He let out a cry of admiration when he saw the car. (*Kare wa sono kuruma o mite kañtañ no koe o ageta.*) 彼はその車を見て感嘆の声を上げた。
2 (an object admired) a「kogare no mato あこがれの的: She is the subject of admiration of young people. (*Kanojo wa wakai hito-tachi no akogare no mato da.*) 彼女は若い人

たちのあこがれの的だ。

admire *vt.* **1** (feel admiration for) ... ni ka「ñshiñ suru ...に感心する ①.
2 (praise) ... o ho「me「ru ...をほめる ⑤: He admired her painting. (*Kare wa kanojo no e o hometa.*) 彼は彼女の絵をほめた。

admission *n.* **1** (of a society) nyu「ukai 入会; (of a school) nyu「u-gaku 入学: gain admission into a club (*kurabu e no nyuukai o yuru-sareru*) クラブへの入会を許される。
2 (price) nyu「ujo「o-ryoo 入場料: Admission to the museum is 800 yen. (*Bijutsukañ no nyuujoo-ryoo wa happyaku-eñ desu.*) 美術館の入場料は800円です。
3 (acknowledging) mi「tomeru koto「 認めること; sho「oniñ 承認: He made an admission that he had told a lie. (*Kare wa uso o tsuita koto o mitometa.*) 彼はうそをついたことを認めた。

admit *vt.* **1** (acknowledge) ... o mi「tomeru ...を認める ⑤: admit one's mistakes (*jibuñ no ayamari o mi-tomeru*) 自分の誤りを認める。
2 (allow entrance) ... ni ha「iru koto o yu「ru「su ...に入ることを許す ©; ... o to「osu ...を通す ©: He was admitted to the school. (*Kare wa sono gakkoo ni hairu koto o yurusareta.*) 彼はその学校に入ることを許された。

admittance *n.* nyu「ujoo 入場: No admittance. (*Tachiiri kiñshi.*) 立ち入り禁止。

adopt *vt.* **1** (of a person) ... o yo「oshi ni suru ...を養子にする ①: He adopted the child. (*Kare wa sono ko o yooshi ni shita.*) 彼はその子を養子にした。
2 (of a plan) ... o sa「iyoo suru ...を採用する ①: I decided to adopt your idea. (*Anata no aidea o sai-yoo suru koto ni shimashita.*) あなたのアイデアを採用することにしました。

adore *vt.* **1** (worship) ... o a「game「ru ...をあがめる ⑤: adore God (*kami o agameru*) 神をあがめる。
2 (love greatly) ... ni a「kogareru ...

にあこがれる V: adore one's teacher (*señsee ni akogareru*) 先生にあこがれる.

3 (like very much) ... ga da¹isuki da ...が大好きだ: I adore listening to music. (*Watashi wa oñgaku o kiku no ga daisuki desu.*) 私は音楽を聞くのが大好きです.

adult *adj.* (fully grown) se¹ejiñ no 成人の: an adult man (*seejiñ dañshi*) 成人男子.
— *n.* se¹ejiñ 成人; o¹tona 大人.

advance *vt.* **1** (bring forward) ... o su¹sumeru ...を進める V; ha¹yame¹ru 早める V: advance a plan (*keekaku o susumeru*) 計画を進める / advance the date of departure (*shuppatsu no hi o hayameru*) 出発の日を早める.

2 (pay, loan) ... o ma¹eba¹rai suru ...を前払いする I; ma¹egashi suru 前貸しする I: advance wages to workers (*roodoosha ni chiñgiñ o maebarai suru*) 労働者に賃金を前払いする.
— *vi.* **1** (move forward) su¹sumu 進む C; ze¹ñshiñ suru 前進する I: advance against the enemy (*teki ni mukatte zeñshiñ suru*) 敵に向かって前進する.

2 (of prices) a¹garu 上がる C: Prices are advancing. (*Bukka wa agatte imasu.*) 物価は上がっています.
— *n.* **1** (progress) shi¹ñpo 進歩: an advance in civilization (*buñmee no shiñpo*) 文明の進歩.

2 (payment) ma¹eba¹rai 前払い: an advance payment (*maebarai*) 前払い.

in advance *adv.* ma¹emo¹tte 前もって; a¹rakajime 予め: I'll let you know in advance. (*Maemotte o-shirase shimasu.*) 前もってお知らせします.

advantage *n.* yu¹uri 有利; ko¹tsu¹goo 好都合; to¹ku 得: It is a great advantage to live near the station. (*Eki no soba ni sumu no wa totemo beñri desu.*) 駅のそばに住むのはとても便利です.

take advantage of ... vt. ... o ri¹ryoo suru ...を利用する I: He took advantage of the opportunity. (*Kare wa sono kikai o riyoo shita.*) 彼はその機会を利用した.

adventure *n.* bo¹okeñ 冒険; a¹bunai keekeñ 危ない経験: have a lot of adventures (*iroiro abunai keekeñ o suru*) いろいろ危ない経験をする.

adverb *n.* fu¹kushi 副詞.

advertise *vt.* ... o ko¹okoku suru ...を広告する I; se¹ñdeñ suru 宣伝する I: advertise a house for sale (*uriya no kookoku o suru*) 売り家の広告をする.
— *vi.* ko¹okoku o da¹su 広告を出す C: That store advertised in a newspaper. (*Sono mise wa shiñbuñ ni kookoku o dashita.*) その店は新聞に広告を出した.

advertisement *n.* ko¹okoku 広告; se¹ñdeñ 宣伝: put an advertisement in a magazine (*zasshi ni kookoku o dasu*) 雑誌に広告を出す.

advice *n.* chu¹ukoku 忠告; jo¹geñ 助言; a¹dobaisu アドバイス: give advice (*adobaisu o ataeru*) アドバイスを与える / I followed his advice. (*Watashi wa kare no chuukoku ni shitagatta.*) 私は彼の忠告に従った.

advise *vt.* ... ni chu¹ukoku suru ...に忠告する I; jo¹geñ suru 助言する I; ... o su¹sumeru ...を勧める I: No one advised me. (*Dare mo watashi ni chuukoku shite kurenakatta.*) だれも私に忠告してくれなかった. / The doctor advised a change of air. (*Isha wa teñchi o susumeta.*) 医者は転地を勧めた.

aeroplane *n.* ⇨ airplane.

affair *n.* **1** (event) ji¹keñ 事件; de¹ki¹goto でき事: a strange affair (*fushigi na dekigoto*) 不思議なでき事 / current affairs (*geñzai no jookyoo*) 現在の状況.

2 (business) ji¹mu 事務; yo¹oji 用事: private affairs (*shiji*) 私事.

3 (love affair) jo¹oji 情事.

affect[1] *vt.* **1** (produce an effect) ... ni e¹ekyoo o ataeru ...に影響を与え

る Ⅴ: The weather greatly affects the growth of crops. (*Teñkoo wa noosakubutsu no seeiku ni ookina eekyoo o ataeru.*) 天候は農作物の生育に大きな影響を与える.

2 (touch) ... o ka¹ñdoo saseru ...を感動させる Ⅴ: We were deeply affected by his story. (*Watashi-tachi wa kare no hanashi ni fukaku kañdoo shita.*) 私たちは彼の話に深く感動した.

affect² *vt.* fu¹ri¹ o suru ふりをする Ⅰ: He affected ignorance. (*Kare wa shiranai furi o shita.*) 彼は知らないふりをした.

affected *adj.* ki¹dotta 気取った; ki¹za na きざな: an affected way of talking (*kidotta hanashikata*) 気取った話し方.

affection *n.* a¹ijoo 愛情: feel affection for a person (*hito ni aijoo o idaku*) 人に愛情を抱く.

affectionate *adj.* a¹ijoo no komo¹tta [komo¹tte iru] 愛情のこもった [こもっている]; ya¹sashii 優しい: He's affectionate to his wife. (*Kare wa tsuma ni yasashii.*) 彼は妻に優しい.

affirm *vt.* ... to da¹ñge¹ñ suru ...と断言する Ⅰ; i¹iki¹ru 言い切る Ⅽ: He affirmed that she was innocent. (*Kare wa kanojo wa mujitsu da to dañgeñ shita.*) 彼は彼女は無実だと断言した.

affirmation *n.* da¹ñge¹ñ 断言; ko¹otee 肯定.

afford *vt.* 〈verb〉 yo¹yuu ga a¹ru ... 余裕がある Ⅽ: I can't afford a new car. (*Shiñsha o kau yoyuu ga nai.*) 新車を買う余裕はない.

afloat *adj., adv.* (floating) u¹kañde (iru) 浮かんで(いる); (at sea) ka¹ijoo ni 海上に: get a boat afloat (*booto o ukabaseru*) ボートを浮かばせる.

afraid *adj.* **1** (frightened) o¹so¹rete (iru) 恐れて(いる); ... ga ko¹wa¹i ...が怖い: I am afraid of going up to high places. (*Watashi wa takai tokoro e agaru no ga kowai.*) 私は高い所へ上がるのが怖い.

2 (fear) shi¹ñpai shite (iru) 心配して

(iru): She is afraid her child might become ill. (*Kanojo wa kodomo ga byooki ni naru ka mo shirenai to shiñpai shite iru.*) 彼女は子どもが病気になるかもしれないと心配している.

I'm afraid ... de wa na¹i ka to o¹mo¹u ...ではないかと思う Ⅽ; ... ka¹ mo shi¹renai ...かもしれない: I'm afraid you are wrong. (*Anata wa machigatte iru ka mo shirenai.*) あなたは間違っているかもしれない.

after *prep.* **1** (of time) ... no a¹to de ...の後で; ... -go¹ ni ...後に: After that, I'll have coffee. (*Sono ato de koohii o moraimasu.*) その後でコーヒーをもらいます. / He went out after dinner. (*Kare wa yuushoku-go ni gaishutsu shimashita.*) 彼は夕食後に外出しました.

2 (of place, order) ... no u¹shiro ni ...の後ろに; ... no a¹to ...の後: I entered the room after him. (*Watashi wa kare no ushiro ni tsuite heya ni haitta.*) 私は彼の後ろについて部屋に入った.

3 (pursuit) ... o o¹tte ...を追って; ... o mo¹to¹mete ...を求めて: The police are after the thief. (*Keesatsu wa sono doroboo o otte iru.*) 警察はそのどろぼうを追っている.

4 (of a clock) su¹gi¹ 過ぎ: fifteen minutes after two (*ni-ji juugo-fuñ sugi*) 2時15分過ぎ.

— *conj.* 〈verb〉 a¹to ni ...後に: He arrived after you left. (*Kare wa anata ga deta ato ni tsukimashita.*) 彼はあなたが出た後に着きました.

— *adv.* a¹to ni [de] 後に[で]: She returned home soon after. (*Kanojo wa sugu ato ni kitaku shimashita.*) 彼女はすぐ後に帰宅しました.

after all *adv.* ke¹kkyoku 結局: He didn't come after all. (*Kare wa kekkyoku konakatta.*) 彼は結局来なかった.

After you. (*O-saki ni doozo.*) お先にどうぞ.

afternoon *n.* go¹go 午後; hi¹ru sugi¹ 昼過ぎ: I'll visit you on Monday afternoon. (*Getsuyoobi no* gogo o-tazune shimasu.) 月曜日の午後お訪ねします。/ Is there an afternoon tour? (*Gogo no koosu wa arimasu ka?*) 午後のコースはありますか。

afterward *adv.* aˈto de 後で; noˈchiˈ ni 後に: He told me afterward that he had refused the offer. (*Kare wa sono mooshide o kotowatta to ato de itta.*) 彼はその申し出を断わったと後で言った。

again *adv.* (once more) fuˈtatabi 再び; maˈta また; moˈo ichido もう一度: Come again tomorrow. (*Ashita mata kite kudasai.*) あしたまた来てください。/ I'll phone again later. (*Ato de mata deñwa shimasu.*) あとでまた電話します。/ Please come again. (*Mata doozo.*) またどうぞ.

against *prep.* 1 (opposition) ... ni haˈñtai shite ...に反対して: I am against war. (*Watashi wa señsoo ni hañtai desu.*) 私は戦争に反対です。
2 (contact) ... ni buˈtsukete) ...に (ぶつけて): He hit his head against a pillar. (*Kare wa hashira ni atama o butsuketa.*) 彼は柱に頭をぶつけた。
3 (contrast) ... o haˈikee ni ...を背景に: The castle looked beautiful against the blue sky. (*Sono shiro wa aozora o haikee ni utsukushiku mieta.*) その城は青空を背景に美しく見えた。

age *n.* 1 (time of life) neˈñree 年齢; toˈshiˈ 年; -sai 歳: Write your name and age here, please. (*Koko ni anata no namae to neñree o kaite kudasai.*) ここにあなたの名前と年齢を書いてください。/ She got married at the age of 22. (*Kanojo wa nijuuni-sai no toki kekkoñ shita.*) 彼女は22歳のとき結婚した。
2 (period) jiˈdai 時代: the golden age (*oogoñ jidai*) 黄金時代.

agency *n.* daˈiriˈteñ 代理店: an advertising agency (*kookoku dairiteñ*) 広告代理店.

agent *n.* daˈiriniñ 代理人; gyoˈosha 業者; eˈejeñto エージェント: a real estate agent (*fudoosañ gyoosha*) 不動産業者.

aggressive *adj.* 1 (energetic) seˈkkyoku-teki na 積極的な; kaˈppatsu na 活発な: You must be aggressive to succeed in business. (*Jigyoo ni seekoo suru ni wa sekkyoku-teki de nakereba naranai.*) 事業に成功するには積極的でなければならない。
2 (ready to attack) koˈogeki-teki na 攻撃的な; shiˈñryaku-teki na 侵略的な: an aggressive war (*shiñryaku-señsoo*) 侵略戦争.

ago *adv.* ... maˈe ni [no] ...前に[の]: He went out five minutes ago. (*Kare wa go-fuñ mae ni gaishutsu shimashita.*) 彼は5分前に外出しました。/ I saw her three days ago. (*Watashi wa mikka mae ni kanojo ni aimashita.*) 私は三日前に彼女に会いました。

long ago *adv.* zuˈtto maˈe ni ずっと前に; muˈkashi 昔.

agree *vi.*, *vt.* 1 (consent) (... ni) doˈoi suru (...に)同意する ①; saˈñsee suru 賛成する ①: I agree to your proposal. (*Anata no teeañ ni sañsee shimasu.*) あなたの提案に賛成します。
2 (match) (... to) iˈtchi suru (...と) 一致する ①: What you say does not agree with the facts. (*Kimi ga itte iru koto wa jijitsu to itchi shinai.*) 君が言っていることは事実と一致しない。

agreeable *adj.* 1 (pleasant) koˈkochi yoˈi 心地よい; kaˈñji no yoˈi 感じのよい: an agreeable voice (*kañji no yoi koe*) 感じのよい声。
2 (willing) ... ni saˈñsee shite (iru) ...に賛成して(いる): I am quite agreeable to the plan. (*Watashi wa sono añ ni mattaku sañsee desu.*) 私はその案にまったく賛成です。

agreement *n.* 1 (contract) kyoˈotee 協定; keˈeyaku 契約: make an agreement (*kyootee o musubu*) 協定を結ぶ。
2 (agreeing) iˈtchi 一致; doˈoi 同意: We are in agreement with their proposal. (*Watashi-tachi wa karera no teeañ ni dooi shite iru.*) 私たちは彼らの提案に同意している。

agriculture *n.* no͞ogyoo 農業.

ahead *adv.* **1** (in front) ze͞npoo ni 前方に; sa͞ki ni 先に: We saw a light ahead of us. (*Ze͞npoo ni akari ga mieta.*) 前方に明かりが見えた. / He walked ahead of us. (*Kare wa watashi-tachi no saki ni tatte aruita.*) 彼は私たちの先に立って歩いた.
2 (forward) sa͞ki 先: Our wedding is two weeks ahead. (*Watashi-tachi no kekko͞nshiki wa ni-shuu-ka͞n saki desu.*) 私たちの結婚式は 2 週間先です.
go ahead *vi.* sa͞ki e su͞sumu 先へ進む Ⓒ: Go ahead. (*Doozo o-saki ni.*) どうぞお先に.

aid *n.* e͞njo 援助; kyu͞ue͞n 救援: ask a person for aid (*hito ni e͞njo o motomeru*) 人に援助を求める.
— *vt.* ... o ta͞suke͞ru ...を助ける Ⓥ; te͞tsuda͞u 手伝う Ⓒ; e͞njo suru 援助する Ⓘ: He aided me in my work. (*Kare wa watashi no shigoto o tetsudatte kureta.*) 彼は私の仕事を手伝ってくれた.

aim *vi.* (... o) me͞za͞su ...を目指す Ⓒ; ne͞rau ねらう Ⓒ: He is aiming to be a lawyer. (*Kare wa be͞ngoshi o mezashite iru.*) 彼は弁護士を目指している. / aim at a target (*mato o nerau*) 的をねらう.
— *vt.* ... o (... ni) mu͞keru ...を(...に)向ける Ⓥ: He aimed a gun at me. (*Kare wa juu o watashi ni muketa.*) 彼は銃を私に向けた.
— *n.* mo͞kuteki 目的; ne͞rai ねらい: achieve one's aim (*mokuteki o tassee suru*) 目的を達成する.

air *n.* **1** (gas) ku͞uki 空気: breathe air (*kuuki o suu*) 空気を吸う.
2 (space) ku͞uchuu 空中; so͞ra 空: a balloon floating in the air (*kuuchuu ni tadayou fuuse͞n*) 空中に漂う風船.
3 (appearance) ga͞ike͞n 外見; ta͞ido 態度: assume an air of indifference (*muka͞nshi͞n na taido o toru*) 無関心な態度をとる.
be on the air *vi.* ho͞osoo sareru 放送される Ⓥ.

air conditioner *n.* e͞ako͞n エアコン; ku͞uraa クーラー.

aircraft *n.* ko͞oku͞uki 航空機.

airfield *n.* hi͞koojoo 飛行場.

air force *n.* ku͞ugu͞n 空軍.

airline *n.* ko͞oku͞uro 航空路; ko͞okuuga͞isha 航空会社: Please check other airlines' flights. (*Hoka no kookuugaisha no bi͞n o shirabete kudasai.*) ほかの航空会社の便を調べてください.

airmail *n.* ko͞okuu yu͞ubi͞n 航空郵便; ko͞okuubi͞n 航空便: What is the airmail postage for America? (*Amerika made no kookuubi͞n wa ikura desu ka?*) アメリカまでの航空便はいくらですか.

airplane *n.* hi͞ko͞oki 飛行機: get on [off] an airplane (*hikooki ni noru [o oriru]*) 飛行機に乗る[を降りる].

airport *n.* ku͞ukoo 空港: transportation to the airport (*kuukoo made no kootsuukika͞n*) 空港までの交通機関 / domestic airport (*kokunai-kuukoo*) 国内空港 / international airport (*kokusai-kuukoo*) 国際空港.

aisle *n.* tsu͞uro 通路: Aisle seat, please. (*Tsuuro gawa no seki ni shite kudasai.*) 通路側の席にしてください.

alarm clock *n.* me͞zamashi-do͞kee 目覚まし時計.

album *n.* **1** (book) a͞rubamu アルバム; (holder) -choo 帳: a photo album (*shashi͞n-choo*) 写真帳.
2 (record) a͞rubamu アルバム.

alcohol *n.* a͞rukooru アルコール; (drinks) a͞rukooru-i͞nryoo アルコール飲料.

alike *adj.* do͞oyoo na 同様な; yo͞ku ni͞te (iru) よく似て(いる): The two of them look alike. (*Futari wa yoku nite iru.*) 二人はよく似ている.
— *adv.* o͞naji yo͞o ni 同じように: treat all pupils alike (*seeto o mi͞nna onaji yoo ni atsukau*) 生徒をみんな同じように扱う.

alive *adj.* **1** i͞kite i͞ru 生きている: This fish is still alive. (*Kono sa-*

kana wa mada ikite iru.) この魚はまだ生きている.

2 ni'giwa'tte (iru) にぎわって(いる): The department store was alive with shoppers. (*Depaato wa kaimono-kyaku de nigiwatte ita.*) デパートは買い物客でにぎわっていた.

all *adj.* ze'nbu (no) 全部(の); su'bete (no) すべての; mi'nna みんな: I'd like coins of all types, please. (*Zenbu no shurui no koin ga hoshii.*) 全部の種類のコインが欲しい. / These are all my personal effects. (*Kore wa zenbu watashi no minomawari-hin desu.*) これは全部私の身の回り品です.

— *pron.* su'bete no mo'no' [hi'to'] すべてのもの[人]: I'll give you all you want. (*Hoshii mono wa subete agemasu.*) 欲しいものはすべてあげます. / All is over. (*Subete wa owatta.*) すべては終わった.

all together *adv.* ze'nbu de 全部で: How much is it all together? (*Zenbu de ikura desu ka?*) 全部でいくらですか.

allergic *adj.* a're'rugii no アレルギーの: I am allergic to antibiotics. (*Watashi wa kooseebusshitsu no arerugii ga arimasu.*) 私は抗生物質のアレルギーがあります.

allergy *n.* a're'rugii アレルギー: I have allergies. (*Watashi wa arerugii-taishitsu desu.*) 私はアレルギー体質です.

alliance *n.* do'omee 同盟; do'ome'e-koku 同盟国.

alligator *n.* wa'ni わに(鰐): alligator skin [leather] (*wani-gawa*) わに皮.

allot *vt.* ... o wa'riate'ru ...を割り当てる Ⅴ: I was alloted the difficult work. (*Watashi wa sono muzukashii shigoto o wariaterareta.*) 私はその難しい仕事を割り当てられた.

allow *vt.* **1** (permit) ... o yu'ru'su ...を許す Ⅽ; kyo'ka suru 許可する Ⅰ: We were allowed into the room. (*Watashi-tachi wa heya e hairu koto o yurusareta.*) 私たちは部

屋へ入ることを許された. / You are not allowed to take pictures here. (*Koko de shashin o totte wa ikemasen.*) ここで写真を撮ってはいけません.

2 (give) ... ni shi'kyuu suru ...に支給する Ⅰ; a'taeru 与える Ⅴ: He allows his son ten thousand yen a month. (*Kare wa musuko ni tsuki ichiman-en ataete iru.*) 彼は息子に月1万円与えている.

allowance *n.* te'ate 手当; ko'zukai こづかい; ne'biki 値引き: a weekly allowance (*is-shuukan no kozukai*) 1週間の小遣い / make an allowance of 10 per cent (*jup-paasento no nebiki o suru*) 10パーセントの値引きをする.

make allowance(s) for ... *vt.* ... o ko'ryo ni i'reru ...を考慮に入れる Ⅴ: We have to make allowances for his age. (*Kare no toshi no koto o kooryo ni irenakereba ikenai.*) 彼の年のことを考慮に入れなければいけない.

all right *adj.* **1** (satisfactory) ke'kkoo na 結構な; i'i いい: That's quite all right. (*Kekkoo desu.*) 結構です. / Is this all right? (*Kore de ii desu ka?*) これでいいですか.

2 (safe) bu'ji na 無事な; da'ijo'obu na 大丈夫な: Are you all right? (*Daijoobu desu ka?*) 大丈夫ですか.

— *adv.* **1** (yes) yo'roshii よろしい; i'i いい: " Please shut the window. " "All right. " (*"Mado o shimete kudasai." "Ii desu yo."*) 「窓を閉めてください」「いいですよ」.

2 (certainly) ta'shika ni 確かに; ma'chigai na'ku 間違いなく: I paid him all right. (*Watashi wa tashika ni kare ni haraimashita.*) 私は確かに彼に払いました.

ally *vt.* (... to) do'omee suru (...と)同盟する Ⅰ: Japan allied itself with the United States. (*Nihon wa Beekoku to doomee shita.*) 日本は米国と同盟した.

— *n.* do'ome'ekoku 同盟国.

almost *adv.* **1** (for the most part) ho'to'ndo ほとんど; ta'itee たいてい: I

almost always go to bed at eleven. (*Watashi wa hotoñdo itsu-mo juuichi-ji ni nemasu.*) 私はほとんどいつも11時に寝ます.
2 (nearly) moˈo sukoˈshi de ...⟨verb⟩ tokoro da もう少しで…ところだ: The cat was almost run over by a car. (*Sono neko wa moo sukoshi de kuruma ni hikareru tokoro datta.*) その猫はもう少しで車にひかれるところだった.

alone *adj.* taˈda hiˈtoˈri no ただひとりの; taˈñdoku no 単独の: He stayed alone at home. (*Kare wa tada hitori de ie ni ita.*) 彼はただひとりで家にいた.
— *adv.* hiˈtoˈri de ひとりで; taˈñdoku de 単独で: She came alone. (*Kanojo wa hitori de kita.*) 彼女はひとりで来た.

along *prep.* ...o toˈoˈtte ...を通って; ...ni soˈtte ...に沿って: walk along the river (*kawa ni sotte aruku*) 川に沿って歩く.
— *adv.* (onward) maˈe e 前へ; zuˈtto ずっと: Move along, please! (*Mae e susuñde kudasai.*) 前へ進んでください.

aloud *adv.* koˈe o dashite 声を出して: read aloud (*koe o dashite yomu*) 声を出して読む.

already *adv.* suˈde ni すでに; moˈo もう: I've already paid. (*Daikiñ wa moo haraimashita.*) 代金はもう払いました.

also *adv.* ...mo ...も; doˈoyoo ni 同様に: Also give me an entertainment guide, please. (*Moyooshi-mono no añnai mo kudasai.*) 催し物の案内もください.

altar *n.* saˈidañ 祭壇.

alter *vt.* ...o heˈñkoo suru ...を変更する ⎁; naˈoˈsu 直す ⎄: He altered his plans. (*Kare wa keekaku o heñkoo shita.*) 彼は計画を変更した.

alternate *vi.* koˈotai de ⟨verb⟩ 交替で…: My sister and I alternate in doing the dishes. (*Imooto to watashi wa kootai de sara o araimasu.*) 妹と私は交替で皿を洗います.

— *vt.* ...o koˈogo ni ⟨verb⟩ ...を交互に…: alternate work and play (*beñkyoo to asobi o koogo ni suru*) 勉強と遊びを交互にする.
— *adj.* koˈogo no 交互の; hiˈtotsu okiˈ no 一つおきの: I go to the hospital on alternate days. (*Watashi wa ichi-nichi oki ni byooiñ e ikimasu.*) 私は1日おきに病院へ行きます.

alternative *adj.* kaˈwari no 代[替]わりの; doˈchira ka hiˈtoˈtsu no どちらか一つの: an alternative plan (*daiañ*) 代案.
— *n.* fuˈtatsu ni hiˈtoˈtsu 二つに一つ: the alternative of going or staying (*iku ka todomaru ka futatsu ni hitotsu*) 行くかとどまるか二つに一つ.

although *conj.* ...ga ...が; ...keˈredo mo ...けれども: Although it was raining, we went out. (*Ame ga futte ita keredo mo watashi-tachi wa dekaketa.*) 雨が降っていたけれども私たちは出かけた.

altitude *n.* taˈkasa 高さ; koˈodo 高度: fly at an altitude of 10,000 meters (*koodo ichimañ meetoru de tobu*) 高度1万メートルで飛ぶ.

altogether *adv.* **1** (entirely) maˈttaku まったく; kaˈñzeñ ni 完全に: He gave it up altogether. (*Kare wa sore o kañzeñ ni akirameta.*) 彼はそれを完全にあきらめた.
2 (on the whole) zeˈñbu de 全部で; goˈokee de 合計で: That comes to 5,000 yen altogether. (*Zeñbu de goseñ-eñ ni narimasu.*) 全部で5千円になります.

always *adv.* iˈtsu-mo いつも; tsuˈne ni 常に: He always comes late. (*Kare wa itsu-mo okurete kuru.*) 彼はいつも遅れて来る. / I got up at six as always. (*Watashi wa itsu-mo no yoo ni roku-ji ni okita.*) 私はいつものように6時に起きた.
not always *adv.* kaˈnarazuˈshimo ... to wa kaˈgiraˈnai 必ずしも…とは限らない: The rich are not always happy. (*Kanemochi ga kanarazu shimo shiawase da to wa kagira-nai.*) 金持ちが必ずしも幸せだとは限らな

い.

a.m. goˈzeñ 午前; aˈsa 朝: I'm leaving at 8 a.m. tomorrow. (*Watashi wa asu no asa hachi-ji ni tachimasu.*) 私は明日の朝8時に発ちます.

amateur *n.* aˈmachua アマチュア; shiˈrooto しろうと.

amaze *vt.* ... o biˈkkuri saseru ...をびっくりさせる ▽: I was amazed to learn that he won the prize. (*Kare ga sono shoo o totta koto o shitte, bikkuri shita.*) 彼がその賞を取ったことを知って、びっくりした.

amazement *n.* oˈdorokiˈ 驚き; kyoˈotañ 驚嘆: in amazement (bikkuri shite) びっくりして / to one's amazement (*odoroita koto ni wa*) 驚いたことには.

ambassador *n.* taˈishi 大使: an ambassador to Japan (*chuunichi taishi*) 駐日大使.

ambition *n.* taˈimoo 大望; yaˈshiñ 野心: I have no ambition to be a politician. (*Watashi ni wa seejika ni naru yashiñ wa arimaseñ.*) 私には政治家になる野心はありません.

ambitious *adj.* taˈimoo [yaˈshiñ] ga aru 大望[野心]がある; yaˈshiñ-teki na 野心的な: He is ambitious for fame. (*Kare ni wa yuumee ni naritai to iu yashiñ ga aru.*) 彼には有名になりたいという野心がある.

ambulance *n.* kyuˈukyuuˈusha 救急車: call for an ambulance (*kyuukyuusha o yobu*) 救急車を呼ぶ.

amend *vt.* ... o kaˈisee [shuˈusee] suru ...を改正[修正]する ▽: amend the constitution (*keñpoo o kaisee suru*) 憲法を改正する.

America *n.* Aˈmerika アメリカ; Beˈekoku 米国: the United States of America (*Amerika gasshuukoku*) アメリカ合衆国.

American *n.* Aˈmerikaˈjiñ アメリカ人; Beˈekokuˈmiñ 米国民.
— *adj.* Aˈmerika no アメリカの; Beˈekoku no 米国の: the American language (*beego*) 米語.

among *prep.* **1** (surrounded by) ... ni kaˈkomarete (iru) ...に囲まれて(いる): a village among the mountains (*yama ni kakomareta mura*) 山に囲まれた村.
2 (in the group of) ... no naˈka [aˈida] de ...の中[間]で: Among all the flowers, I like the rose best. (*Hana no naka de watashi wa bara ga ichibañ suki desu.*) 花の中で私はバラがいちばん好きです.

amount *n.* **1** (of money) gaˈku 額; (quantity) ryoˈo 量: spend a large amount of money (*tagaku no o-kane o tsukau*) 多額のお金を使う / a small amount of butter (*shooryoo no bataa*) 少量のバター.
2 (total) soˈogaku 総額; soˈosuˈu 総数: The amount of the bill comes to 5,000 yen. (*Kañjoo no soogaku wa go-señ-eñ ni narimasu.*) 勘定の総額は5千円になります.
— *vi.* (... ni) taˈssuru (...に)達する ▽; naˈru なる ▣: His debts amount to a million yen. (*Kare no shakkiñ wa hyaku-mañ-eñ ni tassuru.*) 彼の借金は100万円に達する.

ample *adj.* juˈubuˈñ na 十分な; hoˈofu na 豊富な: ample food (*juubuñ na shokuryoo*) 十分な食料.

amuse *vt.* ... o taˈnoshimaseˈru ...を楽しませる ▽; oˈmoshirogaraseˈru おもしろがらせる ▽: His story amused everyone. (*Kare no hanashi wa miñna o tanoshimaseta.*) 彼の話はみんなを楽しませました.

amusement *n.* taˈnoshiˈmi 楽しみ; goˈraku 娯楽: I play the piano for amusement. (*Watashi wa tanoshimi ni piano o hikimasu.*) 私は楽しみにピアノを弾きます. / There are plenty of amusements in this town. (*Kono machi ni wa goraku ga takusañ aru.*) この町には娯楽がたくさんある.

amusement park *n.* yuˈueˈñchi 遊園地.

amusing *adj.* oˈmoshiroˈi おもしろい; oˈkashiˈi おかしい: an amusing story (*omoshiroi hanashi*) おもしろい話.

analogy *n.* ruˈiji 類似: He drew an

analogy between the two events. (*Kare wa futatsu no jikeñ no ruiji o shiteki shita.*) 彼は二つの事件の類似を指摘した.

analysis *n.* buⁿseki 分析: make an analysis of the situation (*joosee no buñseki o suru*) 情勢の分析をする.

analyze *vt.* ... o buⁿseki suru ...を分析する Ⅰ; keⁿtoo suru 検討する Ⅰ: He analyzed the sales figures. (*Kare wa uriage no suuji o buñseki shita.*) 彼は売り上げの数字を分析した.

ancestor *n.* seⁿzo 先祖; soⁿseñ 祖先.

anchor *n.* iⁿkari いかり: cast anchor (*ikari o orosu*) いかりを下ろす.

ancient *adj.* koⁿdai no 古代の; muⁿkashi no 昔の: ancient civilization (*kodai-buñmee*) 古代文明.

and *conj.* **1** (*n. and n.*) to と: a chair and table (*isu to teeburu*) いすとテーブル / 3 and 2 makes 5. (*Sañ to ni de go ni naru.*) 3と2で5になる. **2** (*v. and v.*) ⟨verb⟩-tari ⟨verb⟩-tari ...たり...たり: We sang and danced. (*Watashi-tachi wa utattari odottari shita.*) 私たちは歌ったり踊ったりした. **3** (phrase and phrase) soⁿshite そして; ⟨verb⟩-te[de] ...て[で]: She played the piano and I sang. (*Kanojo ga piano o hiite watashi ga utatta.*) 彼女がピアノを弾いて私が歌った. / I opened the door and went inside. (*Watashi wa doa o akete naka e haitta.*) 私はドアを開けて中へ入った. **4** (as a result) ⟨verb⟩-ba ...ば: Work hard and you will succeed. (*Isshoo-keñmee yareba seekoo shimasu.*) 一生懸命やれば成功します.

anecdote *n.* iⁿtsuwa 逸話.

angel *n.* teⁿnshi 天使.

anger *n.* iⁿkari 怒り: hold back one's anger (*ikari o osaeru*) 怒りを抑える.
in anger *adv., adj.* oⁿkotte 怒って: She tore up the letter in anger. (*Kanojo wa okotte sono tegami o*

yabuita.) 彼女は怒ってその手紙を破いた.

angle *n.* kaⁿku 角; kaⁿkudo 角度: a right angle (*chokkaku*) 直角 / consider from various angles (*iroiro na kakudo kara kañgaeru*) いろいろな角度から考える.

angry *adj.* oⁿkotte (iru) 怒って(いる); haⁿra o taⁿtete (iru) 腹を立てて(いる): He soon gets angry. (*Kare wa sugu okoru.*) 彼はすぐ怒る. / She looked angry. (*Kanojo wa okotta kao o shita.*) 彼女は怒った顔をした.

animal *n.* doⁿobutsu 動物.

ankle *n.* aⁿshiⁿkubi 足首; kuⁿruⁿbushi くるぶし: I think I sprained my ankle. (*Ashikubi o kujiita rashii.*) 足首をくじいたらしい.

annex *n.* beⁿkkañ 別館.

anniversary *n.* kiⁿneⁿñbi 記念日: a wedding anniversary (*kekkoñ kineñbi*) 結婚記念日.

announce *vt.* ... o haⁿppyoo suru ...を発表する Ⅰ; shiⁿraseru 知らせる Ⅴ: They announced their engagement. (*Futari wa koñyaku o happyoo shita.*) 二人は婚約を発表した.

announcement *n.* haⁿppyoo 発表; tsuⁿuchi 通知: I read the announcement in a newspaper. (*Sono happyoo o shiñbuñ de yomimashita.*) その発表を新聞で読みました.

announcer *n.* aⁿnauⁿñsaa アナウンサー.

annoy *vt.* ... o koⁿmaraseⁿru 困らせる Ⅴ; naⁿyamaⁿsu 悩ます Ⓒ: The crying baby annoyed her. (*Naite iru akañbo ga kanojo o komaraseta.*) 泣いている赤ん坊が彼女を困らせた.

annual *adj.* maⁿitoshi no 毎年の; iⁿchi-neⁿñkañ no 1年間の: an annual income (*neñshuu*) 年収.

annul *vt.* ... o haⁿrikesu ...を取り消す Ⓒ; muⁿkoo ni suru 無効にする Ⅰ: annul a contract (*keeyaku o mukoo ni suru*) 契約を無効にする.

anonymous *adj.* toⁿkumee no 匿名の; (of a book) saⁿkusha fuⁿmee no 作者不明の: an anonymous let-

ter (*tokumee no tegami*) 匿名の手
紙.

another *adj.* **1** (one more) moﾌ
hitoﾑtsu [hitoﾑri] no もう一つ[一人]の:
How about another cup of tea?
(*Ocha o moo ip-pai ikaga desu
ka?*) お茶をもう1杯いかがですか.
2 (different) beﾑtsu no 別の; hoﾑka
no ほかの: Can you recommend another hotel? (*Hoka no hoteru o
shookai shite kuremaseñ ka?*) ほか
のホテルを紹介してくれませんか. / Show
me another one, please. (*Hoka no o
misete kudasai.*) ほかのを見せてくださ
い.

answer *n.* koﾑtaeﾑru 答え; heﾑñji 返
事: This answer is wrong. (*Kono
kotae wa machigatte iru.*) この答え
は間違っている. / Please give me
your answer soon. (*Go-heñji o sugu ni kudasai.*) ご返事をすぐに下さ
い.
— *vt.* ... ni koﾑtaeﾑru 答える Ⅴ; he-
ﾑñji o suru 返事をする Ⅰ: Nobody
answered the question. (*Dare mo
sono shitsumoñ ni kotaenakatta.*)
だれもその質問に答えなかった. / I will
answer you later. (*Ato de heñji o
shimasu.*) あとで返事をします.
— *vi.* koﾑtaeﾑru 答える Ⅴ; heﾑñji o
suru 返事をする Ⅰ: Please answer in
English. (*Eego de kotaete kudasai.*)
英語で答えてください.

ant *n.* aﾑri あり.

Antarctic *adj.* naﾑñkyoku no 南極
の: an Antarctic expedition (*nañkyoku tañkeñ*) 南極探検.
— *n.* naﾑñkyoku 南極.

anticipate *vt.* **1** (expect) ... to yo-
ﾑsoo suru ...を予想する Ⅰ: I'm an-
ticipating a large attendance today.
(*Kyoo wa shussekisha ga ooi to
yosoo shite imasu.*) きょうは出席者が
多いと予想しています.
2 (act in advance) ... ni seﾑñte o
uﾑtsu ...に先手を打つ Ⓒ: I anticipated his questions. (*Watashi wa
kare no shitsumoñ ni señte o utta.*)
私は彼の質問に先手を打った.

antique *n.* koﾑttoohiñ 骨董品;
aﾑñtiﾑiku アンティーク: Is there an an-

tiques dealer near here? (*Kono chikaku ni kottoo-ya wa arimasu
ka?*) この近くに骨董屋はありますか.

anxiety *n.* shiﾑñpai 心配; fuﾑañ 不
安: cause a person anxiety (*hito ni
shiñpai o kakeru*) 人に心配をかける.

anxious *adj.* **1** (feeling uneasy)
shiﾑñpai shite (iru) 心配して(いる): I
am anxious about his health. (*Kare
no keñkoo no koto ga shiñpai
desu.*) 彼の健康のことが心配です.
2 (eager) seﾑtsuboo shite (iru) 切望
して(いる); <verb>-tagaﾑtte iru ...た
がっている: She is anxious to meet
you. (*Kanojo wa anata ni aitagatte
iru.*) 彼女はあなたに会いたがっている.

any *adj.* **1** (some) iﾑkuraﾑka no いく
らかの. ★ Not translated in Japa-
nese: Do you have any children?
(*O-ko-sañ wa o-ari desu ka?*) お子
さんはおありですか. / Are there any letters for me? (*Watashi ate no tegami ga todoite imasu ka?*) 私あて
の手紙が届いていますか.
2 (every) doﾑno [doﾑñna] ... de mo
どの[どんな]...でも: Any dictionary
will do. (*Dono jisho de mo kekkoo
desu.*) どの辞書でも結構です.

anybody *pron.* **1** [in negative] da-
ﾑre mo だれも; [interrogative] daﾑre-
ka だれか: I have't seen anybody.
(*Watashi wa dare mo mimaseñ
deshita.*) 私はだれも見ませんでした. / Is
there anybody who can help me?
(*Dare-ka tetsudatte kureru hito
wa imaseñ ka?*) だれか手伝ってくれる
人はいませんか.
2 [in affirmative] daﾑre de mo だれ
でも: Anybody can do a thing like
that. (*Soñna koto wa dare de mo
dekimasu.*) そんなことはだれでもできます.

anyhow *adv.* toﾑnikaku とにかく;
iﾑzure ni shiteﾑ mo いずれにしても:
Anyhow, let's begin. (*Tonikaku
hajimeyoo.*) とにかく始めよう.

anything *pron.* **1** (something)
naﾑni-ka 何か; naﾑni mo 何も: I
don't know anything about it.
(*Sore ni tsuite watashi wa nani
mo shirimaseñ.*) それについて私は何も

知りません.

2 (thing) mo｢no｣ 物: Is there anything cheaper? (*Motto yasui mono wa arimasu ka?*) もっと安い物はありますか.

anyway *adv.* to｢nikaku とにかく; i｢zure ni se｣yo いずれにせよ: Anyway, let's get to work. (*Tonikaku shigoto o hajimeyoo.*) とにかく仕事を始めよう.

anywhere *adv.* **1** [in negative] do｢ko e mo どこへも; [interrogative] do｢ko-ka ni [de] どこかに[で]: Did you see my glasses anywhere? (*Doko-ka de watashi no megane o mimashita ka?*) どこかで私の眼鏡をみましたか. / I didn't go anywhere yesterday. (*Kinoo wa doko e mo ikanakatta.*) きのうはどこへも行かなかった. **2** [in affirmative] do｢ko e de mo どこへでも: You can go anywhere you like. (*Doko e de mo suki na tokoro e itte ii desu yo.*) どこへでも好きな所へ行っていいですよ.

apart *adv.* ha｢na｣rete 離れて; ba｢rabara ni ばらばらに: They live apart. (*Kare-ra wa hanarete kurashite iru.*) 彼らは離れて暮らしている.

apartment *n.* a｢pa｣ato アパート; ma｢nshoñ マンション. ★ In Japan 'apaato' usually refers to an apartment house. 'Apaato' customarily refers to one- or two-storied wooden structures and is less prestigious than 'mañshoñ,' which often refers to a condominium.

apologize *vi.* a｢yama｣ru 謝る ⓒ; wa｢biru わびる Ⓥ: He apologized to her for being late. (*Kare wa okureta koto o kanojo ni ayamatta.*) 彼は遅れたことを彼女に謝った.

apology *n.* wa｢bi わび; sha｢zai 謝罪: make an apology (*wabi o iu*) わびを言う.

apparatus *n.* ki｢gu 器具; so｢ochi 装置: a heating apparatus (*dañboo soochi*) 暖房装置.

apparent *adj.* a｢ki｣raka na 明らかな; ha｢kki｣ri shite iru はっきりしている: This fact is apparent to everybody.

(*Kono jijitsu wa dare no me ni mo akiraka desu.*) この事実はだれの目にも明らかです.

apparently *adv.* mi｢ta tokoro ... ra｢shi｣i 見たところ...らしい: She was apparently happy. (*Kanojo wa mita tokoro shiawase rashikatta.*) 彼女は見たところ幸せらしかった.

appeal *n.* **1** (request) o-｢nega｣i お願い; u｢ttae 訴え: an appeal for help (*eñjo no o-negai*) 援助のお願い. **2** (of a law) ko｢oso 控訴.
— *vi.* **1** (ask for) (... ni) (... o) ta｢no｣mu (...に)(...を)頼む ⓒ: We appealed to him for support. (*Watashi-tachi wa kare ni shiji o tanoñda.*) 私たちは彼に支持を頼んだ. **2** (attract) (... ni) u｢ke｣ru (...に)受ける Ⓥ: The novel appealed to young people. (*Sono shoosetsu wa wakai hito-tachi ni uketa.*) その小説は若い人たちに受けた. **3** (against a legal judgment) ko｢oso suru 控訴する Ⓘ.

appear *vi.* **1** (become visible) a｢raware｣ru 現れる Ⓥ: The moon appeared from behind the mountain. (*Tsuki ga yama no kage kara arawareta.*) 月が山の影から現れた. **2** (present oneself) ... ni de｢ru ...に出る; shu｢tsueñ suru 出演する: appear on television (*terebi ni deru*) テレビに出る. **3** (seem likely) ... ra｢shiku mi｢e｣ru ...らしく見える Ⓥ; ... yo｢o da ...ようだ: He appears to have caught a cold. (*Kare wa kaze o hiite iru yoo da.*) 彼はかぜをひいているようだ.

appearance *n.* **1** (act of appearing) shu｢sseki 出席; shu｢tsujoo 出場: make an appearance at a party (*paatii ni shusseki suru*) パーティーに出席する. **2** (outward form) ga｢ikañ 外観; mi｢kake 見かけ: You should not judge by appearances. (*Mikake de hañdañ shite wa ikenai.*) 見かけで判断してはいけない.

appendicitis *n.* [technically] chu｢usu｣ieñ 虫垂炎; [popularly] moˈochoˌloeñ 盲腸炎: have appendicitis (*moochoo ni naru*) 盲腸になる.

appendix *n.* 1 (of a book) fuˈroku 付録.

2 (bodily organ) chuˈusui 虫垂; [popularly] moˌlochoo 盲腸.

appetite *n.* shoˈkuyoku 食欲: I have a good [poor] appetite. (*Watashi wa shokuyoku ga aru [nai].*) 私は食欲がある[ない].

applaud *vt.* ... ni haˈkushu o oˈkuru ...に拍手を送る Ⓒ: The audience applauded the actor. (*Kañkyaku wa sono haiyuu ni hakushu o okutta.*) 観客はその俳優に拍手を送った.
— *vi.* haˈkushu suru 拍手する Ⓘ; hoˈlmeˈlru ほめる Ⓥ.

applause *n.* haˌlkushu 拍手: win the applause of the audience (*kañshuu no hakushu o abiru*) 観衆の拍手を浴びる.

apple *n.* riˈlñgo りんご: peel an apple (*riñgo no kawa o muku*) りんごの皮をむく.

applicant *n.* oˈobolsha 応募者; moˈoshikomiˈlsha 申込者: an applicant for a job (*kyuushokusha*) 求職者.

application *n.* 1 (formal request) moˈoshikomi 申し込み; shiˈlñsee 申請: make an application for a job (*shigoto no mooshikomi o suru*) 仕事の申し込みをする.

2 (use) teˈlkiyoo 適用; oˈoyoo 応用: the application of law (*hoo no tekiyoo*) 法の適用.

apply *vi.* 1 (formally request) (... ni) (... o) moˈoshikomu (...に)(...を) 申し込む Ⓒ; shiˈlñsee suru 申請する Ⓘ: I applied for a visa. (*Watashi wa biza no shiñsee o shita.*) 私はビザの申請をした.

2 (fit) (... ni) aˈltehamaˈlru ...に当てはまる Ⓒ; teˈlkigoo suru 適合する Ⓘ: The rule does not apply to this case. (*Sono kisoku wa kono baai atehamaranai.*) その規則はこの場合当てはまらない.
— *vt.* 1 (make use of) ... o (... ni)

oˈoyoo suru ...を(...に)応用する Ⓘ; teˈlkiyoo suru 適用する Ⓘ: apply new technology to industry (*atarashii gijutsu o sañgyoo ni ooyoo suru*) 新しい技術を産業に応用する.

2 (put) ... o aˈlteru ...を当てる Ⓥ; haˈlru はる Ⓒ: apply plaster to a wound (*kizuguchi ni kooyaku o haru*) 傷口にこう薬をはる.

appoint *vt.* 1 (assign) ... o (... ni) niˈlñmee suru ...を(...に)任命する Ⓘ; shiˈlmee suru 指名する Ⓘ: They appointed Mr. Yamada chairman. (*Kare-ra wa Yamada-sañ o gichoo ni shimee shita.*) 彼らは山田さんを議長に指名した. / He was appointed professor. (*Kare wa kyooju ni niñmee sareta.*) 彼は教授に任命された.

2 (fix) ... o shiˈltee suru ...を指定する Ⓘ: appoint the date and place for a meeting (*kaigi no nichiji to basho o shitee suru*) 会議の日時と場所を指定する.

appointment *n.* yaˈlkusoku 約束; yoˈlyaku 予約; aˈlpolñtomeñto アポイントメント: I'd like an appointment for 3 p.m. today. (*Kyoo no sañ-ji ni yoyaku o onegai shitai ñ desu ga.*) きょうの3時に予約をお願いしたいんですが. / make an appointment (*apoiñtomeñto o toru*) アポイントメントをとる.

appreciate *vt.* 1 (be grateful) ... ni kaˈlñsha suru ...に感謝する Ⓘ; ... o aˈlrigataˈlku oˈlmolu ...をありがたく思う Ⓒ: I do appreciate your kindness. (*Anata no go-shiñsetsu ni kañsha shimasu.*) あなたのご親切に感謝します.

2 (enjoy) ... o kaˈlñshoo suru ...を鑑賞する Ⓘ: appreciate good music (*yoi oñgaku o kañshoo suru*) よい音楽を鑑賞する.

appreciation *n.* 1 (grateful recognition) kaˈlñsha 感謝: I'd like to express my appreciation for your help. (*Go-eñjo ni taishite kañsha mooshiagemasu.*) ご援助にたいして感謝申し上げます.

2 (sensitive awareness) kaˈlñshoo

鑑賞: appreciation of music (*on-gaku no kanshoo*) 音楽の鑑賞.

approach *vt.* ... ni chiʳkazuʰku ...に近づく C; seʳkkin suru 接近する I: A typhoon is approaching Kyushu. (*Taifuu ga Kyuushuu ni sekkin shite iru.*) 台風が九州に接近している.

— *vi.* chiʳkazuʰku 近づく C: Christmas is approaching. (*Kurisumasu ga chikazuite iru.*) クリスマスが近づいている.

appropriate *adj.* teʳkitoo na 適当な; teʳkisetsu na 適切な: take appropriate measures (*tekisetsu na shochi o toru*) 適切な処置をとる.
— *vt.* ... o aʳteru ...（...に）充てる V: appropriate the money for repaying a loan (*sono o-kane o roon hensai ni ateru*) そのお金をローン返済に充てる.

approval *n.* saʳnsee 賛成; doʰoi 同意: receive a person's approval (*hito no sansee o eru*) 人の賛成を得る.

approve *vt.* ... ni saʳnsee suru ...に賛成する I; ... o shoʳonin suru ...を承認する I: The committee approved the budget. (*linkai wa yosanan o shoonin shita.*) 委員会は予算案を承認した.

April *n.* shi-ʳgatsuʰ 四月.

apron *n.* eʰpuron エプロン: put on an apron (*epuron o kakeru*) エプロンをかける.

apt *adj.* ⟨verb⟩-ʳgachi da ...がちだ; yoʰku ⟨verb⟩ よく...: We are apt to waste time. (*Watashi-tachi wa jikan o muda ni shi-gachi da.*) 私たちは時間を無益にしがちだ. / I am apt to forget people's names. (*Watashi wa yoku hito no namae o wasureru.*) 私はよく人の名前を忘れる.

aquarium *n.* suʳizoku¹kan 水族館.

arbitrary *adj.* niʰni no 任意の; kaʳtte na 勝手な: an arbitrary choice (*katte na sentaku*) 勝手な選択.

arcade *n.* aʳake¹edo アーケード.

arch *n.* aʰachi アーチ.

architect *n.* keʳnchikuka 建築家.

architecture *n.* (art) keʳnchiku-gaku 建築学; keʳnchiku-giʰjutsu 建築技術; (style) keʳnchiku-yoʰoshiki 建築様式: a church of ancient architecture (*kodai kenchiku-yooshiki no kyookai*) 古代建築様式の教会.

Arctic *adj.* hoʳkkyoku no 北極の: an Arctic expedition (*hokkyoku tanken*) 北極探検.
— *n.* hoʳkkyoku 北極; hoʳkkyoku chiʰhoo 北極地方.

ardent *adj.* neʰsshin na 熱心な; neʳtsuretsu na 熱烈な: an ardent supporter of the ruling party (*yotoo no netsuretsu na shijisha*) 与党の熱烈な支持者.

area *n.* **1** (space) meʰnseki 面積: The area of this floor is 30 square meters. (*Kono yuka no menseki wa sanjuu heehoo meetoru desu.*) この床の面積は30平方メートルです. **2** (region) chiʰiki 地域; chiʰhoo 地方: What type of cooking is this area known for? (*Kono chihoo no meebutsu ryoori wa nan desu ka?*) この地方の名物料理は何ですか.

argue *vi.* (quarrel) koʰoron suru 口論する I; (discuss) giʰron suru 議論する I: I argued with him about the novel. (*Watashi wa sono shoosetsu ni tsuite kare to giron shita.*) 私はその小説について彼と議論した.
— *vt.* ... o roʳnjiru ...を論じる V; seʳttoku suru 説得する I: We argued politics. (*Watashi-tachi wa seeji o ronjita.*) 私たちは政治を論じた.

argument *n.* (quarrel) koʰoron 口論; (discussion) giʰron 議論: They had an argument about the plan. (*Kare-ra wa sono keekaku ni tsuite giron shita.*) 彼らはその計画について議論した.

arise *vi.* oʰkoʰru 起こる C; shoʳojiru 生じる V: A difficult problem has arisen. (*Muzukashii mondai ga okotta.*) むずかしい問題が起こった.

arithmetic *n.* saʰnsuʰu 算数.

arm[1] *n.* uʰde¹ 腕: The couple were walking arm in arm. (*Futari wa* *ude o kuñde aruite ita.*) 二人は腕を組んで歩いていた.

arm² *vt.* ... de bu「soo suru ...で武装する ⓣ: arm oneself with a gun (*juu de busoo suru*) 銃で武装する.

arms *n.* he「eki 兵器; bu」ki 武器: bear arms (*buki o motsu*) 武器を持つ.

army *n.* ri「ku」guñ 陸軍; gu「ñtai 軍隊.

around *prep.* **1** (circuit) ... no ma「wari o [ni] ...の周りを[に]; ... o ka「koñde ...を囲んで: run around a tree (*ki no mawari o hashiru*) 木の周りを走る / sit around a fire (*hi o kakoñde suwaru*) 火を囲んで座る. **2** (here and there) a「chi-ko」chi あちこち: travel around the country (*kuni-juu achi-kochi tabi o suru*) 国中あちこち旅をする. **3** (near) ... no a「tari no ...の辺りに: Her house is around here. (*Kanojo no uchi wa kono atari desu.*) 彼女の家はこの辺りです.
— *adv.* ma「wari ni 周りに; a」tari ni 辺りに; gu「ru」ri to くるりと: the scenery around (*mawari no keshiki*) 周りの景色 / look around (*atari o mimawasu*) 辺りを見回す / go around (*mawarimichi o suru*) 回り道をする / hand the papers around (*shorui o mawasu*) 書類を回す.

arouse *vt.* ... o hi「kioko」su ...を引き起こす ⓒ; ma「ne」ku 招く ⓒ: arouse a person's anger (*hito no ikari o maneku*) 人の怒りを招く.

arrange *vt.* **1** (put into order) ... o ki「chi」ñto na「raberu ...をきちんと並べる Ⓥ: arrange the chairs (*isu o kichiñto naraberu*) 椅子をきちんと並べる / arrange flowers (*hana o ikeru*) 花を生ける. **2** (plan) ... o ki「meru ...を決める Ⓥ; te「hai suru 手配する ⓣ: We will arrange the details later. (*Komakai koto wa ato de kimemasu.*) 細かいことは後で決めます. / arrange a car (*kuruma o tehai suru*) 車を手配する.

arrangement *n.* kyo「otee 協定; ju「ñbi 準備; ha「iretsu 配列: come

to an arrangement (*kyootee ga seeritsu suru*) 協定が成立する / make the arrangements for one's trip (*ryokoo no juñbi o suru*) 旅行の準備をする.

arrest *vt.* ... o ta「iho suru ...を逮捕する ⓣ: arrest a thief (*doroboo o taiho suru*) 泥棒を逮捕する.
— *n.* ta「iho 逮捕.

arrival *n.* to「ochaku 到着: arrival time (*toochaku jikañ*) 到着時間.

arrive *vi.* **1** (get to) (... ni) tsu「ku (...に)着く ⓒ; to「ochaku suru 到着する ⓣ: This train arrives at Kyoto at three. (*Kono ressha wa sañ-ji ni Kyooto ni tsukimasu.*) この列車は3時に京都に着きます. / When did the letter arrive? (*Sono tegami wa itsu tsukimashita ka?*) その手紙はいつ着きましたか. **2** (reach) (... ni) ta「ssuru (...に)達する ⓣ: arrive at a conclusion (*ketsuroñ ni tassuru*) 結論に達する.

art *n.* ge「ejutsu 芸術; bi「jutsu 美術: an art museum (*bijutsu-kañ*) 美術館.

article *n.* **1** (account) ki「ji 記事; ro「ñbuñ 論文: an article in a magazine (*zasshi no kiji*) 雑誌の記事. **2** (thing) shi「namono 品物; -hiñ 品: prohibited articles (*mochikomi kiñshi-hiñ*) 持込み禁止品. **3** (clause) jo「okoo 条項: the articles of an agreement (*kyootee no jookoo*) 協定の条項. **4** (of grammar) ka「ñshi 冠詞: a definite [an indefinite] article (*tee [futee]-kañshi*) 定[不定]冠詞.

artificial *adj.* ji「ñkoo no 人工の; ji「ñzoo no 人造の: artificial respiration (*jiñkoo kokyuu*) 人工呼吸 / an artificial flower (*zooka*) 造花.

artist *n.* **1** ge「ejutsuka 芸術家. **2** (painter) ga「ka 画家; e「kaki」 絵かき.

artistic *adj.* ge「ejutsu-teki na 芸術的な: artistic beauty (*geejutsu-teki na utsukushisa*) 芸術的な美しさ.

as *conj.* **1** (in the way) ... no yo」o ni ...のように; to「ori ni とおりに: Do as

you are told. (*Iwareta toori ni shi nasai.*) 言われたとおりにしなさい.
2 (when) ⟨verb⟩ to「ki (ni) …とき(に); (verb) ni tsu「rete …につれて: Just as I was going to bed, there was an earthquake. (*Choodo neyoo to shita toki jishiñ ga atta.*) ちょうど寝ようとしたとき地震があった. / As we grow older, we become forgetful. (*Toshi o toru ni tsurete wasureppoku naru.*) 年をとるにつれて忘れっぽくなる.
3 (because) … no de …ので; … kara …から: As it rained, I didn't go. (*Ame ga futta no de, watashi wa ikanakatta.*) 雨が降ったので私は行かなかった.
— *prep.* (role) … to shi「te …として: He attended the meeting as an observer. (*Kare wa sono kaigi ni obuzaabaa to shite shusseki shita.*) 彼はその会議にオブザーバーとして出席した.
— *pron.* … no yo「o na …のような: Give me the same thing as this. (*Kore to onaji yoo na mono o kudasai.*) これと同じようなものを下さい.
as … as … to o「naji ku「rai …と同じくらい: He is as tall as I am. (*Kare no se no takasa wa watashi to onaji kurai desu.*) 彼の背の高さは私と同じくらいです.

ascertain *vt.* … o ta「shikame「ru …を確かめる Ⓥ: I ascertained the facts. (*Watashi wa sono jijitsu o tashikameta.*) 私はその事実を確かめた.

ash *n.* ha「i 灰: cigarette ash (*tabako no hai*) たばこの灰.

ashamed *adj.* ha「zukashi「i 恥ずかしい: I am ashamed of myself for having done such a thing. (*Watashi wa soñna koto o shite hazukashiku omou.*) 私はそんなことをして恥ずかしく思う.

ashtray *n.* ha「izara 灰皿.

aside *adv.* wa「ki「i わきに: pull a curtain aside (*kaateñ o waki ni hiku*) カーテンをわきに引く / lay a book aside (*hoñ o waki ni oku*) 本をわきに置く.

ask *vt.* **1** (inquire) … ni ki「ku …に聞く Ⓒ; ta「zune「ru 尋ねる Ⓥ: Let's ask him about it. (*Sono koto ni tsuite kare ni kiite mimashoo.*) そのことについて彼に聞いてみましょう. / I asked her her address. (*Watashi wa kanojo ni juusho o tazuneta.*) 私は彼女に住所を尋ねた.
2 (request) … ni (… o) ta「no「mu …に(…を)頼む Ⓒ: I asked him to reserve a room at a hotel. (*Watashi wa kare ni hoteru no heya no yoyaku o tanoñda.*) 私は彼にホテルの部屋の予約を頼んだ.

ask for … *vt.* … o mo「tome「ru …を求める Ⓥ: ask for his advice (*kare no jogeñ o motomeru*) 彼の助言を求める.

asleep *adj.* **1** (sleep) ne「mutte (iru) 眠って(いる): The baby is fast asleep. (*Akañboo wa gussuri nemutte iru.*) 赤ん坊はぐっすり眠っている.
2 (of a limb) shi「bi「rete (iru) しびれて(いる): My left foot is asleep. (*Hidari ashi ga shibireta.*) 左足がしびれた.

aspire *vi.* (… o) ne「tsuboo suru (…を熱望する Ⓘ; no「zomu 望む Ⓒ: He aspired to the position. (*Kare wa sono chii o nozoñde ita.*) 彼はその地位を望んでいた.

aspirin *n.* a「supiriñ アスピリン: take two aspirins (*asupiriñ o ni-joo nomu*) アスピリンを2錠飲む.

assault *vt.* … o shu「ugeki suru …を襲撃する Ⓘ; o「so「u 襲う Ⓒ: The robber assaulted the guard. (*Gootoo ga keebiiñ o osotta.*) 強盗が警備員を襲った.
— *n.* shu「ugeki 襲撃; (rape) bo「okoo 暴行.

assemble *vt.* **1** (gather) … o a「tsume「ru …を集める Ⓥ: assemble the students in a hall (*seeto o hooru ni atsumeru*) 生徒をホールに集める.
2 (put together) … o ku「mitate「ru …を組み立てる Ⓥ: assemble a bicycle (*jiteñsha o kumitateru*) 自転車を組み立てる.
— *vi.* a「tsuma「ru 集まる Ⓒ.

assembly n. 1 (of people) shu「ukai 集会; ka「igoo 会合: The assembly will be held tomorrow. (Shuukai wa ashita hirakaremasu.) 集会はあした開かれます.
2 (legislative body) gi「kai 議会: the city assembly (shi-gikai) 市議会.
3 (of parts) ku「mitate 組立: assembly plant (kumitate-koojoo) 組立工場.

assert vt. 1 (insist) ... o shu「choo suru ...を主張する Ⓣ: assert one's rights (jibuñ no keñri o shuchoo suru) 自分の権利を主張する.
2 (declare) ... to da「ñgeñ suru ...と断言する Ⓣ; ha「kki「ri i「u はっきり言う Ⓒ: He asserted that he had seen it. (Kare wa sore o mita to dañgeñ shita.) 彼はそれを見たと断言した.

assign vt. 1 (allot) ... o wa「riate」ru ...を割り当てる Ⓥ: I assigned the room to them. (Watashi wa sono heya o kare-ra ni wariateta.) 私はその部屋を彼らに割り当てた.
2 (fix) ... o shi「tee suru ...を指定する Ⓣ; ki「meru 決める Ⓥ: assign a day for the meeting (kaigi no hi o kimeru) 会議の日を決める.

assignment n. shu「kudai 宿題; wa「riate 割り当て: a summer assignment (natsuyasumi no shukudai) 夏休みの宿題.

assist vt. ... o te「tsuda」u ...を手伝う Ⓒ; e「ñjo suru 援助する Ⓣ: I assisted him with his work. (Watashi wa kare no shigoto o tetsudatta.) 私は彼の仕事を手伝った.
— vi. jo「ryoku suru 助力する Ⓣ.

assistance n. e「ñjo 援助; jo「ryoku 助力: give economic assistance (keezai eñjo o suru) 経済援助をする.

assistant n. jo「shu 助手.

assistant professor n. jo-「kyo「oju 助教授.

associate vi. ko「osai suru 交際する Ⓣ: associate with many people (ooku no hito to koosai suru) 多くの人と交際する.
— vt. ... o re「ñsoo suru ... を連想

する Ⓣ: We associate Mt. Fuji with Japan. (Fuji-sañ to ieba Nihoñ o reñsoo suru.) 富士山といえば日本を連想する.

associate professor n. ju「ñ-kyo「oju 準教授.

association n. 1 (society) kyo「okai 協会; ku「miai 組合.
2 (companionship) ko「osai 交際.

assume vt. 1 (suppose) to「ozeñ ... to o「mou 当然...と思う Ⓒ: I assumed that he would come. (Kare wa toozeñ kuru mono to omotte ita.) 彼は当然来るものと思っていた.
2 (undertake) ... o hi「kiuke」ru ...を引き受ける Ⓥ; to「ru とる Ⓒ: Who will assume the responsibility? (Dare ga sono sekiniñ o toru no desu ka?) だれがその責任をとるのですか.

assumption n. ka「tee 仮定: It is a mere assumption. (Sore wa tañnaru katee desu.) それは単なる仮定です.

assurance n. (guarantee) ho「shoo 保証; ka「kuyaku 確約; (confidence) ka「kushiñ 確信: receive assurance (hoshoo [kakuyaku] o eru) 保証[確約]を得る.

assure vt. (promise) ... ni (... o) ka-「kuyaku suru ...に(...を)確約する Ⓣ; ho「shoo suru 保証する Ⓣ: I assured her of my assistance. (Watashi wa kanojo ni eñjo o kakuyaku shita.) 私は彼女に援助を確約した.

assured adj. (... o) ka「kushiñ shite (iru) (...を)確信して(いる): I am assured of his innocence. (Watashi wa kare no mujitsu o kakushiñ shite iru.) 私は彼の無実を確信している.

asthma n. ze「ñsoku ぜんそく: suffer from asthma (zeñsoku ni kakaru) ぜんそくにかかる.

astonish vt. ... o o「doroka」su ...を驚かす Ⓒ; bi「kku」ri saseru びっくりさせる Ⓥ: I was astonished to hear the news. (Watashi wa sono shirase o kiite bikkuri shita.) 私はその知らせを聞いてびっくりした.

astonishment n. o「doroki」驚き; bi「kku」ri びっくり: She looked at me in astonishment. (*Kanojo wa odoroite watashi o mita.*) 彼女は驚いて私を見た.

astound *vt.* ... o biˈkkuˈri gyooteñ saˈseru ...をびっくり仰天させる Ⓥ: I was astounded by the news. (*Watashi wa sono shirase ni bikkuri gyooteñ shita.*) 私はその知らせにびっくり仰天した.

astronomy *n.* teˈñmoˈñgaku 天文学.

at *prep.* **1** (position) ... de [ni] ...で [に]: I bought this at that store. (*Watashi wa kore o ano mise de kaimashita.*) 私はこれをあの店で買いました. / At that traffic signal turn left. (*Ano shiñgoo de hidari ni magari nasai.*) あの信号で左に曲がりなさい.
2 (time) ... ni [de] ...に[で]: Please wake me up at six tomorrow morning. (*Ashita no asa roku-ji ni okoshite kudasai.*) あしたの朝6時に起こしてください. / She got married at the age of twenty. (*Kanojo wa hatachi de kekkoñ shita.*) 彼女は20歳で結婚した.
3 (direction) ... o ...を: The boy stared at me. (*Sono otoko-no-ko wa watashi o jirojiro to mita.*) その男の子は私をじろじろと見た.
4 (cost) ... de ...で: I bought this bag at 5,000 yen. (*Watashi wa kono kabañ o goseñ-eñ de katta.*) 私はこのかばんを5千円で買った.

athlete *n.* uˈñdoo seˈñshu 運動選手; suˈpootsu seˈñshu スポーツ選手.

athletics *n.* uˈñdoo kyoˈogi 運動競技.

Atlantic Ocean *n.* Taˈiseˈeyoo 大西洋.

atlas *n.* chiˈzuchoo 地図帳.

atmosphere *n.* **1** (feeling) fuˈñiˈiki 雰囲気; kiˈbuñ 気分; muˈudo ムード: This restaurant has a nice atmosphere. (*Kono resutorañ wa muudo ga ii.*) このレストランはムードがいい. ★ In this sense, Japanese people often use '*muudo*' (mood).
2 (air) taˈiki 大気; kuˈuki 空気: The atmosphere in the city is pol-luted. (*Toshi no kuuki wa yogorete iru.*) 都市の空気は汚れている.

atom *n.* geˈñshi 原子.

attach *vt.* **1** (fasten) ... o toˈritsukeru ...を取り付ける Ⓥ: attach a rope to a boat (*booto ni roopu o toritsukeru*) ボートにロープを取り付ける.
2 (affix) ... o soˈeru ...を添える Ⓥ; tsuˈkekuwaeru つけ加える Ⓥ: I attached my comments to the document. (*Watashi no ikeñ o sono shorui ni soeta.*) 私の意見をその書類に添えた.

attack *vt.* **1** (use force) ... o koˈogeki suru ...を攻撃する Ⓘ; seˈmeˈru 攻める Ⓥ: attack the enemy (*teki o koogeki suru*) 敵を攻撃する.
2 (speak or write against) ... o koˈogeki suru ...を攻撃する Ⓘ; hiˈnañ suru 非難する Ⓘ: attack the government (*seefu o koogeki suru*) 政府を攻撃する.
— *n.* koˈogeki 攻撃; hiˈnañ 非難: a personal attack (*kojiñ-koogeki*) 個人攻撃.

attain *vt.* **1** (achieve) ... o taˈssee suru ...を達成する Ⓘ: attain one's hopes (*nozomi o tassee suru*) 望みを達成する.
2 (reach) ... ni taˈssuru ...に達する Ⓘ: attain the top of a mountain (*yama no choojoo ni tassuru*) 山の頂上に達する.

attempt *vt.* ⟨verb⟩-(y)oo to suru ...(よ)うとする Ⓘ; kuˈwadateˈru 企てる Ⓥ: He attempted to climb the mountain. (*Kare wa sono yama ni noboroo to shita.*) 彼はその山に登ろうとした. / He attempted to stop smoking. (*Kare wa tabako o yameyoo to shita.*) 彼はたばこをやめようとした.
— *n.* koˈkoromiˈ 試み; kuˈwadate 企て: His attempt failed. (*Kare no kuwadate wa shippai shita.*) 彼の企ては失敗した.

attend *vt.* **1** (be present) ... ni shuˈsseki suru ...に出席する Ⓘ: I attended the party. (*Watashi wa sono kai ni shusseki shita.*) 私はそ

の会に出席した.
2 (nurse) ... o ka⌐ngo suru ...を看護する①; ... ni tsu⌐kiso┐u ...に付き添う©: Who is attending your mother? (*Dare ga o-kaasañ o kañgo shite iru ñ desu ka?*) だれがお母さんを看護しているんですか.
── *vi.* (apply oneself to) ... ni se⌐le o dasu ...に精を出す©; se⌐ñneñ suru 専念する①: attend to one's business (*shigoto ni see o dasu*) 仕事に精を出す.

attendance *n.* **1** (attending) shu⌐sseki 出席: attendance at a meeting (*kai e no shusseki*) 会への出席.
2 (number present) shu⌐sseki┐sha 出席者; sa⌐ñka┐sha 参加者: There was a large attendance at the party. (*Paatii ni wa shussekisha ga oozee ita.*) パーティーには出席者が大勢いた.

attendant *adj.* tsu⌐kisoi no 付き添いの: an attendant nurse (*tsukisoi no kañgofu*) 付き添いの看護婦.
── *n.* tsu⌐kisoi 付き添い; ka⌐kari 係: a parking lot attendant (*chuushajoo no kakari*) 駐車場の係.

attention *n.* **1** (notice) chu⌐ui 注意; chu⌐umoku 注目: attract attention (*chuui o hiku*) 注意を引く / Nobody paid attention to what he said. (*Dare mo kare ga itta koto ni chuui o harawanakatta.*) だれも彼が言ったことに注意を払わなかった.
2 (care) se⌐wa 世話; (consideration) ko⌐koroku┐bari 心配り.

attic *n.* ya⌐neura(beya) 屋根裏(部屋).

attitude *n.* **1** (behavior) ta⌐ido 態度: He took a defiant attitude. (*Kare wa hañkoo-teki na taido o totta.*) 彼は反抗的な態度を取った.
2 (thinking) ka⌐ñga┐e 考え: What is your attitude to this problem? (*Kono moñdai ni taisuru anata no kañgae wa doo desu ka?*) この問題に対するあなたの考えはどうですか.

attorney *n.* be⌐ñgo┐shi 弁護士: consult one's attorney (*beñgoshi ni

soodañ suru) 弁護士に相談する.

attract *vt.* ... o hi⌐kitsuke┐ru ...を引き付ける Ⓥ; hi⌐ku 引く ©: A magnet attracts iron. (*Jishaku wa tetsu o hikitsukeru.*) 磁石は鉄を引き付ける. / He tried to attract her attention. (*Kare wa kanojo no chuui o hikoo to shita.*) 彼は彼女の注意を引こうとした.

attraction *n.* mi⌐ryoku 魅力: This painting has no attraction for me. (*Kono e wa watashi ni wa miryoku ga nai.*) この絵は私には魅力がない.

attractive *adj.* mi⌐ryoku-teki na 魅力的な; hi⌐to┐ o hi⌐kitsuke┐ru 人を引き付ける: an attractive woman (*miryoku-teki na josee*) 魅力的な女性.

attribute *vt.* ... o (... no) se⌐le ni suru ...を(...の)せいにする①: He attributed his failure to illness. (*Kare wa shippai o byooki no see ni shita.*) 彼は失敗を病気のせいにした.

audience *n.* (of a concert) cho⌐o-shuu 聴衆; (of a performance) ka⌐ñ-kyaku 観客; (of a radio) cho⌐oshu┐sha 聴取者; (of a TV) shi⌐cho┐osha 視聴者; (of a book) do⌐kusha 読者.

August *n.* ha⌐chi-gatsu┐ 八月.

aunt *n.* (one's own) o⌐ba おば; (another's) o⌐ba-sañ おばさん. ★ Often sounds derogatory.

Australia *n.* O⌐osutora┐ria オーストラリア.

Australian *n.* (person) O⌐osuto-raria┐jiñ オーストラリア人.
── *adj.* O⌐osutora┐ria no オーストラリアの: the Australian flag (*Oosutoraria no kokki*) オーストラリアの国旗.

author *n.* cho⌐osha 著者; sa⌐kusha 作者; (novelist) sa⌐kka 作家.

authority *n.* **1** (right) ke⌐ñge┐ñ 権限; ke⌐ñryoku 権力: I have no authority to do this. (*Watashi ni wa kono koto o suru keñgeñ wa arimaseñ.*) 私にはこのことをする権限はありません.
2 [*pl.*] to⌐okyoku 当局: the govern-

ment authorities (*seefu tookyoku*) 政府当局.

3 (expert) ta⌐ika 大家; ke⌐ñi 権威: He is an authority on Japanese history. (*Kare wa Nihoñshi no keñi desu.*) 彼は日本史の権威です.

authorize *vt.* **1** (give right) ... ni ke⌐ñge⌐ñ o a⌐ataeru ...に権限を与える V: The committee authorized him to negotiate. (*Iiñkai wa kare ni kooshoo suru keñgeñ o ataeta.*) 委員会は彼に交渉する権限を与えた. **2** (give permission) ... o ni⌐ñka suru 認可する 1; ko⌐oniñ suru 公認する 1: an authorized money changer (*kooniñ ryoogaeshoo*) 公認両替商.

automatic *adj.* ji⌐doo-teki na 自動的な: This washing machine is automatic. (*Kono señtakuki wa jidoo desu.*) この洗濯機は自動です.

automobile *n.* ji⌐doosha 自動車; ku⌐ruma 車: drive an automobile (*jidoosha o uñteñ suru*) 自動車を運転する.

autumn *n.* a⌐ki 秋.

avenue *n.* (wide street) o⌐odo⌐ori 大通り; (with trees on both sides) na⌐miki⌐-michi 並木道.

average *n.* he⌐ekiñ 平均: work out an average (*heekiñ o dasu*) 平均を出す.
— *adj.* he⌐ekiñ no 平均の; na⌐mi no 並の: the average temperature (*heekiñ kioñ*) 平均気温 / an average mark (*heekiñ teñ*) 平均点.

avoid *vt.* ... o sa⌐ke⌐ru ...を避ける V: He seems to be avoiding me. (*Kare wa watashi o sakete iru mitai da.*) 彼は私を避けているみたいだ.

await *vt.* ... o ma⌐tsu ...を待つ C: I am awaiting your reply. (*Anata no heñji o matte imasu.*) あなたの返事を待っています.

awake *vt.* me⌐ o sa⌐ma⌐su 目を覚ます C: The noise awoke me. (*Sono monooto de me ga sameta.*) その物音で目が覚めた.
— *vi.* ... ni me⌐zame⌐ru ...目覚める V; ... o ji⌐kaku suru ...を自覚する

V: He awoke to his responsibilities. (*Kare wa jibuñ no sekiniñ o jikaku shita.*) 彼は自分の責任を自覚した.
— *adj.* (not asleep) ne⌐murana⌐i de (iru) 眠らないで(いる); o⌐kite iru 起きている: He is still awake. (*Kare wa mada okite imasu.*) 彼はまだ起きています.

awaken *vt.* ... o yo⌐bioko⌐su ...を呼び起こす C: awaken a person's interest (*hito no kyoomi o yobi-okosu*) 人の興味を呼び起こす.

award *n.* sho⌐o 賞; (thing) sho⌐o-hiñ 賞品: grant an award (*shoo o ataeru*) 賞を与える / receive an award (*shoo o morau*) 賞をもらう.
— *vt.* ... o a⌐ataeru ...を与える V: A gold medal was awarded to her. (*Kiñ medaru ga kanojo ni atae-rareta.*) 金メダルが彼女に与えられた.

aware *adj.* ... ni ki ga tsu⌐ite (iru) ...に気がついて(いる); ... o ka⌐ñzu⌐ite (iru) ...を感づいて(いる): I was aware of the danger. (*Watashi wa sono kikeñ ni ki ga tsuite ita.*) 私はその危険に気がついていた.

away *adj.* (absent) fu⌐zai de [da] 不在で[だ]; (at a distance) ha⌐na⌐rete (iru) 離れて(いる): He is away on a trip. (*Kare wa ryokoo de fuzai desu.*) 彼は旅行で不在です. / How far away is Kobe from Kyoto? (*Koobe wa Kyooto kara dono kurai hanarete imasu ka?*) 神戸は京都からどのくらい離れていますか.
— *adv.* a⌐chira e あちらへ; sa⌐tte 去って: drive away (*oiharau*) 追い払う / fly away (*tobi-saru*) 飛び去る / melt away (*toke-saru*) 解け去る / take away (*mochi-saru*) 持ち去る.

awful *adj.* hi⌐do⌐i ひどい; ta⌐iheñ na 大変な; su⌐go⌐i すごい: an awful pain (*hidoi itami*) ひどい痛み / It was awful yesterday. (*Kinoo wa taiheñ deshita.*) きのうは大変でした.

awfully *adv.* to⌐temo とても; hi⌐doku ひどく: It is awfully cold. (*Totemo samui.*) とても寒い.

awkward *adj.* **1** (clumsy) bu⌐ki⌐

yoo na 不器用な; gi「kochina」i ぎこち
ない: an awkward person (*bukiyoo
na hito*) 不器用な人.
2 (difficult to deal with) ya「kkai
na やっかいな; a「tsukainiku」i 扱いにく
い: an awkward problem (*yakkai*

na moñdai) やっかいな問題.
3 (embarrassing) ba「tsu no waru」i
ばつの悪い; ki「mazui 気まずい: I felt
awkward. (*Watashi wa kimazui
omoi o shita.*) 私は気まずい思いをした.

B

baby *n.* **1** a「kañboo 赤ん坊; [pet
word] a「kachañ 赤ちゃん: a baby
boy [girl] (*otoko* [*oñna*] *no akañboo*) 男[女]の赤ん坊 / have a baby
(*akañboo o umu*) 赤ん坊を生む.
2 ko「domo 子ども: a baby elephant
(*zoo no kodomo*) 象の子ども.
baby-sitter *n.* ko「mo」ri 子守; be-
「bii-shi」ttaa ベビーシッター.
bachelor *n.* do「kushi」ñsha 独身
者; hi「torimono ひとり者: a bachelor
girl (*dokushiñ no josee*) 独身の女
性.
back *n.* **1** (of the body) se「naka 背
中: scratch one's back (*senaka o
kaku*) 背中をかく.
2 (the rear) u「shiro 後ろ; o「ku 奥:
the back seat (*ushiro no zaseki*) 後
ろの座席 / the back of a room (*heya
no oku*) 部屋の奥.
3 (reverse side) u「ra 裏: back and
front (*ura to omote*) 裏と表.
— *vt.* **1** (support) ... o ko「oeñ
suru ...を後援する Ⓣ; shi「ji suru 支
持する Ⓣ: back his plan (*kare no
keekaku o shiji suru*) 彼の計画を支
持する.
2 (cause to go backward) ... o
ko「otai saseru ...を後退させる Ⓥ.
— *vi.* u「shiro e saga」ru 後ろへ下が
る Ⓒ: The car backed up slowly.
(*Kuruma wa yukkuri ushiro e
sagatta.*) 車はゆっくり後ろへ下がった.
— *adv.* u「shiro ni [e] 後ろに[へ];
mo「to no to「koro」ni [e] 元の所に
[へ]: Put my books back where you
got them. (*Watashi no hoñ o moto
atta tokoro e modoshi nasai.*) 私の
本を元あった所へ戻しなさい. / go back

home (*uchi e kaeru*) 家へ帰る.
background *n.* **1** (of scenery)
ha「ikee 背景: high mountains in
the background (*haikee no takai
yama*) 背景の高い山.
2 (of conditions) ha「ikee 背景;
jo「okyoo 状況: the economic and
social background (*keezai-teki,
shakai-teki haikee*) 経済的, 社会的
背景.
3 (of a pattern) ji 地: blue spots on
a white background (*shiro-ji ni aoi
teñ no moyoo*) 白地に青い点の模様.
backward *adj.* **1** u「shiro e」no 後
ろへの; ko「ohoo e」no 後方への: a
gentle backward and forward movement (*zeñpoo to koohoo e no yukkuri shita ugoki*) 前方と後方へのゆっ
くりした動き.
2 o「kureta 遅れた; o「kurete iru 遅れ
ている: a backward region of a rich
country (*yutaka na kuni no okureta chiiki*) 豊かな国の遅れた地域.
— *adv.* u「shiro ni [e] 後ろに[へ];
gya「ku ni 逆に: The policeman
slowly moved backward. (*Keekañ
wa yukkuri ushiro e sagatta.*) 警官
はゆっくり後ろへ下がった. / I can say
the alphabet backward. (*Watashi
wa arufabetto o gyaku ni iemasu.*)
私はアルファベットを逆に言えます.
bacon *n.* be「koñ ベーコン.
bacteria *n.* ba「kuteria バクテリア.
bad *adj.* **1** wa「ru」i 悪い; yo「ku nai
よくない: bad news (*warui shirase*)
悪い知らせ / bad weather (*warui teñki*) 悪い天気 / My luck was bad.
(*Watashi wa uñ ga warukatta.*) 私
は運が悪かった.

2 hi⌐do¹i ひどい: a bad headache (*hidoi zutsuu*) ひどい頭痛.

3 he⌐ta¹ na 下手な; ma⌐zu¹i まずい: I wish I weren't so bad at sports. (*Supootsu ga koñna ni heta de nakereba ii ñ da kedo.*) スポーツがこんなに下手でなければいいんだけど.

4 ... ni wa mu⌐kanai ...には向かない: Yesterday was a bad day for the marathon. (*Kinoo wa marasoñ ni wa mukanai hi datta.*) きのうはマラソンには向かない日だった.

badge *n.* ba⌐jji バッジ; ki⌐shoo 記章: wear a badge (*bajji o tsukeru*) バッジをつける.

badly *adv.* ma⌐zuku まずく; hi⌐doku ひどく; to⌐temo とても: He did his work badly. (*Kare no shigoto wa mazukatta.*) 彼の仕事はまずかった. / I was badly hurt. (*Watashi wa hidoi kega o shita.*) 私はひどいけがをした. / I want this badly. (*Watashi wa kore ga totemo hoshii.*) 私はこれがとても欲しい.

bag *n.* **1** fu⌐kuro¹ 袋: a paper bag (*kami no fukuro*) 紙の袋.
2 (handbag) ha⌐ñdoba¹ggu ハンドバッグ.

baggage *n.* te⌐ni¹motsu 手荷物: check in one's baggage (*tenimotsu o chekku-iñ suru*) 手荷物をチェックインする.

bake *vt.* ... o ya¹ku ...を焼く ⧉: bake bread in the oven (*oobuñ de pañ o yaku*) オーブンでパンを焼く.

bakery *n.* pa¹ñya パン屋; se⌐epañjo 製パン所.

balance *n.* **1** (scales) ha⌐kari はかり; te⌐ñbiñba¹kari てんびんばかり: weigh something on a balance (*hakari ni kakeru*) はかりにかける.
2 (equilibrium) tsu⌐riai つり合い; ki⌐ñkoo 均衡; he⌐ekoo 平衡; ba⌐rañsu バランス: preserve the balance of power (*chikara no kiñkoo o tamotsu*) 力の均衡を保つ / lose one's balance and fall over (*barañsu o ushinatte taoreru*) バランスを失って倒れる.
3 (remainder) za⌐ñgaku 残額: a bank balance (*giñkoo no zañgaku*)

銀行の残額.
— *vt.* (match) ... o hi⌐kaku suru ...を比較する ⧉; ku⌐raberu 比べる ⧊: balance the advantages against the disadvantages (*yuuri na teñ to furi na teñ o hikaku suru*) 有利な点と不利な点を比較する.
— *vi.* (keep steady) tsu⌐riai o to¹ru 釣り合いを取る ⧇: balance on one's toes (*tsumasaki de tsuriai o toru*) つま先で釣り合いをとる.

balcony *n.* ba⌐ruko¹nii バルコニー.

bald *adj.* ha⌐geta はげた; ha⌐gete iru はげている; ke¹no na¹i 毛のない: Mr. Yamaguchi is bald. (*Yamaguchi-sañ wa atama ga hagete iru.*) 山口さんは頭がはげている.

ball *n.* bo¹oru ボール; ta¹ma 球; kyu¹u 球: throw a ball (*booru o nageru*) ボールを投げる / a ball of wool (*keito no tama*) 毛糸の球.

ballet *n.* ba⌐ree バレエ.

balloon *n.* ki⌐kyuu 気球; fu⌐useñ 風船: a hot-air balloon (*netsuki-kyuu*) 熱気球 / blow up a balloon (*fuuseñ o fukuramasu*) 風船をふくらます.

ballpoint (pen) *n.* bo⌐orupeñ ボールペン.

bamboo *n.* ta⌐ke 竹: bamboo shoots and rice (*take-no-ko gohañ*) たけの子飯 / a bamboo thicket (*take-yabu*) 竹やぶ.

ban *n.* ki⌐ñshi 禁止: a ban on parking (*chuusha kiñshi*) 駐車禁止.
— *vt.* ... o ki⌐ñshi suru ...を禁止する ⧉: ban a protest march (*koogi-demo o kiñshi suru*) 抗議デモを禁止する.

banana *n.* ba¹nana バナナ.

band¹ *n.* **1** ga⌐kudañ 楽団; ba¹ñdo バンド: a jazz band (*jazu bañdo*) ジャズバンド.
2 i⌐chi-dañ 一団: a band of robbers (*toozoku no ichi-dañ*) 盗賊の一団.

band² *n.* hi¹mo ひも; ta¹ga たが; ba⌐ñdo バンド; ri¹boñ リボン: a band made of iron (*tetsu no taga*) 鉄のたが / a hat with a blue silk band (*aoi*

kinu no ribon o tsuketa booshi) 青
い絹のリボンをつけた帽子.

bandage n. ho⌐otai 包帯: a clean
bandage (*kiree na hootai*) きれいな包
帯.
— vt. …ni ho⌐otai o suru …に包
帯をする 1: bandage up a wound (*kizu ni hootai o suru*) 傷に包帯をする.

banister n. te⌐suri 手すり.

bank[1] n. gi⌐ŋkoo 銀行; ba⌐ŋku バン
ク: a bank account (*ginkoo kooza*)
銀行口座 / withdraw money from a
bank (*ginkoo kara o-kane o orosu*)
銀行からお金を下ろす / I deposited a
million yen in the bank. (*Watashi
wa ginkoo ni hyakumaŋ-eŋ azuketa.*) 私は銀行に 100 万円預けた.

bank[2] n. do⌐te 土手; tsu⌐tsumi 堤:
the north bank of a river (*kawa no
kita-gawa no dote*) 川の北側の土手.

banker n. gi⌐ŋkooka 銀行家.

bank note n. sa⌐tsu 札; shi⌐hee
紙幣.

bankrupt adj. ha⌐isaŋ shita [shite
iru] 破産した[している]: go bankrupt
(*hasaŋ suru*) 破産する.

bankruptcy n. ha⌐isaŋ 破産; to⌐o-
saŋ 倒産: His company is on the
brink of bankruptcy. (*Kare no kaisha wa toosaŋ shi-soo da.*) 彼の会
社は倒産しそうだ.

banquet n. e⌐ŋkai 宴会: give a
banquet (*eŋkai o hiraku*) 宴会を開
く.

bar[1] n. ba⌐a バー; sa⌐kaba 酒場.

bar[2] n. bo⌐o 棒; no⌐beboo 延べ棒: a
bar of gold (*kiŋ no noboboo*) 金の延
べ棒 / an iron bar (*tetsuboo*) 鉄棒 /
a bar of chocolate (*ita-choko*) 板
チョコ.

bar[3] vt. 1 (fasten) …ni ka⌐nnuki o
ka⌐ke⌐ru …にかんぬきを掛ける Ⅴ: bar
a door (*doa ni kannuki o kakeru*)
ドアにかんぬきを掛ける.
2 (prevent) … o sa⌐matage⌐ru …を
妨げる Ⅴ; bo⌐ogai suru 妨害する 1:
bar someone's progress (*hoka no
hito ga zeŋshiŋ suru no o samata-
geru*) ほかの人が前進するのを妨げる.

barber n. to⌐koya 床屋: go to the

barber (*tokoya e iku*) 床屋へ行く.

barbershop n. to⌐koya 床屋.

bare adj. 1 (naked, uncovered)
mu⌐kidashi no むき出しの; ha⌐daka
no 裸の: bare feet (*hadashi*) はだし /
a bare head (*muboo*) 無帽 / The
trees are already bare. (*Ko no ha
wa moo chitte shimatta.*) 木の葉はも
う散ってしまった.
2 (empty) ka⌐ra no からの: a bare
cupboard (*karappo no todana*) か
らっぽの戸棚.
3 (minimum) gi⌐rigiri no ぎりぎりの:
a bare majority (*girigiri no kahaŋ-
suu*) ぎりぎりの過半数.
4 (unadorned) a⌐rinomama[1] no (あ
りのままの): the bare facts (*arinomama no jijitsu*) ありのままの事実.

barefoot adj. ha⌐dashi no はだしの:
barefoot children (*hadashi no
kodomo-tachi*) はだしの子どもたち.
— adv. ha⌐dashi de はだしで: walk
barefoot (*hadashi de aruku*) はだし
で歩く.

barely adv. ya⌐tto やっと; ka⌐ro⌐o-
jite かろうじて: We barely got to
Narita in time. (*Watashi-tachi wa
karoojite jikan made ni Narita ni
tsuita.*) 私たちはかろうじて時間までに成
田に着いた.

bargain n. 1 (cheap goods, good
buy) ya⌐su⌐i ka⌐imono 安い買い物;
(o-)ka⌐idokuhiŋ (お)買い得品: make
a good bargain (*toku na kaimono o
suru*) 得な買い物をする.
2 (agreement) ba⌐ibai-ke⌐eyaku 売
買契約; to⌐ri⌐hiki 取り引き; ya⌐ku-
soku 約束: make a bargain (*keeyaku o musubu*) 契約を結ぶ / drive
a hard bargain (*yuuri na jookeŋ de
torihiki suru*) 有利な条件で取り引き
する.
— vi. ne⌐biki no kooshoo o suru
値引きの交渉をする 1; ne⌐gi⌐ru 値切
る C: I bargained with the shop-
keeper over the price. (*Watashi wa
mise no shujiŋ to nebiki no kooshoo o shita.*) 私は店の主人と値引き
の交渉をした.
— vt. … o to⌐rikimeru …を取り決め

る ⓥ; koˈoshoo suru 交渉する ⓘ: We bargained that we would have no work on Sundays. (*Nichiyoo wa kiˈnmu shinakute mo yoi yoo ni kooshoo shita.*) 日曜は勤務しなくてもよいように交渉した.

bark *vi.* hoˈeˈru ほえる ⓥ: The dog was barking. (*Sono inu wa hoete ita.*) その犬はほえていた.

barn *n.* naˈya 納屋; kaˈchikugoya 家畜小屋.

barrel *n.* taˈru たる: a wooden barrel (*ki no taru*) 木のたる / a barrel of beer (*hito taru no biiru*) 一たるのビール.

barren *adj.* **1** (of land) fuˈmoo no 不毛の; saˈkuˈmotsu no deˈkiˈnai 作物のできない: a barren land (*fumoo no tochi*) 不毛の土地.
2 (of animals) fuˈniˈn no 不妊の; ko o uˈmanai 子を生まない.

barrier *n.* saˈku さく; shoˈoheki 障壁; shoˈogai 障害: a natural barrier formed by mountains (*yama de tsukurareta shizeˈn no kabe*) 山でつくられた自然の壁 / a language barrier (*kotoba no shooheki*) 言葉の障壁.

base *n.* **1** (bottom) soˈko 底; doˈdai 土台: the base of a mountain (*yama no fumoto*) 山のふもと / the base of a pillar (*hashira no dai*) 柱の台.
2 (foundation) kiˈso 基礎; kiˈbaˈn 基盤: a country with a strong economic base (*keezai-teki kibaˈn ga shikkari shita kuni*) 経済的基盤がしっかりした国.
3 (starting-place) kiˈchi 基地: a military [naval] base (*rikuguˈn [kai-guˈn] kichi*) 陸軍[海軍]基地.
4 (of baseball) ruˈi 塁; beˈesu ベース: third base (*saˈn rui*) 三塁 / home base (*hoomu beesu*) ホームベース.
— *vt.* ... ni ki o oku (...に)基礎を置く; ... ni moˈtozuˈku ...に基づく ⓒ: an argument based on sound facts (*shikkari shita jijitsu ni motozuku giroˈn*) しっかりした事実に基づく議論.

baseball *n.* yaˈkyuu 野球; beˈesuboˈoru ベースボール: play baseball (*yakyuu o suru*) 野球をする.

basin *n.* **1** (container) seˈnmeˈnki 洗面器; haˈchiˈ 鉢.
2 (area) boˈnchi 盆地.

basis *n.* kiˈso 基礎; kiˈjuˈn 基準: a basis for negotiations (*kooshoo no kiso*) 交渉の基礎 / We work on a five-day week basis. (*Watashi-tachi wa shuu itsuka-see desu.*) 私たちは週5日制です.

basket *n.* kaˈgo かご; zaˈru ざる: fill [empty] a basket (*kago o ippai [kara] ni suru*) かごをいっぱい[から]にする / a shopping basket (*kaimono kago*) 買い物かご / a wastebasket (*kuzu-kago*) くずかご.

bath *n.* fuˈro ふろ; nyuˈuyoku 入浴: take a bath (*furo ni hairu*) ふろに入る / This bath is too hot. (*Kono furo wa atsu-sugiru.*) このふろは熱すぎる.

bathe *vt.* ... o fuˈroˈ ni iˈreru ...をふろに入れる ⓥ; aˈrau 洗う ⓒ: How often do you bathe yourself a week? (*Shuu ni naˈn-kai gurai o-furo ni hairimasu ka?*) 週に何回ぐらいおふろに入りますか. / You should bathe that cut in hot water. (*Sono kizu wa o-yu de aratta hoo ga yoi.*) その傷はお湯で洗ったほうがよい.

bathroom *n.* yoˈkushitsu 浴室; fuˈroba ふろ場. ★ Japanese bathrooms are not equipped with toilets, and the word 'bathroom' is never used to mean 'toilet.'

battery *n.* deˈnchi 電池: This battery is dead. (*Kono deˈnchi wa kirete iru.*) この電池は切れている. ★ A car battery is called 'batterii' バッテリー.

battle *n.* **1** (war) taˈtakai 戦い; seˈnsoo 戦争: win [lose] a battle (*tatakai ni katsu [makeru]*) 戦いに勝つ[負ける] / He was wounded in battle. (*Kare wa seˈnsoo de fushoo shita.*) 彼は戦争で負傷した.
2 (struggle) toˈosoo 闘争; taˈtakai 戦い; kyoˈosoo 競争: a battle

against corruption (*oshoku to no tatakai*) 汚職との戦い / the battle for existence (*seezoñ kyoosoo*) 生存競争.

bay *n.* waˈñ 湾; iˈrie 入り江: Tokyo Bay (*Tookyoo wañ*) 東京湾.

be¹ *vi.* **1** [expressing relation] da だ; [polite] desu です: Today is Monday. (*Kyoo wa getsuyoo da.*) 今日は月曜だ. / Miss Yamakawa is a teacher. (*Yamakawa-sañ wa señsee desu.*) 山川さんは先生です.
2 [expressing quality, state, etc.] da だ; [polite] desu です: The room was very quiet. (*Heya wa hijoo ni shizuka datta.*) 部屋は非常に静かだった. / Junko is very happy. (*Juñko-sañ wa totemo shiawase desu.*) 淳子さんはとても幸せです. / I am busy today. (*Watashi wa kyoo isogashii.*) 私はきょう忙しい. ★ An adjective can stand by itself as a complete sentence. The addition of ‘*desu*’ does not change the meaning, but merely makes the sentence more polite.
3 [expressing existence or location of people, animals, and sometimes vehicles] iˈru いる Ⓥ: I was in the garden all afternoon. (*Watashi wa gogo wa zutto niwa ni imashita.*) 私は午後はずっと庭にいました. / There is a cat under the desk. (*Tsukue no shita ni neko ga iru.*) 机の下に猫がいる.
4 [expressing existence or location of inanimate objects] aˈru ある Ⓒ: The pen is in the top drawer. (*Peñ wa ichibañ ue no hikidashi no naka ni arimasu.*) ペンはいちばん上の引き出しの中にあります. / In this country there aren't any high mountains. (*Kono kuni ni wa takai yama wa arimaseñ.*) この国には高い山はありません.
5 [result] ⟨verb⟩-te[de] iˈru …て[で]いる Ⓥ: The light is on. (*Deñki ga tsuite iru.*) 電気がついている. / The window is open. (*Mado ga aite iru.*) 窓が開いている.

be² *aux.* **1** [in a progressive tense] ⟨verb⟩-te[de] iˈru …て[で]いる Ⓥ: He is studying very hard. (*Kare wa isshookeñmee beñkyoo shite imasu.*) 彼は一生懸命勉強しています. / What were you doing while I was sleeping? (*Watashi ga nete iru aida anata wa nani o shite imashita ka?*) 私が寝ている間あなたは何をしていましたか.
2 [in the passive] ⟨verb⟩-(ra[sa]) reru …(ら[さ])れる Ⓥ: My husband and I were invited to her wedding. (*Shujiñ to watashi wa kanojo no kekkoñ-shiki ni shootai sareta.*) 主人と私は彼女の結婚式に招待された. / The boy was scolded by his teacher. (*Sono otoko-no-ko wa señsee ni shikarareta.*) その男の子は先生にしかられた.

beach *n.* haˈmabe 浜辺; kaˈisui-yoˈkujoo 海水浴場: a sandy beach (*suna-hama*) 砂浜.

beam *n.* **1** (ray of light) koˈroseñ 光線; hiˈkariˈ 光: The flashlight beam was clearly visible. (*Kaichuu-deñtoo no hikari ga hakkiri mieta.*) 懐中電灯の光がはっきり見えた.
2 (timber) haˈriˈ はり; keˈta けた: This beam cannot hold up the ceiling. (*Kono hari wa teñjoo o sasaeru koto ga dekinai.*) このはりは天井を支えることができない.

bean *n.* maˈme 豆: soya beans (*daizu*) 大豆 / kidney beans (*iñgeñ mame*) いんげん豆 / string beans (*saya eñdoo*) さやえんどう / coffee beans (*koohii mame*) コーヒー豆.

bear¹ kuˈmaˈ 熊: a polar bear (*shirokuma*) 白熊.

bear² *vt.* **1** (support) … o saˈsaeru …を支える Ⓥ: The ice is thick enough to bear your weight. (*Sono koori wa kimi no taijuu o sasaerareru dake no atsumi ga aru.*) その氷はきみの体重を支えられるだけの厚みがある.
2 (give birth to) ko o uˈmu 子を産む Ⓒ; (produce) mi ˈo musubu 実を結ぶ Ⓒ: My sister bore twins. (*Watashi no ane wa futago o uñda.*) 私の

姉は双子を産んだ. / I was born in 1950. (*Watashi wa señ-kyuu-hyaku-gojuu-neñ ni umaremashita.*) 私は1950年に生まれました. / Do you think this tree will bear fruit this year? (*Kono ki wa kotoshi mi ga naru to omoimasu ka?*) この木はことし実がなると思いますか.

3 (endure) ... o ga⌐mañ suru ...を我慢する Ⓣ; ... ni ta⌐e¬ru ...に耐える Ⓥ: I couldn't bear to listen to his complaints. (*Watashi wa kare no fuhee o kiku no o gamañ suru koto ga dekinakatta.*) 私は彼の不平を聞くのを我慢することができなかった. / I calmly bore their insults. (*Watashi wa kare-ra no bujoku ni jitto taeta.*) 私は彼らの侮辱にじっと耐えた.

beard *n.* a⌐go¬hige あごひげ: grow a beard (*agohige o hayasu*) あごひげを生やす.

beat *vt.* **1** (hit) ... o ta⌐ta¬ku ...をたたく Ⓒ; u⌐tsu 打つ Ⓒ: He beat me on the head. (*Kare wa watashi no atama o tataita.*) 彼は私の頭をたたいた. / beat a drum (*taiko o utsu*) たいこを打つ.

2 (defeat) ... o ma⌐kasu ...を負かす Ⓒ: We stand no chance of defeating them. (*Kare-ra o makasu mikomi wa nai.*) 彼らを負かす見込みはない.

3 (mix vigorously) ... o ka⌐kimaze¬ru ...をかき混ぜる Ⓥ: beat the milk and eggs together (*gyuunyuu to tamago o issho ni kakimazeru*) 牛乳と卵をいっしょにかき混ぜる.

— *vi.* **1** (hit) (... o) do⌐ñdoñ (to) ta⌐ta¬ku (...を)どんどん(と)たたく Ⓒ: I beat on the door. (*Watashi wa to o doñdoñ tataita.*) 私は戸をどんどんたたいた.

2 (of a heart) do⌐kidoki na¬ru どきどき鳴る Ⓒ: Her heart beat with excitement. (*Koofuñ de kanojo no shiñzoo wa dokidoki natta.*) 興奮で彼女の心臓はどきどき鳴った.

— *n.* u⌐tsu o¬to¬ 打つ音; (of a heart) do⌐oki どうき(動悸): the beat of a drum (*taiko o utsu oto*) たいこを打つ音 / the beat of a heart (*shiñ-*

zoo no dooki) 心臓のどうき.

beautiful *adj.* **1** (of looks, etc.) ki⌐ree na きれいな; u⌐tsukushi¬i 美しい: a beautiful woman (*kiree na oñna no hito*) きれいな女の人 / a beautiful voice (*utsukushii koe*) 美しい声 / What a beautiful flower! (*Nañte kiree na hana daroo!*) 何てきれいな花だろう.

2 (splendid) su⌐barashi¬i すばらしい; su⌐teki na すてきな: It's a beautiful day today. (*Kyoo wa subarashii hi da.*) きょうはすばらしい日だ.

beauty *n.* u⌐tsuku¬shisa 美しさ; bi⌐美; su⌐bara¬shisa すばらしさ: the beauty of nature (*shizeñ no bi*) 自然の美.

beauty parlor *n.* bi⌐yo¬oiñ 美容院.

because *conj.* **1** (reason) ... kara ...から; ... no de ...ので: "Why are you late?" "The train was late." (*"Doo shite okureta no?" "Deñsha ga okureta kara desu."*) 「どうして遅れたの」「電車が遅れたからです」/ I took my umbrella because it was raining. (*Ame ga futte ita kara kasa o motte itta.*) 雨が降っていたから傘を持って行った.

2 (just because) ... da⌐ kara to i⌐tte (... nai) ...だからといって(...ない): It isn't because you are my cousin that I promoted you. (*Itoko da kara to itte shooshiñ saseta no de wa nai.*) いとこだからといって昇進させたのではない.

because of ... *prep.* ... no ta⌐me¬ ni ...のために; ... ga ge⌐ñiñ de ...が原因で: He failed the interview because of his casual attitude. (*Kare wa iikageñ na taido ga geñiñ de meñsetsu ni shippai shita.*) 彼はいいかげんな態度が原因で面接に失敗した.

become *vi.* ⟨noun⟩ ni na¬ru ...になる Ⓒ; ⟨adjective⟩-ku naru ...くなる Ⓒ: Our daughter became a nurse. (*Uchi no musume wa kañgofu ni natta.*) うちの娘は看護婦になった. / It will become hot today. (*Kyoo wa atsuku naru deshoo.*) きょうは暑くな

るでしょう. / What has become of Yamamoto? (*Yamamoto wa doo natta deshoo ka?*) 山本はどうなってしょうか.

becoming *adj.* niˈaˈu 似合う; fuˈsawashiˈi ふさわしい: The necklace is very becoming on you. (*Sono nekkuresu wa anata ni yoku niau.*) そのネックレスはあなたによく似合う.

bed *n.* **1** beˈddo ベッド; neˈdoko 寝床: get into bed (*beddo ni hairu*) ベッドに入る / You should not smoke in bed. (*Nedoko de tabako o sutte wa ikemaseñ.*) 寝床でたばこを吸ってはいけません.
2 toˈko 床; soˈko 底: the bed of a river (*kawadoko*) 川床 / the bed of a lake (*kotee*) 湖底.
go to bed *vi.* neˈru 寝る ⓥ; toˈko ni tsuˈku 床につく ⓒ: It's time you went to bed. (*Moo neru jikañ desu.*) もう寝る時間です.

bedroom *n.* shiˈñshitsu 寝室.

bee *n.* haˈchi はち; miˈtsuˈbachi みつばち: be stung by a bee (*hachi ni sasareru*) はちに刺される.

beef *n.* gyuˈuniku 牛肉.

beer *n.* biˈiru ビール: a bottle of beer (*biiru ip-poñ*) ビール1本 / canned beer (*kañ biiru*) 缶ビール / draft beer (*nama biiru*) 生ビール.

beet *n.* biˈito ビート; saˈtoo-daˈikoñ 砂糖大根.

before *prep.* **1** (earlier than; prior to) ... no maˈe (ni) ...の前(に): Can you come before five o'clock? (*Go-ji mae ni koraremasu ka?*) 5時前に来られますか.
2 (in front of) ... no maˈe ni [de] ...の前に[で]: the plaza before the station (*eki no mae no hiroba*) 駅の前の広場 / He walked before me. (*Kare wa watashi no mae o aruita.*) 彼は私の前を歩いた.
— *adv.* (earlier) maˈe ni 前に; iˈzeñ (ni) 以前(に): I think I met him before. (*Kare ni wa mae ni atta yoo ni omoimasu.*) 彼には前に会ったように思います.
— *conj.* (earlier than) 〈verb〉maˈe

ni ...前に; 〈verb〉-nai uˈchi ni ...ないうちに: You must think carefully before you decide. (*Kimeru mae ni shiñchoo ni kañgae nasai.*) 決める前に慎重に考えなさい. / Let's leave before it starts raining. (*Ame ga furi-dasanai uchi ni dekakemashoo.*) 雨が降り出さないうちに出かけましょう.

beg *vt., vi.* **1** (ask for) (... o) (kuˈre to) taˈnoˈmu (...を)(くれと)頼む ⓒ: beg for something to eat (*nani-ka tabemono o kure to tanomu*) 何か食べ物をくれと頼む / I beg you to keep silent. (*Tanomu kara damatte ite kudasai.*) 頼むから黙っていてください.
2 (implore) (... o) koˈlu (...を)請う ⓒ: beg for forgiveness (*yurushi o kou*) 許しを請う.
I beg your pardon. (*Shitsuree shimashita.*) 失礼しました; [repeat] (*Moo ichido osshatte kudasai.*) もう一度おっしゃってください.

beggar *n.* koˈjikiˈ 乞食.

begin *vi.* haˈjimaru 始まる ⓒ; 〈verb〉-daˈsu ...だす ⓒ: School begins at eight and ends at four. (*Gakkoo wa hachi-ji ni hajimari yo-ji ni owaru.*) 学校は8時に始まり4時に終わる. / It began to rain on the way home. (*Uchi e kaeru to-chuu de ame ga furi-dashita.*) 家へ帰る途中で雨が降り出した.
— *vt.* ... o haˈjimeru ...を始める ⓥ; 〈verb〉-haˈjimeru ...始める ⓥ: When did you begin work this morning? (*Kesa wa shigoto o nañ-ji ni haji-memashita ka?*) けさは仕事を何時に始めましたか. / I hear that Bob has begun learning Japanese. (*Bobu wa Nihoñgo o narai-hajimeta ra-shii.*) ボブは日本語を習い始めたらしい.

beginner *n.* shoˈshiˈñsha 初心者; shoˈgaˈkusha 初学者: a beginners' Japanese class (*Nihoñgo shokyuu kurasu*) 日本語初級クラス.

beginning *n.* haˈjime 初め; saˈisho 最初: the beginning of the month (*tsuki no hajime*) 月の初め / I read the book from beginning to end. (*Watashi wa sono hoñ o sai-*

sho kara saigo made yomimashita.) 私はその本を最初から最後まで読みました.

behave *vi.* **1** (conduct oneself) fuˈrumaˈu ふるまう C: He behaved like a gentleman. (*Kare wa shiñshirashiku furumatta.*) 彼は紳士らしくふるまった.

2 (act politely) gyoˈogi yoˈku suru 行儀よくする I: The children behaved well at the party. (*Kodomotachi wa paatii de gyoogi ga yokatta.*) 子どもたちはパーティーで行儀がよかった.

behavior *n.* **1** (way of acting) fuˈrumai ふるまい; taˈido 態度: selfish behavior (*jibuñ katte na furumai*) 自分勝手なふるまい / arrogant behavior (*oohee na taido*) おうへいな態度.

2 (manners) gyoˈogi 行儀: Junko's behavior at the party was good. (*Paatii de Juñko-sañ wa gyoogi ga yokatta.*) パーティーで純子さんは行儀が良かった.

behind *prep.* **1** (at or toward the rear of) ... no uˈshiro ni [e; de] ...の後ろに[へ; で]: The boy was hiding behind a curtain. (*Sono otoko-no-ko wa kaateñ no ushiro ni kakurete ita.*) その男の子はカーテンの後ろに隠れていた.

2 (later than) ... ni oˈkurete ...に遅れて: The Shinkansen trains are behind schedule. (*Shiñkañseñ wa teekoku yori okurete iru.*) 新幹線は定刻より遅れている.

— *adv.* (at or to the back) uˈshiro ni [e, de] 後ろに[へ, で]; aˈto ni [e] あとに[へ]: an apartment building with a park behind (*ushiro ni kooeñ no aru apaato*) 後ろに公園のあるアパート / I stayed behind. (*Watashi wa ato ni nokotta.*) 私はあとに残った.

belief *n.* **1** (faith) shiˈñkoo 信仰; shiˈñjiˈñ 信心: belief in Christianity (*Kirisuto-kyoo no shiñkoo*) キリスト教の信仰.

2 (opinion) shiˈñneñ 信念; kaˈñgaˈe 考え; iˈkeñ 意見: To the best of my belief there is no danger.

(*Watashi no kañgae de wa kikeñ wa nai to omoimasu.*) 私の考えでは危険はないと思います.

3 (trust) shiˈñyoo 信用; shiˈñrai 信頼: I have no belief in his ability. (*Watashi wa kare no nooryoku ni shiñrai o oite imaseñ.*) 私は彼の能力に信頼を置いていません.

believe *vt.* **1** (consider to be true) ... o shiˈñjiru ...を信じる V: We believed her story. (*Wareware wa kanojo no hanashi o shiñjita.*) われDRわれは彼女の話を信じた.

2 (think) ... to kaˈñgaeˈru ...と考える V; oˈmoˈu 思う C: I believe that he is honest. (*Kare wa shoojiki da to omoimasu.*) 彼は正直だと思います.

believe in ... *vt.* ... no soˈñzai o shiˈñjiˈru ...の存在を信じる V; ... o shiˈñrai suru ...を信頼する I: believe in God (*kami no soñzai o shiñjiru*) 神の存在を信じる / I believe in you. (*Watashi wa anata no shiñrai shimasu.*) 私はあなたを信頼します.

bell *n.* **1** (of a church) kaˈne 鐘: I hear the ringing of a temple bell. (*O-tera no kane ga naru no ga kikoeru.*) お寺の鐘が鳴るのが聞こえる.

2 (doorbell) beˈru ベル: ring a bell (*beru o narasu*) ベルを鳴らす / answer a bell (*beru ni kotaeru*) ベルにこたえる.

3 (sound of a bell) beˈru no oˈtoˈ ベルの音: I thought I heard the bell. (*Beru no oto o kiita yoo ni omou.*) ベルの音を聞いたように思う.

belong *vi.* **1** (be the property of) (... no) moˈnoˈ da (...の)ものだ: Who does this umbrella belong to? (*Kono kasa wa dare no mono desu ka?*) この傘はだれのものですか.

2 (be a member of) (... ni) zoˈkusuˈru (...に)属する I; haˈitte iru 入っている V: Did you belong to any college societies? (*Nani-ka daigaku no kurabu ni haitte imashita ka?*) 何か大学のクラブに入っていましたか.

below *prep.* **1** (in a lower place, level, etc.) ... no shiˈta ni ...の下に: Write your name below the line,

please. (*Señ no shita ni o-namae o
kaite kudasai.*) 線の下にお名前を書い
てください.
2 (downstream) ... no ka⌐ryuu ni ...
の下流に: The bridge is a kilometer
below the waterfall. (*Hashi wa taki no ichi-kiro karyuu ni arimasu.*)
橋は滝の1キロ下流にあります.
3 (less than) mi⌐mañ 未満: Anyone
here below 16 must leave. (*Juu-
roku-sai mimañ no hito wa koko
kara dete ikanakereba narimaseñ.*)
16歳未満の人はここから出ていかなければ
なりません.
— *adv.* (beneath; in lower place)
shi⌐ta no [ni] 下の[に]: Miss Ishii
lives in the room below. (*Ishii-sañ
wa shita no heya ni suñde imasu.*)
石井さんは下の部屋に住んでいます.

belt *n.* **1** (band) be⌐ruto ベルト: a
leather belt (*kawa no beruto*) 革の
ベルト / a safety belt (*añzeñ beruto*)
安全ベルト / wear [loosen] one's belt
(*beruto o shimeru [yurumeru]*) ベル
トを締める[緩める].
2 (area) chi⌐tai 地帯: an earthquake belt (*jishiñ-tai*) 地震帯.

bench *n.* be⌐ñchi ベンチ: sit down
on a bench (*beñchi ni suwaru*) ベン
チに座る.

bend *vt.* (curve) ... o ma⌐geru ...を
曲げる Ⅴ: bend one's back (*senaka
o mageru*) 背中を曲げる / It is impossible to bend this iron bar.
(*Kono tetsuboo o mageru no wa
fukanoo da.*) この鉄棒を曲げるのは不
可能だ.
— *vi.* ma⌐garu 曲がる Ⅽ; o⌐re⌐ru
折れる Ⅴ: Just up ahead the road
bends sharp left. (*Chotto saki de
michi wa kyuu ni hidari ni maga-
rimasu.*) ちょっと先で道は急に左に曲が
ります.

beneath *prep.* **1** (under) ... no
shi⌐ta ni [de] ...の下に[で]: A dog is
sleeping beneath the tree. (*Inu ga
ki no shita de nete iru.*) 犬が木の下
で寝ている.
2 (not worthy of) ... ni fu⌐sawa-
shi⌐ku nai ...にふさわしくない; a⌐tai

shinai 値しない: A job like that is
clearly beneath a man like him.
(*Sono yoo na shigoto wa akiraka
ni kare no yoo na otoko ni fusawashiku nai.*) そのような仕事は明らかに彼
のような男にふさわしくない.

benefit *n.* **1** (advantage; profit)
ri⌐eki 利益; o⌐ñkee 恩恵: a public
benefit (*kooeki*) 公益 / The bene-
fits of nuclear energy are great.
(*Geñshiryoku enerugii no oñkee
wa ookii.*) 原子力エネルギーの恩恵は
大きい.
2 (allowance) te⌐ate 手当; kyu⌐ufu
給付: unemployment benefit (*shitsugyoo teate*) 失業手当 / a medical benefit (*iryoo kyuufu*) 医療給付.
be of benefit to ... *vt.* ... no ta-
⌐me⌐ ni na⌐ru ...のためになる Ⅽ: This
book was of great benefit to me.
(*Kono hoñ wa totemo tame ni
natta.*) この本はとてもためになった.
— *vi.* ri⌐eki o eru 利益を得る Ⅴ;
ya⌐ku⌐ ni tatsu 役に立つ Ⅽ: I ben-
efited from the experience. (*Sono
keekeñ ga yaku ni tatta.*) その経験が
役に立った.
— *vt.* ... no ta⌐me⌐ ni naru ...のため
になる Ⅽ; ... ni yo⌐i ...によい: That
investment will benefit the company. (*Sono tooshi wa kaisha no
tame ni naru deshoo.*) その投資は会
社のためになるでしょう.

beside *prep.* **1** (close to) ... no
so⌐ba ni ...のそばに; chi⌐kaku ni 近く
に: There is a park beside the
house. (*Uchi no soba ni kooeñ ga
aru.*) 家のそばに公園がある.
2 (compared to) ... no ku⌐raberu to
...と比べると: Beside the artist's earlier work, this picture is rather inferior. (*Sono gaka no shoki no
sakuhiñ to kuraberu to kono e wa
yaya otoru.*) その画家の初期の作品と
比べるとこの絵はやや劣る.

besides *prep.* **1** (in addition to)
... no ho⌐ka ni ...のほかに; ... ni ku-
⌐waete ...に加えて: Besides John,
who else did you invite? (*Joñ no
hoka ni dare o yobimashita ka?*)

ジョンのほかにだれを呼びましたか. / You should try to do something besides watching television. (*Terebi o miru hoka ni nani-ka shitara doo desu ka.*) テレビを見るほかに何かしたらどうですか.

2 (apart from) ... i⌐gai ni ...以外に: I can trust no one besides you. (*Anata igai ni dare mo shiñyoo dekimaseñ.*) あなた以外にだれも信用できません.

— *adv.* (in addition) so⌐no ue そのうえ; sa⌐ra ni さらに; ho⌐ka ni ほかに: This is my favorite picture but I have two more besides. (*Kore wa watashi ga ki ni itte iru e desu ga watashi wa hoka ni ato ni sakuhiñ motte imasu.*) これは私が気に入っている絵ですが私はほかにあと 2 作品持っています.

best *adj.* mo⌐tto⌐mo yo⌐i 最もよい; sa⌐iryoo no 最良の; i⌐chi⌐bañ no いちばんの: my best friend (*watashi no ichibañ no shiñyuu*) 私のいちばんの親友 / It is the best book I have ever read. (*Sono hoñ wa watashi ga ima made ni yoñda naka de ichibañ yoi hoñ desu.*) その本は私が今までに読んだ中でいちばんよい本です.

— *adv.* i⌐chibañ いちばん: What Japanese food do you like best? (*Ichibañ suki na Nihoñ ryoori wa nañ desu ka?*) いちばん好きな日本料理は何ですか / Tell me which day will suit you best. (*Ichibañ tsugoo no yoi hi o oshiete kudasai.*) いちばん都合のよい日を教えてください.

— *n.* i⌐chibañ yo⌐i mono いちばんよいもの: I did it all for the best. (*Sore ga ichibañ yoi to omotte yarimashita.*) それがいちばんよいと思ってやりました.

do one's best *vi.* ze⌐ñryoku o⌐ tsu⌐ku⌐su 全力を尽くす ⒸⒸ: I did my best to rebuild my business. (*Watashi wa kee-ee no tatenaoshi ni zeñryoku o tsukushita.*) 私は経営の建て直しに全力を尽くした.

make the best of ... *vt.* ...o de⌐kiru dake⌐ ri⌐ryoo suru ...をできる

だけ利用する Ⓘ: I made the best of the time left. (*Watashi wa nokosareta jikañ o dekiru dake katsuyoo shita.*) 私は残された時間をできるだけ活用した.

bet *vt.* ... ni ka⌐ke⌐ru ...に賭ける Ⓥ: I'll bet you ¥1,000 that I am right. (*Watashi ga tadashii hoo ni señ-eñ kakeru yo.*) 私が正しい方に千円賭けるよ.

— *vi.* (... ni) ka⌐ke⌐ru (...に)賭ける Ⓥ: bet on horses (*uma ni kakeru*) 馬に賭ける.

— *n.* ka⌐ke⌐ 賭け: make a bet (*kake o suru*) 賭けをする / win [lose] a bet (*kake ni katsu [makeru]*) 賭けに勝つ[負ける].

betray *vt.* **1** (be disloyal) ... o u⌐ragi⌐ru ...を裏切る Ⓒ; u⌐ru 売る Ⓒ: You have betrayed me. (*Anata wa watashi o uragitta.*) あなたは私を裏切った. / The man betrayed his country to the enemy. (*Sono otoko wa jibuñ no kuni o teki ni utta.*) その男は自分の国を敵に売った.

2 (reveal) ... o mo⌐ra⌐su ...を漏らす Ⓒ: He betrayed our secrets to her. (*Kare wa wareware no himitsu o kanojo ni morashita.*) 彼はわれわれの秘密を彼女に漏らした.

better *adj.* **1** (more good) yori [mo⌐tto; sa⌐ra ni] yo⌐i より[もっと; さらに]よい: Your school grades are better than before. (*Kimi no seeseki wa mae yori mo yoi.*) 君の成績は前よりもよい.

2 (of health, etc.) yo⌐ku natte (iru) よくなって(いる); ge⌐ñki na 元気な: I feel a little better. (*Kibuñ wa sukoshi yoku narimashita.*) 気分は少しよくなりました. / You are looking much better now. (*Kaoiro ga zutto yoku narimashita ne.*) 顔色がずっとよくなりましたね.

— *adv.* mo⌐tto umaku もっとうまく; yo⌐ri yo⌐ku よりよく: I speak Japanese better than I used to. (*Watashi wa Nihoñgo ga mae yori mo umaku hanaseru yoo ni natta.*) 私は日本語が前よりもうまく話せるようになっ

た。/ Which do you like better, sushi or tempura? (*Sushi to teñpura de wa dochira ga suki desu ka?*) すしとてんぷらではどちらが好きですか.

had better ⇨ had better.

between *prep.* **1** (space or time) ... no aⁱida ni [de] ...の間に[で]: an old house standing between two skyscrapers (*futatsu koosoobiru no aida ni hasamareta furui ie*) 二つの高層ビルの間に挟まれた古い家 / Please come between five and six in the evening. (*Yuugata go-ji to roku-ji no aida ni kite kudasai.*) 夕方5時と6時の間に来てください.
2 (range) ... no chuⁱkañ ...の中間; ... no aⁱida ...の間: The price is between ¥10,000 and ¥15,000. (*Nedañ wa ichimañ-eñ to ichimañ-goseñ-eñ no aida desu.*) 値段は1万円と1万5千円の間です.
3 (connection) -ⁱkañ no 間の: a Shinkansen journey between Tokyo and Osaka (*Tookyoo Oosaka-kañ no Shiñkañseñ no tabi*) 東京大阪間の新幹線の旅.
4 (dividing) ... no uⁱchi kara hitoⁱtsu ...のうちから一つ: I don't know how to choose between these neckties. (*Kono nekutai no uchi dore o erañdara yoi ka wakaranai.*) このネクタイのうちどれを選んだらよいかわからない.
— *adv.* aⁱima ni 合間に: I had two classes and there was no time to go to the toilet between. (*Jugyoo ga futatsu atta ga aima ni toire e iku hima mo nakatta.*) 授業が二つあったが合間にトイレへ行く暇もなかった.

beverage *n.* noⁱmiⁱmono 飲み物; iⁱñryoⁱo 飲料.

beware *vi.* (... ni) chuⁱi suru (...に)注意する 工; ki ⁱo tsukeⁱru 気をつける 図: Beware of the dog. (*Inu ni ki o tsuke nasai.*) 犬に気をつけなさい.

beyond *prep.* **1** (position) ... no muⁱkoo ni ...の向こうに: The village was visible beyond the lake. (*Mizuumi no mukoo ni mura ga mieta.*) 湖の向こうに村が見えた.

2 (time) ... o suⁱgite ...を過ぎて: We can't wait beyond 10:30. (*Juuji-hañ o sugite wa matemaseñ.*) 10時半を過ぎては待てません.
3 (ability; extent) ... o koⁱete ...を越えて; ... iⁱjoo ni ...以上に: It's beyond me. (*Watashi ni wa wakaranai.*) 私にはわからない.
— *adv.* muⁱkoo ni 向こうに: The explorer crossed the ocean and discovered the continent beyond. (*Tañkeñka wa taiyoo o watari sono mukoo ni tairiku o hakkeñ shita.*) 探検家は大洋を渡りその向こうに大陸を発見した.

bicycle *n.* jiⁱteⁱñsha 自転車: ride [get on] a bicycle (*jiteñsha ni noru*) 自転車に乗る / get off a bicycle (*jiteñsha kara oriru*) 自転車から下りる / bicycles for rent (*kashi jiteñsha*) 貸し自転車.

bid *n.* nyuⁱusatsu 入札; tsuⁱkeⁱne 付け値: enter a bid for old books (*kosho no nyuusatsu o suru*) 古書の入札をする.

big *adj.* **1** (of great size) oⁱkiⁱi 大きい; oⁱoki-na 大きな: Do you have a bigger desk? (*Motto ookii tsukue wa arimasu ka?*) もっと大きい机はありますか. / This sweater is too big. (*Kono seetaa wa ooki-sugiru.*) このセーターは大きすぎる. / a big baby (*ooki-na akañboo*) 大きな赤ん坊.
2 (elder) toⁱshiue no 年上の: a big brother (*ani*) 兄 / a big sister (*ane*) 姉.
3 (important; great) juⁱuyoo na 重要な; taⁱiheñ na 大変な; oⁱo- 大; daⁱi- 大: a big decision (*juuyoo na kettee*) 重要な決定 / a big mistake (*oo-machigai*) 大間違い / a big incident (*dai-jikeñ*) 大事件.

bike *n.* (bicycle) jiⁱteⁱñsha 自転車; (motorbike) oⁱotoⁱbai オートバイ.
★ Japanese '*baiku*' refers to a motorbike, not to a bicycle.

bill *n.* **1** (payment) seⁱekyuusho 請求書; kaⁱñjoⁱo 勘定: the electricity bill (*deñki-ryoo no seekyuusho*) 電気料の請求書 / It's my treat. I'll pay the bill. (*Watashi no ogori desu. Kañjoo wa watashi ga haraimasu.*) 私のおごりです. 勘定は私が払います.

2 (paper money) shiˈhee 紙幣; saˈtsu 札: a thousand-yen bill (*señ-eñ satsu*) 千円札.

billion *n.* (one thousand million) juˈu-oku 10 億.

bind *vt.* **1** (tie up; bandage) ... o shiˈbaˈru ...を縛る C; maˈku 巻く C: bind a package with a ribbon (*tsutsumi o riboñ de shibaru*) 包みをリボンで縛る / The doctor bound my wound with a bandage. (*Isha wa watashi no kizuguchi o hootai de maita.*) 医者は私の傷口を包帯で巻いた.

2 (of friendship) ... o muˈsubu ...を結ぶ C: Tom and I are bound together by our friendship. (*Tomu to watashi wa yuujoo de musubarete iru.*) トムと私は友情で結ばれている.

3 (of a book) ... o seˈehoñ suru ...を製本する I: bind a book (*hoñ o seehoñ suru*) 本を製本する.

bird *n.* toˈri 鳥: a small bird (*kotori*) 小鳥.

birth *n.* taˈñjoo 誕生; uˈmare 生まれ; shuˈsshoo 出生: the birth of a new nation (*atarashii kuni no tañjoo*) 新しい国の誕生 / Breeding is more important than birth. (*Umare yori mo sodachi no hoo ga taisetsu da.*) 生まれよりも育ちのほうが大切だ. / the date of one's birth (*seeneñ gappi*) 生年月日 / a birth certificate (*shusshoo shoomee*) 出生証明.

birthday *n.* taˈñjoˈobi 誕生日: Happy birthday! ((*O-)tañjoobi omedetoo.*) (お)誕生日おめでとう.

biscuit *n.* (U.S.) paˈñ パン; (U.K.) biˈsukeˈtto ビスケット; kuˈraˈkkaa クラッカー.

bishop *n.* (Church of England) shuˈkyoˈo 主教; (Catholic) shiˈˈkyoo 司教.

bit *n.* **1** (fragment) shoˈoheñ 小片; kaˈkera かけら: bits of glass (*garasu no haheñ*) ガラスの破片 / tear to bits (*biribiri ni saku*) びりびりに裂く.

2 (small amount) suˈkoˈshi 少し; choˈtto ちょっと: I'd like a bit of that ham. (*Sono hamu o sukoshi kudasai.*) そのハムを少し下さい. / Can you just wait a bit? (*Chotto matte moraemasu ka?*) ちょっと待ってもらえますか.

3 (degree) suˈkoˈshi 少し; choˈtto ちょっと: I'm a bit tired. (*Sukoshi tsukaremashita.*) 少し疲れました. / Please turn the volume down a bit. (*Chotto boryuumu o sagete kudasai.*) ちょっとボリュームを下げてください.

bite *vt.* **1** (with teeth) ... o kaˈmu ...をかむ C; ... ni kaˈmitsuku ...にかみつく C: bite one's nails (*tsume o kamu*) つめをかむ / The big dog bit the girl. (*Ooki-na inu ga oñna-no-ko ni kamitsuita.*) 大きな犬が女の子にかみついた.

2 (of an insect) ... o saˈsu ...を刺す C; kuˈu 食う C: I was badly bitten by mosquitoes. (*Watashi wa hidoku ka ni kuwareta.*) 私はひどく蚊に食われた.

— *vi.* kaˈmu かむ C; kaˈmitsuku かみつく C: This dog doesn't bite. (*Kono inu wa kamitsukimaseñ.*) この犬はかみつきません.

— *n.* hiˈtoˈkajiri ひとかじり; hiˈtoˈkuchi ひと口; saˈshiˈkizu 刺し傷: take a bite from an apple (*riñgo o hitokajiri suru*) りんごをひとかじりする / a bite of bread (*hitokuchi no pañ*) ひと口のパン / an insect bite (*mushi no sashikizu*) 虫の刺し傷.

bitter *adj.* **1** (taste) niˈgaˈi 苦い: bitter coffee (*nigai koohii*) 苦いコーヒー.

2 (emotions; experience) tsuˈrai 辛い; kuˈrushiˈi 苦しい: a bitter memory (*tsurai omoide*) 辛い思い出 / suffer a bitter experience (*kurushii taikeñ o suru*) 苦しい体験をする.

3 (very cold) mi ˈo kiˈru yoo na 身を切るような: a bitter wind (*mi o kiru yoo na kaze*) 身を切るような風.

bitterness *n.* **1** (taste) niˈgami 苦み: chocolate with a touch of bitterness (*chotto nigami no aru cho-*

koreeto) ちょっと苦みのあるチョコレート.
2 (emotions; experience) ku⌐ru-shimi 苦しみ: a man with bitterness in his heart (*kokoro ni kurushimi o idaku hito*) 心に苦しみを抱く人.

black *adj.* **1** (color) ku⌐ro⌐i 黒い: black shoes (*kuroi kutsu*) 黒い靴 / black clouds (*kuroi kumo*) 黒い雲.
2 (race) ko⌐kujiñ no 黒人の: black people (*kokujiñ*) 黒人.
3 (of coffee) bu⌐ra⌐kku no ブラックの: drink one's coffee black (*koohii o burakku de nomu*) コーヒーをブラックで飲む.
4 (bad; threatening) ku⌐rai 暗い: The situation is black. (*Jookyoo wa kurai.*) 状況は暗い.
— *n.* **1** (color) ku⌐ro 黒: Mr. Yamauchi likes dressing in black. (*Yamauchi-sañ wa kuro no fukusoo ga konomi da.*) 山内さんは黒の服装が好みだ.
2 (race) ko⌐kujiñ 黒人: The blacks demanded freedom in South Africa. (*Minami Afurika de kokujiñ-tachi wa jiyuu o yookyuu shita.*) 南アフリカで黒人たちは自由を要求した.
be in the black *vi.* ku⌐roji da 黒字だ.

black-and-white *adj.* ku⌐ro to ⌐shi⌐ro no 黒と白の; shi⌐ro-kuro no 白黒の: a black-and-white roll of film (*shiro-kuro no firumu*) 白黒のフィルム / a black-and-white TV (*shiro-kuro no terebi*) 白黒のテレビ.
★ Note that English and Japanese word orders are opposite.

blade *n.* ha⌐ 刃: the blade of a knife (*naifu no ha*) ナイフの刃 / a razor blade (*kamisori no ha*) かみそりの刃.

blame *vt.* ... no se⌐e ni suru ...のせいにする ⊡; ... o se⌐me⌐ru ...を責める Ⓥ: He blamed me for the failure. (*Kare wa sono shippai o watashi no see ni shita.*) 彼はその失敗を私のせいにした. / I don't blame you. (*Kimi o semetari shinai yo.*) きみを責めたりしないよ.

blank *adj.* **1** (not written or

printed) na⌐ni mo ka⌐ite nai 何も書いてない; ha⌐kushi no 白紙の: a blank page (*nani mo kaite nai peeji*) 何も書いてないページ / a blank tape (*nani mo rokuoñ sarete inai teepu*) 何も録音されていないテープ.
2 (expressionless) bo⌐ñya⌐ri shita [shite iru] ぼんやりした[している]; hyo⌐o-jo⌐o no na⌐i 表情のない: He looked blank. (*Kare wa hyoojoo no nai kao o shite ita.*) 彼は表情のない顔をしていた.
— *n.* ku⌐usho 空所; ku⌐urañ 空欄; yo⌐haku 余白: Fill in the blanks with a suitable word. (*Kuusho ni tekitoo na go o ire nasai.*) 空所に適当な語を入れなさい.

blanket *n.* mo⌐ofu 毛布: wrap a baby up in a blanket (*akañboo o moofu de kurumu*) 赤ん坊を毛布でくるむ.

blast *n.* **1** (wind) i⌐chijiñ no kaze 一陣の風; to⌐ppuu 突風: a blast of wind (*ichijiñ no kyoofuu*) 一陣の強風.
2 (explosion) ba⌐kuhatsu 爆発; ba⌐kufuu 爆風: the blast of a bomb (*bakudañ no bakuhatsu*) 爆弾の爆発.
— *vt.* (blow up) ... o ba⌐kuha suru ...を爆破する ⊡: The door was blasted by someone. (*Doa ga dareka ni bakuha sareta.*) ドアがだれかに爆破された.

bleed *vi.* chi ⌐ga de⌐ru 血が出る Ⓥ; shu⌐kketsu suru 出血する ⊡: His cut was bleeding. (*Kare no kizuguchi kara chi ga dete ita.*) 彼の傷口から血が出ていた.

blend *vt.* ... o ma⌐ze⌐ru ...を混ぜる Ⓥ; ko⌐ñgoo suru 混合する ⊡: blend milk and eggs (*gyuunyuu to tamago o mazeru*) 牛乳と卵を混ぜる.
— *vi.* ma⌐za⌐ru 混ざる Ⓒ: Oil does not blend with water. (*Abura wa mizu to mazaranai.*) 油は水と混ざらない.
— *n.* ko⌐ñgo⌐obutsu 混合物; bu⌐reñdo ブレンド.

bless *vt.* ... o shu⌐kufuku suru ...を

祝福する ⊤: The priest blessed the people. (*Shisai wa hitobito o shukufuku shita.*) 司祭は人々を祝福した.
be blessed with ... *vt.* ...ni me｢gumareru ...に恵まれる Ⅴ: We were blessed with good fortune [weather]. (*Watashi-tachi wa koouñ [kooteñ] ni megumareta.*) 私たちは好運[好天]に恵まれた.

blessing *n.* ka｢mi no me｢gumi 神の恵み; shu｢kufuku 祝福; i｢nori 祈り: ask a blessing before [after] a meal (*shokuzeñ [shokugo] no inori o suru*) 食前[食後]の祈りをする.

blind *adj.* **1** (unable to see) me｢ no fu｢ji¹yuu na 目の不自由な; mo｢omoku no 盲目の: a blind man (*me no mienai hito*) 目の見えない人.
2 (unable to understand) ...ni ki｢ga tsuka¹nai ...に気がつかない; wa｢kara¹nai わからない: He was blind to the dangers. (*Kare wa kikeñ ni ki ga tsukanakatta.*) 彼は危険に気がつかなかった.
— *n.* bu｢raiñdo ブラインド; hi｢yoke 日よけ: draw up [pull down] the blinds (*buraiñdo o ageru [orosu]*) ブラインドを上げる[下ろす].

blindness *n.* mo｢omoku 盲目: color blindness (*shikimoo*) 色盲.

block *n.* **1** (material) ka｢tamari 塊: a block of ice (*koori no katamari*) 氷の塊 / a block of wood (*mokuzai*) 木材.
2 (between streets) bu｢ro¹kku ブロック; ku｢kaku 区画.
3 (large building) mu｢ne 棟: an apartment block (*apaato no mune*) アパートの棟.
— *vt.* ...o fu｢sagu ...をふさぐ ©; bo｢ogai suru 妨害する ⊤: They blocked the entrance with barricades. (*Kare-ra wa iriguchi o barikeedo de fusaida.*) 彼らは入り口をバリケードでふさいだ.

blood *n.* chi 血; [technical] ke｢tsu-eki 血液: My blood type is B. (*Watashi no ketsueki-gata wa bii desu.*) 私の血液型はBです. / blood pressure (*ketsuatsu*) 血圧.

bloom *n.* ha｢na¹ 花: a bloom of a rose (*bara no hana*) バラの花.
be in bloom *vi.* sa｢ite iru 咲いている Ⅴ: The cherry blossoms are now in full bloom. (*Sakura wa ima ga mañkai desu.*) 桜は今が満開です.
— *vi.* ha｢na¹ ga sa｢ku 花が咲く ©: Our roses will be blooming in June. (*Uchi no bara wa roku-gatsu ni wa saku deshoo.*) うちのバラは6月には咲くでしょう.

blossom *n.* ha｢na¹ 花: apple blossoms (*ringo no hana*) りんごの花.
— *vi.* ha｢na¹ ga sa｢ku 花が咲く ©: This tree will blossom next week. (*Kono ki wa raishuu saku deshoo.*) この木は来週咲くでしょう.

blotter *n.* su｢itori¹gami 吸い取り紙.

blouse *n.* bu｢ra¹usu ブラウス: wear a blouse (*burausu o kiru*) ブラウスを着る.

blow[1] *vi.* (wind) fu｢ku 吹く ©: The wind is blowing hard. (*Kaze ga hidoku fuite iru.*) 風がひどく吹いている.
— *vt.* (instrument) ...o fu｢ku ...を吹く ©; (horn) na｢rasu 鳴らす ©: blow a trumpet (*torañpetto o fuku*) トランペットを吹く / blow a car horn (*keeteki o narasu*) 警笛を鳴らす.
blow one's nose *vi.* ha｢na o ka-mu 鼻をかむ ©.

blow[2] *n.* **1** (hard stroke) kyo｢oda 強打; i｢chigeki 一撃: I received a blow on the head. (*Watashi wa atama ni ichigeki o kuratta.*) 私は頭に一撃をくらった.
2 (shock) da｢geki 打撃: My father's death was a great blow to me. (*Chichi no shi wa watashi ni totte ooki-na dageki datta.*) 父の死は私にとって大きな打撃だった.

blue *adj.* a｢o¹i 青い: the blue sky (*aoi sora*) 青い空 / The lake was blue. (*Mizuumi wa aokatta.*) 湖は青かった.
— *n.* a¹o 青: dark [light] blue (*koi [akarui] ao*) 濃い[明るい]青.

blunt *adj.* **1** (of a knife) ni｢bu¹i 鈍い; ki｢re¹nai 切れない: a blunt knife (*kirenai naifu*) 切れないナイフ.

2 (of people) bu「kkira」boo na ぶっき らぼうな; so「kkena」i そっけない: a blunt manner (*sokkenai taido*) そっ けない態度.

blush *vi.* ka「o o akarameru 顔を赤 らめる Ⅴ; a「kaku na」ru 赤くなる Ⓒ; se「kimeñ suru 赤面する Ⅰ: The boy blushed for shame. (*Sono otoko-no-ko wa hazukashisa de akaku natta.*) その男の子は恥ずかしさ で赤くなった.

— *n.* se「kimeñ 赤面; ha「jirai no iro 恥じらいの色: hide one's blushes (*hajirai no iro o kakusu*) 恥じらいの 色を隠す.

board *n.* **1** (timber) i「ta 板: a cut- ting board (*manaita*) まな板.

2 (a official group) i「i」ñkai 委員会: a board of education (*kyooiku iiñ- kai*) 教育委員会.

— *vt.* **1** (get on) ... ni no「ru ...に乗 る Ⓒ: We boarded a plane at Nari- ta. (*Watashi-tachi wa Narita de hikooki ni notta.*) 私たちは成田で飛 行機に乗った. / Where can I board the ship to Oshima? (*Ooshima e no fune wa doko de noru ñ desu ka?*) 大島への船はどこで乗るんですか.

2 (cover with boards) ... ni i「ta o ha「ru ...に板を張る Ⓒ: board up a broken window (*kowareta mado ni ita o haru*) 壊れた窓に板を張る.

on board *adv.* (plane) ki「nai de 機内で; (ship) se「ñnai de 船内で: Do they sell tax-free goods on board? (*Kinai de meñzeehiñ no hañbai o shite imasu ka?*) 機内で免 税品の販売をしていますか.

boardinghouse *n.* ge「shukuya 下宿屋.

boast *vi.* ji「mañ suru 自慢する Ⅰ: He boasted about his new house. (*Kare wa shiñchiku no ie o jimañ shita.*) 彼は新築の家を自慢した.

— *vt.* ... to ji「mañ suru ...と自慢す る Ⅰ: She boasted that she could read Chinese characters. (*Kanojo wa kañji ga yomeru to jimañ shita.*) 彼女は漢字が読めると自慢した.

— *n.* ji「mañ no ta」ne 自慢の種; ho「kori 誇り.

make a boast of ... *vt.* ... o ji- 「mañ suru ...を自慢する Ⅰ.

boat *n.* **1** (small vessel) bo「oto ボー ト: row a boat (*booto o kogu*) ボート をこぐ.

2 (ship) fu「ne 船: get on a boat (*fune ni noru*) 船に乗る / get off a boat (*fune kara oriru*) 船から降りる / a fishing boat (*gyoseñ*) 漁船 / a sightseeing boat (*yuurañseñ*) 遊覧 船. ★ 'Ship' is also called *'fune'*.

body *n.* **1** (including head and limbs) ka「rada 体; shi「ñtai 身体: a strong body (*joobu na karada*) じょ うぶな体 / I have aches all over my body. (*Karada-juu ga itai.*) 体中が 痛い.

2 (excluding head and limbs) do「o- (tai) 胴(体); bo「dii ボディー: He was hit twice in the body. (*Kare wa bodii o ni-do utareta.*) 彼はボディーを 2度打たれた.

3 (corpse) shi「tai 死体; i「tai 遺体: an unidentified body (*mimoto fumee no itai*) 身元不明の遺体.

4 (main part) shu「yoobu 主要部; -tai 体: a car body (*shatai*) 車体 / the body of an airplane (*kitai*) 機体 / the body of a letter (*tegami no hoñbuñ*) 手紙の本文.

5 (group) da「ñtai 団体; a「tsuma」ri 集まり: a diplomatic body (*gaikoo- dañ*) 外交団.

boil *vi.* wa「ku 沸く Ⓒ; fu「ttoo suru 沸騰する Ⅰ: Water boils at 100℃. (*Mizu wa sesshi hyaku-do de fut- too suru.*) 水は摂氏 100 度で沸騰する.

— *vt.* ... o wa「kasu ...を沸かす Ⓒ; ni「ru 煮る Ⅴ; ta「ku 炊く Ⓒ; yu「de」ru ゆでる Ⅴ: boil water (*o-yu o waka- su*) お湯を沸かす / boil vegetables (*yasai o niru*) 野菜を煮る / boil rice (*gohañ o taku*) ご飯を炊く / Please boil the eggs soft. (*Tamago o hañ- juku ni shite kudasai.*) 卵を半熟に してください. / a boiled egg (*yude tamago*) ゆで卵.

boiler *n.* bo「iraa ボイラー.

bold adj. daｒitaｎ na 大胆な: a bold plan (daitañ na keekaku) 大胆な計画.

bomb n. baｒkudañ 爆弾: drop a bomb (bakudañ o otosu) 爆弾を落とす.
— vt. ... o baｒkugeki suru ...を爆撃する ①: bomb a city (toshi o bakugeki suru) 都市を爆撃する.

bond n. 1 (ties) muｒsubitsuki 結びつき; kiｒzuna きずな: a bond of friendship (yuujoo no kizuna) 友情のきずな.
2 (restriction) soｒkubaku 束縛: break one's bonds (sokubaku o tachikiru) 束縛を断ち切る.
3 (written promise) shoｒosho 証書; shoｒomoñ 証文: He signed the bond. (Kare wa shoomoñ ni shomee shita.) 彼は証文に署名した.
4 (interest-bearing certificate) saｒikeñ 債券: a public bond (koosai) 公債.

bone n. hoｒneｌ 骨: break a bone in one's arm (ude no hone o oru) 腕の骨を折る / A fish bone got stuck in my throat. (Sakana no hone ga nodo ni sasatta.) 魚の骨がのどに刺さった.

book[1] n. hoｎ 本: read [write] a book (hoñ o yomu [kaku]) 本を読む[書く] / I bought three books. (Watashi wa hoñ o sañ-satsu katta.) 私は本を3冊買った / an instruction book (shiyoo setsumeesho) 使用説明書 / a phone book (deñwachoo) 電話帳.

book[2] vt. ... o yoｒyaku suru ...を予約する ①: book a room at a hotel (hoteru no heya o yoyaku suru) ホテルの部屋を予約する.

bookseller n. hoｒñya 本屋.

bookstore n. hoｒñya 本屋; shoｒteñ 書店: a second-hand bookstore (furuhoñya) 古本屋.

boots n. naｒgagutsu 長靴; buｒutsu ブーツ: rubber boots (gomunaga) ゴム長.

border n. 1 (boundary) koｒkkyoo 国境; kyoｒokai 境界: cross the border (kokkyoo o koeru) 国境を越える.
2 (edge) heｒriｌ へり; haｒshi 端; fuｒchiｌ 縁: a tablecloth with a lace border (reesu no heri ga aru teeburu-kurosu) レースのへりがあるテーブルクロス / There was a border of flowers around the lawn. (Shibafu no mawari wa hana de fuchidorarete ita.) 芝生の周りは花で縁どられていた.
— vt. ... to saｒkaｌi o seｒssuru ...と境を接する ①: Japan borders no other countries. (Nihoñ wa ta no kuni to sakai o sesshite inai.) 日本は他の国と境を接していない.

bore[1] vt. (make a hole) ... ni aｒnaｌ o aｒkeru ...に穴をあける Ⓥ: bore a hole in a board (ita ni ana o akeru) 板に穴をあける.

bore[2] vt. (weary) ... o uｒñzaｌri saseru ...をうんざりさせる Ⓥ; taｒikutsu saseru 退屈させる Ⓥ: Prof. Yamazaki's lecture bored us. (Yamazaki kyooju no koogi wa taikutsu datta.) 山崎教授の講義は退屈だった.

boring adj. taｒikutsu na 退屈な; tsuｒmaraｌnai つまらない: a boring job (taikutsu na shigoto) 退屈な仕事 / The week-end was really boring. (Shuumatsu wa hoñtoo ni tsumaranakatta.) 週末はほんとうにつまらなかった.

born adj. 1 uｒmareta 生まれた: I was born on May 5, 1965. (Watashi wa señ-kyuuhyaku-rokujuugo-neñ no go-gatsu itsuka ni umaremashita.) 私は1965年の5月5日に生まれました.
2 uｒmarenagara no 生まれながらの: a born painter (umarenagara no gaka) 生まれながらの画家.

borrow vt. ... o kaｒriru ...を借りる Ⓥ: Is it okay if I borrow your notebook? (Kimi no nooto o karite mo ii desu ka?) きみのノートを借りてもいいですか / Mr. Ito borrowed two million yen from the bank. (Itoo-sañ wa giñkoo kara nihyakumañ-eñ karita.) 伊藤さんは銀行から200万円

借りた.

both *adj.* ryo「ohoo no 両方の; fu-「tari tomo 二人とも: I don't need both maps. Just give me one. (*Ryoohoo no chizu wa irimaseñ. Ichi-mai dake kudasai.*) 両方の地図 はいりません. 1 枚だけ下さい. / Both my parents are getting along very well. (*Ryooshiñ wa futari tomo geñki ni kurashite imasu.*) 両親は二人とも元 気に暮らしています.
— *pron.* ryo「ohoo 両方; fu「tari 二 人: There's chocolate and cake. Take both if you want to. (*Chokoreeto to keeki ga arimasu. Yokattara ryoohoo doozo.*) チョコレート とケーキがあります. よかったら両方どうぞ. / Both of us went to the same university. (*Watashi-tachi wa futari tomo onaji daigaku ni kayoimashita.*) 私たちは二人とも同じ大学に通 いました.
— *conj.* (both ... and ...) ... mo ... mo ...も...も: He speaks both Chinese and Japanese. (*Kare wa Chuugokugo mo Nihoñgo mo hanashimasu.*) 彼は中国語も日本語 も話します.

bother *vt.* ... o na「yama」su ...を悩 ます ⓒ; u「rusagarase」ru うるさがらせる Ⓥ; ... ni me「waku o ka「ke」ru ...に 迷惑をかける Ⓥ: The noise of the passing trains really bothers me. (*Ressha ga tsuuka suru oto wa hoñtoo ni urusai.*) 列車が通過する音 はほんとうにうるさい. / I am sorry to bother you at this time of night, but I need some information. (*Yabuñ go-meewaku o kakemasu ga chotto oshiete kudasai.*) 夜分に 迷惑をかけますがちょっと教えてください.
— *vi.* o「moinaya」mu 思い悩む ⓒ; ku「 ni suru 苦にする Ⓘ: Don't bother about such a trifling matter. (*Soñna tsumaranai koto de omoinayamu no wa yoshi nasai.*) そんな つまらないことで思い悩むのはよしなさい.
— *n.* me「ñdo」o 面倒; ya「kkai やっ かい: cause a person bother (*hito ni meñdoo o kakeru*) 人に面倒をかける.

bottle *n.* **1** (container) bi「ñ びん: fill [empty] a bottle (*biñ o ippai [kara] ni suru*) びんをいっぱい[から]にす る / a bottle full of water (*mizu ga ippai haitta biñ*) 水がいっぱい入ったび ん / a milk bottle (*gyuunyuu-biñ*) 牛乳びん.
2 (amount) -hoñ [-boñ; -poñ] 本 《⇒ appendix》: I have 2 bottles of whisky. (*Uisukii o ni-hoñ motte imasu.*) ウイスキーを 2 本持っています.

bottle opener *n.* se「ñnuki 栓抜 き.

bottom *n.* **1** (lowest part) so「ko 底: the bottom of a glass (*koppu no soko*) コップの底 / I found my address book at the bottom of my suitcase. (*Juushoroku ga suutsukeesu no soko ni atta.*) 住所録がスー ツケースの底にあった.
2 (of a mountain) fu「moto ふもと; (base) shi「ta 下: a house at the bottom of the mountain (*yama no fumoto no ie*) 山のふもとの家 / Your mistake is on the third line from the bottom. (*Kimi no machigai wa shita kara sañ-gyoome ni aru.*) 君 のまちがいは下から 3 行目にある.
3 (lowest) sa「itee no 最低の; (last) sa「igo no 最後の; bi「ri no びりの: the bottom price (*saitee nedañ*) 最 低値段 / He was at the bottom of the class. (*Kare wa kurasu no biri datta.*) 彼はクラスのびりだった.
4 (buttocks) shi「ri」 尻: She wiped her baby's dirty bottom. (*Kanojo wa akañboo no yogoreta o-shiri o fuita.*) 彼女は赤ん坊の汚れたお尻を拭い た.

bounce *vi.* ha「zumu 弾む ⓒ; ba「uñ-do suru バウンドする Ⓘ: This ball bounces well. (*Kono booru wa yoku hazumu.*) このボールはよく弾む.
— *vt.* ... o ha「zumaseru ...を弾ませ る Ⓥ; ba「uñdo saseru バウンドさせる Ⓥ: bounce a ball (*booru o bauñdo saseru*) ボールをバウンドさせる.

bowl *n.* **1** (container) wa「ñ わん; cha「wañ 茶わん; ha「chi」 鉢; bo「oru ボール: a rice bowl (*gohañ no cha-*

wañ) ご飯の茶わん / a goldfish bowl (*kiñgyo-bachi*) 金魚鉢 / a salad bowl (*sarada booru*) サラダボール.
2 (amount) -hai [-bai; -pai] 杯 《⇨ appendix》: two bowls of rice (*gohañ ni-hai*) ご飯 2 杯.

box *n.* **1** (container) ha⌐ko 箱: a wooden box (*ki no hako*) 木の箱 / a lunch box (*beñtoobako*) 弁当箱 / a match box (*matchibako*) マッチ箱.
2 (amount) -hako [-bako; -pako] 箱 《⇨ appendix》: two boxes of tangerines (*mikañ futa-hako*) みかん 2 箱 / How much do these peaches cost per box? (*Kono momo wa hito-hako ikura desu ka?*) この桃は 1 箱いくらですか.

boy *n.* o⌐toko⌐-no-ko 男の子; sho⌐o-neñ 少年: Will the boys please line up here? (*Otoko-no-ko-tachi wa koko ni narañde choodai.*) 男の子たちはここに並んでちょうだい. / boys and girls (*shooneñ shoojo*) 少年少女.

bra *n.* bu⌐ra⌐jaa ブラジャー: put on a bra (*burajaa o tsukeru*) ブラジャーをつける.

braid *vt.* ... o a⌐mu ...を編む ©: braid hair (*kami o amu*) 髪を編む.
— *n.* (hair) o⌐sage⌐gami おさげ髪; (band) ku⌐mi⌐himo 組みひも; mo⌐oru モール: wear one's hair in braids (*kami o osage ni suru*) 髪をおさげにする / gold braid (*kiñ mooru*) 金モール.

brain *n.* **1** (organ) no⌐o 脳; no⌐ozui 脳髄.
2 (intelligence) zu⌐noo 頭脳; a⌐tama 頭; chi⌐ryoku 知力: have good [no] brains (*atama ga yoi [warui]*) 頭がよい[悪い] / use one's brains (*atama o tsukau*) 頭を使う.
3 (intelligent person) chi⌐teki shido⌐osha 知的指導者; bu⌐re⌐eñ ブレーン; (clever person) a⌐tama no i⌐i hito 頭のいい人: He is the brains of the company. (*Kare wa kaisha no bureeñ da.*) 彼は会社のブレーンだ.

brake *n.* bu⌐re⌐eki ブレーキ: put on [take off] the brakes (*bureeki o kakeru [yurumeru]*) ブレーキをかける

[緩める].
— *vt.* ... ni bu⌐re⌐eki o ka⌐ke⌐ru ...にブレーキをかける Ⓥ: He braked the car. (*Kare wa kuruma ni bureeki o kaketa.*) 彼は車にブレーキをかけた.
— *vi.* bu⌐re⌐eki o ka⌐ke⌐ru ブレーキをかける Ⓥ: The bus braked suddenly. (*Basu ga kyuu-bureeki o kaketa.*) バスが急ブレーキをかけた.

branch *n.* **1** (tree) e⌐da 枝: break a branch (*eda o oru*) 枝を折る.
2 (office) shi⌐teñ 支店; shi⌐bu 支部: the Iidabashi branch of the Sakura Bank (*Sakura giñkoo no Iidabashi shiteñ*) さくら銀行の飯田橋支店.
3 (part) bu⌐moñ 部門; bu⌐ñka 分科: Geometry is a branch of mathematics. (*Kika wa suugaku no ichi-bumoñ desu.*) 幾何は数学の一部門です.
— *vi.* wa⌐kare⌐ru 分かれる Ⓥ; bu⌐ñki suru 分岐する Ⓘ: This road branches up ahead. (*Kono michi wa saki e itte wakaremasu.*) この道は先へ行って分かれます.

branch line *n.* shi⌐señ 支線.

brassiere *n.* bu⌐ra⌐jaa ブラジャー.

brave *adj.* yu⌐ukañ na 勇敢な; yu⌐uki no [ga] aru 勇気の[が]ある: a brave policeman (*yuukañ na keesatsukañ*) 勇敢な警察官 / It was brave of him to jump into the river to save the child. (*Kodomo o sukuu tame ni kawa ni tobikomu to wa kare mo yuukañ datta.*) 子どもを救うために川に飛び込むとは彼も勇敢だった.

bread *n.* pa⌐ñ パン: a loaf [slice] of bread (*pañ hito katamari [hito kire]*) パンひと塊[ひと切れ] / cut [toast] bread (*pañ o kiru [yaku]*) パンを切る[焼く] / butter bread (*pañ ni bataa o nuru*) パンにバターを塗る.

break[1] *vt.* **1** (destroy) ... o ko⌐wa⌐su ...を壊す ©: Who broke the toy? (*Omocha o kowashita no wa dare desu ka?*) おもちゃを壊したのはだれか.
2 (divide) ... o wa⌐ru ...を割る: break an egg (*tamago o w*

割る / She broke the glass into pieces. (*Kanojo wa koppu o kona-gona ni watte shimatta.*) 彼女はコップを粉々に割ってしまった.

3 (snap) ... o o¹ru ...を折る C: break a branch from a tree (*ki no eda o oru*) 木の枝を折る / Taro broke his leg. (*Taroo wa ashi o otta.*) 太郎は脚を折った.

4 (smash) ... o ku¹da¹ku ...を砕く C: break a rock with a hammer (*hañmaa de iwa o kudaku*) ハンマーで岩を砕く.

5 (violate) ... o ya¹bu¹ru ...を破る C: break the law (*hooritsu o yaburu*) 法律を破る / He never breaks a promise. (*Kare wa kesshite yakusoku o yaburanai.*) 彼は決して約束を破らない.

6 (better) ... o ya¹bu¹ru ...を破る C: break the world record (*sekai kiroku o yaburu*) 世界記録を破る.

— *vi.* ko¹ware¹ru 壊れる V; wa¹reru 割れる V; o¹re¹ru 折れる V; ku¹dake¹ru 砕ける V; ya¹bure¹ru 破れる V: This camera has broken. (*Kono kamera wa kowarete shimatta.*) このカメラは壊れてしまった. / My precious vase broke. (*Watashi no daiji na kabiñ ga wareta.*) 私の大事な花びんが割れた.

break² *n.* ya¹sumi 休み; kyu¹ukee 休憩: a coffee [tea] break (*nakayasumi*) 中休み / Let's take a quick break. (*Chotto kyuukee shimashoo.*) ちょっと休憩しましょう.

breakfast *n.* cho¹oshoku 朝食; a¹sa-go¹hañ 朝ご飯: have an early breakfast (*hayai chooshoku o toru*) 早い朝食をとる.

breast *n.* **1** (female) chi¹busa 乳房; chi¹chi 乳: suck the breast (*chichi [oppai] o shaburu*) 乳[おっぱい]をしゃぶる.

2 (chest) mu¹ne¹ 胸: have a pain in one's breast (*mune ga itamu*) 胸が痛む.

breath *n.* i¹ki 息; ko¹kyuu 呼吸: take in [give out] breath (*iki o suu ⌜haku⌝*) 息を吸う[吐く] / have bad

breath (*iki ga kusai*) 息が臭い / hold one's breath (*iki o korasu*) 息をこらす / take a deep breath (*shiñkokyuu o suru*) 深呼吸をする.

breathe *vi.* i¹ki o suru 息をする I; ko¹kyuu suru 呼吸する I: Please breathe in, and then breathe out slowly. (*Iki o sutte sore kara yukkuri haite kudasai.*) 息を吸ってそれからゆっくり吐いてください.

— *vt.* ... o su¹iko¹mu ...を吸い込む C: breathe fresh air (*shiñseñ na kuuki o suikomu*) 新鮮な空気を吸い込む.

breeze *n.* so¹yo¹kaze そよ風; bi¹fuu 微風: a cool breeze (*suzushii kaze*) 涼しい風 / a pleasant spring breeze (*kimochi no yoi haru no kaze*) 気持ちのよい春の風.

bribe *n.* wa¹iro わいろ: offer [accept] a bribe (*wairo o sashidasu [uketoru]*) わいろを差し出す[受け取る].
— *vt.* (hito) ni wa¹iro o tsu¹kau (人)にわいろを使う C; ... o ba¹ishuu suru ...を買収する I: attempt to bribe a mayor (*shichoo o baishuu shiyoo to suru*) 市長を買収しようとする.

brick *n.* re¹ñga れんが: a house built of red bricks (*akai reñga de dekita uchi*) 赤いれんがでできた家.

bride *n.* ha¹na¹yome 花嫁; shi¹ñpu 新婦.

bridegroom *n.* ha¹namu¹ko 花婿; shi¹ñroo 新郎.

bridge *n.* ha¹shi¹ 橋: build a bridge (*hashi o kakeru*) 橋をかける / cross a bridge (*hashi o wataru*) 橋を渡る / a railway bridge (*tekkyoo*) 鉄橋 / a suspension bridge (*tsuribashi*) つり橋.
— *vt.* ... ni ha¹shi¹ o ka¹ke¹ru ...に橋を架ける V: We bridged the stream. (*Watashi-tachi wa sono ogawa ni hashi o kaketa.*) 私たちはその小川に橋を架けた.

brief *adj.* mi¹jika¹i 短い; wa¹zuka no わずかの; ta¹ñji¹kañ no 短時間の: a brief speech (*mijikai eñzetsu*) 短い演説 / take a brief rest (*tanjikan*

no kyuusoku o toru) 短時間の休息
を取る.
—— n. te「kiyoo 摘要; ga「iyoo 概要.
in brief adv. yo「o-su」ru ni 要する
に: In brief, he has failed. (Yoosuru ni kare wa shippai shita.) 要
するに彼は失敗した.

briefcase n. bu「riifu-ke」esu ブリー
フケース; ka「bañ かばん: I left my
briefcase on the train. (Deñsha no
naka ni kabañ o wasuremashita.)
電車の中にかばんを忘れました.

bright adj. **1** (light) a「karui 明るい;
ka「gaya」ite (iru) 輝いて(いる): a
bright morning (akaruku hareta
asa) 明るく晴れた朝 / The sun is
bright. (Taiyoo ga akaruku kagayaite iru.) 太陽が明るく輝いている.
2 (color) a「za」yaka na 鮮やかな:
The roses were bright red. (Bara
wa azayaka na akadatta.) バラは鮮や
かな赤だった.
3 (cheerful) ha「re」yaka na 晴れやか
な; ka「gaya」ite (iru) 輝いて(いる): a
bright, smiling face (hareyaka na
egao) 晴れやかな笑顔 / His eyes were
bright with excitement. (Kare no
me wa koofuñ de kagayaite ita.)
彼の目は興奮で輝いていた.
4 (clever) ri「koo na 利口な; a「tama」
ga i「i 頭がいい: a bright boy (atama
ga ii otoko-no-ko) 頭がいい男の子.

brighten vt. ... o a「karuku suru ...
を明るくする ①; ka「gayakase」ru 輝か
せる Ⅴ: A vase of flowers will
brighten the room. (Kabiñ ni hana
ga areba heya ga akaruku naru
daroo.) 花びんに花があれば部屋が明るく
なるだろう.
—— vi. a「karuku na」ru 明るくなる ©:
The sky brightened. (Sora ga akaruku natta.) 空が明るくなった.

brilliant adj. **1** (very bright) hi-
「kari-kagaya」ku 光り輝く: a bril-
liant diamond (hikari-kagayaku
daiyamoñdo) 光り輝くダイヤモンド.
2 (clever) su「gu」rete iru 優れている;
su「barashi」i すばらしい: a brilliant
student (sugurete iru gakusee) 優
れている学生 / a brilliant idea (su-

barashii kañgae) すばらしい考え.

bring vt. **1** (a thing) ... o mo「tte
ku」ru ...を持ってくる ①: Please bring
me some ice and water. (Koori to
mizu o motte kite kudasai.) 氷と水
を持ってきてください.
2 (a person) ... o tsu「rete ku」ru ...を
連れてくる ①: I will bring my
brother along with me. (Otooto o
issho ni tsurete kimasu.) 弟をいっ
しょに連れてきます.
3 (cause) ... o mo「tara」su ...をもたら
す ©; ma「ne」ku 招く ©: Our action
brought protests from the neighbors. (Watashi-tachi no koodoo
wa kiñjo kara koogi o maneita.) 私
たちの行動は近所から抗議を招いた.

bring up vt. ... o so「date」ru ... を
育てる Ⅴ: I was brought up in the
country. (Watashi wa inaka de
sodatta.) 私はいなかで育った.

Britain n. 「girisu イギリス; E「ekoku
英国.

British adj. 「girisu no イギリスの;
E「ekoku no 英国の: the British (Igi-
risujiñ) イギリス人; (Eekokujiñ) 英国
人.

broad adj. **1** (wide) ha「ba no hiro」i
幅の広い; (extensive) hi「robi」ro to
shita [shite iru] 広々とした[している]:
a broad river (haba no hiroi kawa)
幅の広い川 / a broad ocean (hirobiro to shita umi) 広々とした海 /
broad shoulders (hiroi katahaba)
広い肩幅.
2 (general) hi「ro」i 広い; o「oza」ppa
na おおざっぱな: a broad knowledge
of world events (sekai no dekigoto
ni tsuite no hiroi chishiki) 世界の
出来事についての広い知識 / Just give
me the broad outline of the plan.
(Sono keekaku no oozappa na gaiyoo o oshiete kudasai.) その計画のお
おざっぱな概要を教えてください.

broadcast n. ho「osoo 放送: a
broadcast program (hoosoo bañgumi) 放送番組 / a live broad̚st
(nama-hoosoo) 生放送 / a sa̚
broadcast (eesee hoosoo) ̚
—— vt. ... o ho「osoo suru

する①: The game will be broadcast on television tonight. (*Sono shiai wa koñya terebi de hoosoo saremasu.*) その試合は今夜テレビで放送されます。

brochure *n.* paˈnfuretto パンフレット; shoˈosaˈsshi 小冊子: I'd like a sightseeing brochure for this town. (*Kono machi no kañkoo pañfuretto o itadakitai ñ desu ga.*) この町の観光パンフレットをいただきたいんですが。

broil *vt.* ... o yaˈku ...を焼く ©; aˈbuˈru あぶる ©: broil chicken legs (*tori no ashi o yaku*) 鶏の脚を焼く。

broken *adj.* **1** (thing) koˈwaˈreta 壊れた: a broken cup (*kowareta chawañ*) 壊れた茶碗。
2 (bone) oˈreta 折れた; (body part) keˈgaˈo shita けがをした: a broken leg (*kossetsu shita ashi*) 骨折した脚。
3 (agreement) yaˈbuˈreta 破られた; oˈkasaˈreta 犯された: a broken promise (*yaburareta yakusoku*) 破られた約束 / a broken law (*okasareta hooritsu*) 犯された法律。

brooch *n.* buˈroˈochi ブローチ。

brook *n.* oˈgawa 小川。

broom *n.* hoˈoki ほうき: sweep a room with a broom (*hooki de heya o haku*) ほうきで部屋を掃く。

brother *n.* (older) aˈni 兄; (someone else's older brother) (o-)niˈi-sañ (お)兄さん; (younger) oˈtooto 弟; (someone else's younger brother) oˈtooto-sañ 弟さん; brothers (*kyoodai*) 兄弟。★ There is no direct Japanese equivalent to 'brother'.

brother-in-law *n.* (older) giˈri no aˈni [giˈkee] 義理の兄[義兄]; (younger) giˈri no otooto [giˈtee] 義理の弟[義弟]。

brow *n.* (eyebrow) maˈyu まゆ; maˈyuge まゆ毛; (forehead) hiˈtai 額: He has strong brows. (*Kare wa futoi mayu o shite iru.*) 彼は太いまゆをしている。

brown *adj.* chaˈiro no 茶色の; kaˈsshoku no 褐色の: Hiroko has brown eyes [hair]. (*Hiroko-sañ wa chairo*

no me [*kami no ke*] *o shite iru.*) 広子さんは茶色の目[髪の毛]をしている。/ I painted the chairs and tables brown. (*Watashi wa isu to teeburu o chairo ni nutta.*) 私はいすとテーブルを茶色に塗った。
— *n.* chaˈiro 茶色; kaˈsshoku 褐色: light brown (*usuchairo*) 薄茶色 / dark brown (*kogechairo*) 焦げ茶色。

bruise *vt.* ... ni aˈzaˈo tsuˈkeˈru ...にあざをつける Ⓥ; daˈbokuˈshoo o aˈtaeru 打撲傷を与える Ⓥ; kiˈzu o tsukeˈru 傷をつける Ⓥ: Your blow bruised my cheek. (*Kimi no pañchi de watashi no hoo ni aza ga dekita.*) 君のパンチで私のほおにあざができた。/ bruised fruit (*kizu no tsuita kudamono*) 傷のついた果物。
— *vi.* aˈzaˈni naˈru あざになる ©; kiˈzuato ga tsuˈku 傷あとがつく ©: I bruise easily. (*Watashi wa sugu aza ni naru.*) 私はすぐあざになる。
— *n.* aˈza あざ; kiˈzu 傷; daˈbokuˈshoo 打撲傷: She was covered with bruises. (*Kanojo wa aza darake datta.*) 彼女はあざだらけだった。

brush *n.* buˈrashi ブラシ; haˈkeˈ はけ; fuˈde 筆: Use this brush to clean the tiles. (*Tairu o sooji suru no ni kono burashi o tsukai nasai.*) タイルを掃除するのにこのブラシを使いなさい。/ I wrote Chinese characters with a brush. (*Fude de kañji o kaita.*) 筆で漢字を書いた。
— *vt.* ... ni buˈrashi o kaˈkeˈru ...にブラシをかける Ⓥ; ... o buˈrashi de miˈgaku ...をブラシで磨く ©: Will you please brush this coat? (*Kono kooto ni burashi o kakete kuremasu ka?*) このコートにブラシをかけてくれますか。/ I brush my teeth before going to bed. (*Watashi wa neru mae ni ha o migakimasu.*) 私は寝る前に歯を磨きます。

bubble *n.* aˈwaˈ 泡; aˈbuku あぶく: blow (soap) bubbles (*shabondama o fuku*) シャボン玉を吹く。

bucket *n.* baˈketsu バケツ; teˈoke 手おけ: carry water in a bucket (*baketsu de mizu o hakobu*) バケツで水を運ぶ.

buckle *n.* ba¹kkuru バックル; shi¹megane 締め金: fasten [unfasten] one's belt buckle (*beruto no bakkuru o shimeru* [*hazusu*]) ベルトのバックルを締める[はずす].
— *vt.* ...o ba¹kkuru de shime¹ru ...をバックルで締める Ⓥ: buckle a belt (*beruto o bakkuru de shimeru*) ベルトをバックルで締める.

bud *n.* me¹ 芽; tsu¹bomi¹ つぼみ: a leaf bud (*ha no me*) 葉の芽 / a flower bud (*hana no tsubomi*) 花のつぼみ / The trees are in bud. (*Ki ga me o dashi-hajimeta.*) 木が芽を出し始めた.
— *vi.* me¹ o dasu 芽を出す Ⓒ; tsu¹bomi¹ o tsu¹ke¹ru つぼみをつける Ⓥ: The cherry trees are budding early this year. (*Kotoshi wa sakura ga hayaku tsubomi o tsuke-hajimeta.*) ことしは桜が早くつぼみをつけ始めた.

Buddha *n.* ho¹toke¹ 仏; Bu¹dda ブッダ.

Buddhism *n.* bu¹kkyoo 仏教: believe in Buddhism (*bukkyoo o shiñkoo suru*) 仏教を信仰する.

budget *n.* yo¹sañ 予算: make a monthly budget (*maitsuki no yosañ o tateru*) 毎月の予算を立てる / carry out a project within the budget (*yosañ-nai de keekaku o jikkoo suru*) 予算内で計画を実行する.
— *vi.* yo¹sañ o ta¹te¹ru 予算を立てる Ⓥ: We budgeted for the coming year. (*Yokuneñ no yosañ o tateta.*) 翌年の予算を立てた.

build *vt.* **1** (construct) ...o ta¹te¹ru ...を建てる Ⓥ; ke¹ñchiku suru 建築する Ⓘ; ke¹ñsetsu suru 建設する Ⓘ: The Satos built a new house. (*Satoo-sañ no uchi de wa atarashii uchi o tateta.*) 佐藤さんの家では新しい家を建てた. / Another skyscraper has been built in Shinjuku. (*Moo hitotsu no koosoobiru ga Shiñjuku ni keñsetsu sareta.*) もう一つの高層ビルが新宿に建設された.
2 (develop) ...o ki¹zu¹ku ...を築く

Ⓒ; tsu¹ku¹ru 作る Ⓒ: build a business relationship (*torihiki kañkee o kizuku*) 取り引き関係を築く / I would like to build up my stamina. (*Watashi wa sutamina o tsuketai.*) 私はスタミナをつけたい.
— *n.* ta¹ikaku 体格: a man with a fine build (*rippa na taikaku o shita otoko no hito*) 立派な体格をした男の人.

builder *n.* ke¹ñchiku gyo¹osha 建築業者.

building *n.* ta¹temo¹no 建物; bi¹ru ビル: a ten-year old building (*tatete juu-neñ ni naru biru*) 建てて10年になるビル.

bullet *n.* da¹ñgañ 弾丸; ta¹ma¹ 弾: The bullet hit the wall. (*Tama wa kabe ni atatta.*) 弾は壁に当たった.

bulletin *n.* **1** (official statement) ko¹ohoo 公報; ko¹kuji 告示: issue a bulletin (*koohoo o dasu*) 公報を出す. **2** (printed sheet) ka¹ihoo 会報.

bulletin board *n.* ke¹ejibañ 掲示板.

bundle *n.* ta¹ba 束; tsu¹tsumi¹ 包み: a bundle of firewood (*maki no taba*) まきの束 / a bundle of clothes (*irui no tsutsumi*) 衣類の包み.
— *vt.* ...o ta¹bane¹ru 束ねる Ⓥ; tsu¹tsumi¹ ni suru 包みにする Ⓘ: She bundled all her possessions up. (*Kanojo wa mochimono o zeñbu hitomatome ni shita.*) 彼女は持ち物を全部ひとまとめにした.

burden *n.* **1** (load) ni¹motsu 荷物: She was carrying a heavy burden. (*Kanojo wa omoi nimotsu o hakoñde ita.*) 彼女は重い荷物を運んでいた. **2** (encumbrance) o¹moni 重荷: The sick child was a burden to her. (*Byooki no kodomo ga kanojo no omoni datta.*) 病気の子どもが彼女の重荷だった.

burn *vt.* **1** (of wood, coal) ...o mo¹yasu ...を燃やす Ⓒ; ya¹ku 焼く Ⓒ: Please burn those old papers. (*Kono furui shorui wa moyashite kudasai.*) この古い書類は燃やしてください. **2** (char; damage) ...o ko¹ga¹su ...を

焦がす C; ya「kedo saseru やけどさせ
る V: You've gone and burned the
bread. (*Pañ o kogashite shimaimashita yo.*) パンを焦がしてしまいました
よ. / I burned my hand lighting the
fire. (*Watashi wa hi o tsukete ite
te ni yakedo shita.*) 私は火をつけてい
て手にやけどした.
— *vi.* mo「eru 燃える V; ko「ge」ru
焦げる V: Paper burns easily.
(*Kami wa sugu moeru.*) 紙はすぐ燃
える. / The cake is burning. (*Keeki
ga kogete iru.*) ケーキが焦げている.

burst *vi.* **1** (explode; break open)
ha「retsu suru 破裂する I; wa「reru
割れる V: The bomb burst. (*Bakudañ wa haretsu shita.*) 爆弾が破裂し
た. / The balloon burst. (*Fuuseñ ga
wareta.*) 風船が割れた.
2 (of a bank, dam) ke「kkai suru 決
壊する I: The water level rose and
the dam burst. (*Suii ga agari damu wa kekkai shita.*) 水位が上がり
ダムは決壊した.
— *vt.* ... o ha「retsu saseru ...を破
裂させる V; wa「ru 割る C: The
child burst the soap bubble with a
pencil. (*Kodomo wa shaboñdama
o eñpitsu de watta.*) 子どもはシャボン
玉を鉛筆で割った.
burst into ... *vt.* to「tsuzeñ ⟨verb⟩
突然...: She burst into tears. (*Kanojo wa totsuzeñ naki-dashita.*) 彼
女は突然泣き出した.

bus *n.* ba「su バス: get on a bus (*basu
ni noru*) バスに乗る / get off a bus
(*basu o oriru*) バスを降りる / Does
this bus go to the airport? (*Kono
basu wa kuukoo e ikimasu ka?*) こ
のバスは空港へ行きますか. / a sight-
seeing bus (*kañkoo basu*) 観光バス.

bush *n.* hi「ku」i ki 低い木; ka「ñboku
灌木; ya「bu やぶ: a rose bush (*bara
no ki*) ばらの木.

business *n.* **1** (occupation) sho-
「ku」gyoo 職業: What business are
you in? (*Go-shokugyoo wa nañ
desu ka?*) ご職業は何ですか.
2 (trade) sho「obai 商売; to「ri」hiki
取り引き: Business is doing well.

(*Shoobai wa umaku itte imasu.*)
商売はうまくいっています.
3 (work) shi「goto 仕事; yo「oji 用
事: Are you here on business or
pleasure? (*Koko ni kita no wa shigoto desu ka asobi desu ka?*) ここ
に来たのは仕事ですか遊びですか. / He
went to Osaka on business. (*Kare
wa yooji ga atte Oosaka e ikimashita.*) 彼は用事があって大阪へ行きまし
た.
4 (activity) gyo「omu 業務; ji「mu 事
務: Business as usual. (*Gyoomu wa
heejoo-doori.*) 業務は平常どおり.
5 (shop) mi「se」 店; (firm) ka「isha
会社: My father owns five businesses. (*Chichi wa mise o itsutsu
motte iru.*) 父は店を五つ持っている.
6 (concern) ko「togara 事柄: It's
none of your business. (*Sore wa
anata ni wa kañkee no nai koto
desu.*) それはあなたには関係のないことで
す.

businessman *n.* ji「tsugyooka 実
業家; ji「tsumuka 実務家. ★ A male
office worker is usually called '*bijinesumañ*' (businessman) in Japan.

businesswoman *n.* jo「see no jitsugyooka 女性の実業家; jo「see no
jitsumuka 女性の実務家.

bus stop *n.* ba「su no te「eryuujo バ
スの停留所. ★ Often abbreviated to
'*basu-tee*' バス停: Where is the bus
stop for Shibuya? (*Shibuya-yuki
no basu no teeryuujo wa doko
desu ka?*) 渋谷行きのバスの停留所は
どこですか.

busy *adj.* **1** (actively engaged)
i「sogashi」i 忙しい: a busy person
(*isogashii hito*) 忙しい人 / I am
afraid the manager is too busy to
see you. (*Mooshiwake arimaseñ
ga buchoo wa isogashikute o-ai
suru koto ga dekimaseñ.*) 申し訳あ
りませんが部長は忙しくてお会いすることが
できません.
2 (full of activity; crowded) ni「gi」-
yaka na にぎやかな; ko「ñzatsu shite
iru 混雑している: a busy street (*nigi-
yaka na toori*) にぎやかな通り / Shin-

juku is the busiest station in Tokyo. (*Shiñjuku wa Tookyoo de ichibañ koñzatsu shite iru eki desu.*)
新宿は東京でいちばん混雑している駅です.
The line is busy. (*O-hanashi-
chuu desu.*) お話中です.

but *conj.* (yet, however) shiˈkaˈshi
しかし; deˈ mo でも; daˈ ga だが; keˈ-
redomo けれども: Our family are
poor, but happy. (*Watashi-tachi
ikka wa mazushii. De mo shiawase desu.*) 私たち一家は貧しい. でも
幸せです. / This dress is cheap but
well made. (*Kono doresu wa yasui
ga yoku dekite iru.*) このドレスは安い
がよくできている. / I would like to
watch the movie, but I am now
busy. (*Eega o mitai keredomo ima
wa isogashii.*) 映画を見たいけれども今
は忙しい.

not ... but ... ... de wa naˈku(te)
mushiro ...: The real job of a policeman is not
to catch criminals, but to prevent
crime. (*Keesatsukañ no hoñrai no
shigoto wa hañzaisha o tsukamaeru koto de wa naku mushiro
hañzai o fusegu koto desu.*) 警察官
の本来の仕事は犯罪者を捕まえることで
はなくむしろ犯罪を防ぐこと.

— *prep.* ... o noˈzoite ...を除いて;
... no hoˈka ni ...のほかに: Any day
but Friday is okay. (*Kiñyoo o nozoite itsu de mo kekkoo desu.*) 金
曜を除いていつでも結構です. / There
was no one there but me. (*Soko ni
wa watashi no hoka dare mo inakatta.*) そこには私のほかだれもいなかった.

butcher *n.* niˈkuˈya 肉屋: buy
meat at the butcher's (*nikuya de
niku o kau*) 肉屋で肉を買う / a
butcher shop (*nikuya*) 肉屋.

butter *n.* baˈtaa バター: I spread
the butter on my bread. (*Pañ ni
bataa o nutta.*) パンにバターを塗った.

butterfly *n.* choˈo ちょう; choˈo-
choo ちょうちょう.

button *n.* **1** (clothing) boˈtañ ボタ
ン: sew on a button (*botañ o tsukeru*) ボタンをつける / A button has

come off. (*Botañ ga toreta.*) ボタンが
とれた.
2 (machine) boˈtañ ボタン; oˈshi-
boˈtañ 押しボタン: Push the button
for the third floor, please. (*Sañ-gai
no botañ o oshite kudasai.*) 3階のボ
タンを押してください.
— *vt.* boˈtañ o kakeˈru ボタンを掛
ける ⓥ: button up a shirt (*shatsu
no botañ o kakeru*) シャツのボタンをか
ける.

buy *vt.* **1** (purchase) ... o kaˈu ...を
買う ⓒ; koˈonyuu suru 購入する Ⓘ:
I want to buy a new television.
(*Atarashii terebi o kaitai.*) 新しいテ
レビを買いたい. / I bought this shirt
for five thousand yen. (*Watashi
wa kono shatsu o go-señ-eñ de
katta.*) 私はこのシャツを5千円で買った.
2 (treat) ... o oˈgoru ...をおごる ⓒ:
Bill said he would buy me lunch.
(*Biru wa watashi ni o-hiru o
ogotte kureru to itta.*) ビルは私にお昼
をおごってくれると言った.
— *vi.* kaˈu 買う ⓒ; koˈonyuu suru
購入する Ⓘ: buying and selling (*baibai*) 売買.

buyer *n.* kaˈite 買い手; shiˈiregaˈ-
kari 仕入れ係; baˈiyaa バイヤー.

by *prep.* **1** (passive) ... ni yoˈtte ...に
よって: This book was written by a
famous author. (*Kono hoñ wa yuumee na sakka ni yotte kakarema-
shita.*) この本は有名な作家によって書か
れました.
2 (means) ... de ...で; ... ni yoˈtte
...によって: How long does it take to
go to the airport by taxi? (*Kuukoo
made takushii de dono kurai kakarimasu ka?*) 空港までタクシーでどの
くらいかかりますか. / Please send this
letter by airmail. (*Kono tegami o
kookuubiñ de okutte kudasai.*) この
手紙を航空便で送ってください. / This
machine works by electricity.
(*Kono kikai wa deñki de ugoku.*)
この機械は電気で動く.
3 (next to) ... no soˈba ni [no; o]
...のそばに[の;を]: a house by the railroad tracks (*señro no soba no uchi*)

線路のそばの家 / She sat by me.
(*Kanojo wa watashi no soba ni
suwatta.*) 彼女は私のそばに座った.
4 (not later than) ... ma᷉de ni ...ま
でに: Make sure you are here by 8
o'clock tomorrow morning. (*Asu
no asa hachi-ji made ni kanarazu
koko ni kite kudasai.*) 明日の朝 8
時までに必ずここに来てください.
5 (in accordance with) ... ni shi᷉ta-
gatte ...に従って; ... ni yo᷉tte ...に
よって: play by the rules (*ruuru ni
shitagatte puree suru*) ルールに従っ
てプレーする / The next song is by request. (*Tsugi no uta wa go-yooboo
ni yorimasu.*) 次の歌はご要望によりま
す.
6 (degree; amount) ... dake ...だけ:
Land prices have fallen by 10%.
(*Tochi no kakaku ga jup-paasento
dake sagatta.*) 土地の価格が 10%だけ

下がった.
7 (to show the part) ... o ... を: He
pulled me by the hair. (*Kare wa
watashi no kami no ke o hippatta.*)
彼は私の髪の毛を引っ張った. / The
mother held the child by the arm.
(*Hahaoya wa kodomo no ude o
totta.*) 母親は子どもの腕を取った.
8 (measurements) ta᷉te ... yo᷉ko ...
縦...横...: a room 5 meters by 10
meters (*tate go-meetoru yoko juu-
meetoru no heya*) 縦 5 メートル横 10
メートルの部屋.
9 (rate; size of units) ... de ...で: ...
ta᷉ni de ...単位で: buy eggs by the
dozen (*tamago o ichi-daasu tani
de kau*) 卵を 1 ダース単位で買う. /
How much is it by the hour? (*Ichi-
jikan ikura desu ka?*) 1 時間いくら
ですか.

C

cab *n.* **1** (taxi) ta᷉kushii タクシー.
 2 (of a truck) u᷉nteñdai 運転台:
The driver climbed into the cab.
(*Unteñshu wa unteñdai ni agatta.*)
運転手は運転台に上がった.
cabaret *n.* kya᷉baree キャバレー.
cabbage *n.* kya᷉betsu キャベツ: a
Chinese cabbage (*hakusai*) 白菜.
cabin *n.* **1** (small house) ko᷉ya 小
屋: a log cabin (*maruta-goya*) 丸太
小屋.
 2 (mountain lodge) ya᷉magoya 山
小屋.
 3 (on a ship) se᷉ñshitsu 船室; (on
an airplane) jo᷉omui᷉ñshitsu 乗務員
室.
cabin crew *n.* (on an airplane)
jo᷉omuiñ 乗務員.
cabinet *n.* **1** (furniture) to᷉dana
戸棚; kya᷉binetto キャビネット:
filing cabinet (*fairiñgu kyabinetto*)
ファイリング・キャビネット.
 2 (of a government) na᷉ikaku 内
閣: form [reshuffle] a cabinet (*nai-

kaku o soshiki [kaizoo] suru*) 内閣
を組織[改造]する / a cabinet member
(*kakuryoo*) 閣僚.
cable *n.* **1** (thick wire) fu᷉toli ke᷉-
buru 太いケーブル; (thick rope) fu-
᷉toli tsu᷉na 太い綱: an undersea
cable (*kaitee keeburu*) 海底ケーブル.
 2 (telegram) de᷉ñpoo 電報.
cable car *n.* ke᷉eburu᷉l-kaa ケーブル
カー: The cable car went up the
mountainside. (*Keeburu-kaa wa
yama no shameñ o nobotta.*) ケーブ
ルカーは山の斜面を登った.
cable television *n.* yu᷉useñ te᷉l-
rebi 有線テレビ.
cactus *n.* (plant) sa᷉boteñ サボテン.
caddie *n.* (of golf) kya᷉dii キャディー.
 — *vi.* (... no) kya᷉dii o suru (...の)
キャディーをする ①: caddie for a per-
son (*hito no kyadii o suru*) 人のキャ
ディーをする.
café *n.* ki᷉ssa᷉teñ 喫茶店. ★ A '*kissateñ*' serves coffee, black tea and
may have light meals. For a place

where regular meals are served, use '*resutorañ*' レストラン (usually Western food) or '*taishuu shokudoo*' 大衆食堂 (cheap Japanese family-type meals).

cafeteria *n.* ka「fete¬ria カフェテリア.
★ A cafeteria in a school or institution may be called '*shokudoo*' 食堂.

caffeine *n.* ka「fe¬iñ カフェイン: caffeine-free coffee (*kafeiñ nuki no koohii*) カフェイン抜きのコーヒー.

cage *n.* **1** (small one for birds, rodents) ka「go かご: a birdcage (*torikago*) 鳥かご.
2 (large one for bigger animals) o「ri¬ 檻.

cake *n.* **1** (as a whole) ke「eki ケーキ; (fancy) de「koreeshoñ-ke¬eki デコレーションケーキ; (when sold as individual pieces) yo「oga¬shi 洋菓子: a birthday cake (*baasudee keeki*) バースデーケーキ / bake a cake (*keeki o yaku*) ケーキを焼く.
2 (when counting items) -ko 個: a cake of soap (*sekkeñ ik-ko*) せっけん1個.

calamity *n.* (disaster) sa「igai 災害; (unforeseen occurrence) sa「ina¬iñ 災難.

calcium *n.* ka「rushi¬umu カルシウム.

calculate *vt.* **1** (figure) ... o ke「esañ suru ...を計算する ①: The accounting department calculated the profit for the fiscal year. (*Keeribu wa sono neñdo no rieki o keesañ shita.*) 経理部はその年度の利益を計算した.
2 (estimate) ... o su「isoku suru ...を推測する ①; yo「soku suru 予測する ①: calculate the results of an election (*señkyo no kekka o yosoku suru*) 選挙の結果を予測する.

calculating *adj.* da「sañ-teki na 打算的な; nu「keme no na¬i 抜け目のない: a calculating politician (*dasañ-teki na seejika*) 打算的な政治家.

calculation *n.* **1** (act of figuring) ke「esañ 計算: make a calculation (*keesañ o suru*) 計算をする.
2 (planning) da「sañ 打算; ke「e-

kaku 計画.

calculator *n.* ke「esa¬ñki 計算機: a pocket calculator (*deñtaku*) 電卓.

calendar *n.* ka「re¬ñdaa カレンダー. hang a calendar on the wall (*kabe ni kareñdaa o kakeru*) 壁にカレンダーをかける.

calf *n.* **1** (young cow) ko「ushi 子牛.
★ The calves of other animals are indicated by the name of the animal to which is added '... *no ko*' ...の子: a whale calf (*kujira no ko*) 鯨の子.
2 (part of the leg) fu「kurahagi ふくらはぎ.

caliber *n.* **1** (bore) ko「okee 口径: a 22-caliber rifle (*nijuu-ni kookee raifuru-juu*) 22口径ライフル銃.
2 (ability) ri「kiryoo 力量; shu「wañ 手腕: a man of excellent caliber (*shuwañka*) 手腕家.

call *vt.* **1** (telephone) ... ni [e] de「ñwa suru ...に[へ]電話する ①; de「ñwa o kake¬ru 電話をかける Ⅴ: I want to call Hawaii. (*Hawai e deñwa shitai ñ desu ga.*) ハワイへ電話したいんですが. / Please tell me how to call this number. (*Kono bañgoo ni deñwa suru hoohoo o oshiete kudasai.*) この番号に電話する方法を教えてください.
2 (ask to come) ... o yo「bu ...を呼ぶ ©; ma「ne¬ku 招く ©: Call a doctor, please. (*Isha o yoñde kudasai.*) 医者を呼んでください. / Please call a taxi for me. (*Takushii o yoñde kudasai.*) タクシーを呼んでください.
3 (utter loudly) ... o yo「bu ...を呼ぶ ©: He called Masao's name in a loud voice. (*Kare wa Masao no namae o oogoe de yoñda.*) 彼は正雄の名前を大声で呼んだ.
4 (name) ... to yo「bu ...と呼ぶ ©; i「u いう ①: What is this place called? (*Koko wa nañ to iimasu ka?*) ここは何といいますか.
5 (summon) ... o yo「bida¬su ...を呼び出す ©: He was called to the police station. (*Kare wa keesatsusho ni yobidasareta.*) 彼は警察

署に呼び出された.
— vi. 1 (shout) yoˈbu 呼ぶ ©; saˈ「keˈbu 叫ぶ ©: Someone is calling from upstairs. (*Dare-ka ga ni-kai kara yoñde imasu.*) だれかが 2 階から呼んでいます.
2 (telephone) deˈñwa suru 電話する Ⓘ: I'll call again later. (*Mata ato de deñwa shimasu.*) また後で電話します.

call by *vi.* taˈchiyoru 立ち寄る ©: Call by if you happen to be in the neighborhood. (*Kiñjo ni oide no toki wa tachiyotte kudasai.*) 近所においての時は立ち寄ってください.

call on *vt.* (visit) ... o hoˈomoñ suru ...を訪問する Ⓤ; taˈzuneˈru 訪ねる Ⓥ: call on a person (*hito o tazuneru*) 人を訪ねる.
— n. 1 (telephone) deˈñwa 電話; tsuˈuwa 通話: I'd like to make a long-distance call. (*Chookyori deñwa o o-negai shimasu.*) 長距離電話をお願いします. / a local call (*shinai deñwa*) 市内電話.
2 (paging) yoˈbidashi 呼び出し.

calligraphy *n.* (art) shoˈodoo 書道; shuˈuji 習字; ; (handwriting) hiˈsseki 筆跡.

calm *adj.* **1** (not rough) oˈdaˈyaka na 穏やかな: a calm sea (*odayaka na umi*) 穏やかな海.
2 (not nervous) oˈchitsuita 落ち着いた; oˈchitsuite iru 落ち着いている: Be calm. (*Ochitsuki nasai.*) 落ち着きなさい.
— n. shiˈzukeˈsa 静けさ: the calm before the storm (*arashi no mae no shizukesa*) あらしの前の静けさ.
— vt. ... o shiˈzumeˈru ...を静める Ⓥ: The teacher calmed her pupils. (*Señsee wa seeto-tachi o shizuka ni saseta.*) 先生は生徒たちを静かにさせた.

calmly *adv.* **1** (quietly) shiˈzuka ni 静かに: walk calmly (*shizuka ni aruku*) 静かに歩く.
2 (mentally composed) reˈesee ni 冷静に: Make your decisions calmly. (*Hañdañ wa reesee ni shi nasai.*)

判断は冷静にしなさい.

calorie *n.* kaˈrorii カロリー: This food is high [low] in calories. (*Kono shokuhiñ wa karorii ga takai [hikui].*) この食品はカロリーが高い[低い].

camel *n.* raˈkuda らくだ.

camellia *n.* tsuˈbaki 椿.

camera *n.* kaˈmera カメラ: load a camera (*kamera ni firumu o ireru*) カメラにフィルムを入れる) / a camera shop (*kamera-teñ*) カメラ店.

camp *n.* **1** (hobby) kyaˈñpu キャンプ: a base camp (*beesu kyañpu*) ベースキャンプ.
2 (military) yaˈee 野営: soldiers in a camp (*yaee shite iru heeshi-tachi*) 野営している兵士たち.
3 (for prisoners, refugees) shuˈuyoojo 収容所; kyaˈñpu キャンプ: a refugee camp (*nañmiñ kyañpu*) 難民キャンプ.
— vi. 1 (recreation) kyaˈñpu suru キャンプする Ⓘ; kyaˈñpu-seˈekatsu o suru キャンプ生活をする Ⓘ.
2 (military) yaˈee suru 野営する Ⓘ.

campaign *n.* **1** (for a certain purpose) uˈñdoo 運動; kaˈtsudoo 活動; kyaˈñpeˈeñ キャンペーン: launch an election campaign (*señkyo-uñdoo o hajimeru*) 選挙運動を始める / an advertising campaign (*señdeñ-katsudoo*) 宣伝活動.
2 (military) seˈñtoo 戦闘; seˈñeki 戦役.
— vi. 1 (for a certain purpose) uˈñdoo o okoˈsu [okonau] 運動を起こす © [行う ©]: The labor union campaigned against the law. (*Roo-doo-kumiai wa sono hooritsu ni hañtai suru uñdoo o okonatta.*) 労働組合はその法律に反対する運動を行った.
2 (military) juˈuguñ suru 従軍する Ⓘ; shuˈssee suru 出征する Ⓘ.

campus *n.* **1** (school site) koˈonai 構内; gaˈkuˈnai 学内; kyaˈñpasu キャンパス: a college campus (*dai-gaku no koonai*) 大学の構内 / campus activities (*gakusee-katsudoo*)

学生活動.

2 (branch of a school) bu⸢ñkoo 分校; -koo 校. ★ '*Buñkoo*' is used generically and '*koo*' is used in compounds with proper nouns.

can[1] *aux.* **1** (be able to) de⸢ki˩ru できる ⓥ; ⟨consonant-stem verb⟩-e⸢ru …える; ⟨vowel-stem verb⟩-rare⸢ru …られる; ⟨verb⟩ ko⸢to˩ ga de⸢ki˩ru …ことができる ⓥ: I can write Chinese characters. (*Watashi wa kañji ga kakemasu.*) 私は漢字が書けます. / Can we eat this? (*Kore wa taberaremasu ka?*) これは食べられますか / I can read Chinese. (*Watashi wa Chuugokugo o yomu koto ga dekimasu.*) 私は中国語を読むことができます. / I cannot drive a car. (*Watashi wa jidoosha o uñteñ suru koto ga dekimaseñ.*) 私は自動車を運転することができません.

2 [asking or giving permission] ⟨verb⟩-te[de] mo yo⸢i [i˩i] …て[で]もよい[いい]; ⟨verb⟩-te[de] mo ka⸢mawa˩nai …て[で]もかまわない: Can one take photographs here? (*Koko de shashiñ o totte mo ii desu ka?*) ここで写真を撮ってもいいですか. / You can do your homework later. (*Shukudai wa ato de shite mo kamaimaseñ.*) 宿題は後でしてもかまいません.

3 [commands] ⟨verb⟩ na⸢sa˩i …なさい: If you don't behave, you can leave. (*Otonashiku shinai nara, dete iki nasai.*) おとなしくしないなら, 出て行きなさい.

4 [negative commands] ⟨verb⟩-te [de] wa i⸢kenai …て[で]はいけない: You can't smoke here. (*Koko de tabako o sutte wa ikenai.*) ここでたばこを吸ってはいけない.

5 [habit or custom] ⟨verb⟩ ko⸢to˩ ga a⸢ru …ことがある ⓒ: Mr. Tanaka can be very unpleasant sometimes. (*Tanaka-sañ wa toki ni hidoku iya na taido o toru koto ga aru.*) 田中さんはときにひどくいやな態度をとることがある.

6 [literary form showing possibil-ity] ⟨verb⟩-u⸢ru …得る ⓥ: Accidents can happen. (*Jiko wa okoriuru.*) 事故は起こり得る.

7 [negative possibility] … no ha⸢zu ga na˩i …のはずがない: His story can't be false. (*Kare no hanashi wa uso no hazu ga arimaseñ.*) 彼の話はうそのはずがありません.

as … as … can de⸢kiru dake できるだけ: Try to be as polite as you can in front of the principal. (*Koochoo señsee no mae de wa dekiru dake reegi tadashiku suru yoo ni shi nasai.*) 校長先生の前ではできるだけ礼儀正しくするようにしなさい.

Can you …? ⟨verb⟩-te[de] ku⸢remase˩ñ ka? …て[で]くれませんか: Can you hold a minute, please? (*Chotto matte kuremaseñ ka?*) ちょっと待ってくれませんか.

can[2] *n.* **1** (container) ka⸢ñ 缶: three cans of beer (*kañ biiru sañ-ko*) 缶ビール 3 個 / a trash [garbage] can (*gomibako*) ごみ箱.

2 (canned goods) ka⸢ñzume 缶詰め: a can of pineapples (*paiñ no kañzume*) パインの缶詰め.

Canada *n.* Ka⸢nada カナダ.

Canadian *adj.* Ka⸢nada no カナダの. — *n.* (inhabitant) Ka⸢nada˩jiñ カナダ人.

canal *n.* u⸢ñga 運河: the Suez Canal (*Suezu uñga*) スエズ運河 / an irrigation canal (*yoosuiro*) 用水路.

cancel *vt.* **1** (revoke) … o to⸢ri-kesu …を取り消す ⓒ; kya⸢ñseru suru キャンセルする Ⓣ: Cancel this reservation, please. (*Kono yoyaku o torikeshite kudasai.*) この予約を取り消してください.

2 (cross out) … o ke⸢su …を消す ⓒ: cross out the mistakes (*machigai o kesu*) 間違いを消す.

3 (annul) … o mu⸢koo ni suru …を無効にする Ⓣ: The regulations were canceled. (*Sono kisoku wa mukoo ni natta.*) その規則は無効になった.

cancer *n.* **1** (disease) ga⸢ñ 癌: stomach cancer (*igañ*) 胃癌.

2 (zodiacal sign) ka⸢niza かに座.

candidate *n.* ko⌈oho⌉sha 候補者: a candidate for mayor (*shichoo señkyo no koohosha*) 市長選挙の候補者.

candle *n.* ro⌈osoku⌉ ろうそく: light [put out] a candle (*roosoku o tsukeru [kesu]*) ろうそくをつける[消す].

candy *n.* **1** (Western-style sweets) kya⌉ñdee キャンデー.
2 (Japanese-style hard sweets) a⌈me⌉ 飴. ★ Another word for candy, '*kashi*' 菓子, can also include baked goods such as cookies, crackers, and pastries.

cane *n.* **1** (of a plant) ku⌈ki⌉ 茎.
2 (for walking) su⌈te⌉kki ステッキ; tsu⌉e つえ: walk with a cane (*tsue o tsuite aruku*) つえをついて歩く.

cannon *n.* ta⌈ihoo 大砲: fire a cannon (*taihoo o utsu*) 大砲を撃つ.

canoe *n.* ka⌉nuu カヌー: get into [out of] a canoe (*kanuu ni noru [kara oriru]*) カヌーに乗る[から降りる].

can opener *n.* ka⌈ñki⌉ri 缶切り.

canvas *n.* **1** (cloth) zu⌉kku ズック.
2 (painting) ka⌉ñbasu カンバス: paint a picture on canvas (*kañbasu ni e o egaku*) カンバスに絵を描く.

cap *n.* **1** (for the head) bo⌈oshi 帽子: put on [take off] a cap (*booshi o kaburu [nugu]*) 帽子をかぶる[脱ぐ]) / She wore a navy blue cap. (*Kanojo wa koñ no booshi o kabutte ita.*) 彼女は紺の帽子をかぶっていた.
★ 'Hat' is also called '*booshi*'.
2 (for a bottle, etc.) kya⌉ppu キャップ; fu⌈ta ふた: a bottle cap (*biñ no futa*) びんのふた.

capable *adj.* **1** (of people) yu⌈unoo na 有能な: a capable secretary (*yuunoo na hisho*) 有能な秘書.
2 (of things) ... ga de⌈ki⌉ru …ができる; ka⌈noo na 可能な: This elevator is capable of carrying 30 persons at a time. (*Kono erebeetaa wa ichido ni sañ-juu-ñiñ o hakobu koto ga dekimasu.*) このエレベーターは一度に30人を運ぶことができます.

capacity *n.* **1** (ability to do something) sa⌈inoo 才能; no⌉oryoku 能力: a man of great capacity (*sainoo yutaka na hito*) 才能豊かな人 / This factory doesn't have the capacity to do such a job. (*Kono koojoo ni wa soñna shigoto o konasu nooryoku wa nai.*) この工場にはそんな仕事をこなす能力はない.
2 (maximum amount that can be contained) yo⌉oseki 容積; shu⌈uyo⌉oryoku 収容力: a barrel with a capacity of 20 liters (*yooseki nijuu-rittoru no taru*) 容積 20 リットルのたる / a room with a seating capacity of 50 (*gojuu-niñ buñ no zaseki no aru heya*) 50 人分の座席のある部屋.
3 (position) ta⌈chiba⌉ 立場; shi⌈kaku 資格: in one's individual capacity (*kojiñ no shikaku de*) 個人の資格で.

cape *n.* **1** (land) mi⌈saki 岬.
2 (garment) ke⌉epu ケープ.

capital *n.* **1** (of a nation) shu⌉to 首都; shu⌉fu 首府: Tokyo is the capital of Japan. (*Tookyoo wa Nihoñ no shuto desu.*) 東京は日本の首都です.
2 (letter) o⌈omoji 大文字.
3 (financial resources) shi⌈ki⌉ñ 資金: We are short of capital. (*Shikiñ ga tarinai.*) 資金が足りない.
4 (assets) shi⌈hoñ 資本; ga⌉ñkiñ 元金: capital and interest (*gañkiñ to rishi*) 元金と利子.

capitalism *n.* shi⌈hoñshu⌉gi 資本主義.

capital punishment *n.* shi⌈ke⌉e 死刑: The sentence of capital punishment was handed down. (*Shikee no hañketsu ga iiwatasareta.*) 死刑の判決が言い渡された.

capricious *adj.* (spoiled) ki⌈magurena 気まぐれな; (changeable) ka⌈wariyasu⌉i 変わりやすい; (unstable) fu⌈a⌉ñtee na 不安定な: capricious weather (*kimagure na teñki*) 気まぐれな天気.

captain *n.* **1** (of a ship) señ⌉choo 船長; (of an airplane) ki⌉choo 機長.
2 (of a sports team) kya⌉puteñ キャプテン.

3 (army rank) riˈkuguń taˈii 陸軍大尉; (navy rank) kaˈiguń taˈisa 海軍大佐.

captive *n.* hoˈryo 捕虜: take a person captive (*hito o horyo ni suru*) 人を捕虜にする.

capture *vt.* (people) ... o toˈraeˈru ...を捕える Ⅴ; tsuˈkamaeru 捕まえる Ⅴ: The police captured the thief. (*Keesatsu wa sono doroboo o tsukamaeta.*) 警察はその泥棒を捕まえた.

car *n.* **1** (automobile) kuˈruma 車; jiˈdoˈosha 自動車; joˈoyoˈosha 乗用車. ★ 'Kuruma' can conceivably be anything on wheels; a '*jooyoosha*' is an automobile, especially one for passengers: I'd like to rent a car. (*Kuruma o ichi-dai karitai no desu ga.*) 車を1台借りたいのですが. / My car has broken down. (*Kuruma ga koshoo shita.*) 車が故障した. / a hired car (*haiyaa*) ハイヤー.

2 (private car) maˈikaˈa マイカー.

3 (of a train) shaˈryoo 車両; -sha 車: Is there a dining car? (*Shokudoosha wa tsuite imasu ka?*) 食堂車はついていますか. / a non-smoking car (*kiñeñsha*) 禁煙車.

caravan *n.* **1** (mobile home) iˈdoo-juˈutaku 移動住宅.

2 (of camels) kyaˈrabań キャラバン.

carbon *n.* taˈñso 炭素.

carbon paper *n.* kaˈaboˈñshi カーボン紙.

carburetor *n.* kyaˈbureˈtaa キャブレター.

card *n.* **1** kaˈado カード; (tag) fuˈda 札; (ticket) keˈń 券: a credit [charge] card (*kurejitto kaado*) クレジットカード / a bank [cash] card (*kyasshu kaado*) キャッシュカード / a disembarkation [embarkation] card (*nyuukoku [shukkoku] kaado*) 入国[出国]カード / an identification card (*mibuñ-shoomeesho*) 身分証明書 / a business card (*meeshi*) 名刺.

2 (postcard) haˈgaki 葉書: a picture postcard (*ehagaki*) 絵葉書.

3 (playing) toˈraˈñpu トランプ: a deck of cards (*toranpu hito-kumi*) トランプ1組 / play cards (*toranpu o suru [yaru]*) トランプをする[やる].

cardboard *n.* boˈorugami ボール紙; aˈtsugami 厚紙: a corrugated cardboard (*dañ-booru*) 段ボール / a cardboard box (*dañboorubako*) 段ボール箱.

cardinal *adj.* kiˈhoń-teki na 基本的な: a cardinal principle (*kihoñ-geñsoku*) 基本原則.

care *n.* **1** (mental distress) shiˈñpai 心配; naˈyami 悩み; kuˈroo 苦労: a life free from care (*kuroo no nai seekatsu*) 苦労のない生活.

2 (object of attention) yoˈojiñ 用心; chuˈui 注意: This needs special care. (*Kore wa tokubetsu no chuui ga hitsuyoo desu.*) これは特別の注意が必要です.

3 (help) seˈwaˈ 世話: The care of elderly people was discussed at the meeting. (*Roojiñ no sewa ni tsuite kaigoo de hanaˈshiawareta.*) 老人の世話について会合で話し合われた.

in care of (c/o) ... *prep.* kiˈzuke 気付: c/o Mr. Kazuo Nakamura (*Nakamura Kazuo-sama kizuke*) 中村和夫様気付.

take care *vi.* kiˈo tsukeˈru 気をつける Ⅴ: Take care not to fall. (*Korobanai yoo ni kiˈo tsuke nasai.*) 転ばないように気をつけなさい.

take care of ... *vt.* ... no seˈwa o suru ...の世話をする Ⅰ: I'll take care of the birds. (*Watashi ga tori no sewa o shimashoo.*) 私が鳥の世話をしましょう.

take care of yourself *vi.* daˈiji ni suru 大事にする Ⅰ: Please take good care of yourself. (*Kuregure mo o-karada o odaiji ni.*) くれぐれもお体をお大事に.

career *n.* **1** (occupation) shoˈkuˈgyoo 職業: careers open to women (*josee ni kaihoo sarete iru shokugyoo*) 女性に開放されている職業. ★ '*Kyaria*' キャリア is sometimes used for this sense but not in the sense of 'present occupation.'

2 (life) ke⌐reki 経歴: an academic career (*gakureki*) 学歴 / one's professional career (*shokureki*) 職歴. — *adj.* ho⌐nshoku no 本職の、ha-⌐enuki no 生え抜きの: a career diplomat (*haenuki no gaikookan*) 生え抜きの外交官 / a career woman (*kyaria uuman*) キャリアウーマン.

careful *adj.* **1** (cautious) chu⌐uibuka⌐i 注意深い; shi⌐nchoo na 慎重な: He is very careful with his work. (*Kare wa shigoto ni kan-shite hijoo ni chuuibukai.*) 彼は仕事に関して非常に注意深い. / a careful driver (*shinchoo na untenshu*) 慎重な運転手.
2 (thorough) ne⌐niri na 念入りな; me⌐nmitsu na 綿密な: a careful study of Japanese history (*Nihon-shi no menmitsu na kenkyuu*) 日本史の綿密な研究.

be careful *vi.* ki ⌐o tsuke⌐ru 気をつける Ⓥ: Be careful not to make any noise. (*Oto o tatenai yoo ni ki o tsuke nasai.*) 音を立てないように気をつけなさい.

carefully *adv.* chu⌐uibu⌐kaku 注意深く; shi⌐nchoo ni 慎重に: Handle it carefully. (*Shinchoo ni toriatsu-katte kudasai.*) 慎重に取り扱ってください.

careless *adj.* **1** (lack of thought) fu⌐chu⌐ui na 不注意な: a careless mistake (*kearesu misu*) ケアレスミス.
2 (inattentive) mu⌐to⌐nchaku na むとんちゃくな: He is careless about how he dresses. (*Kare wa fukusoo ni mutonchaku da.*) 彼は服装にむとんちゃくだ.
3 (free from cares) no⌐nki na のんきな: a careless life (*nonki na kura-shi*) のんきな暮らし.

caress *n.* a⌐ibu 愛撫; ho⌐oyoo 抱擁. — *vt.* ... o a⌐ibu suru ...を愛撫する Ⓣ; na⌐de⌐ru なでる Ⓥ: caress a horse's neck (*uma no kubi o na-deru*) 馬の首をなでる.

cargo *n.* (freight in general) tsu⌐mi-ni 積み荷; (specific load) ni⌐motsu 荷物: a ship loaded with cargo

(*nimotsu o tsunda fune*) 荷物を積んだ船.

caries *n.* mu⌐shiba 虫歯.

carnation *n.* (plant) ka⌐rane⌐eshon カーネーション; (flower) ka⌐rane⌐eshon no ha⌐na カーネーションの花.

carnival *n.* (festive occasion) ka⌐a-nibaru カーニバル; (religious occasion) sha⌐niku⌐sai 謝肉祭.

carol *n.* (for Christmas) Ku⌐risu-masu kya⌐roru クリスマスキャロル.

carousel *n.* **1** (merry-go-round) ka⌐iten-mo⌐kuba 回転木馬; me⌐rii-goora⌐undo メリーゴーラウンド.
2 (airport luggage pickup) ta⌐an-te⌐eburu ターンテーブル; ka⌐itendai 回転台.

carp *n.* (fish) ko⌐i こい(鯉): a carp streamer (*koinobori*) 鯉のぼり.

carpenter *n.* da⌐iku 大工: carpenter's tools (*daiku-doogu*) 大工道具.

carpet *n.* ju⌐utan じゅうたん; ka⌐a-petto カーペット: The floor is covered with a thick carpet. (*Yuka ni wa atsui juutan ga shiite aru.*) 床には厚いじゅうたんが敷いてある.

carrier *n.* **1** (transport company) u⌐nsoo gyo⌐osha 運送業者.
2 (mail) yu⌐ubin haitatsunin 郵便配達人.
3 (HIV, etc.) ka⌐nse⌐nsha 感染者: an HIV carrier (*eichi-ai-bui no kansensha*) HIV の感染者.
4 (naval) ku⌐ubo 空母: a nuclear aircraft carrier (*genshiryoku kuubo*) 原子力空母.

carrot *n.* ni⌐njin にんじん(人参): the carrot and the stick (*ame to muchi*) あめとむち.

carry *vt.* **1** (hold and walk) ... o mo⌐chiaru⌐ku ...を持ち歩く Ⓒ; ke⌐e-tai suru 携帯する Ⓣ: He always carries a camera with him. (*Kare wa itsu-mo kamera o mochiaruite iru.*) 彼はいつもカメラを持ち歩いている. / carry a baby on one's back (*akan-boo o onbu suru*) 赤ん坊をおんぶする.
2 (from one place to another) ... o ha⌐kobu ...を運ぶ Ⓒ; mo⌐tte iku 持って行く Ⓒ: I'll carry this one.

(*Kore wa watashi ga mochimasu.*) これは私が持ちます.

3 (reach) ... o tsuˈtaeru ...を伝える V; toˈtosu 通す C: Copper wires carry electricity. (*Dooseñ wa deñki o tooshimasu.*) 銅線は電気を通します.

carry on *vi.* ... o tsuˈtsukeru ...を続ける V: Carry on, please. (*Doozo tsuzukete kudasai.*) どうぞ続けてください.

carry out *vt.* ... o jiˈtkkoo suru ...を実行する I: carry out a plan (*keekaku o jikkoo suru*) 計画を実行する.

carry-on *n.* kiˈnai moˈchikomi teˈniˈmotsu 機内持ち込み手荷物.

carsick *adj.* kuˈruma ni yoˈtta [yoˈtte iru] 車に酔った[酔っている]: Michiko gets carsick easily. (*Michiko-sañ wa sugu kuruma ni yotte shimau.*) 美智子さんはすぐ車に酔ってしまう.

cart *n.* teˈoshiguˈruma 手押し車: a shopping cart (*shoppiñgu kaato*) ショッピングカート / a golf cart (*gorufu kaato*) ゴルフカート.

cartel *n.* kaˈruteru カルテル: form a cartel (*karuteru o tsukuru*) カルテルを作る.

cartoon *n.* **1** (comic book) maˈñga 漫画; (comic strip) reˈñzokumaˈñga 連続漫画.
2 (animated features) aˈnime アニメ; doˈroga 動画.

carve *vt.* **1** (inscribe) ... o kiˈzamu ...を刻む C: carve a name on a tree (*namae o ki ni kizamu*) 名前を木に刻む.
2 (form) ... o hoˈru 彫る C; choˈrokoku suru 彫刻する I: carve a Buddhist image out of wood (*ki de butsuzoo o horu*) 木で仏像を彫る.
3 (meat, etc.) ... o kiˈru ...を切る C; kiˈriwakeˈru 切り分ける V: I carved the turkey for the guests. (*Watashi wa shichimeñchoo o o-kyaku no tame ni kiriwaketa.*) 私は七面鳥をお客のために切り分けた.

carving *n.* choˈrokoku 彫刻; hoˈrimoˈno 彫り物.

case[1] *n.* **1** (instance) baˈai 場合: Please give me somewhere to call in case of trouble. (*Jiko no baai no reñrakusaki o oshiete kudasai.*) 事故の場合の連絡先を教えてください.
2 (example) jiˈtsuree 実例; moˈñdai 問題: a case of life and death (*shikatsu moñdai*) 死活問題.
3 (legal) jiˈkeñ 事件: an unsolved case (*meekyuuiri no jikeñ*) 迷宮入りの事件 / a civil [criminal] case (*miñji [keeji] jikeñ*) 民事[刑事]事件.
4 (medical) kaˈñja 患者: There has been another case of cholera in the neighborhood. (*Kiñjo de moo hitori korera kañja ga deta.*) 近所でもう一人コレラ患者が出た.

in case *adv.* maˈñichi ni soˈnaˈete 万一に備えて: I don't think it will rain, but I'll take an umbrella in case. (*Ame wa furanai to omou ga, mañichi ni sonaete kasa o motte ikoo.*) 雨は降らないと思うが, 万一に備えて傘を持って行こう.
— *conj.* ⟨verb⟩ to iˈkenaˈi kara ...といけないから: Take an umbrella with you in case it rains. (*Ame ga furu to ikenai kara kasa o motte iki nasai.*) 雨が降るといけないから傘を持って行きなさい.

case[2] *n.* **1** (container) iˈremono 入れ物; keˈesu ケース: a pencil case (*fudebako*) 筆箱 / an attaché case (*tesage kabañ*) 手さげかばん.
2 (box) haˈko 箱: a case of wine (*budooshu hito-hako*) ぶどう酒一箱.

cash *n.* **1** (currency) geˈñkiˈñ 現金: pay in cash (*geñkiñ de harau*) 現金で払う.
2 (money) oˈ-kane お金: I'm out of cash now. (*Ima o-kane ga arimaseñ.*) いまお金がありません.
— *vt.* ... o geˈñkiˈñ ni suru ...を現金にする I: I'd like to have this cashed, please. (*Kore o geñkiñ ni shitai no desu ga.*) これを現金にしたいのですが.

cashier *n.* **1** (restaurant, etc.) kaˈikee-gaˈkari 会計係; reˈji-gaˈkari レジ係; reˈji レジ.
2 (bank, commercial establish-

ment, etc.) su⌐itoo-ga⌐kari 出納係.

cash register *n*. re⌐jisutaa レジス
ター; ki⌐ñseñ-tooroku⌐ki 金銭登器器.
★ Or, more commonly, simply
'*reji*' レジ.

cassette *n*. ka⌐se⌐tto カセット: put
a cassette into a tape recorder (*kasetto o teepurekoodaa ni ireru*) カ
セットをテープレコーダーに入れる / play a
cassette (*kasetto o kakeru*) カセット
をかける / take out a cassette (*kasetto o toridasu*) カセットを取り出す.

cast *vt*. **1** (vote) ... ni to⌐ohyoo
suru ...に投票する ⓘ: I cast a vote
for him. (*Watashi wa kare ni toohyoo shita.*) 私は彼に投票した.
2 (direct) ... o mu⌐keru ...を向ける
Ⓥ; na⌐gekake⌐ru 投げかける Ⓥ: cast
suspicion on a person (*hito ni utagai o kakeru*) 人に疑いをかける.
3 (assign) ya⌐ku⌐ o wa⌐riate⌐ru 役を
割り当てる Ⓥ: cast Takeshi in the
role of Benkee (*Takeshi ni Beñkee
no yaku o wariateru*) 健に弁慶の役
を割り当てる.
4 (throw) ... o na⌐ge⌐ru ...を投げる
Ⓥ: cast a stone at a dog (*inu ni
ishi o nageru*) 犬に石を投げる.
— *n*. **1** (performers) kya⌐suto キャ
スト; ha⌐iyuu 俳優: the whole cast
of a film (*eega no kyasuto zeñiñ*)
映画のキャスト全員.
2 (dressing) gi⌐pusu ギブス: Tony's
arm was in a (plaster) cast. (*Tonii
wa ude ni gipusu o shite ita.*) トニ
ーは腕にギブスをしていた.

castle *n*. shi⌐ro 城. ★ In compounds with proper nouns, the
Chinese reading, '*joo*' is often
used: Himeji Castle (*Himeji-joo*)
姫路城.

casual *adj*. **1** (by chance) na⌐ni-
gena⌐i 何気ない: Tom asked a
casual question. (*Tomu wa nani-
genai shitsumoñ o shita.*) トムは何
気ない質問をした.
2 (clothes) fu⌐da⌐ñgi no 普段着の;
ka⌐juaru na カジュアルな: casual
clothes (*fudañgi*) 普段着 / a casual
dress (*kajuaru na doresu*) カジュアル

なドレス / shoes for casual wear
(*fudañbaki no kutsu*) 普段ばきの靴.
3 (occasional) cho⌐tto shita ちょっと
した: a casual acquaintance (*chotto
shita shiriai*) ちょっとした知り合い.

casualty *n*. **1** (injured) fu⌐sho⌐o-
sha 負傷者; (dead) shi⌐sha 死者:
casualties (*shishoosha*) 死傷者.
2 (dead from war) se⌐ñshi⌐sha 戦
死者.

cat *n*. ne⌐ko 猫: She has a cat.
(*Kanojo wa neko o katte iru.*) 彼女
は猫を飼っている.

catalog *n*. **1** (of sales) ka⌐tarogu カ
タログ: Please give us copies of your
catalog. (*O-taku no katarogu o kudasai.*) お宅のカタログを下さい.
2 (of a library, museum, etc.) mo-
⌐kuroku 目録: compile a catalog
(*mokuroku o sakusee suru*) 目録を
作成する / include in a catalog (*mokuroku ni noseru*) 目録に載せる.
3 (of a university, etc.) da⌐igaku
no yoorañ 大学の要覧; nyu⌐ugaku-
a⌐ññai 入学案内.

cataract *n*. **1** (waterfall) o⌐oki-na
ta⌐ki 大きな滝.
2 (of the eye) ha⌐kuna⌐ishoo 白内
障.

catarrh *n*. (medical) ka⌐taru カタル;
[popular term] ha⌐nakaze 鼻かぜ.

catastrophe *n*. da⌐isa⌐igai 大災
害: suffer a catastrophe (*daisaigai
o koomuru*) 大災害を被る.

catch *vt*. **1** (grasp) ... o tsu⌐ka-
maeru ...を捕まえる Ⓥ; to⌐ru とる Ⓒ:
Catch that man! (*Ano hito o tsuka-
maete.*) あの人を捕まえて. / Catch the
ball with both hands. (*Booru wa
ryoote de tore.*) ボールは両手でとれ.
2 (see) ... o mi⌐tsukeru ...を見つける
Ⓥ: The teacher found Yamamoto
cheating on a test. (*Señsee wa Yamamoto ga shikeñ de kañniñgu
shite iru no o mitsuketa.*) 先生は山
本が試験でカンニングしているのを見つけた.
3 (be on time) ... ni ma⌐nia⌐u ...に
間に合う Ⓒ; re⌐ñraku suru 連絡する
ⓘ: I caught the 10 o'clock train.
(*Juu-ji no deñsha ni maniatta.*) 10

時の電車に間に合った. / Where can I catch a taxi? (*Doko de takushii ni noremasu ka?*) どこでタクシーに乗れますか.
4 (contract) ... ni ka⌐ka¬ru ...にかかる C: Hanako caught pneumonia. (*Hanako-sañ wa haieñ ni kakatta.*) 花子さんは肺炎にかかった. / catch a cold (*kaze o hiku*) かぜをひく.

catch up with [to] ... ni o⌐itsu¬ku ... に追いつく C: He caught up with us later. (*Kare wa ato de watashi-tachi ni oitsuita.*) 彼は後で私達に追いついた.

catcher *n.* kya⌐tchaa キャッチャー; ho⌐shu 捕手: play (the position of) catcher (*kyatchaa o suru*) キャッチャーをする.

category *n.* **1** (division) bu⌐moñ 部門: The materials are classified into two categories. (*Shiryoo wa futatsu no bumoñ ni buñrui sarete iru.*) 資料は二つの部門に分類されている. **2** (philosophy, theory, etc.) ha⌐ñchuu 範疇; ka⌐te¬gorii カテゴリー: a grammatical category (*buñpoo-hañchuu*) 文法範疇.

caterpillar *n.* **1** (insect) ke⌐mushi 毛虫. **2** (tractor) kya⌐ta¬piraa キャタピラー.

catfish *n.* na⌐mazu なまず(鯰).

cathedral *n.* da⌐ise¬edoo 大聖堂; da⌐iji¬iñ 大寺院.

Catholic *n.* (believer) (Ro⌐oma) Ka⌐torikku-kyo¬oto (ローマ)カトリック教徒.
— *adj.* (of the Roman Catholic Church) (Ro⌐oma) Katori⌐kku (kyookai) no (ローマ)カトリック(教会)の; kyu⌐ukyoo no 旧教の.

catsup *n.* ke⌐cha¬ppu ケチャップ.

cattle *n.* **1** (livestock) ka⌐chiku 家畜. **2** (cow) u⌐shi 牛: raise cattle (*ushi o kau*) 牛を飼う / beef cattle (*niku-gyuu*) 肉牛 / dairy cattle (*nyuu-gyuu*) 乳牛.

cauliflower *n.* ka⌐rifura¬waa カリフラワー.

cause *n.* **1** (responsible for action) ge⌐ñiñ 原因: cause and effect (*geñiñ to kekka*) 原因と結果 / The police are trying to find the cause of the fire. (*Keesatsu wa sono kaji no geñiñ o tsukitomeyoo to shite iru.*) 警察はその火事の原因を突き止めようとしている. **2** (reason) ri⌐yuu 理由: You cannot be absent from the meeting without good reason. (*Seetoo na riyuu naku kaigi o kesseki suru koto wa dekimaseñ.*) 正当な理由なく会議を欠席することはできません. **3** (principle) mo⌐kuhyoo 目標; shu⌐choo 主張.
— *vt.* (bring about) ...no ge⌐ñiñ to na¬ru ...の原因となる C; ... o hi⌐ki-oko¬su ...を引き起こす C: Careless driving causes accidents. (*Fuchuui na uñteñ wa jiko o hikiokosu.*) 不注意な運転は事故を引き起こす.

caution *n.* **1** (care) chu⌐ui 注意; yo⌐ojiñ 用心: Exercise extreme caution when crossing this street. (*Kono toori o wataru toki ni wa juubuñ ni chuui suru koto.*) この通りを渡る時には十分に注意すること. **2** (warning) ke⌐ekoku 警告: give a person a caution (*hito ni keekoku o ataeru*) 人に警告を与える.
with caution *adv.* yo⌐ojiñ shite 用心して; shi⌐ñchoo ni 慎重に.
— *vt.* ... ni ke⌐ekoku suru ...に警告する C; chu⌐ui suru 注意する C: He cautioned me not to be late. (*Kare wa watashi ni okurenai yoo ni chuui shita.*) 彼は私に遅れないように注意した.

cautious *adj.* shi⌐ñchoo na 慎重な; chu⌐ui shite iru 注意している: Mr. Yamada is a cautious driver. (*Yamada-sañ wa shiñchoo na doraibaa da.*) 山田さんは慎重なドライバーだ. / I was cautious not to overeat. (*Watashi wa tabe-suginai yoo ni chuui shita.*) 私は食べすぎないように注意した.

cave *n.* ho⌐ra-ana ほら穴; do⌐okutsu 洞くつ.

cave-in *n.* (land) ka⌐ñbotsu 陥没;

(mining) ra「kubañ 落盤.

cavity n. 1 (of a tooth) mu「shiba (no a「na̍) 虫歯(の穴).

2 (hole) a「na̍ 空洞; a「na̍ 穴.

CD n. (compact disc) shi「idi̍i シーディ −: play a CD (shiidii o kakeru) CD をかける.

cease vt. ... o ya「meru ...をやめる Ⓥ; o「eru 終える Ⓥ: cease work [talking] (shigoto [shaberu no] o yameru) 仕事[しゃべるの]をやめる.

— vi. ya「mu やむ Ⓒ; o「waru 終わる Ⓒ: The cheering ceased suddenly. (See-eñ ga pitari to yañda.) 声援がぴたりとやんだ.

without ceasing adv. ta「ema na̍ku 絶え間なく.

cease-fire n. te「eseñ 停戦: a cease-fire order (teeseñ-meeree) 停戦命令.

cedar n. su「gi 杉. ★ Strictly speaking 'sugi' is cryptomeria, the Japanese cedar. 'Seeyoosugi' 西洋杉 may be used to explain any kind of cedar that is not Japanese.

ceiling n. te「ñjoo 天井: There are a lot of flies on the ceiling. (Teñjoo ni takusañ no hae ga tomatte iru.) 天井にたくさんのはえが止まっている.

celebrate vt. ... o i「wa̍u ...を祝う Ⓒ: celebrate his 60th birthday (kare no kañreki o iwau) 彼の還暦を祝う.

celebration n. i「wai 祝い; shu「ku-teñ 祝典: a birthday celebration (tañjoobi no o-iwai) 誕生日のお祝い.

celebrity n. yu「ume̍ejiñ 有名人.

celery n. se「rori セロリ.

cell n. 1 (battery) de「ñchi 電池.

2 (biology) sa「iboo 細胞: brain cells (noosaiboo) 脳細胞.

3 (prison) do「kuboo 独房; (small room) ko「beya 小部屋.

cellar n. chi「ka̍shitsu 地下室; chi-「ka-chozo̍oko 地下貯蔵庫: wine cellar (budooshu no chozooko) ぶどう酒の貯蔵庫.

cello n. che「ro チェロ: play the cello (chero o hiku) チェロを弾く.

cellular phone n. i「doo-de̍ñwa

移動電話; ke「etai-de̍ñwa 携帯電話. ★ The latter term is more common.

Celsius adj. se「sshi no 摂氏の: twenty degrees Celsius (sesshi nijuu-do) 摂氏20度. ★ In Japan the Celsius system is used instead of the Fahrenheit system.

cement n. se「meñto セメント: a bag of cement (semeñto hito fukuro) セメント一袋.

— vt. 1 (cover) ... ni se「meñto o nuru ...にセメントを塗る Ⓒ: cement a floor (yuka ni semeñto o nuru) 床にセメントを塗る.

2 (bring together) ... o se「meñto de kuttsuke̍ru ...をセメントでくっつける Ⓥ: cement bricks (reñga o semeñto de kuttsukeru) れんがをセメントでくっつける.

3 (of a friendship, etc.) ... o ka「tameru ...を固める Ⓥ: cement a friendship (yuujoo o katameru) 友情を固める.

cemetery n. bo「chi 墓地: bury in a cemetery (bochi ni hoomuru) 墓地に葬る.

censor n. (government official) ke「ñetsu̍kañ 検閲官.

— vt. ... o ke「ñetsu suru ...を検閲する Ⓘ: Japan censors imported magazines. (Nihoñ wa yunyuu zasshi o keñetsu suru.) 日本は輸入雑誌を検閲する.

censorship n. ke「ñetsu 検閲.

censure n. hi「nañ 非難.

— vt. ... o hi「nañ suru ...を非難する Ⓘ: The prime minister was censured in parliament. (Shushoo wa kokkai de hinañ sareta.) 首相は国会で非難された.

census n. (of a country) ko「kusee cho̍osa 国勢調査: take a census (jiñkoo choosa o suru) 人口調査をする.

cent n. se「ñto セント: 15¢ (juugo-señto) 15セント.

center n. 1 (middle) chu「ushiñ 中心; chu「uo̍o 中央: the center of a circle (eñ no chuushiñ) 円の中心 /

the center of a room (*heya no chuuoo*) 部屋の中央 / the center of gravity (*juushiñ*) 重心.

2 (place) chuʹushiñʹchi 中心地: the center of American theatrical activity (*Amerika no eñgeki katsudoo no chuushiñchi*) アメリカの演劇活動の中心地.

3 (of interest, etc.) chuʹushiñ 中心; chuʹushiñ jiʹñbutsu 中心人物: the center of attention (*chuumoku no mato*) 注目の的 / He is the center of the project. (*Kare wa sono keekaku no chuushiñ jiñbutsu da.*) 彼はその計画の中心人物だ.

4 (facility) -sho[jo] 所; seʹñtaa センター: a community center (*chiiki shakai señtaa*) 地域社会センター / a day-care center (*hoikusho*) 保育所 / a shopping center (*shoppingu señtaa*) ショッピングセンター / a space center (*uchuukichi*) 宇宙基地.

5 (baseball) seʹñtaa センター; chuʹukeñ 中堅: play center field (*señtaa o mamoru*) センターを守る / a center fielder (*chuukeñshu*) 中堅手.

— *vt.* **1** (place) ... o chuʹuoo ni oʹku ...を中央に置く ⓒ: center a table in the room (*teeburu o heya no chuuoo ni oku*) テーブルを部屋の中央に置く.

2 (concentrate) ... ni shuʹuchuu saseru ...に集中させる Ⓥ: All eyes were centered on him. (*Miñna no me ga kare ni shuuchuu shita.*) みんなの目が彼に集中した.

— *vi.* (... ni) shuʹuchuu suru (...に)集中する Ⓘ; aʹtsumaʹru 集まる ⓒ: The debate centered on the gasoline tax. (*Tooroñ wa gasoriñ no zeekiñ ni shuuchuu shita.*) 討論はガソリンの税金に集中した.

centigrade *adj.* seʹsshi no 摂氏の: 50° centigrade [Celsius] (*sesshi gojuu-do*) 摂氏 50 度.

centimeter *n.* seʹñchi-meʹetoru センチメートル. ★ Usually abbreviated in speech and writing to 'señchi': 15 cm (*juugo-señchi*) 15 センチ.

central *adj.* chuʹushiñ no 中心の; chuʹuoʹo no 中央の: the central part of Australia (*Oosutoraria no chuushiñbu*) オーストラリアの中心部 / Central Post Office (*chuuoo yuubiñkyoku*) 中央郵便局 / central heating (*señtoraru hiitiñgu*) セントラルヒーティング.

century *n.* seʹeki 世紀: Japan became a modern nation at the end of the 19th century. (*Nihoñ wa juukyuu-seeki matsu ni kiñdai kokka to natta.*) 日本は 19 世紀末に近代国家となった.

ceramics *n.* (art) toʹogee 陶芸; (articles) toʹojikiʹrui 陶磁器類.

cereal *n.* **1** (commodity) koʹkuʹmotsu 穀物; (grain) koʹkuʹrui 穀類; (plant) koʹkusoo 穀草.

2 (breakfast food) shiʹriaru シリアル.

ceremony *n.* giʹshiki 儀式; -ʹshiki 式: an opening [a closing] ceremony (*kaikai[heekai]-shiki*) 開[閉]会式 / a graduation ceremony (*sotsugyoo-shiki*) 卒業式 / a tea ceremony (*cha no yu*) 茶の湯.

certain *adj.* **1** (limited) aʹru teedo no ある程度の; iʹttee no 一定の: a certain rate (*ittee no hiritsu*) 一定の比率.

2 (not specified but known) aʹru ある: Imai didn't come for a certain reason. (*Imai wa aru riyuu de konakatta.*) 今井はある理由で来なかった.

3 (definite) kaʹkujitsu na 確実な; maʹchigai naʹi 間違いない: He is certain to win. (*Kare ga katsu no wa machigai nai.*) 彼が勝つのは間違いない.

4 (sure) kaʹkushiñ shite (iru) 確信して(いる); shiʹñjite (iru) 信じて(いる): I'm certain of his success. (*Watashi wa kare no seekoo o kakushiñ shite imasu.*) 私は彼の成功を確信しています.

5 (indisputable) kaʹkujitsu na 確実な; taʹshika na 確かな: certain evidence (*tashika na shooko*) 確かな証拠 / a certain cure (*kakujitsu na chiryoohoo*) 確実な治療法.

certainly *adv.* **1** [affirmative reply for permission to ask a question] e˥e, do˥ozo ええ, どうぞ: "May I ask you a question?" "Certainly." ("*Shitsumoñ shite mo yoroshii desu ka?*" "*Ee, doozo.*")「質問してもよろしいですか」「ええ, どうぞ」
2 (without doubt) ta˥shika ni 確かに; ki˥tto きっと: John will certainly come. (*Joñ wa kitto kuru yo.*) ジョンはきっと来るよ.

certainty *n.* ka˥kujitsu na mono˥ [koto˥] 確実なもの[こと]: It's a certainty that an earthquake will hit Tokyo someday. (*Tookyoo ni itsuka jishiñ ga kuru no wa kakujitsu da.*) 東京にいつか地震が来るのは確実だ.

certificate *n.* (of attainment) sho˥omeesho 証明書; (license) me˥ñkyo˥joo 免許状: a birth certificate (*shussee shoomeesho*) 出生証明書 / a death certificate (*shiboo shiñdañsho*) 死亡診断書.

certified check *n.* shi˥harai-hoshoo-kogi˥tte 支払保証小切手.

certified public accountant *n.* ko˥oniñ-kaike˥eshi 公認会計士.

certify *vt.* ... o sho˥omee suru ...を証明する Ⓣ; ho˥shoo suru 保証する Ⓣ: I hereby certify that the documents are correct. (*Shorui ni machigai no nai koto o koko ni shoomee shimasu.*) 書類に間違いのないことをここに証明します.

chain *n.* ku˥sari 鎖; che˥eñ チェーン: a bicycle chain (*jiteñsha no cheeñ*) 自転車のチェーン / put chains on the tires of a car (*kuruma no taiya ni cheeñ o tsukeru*) 車のタイヤにチェーンをつける.
— *vt.* ... o ku˥sari de tsunagu ...を鎖でつなぐ Ⓒ: Keep your dog chained. (*Inu o kusari de tsunaide oki nasai.*) 犬を鎖でつないでおきなさい.

chain store *n.* che˥eñ-suto˥a チェーンストア; ka˥me˥eteñ 加盟店.

chair *n.* **1** (furniture) i˥su いす; ko˥shika˥ke 腰掛け: sit in a chair (*isu ni suwaru*) いすに座る / rise from a chair (*isu kara tachiagaru*) いすから

立ち上がる.
2 (position) gi˥cho˥oseki 議長席: take the chair (*gichooseki ni tsuku*) 議長席に着く.
— *vt.* gi˥choo o tsu˥tome˥ru 議長を務める Ⓥ: He chaired the committee. (*Kare wa sono iiñkai no gichoo o tsutometa.*) 彼はその委員会の議長を務めた.

chairman *n.* ⇨ chairperson.

chairperson *n.* **1** (of a business meeting) gi˥choo 議長; (of a committee) i˥i˥ñchoo 委員長.
2 (of a social event) shi˥ka˥isha 司会者.

chairwoman *n.* jo˥see no gi˥choo [ii˥ñchoo] 女性の議長[委員長].

chalk *n.* cho˥oku チョーク; ha˥kuboku 白墨: write with a piece of chalk (*chooku de kaku*) チョークで書く.

challenge *vt.* **1** (call to contest) ... ni cho˥oseñ suru ...に挑戦する Ⓣ; i˥do˥mu 挑む Ⓒ: I challenged him to a game of tennis. (*Watashi wa kare ni tenisu no shiai o idoñda.*) 私は彼にテニスの試合を挑んだ.
2 (stimulate) ... ni (... o) hi˥tsuyoo to suru ...に(...を)必要とする Ⓣ; yo˥osu˥ru 要する Ⓣ: This task challenges us to further effort. (*Kono shigoto wa wareware no issoo no doryoku o yoosuru.*) この仕事はわれわれの一層の努力を要する.
3 (object) ... ni i˥gi o to˥nae˥ru ...に異議を唱える Ⓥ: I challenged his statement. (*Watashi wa kare ga nobeta koto ni igi o tonaeta.*) 私は彼が述べたことに異議を唱えた.
— *n.* **1** (call to contest) cho˥oseñ 挑戦: a challenge to violence (*booryoku e no chooseñ*) 暴力への挑戦 / accept a challenge to run a race (*kyoosoo shiyoo to iu chooseñ ni oojiru*) 競走しようという挑戦に応じる.
2 (that which requires ability) ya˥rigai やりがい; ha˥riai 張り合い: a job with challenge (*hariai no aru shigoto*) 張り合いのある仕事.
3 (objection) i˥gi 異議.

chamber *n.* **1** (conference room)

ka｢igi｣shitsu 会議室.

2 (judge's) ha｢ŋji｣shitsu 判事室.
chamber of commerce sho｢o-koo-kaigisho 商工会議所.
chambermaid n. me｢edo メイド.
chamber music n. shi｢tsunai｣igaku 室内楽.
champagne n. sha｢ŋpeｎ シャンペン.
champion n. **1** (sports) yu｢ushoo｣-sha 優勝者; cha｢ŋpioｎ チャンピオン: the new world champion (atarashii sekai chaŋpioń) 新しい世界チャンピオン.

2 (of a cause, etc.) yo｢ogo｣sha 擁護者; shi｢ji｣sha 支持者: a champion of liberty (jiyuu no yoogosha) 自由の擁護者.

3 [adjectivally] yu｢ushoo- 優勝: a champion team (yuushoo-chiimu) 優勝チーム / a champion horse (yuushoo-ba) 優勝馬.

championship n. **1** (position) se｢ŋshu｣keń 選手権; cha｢ŋpioŋ-shi｣ppu チャンピオンシップ: win 3 championships (mittsu no seńshu-keń o kakutoku suru) 三つの選手権を獲得する.

2 (competition) se｢ŋshukeń-jiｌai [tai｣kai] 選手権試合[大会]; ke｢ssho｣oseń 決勝戦.

chance n. **1** (coincidence) gu｢uzeń 偶然: It was a mere chance that I met him. (Kare ni atta no wa guuzeń no koto datta.) 彼に会ったのは偶然のことだった.

2 (opportunity) ki｢ka｣i 機会; cha｢ŋ-su チャンス: I finally got a chance to go skiing. (Yooyaku sukii ni iku chańsu ni megumareta.) ようやくスキーに行くチャンスに恵まれた.

3 (probability) mi｢komi 見込み: We have a good chance of winning. (Wareware ni wa kateru mikomi ga juubuń ni aru.) われわれには勝てる見込みが十分にある.

by any chance adv. hyo｢tto shita｣ra ひょっとしたら: Are you Mr. Yamada, by any chance? (Hyotto shitara, Yamada-sań de wa arima-señ ka?) ひょっとしたら、山田さんではありませんか.

take a chance vi. i｢chi｣i ka ba-｢chi｣i ka ya｢tte mi｣ru 一か八かやってみる V.

change n. **1** (unintentional) he｢ŋ-ka 変化: a change in temperature (kioń no heńka) 気温の変化 / change in the town (machi no heńka) 町の変化.

2 (intentional) he｢ŋkoo 変更: the change of schedule (yotee [kee-kaku] no heńkoo) 予定[計画]の変更.

3 (return of excess payment) o-｢tsuri お釣り; tsu｢riseń つり銭: Keep the change. (O-tsuri wa totte oite kudasai.) お釣りはとっておいてください.

4 (small coins) ko｢zeni 小銭; ko-｢maka｣i o-｣kane 細かいお金: I'd like to be paid the balance in change. (Nokori wa kozeni de itadaki ma-shoo.) 残りは小銭でいただきましょう.

5 (of clothes) ki｢gae 着替え: Take a change of clothes with you. (Kigae o motte iki nasai.) 着替えを持って行きなさい.

6 (transfer transportation) no｢ri-kae 乗り換え: Make a change at Tokyo for Sendai. (Seńdai e wa Tookyoo de norikae nasai.) 仙台へは東京で乗り換えなさい.

― vt. 1 (make different) ... o ka-｢eru ...を変える V; he｢ŋkoo suru 変更する I: change one's mind (kań-gae o kaeru) 考えを変える / I want to change my reservation. (Yoyaku o heńkoo shitai no desu ga.) 予約を変更したいのですが.

2 (replace) ... o ka｢ŋkań suru ...を交換する I; to｢rikaeru 取り替える V: I changed my car for a bigger one. (Watashi wa kuruma o ookii no to torikaeta.) 私は車を大きいのと取り替えた.

3 (transfer) ... ni no｢rikae｣ru ...に乗り換える V: change trains for Narita at Ueno (Ueno de Narita-yuki ni norikaeru) 上野で成田行きに乗り換える.

4 (money) ... o ryoꜛogae suru ...を両替する Ⓣ; kuꜜzuꜜsu くずす Ⓒ: I'd like to change 100 dollars. (*Hyakudoru o ryoꜛogae shite kudasai.*) 100ドルを両替してください. / change a ¥1,000 bill (*señ-eñ satsu o kuzusu*) 千円札をくずす.

— vi. 1 (become different) (... ni) kaꜛwaru (...に)変わる Ⓒ; heꜜñka suru 変化する Ⓣ: The traffic light changed from red to green. (*Shiñgoo ga aka kara ao ni kawatta.*) 信号が赤から青に変わった.

2 (clothes) (... ni) kiꜛgaeꜜru (...に)着替える Ⓥ: change into a new dress (*atarashii doresu ni kigaeru*) 新しいドレスに着替える.

3 (transportation) (... ni) noꜛrikaeꜜru (...に)乗り換える Ⓥ: change to a bus (*basu ni norikaeru*) バスに乗り換える.

channel n. **1** (waterway) suꜛiro 水路: The Canberra followed the channel into port. (*Kyañbera-goo wa sono suiro o tootte nyuukoo shita.*) キャンベラ号はその水路を通って入港した.

2 (official routes of communication) keꜛero 経路; shuꜜdañ 手段: diplomatic channels (*gaikoo ruuto*) 外交ルート.

3 (of a TV, radio, etc.) chaꜛññeru チャンネル: watch the game on Channel 4 (*yoñ chañneru de shiai o miru*) 4チャンネルで試合を見る.

4 (strait) kaꜛikyoo 海峡: The English Channel (*Igirisu Kaikyoo*) イギリス海峡.

chaos n. (confusion) daꜛikoꜜñrañ 大混乱: The two-car collision left the street in chaos. (*Ni-dai no kuruma no shoototsu de toori wa daikoñrañ datta.*) 2台の車の衝突で通りは大混乱だった.

chapel n. reꜛehaidoo 礼拝堂; chaꜜperu チャペル.

chapter n. **1** (of a book) shoꜜo 章: chapter 10 (*dai jus-shoo*) 第10章.

2 (period) iꜛchijiꜜki 一時期: open a new chapter in the theater's history (*gekijoo no rekishi ni atarashii ichijiki o kakusu*) 劇場の歴史に新しい一時期を画す.

3 (of an association) shiꜜbu 支部.

character n. **1** (moral structure) seꜛekaku 性格; jiꜛñkaku 人格; hiꜛtogara 人柄; hiꜜñsee 品性: He has a weak character. (*Kare wa seekaku ga yowai.*) 彼は性格が弱い. / improve one's character (*hiñsee o migaku*) 品性を磨く.

2 (distinguishing feature) toꜛkushitsu 特質: Each town has a character of its own. (*Dono machi ni mo sorezore no tokushitsu ga aru.*) どの町にもそれぞれの特質がある.

3 (of a play, history, etc.) toꜛojoo jiꜜñbutsu 登場人物: a main character in the play (*shibai no shuyoo na toojoo jiñbutsu*) 芝居の主要な登場人物.

4 (writing) moꜜji 文字: Chinese characters (*kañji*) 漢字.

characteristic n. toꜛkuchoo 特徴: Nara even now preserves its old characteristics. (*Nara wa mukashi nagara no tokuchoo o ima mo nokoshite iru.*) 奈良は昔ながらの特徴を今も残している.

— adj. doꜛkutoku no 独特の; ...-rashiꜜi ...らしい: It's characteristic of Yamada to behave like that. (*Añna furumai o suru to wa ika ni mo Yamada-rashii.*) あんな振る舞いをするとはいかにも山田らしい.

charcoal n. suꜛmiꜜi 炭; moꜛkutaꜜñ 木炭.

charge n. **1** (payment) ryoꜜokiñ 料金; (commission) teꜛsuꜜuryoo 手数料: How much is the excess charge? (*Chooka ryookiñ wa ikura desu ka?*) 超過料金はいくらですか. / There is no charge. (*Muryoo desu.*) 無料です. / a rental charge (*shakuyoo-ryoo*) 借用料.

2 (public accusation) hiꜜnañ 非難: deny the charge (*hinañ o hitee suru*) 非難を否定する.

3 (legal accusation) koꜜkuso 告訴.

4 (management) kaꜜñri 管理; seꜛkiniñ 責任: a person in charge ((*kañri*) *sekiniñsha*) (管理) 責任者.

5 (electricity) deｎka 電荷: a positive [negative] charge (*see* [*fu*] *deñka*) 正[負]電荷.

6 (attack) koｒogeki 攻撃: The dog made a charge at the bear. (*Inu wa kuma ni tobikakatta.*) 犬は熊に飛びかかった.

in charge of … *prep.* … o taｒñtoo shite iru …を担当している Ⓥ: the teacher in charge of our class (*watashi-tachi no kurasu tañtoo no señsee*) 私たちのクラス担当の先生.

— *vt.* **1** (demand payment) … o seｒekyuu suru …を請求する Ⓣ: charge 20,000 yen for a room (*heya-dai to shite ni-mañ-eñ o seekyuu suru*) 部屋代として2万円を請求する.

2 (record as a debt) … o kuｒejitto kaｒado de haｒraｌu …はクレジットカードで払う Ⓒ; … o (… no) tsuｒke¹ ni suru …を(…の)つけにする Ⓣ: Please charge it to my account. (*Sore o watashi no kañjoo no tsuke ni shite kudasai.*) それを私の勘定のつけにしてください.

3 (accuse publicly) … o hiｒnañ suru …を非難する Ⓣ: He charged that Kimura had let out the secret. (*Kare wa Kimura ga himitsu o morashita to itte hinañ shita.*) 彼は木村が秘密を漏らしたといって非難した.

4 (accuse legally) … o koｒkuso suru …を告訴する Ⓣ: He was charged with theft. (*Kare wa settoozai de kokuso sareta.*) 彼は窃盗罪で告訴された.

5 (with a task, etc.) … ni (… o) meｒezuru …に(…を)命ずる Ⓣ; maｒkaseｌru 任せる Ⓥ: The president charged her secretary with an important task. (*Shachoo wa hisho ni taisetsu na shigoto o makaseta.*) 社長は秘書に大切な仕事を任せた.

6 (energize a battery, etc.) … o juｒudeñ suru …を充電する: charge a battery (*deñchi o juudeñ suru*) 電池を充電する.

charitable *adj.* kaｒñdai na 寛大な; jiｒhibukaｌi 慈悲深い: She was charitable toward him. (*Kanojo wa kare ni kañdai datta.*) 彼女は彼に寛大だった.

charity *n.* **1** (benevolence) oｒmoiyari 思いやり: charity toward one's neighbors (*kiñjo no hito e no omoi-yari*) 近所の人への思いやり.

2 (organization) jiｒzeñ-daｌñtai 慈善団体.

charm *n.* **1** (attraction) miｒryoku 魅力: the charm of her smile (*kanojo no egao no miryoku*) 彼女の笑顔の魅力.

2 (magical formula) maｒjinai まじない; juｒmoñ 呪文: lay a charm on a person (*hito ni majinai o kakeru*) 人にまじないをかける.

3 (talisman) oｒmamori お守り: He always wears a charm. (*Kare wa itsu-mo omamori o motte iru.*) 彼はいつもお守りを持っている.

charming *adj.* (attractive) miｒryoku-teki na 魅力的な; chaｒamiñgu na チャーミングな: a charming woman (*miryoku-teki* [*chaamiñgu*] *na josee*) 魅力的[チャーミング]な女性.

chart *n.* **1** (sheet of information) zuｒhyoo 図表; zu 図; guｒrafu グラフ: a weather chart (*teñkizu*) 天気図 / a bar chart (*boo-gurafu*) 棒グラフ / a pie chart (*eñ-gurafu*) 円グラフ.

2 (nautical) kaｒizu 海図: make a chart of the bay (*wañ no kaizu o tsukuru*) 湾の海図を作る.

3 (medical) kaｒrute カルテ.

charter *n.* **1** [adjectively] kaｒrikiri no 借り切りの; chaｒataa no チャーターの: a charter flight (*chaataa-biñ*) チャーター便.

2 (of an organization) keｒñshoo 憲章: the United Nations Charter (*Kokusaireñgoo Keñshoo*) 国際連合憲章.

— *vt.* **1** (hire) … o chaｒataa suru …をチャーターする Ⓣ; kaｒrikiｌru 借り切る Ⓒ: charter a bus (*basu o chaataa suru*) バスをチャーターする.

2 (approve) … ni toｒkkyoｌjoo o

a「taeru …に特許状を与える Ⅴ.

chartered accountant *n.*
ko「oniñ-kaike」eshi 公認会計士.

chase *vt.* **1** (pursue) …o o「ikake」-
ru …を追いかける Ⅴ; tsu「iseki suru
追跡する Ⅰ: The policeman chased
the pickpocket. (*Keekañ wa suri o
oikaketa.*) 警官はすりを追いかけた.
2 (drive away) …o o「ihara」u を追い
払う Ⅽ: The farmer chased the cattle from his field. (*Noofu wa hatake kara ushi o oiharatta.*) 農夫は
畑から牛を追い払った.
── *vi.* (…o) o「ikake」ru (…を)追いか
ける Ⅴ: The girls chased after the
singer. (*Oñna-no-ko-tachi wa sono
kashu no ato o oikaketa.*) 女の子た
ちはその歌手の後を追いかけた.
── *n.* tsu「iseki 追跡; tsu「ikyuu 追
求: a car chase (*kuruma de no tsuiseki*) 車での追跡.

chassis *n.* (of a car) sha「dai 車台;
sha」shii シャシー.

chat *n.* (light talk) o「sha」beri おしゃ
べり; (about various topics) za「tsu-
dañ 雑談: Ellen likes to have a
chat with me after dinner. (*Ereñ
wa shokugo ni watashi to sekeñ-
banashi o suru no ga suki da.*) エレ
ンは食後に私と世間話をするのが好きだ.
── *vi.* o「sha」beri suru おしゃべりする
Ⅰ; sha「be」ru しゃべる Ⅽ; za「tsudañ
o suru 雑談をする Ⅰ: The pupils
were chatting about their school
trip. (*Seeto-tachi wa shuugaku
ryokoo no koto o shabette ita.*) 生
徒たちは修学旅行のことをしゃべっていた.

chatter *vi.* **1** (of people) pe「cha-
kucha sha「be」ru ぺちゃくちゃしゃべる
Ⅽ: The old ladies chattered away
without regard to the people
around. (*Obaasañ-tachi wa mawari no hito o ki ni shinaide
pecha-kucha shabette ita.*) おばあさ
んたちは周りの人を気にしないでぺちゃく
ちゃしゃべっていた.
2 (of animals) kya「kkya to na「ku
きゃっきゃと鳴く Ⅽ: The monkeys
chattered in the trees. (*Saru ga ki
no ue de kyakkya to naita.*) 猿が木

の上できゃっきゃと鳴いた.
3 (of objects) ga「tagata i「u がたがた
いう Ⅽ: Jim's teeth were chattering
with fear. (*Jimu no ha wa kyoofu
de gatagata itta.*) ジムの歯は恐怖でが
たがたいった.
── *n.* **1** (of people) sha「berigo」e
しゃべり声: The chatter of the
pupils drowned out the voice of
the teacher. (*Seeto no shaberigoe
ga señsee no hanashi o keshita.*)
生徒のしゃべり声が先生の話を消した.
2 (of animals) kya「kkya to iu na-
「kigo」e きゃっきゃという鳴き声.
3 (of objects) ga「tagata suru o「to」
がたがたする音: the chatter of machines (*kikai no gatagata suru
oto*) 機械のがたがたする音.

cheap *adj.* **1** (inexpensive) ya「su」i
安い: a cheap book (*yasui hoñ*) 安い
本 / Do you have something a little
cheaper? (*Moo sukoshi yasui no
wa arimasu ka?*) もう少し安いのはあり
ますか.
2 (inferior) ya「suppo」i 安っぽい;
ya「sumono no 安物の: a cheap hat
(*yasumono no booshi*) 安物の帽子.
3 (mean) ge「hi」ñ na 下品な: His
cheap jokes make me sick. (*Kare
no gehiñ na joodañ ni wa mukamuka suru.*) 彼の下品な冗談にはむか
むかする.

cheat *vt.* …o da「ma」su …をだます
Ⅽ: He cheated me out of my money. (*Kare wa watashi o damashite
o-kane o totta.*) 彼は私をだましてお金
をとった.
── *vi.* (…o) go「maka」su (…を)ごまか
す Ⅽ; (on examinations) ka「ññiñgu
o suru カンニングをする Ⅰ: cheat on
taxes (*zeekiñ o gomakasu*) 税金をご
まかす / He cheated on the examination. (*Kare wa sono shikeñ de kañniñgu o shita.*) 彼はその試験でカンニン
グをした.

check *n.* **1** (inspection) sho「ogoo
照合; te「ñkeñ 点検; che「kku チェッ
ク: a check of a student's grades
(*gakusee no seeseki no shoogoo*)
学生の成績の照合 / a safety check

(*añzeñ no teñkeñ*) 安全の点検.

2 (financial instrument) ko「gi」tte 小切手: pay a bill by check (*see-kyuusho o kogitte de harau*) 請求書を小切手で払う / a traveler's check (*toraberaazu chekku*) トラベラーズチェック.

3 (bill) ka「ñjo」o 勘定; (on a piece of paper) ka「ñjoogaki 勘定書; de「ñpyoo 伝票: The bill, please. (*Kañjoo o onegai shimasu.*) 勘定をお願いします.

4 (mark) che「kku no shi」rushi チェックの印.

5 (control) yo「kusee 抑制; (stop) bo「oshi 防止: a check on labor union activity (*roodoo-kumiai-katsudoo no yokusee*) 労働組合活動の抑制.

6 (pattern) che「kku[i「chimatsu]-mo「yoo チェック[市松]模様: a check shirt (*chekku no waishatsu*) チェックのワイシャツ.

— *vt.* **1** (inspect) ...o shi「rabe」ru ...を調べる Ⅴ; te「ñkeñ suru 点検する Ⅰ; ke「ñsa suru 検査する Ⅰ: Passports are checked here. (*Pasupooto wa koko de keñsa saremasu.*) パスポートはここで検査されます. / check a car's engine (*kuruma no eñjiñ o teñkeñ suru*) 車のエンジンを点検する.

2 (mark) ...o che「kku suru ...をチェックする Ⅰ; ...ni che「kku no shi「rushi o tsuke」ru ...にチェックの印を付ける Ⅴ.

3 (stop) ...o bo「oshi suru ...を防止する Ⅰ; ku「itome」ru 食い止める Ⅴ: check the spread of cholera (*korera no deñseñ o kuitomeru*) コレラの伝染を食い止める.

check in *vi.* che「kku」iñ suru チェックインする Ⅰ: The couple checked in to the hotel at four. (*Futari wa yo-ji ni hoteru ni chekkuiñ shita.*) 二人は4時にホテルにチェックインした.

check out *vi.* che「kkua」uto suru チェックアウトする Ⅰ: I'd like to check out at nine tomorrow morning. (*Asu no asa ku-ji ni chek-kuauto shitai to omoimasu.*) あすの

朝9時にチェックアウトしたいと思います.

checkbook *n.* ko「gittechoo 小切手帳.

checkers *n.* (draughts) che「kkaa チェッカー: play checkers (*chekkaa o suru*) チェッカーをする.

check-in *n.* che「kku」iñ チェックイン.

checking account *n.* to「oza-yo」kiñ 当座預金: open a checking account (*tooza-yokiñ no kooza o hiraku*) 当座預金の口座を開く.

checkout *n.* che「kkua」uto チェックアウト.

checkup *n.* **1** (of health) ke「ñkoo-shi」ñdañ 健康診断: have a checkup (*keñkooshiñdañ o ukeru*) 健康診断を受ける.

2 (of a car, etc.) ke「ñsa 検査.

cheek *n.* **1** (applause) ka「ssai かっさい: receive cheers from the audience (*chooshuu no kassai o ukeru*) 聴衆のかっさいを受ける.

2 (encouragement) ha「gemashi 励まし: words of cheer (*hagemashi no kotoba*) 励ましのことば.

give three cheers *vi.* ba「ñza」i o sa「ñshoo suru 万歳を三唱する.

— *vt.* **1** (encourage) ...o ge「ñki-zuke」ru ...を元気づける Ⅴ; ha「gema」su 励ます Ⓒ: Her word cheered him. (*Kanojo no kotoba wa kare o geñkizuketa.*) 彼女の言葉は彼を元気づけた.

2 (shout) ...o se「e-eñ suru ...を声援する Ⅰ: cheer the weaker team (*yowai hoo no chiimu o see-eñ suru*) 弱い方のチームを声援する.

cheerful *adj.* **1** (of a person) ge「ñki no [ga] ii 元気の[が]いい; ka「ikatsu na 快活な: a cheerful old man (*geñki no ii roojiñ*) 元気のいい老人.

2 (happy) ta「noshi」i 楽しい; a「karui 明るい: cheerful news (*tanoshii shirase*) 楽しい知らせ.

cheese *n.* chi「izu チーズ.

chef *n.* ko「kku」choo コック長; she「fu シェフ: Chef's Special (*Hoñjitsu no* o-susumehiñ) 本日のお勧め品.

chemical adj. kaʹgaku no 化学の; kaʹgaku-teki na 化学的な: chemical change (kagaku heñkà) 化学変化 / a chemical formula (kagakushiki) 化学式 / chemical weapons (kagaku heeki) 化学兵器.

chemicals n. (industrial) kaʹgaku-seʹehiñ 化学製品; (medicinal) kaʹgaku-yaʹkuhiñ 化学薬品.

chemist n. 1 (scientist) kaʹgaʹkusha 化学者.
2 (druggist) yaʹkuzaʹishi 薬剤師.

chemistry n. kaʹgaku 化学: organic [inorganic] chemistry (yuu-[mu]ki kagaku) 有[無]機化学.
★ When speaking of 'kagaku,' (chemistry) Japanese speakers will often add parenthically, 'bakegaku,' (from 'bakeru' 化ける) to distinguish it from 'kagaku' 科学 (science).

cheque n. ⇨ check n. (Sense 2)

cherish vt. 1 (protect) ... o taʹisetsu ni suru …を大切にする [T]: The mother cherished her baby. (Hahaoya wa akañboo o taisetsu ni shita.) 母親は赤ん坊を大切にした.
2 (hold dear) ... o muʹneʹ ni hiʹmeʹru …を胸に秘める [V]: For many years Sally cherished the hope that her son would return. (Sarii wa naganeñ musuko ga modotte kuru kiboo o mune ni himete ita.) サリーは長年息子が戻ってくる希望を胸に秘めていた.

cherry n. 1 (tree) saʹkura no ki 桜の木.
2 (fruit) saʹkurañbo さくらんぼ.
3 (blossom) saʹkura no hana 桜の花. ★ The cherry blossom is Japan's national flower. Japanese often get together for picnics around cherry trees in blossom, and enjoy merrymaking.

chess n. 1 (Western) cheʹsu チェス: play chess (chesu o suru) チェスをする.
2 (Japanese) shoʹogi 将棋: play Japanese-style chess (shoogi o sa-

su) 将棋を指す.

chest n. 1 (breast) muʹneʹ 胸: I have a pain in my chest. (Mune ga itai.) 胸が痛い.
2 (box) haʹko 箱: a chest of drawers (tañsu) たんす.

chestnut n. 1 (nut) kuʹri no mi 栗の実; (tree) kuʹri noʹ ki 栗の木.
2 (color) kuʹri-iro 栗色.

chew vt. kaʹmu 嚙む C: Chew your food well. (Tabemono wa yoku kami nasai.) 食べ物はよくかみなさい.

chicken n. 1 (adult bird) niʹwatori 鶏: keep chickens (niwatori o kau) 鶏を飼う.
2 (meat) toʹriniku 鶏肉: cook some chicken (toriniku o ryoori suru) 鶏肉を料理する / fried chicken (furai-do chikiñ) フライドチキン.
3 (coward) oʹkubyoomono おくびょう者; yoʹwaʹmushi 弱虫.

chief n. (of an organization) -choo 長: chief of police (keesatsu-sho-choo) 警察署長.
— adj. (principle) oʹmo-na 主な; shuʹyoo na 主要な: the chief rivers of Japan (Nihoñ no omo-na kawa) 日本の主な川 / the chief aim of the society (kyookai no shuyoo na mokuteki) 協会の主要な目的.

chiefly adv. shuʹ to shite 主として: The guests were chiefly women. (O-kyaku wa shu to shite josee datta.) お客は主として女性だった.

child n. 1 (opposite of an adult) koʹdomo 子ども: children (kodomo-tachi) 子どもたち / This book is interesting for both children and adults. (Kono hoñ wa kodomo ni mo otona ni mo omoshiroi.) この本は子どもにもおとなにもおもしろい.
2 (son or daughter) ko 子; koʹdomo 子ども: How many children do you have? (O-kosañ wa nañ-niñ imasu ka?) お子さんは何人いますか.

childbirth n. shuʹssañ 出産; [technical] buʹñbeñ 分娩.

childhood n. koʹdomo no toʹki [koʹro] 子供のとき[ころ]: In my childhood, my family lived in Sydney. (*Kodomo no koro, kazoku wa Shidonii ni suōde imashita.*) 子どものころ、家族はシドニーに住んでいました。

childish *adj.* **1** (like a child) koˈdomo-rashiˈi 子どもらしい; koˈdomo no 子どもの: childish games (*kodomo no asobi*) 子どもの遊び.
2 (silly) koˈdomoppoˈi 子供っぽい; yoˈochi na 幼稚な: make childish errors (*yoochi na machigai o suru*) 幼稚な間違いをする.

chill *vt.* ... o hiˈyaˈsu ...を冷やす C: chill wine (*waiō o hiyasu*) ワインを冷やす.
— *n.* **1** (outside temperature) hiˈeˈ 冷え; reˈeki 冷気: autumn chill (*aki no reeki*) 秋の冷気.
2 (body temperature) saˈmuke 寒気: I have a slight chill. (*Watashi wa sukoshi samuke ga suru.*) 私は少し寒気がする.

chilly *adj.* **1** (of weather) saˈmuˈi 寒い; haˈdasamuˈi 肌寒い: a chilly room (*samui heya*) 寒い部屋.
2 (of a response) tsuˈmetai 冷たい: a chilly attitude (*tsumetai taido*) 冷たい態度.

chimney *n.* eˈōtotsu 煙突: clean a chimney (*eōtotsu o sooji suru*) 煙突を掃除する.

chin *n.* aˈgoˈ あご: beard on the chin (*ago no hige*) あごのひげ.

china *n.* jiˈki 磁器; seˈtomono 瀬戸物: a china cup (*setomono no chawaō*) 瀬戸物の茶わん.

China *n.* Chuˈugoku 中国: People's Republic of China (*Chuukajiōmiō kyoowakoku*) 中華人民共和国 / Republic of China (*Chuukamiōkoku*) 中華民国.

Chinese *n.* (people) Chuˈugokuˈjiō 中国人; (language) Chuˈugokugo 中国語.
— *adj.* Chuˈugoku no 中国の; Chuˈugokuˈjiō no 中国人の; Chuˈugokugo no 中国語の: Chinese cooking (*Chuugoku ryoori*) 中国料理.

chip *n.* **1** (of wood, glass, china, etc.) kaˈkera かけら: a wood chip

(*koppa*) こっぱ.
2 (potato chips, crisps) poˈteto chiˈppusu ポテトチップス.
— *vt.* **1** (break) ... o kaˈku ...を欠く C: chip a teacup (*chawaō o kaku*) 茶わんを欠く.
2 (carve) ... o keˈzuru ...を削る C; keˈzuritoˈru 削り取る C: chip the ice off the sidewalk (*hodoo kara koori o kezuritoru*) 歩道から氷を削り取る.

chirp *vi.* (of a bird, insect) naˈku 鳴く C: The crickets are chirping in the garden. (*Koorogi ga niwa de naite iru.*) こおろぎが庭で鳴いている.
— *n.* naˈkigoˈe 鳴き声.

chisel *n.* (for wood and stone) noˈmi のみ; (for metal) taˈgane たがね.

chocolate *n.* **1** (sweet) choˈkoreˈeto チョコレート: a box of chocolates (*chokoreeto hito hako*) チョコレート一箱.
2 (drink) koˈkoa ココア: a cup of chocolate (*kokoa ip-pai*) ココア 1 杯.

choice *n.* **1** (act of choosing) eˈraˈbu koˈtoˈ 選ぶこと; seˈōtaku 選択: make a careful choice of occupations (*shokugyoo o shiōchoo ni erabu*) 職業を慎重に選ぶ.
2 (person) eˈraˈōda hiˈtoˈ 選んだ人; (thing) eˈraˈōda moˈnoˈ 選んだ物: Which is your choice? (*Eraōda no wa dore desu ka?*) 選んだのはどれですか.
3 (collection to choose from) seˈōtaku no shuˈrui 選択の種類: a great choice of roses (*iroiro na shurui no bara*) いろいろな種類のばら.
— *adj.* (of food, drink) goˈkujoo no 極上の: choice grapes (*gokujoo no budō*) 極上のぶどう.

choke *vt.* **1** (smother) ... o chiˈssoku saseru ...を窒息させる V: The baby swallowed a coin and was almost choked. (*Akaōboo wa kooka o nomikoōde, moo sukoshi de chissoku suru tokoro datta.*) 赤ん坊は硬貨を飲み込んで、もう少しで窒息するところだった.
2 (block up) ... o fuˈsagu ...をふさぐ

C: The road was choked with cars.
(*Dooro wa kuruma de fusagarete ita.*) 道路は車でふさがれていた.
— *vi.* i「ki ga tsu「ma」ru 息が詰まる
C: We almost choked in the dust.
(*Hokori de iki ga tsumari-soo datta.*) ほこりで息が詰まりそうだった.

cholera *n.* ko「rera コレラ: contract cholera (*korera ni kakaru*) コレラにかかる.

choose *vt.* (select) ... o e「ra」bu 選ぶ C; se「ntaku suru 選択する I:
Choose the cake you like best.
(*Ichiban suki na keeki o erabi nasai.*) いちばん好きなケーキを選びなさい. /
He was chosen chairman. (*Kare wa gichoo ni erabareta.*) 彼は議長に選ばれた.
— *vi.* e「ra」bu 選ぶ C; se「ntaku suru 選択する I: choose between the two (*futatsu no naka kara erabu*) 二つの中から選ぶ.

chop *vt.* 1 (with an ax) ... o ta「takiki」ru ...をたたき切る C; wa「ru 割る C: chop wood (*maki o waru*) まきを割る.
2 (of vegetables) ... o ki「zamu ...を刻む C: I chopped up the green onions. (*Watashi wa negi o kizanda.*) 私はねぎを刻んだ.
— *vi.* (... o) ta「takiki」ru (...を)たたき切る C: He chopped at the tree.
(*Kare wa sono ki o tatakikitta.*) 彼はその木をたたき切った.
— *n.* a「tsugiri no niku」 厚切りの肉; cho「ppu チョップ: a pork chop (*butaniku no atsugiri*) 豚肉の厚切り.

chopsticks *n.* ha「shi 箸: eat with chopsticks (*hashi de taberu*) 箸で食べる / throwaway chopsticks (*waribashi*) 割りばし.

chore *n.* 1 (duty) za「tsuyoo 雑用: daily chores (*mainichi no zatsuyoo*) 毎日の雑用.
2 (burdensome task) me「ndo」o na shi「goto めんどうな仕事.

chorus *n.* 1 (singing together) ga「sshoo 合唱; ko「orasu コーラス.
2 (group) ga「sshoo」dan 合唱団: join a chorus (*gasshoodan ni*

hairu) 合唱団に入る.
3 (composition) ga「sshoo」kyoku 合唱曲.

Christ *n.* Ki「risuto キリスト: Jesus Christ (*Iesu Kirisuto*) イエスキリスト / Before Christ (B.C.) (*kigen-zen*) 紀元前.

Christian *n.* Ki「risuto-kyo」oto キリスト教徒; Ku「ri」suchan クリスチャン.
— *adj.* Ki「risuto-kyo」o no キリスト教の; Ku「ri」suchan no クリスチャンの: the Christian church (*Kirisuto-kyookai*) キリスト教会.

Christmas *n.* Ku「risu」masu クリスマス; Ki「risuto-koota」nsai キリスト降誕祭: celebrate Christmas (*Kurisumasu o iwau*) クリスマスを祝う / Christmas Eve (*Kurisumasu ibu*) クリスマスイブ.

chronic *adj.* (of disease) ma「nsee no 慢性の: a chronic disease (*manseebyoo*) 慢性病.
2 (long time) na「gabi」ku 長引く: a chronic recession (*nagabiku fukyoo*) 長引く不況.

chrysanthemum *n.* ki「ku」 菊.

chuckle *vi.* ku「sukusu wa「rau くすくす笑う C: He chuckled over a comic strip. (*Kare wa manga o mite kusukusu waratta.*) 彼は漫画を見てくすくす笑った.

church *n.* 1 (the body of Christians) kyo「okai 教会: members of the church (*kyookai no shinto*) 教会の信徒.
2 (building) kyo「okai 教会; kyo「o-kaidoo 教会堂.
3 (service) re「ehai 礼拝: Church begins at 10:00. (*Reehai wa juu-ji ni hajimarimasu.*) 礼拝は10時に始まります.

cider *n.* 1 (alcoholic) ri「ngo」shu りんご酒.
2 (non-alcoholic) ri「ngo ju」usu りんごジュース. ★ Be careful not to confuse either of these with the generic name for fruit-flavored carbonated drinks in Japan, '*saidaa*' サイダー.

cigar *n.* ha「maki 葉巻き.

cigarette *n.* ta「bako たばこ; ka「mi-maki-ta「bako 紙巻きたばこ: smoke a cigarette (*tabako o suu*) たばこを吸う. ★ In Japanese, cigarettes, cigar and tobacco are all called '*tabako*.'

cinema *n.* (theater) e「ega¬-kañ 映画館; (films) e「ega 映画: go to the cinema (*eega o mi ni iku*) 映画を見に行く.

circle *n.* 1 (figure) e「ñ 円; ma「ru ま る; wa「 輪: draw a circle (*eñ o ega-ku*) 円を描く.
2 (company) na「kama¬ 仲間; -sha¬-kai 社会; -kai 界: the upper circles (*jooryuu-shakai*) 上流社会 / business circles (*jitsugyoo-kai*) 実業界.
3 (cycle) ju「ñkan 循環; shu¬uki 周期: the circle of seasons (*shiki no juñkan*) 四季の循環.
— *vi.* ma「waru 回る Ⓒ; se「ñkai suru 旋回する Ⓘ: The airplane circled over the airfield. (*Hikooki wa hikoojoo no ue ni señkai shita.*) 飛行機は飛行場の上を旋回した.
— *vt.* (draw a circle) ... o ma「ru de kakomu ...を丸で囲む Ⓒ: circle the correct answers (*tadashii kotae o maru de kakomu*) 正しい答を丸で囲む.

circuit *n.* 1 (motion) i「s-shuu 一周; ju「ñkai 巡回: The earth makes the circuit of the sun in one year. (*Chikyuu wa ichi-neñ de taiyoo o is-shuu suru.*) 地球は一年で太陽を一周する.
2 (round) ju「ñkai chi「iki 巡回地域: a postman's circuit (*yuubiñ no haitatsu chiiki*) 郵便の配達地域.
3 (race-track) sa「akitto サーキット; shu「ukai ko¬osu 周回コース.
4 (of electricity) ka「iro 回路; ka「i-señ 回線: a short circuit (*shooto*) ショート.

circular *adj.* 1 (round) ma「rui 丸い; e「ñ no 円の: a circular movement (*eñ uñdoo*) 円運動.
2 (of a ticket) shu「uyuu no 周遊の: a circular ticket (*shuuyuukeñ*) 周遊券.
— *n.* (notice) a「ñnaijoo 案内状;

chi「rashi ちらし.

circulate *vi.* 1 (go round) ju「ñ-kañ suru 循環する Ⓘ: Blood circulates through the body. (*Chi wa karada-juu o juñkañ suru.*) 血は体中を循環する.
2 (spread) hi「roma¬ru 広まる Ⓒ; tsu「tawaru 伝わる Ⓒ: The rumor circulated quickly. (*Sono uwasa wa sugu ni hiromatta.*) そのうわさはすぐに広まった.
3 (move from place to place) u「go-kimawa¬ru 動き回る Ⓒ: circulate among the guests at a party (*paatii de o-kyaku no aida o ugokima-waru*) パーティーでお客の間を動き回る.
— *vt.* (cause to circulate) ... o ju「ñ-kañ saseru ...を循環させる Ⓥ; ka「i-rañ suru 回覧する Ⓘ: circulate a magazine (*zasshi o ka¬irañ suru*) 雑誌を回覧する.

circulation *n.* 1 (of blood) ju「ñ-kañ 循環; ke「kkoo 血行: have a good [bad] circulation (*kekkoo ga yoi [warui]*) 血行がよい[悪い].
2 (of money) ryu「utsuu 流通: the circulation of money (*kahee no ryuutsuu*) 貨幣の流通.
3 (number of copies) ha「kkoo-bu-su¬u 発行部数: have a large [small] circulation (*hakkoo-busuu ga ooi [sukunai]*) 発行部数が多い[少ない].

circumstance *n.* ji「joo 事情; jo¬o-kyoo 状況: It depends on circumstances. (*Sore wa jijoo ni yori-masu.*) それは事情によります. / Under the present circumstances I can do nothing. (*Geñzai no jookyoo de wa watashi wa nani mo suru koto ga dekimaseñ.*) 現在の状況では私は何もすることができません.

circus *n.* sa「akasu サーカス.

cite *vt.* ... o i「ñyoo suru ...を引用する Ⓘ; a「geru 挙げる Ⓥ: cite an example (*ree o ageru*) 例を挙げる.

citizen *n.* (of a city) shi「miñ 市民; (of a state) ko「kumiñ 国民: the citizens of Kobe (*Koobe no shimiñ*) 神戸の市民.

city *n.* to「shi 都市; to「kai 都会; shi¬

市: Nara is an ancient city. (*Nara wa furui toshi desu.*) 奈良は古い都市です. / I'd like to reserve a hotel room in the city. (*Shinai no hoteru o yoyaku shitai no desu ga.*) 市内のホテルを予約したいのですが.

city hall *n.* shi'ya¹kusho 市役所.

civil *adj.* **1** (of citizens) shi¹miñ no 市民の: civil duties (*shimiñ no gimu*) 市民の義務.

2 (not of the armed forces) mi¹ñkañ no 民間の: civil aviation (*miñkañ-kookuu*) 民間航空.

3 (polite) re¹egi tadashi¹i 礼儀正しい; te¹enee na 丁寧な: make a civil reply (*teenee na heñji o suru*) 丁寧な返事をする.

civilization *n.* bu¹ñmee 文明: Western civilization (*seeyoo buñmee*) 西洋文明.

civilize *vt.* ... o bu¹ñmeeka suru ...を文明化する ①; kyo¹oka suru 教化する ①: Europe was civilized by the Roman Empire. (*Yooroppa wa Rooma teekoku ni yotte buñmeeka sareta.*) ヨーロッパはローマ帝国によって文明化された.

civilized *adj.* bu¹ñmeeka shita 文明化した; kyo¹oka sareta 教化された: civilized society (*buñmee shakai*) 文明社会.

claim *vt.* **1** (maintain) ... to shu¹choo suru ...と主張する ①; i¹iha¹ru 言い張る ©: He claimed that he is the owner of the land. (*Kare wa sono tochi no shoyuusha da to shuchoo shita.*) 彼はその土地の所有者だと主張した.

2 (demand) ... o yo¹okyuu suru ...を要求する ①; se¹ekyuu suru 請求する ①: I claimed traveling expenses. (*Watashi wa kootsuuhi o seekyuu shita.*) 私は交通費を請求した.

— *n.* **1** (statement) shu¹choo 主張: His claim is groundless. (*Kare no shuchoo wa koñkyo ga nai.*) 彼の主張は根拠がない.

2 (demand) yo¹okyuu 要求; se¹ekyuu 請求: make a claim for damages (*soñgai-baishoo o seekyuu suru*) 損害賠償を請求する.

3 (right) yo¹okyuu suru ke¹ñri 要求する権利: He has a claim to the money. (*Kare wa sono o-kane o yookyuu suru keñri ga aru.*) 彼はそのお金を要求する権利がある.

clamor *n.* sa¹kebi¹ 叫び; ko¹e 声: a clamor against war (*señsoo hañtai no koe*) 戦争反対の声.

— *vi.* sa¹wagitate¹ru 騒ぎ立てる ©; yo¹okyuu suru 要求する ①: They clamored for higher wages. (*Kare-ra wa chiñage o yookyuu shita.*) 彼らは賃上げを要求した.

clap *vt.* ... o ta¹ta¹ku ...をたたく ©; po¹ñ to ta¹ta¹ku ぽんとたたく ©: clap one's hands (*te o tataku*) 手をたたく / He clapped me on the back. (*Kare wa watashi no senaka o poñ to tataita.*) 彼は私の背中をぽんとたたいた.

— *vi.* ha¹kushu suru 拍手する ①: When he appeared on the stage, the audience clapped. (*Kare ga butai ni arawareru to chooshuu wa hakushu shita.*) 彼が舞台に現れると聴衆は拍手した.

— *n.* (clapping) ha¹kushu 拍手; (noise) ba¹ribari [pa¹chipachi] to iu o¹to¹ ばりばり[ぱちぱち]という音: a clap of thunder (*raimee*) 雷鳴.

clash *vi.* **1** (fight) sho¹ototsu suru 衝突する ①: The students and the riot police clashed. (*Gakusee to kidootai ga shoototsu shita.*) 学生と機動隊が衝突した.

2 (conflict) ku¹ichigau 食い違う ©: Their opinions always clash. (*Kare-ra no ikeñ wa itsu-mo kuichigau.*) 彼らの意見はいつも食い違う.

— *n.* sho¹ototsu 衝突; fu¹i¹tchi 不一致: a clash of interests (*rigai no shoototsu*) 利害の衝突.

clasp *n.* to¹megane 留め金: fasten the clasp of a necklace (*nekkuresu no tomegane o tomeru*) ネックレスの留め金を留める.

— *vt.* (with the hand) ... o ni¹giri-shime¹ru ...を握りしめる ⊻; (in the arms) ... o da¹kishime¹ru ...を抱きしめる ⊻: The mother clasped her baby to her breast. (*Hahaoya wa akañboo o mune ni dakishimeta.*) 母親は赤ん坊を胸に抱きしめた.

class *n.* **1** (group of students) ku⌐rasu クラス; ga⌐kkyuu 学級: He and I are in the same class. (*Kare to watashi wa onaji kurasu desu.*) 彼と私は同じクラスです. ★ Japanese 'kurasu' usually means a specific homeroom.
2 (lesson) ju⌐gyoo 授業: How many classes do you have today? (*Kyoo wa nañ-jikañ jugyoo ga arimasu ka?*) きょうは何時間授業がありますか.
3 (social group) ka⌐ikyuu 階級; ka⌐isoo 階層: the upper class (*jooryuu-kaikyuu no shina*) 上流階級.
4 (division) bu⌐rui 部類; shu⌐rui 種類: These two things belong to the same class. (*Kore-ra futatsu no mono wa onaji burui ni zokushimasu.*) これら二つの物は同じ部類に属します.
5 (grade) to⌐okyuu 等級; ku⌐rasu クラス: goods of the highest class (*saikookyuu no shina*) 最高級の品 / first class (*faasuto kurasu*) ファーストクラス.

classic *adj.* **1** (traditional) de⌐ñtoo-teki na 伝統的な; ko⌐teñ-teki na 古典的な: a classic event (*deñtoo-teki na gyooji*) 伝統的な行事.
2 (first-rate) i⌐chi-ryuu no 一流の: a classic author (*ichi-ryuu no sakka*) 一流の作家.
3 (of literature, art, etc.) ko⌐teñ no 古典の: classic culture (*koteñ buñka*) 古典文化.
— *n.* (of literature) ko⌐teñ 古典: the Japanese classics (*Nihoñ no koteñ*) 日本の古典.

classical *adj.* **1** (of music) ko⌐teñ-shu⌐gi no 古典主義の; ku⌐rashi⌐kku no クラシックの: classical music (*kurashikku oñgaku*) クラシック音楽.
2 (of literature) ko⌐teñ bu⌐ñgaku no 古典文学の: the classical languages (*koteñgo*) 古典語.

classification *n.* bu⌐ñrui 分類; buñruihoo 分類法: the classification of animals (*doobutsu no buñrui*) 動物の分類.

classify *vt.* ... o bu⌐ñrui suru ...を分類する □; to⌐okyuu ni wake⌐ru 等級に分ける Ⅴ: I classified the books by subject. (*Watashi wa hoñ o teema-betsu ni buñrui shita.*) 私は本をテーマ別に分類した.

classmate *n.* do⌐okyu⌐usee 同級生; do⌐oki⌐see 同期生; ku⌐rasume⌐eto クラスメート: He is a classmate from high school. (*Kare wa watashi no kookoo kara no dookyuusee desu.*) 彼は私の高校からの同級生です.

classroom *n.* kyo⌐oshitsu 教室.

clause *n.* **1** (of grammar) se⌐tsu 節.
2 (of a legal document) jo⌐okoo 条項; ka⌐joo 箇条: amend the third clause of the contract (*keeyaku no dai-sañ-joo o teesee suru*) 契約の第3条を訂正する.

claw *n.* (hooked nail) tsu⌐me つめ; ka⌐gi⌐tsume かぎつめ; (of a crab) ha⌐sami⌐ はさみ.

clay *n.* ne⌐ñdo 粘土.

clean *adj.* **1** (free from dirt) se⌐eketsu na 清潔な; ki⌐ree na きれいな; yo⌐gorete inai 汚れていない: keep one's room clean (*heya o seeketsu ni shite oku*) 部屋を清潔にしておく / clean water (*kiree na mizu*) きれいな水.
2 (unused) na⌐ni mo ka⌐ite nai 何も書いてない; mi⌐shi⌐yoo no 未使用の: Please give me a clean sheet of paper. (*Nani mo kaite nai kami o ichi-mai kudasai.*) 何も書いてない紙を1枚下さい.
3 (free from offense) ke⌐ppaku na 潔白な; ki⌐ree na きれいな: a clean record (*kiree na rireki*) きれいな履歴.
— *adv.* (completely) su⌐kka⌐ri すっかり; ma⌐ttaku まったく: I clean forgot about it. (*Sono koto wa sukkari wasurete ita.*) そのことはすっかり忘れていた.
— *vt.* ... o se⌐eketsu ni suru ...を清

潔にする T; mi「gaku 磨く C; so「oji
suru 掃除する T; se「ntaku suru 洗
濯する T: clean one's teeth (*ha o
migaku*) 歯を磨く / Please clean the
room. (*Heya o sooji shite kudasai.*)
部屋を掃除してください. / This is to
be cleaned. (*Kore wa señtaku suru
mono desu.*) これは洗濯するものです.

cleaner *n.* **1** (person) so「oji o suru
hito¹ 掃除をする人; ku「riiniñgu-ya ク
リーニング屋: take one's coat to the
cleaner's (*kooto o kuriiniñgu-ya e
motte iku*) コートをクリーニング屋へ
持っていく.
2 (machine) so「oji¹ki 掃除機.

cleaning *n.* **1** (of a room) so「oji 掃
除; (of clothes) se「ntaku 洗濯: do
the cleaning (*sooji [señtaku] o
suru*) 掃除[洗濯]をする.

clear *adj.* **1** (distinct) ha「kki¹ri
shita [shite iru] はっきりした[している];
se「ñmee na 鮮明な: write in clear
letters (*hakkiri shita ji de kaku*)
はっきりした字で書く / a clear photograph (*señmee na shashiñ*) 鮮明な
写真.
2 (obvious) a「ki¹raka na 明かな;
me「ehaku na 明白な: It is clear that
you are wrong. (*Kimi ga machigatte iru no wa meehaku desu.*) 君
が間違っているのは明白です.
3 (bright) a「karui 明るい; ha「reta
晴れた; ha「rete iru 晴れている: clear
sunshine (*akarui nikkoo*) 明るい日
光 / clear weather (*hareta teñki*) 晴
れた天気.
4 (transparent) su「ñda 澄んだ;
su「ñde iru 澄んでいる; to「omee na 透
明な: clear water (*suñda mizu*) 澄ん
だ水.
5 (free from obstacles) ja「ma ga
na¹i じゃまがない; a「ita 空いた; a「ite-
iru 空いている: a clear space (*akichi*)
空き地 / a clear passage (*jiyuu ni
tooreru michi*) 自由に通れる道.
— *vt.* **1** (make clear) ... o ki¹ree
ni suru ...をきれいにする T: clear a
mirror (*kagami o kiree ni suru*) 鏡
をきれいにする.
2 (remove) ... o to「rinozoku ...を取

り除く C: clear the snow from the
road (*michi kara yuki o torinozoku*) 道から雪を取り除く.
3 (free from blame) ... o ha「ra¹su
...を晴らす C: clear a suspect of a
crime (*hañzai no utagai o harasu*)
犯罪の疑いを晴らす.
— *vi.* (of the weather) ha「re¹ru 晴
れる V: The sky is clearing. (*Sora
ga harete kita.*) 空が晴れてきた.

clearly *adv.* ha「kki¹ri (to) はっきり
(と): I can't hear you clearly. (*Hakkiri kikoemaseñ.*) はっきり聞こえませ
ん.

clergyman *n.* bo「kushi 牧師;
se「eshoku¹sha 聖職者.

clerk *n.* **1** (of an office) ji「mu¹iñ 事
務員; sho「ku¹iñ 職員; -in 員: a
bank clerk (*giñkooiñ*) 銀行員 / a
front desk clerk (*furoñtogakari*) フ
ロント係 / a government clerk
(*koomuiñ*) 公務員.
2 (of a shop) te「ñ'iñ 店員: a grocery
clerk (*shokuryoohiñteñ no teñiñ*)
食料品店の店員.

clever *adj.* **1** (showing ability)
u「ma¹i うまい; ta「kumi na 巧みな: a
clever idea (*umai kañgae*) うまい考
え.
2 (skillful) ki¹yoo na 器用な: He is
clever with his hands. (*Kare wa
tesaki ga kiyoo da.*) 彼は手先が器用
だ.
3 (intelligent) a「tama¹ ga i¹i 頭がい
い; ri「koo na 利口な; ka「shiko¹i 賢
い: a clever child (*rikoo na kodomo*) 利口な子ども.

client *n.* i「rainiñ 依頼人; (of a
shop) o-「kyaku お客.

cliff *n.* ga「ke がけ; ze「ppeki 絶壁.

climate *n.* **1** (weather conditions)
ki「koo 気候: The climate of Japan
agrees with me. (*Nihoñ no kikoo
wa watashi ni atte imasu.*) 日本の
気候は私に合っています.
2 (area) chi「hoo 地方; fu「udo 風土:
live in a warmer climate (*atatakai
chihoo de kurasu*) 暖かい地方で暮ら
す.

climb *vt.* ... ni no「boru ...に登る C:

climb a tree (*ki ni noboru*) 木に登る / Have you ever climbed that mountain? (*Ano yama ni nobotta koto wa arimasu ka?*) あの山に登ったことはありますか.
— *vi.* **1** (go up) (... o) no⌐boru (... を)登る C: climb up a ladder (*hashigo o noboru*) はしごを登る.
2 (rise) no⌐boru 昇る C; a⌐garu 上がる C: The moon climbed above the horizon. (*Tsuki ga chiheeseñ no ue ni nobotta.*) 月が地平線の上に昇った. / Prices are climbing. (*Bukka wa agatte iru.*) 物価は上がっている.
— *n.* no⌐boru koto 登ること; jo⌐shoo 上昇; (of a mountain) to⌐zañ 登山: make a climb (*noboru*) 登る.

cling *vi.* (grip) (... ni) shi⌐gamitsu⌐ku (...に)しがみつく C; (stick) ku⌐t-tsu⌐ku くっつく C: The mud clung to my shoes. (*Doro ga kutsu ni kuttsuita.*) 泥が靴にくっついた.

clinic *n.* shi⌐ñryoojo 診療所; ku⌐ri⌐nikku クリニック.

clinical thermometer *n.* ta⌐io⌐ñkee 体温計.

clip[1] *n.* ku⌐ri⌐ppu クリップ; ka⌐mibasami 紙ばさみ: fasten papers with a clip (*shorui o kurippu de tomeru*) 書類をクリップで留める.
— *vt.* ... o to⌐meru ...を留める V: clip a brooch to the lapel (*buroochi o eri ni tomeru*) ブローチをえりに留める.

clip[2] *vt.* (cut) ... o ha⌐sami⌐ de kiru ...をはさみで切る C; (trim) ka⌐riko⌐mu 刈り込む C: clip an article out of a newspaper (*kiji o shiñbuñ kara kirinuku*) 記事を新聞から切り抜く / She clipped her hair close. (*Kanojo wa kami o mijikaku kari-koñda.*) 彼女は髪を短く刈り込んだ.
— *n.* ka⌐rikomi 刈り込み; (clipping) ki⌐rinuki 切り抜き.

cloakroom *n.* ku⌐ro⌐oku(ruumu) クローク(ルーム); ke⌐itaihiñ-azukarijo 携帯品預かり所.

clock *n.* to⌐kee 時計: This clock is five minutes fast [slow]. (*Kono to-*

kee wa go-fuñ susuñde [oku-rete] iru.*) この時計は5分進んで[遅れて]いる. ★ 'Watch' is also called *'tokee.'*

close[1] *vt.* **1** (shut) ... o to⌐jiru ...を閉じる V; shi⌐me⌐ru 閉める V: close one's eyes (*me o tojiru*) 目を閉じる / close a window (*mado o shimeru*) 窓を閉める.
2 (stop up) ... o tsu⌐ukoodome ni suru ...を通行止めにする T: The bridge is closed to traffic. (*Hashi wa tsuukoodome ni natte imasu.*) 橋は通行止めになっています.
3 (bring to an end) ... o o⌐eru ...を終える V; shu⌐uryoo suru 終了する T: close a discussion (*tooroñ o oeru*) 討論を終える.
— *vi.* o⌐waru 終わる C; shi⌐ma⌐ru 閉まる C: What time does the bank close? (*Giñkoo wa nañ-ji ni shima-rimasu ka?*) 銀行は何時に閉まりますか.

close[2] *adj.* **1** (near) se⌐kkiñ shita [shite iru] 接近した[している]; su⌐gu soba (ni) すぐそば(に): His house is close to the station. (*Kare no uchi wa eki no sugu soba desu.*) 彼の家は駅のすぐそばです.
2 (dear) shi⌐tashii⌐ 親しい; shi⌐ñmi-tsu na 親密な: a close friend (*shiñ-yuu*) 親友.
3 (careful) sa⌐ishiñ no 細心の: pay close attention (*saishiñ no chuui o harau*) 細心の注意を払う.
— *adv.* su⌐gu so⌐ba ni すぐそばに; chi⌐kaku ni 近くに: Come closer to me. (*Motto chikaku ni ki nasai.*) もっと近くに来なさい.

closed *adj.* shi⌐mera⌐reta 閉められた; shi⌐ma⌐tte iru 閉まっている; kyu⌐u-gyoo no 休業の: Closed today. (*Hoñjitsu kyuugyoo.*) 本日休業.

closely *adv.* **1** (tightly) pi⌐tta⌐ri (to) ぴったり(と); gi⌐sshi⌐ri (to) ぎっしり(と): Her coat fits closely. (*Ka-nojo no kooto wa pittari atte iru.*) 彼女のコートはぴったり合っている.
2 (carefully) chu⌐ui shite 注意して; me⌐ñmitsu ni 綿密に: listen closely

(chuui shite kiku) 注意して聞く.

closet n. oˈshiire 押し入れ; toˈdana 戸棚; kuˈroˌzetto クロゼット.

cloth n. nuˈno 布; kiˈji 生地; kuˈroˌsu クロス: cloth for a dress (fuku no kiji) 服の生地 / a tablecloth (teeburu kurosu) テーブルクロス.

clothe vt. ... ni fuˈku o kiˈseru ...に服を着せる V: He was clothed in wool. (Kare wa uuru no fuku o kite ita.) 彼はウールの服を着ていた.

clothes n. fuˈkuˌ 服; iˈfuku 衣服; kiˈmono 着物: put on [take off] one's clothes (fuku o kiru [nugu]) 服を着る[脱ぐ].

clothing n. iˈrui 衣類; fuˈkuˌ 服; iˈryoohiˌn 衣料品: children's clothing (kodomo-fuku) 子供服 / food, clothing, and shelter (ishokujuu) 衣食住.

cloud n. kuˈmo 雲: The sun was hidden by a cloud. (Taiyoo ga kumo ni kakureta.) 太陽が雲に隠れた.

cloudy adj. kuˈmoˌtta 曇った; kuˈmoˌtte iru 曇っている; kuˈmori no 曇りの: a cloudy day (kumori no hi) 曇りの日 / a cloudy sky (kumorizora) 曇り空 / It is cloudy today. (Kyoo wa kumotte iru.) きょうは曇っている.

clover n. kuˈroˌobaa クローバー: four-leaf clover (yotsuba no kuroobaa) 四つ葉のクローバー.

club n. 1 (group of people) kuˈrabu クラブ; doˈokoˌkai 同好会: join a golf club (gorufu kurabu ni hairu) ゴルフクラブに入る.
2 (stick) koˈnˌboo こん棒.

clue n. teˈgaˌkari 手がかり; iˈtoˌguchi 糸口: find [miss] an important clue (juuyoo na tegakari o mitsukeru [miotosu]) 重要な手がかりを見つける [見落とす].

clumsy adj. buˈkiˌyoo na 不器用な; giˈkochinaˌi ぎこちない: He is clumsy with his hands. (Kare wa tesaki ga bukiyoo da.) 彼は手先が不器用だ.

cluster n. 1 (bunch) fuˈsaˌ 房: a cluster of grapes (hito-fusa no budoo) 1 房のぶどう.

2 (group) muˈreˌ 群れ; shuˈudañ 集団: a cluster of onlookers (keñbutsuniñ no mure) 見物人の群れ.

clutch vt. ... o shiˈkkaˌri to niˈgiru ...をしっかりと握る C; guˈi to tsuˈkaˌmu ぐいとつかむ C: He clutched my arm firmly. (Kare wa watashi no ude o shikkari to tsukañda.) 彼は私の腕をしっかりとつかんだ.
— n. 1 (grasp) tsuˈkaˌmu koˈtoˌ つかむこと: The pickpocket made a clutch at her bag. (Suri wa kanojo no baggu o tsukamoo to shita.) すりは彼女のバッグをつかもうとした.
2 (control) shiˈhai 支配; shuˈchuu 手中: fall into the clutches of the enemy (teki no shuchuu ni ochiiru) 敵の手中に陥る.

coach n. 1 (person) koˈochi コーチ; shiˈdoˌiñ 指導員: a baseball coach (yakyuu no koochi) 野球のコーチ.
2 (railroad car) kyaˈkusha 客車; (bus) oˈogata baˌsu 大型バス.
3 (carriage) yoˈñriñ oogata baˌsha 四輪大型馬車.
— vt. ... o shiˈdoo suru ...を指導する I; koˈochi suru コーチをする I: I coached her in Japanese. (Watashi wa kanojo ni Nihoñgo o shidoo shita.) 私は彼女に日本語を指導した.

coal n. seˈkitañ 石炭: burn coal (sekitañ o taku) 石炭をたく.

coarse adj. 1 (not fine) tsuˈbu no [ga] oˈokiˌi 粒の[が]大きい: coarse sand (tsubu no ookii suna) 粒の大きい砂.
2 (rough) kiˈmeˌ no [ga] aˈraˌi きめの [が]粗い: coarse cloth (kime no arai nuno) きめの粗い布.
3 (not refined) soˈya na 粗野な; (vulgar) geˈhiˌñ na 下品な: coarse taste (gehiñ na shumi) 下品な趣味.

coast n. kaˈigañ 海岸; eˈñgañ 沿岸: His house is on the coast. (Kare no ie wa kaigañ ni aru.) 彼の家は海岸にある.

coat n. 1 (outer garment) koˈoto コート; (jacket) uˈwagi 上着.
2 (of an animal) keˈgawa 毛皮.
3 (of paint) nuˈri 塗り; toˈsoo 塗装.

— *vt.* (cover) ... o o¹ou ...を覆う C: The furniture was coated with dust. (*Kagu wa hokori de oowarete ita.*) 家具はほこりで覆われていた.

cock *n.* **1** (rooster) o¹ñdori おんどり. **2** (tap) se¹ñ 栓; ko¹kku コック: turn on [off] a cock (*señ o akeru [shimeru]*) 栓を開ける[閉める].

cocktail *n.* ka¹kuteru カクテル.

cocoa *n.* ko¹koa ココア.

code *n.* **1** (secret words) a¹ñgoo 暗号; (symbols) fu¹goo 符号: zip code (*yuubiñ bañgoo*) 郵便番号. **2** (set of laws) ho¹oteñ 法典: the civil code (*miñpoo*) 民法 / the criminal code (*keehoo*) 刑法. **3** (set of rules) o¹kite おきて; ki¹soku 規則: the code of a school (*koosoku*) 校則.

coffee *n.* **1** (drink) ko¹ohi¹i コーヒー: make coffee (*koohii o ireru*) コーヒーをいれる / weak [strong] coffee (*usui [koi] koohii*) 薄い[濃い]コーヒー / a coffee cup (*koohii-jawañ [-kappu]*) コーヒー茶碗[カップ] / a coffee pot (*koohii potto*) コーヒーポット. **2** (shrub) ko¹ohi¹i no ki¹ コーヒーの木; (beans) ko¹ohi¹i ma¹me¹ コーヒー豆.

coffee shop *n.* ko¹ohii sho¹ppu コーヒーショップ; ki¹ssa¹teñ 喫茶店.

★ A '*kissateñ*' serves only coffee, black tea, and other refreshments.

coffin *n.* hi¹tsugi ひつぎ; ka¹ño¹ke 棺おけ.

cognac *n.* ko¹ñya¹kku コニャック.

coil *vt.* ... o gu¹ruguru ma¹ku ...をぐるぐる巻く C: coil a rope (*roopu o guruguru maku*) ロープをぐるぐる巻く. — *vi.* (... ni) ma¹kitsu¹ku (...に)巻きつく C; (of a snake) to¹guro¹ o ma¹ku とぐろを巻く C: The vine coiled around the tree. (*Tsuru ga ki ni makitsuita.*) つるが木に巻きついた. — *n.* **1** (something coiled) ma¹ita mono¹ 巻いたもの; wa¹ 輪: a coil of wire (*hito-maki no harigane*) 一巻きの針金. **2** (for an electric current) ko¹iru コイル.

coin *n.* ko¹oka 硬貨; ko¹iñ コイン.

coincide *vi.* **1** (happen) do¹oji ni o¹ko¹ru 同時に起こる C: The fire coincided with the earthquake. (*Jishiñ to dooji ni kaji ga okotta.*) 地震と同時に火事が起こった. **2** (agree) i¹tchi suru 一致する I: Their tastes in music coincide. (*Kare-ra no oñgaku no shumi wa itchi shite iru.*) 彼らの音楽の趣味は一致している.

Coke *n.* ko¹ora コーラ.

cold *adj.* **1** (of a thing) tsu¹metai 冷たい; (of weather) sa¹mu¹i 寒い: cold milk (*tsumetai gyuunyuu*) 冷たい牛乳 / It is cold today. (*Kyoo wa samui.*) きょうは寒い. **2** (unkind) re¹eta¹ñ na 冷淡な; tsu¹metai 冷たい: a cold answer (*reetañ na heñji*) 冷淡な返事. — *n.* **1** (illness) ka¹ze かぜ: catch a cold (*kaze o hiku*) かぜをひく / I have a cold. (*Watashi wa kaze o hiite imasu.*) 私はかぜをひいています. **2** (low temperature) sa¹musa 寒さ: shiver with cold (*samusa de furueru*) 寒さで震える.

coldness *n.* (of weather) sa¹musa 寒さ; (of a thing) tsu¹meta¹sa 冷たさ.

collaborate *vi.* kyo¹odoo de suru 共同でする I; kyo¹oryoku suru 協力する I: I collaborated with him on writing the book. (*Watashi wa kare to kyoodoo shite sono hoñ o kaita.*) 私は彼と共同してその本を書いた.

collapse *vi.* **1** (break down) ku¹zure¹ru 崩れる V; ho¹okai suru 崩壊する I: The bridge collapsed suddenly. (*Sono hashi wa totsuzeñ kuzureta.*) その橋は突然崩れた. **2** (fall down) ta¹ore¹ru 倒れる V: He collapsed on the job. (*Kare wa shigoto-chuu taoreta.*) 彼は仕事中倒れた. **3** (fail) tsu¹bureru つぶれる V: The project collapsed for lack of funds. (*Sono keekaku wa shikiñ-busoku de tsubureta.*) その計画は資金不足でつぶれた. — *vt.* (fold together) ... o or¹itatamu ...を折り畳む C : collapse an umbrella (*kasa o oritatamu*) 傘を折り畳む.

collar *n.* **1** (of a shirt) ka¹raa カラー; (of a jacket) e¹ri¹ 襟.

2 (of a dog) ku¹biwa 首輪.

colleague *n.* do¹oryoo 同僚; na-¹kama¹ 仲間: He is one of my colleagues. (*Kare wa watashi no dooryoo no hitori desu.*) 彼は私の同僚の一人です.

collect *vt.* ... o a¹tsume¹ru ...を集める V ; shu¹ushuu suru 収集する T : collect garbage (*gomi o atsumeru*) ごみを集める / collect stamps (*kitte o shuushuu suru*) 切手を収集する.

— *vi.* a¹tsuma¹ru 集まる C : Crowds of people collected in front of the building. (*Oozee no hito ga biru no mae ni atsumatta.*) 大勢の人がビルの前に集まった.

collect call *n.* ko¹rekuto ko¹oru コレクトコール; ryo¹okiñ ju¹shiñniñ-barai tsu¹uwa 料金受信人払い通話: Make this a collect call. (*Kono deñwa wa korekuto kooru ni shite kudasai.*) この電話はコレクトコールにしてください.

collection *n.* **1** (collecting) shu¹ushuu 収集; ka¹ishuu 回収; cho¹oshuu 徴収: garbage collection (*gomi no kaishuu*) ごみの回収 / tax collection (*zeekiñ no chooshuu*) 税金の徴収.

2 (something collected) ko¹re¹kushoñ コレクション; shu¹ushuu¹butsu 収集物.

college *n.* da¹igaku 大学; ta¹ñka-da¹igaku 単科大学: go to¹college (*daigaku ni kayou*) 大学に通う.

★ 'University' is also called '*daiga-ku*.'

collide *vi.* **1** (hit) sho¹ototsu suru 衝突する T ; bu¹tsukaru ぶつかる C : The bus collided with a truck. (*Sono basu wa torakku to shoototsu shita.*) そのバスはトラックと衝突した.

2 (disagree) i¹tchi shinai 一致しない; ku¹ichigau 食い違う C : Their views collided over the matter.

(*Kare-ra no ikeñ wa sono moñdai de itchi shinakatta.*) 彼らの意見はその問題で一致しなかった.

collision *n.* **1** (crash) sho¹ototsu 衝突: an automobile collision (*ji-doosha no shoototsu*) 自動車の衝突

2 (disagreement) fu¹i¹tchi 不一致: a collision of interests (*rigai no fui-tchi*) 利害の不一致.

colloquial *adj.* ko¹ogo no 口語の; ha¹nashiko¹toba no 話しことばの: colloquial language (*koogo*) 口語.

colonial *adj.* sho¹kumiñ¹chi no 植民地の: a colonial policy (*shokumiñ-chi seesaku*) 植民地政策.

— *n.* sho¹kumiñ¹chi no ju¹uniñ 植民地の住人.

colony *n.* sho¹kumiñ¹chi 植民地; ka¹itaku¹chi 開拓地: establish a colony (*shokumiñchi o keñsetsu suru*) 植民地を建設する.

color *n.* i¹ro¹ 色; ka¹raa カラー: Do you have this in another color? (*Kore no irochigai no mono wa arimasu ka?*) これの色違いの物はありますか. / 35 mm color film (*sañjuugo-miri no karaa firumu*) 35 mm のカラーフィルム.

— *vt.* ... ni i¹ro¹ o tsu¹ke¹ru ...に色をつける V ; i¹ro¹ o nu¹ru 色を塗る C : The girl colored the sky blue. (*Sono oñna-no-ko wa sora o aoku nutta.*) その女の子は空を青く塗った.

colorful *adj.* shi¹kisai ni to¹ñda 色彩に富んだ; ha¹na¹yaka na 華やかな; ka¹rafuru na カラフルな: colorful folk costumes (*hanayaka na miñzoku ishoo*) 華やかな民族衣装.

column *n.* **1** (of a newspaper) da¹ñ 段; ko¹ramu コラム; ra¹ñ 欄: an advertisement column (*kookokurañ*) 広告欄.

2 (vertical row) ta¹te no retsu 縦の列: add up the column of figures (*suuji no tate no retsu o gookee suru*) 数字の縦の列を合計する.

3 (pillar) e¹ñchuu 円柱; ha¹shira 柱.

comb *n.* ku¹shi¹ くし.

— *vt.* ... o ku¹shi¹ de to¹ka¹su ...をくしでとかす C : comb one's hair (*kami o kushi de tokasu*) 髪をくしでとかす.

combat *n.* se「ntoo 戦闘; ka「kutoo 格闘.
— *vt.* ... to ta「takau ...と戦う C: combat the enemy (*teki to tata-kau*) 敵と戦う.

combination *n.* ke「tsugoo 結合; ku「miawase 組み合わせ: a good combination of Japanese and Western styles (*Nihoñ-fuu to Seeyoo-fuu no umai kumiawase*) 日本風と西洋風のうまい組み合わせ.

combine *vt.* **1** (join) ... o ke「tsugoo suru ...を結合する C; ga「ppee suru 合併する C: combine two businesses (*futatsu no jigyoo o gappee suru*) 二つの事業を合併する.
2 (mix) ... o ma「ze「ru ...を混ぜる V; (of chemistry) ka「goo saseru 化合させる V: combine oxygen and hydrogen (*sanso to suiso o kagoo saseru*) 酸素と水素を化合させる.
— *vi.* **1** (unite) ke「tsugoo suru 結合する C; ga「ppee suru 合併する C: Our company combined with our competitor. (*Watashi-tachi no kaisha wa kyoosoo-aite to gappee shita.*) 私たちの会社は競争相手と合併した.
2 (of chemistry) ka「goo suru 化合する C.

come *vi.* **1** (move toward the speaker) ku「ru 来る C; ya「tte ku「ru やって来る C: When you come to Tokyo, please telephone. (*Tookyoo ni kuru toki wa deñwa o kudasai.*) 東京に来るときは電話をください. / Please come to the hotel tomorrow. (*Ashita hoteru ni kite kudasai.*) あしたホテルに来てください. / He came to see me. (*Kare wa watashi ni ai ni yatte kita.*) 彼は私に会いにやって来た.
2 (move toward the person whom the speaker addresses) i「ku [yu「ku] 行く C ★ '*Yuku*' is somewhat formal and old-fashioned; [polite] u「kagau 伺う C: I'm coming now. (*Ima ikimasu.*) いま行きます. / I'll come to your hotel tomorrow after-

noon. (*Asu no gogo hoteru ni o-ukagai shimasu.*) あすの午後ホテルにお伺いします.
3 (arrive) tsu「ku 着く C; to「ochaku suru 到着する C: At last they came to the town. (*Yatto kare-ra wa sono machi ni tsuita.*) やっと彼らはその町に着いた.
4 (reach) (... ni) na「ru (...に)なる C; ta「ssuru 達する C: The total comes to 5,000 yen. (*Gookee wa goseñ-eñ ni narimasu.*) 合計は5千円になります.

come back *vi.* mo「do「ru 戻る C: I'll come back right away. (*Sugu modorimasu.*) すぐ戻ります.

come from ... *vt.* ... no shu「sshiñ da ...の出身だ: He comes from Kyushu. (*Kare wa Kyuushuu shusshiñ desu.*) 彼は九州出身です.

come in *vi.* ha「iru 入る C: Please come in. (*Doozo o-hairi kudasai.*) どうぞお入りください.

come into ... *vt.* ... e [ni] ha「itte kuru ...へ[に]入って来る C: He came into my room. (*Kare wa watashi no heya e haitte kita.*) 彼は私の部屋へ入って来た.

comedy *n.* ki「geki 喜劇.

comet *n.* su「isee 彗星; ho「oki「bo-shi ほうき星.

comfort *n.* **1** (consolation) na「gusame 慰め: His letter gave me great comfort. (*Kare no tegami wa watashi ni ooki-na nagusame to natta.*) 彼の手紙は私に大きな慰めとなった.
2 (freedom from worries) ka「iteki 快適; a「ñraku 安楽: live in comfort (*añraku de kurasu*) 安楽に暮らす.
— *vt.* ... o na「gusame「ru ...を慰める V: I comforted the crying girl. (*Watashi wa naite iru oñna-no-ko o nagusameta.*) 私は泣いている女の子を慰めた.

comfortable *adj.* **1** (giving comfort) ka「iteki na 快適な; ko「kochi yo「i 心地よい: I had a comfortable journey. (*Watashi wa kaiteki na tabi o shita.*) 私は快適な旅をした.
2 (at ease) ki「raku na 気楽な; ku-

ˈtsuroˌida くつろいだ: Please make yourself comfortable. (*Doozo o-raku ni.*) どうぞお楽に.

comic *adj.* kiˈgeki no 喜劇の: a comic picture (*kigeki-eega*) 喜劇映画.
— *n.* **1** (comedian) kiˈgeki-haˌi-yuu 喜劇俳優.
2 (in a newspaper) maˈngaˌran 漫画欄.

coming *n.* kuˈru koˈto 来ること; toˈorai 到来: wait for the coming of spring (*haru ga kuru no o ma-tsu*) 春が来るのを待つ.
— *adj.* tsuˈgi no 次の; koˈndo no 今度の: the coming generation (*tsugi no sedai*) 次の世代 / the coming summer (*kondo no natsu*) 今度の夏.

command *vt.* **1** (give an order) ... ni (... to) meˈjiru ...に(...と)命じる V: He commanded us to halt. (*Kare wa watashi-tachi ni tomare to meejita.*) 彼は私たちに止まれと命じた.
2 (have authority over) ... o shiˈkiˌ suru ...を指揮する I; shiˈhai suru 支配する I: The captain commands his ship. (*Senchoo wa fune o shiki suru.*) 船長は船を指揮する.
— *n.* **1** (order) meˈeree 命令; saˈshizu 指図: give a command (*meeree o kudasu*) 命令を下す / obey a command (*meeree ni shita-gau*) 命令に従う.
2 (ability to control) jiˈyuuˌ ni tsu-ˈkaeru chikara 自由に使える力: She has a good command of French. (*Kanojo wa Furansugo o jiyuu ni tsukaeru.*) 彼女はフランス語を自由に使える.

commander *n.* shiˈkiˌsha 指揮者; shiˈreˌekan 司令官.

commemoration *n.* kiˈnen 記念; shuˈkuga 祝賀.

commemorative *adj.* kiˈnen no 記念の: a commemorative stamp (*kinen-kitte*) 記念切手.

commence *vt.* ... o kaˈishi suru ...を開始する I; haˈjimeru 始める V:

commence an investigation (*choo-sa o kaishi suru*) 調査を開始する.

comment *n.* **1** (remark) roˈnpyoo 論評; iˈken 意見; hiˈhyoo 批評: He gave favorable comments on the book. (*Kare wa sono hon ni tsuite kooi-teki na hihyoo o shita.*) 彼はその本について好意的な批評をした.
2 (explanation) kaˈisetsu 解説; seˈtsumee 説明.
— *vi.* roˈnpyoo suru 論評する I; hiˈhyoo suru 批評する I: comment on a new novel (*shinkan no shoose-tsu o hihyoo suru*) 新刊の小説を批評する.

commerce *n.* shoˈogyoo 商業; (trade) boˈoeki 貿易: foreign commerce (*gaikoku-booeki*) 外国貿易.

commercial *adj.* **1** (of commerce) shoˈogyoo no 商業の; boˈo-eki no 貿易の: a commercial firm (*shoosha*) 商社.
2 (profit-making) eˈeri no 営利の; shoˈogyoo-teki na 商業的な: a commercial enterprise (*eeri jigyoo*) 営利事業.
— *n.* koˈmaˌasharu コマーシャル; koˈrokuku-hoˌosoo 広告放送.

commission *n.* **1** (money) teˈsuˌuryoo 手数料; buˈai 歩合: receive a commission of 10 % on sales (*uriage no jup-paasento no tesuuryoo o morau*) 売上の10パーセントの手数料をもらう.
2 (group of persons) iˈiˌnkai 委員会: a commission of inquiry (*choosa iinkai*) 調査委員会.
3 (giving authority) iˈnin 委任; iˈtaku 委託: commission of powers (*kengen no inin*) 権限の委任.

commit *vt.* **1** (perform) ... o oˈkaˌsu ...を犯す C; oˈkonau 行う C: commit a crime (*hanzai o okasu*) 犯罪を犯す.
2 (hand over) ... o hiˈkiwataˌsu を引き渡す C; iˈtaku suru 委託する I: commit a girl to her uncle (*shoojo o oji ni azukeru*) 少女をおじに預ける.

commitment *n.* (promise) yaˈkusoku 約束; ko⌐oyaku 公約: I made a commitment to help him. (*Watashi wa kare o eñjo suru to yakusoku shita.*) 私は彼を援助すると約束した.

committee *n.* i⌐iñkai 委員会: a member of a committee (*iiñkai no iiñ*) 委員会の委員.

common *adj.* **1** (usual) fu⌐tsuu no 普通の; yo⌐ku aru よくある: a common mistake (*yoku aru machigai*) よくある間違い.
2 (belonging equally to) kyo⌐otsuu no 共通の; kyo⌐odoo no 共同の: common interests (*kyootsuu no rigai*) 共通の利害.
3 (public) ko⌐okyoo no 公共の; ko⌐oshuu no 公衆の: common land (*kookyoo no tochi*) 公共の土地.

commonly *adv.* i⌐ppañ ni 一般に; fu⌐tsuu wa 普通は: Children commonly like video games. (*Kodomotachi wa ippañ ni terebi geemu ga suki da.*) 子どもたちは一般にテレビゲームが好きだ.

commonplace *adj.* a⌐rifu⌐reta ありふれた; a⌐rifu⌐rete iru ありふれている; he⌐eboñ na 平凡な: a commonplace novel (*heeboñ na shoosetsu*) 平凡な小説.

common sense *n.* jo⌐oshiki 常識; ryo⌐oshiki 良識: He has no common sense. (*Kare wa jooshiki ga nai.*) 彼は常識がない.

communicate *vt.* ... o tsu⌐taeru …を伝える Ⅴ; shi⌐raseru 知らせる Ⅴ: I will communicate the answer to you. (*Henji wa anata ni tsutaemasu.*) 返事はあなたに伝えます.
— *vi.* re⌐ñraku suru 連絡する Ⅰ: communicate by telephone (*deñwa de reñraku suru*) 電話で連絡する.

communication *n.* **1** (conveying information) de⌐ñtatsu 伝達; i⌐shi no so⌐tsuu 意思の疎通; ko⌐myunike⌐eshoñ コミュニケーション: mass communication (*taishuu deñtatsu*) 大衆伝達, (*masukomi*) マスコミ.
2 (means of communicating) tsu⌐u-

shiñ (shu⌐dañ) 通信(手段); ko⌐o-tsuu ki⌐kañ 交通機関: All communication was broken by the storm. (*Arashi no tame subete no tsuushiñ wa todaeta.*) 嵐のためすべての通信は途絶えた.

communist *n.* kyo⌐osañ-shugi⌐-sha 共産主義者.

community *n.* **1** (group of people) kyo⌐odoo-sha⌐kai 共同社会; chi⌐iki-sha⌐kai 地域社会: the artists' community (*geejutsuka no shakai*) 芸術家の社会.
2 (the public in general) i⌐ppañ sha⌐kai 一般社会; ko⌐oshuu 公衆: the welfare of the community (*shakai fukushi*) 社会福祉.

commute *vi.* tsu⌐ukiñ suru 通勤する Ⅰ: I commute between Yokohama and Tokyo. (*Watashi wa Yokohama-Tookyoo kañ o tsuukiñ shite imasu.*) 私は横浜—東京間を通勤しています.

compact *adj.* **1** (packed tightly) gi⌐sshi⌐ri tsu⌐ma⌐tta ぎっしり詰まった; mi⌐tsu na 密な: a compact head of cabbage (*gisshiri maita kyabetsu no tama*) ぎっしり巻いたキャベツの玉.
2 (fitted neatly) ko⌐jiñma⌐ri shita [shite iru] こじんまりした[している]; ko⌐ñpakuto na コンパクトな: a compact camera (*koñpakuto kamera*) コンパクトカメラ.
3 (brief) ka⌐ñketsu na 簡潔な: write in a compact style (*kañketsu ni kaku*) 簡潔に書く.

companion *n.* na⌐kama⌐ 仲間; to⌐modachi 友達: He is one of my companions on the journey. (*Kare wa watashi no tabi no nakama no hitori desu.*) 彼は私の旅の仲間の一人です.

company *n.* **1** (business organization) ka⌐isha 会社: What does your company manufacture? (*Anata no kaisha wa nani o tsukutte imasu ka?*) あなたの会社は何を作っていますか. / a trading company (*shooji-gaisha*) 商事会社 / a company employee (*kaishaiñ*) 会社員.

2 (companionship) ko˥osai 交際; do˥oseki 同席; do˥okoo 同行: I was glad to have her company. (*Kanojo to dooseki dekite ureshikatta.*) 彼女と同席できてうれしかった.

3 (friends) na˥kama¹ 仲間; to˥modachi 友達: keep good company (*yoi nakama to tsukiau*) 良い仲間とつき合う.

4 (guests) ra˥ikyaku 来客: I'm expecting company this evening. (*Koñbañ o-kyaku ga kuru koto ni natte imasu.*) 今晩お客が来ることになっています.

5 (group of people) da˥ñtai 団体; i˥kkoo 一行: a theatrical company (*gekidañ*) 劇団.

comparative *adj.* **1** (making a comparison) hi˥kaku no 比較の: a comparative study of Japanese and American culture (*Nihoñ to Amerika no buñka no hikaku-keñkyuu*) 日本とアメリカの文化の比較研究.

2 (relative) hi˥kaku-teki 比較的; ka˥nari no かなりの: The experiment was a comparative success. (*Jikkeñ wa kanari umaku itta.*) 実験はかなりうまくいった.

comparatively *adv.* hi˥kaku-teki 比較的; ka˥nari かなり; wa˥riai (ni) 割合(に): I found the task comparatively easy. (*Sono shigoto wa wariai ni yasashikatta.*) その仕事は割合にやさしかった.

compare *vt.* **1** (examine) ... o hi˥kaku suru ...を比較する Ⅰ; ku˥raberu 比べる Ⅴ: compare the two pictures (*futatsu no e o hikaku suru*) 二つの絵を比較する.

2 (describe as being the same) ... o (... ni) ta˥toe˥ru ...を(...に)たとえる Ⅴ: Life is often compared to a voyage. (*Jiñsee wa yoku kookai ni tatoerareru.*) 人生はよく航海にたとえられる.

comparison *n.* hi˥kaku 比較; ta˥ishoo 対照: make a comparison between the original and the translation (*geñbuñ to hoñyaku o hikaku shite miru*) 原文と翻訳を比較

してみる.

compartment *n.* **1** (separate division) shi˥kiri 仕切り; ku˥kaku 区画: The drawer is divided into compartments. (*Hikidashi wa shikiri de kugirarete imasu.*) 引き出しは仕切りで区切られています.

2 (of a train) ko˥shitsu 個室; ko˥ñpa˥atomeñto コンパートメント.

compass *n.* **1** (instrument for showing direction) ji˥shaku 磁石; ko˥ñpasu コンパス.

2 (instrument for drawing circles) ko˥ñpasu コンパス: draw a circle with compasses (*koñpasu de eñ o egaku*) コンパスで円を描く.

compel *vt.* mu˥ri ni...⟨verb⟩-(sa)seru 無理に...(さ)せる Ⅴ: I was compelled to confess. (*Watashi wa muri ni hakujoo saserareta.*) 私は無理に白状させられた.

compensate *vt.* ... ni ho˥shoo o suru ...に補償をする Ⅰ: The company compensated him for his injury. (*Kaisha wa kare ni shoogai hoshoo o shita.*) 会社は彼に傷害補償をした.

compensation *n.* ho˥shoo 補償; ba˥ishoo 賠償: They made compensation for the damage. (*Kare-ra wa sono soñgai no hoshoo o shita.*) 彼らはその損害の補償をした.

compete *vi.* kyo˥osoo suru 競争する Ⅰ; ki˥so˥u 競う Ⅽ: We competed with each other for the prize. (*Watashi-tachi wa shoo o mezashite tagai ni kyoosoo shita.*) 私たちは賞をめざして互いに競争した.

competence *n.* no˥oryoku 能力; te˥kisee 適性: I doubt his competence for the task. (*Sono shigoto ni taisuru kare no nooryoku wa gimoñ da.*) その仕事に対する彼の能力は疑問だ.

competent *adj.* no˥oryoku no [ga] a˥ru 能力の[がある]; yu˥unoo na 有能な: She is competent as a teacher. (*Kanojo wa kyooshi to shite yuunoo da.*) 彼女は教師として有能だ.

competition *n.* **1** (rivalry) kyo˥o-

soo 競争: They are in competition with each other. (*Kare-ra wa o-tagai ni kyoosoo shite iru.*) 彼らはお互いに競争している.
2 (contest) shiˈai 試合; kyoˈogi 競技; koˈntesuto コンテスト.

competitive *adj.* kyoˈosoo no 競争の; kyoˈosoo ni taerareˈru 競争に耐えられる: a competitive society (*kyoosoo shakai*) 競争社会 / a competitive price (*kyoosoo ni taerareru kakaku*) 競争に耐えられる価格.

competitor *n.* kyoˈosooˈsha 競争者; kyoˈosoo-aˈite 競争相手: business competitors (*shoobai no kyoosoo-aite*) 商売の競争相手.

complain *vi.* **1** (state one's displeasure) fuˈhee [moˈnku] o iˈu 不平[文句]を言う Ⓒ; buˈtsubutsu iˈu ぶつぶつ言う Ⓒ: He is always complaining. (*Kare wa itsu-mo fuhee o itte iru.*) 彼はいつも不平を言っている.
2 (make a report) (... ni)(... o) uˈttaˈeru (…に)(…を)訴える Ⓥ: complain to the police about the noise (*keesatsu ni soo-oñ no koto o uttaeru*) 警察に騒音のことを訴える.
— *vt.* ... to fuˈhee o iu …と不平を言う Ⓒ; koˈboˈsu こぼす Ⓒ: He complains that he has a small income. (*Kare wa shuunyuu ga sukunai to koboshite iru.*) 彼は収入が少ないとこぼしている.

complaint *n.* fuˈhee 不平; fuˈmañ 不満; kuˈjoo 苦情: He made a complaint about the poor service at the hotel. (*Kare wa sono hoteru no saabisu ga warui koto ni tsuite kujoo o itta.*) 彼はそのホテルのサービスが悪いことについて苦情を言った.

complete *adj.* **1** (whole) kaˈnbi shita [shite iru] 完備した[している]; zeˈnbu no 全部の: This room is complete with furniture. (*Kono heya wa kagu ga kañbi shite iru.*) この部屋は家具が完備している.
2 (perfect) kaˈnzeñ na 完全な: a complete victory (*kañzeñ na shoori*) 完全な勝利.
3 (finished) kaˈnsee shita [shite

iru] 完成した[している]: My picture will soon be complete. (*Watashi no e wa moo sugu kañsee shimasu.*) 私の絵はもうすぐ完成します.
— *vt.* ... o kaˈnsee suru [saseru] …を完成する Ⓘ [させる Ⓥ]: The bridge is now completed. (*Hashi wa moo kañsee shimashita.*) 橋はもう完成しました.

completely *adv.* kaˈnzeñ ni 完全に; maˈttaku まったく; suˈkkaˈri すっかり: I completely forgot to thank him. (*Kare ni o-ree o iu no o sukkari wasurete shimatta.*) 彼にお礼を言うのをすっかり忘れてしまった.

completion *n.* kaˈnsee 完成; kaˈnryoo 完了: I will pay you on completion of the work. (*Shigoto ga kañryoo shitara o-shiharai shimasu.*) 仕事が完了したらお支払いします.

complex *adj.* fuˈkuzatsu na 複雑な: a complex problem (*fukuzatsu na moñdai*) 複雑な問題.
— *n.* (abnormal mental state) koˈnpureˈkkusu コンプレックス: an inferiority complex (*rettookañ*) 劣等感.

complicate *vt.* ... o fuˈkuzatsu ni suru …を複雑にする Ⓘ; meˈndoˈo ni suru 面倒にする Ⓘ: That complicates matters. (*Soo naru to koto ga meñdoo ni naru.*) そうなると事が面倒になる.

complicated *adj.* fuˈkuzatsu na 複雑な; koˈmiitta 込み入った: a complicated machine (*fukuzatsu na kikai*) 複雑な機械.

compliment *n.* **1** (praise) hoˈmeko ˈtoba ほめことば; saˈnji 賛辞: His achievement deserves a compliment. (*Kare no gyooseki wa sañji ni atai suru.*) 彼の業績は賛辞に値する.
2 (flattery) oˈseji お世辞: He is always paying her compliments. (*Kare wa itsu-mo kanojo ni oseji o itte iru.*) 彼はいつも彼女にお世辞を言っている.

comply *vi.* (... ni) oˈojiru (…に)応じる Ⓥ; shiˈtagau 従う Ⓒ: We complied with her request. (*Watashi-*

tachi wa kanojo no yookyuu ni oojita.) 私たちは彼女の要求に応じた.

component *n.* koꞋosee-buꞋbuñ 構成部分; buꞋhiñ 部品: the components of a camera (*kamera no buhiñ*) カメラの部品.

compose *vt.* **1** (write) ... o tsuꞋkuꞋru 作る Ⓒ; (of music) saꞋkkyoku suru 作曲する Ⓘ: compose a poem (*shi o tsukuru*) 詩を作る / compose a song (*uta o sakkyoku suru*) 歌を作曲する.
2 (make up) ... o koꞋosee suru ...を構成する Ⓘ; kuꞋmitateꞋru 組み立てる Ⓥ: Six members compose the committee. (*Roku-niñ ga sono iiñkai o koosee shite imasu.*) 6人がその委員会を構成しています.
3 (calm) ... o shiꞋzumeꞋru ...を静める Ⓥ: compose one's mind (*kokoro o shizumeru*) 心を静める.

composer *n.* (of music) saꞋkkyokuka 作曲家.

composition *n.* **1** (writing) saꞋkubuñ 作文; (music) saꞋkkyoku 作曲: I wrote a short composition in Japanese. (*Watashi wa Nihoñgo de mijikai sakubuñ o kaita.*) 私は日本語で短い作文を書いた.
2 (arrangement) koꞋosee 構成; koꞋozoo 構造: the composition of a committee (*iiñkai no koosee*) 委員会の構成.

compound *n.* **1** (mixture) goꞋoseꞋebutsu 合成物; koꞋñgoꞋobutsu 混合物; (word) fuꞋkugoogo 複合語.
2 (chemical substance) kaꞋgoꞋobutsu 化合物: a compound of carbon and oxygen (*tañso to sañso no kagoobutsu*) 炭素と酸素の化合物.

compress *vt.* ... o aꞋsshuku suru ...を圧縮する Ⓘ: compress air (*kuuki o asshuku suru*) 空気を圧縮する.

comprise *vt.* (consist of) ... kara naꞋru ...から成る Ⓒ: The team comprises nine members. (*Sono chiimu wa kyuu-niñ kara naru.*) そのチームは9人から成る.

compromise *n.* daꞋkyoo 妥協; aꞋyumiyori 歩み寄り: arrive at a

compromise (*dakyoo ni tassuru*) 妥協に達する.
— *vi.* daꞋkyoo suru 妥協する Ⓘ; aꞋyumiyoru 歩み寄る Ⓒ: I compromised with him on the matter. (*Watashi wa sono keñ de kare to dakyoo shita.*) 私はその件で彼と妥協した.

compulsory *adj.* kyoꞋosee-teki na 強制的な; giꞋmu-teki na 義務的な: compulsory education (*gimukyooiku*) 義務教育.

computer *n.* koꞋñpyuꞋutaa コンピューター; deꞋñshi-keesaꞋñki 電子計算機.

comrade *n.* naꞋkamaꞋ 仲間; doꞋoryoo 同僚: They are my comrades at school. (*Kare-ra wa watashi no gakkoo no nakama desu.*) 彼らは私の学校の仲間です.

conceal *vt.* ... o kaꞋkuꞋsu ...を隠す Ⓒ: He concealed the truth from me. (*Kare wa sono shiñsoo o watashi ni kakushite ita.*) 彼はその真相を私に隠していた.

concede *vt.* **1** (admit) ... o miꞋtomeru ...を認める Ⓥ: I concede that I am wrong. (*Watashi wa jibuñ ga machigatte iru koto o mitomemasu.*) 私は自分が間違っていることを認めます.
2 (yield) ... o yuꞋzuru ...を譲る Ⓒ: I cannot concede my position in the matter. (*Sono koto ni tsuite wa watashi wa watashi no tachiba o yuzuremaseñ.*) そのことについては私は私の立場を譲れません.

conceit *n.* uꞋnubore うぬぼれ; jiꞋfuꞋshiñ 自負心: He is full of conceit. (*Kare wa unubore ga tsuyoi.*) 彼はうぬぼれが強い.

conceive *vt.* **1** (of feelings) ... o iꞋdaꞋku ...を抱く Ⓒ: He conceived a hatred for them. (*Kare wa kare-ra ni nikushimi o idaita.*) 彼は彼らに憎しみを抱いた.
2 (of a plan) ... o oꞋmoitsuꞋku ...を思いつく Ⓒ: He conceived a good idea. (*Kare wa ii kañgae o omoitsuita.*) 彼はいい考えを思いついた.

concentrate *vt.* **1** (of attention) (... ni) ... o shuʻuchuu suru (…に)…を集中する ☐: You must concentrate your attention on your work. (*Shigoto ni chuui o shuuchuu shinakereba ikemaseñ.*) 仕事に注意を集中しなければいけません.
2 (of people) (... ni) ... o aʻtsumeʻru (…に)…を集める Ⅴ: concentrate troops at one place (*guñtai o ikkasho ni atsumeru*) 軍隊を一か所に集める.
— *vi.* **1** (come together) (... ni) shuʻuchuu suru …に集中する ☐: People concentrate in large cities. (*Jiñkoo wa dai-toshi ni shuuchuu suru.*) 人口は大都市に集中する.
2 (pay attention) (... ni) shuʻuchuu suru (…に)集中する ☐: It was quiet, so I could concentrate on my studies. (*Shizuka datta no de watashi wa beñkyoo ni shuuchuu dekita.*) 静かだったので私は勉強に集中できた.

concentration *n.* **1** (of attention) shuʻuchuuʻuryoku 集中力: Calligraphy requires a great deal of concentration. (*Shodoo wa hijoo ni shuuchuu-ryoku o hitsuyoo to suru.*) 書道は非常に集中力を必要とする.
2 (of things, people) shuʻuchuu 集中: The concentration of businesses in Tokyo has become a problem. (*Kigyoo no Tookyoo e no shuuchuu ga moñdai ni natte iru.*) 企業の東京への集中が問題になっている.

concept *n.* gaʻineñ 概念; kaʻñneñ 観念.

conception *n.* gaʻineñ 概念; niʻshiki 認識: He has no conception of the problem. (*Kare wa sono moñdai ni tsuite niñshiki ga nai.*) 彼はその問題について認識がない.

concern *vt.* **1** (have to do with) ... ni kaʻñkee suru …に関係する ☐: The matter does not concern me. (*Sono koto wa watashi ni wa kañkee arimaseñ.*) そのことは私には関係ありません.

2 (worry) ... o shiʻñpai saseru …を心配させる Ⅴ.

To whom it may concern *adv.* kaʻñkee kaʻkui dono 関係各位殿.
— *n.* **1** (anxiety) shiʻñpai 心配; keʻneñ 懸念: I thank you for your concern. (*Go-shiñpai arigatoo gozaimasu.*) ご心配ありがとうございます.
2 (business) kaʻñshiʻñji 関心事; koʻtoʻ: It's no concern of mine. (*Sore wa watashi no shitta koto de wa nai.*) それは私の知ったことではない.
3 (involvement) kaʻñkee 関係; kaʻkawari かかわり: I have no concern in this matter. (*Watashi wa kono koto ni kañkee ga arimaseñ.*) 私はこのことに関係がありません.

concerned *adj.* **1** (worried) shiʻñpai shite (iru) 心配して(いる): I'm concerned about my son's future. (*Watashi wa musuko no shoorai ga shiñpai desu.*) 私は息子の将来が心配です.
2 (involved) kaʻñkee shite (iru) 関係して(いる): the parties concerned (*kañkeesha*) 関係者.

as far as ... be concerned *adv.* ... ni kaʻñsuʻru kaʻgiri …に関する限り): As far as I'm concerned, I am against the proposal. (*Watashi ni kañsuru kagiri sono teeañ ni wa hañtai desu.*) 私に関する限りその提案には反対です.

concerning *prep.* ... ni kaʻñshite …に関して: If you have any information concerning this matter, please contact us. (*Kono keñ ni kañshite joohoo o o-mochi deshitara go-reñraku kudasai.*) この件に関して情報をお持ちでしたらご連絡ください.

concert *n.* koʻñsaato コンサート; oʻñgaʻkukai 音楽会: give a concert (*oñgakukai o hiraku*) 音楽会を開く.

conclude *vt.* **1** (decide) ... to keʻtsuroñ o kudasu …と結論を下す Ⓒ; daʻñtee suru 断定する ☐: They concluded that his plan was best. (*Kare-ra wa kare no añ ga ichibañ*

yoi to ketsuroñ o kudashita.) 彼ら
は彼の案がいちばんよいと結論を下した.
2 (finish) ... o o「eru 終える V: He
concluded his speech by thanking
his host. (*Kare wa hosuto ni o-ree
o nobete supiichi o oeta.*) 彼はホスト
にお礼を述べてスピーチを終えた.
3 (arrange) ... o mu「subu ...を結ぶ
C: The two countries concluded a
peace treaty. (*Ryookoku wa heewa-jooyaku o musuñda.*) 両国は平
和条約を結んだ.
— *vi.* o「waru 終わる C: The graduation ceremony concluded with
the school song. (*Sotsugyoo-shiki
wa kooka de owatta.*) 卒業式は校歌
で終わった.

conclusion *n.* **1** (decision) ke-
「tsuroñ 結論: come to a conclusion
(*ketsuroñ ni tassuru*) 結論に達する.
2 (end) o「wari 終わり: the conclusion of a speech (*eñzetsu no owari*)
演説の終わり.
3 (arrangement) te「eketsu 締結:
the conclusion of a treaty (*jooyaku
no teeketsu*) 条約の締結.

concrete[1] *n.* (building material)
ko「ñkuri」ito コンクリート: The building is built of concrete. (*Sono biru
wa koñkuriito de dekite iru.*) そのビ
ルはコンクリートでできている.
— *adj.* ko「ñkuri」ito no コンクリート
の: a concrete building (*koñkuriito
no biru*) コンクリートのビル.

concrete[2] *adj.* gu「tai-teki na 具体
的な: a concrete example (*gutai-
teki na jitsuree*) 具体的な実例.

condemn *vt.* **1** (blame) ... o hi「-
nañ suru ...を非難する ⊤; se「me」ru
責める V: Everyone condemns
child abuse. (*Dare mo ga kodomo
no gyakutai o hinañ suru.*) だれもが
子どもの虐待を非難する.
2 (sentence) ... o se「ñkoku suru ...
を宣告する ⊤: He was condemned
to life in prison. (*Kare wa shuu-
shiñkee o señkoku sareta.*) 彼は終
身刑を宣告された.

condense *vt.* **1** (of liquid) ... o
ko「ku suru ...を濃くする ⊤; no「o-

shuku suru 濃縮する ⊤: condense
orange juice (*oreñji juusu o noo-
shuku suru*) オレンジジュースを濃縮す
る.
2 (of writing) ... o yo「oyaku suru
...を要約する ⊤: condense a book
for children (*kodomo no tame ni
hoñ o yooyaku suru*) 子どものために
本を要約する.
— *vi.* gyo「oshuku suru 凝縮する
⊤: Steam condenses into water
when it cools. (*Suijooki wa hieru
to gyooshuku shite mizu ni naru.*)
水蒸気は冷えると凝縮して水になる.

condition *n.* **1** (circumstances)
jo「okyoo 状況; ji「joo 事情: housing
conditions in Kobe (*Koobe no juutaku jijoo*) 神戸の住宅事情.
2 (state) jo「otai 状態; ko「ñdi」shoñ
コンディション: He's in no condition
to travel. (*Kare wa ryokoo dekiru
jootai de wa nai.*) 彼は旅行できる状
態ではない. / My car is in good condition. (*Watashi no kuruma wa
koñdishoñ ga ii.*) 私の車はコンディ
ションがいい.
3 (requirement) jo「oke」ñ 条件: the
conditions of employment (*koyoo
jookeñ*) 雇用条件.
— *vt.* ... o sa「yuu suru ...を左右する
⊤; ke「ttee suru 決定する ⊤: Our
success is conditioned by health.
(*Seekoo wa keñkoo ni sayuu sareru.*) 成功は健康に左右される.

conditional *adj.* jo「okeñ tsuki no
条件付きの; za「ñtee-teki na 暫定的
な: conditional agreements (*jookeñ
tsuki no kyootee*) 条件付きの協定.

conduct *vt.* **1** (carry out) ... o
o「konau ...を行う C; sho「ri suru 処
理する ⊤: conduct negotiations
(*kooshoo o suru*) 交渉をする / conduct business affairs (*gyoomu o
shori suru*) 業務を処理する.
2 (direct) ... o shi「ki」i suru ...を指揮
する ⊤: conduct an orchestra (*ookesutora o shiki suru*) オーケストラを指
揮する.
3 (guide) ... o a「ñna」i suru ...を案内
する ⊤; mi「chibi」ku 導く C: She

conducted the passenger to his seat. (*Kanojo wa jookyaku o seki ni añnai shita.*) 彼女は乗客を席に案内した.
— *n.* **1** (behavior) oˈkonai 行い; koˈloi 行為: The teacher praised the child's conduct. (*Señsee wa sono kodomo no okonai o hometa.*) 先生はその子どもの行いをほめた.
2 (management) uˈñee 運営; kaˈñri 管理: the conduct of a business (*jigyoo no uñee*) 事業の運営.

conductor *n.* **1** (of an orchestra) shiˈkiˈsha 指揮者.
2 (of a bus, train) shaˈshoo 車掌.
3 (guide) aˈñnainiñ 案内人: a tour conductor (*teñjooiñ*) 添乗員.

cone *n.* (ice-cream cone) aˈisu-kuriimu-koˈloñ アイスクリームコーン; soˈfuto-kuriˈimu ソフトクリーム.

confer *vi.* soˈodañ suru 相談する 🅘; uˈchiawaseru 打ち合わせる 🅥: confer with a lawyer (*beñgoshi to soodañ suru*) 弁護士と相談する.

conference *n.* (meeting) kaˈigi 会議: hold a conference (*kaigi o hiraku*) 会議を開く / Mr. Yamada is in conference now. (*Yamada-sañ wa ima kaigi-chuu desu.*) 山田さんは今会議中です.

confess *vt.* ... o jiˈhaku suru ...を自白する 🅘; koˈkuhaku suru 告白する 🅘: He confessed his guilt. (*Kare wa jibuñ no tsumi o kokuhaku shita.*) 彼は自分の罪を告白した.
— *vi.* jiˈhaku suru 自白する 🅘; haˈkujoo suru 白状する 🅘: He refused to confess. (*Kare wa haku-joo shiyoo to shinakatta.*) 彼は白状しようとしなかった.

confession *n.* jiˈhaku 自白; koˈkuhaku 告白: make a confession (*jihaku suru*) 自白する.

confide *vt.* ... o uˈchiakeru ...を打ち明ける 🅥: He confided his secret to his friend. (*Kare wa tomodachi ni himitsu o uchiaketa.*) 彼は友達に秘密を打ち明けた.
— *vi.* hiˈmitsu o uˈchiakeru 秘密を打ち明ける 🅥: Teenagers confide in friends rather than in parents. (*Tiiñeejaa wa ryooshiñ yori mo tomodachi ni himitsu o uchiakeru.*) ティーンエージャーは両親よりも友達に秘密を打ち明ける.

confidence *n.* **1** (self-assurance) jiˈshiñ 自信: I have confidence in myself. (*Watashi wa jibuñ ni jishiñ ga aru.*) 私は自分に自信がある.
2 (belief) kaˈkushiñ 確信: I have confidence that he will succeed. (*Watashi wa kare ga seekoo suru to iu kakushiñ o motte iru.*) 私は彼が成功するという確信を持っている.
3 (trust) shiˈñrai 信頼; shiˈñniñ 信任: He betrayed my confidence in him. (*Kare wa watashi no shiñrai o uragitta.*) 彼は私の信頼を裏切った.

confident *adj.* **1** (sure) kaˈkushiñ shite (iru) 確信して(いる): He is confident that he will pass the examination. (*Kare wa shikeñ ni ukaru to kakushiñ shite iru.*) 彼は試験に受かると確信している.
2 (self-assured) jiˈshiñ o moˈtta [moˈtte iru] 自信を持った[持っている]: Be confident in yourself. (*Jibuñ ni jishiñ o mochi nasai.*) 自分に自信を持ちなさい.

confidential *adj.* hiˈmitsu no 秘密の; naˈinai no 内々の: This information is confidential. (*Kono joohoo wa himitsu desu.*) この情報は秘密です.

confine *vt.* **1** (restrict) ... o kaˈgiˈru ...を限る 🅒; toˈdomeˈru とどめる 🅥: confine a talk to five minutes (*hanashi o go-fuñ ni todomeru*) 話を5分にとどめる.
2 (shut up) ... o toˈjikomeˈru ...を閉じ込める 🅥; kaˈñkiñ suru 監禁する 🅘: We were confined to the cottage by snow. (*Watashi-tachi wa yuki de yamagoya ni tojikome-rareta.*) 私たちは雪で山小屋に閉じ込められた.

confirm *vt.* **1** (verify) ... o taˈshikameˈru ...を確かめる 🅥; (make sure) kaˈkuniñ suru 確認する 🅘: confirm a rumor (*uwasa o tashikameru*) うわさを確かめる / The reservation was confirmed at Narita. (*Yo-yaku wa Narita de kakuniñ shite arimasu.*) 予約は成田で確認してあります.

2 (strengthen) ... o tsu「yome」ru ... を強める Ⓥ; ka「tameru 固める Ⓥ: confirm one's determination (*ketsui o katameru*) 決意を固める.

confirmation *n.* ka「kuniñ 確認; ka「kushoo 確証: the confirmation of news (*nyuusu no kakuniñ*) ニュースの確認.

conflict *n.* **1** (disagreement) sho「ototsu 衝突; fu「i」tchi 不一致: a conflict of opinions (*ikeñ no shoototsu*) 意見の衝突.

2 (fight) a「rasoi 争い; ta「takai 戦い: a conflict between two nations (*ni-koku-kañ no arasoi*) 2国間の争い.
— *vi.* i「tchi shinai 一致しない; mu「juñ suru 矛盾する Ⓘ: Their interests conflicted with each other. (*Kare-ra no rigai wa o-tagai ni itchi shinakatta.*) 彼らの利害はお互いに一致しなかった.

conform *vi.* (... ni) shi「tagau (...に)従う Ⓒ: We must conform to rules. (*Wareware wa kisoku ni shitagawanakereba naranai.*) われわれは規則に従わなければならない.

confront *vt.* ... o (... ni) cho「kumeñ saseru ...を(...に)直面させる Ⓥ: They are confronted with difficulties. (*Kare-ra wa koñnañ ni chokumeñ shite iru.*) 彼らは困難に直面している.

confuse *vt.* **1** (bewilder) ... o to「owaku saseru ...を当惑させる Ⓥ; ma「gotsukaseru まごつかせる Ⓥ: The unexpected questions confused me. (*Yoki shinai shitsumoñ de magotsuite shimatta.*) 予期しない質問でまごついてしまった.

2 (mistake) ... o ko「ñdoo suru ...を混同する Ⓘ; to「richigaeru 取り違える Ⓥ: I confused their names. (*Watashi wa kare-ra no namae o torichigaeta.*) 私は彼らの名前を取り違えた.

confused *adj.* **1** (bewildered)

to「owaku shita [shite iru] 当惑した[している]: He looked confused. (*Kare wa toowaku shita kao o shite ita.*) 彼は当惑した顔をしていた.

2 (mixed up) ko「ñrañ shita [shite iru] 混乱した[している]: confused ideas (*koñrañ shita kañgae*) 混乱した考え.

confusing *adj.* to「owaku saseru 当惑させる; ma「girawashi」i 紛らわしい: confusing names (*magirawashii namae*) 紛らわしい名前.

confusion *n.* **1** (confusing) ko「ñdoo 混同; ko「ñrañ 混乱: Everything was in confusion. (*Subete ga koñrañ shite ita.*) すべてが混乱していた.

2 (bewilderment) to「owaku 当惑; ro「obai ろうばい: He ran away in confusion. (*Kare wa roobai shite nigete itta.*) 彼はろうばいして逃げて行った.

congratulate *vt.* ... ni (... o) i「wa」u ...に(...を)祝う Ⓒ: He congratulated me on my success. (*Kare wa watashi no seekoo o iwatte kureta.*) 彼は私の成功を祝ってくれた.

congratulation *n.* i「wai 祝い; shu「ku」ga 祝賀; (words) i「wai no ko「toba」 祝いのことば: give a speech of congratulation (*shukuji o noberu*) 祝辞を述べる.

Congratulations! O「medetoo. おめでとう: Congratulations on your promotion! (*Go-shooshiñ omedetoo gozaimasu.*) ご昇進おめでとうございます.

congress *n.* ko「kkai 国会; gi「kai 議会.

conjunction *n.* (of grammar) se「tsuzoku」shi 接続詞.

connect *vt.* **1** (join) ... o tsu「nagu ...をつなぐ Ⓒ; se「tsuzoku suru 接続する Ⓘ: connect two wires (*harigane o ni-hoñ tsunagu*) 針金を2本つなぐ.

2 (of a telephone) (... ni)... o tsu「nagu (...に)...をつなぐ Ⓒ: Please connect me to extension 234. (*Naiseñ*

nii-sañ-yoñ ni tsunaide kudasai.)
内線 234 につないでください.

3 (associate) ...o reˈñsoo suru ...を
連想する ⬚: People often connect
Japan with Mt. Fuji. (*Hito wa
yoku Nihoñ to iu to Fujisañ o reñsoo suru.*) 人はよく日本というと富士山
を連想する.

— *vi.* tsuˈnagaru つながる Ⓒ; seˈtsuzoku suru 接続する ⬚: This train
connects with another at Nagoya.
(*Kono ressha wa Nagoya de betsu
no ressha ni setsuzoku shite imasu.*) この列車は名古屋で別の列車に接
続しています.

connection *n.* **1** (relationship)
kaˈñkee 関係; kaˈñreñ 関連: the
connection between smoking and
cancer (*tabako to gañ no kañkee*)
たばことがんの関係.

2 (useful person) koˈne コネ: use
one's connections (*kone o riyoo
suru*) コネを利用する.

3 (train, bus, etc.) reˈñraku 連絡;
seˈtsuzoku 接続; noˈritsugi 乗り継
ぎ: Is there a connection with this
train at Osaka? (*Oosaka de kono
ressha wa setsuzoku ga arimasu
ka?*) 大阪でこの列車は接続がありますか.

4 (of a telephone) seˈtsuzoku 接続:
We have a bad connection. (*Deñwa no setsuzoku ga warui.*) 電話の
接続が悪い.

conquer *vt.* **1** (take by force) ...o
seˈefuku suru ...を征服する ⬚: con-
quer a country (*kuni o seefuku
suru*) 国を征服する.

2 (overcome) ...ni uˈchikaˈtsu ...に
打ち勝つ Ⓒ; ...o koˈkufuku suru ...
を克服する ⬚: conquer obstacles
(*shoogai o kokufuku suru*) 障害を
克服する.

conqueror *n.* seˈefukuˈsha 征服
者; shoˈoriˈsha 勝利者.

conquest *n.* seˈefuku 征服: the
Norman conquest (*Norumañjiñ no
seefuku*) ノルマン人の征服.

conscience *n.* ryoˈoshiñ 良心: I
acted according to my conscience.
(*Watashi wa ryooshiñ ni shita-*

gatte koodoo shita.) 私は良心に従っ
て行動した.

conscious *adj.* **1** (awake) iˈshiki
ga aru 意識がある: The patient is
still conscious. (*Kañja wa mada
ishiki ga aru.*) 患者はまだ意識がある.

2 (aware) kiˈzuˈite (iru) 気づいて(い
る): I was conscious of being followed. (*Watashi wa ato o tsuke-
rarete iru no ni kizuite ita.*) 私は後
をつけられているのに気づいていた.

consciousness *n.* iˈshiki 意識:
lose consciousness (*ishiki o ushinau*) 意識を失う.

consecutive *adj.* reˈñzoku shita
[shite iru] 連続した[している]: It
rained three consecutive days.
(*Mikka reñzoku shite ame ga
futta.*) 三日連続して雨が降った. / consecutive holidays (*reñkyuu*) 連休.

consent *vi.* (... ni) doˈoi suru (...に)
同意する ⬚; shoˈodaku suru 承諾す
る ⬚: I consented to his plan.
(*Watashi wa kare no keekaku ni
dooi shita.*) 私は彼の計画に同意した.

— *n.* doˈoi 同意; shoˈodaku 承諾:
Her parents gave their consent to
her marriage. (*Kanojo no ryooshiñ
wa kanojo no kekkoñ ni shoodaku
o ataeta.*) 彼女の両親は彼女の結婚に
承諾を与えた.

consequence *n.* **1** (result) keˈk-
ka 結果; naˈriyuki 成り行き: The
accident was a consequence of carelessness. (*Sono jiko wa fuchuui no
kekka datta.*) その事故は不注意の結
果だった.

2 (importance) juˈuyoosa 重要さ:
It is a matter of great consequence
to me. (*Sore wa watashi ni totte
hijoo ni jyuuyoo na koto desu.*) そ
れは私にとって非常に重要なことです.

consequently *adv.* soˈno kekka
その結果; shiˈtagatte 従って: The
rain continued for a week, and consequently the road was flooded.
(*Ame ga is-shuukañ tsuzuki, sono
kekka michi ni mizu ga afureta.*)
雨が 1 週間続き, その結果道に水があふ
れた.

conservative *adj.* **1** (dislike changing) ho「shu-teki na 保守的な: He is conservative in views about education. (*Kare wa kyooiku ni tsuite no kañgaekata ga hoshu-teki da.*) 彼は教育についての考え方が保守的だ.
2 (not extreme) ji「mi」na 地味な; hi「kaeme na 控えめな: She is conservative in her dress. (*Kanojo wa kiru mono ga jimi da.*) 彼女は着るものが地味だ.

consider *vt.* **1** (regard) ... o (... to) o「mo」u ...を(...と)思う C; mi「nasu 見なす C: I think him unfit for the job. (*Watashi wa kare wa sono shigoto ni tekishite inai to omou.*) 私は彼はその仕事に適していないと思う.
2 (think carefully) ... o yo「ku ka-「ñga」eru ...をよく考える V; ko「oryo suru 考慮する I: I am considering what to do next. (*Tsugi ni nani o suru ka o kooryo-chuu desu.*) 次に何をするかを考慮中です.
3 (take into account) ... o ko「oryo ni i「reru ...を考慮に入れる V: You must consider other people's feelings. (*Hoka no hito no kimochi o kooryo ni irenakereba ikenai.*) ほかの人の気持ちを考慮に入れなければいけない.

considerable *adj.* ka「nari no かなりの; so「otoo na 相当な: a considerable number of people (*kanari no kazu no hito-tachi*) かなりの数の人たち.

considerably *adv.* ka「nari かなり; so「otoo ni 相当に: He's considerably older than you. (*Kare wa anata yori mo kanari toshiue desu.*) 彼はあなたよりもかなり年上です.

considerate *adj.* o「moiyari no [ga] a「ru 思いやりの[が]ある: She is considerate toward old people. (*Kanojo wa o-toshiyori ni omoi-yari ga aru.*) 彼女はお年寄りに思いやりがある.

consideration *n.* **1** (fact to be considered) ko「oryo su beki ko「to」 考慮すべきこと; mo「ñda」iteñ 問題点:

The cost was our main considera-tion. (*Kosuto ga ooki-na moñdai-teñ datta.*) コストが大きな問題点だった.
2 (careful thought) yo「ku ka「ñga」-eru ko「to」 よく考えること; ko「oryo 考慮: We gave our careful considera-tion to the problem. (*Watashi-tachi wa sono moñdai ni juubuñ na kooryo o haratta.*) 私たちはその問題に十分な考慮を払った.
3 (kindness) o「moiyari 思いやり: He has no consideration for other people. (*Kare wa hoka no hito ni taishite omoiyari ga nai.*) 彼はほかの人に対して思いやりがない.

considering *prep.* ... o ka「ñga」eru to ...を考えると; ... no wa「ri ni ...の割に: She looks young considering her age. (*Kanojo wa toshi no wari ni wakaku mieru.*) 彼女は年の割に若く見える.
— *conj.* ... o ka「ñga」eru to ...を考えると; ... o o「mo」eba ...を思えば: He's done well, considering he has no experience. (*Keekeñ ga nai koto o omoeba kare wa yoku yatta.*) 経験がないことを思えば彼はよくやった.

consist *vi.* **1** (be made up) (... kara) na「ru (...から)成る C: The committee consists of ten mem-bers. (*Iiñkai wa juu-niñ no meñ-baa kara natte iru.*) 委員会は10人のメンバーから成っている.
2 (be contained) (... ni) a「ru (...に)ある C: Happiness consists in being contented. (*Koofuku wa mañzoku suru koto ni aru.*) 幸福は満足することにある.

consistency *n.* ik「kañsee 一貫性: His opinions lack consistency. (*Kare no ikeñ wa ikkañsee ni ka-keru.*) 彼の意見は一貫性に欠ける.

consistent *adj.* **1** (regular) ik-「kañ shita [shite iru] 一貫した[している]; mu「juñ ga na」i 矛盾がない: He is consistent in his argument. (*Kare no roñpoo wa ikkañ shite iru.*) 彼の論法は一貫している.
2 (in agreement) i「tchi shite (iru) 一致して(いる): His words are not

consistent with his acts. (*Kare wa iu koto to suru koto ga itchi shinai.*) 彼は言うこととすることが一致しない.

console *vt.* ... o na「gusame'ru ...を慰める ▽: She consoled the crying child. (*Kanojo wa sono naite iru kodomo o nagusameta.*) 彼女はその泣いている子どもを慰めた.

consonant *n.* shi「iñ 子音.

conspicuous *adj.* me「da'tsu 目立つ; hi「tome o hiku 人目を引く: Her dress was conspicuous at the party. (*Kanojo no doresu wa paatii de hitome o hiita.*) 彼女のドレスはパーティーで人目を引いた.

constant *adj.* **1** (ceaseless) ta「ema (no) na'i 絶え間(の)ない; hi「kkiri na'shi no ひっきりなしの: The constant noise irritated me. (*Taema (no) nai soo-oñ ga watashi o iraira saseta.*) 絶え間(の)ない騒音が私をいらいらさせた. **2** (unchanging) fu「heñ no 不変の; i「ttee no 一定の: keep the room at a constant temperature (*heya o ittee no oñdo ni tamotsu*) 部屋を一定の温度に保つ.

constantly *adv.* ta「ezu 絶えず; i「tsu-mo いつも: The issue is constantly on my mind. (*Sono moñdai wa itsu-mo ki ni kakatte iru.*) その問題はいつも気にかかっている.

constitute *vt.* **1** (make up) ... o ko「osee suru ...を構成する ▽: Seven members constitute the committee. (*Shichi-niñ no meñbaa ga sono iiñkai o koosee shite iru.*) 7 人のメンバーがその委員会を構成している. **2** (set up) ... o se「tee suru ...を制定する ▽; (establish) se「tsuritsu suru 設立する ▽: constitute a school (*gakkoo o setsuritsu suru*) 学校を設立する.

constitution *n.* **1** (supreme laws) ke「ñpoo 憲法: the Constitution of Japan (*Nihoñkoku keñpoo*) 日本国憲法. **2** (structure) ko「osee 構成; ko「ozoo 構造: the constitution of

society (*shakai no koozoo*) 社会の構造. **3** (physical characteristics) ta「ishitsu 体質: He has a strong constitution. (*Kare wa joobu na taishitsu da.*) 彼は丈夫な体質だ.

constitutional *adj.* **1** (legal) ke「ñpoo no 憲法の; ri「kkeñ no 立憲の: constitutional monarchy (*rikkeñ kuñshusee*) 立憲君主制. **2** (of a person) ta「ikaku no 体格の; u「maretsuki no 生まれつきの: a constitutional weakness (*umaretsuki no byoojaku*) 生まれつきの病弱.

construct *vt.* **1** (build) ... o ku「mitate'ru ...を組み立てる ▽; ke「ñsetsu suru 建設する ▽: construct a bridge (*hashi o keñsetsu suru*) 橋を建設する. **2** (put together) ... o ko「osee suru ...を構成する ▽; ku「mitate'ru 組み立てる ▽: construct a theory (*riroñ o kumitateru*) 理論を組み立てる.

construction *n.* **1** (constructing) ke「ñzoo 建造; ke「ñsetsu 建設: a building under construction (*keñsetsu-chuu no biru*) 建設中のビル. **2** (something built) ke「ñzo'obutsu 建造物; ta「te'mono 建物.

consul *n.* ryo「o'ji 領事.

consulate *n.* ryo「oji'kañ 領事館.

consult *vt.* **1** (seek advice) ... ni so「odañ suru ...に相談する ▽; (of a doctor) mi「te morau 診てもらう ©: consult one's lawyer (*beñgoshi ni soodañ suru*) 弁護士に相談する / consult a doctor (*isha ni mite morau*) 医者に診てもらう. **2** (seek information) ... o shi「ra'beru ...を調べる ▽; (of a dictionary) hi「ku 引く ©: consult a dictionary (*jisho o hiku*) 辞書を引く. — *vi.* so「odañ suru 相談する ▽: I consulted with him about the issue. (*Watashi wa sono moñdai ni tsuite kare to soodañ shita.*) 私はその問題について彼と相談した.

consultant *n.* ko「moñ 顧問; ko「ñsa'rutañto コンサルタント: a legal consultant (*hooritsu komoñ*) 法律顧問

/ a management consultant (*kee-ee koñsarutañto*) 経営コンサルタント.

consultation *n.* 1 (meeting) ka¹igi 会議: They held a consultation on a new project. (*Kare-ra wa atarashii kikaku ni tsuite kaigi o hiraita.*) 彼らは新しい企画について会議を開いた.
2 (consulting) so¹odañ 相談; kyo¹ogi 協議: I decided in consultation with him. (*Watashi wa kare to soodañ shite kimeta.*) 私は彼と相談して決めた.

consume *vt.* 1 (use up) ... o sho¹ohi suru ...を消費する ⨂; sho¹omoo suru 消耗する ⨂: How much electricity do you consume a month? (*Ik-kagetsu ni dono kurai deñki o shoohi shimasu ka?*) 1か月にどのくらい電気を消費しますか.
2 (eat) ... o ta¹be¹ru ...を食べる ⨂; (drink) no¹mu 飲む ⨂: He consumed a bottle of whisky. (*Kare wa uisukii o ip-poñ noñde shimatta.*) 彼はウイスキーを1本飲んでしまった.

consumer *n.* sho¹ohi¹sha 消費者.

consumption *n.* sho¹ohi 消費; (amount consumed) sho¹ohi¹ryoo 消費量: consumption tax (*shoohizee*) 消費税.

contact *n.* 1 (touching) fu¹reai 触れ合い; se¹sshoku 接触: This disease is passed on by contact. (*Kono byooki wa sesshoku ni yotte deñseñ suru.*) この病気は接触によって伝染する.
2 (communication) re¹ñraku 連絡; ko¹oshoo 交渉: I keep in contact with him. (*Watashi wa kare to reñraku o totte imasu.*) 私は彼と連絡をとっています.
3 (business connection) e¹ñko 縁故; ko¹ne コネ: I have made good contacts in China. (*Watashi wa Chuugoku de yoi kone o eta.*) 私は中国でよいコネを得た.
— *vt.* ... ni [to] re¹ñraku suru ...に[と]連絡する ⨂; se¹sshoku suru 接触する ⨂: I contacted him on the telephone. (*Watashi wa kare ni deñ-*

wa de reñraku shita.) 私は彼に電話で連絡した.

contagious *adj.* de¹ñseñsee no 伝染性の: a contagious disease (*deñseñbyoo*) 伝染病.

contain *vt.* 1 (have inside) ... o fu¹ku¹mu ...を含む ⨂; ... ga ha¹itte iru ...が入っている ⨅: This book contains many illustrations. (*Kono hoñ ni wa sashie ga takusañ haitte iru.*) この本には挿し絵がたくさん入っている.
2 (hold) ha¹iru 入る ⨅: How much does this bottle contain? (*Kono biñ wa dono kurai hairimasu ka?*) このびんはどのくらい入りますか.
3 (be equal to) ... ni hi¹toshi¹i ...に等しい: A meter contains 100 centimeters. (*Ichi-meetoru wa hyaku-señchi ni hitoshii.*) 1メートルは100センチに等しい.

container *n.* 1 i¹remono 入れ物; yo¹oki 容器: put into a container (*yooki ni ireru*) 容器に入れる.
2 (metal box) ko¹ñtena コンテナ.

contemplate *vt.* 1 (think seriously) ... o ji¹kku¹ri ka¹ñgae¹ru ...をじっくり考える ⨂; ju¹kkoo suru 熟考する ⨅: I contemplated my future. (*Watashi wa shoorai no koto o jikkuri kañgaeta.*) 私は将来のことをじっくり考えた.
2 (look at) ... o ji¹tto mitsume¹ru ...をじっと見つめる ⨂; ju¹kushi suru 熟視する ⨅: She contemplated herself in the mirror. (*Kanojo wa kagami no naka no jibuñ o jitto mitsumeta.*) 彼女は鏡の中の自分をじっと見つめた.

contemporary *adj.* 1 (modern) ge¹ñdai no 現代の: contemporary music (*geñdai oñgaku*) 現代音楽.
2 (living at the same time) so¹no too¹ji no その当時の; do¹o ji¹dai no 同時代の: He was contemporary with Shakespeare. (*Kare wa Sheekusupia to doo jidai no hito datta.*) 彼はシェークスピアと同時代の人だった.

contempt *n.* ke¹ebetsu 軽蔑; bu¹joku 侮辱: I feel contempt for those who are cruel to animals.

(*Watashi wa doobutsu o gyakutai suru hito o keebetsu suru.*) 私は動物を虐待する人を軽蔑する.

contend *vi.* **1** (be in rivalry) (... to) kyoosoo suru (...と)競争する ①; arasou 争う ©: I contended with him for the prize. (*Watashi wa sono shookiñ o neratte kare to arasotta.*) 私はその賞金をねらって彼と争った.
2 (struggle) (... to) tatakau (...と)闘う ©: contend with difficulties (*koñnañ to tatakau*) 困難と闘う.
— *vt.* (maintain) ... o shuchoo suru ...を主張する ①: He contended that I was wrong. (*Kare wa watashi ga machigatte iru to shuchoo shita.*) 彼は私が間違っていると主張した.

content[1] *n.* **1** (subject matter) shui 趣意; yooshi 要旨: the content of a speech (*eñzetsu no shui*) 演説の趣意.
2 (substance) naiyoo 内容: a speech with little content (*naiyoo no toboshii eñzetsu*) 内容の乏しい演説.

content[2] *adj.* mañzoku shite (iru) 満足して(いる): I am content with my present salary. (*Watashi wa ima no kyuuryoo de mañzoku shite imasu.*) 私は今の給料で満足しています.
— *n.* mañzoku 満足: She smiled with content. (*Kanojo wa mañzoku shite hohoeñda.*) 彼女は満足してほほ笑んだ.
— *vt.* ... o mañzoku saseru ...を満足させる ⊻: Nothing can content him. (*Nanigoto mo kare o mañzoku saseru koto wa dekinai.*) 何事も彼を満足させることはできない.

contented *adj.* mañzoku shita [shite iru] 満足した[している]: He looked contented. (*Kare wa mañzoku shita yoo ni mieta.*) 彼は満足したように見えた.

contents *n.* **1** (that which is contained) nakami 中身; naiyoo 内容: the contents of one's purse (*saifu no nakami*) 財布の中身.
2 (of a book) mokuji 目次: table of contents (*mokuji*) 目次.

contest *n.* kyoosoo 競争; koñtesuto コンテスト: win a speech contest (*beñroñ taikai de yuushoo suru*) 弁論大会で優勝する.
— *vt.* ... o arasou ...を争う ©: contest a prize (*shoo o arasou*) 賞を争う.

context *n.* buñmyaku 文脈; koñtekusuto コンテクスト; zeñgo-kañkee 前後関係: guess the meaning of a word from the context (*buñmyaku kara tañgo no imi o suisoku suru*) 文脈から単語の意味を推測する.

continent *n.* tairiku 大陸: the African Continent (*Afurika-tairiku*) アフリカ大陸.

continental *adj.* tairiku no 大陸の; tairikusee no 大陸性の: a continental climate (*tairikusee kikoo*) 大陸性気候.

continual *adj.* reñzoku-teki na 連続的な; taema no nai 絶え間のない: There's continual trouble on the border. (*Kokkyoo de taema no nai fuñsoo ga okite iru.*) 国境で絶え間のない紛争が起きている.

continually *adv.* taema naku 絶え間なく; shotchuu しょっちゅう: That child is continually crying. (*Ano ko wa shotchuu naite iru.*) あの子はしょっちゅう泣いている.

continue *vt.* ... o tsuzukeru ...を続ける ⊻; ⟨verb⟩-tsuzukeru 続ける ⊻: We continued our journey. (*Watashi-tachi wa ryokoo o tsuzuketa.*) 私たちは旅行を続けた. / He continued to run. (*Kare wa hashiri-tsuzuketa.*) 彼は走り続けた.
— *vi.* tsuzuku 続く ©; ⟨verb⟩-tsuzuku 続く ©: His speech continued for two hours. (*Kare no eñzetsu wa ni-jikañ tsuzuita.*) 彼の演説は2時間続いた. / The rain continued all day. (*Ame wa ichinichijuu furi-tsuzuita.*) 雨は一日中降り続いた.

continuity *n.* reñzoku 連続;

i「kka¬see 一貫性: a continuity of rainy days (amefuri no re¬zoku) 雨降りの連続 / continuity in government policy (seesaku no ikka¬see) 政策の一貫性.

continuous adj. ki「reme no na¬i 切れ目のない; re「¬zoku-teki na 連続的な: a continuous procession of cars (kireme no nai kuruma no retsu) 切れ目のない車の列.

continuously adv. ta「emana¬ku 絶え間なく; re「¬zoku-teki ni 連続的に: It rained continuously all day. (Ichinichi-juu taemanaku ame ga futta.) 一日中絶え間なく雨が降った.

contour n. ri「¬kaku 輪郭; ga「ikee 外形: the contours of a mountain (yama no ri¬kaku) 山の輪郭.

contract[1] n. 1 (agreement) ke「e-yaku 契約: make a contract (kee-yaku o musubu) 契約を結ぶ. 2 (written agreement) ke「eyaku-sho 契約書: sign a contract (keeya-kusho ni shomee suru) 契約書に署名する.
— vt. 1 (agree by contract) ke「e-yaku o suru 契約をする ⓒ: I contracted to pay cash for the car. (Watashi wa kuruma no daiki¬ o ge¬-ki¬ de harau keeyaku o shita.) 私は車の代金を現金で払う契約をした. 2 (of disease) ... ni ka「ka¬ru ...にかかる ⓒ: contract pneumonia (haie¬ ni kakaru) 肺炎にかかる.

contract[2] vi. (become smaller) chi「jimaru 縮まる ⓒ: Metals contract when cooled. (Ki¬zoku wa hieru to chijimaru.) 金属は冷えると縮まる.

contractor n. ke「eyaku¬sha 契約者; u「keoini¬ 請負人.

contradict vt. 1 (deny) ... o hi「tee suru ...を否定する ⓣ: He contradicted the fact. (Kare wa sono jiji-tsu o hitee shita.) 彼はその事実を否定した. 2 (go against) ... to mu「ju¬ suru ...と矛盾する ⓣ: His account contradicts yours. (Kare no setsumee wa kimi no muju¬ suru.) 彼の説明は

君のと矛盾する.

contradiction n. 1 (contradict-ing) ha「¬ro¬ 反論; hi「tee 否定: He said nothing in contradiction. (Kare wa nani mo ha¬ro¬ shina-katta.) 彼は何も反論しなかった. 2 (absence of agreement) mu「ju¬ 矛盾.

contradictory adj. mu「ju¬ shita [shite iru] 矛盾した[している]: a ru-mor contradictory to fact (jijitsu to muju¬ shita uwasa) 事実と矛盾したうわさ.

contrary adj. 1 (opposite) ha「¬tai no 反対の; gya「ku no 逆の: They hold contrary opinions. (Kare-ra wa hantai no ike¬ o motte iru.) 彼らは反対の意見を持っている. 2 (opposed) ... ni ha「¬su¬ru ...に反する: an act contrary to the law (hooritsu ni ha¬suru kooi) 法律に反する行為.
— n. se「eha¬¬tai 正反対.
contrary to ... prep. ... ni ha「¬shite ...に反して: contrary to one's expectation (yosoo ni ha¬shite) 予想に反して.

contrast n. 1 (comparison) ta「i-shoo 対照; ta「ihi 対比; ko「¬tora¬-suto コントラスト: the contrast be-tween light and shade (hikari to kage no taishoo) 光と陰の対照. 2 (difference) sa「i 差異; chi「gai 違い: The contrast between winter and summer is great. (Fuyu to natsu no chigai wa ookii.) 冬と夏の違いは大きい.
— vt. ... o ta「ishoo saseru ...を対照させる ⓥ; ku「raberu 比べる ⓥ: con-trast a recent painting with an older one (saiki¬ no e o mukashi no to kuraberu) 最近の絵を昔のと比べる.
— vi. ta「ishoo-teki da 対照的だ: Black and white contrasts sharply. (Kuro to shiro wa kiwamete tai-shoo-teki da.) 黒と白はきわめて対照的だ.

contribute vt. 1 (give) (... ni) ... o ki「fu suru (...に)...を寄付する ⓣ:

She contributed money to the school. (*Kanojo wa gakkoo ni o-kane o kifu shita.*) 彼女は学校にお金を寄付した.
2 (write) ... o (... ni) ki⌐koo suru ...を(...に)寄稿する ⊤: He contributed a story to the magazine. (*Kare wa monogatari o sono zasshi ni kikoo shita.*) 彼は物語をその雑誌に寄稿した.
— *vi.* **1** (give) (... ni) ki⌐fu suru (...に)寄付する ⊤: contribute to a community chest (*kyoodoo-bokiñ ni kifu suru*) 共同募金に寄付する.
2 (write) (... ni) ki⌐koo suru (...に)寄稿する ⊤: contribute to a newspaper (*shiñbuñ ni kikoo suru*) 新聞に寄稿する.
3 (help) (... ni) ya⌐ku˩ ni tatsu (...に)役に立つ Ⓒ; ko⌐okeñ suru 貢献する ⊤: His discovery contributed to the development of science. (*Kare no hakkeñ wa kagaku no hatteñ ni kookeñ shita.*) 彼の発見は科学の発展に貢献した.

contribution *n.* ki⌐fu 寄付; ki⌐zoo 寄贈: make a contribution to a hospital (*byooiñ ni kifu suru*) 病院に寄付する.

control *n.* **1** (directing) shi˩hai 支配; to⌐osee 統制; (managing) ka⌐ñri 管理: price control (*bukka toosee*) 物価統制 / quality control (*hiñshitsu kañri*) 品質管理.
2 (holding back) yo⌐kusee 抑制; se⌐ege˩ñ 制限: arms control (*guñbi-seegeñ*) 軍備制限 / birth control (*sañji-seegeñ*) 産児制限.
— *vt.* **1** (direct) ... o to⌐osee suru ...を統制する ⊤; (manage) ka⌐ñri suru 管理する ⊤: control a business (*gyoomu o kañri suru*) 業務を管理する.
2 (hold back) ... o o⌐sae˩ru ...を抑える Ⓥ: control one's anger (*ikari o osaeru*) 怒りを抑える.

controversy *n.* ro⌐ñsoo 論争; gi˩-roñ 議論: The problem is beyond controversy. (*Sono moñdai wa gi-roñ no yochi ga nai.*) その問題は議論

の余地がない.

convenience *n.* **1** (suitability) ko⌐otsu˩goo 好都合; be⌐ñri 便利: I bought my present house for its convenience. (*Watashi wa beñri ga ii no de ima no ie o kaimashita.*) 私は便利がいいので今の家を買いました.
2 (apparatus) be⌐ñri na mo⌐no˩ 便利な物; (facilities) be⌐ñri na setsubi 便利な設備: a hotel with modern conveniences (*kiñdai setsubi no totonotta hoteru*) 近代設備の整ったホテル.

convenient *adj.* **1** (suitable) tsu-⌐goo no yo˩i 都合のよい; (useful) be⌐ñri na 便利な: Is Monday convenient for you? (*Getsuyoo wa go-tsugoo yoroshii desu ka?*) 月曜はご都合よろしいですか. / a convenient kitchen (*beñri na daidokoro*) 便利な台所.
2 (near) chi⌐ka˩kute beñri ga yoi 近くて便利がよい: His house is convenient for the station. (*Kare no ie wa eki ni chikakute beñri da.*) 彼の家は駅に近くて便利だ.

conveniently *adv.* tsu⌐goo yo˩ku 都合よく; be⌐ñri ni 便利に: Conveniently, I live near my school. (*Tsugoo yoku watashi wa gakkoo no soba ni suñde imasu.*) 都合よく私は学校のそばに住んでいます.

convention *n.* **1** (meeting) ta⌐i-kai 大会: the national convention of a political party (*too no zeñkoku taikai*) 党の全国大会.
2 (custom) shi⌐kitari しきたり; ka⌐ñ-shuu 慣習: He did not care about convention. (*Kare wa shikitari o ki ni kakenakatta.*) 彼はしきたりを気にかけなかった.

conventional *adj.* ka⌐ta˩ ni ha-⌐matta [ha⌐matte iru] 型にはまった[はまっている]; i˩ñshuu-teki na 因習的な: conventional ideas (*kata ni hamatta kañgae*) 型にはまった考え.

conversation *n.* ka⌐iwa 会話; da⌐ñwa 談話: Japanese conversation (*Nihoñgo-kaiwa*) 日本語会話 / have a conversation with a person (*hito to hanashi o suru*) 人と話をする.

conversion *n.* he「ńkań 変換; ka「ń-sań 換算: a conversion table (*kań-sańhyoo*) 換算表.

converse *vi.* ha「nashia」u 話し合う C; ka「iwa suru 会話する I: We conversed on the matter. (*Watashi-tachi wa sono koto ni tsuite hanashiatta.*) 私たちはそのことについて話し合った.

convert *vt.* **1** (change) ... o (... ni) ka「eru ...を(...に)換える V; te「ńkań suru 転換する I: convert coal to gas (*sekitań o gasu ni kaeru*) 石炭をガスに変える.
2 (of money) ... o (... ni) ka「eru ...を(...に)換える V: Can I convert dollars into yen here? (*Koko de doru o eń ni kaeraremasu ka?*) ここでドルを円に換えられますか.
3 (of religion) ... o (... ni) ka「ishuu saseru ...を(...に)改宗させる V: He tried to convert me to Christianity. (*Kare wa watashi o kirisutokyoo ni kaishuu saseyoo to shita.*) 彼は私をキリスト教に改宗させようとした.
— *vi.* **1** (change) ... ni ka「waru (...に)変わる C: This sofa converts into a bed. (*Kono sofaa wa beddo ni kawarimasu.*) このソファーはベッドに変わります.
2 (of religion) (... ni) ka「ishuu suru (...に)改宗する I: She converted to Christianity. (*Kanojo wa kirisuto-kyoo ni kaishuu shita.*) 彼女はキリスト教に改宗した.

convey *vt.* **1** (carry) ... o ha「kobu ...を運ぶ C; u「ńpań suru 運搬する I: convey goods by truck (*shina-mono o torakku de hakobu*) 品物をトラックで運ぶ.
2 (make known) (... ni) ... o tsu-「taeru (...に)...を伝える V; de「ńtatsu suru 伝達する I: Did you convey my message to him? (*Kare ni wata-shi no messeeji o tsutaemashita ka?*) 彼に私のメッセージを伝えましたか.

convict *vt.* ... o yu「uzai to se「ńko-ku suru ...を有罪と宣告する I: He was convicted of theft. (*Kare wa settoo no tsumi de yuuzai to señ-koku sareta.*) 彼は窃盗の罪で有罪と宣告された.
— *n.* shu「ujiń 囚人; za「iniń 罪人.

conviction *n.* **1** (strong belief) ka「kushiń 確信; shi「ńneń 信念: I have a strong conviction that I am right. (*Watashi wa tadashii to iu tsuyoi kakushiń o motte iru.*) 私は正しいという強い確信を持っている.
2 (being convicted) yu「uzai no hańketsu 有罪の判決: a previous conviction (*zeńka*) 前科.

convince *vt.* ... o ka「kushiń sa-seru ...を確信させる V; ... o na「ttoku saseru ...を(...に)納得させる V: I am convinced that he told the truth. (*Kare wa hońtoo no koto o hanashita to kakushiń shite imasu.*) 彼は本当の事を話したと確信しています. / I convinced him of my innocence. (*Watashi wa jibuń no muzai o kare ni nattoku saseta.*) 私は自分の無罪を彼に納得させた.

cook *vt.* ... o ryo「ori suru ...を料理する I; ni「ru 煮る V: She cooked some chicken. (*Kanojo wa toriniku o ryoori shita.*) 彼女はとり肉を料理した.
— *vi.* ryo「ori suru 料理する I; ni-「eru 煮える V: These vegetables cook quickly. (*Kore-ra no yasai wa hayaku niemasu.*) これらの野菜は早く煮えます.
— *n.* ryo「oriniń 料理人; ko「kku コック: She is a good cook. (*Kanojo wa ryoori ga joozu da.*) 彼女は料理がじょうずだ.

cookie *n.* ku「kkii クッキー.

cooking *n.* ryo「ori 料理: do the cooking (*ryoori o suru*) 料理をする.
— *adj.* ryo「oriyoo no 料理用の: a cooking apple (*ryooriyoo no rińgo*) 料理用のりんご / cooking utensils (*choori kigu*) 調理器具.

cool *adj.* **1** (slightly cold) su「zushi」i 涼しい; (of a thing) tsu「metai 冷たい: a cool breeze (*suzushii kaze*) 涼しい風 / a cool drink (*tsumetai no-*

mimono) 冷たい飲物.

2 (calm) re｢esee na 冷静な; o｢chitsuita 落ち着いた; o｢chitsuite iru 落ち着いている: *He was cool in the face of danger.* (*Kare wa kikeñ ni chokumeñ shite mo reesee datta.*) 彼は危険に直面しても冷静だった.

3 (indifferent) re｢eta¹ñ na 冷淡な; ha｢kujoo na 薄情な: *She was cool toward me.* (*Kanojo wa watashi ni taishite reetañ datta.*) 彼女は私に対して冷淡だった.

— *vt.* **1** (make cool) … o hi｢ya¹su …を冷やす; (of temperature) su｢zu¹shiku suru 涼しくする ⓣ: *cool a beer in the refrigerator* (*biiru o reezooko de hiyasu*) ビールを冷蔵庫で冷やす / *I opened the windows to cool the room.* (*Watashi wa heya o suzushiku suru tame ni mado o aketa.*) 私は部屋を涼しくするために窓を開けた.

2 (make calm) … o re｢esee ni suru …を冷静にする ⓣ; shi｢zume¹ru 静める ⓥ: *cool one's anger* (*ikari o shizumeru*) 怒りを静める.

— *vi.* **1** (become cool) hi｢e¹ru 冷える ⓥ; su｢zu¹shiku naru 涼しくなる ⓒ.

2 (become calm) re｢esee ni na¹ru 冷静になる ⓒ; o｢chitsuku 落ち着く ⓒ.

co-op *n.* se｢ekyoo 生協; se｢ekatsu kyoodoo-ku¹miai 生活協同組合.

cooperate *vi.* kyo｢oryoku suru 協力する ⓣ; kyo｢odoo suru 協同する ⓣ: *If we cooperate, we can finish the work quickly.* (*Moshi mo watashi-tachi ga kyooryoku sureba shigoto o hayaku oeru koto ga dekimasu.*) もしも私たちが協力すれば仕事を早く終えることができます.

cooperation *n.* kyo｢oryoku 協力; kyo｢odoo 協同: *We would be grateful for your cooperation.* (*Go-kyooryoku itadakereba arigatai to omoimasu.*) ご協力いただければありがたいと思います.

cooperative *adj.* kyo｢oryoku-teki na 協力的な; kyo｢odoo no 協同の: *They were very cooperative.*

(*Kare-ra wa hijoo ni kyooryoku-teki datta.*) 彼らは非常に協力的だった.

coordinate *vt.* … o cho｢owa saseru …を調和させる ⓥ; cho｢osee suru 調整する ⓣ: *We have to coordinate the two plans.* (*Sono futatsu no keekaku o choosee shinakereba naranai.*) その二つの計画を調整しなければならない.

cope *vi.* u¹maku taisho suru うまく対処する ⓣ; ki¹rinuke¹ru 切り抜ける ⓥ: *cope with difficulties* (*nañkyoku ni taisho suru*) 難局に対処する.

copper *n.* do¹o 銅.

copy *n.* **1** (of a book) bu 部; sa｢tsu 冊: *I bought a copy of his book.* (*Watashi wa kare no hoñ o issatsu katta.*) 私は彼の本を1冊買った.

2 (imitation) u｢tsushi¹ 写し; (reproduction) fu｢kusee 複製: *a copy of a contract* (*keeyakusho no utsushi*) 契約書の写し / *a copy of a famous painting* (*yuumee na e no fukusee*) 有名な絵の複製.

3 (photocopy) ko¹pii コピー; fu｢sha 複写: *make two copies of a letter* (*tegami o ni-bu kopii suru*) 手紙を2部コピーする.

4 (written material) ko¹pii コピー; ge｢ñkoo 原稿; (of an advertisement) ko｢okoku-bu¹ñañ 広告文案.

— *vt.* **1** (imitate) … o u｢tsu¹su …を写す ⓒ; (reproduce) fu｢kusee suru 複製する ⓣ: *copy a passage into a notebook* (*buñshoo o nooto ni utsusu*) 文章をノートに写す.

2 (make a copy) … o ko¹pii suru …をコピーする ⓣ; fu｢kusha suru 複写する ⓣ: *copy a letter* (*tegami o kopii suru*) 手紙をコピーする.

cord *n.* **1** (string) hi｢mo ひも; (rope) tsu｢na¹ 綱; na｢wa¹ 縄: *tie with a cord* (*himo de shibaru*) ひもで縛る.

2 (electric cable) ko¹odo コード.

core *n.* shi¹ñ 芯: *remove a core from an apple* (*riñgo no shiñ o toru*) りんごのしんを取る.

cork *n.* ko¹ruku コルク: *pull out a cork* (*koruku no señ o nuku*) コルクの栓を抜く.

corn n. 1 (maize) to「omo」rokoshi とうもろこし: grow corn (*toomorokoshi o tsukuru*) とうもろこしを作る.
2 (wheat) ko「mu」gi 小麦.
3 (grain) ko「ku」motsu 穀物.

corner n. 1 (angle) ka「do 角; ma-「garikado 曲がり角: I went to a store on the corner. (*Watashi wa kado no mise e itta.*) 私は角の店へ行った.
2 (hidden place) su「mi 隅; ka「ta-sumi 片隅: the corner of a room (*heya no sumi*) 部屋の隅.

corporation n. ho「ojiñ 法人; ka-「isha 会社: a trading corporation (*shooji-gaisha*) 商事会社.

correct adj. 1 (right) ta「dashi」i 正しい; se「ekaku na 正確な: Can you give me the correct time? (*Tadashii jikañ wa nañ-ji deshoo ka?*) 正しい時間は何時でしょうか.
2 (proper) te「kisetsu na 適切な; re「egi」ni ka「na」tta [ka「na」tte iru] 礼儀にかなった[かなっている]: correct behavior (*reegi ni kanatta furumai*) 礼儀にかなった振る舞い.
— vt. (make right) ... o te「esee suru ...を訂正する ①; na「o」su 直す ©: Please correct me if I'm wrong. (*Watashi ga machigatte itara tee-see shite kudasai.*) 私が間違っていたら訂正してください.
2 (punish) ... o shi「karu ...をしかる ©; ko「rashime」ru こらしめる ⑫: correct a child for disobedience (*iu-koto o kikanai kodomo o shikaru*) 言うことをきかない子どもをしかる.

correction n. te「esee 訂正; shu「u-see 修正: make corrections in an estimate (*mitsumori o teesee suru*) 見積もりを訂正する.

correspond vi. 1 (agree) (... to) i「tchi suru (...と)一致する ①; cho「ro-wa suru 調和する ①: This does not correspond to the sample. (*Kore wa mihoñ to itchi shinai.*) これは見本と一致しない.
2 (be similar) (... ni) so「otoo suru (...に)相当する ①; ga「itoo suru 該当する ①: The Japanese Diet corres-ponds to the American Congress. (*Nihoñ no kokkai wa Amerika no gikai ni sootoo shimasu.*) 日本の国会はアメリカの議会に相当します.
3 (exchange letters) bu「ñtsuu suru 文通する ①: We are corresponding with each other. (*Watashi-tachi wa o-tagai ni buñtsuu shite imasu.*) 私たちはお互いに文通しています.

correspondence n. 1 (exchanging letters) bu「ñtsuu 文通; tsu「u-shiñ 通信: a correspondence course (*tsuushiñ kyooiku*) 通信教育.
2 (letters) te「gami 手紙; sho「kañ 書簡: a pile of correspondence (*te-gami no yama*) 手紙の山.
3 (agreement) i「tchi 一致; cho「ro-wa 調和.

correspondent n. 1 (of a news-paper) tsu「ushi」ñiñ 通信員; to「ku-ha」iñ 特派員: a foreign correspon-dent (*kaigai tokuhaiñ*) 海外特派員.
2 (of a letter) bu「ñtsu」usha 文通者.

corresponding adj. (... ni) ta「ioo suru (...に)対応する; so「otoo suru 相当する: duties corresponding to rights (*keñri ni taioo suru gimu*) 権利に対応する義務.

corridor n. (indoor) ro「oka 廊下; tsu「uro 通路: walk along a corridor (*rooka o aruku*) 廊下を歩く.

corrupt vt. 1 (debase) ... o da「raku saseru ...を堕落させる ⑫: He was corrupted by evil friends. (*Kare wa warui tomodachi ni yotte daraku saserareta.*) 彼は悪い友だちによって堕落させられた.
2 (bribe) ... o ba「ishuu suru ...を買収する ①: corrupt a politician (*see-jika o baishuu suru*) 政治家を買収する.
— adj. 1 (rotten) da「raku shita [shite iru] 堕落した[している]; fu「hai shita [shite iru] 腐敗した[している]: The government is corrupt. (*Seefu wa fuhai shite iru.*) 政府は腐敗している.
2 (impure) yo「goreta 汚れた; yo-「gorete iru 汚れている; o「señ sareta [sarete iru] 汚染された[されている]:

corrupt air (*yogoreta kuuki*) 汚れた空気.

corruption *n.* (corrupting) da「ra-ku 堕落; (bribery) o「shoku 汚職; (decay) fu「hai 腐敗.

cost *n.* **1** (price) da「ika 代価; ka-「kaku 価格; hi「yoo 費用: sell below cost (*geñka o watte uru*) 原価を割って売る / cost of living (*seekatsuhi*) 生活費.

2 (sacrifice) gi「see 犠牲; (loss) so「ñshitsu 損失: The cost of war is great. (*Señsoo no soñshitsu wa ookii.*) 戦争の損失は大きい.

— *vt.* **1** (of money) (... ga) ka「ka-ru (…が)かかる C; ... suru …する I: About how much will it cost? (*Sore wa ikura-gurai kakarimasu ka?*) それはいくらぐらいかかりますか. / This book cost 3,000 yen. (*Kono hoñ wa sañzeñ-eñ shimashita.*) この本は3千円しました.

2 (of hour, labor) ... ga ka「ka-ru …がかかる C; ... o yo「osu「ru …を要する I: This work cost much time and patience. (*Kono shigoto wa ooku no jikañ to koñki o yooshita.*) この仕事は多くの時間と根気を要した.

costly *adj.* **1** (expensive) ko「oka na 高価な; ne「dañ ga taka「i 値段が高い: costly jewels (*kooka na hoo-seki*) 高価な宝石.

2 (gained at a great loss) gi「see [so「ñshitsu] no [ga] ooki「i 犠牲[損失]の[が]大きい: a costly victory (*gisee no ookii shoori*) 犠牲の大きい勝利.

costume *n.* i「shoo 衣装; fu「kusoo 服装: Japanese costume (*wasoo*) 和装.

cottage *n.* i「nakaya いなか家; sho「o-ju「utaku 小住宅.

cotton *n.* (plant) wa「ta「 綿; (fibers) mo「meñ 木綿; me「ñ 綿; (thread) me「ñshi 綿糸: a cotton shirt (*mo-meñ no shatsu*) 木綿のシャツ / cotton goods (*meñ-seehiñ*) 綿製品 / absorbent cotton (*dasshimeñ*) 脱脂綿.

couch *n.* ne「isu 寝いす; na「gaisu 長いす; ka「uchi カウチ: lie on a couch (*nagaisu ni neru*) 長いすに寝る.

cough *vi.* se「ki o suru せきをする: He coughed badly. (*Kare wa hi-doku seki o shita.*) 彼はひどくせきをした.

— *n.* se「ki せき; se「kiba「rai せき払い: I have a cough. (*Seki ga de-masu.*) せきが出ます. / give a cough (*sekibarai o suru*) せき払いをする / cough drops (*seki-dome*) せき止め.

could *aux.* **1** [past tense of can] de「kita できた: When I was a child, we could swim in this pond. (*Watashi ga kodomo no koro, kono ike de oyogu koto ga dekimashita.*) 私が子どものころ、この池で泳ぐことができました.

2 [in a subordinate clause] de「ki「ru できる: He asked me if I could drive a car. (*Kare wa watashi ni kuruma no uñteñ ga dekiru ka kiita.*) 彼は私に車の運転ができるか聞いた.

3 [express a possibility] de「ki「ru daroo できるだろう: I could come tomorrow. (*Ashita kuru koto ga dekiru [korareru] deshoo.*) あした来ることができる[来られる]でしょう.

Could I ...? <verb>-te[de] mo i「i desu ka? …て[で]もいいですか: Could I smoke here? (*Koko de tabako o sutte mo ii desu ka?*) ここでたばこを吸ってもいいですか.

Could you ...? <verb>-te[de] ku-「dasaimase「ñ [i「tadakemase「ñ] ka? …て[で]くださいません[いただけません]か: Could you tell me the way to the station? (*Eki e iku michi o oshiete kudasaimaseñ ka?*) 駅へ行く道を教えてくださいませんか.

council *n.* shi「ñgi「kai 審議会; kyo「ogi「kai 協議会.

counselor *n.* **1** (adviser) ka「uñ-seraa カウンセラー; jo「geñsha 助言者.

2 (lawyer) be「ñgo「shi 弁護士.

count *vt.* **1** (calculate) ... o ka「zo-e「ru …を数える V; ka「ñjo「o suru 勘定する I: I counted the number of people present. (*Watashi wa shus-sekisha no kazu o kazoeta.*) 私は出席者の数を数えた.

2 (include) ... o ka「ñjo」o ni i「reru …を勘定に入れる Ⅴ: There were six people, counting him. (*Kare o kañ- joo ni irete roku-niñ ita.*) 彼を勘定 に入れて6人いた.

3 (consider) ... o (... to) o「mo」u …を (…と)思う Ⅽ: I count myself lucky. (*Watashi wa koouñ da to omou.*) 私は幸運だと思う.

— *vi.* **1** (say numbers) ka「zu o ka「zoe」ru 数を数える Ⅴ: count from 1 to 100 (*ichi kara hyaku made ka- zoeru*) 1から100まで数える.

2 (be important) ju「uyoo da 重要 だ: What he says doesn't count. (*Kare ga iu koto wa juuyoo de wa nai.*) 彼が言うことは重要ではない.

count on ... *vt.* ... o a「te ni suru …を当てにする Ⅰ: I counted on him. (*Watashi wa kare o ate ni shite ita.*) 私は彼を当てにしていた.

— *n.* **1** (counting) ke「esañ 計算; ka「ñjo」o 勘定: I made three counts. (*Watashi wa sañ-kai keesañ shita.*) 私は3回計算した.

2 (the sum total) so「osu」u 総数: the death count (*shisha soosuu*) 死 者総数.

counter *n.* (long table) ka「uñtaa カ ウンター; u「ridai 売り台: Take this baggage to the JAL counter, please. (*Kono nimotsu o Nihoñ kookuu no kauñtaa e hakoñde kudasai.*) この 荷物を日本航空のカウンターへ運んでくだ さい.

countless *adj.* ka「zoekire」nai 数え きれない; mu「su」u no 無数の: the countless stars (*musuu no hoshi*) 無数の星.

country *n.* **1** (nation) ku「ni 国; ko「kka 国家; -koku 国: Which country are you from? (*Dochira no kuni kara oide desu ka?*) どちらの国 からおいでですか. / an agricultural country (*noogyoo-koku*) 農業国 / a developing country (*hatteñ-tojoo- koku*) 発展途上国.

2 (one's native land) so「koku 祖国: I love my country. (*Watashi wa sokoku o aisuru.*) 私は祖国を愛する.

3 (land outside town) i「naka 田舎; de「ñeñ 田園: I want to live in the country. (*Watashi wa inaka ni sumitai.*) 私はいなかに住みたい.

4 (land with special character) chi「iki 地域; chi「hoo 地方: wooded country (*shiñriñ chihoo*) 森林地方.

county *n.* (in the U.S.) gu「ñ 郡; (in England and Wales) shu「u 州.

couple *n.* **1** (of things) fu「tatsu 二 つ; (of people) fu「tari 二人: I gave him a couple of apples. (*Watashi wa kare ni riñgo o futatsu ageta.*) 私は彼にりんごを二つあげた.

2 (a man and a woman) ka「ppuru カップル; (a man and wife) fu「ufu 夫 婦: They will make a good couple. (*Kare-ra wa niai no fuufu ni naru daroo.*) 彼らは似合いの夫婦になるだろう.

a couple of ... *adj.* ni- 2: a cou- ple of weeks (*ni-shuukañ*) 2週間 / a couple of shirts (*shatsu ni-mai*) シャツ2枚.

coupon *n.* **1** (of a discount) ku「u- po「ñ-keñ クーポン券.

2 (of a ticket) ka「isu」ukeñ 回数券.

3 (of a bond) ri「fuda 利札.

courage *n.* yu「uki 勇気; do「kyoo 度胸: a person of courage (*yuuki no aru hito*) 勇気のある人 / take courage (*yuuki o dasu*) 勇気を出す.

courageous *adj.* yu「uki no [ga] aru 勇気の[が]ある; yu「ukañ na 勇敢 な: a courageous person (*yuuki no aru hito*) 勇気のある人.

course *n.* **1** (direction) ho「okoo 方向; shi「ñro 進路: The ship changed its course. (*Fune wa shiñ- ro o kaeta.*) 船は進路を変えた.

2 (series of studies) ka「tee 課程; ka「moku 科目: What course are you taking at the college? (*Dai- gaku de wa doñna kamoku o totte imasu ka?*) 大学ではどんな科目を取っ ていますか.

3 (of a meal) ko「osu コース; ryo「ori 料理: a dinner of five courses (*go- shina no ryoori*) 5品の料理.

4 (racecourse) ko「osu コース; so「oro 走路.

of course adv. moˈchiˈroń もちろん: Of course I'll come. (*Mochiroń watashi wa ukagaimasu.*) もちろん私は伺います.

court n. **1** (of a law trial) hoˈotee 法廷; saˈibańsho 裁判所: the Supreme Court (*saikoo saibańsho*) 最高裁判所.
2 (of a game) koˈoto コート: a tennis court (*tenisu kooto*) テニスコート.
3 (courtyard) naˈkaniwa 中庭.

courteous adj. reˈegi tadashiˈi 礼儀正しい; teˈechoo na 丁重な: courteous greetings (*teechoo na aisatsu*) 丁重なあいさつ.

courtesy n. reˈegi (tadaˈshisa) 礼儀(正しさ); teˈechoosa 丁重さ: a courtesy visit (*hyookee hoomoń*) 表敬訪問.

courtyard n. naˈkaniwa 中庭.

cousin n. iˈtoˈko いとこ: a second cousin (*mata itoko*) またいとこ.

cover vt. **1** (spread over) ... o oˈou ...を覆う C; kaˈkeˈru かける V: She covered the table with a tablecloth. (*Kanojo wa teeburu ni teeburu-kurosu o kaketa.*) 彼女はテーブルにテーブルクロスをかけた.
2 (of wallpaper) ... o haˈru ...を張る C; (of paint) nuˈru 塗る C: I covered the wall with white paint. (*Watashi wa kabe o shiroi peńki de nutta.*) 私は壁を白いペンキで塗った.
3 (hide) ... o kaˈkuˈsu ...を隠す C: She covered her face with her hands. (*Kanojo wa te de kao o kakushita.*) 彼女は手で顔を隠した.
4 (extend over) ... ni waˈtaru ...にわたる C; oˈyobu 及ぶ C: His land covers five square kilometers. (*Kare no tochi wa go-heehoo-kiro-meetoru ni oyobu.*) 彼の土地は5平方キロメートルに及ぶ.
5 (travel) ... o iˈku ...を行く C; tsuˈuka suru 通過する I: You can cover the distance in an hour. (*Sono kyori nara ichi-jikań de ikemasu.*) その距離なら1時間で行けます.
6 (of insurance) ... o kaˈkeˈru ...をかける V: This car is covered by insurance. (*Kono kuruma ni wa hokeń ga kakete arimasu.*) この車には保険がかけてあります.
7 (report) ... o hoˈodoo suru ...を報道する I; shuˈzai suru 取材する I: The reporter covered the trial. (*Sono kisha wa saibań o shuzai shita.*) その記者は裁判を取材した.
— n. **1** (something which covers) oˈoi 覆い; kaˈbaa カバー: put a cover on a chair (*isu ni kabaa o kakeru*) いすにカバーをかける.
2 (of a book) hyoˈoshi 表紙. ★ In Japan, a dust jacket is usually called '*kabaa*' カバー (cover).
3 (shelter) hiˈnańbasho 避難場所; kaˈkurebasho 隠れ場所: cover from a storm (*arashi kara no hinańbasho*) あらしからの避難場所.

cow n. meˈushi 雌牛; nyuˈugyuu 乳牛.

coward n. oˈkubyoomono おくびょう者; hiˈkyoomono ひきょう者.

crab n. kaˈni かに(蟹): the Crab (*kaniza*) かに座.

crack vi. **1** (break) hiˈbiˈ ga haˈiru ひびが入る C: The glass cracked when I poured hot water into it. (*Atsui o-yu o iretara koppu ni hibi ga haitta.*) 熱いお湯を入れたらコップにひびが入った.
2 (make a sharp sound) paˈań [gaˈragara, gaˈchaˈń] to naˈru パーン[ガラガラ, ガチャン]と鳴る C: The fireworks cracked overhead. (*Hanabi ga zujoo de paań to natta.*) 花火が頭上でパーンと鳴った.
— vt. **1** (cause to break) ... ni hiˈbiˈ o iˈreru ...にひびを入れる V; ... o waˈru ...を割る C: crack a walnut (*kurumi o waru*) くるみを割る.
2 (cause to make a sharp sound) ... o paˈchiˈtto [piˈshiˈtto] naˈrasu ...をパチッと[ピシッと]鳴らす C: crack a whip (*muchi o pishitto narasu*) むちをピシッと鳴らす.
— n. **1** (split) waˈreme 割れ目; hiˈbiˈ ひび: a crack in a plate (*sara no hibi*) 皿のひび.
2 (sound) gaˈragara [gaˈchaˈń] to

iu o⌐to ガラガラ[ガチャン]という音: a crack of thunder (*kaminari no bari-bari to iu oto*) 雷のバリバリという音.

cracker *n.* ku⌐ra⌐kkaa クラッカー: a rice cracker (*señbee*) せんべい.

cradle *n.* yu⌐rikago 揺りかご: from the cradle to the grave (*yurikago kara hakaba made*) 揺りかごから墓場まで.

— *vt.* ... o da⌐ite aya⌐su ...を抱いてあやす ©: cradle a baby in one's arms (*akañboo o ude ni daite ayasu*) 赤ん坊を腕に抱いてあやす.

craft *n.* (skill) gi⌐jutsu 技術; gi⌐noo 技能: the craft of a wood block printing (*mokuhañga no gijutsu*) 木版画の技術 / arts and crafts (*bijutsu koogee*) 美術工芸.

crane *n.* 1 (machine) ki⌐ju⌐uki 起重機; ku⌐re⌐eñ クレーン: operate a crane (*kureeñ o ugokasu*) クレーンを動かす.
2 (bird) tsu⌐ru つる(鶴).

crank *n.* ku⌐ra⌐ñku クランク.

crash *vi.* 1 (of a car) sho⌐ototsu suru 衝突する 🄘; (of aircraft) tsu⌐iraku suru 墜落する 🄘: The car and the bus crashed. (*Kuruma to basu ga shoototsu shita.*) 車とバスが衝突した. / The plane crashed into the sea. (*Sono hikooki wa umi ni tsuiraku shita.*) その飛行機は海に墜落した.
2 (make a noise) ga⌐cha⌐ñ [ga⌐ra-gara] to o⌐oki-na o⌐to⌐ o ta⌐te⌐ru ガチャン[ガラガラ]と大きな音を立てる 🄥: The plate crashed to the floor. (*Sara ga gachañ to yuka ni ochita.*) 皿がガチャンと床に落ちた.

— *vt.* (of a car) ... o sho⌐ototsu saseru ...を衝突させる 🄥; (of an aircraft) tsu⌐iraku saseru 墜落させる 🄥: He crashed his car into the wall. (*Kare wa kuruma o kabe ni shoototsu saseta.*) 彼は車を壁に衝突させた.

— *n.* 1 (of a car) sho⌐ototsu 衝突; (of an aircraft) tsu⌐iraku 墜落: Five people were killed in the plane crash. (*Hikooki no tsuiraku*

jiko de go-niñ ga shiñda.) 飛行機の墜落事故で5人が死んだ.
2 (noise) ga⌐cha⌐ñ ガチャン; ga⌐ra-gara ガラガラ; do⌐shi⌐ñ ドシン: fall with a crash (*doshiñ to taoreru*) ドシンと倒れる.

crawl *vi.* 1 (drag one's body) ha⌐u はう ©; ha⌐tte su⌐sumu はって進む ©: He crawled out of the hole. (*Kare wa ana kara hatte deta.*) 彼は穴からはって出た.
2 (move slowly) no⌐ronoro su⌐sumu のろのろ進む ©: The truck crawled up the steep hill. (*Torakku wa kyuuzaka o noronoro to susuñ-da.*) トラックは急坂をのろのろと進んだ.

crazy *adj.* 1 (sick in mind) ki⌐ga kuru⌐tta [kuru⌐tte iru] 気が狂った[狂っている]: He must be crazy to do that. (*Soñna koto o suru nañte kare wa ki ga kurutta ni chigai nai.*) そんなことをするなんて彼は気が狂ったにちがいない.
2 (very eager) ne⌐kkyoo shita [shite iru] 熱狂した[している]; mu⌐chuu no 夢中の: He is crazy about video games. (*Kare wa terebi geemu ni muchuu da.*) 彼はテレビゲームに夢中だ.

cream *n.* 1 (of a cosmetic) ku⌐ri⌐i-mu クリーム: shaving cream (*hige-sori-yoo kuriimu*) ひげそり用クリーム.
2 (of milk) ku⌐ri⌐imu クリーム: ice cream (*aisu kuriimu*) アイスクリーム.

create *vt.* 1 (cause to exist) ... o so⌐ozoo suru ...を創造する 🄘; tsu⌐kuridasu 作り出す ©: create a peaceful world (*heewa na sekai o tsukuridasu*) 平和な世界を作り出す.
2 (produce) ... o hi⌐kioko⌐su ...を引き起こす ©; ma⌐kioko⌐su 巻き起こす ©: create a sensation (*señseeshoñ o makiokosu*) センセーションを巻き起こす.

creation *n.* 1 (creating) so⌐ozoo 創造; so⌐osetsu 創設: the creation of a new city (*atarashii toshi no soosetsu*) 新しい都市の創設.
2 (something created) so⌐osaku 創作; sa⌐kuhiñ 作品: This is his latest

creation. (*Kore wa kare no sai-shiñ-saku desu.*) これは彼の最新作です.

creative *adj.* soˈozoo-teki na 創造的な; doˈkusoo-teki na 独創的な: a creative design (*dokusoo-teki na dezaiñ*) 独創的なデザイン.

creator *n.* soˈozoˈosha 創造者; soˈosaˈkusha 創作者.

creature *n.* (living being) iˈkiˈmono 生き物; (animal) doˈobutsu 動物; (human being) niˈñgeñ 人間.

credit *n.* **1** (of payment) kuˈreˈjitto クレジット; tsuˈkeˈ 付け: buy a thing on credit (*mono o kurejitto de kau*) 物をクレジットで買う.
2 (account at a bank) yoˈkiñ(zaˈñ-daka) 預金(残高): I have credit at this bank. (*Watashi wa kono giñ-koo ni yokiñ ga arimasu.*) 私はこの銀行に預金があります.
3 (money loaned) kaˈshitsukekiñ 貸付金; yuˈushi 融資.
4 (trust) shiˈñrai 信頼; shiˈñyoo 信用: I cannot give credit to his story. (*Kare no hanashi wa shiñyoo de-kinai.*) 彼の話は信用できない.
5 (praise) meˈesee 名声; hyoˈobañ 評判: a person of credit (*hyoobañ no yoi hito*) 評判のよい人.
— *vt.* (believe) ... o shiˈñjiˈru ...を信じる Ⓥ; (trust) shiˈñyoo suru 信用する Ⓘ: I cannot credit a rumor like that. (*Soñna uwasa wa shiñ-yoo dekinai.*) そんなうわさは信用できない.

credit card *n.* kuˈrejitto kaˈado クレジットカード: May I use this credit card? (*Kono kurejitto kaado wa tsukaemasu ka?*) このクレジットカードは使えますか.

creditor *n.* saˈikeˈñsha 債権者; kaˈshiˈnushi 貸し主.

creep *vi.* **1** (move quietly) koˈsso-soˈri [yuˈkkuˈri] こっそり[ゆっくり]進む Ⓒ: He crept out of the room. (*Kare wa heya kara kossori dete itta.*) 彼は部屋からこっそり出て行った.
2 (move on hands and knees) haˈu

はう Ⓒ: The baby crept toward the chair. (*Akañboo wa isu no hoo e hatte itta.*) 赤ん坊はいすのほうへはって行った.

crew *n.* (of a ship) seˈñiñ 船員; noˈrikumiˈiñ 乗組員; (of an aircraft) joˈomuˈiñ 乗務員.

crime *n.* tsuˈmi 罪; haˈñzai 犯罪: commit a crime (*tsumi o okasu*) 罪を犯す / prevent crime (*hañzai o booshi suru*) 犯罪を防止する.

criminal *adj.* haˈñzai no 犯罪の: a criminal act (*hañzai kooi*) 犯罪行為 / He has a criminal record. (*Kare wa zenka ga aru.*) 彼は前科がある.
— *n.* haˈñniñ 犯人: arrest a criminal (*hañniñ o taiho suru*) 犯人を逮捕する.

crisis *n.* **1** (time of difficulty) kiˈki 危機; naˈñkyoku 難局: an oil crisis (*sekiyu kiki*) 石油危機 / an economic crisis (*keezai kiki*) 経済危機.
2 (turning-point) waˈkareme 分かれ目; toˈogeˈ 峠: He was seriously ill, but he passed the crisis. (*Kare wa juubyoo datta ga tooge wa ko-shita.*) 彼は重病だったが峠は越した.

crisp *adj.* **1** (of food) paˈripari [kaˈrikari] no パリパリ[カリカリ]の: crisp lettuce (*paripari no retasu*) パリパリのレタス / crisp toast (*karikari ni yaita toosuto*) カリカリに焼いたトースト.
2 (of manner) teˈkipaki shita [shite iru] てきぱきした[している]; haˈgire no yoˈi 歯切れのよい: a crisp way of speaking (*hagire no yoi hanashikata*) 歯切れのよい話し方.
3 (bracing) saˈwaˈyaka na さわやかな; suˈgasugashiˈi すがすがしい: a crisp morning (*sugasugashii asa*) すがすがしい朝.

critic *n.* hiˈhyooka 批評家; hyoˈo-roñka 評論家: an art critic (*bijutsu hyoorooñka*) 美術評論家.

critical[1] *adj.* **1** (fault-finding) hiˈhañ-teki na 批判的な; aˈrasaˈgashi o suru あら探しをする: He is too critical of others. (*Kare wa hoka no hito no arasagashi bakari suru.*) 彼

はほかの人のあら探しばかりする.
2 (of work) hiʼhyoo no 批評の;
hyoʼoroñ no 評論の: a critical essay
(hyooroñ) 評論.

critical[2] adj. (dangerous) kiʼki no
危機の; kiʼtoku no 危篤の; aʼbunai
危ない: He is in critical condition.
(Kare wa kitoku jootai da.) 彼は危
篤状態だ.

criticism n. **1** (disapproval) hi-
ʼhañ 批判; hiʼnañ 非難: His con-
duct drew a lot of criticism. (Kare
no okonai wa ooku-no hinañ o maneita.) 彼の行いは多くの非難を招いた.
2 (judgment) hiʼhyoo 批評; hyoʼoroñ 評論: literary criticism (buñ-
gee-hyooroñ) 文芸評論.

criticize vt. **1** (find fault with) ...
o hiʼhañ suru ...を批判する①; hiʼ-
nañ suru 非難する①: He criticizes
everything I do. (Kare wa watashi
ga suru koto o nañ de mo hinañ
suru.) 彼は私がすることを何でも非難す
る.
2 (judge) ... o hiʼhyoo suru ...を批
評する①; hyoʼoroñ suru 評論する
①: His new book was criticized in
newspapers and magazines. (Kare
no shiñkañ wa shiñbuñ ya zasshi
de hihyoo sareta.) 彼の新刊は新聞や
雑誌で批評された.

crocodile n. waʼni わに(鰐).

crooked adj. **1** (not straight) ma-
ʼgatta 曲がった; maʼgatte iru 曲がっ
ている: a crooked road (magatta
michi) 曲がった道.
2 (dishonest) fuʼsee na 不正な: a
crooked business deal (fusee na
shootorihiki) 不正な商取り引き.

crop n. **1** (farm product) noʼosa-
kuʼbutsu 農作物; saʼkuʼmotsu 作物:
gather in a crop (sakumotsu o toriireru) 作物を取り入れる.
2 (harvest) shuʼukaku 収穫; saʼku-
gara 作柄: The potato crop was
large this year. (Kotoshi wa jagaimo no shuukaku ga ookatta.) こと
しはじゃがいもの収穫が多かった.
— vt. (cut short) ... o miʼjikaʼku
kiru ...を短く切る©; kaʼrikoʼmu 刈

り込む©: crop one's hair (kami o
mijikaku karikomu) 髪を短く刈り込
む.

cross vt. **1** (go across) ... o yoʼko-
ʼgiru ...を横切る©: cross a street
(michi o yoko-
giru) 道を横切る / cross a bridge
(hashi o wataru) 橋を渡る.
2 (place crosswise) ... o koʼosa
saseru ...を交差させる♡: cross a
knife and fork (naifu to fooku o
koosa saseru) ナイフとフォークを交差
させる.
3 (meet and pass) ... to yuʼkichi-
gaʼu ...と行き違う©: Your letter
crossed mine. (Kimi no tegami wa
watashi no to yukichigai ni natta.)
君の手紙は私のと行き違いになった.
— vi. **1** (go across) yoʼkogiʼru 横
切る©; oʼodañ suru 横断する①:
He crossed while the signal was
red. (Kare wa shiñgoo ga aka na
no ni oodañ shita.) 彼は信号が赤な
のに横断した.
2 (extend across) koʼosa suru 交差
する①; maʼjiwaʼru 交わる©: The
roads cross in the center of town.
(Dooro wa machi no chuushiñ de
koosa shite imasu.) 道路は町の中心
で交差しています.
3 (pass each other) yuʼkichigai ni
naʼru 行き違いになる©.
— n. **1** (two lines placed across)
juʼujikee 十字形; baʼtsu-jiʼrushi ×
印: mark a place with a cross (basho ni batsu-jirushi o tsukeru) 場
所に×印をつける.
2 (symbol of crucifixion) juʼujika
十字架.
— adj. (having a bad temper) fu-
ʼkiʼgeñ na 不機嫌な; (angry) oʼkoʼt-
te (iru) 怒って(いる): Since I was late
he was cross. (Watashi ga okureta
no de kare wa fukigeñ datta.) 私が
遅れたので彼は不機嫌だった.

crossing n. (of roads) koʼosateñ
交差点; (of a railway) fuʼmikiri 踏
切.

crouch vi. kaʼgamu かがむ©; sha-
ʼgamu しゃがむ©: He crouched and

hid behind the curtain. (*Kare wa shagañde kaateñ no kage ni kakureta.*) 彼はしゃがんでカーテンの陰に隠れた.

crow *n.* ka¹rasu からす(鳥).

crowd *n.* **1** (a large group of people) gu¹ñshuu 群衆; hi¹togomi 人込み: He disappeared into the crowd. (*Kare wa hitogomi no naka ni sugata o keshita.*) 彼は人込みの中に姿を消した.
2 (the masses) ta¹ishuu 大衆; miñ「shuu 民衆: appeal to the crowd (*taishuu ni uttaeru*) 大衆に訴える.
a crowd of ... *adj.* o¹ozee no 大勢の: There was a crowd of people in the park. (*Kooen ni wa oozee no hito ga ita.*) 公園には大勢の人がいた.
— *vt.* **1** (gather) ... ni mu¹raga¹ru ...に群がる C; o¹shikake¹ru 押しかける V: Girls crowded the theater. (*Oñna-no-ko-tachi ga gekijoo ni oshikaketa.*) 女の子たちが劇場に押しかけた.
2 (fill) ... o i¹ppai ni suru ...をいっぱいにする I; (... ni) ... o o¹shiko¹mu (...に)...を押し込む C: crowd people into a room (*heya ni hito o oshikomu*) 部屋に人を押し込む.
— *vi.* (come together) (... ni) mu¹raga¹ru (...に)群がる C; a¹tsuma¹ru 集まる C: The children crowded around the player. (*Kodomo-tachi wa sono señshu no mawari ni atsumatta.*) 子どもたちはその選手の周りに集まった.

crowded *adj.* ko¹miatta 込み合った; ko¹miatte iru 込み合っている; ko¹ñzatsu shita [shite iru] 混雑した[している]: a crowded bus (*komiatta basu*) 込み合ったバス.

crown *n.* **1** (headdress) ka¹ñmuri 冠; o¹okañ 王冠: wear a crown (*kañmuri o kaburu*) 冠をかぶる.
2 (royal position) o¹oi 王位: succeed to the crown (*ooi o tsugu*) 王位を継ぐ.
3 (head) a¹tama 頭; no¹ote¹ñ 脳天; (of a mountain) cho¹ojo¹o 頂上.

— *vt.* **1** (make a king or queen) o¹oi ni tsu¹kase¹ru 王位につかせる V: She was crowned in 1558. (*Kanojo wa señ-gohyaku-gojuu-hachi-neñ ni ooi ni tsuita.*) 彼女は 1558 年に王位についた.
2 (cover) ... no u¹e o oo¹u ...の上を覆う C: Snow crowned the mountain. (*Yuki ga yama no ue o ootte ita.*) 雪が山の上を覆っていた.

crucial *adj.* ju¹udai na 重大な; ke¹ttee-teki na 決定的な: a crucial problem (*juudai na mondai*) 重大な問題.

crude *adj.* **1** (unrefined) te¹ñneñ no mama¹ no 天然のままの; ka¹koo shite inai 加工していない: crude oil (*geñyu*) 原油.
2 (rough) so¹ya na 粗野な; ge¹hi¹ñ na 下品な: crude behavior (*soya na furumai*) 粗野なふるまい.

cruel *adj.* **1** (merciless) za¹ñkoku na 残酷な; za¹ñgyaku na 残虐な: It is cruel to beat a dog. (*Inu o butsu no wa zañkoku da.*) 犬をぶつのは残酷だ.
2 (painful) hi¹sañ na 悲惨な; mu¹zañ na 無惨な: meet with a cruel death (*hisañ na saigo o togeru*) 悲惨な最期を遂げる.

cruelty *n.* za¹ñkoku 残酷; za¹ñgyaku 残虐: treat animals with cruelty (*doobutsu o zañkoku ni atsukau*) 動物を残酷に扱う.

crumb *n.* pa¹ñ ku¹zu パンくず; pa¹ñko¹ パン粉.

crumble *vi.* (bo¹roboro ni) ku¹zure¹ru (ぼろぼろに)崩れる V; ku¹dake¹ru 砕ける V: The old wall crumbled down. (*Furui hee ga kuzureochita.*) 古い塀が崩れ落ちた.

crush *vt.* **1** (press) ... o o¹shitsubu¹su ...を押しつぶす C: crush an empty beer can (*biiru no akikañ o oshitsubusu*) ビールの空き缶を押しつぶす.
2 (grind) ... o ku¹da¹ku ...を砕く C: crush ice (*koori o kudaku*) 氷を砕く.
3 (defeat) ... o ka¹imetsu saseru ...を壊滅させる V: crush one's enemies (*teki o kaimetsu saseru*) 敵を

壊滅させる.

— *vi.* (become wrinkled) shi「wa ni na「ru しわになる C: This material crushes easily. (*Kono kiji wa sugu ni shiwa ni naru.*) この生地はすぐにしわになる.

— *n.* 1 (crushing) o「shitsubu「su ko「to」 押しつぶすこと; fu「nsai 粉砕.
2 (crowded people) za「ttoo 雑踏; gu「nshuu 群衆: a crush in the subway (*chikatetsu no zattoo*) 地下鉄の雑踏.

crust *n.* pa「n no ka「wa」 パンの皮.

cry *vi.* 1 (weep) na「ku 泣く C: She cried when she heard the sad news. (*Sono kanashii shirase o kiite kanojo wa naita.*) その悲しい知らせを聞いて彼女は泣いた.
2 (shout) ko「e o a「geru 声を上げる V; sa「ke「bu 叫ぶ C: She cried for help. (*Kanojo wa koe o agete tasuke o motometa.*) 彼女は声を上げて助けを求めた.

— *vt.* ... to sa「ke「bu ...と叫ぶ C: "Fire!" he cried. (*"Kaji da" to kare wa sakenda.*) 「火事だ」と彼は叫んだ.

— *n.* 1 (shout) sa「kebi(go「e) 叫び(声); o「ogo「e 大声: give a cry of pain (*kutsuu no sakebigoe o ageru*) 苦痛の叫び声をあげる.
2 (of a bird) na「kigo「e 鳴き声; (of a beast) ho「e「ru koe ほえる声: the cries of wolves (*ookami no hoeru koe*) おおかみのほえる声.

cube *n.* 1 (solid body) ri「ppootai 立方体: a cube of sugar (*kakuzatoo*) 角砂糖.
2 (of multiplying) sa「njoo 3 乗.

— *vt.* ...o sa「njoo suru ...を3乗する ①: If you cube 2, you will get the answer 8. (*Ni o sañjoo suru to kotae wa hachi desu.*) 2を3乗すると答は8です.

cuff links *n.* ka「fusu bo「tañ カフスボタン.

cultivate *vt.* 1 (till) ...o ta「gaya「su ...を耕す C; ko「osaku suru 耕作する ①: cultivate a field (*hatake o tagayasu*) 畑を耕す.

2 (grow) ...o sa「ibai suru ...を栽培する ①: cultivate mushrooms (*kinoko o saibai suru*) きのこを栽培する.
3 (train) ...o ya「shina」u ...を養う C; mi「gaku 磨く C: cultivate one's mind (*seeshiñ o yashinau*) 精神を養う.

cultural *adj.* bu「nka no 文化の; kyo「oyoo no 教養の: cultural exchange (*buñka no kooryuu*) 文化の交流.

culture *n.* 1 (civilization) bu「nka 文化: Japanese culture (*Nihoñ buñka*) 日本文化.
2 (refinement) kyo「oyoo 教養: a person of culture (*kyooyoo no aru hito*) 教養のある人.
3 (of plants) sa「ibai 栽培; (of fish, etc.) yo「oshoku 養殖: the culture of roses (*bara no saibai*) ばらの栽培 / the culture of pearls (*shiñju no yooshoku*) 真珠の養殖.

cunning *adj.* zu「ru」i ずるい; wa「rugashiko」i 悪賢い: I was fooled by his cunning tricks. (*Watashi wa kare no zurui yarikata ni damasareta.*) 私は彼のずるいやりかたにだまされた.

cup *n.* 1 (of Japanese tea) cha「wañ 茶わん; (of coffee) ka「ppu カップ.
2 (cupful) cha「wañ [ka「ppu] i」ppai 茶わん[カップ] 1杯; -hai 杯: two cups of tea (*koocha ni-hai*) 紅茶2杯. 《⇒ appendix》
3 (ornamental vessel) yu「usho「ohai 優勝杯; ka「ppu カップ: win the cup (*yuushoo suru*) 優勝する.

cupboard *n.* (cabinet) sho「kki」dana 食器棚; (closet) to「dana 戸棚.

curb *n.* (of a street) e「nseki 縁石.

cure *vt.* 1 (heal) ...o chi「ryoo suru ...を治療する ①; na「o」su 治す C: The doctor cured him of his illness. (*Isha wa kare no byooki o naoshita.*) 医者は彼の病気を治した.
2 (make better) ...o na「o」su ...を直す C: cure bad habits (*warui kuse o naosu*) 悪い癖を直す.

— *n.* 1 (remedy) chi「ryoo 治療; ryo「oyoo 療養: undergo a cure (*chiryoo o ukeru*) 治療を受ける.

2 (method) chi⌐ryoohoo 治療法; (medicine) chi⌐ryo⌐oyaku 治療薬: a cure for cancer (gañ no chiryoo-yaku) がんの治療薬.

curiosity n. ko⌐oki¹shiñ 好奇心: satisfy one's curiosity (kookishiñ o mañzoku saseru) 好奇心を満足させる.

curious adj. **1** (eager) shi⌐ritaga¹-ru 知りたがる; ko⌐oki¹shiñ no [ga] tsu⌐yo¹i 好奇心の[が]強い: She is curious to know everything. (Ka-nojo wa nañ de mo shiritagaru.) 彼女は何でも知りたがる.
2 (strange) ki⌐myoo na 奇妙な; me⌐zurashi¹i 珍しい: It is curious that you have heard nothing from him. (Kimi ga kare kara nani mo kiite inai no wa kimyoo da.) 君が彼から何も聞いていないのは奇妙だ.

curiously adv. me⌐zurashi-so¹o ni 珍しそうに: He looked curiously at the insect. (Kare wa mezurashi-soo ni sono mushi o mita.) 彼は珍しそうにその虫を見た.

curl vt. ... o ka⌐aru saseru …をカールさせる Ⓥ; ma⌐kiage¹ru 巻き上げる Ⓥ: curl one's hair (kami o kaaru saseru) 髪をカールさせる.
—— vi. ka⌐aru suru カールする Ⓘ; u⌐zu o ma¹ku 渦を巻く Ⓒ: The smoke curled into the air. (Kemuri wa uzu o maite kuuchuu ni no-botta.) 煙は渦を巻いて空中に昇った.
—— n. ka⌐aru カール; ma⌐kige 巻き毛.

currency n. **1** (money) tsu⌐uka 通貨; ka⌐hee 貨幣: paper currency (shihee) 紙幣 / foreign currency (gaika) 外貨.
2 (being in common) tsu⌐uyoo 通用; ru⌐fu 流布: The rumor soon gained currency. (Sono uwasa wa sugu ni rufu shita.) そのうわさはすぐに流布した.

current n. **1** (stream) na⌐gare¹ 流れ; (of the sea) ka⌐iryuu 海流: the current of a river (kawa no naga-re) 川の流れ / the Japan Current (Nihoñ-kairyuu) 日本海流.
2 (of electricity) de⌐ñryuu 電流:

alternating current (kooryuu) 交流 / direct current (chokuryuu) 直流.
3 (of the times) ji⌐ryuu 時流; to⌐ki no nagare¹ 時の流れ: swim with the current (jiryuu ni shitagau) 時流に従う.
—— adj. **1** (generally accepted) ge⌐ñzai tsu⌐kawarete iru 現在使われている: That word is no longer current. (Sono kotoba wa geñzai wa tsukawarete inai.) そのことばは現在は使われていない. / current fashions (geñzai no ryuukoo) 現在の流行
2 (of the present time) ge⌐ñzai no 現在の; i¹ma no 今の: the current month (koñgetsu) 今月 / the current year (kotoshi) ことし / the current number one CD (ima ichibañ urete iru shii dii) 今いちばん売れているCD.

curse vt. ... o no⌐noshi¹ru …をののしる Ⓒ: curse a barking dog (hoete iru inu o nonoshiru) ほえている犬をののしる.
—— vi. (... o) no⌐ro¹u (…を)のろう Ⓒ: He cursed at his ill luck. (Kare wa jibuñ no fuuñ o norotta.) 彼は自分の不運をのろった.
—— n. no⌐roi のろい; ak⌐uta¹i 悪態: shout curses at a person (hito ni akutai o tsuku) 人に悪態をつく.

curtain n. **1** (at a window) ka⌐a-teñ カーテン: draw a curtain (kaateñ o hiku) カーテンを引く.
2 (in a theater) ma⌐ku 幕: The curtain rises [falls] at eight. (Maku wa hachi-ji ni aku [oriru].) 幕は8時に開く[下りる].

curve n. ka⌐abu カーブ; (line) kyo-⌐kuseñ 曲線: a curve in the road (dooro no kaabu) 道路のカーブ / draw a curve (kyokuseñ o egaku) 曲線を描く.
—— vi. ka⌐abu suru カーブする Ⓘ; ma⌐garu 曲がる Ⓒ; kyo⌐kuseñ o ega¹ku 曲線を描く Ⓒ: The road curves to the right. (Michi wa migi ni kaabu shite iru.) 道は右にカーブしている.

cushion n. ku⌐sshoñ クッション; za-

「bu¹ton 座ぶとん: sit on a cushion (*zabuton no ue ni suwaru*) 座ぶとんの上に座る.

custom *n.* **1** (tradition) ka「ñshuu 慣習; fu「ushuu 風習: follow an old custom (*furuku kara no kañshuu ni shitagau*) 古くからの慣習に従う. **2** (habit) shu「ukañ 習慣: It is my custom to get up early. (*Hayaoki wa watashi no shuukañ desu.*) 早起きは私の習慣です.

customary *adj.* shu「ukañ-teki na 習慣的な; ka「ñree no 慣例の: It is customary for me to take a walk. (*Sañpo o suru no wa watashi no shuukañ desu.*) 散歩するのは私の習慣です. / customary law (*kañshuuhoo*) 慣習法.

customer *n.* (of a shop) o-「kyaku お客; ko「kyaku 顧客; (of business) to「rihikisaki 取引先.

customs *n.* **1** (department) ze「e-kañ 税関: get through customs (*zeekañ o tsuuka suru*) 税関を通過する / a customs declaration form (*zeekañ shiñkokusho*) 税関申告書. **2** (taxes) ka「ñzee 関税: pay customs (*kañzee o harau*) 関税を払う.

cut *vt.* **1** (sever) ... o ki「ru ...を切る Ⓒ; ki「rito「ru 切り取る Ⓒ: cut a cake into six (*keeki o muttsu ni kiru*) ケーキを六つに切る / cut a branch from a tree (*ki kara eda o kiritoru*) 木から枝を切りとる. **2** (with a sharp edge) ... o ki「ru ...を切る Ⓒ: I cut my finger with a knife. (*Watashi wa naifu de yubi o kitta.*) 私はナイフで指を切った. **3** (delete) ... o sa「kujo suru ...を削除する Ⓣ; ke「zuru 削る Ⓒ; ka「tto suru カットする Ⓣ: The editor cut the article. (*Heñshuusha wa sono kiji o sakujo shita.*) 編集者はその記事を削除した. **4** (reduce) ... o sa「kugeñ suru ...を削減する Ⓣ; ki「ritsume「ru 切り詰める Ⓥ: cut one's traveling expenses (*ryohi o kiritsumeru*) 旅費を切り詰める.

5 (shorten) ... o ki「ru ...を切る Ⓒ; (of hair) ka「ru 刈る Ⓒ; ka「tto suru カットする Ⓣ: cut one's nails (*tsume o kiru*) つめを切る / Cut my hair short, please. (*Kami o mijikaku katte [kitte] kudasai.*) 髪を短く刈って[切って]ください.

— *vi.* **1** (of a knife, etc.) ki「re「ru 切れる Ⓥ: This razor cuts well. (*Kono kamisori wa yoku kireru.*) このかみそりはよく切れる. **2** (of a road) (... o) tsu「kki「tte su「sumu (...を)突っ切って進む Ⓒ; yo「kogi「ru 横切る Ⓒ: I cut through the woods. (*Watashi wa mori o tsukkitte itta.*) 私は森を突っ切って行った.

— *n.* **1** (wound) ki「ri「kizu 切り傷: I got a cut on my hand. (*Watashi wa te ni kirikizu o koshiraeta.*) 私は手に切り傷をこしらえた. **2** (deletion) sa「kujo 削除; ka「tto カット: make several cuts in a film (*firumu o suu-kasho katto suru*) フィルムを数か所カットする. **3** (reduction) sa「kugeñ 削減: a tax cut (*geñzee*) 減税. **4** (style) ka「ta 型: change the cut of one's hair (*kamigata o kaeru*) 髪型を変える. **5** (of meat) ki「rimi 切り身; hi「to「-kire ひと切れ: a tender cut of beef (*gyuuniku no yawarakai kirimi*) 牛肉の柔らかい切り身.

cute *adj.* ka「wai「i かわいい; ki「ree na きれいな: a cute baby (*kawaii akañ-boo*) かわいい赤ん坊.

cycle *n.* **1** (period of time) shu「uki 周期; ju「ñkañ 循環; u「tsurikawari 移り変わり: the cycle of the seasons (*kisetsu no utsurikawari*) 季節の移り変わり. **2** (bicycle) ji「te「ñsha 自転車: get on a cycle (*jiteñsha ni noru*) 自転車に乗る / get off a cycle (*jiteñsha kara oriru*) 自転車から降りる.

cycling *n.* sa「ikuriñgu サイクリング.

cylinder *n.* e「ñtoo 円筒; e「ñchuu 円柱; shi「ri「ñdaa シリンダー.

D

dagger n. taˈntoˈo 短刀; taˈnkeñ 短剣.

daily adj. maˈinichi no 毎日の: one's daily work (*mainichi no shigoto*) 毎日の仕事.
— adv. maˈinichi 毎日: Traffic accidents happen daily. (*Kootsuu jiko wa mainichi okoru.*) 交通事故は毎日起こる.

dairy n. 1 (farm) raˈkunoojoo 酪農場.
2 (store) nyuˈuseˈehiñ haˈnbaˈiteñ 乳製品販売店.

dairy cattle n. nyuˈugyuu 乳牛.

dam n. daˈmu ダム: build a dam (*damu o tsukuru*) ダムを造る.

damage n. soˈñgai 損害; hiˈgai 被害: The fire caused a lot of damage. (*Sono kaji wa ooki-na soñgai o ataeta.*) その火事は大きな損害を与えた.
— vt. ... ni soˈñgai o aˈtaeru …に損害を与える Ⓥ; ... o kiˈzutsukeˈru …を傷つける: damage a person's reputation (*hito no meesee o kizutsukeru*) 人の名声を傷つける.

damp adj. shiˈkke no aˈru 湿気のある; jiˈmejime shita [shite iru] じめじめした[している]; nuˈreta ぬれた; nuˈrete iru ぬれている: damp weather (*jimejime shita teñki*) じめじめした天気 / a damp towel (*nureta taoru*) ぬれたタオル.
— n. shiˈkke 湿気.

dampen vt. ... o shiˈmeraseru …を湿らせる Ⓥ: dampen the clothes before ironing (*airoñ o kakeru mae ni fuku o shimeraseru*) アイロンをかける前に服を湿らせる.

dance n. daˈñsu ダンス; oˈdori 踊り; daˈñsu paˈatii ダンスパーティー: give a dance (*dañsu paatii o moyoosu*) ダンスパーティーを催す.
— vi. oˈdoru 踊る Ⓒ: I danced with his daughter. (*Watashi wa kare no musume-sañ to odotta.*) 私は彼の娘さんと踊った.

dandruff n. fuˈke ふけ: I have dandruff. (*Watashi wa fukeshoo desu.*) 私はふけ症です.

danger n. kiˈkeñ 危険; kiˈki 危機: This bridge is in danger. (*Kono hashi wa kikeñ da.*) この橋は危険だ. / He is out of danger now. (*Kare wa ima wa kiki o dasshita.*) 彼は今は危機を脱した.

dangerous adj. kiˈkeñ na 危険な; aˈbunai 危ない: This river is dangerous to cross. (*Kono kawa o wataru no wa kikeñ da.*) この川を渡るのは危険だ. / It is dangerous to play here. (*Koko de asobu no wa abunai.*) ここで遊ぶのは危ない.

dare vt., aux. (be brave enough to do) oˈmoikiˈtte ⟨verb⟩ 思い切って…; aˈete ⟨verb⟩ あえて…: He dared to call on his teacher. (*Kare wa omoikitte señsee o tazuneta.*) 彼は思い切って先生を訪ねた. / I dared not tell her the sad news. (*Watashi wa sono kanashii shirase o totemo kanojo ni ienakatta.*) 私はその悲しい知らせをとても彼女に言えなかった.

dark adj. 1 (without light) kuˈrai 暗い: a dark night (*kurai yoru*) 暗い夜.
2 (of color) koˈi 濃い; (of hair) kuˈroˈi 黒い: dark brown (*koi chairo*) 濃い茶色 / He has dark hair. (*Kare wa kuroi kami o shite iru.*) 彼は黒い髪をしている.

darkness n. kuˈrayami 暗やみ: The room was in darkness. (*Heya wa kurayami datta.*) 部屋は暗やみだった.

dash vi. (rush) toˈsshiñ suru 突進する Ⓘ; iˈsoˈide iˈku 急いで行く Ⓒ: He dashed for the bus. (*Kare wa basu ni noroo to isoida.*) 彼はバスに乗ろうと急いだ.
— n. taˈñkyori-kyoˈosoo 短距離競

走: a 100 meter dash (*hyaku-mee-toru kyoosoo*) 100 メートル競走.

data n. shi「ryoo¹ 資料; de「eta データ: collect data (*deeta o atsumeru*) データを集める / analyze data (*deeta o buñseki suru*) データを分析する.

date n. **1** (day) hi「zuke¹ 日付; ki「-jitsu¹ 期日: This letter has no date. (*Kono tegami wa hizuke ga nai.*) この手紙は日付がない. / set the date for departure (*shuppatsu no kijitsu o kimeru*) 出発の期日を決める.
2 (appointment) de「eto¹ デート: have a date with a girlfriend (*gaaru-fureñdo to deeto suru*) ガールフレンドとデートする.
date of birth n. se「eneñ ga¹ppi 生年月日.

daughter n. mu「sume¹ 娘; (someone else's) o「jo¹o-sañ お嬢さん: one's only daughter (*hitori musume*) 一人娘.

daughter-in-law n. (your own) yo「me¹ 嫁; (someone else's) o-「yo¹-me-sañ お嫁さん.

dawn n. yo「ake¹ 夜明け; a「kegata 明け方: They departed at dawn. (*Kare-ra wa akegata ni shuppatsu shita.*) 彼らは明け方に出発した.
— vi. yo¹ ga a「keru 夜が明ける ⊻: The day dawned. (*Yo ga aketa.*) 夜が明けた.

day n. **1** (24 hours) hi 日; i「chi-nichi¹ 一日: What is the fee per day? (*Ichi-nichi no ryookiñ wa ikura desu ka?*) 一日の料金はいくらですか. / What day will it be ready? (*Sore wa nañ nichi ni dekimasu ka?*) それは何日にできますか. / I am staying here three days. (*Koko ni mikka taizai shimasu.*) ここに三日滞在します.
2 (daytime) hi「ruma¹ 昼間; ni「tchuu 日中: It was very warm during the day. (*Hiruma wa totemo atataka datta.*) 昼間はとても暖かった.
the day after tomorrow n. a「sa¹tte あさって.
the day before yesterday n. o「totoi おととい; is「saku¹jitsu 一昨日.

daytime n. hi「ruma¹ 昼間; hi「ru¹ 昼; ni「tchuu 日中.

dazzle vt. ... no me¹ o ku「ramase¹ru ...の目をくらませる ⊻: I was dazzled by the car's headlights. (*Watashi wa sono kuruma no heddoraito de me ga kurañda.*) 私はその車のヘッドライトで目がくらんだ.

dead adj. **1** (of an animal) shi「ñda 死んだ; shi「ñde iru 死んでいる: The rat is dead. (*Nezumi wa shiñde iru.*) ねずみは死んでいる.
2 (of a plant) ka「reta 枯れた; ka「rete iru 枯れている: dead leaves (*kareha*) 枯れ葉.
3 (of a telephone line) tsu「ujinai 通じない: The telephone line went dead after the earthquake. (*Jishiñ no ato de deñwa ga tsuujinaku natta.*) 地震の後で電話が通じなくなった.
4 (of a battery) ki「reta 切れた; ki「rete iru 切れている: The battery is dead. (*Deñchi ga kirete iru.*) 電池が切れている.
5 (no longer used) su「tareta 廃れた; su「tarete iru 廃れている: a dead custom (*sutareta shuukañ*) 廃れた習慣.

dead end n. (of a road) yu「kido-mari 行き止まり; (of work) yu「kizu-mari 行き詰まり: come to a dead end (*yukizumaru*) 行き詰まる.

deadline n. shi「mekiri 締め切り: meet the deadline (*shimekiri ni maniau*) 締め切りに間に合う.

deaf adj. mi「mi¹ ga fu「ji¹yuu na 耳が不自由な; mi「mi¹ ga to「oi 耳が遠い: My grandfather is rather deaf. (*Watashi no ojii-sañ wa mimi ga tooi.*) 私のおじいさんは耳が遠い.

deal vt. **1** (distribute) ... o ku「ba¹ru ...を配る ⊡: deal the cards (*kaado o kubaru*) カードを配る.
2 (give) ... o ku「waeru ...を加える ⊻: deal a blow to a person (*hito ni dageki o kuwaeru*) 人に打撃を加える.
— vi. **1** (treat) (... o) a「tsukau (...を)扱う ⊡; sho「ri suru 処理する ⊡: deal with pupils fairly (*seeto o koo-hee ni atsukau*) 生徒を公平に扱う /

deal with a difficult problem (*mu-zukashii moñdai o shori suru*) 難しい問題を処理する.
2 (do business) (... o) aˈkinaˈu (...を)商う C; (... no) shoˈobai o suru (...の)商売をする I: He deals in furniture. (*Kare wa kagu no shoobai o shite iru.*) 彼は家具の商売をしている.
— *n.* toˈriˈhiki 取り引き; keˈeyaku 契約: make a deal with a company (*kaisha to keeyaku o musubu*) 会社と契約を結ぶ.

dealer *n.* shoˈoniñ 商人; haˈñbai gyoˈosha 販売業者: a car dealer (*jidoosha hañbai gyoosha*) 自動車販売業者.

dear *adj.* (much loved) shiˈñai na 親愛な: one's dearest friend (*shiñ-yuu*) 親友. ★ The greeting in a formal Japanese letter is '*haikee*' 拝啓. However, '*haikee*' requires the use of many other formal expressions at the same time. For an easy-to-use equivalent of the English 'Dear ...,' use '*zeñryaku*' 前略.

death *n.* shiˈ 死; shiˈboo 死亡: Carelessness caused his death. (*Fuchuui ga kare no shi o maneita.*) 不注意が彼の死を招いた. / death penalty (*shikee*) 死刑.

debate *vt.* ... o toˈoroñ suru ...を討論する I; toˈogi suru 討議する I: debate a problem (*moñdai o too-roñ suru*) 問題を討議する.
— *vi.* toˈoroñ suru 討論する I; toˈogi suru 討議する I: They debated all night. (*Kare-ra wa hitobañ-juu tooroñ shita.*) 彼らは一晩中討論した.
— *n.* toˈoroñ 討論; toˈogi 討議.

debt *n.* (financial) shaˈkkiˈñ 借金; fuˈsai 負債; (moral) oˈñgi 恩義: pay back a debt (*shakkiñ o kaesu*) 借金を返す / I am in debt to him. (*Watashi wa kare ni kari ga aru.*) 私は彼に借りがある. ★ '*Kari*' means both financial and moral debt.

debtor *n.* kaˈriˈnushi 借り主; saˈi-muˈsha 債務者.

decade *n.* juˈuneˈñ-kañ 十年間: the past decade (*koko juuneñ-kañ*) ここ

10 年間.

decay *vi.* **1** (rot) kuˈsaˈru 腐る C: This tree began to decay inside. (*Kono ki wa naka ga kusari-hajimeta.*) この木は中が腐り始めた.
2 (decline) oˈtoroeˈru 衰える V: The state's power decayed. (*Koku-ryoku ga otoroeta.*) 国力が衰えた.
— *n.* fuˈshoku 腐食; oˈtoroe 衰え: tooth decay (*mushiba*) 虫歯.

deceased *adj.* shiˈkyo shita 死去した; boˈo- 亡-: his deceased father (*kare no boofu*) 彼の亡父 / the will of the deceased (*kojiñ no isho*) 故人の遺書.

deceit *n.* daˈmaˈsu koˈtoˈ だますこと; saˈgi 詐欺; kyoˈgi 虚偽: practice deceit on a person (*hito o damasu*) 人をだます.

deceive *vt.* ... o daˈmaˈsu ...をだます C; aˈzamuˈku 欺く C: The advertisement deceived us. (*Sono koo-koku wa watashi-tachi o dama-shita.*) その広告は私たちをだました.

December *n.* juˈuni-gatsuˈ 12 月.

decent *adj.* **1** (suitable) miˈguru-shiˈku nai 見苦しくない; kiˈchiˈñto shita [shite iru] きちんとした[している]: He appeared in decent clothes. (*Kare wa kichiñto shita fukusoo de arawareta.*) 彼はきちんとした服装で現れた.
2 (good enough) waˈruˈku nai 悪くない; kaˈnari yoi かなりよい: He makes a decent living. (*Kare wa kanari yoi seekatsu o shite iru.*) 彼はかなりよい生活をしている.

decide *vt.* **1** (resolve) ... to keˈs-shiñ suru ...と決心する I: He decided to be a lawyer. (*Kare wa beñ-goshi ni naroo to kesshiñ shita.*) 彼は弁護士になろうと決心した.
2 (settle) ... ni kiˈmeru ...に決める V: I decided to postpone my departure. (*Watashi wa shuppatsu o nobasu koto ni kimeta.*) 私は出発を延ばすことに決めた.
— *vi.* (... o) keˈttee suru (...を)決定する I: We have to decide on our next plan. (*Tsugi no keekaku o ket-*

tee shinakereba naranai.) 次の計画を決定しなければならない.

decision *n.* ke⌐ttee 決定; ke⌐tsu-roñ 結論: decision by majority (*tasuuketsu*) 多数決 / come to a decision (*ketsuroñ ni tassuru*) 結論に達する.

decisive *adj.* ke⌐ttee-teki na 決定的な; ki⌐ppa⌐ri shita [shite iru] きっぱりした[している]: decisive evidence (*kettee-teki na shooko*) 決定的な証拠 / a decisive answer (*kippari shita kotae*) きっぱりした答え.

deck *n.* **1** (of a ship) de⌐kki デッキ; ka⌐ñpañ 甲板.
2 (of a tape) de⌐kki デッキ: a cassette deck (*kasetto dekki*) カセットデッキ.
3 (of playing cards) hi⌐to⌐-kumi 一組: a deck of cards (*toranpu hito-kumi*) トランプ一組.

declaration *n.* **1** (announcement) se⌐ñge⌐ñ 宣言; fu⌐koku 布告: the Declaration of Independence (*dokuritsu señgeñ*) 独立宣言 / a declaration of war (*señseñ fukoku*) 宣戦布告.
2 (formal statement) shi⌐ñkoku 申告: a customs declaration form (*zeekañ shiñkokusho*) 税関申告書.

declare *vt.* **1** (affirm) ... to ge⌐ñ-mee suru ...と言明する ⓘ; da⌐ñge⌐ñ suru 断言する ⓘ: He declared that he was innocent. (*Kare wa jibuñ wa keppaku da to geñmee shita.*) 彼は自分は潔白だと言明した.
2 (say openly) ... o se⌐ñge⌐ñ suru ...を宣言する ⓘ: declare independence (*dokuritsu o señgeñ suru*) 独立を宣言する.
3 (make a statement) ... o shi⌐ñ-koku suru ...を申告する ⓘ: I have nothing to declare. (*Shiñkoku suru mono wa nani mo arimaseñ.*) 申告するものは何もありません.

decline *vt.* ... o ko⌐towa⌐ru ...を断る ⓒ: She declined my invitation. (*Kanojo wa watashi no shootai o kotowatta.*) 彼女は私の招待を断った.
— *vi.* o⌐toroe⌐ru 衰える ⓥ; sa⌐ga⌐-

ru 下がる ⓒ: His health is gradually declining. (*Kare no keñkoo wa jojo ni otoroete iru.*) 彼の健康は徐徐に衰えている. / Prices have declined a little. (*Bukka ga sukoshi sagatta.*) 物価が少し下がった.

decorate *vt.* ... o ka⌐zaru ...を飾る ⓒ: She decorated her room with flowers. (*Kanojo wa heya o hana de kazatta.*) 彼女は部屋を花で飾った.

decoration *n.* so⌐oshoku 装飾; ka⌐zari 飾り: interior decoration (*shitsunai sooshoku*) 室内装飾 / Christmas tree decorations (*Kurisu-masu-tsurii no kazari*) クリスマスツリーの飾り.

decrease *vi.* he⌐ru 減る ⓒ; su⌐ku-na⌐ku naru 少なくなる ⓒ: The population of Tokyo is decreasing. (*Too-kyoo no jiñkoo wa hette iru.*) 東京の人口は減っている.
— *vt.* ... o he⌐rasu ...を減らす ⓒ: decrease the number of accidents (*jiko no kazu o herasu*) 事故の数を減らす.
— *n.* ge⌐ñshoo 減少; shu⌐kushoo 縮小.

decree *n.* (law) ho⌐oree 法令; se⌐e-ree 制令; (ruling) ha⌐ñketsu 判決: issue a decree (*hooree o happu suru*) 法令を発布する.

dedicate *vt.* (... ni) ... o sa⌐sageru (...に)...をささげる ⓥ: He dedicated his life to his work. (*Kare wa shi-goto no tame ni isshoo o sasageta.*) 彼は仕事のために一生をささげた.

deed *n.* o⌐konai 行い; ko⌐oi 行為: a good deed (*rippa na kooi*) 立派な行為.

deep *adj.* **1** fu⌐ka⌐i 深い; fu⌐kasa ga ... a⌐ru 深さが...ある: a deep river (*fukai kawa*) 深い川 / This well is 10 meters deep. (*Kono ido wa fukasa ga juu-meetoru aru.*) この井戸は深さが10メートルある. / a deep breath (*shiñ-kokyuu*) 深呼吸.
2 (color) ko⌐i 濃い; (voice) fu⌐to⌐i 太い: a deep red (*koi aka*) 濃い赤 / have a deep voice (*futoi koe o shite iru*) 太い声をしている.

3 (absorbed) muᵓchuu ni naᵓtte (iru) 夢中になって(いる): He was deep in thought. (*Kare wa kañgaegoto ni muchuu ni natte ita.*) 彼は考え事に夢中になっていた.

deepen *vi.* fuᵓkaᵓku naru 深くなる ©; fuᵓkamaᵓru 深まる ©: The autumn colors have deepened. (*Aki no iro ga fukamatta.*) 秋の色が深まった.

deeply *adv.* fuᵓkaku 深く; koᵓkoᵓro kara 心から: breathe deeply (*iki o fukaku suu*) 息を深く吸う / I am deeply grateful to you. (*Watashi wa kokoro kara anata ni kañsha shite orimasu.*) 私は心からあなたに感謝しております.

deer *n.* shiᵓka しか(鹿): deerskin (*shikagawa*) 鹿皮.

defeat *vt.* ... o maᵓkasu ...を負かす ©; yaᵓbuᵓru 破る ©: We defeated our opponent by three to one. (*Wareware wa aite o sañ-tai ichi de makashita.*) われわれは相手を 3 対 1 で負かした. / be defeated (*makeru*) 負ける.
— *n.* (failure) maᵓke 負け; shiᵓppai 失敗; (in war) haᵓiboku 敗北: four victories and two defeats (*yoñ shoo ni hai*) 4 勝 2 敗.

defect *n.* (flaw) keᵓkkañ 欠陥; (fault) keᵓteᵓñ 欠点: a defect in a car (*kuruma no kekkañ*) 車の欠陥.

defend *vt.* **1** (guard) ... o maᵓmoᵓru ...を守る ©; fuᵓseᵓgu 防ぐ ©: defend oneself from dangers (*kikeñ kara mi o mamoru*) 危険から身を守る.
2 (legal) ... o beᵓñgo suru ...を弁護する ©; yoᵓogo suru 擁護する Ⅰ: I defended his opinions. (*Watashi wa kare no ikeñ o beñgo shita.*) 私は彼の意見を弁護した.

defendant *n.* (person accused) hiᵓkoku(niñ) 被告(人).

defense *n.* **1** (protection) boᵓogyo 防御; boᵓoee 防衛: fight in defense of one's country (*kuni no booee no tame ni tatakau*) 国の防衛のために戦う.

2 (argument) beᵓñgo 弁護; beᵓñmee 弁明: He made no defense for his behavior. (*Kare wa jibuñ no kooi ni tsuite nani mo beñmee shinakatta.*) 彼は自分の行為について何も弁明しなかった.

deference *n.* keᵓei 敬意; soᵓñkee 尊敬: pay deference to a person (*hito ni keei o harau*) 人に敬意を払う.

deficiency *n.* (shortage) fuᵓsoku 不足; keᵓtsuboo 欠乏: a deficiency of vitamin C (*bitamiñ shii no fusoku*) ビタミン C の不足.

deficit *n.* (loss) keᵓssoñ 欠損; (of accounting) aᵓkaji 赤字: a trade deficit (*booeki-akaji*) 貿易赤字.

define *vt.* **1** (explain) ... o teᵓegi suru ...を定義する Ⅰ: define a word (*kotoba o teegi suru*) 言葉を定義する.
2 (fix the limits) ... o geᵓñtee suru ...を限定する Ⅰ; saᵓdameᵓru 定める Ⅴ: define a boundary (*kyookai o sadameru*) 境界を定める.

definite *adj.* **1** (fixed) iᵓttee no 一定の: a definite period of time (*ittee kikañ*) 一定期間.
2 (clear) meᵓekaku na 明確な; kaᵓkujitsu na 確実な: a definite answer (*kakutoo*) 確答.

definitely *adv.* taᵓshika ni 確かに; meᵓekaku ni 明確に: He is definitely the best player in the team. (*Kare wa tashika ni chiimu de ichibañ sugureta señshu desu.*) 彼は確かにチームでいちばん優れた選手です.

definition *n.* teᵓegi 定義.

defrost *vt.* **1** (unfreeze) shiᵓmoᵓ [koᵓori] o toᵓru 霜[氷]をとる ©: defrost a refrigerator (*reezoko no shimo o toru*) 冷蔵庫の霜をとる.
2 (of frozen food) ... o kaᵓitoo suru ...を解凍する Ⅰ: defrost the meat (*niku o kaitoo suru*) 肉を解凍する.

defy *vt.* **1** (challenge) ... ni iᵓdoᵓmu ...に挑む ©: I defied him to solve the problem. (*Watashi wa sono moñdai o toite miro to kare ni idoñda.*) 私はその問題を解いてみろと彼

に挑んだ.

2 (resist) ... ni ha｢nkoo suru ...に反抗する ①; ... o mu｣shi suru ...を無視する ①: defy public opinion (*yoroñ o mushi suru*) 世論を無視する.

degree *n*. **1** (unit of measure) do 度: 10 degrees below zero (*reeka juu do*) 零下 10 度. ★ The Celsius scale is used in Japan.

2 (extent) te｣edo 程度; da｢nkai 段階: It is a matter of degree. (*Sore wa teedo no moñdai desu.*) それは程度の問題です.

3 (title) ga｢kui 学位: get a master's degree (*shuushi no gakui o toru*) 修士の学位をとる.

delay *vt*. **1** (put off) ... o no｢ba｣su ...を延ばす ⓒ; e｢nki suru 延期する ①: delay one's departure (*shuppatsu o nobasu*) 出発を延ばす.

2 (make late) ... o o｢kuraseru ...を遅らせる ⓥ: How long will it be delayed? (*Dono kurai okuremasu ka?*) どのくらい遅れますか.

delegate *n*. da｢ihyoo 代表: send a delegate to a convention (*taikai e daihyoo o okuru*) 大会へ代表を送る. — *vt*. ... o da｢ihyoo to shite o｢kuru ...を代表として送る ⓒ; ha｢keñ suru 派遣する ①: The union delegated me to attend the meeting. (*Kumiai wa daihyoo to shite watashi o sono kaigi ni hakeñ shita.*) 組合は代表として私をその会議に派遣した.

delegation *n*. da｢ihyo｣odañ 代表団.

delete *vt*. ... o sa｢kujo suru ...を削除する ①: delete two lines (*ni-gyoo sakujo suru*) 2 行削除する.

deliberate *adj*. **1** (intentional) ko｢i no 故意の; ke｢ekaku-teki na 計画的な: a deliberate lie (*koi no uso*) 故意のうそ.

2 (careful) shi｢ñchoo na 慎重な: We took deliberate action. (*Watashi-tachi wa shiñchoo na koodoo o totta.*) 私たちは慎重な行動をとった.

deliberately *adv*. **1** (on purpose) wa｣zato わざと; ko｢i ni 故意に:

I deliberately told a lie. (*Watashi wa wazato uso o itta.*) 私はわざとうそを言った.

2 (carefully) shi｢ñchoo ni 慎重に: He climbed the stairs deliberately. (*Kare wa shiñchoo ni kaidañ o nobotta.*) 彼は慎重に階段を上った.

delicate *adj*. **1** (fine and beautiful) se｢ñsai na 繊細な; yu｢ubi na 優美な: a delicate piece of silk (*señsai na kinu no orimono*) 繊細な絹の織物.

2 (fragile) kya｢sha na きゃしゃな; ko｢ware-yasu｣i 壊れやすい: a delicate little girl (*kyasha na oñna-no-ko*) きゃしゃな女の子 / a delicate vase (*koware-yasui kabiñ*) 壊れやすい花びん.

3 (needing careful handling) bi｢myoo na 微妙な; a｢tsukai-niku｣i 扱いにくい: a very delicate question (*hijoo ni bimyoo na moñdai*) 非常に微妙な問題.

delicious *adj*. o｢ishii おいしい: It's delicious! (*Oishii desu ne.*) おいしいですね.

delight *n*. o｢oyo｣rokobi 大喜び; u｢re｣shisa うれしさ: She received the present with delight. (*Kanojo wa ooyorokobi de sono okurimono o uketotta.*) 彼女は大喜びでその贈り物を受け取った.

delightful *adj*. ta｢noshii｣ 楽しい; yu｢kai na 愉快な: a delightful summer vacation (*tanoshii natsuyasumi*) 楽しい夏休み.

deliver *vt*. **1** (distribute) ... o ha｢itatsu suru ...を配達する ①; to｢dokeru ⓥ届ける ⓥ: Newspapers are delivered twice a day. (*Shiñbuñ wa ichinichi ni ni-do haitatsu sareru.*) 新聞は 1 日に 2 度配達される. / Please deliver this package to him. (*Kono tsutsumi o kare ni todokete kudasai.*) この包みを彼に届けてください.

2 (hand over) ... o hi｢kiwata｣su ...を引き渡す ⓒ: deliver a thief to the police (*doroboo o keesatsu ni hikiwatasu*) どろぼうを警察に引き渡す.

3 (speak) ... o ha｢na｣su 話す ⓒ; no-

「be¹ru 述べる Ⅴ: He delivered a long speech. (*Kare wa nagai eñzetsu o shita.*) 彼は長い演説をした.

delivery *n.* **1** (distribution) ha¹itatsu 配達: delivery of goods (*shinamono no haitatsu*) 品物の配達 / express [special] delivery (*sokutatsu*) 速達.
2 (birth of a child) shu¹ssañ 出産: an easy [a difficult] delivery (*añ-[nañ]zañ*) 安[難]産.

delusion *n.* mo¹osoo 妄想; sa¹kkaku 錯覚: suffer from delusions (*moosoo ni nayamu*) 妄想に悩む.

deluxe *adj.* go¹oka na 豪華な; ze¹eta¹ku na ぜいたくな: a deluxe hotel (*gooka na hoteru*) 豪華なホテル / a deluxe edition (*gookabañ*) 豪華版.

demand *vt.* **1** (request) ... o yo¹okyuu suru ...を要求する Ⅰ; mo¹tome¹ru 求める Ⅴ: The union demanded higher wages. (*Kumiai wa chiñage o yookyuu shita.*) 組合は賃上げを要求した.
2 (need) ... o yo¹osu¹ru ...を要する Ⅰ: This problem demands careful attention. (*Kono moñdai wa saishiñ no chuui o yoosuru.*) この問題は細心の注意を要する.
— *n.* **1** (request) yo¹okyuu 要求: He turned down our demands. (*Kare wa wareware no yookyuu o shirizoketa.*) 彼はわれわれの要求を退けた.
2 (desire) ju¹yoo 需要: demand and supply (*juyoo to kyookyuu*) 需要と供給.

democracy *n.* (system) mi¹ñshushu¹gi 民主主義; mi¹ñshuse¹eji 民主政治; (nation) mi¹ñshushugi¹koku 民主主義国.

democratic *adj.* mi¹ñshushu¹gi no 民主主義の; mi¹ñshu-teki na 民主的な: His way of doing things is democratic. (*Kare no yarikata wa miñshu-teki da.*) 彼のやり方は民主的だ.

demonstrate *vt.* **1** (show) ... o ji¹ssai ni yatte mise¹ru ...を実際にやって見せる Ⅴ: He demonstrated

how to operate the machine. (*Kare wa sono kikai no ugokashikata o jissai ni yatte miseta.*) 彼はその機械の動かし方を実際にやって見せた.
2 (prove) ... o sho¹omee suru ...を証明する Ⅰ: I demonstrated the correctness of the theory. (*Watashi wa sono riroñ ga tadashii koto o shoomee shita.*) 私はその理論が正しいことを証明した.
— *vi.* (parade) de¹mo o suru デモをする Ⅰ: They demonstrated against the new taxes. (*Kare-ra wa atarashii zee ni hañtai shite demo o shita.*) 彼らは新しい税に反対してデモをした.

demonstration *n.* **1** (advertising) ji¹tsubutsu-se¹ñdeñ 実物宣伝.
2 (teaching) ji¹tsubutsu-kyo¹oiku 実物教育: a demonstration of a new computer (*atarashii koñpyuutaa no jitsubutsu-kyooiku*) 新しいコンピューターの実物教育.
3 (parade) de¹mo デモ: We took part in the demonstrations. (*Watashi-tachi wa sono demo ni sañka shita.*) 私たちはそのデモに参加した.

denial *n.* hi¹tee 否定; hi¹niñ 否認: He made a denial of his connection with the matter. (*Kare wa sono keñ to no kakawari o hitee shita.*) 彼はその件とのかかわりを否定した.

denounce *vt.* ... o hi¹nañ suru ...を非難する Ⅰ: She denounced me as a liar. (*Kanojo wa watashi o usotsuki da to hinañ shita.*) 彼女は私をうそつきだと非難した.

dense *adj.* mi¹sshuu shita [shite iru] 密集した[している]; ko¹i 濃い: a dense forest (*mitsuriñ*) 密林 / a dense fog (*noomu*) 濃霧.

density *n.* mi¹tsudo 密度: the density of population (*jiñkoo mitsudo*) 人口密度.

dent *n.* he¹komi へこみ: I put a dent in my car. (*Watashi wa kuruma ni hekomi o tsukutte shimatta.*) 私は車にへこみをつくってしまった.
— *vt.* ... o he¹komaseru ...をへこま

せる Ⓥ: He dented my car. (*Kare wa watashi no kuruma o hekomaseta.*) 彼は私の車をへこませた.

dentist *n.* haˈisha 歯医者; shiˈkaˈi 歯科医: consult a dentist (*haisha ni mite morau*) 歯医者に診てもらう.

deny *vt.* 1 (declare to be untrue) ... o hiˈtee suru ...を否定する Ⓘ; uˈchikesu 打ち消す Ⓒ: He denied the rumor. (*Kare wa sono uwasa o hitee shita.*) 彼はそのうわさを否定した. 2 (refuse) ... o koˈbaˈmu ...を拒む Ⓒ; koˈtowaˈru 断る Ⓒ: The company denied the employees' requests. (*Kaisha wa juugyooiñ no yookyuu o kobañ da.*) 会社は従業員の要求を拒んだ.

depart *vi.* 1 (leave) shuˈppatsu suru 出発する Ⓘ; deˈru 出る Ⓥ: They departed early in the morning. (*Kare-ra wa asa hayaku shuppatsu shita.*) 彼らは朝早く出発した. / The train departs at 8:15. (*Ressha wa hachi-ji juugo-fuñ ni demasu.*) 列車は8時15分に出ます. 2 (change) ... kara) haˈzureru (...から)外れる Ⓥ; soˈreˈru それる Ⓥ: depart from an original plan (*moto no keekaku kara soreru*) もとの計画からそれる.

department *n.* 1 (office) buˈmoñ 部門, -bu 部: the sales department (*hañbaibu*) 販売部. 2 (store) uˈriba 売場: the toy department (*omocha-uriba*) おもちゃ売場. 3 (university) gaˈkka 学科: the department of English (*eebuñka*) 英文科. 4 (government) -shoo 省: the Department of Agriculture (*Noomushoo*) 農務省.

department store *n.* deˈpaˈato デパート: go shopping at a department store (*depaato e kaimono ni iku*) デパートへ買い物に行く.

departure *n.* (general) shuˈppatsu 出発; (of a train, etc.) haˈssha 発車: What is the departure time of the next flight? (*Tsugi no biñ no*

shuppatsu jikoku wa nañ-ji desu ka?*) 次の便の出発時刻は何時ですか.

depend *vi.* 1 (rely on) (... o taˈyori ni suru (...を)頼りにする Ⓘ; aˈte ni suru 当てにする Ⓘ: We depend on you. (*Watashi-tachi wa anata o tayori ni shite imasu.*) 私たちはあなたを頼りにしています. 2 (be controlled by) (... ni) yoˈru (...に)よる Ⓒ; ... shiˈdai da ...次第だ: Our departure depends on the weather. (*Wareware no shuppatsu wa teñki shidai desu.*) われわれの出発は天気次第です. / It depends. (*Baai ni yorimasu.*) 場合によります.

dependent *adj.* 1 (relying) ... ni taˈyoˈtte iru ...に頼っている: He is still dependent on his parents. (*Kare wa mada oya ni tayotte iru.*) 彼はまだ親に頼っている. 2 (being controlled) ... shiˈdai no ...次第の: Your success is dependent on your efforts. (*Anata no seekoo wa doryoku shidai desu.*) あなたの成功は努力次第です. — *n.* (family member) fuˈyoo kaˈzoku 扶養家族.

deplore *vt.* 1 (lament) ... o naˈgeˈku ...を嘆く Ⓒ; naˈgekikanashiˈmu 嘆き悲しむ Ⓒ: deplore the death of a close friend (*shiñyuu no shi o nageku*) 親友の死を嘆く. 2 (express regret) ... o zaˈñneˈñ [iˈkañ] ni oˈmoˈu ...を残念[遺憾]に思う Ⓒ: I deplore the use of violence. (*Watashi wa booryoku no kooshi o zañneñ ni omou.*) 私は暴力の行使を残念に思う.

deport *vt.* ... o tsuˈihoo suru ...を追放する Ⓘ; kyoˈosee-soˈokañ suru 強制送還する Ⓘ: He was deported for having entered the country illegally. (*Kare wa fuhoo nyuukoku no tame ni kyoosee sookañ sareta.*) 彼は不法入国のために強制送還された.

deposit *vt.* ... o yoˈkiñ suru ...を預金する Ⓘ; aˈzukeˈru 預ける Ⓥ: deposit money in a bank (*giñkoo ni o-kane o azukeru*) 銀行にお金を預ける.

— n. (of bank) yoʳkiñ 預金；(of housing) shiʳkiʳkiñ 敷金；(part payment) teʳtsukekiñ 手付け金；aʳtamakiñ 頭金：pay a deposit (*tetsukekiñ o harau*) 手付け金を払う.

depress *vt.* ... o kiʳochi saseru ...を気落ちさせる V；gaʳkkaʳri saseru がっかりさせる V：The news depressed us. (*Sono shirase wa watashi-tachi o gakkari saseta.*) その知らせは私たちをがっかりさせた.

depression *n.* **1** (slump) fuʳkyoo 不況；fuʳkeʳeki 不景気：The industry is now in a depression. (*Sañgyoo-kai wa ima fukyoo desu.*) 産業界は今不況です.

2 (sadness) yuʳu-utsu ゆううつ；raʳkutañ 落胆：mental depression (*ikishoochiñ*) 意気消沈.

deprive *vt.* ... o ubaʳu ...を奪う C：They were deprived of their lands. (*Kare-ra wa tochi o ubawareta.*) 彼らは土地を奪われた.

depth *n.* **1** (deepness) fuʳkaʳsa 深さ：measure the depth of a river (*kawa no fukasa o hakaru*) 川の深さを測る.

2 (from front to back) oʳkuyuki 奥行き：the depth of a building (*tatemono no okuyuki*) 建物の奥行き.

deputy *n.* daʳiri 代理；daʳiriniñ 代理人：I acted as his deputy. (*Watashi wa kare no dairi o tsutometa.*) 私は彼の代理を務めた.

derive *vt.* **1** (obtain) ... o eʳru ...を得る V：derive pleasure from music (*oñgaku kara tanoshimi o eru*) 音楽から楽しみを得る.

2 (originate) ... ni yuʳrai suru ...に由来する I；(... kara) kiʳte iru (...から)来ている V：This word is derived from Latin. (*Kono tañgo wa Rateñgo kara kite iru.*) この単語はラテン語から来ている.

descend *vi.* **1** (go down) kuʳdaru 下る C；oʳriʳru 降りる V：We descended from the hilltop. (*Watashi-tachi wa oka no choojoo kara kudatta.*) 私たちは丘の頂上から下った. / The hot-air balloon descended in a field. (*Sono netsukikyuu wa hatake ni orita.*) その熱気球は畑に降りた.

2 (be handed down) tsuʳtawaru 伝わる C：The business descended from father to son. (*Sono shoobai wa chichioya kara musuko e to tsutawatta.*) その商売は父親から息子へと伝わった.

— vt. ... o oʳriʳru ...を下りる V：descend the steps (*kaidañ o oriru*) 階段を下りる.

descendant *n.* shiʳsoñ 子孫：a descendant of a famous writer (*yuumee na sakka no shisoñ*) 有名な作家の子孫.

describe *vt.* **1** (give an account) ... o noʳbeʳru ...を述べる V；iʳi arawaʳsu 言い表す C：He described his experiences. (*Kare wa jibuñ no taikeñ o nobeta.*) 彼は自分の体験を述べた.

2 (tell) ... to iʳu ...と言う C：They described my plan as a failure. (*Kare-ra wa watashi no keekaku wa shippai da to itta.*) 彼らは私の計画は失敗だと言った.

description *n.* kiʳjutsu 記述；byoʳosha 描写；(of a person) niʳñsoo 人相：give a full description (*kuwashiku setsumee suru*) 詳しく説明する.

desert[1] *n.* saʳbaku 砂漠.

desert[2] *vt.* **1** (abandon) ... o miʳsuteru ...を見捨てる V：desert one's wife and children (*saishi o misuteru*) 妻子を見捨てる.

2 (leave) ... o suʳteru ...を捨てる V；daʳssoo suru 脱走する I：desert a ship (*fune o suteru*) 船を捨てる / The soldiers deserted their posts. (*Heetai-tachi wa mochiba kara dassoo shita.*) 兵隊たちは持ち場から脱走した.

deserve *vt.* ... ni aʳtai suru ...に値する I：His conduct deserves praise. (*Kare no kooi wa shoosañ ni atai suru.*) 彼の行為は称賛に値する.

design *vt.* **1** (draw up a plan) ... o deʳzaʳiñ suru ...をデザインする I；seʳk-

kee suru 設計する ⓉⒾ: design a new
dress (atarashii doresu o dezaiñ
suru) 新しいドレスをデザインする / Who
designed this house? (Dare ga
kono uchi o sekkee shimashita
ka?) だれがこの家を設計しましたか.
2 (purpose) ... ni yoᶠtee suru ...に予
定する ⓉⒾ: This plot is designed as a
parking lot. (Kono tochi wa chuushajoo ni suru yotee desu.) この土
地は駐車場にする予定です.
— **n. 1** (pattern) moᶠyoo 模様: a
curtain with a design of roses (bara
no moyoo no kaateñ) ばらの模様のカ
ーテン.
2 (sketch) deᶠzaᶦiñ デザイン; zuᶠañ
図案: a design for an advertisement (kookoku no zuañ) 広告の図
案.
3 (plan) seᶠkkee 設計: a building
under design (sekkee-chuu no tatemono) 設計中の建物.

designer n. deᶠzaᶦinaa デザイナー;
seᶠkkeᶦesha 設計者: a fashion designer (fasshoñ dezainaa) ファッショ
ンデザイナー.

desirable adj. noᶠzomashiᶦi 望まし
い; koᶠnomashiᶦi 好ましい: desirable
surroundings (nozomashii kañkyoo) 望ましい環境.

desire vt. ... o noᶠzomu 望む Ⓒ:
neᶠgaᶦu 願う Ⓒ: I desire your presence. (Anata no shusseki o nozomimasu.) あなたの出席を望みます. /
I desire that you answer my letter as
soon as possible. (Dekiru dake
hayaku watashi no tegami ni heñji
o kudasaru koto o negatte imasu.)
できるだけ早く私の手紙に返事を下さるこ
とを願っています.
— n. noᶠzomi 望み; neᶠgaᶦi 願い;
yoᶠkuboo 欲望: My desire is to
visit your country. (Watashi no
nozomi wa anata no kuni o tazuneru koto desu.) 私の望みはあなたの国
を訪ねることです.

desk n. **1** (furniture) tsuᶠkue 机:
The letters are all on your desk.
(Tegami wa zeñbu tsukue no ue
ni arimasu.) 手紙は全部机の上にあり

ます.
2 (of a hotel, etc.) uᶠketsuke 受付.

despair n. zeᶠtsuboo 絶望; shiᶦtsu-
boo 失望: She tried to kill herself
out of despair. (Kanojo wa zetsuboo no amari jisatsu shiyoo to
shita.) 彼女は絶望のあまり自殺しようと
した.
— vi. zeᶠtsuboo suru 絶望する Ⓘ;
aᶠkirameᶦru あきらめる Ⓥ: We de-
spaired of success. (Seekoo wa
akirameta.) 成功はあきらめた.

desperate adj. **1** (reckless) hiᶠs-
shi no 必死の: He was desperate to
escape. (Kare wa nigeyoo to hisshi
datta.) 彼は逃げようと必死だった.
2 (hopeless) zeᶠtsuboo-teki na 絶
望的な: The situation is desperate.
(Jookyoo wa zetsuboo-teki desu.)
状況は絶望的です.

despise vt. ... o keᶠebetsu suru ...
を軽蔑する Ⓘ: Don't despise the
poor. (Mazushii hito-tachi o keebetsu shite wa ikenai.) 貧しい人たちを
軽蔑してはいけない.

despite prep. ... ni mo kaᶠkawaᶦ-
razu ...にもかかわらず: I attended the
meeting despite my illness. (Watashi wa byooki ni mo kakawarazu
sono kai ni shusseki shita.) 私は病
気にもかかわらずその会に出席した.

dessert n. deᶠzaᶦato デザート: I'd
like some fruit for dessert. (Dezaato ni kudamono o kudasai.) デザ
ートに果物を下さい.

destination n. moᶠkutekiᶦchi 目的
地; yuᶠkisaki 行き先: We arrived at
our destination at five. (Watashi-
tachi wa mokutekichi no go-ji ni
tsuita.) 私たちは目的地に5時に着いた.

destiny n. uᶠñmee 運命: It was his
destiny to die on the mountain.
(Yama de shinu no ga kare no
uñmee datta.) 山で死ぬのが彼の運命
だった.

destroy vt. **1** (damage) ... o ha-
ᶠkai suru ...を破壊する Ⓘ; koᶠwaᶦsu
壊す Ⓒ: Three houses were destroyed by a landslide. (Jisuberi
de sañ-geñ no uchi ga hakai sa-

reta.) 地滑りで３軒の家が破壊された.
2 (ruin) ... o uʼchikudaʼku ...を打ち砕く C: His dreams were destroyed by the failure in the examination. (*Shikeñ ni shippai shite kare no yume wa uchikudakareta.*) 試験に失敗して彼の夢は打ち砕かれた.

destruction *n.* haʼkai 破壊: environmental destruction (*kañkyoo hakai*) 環境破壊.

detach *vt.* (... kara) ... o toʼrihazusu (…から)…を取り外す C: detach a key from its chain (*kusari kara kagi o torihazusu*) 鎖から鍵を取り外す.

detail *n.* (small item) koʼmakaʼi teʼñʼ 細かい点; saʼibu 細部; shoʼo-sai 詳細: I will tell you the details of my plan later. (*Watashi no kee-kaku no shoosai wa nochi-hodo o-shirase shimasu.*) 私の計画の詳細は後ほどお知らせします.

detain *vt.* **1** (hold back) ... o hiʼki-tomeʼru ...を引き止める V: I won't detain you. (*O-hikitome wa itashi-maseñ.*) お引き止めはいたしません.
2 (of the police) ... o ryuʼuchi [koʼochi] suru ...を留置[拘置]する I: He was detained at the police station. (*Kare wa keesatsu ni ryuu-chi sareta.*) 彼は警察に留置された.

detect *vt.* ... o miʼtsukeru ...を見つける V; haʼkkeñ suru 発見する I: I detected a slight flaw in the lens. (*Reñzu ni kasuka na kizu o mitsu-keta.*) レンズにかすかな傷を見つけた.

detective *n.* (police) keʼeji 刑事; (civilian) taʼñtee 探偵: a private detective (*shiritsu tañtee*) 私立探偵.

detergent *n.* seʼñzai 洗剤: wash with detergent (*señzai de arau*) 洗剤で洗う.

determination *n.* **1** (resolution) keʼsshiñ 決心; keʼtsudaʼñryoku 決断力: a person of determination (*ketsudañryoku no aru hito*) 決断力のある人.
2 (decision) keʼttee 決定: the determination of the date (*hidori no ket-tee*) 日取りの決定.

determine *vt.* **1** (resolve) ⟨verb⟩ keʼsshiñ o suru ...決心をする I; keʼtsui o suru 決意をする I: I determined to go to Japan. (*Watashi wa Nihoñ e iku kesshiñ o shita.*) 私は日本へ行く決心をした.
2 (decide) ... o kiʼmeru ...を決める V; keʼttee suru 決定する I: We have to determine the date for the next meeting. (*Tsugi no kaigi no hi o kimenakereba naranai.*) 次の会議の日を決めなければならない.

determined *adj.* kaʼtaku keʼsshiñ shita [shite iru] 堅く決心した[している]; daʼñko to shita [shite iru] 断固とした[している]: He was firmly determined to become a painter. (*Kare wa gaka ni naroo to kataku kes-shiñ shite ita.*) 彼は画家になろうと堅く決心していた.

detest *vt.* ... o hiʼdoku kiʼrau ...をひどく嫌う C; ... ga kiʼrai da ...が嫌いだ: I detest speaking in public. (*Watashi wa hito-mae de hanasu no ga kirai da.*) 私は人前で話すのが嫌いだ.

detour *n.* maʼwariʼmichi 回り道: make a detour (*mawarimichi o suru*) 回り道をする.

develop *vt.* **1** ... o haʼttatsu sa-seru ...を発達させる V; haʼtteñ sase-ru 発展させる V: He developed the little shop into a large supermarket. (*Kare wa sono chiisa-na mise o hatteñ sasete ooki-na suupaa ni shita.*) 彼はその小さな店を発展させて大きなスーパーにした.
2 (of photograph) ... o geʼñzoo suru ...を現像する I: Please develop this film. (*Kono firumu o geñ-zoo shite kudasai.*) このフィルムを現像してください.

development *n.* **1** (growth) haʼttatsu 発達; haʼtteñ 発展: industrial development (*sañgyoo no hat-tatsu*) 産業の発達 / I was surprised at the unexpected development in the case. (*Jikeñ no igai na hatteñ ni watashi wa odoroita.*) 事件の意外な発展に私は驚いた.

2 (of photograph) geⁿzoo 現像.

device n. soˡochi 装置; shiˡkake 仕掛け: a safety device (anˈzeñ soochi) 安全装置.

devil n. (evil) aˡkuma 悪魔; (ogre) oˡni 鬼: speaking of the devil ... (uwasa o sureba ...) うわさをすれば….

devise vt. ... o koˈroañ suru ...を考案する Ⓣ; kaˈñgaedaˡsu 考え出す Ⓒ: He devised a new system of classification. (Kare wa atarashii buñrui hoohoo o kañgaedashita.) 彼は新しい分類方法を考え出した.

devoid adj. ... ga naˡi ...ない; kaˈkete iru 欠けている: He is devoid of common sense. (Kare wa jooshiki ga nai.) 彼は常識がない.

devote vt. ... ni seˈñneñ suru ...に専念する Ⓣ; ... o (... ni) saˈsageru ...を(...に)ささげる Ⓥ: He devoted his fortune to the study of cancer. (Kare wa jibuñ no zaisañ o gañ no keñkyuu ni sasageta.) 彼は自分の財産をがんの研究にささげた.

dew n. tsuˡyu 露: The grass was wet with dew. (Kusa no ue ni tsuyu ga orite ita.) 草の上に露が降りていた.

diabetes n. toˈonyoobyoo 糖尿病.

diagnose vt. ... o shiˈñdañ suru ...を診断する Ⓣ: The doctor diagnosed my illness as pneumonia. (Isha wa watashi no byooki o haieñ to shiñdañ shita.) 医者は私の病気を肺炎と診断した.

diagnosis n. shiˈñdañ 診断: What diagnosis did the doctor make? (Isha wa doñna shiñdañ o shimashita ka?) 医者はどんな診断をしましたか.

diagram n. zu 図; zuˡkee 図形: draw a diagram (zu o kaku) 図をかく.

dial n. (telephone) daˈiyaru ダイヤル; (watch) moˡjibañ 文字盤: turn a dial (daiyaru o mawasu) ダイヤルを回す.

— vt. ... ni deˈñwa o kaˈkeˡru ...に電話をかける Ⓥ: dial the police (keesatsu ni deñwa o kakeru) 警察に電話をかける.

dialect n. hoˈogeˡñ 方言: speak in a dialect (hoogeñ de hanasu) 方言で話す.

dialogue n. taˈiwa 対話: a dialogue between the mayor and citizens (shichoo to shimiñ to no taiwa) 市長と市民との対話.

diameter n. choˈkkee 直径: This circle is one meter in diameter. (Kono eñ wa chokkee ga ichi-meetoru aru.) この円は直径が1メートルある.

diamond n. daˈiyamoˡñdo ダイヤモンド. ★ Often shortened to 'daiya.': a diamond ring (daiya no yubiwa) ダイヤの指輪.

diarrhea n. geˈri 下痢: I have diarrhea. (Watashi wa geri o shite imasu.) 私は下痢をしています.

diary n. niˡkki 日記: keep a diary (nikki o tsukete iru) 日記をつけている.

dictate vt. **1** (secretarial) ... o kaˈkitoraseru ...を書き取らせる Ⓥ; koˈojutsu suru 口述する Ⓣ: dictate a letter to one's secretary (hisho ni tegami o koojutsu suru) 秘書に手紙を口述する.

2 (order) ... o oˈshitsukeˡru ...を押しつける Ⓥ: dictate the terms of a treaty (jooyaku no jookeñ o oshitsukeru) 条約の条件を押しつける.

dictation n. kaˈkitori 書き取り; koˈojutsu 口述: take a dictation (koojutsu o kakitoru) 口述を書き取る.

dictator n. doˈkusaˡisha 独裁者.

dictionary n. jiˈisho 辞書; jiˈiteñ 辞典: consult a dictionary (jisho o hiku) 辞書を引く. ★ English-Japanese dictionaries for Japanese are called 'ee-wa jiteñ' 英和辞典, and for foreigners 'ee-nichi jiteñ' 英日辞典; Japanese-English dictionaries for Japanese are called 'wa-ee jiteñ' 和英辞典, and for foreigners 'nichi-ee jiteñ' 日英辞典.

die vi. (animal) shiˈnu 死ぬ Ⓒ;

(plant) ka⌐reru 枯れる Ⅴ: He died from overwork. (*Kare wa karoo de shiⁿda.*) 彼は過労で死んだ. / This pine tree has died. (*Kono matsu no ki wa karete shimatta.*) この松の木は枯れてしまった.

diet *n.* **1** (regular food) ni⌐chijoo no tabemo⌐no 日常の食べ物; sho⌐ᵗkuji 食事; sho⌐ku-se⌐ekatsu 食生活: a well-balanced diet (*baraⁿsu no toreta shokuji*) バランスのとれた食事.
2 (restricted food) da⌐ietto ダイエット; sho⌐ᵗkujiryo⌐ohoo 食事療法; ge⌐ⁿshoku 減食: I am on a diet. (*Watashi wa daietto o shite imasu.*) 私はダイエットをしています.

Diet *n.* ko⌐ᵗkkai 国会; gi⌐ᵗkai 議会: The Diet is in session. (*Kokkai wa kaikai-chuu desu.*) 国会は開会中です.

differ *vi.* **1** (be unlike) chi⌐gau 違う Ⅽ; ko⌐ᵗtona⌐ru 異なる Ⅽ: His brothers differ in character. (*Kare no kyoodai wa seekaku ga chigau.*) 彼の兄弟は性格が違う.
2 (disagree) i⌐ᵗkeⁿ ga a⌐ᵗwa⌐nai 意見が合わない: I differed with him on the matter. (*Watashi wa sono keⁿ de kare to ikeⁿ ga awanakatta.*) 私はその件で彼と意見が合わなかった.

difference *n.* **1** (being different) chi⌐gai 違い; sa 差: I cannot see any difference in these sentences. (*Kono futatsu no buⁿ no chigai ga wakarimaseⁿ.*) この二つの文の違いがわかりません. / the difference in temperature (*kioⁿ no sa*) 気温の差.
2 (disagreement) so⌐oi 相違: differences of opinion (*ikeⁿ no sooi*) 意見の相違.

different *adj.* **1** (unlike) chi⌐gatta 違った; chi⌐ᵗgatte iru 違っている; ko⌐ᵗtona⌐ᵗtta 異なった; ko⌐ᵗtona⌐ᵗtte iru 異なっている: The article was different from the sample. (*Shinamono wa mihoⁿ to chigatte ita.*) 品物は見本と違っていた.
2 (separate) be⌐ᵗtsu no 別の: I consulted a different doctor. (*Watashi*

wa betsu no isha ni mite moratta.) 私は別の医者に診てもらった.

difficult *adj.* mu⌐ᵗzukashi⌐i 難しい; ko⌐ᵗnnaⁿ na 困難な: Japanese grammar is difficult for me. (*Nihoⁿgo no buⁿpoo wa watashi ni wa muzukashii.*) 日本語の文法は私には難しい. / It is difficult to go across this mountain. (*Kono yama o koeru no wa koⁿnaⁿ desu.*) この山を越えるのは困難です.

difficulty *n.* mu⌐ᵗzuka⌐shisa 難しさ; ko⌐ᵗnnaⁿ 困難: I understood the difficulty of this job. (*Kono shigoto no muzukashisa ga wakarimashita.*) この仕事の難しさがわかりました.

dig *vt.* ... o ho⌐ᵗru ...を掘る Ⅽ; ho⌐ᵗrida⌐su 掘り出す Ⅽ: dig a well (*ido o horu*) 井戸を掘る / dig potatoes (*imo o horidasu*) いもを掘り出す.

digest *vt.* ... o sho⌐ᵗoka suru ...を消化する Ⅰ: Food is digested in the stomach. (*Tabemono wa i de shooka sareru.*) 食べ物は胃で消化される.
— *vi.* sho⌐ᵗoka suru 消化する Ⅰ: He had food that was easy to digest. (*Kare wa shooka no yoi mono o tabeta.*) 彼は消化のよいものを食べた.

digestion *n.* sho⌐ᵗoka 消化: I have a good [poor] digestion. (*Watashi wa i ga joobu da [yowai].*) 私は胃がじょうぶだ[弱い].

digit *n.* **1** (number) su⌐ᵗuji 数字.
2 (place) ke⌐ᵗta 桁: a five-digit number (*go-keta no suu*) 5 桁の数 / the 4th digit (*yoⁿ-baⁿme no keta*) 4 番目の桁.

dignity *n.* ki⌐ᵗhiⁿ 気品; i⌐ᵗgeⁿ 威厳: a person of dignity (*kihiⁿ no aru hito*) 気品のある人 / maintain one's dignity (*igeⁿ o tamotsu*) 威厳を保つ.

dilemma *n.* ji⌐ᵗre⌐ⁿma ジレンマ; i⌐ᵗtaba⌐ᵗsami 板ばさみ: be in a dilemma (*jireⁿma ni ochiiru*) ジレンマに陥る.

diligent *adj.* ki⌐ᵗnbeⁿ na 勤勉な; ne⌐ᵗsshiⁿ na 熱心な: a diligent student (*kiⁿbeⁿ na gakusee*) 勤勉な学

生 / He is diligent in work. (*Kare wa shigoto nesshiñ desu.*) 彼は仕事熱心です.

dim *adj.* **1** (not bright) u⸢sugurai 薄暗い: a dim room (*usugurai heya*) 薄暗い部屋.

2 (unclear) bo⸢ñya¹ri shita [shite iru] ぼんやりした[している]; ha⸢kki¹ri shi⸢nai はっきりしない: I have only a dim memory of the event. (*Sono koto wa boñyari to shika oboete inai.*) そのことはぼんやりとしか覚えていない.

dimension *n.* **1** (size) su⸢ñpoo 寸法: measure the dimensions of a box (*hako no suñpoo o hakaru*) 箱の寸法を測る.

2 (aspect) kyo⸢kumeñ 局面: a new dimension to politics (*seeji no atarashii kyokumeñ*) 政治の新しい局面.

3 (physics) ji⸢geñ 次元: the third dimension (*dai-sañ jigeñ*) 第3次元.

diminish *vi.* he⸢ru 減る C; ge⸢ñ-shoo suru 減少する Ⓘ: The water in the dam is diminishing. (*Damu no mizu ga hette iru.*) ダムの水が減っている.

— *vt.* ... o he⸢rasu ...を減らす C; ge⸢ñshoo saseru 減少させる Ⓥ: diminish the risk of war (*señsoo no kikeñ o herasu*) 戦争の危険を減らす.

dine *vi.* sho⸢kuji o suru 食事をする Ⓘ: What time can I dine? (*Shokuji no jikañ wa nañ-ji desu ka?*) 食事の時間は何時ですか.

dining room *n.* sho⸢kudoo 食堂: What time does the dining room open? (*Shokudoo wa nañ-ji ni hirakimasu ka?*) 食堂は何時に開きますか.

dinner *n.* yu⸢ushoku 夕食; sho⸢kuji 食事: Dinner is ready. (*Yuushoku no yooi ga dekimashita.*) 夕食の用意ができました. / I'd like a drink before dinner. (*Shokuji no mae ni nomimono o kudasai.*) 食事の前に飲み物を下さい.

dip *vt.* **1** (put in) ... o cho⸢tto hi-⸢tasu ...をちょっと浸す C: dip a brush into paint (*hake o peñki ni chotto hitasu*) はけをペンキにちょっと浸す

2 (take out) ... o su⸢kuida¹su ...をすくい出す C; ku⸢mida¹su くみ出す C: dip water from a bucket (*baketsu kara mizu o kumidasu*) バケツから水をくみ出す.

diploma *n.* me⸢ñjoo 免状; (of graduation) so⸢tsugyoo sho¹osho 卒業証書.

diplomacy *n.* ga⸢ikoo 外交.

diplomat *n.* ga⸢iko¹okañ 外交官.

direct *adj.* **1** (straight) ma⸢ssu¹gu na 真っすぐな; i⸢tcho¹kuseñ no 一直線の: a direct road to the station (*eki e tsuujiru massugu na michi*) 駅へ通じる真っすぐな道 / a direct flight from Tokyo to New York (*Tookyoo kara Nyuu Yooku e no chokkoo-biñ*) 東京からニューヨークへの直行便.

2 (immediate) cho⸢kusetsu no 直接の; ji⸢ka no じかの: a direct influence (*chokusetsu no eekyoo*) 直接の影響.

— *adv.* ma⸢ssu¹gu ni 真っすぐに; cho⸢kusetsu ni 直接に; cho⸢kkoo shite 直行して: This plane flies direct to London. (*Kono hikooki wa Roñdoñ e chokkoo shimasu.*) この飛行機はロンドンへ直行します.

— *vt.* **1** (guide) ... ni mi⸢chi o o⸢shieru ...に道を教える Ⓥ: Can you direct me to the station? (*Eki made no michi o oshiete itadakemasu ka?*) 駅までの道を教えていただけますか.

2 (order) ... ni sa⸢shizu suru ...に指図する Ⓘ; me⸢ejiru 命じる Ⓥ: The policeman directed the driver to proceed slowly. (*Keekañ wa uñteñ-sha ni yukkuri susumu yoo meejita.*) 警官は運転者にゆっくり進むよう命じた.

3 (conduct) ... o shi⸢ki¹ suru ...を指揮する Ⓘ; e⸢ñshutsu suru 演出する Ⓘ: direct a choir (*gasshoo o shiki suru*) 合唱を指揮する / direct a play (*geki o eñshutsu suru*) 劇を演出する.

direction *n.* **1** (course) ho⸢rokoo

方向; ho「ogaku 方角: He went in the opposite direction. (*Kare wa hañtai no hookoo e ikimashita.*) 彼は反対の方向へ行きました.

2 (order) shi「ji 指示; sa「shizu 指図: We obeyed the teacher's directions. (*Watashi-tachi wa señsee no shiji ni shitagatta.*) 私たちは先生の指示に従った.

directly *adv.* **1** (straight) ma「ssu⌐gu ni 真っすぐに: I went directly to the hall. (*Watashi wa massugu ni sono kaijoo e itta.*) 私は真っすぐにその会場へ行った.

2 (immediately) cho「kusetsu (ni) 直接(に): I bought the goods directly from the wholesaler. (*Watashi wa sono shina o toñya kara chokusetsu katta.*) 私はその品を問屋から直接買った.

director *n.* (company) ju「uyaku 重役; to「rishimari」yaku 取締役; (screen) ka「ñtoku 監督; (institution) sho「choo 所長; (project) se「kini」ñsha 責任者: a board of directors (*juuyaku-kai*) 重役会.

directory *n.* (name list) ji「ñme」ebo 人名簿: a telephone directory (*deñwachoo*) 電話帳.

dirt *n.* (soil) tsu「chi」 土; (mud) do「ro」 泥; (dust) ho「kori ほこり: remove dirt from trousers (*zuboñ no doro o otosu*) ズボンの泥を落とす.

dirty *adj.* (morally and physically) ki「tana」i 汚い; (physically) yo「goreta 汚れた; yo「gorete iru 汚れている; (covered with mud) do「roda」rake no 泥だらけの: a dirty hand (*kitanai te*) 汚い手 / He wore a dirty shirt. (*Kare wa yogoreta shatsu o kite ita.*) 彼は汚れたシャツを着ていた.

disability *n.* (physical) shi「ñtaisho」ogai 身体障害: mental disability (*seeshiñ-shoogai*) 精神障害.

disabled *adj.* shi「ñtai-sho」ogai no aru 身体障害のある: the disabled (*shiñtai shoogaisha*) 身体障害者.

disadvantage *n.* fu「ri na ta「chiba」 不利な立場; fu「ri na ko「to」 不利なこと: have the disadvantage of being in a bad location (*ritchi joo-keñ ga yokunai to iu furi na teñ ga aru*) 立地条件がよくないという不利な点がある.

disagree *vi.* i「keñ ga a「wa」nai 意見が合わない; i「tchi shinai 一致しない: I disagreed with her. (*Watashi wa kanojo to ikeñ ga awanakatta.*) 私は彼女と意見が合わなかった. / What you say disagrees with the facts. (*Kimi ga itte iru koto wa jijitsu to itchi shinai.*) 君が言っていることは事実と一致しない.

disagreeable *adj.* fu「yu」kai na 不愉快な; i「ya」 na いやな: a disagreeable smell (*iya na nioi*) いやなにおい.

disagreement *n.* fu「i」tchi 不一致; i「keñ no so「oi 意見の相違: There was disagreement between the two reports. (*Futatsu no hookoku no aida ni wa ikeñ no sooi ga atta.*) 二つの報告の間には意見の相違があった.

disappear *vi.* **1** (from sight) mi「e」naku naru 見えなくなる Ⓒ; su「gata o ke「su 姿を消す Ⓒ: The moon disappeared behind a cloud. (*Tsuki wa kumo ni kakurete mienaku natta.*) 月は雲に隠れて見えなくなった.

2 (existence) ki「ete nakunaru 消えてなくなる Ⓒ: The snow soon disappeared. (*Yuki wa sugu ni kiete nakunatta.*) 雪はすぐに消えてなくなった.

disappoint *vt.* ... o ga「kka」ri sa「seru ...をがっかりさせる Ⓥ; shi「tsuboo saseru 失望させる Ⓥ: His remarks disappointed me. (*Kare no hatsugeñ wa watashi o gakkari saseta.*) 彼の発言は私をがっかりさせた.

disappointed *adj.* ga「kka」ri shita [shite iru] がっかりした[している]; shi「tsuboo shita [shite iru] 失望した[している]: I am disappointed with the result. (*Watashi wa sono kekka ni shitsuboo shite imasu.*) 私はその結果に失望しています.

disappointment *n.* shi「tsuboo 失望; ki「tai-ha」zure 期待外れ: The team was a disappointment to us.

(*Sono chiimu wa kitai-hazure datta.*) そのチームは期待外れだった.

disapproval *n.* (non-agreement) fuʃshoʾochi 不承知; fuʃsaʾnsee 不賛成: express one's disapproval (*fusañsee no i o shimesu*) 不賛成の意を示す.

disapprove *vi.* saʾnsee shinai 賛成しない; naʾnshoku o shimeʾsu 難色を示す Ⓒ: My father disapproved of my going abroad. (*Chichi wa watashi ga gaikoku e iku koto ni sañsee shinakatta.*) 父は私が外国へ行くことに賛成しなかった.

disarmament *n.* guʾnbi shuʾkushoo 軍備縮小: nuclear disarmament (*kaku guñshuku*) 核軍縮.

disaster *n.* (literal) saʾigai 災害: a disaster area (*hisaichi*) 被災地 / A lot of people died in the disaster. (*Sono saigai de ooku no hito ga nakunatta.*) その災害で多くの人が亡くなった.

disastrous *adj.* daʾi-saʾigai no 大災害の; hiʾsañ na 悲惨な: a disastrous war (*hisañ na señsoo*) 悲惨な戦争.

discharge *vt.* 1 (release) ... o kaʾihoo suru ...を解放する Ⓘ; shaʾkuhoo suru 釈放する Ⓘ: discharge a prisoner (*shuujiñ o shakuhoo suru*) 囚人を釈放する.
2 (dismiss) ... o kaʾiko suru ...を解雇する Ⓘ: He discharged his secretary. (*Kare wa hisho o kaiko shita.*) 彼は秘書を解雇した.

discipline *n.* 1 (training) kuʾnreñ 訓練; shiʾtsuke しつけ: Home discipline is important. (*Katee no shitsuke ga daiji desu.*) 家庭のしつけが大事です.
2 (order) kiʾritsu 規律; toʾosee 統制: keep [break] discipline (*kiritsu o mamoru [yaburu]*) 規律を守る[破る].

disclose *vt.* ... o aʾkiʾraka ni suru ...を明らかにする Ⓘ; haʾppyoo suru 発表する Ⓘ: disclose a secret (*himitsu o akiraka ni suru*) 秘密を明らかにする.

disco *n.* diʾsuko ディスコ.

discomfort *n.* fuʾkai 不快; fuʾañ 不安.

disconnect *vt.* (pipe, etc.) ... o haʾzusu ...を外す; (telephone, etc.) ... o kiʾru ...を切る Ⓒ: disconnect a plug (*puragu o nuku*) プラグを抜く / I've been disconnected. (*Deñwa ga kirete shimatta.*) 電話が切れてしまった.

discontent *n.* fuʾhee 不平; fuʾmañ 不満.

discord *n.* 1 (disagreement) fuʾiʾtchi 不一致: discord among committee members (*iiñ no aida no ikeñ no fuitchi*) 委員の間の意見の不一致.
2 (argument) fuʾwa 不和: marital discord (*fuufu kañ no fuwa*) 夫婦間の不和.

discount *n.* waʾribiki 割引: Can you give me a discount on this? (*Kore wa waribiki shite morae-masu ka?*) これは割引してもらえますか.
— *vt.* 1 ... o waʾribiʾku ...を割り引く Ⓒ: discount the price 5 percent (*nedañ o go-paaseñto waribiku*) 値段を5%割り引く.
2 (ignore) ... o muʾshi suru ...を無視する Ⓘ: You should discount his story. (*Kare no hanashi wa mushi shita hoo ga ii.*) 彼の話は無視したほうがいい.

discourage *vt.* ... o gaʾkkaʾri saʾseru ...をがっかりさせる Ⓥ; raʾkutañ saseru 落胆させる Ⓥ: The failure discouraged him. (*Sono shippai wa kare o gakkari saseta.*) その失敗は彼をがっかりさせた.

discover *vt.* ... o haʾkkeñ suru ...を発見する Ⓘ; miʾtsukeru 見つける Ⓥ: He discovered a new species of a plant. (*Kare wa shokubutsu no shiñshu o hakkeñ shita.*) 彼は植物の新種を発見した. / I discovered my name on the list. (*Watashi wa meebo ni watashi no namae o mitsuketa.*) 私は名簿に私の名前を見つけた.

discovery *n.* haʾkkeñ 発見: He

made some important discoveries. (*Kare wa ikutsu-ka no juuyoo na hakkeñ o shita.*) 彼はいくつかの重要な発見をした.

discreet *adj.* shi「ryo no aru 思慮のある; fu「ñbetsu no aru 分別のある; shi「ñchoo na 慎重な: He's discreet in his behavior. (*Kare wa koodoo ga shiñchoo da.*) 彼は行動が慎重だ.

discriminate *vt.* (distinguish) ...o ku「betsu suru ...を区別する ⓉⒿ: discriminate synonyms (*dooigo o kubetsu suru*) 同意語を区別する.
— *vi.* (against) sa「betsu suru 差別する ⓉⒿ: discriminate between men and women (*dañsee to josee o sabetsu suru*) 男性と女性を差別する.

discrimination *n.* (prejudice) sa「betsu 差別: racial discrimination (*jiñshu sabetsu*) 人種差別.

discuss *vt.* ... o ha「nashia」u ...を話し合う Ⓒ; to「ogi suru 討議する ⓉⒿ: I discussed the problem with him. (*Watashi wa sono moñdai o kare to hanashiatta.*) 私はその問題を彼と話し合った.

discussion *n.* to「ogi 討議; gi「roñ 議論; ha「nashiai 話し合い: hold a discussion about future plans (*shoorai no keekaku ni tsuite toogi suru*) 将来の計画について討議する.

disease *n.* byo「oki 病気: catch [suffer from] a disease (*byooki ni kakaru*) 病気にかかる / prevent [cure] a disease (*byooki o fusegu [naosu]*) 病気を防ぐ[治す] / a heart disease (*shiñzoo-byoo*) 心臓病.

disembark *vi.* (from a boat) jo「oriku suru 上陸する ⓉⒿ; (from an airplane) o「ri」ru 降りる Ⓒ.

disgrace *n.* (dishonor) fu「me」eyo 不名誉; (shame) ha「ji」 恥: Poverty is no disgrace. (*Mazushii koto wa kesshite haji de wa nai.*) 貧しいことは決して恥ではない.

disguise *vt.* ... o he「ñsoo saseru ...を変装させる Ⓥ: He disguised himself as a policeman. (*Kare wa keekañ ni heñsoo shita.*) 彼は警官に変装した.

— *n.* he「ñsoo 変装; ka「soo 仮装.

disgust *vt.* ... o mu「kamuka sa「seru ...をむかむかさせる Ⓥ; u「ñza」ri sa「seru うんざりさせる Ⓥ: I was disgusted at his behavior. (*Kare no taido ni mukamuka shita.*) 彼の態度にむかむかした.
— *n.* ke「ño 嫌悪; i「yake 嫌気: I left the room in disgust. (*Watashi wa iyake ga sashite heya o deta.*) 私は嫌気がさして部屋を出た.

disgusting *adj.* i「ya」 na いやな: a disgusting smell (*iya na nioi*) いやなにおい.

dish *n.* **1** (plate) sa「ra 皿: serve fruit in a dish (*kudamono o sara ni irete dasu*) 果物を皿に入れて出す. **2** (food) ryo「ori 料理; ta「bemo」no 食べ物: This is my favorite French dish. (*Kore wa watashi no ichibañ suki na Furañsu ryoori desu.*) これは私のいちばん好きなフランス料理だ.

dishonest *adj.* fu「sho」ojiki na 不正直な; fu「see na 不正な: a dishonest transaction (*fusee na tori-hiki*) 不正な取り引き.

dishonor *n.* fu「me」eyo 不名誉; ku「tsujoku 屈辱; ha「ji」 恥: live in dishonor (*kutsujoku no seekatsu o okuru*) 屈辱の生活を送る / a dishonor to one's family (*ie no haji*) 家の恥.

dishwasher *n.* sho「kki-arai」ki 食器洗い機.

disinfect *vt.* ... o sho「odoku suru ...を消毒する ⓉⒿ: disinfect a room (*heya o shoodoku suru*) 部屋を消毒する.

disinfectant *n.* sho「odoku」zai 消毒剤.

disk *n.* e「ñbañ 円盤: disk drive (*disuku doraibu*) ディスクドライブ / a hard disk (*haado disuku*) ハードディスク.

dislike *vt.* ... o ki「rau ...を嫌う Ⓒ; i「yaga」ru いやがる Ⓒ: He seems to dislike me. (*Kare wa watashi o kiratte iru mitai da.*) 彼は私を嫌っているみたいだ. / I dislike living in a large city. (*Dai-toshi ni sumu no* *wa iya da.*) 大都市に住むのはいやだ.

disloyal *adj.* chuᵘjitsu de naˈi 忠
実でない; fuˈjitsu na 不実な.

dismiss *vt.* **1** (discharge) ... o ku-
ˈbi ni suru ...を首にする Ⓣ; kaˈiko
suru 解雇する Ⓣ: He dismissed his
lazy secretary. (*Kare wa namakemono no hisho o kubi ni shita.*) 彼
は怠け者の秘書を首にした.
2 (send away) ... o kaˈisañ suru ...
を解散する Ⓣ: The class was dismissed early today. (*Kyoo wa jugyoo ga hayaku owatta.*) きょうは授
業が早く終わった.

disobey *vt.* ... ni shiˈtagawaˈnai
...に従わない; soˈmuˈku 背く Ⓒ: disobey a superior (*jooshi ni somuku*)
上司に背く.

disorder *n.* **1** (confusion) koˈñrañ
混乱; raˈñzatsu 乱雑: The room is
in disorder. (*Heya ga chirakatte
iru.*) 部屋が散らかっている.
2 (disturbance) soˈodoo 騒動;
boˈodoo 暴動.

dispatch *vt.* (a person) ... o haˈkeñ
suru ...を派遣する Ⓣ: He was dis-
patched to China. (*Kare wa Chuugoku e hakeñ sareta.*) 彼は中国へ派
遣された.

display *vt.* ... o teˈñji suru ...を展示
する Ⓣ; chiˈñretsu suru 陳列する Ⓣ:
display goods for sale (*shoohiñ o
chiñretsu suru*) 商品を陳列する.
— *n.* teˈñji 展示; chiˈñretsu 陳列:
His works are now on display.
(*Kare no sakuhiñ ga ima chiñretsu sarete iru.*) 彼の作品が今陳列され
ている.

displease *vt.* ... o oˈkoraseˈru ...を
怒らせる Ⓥ; fuˈkiˈgeñ ni suru 不機嫌
にする Ⓣ: His remarks displeased
her. (*Kare no hatsugeñ wa kanojo
o okoraseta.*) 彼の発言は彼女を怒らせ
た.

disposable *adj.* tsuˈkaisute no 使
い捨ての: a disposable lighter (*tsu-
kaisute no raitaa*) 使い捨てのライター.

disposal *n.* shoˈbuñ 処分; shoˈri
処理: the disposal of garbage
(*gomi no shori*) ごみの処理.

be at one's disposal *vi.* jiˈyuˈu
ni tsuˈkaeru 自由に使える Ⓥ: This
car is at your disposal. (*Kono
kuruma o jiyuu ni o-tsukai kudasai.*) この車を自由にお使いください.

dispose *vi.* (... o) shoˈbuñ suru (...
を)処分する Ⓣ; kaˈtazukeˈru 片づける
Ⓥ: dispose of garbage [old newspa-
pers] (*gomi [furu-shiñbuñ] o sho-
buñ suru*) ごみ[古新聞]を処分する.

disposition *n.* seˈeshitsu 性質;
kiˈshitsu 気質: a man with a cheerful disposition (*yooki na kihitsu
no hito*) 陽気な気質の人.

dispute *vi.* roˈñsoo suru 論争する
Ⓣ; giˈroñ suru 議論する Ⓣ: dispute
over a problem (*mondai ni tsuite
roñsoo suru*) 問題について論争する.
— *n.* roˈñsoo 論争; fuˈñsoo 紛争:
a labor dispute (*roodoo soogi*) 労働
争議 / a territorial dispute (*ryoodo
fuñsoo*) 領土紛争.

disqualify *vt.* ... no shiˈkaku o to-
ˈriageru ...の資格を取り上げる Ⓥ: He
was disqualified from taking part
in the contest. (*Kare wa sono
kyoogi no shutsujoo shikaku o
toriagerareta.*) 彼はその競技の出場資
格を取り上げられた.

disrupt *vt.* (break up) ... o buˈñre-
tsu saseru ...を分裂させる Ⓥ; (throw
into disorder) koˈñrañ saseru 混乱
させる Ⓥ: Train service was dis-
rupted by an accident. (*Ressha no
unkoo ga jiko no tame ni koñrañ
shita.*) 列車の運行が事故のために混乱
した.

dissatisfaction *n.* fuˈmañ 不満;
fuˈhee 不平: express one's dissatisfaction (*fumañ o noberu*) 不満を述
べる.

dissatisfied *adj.* fuˈmañ na 不満
な; fuˈhee na 不平な: He seemed
dissatisfied with the terms. (*Kare
wa sono jookeñ ni fumañ no yoo
datta.*) 彼はその条件に不満のようだった.

dissent *vi.* doˈoi shinai 同意しない;
haˈñtai suru 反対する Ⓣ: Two members dissented from our conclusion.
(*Futari ga watashi-tachi no ketsu-*

roñ ni hañtai shita.) 二人が私たちの
結論に反対した.

dissident adj. (opinion) iˈkeñ ga
chiˈgau 意見が違う; (anti-regime)
haˈñtaˈisee no 反体制の.
— n. iˈkeñ no chiˈgau hitoˈ 意見の
違う人; haˈñtaˈisee no hiˈtoˈ 反体制
の人.

dissolve vt. **1** (make liquid) ... o
toˈkaˈsu ...を溶かす Ⓒ: dissolve salt
in water (shio o mizu ni tokasu) 塩
を水に溶かす.
2 (break up) ... o kaˈisañ suru ...を
解散する Ⓣ: dissolve a parliament
(gikai o kaisañ suru) 議会を解散す
る.
— vi. toˈkeˈru 溶ける Ⓥ; kaˈisañ
suru 解散する Ⓣ.

distance n. kyoˈri 距離: The distance from here to the station is
two kilometers. (Koko kara eki
made no kyori wa ni-kiro desu.) こ
こから駅までの距離は2キロです.

distant adj. toˈoi 遠い; haˈnaˈreta
離れた; haˈnaˈrete iru 離れている: a
distant country (tooi kuni) 遠い国 /
The town is distant from Tokyo.
(Sono machi wa Tookyoo kara
hanarete iru.) その町は東京から離れて
いる.

distinct adj. **1** (different) beˈtsu
no 別の; chiˈgatta 違った; chiˈgatte
iru 違っている: His method is quite
distinct from ours. (Kare no yarikata wa wareware no to mattaku
chigatte iru.) 彼のやり方はわれわれのと
まったく違っている.
2 (clear) haˈkkiˈri shita [shite iru]
はっきりした[している]; meˈeryoo na 明
瞭な: She gave me a distinct refusal. (Kanojo wa hakkiri to watashi
ni kotowatta.) 彼女ははっきりと私に
断った.

distinction n. kuˈbetsu 区別; chi-
ˈgai 違い; toˈkuchoo 特徴: It is
important to draw a distinction between official and personal affairs.
(Kooshi no kubetsu o tsukeru koto
ga taisetsu desu.) 公私の区別をつける
ことが大切です. / I can see no dis-

tinction between these plants.
(Kore-ra no shokubutsu no chigai
ga wakaranai.) これらの植物の違いが
わからない.

distinguish vt. ... o kuˈbetsu suru
...を区別する Ⓣ; miˈwakeru 見分ける
Ⓥ: The uniforms are so alike that
it is diffiuclt to distinguish the two
teams. (Yunifoomu ga amari nite
iru no de ryoo chiimu no kubetsu
ga muzukashii.) ユニフォームがあまり
似ているので両チームの区別が難しい.

distinguished adj. **1** (of a person) yuˈumee na 有名な; choˈmee
na 著名な: a distinguished writer
(chomee na sakka) 著名な作家.
2 (of quality) suˈguˈreta 優れた;
suˈguˈrete iru 優れている: a distinguished performance (sugureta
eñgi) 優れた演技.

distort vt. **1** (twist) ... o yuˈga-
meru ...をゆがめる Ⓥ; neˈjiˈru ねじる
Ⓒ: His face was distorted with
pain. (Kare no kao wa kutsuu de
yugañda.) 彼の顔は苦痛でゆがんだ.
2 (of truth, etc.) ... o maˈgeru ...を
曲げる Ⓥ: distort the truth (shiñjitsu o mageru) 真実を曲げる.

distract vt. ... o soˈraˈsu ...をそらす
Ⓒ; maˈgiraˈsu 紛らす Ⓒ: The noise
distracted his attention. (Sono soo-
oñ ga kare no chuui o sorashita.)
その騒音が彼の注意をそらした.

distress n. (worry) naˈyamiˈ 悩み;
kuˈrushimi 苦しみ; (sorrow) kaˈna-
shimi 悲しみ.
— vt. ... o naˈyamaˈsu ...を悩ます
Ⓒ; kuˈrushimeˈru 苦しめる Ⓥ;
kaˈnashimaseˈru 悲しませる Ⓥ: I
was distressed at the bad news.
(Watashi wa sono warui shirase
ni kokoro o itameta.) 私はその悪い知
らせに心を痛めた.

distribute vt. ... o kuˈbaˈru ...を配
る Ⓒ; buˈñpai suru 分配する Ⓣ:
The teacher distributed handouts
to the students. (Señsee wa seeto
ni puriñto o kubatta.) 先生は生徒に
プリントを配った.

distribution n. buˈñpai 分配;

haˈifu 配布: distribution of profit (*rieki no buñpai*) 利益の分配.

district *n.* 1 (region of a country) chiˈhoˈo 地方: the Kantoo district (*Kañtoo chihoo*) 関東地方.

2 (area of a city) chiˈku 地区: the business district of a city (*shi no shoogyoo chiku*) 市の商業地区 / an electoral district (*señkyoku*) 選挙区 / a shopping district (*shooteñgai*) 商店街.

distrust *vt.* ... o shiˈñyoo shinai ... を信用しない; uˈtagau 疑う C: distrust one's own eyes (*jibuñ no me o utagau*) 自分の目を疑う.
— *n.* fuˈshiñ 不信; giˈwaku 疑惑: I have a distrust of what he says. (*Kare ga iu koto wa shiñyoo shimaseñ.*) 彼が言うことは信用しません.

disturb *vt.* 1 (interrupt) ... o jaˈma suru ...をじゃまする ①; saˈmatageˈru 妨げる Ⓥ: Don't disturb me while I'm working. (*Shigoto o shite iru toki jama o shinaide kudasai.*) 仕事をしているときじゃまをしないでください.

2 (worry) ... o shiˈñpai saseru ...を心配させる Ⓥ; fuˈañ ni suru 不安にする ①: The news of the accident disturbed her. (*Sono jiko no shirase wa kanojo o fuañ ni shita.*) その事故の知らせは彼女を不安にした.

3 (stir up) ... o kaˈkimidaˈsu ...をかき乱す C: The wind disturbed the papers on the desk. (*Kaze ga tsukue no ue no shorui o kakimidashita.*) 風が机の上の書類をかき乱した.

ditch *n.* miˈzo 溝; doˈbu どぶ; haˈisuˈikoo 排水溝: an irrigation ditch (*yoosuiro*) 用水路.

dive *vi.* 1 (plunge) (... ni) toˈbikoˈmu (...に)飛び込む C: He dived into the river. (*Kare wa kawa ni tobikoñda.*) 彼は川に飛び込んだ.

2 (go under) (... ni) moˈguˈru (...に)潜る C: dive for pearls (*shiñju o toru tame ni mizu ni moguru*) 真珠を採るために水に潜る.

diverse *adj.* saˈmaˈzama na さまざまな; iˈroiro na いろいろな: He has

diverse interests. (*Kare wa samazama na shumi o motte iru.*) 彼はさまざまな趣味をもっている.

diversity *n.* taˈyoosee 多様性; saˈmaˈzama na koˈtoˈ さまざまなこと; soˈoi 相違: a diversity of opinions (*samazama na ikeñ*) さまざまな意見.

divide *vt.* 1 (separate) ... o waˈkeˈru ...を分ける Ⓥ; buˈñkatsu suru 分割する ①: divide a large room into four (*ooki-na heya o yottsu ni wakeru*) 大きな部屋を四つに分ける.

2 (distribute) ... o waˈkeˈru ...を分ける Ⓥ; buˈñpai suru 分配する ①: They divided the money among themselves. (*Kare-ra wa sono okane o jibuñ-tachi de waketa.*) 彼らはそのお金を自分たちで分けた.

3 (of mathematics) ... o waˈru ...を割る C: divide 8 by 2 (*hachi o ni de waru*) 8 を 2 で割る.
— *vi.* waˈkareˈru 分かれる Ⓥ; waˈreru 割れる Ⓥ: The road divides into two here. (*Michi wa koko de futatsu ni wakaremasu.*) 道はここで二つに分かれます.

dividend *n.* haˈitookiñ 配当金.

divine *adj.* (absolute) kaˈmi no 神の; (holy) shiˈñsee na 神聖な: divine grace (*kami no megumi*) 神の恵み.

diving *n.* toˈbikomi 飛び込み; daˈibiñgu ダイビング: scuba diving (*sukyuuba daibiñgu*) スキューバダイビング.

diving board *n.* toˈbi-ita 飛び板; toˈbikomidai 飛び込み台.

division *n.* 1 (separation) buˈñkatsu 分割; (distribution) buˈñpai 分配: a division of profits (*rieki no buñpai*) 利益の分配.

2 (section) kyoˈku 局; bu 部; ka 課: the sales division (*hañbai-bu*) 販売部.

3 (mathematics) waˈriˈzañ 割り算: problems in division (*warizañ no moñdai*) 割り算の問題.

divorce *n.* riˈkoñ 離婚: get a divorce from one's husband (*otto to rikoñ suru*) 夫と離婚する.

— vt. ... to ri「koń suru ...と離婚する ①: We got divorced two years ago. (*Watashi-tachi wa ni-neń mae ni rikoń shimashita.*) 私たちは 2 年前に離婚しました.

dizzy *adj.* me「ma」i ga suru めまいがする: I feel dizzy. (*Watashi wa me-mai ga shimasu.*) 私は目まいがします.

do *vt.* ... o su「ru ...をする ①; o「konau 行う ②: do the shopping [cooking] (*kaimono [ryoori] o suru*) 買い物[料理]をする / What are you doing now? (*Anata wa ima nani o shite imasu ka?*) あなたは今何をしていますか. / What should I do? (*Doo sureba ii deshoo ka?*) どうすればいいでしょうか.
— vi. su「ru する ①; ya「ru やる ②: You have done well. (*Yoku yarima-shita.*) よくやりました.

dock *n.* do「kku ドック: a floating dock (*uki dokku*) 浮きドック.

doctor *n.* **1** (physician) i「sha 医者: see a doctor (*isha ni mite morau*) 医者に診てもらう / Can you get a doctor? (*Isha o yońde moraemasu ka?*) 医者を呼んでもらえますか.
2 (a person with a degree) ha「kase [ha「kushi] 博士: a Doctor of Science (*rigaku hakase*) 理学博士.

doctrine *n.* (politics) shu「gi 主義; (religion) kyo「ogi 教義: preach a doctrine (*kyoogi o toku*) 教義を説く.

document *n.* bu「ńsho 文書; sho「rui 書類: draw up a document (*shorui o sakusee suru*) 書類を作成する / an official document (*koobuń-sho*) 公文書.

documentary *n.* (film) ki「roku-e「lega 記録映画.

dodge *vt.* ... o yo「ke」ru ...をよける ⑤; sa「ke」ru 避ける ⑤: dodge a ball (*booru o yokeru*) ボールをよける.

dog *n.* i「nu」犬: He keeps two dogs. (*Kare wa inu o ni-hiki katte iru.*) 彼は犬を 2 匹飼っている. / I was bitten by a dog. (*Watashi wa inu ni kamareta.*) 私は犬にかまれた.

doghouse *n.* i「nugoya 犬小屋.

doings *n.* o「konai 行い; ko「odoo 行動; ko「oi 行為.

doll *n.* ni「ńgyoo 人形: play with a doll (*ńgyoo de asobu*) 人形で遊ぶ.

dollar *n.* do「ru ドル: Can I change dollars here? (*Koko de doru o kaeraremasu ka?*) ここでドルを換えられますか. / What is the dollar rate? (*Doru wa ikura desu ka?*) ドルはいくらですか.

dolphin *n.* i「ruka いるか.

dome *n.* ma「ruyane 丸屋根; ma-「rute」ńjoo 丸天井; do「omu ドーム.

domestic *adj.* **1** (of the home) ka「tee no 家庭の; ka「tee-teki na 家庭的な: domestic chores (*kaji*) 家事.
2 (not foreign) ko「ku」nai no 国内の; ji「koku no 自国の: domestic news (*kokunai nyuusu*) 国内ニュース / a domestic flight (*kokunai-biń*) 国内便 / a domestic animal (*kachiku*) 家畜.

dominant *adj.* shi「hai-teki na 支配的な; yu「usee na 優勢な: dominant opinion against the tax increase (*zoozee ni hańtai suru shi-hai-teki na ikeń*) 増税に反対する支配的な意見.

dominate *vt.* ... o shi「hai suru ...を支配する ①: The stronger person dominates the weaker. (*Tsuyoi mono ga yowai mono o shihai suru.*) 強い者が弱い者を支配する.

donate *vt.* **1** (money, etc.) ... o ki「fu suru ...を寄付する ①; ki「zoo suru 寄贈する ①: I donated some money to the fund. (*Watashi wa o-kane o ikura-ka sono kikiń ni kifu shita.*) 私はお金をいくらかその基金に寄付した.
2 (organs) ... o te「ekyoo suru ...を提供する ①; (blood) keńketsu suru 献血する ①.

donation *n.* ki「fu 寄付; (especially money) ki「fu」kiń 寄付金: blood donation (*keńketsu*) 献血.

donkey *n.* ro「ba ろば.

donor *n.* ki「zo」osha 寄贈者; te「e-kyo」osha 提供者: a heart donor (*shińzoo teekyoosha*) 心臓提供者 / a blood donor (*keńketsusha*) 献血者.

donut n. do.onatsu ドーナツ.

door n. d.oa ドア; to 戸; to.bira 扉:
open [close] a door (doa o akeru
[shimeru]) ドアを開ける[閉める] / Did
you lock the door? (Doa ni kagi o
kakemashita ka?) ドアに鍵をかけまし
たか. / a front door (geñkañ) 玄関 /
a back door (katteguchi) 勝手口.

dormitory n. ryo.o 寮.

dose n. (of medicine) i.ppuku 1 服;
(quantity) fu.kuyoo.ryoo 服用量:
Take three doses a day. (Ichi-nichi
sañ-kai fukuyoo no koto.) 1 日 3 回
服用のこと.

dot n. te.ñ 点: put a dot over the letter i (ai no ji no ue ni teñ o utsu) I
の字の上に点を打つ.

on the dot adv. ki.kka.ri ni きっか
りに.

double adj. **1** (twice) ni-.bai no 2
倍の: His pay is double my pay.
(Kare no kyuuryoo wa watashi no
ni-bai da.) 彼の給料は私の 2 倍だ.
2 (layers) ni-.juu no 二重の: dou-
ble-glazed windows (ni-juu mado)
二重窓.
— adv. ni-.bai 2 倍: I'll pay double. (Watashi wa ni-bai haraimasu.)
私は 2 倍払います.
— vt. ... o ni-.bai ni suru ...を 2 倍
にする □; ni-.juu ni suru 二重にする
□: double the sales (uriage o ni-
bai ni suru) 売り上げを 2 倍にする.
— vi. ni-.bai ni na.ru 2 倍になる ©:
The population of this town has
doubled. (Kono machi no jiñkoo
wa ni-bai ni natta.) この町の人口は 2
倍になった.

doubt vt. ... o u.tagau ...を疑う ©:
gi.moñ ni omo.u 疑問に思う ©: I
doubt his innocence. (Watashi wa
kare no mujitsu o utagau.) 私は彼の
無実を疑う. / I doubt if she will
come. (Kanojo ga kuru ka doo ka
gimoñ ni omou.) 彼女が来るかどうか
疑問に思う.
— n. u.tagai 疑い; gi.moñ 疑問:
There is some doubt whether he
will succeed. (Kare ga seekoo suru
ka doo ka gimoñ da.) 彼が成功する

かどうか疑問だ.

no doubt adv. o.so.raku 恐らく;
ki.tto きっと: No doubt he will win.
(Osoraku kare wa katsu deshoo.)
恐らく彼は勝つでしょう.

doubtful adj. u.tagawashi.i 疑わし
い; ka.kushiñ ga na.i 確信がない: I
am doubtful whether he will agree
to our suggestions. (Kare ga wareware no teeañ ni sañsee suru ka
doo ka utagawashii.) 彼がわれわれの
提案に賛成するかどうか疑わしい.

doubtless adv. ta.buñ たぶん; ta.-
shika ni 確かに: He will doubtless
come later. (Kare wa tabuñ ato
kara kuru deshoo.) 彼はたぶん後から
来るでしょう.

dove n. ha.to はと. ★ 'Pigeon' is
also called 'hato.'

down adv. shi.ta e 下へ; hi.ku.i hoo
e 低い方へ: jump down from a tree
(ki kara tobioriru) 木から跳び下りる
/ pull the blinds down (buraiñdo o
orosu) ブラインドを下ろす.
— prep. ... no shi.ta e ...の下へ; ...
no ka.hoo ni ...の下方に: go down a
hill (oka o kudaru) 丘を下る / The
bridge is about two kilometers
down the stream. (Sono hashi wa
nagare no yaku ni-kiro karyuu ni
aru.) その橋は流れの約 2 キロ下流にある.
— adj. ka.hoo e no 下方への; ku.-
dari no 下りの: a down elevator
(kudari no erebeetaa) 下りのエレベー
ター / a down train (kudari ressha)
下り列車.

downstairs adv. ka.ika e 階下へ:
go downstairs (kaika e oriru) 階下
へ降りる.
— adj. ka.ika no 階下の: a downstairs room (kaika no heya) 階下の
部屋.

downtown n. (commercial center) ha.ñka.gai 繁華街; (city center) to.shi.ñbu 都心部: go downtown shopping (hañkagai e kaimono ni iku) 繁華街へ買い物に行く.

downward adv. shi.ta no ho.o e
下の方へ; shi.tamuki ni 下向きに:
The elevator went downward. (Ere-

beetaa wa shita e ikimashita.) エレベーターは下へ行きました.

— *adj.* ka「hoo e no 下方への; shi「tamuki no 下向きの: a downward slope (*kudarizaka*) 下り坂.

doze *vi.* i「nemu」ri suru 居眠りする ①; u「touto suru うとうとする ①: I dozed off during the lecture. (*Watashi wa koogi no aida utouto shite shimatta.*) 私は講義の間うとうとしてしまった.

dozen *n.* da「asu ダース: one [two] dozen (*ichi* [*ni*] *daasu*) 1 [2]ダース.

draft *n.* **1** (rough copy) shi「tagaki 下書き; so「oañ 草案: make a draft of a report (*repooto no shitagaki o suru*) レポートの下書きをする.

2 (current of air) su「kima」kaze すきま風; tsu「ufuu 通風: keep out drafts (*sukimakaze o fusegu*) すきま風を防ぐ.

3 (order for payment) ka「wase-te」gata 為替手形: draw a draft on a bank (*giñkoo ate ni tegata o furi-dasu*) 銀行宛に手形を振り出す.

drag *vt.* **1** (physically) ... o hi「ppa」ru ...を引っぱる ©; hi「kizuru 引きずる ©: We dragged the heavy table across the floor. (*Watashi-tachi wa sono omoi teeburu o hikizutte yuka no ue o ugokashita.*) 私たちはその重いテーブルを引きずって床の上を動かした.

2 (figuratively) ... ni hi「kiko」mu ...に引き込む ©: He was dragged into a fight. (*Kare wa keñka ni hiki-komareta.*) 彼はけんかに引き込まれた.

drain *vt.* **1** (make flow away) ... no ha「isui o suru ...の排水をする ①: drain the water away from the playground (*uñdoojoo no haisui o su-ru*) 運動場の排水をする.

2 (remove water) ... no mi「zu o ki」ru ...の水を切る ©: She washed the spinach and drained it. (*Ka-nojo wa hooreñsoo o aratte mizu o kitta.*) 彼女はほうれんそうを洗って水を切った.

drama *n.* (play) ge「ki 劇; shi「bai 芝居; do「rama ドラマ; (study) e「ñgeki

演劇: act a drama (*shibai o jooeñ suru*) 芝居を上演する.

dramatic *adj.* **1** (of a play) e「ñgeki no 演劇の: dramatic works (*eñgeki sakuhiñ*) 演劇作品.

2 (exciting) ge「kiteki na 劇的な: a dramatic incident (*gekiteki na jikeñ*) 劇的な事件.

drastic *adj.* o「mo」ikitta 思い切った; te「ttee-teki na 徹底的な: adopt drastic measures (*omoikitta shu-dañ o toru*) 思い切った手段をとる.

draw *vt.* **1** (sketch) ... o e「ga」ku ...を描く ©; ka「ku かく ©; (of a line) hi「ku 引く ©: Please draw a map here. (*Koko ni chizu o kaite kuda-sai.*) ここに地図をかいてください / draw a straight line (*chokuseñ o hiku*) 直線を引く.

2 (pull) ... o hi「ku ...を引く ©; hi「ppa」ru 引っぱる ©: draw a curtain (*kaateñ o hiku*) カーテンを引く.

3 (attract) ... o hi「kitsuke」ru ...を引きつける Ⓥ; hi「ku 引く ©: He tried to draw her attention. (*Kare wa kanojo no chuui o hikoo to shita.*) 彼は彼女の注意を引こうとした.

4 (get) ... o hi「kida」su ...を引き出す ©; o「ro」su おろす ©: I have to draw some money from the bank. (*Wata-shi wa giñkoo kara ikura-ka o-kane o orosanakereba naranai.*) 私は銀行からいくらかお金を下ろさなければならない.

5 (breathe) ... o su「u ...を吸う ©: draw a deep breath (*iki o fukaku suu*) 息を深く吸う.

drawer *n.* hi「kidashi 引き出し: open [shut] a drawer (*hikidashi o akeru* [*shimeru*]) 引き出しを開ける [閉める].

drawing *n.* e「 絵; zu 図: She made a drawing of vegetables. (*Kanojo wa yasai no e o kaita.*) 彼女は野菜の絵をかいた.

dread *vt.* ... o o「sore」ru ...を恐れる Ⓥ; ko「waga」ru 怖がる ©: The boy dreaded visiting the dentist. (*Sono otoko-no-ko wa haisha e iku no o kowagatta.*) その男の子は歯医者へ行

くのを怖がった.
— *n.* kyo「ofu 恐怖; fu「añ 不安.

dreadful *adj.* o「soroshi¹i 恐ろしい;
ko「wa¹i 怖い: a dreadful accident
(*osoroshii jiko*) 恐ろしい事故.

dream *n.* yu「me¹i 夢: I had a
curious dream last night. (*Yuube
wa omoshiroi yume o mita.*) ゆうべ
はおもしろい夢を見た. / It is my dream
to live in the country. (*Inaka de
kurasu no ga watashi no yume
desu.*) 田舎で暮らすのが私の夢です.
— *vi.* yu「me¹ o miru 夢を見る 図: I
seldom dream. (*Watashi wa metta
ni yume o minai.*) 私はめったに夢を見
ない.

dreamer *n.* yu「memi¹ru hi「to¹ 夢見
る人; ku「usooka 空想家.

dress *n.* **1** (women's garment) fu-
「ji¹ñfuku 婦人服; do「resu ドレス;
wa「ñpi¹isu ワンピース: She wore a
pretty dress. (*Kanojo wa kiree na
wañpiisu o kite ita.*) 彼女はきれいな
ワンピースを着ていた.
2 (clothes) fu「kusoo 服装; i¹fuku 衣
服: full [formal] dress (*seesoo*) 正
装 / casual dress (*fudañgi*) 普段着
— *vt.* ... ni fu「ku¹ o ki「seru ...に服を
着せる 図: dress a doll (*niñgyoo ni
fuku o kiseru*) 人形に服を着せる.
— *vi.* fu「ku¹ o ki「ru 服を着る 図: I
dressed in my best suit. (*Watashi
wa ichibañ ii sebiro o kita.*) 私はい
ちばんいい背広を着た.

dressing *n.* **1** (bandage) ho「otai
包帯.
2 (salad dressing) do「re¹sshiñgu ド
レッシング.

dressmaker *n.* do「resu me¹ekaa
ドレスメーカー; yo「osa¹ishi 洋裁師.

drift *vi.* **1** (being driven) hyo「o-
ryuu suru 漂流する 囗; ta「dayo¹u 漂
う 囨: The boat was drifting on the
sea. (*Sono booto wa umi no ue o
hyooryuu shite ita.*) そのボートは海の
上を漂流していた.
2 (without purpose) ma「ñzeñ to
sugo¹su 漫然と過ごす 囨: drift
through life (*jiñsee o mañzeñ to
sugosu*) 人生を漫然と過ごす.

— *vt.* (snow) ... o fu「kitsumorase-
ru ...を吹き積もらせる 図: The wind
drifted the snow. (*Kaze ga yuki o
fukitsumoraseta.*) 風が雪を吹き積も
らせた.

drill *n.* **1** (tool) ki「ri¹ きり; do「riru ド
リル: use a drill to make a hole (*ana
o akeru no ni kiri o tsukau*) 穴を開
けるのにきりを使う.
2 (exercise) re「ñshuu 練習; ku「ñreñ
訓練: drills in Japanese pronunciation (*Nihoñgo no hatsuoñ reñshuu*) 日本語の発音練習.
— *vt.* **1** (make a hole) ... ni a「na¹
o a「keru ...に穴を開ける 図: drill a
hole in the wall (*kabe ni ana o
akeru*) 壁に穴を開ける.
2 (train) ... o re「ñshuu saseru ...を
練習させる 図; o「shieko¹mu 教え込む
囮: The teacher drilled the class in
sentence patterns. (*Señsee wa
kurasu ni buñkee o oshiekoñda.*)
先生はクラスに文型を教え込んだ.

drink *vt.* ... o no¹mu ...を飲む 囮:
Can I drink this water? (*Kono mizu wa nomemasu ka?*) この水は飲め
ますか. / I want something to drink.
(*Nani-ka nomimono ga hoshii.*) 何
か飲み物が欲しい.
— *vi.* no¹mu 飲む 囮; sa「ke o no¹-
mu 酒を飲む 囮: I drank too much.
(*Nomi-sugimashita.*) 飲み過ぎました.
— *n.* no「mimono 飲み物; sa「ke
酒: I'd like a drink before dinner.
(*Shokuzeñshu o kudasai.*) 食前酒を
下さい.

drip *vi.* po「tapota o「chi¹ru ぽたぽた落
ちる 図: The faucet is dripping.
(*Jaguchi kara mizu ga potapota
ochite iru.*) 蛇口から水がぽたぽた落ち
ている.
— *n.* shi「tatari したたり; shi「zuku¹
しずく: drips of sweat (*ase no shizuku*) 汗のしずく.

drive *vt.* **1** (control) ... o u「ñteñ
suru ...を運転する 囗: I can drive a
bus. (*Watashi wa basu o uñteñ dekiru.*) 私はバスを運転できる.
2 (urge) ... o o「itate¹ru 追い立てる
図; ka「ritate¹ru 駆り立てる 図: drive

the cattle to the fields (*ushi o no-hara e oiyaru*) 牛を野原へ追いやる.
— *vi*. (car) ku⌐ruma o uñteñ suru 車を運転する Ⅰ; do⌐ra¬ibu suru ドライブする Ⅰ: We drove around the city. (*Watashi-tachi wa shinai o doraibu shita.*) 私たちは市内をドライブした.

driver *n*. u⌐ñte¬ñshu 運転手: a taxi driver (*takushii no uñteñshu*) タクシーの運転手.

driveway *n*. sha⌐doo 車道. ★ Japanese does not have a word for 'driveway' especially in its North American sense. A road on private property leading for a public street '*koodoo*' 公道 is a '*shidoo*' 私道 but this can refer to a road on a farm as well. '*Shadoo*' can refer to any public or private street.

droop *vi*. (person) u⌐nadareru うなだれる Ⅴ; (plant) shi⌐oreru しおれる Ⅴ: Her head drooped sadly. (*Kanojo wa kanashi-soo ni unadareta.*) 彼女は悲しそうにうなだれた. / The flowers drooped because they had no water. (*Mizu ga nai no de hana ga shiorete shimatta.*) 水がないので花がしおれてしまった.

drop *vi*. (thing) o⌐chi¬ru 落ちる Ⅴ; (price, temperature) sa⌐ga¬ru 下がる Ⓒ: The boy dropped from a tree. (*Sono otoko-no-ko wa ki kara ochita.*) その男の子は木から落ちた. / Stock prices dropped sharply. (*Kabuka ga kyuugeki ni sagatta.*) 株価が急激に下がった.
— *vt*. ... o o⌐to¬su ...を落とす Ⓒ: You dropped your notebook. (*Techoo o otoshimashita yo.*) 手帳を落としましたよ.

drop out *vi*. (of school) chu⌐uto ta¬igaku suru 中途退学する Ⅰ.
— *n*. (water) shi⌐zuku¬ しずく; i⌐t-teki 一滴; (price) ge⌐raku 下落; (temperature) ka⌐koo 下降: drops of rain (*ame no shizuku*) 雨のしずく / There was not a drop of water. (*Mizu wa it-teki mo nakatta.*) 水は一滴もなかった. / a sudden drop of

temperature (*oñdo no totsuzeñ no kakoo*) 温度の突然の下降.

drown *vi*. o⌐boreshi¬nu おぼれ死ぬ Ⓒ; su⌐ishi suru 水死する Ⅰ: He almost drowned in the river. (*Kare wa kawa de oboreshinu tokoro datta.*) 彼は川でおぼれ死ぬところだった.

drug *n*. (narcotic) ma⌐yaku 麻薬; (medicine) ku⌐suri 薬: a drug addict (*mayaku jooshuusha*) 麻薬常習者 / take drugs (*mayaku o utsu*) 麻薬を打つ.

drugstore *n*. do⌐raggusuto¬a ドラッグストア. ★ In Japan, there are pharmacies, but no stores equivalent to drugstores.

drum *n*. **1** (musical instrument) ta⌐iko 太鼓: beat a drum (*taiko o tataku*) 太鼓をたたく.
2 (for oil, etc.) do⌐ramukañ ドラム缶.

drunk *adj*. yo⌐tta 酔った; yo⌐tte iru 酔っている; yo⌐ppa-ratta 酔っぱらった; yo⌐pparatte iru 酔っぱらっている: drunk driving (*yopparai uñteñ*) 酔っぱらい運転 / I got drunk on whisky. (*Watashi wa uisukii de yopparatta.*) 私はウイスキーで酔っぱらった.

dry *adj*. **1** (not wet) ka⌐waita 乾いた; ka⌐wa¬itte iru 乾いている; ka⌐ñ-soo shita [shite iru] 乾燥した[している]: dry air (*kawaita kuuki*) 乾いた空気 / The clothes are dry now. (*Fuku wa moo kawaite imasu.*) 服はもう乾いています.
2 (wine) ka⌐rakuchi no 辛口の: I like dry white wine. (*Watashi wa karakuchi no shiro-waiñ ga suki desu.*) 私は辛口の白ワインが好きです.
— *vt*. ... o ka⌐waka¬su ...を乾かす Ⓒ; ho⌐¬su 干す Ⓒ: He dried his wet trousers in front of the fire. (*Kare wa nureta zuboñ o hi no mae de kawakashita.*) 彼はぬれたズボンを火の前で乾かした.

dry cleaner *n*. do⌐rai-kuriiniñgu-ya ドライクリーニング屋. ★ In every-day conversation, the dry cleaner's will often be called '*señtakuya*' 洗濯屋.

duck *n*. (domestic) a⌐hiru あひる(家

鴨); (wild) ka⌐mo かも(鴨).

due adj. **1** (payable) shi⌐harawana⌐kereba na⌐ra⌐nai 支払わなければならない; shi⌐harai kijitsu ga ki⌐te iru 支払期日がきている: The bill is due today. (Sono seekyuusho wa kyoo shiharawanakereba narimaseñ.) その請求書はきょう支払わなければなりません.

2 (proper) to⌐ozeñ no 当然の; se⌐etoo na 正当な: I drove with due care. (Watashi wa toozeñ no chuui o haratte uñteñ shita.) 私は当然の注意を払って運転した.

3 (expected) ...koto ni na⌐tte iru ...ことになっている; ...ha⌐zu da ...はずだ: He is due to come at seven. (Kare wa shichi-ji ni kuru hazu ni natte iru.) 彼は7時に来るはずになっている.

due to ... prep. ... no ta⌐me⌐ ni ...のために: Due to the snow the train was delayed. (Yuki no tame ni ressha ga okureta.) 雪のために列車が遅れた.

dull adj. **1** (uninteresting) tsu⌐mara⌐nai つまらない; o⌐moshi⌐roku nai おもしろくない: a dull book (tsumaranai hoñ) つまらない本.

2 (weak) ni⌐bu⌐i 鈍い: a dull pain (nibui itami) 鈍い痛み.

3 (blunt) ki⌐re⌐aji no wa⌐ru⌐i 切れ味の悪い; na⌐makura na なまくらな: a dull knife (kireaji no warui naifu) 切れ味の悪いナイフ.

4 (stupid) a⌐tama no nibu⌐i 頭の鈍い: a dull pupil (atama no nibui seeto) 頭の鈍い生徒.

5 (not clear) ha⌐kki⌐ri shinai はっきりしない: dull weather (hakkiri shinai teñki) はっきりしない天気.

dumb adj. **1** (mute) ku⌐chi no [ga] kikenai 口の[が]きけない; mo⌐no⌐ o i⌐enai 物を言えない: The child was born dumb. (Sono ko wa umare nagara kuchi ga kikenakatta.) その子は生まれながら口がきけなかった.

2 (silent) da⌐ma⌐tte iru 黙っている: He remained dumb about his activities. (Kare wa jibuñ no koodoo ni tsuite damatte ita.) 彼は自分の行動について黙っていた.

dump vt. ... o na⌐gesuteru ...を投げ捨てる Ⓥ: Don't dump rubbish into the river. (Gomi o kawa e nagesutete wa ikemaseñ.) ごみを川へ投げ捨ててはいけません.
— n. go⌐misuteba ごみ捨て場.

duplicate n. (document) u⌐tsushi⌐ 写し; (key) a⌐ikagi 合い鍵.

durable adj. na⌐gamochi⌐ suru 長持ちする; jo⌐obu na じょうぶな: These trousers are made of durable material. (Kono zuboñ wa joobu na kiji de dekite iru.) このズボンはじょうぶな生地でできている.

during prep. **1** (throughout) ... no a⌐ida zutto ...の間ずっと; ... chuu ...中: I was in Hokkaido during the whole summer. (Watashi wa natsu no aida zutto Hokkaidoo ni imashita.) 私は夏の間ずっと北海道にいました.

2 (in the course of) ... no a⌐ida ni ...の間に: During the night the rain changed to snow. (Yoru no aida ni ame ga yuki ni kawatta.) 夜の間に雨が雪に変わった.

dust n. ho⌐kori ほこり; chi⌐ri ちり: The desk is covered with dust. (Tsukue ni hokori ga tamatte iru.) 机にほこりがたまっている.
— vt. ... no ho⌐kori [chi⌐ri] o ha⌐ra⌐u ...のほこり[ちり]を払う Ⓒ: dust the furniture (kagu no hokori o harau) 家具のほこりを払う.

dusty adj. ho⌐korippo⌐i ほこりっぽい; ho⌐korida⌐rake no ほこりだらけの: a dusty room (hokoridarake no heya) ほこりだらけの部屋.

Dutch adj. Ora⌐ñda no オランダの; (language) Ora⌐ñdago no オランダ語の; (people) Ora⌐ñda⌐jiñ no オランダ人の.
— n. (language) Ora⌐ñdago オランダ語; (people) Ora⌐ñda⌐jiñ オランダ人.

duty n. **1** (what one ought to do) gi⌐mu 義務: carry out [shirk] one's duty (jibuñ no gimu o hatasu [nogareru]) 自分の義務を果たす[逃れ

る].

2 (job) ni⌐nmu 任務; sho⌐kumu 職務: the duties of a policeman (*keekañ no niñmu*) 警官の任務.

3 (tax) ze⌐e 税; ka⌐ñzee 関税: a duty on foreign goods (*gaikoku shoohiñ ni taisuru kañzee*) 外国商品に対する関税.

duty-free shop *n.* me⌐ñze⌐eteñ 免税店.

dwarf *n.* ko⌐bito 小人: a dwarf tree (*boñsai*) 盆栽.

dwell *vi.* su⌐mu 住む Ⓒ; kyo⌐juu suru 居住する Ⓘ: dwell in the country (*inaka ni sumu*) 田舎に住む.

dye *n.* se⌐ñryo⌐o 染料: synthetic dyes (*goose señryoo*) 合成染料.
— *vt.* … o so⌐meru …を染める Ⓥ: He dyed his hair brown. (*Kare wa kami no ke o chairo ni someta.*) 彼は髪の毛を茶色に染めた.

dynamic *adj.* (energetic) ka⌐tsu-doo-teki na 活動的な; (great) da⌐i-nami⌐ku na ダイナミックな: a dynamic person (*katsudoo-teki na hito*) 活動的な人.

dynamite *n.* da⌐inama⌐ito ダイナマイト: explode the dynamite (*dainamaito o bakuha suru*) ダイナマイトを爆破する.

E

each *adj.* so⌐re⌐zore no それぞれの; me⌐eme⌐e no めいめいの: Each student stood up and gave a speech. (*Sorezore no gakusee ga tachiagatte supiichi o shita.*) それぞれの学生が立ち上がってスピーチをした.
— *pron.* so⌐re⌐zore それぞれ; me⌐e-me⌐e めいめい: I gave a small tip to each. (*Watashi wa meemee ni chippu o sukoshi yatta.*) 私はめいめいにチップを少しやった.
— *adv.* so⌐re⌐zore それぞれ; me⌐e-me⌐e めいめい: I gave the children a slice of cake each. (*Watashi wa kodomo-tachi ni meemee keeki o hito-kire zutsu ageta.*) 私は子どもたちにめいめいケーキを一切れずつあげた.

each other *pron.* ta⌐gai ni 互いに: We looked at each other. (*Watashi-tachi wa o-tagai ni kao o miawaseta.*) 私たちはお互いに顔を見合わせた.

eager *adj.* shi⌐kiri ni ⟨verb⟩-taga⌐t-te iru しきりに…たがっている; ne⌐tsu-boo shite iru 熱望している; ne⌐sshiñ na 熱心な: He is eager to climb the mountain. (*Kare wa shikiri ni sono yama ni noboritagatte iru.*) 彼はしきりにその山に登りたがっている. / She is eager in her study of Japa-

nese. (*Kanojo wa Nihoñgo no beñ-kyoo ga nesshiñ da.*) 彼女は日本語の勉強が熱心だ.

eagle *n.* wa⌐shi わし.

ear *n.* **1** (body part) mi⌐mi⌐ 耳: My ears are ringing. (*Watashi wa miminari ga suru.*) 私は耳鳴りがする.

2 (hearing) cho⌐oryoku 聴力; cho⌐okaku 聴覚: have keen ears (*chookaku ga surudoi*) 聴覚が鋭い / I have no ear for music. (*Watashi wa oñgaku ga wakaranai.*) 私は音楽がわからない.

earache *n.* mi⌐mi no itami⌐ 耳の痛み: have an earache (*mimi ga itai*) 耳が痛い.

ear doctor *n.* ji⌐bika⌐-i 耳鼻科医.

eardrum *n.* ko⌐maku 鼓膜.

early *adj.* **1** (before the usual time) ha⌐ya⌐i 早い: I had an early lunch. (*Watashi wa hayai chuu-shoku o totta.*) 私は早い昼食をとった.

2 (beginning of) ha⌐ya⌐i 早い; ha⌐jime no 初めの: early spring (*soo-shuñ*) 早春 / early summer (*shoka*) 初夏 / She got married in her early twenties. (*Kanojo wa nijuu-dai no hajime ni kekkoñ shita.*) 彼女は20代の初めに結婚した.
— *adv.* ha⌐yaku 早く; ha⌐yame ni

早めに: Get up early. (*Hayaku oki nasai.*) 早く起きなさい.

earn *vt.* **1** (money) ... o ka「se1gu ... を稼ぐ C: He earns more than ten million yen a year. (*Kare wa ichi-neñ ni is-señ-mañ-eñ ijoo kasegu.*) 彼は1年に1千万円以上稼ぐ. **2** (gain) ... o e「ru ...を得る V; to「ru 取る C: earn a reputation for honesty (*shoojiki no hyoobañ o toru*) 正直の評判を取る.

earnest *adj.* (serious) ma「jime na まじめな; (eager) ne1sshiñ na 熱心な: an earnest student (*majime na ga-kusee*) まじめな学生 / He refused her earnest request. (*Kare wa ka-nojo no nesshiñ na tanomi o koto-watta.*) 彼は彼女の熱心な頼みを断わった.

earth *n.* **1** (globe) chi「kyuu 地球: The spaceship left the earth. (*Uchuuseñ wa chikyuu o hanareta.*) 宇宙船は地球を離れた. **2** (ground) ji「meñ 地面; da「ichi 大地: Snow covered the earth. (*Yuki ga daichi o ootte ita.*) 雪が大地を覆っている. **3** (soil) tsu「chi1 土; do「joo 土壌: There is not enough earth here to grow a tree. (*Koko wa ki o soda-teru no ni juubuñ na dojoo ga nai.*) ここは木を育てるのに十分な土壌がない.

earthquake *n.* ji「shiñ 地震: A strong earthquake hit the island. (*Tsuyoi jishiñ ga shima o osotta.*) 強い地震が島を襲った.

ease *vt.* **1** (relieve) ... o ya「wara-ge1ru ...を和らげる V; ka「ruku suru 軽くする T: This medicine should ease your pain. (*Kono kusuri wa itami o yawarageru hazu desu.*) この薬は痛みを和らげるはずです. **2** (loosen) ... o yu「rume1ru ...を緩める V: Ease your belt a little. (*Be-ruto o sukoshi yurume nasai.*) ベルトを少し緩めなさい. **3** (carefully move) ... o so「tto ugoka1su ...をそっと動かす C: He eased the car to a stop. (*Kare wa kuruma o sotto tometa.*) 彼は車を

そっと止めた.

― *vi.* (lighten) ka「ruku na1ru 軽くなる C; ra「ku1 ni naru 楽になる C: The pain eased. (*Itami wa karuku natta.*) 痛みは軽くなった.

― *n.* (comfort) ki「raku 気楽; a「ñ-raku 安楽: a life of ease (*kiraku na seekatsu*) 気楽な生活 / The whole family lives in ease. (*Ikka wa añ-raku ni kurashite imasu.*) 一家は安楽に暮らしています.

with ease *adv.* ya「suya1su to やすやすと: He did the task with ease. (*Kare wa sono shigoto o yasuyasu to yatta.*) 彼はその仕事をやすやすとやった.

easily *adv.* **1** (without difficulty) yo「oi ni 容易に; ta「ya1suku たやすく: He easily solved the problem. (*Kare wa sono moñdai o tayasuku toita.*) 彼はその問題をたやすく解いた. **2** (without doubt) u「tagai na1ku 疑いなく; ta「shika ni 確かに: Buy this one. It's easily the best. (*Kore o kai nasai. Sore wa tashika ni ichi-bañ ii mono desu.*) これを買いなさい. それは確かにいちばんいい物です.

east *n.* **1** (direction) hi「gashi 東: Chiba is to the east of Tokyo. (*Chiba wa Tookyoo no higashi no hoo ni aru.*) 千葉は東京の東の方にある. / North, South, East, West (*too-zai-nañ-boku*) 東西南北. ★ The Japanese order is east, west, south, north. **2** (Orient) To「oyoo 東洋: the Far East (*Kyoku-too*) 極東 / the Mid-dle East (*Chuu-too*) 中東. ― *adj.* hi「gashi no 東の: an east wind (*higashi kaze*) 東風. ― *adv.* hi「gashi e [ni] 東へ[に]: Our balcony faces east. (*Watashi-tachi no barukonii wa higashi ni muite iru.*) 私たちのバルコニーは東に向いている.

Easter *n.* fu「kkatsu1sai 復活祭.

eastern *adj.* **1** (direction) hi「gashi no 東の: the eastern sky (*higashi no sora*) 東の空. **2** (Oriental) To「oyoo no 東洋の:

Eastern culture (*Tooyoo no buñka*) 東洋の文化.

easy *adj*. **1** (not difficult) ya「sashii やさしい; yo「oi na 容易な: The problem was easy to solve. (*Sono moñdai wa toku no ga yasashikatta*.) その問題は解くのがやさしかった.

2 (comfortable) ki「raku na 気楽な; a「ñraku na 安楽な: a person with an easy manner (*kiraku na taido no hito*) 気楽な態度の人 / She leads an easy life. (*Kanojo wa kiraku na seekatsu o okutte iru*.) 彼女は気楽な生活を送っている.

eat *vt*. **1** (consume) ... o ta「be「ru ...を食べる Ⓥ; [honorific] me「shiagaru 召し上がる Ⓒ; [humble] i「tadaku いただく Ⓒ; [rude] ku「u 食う Ⓒ: eat an apple (*riñgo o taberu*) りんごを食べる / What did you eat for breakfast? (*Chooshoku ni nani o tabemashita ka?*) 朝食に何を食べましたか? (*Nani o meshiagarimasu ka?*) 何を召し上がりますか.

2 (corrode) ... o fu「shoku suru ...を腐食する Ⓘ: The iron bar was eaten away. (*Sono tetsuboo wa fushoku shite shimatta*.) その鉄棒は腐食してしまった.

—— *vi*. ta「be「ru 食べる Ⓥ: Shall we eat out? (*Soto de tabemasu ka?*) 外で食べますか.

echo *n*. (sound) ha「ñkyoo 反響; ko「dama こだま: I heard the echo of my voice in the cave. (*Hora-ana no naka de jibuñ no koe no hañkyoo o kiita*.) 洞穴の中で自分の声の反響を聞いた.

—— *vi*. ha「ñkyoo suru 反響する Ⓘ: The music echoed in the hall. (*Oñgaku ga hooru ni hañkyoo shita*.) 音楽がホールに反響した.

ecology *n*. (study) se「eta「igaku 生態学; (environment) shi「zeñ kañ「kyoo 自然環境.

economic *adj*. ke「ezaijoo no 経済上の: economic assistance (*keezai eñjo*) 経済援助 / the economic policy of the government (*seefu no keezai-seesaku*) 政府の経済政策.

economical *adj*. ke「ezai-teki na 経済的な; se「tsuyaku ni na「ru 節約になる: an economical car (*keezai-teki na kuruma*) 経済的な車 / He is economical with money. (*Kare wa o-kane o setsuyaku shite iru*.) 彼はお金を節約している.

economics *n*. ke「eza「igaku 経済学: I study economics at Waseda University. (*Watashi wa Wasedadaigaku de keezaigaku o beñkyoo shite imasu*.) 私は早稲田大学で経済学を勉強しています.

economize *vi*. (... o) se「tsuyaku suru (...を)節約する Ⓘ; mu「da na「ku tsu「kau むだなく使う Ⓒ: economize on water (*mizu o setsuyaku suru*) 水を節約する / Make every effort to economize. (*Muda o nakusu yoo ni arayuru doryoku o shi nasai*.) むだをなくすようにあらゆる努力をしなさい.

economy *n*. **1** (saving) se「tsuyaku 節約; ke「ñyaku 倹約: make economies (*setsuyaku o suru*) 節約をする / try to practice economy (*keñyaku o kokorogakeru*) 倹約を心がける.

2 (system) ke「ezai 経済: domestic economy (*katee keezai*) 家庭経済 / the world economy (*sekai keezai*) 世界経済.

—— *adj*. ke「ezai-teki na 経済的な; ya「su「i 安い; e「ko「nomii no エコノミ: economy passengers (*ekonomii-kurasu no jookyaku*) エコノミークラスの乗客.

edge *n*. **1** (border) ha「shi 端; fu「chi「 縁; he「ri「 へり: the edge of a table (*teeburu no hashi*) テーブルの端 / the edge of a cup (*chawañ no fuchi*) 茶わんの縁 / the edge of a tatami (*tatami no heri*) 畳のへり.

2 (of a blade) ha「 刃; ha「saki「 刃先: the edge of a razor (*kamisori no ha*) かみそりの刃 / a knife with a sharp edge (*surudoi hasaki o motta naifu*) 鋭い刃先を持ったナイフ.

edit *vt*. ... o he「ñshuu suru ...を編集する Ⓘ: edit a magazine (*zasshi o heñshuu suru*) 雑誌を編集する.

edition *n.* ha⌈ń 版: the first edition (*sho-hań*) 初版 / a revised edition (*kaitee-bań*) 改訂版.

editor *n.* he⌈ńshu⌉usha 編集者: the editor in chief (*heńshuu shukań*) 編集主幹.

editorial *n.* sha⌈setsu 社説; ro⌈ńse-tsu 論説: Did you read yesterday's editorial in the Asahi? (*Kinoo no Asahi-shińbuń no shasetsu o yomi-mashita ka?*) きのうの朝日新聞の社説を読みましたか.

educate *vt.* **1** (teach) ... o kyo⌈o-iku suru ...を教育する ①: It costs a lot to educate children. (*Kodomo o kyooiku suru no ni wa o-kane ga kakaru.*) 子どもを教育するのにはお金がかかる. **2** (train) ... o ya⌈shinau ...を養う ②; ku⌈ńreń suru 訓練する ①: edu-cate one's ear to appreciate good music (*yoi ońgaku o kańshoo suru mimi o yashinau*) よい音楽を鑑賞する耳を養う.

education *n.* kyo⌈oiku 教育: com-pulsory education (*gimu-kyooiku*) 義務教育 / receive a good educa-tion (*yoi kyooiku o ukeru*) よい教育を受ける.

effect *n.* **1** (result produced) ko⌈o-ka 効果; e⌈ekyoo 影響; sa⌈yoo 作用: The PR campaign has had no effect. (*Pii aaru kyańpeeń wa koo-ka ga nakatta.*) PR キャンペーンは効果がなかった. / a side effect (*fukusa-yoo*) 副作用. **2** (result) ke⌈kka 結果: cause and effect (*geńiń to kekka*) 原因と結果. **3** (meaning) i⌈mi 意味; shu⌈shi 趣旨: I received a letter to the effect that he would resign his post. (*Ka-re kara jishoku suru to iu imi no tegami o uketotta.*) 彼から辞職するという意味の手紙を受け取った.

come into effect *vi.* ha⌈kkoo suru 発効する ①: The law comes into effect next month. (*Sono hoo-ritsu wa raigetsu hakkoo shimasu.*) その法律は来月発効します.

personal effects *n.* mi ⌈no ma-

warihiń 身の回り品.

take effect *vi.* ki⌈ku 効く ②: This medicine soon takes effect. (*Kono kusuri wa sugu kikimasu.*) この薬はすぐ効きます.

effective *adj.* **1** (producing a re-sult) ko⌈oka no aru 効果のある; ko⌈oka-teki na 効果的な: His speech was very effective. (*Kare no eńzetsu wa hijoo ni kooka ga atta.*) 彼の演説は非常に効果があった. / make effective use of light and shade (*hikari to kage o kooka-teki ni tsu-kau*) 光と陰を効果的に使う. **2** (actual) ji⌈ssai no 実際の; ji⌈jitsu-joo no 事実上の: He is the effective leader of the group. (*Kare wa sono guruupu no jijitsujoo no shidoo-sha desu.*) 彼はそのグループの事実上の指導者です.

efficiency *n.* no⌈oritsu 能率: raise [lower] efficiency (*nooritsu o ageru [sageru]*) 能率を上げる[下げる].

efficient *adj.* **1** (of people) yu⌈u-noo na 有能な; no⌈oryoku no aru 能力のある: an efficient secretary (*yuunoo na hisho*) 有能な秘書 / The teacher was very efficient. (*Sono seńsee wa totemo yuunoo datta.*) その先生はとても有能だった. **2** (of methods) ko⌈oka-teki na 効果的な; (of machines) no⌈oritsu-teki na 能率的な: The machines in this factory are very efficient. (*Ko-no koojoo no kikai wa totemo noo-ritsu-teki da.*) この工場の機械はとても能率的だ.

effort *n.* **1** (endeavor) do⌈ryoku 努力; ho⌈neori⌉ 骨折り: We made every effort to find the child. (*Watashi-tachi wa sono ko o sa-gasu tame ni arayuru doryoku o shita.*) 私たちはその子を捜すためにあらゆる努力をした. **2** (achievement) se⌈eka 成果; (work) ro⌈osaku 労作: It is a pretty good effort. (*Sore wa nakanaka yoku dekite iru.*) それはなかなかよくできている.

egg *n.* ta⌈ma⌉go 卵: a raw egg (*na-*

ma-tamago) 生卵 / a boiled egg (*yude-tamago*) ゆで卵 / a fried egg (*tamagoyaki*) 卵焼き / scrambled eggs (*iri-tamago*) いり卵 / break an egg (*tamago o waru*) 卵を割る / This egg is soft-boiled [hard-boiled]. (*Kono tamago wa hañjuku* [*kata-yude*] *da.*) この卵は半熟[固ゆで]だ.

egoism *n.* ri「koshu¬gi 利己主義.

eight *pron.* ya「ttsu¬ 八つ; (people) ha「chi¬-niñ 8 人; (things) ha「chi¬-ko [ha¬k-ko] 8 個: I bought eight apples. (*Ringo o yattsu* [*hachi-ko*] *katta.*) りんごを八つ[8 個]買った.
— *n.* (figure) ha「chi¬ 8; (hour) ha「chi¬-ji 8 時; (minute) ha「chi¬-fuñ 8 分; (age) ha¬s-sai 8 歳.
— *adj.* ha「chi¬ no 8 の; ya「ttsu¬ no 八つの; (people) ha「chi¬-niñ no 8 人の; (things) ha¬k-ko no 8 個の; (age) ha¬s-sai no 8 歳の.

eighteen *pron.* ju「uhachi¬-niñ 18; (people) ju「uhachi¬-niñ 18 人; (things) ju「uhachi¬-ko [ju「u-ha¬k-ko] 18 個; (age) ju「u-has¬sai 18 歳.
— *n.* (figure) ju「uhachi¬ 18; (hour) ju「uhachi¬-ji 18 時; (minute) ju「uha¬p-puñ 18 分; (age) ju「uha¬ssai 18 歳.
— *adj.* ju「u-hachi¬ no 18 の; (people) ju「uhachi¬-niñ no 18 人の; (things) ju「uhachi¬-ko [ju「u-ha¬k-ko] no 18 個の; (age) ju「uha¬s-sai no 18 歳の.

eighteenth *adj.* ju「uhachi-bañme¬ no 18 番目の; da¬i-ju「uhachi¬ no 第 18 の.
— *n.* **1** (people) ju「uhachi-bañme¬ no hi「to¬ 18 番目の人; (things) ju「uhachi-bañme¬ no mo「no¬ 18 番目のもの.
2 (day) ju「uhachi-nichi¬ 18 日.
3 (fraction) ju「uhachi-buñ no ichi¬ 18 分の1.

eighth *adj.* ha「chi-bañme¬ no 8 番目の; da¬i-ha「chi¬ no 第 8 の.
— *n.* **1** (people) ha「chi-bañme¬ no hi「to¬ 8 番目の人; (things) ha「chi-bañme¬ no mo「no¬ 8 番目のもの.

2 (day) yo「oka 8 日.
3 (fraction) ha「chi-buñ no ichi¬ 8 分の1.

eightieth *adj.* ha「chijuu-bañme¬ no 80 番目の; da¬i-ha「chiju¬u no 第 80 の.
— *n.* **1** (people) ha「chijuu-bañ- me¬ no hi「to¬ 80 番目の人; (things) ha「chijuu-bañme¬ no mo「no¬ 80 番目のもの.
2 (fraction) ha「chijuu-buñ no ichi¬ 80 分の1.

eighty *pron.* ha「chiju¬u 80; (people) ha「chiju¬u-niñ 80 人; (things) ha「chiju¬k-ko 80 個.
— *n.* (figure) ha「chiju¬u 80; (age) ha「chiju¬s-sai 80 歳.
— *adj.* ha「chiju¬u no 80 の; (people) ha「chiju¬u-niñ no 80 人の; (things) ha「chiju¬k-ko no 80 個の; (age) ha「chiju¬s-sai no 80 歳の.

either *adj.* **1** (one or the other) do「chira ka hi「to¬tsu no どちらか一つの; [in the negative] do「chira no ... mo (... de na¬i) どちらの...も(...でない): Please take either slice of cake. (*Keeki o dochira ka hitotsu tori nasai.*) ケーキをどちらか一つとりなさい. / I don't like either Tokyo or Osaka. (*Tookyoo mo Oosaka mo dochira mo suki ja arimaseñ.*) 東京も大阪もどちらも好きじゃありません.
2 (one and the other) do「chira no どちらの: There were candles at either end of the table. (*Teeburu no dochira no hashi ni mo roosoku ga atta.*) テーブルのどちらの端にもろうそくがあった.
— *pron.* (one or the other) do「chi- ra de mo どちらでも; [in the negative] do「chira mo (... de nai) どちらも(...でない): You can choose either of them. (*Sono uchi no dochira de mo erabu koto ga dekimasu.*) そのうちのどちらでも選ぶことができます. / She didn't want either. (*Kanojo wa dochira mo nozomanakatta.*) 彼女はどちらも望まなかった.
— *adv.* [in the negative] ... mo ma「ta (... nai) ...もまた(...ない): I

don't like sushi, and I don't like tempura either. (*Watashi wa sushi wa suki ja arimaseñ shi, teñpura mo mata suki ja arimaseñ.*) 私はすしは好きじゃありませんし、てんぷらもまた好きじゃありません. / "I can't speak Chinese." "I can't either." (*"Watashi wa Chuugokugo o hanasemaseñ." "Watashi mo hanasemaseñ."*)「私は中国語を話せません」「私も話せません」

— *conj.* ... ka ma¹ta¹ wa ... ka ...か または...か; [in the negative] ... mo ... mo (... nai) ...も...も(...ない): You can have either coffee or tea. (*Koohii ka mata koocha ga arimasu.*) コーヒーかまたは紅茶があります. / I cannot write either hiragana or katakana. (*Watashi wa hiragana mo katakana mo kakemaseñ.*) 私はひらがなもカタカナも書けません.

elastic *adj.* da¹ñryoku no a¹ru 弾力のある: an elastic band (*wagomu*) 輪ゴム.

— *n.* go¹mu¹himo ゴムひも: a piece of elastic (*gomuhimo ip-poñ*) ゴムひも 1本.

elbow *n.* hi¹ji¹ ひじ: lean forward on one's elbows (*hiji ni yorikakaru*) ひじに寄り掛かる.

— *vt.* ... o hi¹ji¹ de o¹su ...をひじで押す ©: He elbowed me out of the way. (*Kare wa watashi o oshinoketa.*) 彼は私を押しのけた.

elder *adj.* to¹shiue no 年上の: my elder brother [sister] (*watashi no ani [ane]*) 私の兄[姉].

— *n.* ne¹ñcho¹osha 年長者; to¹shiue no hito¹ 年上の人: Be polite to your elders. (*Toshiue no hito ni wa reegi tadashiku shi nasai.*) 年上の人には礼儀正しくしなさい.

elderly *adj.* ne¹ñpai no 年配の; o¹toshiyori no お年寄りの: an elderly gentleman [lady] (*neñpai no shiñshi [josee]*) 年配の紳士[女性].

eldest *adj.* i¹chibañ toshiue no いちばん年上の; sa¹ine¹ñcho¹no 最年長の: my eldest brother [sister] (*watashi no ichibañ toshiue no ani*

elect *vt.* ... o se¹ñkyo suru ...を選挙する □; e¹ra¹bu 選ぶ ©: We have to elect a chairman. (*Gichoo o señkyo shinakereba naranai.*) 議長を選挙しなければならない. / The voters elected Mrs. Yasukawa mayor. (*Toohyoosha wa Yasukawa-sañ o shichoo ni erañda.*) 投票者は安川さんを市長に選んだ.

election *n.* se¹ñkyo 選挙: a general election (*soo-señkyo*) 総選挙 / an election campaign (*señkyo-uñdoo*) 選挙運動 / Our candidate won [lost] the election. (*Wareware no koohosha wa señkyo ni katta [maketa].*) われわれの候補者は選挙に勝った [負けた].

electric *adj.* de¹ñki de u¹go¹ku 電気で動く; de¹ñki no 電気の: an electric clock (*deñki-dokee*) 電気時計 / an electric shaver (*deñki-kamisori*) 電気かみそり / electric current (*deñryuu*) 電流.

electrical *adj.* de¹ñki no 電気の: an electrical engineer (*deñki gishi*) 電気技師.

electrician *n.* de¹ñki gi¹shi 電気技師; de¹ñki¹koo 電気工.

electricity *n.* de¹ñki 電気; (current) de¹ñryuu 電流: turn on [off] the electricity (*deñki o ireru [kiru]*) 電気を入れる[切る] / install electricity (*deñki o hiku*) 電気を引く.

electronic *adj.* de¹ñshi no 電子の; de¹ñshi-koo¹gaku no 電子工学の; e¹rekutoroni¹kusu no エレクトロニクスの: an electronic computer (*deñshi keesañki*) 電子計算機 / electronic industries (*erekutoronikusu-sañgyoo*) エレクトロニクス産業.

electronics *n.* de¹ñshi-ko¹ogaku 電子工学.

elegant *adj.* jo¹ohiñ¹ na 上品な; hi¹ñ no yo¹i 品のよい: an elegant lady (*joohiñ na fujiñ*) 上品な婦人 / She was wearing elegant clothes. (*Kanojo wa hiñ no yoi fuku o kite ita.*) 彼女は品のよい服を着ていた.

element *n.* **1** (essential part) yo¹loso 要素; se˥ebuñ 成分: An essential element of success is hard work. (Seekoo ni nakute wa naranai yooso wa kiñbeñ desu.) 成功になくてはならない要素は勤勉です.

2 (of chemistry) ge˥ñso 元素.

elementary adj. sho˥ho no 初歩の; ki˥hoñ no 基本の: the elementary Japanese course (shokyuu Nihoñgo koosu) 初級日本語コース.

elementary school n. sho˥ogakkoo 小学校: enter [leave] an elementary school (shoogakkoo ni nyuugaku [o sotsugyoo] suru) 小学校に入学[を卒業]する.

elephant n. zo˥o 象.

elevator n. e˥rebe˥etaa エレベーター: get on [off] an elevator (erebeetaa ni noru [kara oriru]) エレベーターに乗る[から降りる] / take the elevator to the fifth floor (erebeetaa ni go-kai made noru) エレベーターに5階まで乗る.

eleven pron. ju˥uichi˥ 11; (people) ju˥uichi˥-niñ 11 人; (things) ju˥uik-ko 11 個.

— n. (figure) ju˥uichi˥ 11; (hour) ju˥uichi˥-ji 11 時; (minute) ju˥ui˥p-puñ 11 分; (age) ju˥ui˥s-sai 11 歳.

— adj. ju˥uichi˥ no 11 の; (people) ju˥uichi˥-niñ no 11 人の; (things) ju˥uik-ko no 11 個の; (age) ju˥ui˥s-sai no 11 歳の.

eleventh adj. ju˥uichi-bañme˥ no 11 番目の; da˥i-ju˥uichi˥ no 第 11 の.

— n. **1** (people) ju˥uichi-bañme˥ no h˥ito˥ 11 番目の人; (things) ju˥uichi-bañme˥ no mo˥no˥ 11 番目のもの.

2 (date) ju˥uichi-nichi˥ 11 日.

3 (fraction) ju˥uichi-buñ no ichi˥ 11 分の1.

eliminate vt. ... o no˥zoku ...を除く C; sa˥kujo suru 削除する I: It is not easy to eliminate hunger. (Ue o nozoku no wa yooi de nai.) 飢えを除くのは容易でない. / eliminate useless words from sentences (fuyoo na go o buñshoo kara sakujo suru) 不要な語を文章から削除する.

eloquence n. yu˥ubeñ 雄弁: a person of eloquence (yuubeñka) 雄弁家.

eloquent adj. yu˥ubeñ na 雄弁な: an eloquent speaker (yuubeñka) 雄弁家.

else adj. so˥no˥ hoka no そのほかの; ta˥ no 他の; be˥tsu no 別の: No one else came yesterday. (Kinoo wa sono hoka no hito wa dare mo kimaseñ deshita.) きのうはそのほかの人はだれも来ませんでした. / I have nothing else to say. (Hoka ni nani mo iu koto wa arimaseñ.) ほかに何も言うことはありません.

— adv. so˥no˥ hoka ni そのほかに; ta˥ ni 他に; be˥tsu ni 別に: It cannot be bought anywhere else. (Sore wa hoka no basho de wa kaemaseñ.) それはほかの場所では買えません.

or else conj. so˥ shinai to そうしないと: Do as we say, or else! (Iu toori ni shi nasai. Soo shinai to.) 言うとおりにしなさい. そうしないと.

elsewhere adv. ho˥ka no basho de ほかの場所で: They are sold out. Let's buy it elsewhere. (Sore wa urikire desu. Hoka de kaimashoo.) それは売り切れです. ほかで買いましょう.

elude vt. ... o sa˥ke˥ru ...を避ける V; no˥gare˥ru 逃れる V: elude one's pursuers (otte o nogareru) 追っ手を逃れる.

embankment n. te˥eboo 堤防; do˥te 土手.

embark vi. (airplane) to˥ojoo suru 搭乗する I; (ship) jo˥oseñ suru 乗船する I: We embark for Okinawa next week. (Watashi-tachi wa raishuu jooseñ shite Okinawa ni mukaimasu.) 私たちは来週乗船して沖縄に向かいます.

embarkation n. (airplane) to˥ojoo 搭乗; (ship) jo˥oseñ 乗船: an embarkation card (shukkoku kaado) 出国カード / an embarkation procedure (shukkoku tetsuzuki) 出国手続き / the port of embarkation (toojoochi) 搭乗地.

embarrass *vt.* ... o to⌈owaku saseru …を当惑させる [V]; ... ni ki⌈mazui omo⌉i o sa⌈seru …に気まずい思いをさせる [V]: He embarrassed me with unexpected questions. (*Kare wa igai na shitsumoñ de watashi o toowaku saseta.*) 彼は意外な質問で私を当惑させた.

embarrassed *adj.* ki⌈mari waru⌉i o⌈mo⌉i o shita [shite iru] きまり悪い思いをした[している]; to⌈owaku shita [shite iru] 当惑した[している]: I was embarrassed when I made the mistake. (*Sono machigai o shita toki kimari warui omoi o shita.*) その間違いをしたときまり悪い思いをした.

embarrassing *adj.* ki⌈mazui omo⌉i o sa⌈seru 気まずい思いをさせる; ya⌉kkai na 厄介な: an embarrassing question (*yakkai na shitsumoñ*) 厄介な質問.

embarrassment *n.* ki⌈mazusa 気まずさ; ko⌈ñwaku 困惑: He tried to hide his embarrassment. (*Kare wa kimazusa o kakusoo to shita.*) 彼は気まずさを隠そうとした.

embassy *n.* ta⌈ishi⌉kañ 大使館: the French embassy in Japan (*Nihoñ no Furañsu taishikañ*) 日本のフランス大使館.

embody *vt.* ... o gu⌈tai-teki ni nobe⌉ru …を具体的に述べる [V]; gu⌈tai-ka suru 具体化する [I]: He embodied his ideas in his speech. (*Kare wa eñzetsu no naka de jibuñ no kañgae o gutai-teki ni nobeta.*) 彼は演説の中で自分の考えを具体的に述べた.

embrace *vt.* ... o da⌈kishime⌉ru …を抱き締める [V]: The mother embraced her child. (*Hahaoya wa kodomo o dakishimeta.*) 母親は子どもを抱き締めた.

— *vi.* da⌈kia⌉u 抱き合う [C]: The two lovers embraced. (*Futari no koibito wa dakiatta.*) 二人の恋人は抱き合った.

— *n.* ho⌈oyoo 抱擁: a close embrace (*katai hooyoo*) 固い抱擁.

embroider *vt.* ... o shi⌈shuu suru …をししゅうする [I]; nu⌈iko⌉mu 縫い込む [C]: embroider initials on a handkerchief (*hañkachi ni inisharu o nuikomu*) ハンカチにイニシャルを縫い込む.

embroidery *n.* shi⌈shuu ししゅう; nu⌈itori 縫い取り.

emerald *n.* e⌈mera⌉rudo エメラルド.

emerge *vi.* **1** (appear) a⌈raware⌉ru 現われる [V]; (come out) de⌉te kuru 出てくる [I]: The fireman emerged from the burning building. (*Shoobooshi ga moete iru biru kara arawareta.*) 消防士が燃えているビルから現われた.

2 (become known) a⌈ki⌉raka ni naru 明かになる [C]; ha⌈ñmee suru 判明する [I]: The true facts are unlikely to ever emerge. (*Shiñsoo wa doomo akiraka ni narisoo mo nai.*) 真相はどうも明らかになりそうもない.

emergency *n.* ki⌈ñkyuu ji⌉tai 緊急事態; hi⌈joo ji⌉tai 非常事態: In an emergency, push this button. (*Hijoo no baai wa kono botañ o oshite kudasai.*) 非常の場合はこのボタンを押してください. / Where is the emergency exit? (*Hijooguchi wa doko ni arimasu ka?*) 非常口はどこにありますか.

eminent *adj.* cho⌈mee na 著名な; ko⌈omee na 高名な: an eminent writer (*chomee na sakka*) 著名な作家.

emotion *n.* **1** (feelings) ka⌈ñjoo 感情: Love and hate are perhaps the strongest emotions. (*Ai to nikushimi wa osoraku mottomo tsuyoi kañjoo de aru.*) 愛と憎しみはおそらくもっとも強い感情である.

2 (excited state) ka⌈ñdoo 感動; ko⌈ofuñ 興奮: His voice was shaking with emotion. (*Kare no koe wa koofuñ de furuete ita.*) 彼の声は興奮で震えていた.

emperor *n.* (of Japan) te⌈ñno⌉o 天皇; (of other empires) ko⌈otee 皇帝: His Majesty the Emperor (*teñnoo heeka*) 天皇陛下 / the present Emperor (*kiñjoo teñnoo*) 今上天皇

/ the Emperor Showa (*Shoowa teñnoo*) 昭和天皇.

emphasis *n.* kyo⌐ochoo 強調; ju⌐ute¹ñ o o⌐ku koto¹ 重点を置くこと: speak with emphasis (*kyoochoo shite hanasu*) 強調して話す / put emphasis on oral practice (*kootoo kuñreñ ni juuteñ o oku*) 口頭訓練に重点を置く.

emphasize *vt.* ... o kyo⌐ochoo suru ...を強調する ⊤; ri⌐kisetsu suru 力説する ⊤: emphasize one's point of view (*jibuñ no ikeñ o kyoochoo suru*) 自分の意見を強調する.

emphatic *adj.* **1** (forceful) kyo⌐ochoo shita [shite iru] 強調した[している]; ki⌐ppa¹ri to shita [shite iru] きっぱりとした[している]: an emphatic denial (*kippari to shita hiniñ*) きっぱりとした否認.

2 (clear) ha⌐kki¹ri to shita [shite iru] はっきりとした[している]; a⌐ki¹raka na 明らかな: an emphatic defeat (*akiraka na haiboku*) 明らかな敗北.

empire *n.* te⌐ekoku 帝国: the Roman Empire (*Rooma teekoku*) ローマ帝国.

employ *vt.* **1** (hire) ... o ya⌐to¹u ...を雇う ⊂: Our family employs three gardeners. (*Uchi de wa niwashi o sañ-niñ yatotte iru.*) うちでは庭師を3人雇っている. / Miss Nomura is employed in a bank. (*Nomurasañ wa giñkoo ni tsutomete iru.*) 野村さんは銀行に勤めている.

2 (use) ... o tsu⌐kau ...を使う ⊂; mo⌐chii¹ru 用いる ⊽: Petroleum is employed for many purposes. (*Sekiyu wa iroiro na mokuteki ni tsukawarete iru.*) 石油はいろいろな目的に使われている.

employee *n.* ya⌐towa¹rete iru hi⌐¹to¹ 雇われている人; ju⌐ugyo¹iñ 従業員: The employees went on strike. (*Juugyooiñ wa sutoraiki ni haitta.*) 従業員はストライキに入った. / government employees (*koomuiñ*) 公務員 / a company employee (*kaishaiñ*) 会社員.

employer *n.* ya⌐toi¹nushi 雇い主;

ko⌐yo¹osha 雇用者: Mr. Hayashi was fired by his employer. (*Hayashi-sañ wa yatoinushi ni kubi ni sareta.*) 林さんは雇い主に首にされた.

employment *n.* **1** (being employed) ko⌐yoo 雇用: full employment (*kañzeñ-koyoo*) 完全雇用 / the system of lifetime employment (*shuushiñ koyoo seedo*) 終身雇用制度.

2 (paid work) sho⌐ku 職; shi⌐goto 仕事: Luckily all our graduates found employment. (*Uñ yoku uchi no sotsugyoosee wa zeñiñ shoku ga mitsukatta.*) 運よくうちの卒業生は全員職が見つかった. / look for employment (*shigoto o sagasu*) 仕事を探す.

empress *n.* (of Japan) ko⌐ogo¹o 皇后; (of other empires) jo⌐tee 女帝: Her Majesty the Empress (*koogoo heeka*) 皇后陛下.

empty *adj.* **1** (containing nothing) ka⌐ra¹ no 空の: an empty glass (*kara no koppu*) 空のコップ / an empty house (*akiya*) 空き家 / an empty stomach (*kuufuku*) 空腹 / I opened the box, but it was empty. (*Hako o aketa ga kara datta.*) 箱を開けたが空だった.

2 (meaningless) mu⌐i¹mi na 無意味な; mu⌐nashi¹i むなしい: an empty promise (*kara-yakusoku*) 空約束 / feel emotionally empty (*munashiku kañjiru*) むなしく感じる.

— *vt.* ... o ka⌐ra¹ ni suru ...を空にする ⊤; a⌐keru 空ける ⊽: empty a glass (*koppu o kara ni suru*) コップを空にする / She emptied the water into the bucket. (*Kanojo wa mizu o baketsu ni aketa.*) 彼女は水をバケツに空けた.

enable *vt.* ... no o⌐kage de ... de⌐¹ki¹ru ...のおかげで...できる ⊽; ... o ka⌐¹noo ni suru ...を可能にする ⊤: The scholarship enabled him to go to college. (*Shoogakukiñ no okage de kare wa daigaku e iku koto ga dekita.*) 奨学金のおかげで彼は大学へ行くことができた. / Proper qualifications will enable you to get a good job. (*Tekitoo na shikaku ga areba yoi shoku ni tsuku koto ga kanoo deshoo.*) 適当な資格があればよい職に就くことが可能でしょう.

enamel *n.* e「nameru エナメル; ho「o-roo ほうろう: an enamel bowl (*hooroo no booru*) ほうろうのボール.

enclose *vt.* **1** (surround) ... o ka-「kou ...を囲う C: The landlord enclosed the vacant lot with a fence. (*Jinushi wa akichi o saku de kakotta.*) 地主は空き地をさくで囲った. **2** (put inside an envelope) ... o do「ofu suru ...を同封する I; fu「u-nyuu suru 封入する I: I am enclosing some family photos with this letter. (*Kazoku no shashiñ o nañ-mai ka kono tegami ni doofuu shi-masu.*) 家族の写真を何枚かこの手紙に同封します.

enclosure *n.* **1** (enclosed materials) do「ofu「ubutsu 同封物. **2** (fence) ka「koi 囲い.

encourage *vt.* **1** (give courage, support) ... o ha「gema「su ...を励ます C; ge「ñkizuke「ru 元気づける V: Our teacher always encourages us to study harder. (*Watashi-tachi no señsee wa motto isshookeñmee beñkyoo suru yoo ni watashi-tachi o itsu-mo hagemashite kureru.*) 私たちの先生はもっと一生懸命勉強するように私たちをいつも励ましてくれる. / We were encouraged by our team's success. (*Chiimu no seekoo de wata-shi-tachi wa geñkizuita.*) チームの成功で私たちは元気づいた. **2** (foster) ... o so「kushiñ suru ...を促進する I; jo「choo suru 助長する I: The warm summer encouraged the growth of rice plants. (*Atsui natsu ga ine no seechoo o soku-shiñ shita.*) 暑い夏が稲の生長を促進した.

encouragement *n.* ge「kiree 激励; sho「oree 奨励: give a person encouragement (*hito o gekiree suru*) 人を激励する.

end *n.* **1** (of a period of time; of a

story) o「wari 終わり; -matsu 末; sa「igo 最後: the end of the week (*shuu no owari*) 週の終わり / the end of the month (*getsu-matsu*) 月末. **2** (end point; tip) sa「ki 先; se「ñtañ 先端; ha「shi 端: the end of a stick (*boo no saki*) 棒の先 / the end of a rope (*roopu no señtañ*) ロープの先端 / sit at the end of a bench (*beñchi no hashi ni suwaru*) ベンチの端に座る. **3** (limit) ge「ñdo 限度: I am at the end of my patience. (*Watashi wa gamañ no geñdo ni kita.*) 私は我慢の限度にきた. **4** (aim) mo「kuteki 目的: He achieved his ends. (*Kare wa moku-teki o tasshita.*) 彼は目的を達した.
— *vi.* (come to an end) o「waru 終わる C: The exhibition ends next week. (*Teñrañkai wa raishuu owa-rimasu.*) 展覧会は来週終わります.
— *vt.* (bring to an end) ... o o「eru ...を終える V; ya「meru やめる V: The two of you must end your quarrel. (*Futari tomo keñka o yamenakereba ikenai.*) 二人ともけんかをやめなければいけない.

endeavor *vi.* do「ryoku suru 努力する I: We will endeavor to meet your request. (*Go-yooboo ni sou yoo ni doryoku itashimasu.*) ご要望に添うように努力いたします.
— *n.* do「ryoku 努力: make every endeavor (*arayuru doryoku o su-ru*) あらゆる努力をする.

ending *n.* o「wari 終わり; ke「tsuma-tsu 結末: the ending of a movie (*eega no ketsumatsu*) 映画の結末.

endless *adj.* o「wari no na「i 終わりのない; ha「teshina「i 果てしない: an endless desert (*hateshinai sabaku*) 果てしない砂漠.

endorse *vt.* ... ni u「ragaki suru ...に裏書きする I: endorse a check (*kogitte ni uragaki suru*) 小切手に裏書きする.

endurance *n.* ni「ñtai 忍耐; ga「-mañ 我慢: I came to the end of my endurance. (*Watashi wa gamañ no* *geñdo ni kita.*) 私は我慢の限度にきた. / be beyond endurance (*gamañ shi-kirenai*) 我慢しきれない.

endure *vt.* 1 (bear) ... o ga˺mañ suru ...を我慢する ①: endure pain (*kutsuu o gamañ suru*) 苦痛を我慢する.

2 (suffer) ... o ta˺eshino˺bu ...を耐え忍ぶ ©: The explorers endured the harsh winter. (*Tañkeñka-tachi wa kibishii fuyu o taeshinoñda.*) 探検家たちは厳しい冬を耐え忍んだ.

enemy *n.* 1 (person one hates) te˺ki 敵; ka˺taki˺ かたき: A politician always has enemies. (*Seejika wa itsu-mo teki o motte iru.*) 政治家はいつも敵を持っている.

2 (enemy forces) te˺kiguñ 敵軍: The enemy army advanced on us. (*Tekiguñ wa wareware ni mukatte zeñshiñ shite kita.*) 敵軍はわれわれに向かって前進して来た.

energetic *adj.* se˺eryoku-teki na 精力的な; ka˺tsudoo-teki na 活動的な: an energetic businessman (*seeryoku-teki na bijinesumañ*) 精力的なビジネスマン.

energy *n.* 1 (vigor) se˺eryoku 精力; ge˺ñki 元気: work with energy (*seeryoku-teki ni hataraku*) 精力的に働く / He seems to have no energy these days. (*Kare wa saikiñ geñki ga nai yoo da.*) 彼は最近元気がないようだ.

2 (effort) ka˺tsudo˺oryoku 活動力; se˺ekoñ 精魂: I devoted all my energy to the task. (*Watashi wa shigoto ni zeñ seekoñ o katamuketa.*) 私は仕事に全精魂を傾けた.

3 (power) e˺ne˺rugii エネルギー: solar [atomic] energy (*taiyoo [geñshiryoku] enerugii*) 太陽[原子力]エネルギー / We must stop wasting energy. (*Enerugii no mudazukai o yamenakereba naranai.*) エネルギーのむだづかいをやめなければならない.

enforce *vt.* ... o ji˺sshi suru ...を実施する ①; shi˺koo suru 施行する ①: The law was enforced immediately. (*Sono hooritsu wa tadachi ni jis-*

shi sareta.) その法律は直ちに実施された.

engage *vt.* 1 (hire; employ) ... o ya˺to˺u ...を雇う ©: We wish to engage an interpreter. (*Tsuuyaku o hitori yatoitai.*) 通訳を一人雇いたい.

2 (reserve) ... o yo˺yaku suru ...を予約する ①: engage seats (*zaseki o yoyaku suru*) 座席を予約する.

3 (attract; occupy) ... o hi˺ku ...を引く ©; ... ni hi˺kiko˺mu ...に引き込む ©: engage a person's attention (*hito no chuui o hiku*) 人の注意を引く.

engaged *adj.* 1 (betrothed) ko˺ñyaku shite (iru) 婚約して(いる): Miss Suzuki is engaged to Mr. Miyashita. (*Suzuki-sañ wa Miyashita-shi to koñyaku shite iru.*) 鈴木さんは宮下氏と婚約している.

2 (be occupied in) ju˺uji shite (iru) 従事して(いる); hi˺ma ga na˺i 暇がない: She is engaged in social work. (*Kanojo wa shakai jigyoo ni juuji shite iru.*) 彼女は社会事業に従事している.

3 (of a telephone) o-ha˺nashi-chuu de お話し中で: The number is engaged. (*Ima o-hanashi-chuu desu.*) 今お話し中です.

engagement *n.* 1 (for marriage) ko˺ñyaku 婚約: break off an engagement (*koñyaku o haki suru*) 婚約を破棄する.

2 (appointment) ya˺kusoku 約束: I have a previous engagement. (*Señyaku ga arimasu.*) 先約があります.

engine *n.* e˺ñjiñ エンジン: start the engine of a car (*jidoosha no eñjiñ o shidoo saseru*) 自動車のエンジンを始動させる.

engineer *n.* gi˺shi 技師: an electrical engineer (*deñki gishi*) 電気技師.

England *n.* I˺ñgurañdo イングランド; (the U.K.) I˺girisu イギリス; E˺ekoku 英国.

English *n.* 1 (language) E˺ego 英語: Do you speak English? (*Anata wa Eego o hanashimasu ka?*) あなたは英語を話しますか.

2 (people) I「girisu」jiń イギリス人; E「e-kokuˌjiń 英国人.

— *adj.* **1** (language) E「ego no 英語の: Is there an English menu? (*Eego no menyuu wa arimasu ka?*) 英語のメニューはありますか.

2 I「ńgurańdo no イングランドの: English folk songs (*Ińgurańdo no mińyoo*) イングランドの民謡.

3 (British) I「girisu no イギリスの; E「ekoku no 英国の: English history (*Eekoku no rekishi*) 英国の歴史.

4 (people) I「girisu」jiń no イギリス人の; E「ekokuˌjiń no 英国人の: My grandmother was English. (*Watashi no obaa-sań wa Igirisujiń deshita.*) 私のおばあさんはイギリス人でした.

Englishman *n.* I「ńgurańdoˌjiń イングランド人; (born in Britain) I「giri-suˌjiń イギリス人; E「ekokuˌjiń 英国人.

Englishwoman *n.* I「ńgurańdo no jo「see イングランドの女性; (born in Britain) I「girisu [E「ekoku] no josee イギリス[英国]の女性.

engrave *vt.* ... o ho「ru ...を彫る C: engrave letters on stone (*ishi ni moji o horu*) 石に文字を彫る.

enjoy *vt.* **1** (get pleasure) ... o ta「noshi」mu ...を楽しむ C; ... wa ta「noshiˌi ...は楽しい: We really enjoyed our holiday. (*Kyuuka wa hońtoo ni tanoshikatta.*) 休暇は本当に楽しかった.

2 (experience) ... o mo「tte iru ... を持っている Ⓥ; ... ni me「gumarete iru ...に恵まれている Ⓥ: Fortunately I enjoy good health. (*Saiwai na koto ni watashi wa keńkoo ni megumarete iru.*) 幸いなことに私は健康に恵まれている.

enjoyable *adj.* ta「noshiˌi 楽しい; yu「kai na 愉快な: The play was very enjoyable. (*Shibai wa totemo tanoshikatta.*) 芝居はとても楽しかった.

enjoyment *n.* ta「noshiˌmi 楽しみ; yu「kai 愉快; yo「rokobi 喜び: Reading is a great enjoyment to me. (*Dokusho wa watashi ni totte ooki-na tanoshimi desu.*) 読書は私

にとって大きな楽しみです.

enlarge *vt.* **1** (make larger) ... o o「okiku suru ...を大きくする Ⓘ; ka「kuchoo suru 拡張する Ⓘ: Our neighbors are planning to enlarge their garden. (*Uchi no tonari no hito wa niwa o kakuchoo suru koto o keekaku shite iru.*) うちの隣の人は庭を拡張することを計画している. **2** (of a photograph) ... o hi「kino-ba」su ...を引き伸ばす C: enlarge a photograph (*shashiń o hikinobasu*) 写真を引き伸ばす.

enlargement *n.* (sha「shiń no) hi-「kinobashi (写真の) 引き伸ばし: I'd like to have an enlargement made. (*Hikinobashi o shite moraitai no desu ga.*) 引き伸ばしをしてもらいたいのですが.

enlist *vi.* (... ni) nyu「utai suru (...に) 入隊する Ⓘ: enlist in the army (*rikuguń ni nyuutai suru*) 陸軍に入隊する.

enormous *adj.* kyo「dai na 巨大な; ba「kudai na 莫大な: an enormous building (*kyodai na tatemono*) 巨大な建物 / an enormous amount of money (*bakudai na kińgaku*) 莫大な金額.

enough *adj.* ju「ubuń na 十分な: We don't have enough players to make two teams. (*Chiimu o futatsu tsukuru hodo juubuń na seńshu ga inai.*) チームを二つ作るほど十分な選手がいない.

— *adv.* **1** (to the required degree) ju「ubuń ni 十分に: This apartment is large enough for our family. (*Kono apaato wa watashi-tachi kazoku ni wa juubuń hiroi.*) このアパートは私たち家族には十分広い. **2** (to a certain degree) ka「nari かなり: The situation is serious enough, but it will get worse. (*Jookyoo wa kanari kibishii ga sara ni waruku naru deshoo.*) 状況はかなり厳しいがさらに悪くなるでしょう.

— *pron.* ju「ubuń 十分: I can't eat anymore. I've had enough. (*Kore ijoo wa taberaremaseń. Moo juu-*

buñ itadakimashita.) これ以上は食べられません. もう十分いただきました.

enquire *v.* = inquire.

enroll *vi.* ka⌐iiñ ni na⌐ru 会員になる C; (... ni) ha⌐iru (…に) 入る C: enroll in the advanced Japanese course (*Nihoñgo jookyuu koosu ni hairu*) 日本語上級コースに入る.

enter *vt.* **1** (go into; come into) ... ni ha⌐iru …に入る C: Can I enter the room now? (*Ima sugu heya ni hairemasu ka?*) 今すぐ部屋に入れますか.
2 (join; take part in) ... ni nyu⌐ugaku suru …に入学する I; sa⌐ñka suru 参加する I: enter a university (*daigaku ni nyuugaku suru*) 大学に入学する / enter a competition (*koñtesuto ni sañka suru*) コンテストに参加する.
3 (cause to take part) ... o (... ni) nyu⌐ugaku saseru …を(…に)入学させる V; sa⌐ñka saseru 参加させる V: enter a child in a school (*kodomo o gakkoo ni nyuugaku saseru*) 子どもを学校に入学させる / I entered my horse in the race. (*Watashi wa watashi no uma o reesu ni sañka saseta.*) 私は私の馬をレースに参加させた.
4 (write down; insert) ... o ki⌐ñnyuu suru …を記入する I; i⌐reru 入れる V: Please enter your name here. (*Koko ni o-namae o kinyuu shite kudasai.*) ここにお名前を記入してください. / enter data into a computer (*deeta o koñpyuutaa ni ireru*) データをコンピューターに入れる.

enterprise *n.* (commercial) ki⌐gyoo 企業; (company) ka⌐isha 会社: private enterprises (*miñkañ kigyoo*) 民間企業.

entertain *vt.* **1** (amuse) ... o ta⌐noshimase⌐ru …を楽しませる V: Her jokes entertained us all. (*Kanojo no jooku wa watashi-tachi miñna o tanoshimaseta.*) 彼女のジョークは私たちみんなを楽しませた. **2** (provide hospitality) ... o mo⌐tena⌐su …をもてなす C; sho⌐otai suru 招待する I: I entertained the guests with refreshments. (*Watashi wa chaka de kyaku o motenashita.*) 私は茶菓で客をもてなした. / entertain friends to dinner (*tomodachi o yuushoku ni shootai suru*) 友だちを夕食に招待する.

entertainment *n.* **1** (providing hospitality) se⌐ttai 接待; mo⌐tenashi もてなし: the entertainment of guests (*o-kyaku no motenashi*) お客のもてなし.
2 (amusement) go⌐raku 娯楽; ta⌐noshimi 楽しみ: watch television for entertainment (*goraku ni terebi o miru*) 娯楽にテレビを見る.
3 (public events) mo⌐yooshimono 催し物; yo⌐kyoo 余興: this week's entertainments (*koñshuu no moyooshimono*) 今週の催し物.

enthusiasm *n.* ne⌐tchuu 熱中; ne⌐kkyoo 熱狂; -netsu 熱: In Japan, young people's enthusiasm for soccer has recently increased. (*Nihoñ de wa saikiñ wakai hito no sakkaa-netsu ga takamatte iru.*) 日本では最近若い人のサッカー熱が高まっている.

enthusiastic *adj.* ne⌐tsuretsu na 熱烈な; ne⌐sshiñ na 熱心な: an enthusiastic fan (*netsuretsu na fañ*) 熱烈なファン / an enthusiastic supporter (*nesshiñ na shijisha*) 熱心な支持者.

entire *adj.* **1** (whole) ze⌐ñtai no 全体の; ma⌐ruma⌐ru no まるまるの: She stayed in bed the entire day. (*Kanojo wa maru ichi-nichi beddo ni ita.*) 彼女はまる1日ベッドにいた.
2 (complete) ma⌐ttaku⌐ no まったくの: We were in entire ignorance of the events. (*Watashi-tachi wa sono dekigoto o mattaku shiranakatta.*) 私たちはその出来事をまったく知らなかった.
3 (not missing) ka⌐ñzeñ na 完全な: an entire set of the author's works (*sono chosha no sakuhiñ no kañzeñ na setto*) その著者の作品の完全なセット.

entirely *adv.* ma「ttaku まったく；su「kka「ri すっかり：I entirely agree with you. (*Watashi wa anata to mattaku onaji ikeñ desu.*) 私はあなたとまったく同じ意見です.

entitle *vt.* **1** (give a right) ... ni ke「ñri o ataeru ...に権利を与える Ⓥ；shi「kaku o ataeru 資格を与える Ⓥ：He is entitled to a pension. (*Kare wa neñkiñ o ukeru shikaku ga aru.*) 彼は年金を受ける資格がある.
2 (give a title) ... ni da「i o tsu「ke「ru ...に題をつける Ⓥ：a book entitled 'A Guide to Japan' (*'Nihoñ Añnai' to dai o tsukerareta hoñ*) 「日本案内」と題をつけられた本.

entrance *n.* **1** (entry) i「riguchi 入り口：I couldn't find the entrance to the car park. (*Chuushajoo no iriguchi ga mitsukaranakatta.*) 駐車場の入り口が見つからなかった.
2 (act of entering) ha「iru ko「to「 入ること；(of an actor) to「ojoo 登場：The security man refused us entrance. (*Gaadomañ wa watashi-tachi ga hairu koto o kotowatta.*) ガードマンは私たちが入ることを断った.
3 (admission) nyu「ugaku 入学：entrance into college (*daigaku nyuugaku*) 大学入学.

entrance examination *n.* (for a school) nyu「ugaku shi「keñ 入学試験 ★ Often abbreviated to '*nyuu-shi*' 入試；(for a company) nyu「u-sha shi「keñ 入社試験：the entrance examination for Kyoto University (*Kyooto daigaku no nyuugaku shi-keñ*) 京都大学の入学試験.

entrust *vt.* ... o (... ni) ma「kase「ru ...を(...に)任せる Ⓥ；a「zuke「ru 預ける Ⓥ：I entrusted the work to him. (*Watashi wa sono shigoto o kare ni makaseta.*) 私はその仕事を彼に任せた. / She entrusted her savings to her best friend. (*Kanojo wa chokiñ o ichibañ naka no yoi tomodachi ni azuketa.*) 彼女は貯金をいちばん仲のよい友達に預けた.

entry *n.* **1** (act of entering) ha「iru ko「to「 入ること；ka「nyuu 加入：the entry of a country into the United Nations (*kuni no kokureñ e no kanyuu*) 国の国連への加入 / No Entry. (*Tachiiri kiñshi.*) 立ち入り禁止.
2 (written information) ki「nyuu 記入；ki「sai 記載：She made an entry in her notebook. (*Kanojo wa nooto ni kinyuu shita.*) 彼女はノートに記入した.
3 (a person in a competition) sa「ñka「sha 参加者.

envelope *n.* fu「utoo 封筒：address an envelope (*fuutoo ni atena o kaku*) 封筒に宛名を書く.

envious *adj.* u「rayamashi-ga「ru うらやましがる；u「rayamashi-so「o na うらやましそうな：an envious look (*ura-yamashi-soo na kaotsuki*) うらやましそうな顔つき / Everyone was envious of her success. (*Miñna ga kanojo no seekoo o urayamashi-gatta.*) みんなが彼女の成功をうらやましがった.

environment *n.* ka「ñkyoo 環境：protect the environment (*kañkyoo o hogo suru*) 環境を保護する.

envy *vt.* ... o urayamu ...をうらやむ Ⓒ：Many people envy him his good fortune. (*Ooku no hito ga kare no koouñ o urayañde iru.*) 多くの人が彼の好運をうらやんでいる.
— *n.* ne「tami「 ねたみ；shi「tto しっと；u「rayami「 うらやみ：I feel envy at his success. (*Watashi wa kare no seekoo ga urayamashii.*) 私は彼の成功がうらやましい.

episode *n.* **1** (event) e「pisoodo エピソード；de「ki「goto 出来事：an interesting episode in history (*reki-shi-joo no kyoomibukai episoodo*) 歴史上の興味深いエピソード.
2 (of a novel) so「owa 挿話.

equal *adj.* **1** (same) o「naji 同じ；hi「toshi「i 等しい：The girls are of equal height. (*Oñna-no-ko-tachi wa onaji se no takasa da.*) 女の子たちは同じ背の高さだ. / He cut the cake into three equal pieces. (*Kare wa keeki o mittsu no hitoshii ookisa ni kitta.*) 彼はケーキを三つの等しい大き

さに切った.

2 (fair) byo「odoo na 平等な; ta「i-too na 対等な: Every person is born equal. (*Dare de mo umareta toki wa byoodoo desu.*) だれでも生まれたときは平等です.

3 (up to) ta「e「ru 耐える; shi「kaku ga a「ru 資格がある: I am not equal to such a task. (*Watashi ni wa sono yoo na shigoto wa taerarenai.*) 私にはそのような仕事は耐えられない.
— *n.* (people) do「otoo no hito「 同等の人: one's social equals (*shakai-teki ni dootoo no hito-tachi*) 社会的に同等の人たち.
— *vt.* **1** (be the same as) ... ni hi「toshi「i ...に等しい: Five plus eight equals thirteen. (*Go tasu hachi wa juusañ desu.*) 5足す8は13です.
2 (reach the same standard) ... ni hi「tteki suru ...に匹敵する⌐; o「tora」-nai 劣らない: Nobody can equal him in mathematics. (*Suugaku de kare ni hitteki suru mono wa inai.*) 数学で彼に匹敵する者はいない.

equality *n.* byo「odoo 平等; ki「ñ-too 均等: equality of the sexes (*danjo byoodoo*) 男女平等 / equality of opportunity (*kikai kiñtoo*) 機会均等.

equator *n.* se「kidoo 赤道: cross the equator (*sekidoo o koeru*) 赤道を越える.

equilibrium *n.* he「ekoo 平衡; ki「ñkoo 均衡: maintain an equilibrium (*kiñkoo o tamotsu*) 均衡を保つ.

equip *vt.* **1** (fit out) ... o so「nae「ru ...を備える⌐; so「obi suru 装備する⌐: The clinic is equipped with an X-ray machine. (*Shiñryoojo wa reñtogeñ shashiñ satsueeki o sonaete iru.*) 診療所はレントゲン写真撮影機を備えている.
2 (prepare) ... o u「kesase「ru ...を受けさせる⌐: Parents should equip their children with a good education. (*Oya wa kodomo ni yoi kyooiku o ukesasenakereba naranai.*) 親は子どもによい教育を受けさせなければならない.

equipment *n.* se「tsubi 設備; yo「o-gu 用具; so「ochi 装置: equipment costs (*setsubi-hi*) 設備費 / camping equipment (*kyañpu yoogu*) キャンプ用具 / video equipment (*bideo soo-chi*) ビデオ装置.

equivalent *adj.* do「otoo no 同等の; hi「toshi「i 等しい; so「otoo no 相当の: These two words are equivalent in meaning. (*Kono futatsu no go wa imi ga hitoshii.*) この二つの語は意味が等しい. / What is one dollar equivalent to in Japanese yen? (*Ichi doru wa Nihoñ eñ de ikura ni sootoo shimasu ka?*) 1ドルは日本円でいくらに相当しますか.
— *n.* do「otoo「obutsu 同等物; (words) so「otoo-go 相当語: The English equivalent of Japanese 'inu' is 'dog.' (*Nihoñgo no 'inu' ni sootoo suru Eego wa 'dog' desu.*) 日本語の「犬」に相当する英語は'dog'です.

era *n.* ji「dai 時代; ki「geñ 紀元: the Showa [Meiji] era (*Shoowa [Meiji] jidai*) 昭和[明治]時代 / the Christian era (*Kirisuto kigeñ*) キリスト紀元.

erase *vt.* **1** (of writing) ... o ke「su ...を消す⌐; sa「kujo suru 削除する⌐: erase the writing on a blackboard (*kokubañ no ji o kesu*) 黒板の字を消す / Please erase all your mistakes. (*Machigai o zeñbu sakujo shite kudasai.*) 間違いを全部削除してください.
2 (of recording) ... o ke「su ...を消す⌐; sho「okyo suru 消去する⌐: erase everything on the tape (*teepu no mono o subete kesu*) テープのものをすべて消す.

eraser *n.* ke「shigomu 消しゴム; ko-「kuba」ñ-fuki 黒板ふき: a pencil with an eraser (*keshigomu-tsuki no eñpitsu*) 消しゴムつきの鉛筆 / a blackboard eraser (*kokubañ-fuki*) 黒板ふき.

erect *adj.* cho「kuritsu no 直立の; ma「ssu」gu no 真っすぐの: an erect posture (*chokuritsu no shisee*) 直

立の姿勢 / hold a flag erect (*hata o massugu ni tateru*) 旗を真っすぐに立てる.
— *vt.* ... o ta｢te¹ru ...を建てる Ⓥ; ke｢ñsetsu suru 建設する Ⓣ: erect a monument (*kineñhi o tateru*) 記念碑を建てる / erect a church (*kyookai o keñsetsu suru*) 教会を建設する.

erotic *adj.* se｢eai no 性愛の; er｢ochi¹kku na エロチックな: a vulgarly erotic film (*poruno eega*) ポルノ映画.

err *vi.* (... o) a｢yama¹ru (...を)誤る Ⓒ; ma｢chiga¹i o suru 間違いをする Ⓣ: err in one's judgment (*hañdañ o ayamaru*) 判断を誤る.

errand *n.* tsu｢kai 使い: go on an errand (*tsukai ni iku*) 使いに行く / send a person on an errand (*hito o tsukai ni dasu*) 人を使いに出す.

error *n.* a｢yamari¹ 誤り; ma｢chiga¹i 間違い: make a serious error (*hidoi machigai o suru*) ひどい間違いをする / I made an error of judgment. (*Watashi wa hañdañ o ayamatta.*) 私は判断を誤った.

erupt *vi.* fu｢ñka suru 噴火する Ⓣ; ba｢kuhatsu suru 爆発する Ⓣ: The volcano erupted. (*Kazañ ga fuñka shita.*) 火山が噴火した.

eruption *n.* fu｢ñka 噴火; ba｢kuhatsu 爆発: a volcanic eruption (*kazañ no fuñka*) 火山の噴火.

escalator *n.* e｢sukare¹etaa エスカレーター: go up [down] an escalator (*esukareetaa de agaru [sagaru]*) エスカレーターで上がる[下がる].

escape *vi.* **1** (get free) ni｢ge¹ru 逃げる Ⓥ: The prisoners escaped from jail. (*Shuujiñ-tachi wa keemusho kara nigeta.*) 囚人たちは刑務所から逃げた.
2 (leak) mo｢re¹ru 漏れる Ⓥ: The gas escaped from the pipe and caused an explosion. (*Gasu ga paipu kara morete bakuhatsu shita.*) ガスがパイプから漏れて爆発した.
— *vt.* (avoid) ... o no｢gare¹ru ...を逃れる Ⓥ; ma｢nugare¹ru 免れる Ⓥ: escape punishment (*batsu o nogareru*) 罰を逃れる / No one can

escape death. (*Dare de mo shi o manugareru koto wa dekinai.*) だれでも死を免れることはできない.
— *n.* **1** (breakout) to｢oboo 逃亡; da｢ssoo 脱走: an escape from jail (*keemusho kara no dassoo*) 刑務所からの脱走.
2 (avoiding) ma｢nugare¹ru ko｢to¹ 免れること: an escape from disaster (*saigai o manugareru koto*) 災害を免れること.
3 (leakage) mo｢re¹ 漏れ: an escape of gas (*gasu-more*) ガス漏れ.

escort *n.* **1** (accompaniment) go｢ee 護衛: A large escort accompanied the premier. (*Oozee no goee ga shushoo ni zuikoo shita.*) 大勢の護衛が首相に随行した.
2 (social companion) tsu｢kisoi 付き添い; do｢oha¹ñsha 同伴者: Who is your escort to tonight's dance? (*Koñya no dañsu paatii no doohañsha wa donata desu ka?*) 今夜のダンスパーティーの同伴者はどなたですか.
— *vt.* **1** (protectively accompany) ... o go｢ee suru ...を護衛する Ⓣ: Those security men always escort the President. (*Sore-ra no keego no hito-tachi wa itsu-mo daitooryoo o goee shite iru.*) それらの警護の人たちはいつも大統領を護衛している.
2 (socially accompany) ... ni tsu｢kiso¹u ...に付き添う Ⓒ; ... o o｢kuritodoke¹ru ...を送り届ける Ⓥ: Please allow me to escort you home. (*Otaku made okurasete kudasai.*) お宅まで送らせてください.

especially *adv.* to｢ku ni 特に; to｢kubetsu ni 特別に: I am especially interested in music. (*Watashi wa toku ni oñgaku ni kyoomi o motte imasu.*) 私は特に音楽に興味を持っています.

essay *n.* zu｢ihitsu 随筆; hyo｢oroñ 評論; sa｢kubuñ 作文: He wrote an essay about the novel. (*Kare wa sono shoosetsu ni tsuite hyooroñ o kaita.*) 彼はその小説について評論を書いた. / I have to finish this essay by tomorrow. (*Watashi wa kono saku-*

buñ o ashita made ni kakanake-reba naranai.) 私はこの作文をあしたまでに書かなければならない.

essential *adj.* **1** (vital) fuˈkaˈketsu na 不可欠な; zeˈhi hiˈtsuyoo na ぜひ必要な: A balanced diet is essential for health. (*Baraǹsu no toreta shokuji wa keñkoo ni fukaketsu desu.*) バランスのとれた食事は健康に不可欠です.

2 (basic) hoˈñshitsu-teki na 本質的な; koˈñpoñ-teki na 根本的な: an essential difference (*hoñshitsu-teki na chigai*) 本質的な違い.

—— *n.* yoˈoteˈñ 要点: the essentials of Japanese grammar (*Nihoñgo-buñpoo no yooteñ*) 日本語文法の要点.

establish *vt.* **1** (found) ... o seˈtsuritsu suru ...を設立する Ⓣ; (create) tsuˈkuˈru 作る Ⓒ: establish a school (*gakkoo o setsuritsu suru*) 学校を設立する / establish a new system (*atarashii soshiki o tsukuru*) 新しい組織を作る.

2 (firmly settle) ... ni oˈchitsuka-seru ...に落ち着かせる Ⓥ: They are established in their new house. (*Kare-ra wa shiñkyo ni ochitsuita.*) 彼らは新居に落ち着いた.

3 (of custom, reputation) ... o kaˈkuritsu suru ...を確立する Ⓣ: That custom is one that was established many years ago. (*Sono shuukañ wa nañ-neñ mo mae ni kakuritsu shita mono desu.*) その習慣は何年も前に確立したものです.

4 (ascertain) ... o shoˈomee suru ...を証明する Ⓣ: establish one's alibi (*jibuñ no aribai o shoomee suru*) 自分のアリバイを証明する.

establishment *n.* seˈtsuritsu 設立; seˈetee 制定: the establishment of a new hospital (*atarashii byooiñ no setsuritsu*) 新しい病院の設立 / the establishment of the constitution (*keñpoo no seetee*) 憲法の制定.

estate *n.* **1** (land) jiˈsho 地所: We have a small estate in the country. (*Watashi-tachi wa inaka ni chiisa-*

na jisho o motte imasu.) 私たちは田舎に小さな地所を持っています.

2 (property) zaˈisañ 財産: real estate (*fudoosañ*) 不動産.

esteem *n.* (of people) soˈñkee 尊敬; (of things) soˈñchoo 尊重: hold a person in esteem (*hito o soñkee suru*) 人を尊敬する.

—— *vt.* (of people) ... o soˈñkee suru ...を尊敬する Ⓣ; (of things) soñchoo suru 尊重する Ⓣ: He is esteemed by everyone. (*Kare wa miñna ni soñkee sarete iru.*) 彼はみんなに尊敬されている. / I esteem your advice highly. (*Watashi wa anata no chuukoku o ooi ni soñchoo ita-shimasu.*) 私はあなたの忠告を大いに尊重いたします.

estimate *vt.* ... o miˈtsumoru ...を見積もる Ⓒ; haˈñdañ suru 判断する Ⓣ: I estimated the cost at a million yen. (*Watashi wa sono hiyoo o hyakumañ-eñ to mitsumotta.*) 私はその費用を100万円と見積もった.

—— *vi.* miˈtsumori o suru 見積もりをする Ⓣ: estimate for repairs (*shuuri no mitsumori o suru*) 修理の見積もりをする.

—— *n.* miˈtsumori 見積もり; miˈkomi 見込み: The carpenter has given us his estimate. (*Daiku wa wata-shi-tachi ni mitsumori o kureta.*) 大工は私たちに見積もりをくれた.

eternal *adj.* eˈe-eñ no 永遠の; eˈekyuu no 永久の: eternal life (*ee-eñ no seemee*) 永遠の生命 / They pledged their eternal love. (*Kare-ra wa ee-eñ no ai o chikatta.*) 彼らは永遠の愛を誓った.

ethical *adj.* doˈotokujoo no 道徳上の; riˈñri-teki na 倫理的な: ethical problems (*dootokujoo no moñdai*) 道徳上の問題.

etiquette *n.* reˈegi-saˈhoo 礼儀作法; eˈchiketto エチケット.

Europe *n.* Yoˈoroˈppa ヨーロッパ; Oˈoshuu 欧州.

European *adj.* Yoˈoroˈppa no ヨーロッパの; Oˈoshuu no 欧州の: European countries (*Yooroppa no kuñi-*

guni) ヨーロッパの国々.
— n. Yo「oroppa¹jiň ヨーロッパ人.

evade vt. **1** (avoid) ... o sa「ke¹ru
...を避ける Ⓥ; no「gare¹ru 逃れる Ⓥ:
evade the issue (moňdai o sakeru)
問題を避ける / evade taxes (datsu-
zee suru) 脱税する.
2 (escape) ... o ma「nugare¹ru ...を免
れる Ⓥ: evade capture (taiho o
manugareru) 逮捕を免れる.

eve n. **1** (day or night before) ze¹-
ňya 前夜; ze「ňjitsu 前日; i¹bu イブ:
Christmas Eve (Kurisumasu ibu)
クリスマスイブ / New Year's Eve
(oomisoka) 大みそか.
2 (time just before) cho「kuzeň 直
前: the eve of an election (seňkyo
no chokuzeň) 選挙の直前.

even[1] adv. **1** [emphasizing a surprising statement] ... de sa¹e ...でさ
え; ... de su¹ra ...ですら: He gets up
at six even on Sundays. (Kare wa
nichiyoo de sae roku-ji ni okiru.)
彼は日曜でさえ6時に起きる. / Even a
child can answer that. (Kodomo de
sura soňna koto wa kotaerareru.)
子どもですらそんなことは答えられる.
2 (still; yet) sa¹ra ni さらに; i¹ssoo
いっそう: This painting is even better than that. (Kono e wa sono e
yori mo sara ni yoi.) この絵はその絵
よりもさらによい. / He made an even
worse mistake. (Kare wa issoo
hidoi machigai o shita.) 彼はいっそう
ひどい間違いをした.
3 (indeed) so「re do¹koro ka それど
ころか: I like Sachiko very much,
even love her. (Watashi wa
Sachiko-saň ga suki desu. Sore
dokoro ka aishite imasu.) 私は幸子
さんが好きです. それどころか愛しています.

even if ... conj. ta「toe ⟨verb⟩-te
[de] mo たとえ...て[で]も: Even if we
fail, it will be a good experience.
(Tatoe shippai shite mo ii keekeň
to naru deshoo.) たとえ失敗してもいい
経験となるでしょう.

even[2] adj. **1** (flat) ta「ira na 平らな:
an even surface (taira na hyoomeň)
平らな表面 / I made the ground

even. (Watashi wa jimeň o taira
ni shita.) 私は地面を平らにした.
2 (equal) o「naji no 同じの; ta「itoo
no 対等の: an even score (dooteň)
同点 / an even bargain (taitoo no
torihiki) 対等の取り引き.
3 (of a number) gu「usu¹u no 偶数
の: even numbers and odd numbers (guusuu to kisuu) 偶数と奇数.
4 (of a level) o「naji ta¹kasa no 同じ
高さの: The water was even with
my knees. (Mizu wa watashi no
hiza to onaji takasa datta.) 水は私の
ひざと同じ高さだった.

evening n. ba¹ň 晩; yu「ugata 夕方:
I met him on Saturday evening.
(Watashi wa doyoobi no baň ni
kare ni atta.) 私は土曜日の晩に彼に
会った. / He came back late in the
evening. (Kare wa yuugata osoku
kaette kita.) 彼は夕方遅く帰って来た.

event n. **1** (important occurrence)
de「ki¹goto 出来事; ji「keň 事件;
gyo¹oji 行事: the major events of
that year (sono toshi no omo na
dekigoto) その年の主な出来事 / a
special event (tokubetsu-gyooji) 特
別行事.
2 (competition) shu「moku 種目;
kyo¹ogi 競技: field [track] events
(fiirudo [torakku] shumoku) フィー
ルド[トラック]種目 / today's main
event (kyoo no shuyoo kyoogi) きょ
うの主要競技.

in the event of ... prep. ... no
ba「ai wa ...の場合は: in the event
of bad weather (teňki no warui
baai wa) 天気の悪い場合は.

ever adv. **1** [in questions] (up to
now) i「ma ma¹de ni 今までに; ka¹l-
tsute かつて: "Have you ever been
to Sapporo?" "Yes, I have." ("Ima
made ni Sapporo e itta koto ga arimasu ka?" "Hai, arimasu.")「今ま
でに札幌へ行ったことがありますか」「はい,
あります」
2 [with negatives] (up to now) ko-
「re ma¹de (... nai) これまで(...ない):
None of us have ever seen it.
(Wareware wa kore made dare

mo sore o mita koto ga arimaseñ.)
われわれはこれまでだれもそれを見たことがありません.

3 [with superlative] (up to now)
i｢ma ma┐de 今まで; ka┐tsute かつて:
This is the most beautiful orchid I have ever seen. (*Kore wa watashi ga ima made mita uchi de ichibañ utsukushii rañ da.*) これは私が今まで見たうちでいちばん美しいらんだ.

4 [used with if] (sometime) i┐tsuka いつか: If you ever come to Kobe, please look us up. (*Itsu-ka Koobe e kita toki wa yotte kudasai.*) いつか神戸へ来たときは寄ってください.

every *adj.* **1** (each; all) do┐no ... mo どの…も; su┐bete no すべての:
Every student wants to win the prize. (*Dono gakusee mo shoo o toritagatte iru.*) どの学生も賞を取りたがっている. / I learned every word in the list. (*Watashi wa risuto ni aru tañgo o subete oboemashita.*) 私はリストにある単語をすべて覚えました.

2 (once in each) ma┐i- 毎; ... go┐to ni …ごとに: every day [week, month, year] (*mainichi* [*maishuu, maitsuki, maitoshi*]) 毎日[毎週, 毎月, 毎年] / I have the car serviced every six months. (*Watashi wa rokkagetsu goto ni kuruma o teñkeñ shite moraimasu.*) 私は6か月ごとに車を点検してもらいます.

3 (sufficient; great) ju┐ubu┐ñ na 十分な; ka┐noo na ka┐giri no 可能限りの: take every possible measure (*kanoo na kagiri no shochi o toru*) 可能な限りの処置をとる.

every other *adj.* hi┐totsu oki no 一つおきの: every other day (*ichi-nichi oki*) 1日おき.

everybody *pron.* ⇨ everyone.

everyday *adj.* **1** (daily) ma┐inichi no 毎日の; ni┐chijoo no 日常の: everyday life (*mainichi no seekatsu*) 毎日の生活 / everyday conversation (*nichijoo-kaiwa*) 日常会話. ★ Adverb 'every day' is 'mainichi' 毎日.

2 (usual) fu┐dañ no ふだんの: We all

attended the party in everyday clothes. (*Watashi-tachi wa miñna fudañgi de paatii ni shusseki shita.*) 私たちはみんなふだん着でパーティーに出席した.

everyone *pron.* mi┐ñna┐ みんな; da┐re de mo mi┐na┐ だれでもみな: Everyone has left. (*Miñna dete iki-mashita.*) みんな出て行きました. / Everyone praises the boy. (*Dare de mo mina sono shooneñ o home-masu.*) だれでもみなその少年をほめます.

everything *pron.* **1** (all things) na┐ñ de mo mi┐na┐ 何でもみな; mi┐ñna┐ みんな; su┐bete すべて: I've tried everything, but it's no use. (*Nañ de mo mina yatte mita ga dame datta.*) 何でもみなやってみたがだめだった. / She told the police everything she knew. (*Kanojo wa shitte iru koto wa subete keesatsu ni hana-shita.*) 彼女は知っていることはすべて警察に話した. / Thank you for everything. (*Iroiro doomo arigatoo gozaimashita.*) いろいろどうもありがとうございました.

2 (the most important thing) mo┐t-to┐mo ta┐isetsu na mono┐ 最も大切なもの; su┐bete すべて: Money isn't everything. (*O-kane ga subete de wa nai.*) お金がすべてではない.

everywhere *adv.* do┐ko de mo どこでも; i┐ta┐ru to┐koro┐ ni 至る所に; do┐ko mo kashiko mo どこもかしこも: Is rice grown everywhere in Japan? (*Nihoñ de wa doko de mo kome ga dekimasu ka?*) 日本ではどこでも米ができますか. / There is mold everywhere. (*Itaru tokoro ni kabi ga haete iru.*) 至る所にかびが生えている.

evidence *n.* **1** (proof) sho┐oko 証拠: I will believe you if you show me the evidence. (*Sono shooko o misete kurereba anata o shiñji-masu.*) その証拠を見せてくれればあなたを信じます.

2 (testimony) sho┐ogeñ 証言: The witness stood up and gave her evidence. (*Shooniñ wa tachiagatte* shoogeñ o nobeta.) 証人は立ち上がって証言を述べた.

evident adj. meˈehaku na 明白な; aˈkiˈraka na 明らかな: an evident mistake (akiraka na machigai) 明らかな間違い / It is evident that he lied to us. (Kare ga uso o tsuita no wa akiraka da.) 彼がうそをついたのは明らかだ.

evil adj. waˈruˈi 悪い; aˈkui no 悪意の: an evil custom (akushuu) 悪習 / an evil tongue (dokuzetsu) 毒舌.
— n. aˈku 悪; aˈkuji 悪事: good and evil (zeñ aku) 善悪 / do evil (akuji o hataraku) 悪事を働く.

evoke vt. ... o yoˈbiokoˈsu ...を呼び起こす Ⓒ: evoke a memory (kioku o yobiokosu) 記憶を呼び起こす.

evolution n. haˈttatsu 発達; haˈtteñ 発展; shiˈñka 進化: the evolution of democracy (miñshushugi no hattatsu) 民主主義の発達 / the theory of evolution (shiñkaroñ) 進化論.

evolve vt. ... o haˈttatsu saseru ...を発達させる Ⓥ; haˈtteñ saseru 発展させる Ⓥ: The Japanese have evolved a very interesting culture. (Nihoñjiñ wa hijoo ni kyoomibukai buñka o hattatsu saseta.) 日本人は非常に興味深い文化を発達させた.
— vi. haˈtteñ suru 発展する Ⓘ; shiˈñka suru 進化する Ⓘ: Man evolved from the apelike creatures. (Niñgeñ wa ruijiñeñ kara shiñka shita.) 人間は類人猿から進化した.

exact adj. 1 (precise) seˈekaku na 正確な: the exact time (seekaku na jikañ) 正確な時間 / I didn't understand the exact meaning of the sentence. (Watashi wa sono buñ no seekaku na imi ga wakaranakatta.) 私はその文の正確な意味がわからなかった.
2 (accurate; careful) geˈñmitsu na 厳密な; seˈemitsu na 精密な: The accounts have to be exact. (Kaikee wa geñmitsu de nakereba ikenai.) 会計は厳密でなければいけない. / the exact sciences (seemitsu kagaku) 精密科学.

exactly adv. 1 (precisely) seˈekaku ni 正確に; (just) choˈodo ちょうど: Explain everything exactly as it happened. (Okotta mama ni seekaku ni setsumee shi nasai.) 起こったままに正確に説明しなさい. / I come at exactly nine o'clock. (Choodo ku-ji ni kimasu.) ちょうど9時に来ます.
2 [emphatic use] (quite) soˈno toˈori ni そのとおりに; maˈttaku まったく: Taro did exactly what I told him to. (Taroo wa watashi ga itta koto o sono toori ni yatta.) 太郎は私が言ったことをそのとおりにやった.

exaggerate vt. ... o oˈogesa ni iˈu ...を大げさに言う Ⓒ; koˈochoo suru 誇張する Ⓘ: You are exaggerating the danger. (Anata wa kikeñ o oogesa ni itte iru.) あなたは危険を大げさに言っている.
— vi. oˈogesa ni iu 大げさに言う Ⓒ: Suzuki tends to exaggerate. (Suzuki wa oogesa ni iu keekoo ga aru.) 鈴木は大げさに言う傾向がある.

exaggeration n. koˈchoo 誇張; oˈogesa 大げさ: What you say is an exaggeration. (Kimi ga itte iru koto wa oogesa da.) 君が言っていることは大げさだ.

examination n. 1 (academic) shiˈkeñ 試験: take an examination (shikeñ o ukeru) 試験を受ける / pass [fail] an examination (shikeñ ni ukaru [ochiru]) 試験に受かる[落ちる] / an entrance examination of a school (nyuugaku shikeñ) 入学試験. ★ Japanese 'shikeñ' also refers to 'test' and 'quiz.'
2 (medical) shiˈñsatsu 診察; shiˈñdañ 診断: undergo a physical examination (keñkoo shiñdañ o ukeru) 健康診断を受ける.
3 (investigation) keˈñsa 検査; choˈosa 調査: carry out an examination of water quality (suishitsu keñsa o suru) 水質検査をする.
4 (legal) jiˈñmoñ 尋問; shiˈñri 審理: the examination of a witness (shooniñ no jiñmoñ) 証人の尋問.

examination paper *n.* shiⁱkeñ-moⁱdai 試験問題; shiⁱkeñ no toⁱoañ 試験の答案.

examine *vt.* **1** (scrutinize) ... o shiⁱrabeⁱru ...を調べる Ⅴ; keⁱñsa suru 検査する Ⅰ: The customs officer examined my bags. (*Zeekañ no kakarikañ wa watashi no kabañ o shirabeta.*) 税関の係官は私のかばんを調べた.
2 (medically check) ... o shiⁱñsatsu suru ...を診察する Ⅰ: The doctor carefully examined the patient. (*Isha wa kañja o teenee ni shiñsatsu shita.*) 医者は患者をていねいに診察した.
3 (test) ... ni shiⁱkeⁱñ o suru ...に試験をする Ⅰ: examine the students in history (*gakusee ni rekishi no shikeñ o suru*) 学生に歴史の試験をする.
4 (question) ... o jiⁱñmoñ suru ...を尋問する Ⅰ: examine a witness (*shooniñ o jiñmoñ suru*) 証人を尋問する.

example *n.* **1** (illustration) reⁱe 例; jiⁱtsuree 実例: an example of a terrible traffic accident (*hisañ na kootsuu jiko no ree*) 悲惨な交通事故の例.
2 (model) teⁱhoⁱñ 手本; moⁱhañ 模範: give a good example to a person (*hito ni yoi tehoñ o shimesu*) 人によい手本を示す.
for example *adv.* taⁱtoⁱeba 例えば.

exceed *vt.* ... o koⁱsu ...を越す Ⅽ; koⁱeru 越える Ⅴ; choⁱoka suru 超過する Ⅰ: This year his income will exceed six million yen. (*Kotoshi kare no shuunyuu wa roppyaku-mañ-eñ o koeru daroo.*) 今年彼の収入は600万円を越えるだろう. / exceed the speed limit (*seegeñ sokudo o chooka suru*) 制限速度を超過する.

excel *vt.* ... yoⁱri suⁱguⁱrete iru ...より優れている Ⅴ; ... ni maⁱsaⁱru ...に勝る Ⅽ: Peter excelled the other students in Japanese. (*Piitaa wa Nihoñgo de wa hoka no gakusee*

yori mo sugurete ita.) ピーターは日本語ではほかの学生よりも優れていた.
— *vi.* suⁱguⁱrete iru 優れている Ⅴ; nuⁱkiñdeⁱru 抜きん出る Ⅴ: Mary excels as an interpreter. (*Mearii wa tsuuyaku to shite sugurete iru.*) メアリーは通訳として優れている. / excel at sports (*supootsu de nukiñdete iru*) スポーツで抜きん出ている.

excellent *adj.* suⁱguⁱreta 優れた; suⁱguⁱrete iru 優れている; yuⁱushuu na 優秀な; suⁱbarashiⁱi すばらしい: an excellent painting (*sugureta e*) 優れた絵 / an excellent meal (*subarashii shokuji*) すばらしい食事.

except *prep.* ... iⁱgai wa ...以外は; ... o noⁱzoiteⁱ wa ...を除いては: everyone except me (*watashi igai wa miñna*) 私以外はみんな / any day except Friday (*kiñyoobi igai wa itsu de mo*) 金曜日以外はいつでも / except the last one (*saigo no mono o nozoite*) 最後のものを除いて / I have nothing to declare except this perfume. (*Kono koosui igai ni wa shiñkoku suru mono wa nani mo arimaseñ.*) この香水以外には申告するものは何もありません.
except for ... *prep.* ... o noⁱzokeⁱ ba ...を除けば: Except for a few kanji mistakes, your composition was excellent. (*Jakkañ no kañji no machigai o nozokeba, kimi no sakubuñ wa yoku dekite imashita.*) 若干の漢字の間違いを除けば, 君の作文はよくできていました.

exception *n.* reⁱegai 例外: an exception to a rule (*kisoku no reegai*) 規則の例外 / In this case we can make no exception. (*Kono baai wa reegai to shimaseñ.*) この場合は例外としません.

exceptional *adj.* **1** (unusual) reⁱegai-teki na 例外的な: an exceptional case (*reegai-teki na baai*) 例外的な場合.
2 (remarkable) suⁱguⁱreta 優れた; suⁱguⁱrete iru 優れている: an exceptional gift for music (*oñgaku ni taisuru sugureta sainoo*) 音楽に対する

優れた才能.

excess¹ *n.* choᵣoka 超過; kaᵣdo 過
度: Any excess in payment will be
returned. (*Shiharai no chooka-buñ
wa heñkyaku shimasu.*) 支払の超過
分は返却します. / go to excess (*do o
sugosu*) 度を過ごす.

excess² *adj.* choᵣoka no 超過の;
yoᵣbuñ no 余分の: excess baggage
(*chooka tenimotsu*) 超過手荷物 /
pay the excess fare (*yobuñ no ryookiñ o harau*) 余分の料金を払う.

excessive *adj.* kaᵣdo no 過度の;
hoᵣogai na 法外な: show an excessive interest (*kado no kyoomi o
shimesu*) 過度の興味を示す / These
prices are certainly excessive. (*Kono nedañ wa tashika ni hoogai da.*)
この値段はたしかに法外だ.

exchange *n.* **1** (of money) kaᵣwa-
se 為替; ryoᵣogae 両替: foreign
exchange (*gaikoku kawase*) 外国為
替 / the exchange rate (*kawase
reeto*) 為替レート / a bill of exchange (*kawase-tegata*) 為替手形.
2 (giving and taking) koᵣokañ 交
換; yaᵣriᵣtori 取り: an exchange
student (*kookañ-gakusee*) 交換学
生 / an exchange of opinions (*ikeñ
no yaritori*) 意見のやり取り.
— *vt.* **1** (give and take) ... o koᵣokañ suru ...を交換する①; ... to toᵣri-
kaeru ...と取り替える▽: exchange
presents (*okurimono o kookañ
suru*) 贈り物を交換する / Excuse me,
but could you exchange seats with
me? (*Shitsuree desu ga watashi to
seki o torikaete itadakemasu ka?*)
失礼ですが私と席を取り替えていただけま
すか.
2 (of money) ... o ryoᵣogae suru ...
を両替する①: Can I exchange dol-
lars for yen here? (*Koko de doru o
eñ ni ryoogae dekimasu ka?*) ここで
ドルを円に両替できますか.

excite *vt.* **1** (stir up) ... o koᵣofuñ
saseru ...を興奮させる▽; waᵣku-
waku saᵣseru わくわくさせる▽: The
news excited us all. (*Sono shirase
wa watashi-tachi miñna o wakuwaku saseta.*) その知らせは私たちみん
なをわくわくさせた.
2 (stimulate) ... o soᵣsoᵣru ...をそそ
る©; oᵣkosaseᵣru 起こさせる▽:
The story excited my curiosity.
(*Sono hanashi wa watashi no
kyoomi o sosotta.*) その話は私の興味
をそそった.

excited *adj.* koᵣofuñ shita [shite
iru] 興奮した[している]; waᵣkuwaku
shita [shite iru] わくわくした[している]:
an excited voice (*koofuñ shita koe*)
興奮した声 / We got excited when
we saw the movie star. (*Sono eega
sutaa o mite watashi-tachi wa wakuwaku shita.*) その映画スターを見て
私たちはわくわくした.

excitement *n.* koᵣofuñ 興奮: I
jumped up in excitement. (*Watashi wa koofuñ shite tobiagatta.*) 私
は興奮して跳び上がった.

exciting *adj.* koᵣofuñ saseru 興奮
させる; waᵣkuwaku saᵣseru yoᵣo na
わくわくさせるような: an exciting story
(*wakuwaku saseru yoo na hanashi*) わくわくさせるような話 / an exciting game (*sugoku omoshiroi shiai*)
すごくおもしろい試合.

exclaim *vi.* saᵣkeᵣbu 叫ぶ©; koᵣe
o aᵣgeru 声をあげる▽: The girl ex-
claimed in joy. (*Sono oñna-no-ko
wa yorokoñde koe o ageta.*) その女
の子は喜んで声をあげた.
— *vt.* ... to saᵣkeᵣbu ...と叫ぶ©:
"I've made a mistake!" he ex-
claimed. (*"Machigaeta" to kare
wa sakeñda.*) 「間違えた」と彼は叫
んだ.

exclamation *n.* saᵣkebigoᵣe 叫び
声: give an exclamation of surprise
(*odoroki no sakebigoe o ageru*) 驚
きの叫び声をあげる.

exclamation mark [point] *n.*
kaᵣñtaᵣñfu 感嘆符.

exclude *vt.* ... o shiᵣmedasu ...を締
め出す©; joᵣgai suru 除外する①:
We decided to exclude him from
the group. (*Kare o nakama kara
shimedasu koto ni kimeta.*) 彼を仲
間から締め出すことに決めた.

excluding *prep.* ... o no⌐zoite ...を
除いて: There were ten members
present excluding him. (*Kare o
nozoite juu-niñ no kaiiñ ga shusseki shita.*) 彼を除いて 10 人の会員が
出席した.

exclusive *adj.* **1** (high class) ko⌐o-
kyuu na 高級な; i⌐chiryuu no 一流
の: an exclusive hotel (*kookyuu
hoteru*) 高級ホテル.
2 (not shared) se⌐ñyoo no 専用の;
do⌐kuseñ-teki na 独占的な: This
car is for the president's exclusive
use. (*Kono kuruma wa shachoo
señyoo no kuruma desu.*) この車は
社長専用の車です. / an exclusive
interview (*dokuseñ-kaikeñ*) 独占会
見.

　exclusive of ... *prep.* ... o no⌐zo-
ite ...を除いて: The book costs
¥5,000, exclusive of postage. (*Sono
hoñ wa sooryoo o nozoite go-señ-
eñ da.*) その本は送料を除いて 5 千円だ.

excursion *n.* e⌐ñsoku 遠足; ka⌐ñ-
koo-ryo⌐koo 観光旅行: a school
excursion (*gakkoo no eñsoku*) 学校
の遠足 / go on an excursion to
Nikko (*Nikkoo e kañkoo-ryokoo
ni iku*) 日光へ観光旅行に行く.

excuse *vt.* **1** (forgive) ... o yu⌐ru⌐-
su ...を許す C: Please excuse me
for my rudeness. (*Shitsuree o o-
yurushi kudasai.*) 失礼をお許しくださ
い.
2 (from obligation) ... o me⌐ñjo
suru ...を免除する I: The teacher
excused me from attending. (*Señsee wa watashi no shusseki o
meñjo shite kureta.*) 先生は私の出席
を免除してくれた.
3 (justify) ... no i⌐iwake o suru ...
の言い訳をする I: He excused him-
self for being late. (*Kare wa okureta koto no iiwake o shita.*) 彼は遅
れたことの言い訳をした.

Excuse me. [disturbing someone]
(*Chotto shitsuree.*) ちょっと失礼. /
[apologizing] (*Gomeñ nasai.*) ごめん
なさい.

Excuse me? [asking for repetition]
(*Sumimaseñ ga moo ichido o-
negai shimasu.*) すみませんがもう一度
お願いします.
Excuse me, but .... [addressing or
interrupting] (*Shitsuree desu ga ....*)
失礼ですが....

----

execute *vt.* **1** (put to death) ... o
sho⌐kee suru ...を処刑する I: The
murderer was executed. (*Sono satsujiñhañ wa shokee sareta.*) その殺
人犯は処刑された.
2 (carry out) ... o ji⌐kko suru ...を
実行する I: execute an order [a
plan] (*meeree [keekaku] o jikko
suru*) 命令[計画]を実行する.

execution *n.* **1** (lawful killing)
sho⌐kee 処刑: the execution of a
murderer (*satsujiñhañ no shokee*)
殺人犯の処刑.
2 (carrying out) su⌐ikoo 遂行: the
proper execution of one's duties
(*jibuñ no shokumu no tadashii sui-
koo*) 自分の職務の正しい遂行.

executive *n.* ya⌐ku⌐iñ 役員; ju⌐u-
yaku 重役; ke⌐e-e⌐esha 経営者.
— *adj.* ka⌐ñri no 管理の; gyo⌐osee-
joo no 行政上の: an executive committee (*shikkoo iiñkai*) 執行委員会.

exempt *vt.* ... o me⌐ñjo suru ...を免
除する I: be exempted from a tax
(*zeekiñ o meñjo sareru*) 税金を免除
される.

exercise *n.* **1** (physical) u⌐ñdoo
運動; ta⌐isoo 体操: I make sure I
get regular exercise. (*Watashi wa
itsu-mo kimatta uñdoo o suru yoo
ni shite imasu.*) 私はいつも決まった運
動をするようにしています.
2 (academic) re⌐ñshuu 練習; re⌐ñ-
shuu-mo⌐ñdai 練習問題: The grammar exercises are after each lesson.
(*Buñpoo no reñshuu-moñdai wa
kaku ka no owari ni tsuite imasu.*)
文法の練習問題は各課の終わりについて
います.
— *vt.* **1** (train) ... o u⌐ñdoo saseru
...を運動させる V: exercise a dog
(*inu o uñdoo saseru*) 犬を運動させる.

2 (use) ... o mo⌐chii¬ru ...を用いる Ⓥ: exercise care (*chuui suru*) 注意 する.

exhaust vt. **1** (tire out) ... o tsu⌐karehate sase¬ru ...を疲れ果てさせる Ⓥ: The walk from the station has exhausted me. (*Eki kara aruitara tsukarehateta.*) 駅から歩いたら疲れ果てた.

2 (use up) ... o tsu⌐kaihata¬su ...を使い果たす Ⓒ: exhaust one's money [strength] (*o-kane [tairyoku] o tsukaihatasu*) お金[体力]を使い果たす.

exhausted adj. tsu⌐kareki¬tta 疲れきった; tsu⌐kareki¬tte iru 疲れきっている; he⌐toheto ni na¬tta [na¬tte iru] へとへとになった[なっている]: We were all absolutely exhausted. (*Watashitachi wa miñna sukkari tsukarekitte ita.*) 私たちはみんなすっかり疲れきっていた.

exhaust gas n. ha⌐ikiga¬su 排気ガス.

exhausting adj. hi⌐doku tsu⌐kare¬ru ひどく疲れる: an exhausting job (*hidoku tsukareru shigoto*) ひどく疲れる仕事 / The climb to the summit was exhausting. (*Choojoo made no yamanobori wa hidoku tsukareta.*) 頂上までの山登りはひどく疲れた.

exhaustion n. **1** (tiredness) hi⌐do¬i tsu⌐kare ひどい疲れ: mental [physical] exhaustion (*atama [karada] no hidoi tsukare*) 頭[体]のひどい疲れ.

2 (using up) tsu⌐kaitsuku¬su ko⌐to¬ 使い尽くすこと: the exhaustion of natural resources (*teññeñ shigeñ o tsukaitsukusu koto*) 天然資源を使い尽くすこと.

exhibit vt. **1** (put on a show) ... o te⌐ñji suru ...を展示する Ⓘ: She is exhibiting some of her photographs next week. (*Kanojo wa raishuu jibuñ no shashiñ o ikutsu-ka teñji shimasu.*) 彼女は来週自分の写真をいくつか展示します.

2 (show) ... o shi⌐me¬su ...を示す Ⓒ: She exhibited no interest. (*Kanojo wa nañ no kyoomi mo shime-*

sanakatta.*) 彼女は何の興味も示さなかった.
— n. te⌐ñjihiñ 展示品; shu⌐ppi¬ñbutsu 出品物: exhibits in a museum (*hakubutsukañ no teñjihiñ*) 博物館の展示品.

exhibition n. **1** (show) te⌐ñra¬ñkai 展覧会; te⌐ñji¬kai 展示会: put on an art exhibition (*bijutsuteñ o hiraku*) 美術展を開く.

2 (act of exhibiting) shi⌐me¬su ko⌐to¬ 示すこと; mi⌐se¬ru ko⌐to¬ 見せること: a good opportunity for the exhibition of one's talents (*sainoo o shimesu yoi kikai*) 才能を示すよい機会.

exile n. **1** (forced absence) tsu⌐ihoo 追放; bo⌐omee 亡命: He was sent into exile. (*Kare wa kokugai ni tsuihoo sareta.*) 彼は国外に追放された. / live in exile (*boomee-seekatsu o okuru*) 亡命生活を送る.

2 (exiled person) tsu⌐ihoo sareta hito¬ 追放された人; bo⌐omee¬sha 亡命者: a political exile (*seeji boomeesha*) 政治亡命者.
— vt. ... o ko⌐ku¬gai ni tsu⌐ihoo suru ...を国外に追放する Ⓘ: be exiled from home (*kokoku kara tsuihoo sareru*) 故国から追放される.

exist vi. **1** (be) i⌐ru¬ いる Ⓥ; so⌐ñzai suru 存在する Ⓘ: No life exists on the moon. (*Tsuki ni wa seebutsu wa inai.*) 月には生物はいない.

2 (stay alive) se⌐ezoñ suru 生存する Ⓘ; i⌐kite iru 生きている Ⓥ: The survivors existed only on water. (*Seezoñsha wa mizu dake de ikite ita.*) 生存者は水だけで生きていた.

existence n. **1** (existing) so⌐ñzai 存在; ji⌐tsuzai 実在: I believe in the existence of God. (*Watashi wa kami no soñzai o shiñjimasu.*) 私は神の存在を信じます.

2 (survival) se⌐ezoñ 生存; i⌐kite iru ko⌐to¬ 生きていること: the struggle for existence (*seezoñ-kyoosoo*) 生存競争 / Oxygen is necessary for our existence. (*Sañso wa watashitachi ga ikite iku tame ni hitsu-*

yoo desu.) 酸素は私たちが生きていくために必要です.

3 (way of life) seʼekatsu 生活; kuʼrashi 暮らし: lead a happy existence (*shiawase na kurashi o okuru*) 幸せな暮らしを送る.

exit *n.* deʼguchi 出口: an emergency exit (*hijooguchi*) 非常口 / The exit is the same as the entrance. (*Deguchi wa iriguchi to onaji desu.*) 出口は入り口と同じです.
—— *vi.* taʼijoo suru 退場する Ⅰ.

expand *vi.* **1** (grow large) oʼokiku naru 大きくなる Ⓒ; (swell) boʼochoo suru 膨張する Ⅰ: This city has expanded rapidly in the last few years. (*Kono toshi wa koko suuneñ de kyuusoku ni ookiku natta.*) この都市はここ数年で急速に大きくなった. / Metals expand when heated. (*Kiñzoku wa nessuru to boochoo suru.*) 金属は熱すると膨張する.

2 (develop) kaʼkuchoo suru 拡張する Ⅰ; haʼtteñ suru 発展する Ⅰ: The store expanded into a large supermarket. (*Sono mise wa kakuchoo shite ooki-na suupaa ni natta.*) その店は拡張して大きなスーパーになった.

3 (explain in detail) kuʼwaʼshiku noʼbeʼru 詳しく述べる Ⅴ: Could you please expand on the last point? (*Saigo no tokoro o kuwashiku nobete itadakemasu ka?*) 最後の所を詳しく述べていただけますか.
—— *vt.* **1** (enlarge) ... o oʼokiku suru ...を大きくする Ⅰ: The wrestler expanded his chest. (*Resuraa wa mune o ookiku shita.*) レスラーは胸を大きくした.

2 (develop) ... o kaʼkuchoo suru ...を拡張する Ⅰ; haʼtteñ saseru 発展させる Ⅴ: expand one's business (*shoobai o kakuchoo suru*) 商売を拡張する / expand an idea into a theory (*aidea o hatteñ sasete riron ni matomeru*) アイデアを発展させて理論にまとめる.

expansion *n.* **1** (in size) kaʼkuchoo 拡張; kaʼkudai 拡大: the expansion of territory (*ryoodo no kakuchoo*) 領土の拡張.

2 (in volume) boʼochoo 膨張: the expansion of gases (*kitai no boochoo*) 気体の膨張.

3 (development) haʼtteñ 発展: the expansion of trade (*booeki no hatteñ*) 貿易の発展.

expect *vt.* **1** (think) ... daroo to oʼmoʼu ...だろうと思う Ⓒ; (anticipate) yoʼki suru 予期する Ⅰ: I expect Mr. Miyamoto to come. (*Miyamoto-sañ wa kuru daroo to omou.*) 宮本さんは来るだろうと思う.

2 (wait for) ... o maʼtsu ...を待つ Ⓒ: The boss is expecting you. (*Kachoo ga anata o matte imasu yo.*) 課長があなたを待っていますよ.

3 (consider reasonable) ... o kiʼtai suru ...を期待する Ⅰ: He expects good pay for the work. (*Kare wa sono shigoto ni taishite yoi kyuuryoo o kitai shite iru.*) 彼はその仕事に対して良い給料を期待している.

be expecting (a baby) *vi.* shuʼssañ yoʼtee da 出産予定だ: I hear that Mary is expecting next month. (*Mearii wa raigetsu shussañ no yotee da soo desu.*) メアリーは来月出産の予定だそうです.

expectation *n.* yoʼsoo 予想; miʼkomi 見込み; (hopes) kiʼtai 期待: The outcome was contrary to expectations. (*Kekka wa yosoo ni hañshite ita.*) 結果は予想に反していた. / Our expectations were finally realized. (*Watashi-tachi no kitai wa tsui ni jitsugeñ sareta.*) 私たちの期待はついに実現された.

expedition *n.* (journey) taʼñkeñ 探検; (group) taʼñkeñtai 探検隊: go on an expedition (*tañkeñ ni iku*) 探検に行く.

expel *vt.* ... o oʼidaʼsu ...を追い出す Ⓒ; tsuʼihoo suru 追放する Ⅰ: The illegal immigrants were expelled from Japan. (*Fuhoo ijuusha wa Nihoñ kara tsuihoo sareta.*) 不法移住者は日本から追放された. / be expelled from school (*taigaku ni naru*) 退学になる.

expense n. 1 (cost) hi'yoo 費用;
shi'shutsu 支出: They built the
church at great expense. (*Kare-ra
wa tagaku no hiyoo o kakete sono
kyookai o tateta.*) 彼らは多額の費用
をかけてその教会を建てた.
2 (necessary costs) ke'ehi 経費:
school expenses (*gakuhi*) 学費 /
traveling expenses (*ryohi*) 旅費 /
My expenses were paid by the
company. (*Watashi no keehi wa kaisha ga haratte kureta.*) 私の経費は
会社が払ってくれた.

expense account n. hi'tsuyoo
ke'ehi 必要経費; se'tta'ihi 接待費.

expensive adj. ko'oka na 高価な;
ta'ka'i 高い: That ring looks very
expensive. (*Sono yubiwa wa taka-
soo ni mieru.*) その指輪は高そうに見え
る. / Do you have a less expensive
watch? (*Motto yasui tokee wa arimasu ka?*) もっと安い時計はありますか.

experience n. 1 (knowledge or
skill) ke'eken 経験; ta'iken 体験:
I have experience in teaching English. (*Watashi wa Eego no kyooiku ni keeken ga arimasu.*) 私は英
語の教育に経験があります.
2 (event) ke'eken [ta'iken] shita
koto' 経験[体験]したこと: I had a lot
of strange experiences when living
abroad. (*Gaikoku ni sunde iru toki
fushigi na keeken o takusan shimashita.*) 外国に住んでいるとき不思議
な経験をたくさんしました.
— vt. ... o ke'eken suru ...を経験す
る ①; ta'iken suru 体験する ①: I
have never before experienced a
hardship like this. (*Kono yoo na
konnan o taiken shita koto wa ima
made ni arimasen.*) このような困難を
体験したことは今までにありません.

experienced adj. ke'eken no
a'ru 経験のある; be'teran no ベテラン
の: an experienced nurse (*beteran
no kangofu*) ベテランの看護婦.

experiment n. ji'kken 実験: conduct a chemical experiment (*kagaku no jikken o suru*) 科学の実験
をする.

— vi. ji'kken suru 実験する ①:
experiment on animals (*doobutsu
jikken o suru*) 動物実験をする.

expert n. se'nmonka 専門家; ju-
'kure'nsha 熟練者; be'teran ベテラ
ン: an expert on the Japanese
economy (*Nihon keezai no sen-
monka*) 日本経済の専門家 / She is
an expert at teaching Japanese.
(*Kanojo wa Nihongo kyooiku no
beteran da.*) 彼女は日本語教育のベテ
ランだ.
— adj. ju'kuren shita [shite iru] 熟
練した[している]; ju'kutatsu shita
[shite iru] 熟達した[している]: an
expert driver (*jukuren shita doraibaa*) 熟練したドライバー.

expiration n. ma'nki 満期; ki'ge-
ngire 期限切れ: the expiration of
one's alien registration certificate
(*gaikokujin toorokusho no kigen-
gire*) 外国人登録書の期限切れ.

expire vi. ma'nki ni naru 満期になる
Ⓒ; ki'gen ga ki're'ru 期限が切れる
Ⓥ: The validity of my passport
has expired. (*Pasupooto no kigen
ga kireta.*) パスポートの期限が切れた.

explain vt. 1 (make clear) ... o
se'tsumee suru ...を説明する ①: explain the structure of a building
(*tatemono no koozoo o setsumee
suru*) 建物の構造を説明する.
2 (account for) ... o be'nmee suru
...を弁明する ①; sha'kumee suru 釈
明する ①: explain one's absence
(*kesseki shita koto o benmee
suru*) 欠席したことを弁明する.

explanation n. se'tsumee 説明;
ka'isetsu 解説; be'nmee 弁明: We
demand a satisfactory explanation
from you. (*Nattoku no yuku setsumee o anata ni yookyuu shimasu.*)
納得のゆく説明をあなたに要求します.

explode vi. 1 (of bombs) ba'kuhatsu suru 爆発する ①; ha'retsu suru
破裂する ①: A bomb exploded.
(*Bakudan ga bakuhatsu shita.*) 爆
弾が爆発した.
2 (of emotions) ka'tto na'ru かっとな
る Ⓒ: He exploded in anger. (*Kare*

wa okotte katto natta.) 彼は怒って
かっとなった.

── *vt.* ... o baʳkuhatsu saseru ...を
爆発させる Ⓥ; haʳretsu saseru 破裂
させる Ⓥ: explode a bomb (*bakudañ o haretsu saseru*) 爆弾を破裂さ
せる.

exploit *vt.* 1 (develop) ... o kaʳiha-
tsu suru ...を開発する Ⓘ: exploit the
natural resources of a country (*kuni no teññeñ shigeñ o kaihatsu suru*) 国の天然資源を開発する.

2 (take advantage of) ... o riʳyoo
suru ...を利用する Ⓘ; saʳkushu suru
搾取する Ⓘ; kuʳimoʳno ni suru 食い
物にする Ⓘ: That company exploits
its employees. (*Ano kaisha wa juugyooiñ o kuimono ni shite iru.*) あ
の会社は従業員を食い物にしている.

explore *vt.* 1 (travel) ... o taʳñkeñ
suru ...を探検する Ⓘ: explore un-
known regions (*michi no chiiki o
tañkeñ suru*) 未知の地域を探検する.

2 (examine) ... o choʳosa suru ...を
調査する Ⓘ: explore all aspects of a
problem (*moñdai no arayuru meñ
o choosa suru*) 問題のあらゆる面を調
査する.

explosion *n.* 1 (of a bomb) baʳkuhatsu 爆発: a nuclear explosion
(*kaku-bakuhatsu*) 核爆発.

2 (of emotions) baʳkuhatsu 爆発:
an explosion of anger (*ikari no
bakuhatsu*) 怒りの爆発 / an explosion of laughter (*bakushoo*) 爆笑.

3 (sudden increase) baʳkuhatsu-
teki na zooka 爆発的な増加: the
population explosion (*jiñkoo no
bakuhatsu-teki na zooka*) 人口の爆
発的な増加.

export *vt.* ... o yuʳshutsu suru ... を
輸出する Ⓘ: import raw materials
and export finished goods (*geñryoo o yunyuu shite kañseehiñ o
yushutsu suru*) 原料を輸入して完成
品を輸出する.

── *n.* (exporting) yuʳshutsu 輸出;
(goods) yuʳshutsuhiñ 輸出品:
Exports exceed imports this year.
(*Kotoshi wa yushutsu ga yunyuu*

o uwamawatte iru.) ことしは輸出が輸
入を上回っている.

expose *vt.* 1 (leave unprotected)
... o saʳrasu ...をさらす Ⓒ: expose
one's skin to the sun (*hada o taiyoo ni sarasu*) 肌を太陽にさらす / be
exposed to danger and hardship
(*kikeñ to koññañ ni sarasareru*) 危
険と困難にさらされる.

2 (disclose) ... o baʳkuro suru ...を
暴露する Ⓘ; aʳbaʳku 暴く Ⓒ: expose
the real facts to the public (*shiñsoo
o kooshuu ni bakuro suru*) 真相を
公衆に暴露する.

exposure *n.* 1 (revelation) baʳkuro 暴露; teʳkihatsu 摘発: the
exposure of corruption (*oshoku no
bakuro*) 汚職の暴露.

2 (exposing) saʳrasu katoʳ さらすこ
と: exposure to the sun (*hi ni
sarasu koto*) 日にさらすこと.

3 (photography) fiʳrumu no hitoʳ-
koma フィルムのひとこま: a 36-
exposure roll of film (*sañjuu-roku-
mai-dori no firumu*) 36枚どりのフィ
ルム.

express *vt.* 1 (state) ... o hyoʳo-
geʳñ suru ...を表現する Ⓘ; iʳiara-
waʳsu 言い表わす Ⓒ: express one's
feelings freely (*kañjite iru koto o
jiyuu ni hyoogeñ suru*) 感じているこ
とを自由に表現する / I don't know
how to express my gratitude.
(*Watashi no kañsha no kimochi o
doo iiarawashite yoi ka wakarimaseñ.*) 私の感謝の気持ちをどう言い表わ
してよいかわかりません.

2 (show) ... o aʳrawaʳsu ...を表わす
Ⓒ; shiʳmeʳsu 示す Ⓒ: Tomoko's
tears expressed how sad she was.
(*Tomoko-sañ no namida wa
kanojo ga doñna ni kanashiñde
iru ka o shimeshite ita.*) 友子さんの
涙は彼女がどんなに悲しんでいるかを示し
ていた.

3 (send by fast delivery) soʳkuta-
tsu de okuru 速達で送る Ⓒ: I'd like
to have this letter expressed. (*Kono
tegami o sokutatsu ni shite itadakitai no desu ga.*) この手紙を速達に

していただきたいのですが.
— *adj*. **1** (especially fast) kyuʼu-
koo no 急行の; soʼkutatsu no 速達
の: an express bus (*kyuukoo basu*)
急行バス / an express letter (*sokutatsu no tegami*) 速達の手紙.
2 (definite) meʼekaku na 明確な;
haʼkkiʼri shita [shite iru] はっきりした
[している]: my father's express wish
(*chichi no meekaku na kiboo*) 父の
明確な希望.
— *n*. (train) kyuʼukoo-reʼssha 急
行列車: the 8:45 express from
Ueno (*Ueno hatsu hachi-ji yoñ-
juugo-fuñ no kyuukoo*) 上野発8:
45の急行.

expression *n*. **1** (showing of
opinions, etc.) hyoʼogeʼñ 表現: the
expression of ideas (*shisoo no hyoogeñ*) 思想の表現 / give expression
to one's feelings (*kañjoo o arawasu*) 感情を表わす.
2 (look) hyoʼojoʼo 表情; kaʼotsuki
顔つき: a serious expression (*shiñkeñ na hyoojoo*) 真剣な表情 /
When I saw her expression, I realized she was angry. (*Kanojo no kaotsuki o mite kanojo ga okotte iru
no ga wakatta.*) 彼女の顔つきを見て
彼女が怒っているのがわかった.
3 (of words) goʼku 語句; iʼimawa-
shi 言い回し: a set expression (*kimari moñku*) 決まり文句 / There
are lots of special polite expressions in Japanese. (*Nihoñgo ni wa
tokubetsu teenee na iimawashi ga
takusañ aru.*) 日本語には特別丁寧な
言い回しがたくさんある.

expressive *adj*. hyoʼojoʼo ni
toʼmu 表情に富む; aʼrawaʼshite (iru)
表わして(いる): an expressive look
(*hyoojoo ni tomu kaotsuki*) 表情に
富む顔つき / be expressive regarding
one's gratitude (*kañsha o arawasu*)
感謝を表わす.

express train *n*. kyuʼukoo-reʼssha 急行列車: a semi-express train
(*juñkyuu-ressha*) 準急列車 / a
super-express train (*tokkyuu-res-
sha*) 特急列車.

expressway *n*. koʼosoku-
jidooshaʼdoo 高速自動車道: the
Tomei Expressway between
Tokyo and Nagoya (*Tookyoo-
Nagoya kañ no Toomee Koosoku*)
東京―名古屋間の東名高速.

exquisite *adj*. **1** (beautiful) hiʼjoo
ni utsukushiʼi 非常に美しい; hiʼjoo
ni subarashiʼi 非常にすばらしい: an
exquisite fragrance (*hijoo ni yoi
kaori*) 非常によい香り / an exquisite
design (*hijoo ni subarashii dezaiñ*)
非常にすばらしいデザイン.
2 (refined) yuʼuga na 優雅な: a person of exquisite taste (*yuuga na
shumi no hito*) 優雅な趣味の人.

extend *vt*. **1** (of time, a line) ... o
eʼñchoo suru ...を延長する ⧇; no-
ʼbaʼsu 延ばす Ⓒ: I decided to extend my stay in Japan for another
year. (*Watashi wa Nihoñ de no
taizai o ato ichi-neñ nobasu koto
ni kimeta.*) 私は日本での滞在をあと1
年延ばすことに決めた. / extend the
road to the next town (*tsugi no
machi made dooro o eñchoo suru*)
次の町まで道路を延長する.
2 (of an area, activity) ... o kaʼ-
kuchoo suru ...を拡張する ⧇; hiʼro-
geru 広げる Ⓥ: This sidewalk is
going to be extended. (*Kono hodoo
wa hirogerareru koto ni natte
imasu.*) この歩道は広げられることになっ
ています. / extend one's business
into a new field (*shigoto o atarashii buñya e kakuchoo suru*) 仕事
を新しい分野へ拡張する.
3 (of limbs) ... o noʼbaʼsu ...を伸ば
す Ⓒ: extend an arm (*ude o nobasu*) 腕を伸ばす.
4 (of friendship, credit) ... o aʼta-
eru 与える Ⓥ; hoʼdokoʼsu 施す Ⓒ:
extend a warm welcome (*atatakaku kañgee suru*) 温かく歓迎する.
— *vi*. **1** (of an area) hiʼrogaru 広
がる Ⓒ; noʼbiʼru 延びる Ⓥ: The
paddy field extends as far as the
eye can see. (*Miwatasu kagiri sui-
deñ ga hirogatte iru.*) 見渡すかぎり
水田が広がっている.

2 (continue to) ke⌐ezoku suru 継続する ①; zu⌐rekomu ずれ込む ⓒ: The conference will extend into next week. (*Kaigi wa raishuu made zurekomu deshoo.*) 会議は来週までずれ込むでしょう.

extension *n.* **1** (of a line, space, time) e⌐ñchoo 延長; (of a building) ta⌐temashi 建て増し; zo⌐ochiku 増築: the extension of a railroad (*te-tsudoo no eñchoo*) 鉄道の延長 / build an extension to a hospital (*byooiñ no tatemashi o suru*) 病院の建て増しをする.

2 (further development) ka⌐ku-choo 拡張; ka⌐kudai 拡大: the extension of foreign trade (*gaikoku-boo-eki no kakudai*) 外国貿易の拡大.

3 (of a telephone line) na⌐iseñ 内線: Please give me extension 476. (*Naiseñ yoñ-nana-roku o o-negai shimasu.*) 内線 476 をお願いします.

extensive *adj.* ko⌐ohañi ni wa-⌐taru 広範囲にわたる; ha⌐ñi ga hi⌐roʼi 範囲が広い: extensive damage (*koo-hañi ni wataru higai*) 広範囲にわたる被害.

extent *n.* **1** (expanse) hi⌐rogari 広がり; o⌐okisa 大きさ: a vast extent of land (*tochi no koodai na hirogari*) 土地の広大な広がり.

2 (degree) te⌐ledo 程度; ha⌐ñi 範囲: To some extent I agree with you. (*Aru teedo made wa anata ni dooi shimasu.*) ある程度まではあなたに同意します.

exterior *adj.* ga⌐ibu no 外部の; so-⌐togawa no 外側の: the exterior walls of a building (*biru no soto-gawa no kabe*) ビルの外側の壁.
　— *n.* ga⌐ibu 外部; so⌐togawa 外側: a house with a marble exterior (*sotogawa ga dairiseki no ie*) 外側が大理石の家.

external *adj.* **1** (outer) ga⌐ibu no 外部の; so⌐to no 外の: the external appearance of a house (*ie no gai-kañ*) 家の外観 / external wounds (*gaishoo*) 外傷.

2 (foreign) ga⌐ikoku no 外国の; ta-⌐igai-teki na 対外的な: external affairs (*gaikoku jijoo*) 外国事情 / external trade (*taigai-booeki*) 対外貿易.

3 (superficial) u⌐wabe dakeʼ no うわべだけの: external politeness (*uwabe dake no reegi*) うわべだけの礼儀.

extinct *adj.* ki⌐eta 消えた; ki⌐ete iru 消えている; ze⌐tsumetsu shita [shite iru] 絶滅した[している]: an extinct volcano (*shikazañ*) 死火山 / an extinct animal (*zetsumetsu shita doobu-tsu*) 絶滅した動物.

extinction *n.* ze⌐tsumetsu 絶滅; sho⌐ometsu 消滅: the complete extinction of a species of bird (*tori no shu no kañzeñ na zetsumetsu*) 鳥の種の完全な絶滅.

extinguish *vt.* ... o chi⌐ñka suru ...を鎮火する ①; ke⌐su 消す ⓒ: extinguish a forest fire (*yamakaji o chiñ-ka suru*) 山火事を鎮火する.

extra *adj.* yo⌐buñ na 余分な; ri⌐ñji no 臨時の: I saved some extra money. (*Yobuñ na o-kane wa cho-kiñ shita.*) 余分なお金は貯金した. / an extra charge (*tokubetsu ryookiñ*) 特別料金 / Wine is not included; it's extra. (*Waiñ wa fukumarete orimaseñ. Sore wa betsu desu.*) ワインは含まれておりません. それは別です.
　— *adv.* yo⌐buñ ni 余分に; to⌐kube-tsu ni 特別に: an extra good meal (*tokubetsu jootoo no shokuji*) 特別上等の食事 / I gave the bellhop an extra large tip. (*Booi ni tokubetsu ni takusañ chippu o yatta.*) ボーイに特別にたくさんチップをやった.
　— *n.* wa⌐rimashi ryoʼokiñ 割り増し料金; tsu⌐ika ryoʼokiñ 追加料金: Breakfast is an extra here. (*Koko de wa chooshoku wa betsu-ryoo-kiñ desu.*) ここでは朝食は別料金です.

extract *vt.* **1** (pull out) ... o nu⌐ku ...を抜く ⓒ; nu⌐kitoʼru 抜き取る ⓒ: have a tooth extracted (*ha o nuite morau*) 歯を抜いてもらう / extract a cork from a bottle (*koruku o biñ kara nuku*) コルクをびんから抜く.

2 (squeeze out) ... o shi「borida¹su ...を搾り出す C; chu「ushutsu suru 抽出する T: extract juice from an orange (ore̅nji kara juusu o shi-boridasu) オレンジからジュースを搾り出す.

3 (of information) ... o hi「kida¹su ...を引き出す C: extract a secret from a person (hito kara himitsu o hikidasu) 人から秘密を引き出す.
— n. ba「ssui 抜粋; i「n̄yo¹oku 引用句: an extract from a work of fiction (shoosetsu kara no in̄yoo) 小説からの引用.

extraordinary adj. **1** (unusual) i「joo na 異常な; na「mihazu¹reta 並外れた; na「mihazu¹rete iru 並み外れている: an extraordinary event (ijoo na dekigoto) 異常な出来事 / a man of extraordinary genius (namiha-zureta te̅n̄sai no hito) 並み外れた天才の人.

2 (unscheduled) to「kubetsu no 特別の; ri「n̄ji no 臨時の: an extraordinary general meeting (rin̄ji-sookai) 臨時総会.

extravagance n. ze「eta¹ku ぜいたく; ro「ohi 浪費: a needless extravagance (fuhitsuyoo na roohi) 不必要な浪費.

extravagant adj. ze「eta¹ku na ぜいたくな; ro「ohi suru 浪費する: an extravagant meal (zeetaku na sho-kuji) ぜいたくな食事.

extreme adj. **1** (very great) kyo¹-kudo no 極度の; hi「joo-na 非常な: extreme poverty (kyokudo no hin̄-kon̄) 極度の貧困 / live to an extreme old age (hijoo-na kooree made ikiru) 非常な高齢まで生きる.

2 (most remote) i「chiban̄ hashi no いちばん端の; se「n̄tan̄ no 先端の: We live on the extreme edge of Tokyo. (Watashi-tachi wa Tookyoo no ichiban̄ hashi ni sun̄de imasu.) 私たちは東京のいちばん端に住んでいます.

3 (drastic) kyo「kuta¹n̄ na 極端な: hold extreme views (kyokutan̄ na

kan̄gae o motsu) 極端な考えを持つ.
— n. kyo「kuta¹n̄ 極端: experience the extremes of heat and cold (kan̄-sho no ryoo kyokutan̄ o keeken̄ suru) 寒暑の両極端を経験する.

extremely adv. kyo「kuta¹n̄ ni 極端に; kyo「kudo ni 極度に; ki「wa¹-mete きわめて; to「temo とても: an extremely difficult problem (kiwa-mete muzukashii mon̄dai) きわめて難しい問題 / He is extremely angry. (Kare wa sugoku okotte iru.) 彼はすごく怒っている.

eye n. **1** (organ) me¹ 目[眼]: have blue [brown, dark] eyes (aoi [chairoi, kuroi] me o shite iru) 青い[茶色い, 黒い]目をしている / shut [open] one's eyes (me o tojiru [akeru]) 目を閉じる[開ける].

2 (sight) shi「ryoku 視力: I have weak eyes. (Watashi wa shiryoku ga yowai.) 私は視力が弱い.

3 (discernment) ka「n̄satsu¹ryoku 観察力; me¹ 目: Mary has an eye for pictures. (Mearii wa e o miru me o motte iru.) メアリーは絵を見る眼を持っている.

4 (something like an eye) the eye of a needle (hari no me) 針の目 / the eye of a typhoon (taifuu no me) 台風の目.

eyeball n. ga「n̄kyuu 眼球.

eyebrow n. ma「yu 眉; ma「yuge 眉毛: knit one's eyebrows (mayu o shikameru) 眉をしかめる.

eye doctor n. ga「n̄ka¹-i 眼科医; me「isha 目医者.

eyeglasses n. me「gane 眼鏡.

eyelash n. ma「tsuge まつげ.

eyelid n. ma「buta まぶた: the upper [lower] eyelid (uwa [shita] mabuta) 上[下]まぶた.

eyesight n. shi「ryoku 視力: a person with good [poor] sight (shi-ryoku no yoi [warui] hito) 視力のよい[悪い]人 / have one's eyesight tested (shiryoku o shirabete mo-rau) 視力を調べてもらう.

F

fable n. guˈuwa 寓話; deˈñsetsu 伝説.

fabric n. **1** (cloth) oˈrimono 織物; kiˈji 生地: woolen fabrics (*keorimono*) 毛織物 / weave a fabric (*orimono o oru*) 織物を織る.
2 (structure) koˈozoo 構造; soˈshiki 組織: the fabric of society (*shakai no koozoo*) 社会の構造.

face n. **1** (the front part of the head) kaˈo 顔: wash one's face (*kao o arau*) 顔を洗う.
2 (look) kaˈotsuki 顔つき; kaˈo 顔: put on a sad face (*kanashii kao o suru*) 悲しい顔をする.
3 (surface) hyoˈomeñ 表面; (front) oˈmoteˈ 表: the face of the earth (*chihyoo*) 地表 / the face of a playing card (*torañpu no omote*) トランプの表.
— vt. **1** (look toward) ... ni meˈñshite iru ...に面している Ⓥ: My room faces the south. (*Watashi no heya wa minami ni meñshite imasu.*) 私の部屋は南に面しています.
2 (meet defiantly) ... ni taˈchimukau ...に立ち向かう Ⓒ: face dangers (*kikeñ ni tachimukau*) 危険に立ち向かう.
3 (present itself to) ... ni shoˈojiru ...に生じる Ⓥ: A new problem faced us. (*Atarashii moñdai ga wareware ni shoojita.*) 新しい問題がわれわれに生じた.

facilitate vt. ... o yoˈoi ni suru ...を容易にする Ⓣ; raˈkuˈ ni suru 楽にする Ⓣ: This computer will facilitate your task. (*Kono koñpyuutaa wa anata no shigoto o raku ni suru deshoo.*) このコンピューターはあなたの仕事を楽にするでしょう.

facility n. **1** (means) seˈtsubi 設備; shiˈsetsu 施設: public facilities (*kookyoo shisetsu*) 公共施設.
2 (conveniences) beˈñ 便: transpor-

tation facilities (*kootsuu no beñ*) 交通の便.
3 (skill) noˈoryoku 能力; saˈinoo 才能: a facility for language (*gogaku no sainoo*) 語学の才能.

fact n. **1** (something that has happened) jiˈjitsu 事実: I told him the facts. (*Watashi wa kare ni jijitsu o hanashita.*) 私は彼に事実を話した.
2 (reality) geˈñjitsu no hanashiˈ 現実の話; jiˈjitsu 事実: a novel based on fact (*jijitsu ni motozuita shoosetsu*) 事実に基づいた小説.

factor n. yoˈoiñ 要因; yoˈoso 要素: Effort was a factor in his success. (*Doryoku ga kare no seekoo no ichi yooiñ datta.*) 努力が彼の成功の一要因だった.

factory n. koˈojoˈo 工場: He works in this factory. (*Kare wa kono koojoo de hataraite imasu.*) 彼はこの工場で働いています.

faculty n. **1** (ability) noˈoryoku 能力; saˈinoo 才能: She has a faculty for music. (*Kanojo wa oñgaku no sainoo ga aru.*) 彼女は音楽の才能がある.
2 (department) gaˈkubu 学部: the faculty of law (*hoogaku-bu*) 法学部.

fade vi. **1** (of a flower) shiˈbomu しぼむ Ⓒ; shiˈoreru しおれる Ⓥ: The roses have faded. (*Bara ga shiorete shimatta.*) ばらがしおれてしまった.
2 (of color) aˈseˈru あせる Ⓒ; saˈmeˈru さめる Ⓥ: The shirt faded when it was washed. (*Shatsu o arattara iro ga sameta.*) シャツを洗ったら色がさめた.
3 (disappear) kiˈesaˈru 消え去る Ⓒ: My hopes faded. (*Watashi no nozomi wa kiesatta.*) 私の望みは消え去った.
— vt. **1** (of a flower) ... o shiˈoresasu ...をしおれさす Ⓒ.
2 (of color) ... o aˈsesaseˈru ...をあ

せさせる Ⅴ: Sunlight fades curtains. (*Nikkoo wa kaateñ no iro o asesaseru.*) 日光はカーテンの色をあせさせる.

Fahrenheit *adj.* ka¹shi no 華氏の: eighty degrees Fahrenheit (*kashi hachijuu-do*) 華氏 80 度. ★ In Japan the Celsius system is used instead of the Fahrenheit system.

fail *vi.* **1** (be unsuccessful) shi¹ppai suru 失敗する Ⅰ; shi¹kuji¹ru しくじる C: All his attempts failed. (*Kare no kokoromi wa subete shippai shita.*) 彼の試みはすべて失敗した. / fail in the examination (*shikeñ ni ochiru*) 試験に落ちる.

2 (neglect) (... o) o¹kota¹ru (...を)怠る ⟨verb⟩-na¹i ...ない: He often fails to keep his word. (*Kare wa yakusoku o mamoranai koto ga yoku aru.*) 彼は約束を守らないことがよくある.

3 (break down) ko¹shoo suru 故障 する Ⅰ; ki¹kanai 利かない: The brakes failed. (*Bureeki ga kikanakatta.*) ブレーキが利かなかった.

4 (be not enough) fu¹soku suru 不足する Ⅰ; fu¹saku ni na¹ru 不作になる C: The crops failed this year. (*Kotoshi wa fusaku datta.*) ことしは不作だった.

5 (become weak) o¹toroe¹ru 衰える Ⅴ; yo¹wa¹ru 弱る C: My sight has failed. (*Watashi wa shiryoku ga otoroeta.*) 私は視力が衰えた.

— *vt.* **1** (disappoint) ... o shi¹tsuboo saseru ...を失望させる Ⅴ; (forsake) mi¹suteru 見捨てる Ⅴ: When I wanted his help he failed me. (*Kare no tasuke ga hoshii toki kare wa watashi o misuteta.*) 彼の助けが欲しいとき彼は私を見捨てた.

2 (of a teacher) ... o ra¹kudai saseru ...を落第させる Ⅴ; (of a student) ... ni o¹chi¹ru ...に落ちる C: The teacher failed five students. (*Señsee wa go-niñ o rakudai saseta.*) 先生は 5 人を落第させた. / He failed his exam. (*Kare wa shikeñ ni ochita.*) 彼は試験に落ちた.

failure *n.* **1** (act of failing) shi¹p-

pai 失敗: His plan ended in failure. (*Kare no keekaku wa shippai ni owatta.*) 彼の計画は失敗に終わった.

2 (unsuccessful person) shi¹ppa¹isha 失敗者; ra¹kuda¹isha 落第者: He is a failure as a politician. (*Kare wa seejika to shite wa rakudai da.*) 彼は政治家としては落第だ.

3 (cessation) te¹eshi 停止; ko¹shoo 故障: a power failure (*teedeñ*) 停電 / a heart failure (*shiñzoo mahi*) 心臓まひ.

faint *adj.* **1** (indistinct) ka¹suka na かすかな; ho¹noka na ほのかな: a faint smell (*kasuka na nioi*) かすかなにおい.

2 (vague) ka¹suka na かすかな; wa¹zuka na わずかな: There is still a faint hope. (*Mada kasuka na nozomi ga arimasu.*) まだかすかな望みがあります.

3 (dizzy) me¹ma¹i ga suru めまいがする: feel faint (*memai ga suru*) めまいがする.

— *vi.* (lose consciousness) shi¹sshiñ suru 失神する Ⅰ: She fainted from the heat. (*Kanojo wa atsusa no tame shisshiñ shita.*) 彼女は暑さのため失神した.

— *n.* shi¹sshiñ 失神; ki¹zetsu 気絶: fall in a faint (*kizetsu shite taoreru*) 気絶して倒れる.

fair¹ *adj.* **1** (just) ko¹osee na 公正な; ko¹ohee na 公平な: a fair judgment (*koosee na hañdañ*) 公正な判断.

2 (considerable) ka¹nari no かなりの; so¹otoo no 相当の: There were a fair number of people in the room. (*Heya ni wa kanari no kazu no hito ga imashita.*) 部屋にはかなりの数の人がいました.

3 (fine) ha¹reta 晴れた; ha¹rete iru 晴れている: a fair sky (*hareta sora*) 晴れた空.

4 (of hair) ki¹ñpatsu no 金髪の: She has fair hair. (*Kanojo wa kiñpatsu desu.*) 彼女は金髪です.

5 (of skin) shi¹ro¹i 白い: She has a fair skin. (*Kanojo wa hada ga shiroi.*) 彼女は肌が白い.

6 (of baseball) feʰa na フェアな: a fair ball (fea booru) フェアボール.
— adv. seʰeseʰe doʰodoʰo to 正々堂々と; koʰomee seedai ni 公明正大に: fight fair (seesee seedai ni tatakau) 正々堂々と戦う.

fair[2] n. **1** (of farm products) hiʰn-pyoʰokai 品評会; kyoʰoshiʰnkai 共進会.

2 (exhibition) haʰkuraʰnkai 博覧会; miʰhoʰnichi 見本市; -feʰa フェア: an international trade fair (kokusai mihonichi) 国際見本市.

fairly adv. **1** (justly) koʰosee ni 公正に; koʰohee ni 公平に: treat pupils fairly (seeto o koohee ni atsukau) 生徒を公平に扱う.

2 (quite) kaʰnari かなり; soʰotoo (ni) 相当(に): He speaks Japanese fairly well. (Kare wa Nihongo o kanari joozu ni hanashimasu.) 彼は日本語をかなりじょうずに話します.

fairy tale n. oʰtogibaʰnashi おとぎ話; doʰowa 童話.

faith n. **1** (belief) shiʰnkoo 信仰; shiʰnnen 信念: a person of strong faith (shinkoo no atsui hito) 信仰のあつい人.

2 (trust) shiʰnrai 信頼; shiʰnyoo 信用: I haven't much faith in his ability. (Watashi wa kare no nooryoku o taishite shinyoo shite imasen.) 私は彼の能力をたいして信用していません.

3 (loyalty) shiʰngi 信義; seʰejitsu 誠実: keep faith with a person (hito to no shingi o mamoru) 人との信義を守る.

faithful adj. **1** (loyal) chuʰujitsu na 忠実な; (sincere) seʰejitsu na 誠実な: He was faithful to his promise. (Kare wa yakusoku ni chuujitsu datta.) 彼は約束に忠実だった.

2 (exact) seʰekaku na 正確な; chuʰujitsu na 忠実な: a faithful copy (seekaku na utsushi) 正確な写し / a translation faithful to the original (genbun ni chuujitsu na yaku) 原文に忠実な訳.

fall[1] n. (autumn) aʰki 秋.

fall[2] vi. **1** (go down) oʰchiʰru 落ちる

V: He fell off a ladder. (Kare wa hashigo kara ochita.) 彼ははしごから落ちた.

2 (of rain, etc.) fuʰru 降る C: The rain began to fall. (Ame ga furi-hajimeta.) 雨が降り始めた.

3 (collapse) taʰoreʰru 倒れる V: I slipped and fell to the ground. (Watashi wa subette jimen ni taoreta.) 私は滑って地面に倒れた.

4 (become lower) saʰgaru 下がる C; hiʰkuku naru 低くなる C: The temperature has fallen five degrees. (Ondo ga go-do sagatta.) 温度が5度下がった.

5 (become) ... ni naʰru ...になる C: fall ill (byooki ni naru) 病気になる / The room fell silent. (Heya ga shizuka ni natta.) 部屋が静かになった.

6 (hang down) taʰreʰru 垂れる V: Her hair fell over her shoulders. (Kanojo no kami no ke wa kata no ue ni tarete ita.) 彼女の髪の毛は肩の上に垂れていた.

fall down vi. koʰrobu 転ぶ C: He fell down on the ice. (Kare wa koori no ue de koronda.) 彼は氷の上で転んだ.

— n. **1** (becoming lower) teʰeka 低下; geʰraku 下落: a fall in temperature (ondo no teeka) 温度の低下 / a fall in prices (bukka no geraku) 物価の下落.

2 (going down to the ground) teʰntoo 転倒: break one's leg in a fall (tentoo shite ashi o oru) 転倒して脚を折る.

3 (dropping) oʰchiʰru koʰtoʰ 落ちること; raʰkka 落下: a fall from a horse (rakuba) 落馬.

4 (rainfall) koʰou 降雨; (snowfall) koʰosetsu 降雪: a heavy fall of snow (ooyuki) 大雪.

5 (downfall) boʰtsuraku 没落; meʰtsuboo 滅亡: the fall of the Heike family (Heeko no metsuboo) 平家の滅亡.

6 (waterfall) taʰki 滝.

false adj. **1** (mistaken) maʰchi-gaʰtta 間違った; maʰchigaʰtte iru 間

違っている: a false account (*machi-gatta keesañ*) 間違った計算.
2 (not true) u˥so no うその; i˥tsu-wari no 偽りの: make a false statement (*uso no chiñjutsu o suru*) うその陳述をする.
3 (not genuine) ho˥ñmono de na˥i 本物でない; ni˥se no 偽の: false teeth (*ireba*) 入れ歯.
4 (not loyal) fu˥se˥ejitsu na 不誠実な; fu˥jitsu na 不実な: a false friend (*fujitsu na tomo*) 不実な友.

fame *n.* **1** (being well-known) me˥esee 名声: come into fame (*yuumee ni naru*) 有名になる.
2 (reputation) hyo˥obañ 評判: good fame (*yoi hyoobañ*) よい評判.

familiar *adj.* **1** (well-known) yo˥ku shi˥rarete iru よく知られている; o-˥najimi no おなじみの: a familiar song (*o-najimi no uta*) おなじみの歌.
2 (knowing about) shi˥tte iru 知っている: I am not very familiar with Japanese history. (*Nihoñ no reki-shi wa amari yoku shirimaseñ.*) 日本の歴史はあまりよく知りません.
3 (too friendly) u˥chitoketa 打ち解けた; u˥chitokete iru 打ち解けている; ku˥da˥keta くだけた; ku˥da˥kete iru くだけている: a familiar greeting (*uchi-toketa aisatsu*) 打ち解けたあいさつ.

familiarity *n.* **1** (close friend-ship) shi˥tashimi 親しみ; shi˥ñkoo 親交: treat one's friend with fami-liarity (*tomodachi o shitashimi o komete atsukau*) 友だちを親しみをこめて扱う.
2 (being familiar) yo˥ku shi˥tte iru koto よく知っていること; se˥etsuu 精通: I admire his familiarity with many languages. (*Kare ga ooku no kotoba o shitte iru no ni kañshiñ suru.*) 彼が多くの言葉を知っているのに感心する.

family *n.* **1** (parents and children) ka˥zoku 家族; se˥ta˥i 世帯: We are a family of five in all. (*Watashi no kazoku wa zeñbu de go-niñ desu.*) 私の家族は全部で5人です. / Six fami-lies live in this apartment house.

(*Kono appaato ni wa roku-setai ga suñde imasu.*) このアパートには6世帯が住んでいます.
2 (children) ko˥domo˥-tachi 子どもたち: He has a large family. (*Kare wa kodomo ga takusañ iru.*) 彼は子どもがたくさんいる.
3 (lineage) i˥egara 家柄: a person of respectable family (*rippa na iegara no hito*) 立派な家柄の人.
— *adj.* ka˥zoku no 家族の; ka˥tee no 家庭の: a family hotel (*kazoku muki no hoteru*) 家族向きのホテル / family life (*katee-seekatsu*) 家庭生活.

family name *n.* se˥e 姓; myo˥oji 名字.

famine *n.* ki˥kiñ ききん: Many peo-ple are suffering from famine. (*Oozee no hito ga kikiñ de kuru-shiñde iru.*) 大勢の人がきんきで苦しんでいる.

famous *adj.* yu˥umee na 有名な: Kyoto is famous for its old temples and shrines. (*Kyooto wa furui tera ya jiñja de yuumee desu.*) 京都は古い寺や神社で有名です. / famous spots (*meesho*) 名所.

fan[1] *n.* (waved in the hand) u˥chi˥wa うちわ; (folding fan) se˥ñsu 扇子; (electric fan) se˥ñpu˥uki 扇風機.
— *vt.* ... o a˥o˥gu ...をあおぐ $\boxed{C}$: He fanned his face with a hat. (*Kare wa booshi de kao o aoida.*) 彼は帽子で顔をあおいだ.

fan[2] *n.* fa˥ñ ファン: a baseball fan (*yakyuu fañ*) 野球ファン.

fancy *adj.* **1** (decorated) so˥osho-ku-teki na 装飾的な; ha˥de˥na 派手な: This dress is too fancy for me. (*Kono doresu wa watashi ni wa hade-sugimasu.*) このドレスは私には派手すぎます. / fancy cakes (*dekoree-shoñ keeki*) デコレーションケーキ.
2 (superior) go˥kujoo no 極上の; to˥kuseñ no 特選の: fancy fruits (*gokujoo no kudamono*) 極上の果物.
— *n.* **1** (fondness) ko˥nomi˥ 好み; a˥ikoo 愛好: This tie suits my fancy. (*Kono nekutai wa watashi*

no konomi ni atte imasu.) このネクタイは私の好みに合っています.
2 (imagination) ku⌐usoo 空想; ge⌐ñsoo 幻想: a story based on fancy (*kuusoo ni motozuita hanashi*) 空想に基づいた話.
—— *vt.* **1** (imagine) ... o so⌐ozoo suru ...を想像する ①; ku⌐usoo suru 空想する ①: I cannot fancy her doing such a thing. (*Kanojo ga soñna koto o suru nañte soozoo dekinai.*) 彼女がそんなことをするなんて想像できない.
2 (think) ... to o⌐mou ...と思う ⓒ: I fancy she is about thirty. (*Kanojo wa sañjuu gurai da to omoimasu.*) 彼女は 30 くらいだと思います.

fantastic *adj.* **1** (marvelous) su⌐barashi⌐i すばらしい; su⌐teki na すてきな: a fantastic view (*subarashii nagame*) すばらしい眺め.
2 (extravagant) to⌐hoo mo na⌐i 途方もない; to⌐tetsu mo na⌐i とてつもない: a fantastic price (*tohoo mo nai nedañ*) 途方もない値段.
3 (wild) fu⌐uga⌐wari na 風変わりな: a fantastic house (*fuugawari na ie*) 風変わりな家.

fantasy *n.* ku⌐usoo 空想; ge⌐ñsoo 幻想: a world of fantasy (*geñsoo no sekai*) 幻想の世界.

far *adv.* **1** (of a place, distance, etc.) to⌐oku⌐ ni [e] 遠くに[へ]: He hasn't gone so far. (*Kare wa soñna ni tooku e wa itte imaseñ.*) 彼はそんなに遠くへは行っていません. / How far is it to the station? (*Eki made dono kurai arimasu ka?*) 駅までどのくらいありますか.
2 (of time, degree, etc.) ha⌐ruka ni はるかに; zu⌐tto ずっと: His car is far better than mine. (*Kare no kuruma wa watashi no yori haruka ni yoi.*) 彼の車は私のよりはるかによい.
as far as ... *prep.* ... ma⌐de ...まで: I drove as far as Nagoya on Sunday. (*Watashi wa nichiyoo ni Nagoya made kuruma de itta.*) 私は日曜に名古屋まで車で行った.
so far *adv.* i⌐ma ma⌐de 今まで: So

far everything has gone off well. (*Ima made no tokoro subete umaku ikimashita.*) 今までのところすべてうまくいきました.
—— *adj.* to⌐oi 遠い: Is the hotel far from here? (*Sono hoteru wa koko kara tooi desu ka?*) そのホテルはここから遠いですか.

fare *n.* u⌐ñchiñ 運賃; ryo⌐okiñ 料金: a taxi fare (*takushii ryookiñ*) タクシー料金 / How much is the fare? (*Ryookiñ wa ikura desu ka?*) 料金はいくらですか.

farewell *n.* wa⌐kare⌐ 別れ: a farewell speech (*wakare no aisatsu*) 別れのあいさつ / a farewell party (*soobetsukai*) 送別会.

farm *n.* **1** (area) no⌐ojoo 農場; no⌐oeñ 農園: work on a farm (*noojoo de hataraku*) 農場で働く.
2 (place where animals are bred) shi⌐ikujoo 飼育場: a chicken farm (*yookeejoo*) 養鶏場.
—— *vt.* ... o ko⌐osaku suru ...を耕作する ①: He farms 50 ares. (*Kare wa gojuu-aaru no tochi o koosaku shite imasu.*) 彼は 50 アールの土地を耕作しています.
—— *vi.* no⌐ogyoo o i⌐tona⌐mu 農業を営む ⓒ.

farmer *n.* no⌐ojo⌐onushi 農場主; no⌐ojoo-kee-e⌐lesha 農場経営者.

farming *n.* no⌐ogyoo 農業.

farther *adv.* sa⌐ra ni to⌐oku⌐ ni さらに遠くに; mo⌐tto sa⌐ki ni もっと先に: I can walk no farther. (*Moo kore ijoo arukemaseñ.*) もうこれ以上歩けません.
—— *adj.* sa⌐ra ni to⌐oku⌐ no さらに遠くの; mo⌐tto sa⌐ki no もっと先の: The station was farther than we had thought. (*Eki wa omotta yori mo sara ni tookatta.*) 駅は思ったよりもさらに遠かった.

farthest *adv.* mo⌐tto⌐mo to⌐oku⌐ もっとも遠くに: He was able to throw the ball farthest. (*Kare ga ichibañ tooku made booru o nagerareta.*) 彼がいちばん遠くまでボールを投げられた.
—— *adj.* mo⌐tto⌐mo to⌐oi もっとも遠

い: the farthest planet (*mottomo tooi wakusee*) もっとも遠い惑星.

fascinate *vt.* ... o mi「ryoo suru ...を魅了する ①; ... no ko「ko「ro o u「ba」u ...の心を奪う ⓒ: He was fascinated with her beauty. (*Kare wa kanojo no utsukushisa ni kokoro o ubawareta.*) 彼は彼女の美しさに心を奪われた.

fascinating *adj.* mi「waku-teki na 魅惑的な; su「go」ku o「moshiro」i すごくおもしろい: I found his story fascinating. (*Kare no hanashi wa sugoku omoshirokatta.*) 彼の話はすごくおもしろかった.

fashion *n.* 1 (style) ryu「ukoo 流行; fa「sshoñ ファッション: She was dressed in the latest fashion. (*Kanojo wa saishiñ ryuukoo no fuku o kite ita.*) 彼女は最新流行の服を着ていた.
2 (manner) ya「rikata やり方; shi「kata 仕方: He has a strange fashion of speaking. (*Kare wa myoo na hanashikata o suru.*) 彼は妙な話し方をする.

fashionable *adj.* ryu「ukoo no 流行の; ha「ikara na ハイカラな: a fashionable hairdo (*ryuukoo no heasutairu*) 流行のヘアスタイル.

fast *adj.* 1 (quick) ha「ya」i 速[早]い; su「baya」i すばやい: a fast horse (*hayai uma*) 速い馬 / a fast worker (*shigoto no hayai hito*) 仕事の早い人. ★ The kanji '速' is used in reference to 'velocity.'
2 (of a clock) su「suñde iru 進んでいる: This clock is five minutes fast. (*Kono tokee wa go-fuñ susuñde iru.*) この時計は5分進んでいる.
3 (firmly fixed) ko「tee shita [shite iru] 固定した[している]; (secure) shi「kka」ri shita [shite iru] しっかりした[している]: make a door fast (*doa o shikkari shimeru*) ドアをしっかり閉める.
4 (of colors) he「ñshoku shinai 変色しない; a「se」nai あせない: a fast color (*asenai iro*) あせない色.
— *adv.* 1 (quickly) ha」yaku 速く: He ran as quickly as possible. (*Ka-*

re wa dekiru dake hayaku ha-shitta.*) 彼はできるだけ速く走った.
2 (securely) ka「taku 堅く; shi「kka」ri to しっかりと: bind a rope fast (*tsuna o shikkari shibaru*) 綱をしっかり縛る.

fasten *vt.* 1 (fix firmly) ... o shi「kka」ri to「meru ...をしっかり留める Ⓥ; shi「me」ru 締める Ⓥ: Please fasten your seat belt. (*Shiito-beruto o shimete kudasai.*) シートベルトを締めてください.
2 (close firmly) ... o shi「kka」ri shi「me」ru ...をしっかり閉める Ⓥ: Have you fastened all the windows? (*Mado wa zeñbu shikkari shimemashita ka?*) 窓は全部しっかり閉めましたか.
3 (direct one's looks) ... o ji「tto mi」ru ...をじっと見る Ⓥ: The child fastened his eyes on me. (*Sono ko wa watashi o jitto mita.*) その子は私をじっと見た.
— *vi.* shi「ma」ru 閉まる ⓒ: This door will not fasten. (*Kono to wa doo shite mo shimaranai.*) この戸はどうしても閉まらない.

fat *adj.* 1 (plump) fu「to」tta 太った; fu「to」tte iru 太っている: a fat man (*futotta otoko no hito*) 太った男の人 / grow fat (*futoru*) 太る.
2 (greasy) shi「boo no [ga] o」oi 脂肪の[が]多い; a「burakko」i 脂っこい: fat meat (*shiboo no ooi niku*) 脂肪の多い肉.
3 (thick) fu「kureta ふくれた; fu「kurete iru ふくれている; bu「atsui 分厚い: a fat wallet (*o-kane de fukureta saifu*) お金でふくれた財布.
— *n.* 1 (used for cooking) a「bura 油: fry potatoes in deep fat (*jagaimo o abura de ageru*) じゃがいもを油で揚げる.
2 (formed on the body) shi「boo 脂肪: put on fat (*shiboo ga tsuku*) 脂肪がつく.

fatal *adj.* 1 (causing death) chi「mee-teki na 致命的な: a fatal wound (*chimee-shoo*) 致命傷.
2 (decisive) u「ñmee no 運命の: the

fatal day (u*ǹmee o kessuru hi*) 運命を決する日.

3 (disastrous) ju「udai na 重大な; to「rikaeshi no [ga] tsuka「nai 取り返しの[が]つかない: make a fatal mistake (*torikaeshi no tsukanai machigai o suru*) 取り返しのつかない間違いをする.

fate *n.* **1** (destiny) u「ǹmee 運命; shu「kumee 宿命: He abandoned himself to his fate. (*Kare wa uǹmee ni mi o makaseta.*) 彼は運命に身を任せた.

2 (future) yu「kusue 行く末; sho「orai 将来: Nobody knows what fate has in store. (*Shoorai doo naru ka dare ni mo wakaranai.*) 将来どうなるかだれにもわからない.

3 (death) shi「 死; sa「igo 最期: meet one's fate (*saigo o togeru*) 最期を遂げる.

father *n.* **1** (male parent) chi「chi 父; chi「chioya 父親; (someone else's) o-「to「osaǹ お父さん: My father is a policeman. (*Watashi no chichi wa keesatsukaǹ desu.*) 私の父は警察官です. / He takes after his father. (*Kare wa o-toosaǹ ni nite iru.*) 彼はお父さんに似ている.

2 (founder) so「oshi「sha 創始者; chi「chi 父: the Father of Medicine (*igaku no chichi*) 医学の父.

3 (priest) shi「ǹpu 神父.

fatigue *n.* tsu「kare「 疲れ; hi「roo 疲労: He became ill with fatigue. (*Kare wa hiroo de byooki ni natta.*) 彼は疲労で病気になった.

faucet *n.* ja「guchi 蛇口; se「ǹ 栓: turn on [off] a faucet (*jaguchi o hinette akeru* [*shimeru*]) 蛇口をひねって開ける[閉める].

fault *n.* **1** (responsibility) (ka「shitsu no) se「kiniǹ (過失の)責任: The fault lies with me. (*Sono sekiniǹ wa watashi ni arimasu.*) その責任は私にあります.

2 (imperfection) ke「tte「ǹ 欠点; ke「kkaǹ 欠陥: Everyone has their faults. (*Dare ni mo ketteǹ wa aru.*) だれにも欠点はある.

3 (error) a「yamari「 誤り; ka「shitsu 過失: a fault in grammar (*buǹpoojoo no ayamari*) 文法上の誤り.

favor *n.* **1** (kindness) ko「oi 好意; shi「ǹsetsu 親切: I have to return his favor. (*Kare no kooi ni mukuinakereba naranai.*) 彼の好意に報いなければならない.

2 (support) shi「ji 支持; sa「ǹsee 賛成: I am in favor of your plan. (*Watashi wa anata no keekaku ni saǹsee desu.*) 私はあなたの計画に賛成です.

3 (unfair partiality) e「kohi「iki えこひいき: show favor to a person (*hito o ekohiiki suru*) 人をえこひいきする.

ask a favor of ... *vt.* ...ni o-「negai suru ...にお願いする ①: I have a favor to ask of you. (*O-negai ga aru no desu ga.*) お願いがあるのですが.
— *vt.* **1** (show favor to) ... ni ko「oi o shi「me「su ...に好意を示す Ⓒ; sa「ǹsee suru 賛成する ①: favor a proposal (*teeaǹ ni saǹsee suru*) 提案に賛成する.

2 (show unfair partiality to) ... o e「kohi「iki suru ...をえこひいきする ①; ka「waiga「ru かわいがる Ⓒ: favor the youngest child (*ichibaǹ shita no ko o kawaigaru*) いちばん下の子をかわいがる.

favorable *adj.* **1** (showing approval) ko「oi-teki na 好意的な; sa「ǹsee suru 賛成する: I got a favorable answer from him. (*Watashi wa kare kara kooi-teki na heǹji o moratta.*) 私は彼から好意的な返事をもらった.

2 (helpful) ko「otsu「goo na 好都合な; (promising) yu「uboo na 有望な: The weather was favorable for hiking. (*Teǹkoo wa haikiǹgu ni kootsugoo datta.*) 天候はハイキングに好都合だった.

favorite *adj.* o-「kiniiri no お気に入りの; i「chibaǹ suki「 na いちばん好きな: Who is your favorite singer? (*Anata no ichibaǹ suki na kashu wa dare desu ka?*) あなたのいちばん好きな歌手はだれですか.

— n. oˈkiniiri お気に入り; (person) niˈnkimono 人気者; (thing) koˈobutsu 好物: Sashimi is a favorite of mine. (Sashimi wa watashi no koobutsu desu.) 刺し身は私の好物です.

fear n. 1 (dread) oˈsore 恐れ; kyoˈofu 恐怖: I trembled in fear. (Watashi wa kyoofu de furueta.) 私は恐怖で震えた.

2 (anxiety) fuˈan 不安; shiˈnpai 心配: There is no fear of rain today. (Kyoo wa ame no shinpai wa nai.) きょうは雨の心配はない.

— vt. 1 (be uneasy) ... o kiˈzukaˈu ...を気づかう ⓒ; shiˈnpai suru 心配する Ⓘ: He feared that he would fail. (Kare wa shippai shinai ka to shinpai datta.) 彼は失敗しないかと心配だった.

2 (be afraid of) ... o oˈsoreˈru ...を恐れる Ⓥ; koˈwagaˈru 怖がる ⓒ: Animals fear fire. (Doobutsu wa hi o kowagaru.) 動物は火を怖がる.

fearful adj. 1 (terrible) oˈsoroshiˈi 恐ろしい; moˈnosugoˈi ものすごい: a fearful accident (osoroshii jiko) 恐ろしい事故.

2 (afraid) (... o) oˈsoˈrete (iru) (...を)恐れて(いる); koˈwagaˈtte (iru) 怖がって(いる): She was fearful of walking in the dark. (Kanojo wa kurayami no naka o aruku no o kowagatta.) 彼女は暗闇の中を歩くのを怖がった.

3 (very bad) hiˈdoˈi ひどい; taˈrihen na 大変な: make a fearful mistake (hidoi machigai o suru) ひどい間違いをする.

fearless adj. oˈsoreˈnai 恐れない; daˈitaˈn na 大胆な: He was fearless of danger. (Kare wa kiken o osorenakatta.) 彼は危険を恐れなかった.

feast n. 1 (banquet) shuˈkuen 祝宴; eˈnkai 宴会: give a gorgeous wedding feast (gooka na kekkon no shukuen o moyoosu) 豪華な結婚の祝宴を催す.

2 (splendid meal) goˈchisoo ごちそう: She prepared a feast for us. (Kanojo wa watashi-tachi ni gochi-

soo o tsukutte kureta.) 彼女は私たちにごちそうを作ってくれた.

3 (religious festival) shuˈkujitsu 祝日; saˈijitsu 祭日.

— vt. 1 (give a feast) ... ni goˈchisoo o suru ...にごちそうをする Ⓘ; ... o moˈtenaˈsu ...をもてなす ⓒ: feast one's guests (o-kyaku o motenasu) お客をもてなす.

2 (give pleasure) ... o taˈnoshimaseˈru ...を楽しませる Ⓥ: feast one's eyes on a painting (e o mite tanoshimu) 絵を見て楽しむ.

feather n. haˈne 羽; uˈmoo 羽毛.

feature n. 1 (characteristic) toˈkuchoo 特徴; toˈkushoku 特色: geographical features (chiri-teki tokuchoo) 地理的特徴.

2 (special article) toˈkushuu kiˈji 特集記事: a feature in a magazine (zasshi no tokushuu kiji) 雑誌の特集記事.

3 (of a movie, TV, etc.) yoˈbimono 呼び物: a main feature on the program (puroguramu no yobimono) プログラムの呼び物.

4 (the face as a whole) kaˈodachi 顔立ち; yoˈoboo 容貌: a man of regular features (kaodachi no totonotta otoko no hito) 顔立ちの整った男の人.

— vt. 1 (of an article) ... o toˈkushuu suru ...を特集する Ⓘ: a magazine featuring overseas travel (kaigai-ryokoo o tokushuu shita zasshi) 海外旅行を特集した雑誌.

2 (of a movie, TV, etc.) ... o shuˈen saseru ...を主演させる Ⓥ: The movie featured a new actress. (Sono eega wa shinjin-joyuu o shuen saseta.) その映画は新人女優を主演させた.

February n. ni-ˈgatsu 2 月.

federal adj. reˈngoo no 連合の; reˈnpoo no 連邦の: a federal government (renpoo seefu) 連邦政府.

federation n. reˈnpoo 連邦; reˈnmee 連盟.

fee n. 1 (payment for a professional service) shaˈree 謝礼; hoˈroshuu 報酬; -ryoo 料: a lawyer's fee (*beñgo-ryoo*) 弁護料.

2 (fixed charge) ryoˈokiñ 料金; -ryoo 料: What is the fee per day? (*Ichi-nichi no ryookiñ wa ikura desu ka?*) 1 日の料金はいくらですか. / an admission fee (*nyuujoo-ryoo*) 入場料.

feeble *adj.* **1** (weak) yoˈwaˈi 弱い; yoˈwayowashiˈi 弱々しい: a feeble old man (*yowayowashii roojiñ*) 弱弱しい老人.

2 (faint) kaˈsuka na かすかな: I heard a feeble cry. (*Watashi wa kasuka na sakebigoe o kiita.*) 私はかすかな叫び声を聞いた.

feed *vt.* **1** (give food to) ... ni taˈbemoˈno o aˈtaeru ...に食べ物を与える Ⓥ; (of animals) ... ni eˈsaˈo yaˈru ...にえさをやる Ⓒ: She fed her baby with a spoon. (*Kanojo wa akañboo ni saji de tabesaseta.*) 彼女は赤ん坊にさじで食べさせた. / Do not feed the animals. (*Doobutsu ni esa o yaranaide kudasai.*) 動物にえさをやらないでください.

2 (supply) ... o kyoˈokyuu suru ...を供給する Ⓘ; iˈreru 入れる Ⓥ: feed data into a computer (*koñpyuutaa ni deeta o ireru*) コンピューターにデータを入れる.

— *vi.* (eat) moˈnoˈo taˈbeˈru ものを食べる Ⓥ: The cows are feeding in the pasture. (*Ushi ga bokujoo de kusa o tabete iru.*) 牛が牧場で草を食べている.

— *n.* eˈsaˈえさ; shiˈryoo 飼料.

feel *vi.* **1** (be aware of) kaˈñjiru 感じる Ⓥ: I feel very cold. (*Watashi wa totemo samui.*) 私はとても寒い.

2 (be in a state) kiˈbuñ ga ... da 気分が...だ: How do you feel today? (*Kyoo wa kibuñ wa ikaga desu ka?*) きょうは気分はいかがですか. / I don't feel well. (*Kibuñ ga yoku arimaseñ.*) 気分がよくありません.

3 (think) (... to) oˈmoˈu (...と)思う Ⓒ: I feel sure of his success. (*Kare wa kitto seekoo suru to omoimasu.*) 彼はきっと成功すると思います.

4 (search) (... o) saˈgasu (...を)探す Ⓒ: I felt in my pocket for the key. (*Watashi wa poketto no naka no kii o sagashita.*) 私はポケットの中のキーを捜した.

— *vt.* **1** (touch) ... ni saˈwatte miˈru ...に触ってみる Ⓒ: feel a pulse (*myaku ni sawatte miru*) 脈に触ってみる.

2 (perceive) ... o kaˈñjiru ...を感じる Ⓥ: I felt the house shake. (*Watashi wa ie ga yureru no o kañjita.*) 私は家が揺れるのを感じた.

3 (consider) ... to oˈmoˈu ...と思う Ⓒ; ... yoˈo na ki ga suru ...ような気がする Ⓘ: I feel that he will come. (*Watashi wa kare ga kuru yoo na ki ga suru.*) 私は彼が来るような気がする.

feel like ... *vt.* 〈verb〉-tai ki ga suru ...たい気がする Ⓘ: I don't feel like eating a meal. (*Shokuji wa tabetaku arimaseñ.*) 食事は食べたくありません.

feeling *n.* **1** (state of mind) kaˈñji 感じ; kiˈmochi 気持ち: a feeling of gratitude (*kañsha no kimochi*) 感謝の気持ち.

2 (emotions) kaˈñjoo 感情; kiˈbuñ 気分: hurt a person's feelings (*hito no kañjoo o gaisuru*) 人の感情を害する.

3 (impression) kaˈñji 感じ; iˈñshoo 印象: I have a feeling that he is working too hard. (*Kare wa hatarakisugi no yoo na kañji ga suru.*) 彼は働き過ぎのような感じがする.

4 (power to feel) kaˈñkaku 感覚: I lost all feeling in my fingers. (*Watashi wa yubi no kañkaku ga sukkari nakunatta.*) 私は指の感覚がすっかりなくなった.

fellow *n.* **1** (man) oˈtokoˈ男; yaˈtsu やつ: He is a pleasant fellow. (*Kare wa yukai na otoko da.*) 彼は愉快な男だ. / a stupid fellow (*baka na yatsu*) ばかなやつ.

2 (comrade) naˈkama 仲間; doˈoryoo 同僚: a fellow student (*gakuyuu*) 学友 / a fellow worker (*shi-*

goto nakama) 仕事仲間.

fellowship n. 1 (friendly association) shiˈñkoo 親交; shiˈñboku 親睦: enjoy fellowship with people (hito to shiñkoo o musubu) 人と親交を結ぶ.

2 (group) daˈñtai 団体; kuˈmiai 組合.

3 (money) shoˈogakukiñ 奨学金: receive a fellowship (shoogakukiñ o morau) 奨学金をもらう.

female adj. (of people) joˈsee no 女性の; (of animals) meˈsu¹ no 雌の: a female child (oñna-no-ko) 女の子 / a female dog (mesu-inu) 雌犬.
— n. (of a person) joˈsee 女性; (of an animal) meˈsu¹ 雌.

feminine adj. joˈsee no 女性の; oˈñna-rashiˈi 女らしい: feminine beauty (joseebi) 女性美 / a feminine gesture (oñna-rashii shigusa) 女らしいしぐさ.

fence n. kaˈkoi 囲い; saˈku¹ さく; kaˈki¹ 垣; feˈñsu フェンス: put up a fence around a garden (niwa no mawari ni saku o tateru) 庭の回りにさくを立てる.
— vt. ... ni kaˈkoi o suru ...に囲いをする; saˈku¹ o meˈgurasu さくを巡らす: I fenced my field. (Watashi wa hatake ni kakoi o shita.) 私は畑に囲いをした.

fencing n. (with a sword) feˈñshiñ-gu フェンシング; keˈñjutsu 剣術: Japanese fencing (keñdoo) 剣道.

ferocious adj. doˈomoo na どうもうな; kyoˈoboo na 凶暴な: a ferocious animal (doomoo na doobutsu) どうもうな動物.

ferry n. feˈrii フェリー; reˈñrakuseñ 連絡船; waˈtashibuˈne 渡し船: take a ferry (ferii de iku) フェリーで行く.
— vt. ... o fuˈne de waˈtasu ...を船で渡す; haˈkobu 運ぶ: ferry people across a river (hito o fune de kawa o watasu) 人を船で川を渡す.

fertile adj. 1 (of land) koˈeta 肥えた; koˈete iru 肥えている; hiˈyoku na 肥沃な: fertile land (hiyoku na tochi) 肥沃な土地.

2 (of mind) yuˈtaka na 豊かな: a fertile imagination (yutaka na soozooryoku) 豊かな想像力.

festival n. 1 (day) shuˈkujitsu 祝日; saˈijitsu 祭日.

2 (performances) moˈyooshi 催し; maˈtsuri 祭り; feˈsutibaru フェスティバル; -sai 祭: a music festival (oñgaku-sai) 音楽祭.

fetch vt. (of a thing) ... o toˈtte kuru ...を取って来る; (of a person) ... o tsuˈrete kuru ...を連れて来る: Please fetch me my glasses. (Megane o totte kite kudasai.) 眼鏡を取って来てください. / If you would like to meet her, I will fetch her. (Moshi kanojo ni aitai nara tsurete kimasu yo.) もし彼女に会いたいなら連れて来ますよ.

fever n. 1 (high body temperature) neˈtsu¹ 熱: I have a fever. (Watashi wa netsu ga aru.) 私は熱がある.

2 (excitement) koˈofuñ 興奮; neˈk-kyoo 熱狂: The spectators were in a fever of excitement. (Kañkyaku wa nekkyoo shite ita.) 観客は熱狂していた.

few adj. 1 (not many) suˈko¹shi shika naˈi 少ししかない; hoˈto¹ñdo naˈi ほとんどない: I have few friends. (Watashi wa yuujiñ ga hotoñdo imaseñ.) 私には友人がほとんどいません.

2 (a small number of) shoˈosuˈu no 少数の; waˈzuka no わずかの: A few people were in the room. (Wazuka no hito ga sono heya ni imashita.) わずかの人がその部屋にいました.
— pron. shoˈosuˈu 少数: Few understood his theories. (Hoñ no shoosuu no hito shika kare no riroñ o rikai dekinakatta.) ほんの少数の人しか彼の理論を理解できなかった.

fiancé(e) n. koˈñyaˈkusha 婚約者.

fiber n. seˈñi 繊維: fibers of cotton (momeñ no señi) 木綿の繊維.

fiction n. 1 (novel) shoˈosetsu 小説: a writer of fiction (shoosetsuka) 小説家.

2 (invented story) tsuˈkuri-baˈnashi 作り話: What he says is a fiction. (*Kare ga itte iru koto wa tsukuri-banashi da.*) 彼が言っていることは作り話だ.

field *n.* **1** (for growing crops) haˈtake 畑; taˈ 田: a wheat field (*komugi-batake*) 小麦畑 / a rice field (*tanbo*) たんぼ.
2 (wide area) noˈ 野; haˈra 原; noˈhara 野原: field flowers (*no no hana*) 野の花 / pick flowers in a field (*nohara de hana o tsumu*) 野原で花を摘む.
3 (area for sports) kyoˈogijoo 競技場; fiˈirudo フィールド: a playing field (*undoojoo*) 運動場.
4 (area of study) buˈnya 分野; ryoˈoiki 領域: Many people are working in this field. (*Ooku no hito ga kono bunya de hataraite imasu.*) 多くの人がこの分野で働いています.
5 (area of battle) seˈnjoo 戦場.

fierce *adj.* **1** (violent) kyoˈoboo na 凶暴な; oˈsoroshiˈi 恐ろしい: have a fierce look (*osoroshii kao o suru*) 恐ろしい顔をする.
2 (intense) moˈoretsu na 猛烈な; haˈgeshiˈi 激しい: a fierce storm (*mooretsu na arashi*) 猛烈な嵐.

fifteen *pron.* juˈugo 15; (people) juˈugo-nin 15 人; (things) juˈugo-ko 15 個.
— *n.* (figure) juˈugo 15; (hour) juˈugo-ji 15 時; (minute) juˈugo-fun 15 分; (age) juˈugo-sai 15 歳.
— *adj.* juˈugo no 15 の; (people) juˈugo-nin 15 人の; (things) juˈugo-ko no 15 個の; (age) juˈugo-sai no 15 歳の.

fifteenth *adj.* juˈugo-banme no 15 番目の; daˈi-juugo no 第 15 の.
— *n.* **1** (people) juˈugo-banme no hiˈtoˈ 15 番目の人; (things) juˈugo-banme no moˈnoˈ 15 番目のもの.
2 (day) juˈugo-nichi 15 日.
3 (fraction) juˈugo-bun no ichiˈ 15 分の 1.

fifth *adj.* go-ˈbanme 5 番目の; daˈi-go no 第 5 の.

— *n.* **1** (people) go-ˈbanme no hiˈtoˈ 5 番目の人; (things) go-ˈbanme no mono 5 番目のもの.
2 (day) iˈtsuka 5 日.
3 (fraction) go-ˈbun no ichiˈ 5 分の 1.

fiftieth *adj.* goˈjuu-banme no 50 番目の; daˈi-goˈjuˈu no 第 50 の.
— *n.* **1** (people) goˈjuu-banme no hiˈtoˈ 50 番目の人; (things) goˈjuu-banme no moˈnoˈ 50 番目のもの.
2 (fraction) goˈjuu-bun no ichiˈ 50 分の 1.

fifty *pron.* goˈjuˈu 50; (people) goˈjuˈu-nin 50 人; (things) goˈjuˈk-ko 50 個.
— *n.* (figure) goˈjuˈu 50; (minute) goˈjuˈp-pun 50 分; (age) goˈjuˈs-sai 50 歳.
— *adj.* goˈjuˈu no 50 の; (people) goˈjuˈu-nin no 50 人の; (things) goˈjuˈk-ko no 50 個の; (age) goˈjuˈs-sai no 50 歳の.

fig *n.* (fruit) iˈchiˈjiku いちじく; (tree) iˈchiˈjiku no ki いちじくの木.

fight *vi.* **1** (combat) taˈtakau 戦う C: fight against an enemy (*teki to tatakau*) 敵と戦う.
2 (box) naˈguriaˈu 殴り合う C; keˈnka suru けんかする I: Two men were fighting on the street. (*Futari no otoko ga toori de kenka shite ita.*) 2 人の男が通りでけんかしていた.
3 (quarrel) koˈoron suru 口論する I; iˈiarasoˈu 言い争う C: They are always fighting. (*Kare-ra wa itsumo iiarasotte iru.*) 彼らはいつも言い争っている.
— *vt.* (struggle) ... to taˈtakau ...と戦う C; ... o aˈrasoˈu ...を争う C: fight inflation (*infure to tatakau*) インフレと戦う / fight a losing battle (*makeikusa o tatakau*) 負け戦を戦う.
— *n.* **1** (battle) taˈtakai 戦い: win [lose] a fight (*tatakai ni katsu [makeru]*) 戦いに勝つ[負ける].
2 (struggle) taˈtakai 闘い; toˈosoo 闘争: a fight for higher pay (*chinage-toosoo*) 賃上げ闘争.

fighter *n.* (person who fights) seˈn-

figure 176

shi 戦士; (boxer) se「nshu 選手; (plane) se「nto」oki 戦闘機.

figure n. **1** (shape of a person) su「gata 姿; hi「tokage 人影; ka「kkoo 格好: a slender figure (hossori shita sugata) ほっそりした姿 / I saw a figure in the dark. (Watashi wa kurayami no naka ni hitokage o mita.) 私は暗闇の中に人影を見た.

2 (symbol for a number) su「uji 数字: Arabic figures (Arabia-suuji) アラビア数字 / double [three] figures (futaketa [miketa] no suuji) 2けた[3けた]の数字.

3 (diagram) zu 図; zu「kee 図形: The details are shown in figure 2. (Shoosai wa zu ni ni shimesarete imasu.) 詳細は図2に示されています.

4 (person) ji「nbutsu 人物: a key figure (chuushin jinbutsu) 中心人物.

5 (arithmetic) ke「esan 計算; sa「nsu」u 算数: He is good at figures. (Kare wa keesan ga tokui da.) 彼は計算が得意だ.

— vt. **1** (think) ... to o「mou」 ...と思う C; ka「ngae」eru 考える V: I figured that he would be late. (Kare wa okureru to omotte imashita.) 彼は遅れると思っていました.

2 (calculate) ... o ke「esan suru ...を計算する I: figure up a total (keesan shite gookee o dasu) 計算して合計を出す.

file¹ n. (folder) to「jikomi とじ込み; fa「iru ファイル: a file of newspapers (shinbun no tojikomi) 新聞のとじ込み.

— vt. ... o to「jikomu ...をとじ込む C; fa「iru suru ファイルする I: file away papers (shorui o fairu suru) 書類をファイルする.

file² n. (metal tool) ya「suri やすり.

— vt. ... ni ya「suri o kake「ru ...にやすりをかける V: file one's fingernails (tsume ni yasuri o kakeru) つめにやすりをかける.

fill vt. **1** (make full) ... o i「ppai ni suru ...をいっぱいにする I; mi「ta」su 満たす C: fill a bottle with water

(bin ni mizu o ippai ni ireru) びんに水をいっぱいに入れる / Sorrow filled my heart. (Watashi no mune wa kanashimi de ippai datta.) 私の胸は悲しみでいっぱいだった.

2 (stop up) ... o fu「sagu ...をふさぐ C; u「zumeru うずめる V: fill a crack with cement (sakeme o semento de fusagu) 裂け目をセメントでふさぐ.

— vi. i「ppai ni na」ru いっぱいになる C: The hall soon filled. (Hooru wa sugu ni ippai ni natta.) ホールはすぐにいっぱいになった.

fill in vt. (... ni) ... o ki「nyuu suru (...に)...を記入する I: Fill in your name on this form, please. (Kono shorui ni namae o kinyuu shite kudasai.) この書類に名前を記入してください.

film n. **1** (of a photo) fi「rumu フィルム: put a film into a camera (kamera ni firumu o ireru) カメラにフィルムを入れる / develop a film (firumu o genzoo suru) フィルムを現像する / a 36-exposure roll of film (sanjuu-roku-mai-dori no firumu) 36枚撮りのフィルム / a film for color prints [slides] (karaa-purinto [suraido]-yoo firumu) カラープリント[スライド]用フィルム.

2 (motion picture) e「ega 映画: go to see a film (eega o mi ni iku) 映画を見に行く.

3 (thin covering) u「sumaku 薄膜; u「sukawa 薄皮: a film of oil (abura no usui maku) 油の薄い膜.

— vt. (make a motion picture) ... o sa「tsuee suru ...を撮影する I; e「ega-ka suru 映画化する I: film a novel (shoosetsu o eega-ka suru) 小説を映画化する.

filter n. (machine) ro「ka」ki ろ過器; (paper) fi「rutaa フィルター: clean water with a filter (mizu o rokaki de jooka suru) 水をろ過器で浄化する.

— vt. ... o ro「ka suru ...をろ過する I; ko「su こす C: filter oil (abura o kosu) 油をこす.

— vi. (of liquid) shi「mide」ru しみ出る V; (of light) sa「shiko」mu 差し込

む C: Sunlight filtered through the curtains. (*Hi no hikari ga kaateñ o tooshite sashikoñda.*) 日の光がカーテンを通して差し込んだ。

filthy *adj.* **1** (unclean) fuʳketsu na 不潔な; yoʳgoreta 汚れた; yoʳgorete iru 汚れている: a filthy towel (*yogoreta taoru*) 汚れたタオル.
2 (obscene) miʳdara na みだらな; geʳhiñ na 下品な: a filthy story (*gehiñ na hanashi*) 下品な話.

final *adj.* saʳigo no 最後の; saʳishuu-teki na 最終的な: the final chapter of a book (*hoñ no saigo no shoo*) 本の最後の章 / a final decision (*saishuu-kettee*) 最終決定.
— *n.* (of a game) keʳsshooseñ 決勝戦; (of an exam) saʳishuu shikeñ 最終試験.

finally *adv.* **1** (at last) tsuʳi ni ついに; yoʳoyaku ようやく: The engine finally started. (*Eñjiñ ga yooyaku kakatta.*) エンジンがようやくかかった.
2 (lastly) saʳigo ni 最後に: Finally, I'd like to say a few words. (*Saigo ni hitokoto mooshiagemasu.*) 最後に一言申し上げます.

finance *n.* (management) zaʳisee 財政; (money) zaʳigeñ 財源: an expert in finance (*zaisee no señmoñka*) 財政の専門家 / the Finance Minister (*ookura daijiñ*) 大蔵大臣.
— *vt.* ...ni shiʳkiñ o dasu ...に資金を出す C: The company financed his trip. (*Kaisha ga kare no ryohi o dashite kureta.*) 会社が彼の旅費を出してくれた.

financial *adj.* zaʳisee(joo) no 財政(上)の; kiʳñyuu no 金融の: the financial condition of a company (*kaisha no zaisee jootai*) 会社の財政状態.

find *vt.* **1** (look for and get) ...o miʳtsukeru ...を見つける V; saʳgashidaʳsu 捜し出す C: I found the key I lost. (*Watashi wa nakushita kii o mitsuketa.*) 私はなくしたキーを見つけた. / I can't find my baggage. (*Watashi no nimotsu ga mitsukarimaseñ.*) 私の荷物が見つかりません.

2 (come up by chance) ...o miʳtsukeru ...を見つける V: I found a 100 yen coin on the floor. (*Watashi wa yuka ni hyaku-eñ-dama o mitsuketa.*) 私は床に100円玉を見つけた.
3 (discover) ...o haʳkkeñ suru ...を発見する I: find a solution to a problem (*moñdai no kaiketsuhoo o hakkeñ suru*) 問題の解決法を発見する.
4 (learn) ...o shiʳru ...を知る C; ...ga waʳkaʳru ...がわかる C: I found it difficult to climb the mountain. (*Sono yama ni noboru no wa muzukashii koto ga wakatta.*) その山に登るのは難しいことがわかった.
5 (obtain) ...o teʳ ni iʳreru ...を手に入れる V; ...ga aʳru ...がある C: I cannot find the time to read a book. (*Hoñ o yomu jikañ ga nai.*) 本を読む時間がない.

fine[1] *adj.* **1** (very good) suʳbarashiʳi すばらしい; miʳgoto na 見事な; riʳppa na 立派な: The view from here is fine. (*Koko kara no nagame wa subarashii.*) ここからの眺めはすばらしい.
2 (of weather) haʳreta 晴れた; haʳrete iru 晴れている; yoʳi teñki no よい天気の: It is fine today. (*Kyoo wa yoi teñki da.*) きょうはよい天気だ.
3 (in good health) geʳñki na 元気な: "How are you?" "Fine, thank you." (*"Genki desu ka?" "Okagesama de (geñki desu.)*) 「元気ですか」「おかげさまで(元気です)」
4 (satisfactory) moʳoshibuñ naʳi 申し分ない; keʳkkoo na 結構: "Is this all right?" "That's fine." (*"Kore de yoroshii desu ka?" "Kekkoo desu."*) 「これでよろしいですか」「結構です」
5 (thin) hoʳsoʳi 細い: a fine thread (*hosoi ito*) 細い糸.
— *adv.* uʳmaku うまく; riʳppa ni 立派に: He is doing fine. (*Kare wa umaku yatte imasu.*) 彼はうまくやっています.

fine[2] *n.* baʳkkiñ 罰金; kaʳryoo 科料: pay a fine (*bakkiñ o shiharau*) 罰金を支払う.

finger *n.* yuˈbiˈ 指: the index finger (*hitosashi-yubi*) 人差し指 / the middle finger (*naka-yubi*) 中指 / the ring finger (*kusuri-yubi*) 薬指 / the little finger (*ko-yubi*) 小指.
★ thumb (*oya-yubi*) 親指.

finish *vt.* **1** (bring to an end) ... o oˈeru ...を終える V; suˈmaˈsu 済ます C: I have finished my work. (*Shigoto wa oemashita.*) 仕事は終えました.
2 (consume) ... o taˈirageˈru ...を平らげる V: finish a cake (*keeki o tairageru*) ケーキを平らげる.
3 (make complete) ... no shiˈage o suru ...の仕上げをする I: This painting is beautifully finished. (*Kono e wa utsukushiku shiagatte iru.*) この絵は美しく仕上がっている.
— *vi.* (come to an end) oˈwaru 終わる C; suˈmu 済む C: The play finishes at eight. (*Shibai wa hachiji ni owarimasu.*) 芝居は8時に終わります.

fire *n.* **1** (flame) hiˈ 火; hoˈnoo 炎: Fire burns. (*Hi wa moeru.*) 火は燃える.
2 (destructive burning) kaˈji 火事: A fire broke out in my neighborhood. (*Watashi no kiñjo de kaji ga atta.*) 私の近所で火事があった.
3 (burning fuel) hiˈ 火: build a fire (*hi o okosu*) 火をおこす / put out a fire (*hi o kesu*) 火を消す.
— *vt.* **1** (shoot) ... o haˈssha suru ...を発射する I; haˈppoo suru 発砲する I: fire a gun (*juu o hassha suru*) 銃を発射する.
2 (dismiss) ... o kuˈbi ni suru ...を首にする I; kaˈiko suru 解雇する I: He got fired from his job. (*Kare wa shigoto o kubi ni natta.*) 彼は仕事を首になった.
3 (set fire) ... ni hiˈ o tsuˈkeˈru ...に火をつける V: fire a heap of dead leaves (*kareha no yama ni hi o tsukeru*) 枯れ葉の山に火をつける.

fire engine *n.* shoˈoboˈosha 消防車; shoˈoboo-jidoˈosha 消防自動車.

fireman *n.* shoˈoboˈoshi 消防士.

fireplace *n.* daˈñro 暖炉.

fire station *n.* shoˈoboosho 消防署.

fireworks *n.* haˈnabi 花火: set off fireworks (*hanabi o ageru*) 花火を上げる.

firm[1] *adj.* **1** (hard) kaˈtai 堅い; (strong) gaˈñjoo na がんじょうな: firm ground (*katai jimeñ*) 堅い地面 / a firm chair (*gañjoo na isu*) がんじょうないす.
2 (steady) shiˈkkaˈri shita [shite iru] しっかりした[している]; keˈñjitsu na 堅実な: walk with firm steps (*shikkari shita ashidori de aruku*) しっかりした足どりで歩く.
3 (decided) kiˈppaˈri shita [shite iru] きっぱりした[している]; daˈñko to shita [shite iru] 断固とした[している]: I gave a firm refusal. (*Watashi wa kippari kotowatta.*) 私はきっぱり断わった.

firm[2] *n.* shoˈokai 商会; shoˈosha 商社; kaˈisha 会社: I work for this firm. (*Watashi wa kono kaisha ni tsutomete imasu.*) 私はこの会社に勤めています.

firmly *adv.* kaˈtaku 堅く; shiˈkkaˈri (to) しっかり(と): close a door firmly (*doa o shikkari shimeru*) ドアをしっかり閉める.

first *adj.* **1** (of time and place) iˈchibaˈñme no 1番目の; daiˈichi no 第1の: the first lesson (*dai-ik-ka*) 第1課 / the first floor (*ik-kai*) 1階.
★ BrE=ni-kai 2階.
2 (of order) saˈisho no 最初の; seˈñtoo no 先頭の; haˈjime no 初めの: This is her first novel. (*Kore wa kanojo no saisho no shoosetsu desu.*) これは彼女の最初の小説です. / He was first in line. (*Kare wa retsu no señtoo datta.*) 彼は列の先頭だった.
— *n.* **1** (people) saˈisho no hitoˈ 最初の人; (things) saˈisho no monoˈ 最初のもの: He was the first to come. (*Kare ga saisho ni kita hito datta.*) 彼が最初に来た人だった.
2 (date) tsuˈitachiˈ 1日.

— *adv.* dai¹-ichi ni 第 1 に; sa¹isho ni 最初に; ha¹ji¹mete 初めて: He stood first. (*Kare ga dai-ichi-i o shimeta.*) 彼が第 1 位を占めた. / It was ten years ago when I saw him first. (*Kare ni hajimete atta no wa juu-neñ mae desu.*) 彼に初めて会ったのは 10 年前です.

first class *n.* fa¹asuto ku¹rasu ファーストクラス; i¹t-to¹o 一等.

first-class *adj.* i¹chiryuu no 一流の; sa¹iko¹okyuu no 最高級の: a first-class hotel (*ichiryuu no hoteru*) 一流のホテル.

fiscal *adj.* za¹iseejoo no 財政上の; ka¹ikee no 会計の: a fiscal year (*kaikee neñdo*) 会計年度.

fish *n.* sa¹kana 魚; (flesh) gyo¹niku 魚肉: catch a fish (*sakana o toru*) 魚をとる.
— *vi.* sa¹kana o to¹ru 魚をとる ⓒ; tsu¹ri o suru 釣りをする Ⓘ: go fishing (*tsuri ni iku*) 釣りに行く.
— *vt.* ... o tsu¹ru ...を釣る ⓒ: fish trout (*masu o tsuru*) マスを釣る.

fisherman *n.* ryo¹oshi 漁師.

fishery *n.* gyo¹gyoo 漁業; su¹i-sa¹ñgyoo 水産業.

fishing *n.* tsu¹ri 釣り; sa¹kana¹tori 魚捕り: a fishing boat (*tsuri-bune*) 釣り船 / a fishing line (*tsuri-ito*) 釣り糸 / a fishing rod (*tsuri-zao*) 釣りざお.

fist *n.* ni¹giri ko¹bushi 握りこぶし; ge¹ñkotsu げんこつ: clench one's fist (*kobushi o nigirishimeru*) こぶしを握りしめる / He struck me with his fist. (*Kare wa watashi o geñkotsu de nagutta.*) 彼は私をげんこつで殴った.

fit¹ *vt.* **1** (be the right size) ... ni (pi¹tta¹ri) a¹u ...に(ぴったり)合う ⓒ: These shoes fit me very well. (*Kono kutsu wa watashi ni pittari da.*) この靴は私にぴったりだ.
2 (make suitable) ... ni a¹wase¹ru ...に合わせる Ⓥ: I will fit my schedule to yours. (*Watashi no yotee o anata no ni awasemashoo.*) 私の予定をあなたのに合わせましょう.
3 (put in position) ... ni pi¹ta¹ri to

ha¹meru ...にぴたりとはめる Ⓥ; sa¹shi-komu 差し込む ⓒ: fit a key in the lock (*kagi o joo ni sashikomu*) 鍵を錠に差し込む.
4 (equip with) ... o to¹ritsukeru ...を取り付ける Ⓥ: I fitted new tires to my car. (*Watashi wa kuruma ni atarashii taiya o toritsuketa.*) 私は車に新しいタイヤを取り付けた.
— *vi.* a¹u 合う ⓒ; pi¹tta¹ri suru ぴったりする Ⓘ: This door does not fit. (*Kono to wa umaku awanai.*) この戸はうまく合わない.
— *adj.* **1** (suitable) te¹ki¹shita 適した; te¹ki¹shite iru 適している; fu-¹sawashi¹i ふさわしい: This water is not fit to drink. (*Kono mizu wa nomu no ni tekishite imaseñ.*) この水は飲むのに適していません.
2 (proper) to¹o o eta [ete iru] 当を得た[得ている]; o¹ñtoo na 穏当な: It is not fit for you to say so. (*Anata ga soo iu no wa oñtoo de wa nai.*) あなたがそう言うのは穏当ではない.
3 (in good health) ke¹ñkoo na 健康な; ge¹ñki na 元気な: I am feeling very fit. (*Watashi wa totemo geñki desu.*) 私はとても元気です.

fit² *n.* (sudden attack of illness) ho¹s-sa 発作: fall down in a fit (*hossa de taoreru*) 発作で倒れる.

five *pron.* i¹tsu¹tsu 五つ; (people) go-¹ni¹ñ 5 人; (things) go¹-ko 5 個: I want five of these. (*Kore o itsutsu kudasai.*) これを五つ下さい.
— *n.* (figure) go¹ 5; (hour) go¹-ji 5 時; (minute) go¹-fuñ 5 分; (age) go¹-sai 5 歳.
— *adj.* i¹tsu¹tsu no 五つの; (people) go-¹ni¹ñ no 5 人の; (things) go¹-ko no 5 個の; (age) go¹-sai no 5 歳の.

fix *vt.* **1** (mend) ... o shu¹uri suru ...を修理する Ⓘ; na¹o¹su 直す ⓒ: I got the camera fixed. (*Watashi wa kamera o shuuri shite moratta.*) 私はカメラを修理してもらった.
2 (prepare) ... o yo¹oi suru ...を用意する Ⓘ; shi¹taku suru したくする Ⓘ: She fixed a meal for us. (*Kanojo wa watashi-tachi ni shokuji o yooi*

shite kureta.) 彼女は私たちに食事を用意してくれた.
3 (decide on) ... o ke⌐ttee suru ...を決定する ⊡; ki⌐meru 決める Ⅴ: We fixed the time and place for the meeting. (*Watashi-tachi wa kaigi no jikañ to basho o kimeta.*) 私たちは会議の時間と場所を決めた.
4 (make firm) (... ni) ... o ko⌐ttee saseru ...を固定させる Ⅴ; to⌐ri-tsuke⌐ru 取り付ける Ⅴ: fix a shelf to the wall (*kabe ni tana o toritsu-keru*) 壁に棚を取り付ける.

flag *n.* ha⌐ta⌐ 旗: run up a flag (*hata o kakageru*) 旗を掲げる.

flake *n.* u⌐sui kakera 薄いかけら; ha⌐kuheñ 薄片: flakes of snow (*seppeñ*) 雪片.

flame *n.* ho⌐noo 炎; ka⌐eñ 火炎: burst in flames (*patto moeagaru*) ぱっと燃え上がる.
— *vi.* **1** (burn with flames) ho⌐noo o dasu 炎を出す ⊡; mo⌐eaga⌐ru 燃え上がる ⊡: The fire flamed brightly. (*Hi wa aka-aka to moe-agatta.*) 火は赤々と燃え上がった.
2 (become red) a⌐kaku na⌐ru 赤くなる ⊡: Her cheeks flamed. (*Kanojo no hoo ga akaku natta.*) 彼女のほおが赤くなった.

flap *vt.* **1** (move) ... o pa⌐ta pata u⌐goka⌐su ...をばたばた動かす ⊡; (of wings) ha⌐batakase⌐ru 羽ばたかせる Ⅴ: The bird flapped its wings. (*Tori wa hane o habatakaseta.*) 鳥は羽を羽ばたかせた.
2 (give a light blow) ... o ta⌐ta⌐ku ...をたたく ⊡: flap flies away (*hae o tataite oiharau*) はえをたたいて追い払う.
— *vi.* **1** (of a flag) ha⌐tame⌐ku はためく ⊡: The flag was flapping in the wind. (*Hata ga kaze ni hata-meite ita.*) 旗が風にはためいていた.
2 (of a bird) ha⌐bata⌐ku 羽ばたく ⊡: The bird flapped away. (*Tori ga habataite tobisatta.*) 鳥が羽ばたいて飛び去った.

flash *vi.* **1** (shine quickly) pi⌐ka⌐tto hi⌐ka⌐ru ぴかっと光る ⊡; hi⌐rame⌐ku

ひらめく ⊡: Lightning flashed. (*Ina-zuma ga pikatto hikatta.*) 稲妻がぴかっと光った.
2 (come suddenly) pa⌐tto u⌐kabu ぱっと浮かぶ ⊡: A good idea flashed into my mind. (*Yoi kañgae ga patto atama ni ukañda.*) よい考えがぱっと頭に浮かんだ.
— *vt.* **1** (give out light) ... o pa⌐tto te⌐ra⌐su ...をぱっと照らす ⊡: flash a light (*akari o patto terasu*) 明かりをぱっと照らす.
2 (show) ... o chi⌐ra⌐ri to mi⌐se⌐ru ...をちらりと見せる Ⅴ: flash a badge (*bajji o chirari to miseru*) バッジをちらりと見せる.
— *n.* **1** (bright light) se⌐ñkoo 閃光; hi⌐rameki ひらめき.
2 (for taking photographs) fu⌐ra⌐s-shu フラッシュ: Can I use a flash? (*Furasshu o taite mo ii desu ka?*) フラッシュをたいてもいいですか.

flashlight *n.* **1** (torch) ka⌐ichuu-de⌐ñtoo 懐中電灯: switch on [off] a flashlight (*kaichuudeñtoo o tsu-keru [kesu]*) 懐中電灯をつける[消す].
2 (for taking photographs) fu⌐ra⌐s-shu フラッシュ.

flat[1] *adj.* **1** (level) ta⌐ira na 平らな; hi⌐ratai 平たい: a flat floor (*taira na yuka*) 平らな床.
2 (spread out) ba⌐tta⌐ri ta⌐o⌐rete (iru) ばったり倒れて(いる): She fell flat on her face. (*Kanojo wa utsubuse ni battari taoreta.*) 彼女はうつ伏せにばったり倒れた.
3 (of a tire) pa⌐ñku shita [shite iru] パンクした[している]: I have a flat tire. (*Taiya ga pañku shimashita.*) タイヤがパンクしました.
4 (absolute) ki⌐ppa⌐ri shita [shite iru] きっぱりした[している]: give a flat refusal (*kippari to kotowaru*) きっぱりと断わる.
— *n.* (surface) he⌐eme⌐ñ 平面; (land) he⌐echi 平地.
— *adv.* **1** (in a flat manner) ta⌐ira ni 平に.
2 (absolutely) ki⌐ppa⌐ri to きっぱりと; ha⌐kki⌐ri はっきり: I told him flat.

(*Watashi wa kare ni hakkiri itte oita.*) 私は彼にはっきり言っておいた.
3 (exactly) ki¬kka¬ri きっかり; fu¬ra¬tto フラット: run a course in 10 seconds flat (*koosu o juu-byoo furatto de hashiru* コースを10秒フラットで走る.

flat² *n.* (apartment) a¬pa¬ato アパート; ma¬ñshoñ マンション.

flatter *vt.* **1** (praise insincerely) ... ni o¬seji o iu ...にお世辞を言う C: She flattered me about my singing. (*Kanojo wa watashi ni uta ga umai to oseji to itta.*) 彼女は私に歌がうまいとお世辞を言った.
2 (give a feeling of pleasure) ... o u¬reshigarase¬ru ...をうれしがらせる V: I am flattered by your invitation. (*Go-shootai o ureshiku omoimasu.*) ご招待をうれしく思います.

flattery *n.* o¬seji お世辞; o¬be¬kka おべっか.

flavor *n.* **1** (taste) a¬ji¬ 味; (taste and smell) fu¬umi 風味: This soup has a flavor of garlic. (*Kono suupu wa niñniku no aji ga suru.*) このスープはにんにくの味がする.
2 (atmosphere) o¬momuki 趣; a¬ji¬wai 味わい: a castle with the flavor of the Middle Ages (*chuusee no omomuki no aru shiro*) 中世の趣のある城.
—— *vt.* ... ni fu¬umi o tsu¬ke¬ru ...に風味をつける V: flavor the tea with lemon (*koocha ni remoñ no fuumi o tsukeru*) 紅茶にレモンの風味をつける.

flaw *n.* ki¬zu きず: a flaw in a jewel (*hooseki no kizu*) 宝石のきず.

flee *vi.* ni¬ge¬ru 逃げる V; no¬gare¬ru 逃れる V: flee from the enemy (*teki kara nogareru*) 敵から逃れる.

fleet *n.* ka¬ñtai 艦隊; se¬ñdañ 船団.

flesh *n.* **1** (of an animal) ni¬ku¬ 肉; (of a fruit) ka¬niku 果肉: a flesh eating animal (*nikushoku-doobutsu*) 肉食動物.
2 (body) ni¬kutai 肉体.

flexible *adj.* **1** (easily bent) ma¬geyasu¬i 曲げやすい; ji¬fyu¬u ni ma¬garu 自由に曲がる: a flexible cord (*jiyuu*

ni magaru koodo) 自由に曲がるコード.
2 (adaptable) ju¬unañ na 柔軟な; yu¬uzuu no [ga] kiku 融通の[が]きく; fu¬re¬kishiburu na フレキシブルな: a flexible plan (*yuuzuu no kiku keekaku*) 融通の利く計画.

flight *n.* **1** (journey) so¬ra no ta¬bi¬ 空の旅; fu¬raito フライト: How was your flight? (*Sora no tabi wa ikaga deshita ka?*) 空の旅はいかがでしたか.
2 (of a plane) bi¬ñ 便: Will this flight leave on time? (*Kono biñ wa yotee doori demasu ka?*) この便は予定どおり出ますか. / an extra flight (*riñji-biñ*) 臨時便 /a regular flight (*teeki-biñ*) 定期便.
3 (stairs) ka¬idañ 階段.

flight attendant *n.* kya¬kushitsu joomu¬iñ 客室乗務員.

fling *vt.* ... o na¬ge¬ru ...を投げる V; ho¬orida¬su ほうり出す C: He flung his clothes on the floor. (*Kare wa fuku o yuka ni hooridashita.*) 彼は服を床にほうり出した.

flint *n.* (for a lighter) ra¬itaa no i¬shi¬ ライターの石.

flip *vt.* ... o ha¬ji¬ku ...をはじく C; po¬i to na¬ge¬ru ぽいと投げる V: flip a coin on the counter (*kooka o kauñtaa no ue ni poi to nageru*) 硬貨をカウンターの上にぽいと投げる.

float *vi.* **1** (stay on the surface) u¬ku 浮く C: Wood floats on water. (*Ki wa mizu ni uku.*) 木は水に浮く.
2 (drift) ta¬dayo¬u 漂う C: A balloon floated in the air. (*Fuuseñ ga kuuchuu ni tadayotte ita.*) 風船が空中に漂っていた.
—— *vt.* ... o u¬kaberu ...を浮かべる V; u¬kaseru 浮かせる V: float a raft on the river (*ikada o kawa ni ukaberu*) いかだを川に浮かべる.
—— *n.* **1** (on a fishing line) u¬ki¬ 浮き: The float is moving. (*Uki ga ugoite imasu.*) 浮きが動いています.
2 (vehicle in a procession) da¬shi¬ 山車.

flock *n.* mu¬re¬ 群れ: a flock of sheep (*hitsuji no mure*) 羊の群れ.

flood n. **1** (overflow of water) koʼo-zui 洪水; oʼomiʼzu 大水: The typhoon caused a bad flood. (*Taifuu ga hidoi koozui o hikiokoshita.*) 台風がひどい洪水を引き起こした.
2 (outpouring) aʼfureʼru koʼtoʼ あふれること: a flood of tears (*afureru namida*) あふれる涙.
— vt. **1** (of a place) ... o miʼzubitashiʼ ni suru ...を水浸しにする ①; (of a river) haʼnʼran saseru はんらんさせる Ⅴ: The river flooded the village. (*Kawa wa mura o mizubitashi ni shita.*) 川は村を水浸しにした.
2 (fill to overflowing) ... ni saʼttoo suru ...に殺到する ①: Applicants flooded the office. (*Oobosha ga jimusho ni sattoo shita.*) 応募者が事務所に殺到した.
— vi. haʼnʼran suru はんらんする ①; saʼttoo suru 殺到する ①.

floor n. **1** (surface in a room) yuʼka 床: sit on the floor (*yuka ni suwaru*) 床に座る.
2 (of a building) kaʼi 階; fuʼroʼa フロア: the second floor (*ni-kai*) 2 階. ★ BrE=saň-gai 3 階 / I'd like a room on a higher [lower] floor. (*Motto ue [shita] no kai no heya ni shite kudasai.*) もっと上[下]の階の部屋にしてください.
— vt. ... ni yuʼka o haru ...に床を張る ⓒ: floor a room with plastic tiles (*heya ni purasuchikku tairu no yuka o haru*) 部屋にプラスチックタイルの床を張る.

flour n. koʼmugiko 小麦粉.

flourish vi. **1** (grow well) yoʼku soʼdaʼtsu よく育つ ⓒ; haʼnʼmo suru 繁茂する ①: Roses in my garden are flourishing. (*Uchi no niwa no bara wa yoku sodatte imasu.*) うちの庭のばらはよく育っています.
2 (be successful) haʼnʼjoo suru 繁盛する ①: His business is flourishing. (*Kare no shoobai wa hanjoo shite iru.*) 彼の商売は繁盛している.
— vt. (wave) ... o fuʼrimawaʼsu ...を振り回す ⓒ: flourish a sword (*katana o furimawasu*) 刀を振り回す.

flow vi. **1** (move along) naʼgareʼru 流れる Ⅴ: The Sumida River flows through Tokyo. (*Sumida-gawa wa Tookyoo o nagarete imasu.*) 墨田川は東京を流れています.
2 (of the tide) saʼsu 差す ⓒ; miʼchiʼru 満ちる Ⅴ: The tide began to flow. (*Shio ga michite kita.*) 潮が満ちてきた.
— n. naʼgareʼ 流れ: stop the flow of blood (*chi no nagare o tomeru*) 血の流れを止める.

flower n. haʼnaʼ 花; kuʼsaʼbana 草花: arrange flowers (*hana o ikeru*) 花を生ける / plant flowers (*kusabana o ueru*)) 草花を植える / a flower shop (*hana-ya*) 花屋 / flower arrangement (*ikebana*) 生け花.
— vi. haʼnaʼ ga saʼkuʼ 花が咲く ⓒ: Tulips flower in spring. (*Chuurippu wa haru ni saku.*) チューリップは春に咲く.

flu n. iʼnfurueʼnza インフルエンザ; ryuʼukaň 流感: He has the flu. (*Kare wa ryuukaň ni kakatte iru.*) 彼は流感にかかっている.

fluent adj. ryuʼuchoo na 流ちょうな; naʼmeʼraka na 滑らかな: He is fluent in Japanese. (*Kare wa Nihoňgo ga ryuuchoo desu.*) 彼は日本語が流ちょうです.

fluid n. ryuʼutai 流体; ryuʼudootai 流動体.
— adj. ryuʼudoosee no 流動性の; ryuʼudoo-teki na 流動的な: The situation is still fluid. (*Joosee wa mada ryuudoo-teki desu.*) 情勢はまだ流動的です.

flush vi. **1** (of water) doʼtto nagareʼru どっと流れる Ⅴ; hoʼtobashiʼru ほとばしる ⓒ: The water flushed out from the pipe. (*Mizu ga sono kaň kara hotobashiri-deta.*) 水がその管からほとばしり出た.
2 (blush) paʼtto aʼkaku naʼru ぱっと赤くなる ⓒ; koʼochoo suru 紅潮する ①: His face flushed with excitement. (*Kare no kao wa koofuň de akaku natta.*) 彼の顔は興奮で赤くなった.

— *vt.* **1** (of water) ... o doˈtto naˈgaˈsu ...をどっと流す C: flush the toilet (*toire no mizu o nagasu*) トイレの水を流す.

2 (blush) ... o aˈkarameˈru ...を赤める V; koˈochoo saseru 紅潮させる V: She was flushed with fever. (*Kanojo wa netsu de akaku natte ita.*) 彼女は熱で赤くなっていた.

— *n.* koˈochoo 紅潮; seˈkimeñ 赤面.

flutter *vi.* **1** (of a bird) haˈbaˈtaki suru 羽ばたきする I; (of a butterfly) hiˈrahira toˈbu ひらひら飛ぶ C: A butterfly is fluttering about. (*Choo ga ip-piki hirahira toñde iru.*) ちょうが1匹ひらひら飛んでいる.

2 (of a flag, etc.) haˈtameˈku はためく C; hiˈrahira suru ひらひらする I: The curtains are fluttering in the breeze. (*Kaateñ ga kaze ni hirahira shite iru.*) カーテンが風にひらひらしている.

— *vt.* ... o baˈtabata saseru ...をばたばたさせる V; hiˈrahira saseru ひらひらさせる V: The bird fluttered its wings. (*Sono tori wa hane o batabata saseta.*) その鳥は羽をばたばたさせた.

— *n.* haˈbaˈtaki 羽ばたき; haˈtamekiˈ はためき.

fly[1] *vi.* **1** (travel through the air) toˈbu 飛ぶ C: These birds fly south in winter. (*Kore-ra no tori wa fuyu ni minami e toñde ikimasu.*) これらの鳥は冬に南へ飛んで行きます.

2 (travel by aircraft) hiˈkoˈoki de iˈku 飛行機で行く C: We flew from Tokyo to Seoul. (*Watashi-tachi wa Tookyoo kara Souru made hikooki de itta.*) 私たちは東京からソウルまで飛行機で行った.

3 (pass quickly) toˈbu yoˈo ni suˈgiˈsaru 飛ぶように過ぎ去る C: Time flies. (*Toki wa tobu yoo ni sugisaru.*) 時は飛ぶように過ぎ去る.

4 (wave) hiˈrugaˈeru 翻る C: A flag was flying on the mast. (*Masuto ni hata ga hirugaette ita.*) マストに旗が翻っていた.

— *vt.* (in an aircraft) ... o hiˈkoˈoki de toˈbu ...を飛行機で飛ぶ C: fly the Pacific (*Taiheeyoo o hikooki de tobu*) 太平洋を飛行機で飛ぶ.

fly[2] *n.* **1** (insect) haˈe はえ: catch a fly (*hae o tsukamaeru*) はえを捕まえる.

2 (fish-hook) kaˈbari 蚊針; keˈbari 毛針.

foam *n.* aˈwaˈ 泡: the foam of beer (*biiru no awa*) ビールの泡.

— *vi.* aˈwadaˈtsu 泡立つ C: The beer foamed over the top of the glass. (*Biiru ga awadatte koppu kara afureta.*) ビールが泡立ってコップからあふれた.

focus *n.* **1** (meeting point) shoˈoteñ 焦点; piˈñto ピント: the focus of a lens (*reñzu no shooteñ*) レンズの焦点.

2 (center) chuˈushiñ 中心: the focus of interest (*kyoomi no chuushiñ*) 興味の中心.

— *vt.* **1** (adjust) ... ni shoˈoteñ [piˈñto] o aˈwaseˈru ...に焦点[ピント]を合わせる V: I focused my camera on the flower. (*Watashi wa sono hana ni piñto o awaseta.*) 私はその花にピントを合わせた.

2 (concentrate) ... ni shuˈuchuu saseru ...に集中させる V: We focused our efforts on the problem. (*Watashi-tachi wa sono moñdai ni doryoku o shuuchuu saseta.*) 私たちはその問題に努力を集中させた.

fog *n.* kiˈri 霧; moˈya もや: a mountain covered with fog (*kiri ni tsutsumareta yama*) 霧に包まれた山. ★ 'Mist' is also called '*kiri*'.

— *vt.* ... o kiˈri [moˈya] de oˈoˈu ...を霧[もや]で覆う C; kuˈmoraseˈru 曇らせる V: My glasses were fogged up with steam. (*Megane ga yuge de kumotta.*) 眼鏡が湯気で曇った.

foil *n.* aˈrumiˈ-haku はく; hoˈiru ホイル: bake potatoes in aluminum foil (*jagaimo o arumi-haku ni tsutsuñde yaku*) じゃがいもをアルミはくに包んで焼く.

fold *vt.* **1** (double over) ... o oˈritatamu ...を折り畳む C: fold a piece of paper in half (*kami o hañbuñ ni oritatamu*) 紙を半分に折り畳む.

2 (bring in close to the body) ... o da¹kishime¹ru ...を抱き締める V: She folded her arms around her child. (*Kanojo wa kodomo o ryoouude de dakishimeta.*) 彼女は子どもを両腕で抱き締めた.

3 (enclose) ... o tsu¹tsu¹mu ...を包む C; ku¹ru¹mu くるむ C: fold a present in paper (*okurimono o kami de tsutsumu*) 贈物を紙で包む.

— *vi.* o¹ritatameru 折り畳める V: This chair folds easily. (*Kono isu wa kañtañ ni oritatamemasu.*) このいすは簡単に折り畳めます.

— *n.* o¹rime¹ 折り目; hi¹da ひだ: the folds of a skirt (*sukaato no hida*) スカートのひだ.

foliage *n.* ha 葉.

folk *n.* **1** (people) hi¹to¹bito 人々; hi¹to¹-tachi 人たち: country [town] folk (*inaka [machi] no hito-tachi*) いなか[町]の人たち.

2 (family) ka¹zoku 家族; (relatives) shi¹ñzoku 親族: How are your folks? (*O-taku no minasañ wa ikaga desu ka?*) お宅のみなさんはいかがですか.

— *adj.* mi¹ñkañ no 民間の; mi¹ñzoku no 民族の: a folk dance (*miñzoku buyoo*) 民族舞踊 / a folk music (*miñzoku oñgaku*) 民族音楽.

folk song *n.* fo¹oku-so¹ñgu フォークソング; mi¹ñyoo 民謡.

follow *vt.* **1** (go after) ... no a¹to ni tsuite i¹ku ...の後について行く C: You go first and I will follow you. (*Anata ga saki ni ikeba ato ni tsuite ikimasu.*) あなたが先に行けば後について行きます.

2 (come after) a¹to ni kuru 後に来る I: Summer follows spring. (*Haru no ato ni natsu ga kuru.*) 春の後に夏が来る.

3 (go along) ... o ta¹do¹ru ...をたどる C; i¹ku 行く C: Follow this road until you get to the station. (*Eki ni tsuku made kono michi o iki na-*

sai.*) 駅に着くまでこの道を行きなさい.

4 (obey) ... ni shi¹tagau ...に従う C; ... o ma¹mo¹ru ...を守る C: He didn't follow my instructions. (*Kare wa watashi no shiji ni shita-gawanakatta.*) 彼は私の指示に従わなかった.

5 (pursue) ... o o¹u ...を追う C; tsu¹iseki suru 追跡する I: We followed the car. (*Watashi-tachi wa sono kuruma o otta.*) 私たちはその車を追った.

6 (understand) ... o ri¹kai suru ...を理解する I: I was unable to follow his explanation. (*Watashi wa kare no setsumee ga rikai dekinakatta.*) 私は彼の説明が理解できなかった.

— *vi.* **1** (go [come] after) (... ni) tsu¹ite iku [kuru] (...に)ついて行く C [来る I]: The dog followed behind me. (*Sono inu wa watashi ni tsuite kita.*) その犬は私についてきた.

2 (happen) tsu¹gi¹ ni o¹ko¹ru 次に起こる C: No one knows what will follow. (*Tsugi ni nani ga okoru ka dare ni mo wakaranai.*) 次に何が起こるかだれにもわからない.

3 (come as a result) to¹ozeñ ... to na¹ru 当然...となる C: It follows from this fact that he knows the truth. (*Kono jijitsu kara kare wa toozeñ sono shiñsoo o shitte iru koto ni naru.*) この事実から彼は当然その真相を知っていることになる. / It does not follow that poor people are unhappy. (*Mazushii hito ga fukoo da to wa kagiranai.*) 貧しい人が不幸だとは限らない.

follower *n.* ju¹usha 従者; shi¹ñpo¹osha 信奉者.

following *adj.* tsu¹gi¹ no 次の; i¹ka no 以下の: read the following chapter (*tsugi no shoo o yomu*) 次の章を読む.

— *n.* tsu¹gi¹ no ko¹to¹ 次のこと; i¹ka 以下: The following is his answer. (*Ika ga kare no heñji desu.*) 以下が彼の返事です.

fond *adj.* **1** (like) su¹ki¹ da 好きだ: She is fond of music. (*Kanojo wa* *oñgaku ga suki da.*) 彼女は音楽が好きだ.

2 (loving) a「ijoo no fuka「i 愛情の深い; a「mai 甘い: a fond mother (*kodomo ni amai hahaoya*) 子どもに甘い母親.

food *n.* **1** (what is eaten) ta「bemo「no 食べ物; sho「ku」motsu 食物: The food is delicious. (*Tabemono ga oishii.*) 食べ物がおいしい. / food and drink (*iñshokubutsu*) 飲食物.

2 (particular kind of food) sho「kuhiñ 食品: frozen food (*reetoo-shokuhiñ*) 冷凍食品 / natural foods (*shizeñ-shokuhiñ*) 自然食品.

3 (cooked food) ryo「ori 料理: Japanese [Chinese] food (*Nihoñ [Chuuka] ryoori*) 日本[中華]料理 / local food (*kyoodo ryoori*) 郷土料理.

fool *n.* ba「kamono ばか者; o「rokamono 愚か者: I was a fool to believe him. (*Kare o shiñjiru nañte watashi mo baka datta.*) 彼を信じるなんて私もばかだった.

— *vt.* ... o da「ma」su ...をだます ©: He fooled her out of her money. (*Kare wa kanojo o damashite o-kane o makiageta.*) 彼は彼女をだましてお金を巻き上げた.

foolish *adj.* ba「ka na ばかな; o「roka na 愚かな: It is foolish of you to do a thing like that. (*Soñna koto o suru nañte kimi mo baka da.*) そんなことをするなんて君もばかだ.

foot *n.* **1** (the part of a leg) a「shi」足: My feet are sore from walking. (*Aruita no de ashi ga itai.*) 歩いたので足が痛い.

2 (bottom) shi「ta no bu」buñ 下の部分; ne「moto」根元; (of a mountain) fu「moto」ふもと: the foot of a page (*peeji no shita no bubuñ*) ページの下の部分 / the foot of a mountain (*yama no fumoto*) 山のふもと.

3 (measure of length) fi「ito フィート: He is six feet tall. (*Kare wa shiñchoo ga roku-fiito aru.*) 彼は身長が6フィートある. ★ Japanese use the metric system and 'foot' is not used.

football *n.* **1** (American football) fu「ttobo「oru フットボール; (association football) sa「kkaa サッカー.

2 (ball) fu「ttobooru-yoo no booru フットボール用のボール.

footstep *n.* (sound) a「shio」to 足音: I heard somebody's footsteps. (*Watashi wa dare-ka no ashioto o kiita.*) 私はだれかの足音を聞いた.

for *prep.* **1** (in order to) ... no ta「me」ni ...のために: We held a party for him. (*Watashi-tachi wa kare no tame ni paatii o hiraita.*) 私たちは彼のためにパーティーを開いた. / He went out for a walk. (*Kare wa sañpo ni ikimashita.*) 彼は散歩に行きました.

2 (sent to) ... a「te no ...あての: Are there any letters for me? (*Watashi ate no tegami wa todoite imasu ka?*) 私あての手紙は届いていますか.

3 (during) ... no a「ida ...の間; -kañ 間: I stayed in Kyoto for three days. (*Watashi wa Kyooto ni mikka-kañ taizai shimashita.*) 私は京都に3日間滞在しました. / I'd like to rent this car for 24 hours. (*Kono kuruma o nijuu-yo-jikañ karitai no desu ga.*) この車を24時間借りたいのですが.

4 (as far as) ... no ai「da ...の間: I walked for four kilometers. (*Watashi wa yoñ-kiro aruita.*) 私は4キロ歩いた.

5 (suiting) ... muki no ...向きの; ... ni te「ki」shita ...に適した: This is a car for young people. (*Kore wa wakamono muki no kuruma desu.*) これは若者向きの車です.

6 (in return) ... to hi「kikae ni ...と引き換えに; ... ni ta「ishite ...に対して: I paid five thousand yen for the tie. (*Watashi wa sono nekutai ni go-señ-eñ haratta.*) 私はそのネクタイに5千円払った.

7 (toward) ... ni mu「katte ...に向かって; ... e i「ku tame」ni ...へ行くために: He left Tokyo for London. (*Kare wa Roñdoñ ni mukatte Too-*

kyoo o tatta.) 彼はロンドンに向かって
東京を立った.

8 (in favor of) ... ni saˈñsee no ...
に賛成の: Are you for the proposal?
(*Anata wa teeañ ni sañsee desu
ka?*) あなたは提案に賛成ですか.

9 (on behalf of) ... no kaˈwari ni
...の代わりに; ... o daˈihyoo shite ...
を代表して: He spoke for his classmates. (*Kare wa kurasu o daihyoo
shite shabetta.*) 彼はクラスを代表して
しゃべった.

10 (with regard to) ... ni taˈishite
...に対して: I felt no regret for what
I have done. (*Watashi wa jibuñ
no shita koto ni taishite kookai
shinakatta.*) 私は自分のしたことに対し
て後悔しなかった.

11 (because of) ... no riˈyuu de ...の
理由で; ... de ...で: This place is
famous for its cherry blossoms.
(*Koko wa sakura de yuumee desu.*)
ここは桜で有名です.

12 (as) ... to shiˈte ...として: You
mustn't give him up for dead.
(*Kare o shiñda mono to shite
akiramete wa ikenai.*) 彼を死んだも
のとしてあきらめてはいけない.

13 (considering) ... no waˈri ni ...
の割に: He looks young for his age.
(*Kare wa toshi no wari ni wakaku
mieru.*) 彼は年の割に若く見える.

forbid *vt.* ... o kiˈñjiru ...を禁じる ▽;
kiˈñshi suru 禁止する ▣: Smoking
is forbidden here. (*Kitsueñ wa
koko de wa kiñjirarete imasu.*) 喫
煙はここでは禁じられています.

force *n.* **1** (violence) boˈoryoku 暴
力: resort to force (*booryoku ni
uttaeru*) 暴力に訴える.

2 (power) chiˈkara 力: the force of
the wind (*kaze no chikara*) 風の力.

3 (organized body) taˈi 隊: the
armed forces (*guñtai*) 軍隊 / an ex-
ploration force (*tañkeñtai*) 探検隊.

4 (influence) eˈekyoˈoryoku 影響
力; chiˈkara 力: the force of public
opinion (*yoroñ no chikara*) 世論の
力.

— *vt.* **1** (compel) ... ni [o] muˈri-

yari ⟨verb⟩-(sa)seru ...に[を]無理やり
...(さ)せる ▽: They forced him to
accept the offer. (*Kare-ra wa kare
ni muriyari sono mooshide o uke-
saseta.*) 彼らは彼に無理やりその申し出
を受けさせた.

2 (do by force) ... o muˈri ni ⟨verb⟩
...を無理に...: He forced the door
open. (*Kare wa muri ni sono doa o
aketa.*) 彼は無理にそのドアを開けた.

forecast *vt.* ... o yoˈhoo suru ...を
予報する ▣; yoˈsoo suru 予想する
▣: forecast the weather (*teñki o
yohoo suru*) 天気を予報する.
— *n.* yoˈhoo 予報: weather forecast (*teñki-yohoo*) 天気予報.

forefinger *n.* hiˈtosashiˈ-yubi 人
差し指.

forehead *n.* hiˈtai 額: a high [low]
forehead (*hiroi* [*semai*] *hitai*) 広い
[狭い]額.

foreign *adj.* gaˈikoku no 外国の;
(of people) gaˈikokuˈjiñ no 外国人
の: a foreign language (*gaikokugo*)
外国語 / foreign trade (*gaikoku-
booeki*) 外国貿易.

foreigner *n.* gaˈikokuˈjiñ 外国人;
gaˈijiñ 外人.

foresee *vt.* ... o miˈtoosu ...を見通
す ▣; yoˈchi suru 予知する ▣: No-
body can foresee what will happen.
(*Nani ga okoru ka dare ni mo
yochi dekinai.*) 何が起こるかだれにも
予知できない.

forest *n.* moˈri 森; shiˈñriñ 森林.
★ A wood is often called '*hayashi*'
林.

forever *adv.* iˈtsu made mo いつまで
も; eˈekyuu ni 永久に: I will remember you forever. (*Anata no
koto wa itsu made mo wasuremaseñ.*) あなたのことはいつまでも忘れません.

forget *vt.* **1** (fail to remember) ...
o waˈsureru ...を忘れる ▽; oˈmoi-
dasenai 思い出せない: I've forgotten
her name. (*Kanojo no namae o wasurete shimatta.*) 彼女の名前を忘れ
てしまった.

2 (leave behind) ... o oˈkiwasureˈru
...を置き忘れる ▽: I often forget my

umbrella. (*Watashi wa yoku kasa o okiwasureru.*) 私はよく傘を置き忘れる.

— *vi.* wa「sureru 忘れる V: Don't forget! (*Wasurenaide.*) 忘れないで.

forgetful *adj.* wa「sure-yasu」i 忘れやすい; wa「sureppo」i 忘れっぽい: a forgetful person (*wasureppoi hito*) 忘れっぽい人.

forgive *vt.* **1** (pardon) ... o yu「ru」su ...を許す C; ka「nben suru 勘弁する I: I forgave him for his negligence. (*Watashi wa kare no taiman o yurushite yatta.*) 私は彼の怠慢を許してやった.

2 (let go without payment) ... o me「njo suru ...を免除する I: forgive a debt (*shakkin o menjo suru*) 借金を免除する.

fork *n.* **1** (for food) fo「oku フォーク.

2 (gardening tool) ku「made」 くま手.

3 (place of division) bu「nki」ten 分岐点: a fork in the road (*michi no bunkiten*) 道の分岐点.

— *vi.* (divide) bu「nki suru 分岐する I; wa「kare」ru 分かれる V: The river forks here. (*Kawa wa koko de futatsu ni wakaremasu.*) 川はここで二つに分かれます.

form *n.* **1** (shape) ka「tachi 形; (appearance) ga「ikan 外観: That rock has the form of an animal. (*Ano iwa wa doobutsu no katachi o shite iru.*) あの岩は動物の形をしている.

2 (type) ke「itai 形態; (kind) shu」rui 種類: There are various forms of government. (*Seeji ni wa iroiro na keetai ga arimasu.*) 政治にはいろいろな形態があります.

3 (printed paper) yo「oshi 用紙; (document) sho「rui 書類; sho「shiki 書式: an application form (*mooshikomi yooshi*) 申し込み用紙.

4 (condition) cho「oshi 調子: He is in good form. (*Kare wa chooshi ga ii.*) 彼は調子がいい.

— *vt.* **1** (give shape) ... o ka「tachizuku」ru ...を形作る C; (produce) ... o tsu「ku」ru ...を作る C: form a doll

out of clay (*nendo de ningyoo o tsukuru*) 粘土で人形を作る.

2 (organize) ... o so」shiki suru ...を組織する I; ko「osee suru 構成する I: form a committee (*iinkai o soshiki suru*) 委員会を組織する.

3 (conceive) ... o ma「tomeru ...をまとめる V: form ideas (*kangae o matomeru*) 考えをまとめる.

— *vi.* **1** (take shape) ka「tachi o na」su 形を成す C; de「ki」ru てきる V: Icicles formed on the eaves. (*Noki ni tsurara ga dekita.*) 軒につららができた.

2 (come into existence) u「mareru 生まれる V; u「kabu 浮かぶ C: A good idea formed in my mind. (*Atama ni ii kangae ga ukanda.*) 頭にいい考えが浮かんだ.

formal *adj.* **1** (correct for the occasion) ko「oshiki no 公式の; se「eshiki no 正式の: a formal visit (*kooshiki no hoomon*) 公式の訪問 / a formal contract (*seeshiki no keeyaku*) 正式の契約.

2 (not relaxed) ka「kushikiba」tta 格式ばった; ka「kushikiba」tte iru 格式ばっている; a「ratama」tta 改まった: formal behavior (*aratamatta taido*) 改まった態度.

formally *adv.* se「eshiki ni 正式に; ko「oshiki ni 公式に: I was formally invited to the party. (*Watashi wa seeshiki ni sono paatii ni shootai sareta.*) 私は正式にそのパーティーに招待された.

formation *n.* **1** (shaping) ko「osee 構成; ke「esee 形成: the formation of character (*jinkaku no keesee*) 人格の形成.

2 (of troops) ta「ikee 隊形.

former *adj.* **1** (of an earlier time) i「zen no 以前の; ma「e no 前の: He is the former president of our company. (*Kare wa watashi-tachi no kaisha no mae no shachoo desu.*) 彼は私たちの会社の前の社長です.

2 (first-mentioned) ze「nsha no 前者の: I prefer the former painting to the latter. (*Watashi wa zensha*

no e no hoo ga koosha yori mo
suki da.) 私は前者の絵のほうが後者よ
りも好きだ.

formerly adv. i˩zeñ wa 以前は;
mu˩kashi wa 昔は: Formerly there
was a lake here. (Izeñ wa koko ni
mizuumi ga arimashita.) 以前はここ
に湖がありました.

formula n. ko˩oshiki 公式; shi˩ki˩
式: the chemical formula for water
(mizu no kagaku-shiki) 水の化学式.

forsake vt. (abandon) ... o mi˩su-
teru ...を見捨てる Ⅴ: forsake a
friend (yuujiñ o misuteru) 友人を見
捨てる.

fort n. to˩ride とりで; yo˩osai 要塞:
attack a fort (toride o koogeki
suru) とりでを攻撃する.

fortieth adj. yo˩ñjuu-bañme˩ no 40
番目の; da˩i-yoñjuu no 第 40 の.
— n. 1 (things) yo˩ñjuu-bañme˩
no mo˩no˩ 40 番目のもの; (people)
yo˩ñjuu-bañme˩ no hi˩to˩ 40 番目の
人.
2 (fraction) yo˩ñjuu-buñ no ichi˩ 40
分の 1.

fortunate adj. ko˩ouñ na 幸運な;
u˩ñ no yoi 運のよい: I was fortunate
to survive the accident. (Watashi
wa uñ yoku sono jiko de tasu-
katta.) 私は運よくその事故で助かった.

fortunately adv. ko˩ouñ ni˩ mo
幸運にも; u˩ñ yoku 運よく: Fortunately nobody was injured in the
accident. (Koouñ ni mo sono jiko
de dare mo kega o shinakatta.) 幸
運にもその事故でだれもけがをしなかった.

fortune n. 1 (great sum of money) to˩mi 富; za˩isañ 財産: inherit
a large fortune (bakudai na zaisañ
o soozoku suru) 莫大な財産を相続す
る.
2 (luck) u˩ñ 運; ko˩ouñ 幸運: try
one's fortune (uñ o kakeru) 運をかけ
る / He had the good fortune to succeed. (Koouñ ni mo kare wa seekoo shita.) 幸運にも彼は成功した.
3 (fate) u˩ñmee 運命; u˩ñsee 運勢:
tell a persons's fortune (hito no
uñsee o uranau) 人の運勢を占う.

forty pron. yo˩ñjuu 40; (things)
yo˩ñjuk-ko 40 個; (people) yo˩ñju-u-
niñ 40 人.
— n. (figure) yo˩ñjuu 40; (minute)
yo˩ñju˩p-puñ 40 分; (age) yo˩ñju˩s-
sai 40 歳.
— adj. yo˩ñjuu no 40 の; (things)
yo˩ñjuk-ko no 40 個の; (people) yo-
˩ñju-u-niñ no 40 人の; (age) yo˩ñju˩s-
sai no 40 歳の.

forward adv. 1 (toward the
front) ma˩e e [ni] 前へ[に]; ze˩ñpoo
e [ni] 前方へ[に]: go forward (zeñshiñ suru) 前進する / step forward
(mae e susumideru) 前へ進み出る.
2 (toward the future) sa˩ki e 先へ;
sho˩orai ni mu˩katte 将来に向かって:
look forward (shoorai o kañgaeru)
将来を考える.
— adj. 1 (toward the front) ze˩ñ-
poo e˩ no 前方への; ma˩e no hoo no
前のほうの: The seat is too far forward. (Seki ga mae no hoo sugiru.)
席が前のほう過ぎる.
2 (well advanced) ha˩ya˩i 早い;
so˩ojuku na 早熟な; shi˩ñpo-teki na
進歩的な: a forward child (soojuku
na kodomo) 早熟な子ども / forward
opinions (shiñpo-teki na ikeñ) 進歩
的な意見.
— vt. ... o te˩ñsoo suru ...を転送す
る Ⅰ: Please forward my mail to
this address. (Yuubiñ wa kono juusho ni teñsoo shite kudasai.) 郵便
はこの住所に転送してください.

foster vt. 1 (bring up) ... o yo˩oi-
ku suru ...を養育する Ⅰ; so˩date˩ru
育てる Ⅴ: She fostered the orphan.
(Kanojo wa sono koji o sodateta.)
彼女はその孤児を育てた.
2 (encourage) ... o so˩kushiñ suru
...を促進する Ⅰ; jo˩choo suru 助長す
る Ⅰ: foster exports (yushutsu o
sokushiñ suru) 輸出を促進する.
3 (cherish) ... o ko˩koro ni i˩da˩ku
...を心に抱く Ⅽ: foster an ambition
(taimoo o idaku) 大望を抱く.
— adj. yo˩oiku ni yoru 養育による;
yo˩o- 養; sa˩to- 里: a foster mother
(yoobo) 養母 / a foster child (sa-

togo) 里子.

foul *adj.* **1** (causing disgust) iˈyaˌna いやな; fuˈkai na 不快な: a foul smell (*iya na nioi*) いやな臭い.
2 (dirty) kiˈtanaˌi 汚い; yoˈgoreta 汚れた; yoˈgorete iru 汚れている: a foul room (*kitanai heya*) 汚い部屋.
— *vt.* (make foul) ... o kiˈtanaˌku suru …を汚くする Ⓣ; yoˈgosu 汚す ⓒ: This water has been fouled by oil. (*Kono mizu wa abura de yogorete iru.*) この水は油で汚れている.

found *vt.* **1** (establish) ... o seˈtsuritsu suru …を設立する Ⓣ; soˈoritsu suru 創立する Ⓣ: found a school (*gakkoo o sooritsu suru*) 学校を創立する.
2 (base on) ... o koˈnˌkyo to suru …を根拠とする ⓒ; ... ni moˈtozuˌku …に基づく ⓒ: This story is founded upon fact. (*Kono hanashi wa jijitsu ni motozuite iru.*) この話は事実に基づいている.

foundation *n.* **1** (founding) seˈtsuritsu 設立; soˈoritsu 創立: foundation of a hospital (*byooiñ no setsuritsu*) 病院の設立.
2 (base) kiˈso 基礎; doˈdai 土台: lay the foundations of a house (*ie no kiso o sueru*) 家の基礎を据える.
3 (institution) shiˈsetsu 施設; daˈntai 団体; zaˈidaˌñ 財団.

founder *n.* soˈoritsuˌsha 創立者; seˈtsuritsuˌsha 設立者.

fountain *n.* **1** (spring of water) fuˈnsui 噴水.
2 (source) geˈnseñ 源泉; miˈnamoto 源: the fountain of knowledge (*chishiki no minamoto*) 知識の源.

fountain pen *n.* maˈnneˌnˌhitsu 万年筆.

four *pron.* yoˈttsu 四つ; (things) yoˈn-ko 4 個; (people) yoˈniˌñ 4 人.
— *n.* (figure) yoˈñ 4; (hour) yoˈ-ji 4 時; (minute) yoˈn-puñ 4 分; (age) yoˈn-sai 4 歳.
— *adj.* yoˈttsu no 四つの; (things) yoˈn-ko no 4 個の; (people) yo-ˈniˌñ no 4 人の; (age) yoˈn-sai no 4 歳の.

fourteen *pron.* juˈuyoˌñ 14; (things) juˈuyoˌñ-ko 14 個; (people) juˈuyo-niñ 14 人.
— *n.* (figure) juˈuyoˌñ 14; (hour) juˈuyoˌñ-ji 14 時; (minute) juˈuyoˌñ-puñ 14 分; (age) juˈuyoˌñ-sai 14 歳.
— *adj.* juˈuyoˌñ no 14の; (things) juˈuyoˌñ-ko no 14 個の; (people) juˈuyo-niñ no 14 人の; (age) juˈuyoˌñ-sai no 14 歳の.

fourteenth *adj.* juˈuyoñ-baˌnmeˌ no 14 番目の; daˈi-juˈuyoˌñ no 第14の.
— *n.* **1** (things) juˈuyoñ-baˌnmeˌ no moˈnoˌ 14 番目のもの; (people) juˈuyoñ-baˌnmeˌ no hiˈtoˌ 14 番目の人.
2 (date) juˈuyok-ka 14 日.
3 (fraction) juˈuyon-buñ no ichiˌ 14 分の1.

fourth *adj.* yoˈñ-baˌnmeˌ no 4 番目の; daˈi-yoñ no 第4の.
— *n.* **1** (things) yoˈñ-baˌnmeˌ no moˈnoˌ 4 番目のもの; (people) yoˈñ-baˌnmeˌ no hiˈtoˌ 4 番目の人.
2 (date) yoˈk-ka 4 日.
3 (fraction) yoˈñbuñ no ichiˌ 4 分の1.

fowl *n.* **1** (rooster or hen) niˈwatori 鶏; (domestic bird) kaˈkiñ 家禽.
2 (any bird) toˈri 鳥: a waterfowl (*mizudori*) 水鳥.

fox *n.* kiˈtsune きつね(狐).

fragile *adj.* **1** (of a thing) koˈwareyasuˌi 壊れやすい; moˈroˌi もろい: a fragile vase (*koware-yasui kabiñ*) 壊れやすい花びん.
2 (of a person) kyoˈjaku na 虚弱な; hiˈyowa na ひ弱な: a fragile child (*hiyowa na kodomo*) ひ弱な子ども.

fragment *n.* haˈheñ 破片; kaˈkera かけら: The glass broke into fragments. (*Koppu ga konagona ni natta.*) コップが粉々になった.

fragrance *n.* kaˈori 香り; hoˈokoo 芳香; niˈoi におい: Roses have a pleasant fragrance. (*Bara wa ii kaori ga suru.*) ばらはいい香りがする.

fragrant *adj.* kaˈori no [ga] yoˈi 香りの[が]よい: fragrant flowers (*kaori* no yoi hana) 香りのよい花.

frail adj. (weak) ka⌐yowa⌐i 弱い; (fragile) ko⌐ware-yasu⌐i 壊れやすい: a frail child (kayowai ko) 弱い子.

frame n. 1 (border) wa⌐ku⌐ 枠; fu-⌐chi⌐ 縁; fu⌐reemu⌐ フレーム: a window frame (mado-waku) 窓枠 / a picture frame (gaku-buchi) 額縁.
2 (skeleton) ho⌐negumi 骨組み; (of a person) ta⌐ikaku 体格: the frame of a house (ie no honegumi) 家の骨組み / a person of large frame (taikaku no ookii hito) 体格の大きい人.
3 (structure) ko⌐ozoo 構造; ko⌐osee 構成: the frame of society (shakai no koozoo) 社会の構造.
— vt. 1 (enclose) ... o wa⌐ku⌐ ni ha⌐meru ...を枠にはめる Ⅴ: frame a picture (e o gakubuchi ni ireru) 絵を額縁に入れる.
2 (put together) ... o ku⌐mitate⌐ru ...を組み立てる Ⅴ: frame a house (ie o kumitateru) 家を組み立てる / frame a plan (keekaku o tateru) 計画を立てる.

framework n. ho⌐negumi 骨組み; ko⌐osee 構成; ki⌐koo 機構: the framework of a bridge (hashi no honegumi) 橋の骨組み / the framework of a government (seefu no kikoo) 政府の機構.

France n. Fu⌐rañsu フランス.

frank adj. so⌐tchoku na 率直な; za⌐kkubarañ na ざっくばらんな: I'd like to hear your frank opinion. (Anata no sotchoku na ikeñ o o-kiki shitai.) あなたの率直な意見をお聞きしたい.

frankly adv. so⌐tchoku ni 率直に; za⌐kkubarañ ni ざっくばらんに: He admitted his mistake frankly. (Kare wa jibuñ no machigai o sotchoku ni mitometa.) 彼は自分の間違いを率直に認めた. / Frankly, I think you are wrong. (Sotchoku ni itte kimi wa machigatte iru to omoimasu.) 率直に言って君は間違っていると思います.

free adj. 1 (not bound, controlled) ji⌐yuu⌐na 自由な; so⌐kubaku no

[ga] na⌐i 束縛の[が]ない: free speech (jiyuu na geñroñ) 自由な言論 / They were glad to be free. (Karera wa jiyuu ni natte yorokoñda.) 彼らは自由になって喜んだ.
2 (costing nothing) mu⌐ryoo no 無料の; ta⌐da no ただの; (of tax) mu⌐zee no 無税の: Is there a free city map? (Muryoo no shigai chizu wa arimasu ka?) 無料の市街地図はありますか.
3 (not busy) hi⌐ma na 暇な: Are you free tonight? (Koñbañ o-hima desu ka?) 今晩お暇ですか.
4 (not occupied) a⌐ite iru 空いている: Do you have any rooms free? (Aite iru heya wa arimasu ka?) 空いている部屋はありますか.
5 (without) ... no [ga] na⌐i ...の[が]ない: Her life is quite free from care. (Kanojo no seekatsu wa mattaku kuroo ga nai.) 彼女の生活は全く苦労がない.
6 (generous) ki⌐mae no [ga] i⌐i 気前の[が]いい: He is free with his money. (Kare wa kimae yoku o-kane o tsukau.) 彼は気前よくお金を使う.
— vt. 1 (make free) ... o (... kara) ji⌐yuu⌐ni suru ...を(...から)自由にする Ⅰ; ka⌐ihoo suru 解放する Ⅰ: free a bird from a cage (tori o kago kara jiyuu ni shite yaru) 鳥をかごから自由にしてやる.
2 (relieve) ... kara (... o) to⌐rino-zoku ...から(...を)取り除く Ⅽ: free the road of snow (dooro kara yuki o torinozoku) 道路から雪を取り除く.

freedom n. ji⌐yuu⌐ 自由: freedom of speech (geñron no jiyuu) 言論の自由 / I have freedom to do what I like. (Watashi wa yaritai koto ga dekiru jiyuu ga aru.) 私はやりたいことができる自由がある.

freely adv. ji⌐yuu⌐ni 自由に; ka⌐tte ni 勝手に: Everybody can enter this room freely. (Dare de mo kono heya ni jiyuu ni hairemasu.) だれでもこの部屋に自由に入れます.

freeze vi. 1 (become ice) ko⌐oru

凍る Ⓒ; ko「ori ga haru 氷が張る Ⓒ: The lake froze over. (*Mizuumi ichimeñ ni koori ga hatta.*) 湖一面に氷が張った.

2 (be very cold) ko「goeru hodo sa「mu」i 凍えるほど寒い: I am freezing. (*Samukute kogoe-soo da.*) 寒くて凍えそうだ.

3 (become motionless) u「goka」naku naru 動かなくなる Ⓒ; mi ga su「kumu 身がすくむ Ⓒ: I froze at the sight of the snake. (*Watashi wa hebi o mite mi ga sukuñda.*) 私はへびを見て身がすくんだ.

— vt. **1** (make ice) ... o ko「ora-seru ...を凍らせる Ⓥ: The pond was frozen. (*Ike ga kootta.*) 池が凍った.

2 (of food) ... o re「etoo suru ...を冷凍する Ⓣ: freeze meat (*niku o reetoo suru*) 肉を冷凍する.

freezer *n*. re「eto」oki 冷凍庫; fu「ri」izaa フリーザー; re「eto」oki 冷凍器: keep food in a freezer (*shokuhiñ o reetooko ni hozoñ suru*) 食品を冷凍庫に保存する.

freight *n*. **1** (carrying) ka「motsu u「ñsoo 貨物輸送: send by air freight (*kookuu kamotsu de okuru*) 航空貨物で送る.

2 (goods) ka「motsu 貨物; tsu「mini 積み荷.

3 (charge) u「ñchiñ 運賃: freight free (*uñchiñ muryoo*) 運賃無料.

French *adj*. Fu「rañsu no フランスの; (of people) Fu「rañsu」jiñ no フランス人の; (of language) Fu「rañsugo no フランス語の.
— *n*. (language) Fu「rañsugo フランス語; (people) Fu「rañsu」jiñ フランス人.

frequency *n*. **1** (occurrence) shi「bashiba o「ko」ru ko「to」 しばしば起こること; hi「ñ-patsu 頻発: the frequency of earthquakes in Japan (*Nihoñ ni okeru jishiñ no hiñpatsu*) 日本における地震の頻発.

2 (rate) ka「isu」u 回数; hi「ñdo 頻度: the frequency of crime (*hañzai no hassee-ritsu*) 犯罪の発生率.

frequent *adj*. ta「bitabi no たびたびの; shi「bashiba no しばしばの: He

makes frequent trips to China. (*Kare wa Chuugoku e tabitabi ryokoo shimasu.*) 彼は中国へたびたび旅行します.

frequently *adv*. ta「bitabi たびたび; shi「bashiba しばしば: He frequently arrives late. (*Kare wa tabitabi chikoku suru.*) 彼はたびたび遅刻する.

fresh *adj*. **1** (newly made) shi「ñseñ na 新鮮な: fresh vegetables (*shiñseñ na yasai*) 新鮮な野菜.

2 (new) a「tarashi」i 新しい: Is there any fresh news? (*Nani-ka atarashii nyuusu wa arimasu ka?*) 何か新しいニュースはありますか.

3 (refreshing) sa「wa」yaka na さわやかな: I felt fresh after a walk. (*Sañpo no ato sawayaka na kibuñ datta.*) 散歩の後さわやかな気分だった.

4 (bright) a「za」yaka na 鮮やかな: fresh colors (*azayaka na iro*) 鮮やかな色.

5 (without salt) shi「oke no na」i 塩気のない; ta「ñsui no 淡水の: fresh water (*tañsui*) 淡水.

freshman *n*. shi「ñnyu」usee 新入生; i「chi-ne」ñsee 1 年生.

friction *n*. (rubbing) ma「satsu 摩擦; (conflict) fu「wa 不和: trade friction (*booeki masatsu*) 貿易摩擦.

Friday *n*. ki「ñyo」o(bi) 金曜(日).

fridge *n*. re「ezooko 冷蔵庫.

fried *adj*. (pan-fried) a「bura de i「ta」meta 油でいためた; (deep-fried) a「bura de ageta 油で揚げた; fu「rai ni shita フライにした: fried chicken (*furaido chikiñ*) フライドチキン / a fried egg (*medamayaki*) 目玉焼き.

friend *n*. **1** (close companion) to「modachi 友だち; yu「ujiñ 友人: This is a souvenir for a friend. (*Kore wa yuujiñ e no o-miyage desu.*) これは友人へのおみやげです.

2 (helper) mi「kata 味方: a friend of the poor (*mazushii hito-tachi no mikata*) 貧しい人たちの味方.

friendly *adj*. **1** (like a friend) shi「tashi」i 親しい; yu「ukoo-teki na 友好的な: I am on a friendly terms with him. (*Watashi wa kare to wa*

shitashii aidagara desu.) 私は彼とは
親しい間柄です。/ a friendly nation
(*yuukookoku*) 友好国.

2 (kind) shi「ñsetsu na 親切な;
ko「oi-teki na 好意的な: She is
friendly to everybody. (*Kanojo wa
dare ni taishite mo shiñsetsu desu.*)
彼女はだれに対しても親切です.

friendship *n*. yu「ujoo 友情; yu「u-
koo-ka「ñkee 友好関係: The friendship between them lasted long.
(*Kare-ra no yuujoo wa nagaku tsuzuita.*) 彼らの友情は永く続いた.

fright *n*. kyo「ofu 恐怖; ha「geshi「i
o「doroki: 激しい驚き: have a fright
(*kyoofu ni osowareru*) 恐怖に襲われ
る.

frighten *vt*. **1** (make afraid) ... o
ko「wagarase」ru ...を怖がらせる Ⓥ;
gyo「tto saseru ぎょっとさせる Ⓥ: I
was frightened by a snake. (*Watashi wa hebi o mite gyotto shita.*)
私は蛇を見てぎょっとした.

2 (scare) ... o o「dosu ...を脅す Ⓒ:
They frightened him into obedience. (*Kare-ra wa kare o odo-
shite fukujuu saseta.*) 彼らは彼を脅
して服従させた.

frightened *adj*. o「bieta おびえた;
o「biete iru おびえている; gyo「tto
shita ぎょっとした: I was frightened
at the sound. (*Watashi wa sono
oto ni gyotto shita.*) 私はその音に
ぎょっとした.

frightful *adj*. o「soroshi」i 恐ろしい;
mo「nosugo」i ものすごい: a frightful
sight (*osoroshii kookee*) 恐ろしい光
景.

fringe *n*. **1** (ornamental border)
fu「saka」zari 房飾り: the fringe of a
rug (*juutañ no fusakazari*) じゅうた
んの房飾り.

2 (edge) fu「chi」 縁; he「ri」 へり; ma-
「wari 周り: a park with a fringe of
trees (*mawari ni ki no aru kooeñ*)
周りに木のある公園.

frivolous *adj*. (not important) tsu-
「mara」nai つまらない; to「ru ni ta「ra-
nai 取るに足らない: frivolous matters
(*toru ni taranai kotogara*) 取るに足

らない事柄.

frog *n*. ka「eru かえる(蛙).

from *prep*. **1** (starting point) ...
kara ...から: How far is it from
here to the station? (*Koko kara eki
made dono kurai arimasu ka?*) ここ
から駅までどのくらいありますか。/ rise
from a chair (*isu kara tachiagaru*)
いすから立ち上がる.

2 (beginning) ... kara ...から: I
know her from her childhood.
(*Watashi wa kanojo o kodomo no
koro kara shitte imasu.*) 私は彼女を
子どものころから知っています。/ read a
book from cover to cover (*hoñ o
hajime kara owari made yomu*) 本
を初めから終わりまで読む.

3 (distance) ... kara (ha「na」rete) ...
から(離れて): The town is four
kilometers away from here. (*Sono
machi wa koko kara yoñ-kiro
hanareta tokoro ni arimasu.*) その町
はここから４キロ離れた所にあります /
His house is not far from the station. (*Kare no ie wa eki kara
tooku nai.*) 彼の家は駅から遠くない.

4 (origin) ... kara ki「ta ...から来た; ...
shu「sshiñ no ...出身の: Where are
you from? (*Dochira no go-shus-
shiñ desu ka?*) どちらのご出身ですか。
/ I come from Hokkaido. (*Watashi
wa Hokkaidoo shusshiñ desu.*) 私
は北海道出身です.

5 (source) ... kara ...から: A strange
sound was heard from within.
(*Naka kara heñ na mono-oto ga
kikoeta.*) 中から変な物音が聞こえた。/
quotations from the Bible (*seesho
kara no iñyoo*) 聖書からの引用.

6 (material) ... kara ...から: Wine is
made from grapes. (*Budooshu wa
budoo kara tsukurimasu.*) ぶどう酒
はぶどうから造ります.

7 (cause) ... de ...で; ... ga ge「ñiñ
de ...が原因で: I was tired from
overwork. (*Watashi wa shigoto no
shi-sugi de tsukareta.*) 私は仕事のし
過ぎで疲れた / He died from a
wound. (*Kare wa kizu ga geñiñ
de shiñda.*) 彼は傷が原因で死んだ.

front *n.* **1** (part) maˡe 前; zeˡñbu 前部: The front of his car was dented. (*Kare no kuruma no zeñbu wa hekoñde ita.*) 彼の車の前部はへこんでいた. / I sat in the front of the car. (*Watashi wa kuruma no mae no seki ni suwatta.*) 私は車の前の席に座った. ★ Japanese '... *no mae*' is used in two senses, 'in front of' and 'at the front of.'
2 (of a building) shoˡomeˡñ 正面: the front of a house (*ie no shoomeñ*) 家の正面.
3 (in war) zeˡñseñ 前線; seˡñseñ 戦線: go to the front (*señseñ ni deru*) 戦線に出る.
in front of ... *prep.* ... no maˡe ni ...の前に: There is a big tree in front of his house. (*Kare no ie no mae ni wa ooki-na ki ga arimasu.*) 彼の家の前には大きな木があります.
— *adj.* zeˡñbu ni aru 前部にある; shoˡomeˡñ no 正面の: the front garden (*zeñtee*) 前庭.
front desk *n.* fuˡroñto フロント; uˡketsuke 受付: a front desk clerk (*furoñto-gakari*) フロント係.
frontier *n.* **1** (boundary) koˡkkyoo 国境: cross the frontier by car (*kuruma de kokkyoo o koeru*) 車で国境を越える.
2 (the farthest area of land) fuˡroˡñtia フロンティア; heˡñkyoo 辺境.
frost *n.* **1** (frozen dew) shiˡmoˡ 霜: Frost formed on the ground. (*Jimeñ ni shimo ga orita.*) 地面に霜が降りた.
2 (coldness) kaˡñki 寒気; hiˡekomi 冷え込み.
— *vt.* ... o shiˡmoˡ de oˡoˡu ...を霜で覆う C: frosted window panes (*shimo de oowareta madogarasu*) 霜で覆われた窓ガラス.
frown *vi.* maˡyu o hiˡsomeˡru まゆをひそめる V; shiˡkamettsura suru しかめっ面をする I; iˡya na kaˡo o suru いやな顔をする I: She frowns on my smoking. (*Kanojo wa watashi ga tabako o suu to iya na kao o suru.*) 彼女は私がたばこを吸うといやな

顔をする.
— *n.* shiˡkamettsura しかめっ面; shiˡbuˡi kao 渋い顔: He looked at me with a frown. (*Kare wa shibui kao de watashi o mita.*) 彼は渋い顔で私を見た.

frozen *adj.* koˡotta 凍った; koˡotte iru 凍っている; reˡetoo shita [shite aˡru] 冷凍した[してある]: frozen food (*reetoo-shokuhiñ*) 冷凍食品.

fruit *n.* kuˡdamono 果物; kaˡjitsu 果実: I'd like some fruit for dessert. (*Dezaato ni kudamono o kudasai.*) デザートに果物を下さい.

fruitful *adj.* miˡnori no [ga] oˡoi 実りの[が]多い; yuˡueki na 有益な: a fruitful meeting (*yuueki na kaigoo*) 有益な会合.

frustration *n.* yoˡkkyuu-fuˡmañ 欲求不満; fuˡrasutoreˡeshoñ フラストレーション: Her frustration with her job gradually increased. (*Shigoto ni taisuru kanojo no yokkyuu-fumañ wa shidai ni zoodai shita.*) 仕事に対する彼女の欲求不満は次第に増大した.

fry *vt.* (pan-fry) ... o (aˡbura de) iˡtameˡru ...を(油で)いためる V; (deep-fry) (aˡbura de) aˡgeru (油で)揚げる V; (of an egg) yaˡku 焼く C: Fry me an egg. (*Tamago o yaite kudasai.*) 卵を焼いてください.
— *n.* iˡtamemono いため物; aˡgemono 揚げ物; fuˡrai ryoˡori フライ料理.

frying pan *n.* fuˡraipañ フライパン.

fuel *n.* neˡñryoˡo 燃料: We have enough fuel for this winter. (*Kotoshi no fuyu no neñryoo ga juubuñ arimasu.*) ことしの冬は燃料が十分あります.

fugitive *n.* (runaway) toˡoboˡosha 逃亡者; (political refugee) boˡomeˡesha 亡命者.

fulfill *vt.* **1** (perform) ... o haˡtaˡsu ...を果たす C: I fulfilled my duty. (*Watashi wa jibuñ no gimu o hatashita.*) 私は自分の義務を果たした.
2 (satisfy) ... o jiˡtsugeñ suru ...を実現する I; kaˡnaeˡru かなえる V:

He fulfilled his parents' hopes. (*Kare wa ryooshiñ no kiboo o kanaeta.*) 彼は両親の希望をかなえた.

fulfillment *n.* riꜝkoo 履行; jiꜝtsugeñ 実現: fulfillment of a promise (*yakusoku no rikoo*) 約束の履行.

full *adj.* **1** (filled) … de iꜝppai na [no] …でいっぱいな[の]; miꜝchita 満ちた; miꜝchite iru 満ちている: The room was full of people. (*Heya wa hito de ippai datta.*) 部屋は人でいっぱいだった. / a glass full of wine (*waiñ ga ippai haitta gurasu*) ワインがいっぱい入ったグラス.

2 (complete) kaꜝñzeñ na 完全な; maꜝñ- 満-: The flowers are in full bloom. (*Hana wa mañkai desu.*) 花は満開です. / get full marks (*mañteñ o toru*) 満点をとる. / Full tank, please. (*Mañtañ ni shite kudasai.*) 満タンにしてください.

3 (of food) o-ꜝnaka ippai no お腹いっぱいの: I am full. (*O-naka ga ippai desu.*) お腹がいっぱいです.

4 (of time) maꜝru まる: I waited for a full hour. (*Watashi wa maru ichi-jikan matta.*) 私はまる1時間待った. / a full five years (*maru go-neñ-kañ*) まる5年間.

full stop *n.* piꜝriodo ピリオド; shuꜝshiꜝfu 終止符.

fully *adv.* **1** (completely) juꜝubuꜝñ ni 十分に; kaꜝñzeñ ni 完全に: I am fully satisfied. (*Watashi wa juubuñ ni mañzoku shite imasu.*) 私は十分に満足しています.

2 (at least) suꜝkuꜝnaku tomo 少なくとも; taꜝppuꜝri たっぷり: We walked fully five kilometers. (*Watashitachi wa tappuri go-kiro arukimashita.*) 私たちはたっぷり5キロ歩きました.

fun *n.* taꜝnoꜝshisa 楽しさ; oꜝmoshiꜝrosa おもしろさ: We had a lot of fun at the party. (*Paatii wa totemo tanoshikatta.*) パーティーはとても楽しかった. / It was fun riding a horse. (*Uma ni noru no wa omoshirokatta.*) 馬に乗るのはおもしろかった.

function *n.* **1** (special job) haꜝtaraki 働き; kiꜝnoo 機能: the func-

tion of the heart (*shiñzoo no hataraki* [*kinoo*]) 心臓の働き[機能].

2 (ceremony) giꜝshiki 儀式; gyoꜝoji 行事; (party) eꜝñkai 宴会.

— *vi.* uꜝgoꜝku 動く ꜟCꜟ; kiꜝnoo suru 機能する ꜟIꜟ: The elevator is not functioning now. (*Erebeetaa wa ima ugoite imaseñ.*) エレベーターは今動いていません.

functional *adj.* kiꜝnoo-teki na 機能的な; jiꜝtsuyoo-teki na 実用的な: functional furniture (*kinoo-teki na kagu*) 機能的な家具.

fund *n.* **1** (money) kiꜝkiñ 基金; shiꜝkiñ 資金: a relief fund (*kyuusai shikiñ*) 救済資金.

2 (store) taꜝkuwae 蓄え; chiꜝkuseki 蓄積: a fund of information (*joohoo no chikuseki*) 情報の蓄積.

fundamental *adj.* **1** (basic) kiꜝso no 基礎の; kiꜝhoñ-teki na 基本的な: fundamental human rights (*kihoñ-teki jiñkeñ*) 基本的人権.

2 (essential) hiꜝssu no 必須の; juꜝuyoo na 重要な: Moderate exercise is fundamental to good health. (*Tekido na uñdoo wa keñkoo ni hissu desu.*) 適度な運動は健康に必須です.

funeral *n.* soꜝoshiki 葬式; soꜝogi 葬儀: attend a funeral (*soogi ni sañretsu suru*) 葬儀に参列する.

funny *adj.* **1** (amusing) oꜝmoshiꜝroꜝi おもしろい; koꜝkkee na こっけいな: a funny story (*omoshiroi hanashi*) おもしろい話.

2 (strange) kiꜝmyoo na 奇妙な; heꜝñ na 変な: This fish has a funny smell. (*Kono sakana wa heñ na nioi ga suru.*) この魚は変なにおいがする.

fur *n.* **1** (skin) keꜝgawa 毛皮: a fur coat (*kegawa no oobaa*) 毛皮のオーバー.

2 (something made of fur) keꜝgawa-seꜝehiñ 毛皮製品: wear expensive furs (*kooka na kegawa o kiru*) 高価な毛皮を着る.

furious *adj.* **1** (very angry) suꜝgoꜝku oꜝkoꜝtta [oꜝkotꜝte iru] すごく怒った[怒っている]; geꜝkido shita [shite iru] 激怒した[している]: She is furious with you for sexual discrimination. (*Kanojo wa see sabetsu no koto de kimi no koto o sugoku okotte iru.*) 彼女は性差別のことで君のことをすごく怒っている.

2 (violent) moˈoretsu na 猛烈な; moˈnosugoˈi ものすごい: a furious storm (*mooretsu na arashi*) 猛烈なあらし.

furnace *n.* ro 炉; kaˈmado かまど.

furnish *vt.* **1** (equip) ... ni kaˈgu o soˈnaetsukeru ...に家具を備え付ける Ⓥ; toˈritsukeru 取り付ける Ⓥ: His room is luxuriously furnished. (*Kare no heya ni wa zeetaku na kagu ga okarete iru.*) 彼の部屋にはぜいたくな家具が置かれている.

2 (supply) ... ni (... o) kyoˈokyuu suru ...に(...を)供給する Ⓣ: The river furnishes this town with water. (*Sono kawa wa kono machi ni mizu o kyookyuu shite imasu.*) その川はこの町に水を供給しています.

furniture *n.* kaˈgu 家具; biˈhiñ 備品: a furniture store (*kaguya*) 家具屋.

furrow *n.* **1** (long cut in the ground) miˈzo 溝; (rut) waˈdachi わだち.

2 (wrinkle) shiˈwa しわ.
— *vt.* (wrinkle) ... ni shiˈwa o yoseru ...にしわを寄せる Ⓥ: furrow one's brow (*hitai ni shiwa o yoseru*) 額にしわを寄せる.

further *adv.* **1** (more) saˈra ni さらに; naˈo soˈno ueˈ ni なおそのうえに: He spoke further on the issue.

(*Kare wa sono moñdai ni tsuite sara ni hanashita.*) 彼はその問題についてさらに話した.

2 (farther) saˈra ni toˈoku さらに遠く; moˈtto saˈki ni もっと先に: go further away (*motto saki ni iku*) もっと先に行く.

— *adj.* soˈre iˈjoo no それ以上の: We need further information. (*Sore ijoo no joohoo ga hitsuyoo da.*) それ以上の情報が必要だ.

— *vt.* ... o soˈkushiñ suru ...を促進する Ⓣ: further public welfare (*kookyoo no fukushi o sokushiñ suru*) 公共の福祉を促進する.

furthermore *adv.* naˈo なお; soˈno ue そのうえ.

fury *n.* haˈgeshiˈi iˈkari 激しい怒り; geˈkido 激怒: He flew into a fury. (*Kare wa gekido shita.*) 彼は激怒した.

fuss *n.* oˈosaˈwagi 大騒ぎ: make a fuss about trifles (*tsumaranai koto ni oosawagi suru*) つまらないことに大騒ぎする.

future *n.* **1** (the time to come) miˈrai 未来; shoˈorai 将来; koˈñgo 今後: No one can tell what will happen in the future. (*Shoorai nani ga okoru ka dare ni mo wakaranai.*) 将来何が起こるかだれにもわからない. / You must be careful in future. (*Kore kara wa motto ki o tsuke nasai.*) これからはもっと気をつけなさい.

2 (prospect) zeˈñto 前途; shoˈoraisee 将来性: a young man with a bright future (*zeñto no akarui seeneñ*) 前途の明るい青年.

G

gain *vt.* **1** (obtain) ... o eˈru ...を得る Ⓥ; kaˈkutoku suru 獲得する Ⓣ: I have gained a lot from it. (*Watashi wa sore kara ooku no mono o eta.*) 私はそれから多くのものを得た.

2 (add) ... o maˈsu ...を増す Ⓒ: The car gained speed. (*Kuruma*

wa sokudo o mashita.) 車は速度を増した.

3 (run fast) suˈsumu 進む Ⓒ: This watch gains 10 seconds a week. (*Kono tokee wa is-shuukañ ni juu-byoo susumu.*) この時計は1週間に10秒進む.

— *vi.* ri「eki o eru 利益を得る Ⓥ; to 「ku o suru 得をする Ⓘ: How much did you gain in that deal? (*Sono torihiki de ikura mookemashita ka?*) その取り引きでいくらもうけましたか.

— *n.* (profit) ri「eki 利益; (increase) zo「oka 増加: My losses were greater than my gains. (*Rieki yori mo sonshitsu no hoo ga ookikatta.*) 利益よりも損失のほうが大きかった. / a gain in weight (*taijuu no zooka*) 体重の増加.

gallbladder *n.* ta「nnoo 胆のう.

gallant *adj.* i「samashi」i 勇ましい; yu「ukan na 勇敢な: a gallant leader (*yuukan na shidoosha*) 勇敢な指導者.

gallery *n.* (for selling art) ga「roo 画廊; gya「rarii ギャラリー; (for exhibiting art) bi「jutsu」kan 美術館.

gallon *n.* ga「ron ガロン: 30 miles per gallon (*ichi-garon ni tsuki sanjuu mairu*) 1 ガロンにつき 30 マイル.
★ The gallon is not used in Japan; in the example above, the Japanese would use the liter. There are 4.5 liters in a U.S. gallon.

gallstone *n.* ta「nseki 胆石.

gamble *vi.* ka「ke」o suru 賭けをする Ⓘ; ba「kuchi o u」tsu ばくちを打つ Ⓒ: gamble on horses (*keeba ni kane o kakeru*) 競馬に金を賭ける.

— *n.* ka「ke」賭け; ba「kuchi ばくち.

game *n.* 1 (sport) shi「ai 試合; kyo「ogi 競技: win [lose] a game (*shiai ni katsu [makeru]*) 試合に勝つ[負ける].
2 (play) a「sobi 遊び; yu「ugi 遊戯; ge「emu ゲーム: What games do the children play? (*Kodomo-tachi wa donna asobi o shimasu ka?*) 子どもたちはどんな遊びをしますか.

gang *n.* 1 (criminals) bo「oryoku」-dan 暴力団; gya「ngu ギャング.
2 (group) i「chidan 一団; (comrade) na「kama 仲間: a gang of workers (*roodoosha no ichidan*) 労働者の一団.

gap *n.* 1 (opening) sa「keme 裂け目;

su「kima すき間: a gap in the wall (*kabe no sakeme*) 壁の裂け目 / fill a gap (*sukima o fusagu*) すき間をふさぐ.
2 (difference) so「oi 相違; zu「re」ずれ; gya「ppu ギャップ: There is a big gap between their points of view. (*Kare-ra no kangae ni wa ooki-na gyappu ga aru.*) 彼らの考えには大きなギャップがある.

garage *n.* sha「ko 車庫; ga「re」eji ガレージ: put a car into the garage (*kuruma o gareeji ni ireru*) 車をガレージに入れる. ★ Japanese '*gareeji*' is not used in the sense of a place where motor vehicles are repaird.

garbage *n.* go「mi」ごみ; ku「zu くず: take out the garbage (*gomi o dasu*) ごみを出す.

garden *n.* ni「wa 庭; (formal) te「e-en 庭園: play in the garden (*niwa de asobu*) 庭で遊ぶ / a kitchen garden (*katee saien*) 家庭菜園.
★ 'Yard' and 'court' are also called '*niwa.*'

gardener *n.* u「ekiya 植木屋; ni-「wa」shi 庭師.

gargle *vi.* u「gai o suru うがいをする Ⓘ.
— *n.* u「gai うがい.

garlic *n.* ni「nniku にんにく; ga「arikku ガーリック.

garment *n.* (clothes in general) i「rui 衣類; i「fuku 衣服: ladies' garments (*fujin-yoo no irui*) 婦人用の衣類.

gas *n.* 1 (fuel) ga「su ガス: turn on [off] the gas (*gasu o tsukeru [kesu]*) ガスをつける[消す].
2 (air) ki「tai 気体; ga「su ガス: Hydrogen is a gas at normal temperatures. (*Suiso wa joo-on de kitai desu.*) 水素は常温で気体です.
3 (gasoline) ga「sorin ガソリン.

gasoline *n.* ga「sorin ガソリン.

gasp *vi.* a「e」gu あえぐ Ⓒ; i「ki o ki-「ra」su 息を切らす Ⓒ: He went up the stairs gasping for breath. (*Kare wa iki o kirashi-nagara kaidan o nobotta.*) 彼は息を切らしながら階段を上った.

— *n.* a「egi あえぎ; i「kigire 息切れ: give a gasp of surprise (*odoroite iki o nomu*) 驚いて息をのむ.

gas station *n.* ga「soriñ-suta「ñdo ガソリンスタンド; su「tañdo スタンド; kyu「uyujo 給油所.

gas tank *n.* (storage facility) ga-「suta「ñku ガスタンク; (autos, planes, etc.) ga「soriñ ta「ñku ガソリンタンク.

gate *n.* (traditional) mo「ñ 門; (opening in fence, wall) ge「eto ゲート: open [close] a gate (*moñ o akeru [shimeru]*) 門を開ける[閉める].

gather *vt.* **1** (bring together) ... o a「tsume「ru ...を集める V: I gathered fallen leaves and burned them. (*Watashi wa ochiba o atsumete moyashita.*) 私は落ち葉を集めて燃やした.
2 (pick; harvest) ... o tsu「mu ...を摘む C; to「riireru 取り入れる V: gather flowers (*hana o tsumu*) 花を摘む / gather the crops (*sakumotsu o toriireru*) 作物を穫り入れる.
3 (increase) ... o ma「su ...を増す C: The car gathered speed. (*Kuruma wa supiido o mashita.*) 車はスピードを増した.
4 (infer) ... to su「isoku suru ...と推測する I: I gathered that he did not know that fact. (*Kare wa sono jijitsu o shiranai no da to suisoku shita.*) 彼はその事実を知らないのだと推測した.
— *vi.* (assemble) a「tsuma「ru 集まる C: A crowd gathered in the park. (*Kooeñ ni guñshuu ga atsumatta.*) 公園に群集が集まった.

gathering *n.* a「tsumari「 集まり; shu「ukai 集会.

gauge *n.* ke「eki 計器; ge「eji ゲージ: a fuel gauge (*neñryookee*) 燃料計 / a pressure gauge (*atsuryokukee*) 圧力計.

gay *adj.* (homosexual) do「osee「ai no 同性愛の: a gay bar (*geebaa*) ゲイバー.
— *n.* do「oseea「isha 同性愛者.
★ '*Dooseeaisha*' usually connotes a male in Japan. For females use

'*resubiañ*' レスビアン.

gaze *vi.* (... o) ji「tto mi「tsumeru (...を)じっと見つめる V: He gazed into my face. (*Kare wa watashi no kao o jitto mitsumeta.*) 彼は私の顔をじっと見つめた.

gear *n.* **1** (wheels with teeth) gi「ya ギヤ; ha「gu「ruma 歯車: a car with four gears (*yoñdañ giya no kuruma*) 4段ギヤの車.
2 (equipment) yo「ogu 用具; yo「ohiñ 用品: fishing gear (*tsuriyoogu*) 釣り用具 / sports gear (*supootsu yoohiñ*) スポーツ用品.
3 (clothing) fu「kusoo 服装: hunting gear (*shuryoofuku*) 狩猟服.

gear shift *n.* (on an auto) shi「futo シフト.

gem *n.* ho「oseki 宝石.

gender *n.* (in grammar) se「e 性; (distinction of sex) se「ebetsu 性別.

gene *n.* i「de「ñshi 遺伝子.

general *adj.* **1** (not specific) i「ppañ no 一般の; i「ppañ-teki na 一般的な; so「ogoo-teki na 総合的な: This book is intended for the general reader. (*Kono hoñ wa ippañ no dokusha o taishoo ni shite iru.*) この本は一般の読者を対象にしている. / the general public (*ippañ taishuu*) 一般大衆.
2 (not detailed) ga「iryaku no 概略の; da「itai no だいたいの: a general plan (*daitai no keekaku*) だいたいの計画.

in general *adv.* i「ppañ ni 一般に.

generalize *vi.* i「ppañ「roñ o no「beru 一般論を述べる V: generalize from data (*deeta kara ippañroñ o noberu*) データから一般論を述べる.

generally *adv.* **1** (usually) i「ppañ ni 一般に; fu「tsuu (wa) 普通(は): I generally get up at six. (*Watashi wa futsuu (wa) roku-ji ni okimasu.*) 私は普通(は)6時に起きます.
2 (widely) hi「roku 広く: The fact is generally known. (*Sono jijitsu wa hiroku shirarete iru.*) その事実は広く知られている.

general manager *n.* (of a

bureau) kyoˈkuchoo 局長; (of a department) buˈchoo 部長; (of a store) shiˈteˈnchoo 支店長.

generate vt. ... o haˈssee suru ... o 発生する □; oˈkoˈsu 起こす □: Friction generates heat. (Masatsu wa netsu o hassee suru.) 摩擦は熱を発生する.

generation n. daˈi 代; seˈdai 世代: Three generations live in her house. (Kanojo no ie ni wa sañ-sedai ga suñde iru.) 彼女の家には3世代が住んでいる. / We are of the same generation. (Watashi-tachi wa doo sedai da.) 私たちは同世代だ.

generation gap n. seˈdai kañ no daˈñzetsu 世代間の断絶.

generosity n. kiˈmae no yoˈsa 気前のよさ; kaˈñdai 寛大: He showed generosity with his money. (Kare wa o-kane ni kimae no yoi tokoro o miseta.) 彼はお金に気前のよいところを見せた.

generous adj. 1 (free in giving) kˈimae no yoˈi 気前のよい; moˈno-oˈshimi shinai 物惜しみしない: He made a generous donation. (Kare wa kimae no yoi kifu o shita.) 彼は気前のよい寄付をした.
2 (forgiving) kaˈñdai na 寛大な: He was generous regarding my mistake. (Kare wa watashi no machigai ni taishite kañdai datta.) 彼は私の間違いに対して寛大だった.

genetics n. iˈdeˈngaku 遺伝学.

genius n. 1 (person) teˈñsai 天才: He is a genius in mathematics. (Kare wa suugaku no teñsai da.) 彼は数学の天才だ.
2 (ability) saˈinoo 才能: She has a genius for music. (Kanojo wa oñ-gaku no sainoo ga aru.) 彼女は音楽の才能がある.

gentle adj. 1 (tender) yaˈsashii 優しい; oˈtonashiˈi おとなしい: He is gentle with children. (Kare wa kodomo ni yasashii.) 彼は子どもに優しい.
2 (mild) oˈdaˈyaka na 穏やかな; (gradual) yuˈruˈyaka na 緩やかな: a

gentle wind (odayaka na kaze) 穏やかな風 / a gentle slope (yuruyaka na saka) 緩やかな坂.

gentleman n. (well-bred man) shiˈñshi 紳士; (male) daˈñsee 男性: behave like a gentleman (shiñshi-rashiku furumau) 紳士らしく振る舞う.

gently adv. 1 (tenderly) yaˈsa-shiku 優しく; oˈdaˈyaka ni 穏やかに: speak gently (yasashiku hanasu) 優しく話す.
2 (gradually) yuˈruˈyaka ni 緩やかに: This road curves gently to the right. (Kono michi wa yuruyaka ni migi e magatte iru.) この道は緩やかに右へ曲がっている.

genuine adj. 1 (real) hoˈñmono no 本物の; shoˈoshiñ shoomee no 正真正銘の: a genuine diamond (hoñmono no daiyamoñdo) 本物のダイヤモンド.
2 (sincere) seˈejitsu na 誠実な; koˈkoˈro kara no 心からの: genuine sympathy (kokoro kara no doojoo) 心からの同情.

geography n. 1 (study) chiˈriˈga-ku 地理学: physical geography (shi-zeñ chirigaku) 自然地理学.
2 (natural features) chiˈri 地理; chiˈsee 地勢: the geography of Japan (Nihoñ no chiri) 日本の地理.

geology n. chiˈshitsuˈgaku 地質学.

geometry n. kiˈkaˈgaku 幾何学.

geranium n. zeˈranyuˈumu ゼラニューム.

germ n. baˈikiñ ばい菌; saˈikiñ 細菌; byoˈogeˈnkiñ 病原菌.

gesture n. 1 (movement) miˈburi 身ぶり; teˈmane 手まね: I communicated with him with gestures. (Watashi wa kare to temane de hanashita.) 私は彼と手まねで話した.
2 (attitude) soˈburi そぶり; jeˈsu-chaa ジェスチャー: His offer of help was a mere gesture. (Kare no eñjo no mooshide wa tañnaru jesuchaa ni suginakatta.) 彼の援助の申し出は単なるジェスチャーにすぎなかった.
—— vi. miˈburi [teˈburi] o suru 身ぶ

り[手ぶり]をする ①: He gestured to me to keep quiet. (*Kare wa watashi ni damatte iru yoo ni miburi de aizu shita.*) 彼は私に黙っているように身ぶりで合図した.

get *vt.* **1** (receive) ... o uˈkeˈru ...を受ける ⓥ; uˈketoru 受け取る ⓒ: Who is it that got the phone call? (*Sono deñwa o uketa no wa dare desu ka?*) その電話を受けたのはだれですか. / I got the letter this morning. (*Watashi wa sono tegami o kesa uketorimashita.*) 私はその手紙をけさ受け取りました.

2 (buy) ... o kaˈu ...を買う ⓒ: Where did you get that hat? (*Sono booshi o doko de kaimashita ka?*) その帽子をどこで買いましたか.

3 (obtain) ... o eˈru ...を得る ⓥ; toˈru 取る ⓒ; teˈ ni iˈreru 手に入れる ⓥ: He got first prize in the contest. (*Kare wa koñtesuto de it-too-shoo o totta.*) 彼はコンテストで1等賞を取った.

4 (bring) ... o toˈtte kuˈru ...を取ってくる ①; moˈtte kuˈru 持ってくる ①: Get me a chair. (*Isu o motte kite kudasai.*) いすを持ってきてください.

5 (become) ... ni naˈru ...になる ⓒ: He got sick while traveling. (*Kare wa ryokoo saki de byooki ni natta.*) 彼は旅行先で病気になった.

6 (catch) ... o tsuˈkamaeru ...を捕まえる ⓥ: The police failed to get the thief. (*Keesatsu wa doroboo o tsukamaeru koto ga dekinakatta.*) 警察はどろぼうを捕まえることができなかった.

7 (understand) ... ga waˈkaˈru ...がわかる ⓥ: I get you. (*Wakarimashita.*) わかりました.

— *vi.* **1** (become) naˈru なる ⓒ: It's getting warmer. (*Dañdañ atatakaku natte kite iru.*) だんだん暖かくなってきている.

2 (arrive) (... ni) tsuˈku (...に)着く ⓒ: I'll get there by 5 o'clock. (*Go-ji made ni wa soko ni tsukimasu.*) 5時までにはそこに着きます.

3 (passive) ⟨verb⟩-(ra)reru ...(ら)れる ⓥ: He got scolded by his teacher.

(*Kare wa señsee ni shikarareta.*) 彼は先生にしかられた.

get along *vi.* (live) kuˈrashite iku 暮らしていく ⓒ: How are you getting along? (*Ikaga o-kurashi desu ka?*) いかがお暮らしですか.

get away *vi.* niˈgedasu 逃げ出す ⓒ: I could not get away from the meeting. (*Kaigi kara nigedasu koto ga dekinakatta.*) 会議から逃げ出すことができなかった.

get back *vi.* (return) moˈdoˈru 戻る ⓒ: He'll soon get back. (*Kare wa sugu modoru deshoo.*) 彼はすぐ戻るでしょう.

get down *vi.* oˈriˈru 降りる ⓥ; *vt.* oˈroˈsu 下(降)ろす ⓒ: Please get the book down from the shelf. (*Tana kara sono hoñ o oroshite kudasai.*) 棚からその本を下ろしてください.

get in *vi.* naˈka ni hairu 中に入る ⓒ; *vt.* ... ni noˈru ...に乗る ⓒ: I got in a taxi. (*Watashi wa takushii ni notta.*) 私はタクシーに乗った.

get off *vi.* oˈriˈru 降りる ⓥ: I'll get off at the next stop. (*Tsugi no tee-ryuujo de orimasu.*) 次の停留所で降ります.

get on *vt.* ... ni noˈru ...に乗る ⓒ: Where can I get on the bus? (*Sono basu ni wa doko de noru ñ desu ka?*) そのバスにはどこで乗るんですか.

get out of ... kara deˈru ...から出る ⓥ: Get out of bed. (*Beddo kara de nasai.*) ベッドから出なさい.

get up *vi.* oˈkiˈru 起きる ⓥ: I have to get up early tomorrow morning. (*Ashita no asa wa hayaku okinakereba naranai.*) あしたの朝は早く起きなければならない.

ghetto *n.* (where a specific minority lives) kyoˈjuˈuku 居住区; (slum) hiˈñmiˈñgai 貧民街.

ghost *n.* yuˈuree 幽霊: People say a ghost appears at this house. (*Kono uchi ni yuuree ga deru soo da.*) この家に幽霊が出るそうだ.

giant *n.* (person) kyoˈjiñ 巨人; (figuratively) oˈomono 大物: an economic giant (*keezai taikoku*) 経済

大国.

— adj. kyo⌐dai na 巨大な: a giant Christmas tree (*kyodai na Kurisumasu tsurii*) 巨大なクリスマスツリー.

gift n. **1** (present) o⌐kurimono 贈り物; pu⌐re¬zeñto プレゼント: I sent her a birthday gift. (*Watashi wa kanojo ni tañjoobi no okurimono o okutta.*) 私は彼女に誕生日の贈り物を送った.

2 (talent) sa⌐inoo 才能: She has a gift for painting. (*Kanojo wa e no sainoo ga aru.*) 彼女は絵の才能がある.

gift certificate n. sho⌐ohi¬ñkeñ 商品券.

gifted adj. sa⌐inoo no [ga] a⌐ru 才能の[が]ある: a gifted painter (*sainoo no aru gaka*) 才能のある画家.

giggle vi. ku⌐sukusu wa⌐rau くすくす笑う C: The girl started giggling. (*Sono oñna-no-ko wa kusukusu warai-dashita.*) その女の子はくすくす笑い出した.

ginger n. (plant) sho⌐oga しょうが(生姜).

ginkgo n. (tree) i⌐choo いちょう(銀杏).

ginseng n. cho⌐oseñ-ni¬ñjiñ 朝鮮人参.

giraffe n. ki⌐riñ きりん; ji⌐rafu ジラフ.

girl n. o⌐ñna¬-no-ko 女の子; sho⌐ojo 少女: The girls are playing with dolls. (*Oñna-no-ko-tachi wa niñgyoo de asoñde iru.*) 女の子たちは人形で遊んでいる.

girlfriend n. (friend who is a girl) o⌐ñna-to¬modachi 女友達; (in a relationship) ga⌐arufure¬ñdo ガールフレンド; (lover) ko⌐ibito 恋人.

give vt. **1** (to a person) ... o a⌐geru ...をあげる V; (to an inferior recipient) ya⌐ru やる C; (to a superior recipient) sa⌐shiageru 差し上げる V: I'll give you this book. (*Anata ni kono hoñ o agemashoo.*) あなたにこの本をあげましょう. / I gave apples to children. (*Watashi wa kodomotachi ni riñgo o yatta.*) 私は子どもたちにりんごをやった. / She gave water to the flowers. (*Kanojo wa hana ni*

mizu o yatta.*) 彼女は花に水をやった.

2 (to me) ... o ku⌐reru ...をくれる V; [honorific] ku⌐dasa¬ru 下さる C: My father gave me a fountain pen. (*Chichi wa watashi ni mañneñhitsu o kureta.*) 父は私に万年筆をくれた. / My teacher gave me a notebook. (*Señsee wa watashi ni nooto o kudasatta.*) 先生は私にノートを下さった.

3 (ask for) [imperative] ... o ku⌐dasa¬i ...を下さい: Please give me something to drink. (*Nani-ka nomimono o kudasai.*) 何か飲み物を下さい.

4 (provide) ... o a⌐taeru ...を与える V: The results will give you satisfaction. (*Sono kekka wa anata ni mañzoku o ataeru deshoo.*) その結果はあなたに満足を与えるでしょう.

5 (hand over) ... o wa⌐tasu ...を渡す C: I gave my baggage to a porter. (*Watashi wa nimotsu o pootaa ni watashita.*) 私は荷物をポーターに渡した.

6 (show) ... o shi⌐me¬su ...を示す C; (state) no⌐be¬ru 述べる V: He gave us a better example. (*Kare wa motto yoi ree o shimeshita.*) 彼はもっとよい例を示した. / I gave a farewell speech. (*Watashi wa wakare no kotoba o nobeta.*) 私は別れの言葉を述べた.

give up vt. ... o a⌐kirame¬ru ...をあきらめる V: We gave up the plan. (*Watashi-tachi wa sono keekaku o akirameta.*) 私たちはその計画をあきらめた.

given name n. na 名. ★ Japanese 'surname' is followed by 'given name.'

glad adj. u⌐reshi¬i うれしい: I'm very glad to see you. (*Anata ni o-me ni kakarete taiheñ ureshii desu.*) あなたにお目にかかれて大変うれしいです.

be glad to do yo⌐roko¬ñde ⟨verb⟩ 喜んで...: I'd be glad to help you. (*Yorokoñ de o-tetsudai itashimasu.*) 喜んでお手伝いいたします.

gladly adv. yo⌐roko¬ñde 喜んで; ko⌐koroyo¬ku 快く: I will come gladly. (*Yorokoñde o-ukagai shimasu.*) 喜

んでお伺いします.

glamour *n.* mi「ryoku 魅力: the glamour of a beautiful woman (*utsukushii josee no miryoku*) 美しい女性の魅力.

glance *vi.* (... o) chi「ratto mi」ru (...を)ちらっと見る Ⓥ: She glanced at me. (*Kanojo wa chiratto watashi o mita.*) 彼女はちらっと私を見た.
— *n.* hi「to」me ひと目: I recognized him at a glance. (*Watashi wa hitome de kare to wakatta.*) 私はひと目で彼とわかった.

gland *n.* se「ñ 腺: lymph glands (*riñpaseñ*) リンパ腺.

glare *vi.* **1** (shine) gi「ragira ka「gaya」ku ぎらぎら輝く Ⓒ: The sun glared down on us. (*Taiyoo wa giragira to teritsuketa.*) 太陽はぎらぎらと照りつけた.
2 (stare) (... o) ni「ramitsuke」ru (...を)にらみつける Ⓥ: He glared at me. (*Kare wa watashi o niramitsuketa.*) 彼は私をにらみつけた.
— *n.* (light) ma「bushi」i hi「kari」 まぶしい光; (stare) ni「rami」 にらみ.

glass *n.* **1** (clear material) ga「rasu ガラス: a glass door (*garasu-do*) ガラス戸.
2 (vessel) ko「ppu コップ: a glass of water (*koppu ip-pai no mizu*) コップ1杯の水.

glasses *n.* me「gane 眼鏡: I put on glasses when I read. (*Watashi wa hoñ o yomu toki megane o kakemasu.*) 私は本を読むとき眼鏡をかけます.

gleam *n.* ka「suka na hi「kari」 かすかな光; bi「koo 微光: the gleam of distant fishing boats (*tooku no gyoseñ no hikari*) 遠くの漁船の光.

glide *vi.* su「be」ru 滑る Ⓒ: They glided down the slope. (*Kare-ra wa shameñ o subette orita.*) 彼らは斜面を滑って下りた.

glimpse *vt.* ... o chi「ra」ri to mi「ru ...をちらりと見る Ⓥ: I glimpsed him in the crowd. (*Watashi wa hitogomi no naka de kare o chirari to mita.*) 私は人込みの中で彼をちらりと見た.
— *n.* hi「to」me ひと目: I only caught a glimpse of the red car. (*Watashi wa sono akai kuruma o hitome mita dake desu.*) 私はその赤い車をひと目見ただけです.

glitter *vi.* pi「kapika hi「ka」ru ぴかぴか光る Ⓒ; ki「rakira ka「gaya」ku きらきら輝く Ⓒ: Stars are glittering in the sky. (*Sora ni hoshi ga kirakira kagayaite iru.*) 空に星がきらきら輝いている.

global *adj.* **1** (of the earth) chi「kyuu (zeñtai) no 地球(全体)の; (of the world) se「kai-teki na 世界的な: a global depression (*sekai-teki na fukyoo*) 世界的な不況.
2 (complete) ze「ñtai-teki na 全体的な: a global view (*zeñtai o miru kañgae-kata*) 全体を見る考え方.

globe *n.* (of the earth) chi「kyuu」gi 地球儀.

gloomy *adj.* **1** (dark) u「sugurai 薄暗い: a gloomy room (*usugurai heya*) 薄暗い部屋.
2 (low spirited) yu「u-utsu na 憂うつな; fu「sagiko」ñda ふさぎ込んだ: He looked gloomy. (*Kare wa yuu-utsu-soo ni mieta.*) 彼は憂うつそうに見えた.

glorious *adj.* **1** (praiseworthy) e「ekoo a」ru 栄光ある; me「eyo no 名誉の: a glorious victory (*eekoo no shoori*) 栄光の勝利.
2 (wonderful) su「barashi」i すばらしい; su「teki na すてきな: have a glorious holiday (*suteki na kyuujitsu o sugosu*) すてきな休日を過ごす.

glory *n.* **1** (honor) e「ekoo 栄光; me「eyo 名誉: win glory in battle (*tatakai de meeyo o ukeru*) 戦いで名誉を受ける.
2 (splendor) u「tsuku」shisa 美しさ; so「rokañ 壮観: the glory of the setting sun (*yuuhi no utsukushisa*) 夕日の美しさ.

glossary *n.* yo「ogo」shuu 用語集.

glove *n.* **1** (for hands) te「bu」kuro 手袋: put on [take off] gloves (*tebukuro o hameru [nugu]*) 手袋をはめる[脱ぐ].

2 (for sports) guˈrabu グラブ.

glove compartment n. (of a car) koˈmonoˈire 小物入れ.

glow vi. **1** (give bright light) aˈkaku kagayaˈku 赤く輝く ⊂: The hot iron glowed. (Nesshita tetsu wa akaku kagayaita.) 熱した鉄は赤く輝いた.

2 (show rosy color) koˈochoo suru 紅潮する Ⓘ: She glowed with pleasure. (Kanojo wa yorokobi de koochoo shita.) 彼女は喜びで紅潮した.

— n. (brightness) kaˈgayaki 輝き; (redness) aˈkarami 赤らみ: The glow of the fire lighted the room. (Hi no kagayaki ga heya o terashita.) 火の輝きが部屋を照らした.

glue n. (especially for paper) noˈriˈ のり; (bonding agent) seˈtchakuˈzai 接着剤: stick paper together with glue (kami o nori de tsukeru) 紙をのりでつける.

— vt. ... o noˈrizuke ni suru ...をのりづけにする Ⓘ; seˈtchakuˈzai de tsuˈˈkeˈru 接着剤でつける Ⓥ: glue a broken cup together (wareta chawañ o setchakuzai de tsukeru) 割れた茶碗を接着剤でつける.

go vi. **1** (move) (... e) iˈku ...へ行く ⊂: go to school [church] (gakkoo [kyookai] e iku) 学校[教会]へ行く.

2 (travel) (... e) iˈku ...へ行く ⊂: We went to Nikko by bus. (Watashi-tachi wa Nikkoo e basu de itta.) 私たちは日光へバスで行った.

3 (leave) iˈku 行く ⊂; saˈru 去る ⊂: I must be going now. (Moo ikanakereba narimaseñ.) もう行かなければなりません.

4 (proceed) iˈku 行く ⊂; shiˈñkoo suru 進行する Ⓘ: Everything is going well. (Subete wa umaku itte imasu.) すべてはうまくいっています.

5 (attend) kaˈyou 通う ⊂: She goes to work on the subway. (Kanojo wa chikatetsu de shigoto ni kayotte imasu.) 彼女は地下鉄で仕事に通っています.

6 (disappear) naˈkunaru なくなる ⊂; kiˈeru 消える Ⓥ: My pain has gone. (Itami ga nakunatta.) 痛みがなくなった.

7 (sound) naˈru 鳴る ⊂: There goes the bell. (Beru ga natte iru.) ベルが鳴っている.

go away vi. taˈchisaru 立ち去る ⊂: He went away without a word. (Kare wa nani mo iwazu ni tachisatta.) 彼は何も言わずに立ち去った.

go down vi. saˈgaˈru 下がる ⊂: Land prices went down. (Tochi no nedañ ga sagatta.) 土地の値段が下がった.

going to do ⟨verb⟩ toˈkoroˈ da ... ところだ: I was just going to phone you. (Ima choodo deñwa suru tokoro deshita.) 今ちょうど電話するところでした.

go into ... vt. ... ni haˈiru ...に入る ⊂: I went into the room. (Watashi wa sono heya ni haitta.) 私はその部屋に入った.

go on doing vt. ⟨verb⟩-tsuzukeru ... 続ける Ⓥ: I want to go on working. (Watashi wa hataraki-tsuzuketai.) 私は働き続けたい.

go out vi. deˈte iku 出て行く ⊂: She went out of the house. (Kanojo wa uchi kara dete ikimashita.) 彼女は家から出て行きました.

go up vi. aˈgaru 上がる ⊂: The temperature suddenly went up. (Kioñ ga kyuu ni agatta.) 気温が急に上がった.

goal n. **1** (of a game) goˈoru ゴール; toˈkuteñ 得点: get a goal (gooru o kimeru) ゴールを決める.

2 (aim) moˈkuhyoo 目標: reach one's goal (mokuhyoo o tassei suru) 目標を達成する. ★ In Japanese, the finish line in a race is usually called 'gooru' (goal).

goalkeeper n. goˈoru kiˈipaa ゴールキーパー.

goalpost n. goˈoru poˈsuto ゴールポスト.

goat n. yaˈgi やぎ(山羊).

go-between n. **1** (in a negotiation) chuˈukaˈisha 仲介者; aˈsseñniñ 斡旋人.

2 (matchmaker) na「ko¹odo 仲人；ba「ishakuniñ 媒酌人. ★ In Japan marriage is often arranged by a '*nakoodo*.'

god [God] n. ka「mi 神: pray to a god [to God] (*kami ni inoru*) 神に祈る. ★ Christianity in Japan also uses '*kami*' to refer to its deity.

goddess n. me「gami 女神: the goddess of love (*ai no megami*) 愛の女神.

gold n. ki「ñ 金; o「ogoñ 黄金: This ring is made of gold. (*Kono yubiwa wa kiñ de dekite iru.*) この指輪は金でできている.
— adj. ki「ñ no 金の: a gold coin (*kiñka*) 金貨.

golden adj. **1** (color) ki「ñiro no 金色の: golden hair (*kiñpatsu*) 金髪. **2** (made of gold) ki「ñsee no 金製の: a golden cup (*kiñsee no kappu*) 金製のカップ. **3** (favorable) ze「kkoo no 絶好の: a golden opportunity (*zekkoo no kikai*) 絶好の機会.

golden age n. o「ogoñ-ji¹dai 黄金時代; sa「ise¹eki 最盛期.

goldfish n. ki「ñgyo 金魚.

golf n. go「rufu ゴルフ: play golf (*gorufu o suru*) ゴルフをする.

golfer n. go「rufaa ゴルファー: a professional golfer (*puro gorufaa*) プロゴルファー.

good adj. **1** (not bad) yo「i よい: good news (*yoi shirase*) よい知らせ / good weather (*yoi teñki*) よい天気. **2** (suitable) te「ki¹shite iru 適している: This water is good to drink. (*Kono mizu wa nomu no ni tekishite iru.*) この水は飲むのに適している. **3** (skillful) jo「ozu na 上手な; u「ma¹i うまい: You speak good English. (*Anata wa Eego ga o-joozu desu ne.*) あなたは英語がお上手ですね. / He is good at golf. (*Kare wa gorufu ga umai.*) 彼はゴルフがうまい. **4** (kind) shi「ñsetsu na 親切な: She was very good to me. (*Kanojo wa watashi ni totemo shiñsetsu deshita.*) 彼女は私にとても親切でした.

5 (beneficial) ta「me¹ ni naru ためになる; yo「i よい: Early rising is good for the health. (*Hayaoki wa keñkoo ni yoi.*) 早起きは健康によい.
— n. **1** (benefit) ri「eki 利益; ta「me¹ ため: I am saying so for your good. (*Anata no tame ni soo itte iru no desu.*) あなたのためにそう言っているのです. **2** (merit) yo「i teñ よい点; to「rie¹ とりえ: I can find no good in him. (*Kare ni wa nani mo torie ga nai.*) 彼には何もとりえがない.

good afternoon int. ko「ñnichiwa こんにちわ; (when parting) sa「yoonara さよなら.

good-bye int. sa「yoonara さようなら.
— n. wa「kare no a¹isatsu 別れのあいさつ: I had no time to say good-bye. (*Wakare no aisatsu o suru hima mo nakatta.*) 別れのあいさつをする暇もなかった.

good evening int. ko「ñbañwa こんばんは; (when parting) sa「yoonara さようなら.

good-looking adj. ka「odachi no yo¹i 顔立ちのよい: a good-looking woman (*kaodachi no yoi josee*) 顔立ちのよい女性.

good luck n. ko「ouñ 幸運: I wish you good luck! (*Koouñ o o-inori shimasu.*) 幸運をお祈りします.

good morning int. o「hayoo お早う; [polite] o「hayoo-gozaimasu お早うございます; (late morning) ko「ñnichiwa こんにちは; (when parting) sa「yoonara さようなら.

good-natured adj. (of young people and women) ki「date no yo¹i 気だてのよい.

good night int. o「yasumi nasai おやすみなさい; (when parting) sa「yoonara さようなら.

goods n. sho「ohiñ 商品; shi「namono 品物: There are a variety of goods in that supermarket. (*Ano suupaa ni wa iroiro na shinamono ga aru.*) あのスーパーにはいろいろな品物がある.

goodwill *n.* koﾞoi 好意: show goodwill to a person (*hito ni kooi o shimesu*) 人に好意を示す.

goose *n.* gaﾞchoo がちょう.

gorge *n.* kyoﾞokoku 峡谷.

gorgeous *adj.* suﾞbarashiﾞi すばらしい; kaﾞree na 華麗な: The bride appeared in a gorgeous dress. (*Hanayome wa karee na ishoo de arawareta.*) 花嫁は華麗な衣装で現れた.

gorilla *n.* goﾞrira ゴリラ.

gospel *n.* (of Jesus Christ) fuﾞkuiñ 福音; (book) fuﾞkuiñsho 福音書.

gossip *n.* uﾞwasabanaﾞshi うわさ話; goﾞshiﾞppu ゴシップ: The gossip spread at once. (*Sono uwasabanashi wa sugu ni hiromatta.*) そのうわさ話はすぐに広まった.

govern *vt.* **1** (rule) ... o oﾞsameﾞru ...を治める Ⓥ; shiﾞhai suru 支配する Ⓘ: govern a country (*kuni o osameru*) 国を治める.
2 (control) ... o kaﾞñri suru ...を管理する Ⓘ: This university is governed by a board of trustees. (*Kono daigaku wa rijikai ni yotte kañri sarete iru.*) この大学は理事会によって管理されている.
3 (influence) ... o saﾞyuu suru ...を左右する Ⓘ: Newspapers are often governed by public opinion. (*Shiñbun wa shibashiba yoroñ ni sayuu sareru.*) 新聞はしばしば世論に左右される.

government *n.* **1** (body) seﾞefu 政府: The government decided to increase taxes. (*Seefu wa zoozee o kimeta.*) 政府は増税を決めた.
2 (act) seﾞeji 政治: democratic government (*miñshu seeji*) 民主政治.

governor *n.* **1** (elected person) chiﾞji 知事: the governor of a prefecture (*keñchiji*) 県知事.
2 (appointed person) choﾞokañ 長官; soﾞosai 総裁; riﾞji 理事.

grab *vt.* ... o hiﾞtsukaﾞmu ...をひっつかむ Ⓒ; hiﾞttakuﾞru ひったくる Ⓒ: The man grabbed the money and ran away. (*Sono otoko wa o-kane o*

hittakutte nigeta.) その男はお金をひったくって逃げた.

grace *n.* **1** (beauty) yuﾞuga 優雅; joﾞohiﾞñ 上品: She danced with grace. (*Kanojo wa yuuga ni odotta.*) 彼女は優雅に踊った.
2 (prayer) shoﾞkuzeñ no kaﾞñsha no iﾞnori 食前の感謝の祈り: say grace (*shokuzeñ no kañsha no inori o suru*) 食前の感謝の祈りをする.

graceful *adj.* yuﾞuga na 優雅な; shiﾞtoﾞyaka na しとやかな: She is graceful in manner. (*Kanojo wa furumai ga shitoyaka da.*) 彼女は振る舞いがしとやかだ.

gracious *adj.* **1** (kind) yaﾞsashii 優しい; shiﾞñsetsu na 親切な: She is gracious to everyone. (*Kanojo wa dare ni mo yasashii.*) 彼女はだれにも優しい.
2 (elegant) yuﾞuga na 優雅な: gracious living (*yuuga na seekatsu*) 優雅な生活.

grade *n.* **1** (mark) seﾞeseki 成績; hyoﾞoteñ 評点: I got a good grade in mathematics. (*Watashi wa suugaku de yoi seeseki o totta.*) 私は数学でよい成績をとった.
2 (division of a school) gaﾞkuneñ 学年: The child is in the fifth grade of primary school. (*Sono ko wa shoogakkoo go-neñ-see desu.*) その子は小学校5年生です.
3 (rate) toﾞokyuu 等級; teﾞedo 程度: the best grade of meat (*saikookyuu no niku*) 最高級の肉.
— *vt.* ... ni toﾞokyuu o tsuﾞkeﾞru ...に等級をつける Ⓥ: grade eggs by size (*ookisa de tamago ni toﾞokyuu o tsukeru*) 大きさで卵に等級をつける.

gradual *adj.* joﾞjo no 徐々の; daﾞñdañ no だんだんの: a gradual but steady improvement (*jojo de wa aru ga kakujitsu na kaizeñ*) 徐々ではあるが確実な改善.

gradually *adv.* daﾞñdañ to だんだんと; shiﾞdai ni 次第に: His health improved gradually. (*Kare no keñkoo wa jojo ni kaifuku shita.*) 彼の健康は徐々に回復した.

graduate *vi.* (... o) so「tsugyoo suru (...を)卒業する ①: He graduated from college with honors. (*Kare wa daigaku o yuutoo de sotsugyoo shita.*) 彼は大学を優等で卒業した.
— *n.* so「tsugyo¬osee 卒業生.

graduation *n.* so「tsugyoo 卒業; (ceremony) so「tsugyo¬o-shiki 卒業式: He went to college after graduation from high school. (*Kare wa kookoo o sotsugyoo shite kara daigaku e shiñgaku shita.*) 彼は高校を卒業してから大学へ進学した.

grain *n.* **1** (a tiny piece) tsu「bu 粒: a grain of sand (*hito-tsubu no suna*) ひと粒の砂 / grains of wheat (*komugi-tsubu*) 小麦粒.
2 (cereal) ko「ku¬motsu 穀物: harvest the grain (*kokumotsu o shuukaku suru*) 穀物を収穫する.
3 (a tiny bit) sho「oryo¬o 少量: He hasn't a grain of sense. (*Kare wa sukoshi no fuñbetsu mo nai.*) 彼は少しの分別もない.

gram *n.* gu「ramu グラム: This parcel weighs 500 grams. (*Kono tsutsumi wa gohyaku-guramu aru.*) この包みは 500 グラムある.

grammar *n.* bu「ñpoo 文法: Japanese grammar (*Nihoñgo no buñpoo*) 日本語の文法.

grand *adj.* **1** (magnificent) so「odai na 壮大な; yu「udai na 雄大な: The view from the mountain was grand. (*Yama kara no nagame wa yuudai datta.*) 山からの眺めは雄大だった.
2 (dignified) ri「ppa na 立派な; i「dai na 偉大な: a grand gentleman (*rippa na shiñshi*) 立派な紳士.
3 (enjoyable) su「teki na すてきな: We had a grand time at the party. (*Watashi-tachi wa paatii de suteki na toki o sugoshita.*) 私たちはパーティーですてきな時を過ごした.

grandchild *n.* ma「go¬ 孫; (someone else's) o-「mago-sañ お孫さん.

granddaughter *n.* ma「gomu¬sume 孫娘; (someone else's) o「ñna no o-「mago-sañ 女のお孫さん.

grandfather *n.* so「fu 祖父; (someone else's) o-「ji¬i-sañ おじいさん.

grandmother *n.* so「bo 祖母; (someone else's) o-「ba¬a-sañ おばあさん.

grandson *n.* ma「gomu¬suko 孫息子; (someone else's) o「toko no o-「mago-sañ 男のお孫さん.

grant *vt.* **1** (consent) ... o ki「ki-ire¬ru ...を聞き入れる ②; (agree) sho「odaku suru 承諾する ①: He granted us our request. (*Kare wa watashi-tachi no negai o kiki-irete kureta.*) 彼は私たちの願いを聞き入れてくれた.
2 (give) ... ni (... o) a「taeru ...に(...を)与える ②: He didn't grant us permission to use the hall. (*Kare wa sono hooru o tsukau kyoka o watashi-tachi ni ataete kurenakatta.*) 彼はそのホールを使う許可を私たちに与えてくれなかった.
3 (admit) ... o mi「tomeru ...を認める ②: I grant that I was wrong. (*Watashi ga machigatte ita koto o mitomemasu.*) 私が間違っていたことを認めます.

grape *n.* bu「doo ぶどう: a bunch of grapes (*budoo hito-fusa*) ぶどう一房.

grapefruit *n.* gu「reepu-furu¬utsu グレープフルーツ.

graph *n.* gu「rafu グラフ; zu「hyoo 図表: draw a graph (*gurafu o egaku*) グラフを描く.

grasp *vt.* **1** (hold) ... o shi「kka¬ri tsu「ka¬mu ...をしっかりつかむ ©; ni「girishime¬ru 握りしめる ②: I grasped his hand and pulled him up. (*Watashi wa te o shikkari tsukande kare o hippari-ageta.*) 私は手をしっかりつかんで彼を引っ張り上げた.
2 (understand) ... o tsu「ka¬mu ...をつかむ ©; wa「ka¬ru わかる ©: I cannot grasp the meaning of the word. (*Watashi ni wa sono go no imi ga wakaranai.*) 私にはその語の意味がわからない.
— *vi.* (... ni) tsu「kamaru (...に)つかまる ©.
— *n.* **1** (holding) shi「kka¬ri tsu-

「ka¹mu ko¹to¹ しっかりつかむこと: have [get] a firm grasp on a rope (*roopu o shikkari tsukamu*) ローブをしっかりつかむ.

2 (understanding) ri「kai 理解; ha-「aku 把握: have a good grasp of the problem (*mondai o yoku haaku suru*) 問題をよく把握する.

grass n. (plant) ku「sa¹ 草; (lawn) shi「bafu 芝生: Keep off the grass. (*Shibafu ni haitte wa ikenai.*) 芝生に入ってはいけない.

grasshopper n. ba「tta ばった; i「nago いなご.

grass roots n. (ordinary people) i「ppañ taishuu 一般大衆; ku「sa no ne 草の根.

grateful adj. ka「ñsha shite (iru) 感謝して(いる); a「riga¹taku o「mo¹tte (iru) ありがたく思って(いる): I am grateful for your advice. (*Anata no jo-geñ o kañsha shite imasu.*) あなたの助言を感謝しています. / I'd be grateful if you would help me. (*Tasukete itadakereba arigataku omoimasu.*) 助けていただければありがたく思います.

gratitude n. ka「ñsha no ki「mochi 感謝の気持ち; ka「ñsha 感謝: I showed my gratitude by sending her flowers. (*Watashi wa kanojo ni hana o okutte kañsha no kimochi o arawashita.*) 私は彼女に花を送って感謝の気持ちを表した.

grave¹ n. ha「ka¹ 墓; bo「chi 墓地: visit a grave (*hakamairi o suru*) 墓参りをする.

grave² adj. **1** (serious) ju「udai na 重大な: He made a grave mistake. (*Kare wa juudai na machigai o shita.*) 彼は重大な間違いをした.

2 (dignified) i「geñ no a¹ru 威厳のある; (solemn) ma「jime na まじめな: His face was grave. (*Kare no kao wa majime datta.*) 彼の顔はまじめだった.

gravel n. ja「ri 砂利: The road was covered with gravel. (*Dooro ni wa jari ga shiite atta.*) 道路には砂利が敷いてあった.

gravity n. ju「uryoku 重力; i「ñryoku 引力: the center of gravity (*juu-shiñ*) 重心.

gray adj. **1** (of a color) ha「iiro no 灰色の; gu「re¹e no グレーの; ne「zumi iro no ねずみ色の: gray eyes (*haiiro no me*) 灰色の目 / a gray coat (*gu-ree [nezumi iro] no kooto*) グレー[ねずみ色]のコート.

2 (of hair) shi「raga(ma¹jiri) no 白髪(混じり)の: His hair is turning gray. (*Kare no kami no ke wa shiraga ni natte kita.*) 彼の髪の毛は白髪になってきた.

— n. ha「iiro 灰色; ne「zumi iro ねずみ色.

grease n. (lubricant) gu「ri¹isu グリース; (animal fat) ju「ushi 獣脂; a「bura 脂.

great adj. **1** (important) i「dai na 偉大な; ri「ppa na りっぱな: He became a great writer. (*Kare wa idai na sakka ni natta.*) 彼は偉大な作家になった.

2 (nice) su「barashi¹i すばらしい; su-「teki na すてきな: It is a great idea. (*Sore wa subarashii kañgae da.*) それはすばらしい考えだ.

3 (large in degree) o「oki-na 大きな: great joy (*ooki-na yorokobi*) 大きな喜び.

4 (a lot of) ta「su¹u no 多数の; ta「ku-sa¹ñ no たくさんの: A great number of people attended the opening ceremony. (*Oozee no hito ga sono kaikai-shiki ni shusseki shita.*) 大勢の人がその開会式に出席した.

greatness n. i「daisa 偉大さ; e「ra-sa 偉さ: his greatness as a statesman (*kare no seejika to shite no idaisa*) 彼の政治家としての偉大さ.

greedy adj. **1** (avaricious) yo「ku-ba¹ri no 欲ばりの: He is too greedy. (*Kare wa yokubari-sugi da.*) 彼は欲張り過ぎだ.

2 (for food) ga「tsugatsu shita [shite iru] がつがつした[している]; ku-「ishi¹ñboo na 食いしんぼうな: a greedy boy (*kuishiñboo na otoko-no-ko*) 食いしんぼうな男の子.

green *adj.* **1** (color) mi'doriiro no 緑色の; gu'rii'iñ no グリーンの: a green dress (*midori iro no doresu*) 緑色のドレス.
2 (not ripe) u'rete nai 熟れてない; ma'da a'oi まだ青い: green fruit (*urete nai kudamono*) 熟れてない果物.
— *n.* (color) mi'dori 緑.

greenhouse *n.* o'ñshitsu 温室: the greenhouse effect (*oñshitsu kooka*) 温室効果.

green light *n.* (traffic signal) mi'dori no shi'ñgoo 緑の信号.

greet *vt.* ... ni a'isatsu suru ...にあいさつする□: She greeted me with a smile. (*Kanojo wa nikoniko shite watashi ni aisatsu shita.*) 彼女はにこにこして私にあいさつした.

greeting *n.* a'isatsu あいさつ: exchange greetings (*aisatsu o kawasu*) あいさつを交わす.

greeting card *n.* gu'riitiñgu ka'ado グリーティングカード; a'isatsu'joo あいさつ状. ★ In Japan many people send greetings in the form of a postcard: '*neñgajoo*' 年賀状 at the New Year and some people send '*shochuu mimai*' 暑中見舞い during summer.

grief *n.* fu'ka'i ka'nashimi 深い悲しみ: be filled with grief (*fukai kanashimi ni shizumu*) 深い悲しみに沈む.

grieve *vi.* (... o) fu'kaku ka'nashimu (...を)深く悲しむ□: He grieved over the death of his friend. (*Kare wa yuujiñ no shi o fukaku kanashiñda.*) 彼は友人の死を深く悲しんだ.

grim *adj.* **1** (stern) i'kameshi'i いかめしい: a grim face (*ikameshii kao*) いかめしい顔.
2 (unpleasant) i'ya'i na いやな; fu'yu'kai na 不愉快な: a grim task (*iya na shigoto*) いやな仕事.
3 (cruel) za'ññiñ na 残忍な: War is grim. (*Señsoo wa zañniñ da.*) 戦争は残忍だ.

grin *vi.* ni'kko'ri wa'rau にっこり笑う□: He grinned when he saw me. (*Kare wa watashi o mite nikkori*

waratta.) 彼は私を見てにっこり笑った.

grind *vt.* **1** (crush) ... o hi'ku ...をひく□: grind coffee beans (*koohii mame o hiku*) コーヒー豆をひく.
2 (sharpen) ... o to'gu ...を研ぐ□; (polish) mi'gaku 磨く□: grind a knife (*naifu o togu*) ナイフを研ぐ / grind a lens (*reñzu o migaku*) レンズを磨く.
3 (rub together) ... o gi'shigishi ko'suru ...をぎしぎしこする□: grind one's teeth (*hagishiri o suru*) 歯ぎしりをする.

grip *vt.* ... o shi'kka'ri tsu'ka'mu ...をしっかりつかむ□; ni'giru 握る□: He gripped me by the arm. (*Kare wa watashi no ude o shikkari tsukañda.*) 彼は私の腕をしっかりつかんだ.
— *n.* **1** (gripping) tsu'ka'mu ko'to' つかむこと.
2 (handle) ni'giri にぎり; e 柄: a tool with a wooden grip (*ki no nigiri no doogu*) 木のにぎりの道具.

groan *n.* u'mekigo'e うめき声; u'narigo'e うなり声: give a groan (*umekigoe o ageru*) うめき声をあげる.
— *vi.* u'me'ku うめく□: The patient was groaning. (*Sono byooniñ wa umeite ita.*) その病人はうめいていた.

grocery store *n.* sho'kuryoohiñ'teñ 食料品店: I bought salt and sugar at the grocery store. (*Shokuryoohiñteñ de shio to satoo o katta.*) 食料品店で塩と砂糖を買った. ★ '*Shokuryoohiñteñ*' deals in only food and does not sell household supplies.

grope *vi.* (... o) te'sa'guri suru (...を)手探りする□; te'sa'guri de sa'gasu 手探りで捜す□: grope for one's shoes in the dark (*kurayami de kutsu o tesaguri de sagasu*) 暗闇で靴を手探りで捜す.

gross *adj.* **1** (total) so'otai no 総体の: the gross amount (*soogaku*) 総額 / a gross profit (*soorieki*) 総利益.
2 (very bad) hi'do'i ひどい: a gross mistake (*hidoi machigai*) ひどい間違い.

ground *n.* **1** (surface) ji'meñ 地面:

The ground is frozen. (*Jimeñ ga kootte iru.*) 地面が凍っている.

2 (soil) to'chi 土地; do'joo 土壌: rich [poor] ground (*koeta* [*yaseta*] *tochi*) 肥えた[やせた]土地.

3 (for facilities) shi'kichi 敷地; ko'onai 構内: palace grounds (*kyuudeñ no shikichi*) 宮殿の敷地 / school grounds (*gakkoo no koonai*) 学校の構内.

4 (field) ba'sho 場所; u'ñdoojoo 運動場; gu'rañdo グランド: a baseball ground (*yakyuujoo*) 野球場.

5 (reason) ko'ñkyo 根拠; ri'yuu 理由: There are no grounds for fear. (*Osoreru riyuu wa nai.*) 恐れる理由はない.

6 (of coffee) ka'su かす: coffee grounds (*koohii no kasu*) コーヒーのかす.

ground floor *n.* i'k-kai 1 階.

group *n.* mu're¹ 群れ; shu'udañ 集団; gu'ru'upu グループ: A group of birds flew away. (*Tori no mure ga tobisatta.*) 鳥の群れが飛び去った.

—— *vt.* ... o a'tsume'ru ...を集める Ⓥ: The teacher grouped the children for a photograph. (*Señsee wa shashiñ o toru tame ni kodomotachi o atsumeta.*) 先生は写真を撮るために子どもたちを集めた.

grow *vi.* **1** (of a plant) se'echoo suru 生長する Ⓘ; so'da'tsu 育つ Ⓒ: Oranges grow in warm regions. (*Oreñji wa atatakai chihoo de sodatsu.*) オレンジは暖かい地方で育つ.

2 (of people) se'echoo suru 成長する Ⓘ; o'okiku naru 大きくなる Ⓒ: Children grow rapidly. (*Kodomo wa ookiku naru no ga hayai.*) 子どもは大きくなるのが早い.

3 (develop) ha'tteñ suru 発展する Ⓘ; no'bi'ru 伸びる Ⓥ: Our company is growing every year. (*Watashi-tashi no kaisha wa maitoshi nobite iru.*) 私たちの会社は毎年伸びている.

4 (become) (... ni) na'ru (...に)なる Ⓒ: It is growing dark. (*Dañdañ kuraku natte kita.*) だんだん暗くなって

きた.

—— *vt.* **1** (cultivate) ... o sa'ibai suru ...を栽培する Ⓘ; so'date'ru 育てる Ⓥ: He grows roses in a greenhouse. (*Kare wa oñshitsu de bara o saibai shite iru.*) 彼は温室でばらを栽培している.

2 (of hair) no'ba'su 伸ばす Ⓒ; (of a beard) ha'ya'su 生やす Ⓒ: He grew his hair long. (*Kare wa kami no ke o nagaku nobashita.*) 彼は髪の毛を長く伸ばした.

grow up *vi.* o'tona ni na'ru おとなになる Ⓒ.

growth *n.* **1** (increase) zo'oka 増加: a rapid growth of population (*jiñkoo no kyuusoku na zooka*) 人口の急速な増加.

2 (development) ha'tteñ 発展; ha'ttatsu 発達: industrial growth (*sañgyoo no hattatsu*) 産業の発達.

grudge *n.* u'rami' 恨み; ni'kushimi 憎しみ: bear a grudge (*urami o motsu*) 恨みを持つ.

grumble *vi.* fu'hee o iu 不平を言う Ⓒ; ku'joo o nobe'ru 苦情を述べる Ⓥ: Stop grumbling about the food. (*Tabemono no koto de fuhee o iu no wa yoshi nasai.*) 食べ物のことで不平を言うのはよしなさい.

—— *n.* fu'hee 不平; ku'joo 苦情.

guarantee *vt.* ... o ho'shoo suru ...を保証する Ⓘ: He guaranteed that the diamond was genuine. (*Kare wa sono daiyamoñdo ga hoñmono de aru koto o hoshoo shita.*) 彼はそのダイヤモンドが本物であることを保証した.

—— *n.* ho'shoo 保証: This camera has a year guarantee. (*Kono kamera wa ichi-neñ no hoshoo ga tsuite imasu.*) このカメラは 1 年の保証がついています.

guard *vt.* **1** (defend) ... o ma'mo'ru ...を守る Ⓒ: A big dog was guarding the house. (*Ooki-na inu ga uchi o mamotte ita.*) 大きな犬が家を守っていた.

2 (watch) ... o mi'haru ...を見張る Ⓒ: guard a prisoner (*horyo o mi-*

haru) 捕虜を見張る.
— *n.* mi「hari 見張り; ga「adomañ ガードマン: post a guard at the gate (*moñ ni mihari o tateru*) 門に見張りを立てる / a security guard (*keebii-iñ*) 警備員.

guardian *n.* ho「go」sha 保護者; ko「okeñniñ 後見人.

guerilla *n.* ge「rira ゲリラ: guerilla warfare (*gerirasañ*) ゲリラ戦.

guess *vt.* **1** (judge) ... o i「iate」ru ...を言い当てる V; ke「ñto」o o tsu「ke」ru 見当をつける V: He guessed the right answer. (*Kare wa tadashii kotae o iiateta.*) 彼は正しい答えを言い当てた. / I cannot guess how old she is. (*Kanojo ga nañ-sai ka keñ-too ga tsukanai.*) 彼女が何歳か見当がつかない.
2 (think) ... to o「mo」u ...と思う C: I guess he is wrong. (*Kare wa machigatte iru to omou.*) 彼は間違っていると思う.
— *n.* su「isoku 推測; su「iryoo 推量.

guest *n.* kya「ku 客; [polite] o-「kyaku(-sañ) お客(さん): We are having guests for dinner today. (*Kyoo wa o-kyaku o yuuhañ ni maneite imasu.*) 今日はお客を夕飯に招いています.

guidance *n.* shi「doo 指導: Under Mr. Tanaka's guidance, I learned how to ski. (*Watashi wa Tanaka-sañ no shidoo de sukii o naraimashita.*) 私は田中さんの指導でスキーを習いました.

guide *n.* **1** (person) a「ñnainiñ 案内人; ga「ido ガイド: The guide took us around Kyoto. (*Gaido ga Kyooto o añnai shite kureta.*) ガイドが京都を案内してくれた.
2 (book) ga「idobu」kku ガイドブック: a guide to Kamakura (*Kamakura no gaidobukku*) 鎌倉のガイドブック.
— *vt.* **1** (direct) ... o a「ñna」i suru 案内する I; mi「chibi」ku 導く C: He guided me around the city. (*Kare ga machi o añnai shite kureta.*) 彼

が町を案内してくれた.
2 (control) ... o shi「hai suru ...を支配する I; mi「chibi」ku 導く C: I was guided by my conscience. (*Watashi wa ryooshiñ ni shitagatta.*) 私は良心に従った.

guide dog *n.* mo「odookeñ 盲導犬.

guilt *n.* **1** (of crime) yu「uzai 有罪: His guilt was proved by the evidence. (*Kare no yuuzai wa shooko ni yotte risshoo sareta.*) 彼の有罪は証拠によって立証された.
2 (of sense) za「iaku」kañ 罪悪感; tsu「mi no ishiki 罪の意識.

guilty *adj.* yu「uzai no 有罪の: He was declared guilty. (*Kare wa yuuzai to señkoku sareta.*) 彼は有罪と宣告された.

guinea pig *n.* (animal) mo「rumo」tto モルモット; (person) ji「kkeñdai 実験台.

guitar *n.* gi「taa ギター: play the guitar (*gitaa o hiku*) ギターを弾く.

gulf *n.* wa「ñ 湾: the Gulf of Mexico (*Mekishiko wañ*) メキシコ湾.

gum *n.* **1** (chewing gum) chu「uiñ-ga」mu チューインガム: chew gum (*gamu o kamu*) ガムを嚙む.
2 (part of mouth) ha「guki 歯ぐき.

gun *n.* (hand-carried weapon) ju「u 銃; (hand weapon) ke「ñjuu けん銃; pi「sutoru ピストル: fire a gun (*juu o hassha suru*) 銃を発射する.

gunshot *n.* ha「ppoo 発砲; ju「ugeki 銃撃.

gush *vi.* ho「tobashiride」ru ほとばしり出る V; fu「ñshutsu suru 噴出する I: Water gushed out of the pipe. (*Mizu ga kañ kara fuñshutsu shita.*) 水が管から噴出した.

gym *n.* ta「iiku」kañ 体育館; ji「mu ジム.

gymnastics *n.* ta「isoo 体操: rhythmic gymnastics (*shiñtaisoo*) 新体操.

gynecologist *n.* fu「jiñka」-i 婦人科医.

gynecology *n.* fu「jiñ-ka」gaku 婦人科学.

H

habit *n.* **1** (behavior) ku⌐se⌐ 癖: That child has the habit of biting his fingernails. (*Sono ko wa yubi no tsume o kamu kuse ga aru.*) その子は指のつめをかむ癖がある.

2 (custom) shu⌐ukañ 習慣: It is his habit to walk his dog every morning. (*Maiasa inu o sañpo saseru no ga kare no shuukañ da.*) 毎朝犬を散歩させるのが彼の習慣だ.

habitual *adj.* shu⌐ukañ-teki na 習慣的な; i⌐tsu-mo no いつもの: one's habitual breakfast (*itsu-mo no chooshoku*) いつもの朝食.

had better ⟨verb⟩ nasa⌐i …なさい; ⟨verb⟩-ta hoo ga yo⌐i …たほうがよい: You had better do as you are told. (*Iwareta toori ni shi nasai.*) 言われたとおりにしなさい. / You had better not open that door. (*Sono doa wa akenaide oita hoo ga yoi.*) そのドアは開けないでおいたほうがよい.

hail[1] *n.* a⌐rare あられ; hyo⌐o ひょう: A lot of hail fell. (*Hyoo ga takusañ futta.*) ひょうがたくさん降った.

hail[2] *vt.* … o yo⌐bitome⌐ru …を呼び止める Ⓥ: hail a taxi (*takushii o yobitomeru*) タクシーを呼び止める.

hair *n.* **1** (of the head) ka⌐mi no⌐ ke 髪の毛; ka⌐mi⌐ 髪; ke 毛: There is a hair in the soup. (*Suupu ni kami no ke ga ip-poñ haitte iru.*) スープに髪の毛が1本入っている. / I'd like to have my hair cut [set]. (*Kami o katto [setto] shite kudasai.*) 髪をカット[セット]してください.

2 (of the body) ke 毛: a dog hair (*inu no ke*) 犬の毛.

hairbrush *n.* he⌐abu⌐rashi ヘアブラシ.

haircut *n.* sa⌐ñpatsu 散髪: I'd like to have a haircut. (*Sañpatsu o shite moraitai no desu ga.*) 散髪をしてもらいたいのですが.

hairdo *n.* ka⌐migata 髪型; he⌐a-suta⌐iru ヘアスタイル: the latest hairdo (*saishiñ no kamigata*) 最新の髪型.

hairdresser *n.* bi⌐yo⌐oshi 美容師; ri⌐hatsu⌐shi 理髪師: go to the hairdresser's (*biyooiñ e iku*) 美容院へ行く.

hairdryer *n.* do⌐raiyaa ドライヤー.

hairy *adj.* ke⌐buka⌐i 毛深い: a hairy person (*kebukai hito*) 毛深い人.

half *n.* **1** (equal part) ha⌐ñbuñ⌐ 半分; ni-⌐buñ no ichi⌐ 2 分の 1: Cut the apple in half, please. (*Riñgo o hañbuñ ni kitte kudasai.*) りんごを半分に切ってください. / Half of 32 is 16. (*Sañjuu-ni no ni-buñ no ichi wa juuroku desu.*) 32 の 2 分の 1 は 16 です.

2 (of games) ze⌐ñ-[ko⌐o-]hañ 前[後]半: I saw both the first half and the second half of the match. (*Watashi wa shiai no zeñ-hañ to koohañ no ryoohoo o mita.*) 私は試合の前半と後半の両方を見た.

half past *prep.* … ji-ha⌐ñ …時半: I got up at half past six. (*Watashi wa roku-ji-hañ ni okimashita.*) 私は6時半に起きました.

— *adj.* ha⌐ñbuñ⌐ no 半分の; ni-⌐buñ no ichi⌐ no 2 分の 1 の: Half the accidents are due to careless driving. (*Jiko no hañbuñ wa fuchuui na uñteñ ni yoru.*) 事故の半分は不注意な運転による. / Please give me one and a half kilograms of that meat. (*Sono niku o ichi-kiro hañ kudasai.*) その肉を1キロ半下さい.

— *adv.* **1** (partly) ha⌐ñbuñ⌐ (dake) 半分(だけ); na⌐ka⌐ba 半ば: This job is half done. (*Kono shigoto wa nakaba owarimashita.*) この仕事は半ば終わりました.

2 (not completely) fu⌐ju⌐ubuñ ni 不十分に; fu⌐ka⌐ñzeñ ni 不完全に: These potatoes are only half cooked. (*Kono jagaimo wa juubuñ*

ni niete inai.) このじゃがいもは十分に
煮えていない.

hall *n.* **1** (hallway) geⁿkaⁿ 玄関:
an entrance hall (*omote geñkañ*) 表
玄関.

2 (large room) kaⁱkaⁿ 会館; hoⁱo-
ru ホール: a concert hall (*koñsaato
hooru*) コンサートホール / a lecture
hall (*koodoo*) 講堂 / a city hall (*shiyakusho*) 市役所.

ham *n.* haⁱmu ハム: a slice of ham
(*hamu hito-kire*) ハム一切れ.

hammer *n.* kaⁱnazuⁱchi 金づち;
haⁿmaa ハンマー.

— *vt.* ... o kaⁱnazuⁱchi de uⁱchi-
komu …を金づちで打ち込む Ⓒ: ham-
mer nails into a board (*kanazuchi
de ita ni kugi o uchikomu*) 金づちで
板にくぎを打ち込む.

hand *n.* **1** (body part) teⁱ 手: What
are you holding in your hands? (*Te
ni nani o motte iru no desu ka?*)
手に何を持っているのですか. / Raise
your hand if you have a question.
(*Shitsumoñ ga areba te o age
nasai.*) 質問があれば手を挙げなさい.

2 (pointer) haⁱri 針: the hour
[minute, second] hand (*ji*[*fuñ,
byoo*]*-shiñ*) 時[分, 秒]針 / The
hands of the clock pointed to 6:30.
(*Tokee no hari wa roku-ji hañ o
sashite ita.*) 時計の針は 6 時半を指し
ていた.

3 (assistance) teⁱ 手; teⁱdaⁱsuke 手
助け: Give me a hand with the
homework. (*Shukudai ni te o kashite kudasai.*) 宿題に手を貸してくだ
さい.

on the other hand *adv.* taⁱhoⁱo
de wa 他方では.

— *vt.* ... o waⁱtasu …を渡す Ⓒ: I
handed the money to the taxi
driver. (*Watashi wa takushii no
uñteñshu ni o-kane o watashita.*)
私はタクシーの運転手にお金を渡した.

hand in *vt.* ... o teⁱeshutsu suru
…を提出する Ⓘ.

hand out *vt.* ... o kuⁱbaⁱru …を配
る Ⓒ.

handbag *n.* haⁿdobaⁱggu ハンドバッ

グ: a leather handbag (*kawa no hañ-
dobaggu*) 革のハンドバッグ.

hand baggage *n.* teⁱniⁱmotsu 手
荷物.

handful *n.* **1** (amount in the
hand) hiⁱtoⁱ-tsukami ひとつかみ; hi-
ⁱtoⁱ-nigiri ひと握り: a handful of
flour (*hito-tsukami no komugiko*)
ひとつかみの小麦粉.

2 (small number) shoⁱosuⁱu 少数:
a handful of spectators (*shoosuu
no kañkyaku*) 少数の観客.

handkerchief *n.* haⁿkachi ハンカ
チ: blow one's nose into one's handkerchief (*hañkachi de hana o kamu*) ハンカチで鼻をかむ.

handle *n.* toⁱtte 取っ手; e 柄; haⁿ-
doru ハンドル: a door handle (*doa no
totte*) ドアの取っ手 / the handle of a
knife (*naifu no e*) ナイフの柄. ★ Japanese '*hañdoru*' is also used in the
sense of 'steering wheel.'

— *vt.* **1** (hold) ... o teⁱ de aⁱtsu-
kau …を手で扱う Ⓒ; tsuⁱkau 使う
Ⓒ: He handles his chopsticks very
well. (*Kare wa hashi o totemo
joozu ni tsukau.*) 彼は箸をとてもじょ
うずに使う.

2 (deal with) ... o toⁱriatsukau …を
取り扱う Ⓒ; shoⁱri suru 処理する Ⓘ:
handle a customer politely (*o-kyaku o teenee ni atsukau*) お客を丁寧
に扱う / handle a problem (*moñdai
o shori suru*) 問題を処理する.

3 (deal in) ... o toⁱriatsukau …を取
り扱う Ⓒ; aⁱkinaⁱu 商う Ⓒ: handle
electrical goods (*deñki-seehiñ o
toriatsukau*) 電気製品を取り扱う.

handsome *adj.* **1** (good looking)
kaⁱodachi no yoⁱi 顔立ちのよい; haⁱ-
ñsamu na ハンサムな: a handsome
man (*bidañshi*) 美男子.

2 (large) kaⁱnari no かなりの; soⁱo-
too na 相当な: a handsome sum of
money (*kanari no kiñgaku*) かなりの
金額.

3 (generous) kiⁱmae no yoⁱi 気前の
よい: a handsome tip (*kimae no yoi
chippu*) 気前のよいチップ.

handwriting *n.* hiⁱsseki 筆跡;

shoˈtai 書体; jiˈ 字: neat handwriting (*kiree na ji*) きれいな字.

handy *adj.* **1** (easy to use) beˈnri na 便利な; teˈgoro na 手ごろな: a handy camera (*tegoro na kamera*) 手ごろなカメラ.
2 (skillful) kiˈyoo na 器用な; joˈozuˈ na じょうずな: He is handy with tools. (*Kare wa doogu o atsukau no ga kiyoo da.*) 彼は道具を扱うのが器用だ.
3 (nearby) teˈjika na 手近な: Keep this dictionary handy. (*Kono jisho o tejika ni oite oki nasai.*) この辞書を手近に置いておきなさい.

hang *vt.* **1** (support from above) ... o kaˈkeˈru ...を掛ける Ⓥ; tsuˈrusu つるす Ⓒ: Where shall I hang this calendar? (*Kono kareñdaa wa doko ni kakemasu ka?*) このカレンダーはどこに掛けますか. / hang curtains over a window (*mado ni kaateñ o tsurusu*) 窓にカーテンをつるす.
2 (fasten to a wall) ... o kaˈkeˈru ...を掛ける Ⓥ; kaˈzaru 飾る Ⓒ: I hung the picture at eye level. (*Watashi wa sono e o me no takasa ni kaketa.*) 私はその絵を目の高さに掛けた.
3 (execute) ... o koˈoshuˈkee ni suru ...を絞首刑にする Ⓘ; kuˈbi o tsuru 首をつる Ⓒ: be hanged for murder (*satsujiñzai de kooshukee ni naru*) 殺人罪で絞首刑になる / She committed suicide by hanging herself. (*Kanojo wa kubi o tsutte jisatsu shita.*) 彼女は首をつって自殺した.
— *vi.* kaˈkaˈru 掛かる Ⓒ; buˈrasagatte iru ぶら下がっている Ⓥ: The painting hung on the wall. (*Sono e wa kabe ni kakatte ita.*) その絵は壁に掛かっていた. / A long rope was hanging from the ceiling. (*Nagai roopu ga teñjoo kara burasagatte ita.*) 長いローブが天井からぶら下がっていた.

hang up *vi.* deˈñwa o kiˈru 電話を切る Ⓒ: Hang up and wait, please. (*Ittañ kitte o-machi kudasai.*) いったん切ってお待ちください.

happen *vi.* **1** (occur) oˈkoˈru 起こ

る Ⓒ; shoˈojiru 生じる Ⓥ: Please tell us how the accident happened. (*Doo shite sono jiko ga okita no ka hanashite kudasai.*) どうしてその事故が起きたのか話してください. / What happened? (*Doo shita ñ desu ka?*) どうしたんですか.
2 (chance) guˈuzeñ [taˈrmatama] ⟨verb⟩ 偶然[たまたま]...: Luckily, I happened to have enough money on me. (*Watashi wa uñ yoku guuzeñ o-kane o juubuñ ni mochiawasete ita.*) 私は運よく偶然お金を十分に持ち合わせていた. / The customer was a woman I happened to know. (*Sono o-kyaku wa tamatama watashi ga shitte iru josee datta.*) そのお客はたまたま私が知っている女性だった.

happening *n.* deˈkiˈgoto 出来事; jiˈkeñ 事件: an unfortunate happening (*fukoo na dekigoto*) 不幸な出来事.

happily *adv.* koˈofuku ni 幸福に; taˈnoshi-soˈo ni 楽しそうに; yuˈkai ni 愉快に: laugh happily (*tanoshisoo ni warau*) 楽しそうに笑う.

happiness *n.* koˈofuku 幸福; (good luck) koˈouñ 幸運; yuˈkai 愉快: I wish you every happiness. (*Anata no go-takoo o o-inori shimasu.*) あなたのご多幸をお祈りします.

happy *adj.* **1** (pleasurable; contented) koˈofuku na 幸福な; shiˈawase na 幸せな; uˈreshiˈi うれしい: a happy life (*koofuku na seekatsu*) 幸福な生活 / a happy marriage (*shiawase na kekkoñ*) 幸せな結婚 / a happy event (*ureshii dekigoto*) うれしい出来事 / I am most happy to meet you. (*O-me ni kakarete ureshii desu.*) お目にかかれてうれしいです. / Happy birthday! (*O-tañjoobi omedetoo.*) お誕生日おめでとう. / Happy New Year! (*Akemashite omedetoo.*) 明けましておめでとう.
2 (satisfied) maˈñzoku na 満足な; naˈttoku shita [shite iru] 納得した[している]: I am happy in my present job. (*Watashi wa ima no shigoto ni mañzoku shite imasu.*) 私は今の

仕事に満足しています.

3 (lucky) koﾞoun na 幸運な; uﾞn no yoﾞi 運のよい: I met him by a happy chance. (*Watashi wa uñ yoku kare ni atta.*) 私は運よく彼に会った.

harbor *n.* miﾞnato 港: arrive in harbor (*minato ni hairu*) 港に入る.

★ Japanese '*minato*' also refers to 'port.'

hard *adj.* **1** (not soft) kaﾞtai 硬い; (solid) kaﾞtai 堅い; (not easy to break) kaﾞtai 固い: hard ground (*katai jimeñ*) 硬い地面 / hard wood (*katai zaimoku*) 堅い材木 / a hard knot (*katai musubime*) 固い結び目 / She boiled the eggs hard. (*Kanojo wa tamago o kataku yudeta.*) 彼女は卵を固くゆでた.

2 (difficult) muﾞzukashii 難しい; koﾞñnañ na 困難な: a hard question (*muzukashii shitsumoñ*) 難しい質問 / It was hard to understand her explanation. (*Kanojo no setsumee o rikai suru no wa koññañ datta.*) 彼女の説明を理解するのは困難だった.

3 (severe) kiﾞbishiﾞi 厳しい; geﾞñkaku na 厳格な: hard training (*kibishii kuñreñ*) 厳しい訓練 / a hard winter (*kibishii fuyu*) 厳しい冬 / The boss is hard on us all. (*Buchoo wa wareware miñna ni tsuraku ataru.*) 部長はわれわれみんなにつらく当たる.

4 (eager) neﾞsshiñ na 熱心な; kiﾞñbeñ na 勤勉な: a hard worker (*kiñbeñka*) 勤勉家.

— *adv.* **1** (with effort) neﾞsshiñ ni 熱心に; iﾞsshookeﾞñmee (ni) 一生懸命に: He worked hard. (*Kare wa isshookeñmee* (*ni*) *hataraita.*) 彼は一生懸命(に)働いた.

2 (strongly) hiﾞdoku ひどく; haﾞgeﾞshiku 激しく: The wind is blowing hard. (*Kaze ga hageshiku fuite iru.*) 風が激しく吹いている.

harden *vt.* **1** (cause to become hard) ... o kaﾞtaku suru ...を堅くする ⊤; kaﾞtameru 固める Ⅴ: Heat hardens clay. (*Netsu wa neñdo o kataku suru.*) 熱は粘土を固くする.

2 [figurative use] ... o hiﾞjoo ni suru ...を非情にする ⊤: harden one's heart (*kokoro o hijoo ni suru*) 心を非情にする.

— *vi.* kaﾞtaku naﾞru 堅くなる Ⓒ; kaﾞtamaru 固まる Ⓒ: The mud hardened. (*Doro ga katamatta.*) 泥が固まった. / Her face hardened with anger. (*Kare no kao wa ikari de kowabatta.*) 彼の顔を怒りでこわばった.

hardly *adv.* **1** (scarcely) hoﾞtoﾞñdo ... naﾞi ほとんど...ない: The old man could hardly walk. (*Sono roojiñ wa hotoñdo aruku koto ga dekinakatta.*) その老人はほとんど歩くことができなかった. / There is hardly any beer left. (*Biiru wa hotoñdo nokotte inai.*) ビールはほとんど残っていない.

2 (not really) toﾞtemo ... deﾞkiﾞnai とても...できない: I can hardly demand money from him. (*Totemo kare ni o-kane o yookyuu dekinai.*) とても彼にお金を要求できない.

3 (unlikely) oﾞsoﾞraku ... <verb>-soo mo naﾞi 恐らく...そうもない: A typhoon is hardly likely to hit us. (*Taifuu wa osoraku ki-soo mo nai.*) 台風は恐らく来そうもない.

hardly ... when ... <verb> ga haﾞyaﾞi ka ...が早いか: He had hardly seen the policeman when he started running. (*Kare wa keekañ o miru ga hayai ka nigedashita.*) 彼は警官を見るが早いか逃げ出した.

hardship *n.* kuﾞnañ 苦難; kuﾞrushimiﾞ 苦しみ: endure hardship (*kunañ ni taeru*) 苦難に耐える.

hardware *n.* **1** (metal goods) kaﾞnamonoﾞrui 金物類: a hardware store (*kanomono-teñ*) 金物店.

2 (machinery) haﾞadoueﾞa ハードウエア.

hardy *adj.* kuﾞkkyoo na 強健な; gaﾞñkeñ na 頑健な: a hardy young man (*kukkyoo na wakamono*) 屈強な若者.

hare *n.* noﾞuﾞsagi 野うさぎ.

harm *n.* (damage) gaﾞi 害; (wrong) waﾞruﾞi koﾞtoﾞ 悪いこと: do more harm than good (*eki yori mo gai ni naru*) 益よりも害になる / I meant no harm by what I said. (*Warugi ga atte itta no de wa arimaseñ.*) 悪気があって言ったのではありません.

— *vt.* ... o ga⌐isu¬ru ...を害する Ⓣ; ki⌐zutsuke¬ru 傷つける Ⓥ: harm a person's reputation (*hito no meeyo o kizutsukeru*) 人の名誉を傷つける.

harmful *adj.* yu⌐ugai na 有害な; ga⌐i ni naru 害になる: a harmful insect (*yuugai na mushi*) 有害な虫 / Too much alcohol is harmful to the health. (*Arukooru no nomisugi wa keñkoo ni gai ni narimasu.*) アルコールの飲み過ぎは健康に害になります.

harmless *adj.* mu⌐gai na 無害な; a⌐kui no nai 悪意のない: a harmless snake (*mugai na hebi*) 無害なへび / a harmless joke (*akui no nai joodañ*) 悪意のない冗談.

harmonious *adj.* **1** (friendly) na⌐ka no yoi 仲の良い: a harmonious married couple (*naka no yoi fuufu*) 仲の良い夫婦.

2 (tasteful) cho⌐rowa shita [shite iru] 調和した[している]: a harmonious combination of colors (*choowa shita iro no kumiawase*) 調和した色の組み合わせ.

3 (tuneful) u⌐tsukushi¬i 美しい: a harmonious melody (*utsukushii merodii*) 美しいメロディー.

harmony *n.* **1** (pleasing combination) cho⌐rowa 調和: The colors in this picture are in harmony. (*Kono e no iro wa choowa ga torete iru.*) この絵の色は調和がとれている.

2 (agreement) i⌐tchi 一致: Your ideas are in harmony with mine. (*Anata no kañgae wa watashi no to itchi shite iru.*) あなたの考えは私のと一致している.

3 (of music) ha⌐amonii ハーモニー; wa⌐see 和声; wa⌐oñ 和音.

harsh *adj.* **1** (rough) a⌐rai 粗い; te⌐za¬wari ga wa⌐ru¬i 手触りが悪い: This cloth is harsh to the touch. (*Kono kire wa tezawari ga warui.*) このきれは手触りが悪い.

2 (unpleasant to ears) mi⌐miza¬-wari na 耳障りな; (to eyes) do⌐gi-tsui どぎつい: a harsh voice (*mimizawari na koe*) 耳障りな声 / harsh colors (*dogitsui iro*) どぎつい色.

3 (severe) ki⌐bishi¬i 厳しい: a harsh winter (*kibishii fuyu*) 厳しい冬 / a harsh punishment (*geñbatsu*) 厳罰.

harvest *n.* **1** (gathering) shu⌐u-kaku 収穫: a rice harvest (*kome no shuukaku*) 米の収穫.

2 (time) shu⌐ukaku¬ki 収穫期; to⌐ri-ire ji¬ki 取り入れ時期: The villagers are busy during the harvest. (*Nooson no hito-tachi wa toriire jiki wa isogashii.*) 農村の人たちは取り入れ時期は忙しい.

3 (amount) shu⌐ukaku¬daka 収穫高: The harvest was worse than anticipated. (*Shuukakudaka wa yosoo yori mo warukatta.*) 収穫高は予想よりも悪かった. / a good [bad] harvest (*hoosaku [kyoosaku]*) 豊作[凶作].

4 (consequences) se⌐ika 成果: reap the harvest of one's labors (*doryoku no seeka o te ni suru*) 努力の成果を手にする.

— *vt.* ... o shu⌐ukaku suru ...を収穫する Ⓣ; ka⌐ri-ire¬ru 刈り入れる Ⓥ: harvest crops (*sakumotsu o kari-ireru*) 作物を刈り入れる.

haste *n.* i⌐sogi¬ 急ぎ; a⌐wateru ko-to¬ 慌てること: a matter requiring haste (*kyuu o yoosuru koto*) 急を要すること / There is no need for all this haste. (*Koñna ni awateru hi-tsuyoo wa nai.*) こんなに慌てる必要はない.

hasten *vt.* ... o i⌐soga¬su ...を急がす Ⓒ; ha⌐yame¬ru 速める Ⓥ: hasten one's pace (*ashi o hayameru*) 足を速める.

— *vi.* i⌐so¬gu 急ぐ Ⓒ: He hastened home. (*Kare wa isoide uchi e ka-etta.*) 彼は急いで家へ帰った.

hat *n.* bo⌐oshi 帽子: put on [take off] a hat (*booshi o kaburu [nugu]*) 帽子をかぶる[脱ぐ] / wear a hat (*booshi o kabutte iru*) 帽子をかぶっている.

★ 'Cap' is also called 'booshi'.

hatch[1] *n.* sho⌐oko⌐oguchi 昇降口:
an escape hatch (hijooyoo dasshu-
tsuguchi) 非常用脱出口.

hatch[2] *vt.* (ta⌐ma⌐go o) ka⌐esu (卵
を)かえす C; fu⌐ka suru ふ化する I:
The hen hatched the eggs. (Niwatori ga tamago o kaeshita.) にわとり
が卵をかえした.
—— *vi.* (ta⌐ma⌐go ga) ka⌐eru (卵が)か
える C.

hate *vt.* **1** (detest) ... o (hi⌐doku)
ki⌐rau ...を(ひどく)嫌う C; ni⌐ku⌐mu
憎む C: The child hates carrots.
(Sono ko wa niñjiñ ga daikirai da.)
その子はにんじんが大嫌いだ. / I hate
violence. (Watashi wa booryoku o
nikumu.) 私は暴力を憎む.
2 (dislike) ... o i⌐yaga⌐ru ...をいやがる
C; ⟨verb⟩-taku nai ...たくない: She
hates people interrupting her when
she is talking. (Kanojo wa hanashite iru toki hito ga jama suru no
o iyagaru.) 彼女は話しているとき人が
じゃまするのをいやがる. / I hate to
bother you. (Anata o jama shitaku
arimaseñ.) あなたをじゃましたくありませ
ん.
—— *n.* ni⌐kushimi 憎しみ; zo⌐o-o 憎
悪: love and hate (ai to nikushimi)
愛と憎しみ.

hateful *adj.* ni⌐kumu be⌐ki 憎むべき;
i⌐ya⌐ na いやな: a hateful crime
(nikumu beki hañzai) 憎むべき犯罪.

hatred *n.* ni⌐kushimi 憎しみ; zo⌐o-o
憎悪: I feel hatred for people who
tell lies. (Watashi wa uso o tsuku
hito o nikumu.) 私はうそをつく人を憎
む. / He looked at me with hatred.
(Kare wa zoo-o no me de watashi
o mita.) 彼は憎悪の目で私を見た.

haughty *adj.* ko⌐omañ na 高慢な;
o⌐ohee na 横柄な: He looks haughty. (Kare wa koomañ na kao o
shite iru.) 彼は高慢な顔をしている.

have[1] *vt.* **1** (possess) ... o mo⌐tte iru
...を持っている V; (of things) ... ga
a⌐ru ...がある C; (of people) ... ga
i⌐ru ...がいる V: I have a map. (Watashi wa chizu o motte imasu.) 私

は地図を持っています. / We have a factory in Kobe. (Koobe ni koojoo ga
arimasu.) 神戸に工場があります. / Do
you have a smaller one? (Motto
chiisai no wa arimasu ka?) もっと
小さいのはありますか. / I have three
children. (Watashi wa kodomo ga
sañ-niñ imasu.) 私は子どもが 3 人いま
す.
2 (take) ... o to⌐ru ...をとる C; (eat)
ta⌐be⌐ru 食べる V; (drink) no⌐mu 飲
む C: have a meal (shokuji o toru)
食事をとる / have a drink (nomimono o nomu) 飲物を飲む / Can I
have breakfast in my room? (Chooshoku wa heya de toremasu ka?)
朝食は部屋でとれますか. / What did
you have for lunch? (Chuushoku
ni nani o tabemashita ka?) 昼食に
何を食べましたか.
3 (obtain; receive) ... o mo⌐rau ...を
もらう V; u⌐ke⌐ru 受ける V: She had
a letter from her mother. (Kanojo
wa haha-oya kara tegami o moratta.) 彼女は母親から手紙をもらった. /
I'll have that red sweater. (Sono
akai seetaa o moraimasu.) その赤い
セーターをもらいます. / May I have a
receipt? (Reshiito o kudasai.) レシー
トを下さい.
4 (hold) ... o hi⌐ra⌐ku ...を開く C; ...
ga a⌐ru ...がある C: have a party
(paatii o hiraku) パーティーを開く / I
have a meeting this afternoon.
(Gogo ni kaigi ga arimasu.) 午後に
会議があります.
5 (suffer) ... ni ka⌐ka⌐tte i⌐ru ...にか
かっている V. ★ The Japanese verb
used varies according to the kind
of disease, pain, etc: have a headache [toothache] (atama [ha] ga
itai) 頭[歯]が痛い / I have a pain
here. (Koko ga itai.) ここが痛い. /
have a cold (kaze o hiite iru) かぜを
ひいている / have a cough (seki ga
deru) 咳が出る / have a fever (netsu
ga aru) 熱がある / have chills (samuke ga suru) 寒気がする.
6 (think; feel) ... o mo⌐tte iru ...を
持っている V: I have some doubts

about this project. (*Watashi wa kono keekaku ni ikura-ka gimon o motte iru.*) 私はこの計画にいくらか疑問を持っている.

7 [experience] ... o keʼekeñ suru ...を経験する Ⓣ; taʼnoshiʼmu 楽しむ Ⓒ: I hope you have a nice holiday. (*Yoi kyuuka o tanoshimu koto o inorimasu.*) よい休暇を楽しむことを祈ります.

8 [give birth] ... o uʼmu ...を生む Ⓒ: She had a child when she was 35. (*Kanojo wa sañjuu-go-sai no toki akañboo o uñda.*) 彼女は 35 歳のとき赤ん坊を生んだ.

9 [causative use] ⟨verb⟩-(sa)seru (さ)せる Ⓥ; ⟨verb⟩-te[de] moʼrau て[で]もらう Ⓒ: I'll have him come tomorrow. (*Ashita kare o kosasemashoo.*) あした彼を来させましょう. / I'd like to have these shirts ironed. (*Kono shatsu ni airoñ o kakete moraitai no desu ga.*) このシャツにアイロンをかけてもらいたいのですが.

10 [passive use] ⟨verb⟩-[ra]reru ...[ら]れる Ⓥ: Mrs. Tanaka had all her money stolen. (*Tanaka-sañ wa o-kane o zeñbu nusumareta.*) 田中さんはお金を全部盗まれた. / He had his left leg broken in the accident. (*Kare wa sono jiko de hidari ashi o otta.*) 彼はその事故で左足を折った.

have² *aux.* **1** [recent past] ⟨verb⟩-te [de] shiʼmatta ...て[で]しまった: I have already read that book. (*Watashi wa moo sono hoñ o yoñde shimaimashita.*) 私はもうその本を読んでしまいました.

2 [past experience] ⟨verb⟩-ta koʼto ga aru ...たことがある: I have never been to Kyoto. (*Watashi wa Kyooto e itta koto ga arimaseñ.*) 私は京都へ行ったことがありません.

3 [continuing state] ⟨verb⟩-te[de] iʼru ...て[で]いる: We have lived in this house for ten years. (*Watashi-tachi wa kono uchi ni juu-neñ suñde imasu.*) 私たちはこの家に 10 年住んでいます.

haven *n.* (harbor) miʼnato 港; (shel-ter) hiʼnañjo 避難所.

have to 1 [obligation] ⟨verb⟩-naʼ-kereba naʼraʼnai ...なければならない: Excuse me, but I have to leave now. (*Shitsuree desu ga moo ika-nakereba narimaseñ.*) 失礼ですがもう行かなければなりません. / You have to do as you are told. (*Kimi wa iwa-reta toori ni shinakereba naranai.*) 君は言われたとおりにしなければならない.

2 [negative use] hiʼtsuyoo wa naʼi 必要はない: You don't have to go if you don't want to. (*Ikitaku nake-reba iku hitsuyoo wa arimaseñ.*) 行きたくなければ行く必要はありません.

3 [certain inference] ... ni chiʼgai naʼi ...にちがいない: You have to be mistaken. (*Anata wa machigaeta ni chigai arimaseñ.*) あなたは間違えたにちがいありません.

hay *n.* hoʼshikusa 干し草.

hazard *n.* kiʼkeñ 危険: the hazards of mountain-climbing (*tozañ no kikeñ*) 登山の危険.

he *pron.* **1** (male) kaʼre 彼; aʼnoʼ hito あの人; [polite] aʼno kataʼ あの方: He is a businessman. (*Kare wa jitsugyooka desu.*) 彼は実業家です. / "Who is he?" "He is Mr. Tanaka." (*"Ano hito wa dare desu ka?" "(Ano hito wa) Tanaka-sañ desu."*) 「あの人はだれですか」「(あの人は)田中さんです」★ When referring to a person, the occupation or position is used instead of 'he': "Is Mr. Yoshida, the de-partment head, in now?" "He's out on business." (*"Yoshida buchoo wa ima oide desu ka?" "Buchoo wa shigoto de gaishutsu shite orimasu."*) 「吉田部長はいまおいでですか」「部長は仕事で外出しております」

2 (general) ★ Not translated in Japanese: Everybody should do his best. (*Dare mo ga zeñryoku o tsukusu beki da.*) だれもが全力を尽くすべきだ.

head *n.* **1** (body part) aʼtamaʼ 頭: He hit me on the head. (*Kare wa* watashi no atama o nagutta.) 彼は私の頭を殴った. / Mind your head. (Zujoo chuui.) 頭上注意. ★ English 'head' often corresponds to Japanese 'kao' (face) and 'kubi' (neck): / Don't put your head out of the window. (Mado kara kao [kubi] o dashite wa ikemaseñ.) 窓から顔[首]を出してはいけません.

2 (intellect; imagination) a「tama¹ 頭; zu¹noo 頭脳: Come on! Use your head. (Saa, atama o tsukae.) さあ, 頭を使え. / A brilliant idea came into my head. (Umai kañgae ga atama ni ukañda.) うまい考えが頭に浮かんだ.

3 (top) i「chibañ ue いちばん上; se「ñtañ 先端: Your name is at the head of the list. (Anata no namae wa hyoo no ichibañ ue ni arimasu.) あなたの名前は表のいちばん上にあります.

4 (chief) -choo 長; ka「shira¹ 頭: the head of a school (koochoo) 校長 / a department head (buchoo) 部長.

5 (individual) ni「ñzuu 人数; a「tamaka¹zu 頭数: count heads (niñzuu o kazoeru) 人数を数える / twenty head of cattle (ushi nijut-too) 牛20頭.

6 (of a coin) o「mote¹ 表: Heads or tails? (Omote ka ura ka?) 表か裏か.
— vt. **1** (be foremost) ...no se「ñtoo ni ta¹tsu ...の先頭に立つ ©: head a procession (gyooretsu no señtoo ni tatsu) 行列の先頭に立つ. **2** (lead) ...o hi「kii¹ru ...を率いる ▽: head the association (kai o hikiiru) 会を率いる. **3** (direct) ...no ho¹o e mu「keru ...の方へ向ける ▽: head a boat for the shore (booto o kishi no hoo e mukeru) ボートを岸の方へ向ける.
— vi. (... ni mu「katte) su「sumu (...に向かって)進む ©: head south (minami ni mukatte susumu) 南に向かって進む.

headache n. zu「tsuu 頭痛: I have a headache. (Watashi wa zutsuu ga suru.) 私は頭痛がする.

headline n. mi「dashi 見出し: quickly scan the headlines (midashi o isoide satto miru) 見出しを急いでさっと見る.

head office n. ho「ñsha 本社; ho「ñteñ 本店.

headquarters n. ho「ñsha 本社; ho「ñbu 本部: the headquarters of a company (kaisha no hoñsha) 会社の本社.

heal vt. ... o na「o¹su ...を治す ©: It took a long time to heal the broken bone. (Kossetsu o naosu no ni nagai jikañ ga kakatta.) 骨折を治すのに長い時間がかかった.
— vi. na「o¹ru 治る ©: The wound has finally healed. (Kizu ga yatto naotta.) 傷がやっと治った.

health n. **1** (being well) ke「ñkoo 健康: Too much alcohol is bad for the health. (Kado no arukooru wa keñkoo ni warui.) 過度のアルコールは健康に悪い. **2** (physical condition) ke「ñkoo-jo¹otai 健康状態; ka「rada no guai 体の具合: I'm in good [poor] health these days. (Watashi wa saikiñ karada no guai ga yoi [yoku nai].) 私は最近体の具合がよい[よくない].

health insurance n. ke「ñkoo-ho¹keñ 健康保険: join a health insurance scheme (keñkoo-hokeñ ni kanyuu suru) 健康保険に加入する.

healthy adj. **1** (having good health) ke「ñkoo na 健康な; ke「ñzeñ na 健全な: a healthy child (keñkoo na kodomo) 健康な子ども / I feel very healthy these days. (Watashi wa saikiñ totemo keñkoo desu.) 私は最近とても健康です. **2** (producing good health) ke「ñkoo-teki na 健康的な; ke「ñkoo ni yo¹i 健康によい: a healthy lifestyle (keñkoo-teki na seekatsu-yoo-shiki) 健康的な生活様式 / The climate here is not very healthy. (Koko no kikoo wa keñkoo ni amari yoku nai.) ここの気候は健康にあまりよくない.

heap n. tsu「mikasane 積み重ね;

(... no) ya「ma¹ (...の)山: a heap of rubbish (*gomi no yama*) ごみの山 / The magazines and books lay in a heap on the floor. (*Zasshi ya hoñ ga yuka ni tsumikasanete atta.*) 雑誌や本が床に積み重ねてあった.

— *vt.* ... o tsu「miage」ru ...を積み上げる Ⓥ; ya「mamori ni suru 山盛りにする Ⓘ: heap up leaves (*ki no ha o tsumiageru*) 木の葉を積み上げる / heap strawberries on a plate (*ichigo o sara ni yamamori ni suru*) いちごを皿に山盛りにする.

hear *vt.* **1** (perceive sounds) ... ga ki「koeru ...が聞こえる Ⓥ; ... o ki「ku ...を聞く Ⓒ: Can you hear me? (*Kikoemasu ka?*) 聞こえますか. / I heard the door shut. (*Watashi wa doa ga shimaru oto o kiita.*) 私はドアが閉まる音を聞いた.

2 (be told) ... o ki「ku ...を聞く Ⓒ; mi「mi¹ ni suru 耳にする Ⓘ: Have you heard the news? (*Sono nyuusu o kikimashita ka?*) そのニュースを聞きましたか. / I heard a strange rumor last night. (*Watashi wa sakuya heñ na uwasa o mimi ni shita.*) 私は昨夜変なうわさを耳にした.

3 (listen to) ... o ki「ku ...を聞く Ⓒ; ... ni mi「mi¹ o ka「tamuke」ru ...に耳を傾ける Ⓥ: We should hear Miss Watanabe's explanation. (*Wareware wa Watanabe-sañ no setsumee ni mimi o katamukeru beki da.*) われわれは渡辺さんの説明に耳を傾けるべきだ.

— *vi.* mi「mi¹ ga ki「koeru 耳が聞こえる Ⓥ: My grandmother cannot hear very well. (*Watashi no sobo wa amari yoku mimi ga kikoenai.*) 私の祖母はあまりよく耳が聞こえない.

hear from ... *vt.* ... kara te「gami [de「ñwa] o mo「rau ...から手紙[電話]をもらう Ⓒ.

hear of ... *vt.* ... no u「wasa o ki「ku ...のうわさを聞く Ⓒ.

hearing *n.* **1** (sense) cho「oryoku 聴力; cho「okaku 聴覚: lose one's hearing (*mimi ga kikoenaku naru*) 耳が聞こえなくなる / be hard of

hearing (*mimi ga tooi*) 耳が遠い.

2 (enquiry) cho「omo「ñkai 聴聞会: a public hearing (*koochookai*) 公聴会.

heart *n.* **1** (organ) shi「ñzoo 心臓: My heart is beating fast. (*Shiñzoo ga dokidoki shite iru.*) 心臓がどきどきしている.

2 (emotion) ko「koro 心; ka「ñjoo 感情: She has a kind heart. (*Kanojo wa yasashii kokoro o motte iru.*) 彼女は優しい心を持っている.

3 (compassion) a「ijoo 愛情; o「moiyari 思いやり: He has no heart. (*Kare wa omoiyari ga nai.*) 彼は思いやりがない.

4 (the center) chu「ushiñ 中心; ka「kushiñ 核心: the heart of the city (*shi no chuushiñbu*) 市の中心部 / the heart of a problem (*jikeñ no kakushiñ*) 事件の核心.

5 (of cards) ha「ato ハート: the king of hearts (*haato no kiñgu*) ハートのキング.

heart attack *n.* shi「ñzoo-ho「ssa 心臓発作; shi「ñzoo ma「hi 心臓まひ.

heartburn *n.* mu「neyake 胸焼け: have heartburn (*muneyake ga suru*) 胸焼けがする.

heart disease *n.* shi「ñzoobyoo 心臓病.

hearty *adj.* **1** (very friendly) ko「koro kara no 心からの: receive a hearty welcome (*kokoro kara no kañgee o ukeru*) 心からの歓迎を受ける.

2 (very cheerful) ge「ñki na 元気な; o「osee na 旺盛な: have a hearty appetite (*shokuyoku ga oosee da*) 食欲が旺盛だ.

heat *n.* **1** (high temperature) ne「tsu¹ 熱; a「tsusa 暑さ: the heat of the sun (*taiyoo netsu*) 太陽熱 / Don't excercise in the heat of the day. (*Nitchuu no atsusa no naka de uñdoo suru no wa yoshi nasai.*) 日中の暑さの中で運動するのはよしなさい.

2 (excitement) ko「ofuñ 興奮; ne「sshi¹ñsa 熱心さ: take the heat off (*koofuñ o samasu*) 興奮をさます.

3 (preliminary competition) se`n 選; se`n 戦: trial heats (yose`n) 予選.
— vt. ... o ne`ssuru ...を熱する C; a`tatame`ru 暖[温]める V: heat a room (heya o atatameru) 部屋を暖める / heat up soup (suupu o atatameru) スープを温める / heat water (o-yu o wakasu) お湯を沸かす.
— vi. a`tsuku naru 熱くなる C; a`tatama`ru 暖[温]まる C.

heater n. da`nbooki`gu 暖房器具; hi`itaa ヒーター; su`too`bu ストーブ: an electric [oil] heater (de`nki [se-kiyu] sutoobu) 電気[石油]ストーブ.

heave vt. ... o mo`chiageru ...を持ち上げる V: heave a heavy suitcase (omoi suutsukeesu o mochiageru) 重いスーツケースを持ち上げる.

heaven n. **1** (of religion) te`ngoku 天国: God is in heaven. (Kami wa tengoku ni iru.) 神は天国にいる.
2 (state of bliss) go`kuraku 極楽; ra`kuen 楽園: A hot bath would be sheer heaven. (Atatakai o-furo wa masa ni gokuraku da.) 温かいおふろはまさに極楽だ.

heavily adv. **1** (excessively) ta`i-ryoo ni 大量に; ta`kusa`n たくさん; hi`doku ひどく: rain heavily (tairyoo ni ame ga furu) 大量に雨が降る / smoke heavily (hidoku tabako o suu) ひどくたばこを吸う.
2 (densely) mi`tsu ni 密に: a heavily populated area (jinkoo no mitsu na chiiki) 人口の密な地域.
3 (with weight) o`mosoo ni 重そうに; o`moku 重く: The fruit hung heavily from the branches. (Kudamono ga omosoo ni eda ni natte ita.) 果物が重そうに枝になっていた.

heavy adj. **1** (of great weight) o`moi 重い: This sofa is too heavy for me to move. (Kono sofaa wa omokute watashi ni wa ugokasenai.) このソファーは重くて私には動かせない.
2 (of degree of weight) o`mosa ga ... a`ru 重さが...ある C: "How heavy is the suitcase?" "It's twenty kilograms." ("Kono suutsukeesu wa

omosa ga dono kurai arimasu ka?" "Nijuk-kiro arimasu.") 「このスーツケースは重さがどのくらいありますか」「20 キロあります」
3 (of great force, amount, degree) ha`geshi`i 激しい; ta`iryoo no 大量の: a heavy blow (tsuuda) 痛打 / a heavy drinker (oozakenomi) 大酒飲み / a heavy rain (goou) 豪雨.
4 (hard) ho`ne no ore`ru 骨の折れる; tsu`rai つらい: heavy work (hone no oreru shigoto) 骨の折れる仕事 / I had a heavy day yesterday. (Kinoo wa tsurai ichinichi datta.) きのうはつらい 1 日だった.
5 (difficult to digest) shi`tsuko`i しつこい: heavy food (shitsukoi tabemono) しつこい食べ物.
6 (sad) shi`zunda 沈んだ; ka`nashii 悲しい: a heavy heart (shizunda kokoro) 沈んだ心 / heavy news (kanashii shirase) 悲しい知らせ.

heavy industry n. ju`uko`ogyoo 重工業.

hedge n. **1** (bushes) i`kegaki 生け垣: plant a hedge (ikegaki o megurasu) 生け垣を巡らす.
2 (protection) bo`oe`saku 防衛策: a hedge against inflation (infure booeesaku) インフレ防衛策.

heed vt. ... o ko`ko`ro ni to`meru ...を心に留める V: heed advice [a warning] (chuukoku [chuui] o kokoro ni tomeru) 忠告[注意]を心に留める.

heel n. **1** (of a foot) ka`kato かかと: have a blister on one's heel (kakato ni mame ga dekite iru) かかとにまめができている.
2 (of a shoe) ka`kato かかと: shoes with high heels (kakato no takai kutsu) かかとの高い靴.

height n. **1** (being high) ta`kasa 高さ; ko`odo 高度: What is the height of Tokyo Tower? (Tookyoo Tawaa no takasa wa dono kurai arimasu ka?) 東京タワーの高さはどのくらいありますか. / We are now flying at a height of 10,000 meters. (Watashi-tachi wa ima koodo ichiman-meetoru de tonde imasu.) 私たちは

今高度 1 万メートルで飛んでいます.
2 (high place) ta「ka」i to「koro」高い
所; ta「kadai 高台; cho「ojo」o 頂上:
I am afraid of heights. (*Watashi
wa takai tokoro ga kowai.*) 私は高
い所が怖い.
3 (extreme degree) ma「ssa」kari 真
っ盛り; ze「tchoo 絶頂: We arrived
in Rome at the height of the tourist season. (*Watashi-tachi wa kaṅ-
koo shiizuṅ no massakari ni
Rooma ni tsuita.*) 私たちは観光シーズ
ンの真っ盛りにローマに着いた.

heir *n.* so「ozokuniṅ 相続人: a legal
heir (*hootee soozokuniṅ*) 法定相続
人.

heiress *n.* jo「see no soozokuniṅ
女性の相続人.

helicopter *n.* he「riko」putaa ヘリコ
プター: They hurried to the crash
site by helicopter. (*Kare-ra wa
herikoputaa de tsuiraku geṅba e
kyuukoo shita.*) 彼らはヘリコプターで
墜落現場へ急行した.

hell *n.* ji「goku 地獄.

hello *int.* **1** (greeting) ya「a やぁ;
(morning) o「hayoo お早う; (afternoon) ko「ṅnichi wa こんにちは;
(evening) ko「ṅbaṅ wa こんばんは.
2 (over the telephone) mo「shimo」-
shi もしもし: Hello. Is this Mr.
Yamada? (*Moshimoshi. Yamada-
saṅ desu ka?*) もしもし. 山田さんですか.

helmet *n.* he「rume」tto ヘルメット:
put on [take off] a helmet (*heru-
metto o kaburu* [*nugu*]) ヘルメットを
かぶる[脱ぐ].

help *vt.* **1** (assist) ... o te「tsuda」u ...
を手伝う ⓒ: Can you please help
me carry this baggage? (*Kono nimotsu o hakobu no o tetsudatte
moraemasu ka?*) この荷物を運ぶのを
手伝ってもらえますか.
2 (save) ... o ta「suke」ru ...を助ける
Ⓥ: We helped the climbers on
the mountain. (*Watashi-tachi wa to-
zaṅsha o tasuketa.*) 私たちは登山者
を助けた.
3 (be useful) ... ni ya「kuda」tsu ...に
役立つ ⓒ: Your advice helped us

complete the project. (*Anata no
jogeṅ wa keekaku no kaṅsee ni
yakudachimashita.*) あなたの助言は
計画の完成に役立ちました.
4 (relieve) ... o ra「ku」ni suru ...を楽
にする Ⓣ: This medicine will help
your cough. (*Kono kusuri o no-
meba seki ga raku ni narimasu yo.*)
この薬を飲めば咳が楽になりますよ.
5 (serve food) ... o ji「yu」u ni to「tte
ta「be」ru ...を自由に取って食べる Ⓥ:
Help yourself to whatever you
want. (*Tabetai mono wa naṅ de
mo go-jiyuu ni totte o-tabe kudasai.*) 食べたいものは何でもご自由に取っ
てお食べください.
— *vi.* te「tsuda」u 手伝う ⓒ: We
can finish quickly if you will help.
(*Anata ga tetsudatte kurereba
sugu ni owarimasu.*) あなたが手伝っ
てくれればすぐに終わります.
Can I help you? (in a shop)
(*Nani o sashiagemashoo ka?*) 何を
差し上げましょうか.
cannot help doing 〈verb〉-zu ni
wa i「rarenai ...ずにはいられない: I cannot help laughing at him. (*Kare o
warawazu ni wa irarenai.*) 彼を笑わ
ずにはいられない.
— *n.* **1** (assistance) ta「suke」助け:
We need your help. (*Watashi-
tachi wa anata no tasuke ga hitsuyoo desu.*) 私たちはあなたの助けが必要
です.
2 (referring to a person) ta「suke」
ni naru hi「to」助けになる人: You
have been a great help. (*Totemo
tasukarimashita.*) とても助かりました.
Help Wanted. (*Kyuujiṅ.*) 求人.

helper *n.* ta「suke」ru hi「to」助ける人;
te「tsuda」i 手伝い; he「rupaa ヘルパー.

helpful *adj.* yu「ueki na 有益な; ya-
「kuda」tsu 役立つ: helpful advice
(*yuueki na chuukoku*) 有益な忠告 /
The computer manual was very
helpful. (*Koṅpyuutaa no manyu-
aru wa taiheṅ yakudatta.*) コンピュー
ターのマニュアルは大変役だった.

helpless *adj.* **1** (unable to act)
do「o suru ko「to」mo de「ki」nai どうす

るНこともできない: a helpless invalid
(*jibuñ de doo suru koto mo dekinai byooniñ*) 自分でどうすることも
できない病人.
　2 (lacking help) ta「suke no na¹i 助
けのない; ta「yo¹ru mo「no no na¹i 頼る
者のない: a helpless orphan (*tayoru
mono no nai koji*) 頼る者のない孤児.

hem *n.* he「ri¹ へり; fu「chi¹ 縁: the
hem of a shirt (*waishatsu no heri*)
ワイシャツのへり.

hen *n.* me「ñdori めん鳥.

her *pron.* **1** [possessive form] ka¹-
nojo no 彼女の; so「ñna oñna no hito
no その女の人の: I think this is her
pen. (*Kore wa kanojo no peñ da to
omoimasu.*) これは彼女のペンだと思い
ます.
　2 [direct object] ka¹nojo o 彼女を:
Do you know her? (*Anata wa
kanojo o shitte imasu ka?*) あなたは
彼女を知っていますか.
　3 [indirect object] ka¹nojo ni 彼女
に: I gave her flowers. (*Watashi
wa kanojo ni hana o ageta.*) 私は彼
女に花をあげた.
　4 [with a preposition] ka¹nojo 彼
女: I just can't live without her.
(*Watashi wa kanojo nashi ni wa
ikite ikenai.*) 私は彼女なしには生きて
いけない.

herb *n.* ha「abu ハーブ; ko「oryoo-
shoku¹butsu 香料植物: medicinal
herbs (*yakusoo*) 薬草.

herd *n.* mu「re¹ 群れ: a herd of cows
(*ushi no mure*) 牛の群れ.

here *adv.* **1** (at, in, to this place)
ko「ko ni [de, e] ここに[で, へ]: Mr.
Yamada is here. (*Yamada-sañ wa
koko ni imasu.*) 山田さんはここにいま
す. / Wait here a moment, please.
(*Koko de chotto matte ite kudasai.*)
ここでちょっと待っていてください. /
Come here. (*Koko e irasshai.*) ここ
へいらっしゃい. ★ The meaning is con-
veyed by the particle: *koko ni* =
existence here, movement to here;
koko de = action here; *koko ni/e*
= movement to here; *koko kara*
= movement from here.

2 [specifying] ko「ko ここ; ko「chira
こちら: Here's your bag. (*Anata no
kabañ wa koko ni arimasu.*) あなた
のかばんはここにあります. / Here's the
person you were looking for. (*Kochira ga anata ga sagashite ita
kata desu.*) こちらがあなたが捜してい
た方です.
　3 [emphasizing] ko「ko ここ: This
corner here is where the accident
happened. (*Kono koko no kado ga
jiko no okita tokoro desu.*) このここ
の角が事故の起きた所です.
　4 (hereabouts) ko「no この: Is there
a post office near here? (*Kono chikaku ni yuubiñkyoku wa arimasu
ka?*) この近くに郵便局はありますか.
　5 (at this time) i「ma 今; ko「ko de
ここで: Here the story ends. (*Koko
de hanashi wa owarimasu.*) ここで
話は終わります.
　here and there *adv.* a「chi ko¹chi
あちこち.

heritage *n.* i「sañ 遺産; de「ñtoo 伝統.

hero *n.* **1** (brave person) e「eyuu 英
雄; yu¹ushi 勇士: a national hero
(*kokumiñ-teki eeyuu*) 国民的英雄.
　2 (main character) shu「jiñkoo 主
人公: the hero of a play (*geki no
shujiñkoo*) 劇の主人公.

heroic *adj.* e「eyuu-teki na 英雄的
な: heroic acts (*eeyuu-teki na kooi*)
英雄的な行為.

heroin *n.* he「ro¹iñ ヘロイン.

heroine *n.* **1** (brave woman) jo-
「see no eeyuu 女性の英雄; jo「ketsu
女傑.
　2 (main character) o「ñna shuji「ñ-
koo 女主人公; hi「ro¹iñ ヒロイン: the
heroine of the novel (*shoosetsu no
hiroiñ*) 小説のヒロイン.

herring *n.* ni「shiñ にしん: a can of
herrings (*nishiñ no kañzume*) にしん
の缶詰.

hers *pron.* ka「nojo no mo「no¹ 彼女の
もの: This magazine is hers. (*Kono
zasshi wa kanojo no mono da.*) この
雑誌は彼女のものだ.

herself *pron.* **1** [reflexive use] ji-
「buñ ji「shiñ o [ni] 自分自身を[に].

★ Usually not translated: She cut herself with a knife. (*Kanojo wa naifu de kega o shita.*) 彼女はナイフでけがをした.

2 [emphatic use] ji˺buñ de 自分で; ka˹nojo ji˹shiñ de 彼女自身で: Did Mrs. Yamazaki herself tell you that? (*Yamazaki-sañ jishiñ ga soo itta no desu ka?*) 山崎さん自身がそう言ったのですか.

hesitate *vi.* ta˹mera˺u ためらう C; chu˺ucho suru ちゅうちょする ①; ma˹yo˺u 迷う C: He hesitated about what to do. (*Kare wa nani o shitara yoi ka mayotta.*) 彼は何をしたらよいか迷った.

hiccup *n.* sha˹kkuri しゃっくり: have hiccups (*shakkuri o suru*) しゃっくりをする.

hide *vt.* ... o ka˹ku˺su ...を隠す C: I hid the money under the tatami. (*Watashi wa sono o-kane o tatami no shita ni kakushita.*) 私はそのお金を畳の下に隠した.

—— *vi.* ka˹kure˺ru 隠れる Ⓥ: The police know where the criminal is hiding. (*Keesatsu wa hañniñ ga doko ni kakurete iru ka shitte iru.*) 警察は犯人がどこに隠れているか知っている.

hideous *adj.* zo˹tto suru ぞっとする; o˹soroshi˺i 恐ろしい: a hideous sight (*zotto suru kookee*) ぞっとする光景 / a hideous crime (*osoroshii hañzai*) 恐ろしい犯罪.

high *adj.* **1** (distance above the ground) ta˹ka˺i 高い: a high mountain (*takai yama*) 高い山 / The sun was already high. (*Hi wa sude ni takakatta.*) 日はすでに高かった.

2 (in measuring) ta˹kasa ga ... a˺ru 高さが…ある: The pole is five meters high. (*Sono boo wa takasa ga go-meetoru aru.*) その棒は高さが5メートルある. / How high is Mt. Fuji? (*Fuji-sañ no takasa wa dono kurai desu ka?*) 富士山の高さはどのくらいですか.

3 (of degree, amount, etc.) ta˹ka˺i 高い: a high temperature (*takai oñdo*) 高い温度 / He drove at high speed. (*Kare wa koosoku de kuruma o uñteñ shita.*) 彼は高速で車を運転した. / The price is too high for me. (*Sono nedañ wa watashi ni wa taka-suguiru.*) その値段は私には高すぎる.

4 (of a voice) ta˹ka˺i 高い: speak in a high voice (*takai koe de hanasu*) 高い声で話す / sing in a high tone (*takai chooshi de utau*) 高い調子で歌う.

5 (important) ta˹ka˺i 高い: a high status (*takai chii*) 高い地位 / a high official in the government (*seefu no kookañ*) 政府の高官.

—— *adv.* ta˹kaku 高く: The birds are flying high in the sky. (*Tori ga sora takaku toñde iru.*) 鳥が空高く飛んでいる. / aim high (*mokuhyoo o takaku motsu*) 目標を高く持つ / rise high in the world (*shusse suru*) 出世する.

higher *adj.* **1** (far above) yo˹ri ta˹ka˺i より高い: mountains higher than Mt. Fuji (*Fuji-sañ yori (mo) takai yama*) 富士山より(も)高い山.

2 (of a degree) ko˹otoo na 高等な: higher animals (*kootoo-doobutsu*) 高等動物.

high school *n.* ko˹otoo-ga˺kkoo 高等学校; chu˹u-ga˺kkoo 中学校: a junior high school (*chuu-gakkoo*) 中学校 / a senior high school (*kootoo-gakkoo*) 高等学校.

highway *n.* ka˹ñseñ do˹oro 幹線道路; ko˹odoo 公道: a highway linking two cities (*futatsu no toshi o musubu kañseñ dooro*) 2つの都市を結ぶ幹線道路.

hijack *vt.* ... o ha˹ija˺kku suru ...をハイジャックする ①: hijack an aircraft (*hikooki o haijakku suru*) 飛行機をハイジャックする.

hike *vi.* ha˹ikiñgu o suru ハイキングをする ①; to˹horyo˹koo o suru 徒歩旅行をする ①: go hiking (*haikiñgu ni iku*) ハイキングに行く.

—— *n.* ha˹ikiñgu ハイキング; to˹horyo˹koo 徒歩旅行: go on a hike

(*haikiñgu ni iku*) ハイキングに行く.

hill *n.* **1** (high ground) o'ka 丘; ko-「yama 小山: go up a hill (*oka ni noboru*) 丘に登る / go down a hill (*oka o oriru*) 丘を下りる.
2 (slope) sa'ka¹ 坂; sa'ka¹michi 坂道: go up [down] a steep hill (*kyuu na sakamichi o agaru [kudaru]*) 急な坂道を上がる[下る].

him *pron.* **1** [direct object] ka're o 彼を: I don't know him. (*Watashi wa kare o shirimaseñ.*) 私は彼を知りません.
2 [indirect object] ka're ni 彼に: I gave him a dictionary. (*Watashi wa kare ni jisho o ageta.*) 私は彼に辞書をあげた.
3 [with a preposition] ka're 彼: I went with him. (*Watashi wa kare to issho ni itta.*) 私は彼のといっしょに行った.

himself *pron.* **1** [reflexive use] ji-「buñ ji'shiñ o [ni] 自分自身を[に].
★ Usually not translated: He cut himself while shaving. (*Kare wa hige o sotte ite kitte shimatta.*) 彼はひげをそっていて切ってしまった.
2 [emphatic use] ji'buñ de 自分で; ka're ji'shiñ de 彼自身で: Mr. Hoshino said so himself. (*Hoshino-shi wa jibuñ de soo iimashita.*) 星野氏は自分でそう言いました.

hind *adj.* u'shiro no 後ろの; ko'obu no 後部の: the hind legs of a horse (*uma no ushiro ashi*) 馬の後脚.

hinder *vt.* ... o ja'ma suru ...をじゃまする①; o'kuraseru 遅らせる⑤: Don't hinder me in my work. (*Watashi no shigoto o jama shinaide kure.*) 私の仕事をじゃましないでくれ. / Construction was hindered by the bad weather. (*Teñki ga warui no de keñsetsu ga okurete shimatta.*) 天気が悪いので建設が遅れてしまった.

hinge *n.* cho'otsu¹gai ちょうつがい: the hinge of a door (*doa no chootsugai*) ドアのちょうつがい.

hint *n.* **1** (suggestion) hi'ñto ヒント; a'ñji 暗示: drop a hint (*hiñto o ataeru*) ヒントを与える / take a hint (*sore to kañzuku*) それと感づく.
2 (guidance) jo'geñ 助言: hints for newly married couples (*shiñkoñ fuufu e no jogeñ*) 新婚夫婦への助言.
3 (sign) ki'zashi 兆し: a hint of spring (*haru no kizashi*) 春の兆し.
— *vt.* ... to so're to na¹ku i'u ...とそれとなく言う©: He hinted to her that he loved her. (*Kare wa kanojo ni aishite iru to sore to naku itta.*) 彼は彼女に愛しているとそれとなく言った.
— *vi.* (... o) ho'nomeka¹su (...を)ほのめかす©: The boss hinted at my dismissal. (*Buchoo wa watashi ni kaiko o honomekashita.*) 部長は私に解雇をほのめかした.

hip *n.* ko'shi 腰; hi'ppu ヒップ.
★ Japanese '*hippu*' usually refers to the buttocks: with one's hands on one's hips (*ryoote o koshi ni atete*) 両手を腰に当てて.

hire *vt.* **1** (employ) ... o ya'to¹u ...を雇う©: hire a gardener (*niwashi o yatou*) 庭師を雇う / Some workers were hired by the factory. (*Nañniñ ka no roodoosha ga sono koojoo de yatowareta.*) 何人かの労働者がその工場で雇われた.
2 (rent) ... o ka'riru ...を借りる⑤: hire a car (*kuruma o kariru*) 車を借りる / Our society hired a hall for the party. (*Watashi-tachi no kai de wa paatii no tame ni hooru o karita.*) 私たちの会ではパーティーのためにホールを借りた.
— *n.* chi'ñgari 賃借り; chi'ñgashi 賃貸し.

his[1] *pron.* ka're no 彼の; so'no otoko no hito no その男の人の: His wife is a film star. (*Kare no okusañ wa eega sutaa desu.*) 彼の奥さんは映画スターです. / I know him, but I can't remember his name. (*Watashi wa kare o shitte iru ga namae o omoidasenai.*) 私は彼を知っているが名前を思い出せない. ★ Often omitted in Japanese.

his[2] *pron.* ka're no mo'no¹ 彼のもの; so'no otoko no hito no mono¹ その

男の人のもの: Is this car really his? (*Kono kuruma wa hoñtoo ni kare no mono desu ka?*) この車は本当に彼のものですか. / My shoes are old but his are new. (*Watashi no kutsu wa furui ga kare no wa atarashii.*) 私の靴は古いが彼のは新しい.

historian *n.* reˈkishika 歴史家.

historic *adj.* reˈkishi-teki na 歴史的な; reˈkishi-teki ni yuumee na 歴史的に有名な: a historic event (*rekishi-teki na dekigoto*) 歴史的な出来事 / a historic town (*rekishi-teki ni yuumee na machi*) 歴史的に有名な町.

historical *adj.* reˈkishi-joo no 歴史上の: a historical person (*rekishi-joo no jiñbutsu*) 歴史上の人物 / a historical novel (*rekishi-shoosetsu*) 歴史小説 / places of historical interest (*kyuuseki*) 旧跡.

history *n.* **1** (past events; academic subject) reˈkishi 歴史: study history (*rekishi o beñkyoo suru*) 歴史を勉強する.
2 (written account) reˈkishi no hoˈñ 歴史の本: a history of Japan (*Nihoñ no rekishi no hoñ*) 日本の歴史の本.
3 (record) keˈreki 経歴; raˈireki 来歴: He related his life history. (*Kare wa jibuñ no keereki o katatta.*) 彼は自分の経歴を語った. / a personal history (*rirekisho*) 履歴書.

hit *vt.* **1** (strike) ... o uˈtsu ...を打つ C; naˈguˈru 殴る C: hit a ball with a bat (*booru o batto de utsu*) ボールをバットで打つ / hit a boy on the head (*kodomo no atama o naguru*) 子どもの頭を殴る.
2 (strike home) ... ni meˈechuu suru ...に命中する I: The stone hit the window. (*Ishi wa mado ni meechuu shita.*) 石は窓に命中した.
3 (contact forcefully; collide with) ... o buˈtsukeru ...をぶつける V; ... ni butsukaru ...にぶつかる C: I hit my knee on the table. (*Watashi wa hiza o teeburu ni butsuketa.*) 私はひざをテーブルにぶつけた. / The car hit

the wall. (*Kuruma wa hee ni butsukatta.*) 車は塀にぶつかった.
4 (of misfortune, disaster, etc.) ... o oˈsoˈu ...を襲う C: The typhoon is likely to hit us. (*Taifuu ga wareware o osoi-soo da.*) 台風がわれわれを襲いそうだ.
5 (in baseball) ... o uˈtsu ...を打つ C: hit a homerun (*hoomurañ o utsu*) ホームランを打つ.
— *vi.* **1** (strike) (... ni) naˈguri-kakaˈru (...に)殴りかかる C: He hit at me. (*Kare wa watashi ni naguri-kakatta.*) 彼は私に殴りかかった.
2 (contact forcefully) (... ni) buˈtsukaru (...に)ぶつかる C: hit against the wall (*hee ni butsukaru*) 塀にぶつかる.
— *n.* **1** (blow) daˈgeki 打撃: a hard hit (*kyooretsu na dageki*) 強烈な打撃.
2 (successful attempt) aˈtari 当たり; meˈechuu 命中: two hits and three misses (*futatsu atari mittsu hazure*) 二つ当たり三つ外れ.
3 (success) seˈekoo 成功; hiˈtto ヒット: a hit song (*hitto soñgu*) ヒットソング / a big hit (*dai-seekoo*) 大成功.

hives *n.* jiˈñmaˈshiñ じんましん.

hoarse *adj.* shiˈwagareta しわがれた; shiˈwagarete iru しわがれている; kaˈreta かれた; kaˈrete iru かれている: a hoarse voice (*shiwagare-goe*) しわがれ声.

hobby *n.* shuˈmi 趣味; doˈorakuˈ 道楽: Stamp collecting is my hobby. (*Kitte shuushuu ga watashi no shumi desu.*) 切手収集が私の趣味です.

hoe *n.* kuˈwa くわ(鍬).

hog *n.* buˈta 豚.

hold *vt.* **1** (in the hand) teˈ ni moˈtsu 手に持つ C; kaˈkaeru 抱える V; tsuˈkaˈmu つかむ C: Hold this bag, please. (*Kono kabañ o motte kudasai.*) このかばんを持ってください. / hold a parcel with both hands (*tsutsumi o ryoote de kakaeru*) 包みを両手で抱える / hold a strap tightly while in a train (*deñsha no naka de tsuri-kawa o shikkari tsukamu*) 電車の中でつり革をしっかりつかむ.

2 (support) ... o sa⌐sae⌐ru ...を支える V: The chair couldn't hold my weight. (*Isu wa watashi no taijuu o sasaeru koto ga dekinakatta.*) いすは私の体重を支えることができなかった.

3 (keep in a position) ... o ta⌐mo⌐tsu ...を保つ C; ma⌐ma⌐ ni shite oku ままにしておく C: Hold the door open, please. (*Doa o aketa mama ni shite oite kudasai.*) ドアを開けたままにしておいてください. / Please hold the line. (*Sono mama kirazu ni o-machi kudasai.*) そのまま切らずにお待ちください.

4 (contain) ... o shu⌐uyoo suru ...を収容する Ⓣ; i⌐reru koto ga deki⌐ru 入れることができる V: This hall can hold 2,000 people. (*Kono hooru wa niseñ-niñ shuuyoo dekimasu.*) このホールは2千人収容できます. / How many liters does this bottle hold? (*Kono biñ wa nañ rittoru gurai ireru koto ga dekimasu ka?*) このびんは何リットルぐらい入れることができますか.

5 (make; take place) ... o hi⌐ra⌐ku ...を開く C; mo⌐yoo⌐su 催す C: hold a meeting (*kaigoo o hiraku*) 会合を開く.

6 (keep; restrain) ... o o⌐sae⌐ru ...を押さえる V: Hold him! Don't let him escape! (*Kare o osaero! Nigasu na!*) 彼を押さえろ. 逃がすな.

7 (defend) ... o ma⌐mo⌐ru ...を守る C: hold a town against the enemy (*teki kara machi o mamoru*) 敵から町を守る.

8 (think) ... to ka⌐ñgae⌐ru ...と考える: They held that he was guilty. (*Kare-ra wa kare wa yuuzai da to kañgaeta.*) 彼らは彼は有罪だと考えた.

— *vi.* **1** (not break) mo⌐chikotae⌐ru 持ちこたえる V: The rope held. (*Roopu wa mochikotaeta.*) ロープは持ちこたえた.

2 (continue) tsu⌐zuku 続く C: The fine weather held. (*Seeteñ ga tsu-*

zuita.) 晴天が続いた.

3 (apply) a⌐tehama⌐ru 当てはまる C: In this case, that rule does not hold. (*Kono baai, sono kisoku wa atehamaranai.*) この場合その規則は当てはまらない.

— *n.* **1** (grip) tsu⌐ka⌐mu koto つかむこと: release one's hold (*tsukañde iru te o hanasu*) つかんでいる手を離す.

2 (something to hold onto) tsu⌐kamaru tokoro つかまる所: There were no holds for my hands. (*Te de tsukamaru tokoro ga nani mo nakatta.*) 手でつかまる所が何もなかった.

hole *n.* **1** (cavity; depression) a⌐na⌐ 穴; ku⌐bomi くぼみ: dig a hole (*ana o horu*) 穴を掘る / a hole in a wall (*kabe no ana*) 壁の穴 / a road full of holes (*ana-darake no dooro*) 穴だらけの道路.

2 (home of an animal) a⌐na⌐ 穴; su⌐ 巣: the hole of a mouse (*nezumi no ana*) ねずみの穴.

— *vt.* ... ni a⌐na⌐ o a⌐keru ...に穴を開ける V: The iceberg holed the ship. (*Hyoozañ ga fune ni ana o aketa.*) 氷山が船に穴を開けた.

holiday *n.* **1** (official) shu⌐kujitsu 祝日; sa⌐ijitsu 祭日: a national holiday (*kokumiñ no shukujitsu*) 国民の祝日.

2 (vacation; day off) kyu⌐ujitsu 休日; kyu⌐uka 休暇: the summer holidays (*natsu-yasumi*) 夏休み / I didn't take a holiday last month. (*Señgetsu wa kyuuka o toranakatta.*) 先月は休暇をとらなかった.

hollow *adj.* **1** (empty inside) u⌐tsuro no うつろの; ku⌐udoo no 空洞の: a hollow pipe (*naka ga kuudoo no paipu*) 中が空洞のパイプ.

2 (sunken) ku⌐boñda くぼんだ: a person with hollow cheeks (*hoo no kuboñda hito*) ほおのくぼんだ人.

3 (of sounds) u⌐tsuro na うつろな: a hollow voice (*utsuro na koe*) うつろな声.

— *n.* ku⌐bomi くぼみ; a⌐na⌐ 穴: a hollow in the ground (*jimeñ no kubomi*) 地面のくぼみ.

— *vt.* ... o ku⌈rinu⌉ku ...をくりぬく
Ⓒ: hollow out a log (*maruta o kurinuku*) 丸太をくりぬく.

holy *adj.* **1** (sacred) shi⌈n̄see na 神聖な: holy ground (*seechi*) 聖地.
2 (devout) shi⌈n̄jin̄buka⌉i 信心深い: live a holy life (*shin̄koo-seekatsu o okuru*) 信仰生活を送る.

homage *n.* ke⌈ei 敬意; so⌈n̄kee 尊敬: pay homage to a person (*hito ni keei o hyoo suru*) 人に敬意を表する.

home *n.* **1** (abode) ka⌈tee 家庭; ji⌈taku 自宅: a happy home (*tanoshii katee*) 楽しい家庭 / I help out at home. (*Watashi wa jitaku de tetsudai o shite imasu.*) 私は自宅で手伝いをしています.
2 (birthplace; country) ko⌈kyoo 故郷; kyo⌈ori 郷里; ko⌈koku 故国: Where is your home? (*Kyoori wa dochira desu ka?*) 郷里はどちらですか. / My home is in Canada. (*Watashi no kokoku wa Kanada desu.*) 私の故国はカナダです.
3 (property) i⌈e 家; ju⌈utaku 住宅: He bought a home in the suburbs. (*Kare wa koogai ni ie o katta.*) 彼は郊外に家を買った.
4 (special facility) shi⌈setsu 施設; ho⌈omu ホーム: a home for old people (*roojin̄ hoomu*) 老人ホーム.
5 (place of origin) ge⌈n̄sa⌉n̄chi 原産地; ho⌈n̄ba 本場: Scotland is the home of whisky. (*Sukottorando wa uisukii no hon̄ba desu.*) スコットランドはウイスキーの本場です.

make oneself at home *vi.* ku⌈tsuro⌉gu くつろぐ Ⓒ.

— *adj.* ka⌈tee no 家庭の; ji⌈taku no 自宅の; ko⌈ku⌉nai no 国内の: home life (*katee-seekatsu*) 家庭生活 / one's home address (*jitaku no juusho*) 自宅の住所 / home and foreign news (*kokunai narabi ni kokugai no nyuusu*) 国内ならびに国外のニュース.

— *adv.* i⌈e e [ni] 家へ[に]; ko⌈kyoo e 故郷へ; ko⌈koku e 故国へ: write home (*kokyoo e tegami o kaku*) 故

郷へ手紙を書く.

homemade *adj.* ji⌈kasee no 自家製の: a homemade cake (*jikasee no keeki*) 自家製のケーキ.

hometown *n.* u⌈mareko⌉kyoo no ma⌈chi⌉ 生まれ故郷の町; ko⌈kyoo 故郷: return to one's hometown (*umarekokyoo e kaeru*) 生まれ故郷へ帰る.

homework *n.* shu⌈kudai 宿題: do [finish] one's homework (*shukudai o suru [sumaseru]*) 宿題をする[済ませる].

homosexual *adj.* do⌈ose⌉eai no 同性愛の.
— *n.* do⌈ose⌉eai no hi⌈to⌉ 同性愛の人.

honest *adj.* **1** (trustworthy) sho⌈o-ji⌉ki na 正直な; se⌈ejitsu na 誠実な: an honest young man (*shoojiki na wakamono*) 正直な若者 / He is honest in business. (*Kare wa shigoto ni seejitsu da.*) 彼は仕事に誠実だ.
2 (direct; frank) a⌈rinomama⌉ no ありのままの; so⌈tchoku na 率直な: give an honest opinion (*arinomama no iken̄ o noberu*) ありのままの意見を述べる.

honesty *n.* sho⌈oji⌉ki 正直; se⌈ejitsu 誠実: Honesty is the best policy. (*Shoojiki wa saijoo no saku.*) 正直は最上の策.

honey *n.* ha⌈chimitsu はちみつ(蜂蜜).

honor *n.* **1** (high reputation) me⌈e-yo 名誉: gain [lose] honor (*meeyo o eru [ushinau]*) 名誉を得る[失う].
2 (high principle) shi⌈n̄gi 信義: He is a man of honor. (*Kare wa shin̄gi o omon̄jiru hito da.*) 彼は信義を重んじる人だ.
3 (respect) ke⌈ei 敬意; so⌈n̄kee 尊敬: The citizens showed honor to their hero. (*Shimin̄ wa kare-ra no eeyuu ni keei o hyooshita.*) 市民は彼らの英雄に敬意を表した.
4 (degree) yu⌈utoo 優等: graduate from college with honors (*yuutoo de daigaku o sotsugyoo suru*) 優等で大学を卒業する.

— *vt.* ... o so⌐ñkee suru ...を尊敬する ▯; u⌐yama⌐n 敬う C: honor one's parents (*oya o uyamau*) 親を敬う.

honorable *adj.* **1** (worthy of respect) so⌐ñkee su be⌐ki 尊敬すべき; ri⌐ppa na 立派な: honorable conduct (*rippa na kooi*) 立派な行為.

2 (deserving honor) me⌐eyo aru 名誉ある; ko⌐oee na 光栄な: an honorable position (*meeyo aru chii*) 名誉ある地位.

honorific *adj.* so⌐ñkee no 尊敬の; ke⌐ego no 敬語の: There are many honorific verbs in Japanese. (*Nihoñgo ni wa keego no dooshi ga takusañ arimasu.*) 日本語には敬語の動詞がたくさんあります.

— *n.* ke⌐ego 敬語; ke⌐eshoo 敬称.

hood *n.* **1** (head covering) fu⌐udo フード; zu⌐kiñ ずきん: wear a hood (*fuudo o kaburu*) フードをかぶる.

2 (of a car) bo⌐ñne⌐tto ボンネット.

hoof *n.* hi⌐zume ひづめ.

hook *n.* **1** (for hanging things) ka⌐gi⌐ かぎ; to⌐megane 留め金: hang one's hat on a hook (*booshi o kagi ni kakeru*) 帽子をかぎにかける.

2 (fishhook) tsu⌐ribari 釣り針.

3 (fastener) ho⌐kku ホック: the hooks on a dress (*doresu no hokku*) ドレスのホック.

— *vt.* ... o ka⌐gi⌐ [ho⌐kku] de to⌐meru ...をかぎ[ホック]で留める Ⅴ: Please hook this dress at the back for me. (*Kono doresu no ushiro o hokku de tomete kudasai.*) このドレスの後ろをホックで留めてください.

— *vi.* ka⌐gi⌐ [ho⌐kku] de to⌐maru かぎ[ホック]で留まる C: This dress hooks at the neck. (*Kono doresu wa kubi no tokoro ga hokku de tomarimasu.*) このドレスは首の所がホックで留まります.

hop *vi.* **1** (on one leg) ka⌐ta-ashi de tobu 片足で跳ぶ C: hop along on one's left foot (*hidariashi de toñde aruku*) 左足で跳んで歩く.

2 (jump) hyo⌐i to to⌐bu ひょいと跳ぶ C: hop onto a bicycle (*jiteñsha ni*

hyoi to noru) 自転車にひょいと乗る / hop across a stream (*ogawa o hyoi to tobikosu*) 小川をひょいと跳び越す.

hope *vt.* ... o no⌐zomu ...を望む C; ki⌐tai suru 期待する ▯; ki⌐tai to o⌐mo⌐u ...たいと思う C: She's hoping to get into Waseda University. (*Kanojo wa Waseda daigaku e hairu koto o nozoñde imasu.*) 彼女は早稲田大学へ入ることを望んでいます. / I hope to see you next week. (*Raishuu o-ai shitai to omoimasu.*) 来週お会いしたいと思います.

— *vi.* ki⌐boo o mo⌐tsu 希望を持つ C; ki⌐tai suru 期待する ▯: We are still hoping. (*Wareware wa mada kiboo o motte imasu.*) われわれはまだ希望を持っています.

— *n.* **1** (expectation) ki⌐boo 希望; no⌐zomi 望み; mi⌐komi 見込み: I lost all hope. (*Watashi wa subete no kiboo o ushinatta.*) 私はすべての希望を失った. / There is little hope that there are any survivors. (*Seezoñsha ga iru mikomi wa hotoñdo arimaseñ.*) 生存者がいる見込みはほとんどありません.

2 (person or thing) ki⌐boo o ataeru mono⌐ 希望を与えるもの; ho⌐opu ホープ: He is our last hope. (*Kare wa wareware no saigo no tanomi no tsuna da.*) 彼はわれわれの最後の頼みの綱だ.

hopeful *adj.* **1** (having hope) ki⌐boo o mo⌐tta [mo⌐tte iru] 希望を持った[持っている]: I feel hopeful about the future. (*Watashi wa shoorai ni kiboo o motte iru.*) 私は将来に希望を持っている.

2 (promising) yu⌐uboo na 有望な; mi⌐komi no a⌐ru 見込みのある: a hopeful young man (*yuuboo na seeneñ*) 有望な青年.

hopeless *adj.* **1** (full of despair) ki⌐boo o ushinatta [ushinatte iru] 希望を失った[失っている]; ze⌐tsuboo shita [shite iru] 絶望した[している]: feel hopeless (*zetsuboo shite iru*) 絶望している.

2 (unpromising) mi⌐komi no na⌐i

見込みのない; ze˥tsuboo-teki na 絶望
的な: a hopeless situation (*zetsuboo-teki na jitai*) 絶望的な事態.

horizon *n.* **1** (on land) chi˥heeseñ
地平線: The moon rose above the
horizon. (*Tsuki ga chiheeseñ no
ue ni nobotta.*) 月が地平線の上に昇っ
た.

2 (at sea) su˥iheeseñ 水平線.

3 (outlook) ha˥ñi 範囲; shi˥ya 視
野: broaden one's horizons (*shiya
o hiromeru*) 視野を広める.

horizontal *adj.* su˥ihee na 水平な;
yo˥ko no 横の: a horizontal line
(*yokoseñ*) 横線.

horn *n.* **1** (of an animal) tsu˥no˥ 角:
a bull's horns (*ushi no tsuno*) 牛の
角.

2 (substance) tsu˥no-se˥ehiñ 角製
品: These spoons are made of horn.
(*Kono supuuñ wa tsuno-see desu.*)
このスプーンは角製です.

3 (of a car) ke˥eteki 警笛: blow a
horn (*keeteki o narasu*) 警笛を鳴ら
す.

4 (musical instrument) ho˥ruñ ホル
ン: blow a horn (*horuñ o fuku*) ホル
ンを吹く.

horoscope *n.* (diagram) te˥ñkyu˥u-
zu 天宮図; (forecast) se˥ñse˥ejutsu
占星術.

horrible *adj.* **1** (causing horror)
o˥soroshi˥i 恐ろしい: commit a horrible crime (*osoroshii hañzai o
okasu*) 恐ろしい犯罪を犯す.

2 (unpleasant) fu˥yu˥kai na 不愉快
な; (terrible) hi˥do˥i ひどい: horrible
weather (*fuyukai na teñki*) 不愉快
な天気 / a horrible mistake (*hidoi
machigai*) ひどい間違い.

horror *n.* **1** (fear) kyo˥ofu 恐怖;
o˥sore˥ 恐れ: scream in horror
(*kyoofu de himee o ageru*) 恐怖で
悲鳴を上げる.

2 (dislike) ke˥ño 嫌悪: I have a
great horror of snakes. (*Watashi
wa hebi ga dai-kirai desu.*) 私は蛇
が大嫌いです.

hors d'oeuvre *n.* o˥odoburu オー
ドブル.

horse *n.* u˥ma˥ 馬: I like to ride
horses. (*Watashi wa uma ni noru
no ga suki da.*) 私は馬に乗るのが好き
だ. / horse racing (*keeba*) 競馬.

horseback *n.* u˥ma no se 馬の背:
go on horseback (*uma ni notte iku*)
馬に乗って行く.

hose *n.* ho˥osu ホース: use a hose to
water the plants (*shokubutsu ni
mizu o yaru no ni hoosu o tsukau*)
植物に水をやるのにホースを使う.

hospitable *adj.* mo˥tenashi no
yo˥i もてなしのよい; ka˥ñtai suru 歓待
する: He was hospitable to me.
(*Kare wa watashi o kañtai shite
kureta.*) 彼は私を歓待してくれた.

hospital *n.* byo˥oiñ 病院: an emergency hospital (*kyuukyuu-byooiñ*)
救急病院 / a maternity hospital
(*sañka-byooiñ*) 産科病院 / enter
the hospital (*nyuuiñ suru*) 入院する
/ leave the hospital (*taiiñ suru*) 退
院する / Please take me to the hospital. (*Byooiñ e tsurete itte kudasai.*)
病院へ連れて行ってください.

host *n.* **1** (person) shu˥jiñ 主人;
ho˥suto ホスト: act as host at a party
(*paatii de hosuto o tsutomeru*) パー
ティーでホストを務める.

2 (holder of an event) shu˥sa˥isha
主催者: the host city for the Olym-
pic Games (*Oriñpikku no shusai
toshi*) オリンピックの主催都市.

3 (on TV) shi˥ka˥isha 司会者.

— *vt.* ... o shu˥sai suru …を主催す
る ①: Kyoto will host the coming
conference. (*Kyooto ga koñdo no
kaigi o shusai shimasu.*) 京都が今
度の会議を主催します.

hostage *n.* hi˥tojichi 人質: They
kept the passengers as hostages.
(*Kare-ra wa jookyaku o hitojichi
ni shita.*) 彼らは乗客を人質にした.

hostess *n.* **1** (woman who re-
ceives guests) o˥ñna shu˥jiñ 女主人:
act as hostess at a party (*paatii de
shujiñyaku o tsutomeru*) パーティー
で主人役を務める.

2 (of a night-club) ho˥sutesu ホステ
ス.

hostile adj. **1** (unfriendly) te「ki¯ no 敵の; te「ki-i no aru 敵意のある: a hostile country (tekikoku) 敵国 / a hostile look (teki-i o motta kao-tsuki) 敵意を持った顔つき.

2 (disapproving of) ha「ńtai no 反対の: He was hostile to the idea. (Kare wa sono kańgae ni hańtai datta.) 彼はその考えに反対だった.

hostility n. te「ki-i 敵意: feel hostility toward a person (hito ni teki-i o idaku) 人に敵意を抱く.

hot adj. **1** (temperature) a「tsu¯i 暑い; (of heat) a「tsu¯i 熱い: It's hot, isn't it? (Atsui desu ne.) 暑いですね. / I like coffee hot. (Watashi wa atsui koohii ga suki desu.) 私は熱いコーヒーが好きです.

2 (of taste) pi「ri¯tto ka「ra¯i ぴりっと辛い: hot pepper (piritto karai koshoo) ぴりっと辛いこしょう / This curry is too hot for me. (Kono karee wa kara-sugiru.) このカレーは辛すぎる.

3 (excitable; angry) ha「geshi¯i 激しい; o「ko¯tta 怒った: a hot debate (hageshii toorooń) 激しい討論 / a person with a hot temper (tańki na hito) 短気な人.

4 (fresh) sa「ishiń no 最新の: hot news (saishiń nyuusu) 最新ニュース.

hotel n. ho「teru ホテル: I'll stay at Yamanaka Hotel. (Watashi wa Yamanaka hoteru ni tomarimasu.) 私は山中ホテルに泊まります. / I'd like to reserve a hotel room in the city. (Shinai no hoteru o yoyaku shite kudasai.) 市内のホテルを予約してください.

hot spring n. o「ńseń 温泉.

hot water n. o-「yu お湯; yu¯ 湯.

hour n. **1** (60 minutes) ji「kań 時間: I waited for him for two hours. (Watashi wa kare o ni-jikan matta.) 私は彼を 2 時間待った. / The station is an hour from here. (Eki wa koko kara ichi-jikan desu.) 駅はここから 1 時間です.

2 (time of an activity) ji「kań 時間: office hours (kińmu-jikań) 勤務時間 / Our lunch hour is only forty minutes. (Watashi-tachi no chuu-shoku-jikań wa tatta yonjuugo-fuń desu.) 私たちの昼食時間はたった 45 分です.

3 (time) ji「koku 時刻: arrive at the appointed hour (yakusoku no jiko-ku ni tsuku) 約束の時刻に着く.

4 (start of a new hour) sho「oji 正時: The bus leaves every hour on the hour. (Basu wa mai-shooji ni demasu.) バスは毎正時に出ます.

5 (period) to「ki¯ 時; ji「ki¯ 時期: the happiest hours of one's life (jińsee de ichiban tanoshii jiki) 人生でいちばん楽しい時期.

house n. **1** (dwelling) i「e¯ 家; ka「oku 家屋: build a house (ie o ta-teru) 家を建てる / He lives in a large house. (Kare wa ooki-na ie ni sunde iru.) 彼は大きな家に住んでいる. / a house for rent (kashiya) 貸家.

2 (people in a house) i「e no mono¯ 家の者; ka「zoku 家族: The whole house felt the earthquake. (Kazoku mińna no mono ga jishiń o kańjita.) 家族みんなの者が地震を感じた.

3 (legislature) gi「iń 議院; gi「jidoo 議事堂: the House of Councilors (Sańgiiń) 参議院 / the Houses of Parliament (kokkai gijidoo) 国会議事堂.

household n. ka「zoku 家族: a large household (dai-kazoku) 大家族.

— adj. ka「zoku no 家族の: household affairs (kaji) 家事.

housekeeper n. ka「se¯efu 家政婦.

housekeeping n. ka「see 家政; ka「ji 家事: housekeeping money (kakeehi) 家計費.

housewife n. shu「fu 主婦.

how adv. **1** (in what way) do「o yatte どうやって; do「ńna fuu ni どんな風に: How can I get to Hiroshima? (Hiroshima e wa doo yatte iki-masu ka?) 広島へはどうやって行きますか. / Please tell me how to call this number. (Kono bańgoo ni deńwa suru hoohoo o oshiete kudasai.) こ

の番号に電話する方法を教えてください。/ Please show me how to fill in this form. (*Kono shorui no kaki-kata o oshiete kudasai.*) この書類の書き方を教えてください。

2 (to or by what amount or degree) do'no kurai どのくらい; do'no te'edo どの程度: How long will it take to get to Kobe? (*Koobe made iku no ni dono kurai kakarimasu ka?*) 神戸まで行くのにどのくらいかかりますか。/ How much is it? (*Sore wa ikura desu ka?*) それはいくらですか。/ How old is your younger sister? (*Imooto-sañ wa nañ-sai desu ka?*) 妹さんは何歳ですか。

3 (in what condition) i'ka'ga いかが; do'ñna guai どんな具合: How is everyone in your family? (*Go-kazoku no minasañ wa ikaga desu ka?*) ご家族のみなさんはいかがですか。/ "How do you feel today?" "Not so well." (*"Kyoo wa doñna guai desu ka?" "Amari yoku arimaseñ."*) 「きょうはどんな具合ですか」「あまりよくありません」

4 [for emphasis] na'ñ と 何と; na'ñ-te 何て; do'ñna ni どんなに: How pretty this flower is! (*Kono hana wa nañte kiree nañ daroo.*) この花はなんてきれいなんだろう。/ How I wish I could speak Japanese perfectly! (*Nihoñgo ga kañzeñ ni hanasetara doñna ni ii daroo.*) 日本語が完全に話せたらどんなにいいだろう。

5 [in surprised question] do'o shite どうして: How could I have made such a stupid mistake? (*Doo shite añna baka na machigai o shita no daroo?*) どうしてあんなばかな間違いをしたのだろう。

How about ...? ... wa i'ka'ga desu ka? ...はいかがですか: How about a cup of tea? (*O-cha o ip-pai ikaga desu ka?*) お茶を1杯いかがですか。

How about doing? ⟨verb⟩-「mase'ñ ka? ...ませんか: How about playing tennis? (*Tenisu o shima-señ ka?*) テニスをしませんか。

How are you? 1 (when meeting someone) O-「ge'ñki desu ka? お元気ですか。
2 (when meeting for the first time) Ha'jimema'shite. はじめまして。
How do you do? (*Hajimemashite.*) はじめまして。
― *conj.* ... ko'to no shidai ...ことの次第: I told him how it happened. (*Watashi wa sore ga okotta koto no shidai o kare ni hanashita.*) 私はそれが起こったことの次第を彼に話した。

however *adv.* **1** (to whatever degree) do'ñna ni ⟨verb⟩-te[de] mo どんなに...て[で]も: However hard I try, I still can't do it. (*Doñna ni isshookeñmee yatte mo, watashi ni wa mada dekinai.*) どんなに一生懸命にやっても、私にはまだできない。
2 (in whatever way) do'no yoo ni ⟨verb⟩-te[de] mo どのように...て[で]も: However you do it, you are likely to fail. (*Dono yoo ni shite mo kimi wa shippai shi-soo da.*) どのようにしても君は失敗しそうだ。
― *conj.* shi'ka'shi しかし: However, I will do it in my own way. (*Shika-shi watashi wa watashi no yari-kata de yarimasu.*) しかし私は私のやり方でやります。

howl *vi.* ho'e'ru 吠える Ⓥ: A dog is howling in the distance. (*Inu ga tooku de hoete iru.*) 犬が遠くで吠えている。

hug *vt.* ... o da'kishime'ru ...を抱き締める Ⓥ: hug a child (*kodomo o dakishimeru*) 子どもを抱き締める。

huge *adj.* kyo'dai na 巨大な; ba'kudai na 莫大な: a huge airplane (*kyo-dai na hikooki*) 巨大な飛行機 / a huge amount of money (*bakudai na kiñgaku*) 莫大な金額。

human *adj.* **1** (of mankind) ni'ñ-geñ no 人間の; ji'ñrui no 人類の: human nature (*niñgeñsee*) 人間性 / the human race (*jiñrui*) 人類。
2 (typical of ordinary people) ni'ñ-geñ-teki na 人間的な; ni'ñgeñ-rashi'i 人間らしい: human interest (*niñgeñ-teki kyoomi*) 人間的興味 /

human feelings (*niṇgeñ-rashii kañjoo*) 人間らしい感情.
— *n.* = human being.

human being *n.* niⁿgeñ 人間; hiⁿtoⁿ 人.

humane *adj.* niⁿnjoo no aru 人情のある; jiⁿhibukaⁿi 慈悲深い: a man of humane character (*niñjoomi no aru hito*) 人情味のある人.

humanism *n.* jiⁿñbuñshuⁿgi 人文主義. ★ In Japanese 'humanitarianism' is called '*hyuumanizumu*' ヒューマニズム.

humanity *n.* **1** (mankind) jiⁿñrui 人類: crimes against humanity (*jiñrui ni taisuru hañzai*) 人類に対する犯罪.
2 (kindness; human feelings) oⁿmoiyari 思いやり; niⁿñjoo 人情: be lacking in humanity (*niñjoo ni kakeru*) 人情に欠ける.

human relations *n.* niⁿñgeñkaⁿñkee 人間関係.

humble *adj.* **1** (modest) hiⁿkaeme na 控えめな; keⁿñsoñ shita [shite iru] 謙そんした[している]: a humble request (*hikaeme na yookyuu*) 控えめな要求 / a humble attitude (*keñsoñ shita taido*) 謙そんした態度.
2 (low) hiⁿkuⁿi 低い; iⁿyashii 卑しい: a person of humble social standing (*shakai-teki ni mibuñ no hikui hito*) 社会的に身分の低い人.
3 (poor) shiⁿsso na 質素な; soⁿmatsu na 粗末な: a humble house (*shisso na ie*) 質素な家.

humid *adj.* shiⁿmeppoⁿi しめっぽい; shiⁿkke no oⁿoi 湿気の多い: It's humid this evening. (*Koñya wa shimeppoi*.) 今夜はしめっぽい. / a humid climate (*shikke no ooi kikoo*) 湿気の多い気候.

humidity *n.* shiⁿkke 湿気; shiⁿtsuⁿdo 湿度: high [low] humidity (*takai [hikui] shitsudo*) 高い[低い]湿度.

humiliate *vt.* ... ni haⁿjiⁿ o kaⁿkaseⁿru ...に恥をかかせる [V]; ... no jiⁿsoⁿñshiñ o kiⁿzutsukeⁿru ...の自尊心を傷つける [V]: I was humiliated

by my blunder. (*Watashi wa hema o yatte haji o kaita*.) 私はへまをやって恥をかいた.

humility *n.* keⁿñsoñ けんそん; hiⁿge 卑下: speak with humility (*keñsoñ shite hanasu*) けんそんして話す.

humor *n.* **1** (being amusing) yuⁿmoa ユーモア: a story full of humor (*yuumoa ni toñda hanashi*) ユーモアに富んだ話 / He has no sense of humor. (*Kare wa yuumoa no señsu ga nai*.) 彼はユーモアのセンスがない.
2 (mood) kiⁿbuñ 気分; kiⁿgeñ きげん: I am in no humor for driving now. (*Ima wa kuruma o uñteñ suru kibuñ ja nai*.) いまは車を運転する気分じゃない. / He was in a good humor. (*Kare wa joo-kigeñ datta*.) 彼は上きげんだった.

humorous *adj.* koⁿkkee na こっけいな; yuⁿmoa no aru ユーモアのある: a humorous story (*kokkee na hanashi*) こっけいな話 / a humorous writer (*yuumoa sakka*) ユーモア作家.

hundred *n.* hyaⁿkuⁿ 100, 百; (people) hyaⁿkuⁿ-niñ 100 人; (things) hyaⁿk-ko 100 個; (age) hyaⁿkuⁿ-sai 100 歳.
— *adj.* hyaⁿku no 100 の; (people) hyaⁿkuⁿ-niñ no 100 人の; (things) hyaⁿk-ko no 100 個の.

hundredth *adj.* hyaⁿku-bañme no 100 番目の.
— *n.* **1** (people) hyaⁿku-bañmeⁿ no hiⁿtoⁿ 100 番目の人; (things) hyaⁿku-bañmeⁿ no moⁿnoⁿ 100 番目のもの.
2 (fraction) hyaⁿku-buñ no ichiⁿ 100 分の 1.

hunger *n.* **1** (being hungry) kuⁿfuku 空腹: satisfy one's hunger (*kuufuku o mitasu*) 空腹を満たす.
2 (starvation) uⁿeⁿ 飢え: suffer from hunger (*ue ni kurushimu*) 飢えに苦しむ.
3 (strong desire) -yoku 欲; neⁿtsuboo 熱望: a hunger for knowledge (*chishiki-yoku*) 知識欲.

hungry *adj.* **1** (feeling hunger)

uʟeta 飢えた; uʟete iru 飢えている; o-ˈnaka ga suita [suite iru] おなかがすいた[すいている]: I am hungry now. (*Watashi wa ima onaka ga suite iru.*) 私は今おなかがすいている.
2 (eager for) neˈtsuboo shite (iru) 熱望して(いる); tsuˈyoku hoˈshigaˈtte (iru) 強く欲しがって(いる): He is hungry for power. (*Kare wa keñryoku o hoshigatte iru.*) 彼は権力を欲しがっている.

hunt *vt.* **1** (chase) ... o kaˈru ...を狩る Ⓒ: We hunted bears in the mountains. (*Watashi-tachi wa yama de kuma-gari o shita.*) 私たちは山で熊狩りをした.
2 (search) ... o saˈgasu ...を探[捜]す Ⓒ; tsuˈiseki suru 追跡する Ⓘ: hunt a better job (*motto yoi shigoto o sagasu*) もっとよい仕事を探す / The bank robber is being hunted by the police. (*Sono giñkoo gootoo wa keesatsu ni tsuiseki sarete iru.*) その銀行強盗は警察に追跡されている.
— *vi.* **1** (chase) kaˈri o suru 狩りをする Ⓘ: go hunting (*kari ni deka-keru*) 狩りに出かける.
2 (search) (... o) saˈgasu (...を)探[捜]す Ⓒ: hunt for a house to rent (*kashiya o sagasu*) 貸家を探す.

hunter *n.* kaˈri o suru hiˈtoˈ 狩りをする人; ryoˈoshi 猟師; haˈñtaa ハンター.

hurry *vi.* (be quick) iˈsoˈgu 急ぐ Ⓒ; aˈwateru 慌てる Ⓥ: hurry to the station (*eki e isogu*) 駅へ急ぐ / Where are you hurrying? (*Awatete doko e iku no desu ka?*) 慌ててどこへ行くのですか.
— *vt.* **1** (cause to be quick) ... o iˈsogaseˈru 急がせる Ⓥ; seˈkitateru せきたてる Ⓥ: You hurried me into making that mistake. (*Kimi ga iso-gaseta kara añna machigai o shita no da.*) 君が急がせたからあんな間違いをしたのだ.
2 (do quickly) ... o iˈsoˈide ⟨verb⟩ ...を急いで...; aˈwatete ⟨verb⟩ 慌てて...: We have to hurry our work. (*Shigoto o isoide shinakereba na-ranai.*) 仕事を急いでしなければならない.

— *n.* **1** (quick activity) oˈoiˈsogi 大急ぎ; oˈoaˈwate 大慌て: I'm in a hurry. (*Isoide imasu.*) 急いでいます.
2 (need for quickness) iˈsoˈgu hiˈtsuyoo 急ぐ必要: We can take our time. There is no hurry. (*Yukkuri yareba ii. Isogu hitsuyoo wa ari-maseñ.*) ゆっくりやればいい. 急ぐ必要はありません.

hurt *vt.* **1** (injure) ... ni keˈgaˈ o saˈseru ...にけがをさせる Ⓥ; ... o iˈtameˈ-ru ...を痛める Ⓥ: He hurt his knee when he fell. (*Kare wa koroñda toki hiza ni kega o shita.*) 彼は転んだときひざにけがをした.
2 (cause emotional pain) ... o gaˈi-suˈru ...を害する Ⓘ; kiˈzu tsukeˈru 傷つける Ⓥ: His remarks hurt her pride deeply. (*Kare no kotoba wa kanojo no puraido o fukaku kizu-tsuketa.*) 彼の言葉は彼女のプライドを深く傷つけた.
3 (do harm) ... ni gaˈi o aˈtaeru ...に害を与える Ⓥ: The frost hurt the fruit. (*Shimo wa kudamono ni gai o ataeta.*) 霜は果物に害を与えた.
— *vi.* iˈtaˈmu 痛む Ⓒ: My tooth hurts. (*Ha ga itamu.*) 歯が痛む. / Where does it hurt most? (*Doko ga ichibañ itamimasu ka?*) どこがいちばん痛みますか.

husband *n.* oˈtto 夫; shuˈjiñ 主人. ★ The wife refers to her own husband as 'shujiñ' or 'otto' and someone else's husband 'go-shujiñ.': This is a gift for my husband. (*Kore wa shujiñ e no o-miyage desu.*) これは主人へのおみやげです / an ideal husband (*risoo-teki na otto*) 理想的な夫 / husband and wife (*fuufu*) 夫婦.

hush *vt.* ... o shiˈzuka ni saˈseru ...を静かにさせる Ⓥ; daˈmaraseˈru 黙らせる Ⓥ: hush a crying child (*naite iru kodomo o damaraseru*) 泣いている子どもを黙らせる.
— *vi.* shiˈzuka ni naru 静かになる Ⓒ; daˈmaˈru 黙る Ⓒ.

hut *n.* koˈya 小屋: a mountain hut (*yama-goya*) 山小屋.

hyphen *n.* haˈifuñ ハイフン.

hypocrisy *n.* giˈzeñ 偽善; neˈkokaˈburi 猫かぶり.

hypocrite *n.* giˈzeˈnsha 偽善者: play the hypocrite (*neko o kaburu*) 猫をかぶる.

hypothesis *n.* kaˈsetsu 仮説; kaˈtee 仮定: put forward a hypothesis (*kasetsu o tateru*) 仮説を立てる.

I

I *pron.* waˈtashi wa [ga] 私は[が]; boˈku wa [ga] 僕は[が]. ★ '*Boku*' is usually used by boys and young men. Also used by adult men on informal occasions: I'm a tourist. (*Watashi wa kañkookyaku desu.*) 私は観光客です。/ I like dogs. (*Boku wa inu ga suki da.*) 僕は犬が好きだ.

ice *n.* koˈori 氷: Please bring me some ice and water. (*Koori to mizu o motte kite kudasai.*) 氷と水を持ってきてください.

ice cream *n.* aˈisu kuriˈimu アイスクリーム.

icicle *n.* tsuˈrara. つらら.

icy *adj.* **1** (covered with ice) koˈori de oowaˈreta [oowaˈrete iru] 氷でおおわれた[おおわれている]; hyoˈoketsu shita [shite iru] 氷結した[している]: an icy road (*hyooketsu shita dooro*) 氷結した道路.
2 (very cold) koˈori no yoˈo na 氷のような: Her hands were icy cold. (*Kanojo no te wa koori no yoo ni tsumetakatta.*) 彼女の手は氷のように冷たかった.
3 (unfriendly) reˈetaˈñ na 冷淡な: an icy manner (*reetañ na taido*) 冷淡な態度.

idea *n.* **1** (thought) kaˈñgaˈe 考え; aˈideˈa アイデア: That's a good idea. (*Sore wa yoi kañgae da.*) それはよい考えだ。/ I hit on a good idea. (*Watashi wa ii aidea o omoitsuita.*) 私はいいアイデアを思いついた.
2 (opinion) iˈkeñ 意見: We exchanged ideas with each other. (*Watashi-tachi wa o-tagai ni ikeñ o kookañ shita.*) 私たちはお互いに意見を交換した.
3 (imagination) soˈozoo 想像; keˈñtoˈo 見当: I have no idea where he went. (*Kare ga doko e itta no ka keñtoo ga tsukimaseñ.*) 彼がどこへ行ったのか見当がつきません.

ideal *adj.* riˈsoo-teki na 理想的な: an ideal marriage (*risoo-teki na kekkoñ*) 理想的な結婚.
— *n.* riˈsoo 理想: He has high ideals. (*Kare wa takai risoo o motte iru.*) 彼は高い理想を持っている.

idealism *n.* riˈsoo-shuˈgi 理想主義; kaˈñneˈñroñ 観念論.

idealist *n.* riˈsooka 理想家; riˈsoo-shugiˈsha 理想主義者.

identical *adj.* **1** (exactly alike) oˈnaji 同じ; hiˈtoshiˈi 等しい: Her dress is identical with mine. (*Kanojo no doresu wa watashi no to onaji da.*) 彼女のドレスは私のと同じだ.
2 (the very same) doˈoitsu no 同一の: This car is identical to the one that was stolen. (*Kono kuruma wa nusumareta no to dooitsu da.*) この車は盗まれたのと同一だ.

identification *n.* miˈbuñ shoˈomee 身分証明: Do you have any identification? (*Nani-ka mibuñ shoomee o o-mochi desu ka?*) 何か身分証明をお持ちですか.

identify *vt.* **1** (recognize) ... o kaˈkuniñ suru ...を確認する ①; miˈwakeru 見分ける Ⓥ: The body has not been identified. (*Sono itai wa mimoto ga kakuniñ sarete imaseñ.*) その遺体は身元が確認されていません.
2 (regard as the same) ... o doˈoitsuˈshi suru ...を同一視する ①: identify democracy with liberty (*miñshushugi o jiyuu to dooitsu-*

shi suru) 民主主義を自由と同一視する.

identity *n.* (who or what a person is) miˈmoto 身元; shoˈotai 正体: conceal one's identity (*mimoto o kakusu*) 身元を隠す.

idiom *n.* kaˈñyoo goˈku 慣用語句; seˈeku 成句.

idiot *n.* baˈka ばか; maˈnuke まぬけ.

idle *adj.* **1** (doing nothing) naˈni mo shinai 何もしない; aˈsoñde iru 遊んでいる: I spent an idle hour watching TV. (*Watashi wa terebi o minagara nani mo shinai de jikañ o sugoshita.*) 私はテレビを見ながら何もしないで時間を過ごした.
2 (lazy) naˈmaˈkete iru 怠けている: an idle fellow (*namakemono*) 怠け者.

idol *n.* (carved image) guˈuzoo 偶像; (someone admired) aˈidoru アイドル.

if *conj.* **1** (supposing that) (moˈshi mo) ⟨verb⟩ naˈra(ba) (もし も)…なら(ば): If you go, I will go, too. (*Anata ga iku nara(ba) watashi mo ikimasu.*) あなたが行くなら(ば)私も行きます.
2 (provided) kaˈri ni … to ⟨verb⟩-ba 仮に…と…ば: If I were you, I would not do such a thing. (*Kari ni watashi ga anata to sureba soñna koto wa shinai deshoo.*) 仮に私があなたとすればそんなことはしないでしょう.
3 (whether) … ka doˈo ka …かどうか: Do you know if he is at home? (*Kare ga uchi ni iru ka doo ka shitte imasu ka?*) 彼が家にいるかどうか知っていますか.
4 (even though) taˈtoe … -te [de] mo たとえ…て[で]も: We are happy, if poor. (*Tatoe mazushikute mo watashi-tachi wa shiawase desu.*) たとえ貧しくても私たちは幸せです.

ignorance *n.* muˈchi 無知; shiˈranai kotoˈ 知らないこと: Ignorance of the law is no excuse. (*Hooritsu o shiranai to iu koto wa iiwake ni naranai.*) 法律を知らないということは言い訳にならない.

ignorant *adj.* **1** (knowing very little) muˈchi no 無知の; shiˈranai 知らない: I am ignorant about computers. (*Watashi wa koñpyuutaa no koto no koto wa shirimaseñ.*) 私はコンピューターのことは知りません.
2 (uneducated) muˈgaku na 無学な: an ignorant person (*mugaku na hito*) 無学な人.
3 (unaware) kiˈzukaˈnai 気づかない: I was ignorant of the errors. (*Watashi wa sono machigai ni kizukanakatta.*) 私はその間違いに気づかなかった.

ignore *vt.* … o muˈshi suru …を無視する ①: He ignored my advice. (*Kare wa watashi no chuukoku o mushi shita.*) 彼は私の忠告を無視した.

ill *adj.* **1** (sick) byoˈoki de 病気で: He is ill in bed. (*Kare wa byooki de nete imasu.*) 彼は病気で寝ています.
2 (bad) waˈruˈi 悪い; (harmful) gaˈi no aru 害のある: ill news (*warui shirase*) 悪い知らせ.
3 (unlucky) fuˈkitsu na 不吉な: an ill omen (*fukitsu na zeñchoo*) 不吉な前兆.
— *adv.* (badly) waˈruku 悪く: take things ill (*monogoto o waruku toru*) 物事を悪く取る.

illegal *adj.* fuˈhoo na 不法な; hiˈgoˈohoo no 非合法の: an illegal trade (*higoohoo no torihiki*) 非合法の取り引き.

illness *n.* byoˈoki 病気: He is suffering from a serious illness. (*Kare wa omoi byooki ni kakatte imasu.*) 彼は重い病気にかかっています.

illuminate *vt.* … o teˈraˈsu …を照らす ⓒ; aˈkaruku suru 明るくする ①: Candles illuminated the room. (*Roosoku ga heya o akaruku terashita.*) ろうそくが部屋を明るく照らした.

illusion *n.* **1** (false idea) geˈñsoo 幻想; geˈñee 幻影: have illusions about one's future (*jibuñ no mirai ni taishite geñsoo o idaku*) 自分の未来に対して幻想を抱く.
2 (appearance which is not real) saˈkkaku 錯覚: an optical illusion

(*me no sakkaku*) 目の錯覚.

illustrate *vt.* **1** (put drawings) ... ni sa「shie o ireru ...に挿し絵を入れる ⟨V⟩; ... o zu「kai suru ...を図解する ⟨I⟩: an illustrated book (*sashie no haitta hoñ*) 挿し絵の入った本.

2 (explain by example) ... o se「tsumee suru ...を説明する ⟨I⟩; re「eji suru 例示する ⟨I⟩: I illustrated my point with examples. (*Watashi wa yooteñ o ree o agete setsumee shita.*) 私は要点を例を挙げて説明した.

illustration *n.* **1** (drawing) sa「shie 挿絵; zu 図; i「rasuto イラスト.

2 (example) re「e 例; ji「tsuree 実例.

3 (illustrating) re「e ni yoru se「tsumee 例による説明; zu「kai 図解: Illustration is very useful in teaching. (*Ree ni yoru setsumee wa oshieru no ni taiheñ yakudatsu.*) 例による説明は教えるのに大変役だつ.

image *n.* **1** (mental picture) o「mokage 面影; su「gata 姿: The image of her is still fresh in my mind. (*Kanojo no omokage ga mada hakkiri to kokoro ni nokotte iru.*) 彼女の面影がまだはっきりと心に残っている.

2 (general opinion) hyo「obañ 評判; i「meeji イメージ: improve the image of a company (*kaisha o imeeji-appu suru*) 会社をイメージアップする.

3 (close likeness) i「kiutsushi 生き写し: She is the image of her mother. (*Kanojo wa o-kaasañ ni ikiutsushi da.*) 彼女はお母さんに生き写しだ.

4 (reflection) e「ezoo 映像; su「gata 姿: look at one's image in the mirror (*kagami ni utsutta jibuñ no sugata o miru*) 鏡に映った自分の姿を見る.

5 (statue) zo「o 像; sho「ozoo 肖像: worship images (*guuzoo o suuhai suru*) 偶像を崇拝する.

imaginary *adj.* so「ozoo-joo no 想像上の; ka「kuu no 架空の: an imaginary animal (*kakuu no doobutsu*) 架空の動物.

imagination *n.* **1** (ability to imagine) so「ozo「oryoku 想像力:

exercise one's imagination (*soozooryoku o hatarakasu*) 想像力を働かす.

2 (ideas in the mind) so「ozoo 想像; ki no ma「yo「i 気の迷い: It's just your imagination. (*Sore wa kimi no ki no mayoi ni suginai.*) それは君の気の迷いにすぎない.

imagine *vt.* **1** (form a mental picture) ... o so「ozoo suru ...を想像する ⟨I⟩; ko「ko「ro ni e「ga「ku 心に描く ⟨C⟩: She imagined life abroad. (*Kanojo wa gaikoku de no seekatsu o soozoo shita.*) 彼女は外国での生活を想像した.

2 (suppose) ... to su「isatsu suru ...と推察する ⟨I⟩; o「mo「u 思う ⟨C⟩: I imagine that he will come. (*Kare wa kuru to omoimasu.*) 彼は来ると思います.

imitate *vt.* **1** (copy) ... o ma「neru ...をまねる ⟨V⟩; mo「hoo suru 模倣する ⟨I⟩: imitate the song of a bird (*tori no nakigoe o maneru*) 鳥の鳴き声をまねる.

2 (resemble) ... ni ni「seru ...に似せる ⟨V⟩: This floor is painted to imitate marble. (*Kono yuka wa dairiseki ni nisete nurarete iru.*) この床は大理石に似せて塗られている.

imitation *n.* **1** (imitating) ma「ne まね; mo「hoo 模倣: He did an imitation of a monkey. (*Kare wa saru no mane o shita.*) 彼は猿のまねをした.

2 (copy) ni「semono 偽物; mo「zoohiñ 模造品: imitation pearls (*mozoo shiñju*) 模造真珠.

immediate *adj.* **1** (instant) su「gu no su「gu no; so「kuza no 即座の: He gave me an immediate answer. (*Kare wa sugu ni heñji o kureta.*) 彼はすぐに返事をくれた.

2 (direct) cho「kusetsu no 直接の: the immediate cause of death (*chokusetsu no shi-iñ*) 直接の死因.

3 (very near) su「gu to「nari no すぐ隣の: an immediate neighbor (*sugu tonari no hito*) すぐ隣の人.

immediately *adv.* (at once) su「gu ni すぐに; ta「dachi ni 直ちに: The policeman came immediately. (*Keekañ wa sugu ni kita.*) 警官はすぐに来た.

immense *adj.* (very large) ko｢odai na 広大な; (very huge) kyo｢odai na 巨大な: an immense area of desert (*koodai na sabaku chitai*) 広大な砂漠地帯 / an immense statue (*kyodai na zoo*) 巨大な像.

immigrant *n.* i｢juusha 移住者; im｢iñ 移民. ★ Japanese '*imiñ*' means both immigrant and emigrant.

immigration *n.* i｢juu 移住; i｢miñ 移民; nyu｢ukoku 入国: immigration control (*nyuukoku kañri*) 入国管理.

imminent *adj.* sa｢shisema｢tta 差し迫った; sa｢shisema｢tte iru 差し迫っている; se｢ppaku shita [shite iru] 切迫した[している]: imminent danger (*sashisematta kikeñ*) 差し迫った危険.

immoral *adj.* fu｢do｢otoku na 不道徳な; fu｢hi｢ñkoo na 不品行な: immoral conduct (*fudootoku na kooi*) 不道徳な行為.

immorality *n.* fu｢do｢otoku 不道徳; fu｢hi｢ñkoo 不品行.

immortal *adj.* (never dying) fu｢shi no 不死の; (eternal) fu｢kyuu no 不朽の; fu｢metsu no 不滅の: immortal fame (*fukyuu no meesee*) 不朽の名声.

immortality *n.* fu｢shi 不死; fu｢metsu 不滅.

impact *n.* 1 (collision) sho｢ototsu 衝突; sho｢ogeki 衝撃: the impact of two cars (*ni-dai no kuruma no shoototsu*) 2 台の車の衝突.
2 (effect) e｢ekyoo 影響: His death had an impact on them. (*Kare no shi wa kare-ra ni eekyoo o ataeta.*) 彼の死は彼らに影響を与えた.

impartial *adj.* ka｢tayora｢nai 偏らない; ko｢ohee na 公平な: an impartial judge (*koohee na saibañkañ*) 公平な裁判官.

impatience *n.* ta｢ñki 短気; se｢kkachi せっかち; i｢raira いらいら: He waited for her with impatience.

(*Kare wa iraira shi-nagara kanojo o matta.*) 彼はいらいらしながら彼女を待った.

impatient *adj.* 1 (not patient) ki｢mijika na 気短な; i｢raira shite iru いらいらしている: We were impatient at his delay in coming. (*Watashi-tachi wa kare no kuru no ga osoi no de iraira shita.*) 私たちは彼の来るのが遅いのでいらいらした.
2 (eager to do) shi｢kiri ni 〈verb〉-tagaru しきりに…たがる: The children are impatient to go. (*Kodomo-tachi wa shikiri ni ikitagatte iru.*) 子どもたちはしきりに行きたがっている.

imperfect *adj.* fu｢ka｢ñzeñ na 不完全な; fu｢ju｢ubuñ na 不十分な: Their preparations are imperfect. (*Kare-ra no juñbi wa fukañzeñ da.*) 彼らの準備は不完全だ.

imperial *adj.* (of an empire) te｢ekoku no 帝国の; (of an emperor) ko｢otee no 皇帝の: the Imperial Family (*kooshitsu*) 皇室 / the Imperial Palace (in Tokyo) (*Kookyo*) 皇居.

impersonal *adj.* ko｢jiñ-teki de nai 個人的でない; hi-ko｢jiñ-teki na 非個人的な: an impersonal letter (*kojiñ ate de nai tegami*) 個人あてでない手紙.

implicit *adj.* a｢ñ ni shi｢mesa｢reta 暗に示された; a｢ñmoku no 暗黙の: implicit consent (*añmoku no shoodaku*) 暗黙の承諾.

implore *vt.* … ni ne｢sshiñ ni ta｢no｢mu …に熱心に頼む ⓒ; … o ta｢ñgañ suru …を嘆願する ⓘ: She implored her husband to give up smoking. (*Kanojo wa otto ni tabako o yameru yoo nesshiñ ni tanoñda.*) 彼女は夫にたばこをやめるよう熱心に頼んだ.

imply *vt.* … o ho｢nomeka｢su …をほのめかす ⓒ; i｢mi suru 意味する ⓘ: Silence often implies resistance. (*Mugoñ wa shibashiba hañkoo o imi suru.*) 無言はしばしば反抗を意味する.

impolite *adj.* bu⌐sa⌐hoo na 無作法な; shi⌐tsu⌐ree na 失礼な: It is impolite of you not to answer him. (*Ka-re ni heñji o shinai no wa shitsu-ree da.*) 彼に返事をしないのは失礼だ.

import *vt.* ... o yu⌐nyuu suru ...を輸入する Ⓣ: His company imports wine. (*Kare no kaisha wa waiñ o yunyuu shite iru.*) 彼の会社はワインを輸入している.
— *n.* (importing) yu⌐nyuu 輸入; (goods) yu⌐nyuuhiñ 輸入品: Imports this year were greater than exports. (*Kotoshi wa yunyuu no hoo ga yushutsu yori mo ookatta.*) ことしは輸入のほうが輸出よりも多かった.

importance *n.* ju⌐uyoosee 重要性; ju⌐udaisa 重大さ: a matter of great importance (*kiwamete juu-yoo na kotogara*) きわめて重要な事柄 / a person of importance (*juuyoo jiñbutsu*) 重要人物.

important *adj.* **1** (of a matter) ju⌐uyoo na 重要な; ta⌐isetsu na 大切な; ju⌐udai na 重大な: It is important to read good books. (*Yoi hoñ o yomu koto wa juuyoo na koto desu.*) よい本を読むことは重要なことです. / Sleeping is important for our health. (*Suimiñ wa keñkoo ni tai-setsu desu.*) 睡眠は健康に大切です.
2 (of a person) yu⌐uryoku na 有力な; ju⌐uyoo na 重要な: a very important person (*yoojiñ*) 要人.

impose *vt.* **1** (place) ... o (... ni) ka⌐su ...を(...に)課す Ⓒ; o⌐waseru 負わせる Ⓥ: impose a tax on imports (*zeekiñ o yunyuuhiñ ni kasu*) 税金を輸入品に課す.
2 (force) ... o (... ni) o⌐shitsuke⌐ru ...を(...に)押しつける Ⓥ: He tried to impose his opinion on me. (*Kare wa kare no ikeñ o watashi ni oshi-tsukeyoo to shita.*) 彼は彼の意見を私に押しつけようとした.

impossible *adj.* **1** (that cannot be done) fu⌐ka⌐noo na 不可能な: It is impossible to move this stone. (*Kono ishi o ugokasu no wa fuka-noo da.*) この石を動かすのは不可能だ.

2 (that cannot happen) a⌐ri e⌐nai あり得ない; shi⌐ñjirare⌐nai 信じられない: It is impossible that he would break his word. (*Kare ga yaku-soku o yaburu nante ari enai.*) 彼が約束を破るなんてあり得ない.

impractical *adj.* hi-ji⌐ssai-teki na 非実際的な; hi-ge⌐ñjitsu-teki na 非現実的な: an impractical plan (*hi-jissai-teki na keekaku*) 非実際的な計画.

impress *vt.* **1** (move deeply) ... ni ka⌐ñmee o ataeru ...に感銘を与える Ⓥ: I was deeply impressed by his speech. (*Watashi wa kare no eñ-zetsu ni fukai kañmee o uketa.*) 私は彼の演説に深い感銘を受けた.
2 (press upon the mind) ... ni i⌐ñ-shoo o ataeru ...に印象を与える Ⓥ: His manner impressed her favorably. (*Kare no taido wa kanojo ni yoi iñshoo o ataeta.*) 彼の態度は彼女によい印象を与えた.

impression *n.* i⌐ñshoo 印象; ka⌐ñmee 感銘: What are your first impressions of Tokyo? (*Tookyoo no dai-ichi iñshoo wa ikaga desu ka?*) 東京の第一印象はいかがですか.

impressive *adj.* tsu⌐yo⌐i i⌐ñshoo o ataeru 強い印象を与える; i⌐ñshoo-teki na 印象的な; ka⌐ñmee o ataeru 感銘を与える: an impressive speech (*hito ni kañmee o ataeru eñzetsu*) 人に感銘を与える演説.

imprison *vt.* ... o ke⌐emu⌐sho ni i⌐reru ...を刑務所に入れる Ⓥ; to⌐o-goku suru 投獄する Ⓣ: He was imprisoned for the crime. (*Kare wa sono hañzai no tame ni too-goku sareta.*) 彼はその犯罪のために投獄された.

improper *adj.* **1** (not proper) fu⌐te⌐kitoo na 不適当な; fu⌐sawa⌐shi-ku na⌐i ふさわしくない: wear dress improper to the occasion (*sono ba ni fusawashiku nai fukusoo o suru*) その場にふさわしくない服装をする.
2 (wrong) ta⌐da⌐shiku na⌐i 正しくない; a⌐yama⌐tta 誤った; a⌐yama⌐tte iru 誤っている: an improper conclu-

sion (*ayamatta ketsuroñ*) 誤った結論.

improve *vt.* ... o ka⌐izeñ suru ...を改善する Ⅰ; ka⌐iryoo suru 改良する Ⅰ; jo⌐otatsu saseru 上達させる Ⅴ: improve a product (*seehiñ o kairyoo suru*) 製品を改良する / He improved his Japanese. (*Kare wa Nihoñgo ga jootatsu shita.*) 彼は日本語が上達した.
— *vi.* yo⌐ku naru よくなる Ⅽ; shi⌐ñpo suru 進歩する Ⅰ: His health is improving. (*Kare no keñkoo wa yoku natte imasu.*) 彼の健康はよくなっています.

improvement *n.* ka⌐izeñ 改善; ka⌐iryoo 改良; shi⌐ñpo 進歩: There's room for improvement. (*Kairyoo no yochi ga aru.*) 改良の余地がある.

improvise *vi.* (compose) so⌐kuseki ni tsuku⌐ru 即席に作る Ⅽ; (perform) so⌐kkyoo de eñsoo suru 即興で演奏する Ⅰ: improvise on the piano (*piano o sokkyoo de eñsoo suru*) ピアノを即興で演奏する.

imprudence *n.* ke⌐esotsu 軽率; mu⌐fu⌐ñbetsu 無分別.

imprudent *adj.* ke⌐esotsu na 軽率な; mu⌐fu⌐ñbetsu na 無分別な: What he did was imprudent. (*Kare no shita koto wa keesotsu datta.*) 彼のしたことは軽率だった.

impulse *n.* **1** (sudden desire) sho⌐odoo 衝動; de⌐kigo⌐koro でき心: act on impulse (*shoodoo ni kararete koodoo suru*) 衝動に駆られて行動する / impulse buying (*shoodoogai*) 衝動買い.
2 (sudden force) sho⌐ogeki 衝撃: the impulse of a wave (*nami no shoogeki*) 波の衝撃.

impulsive *adj.* sho⌐odoo-teki na 衝動的な: an impulsive action (*shoodoo-teki na koodoo*) 衝動的な行動.

impure *adj.* (not pure) ju⌐ñsui de na⌐i 純粋でない; (dirty) yo⌐goreta 汚れた; yo⌐gorete iru 汚れている; fu⌐ketsu na 不潔な: The air in this

room is impure. (*Kono heya no kuuki wa yogorete iru.*) この部屋の空気は汚れている.

in *prep.* **1** (position) ... ni [de] ...に[で]: I live in Tokyo. (*Watashi wa Tookyoo ni suñde imasu.*) 私は東京に住んでいます. / Let's swim in the lake. (*Mizuumi de oyogoo.*) 湖で泳ごう.
2 (time) ... ni [de] ...に[で]: Cherry blossoms bloom in April. (*Sakura wa shi-gatsu ni sakimasu.*) 桜は4月に咲きます. / I can finish it in one day. (*Watashi wa ichi-nichi de sore o oeru koto ga dekimasu.*) 私は1日でそれを終えることができます.
3 (motion) ... ni ...に: He put his hand in his pocket. (*Kare wa te o poketto ni ireta.*) 彼は手をポケットに入れた.
4 (state) ... no na⌐ka o ...の中を: He went out in the rain. (*Kare wa ame no naka o dete itta.*) 彼は雨の中を出て行った.
5 (be means of) ... de ...で: write in ink (*iñku de kaku*) インクで書く / Please speak in Japanese. (*Nihoñgo de hanashite kudasai.*) 日本語で話してください.
6 (limitation) ... ni oite ...において; ... ga ...が: one meter in length (*nagasa ga ichi-meetoru*) 長さが1メートル / We were five in number. (*Wareware wa niñzuu ga go-niñ datta.*) われわれは人数が5人だった.
7 (wearing) ... o ki⌐te ...を着て: a woman in white (*shiroi fuku o kita fujiñ*) 白い服を着た婦人.
— *adv.* ... no na⌐ka ni [e] ...の中に[へ]: Please come in. (*Doozo naka e o-hairi kudasai.*) どうぞ中へお入りください.
— *adj.* za⌐itaku shite (iru) 在宅して(いる): Is Mr.Tanaka in? (*Tanaka-sañ wa go-zaitaku desu ka?*) 田中さんはご在宅ですか.

inadequate *adj.* fu⌐ju⌐ubuñ na 不十分な; fu⌐te⌐kitoo na 不適当な: an inadequate income (*fujuubuñ na shuunyuu*) 不十分な収入.

inaugurate vt. **1** (install) ... o shu⌐unin saseru ...を就任させる Ⓥ: inaugurate a president (*daitooryoo o shuunin saseru*) 大統領を就任させる.
2 (make a start) ... o ka⌐ishi suru ...を開始する Ⓣ; ho⌐ssoku saseru 発足させる Ⓥ: inaugurate a long-term plan (*chooki keekaku o hossoku saseru*) 長期計画を発足させる.

incapable adj. **1** (not able) de-⌐ki¬nai できない: He's incapable of telling a lie. (*Kare wa uso o tsuku koto ga dekinai.*) 彼はうそをつくことができない.
2 (lacking ability) mu⌐noo na 無能な; mu¬ryoku na 無力な: an incapable person (*munoo na hito*) 無能な人.

inch n. i¬nchi インチ: 6 feet 3 inches (*roku-fiito san-inchi*) 6 フィート 3 インチ. ★ Japanese use the metric system and 'inch' is not used.

incident n. de⌐ki¬goto 出来事; ji-ken 事件: He told us about a recent incident. (*Kare wa watashi-tachi ni saikin no dekigoto ni tsuite hanashite kureta.*) 彼は私たちに最近の出来事について話してくれた.

incidentally adv. to⌐koro¬ de ところで; so⌐re wa so¬o to それはそうと: Incidentally, what time is it now? (*Tokoro de ima nan-ji desu ka?*) ところで今何時ですか.

inclination n. **1** (liking; wish) ko⌐nomi 好み; i⌐koo 意向: I have no inclination to listen to jazz. (*Watashi wa jazu o kiku no wa konomanai.*) 私はジャズを聞くのは好まない.
2 (tendency) ke⌐ekoo 傾向; ku¬se¬ 癖: The boy has an inclination to tell lies. (*Sono otoko-no-ko wa uso o tsuku kuse ga aru.*) その男の子はうそをつく癖がある.
3 (sloping) ka⌐tamuki 傾き; ke⌐e-sha 傾斜; ko⌐obai 勾配: the inclination of a roof (*yane no koobai*) 屋根の勾配.

incline vt. (bend) ... o ka⌐tamuke¬-ru ...を傾ける Ⓥ; ma⌐geru 曲げる Ⓥ: He inclined his head to hear her words. (*Kare wa kanojo no kotoba o kiku tame ni atama o katamuketa.*) 彼は彼女の言葉を聞くために頭を傾けた.
— vi. **1** (lean) ka⌐tamu¬ku 傾く Ⓒ: The tree inclines toward the left. (*Sono ki wa hidari ni katamuite iru.*) その木は左に傾いている.
2 (tend) ⟨verb⟩-gachi da ...がちだ: He inclines to carelessness. (*Kare wa fuchuui ni narigachi da.*) 彼は不注意になりがちだ.

be inclined to do vi. **1** (have a willingness) ... ki ni na⌐tte iru ...気になっている Ⓥ: He is inclined to go. (*Kare wa iku ki ni natte imasu.*) 彼は行く気になっています.
2 (have a tendency) ke⌐ekoo ga a¬-ru 傾向がある Ⓒ: I am inclined to put on weight. (*Watashi wa futoru keekoo ga aru.*) 私は太る傾向がある.

include vt. ... o fu⌐ku¬mu ...を含む Ⓒ; fu⌐kume¬ru 含める Ⓥ: Is the tax included in this? (*Kore ni zeekin wa fukumarete imasu ka?*) これに税金は含まれていますか. / two meals included (*ni-shoku-tsuki*) 2 食付き.

including prep. ... o fu⌐ku¬mete ...を含めて; i⌐rete 入れて: All of us, including me, will attend the meeting. (*Watashi mo fukumete zenin ga kai ni shusseki shimasu.*) 私も含めて全員が会に出席します.

income n. shu⌐unyuu 収入; sho⌐to-ku 所得: He has a high income. (*Kare wa koo-shuunyuu o ete iru.*) 彼は高収入を得ている. / income tax (*shotokuzee*) 所得税.

incomparable adj. hi⌐kaku de-ki¬nai 比較できない; hi⌐rui no na¬i 比類のない; mu¬hi no 無比の: incomparable beauty (*hirui no nai utsu-kushisa*) 比類のない美しさ.

incompatible adj. a⌐i-irenai 相容れない; ryo⌐oritsu shinai 両立しない; mu¬jun shita [shite iru] 矛盾した[している]: a theory incompatible with the facts (*jijitsu to mujun* *shita riroñ*) 事実と矛盾した理論.

incompetent *adj.* mu⌐noo na 無
能な; ya⌐ku⌐ ni ta⌐ta⌐nai 役に立たな
い: He's incompetent as manager.
(*Kare wa kañtoku to shite munoo
da.*) 彼は監督として無能だ.

incomplete *adj.* fu⌐ka⌐ñzeñ na 不
完全な; mi⌐ka⌐ñsee no 未完成の:
The bridge is still incomplete.
(*Sono hashi wa mada mikañsee
desu.*) その橋はまだ未完成です.

inconvenience *n.* fu⌐beñ 不便;
fu⌐tsu⌐goo 不都合; me⌐ewaku 迷惑:
I hope this will not cause you any
inconvenience. (*Kono koto ga go-
meewaku ni naranai koto o nozomimasu.*) このことがご迷惑にならないこ
とを望みます.

inconvenient *adj.* fu⌐beñ na 不便
な; tsu⌐goo no waru⌐i 都合の悪い: It
is inconvenient not to have a car.
(*Kuruma ga nai to fubeñ da.*) 車が
ないと不便だ. / If it is inconvenient
for you, I will put off my visit.
(*Moshi mo go-tsugoo ga waru-
kereba hoomoñ o nobashimasu.*) も
しもご都合が悪ければ訪問を延ばします.

incorporate *vt.* ... o ga⌐ppee saseru ...を合併させる Ⓥ; ku⌐miire⌐ru
組み入れる Ⓥ: incorporate a firm
with another (*shoosha o ta no shoosha to gappee saseru*) 商社を他の商
社と合併させる.

incorrect *adj.* fu⌐se⌐ekaku na 不正
確な; ma⌐chiga⌐tta 間違った; ma⌐chi-
ga⌐tte iru 間違っている: an incorrect
answer (*machigatta kotae*) 間違った
答え / His information is incorrect.
(*Kare no joohoo wa fuseekaku da.*)
彼の情報は不正確だ.

increase *vi.* fu⌐e⌐ru 増える Ⓥ; zo⌐o-
ka suru 増加する Ⓘ: Traffic accidents show a tendency to increase.
(*Kootsuu jiko wa zooka suru keekoo ni aru.*) 交通事故は増加する傾向
にある.
— *vt.* ... o fu⌐ya⌐su ...を増やす Ⓒ;
zo⌐oka saseru 増加させる Ⓥ: The
school increased the number of students. (*Sono gakkoo wa seeto no

kazu o fuyashita.) その学校は生徒の
数を増やした.
— *n.* zo⌐oka 増加; zo⌐odai 増大:
an increase in income (*shuunyuu
no zooka*) 収入の増加.

increasingly *adv.* ma⌐su⌐masu ま
すます; shi⌐dai ni 次第に: It has become increasingly difficult to build
a house. (*Ie o tateru no ga masu-
masu muzukashiku natta.*) 家を建
てるのがますます難しくなった.

incredible *adj.* shi⌐ñjirare⌐nai 信じ
られない; su⌐go⌐i すごい: an incredible
story (*shiñjirarenai hanashi*) 信じら
れない話 / His appetite is incredible.
(*Kare no shokuyoku wa sugoi.*) 彼
の食欲はすごい.

incur *vt.* ... o ma⌐ne⌐ku ...を招く Ⓒ:
incur a person's wrath (*hito no
ikari o maneku*) 人の怒りを招く.

indebted *adj.* o⌐ñ o ukete (iru) 恩
を受けて(いる); ka⌐ñsha shite (iru) 感
謝して(いる): I'm greatly indebted to
you for your help. (*Go-joryoku ni
taiheñ kañsha shite orimasu.*) ご助
力に大変感謝しております.

indeed *adv.* ma⌐ttaku まったく;
ho⌐ñtoo ni 本当に; ji⌐tsu⌐ ni 実に: I
was indeed very tired. (*Watashi
wa mattaku tsukarekitte ita.*) 私は
まったく疲れきっていた. / Thank you
very much indeed. (*Hoñtoo ni arigatoo gozaimashita.*) 本当にありがと
うございました.

independence *n.* do⌐kuritsu 独
立; ji⌐ritsu 自立: live a life of independence (*jiritsu shita seekatsu o
suru*) 自立した生活をする.

independent *adj.* **1** (not ruled)
do⌐kuritsu no 独立の; ji⌐shu no 自主
の: an independent country (*doku-
ritsukoku*) 独立国.
2 (not relying on) ta⌐yora⌐nai 頼ら
ない; ji⌐katsu shita [shite iru] 自活し
た[している]: My daughter is leading
an independent life. (*Musume wa
jikatsu shite imasu.*) 娘は自活してい
ます.
3 (separate) be⌐tsubetsu no 別々の;
(not connected) mu⌐ka⌐ñkee no 無

関係の: These two problems are independent of each other. (*Kono futatsu no moñdai wa o-tagai ni mukañkee desu.*) この二つの問題はお互いに無関係です.

index *n.* **1** (list) sa⌐kuiñ˥ 索引: an index to a book (*hoñ no sakuiñ*) 本の索引.
2 (figure) shi⌐su˥u 指数: a price index (*bukka shisuu*) 物価指数.

index finger *n.* hi⌐tosashi˥-yubi 人さし指.

India *n.* I˥ñdo インド.

indicate *vt.* **1** (point out) ... o sa⌐shishime˥su ...を指し示す Ⓒ; sa˥su 指す Ⓒ: He indicated where Matsue was on the map. (*Kare wa Matsue ga doko ni aru ka o chizu de sashi shimeshita.*) 彼は松江がどこにあるかを地図で指し示した.
2 (be a sign of) ... o shi⌐me˥su ...を示す Ⓒ; a⌐rawa˥su 表す Ⓒ: The arrow indicates the exit. (*Yajirushi wa deguchi o shimeshite imasu.*) 矢印は出口を示しています.

indication *n.* cho⌐rokoo 徴候; ki⌐zashi˥ 兆し: There are indications that business will recover. (*Keeki ga yoku naru kizashi ga aru.*) 景気がよくなる兆しがある.

indifference *n.* mu⌐ka˥ñshiñ 無関心; re⌐eta˥ñ 冷淡: an indifference toward politics (*seeji ni taisuru mukañshiñ*) 政治に対する無関心.

indifferent *adj.* mu⌐ka˥ñshiñ na 無関心な; re⌐eta˥ñ na 冷淡な: He is indifferent to other people's troubles. (*Kare wa hoka no hito no shiñpaigoto ni wa mukañshiñ da.*) 彼はほかの人の心配事には無関心だ.

indigestion *n.* sho⌐okafu˥ryoo 消化不良.

indignant *adj.* fu⌐ñgai shita [shite iru] 憤慨した[している]; o⌐ko˥tta 怒った; o⌐ko˥tte iru 怒っている: He was indignant at the unfair judgment. (*Kare wa sono fukoohee na hañtee ni fuñgai shita.*) 彼はその不公平な判定に憤慨した.

indignation *n.* i⌐kidoori˥ 憤り;

fu⌐ñgai 憤慨: feel indignation about an injustice (*fusee ni taishite ikidoori o kañjiru*) 不正に対して憤りを感じる.

indirect *adj.* **1** (not direct) ma⌐s-su˥gu de nai 真っすぐでない; ma⌐warimichi no 回り道の: take an indirect route (*mawarimichi o suru*) 回り道をする.
2 (not straightforward) to⌐oma˥washi no 遠回しの; so⌐tchoku de na˥i 率直でない: give an indirect answer (*toomawashi no heñji o suru*) 遠回しの返事をする.
3 (not connected directly) ka⌐ñse-tsu no 間接の; ka⌐ñsetsu-teki na 間接的な: an indirect cause (*kañse-tsu-teki na geñiñ*) 間接的な原因.

indiscreet *adj.* fu⌐ñbetsu no na˥i 分別のない; ke⌐esotsu na 軽率な: an indiscreet remark (*keesotsu na hatsugeñ*) 軽率な発言.

indispensable *adj.* ka⌐ku koto no deki˥nai 欠くことのできない; fu⌐ka˥ketsu na 不可欠な; ze⌐ttai ni hi˥tsuyoo na 絶対に必要な: Water is indispensable to life. (*Mizu wa seemee ni fukaketsu desu.*) 水は生命に不可欠です.

individual *adj.* **1** (separate) ko⌐ko no 個々の; so⌐re˥zore no それぞれの: I checked each individual bag. (*Watashi wa sorezore no kabañ o shirabeta.*) 私はそれぞれのかばんを調べた.
2 (of a single person) ko⌐jiñ no 個人の; ko⌐jiñ-teki na 個人的な: an individual matter (*kojiñ-teki na moñdai*) 個人的な問題.
3 (characteristic) ko⌐see-teki na 個性的な; do⌐kutoku na 独特の: an individual style of speaking (*doku-toku no hanashikata*) 独特の話し方.
— *n.* ko⌐jiñ 個人: the rights of the individual (*kojiñ no keñri*) 個人の権利.

indoor *adj.* o⌐ku˥nai no 屋内の: indoor games (*okunai kyoogi*) 屋内競技.

indoors *adv.* o⌐ku˥nai de [e] 屋内で

[へ]; u「chi no na「ka de [e] 家の中で [へ]: It began to rain, so I went indoors. (*Ame ga furi-dashita no de watashi wa uchi no naka e haitta.*) 雨が降りだしたので私は家の中へ入った.

induce *vt.* **1** (lead into doing) ... o ⟨verb⟩-(sa)seru ...を...(さ)せる ☑: Nothing can induce him to change his mind. (*Nanigoto mo kare no kokoro o kaesaseru koto wa dekinai.*) なにごとも彼の心を変えさせることはできない.
2 (cause) ... o hi「kioko「su ...を引き起こす ☐: His illness was induced by overwork. (*Kare no byooki wa karoo ni yotte hikiokosareta.*) 彼の病気は過労によって引き起こされた.

indulge *vt.* **1** (spoil) ... o a「mayaka「su ...を甘やかす ☐; ki「mama ni saseru 気ままにさせる ☑: He indulges his children too much. (*Kare wa kodomo o amayakashi-sugiru.*) 彼は子どもを甘やかし過ぎる.
2 (satisfy) ...o ma「nzoku saseru ...を満足させる ☑: indulge one's desires (*yokuboo o manzoku saseru*) 欲望を満足させる.

industrial *adj.* sa「ngyoo no 産業の; ko「ogyoo no 工業の: an industrial town (*koogyoo toshi*) 工業都市.

industrious *adj.* ki「nben na 勤勉な; yo「ku ha「taraku よく働く: an industrious student (*kinben na gaku-see*) 勤勉な学生.

industry *n.* **1** (business) sa「ngyoo 産業; ko「ogyoo 工業: the automobile industry (*jidoosha-sangyoo*) 自動車産業.
2 (hard work) ki「nben 勤勉: He worked with industry. (*Kare wa kinben ni hataraita.*) 彼は勤勉に働いた.

inevitable *adj.* sa「kerare「nai 避けられない; to「ozen no 当然の: Death is inevitable. (*Shi wa sakerarenai.*) 死は避けられない.

inexpensive *adj.* hi「yoo no ka「kara「nai 費用のかからない; ya「su「i 安

い: an inexpensive restaurant (*ne-dañ no yasui resutorañ*) 値段の安いレストラン.

infant *n.* yo「oji 幼児.
—— *adj.* yo「oji no 幼児の; yo「ojiyoo no 幼児用の: infant food (*yooji-shoku*) 幼児食.

infect *vt.* (give a disease) ... ni ka-「ñseñ saseru ...に感染させる ☑; byo「oki o utsu「su 病気をうつす ☐: His cold infected his child. (*Kare no kaze ga kodomo ni utsutta.*) 彼のかぜが子どもにうつった.

infection *n.* ka「ñseñ 感染; de「ñ-señ 伝染: prevent infection (*kañ-señ o fusegu*) 感染を防ぐ.

infectious *adj.* ka「ñseñ suru 感染する; ka「ñseñsee no 感染性の: Cancer is not infectious. (*Gañ wa kañ-señ shinai.*) がんは感染しない.

infer *vt.* ... to su「iroñ suru ...と推論する ☐; su「isoku suru 推測する ☐: I inferred from his expression that he was angry. (*Kare no hyoojoo kara kare wa okotte iru no da to suisoku shita.*) 彼の表情から彼は怒っているのだと推測した.

inferior *adj.* **1** (poor in quality) o「to「tta 劣った; o「to「tte iru 劣っている; so「aku na 粗悪な: This wine is inferior to that in quality. (*Kono wañ wa sore yori mo shitsu ga ototte iru.*) このワインはそれよりも質が劣っている.
2 (lower in rank) ka「kyuu no 下級の; ka「i no 下位の: an inferior court (*kakyuu saibañsho*) 下級裁判所.

inferiority *n.* o「to「tte iru ko「to「 劣っていること; re「ttoo 劣等; so「aku 粗悪: an inferiority complex (*ret-tookañ*) 劣等感.

infinite *adj.* ka「giri no na「i 限りのない; mu「geñ no 無限の: The universe is infinite. (*Uchuu wa mugeñ desu.*) 宇宙は無限です.

inflation *n.* i「ñfure インフレ; i「ñfu-re「eshoñ インフレーション.

inflict *vt.* ... o a「taeru ...を与える ☑; o「waseru 負わせる ☑: inflict damage (*soñgai o ataeru*) 損害を与える /

inflict a wound (*kizu o owaseru*) 傷を負わせる.

influence *n.* **1** (effect) e「ekyoo 影響; ka「nka 感化: the influence of television on children (*kodomo-tachi ni taisuru terebi no eekyoo*) 子どもたちに対するテレビの影響.

2 (power) se「eryoku 勢力; ke「n-ryoku 権力: a person of influence (*yuuryokusha*) 有力者.

3 (person) e「ekyo「oryoku no aru hi「to「 影響力のある人: a powerful influence in politics (*seekai no oo-mono jitsuryokusha*) 政界の大物実力者.

— *vt.* ... ni e「ekyoo o ataeru …に影響を与える V: The weather influences the crop. (*Tenkoo wa saku-motsu ni eekyoo o ataeru.*) 天候は作物に影響を与える.

influential *adj.* e「ekyo「oryoku no aru 影響力のある; yu「uryoku na 有力な: an influential politician (*yuu-ryoku na seejika*) 有力な政治家.

inform *vt.* ... ni (... o) tsu「uchi suru …に(…を)通知する I; shi「raseru 知らせる V: I informed my parents of my safe arrival. (*Watashi wa ryoo-shin ni buji ni tsuita koto o shira-seta.*) 私は両親に無事に着いたことを知らせた.

informal *adj.* **1** (not formal) hi「ko「oshiki na 非公式の; rya「kushiki no 略式の: informal clothes (*ryaku-shiki no fuku*) 略式の服.

2 (colloquial) ku「da「keta くだけた; ku「da「kete iru くだけている; ko「ogo no 口語の: informal expressions (*kudaketa hyoogen*) くだけた表現.

information *n.* **1** (news) jo「ohoo 情報: We got a valuable piece of information. (*Watashi-tachi wa kichoo na joohoo o eta.*) 私たちは貴重な情報を得た.

2 (knowledge) chi「shiki 知識: This book gives information about animals. (*Kono hon wa doobutsu ni tsuite no chishiki o ataete kureru.*) この本は動物についての知識を与えてくれる.

3 (place) a「nnaijo 案内所: Where is the tourist information office? (*Kankoo annaijo wa doko desu ka?*) 観光案内所はどこですか.

ingenious *adj.* do「kusoo-teki na 独創的な; ri「koo na 利口な: an ingenious theory (*dokusoo-teki na riron*) 独創的な理論.

ingredient *n.* za「iryo「o 材料: a list of the ingredients for making cake (*keeki o tsukuru no ni hitsu-yoo na zairyoo no risuto*) ケーキを作るのに必要な材料のリスト.

inhabit *vt.* ... ni su「mu …に住む C; kyo「juu suru 居住する I: This area is inhabited by rich people. (*Kono chiiki ni wa kanemochi ga sunde iru.*) この地域には金持ちが住んでいる.

inhabitant *n.* ju「umin 住民: the inhabitants of a village (*mura no juumin*) 村の住民.

inherit *vt.* **1** (receive) ... o so「ozo-ku suru …を相続する I; u「ketsu「gu 受け継ぐ C: She inherited considerable property from her father. (*Kanojo wa chichi-oya kara kanari no zaisan o soozoku shita.*) 彼女は父親からかなりの財産を相続した.

2 (get from one's parents) ... o u「ketsu「gu …を受け継ぐ C: a characteristic inherited from one's parents (*ryooshin kara uketsuida tokushitsu*) 両親から受け継いだ特質.

inheritance *n.* (act) so「ozoku 相続; (money) i「san 遺産: He came into a large inheritance from his uncle. (*Kare wa oji kara tagaku no isan o moratta.*) 彼はおじから多額の遺産をもらった.

initial *adj.* ha「jime no 初めの; sa「i-sho no 最初の: the initial stage of a disease (*byooki no hajime no dan-kai*) 病気の初めの段階.

— *n.* (the first letter) ka「shiramo「ji 頭文字.

— *vt.* ... ni ka「shiramo「ji de sho「mee suru …に頭文字で署名する I: initial a letter (*tegami ni kashira-moji de shomee suru*) 手紙に頭文字で署名する.

initiate vt. (start) ... o ka⌐ishi suru ...を開始する Ⓣ; ... ni cha⌐kushu suru ...に着手する Ⓣ: initiate reforms (kaikaku ni chakushu suru) 改革に着手する.

initiative n. shu⌐do⌐okeñ 主導権; i⌐nishia⌐chibu イニシアチブ: take the initiative (inishiachibu o toru) イニシアチブを取る.

injection n. chu⌐usha 注射: I had an injection to stop the pain. (Watashi wa itamidome no chuusha o shite moratta.) 私は痛み止めの注射をしてもらった.

injure vt. ... ni ke⌐ga o sa⌐seru ...にけがをさせる Ⓥ; ... o ki⌐zutsuke⌐ru ...を傷つける Ⓥ: He was slightly injured in the accident. (Kare wa sono jiko de karui kega o shita.) 彼はその事故で軽いけがをした. / injure a person's feelings (hito no kañjoo o kizutsukeru) 人の感情を傷つける.

injurious adj. yu⌐ugai na 有害な: Smoking is injurious to the lungs. (Kitsueñ wa hai ni yuugai desu.) 喫煙は肺に有害です.

injury n. **1** (hurt) fu⌐shoo 負傷; ke⌐ga⌐ けが: suffer injuries to one's head (atama ni kega o suru) 頭にけがをする.
2 (harm) ki⌐zutsuke⌐ru ko⌐to⌐ 傷つけること; bu⌐ree 無礼; bu⌐joku 侮辱: an injury to a person's reputation (meeyo kisoñ) 名誉毀損.

injustice n. fu⌐ko⌐osee 不公正; fu⌐ko⌐ohee 不公平: do a person an injustice (hito o futoo ni atsukau) 人を不当に扱う.

ink n. i⌐ñku インク: He signed his name in ink. (Kare wa namae o iñku de saiñ shita.) 彼は名前をインクでサインした.

inn n. ya⌐doya 宿屋: stay at an inn (yadoya ni tomaru) 宿屋に泊まる / a Japanese inn (ryokañ) 旅館.

inner adj. u⌐chigawa no 内側の; na⌐ibu no 内部の: an inner court (nakaniwa) 中庭.

innocence n. **1** (freedom from guilt) mu⌐zai 無罪: He proved his innocence. (Kare wa jibuñ no muzai o shoomee shita.) 彼は自分の無罪を証明した.
2 (purity) mu⌐jaki 無邪気; ju⌐ñshiñ 純真: childlike innocence (kodomo no yoo na mujakisa) 子どものような無邪気さ.

innocent adj. **1** (not guilty) mu⌐zai no 無罪の; ke⌐ppaku na 潔白な: I am innocent. (Watashi wa keppaku desu.) 私は潔白です.
2 (knowing no evil) mu⌐jaki na 無邪気な; a⌐dokena⌐i あどけない: an innocent child (adokenai kodomo) あどけない子ども.
3 (harmless) mu⌐gai na 無害な; a⌐kui no nai 悪意のない: innocent jokes (akui no nai joodañ) 悪意のない冗談.

innumerable adj. ka⌐zoekire⌐nai 数え切れない; mu⌐su⌐u no 無数の: innumerable stars (musuu no hoshi) 無数の星.

inquire vt. ... o ta⌐zune⌐ru ...を尋ねる Ⓥ; to⌐iawase⌐ru 問い合わせる Ⓥ: He inquired the way to the museum. (Kare wa bijutsukañ e iku michi o tazuneta.) 彼は美術館へ行く道を尋ねた.
— vi. shi⌐tsumoñ suru 質問する Ⓣ; ta⌐zune⌐ru 尋ねる Ⓥ: inquire at the information desk (añnaijo de tazuneru) 案内所で尋ねる.
inquire into ... vt. ... o shi⌐rabe⌐ru ...を調べる Ⓥ: inquire into the cause of an accident (jiko no geñiñ o shiraberu) 事故の原因を調べる.

inquiry n. **1** (asking) to⌐iawase 問い合わせ; sho⌐okai 照会: a letter of inquiry (toiawase no tegami) 問い合わせの手紙.
2 (investigation) cho⌐osa 調査; to⌐rishirabe 取り調べ: They made inquiries into the matter. (Kare-ra wa sono moñdai o choosa shita.) 彼らはその問題を調査した.

insane adj. (mad) sho⌐oki de na⌐i 正気でない; kyo⌐oki no 狂気の; (foolish) hi⌐jo⌐oshiki na 非常識な: an insane scheme (hijooshiki na *keekaku*) 非常識な計画.

insect *n.* ko⌐ñchuu 昆虫 ; mu⌐shi 虫.
★ 'Worm' is also called '*mushi*' in
Japanese.

insecure *adj.* **1** (lacking confidence) ji⌐shiñ ga na⌐i 自信がない;
fu⌐añ na 不安な: I am insecure
about my new job. (*Watashi wa
atarashii shigoto ni jishiñ ga nai.*)
私は新しい仕事に自信がない.
2 (not safe) a⌐ñzeñ de na⌐i 安全でな
い; fu⌐añtee na 不安定な: an insecure footing (*fuañtee na ashiba*) 不
安定な足場.

insensitive *adj.* do⌐ñkañ na 鈍感
な; ka⌐ñji nai 感じない: He is insensitive to other people's feelings. (*Kare wa taniñ no kimochi ni doñkañ
da.*) 彼は他人の気持ちに鈍感だ.

insert *vt.* ... o (... ni) sa⌐shiko⌐mu
...を(...に)差し込む C; so⌐ñyuu suru
挿入する I; i⌐reru 入れる V: insert
a key in a lock (*kagi o joo ni sashikomu*) 鍵を錠に差し込む / insert a
coin into a vending machine
(*kooka o jidoo hañbaiki ni ireru*)
硬貨を自動販売機に入れる.

inside *adv.* na⌐ka ni [de, e, wa] 中
に[で, へ, は]: She went inside.
(*Kanojo wa naka ni haitta*) 彼女は
中に入った.
— *adj.* na⌐ibu no 内部の; u⌐chi-
gawa no 内側の: inside walls (*uchigawa no kabe*) 内側の壁 / an inside
pocket (*uchi poketto*) 内ポケット.
— *n.* na⌐ibu 内部; u⌐chigawa 内
側: the inside of a pocket (*poketto
no uchigawa*) ポケットの内側 / This
door opens from the inside. (*Kono
doa wa uchigawa kara hirakimasu.*) このドアは内側から開きます.

insight *n.* do⌐osatsu⌐ryoku 洞察力;
ga⌐ñshiki 眼識: a person of insight
(*doosatsuryoku no aru hito*) 洞察
力のある人.

insincere *adj.* se⌐iei no nai 誠意の
ない; fu⌐ma⌐jime na ふまじめな: insincere promises (*seei no nai yakusoku*) 誠意のない約束.

insist *vt.* **1** (state) ... to tsu⌐yoku

shu⌐choo suru ...と強く主張する I;
i⌐iha⌐ru 言い張る C: He insisted
that he was right. (*Kare wa jibuñ
ga tadashii to iihatta.*) 彼は自分が正
しいと言い張った.
2 (demand) ... to tsu⌐yoku yo⌐o-
kyuu suru ...と強く要求する I;
kyo⌐oyoo suru 強要する I: He insisted that I go. (*Kare wa watashi
ni iku yoo ni kyooyoo shita.*) 彼は
私に行くように強要した.
— *vi.* (... to) tsu⌐yoku shu⌐choo
suru (...と)強く主張する I; i⌐iha⌐ru
言い張る C: He insisted on his
innocence. (*Kare wa muzai da to
iihatta.*) 彼は無罪だと言い張った.

if you insist *adv.* ze⌐hi tomo to
i⌐u na⌐ra ぜひともというなら: I'll attend if you insist. (*Zehi tomo to iu
nara shusseki shimasu.*) ぜひともとい
うなら出席します.

inspect *vt.* **1** (examine) ... o ke⌐ñ-
sa suru ...を検査する I; shi⌐rabe⌐-
ru 調べる V: I inspected the house
before I bought it. (*Watashi wa
sono ie o kau mae ni shirabeta.*) 私
はその家を買う前に調べた.
2 (view officially) ... o shi⌐satsu
suru ...を視察する I: inspect a factory (*koojoo o shisatsu suru*) 工場
を視察する.

inspection *n.* ke⌐ñsa 検査; te⌐ñ-
keñ 点検; shi⌐satsu 視察: an inspection of plants (*shokubutsu no
keñsa*) 植物の検査 / a tour of inspection (*shisatsu ryokoo*) 視察旅行.

inspiration *n.* **1** (stimulus) re⌐e-
kañ 霊感; i⌐ñspire⌐eshoñ インスピレ
ーション: draw one's inspiration
from nature (*shizeñ kara reekañ o
ukeru*) 自然から霊感を受ける.
2 (bright idea) myo⌐oañ 妙案;
me⌐eañ 名案: I had a sudden
inspiration. (*Totsuzeñ meeañ ga
hirameita.*) 突然名案がひらめいた.

inspire *vt.* **1** (encourage) ... o fu⌐-
⌐ruitase⌐ru ...を奮い立たせる V;
ko⌐bu suru 鼓舞する I: His courage
inspired us. (*Kare no yuuki wa
watashi-tachi o furuitataseta.*) 彼の

勇気は私たちを奮い立たせた.
2 (produce a feeling) ...o fu「kiko¬mu ...を吹き込む C; yo「bioko¬su 呼び起こす C: The news inspired us with hope. (*Sono shirase wa watashi-tachi ni kiboo o yobiokoshita.*) その知らせは私たちに希望を呼び起こした.

install *vt.* **1** (fix) ...o to「ritsukeru ...を取り付ける Ⓥ; se「tchi suru 設置する Ⓘ: I installed a new air conditioner. (*Watashi wa atarashii kuuraa o toritsuketa.*) 私は新しいクーラーを取り付けた.
2 (place in a position) ...o shu「unin saseru ...を就任させる Ⓥ; ni「nmee suru 任命する Ⓘ: He was installed as chairman. (*Kare wa gichoo ni ninmee sareta.*) 彼は議長に任命された.

installment *n.* **1** (of payments) bu「nkatsu-ba¬rai 分割払い: buy a car on the installment plan (*bunkatsu-barai de kuruma o kau*) 分割払いで車を買う.
2 (of a story, drama) i「k-kai¬bun 1回分.

instance *n.* re「e¬ 例; ji「tsuree 実例: He gave many instances. (*Kare wa takusan no jitsuree o shimeshita.*) 彼はたくさんの実例を示した.
for instance *adv.* ta「to¬eba 例えば.

instant *adj.* **1** (immediate) so「kuza no 即座の; so「kuji no 即時の: an instant reply (*sokutoo*) 即答.
2 (of food) i「nsuta¬nto no インスタントの: instant coffee (*insutanto koohii*) インスタントコーヒー.
— *n.* shu「nkan 瞬間; so「kuji 即時: He was back in an instant. (*Kare wa sugu ni modotte kita.*) 彼はすぐに戻ってきた.

instantaneous *adj.* shu「nkan no 瞬間の; so「kuza no 即座の: instantaneous death (*sokushi*) 即死.

instantly *adv.* so「kuza ni 即座に; ta「dachi ni 直ちに: be killed instantly (*sokushi suru*) 即死する.

instead *adv.* so「no kawari ni その代わりに; ka「wari to shite 代わりとして: Give me this instead. (*Sono kawari ni kore o kudasai.*) その代わりにこれを下さい.
instead of ... *prep.* ...no ka「wari ni ...の代わりに: I went by train instead of by car. (*Watashi wa kuruma no kawari ni densha de itta.*) 私は車の代わりに電車で行った.

instinct *n.* ho「nnoo 本能: As winter approaches, swallows fly south by instinct. (*Fuyu ga chikazuku to tsubame wa honnoo ni yotte minami e tonde iku.*) 冬が近づくとつばめは本能によって南へ飛んで行く.

institute *n.* (society) ga「kkai 学会; (building) ke「nkyuujo 研究所.
— *vt.* ...o mo「okeru ...を設ける Ⓥ; se「etee suru 制定する: institute new rules (*atarashii kisoku o seetee suru*) 新しい規則を制定する.

institution *n.* **1** (instituting) se「tsuritsu 設立; se「tchi 設置: the institution of a committee (*iinkai no setchi*) 委員会の設置.
2 (building) shi「setsu 施設; (organization) ki「kan 機関: an institution for the aged (*roojin shisetsu*) 老人施設 / a public institution (*kookyoo kikan*) 公共機関.
3 (established law) ka「nree 慣例; se「edo 制度.

instruct *vt.* **1** (teach) ... ni (... o) o「shieru ...に(...を)教える Ⓥ: Mr. Yagi instructed us in Japanese. (*Yagi sensee ga watashi-tachi ni Nihongo o oshiete kureta.*) 八木先生が私たちに日本語を教えてくれた.
2 (order) ... ni (... o) sa「shizu suru ...に(...を)指図する Ⓘ; shi「ji suru 指示する Ⓘ: I instructed him how to do the work. (*Watashi wa kare ni sono shigoto no yarikata o shiji shita.*) 私は彼にその仕事のやり方を指示した.

instruction *n.* **1** (teaching) o「shie 教え; kyo「oiku 教育: give [receive] instruction in Japanese (*Nihongo no kyooiku o suru [ukeru]*) 日本語の教育をする[受ける].
2 (directions) shi「yoo setsumee(-

sho) 使用説明（書）: the instructions for a watch (tokee no setsumee-sho) 時計の説明書.

3 (order) sa˺shizu 指図; me˺eree 命令: We followed our teacher's instructions. (Watashi-tachi wa señsee no shiji ni shitagatta.) 私たちは先生の指示に従った.

instructive adj. kyo˺oiku-teki na 教育的な; ta˺me˺ni naru ためになる: an instructive book (tame ni naru hoñ) ためになる本.

instructor n. o˺shieru hito˺ 教える人; shi˺do˺osha 指導者; (of a college) se˺ñniñ ko˺oshi 専任講師.

instrument n. **1** (of music) ga˺kki 楽器: He can play several instruments. (Kare wa ikutsu-ka no gakki o hikeru.) 彼はいくつかの楽器を弾ける.

2 (tool) ki˺gu 器具; yo˺ogu 用具; ki˺ka˺i 器械: medical instruments (iryoo kigu) 医療器具.

insufficient adj. fu˺ju˺ubuñ na 不十分な; fu˺soku shite iru 不足している: There are insufficient nurses. (Kañgofu ga fusoku shite iru.) 看護婦が不足している.

insult vt. ... o bu˺joku suru ...を侮辱する ①: insult a person (hito o bujoku suru) 人を侮辱する.

— n. bu˺joku 侮辱; bu˺ree 無礼: What you say is an insult. (Kimi no iu koto wa bujoku da.) 君の言うことは侮辱だ.

insurance n. **1** (contract) ho˺keñ 保険; ho˺keñ-ke˺eyaku 保険契約: take out insurance on one's car (kuruma ni hokeñ o kakeru) 車に保険をかける / fire insurance (kasai-hokeñ) 火災保険 / health insurance (keñkoo-hokeñ) 健康保険.

2 (premium) ho˺ke˺ñryoo 保険料; ho˺keñkiñ 保険金: pay one's insurance (hokeñryoo o shiharau) 保険料を支払う.

insure vt. ... ni ho˺keñ o kake˺ru ...に保険をかける ⑤: He insured his house against fire. (Kare wa ie ni kasai-hokeñ o kaketa.) 彼は家に火

災保険をかけた.

intake n. se˺sshu˺ryoo 摂取量; to˺ri-ire 取り入れ: a daily intake of calcium (karushuumu no ichi-nichi no sesshuryoo) カルシウムの1日の摂取量.

integrate vt. ... o to˺ogoo suru ...を統合する ①; to˺oitsu suru 統一する ①: Some subjects were integrated into one course. (Ikutsu-ka no ka-moku ga hitotsu no koosu ni too-goo sareta.) いくつかの課目が一つのコースに統合された.

intellect n. chi˺see 知性; chi˺-ryoku 知力: a person of intellect (chisee no aru hito) 知性のある人.

intellectual adj. chi˺teki na 知的な; chi˺see no 知性の: Chess is an intellectual game. (Chesu wa chi-teki na geemu desu.) チェスは知的なゲームです.

— n. chi˺shiki˺jiñ 知識人; i˺ñteri インテリ.

intelligence n. **1** (ability to understand) chi˺noo 知能; ri˺ka˺i-ryoku 理解力: an intelligence quotient (chinoo shisuu) 知能指数 / an intelligence test (chinoo keñsa) 知能検査.

2 (information) jo˺ohoo 情報: collect intelligence (joohoo o atsu-meru) 情報を集める.

intelligent adj. **1** (of an animal) chi˺noo no ta˺ka˺i 知能の高い; ri˺koo na 利口な: an intelligent animal (rikoo na doobutsu) 利口な動物.

2 (of a building) jo˺ohooka sareta 情報化された; i˺ñte˺rijeñto na インテリジェントな: an intelligent building (iñterijeñto biru) インテリジェントビル.

intend vt. **1** (plan) ... tsu˺mori da ...つもりだ: I intend to buy a new car. (Watashi wa shiñsha o kau tsumori desu.) 私は新車を買うつもりです.

2 (mean) ... tsu˺mori da ...つもりだ; ... mu˺ke da ...向けだ: That was intended as a joke. (Are wa joodañ no tsumori deshita.) あれは冗談のつ

もりでした. / This book is intended for beginners. (*Kono hoñ wa sho-shiñsha muke desu.*) この本は初心者向けです.

intense *adj.* kyoˈoretsu na 強烈な; moˈoretsu na 猛烈な; haˈgeshiˈi 激しい: intense heat (*mooretsu na atsusa*) 猛烈な暑さ / a person of intense feelings (*kañjoo no hage-shii hito*) 感情の激しい人.

intensity *n.* kyoˈoretsusa 強烈さ; haˈgeˈshisa 激しさ: the intensity of feeling (*kañjoo no hageshisa*) 感情の激しさ.

intensive *adj.* shuˈuchuu-teki na 集中的な; teˈttee-teki na 徹底的な: an intensive investigation (*tettee-teki na choosa*) 徹底的な調査 / intensive reading (*seedoku*) 精読.

intent *adj.* neˈsshiñ na 熱心な; muˈuchuu na 夢中な: He is intent on the video game. (*Kare wa terebi geemu ni muchuu da.*) 彼はテレビゲームに夢中だ.

intention *n.* iˈito 意図; iˈkoo 意向; tsuˈmori つもり: I had no intention of telling a lie. (*Watashi wa uso o tsuku tsumori wa arimaseñ de-shita.*) 私はうそをつくつもりはありませんでした.

intentional *adj.* koˈi no 故意の; iˈto-teki na 意図的な: His mistake was intentional. (*Kare no machi-gai wa ito-teki datta.*) 彼の間違いは意図的だった.

interest *n.* **1** (curiosity) kyoˈomi 興味: I have an interest in sports. (*Watashi wa supootsu ni kyoomi o motte imasu.*) 私はスポーツに興味を持っています.
2 (matter concerned) kaˈñshiˈñji 関心事: One of my greatest interests is gardening. (*Watashi no ichibañ no kañshiñji no hitotsu wa eñgee desu.*) 私のいちばんの関心事の一つは園芸です.
3 (benefit) riˈeki 利益: He is look-ing after only his own interests. (*Kare wa jibuñ no rieki dake o motomete iru.*) 彼は自分の利益だけを求めている.
4 (money) riˈsoku 利息; riˈshi 利子: pay interest of 5 percent (*go-paaseñto no risoku o harau*) 5 パーセントの利息を払う.

interested *adj.* kyoˈomi o moˈtte iru 興味を持っている; kaˈñshiñ ga aˈru 関心がある: We are interested in your products. (*Watashi-domo wa anata no seehiñ ni kyoomi o motte imasu.*) 私どもはあなたの製品に興味を持っています.

interesting *adj.* kyoˈomi no aˈru 興味のある; oˈmoshiroˈi おもしろい: His story was very interesting. (*Kare no hanashi wa totemo omo-shirokatta.*) 彼の話はとてもおもしろかった.

interfere *vi.* **1** (meddle in) (... ni) kaˈñshoo suru (...に)干渉する ①; kuˈchidashi suru 口出しする ①: Don't interfere in other people's affairs. (*Hoka no hito no koto ni kuchidashi shite wa ikemaseñ.*) ほかの人のことに口出ししてはいけません.
2 (prevent) (... o) jaˈma suru (...を)じゃまする ①; boˈogai suru 妨害する ①: He interfered with my plan. (*Kare wa watashi no keekaku o jama shita.*) 彼は私の計画をじゃました.

interference *n.* kaˈñshoo 干渉; boˈogai 妨害: I don't like your interference in my work. (*Watashi no shigoto ni kañshoo shite morai-taku nai.*) 私の仕事に干渉してもらいたくない.

interior *adj.* **1** (inside) naˈibu no 内部の; uˈchigawa no 内側の: an inside wall (*uchikabe*) 内壁.
2 (inland) naˈiriku no 内陸の; koˈkuˈnai no 国内の: interior regions (*nairiku chiiki*) 内陸地域.
— *n.* naˈibu 内部; uˈchigawa 内側: the interior of a house (*ie no naibu*) 家の内部.

intermediate *adj.* chuˈukañ no 中間の; chuˈukyuu no 中級の: an intermediate course (*chuukyuu koosu*) 中級コース.

internal *adj.* **1** (of the inside)

na˩ibu no 内部の: internal organs (*naizoo*) 内臓.

2 (domestic) ko˥ku˩nai no 国内の; na˩isee no 内政の: internal affairs (*kokunai jijoo*) 国内事情.

international *adj.* ko˥kusai no 国際の; ko˥kusai-teki na 国際的な: an international phone call (*kokusai-deñwa*) 国際電話 / an international airport (*kokunai kuukoo*) 国際空港.

interpret *vt.* **1** (understand) ... o ka˩ishaku suru ...を解釈する ▯; (explain) se˥tsumee suru 説明する ▯: How do you interpret this poem? (*Kono shi o doo kaishaku shimasu ka?*) この詩をどう解釈しますか.

2 (translate) ... o tsu˩uyaku suru ...を通訳する ▯: She interpreted his speech into Japanese. (*Kanojo wa kare no eñzetsu o Nihoñgo ni tsuuyaku shita.*) 彼女は彼の演説を日本語に通訳した.

— *vi.* tsu˩uyaku suru 通訳する ▯: She interpreted for me. (*Kanojo ga watashi no tsuuyaku o shite kureta.*) 彼女が私の通訳をしてくれた.

interpretation *n.* **1** (understanding) ka˩ishaku 解釈; (explanation) se˥tsumee 説明: the interpretation of dreams (*yume no kaishaku*) 夢の解釈.

2 (translation) tsu˩uyaku 通訳: simultaneous interpretation (*dooji tsuuyaku*) 同時通訳.

interpreter *n.* tsu˩uyaku 通訳; tsu˥uyaku˩sha 通訳者: He acted as interpreter. (*Kare ga tsuuyaku o shita.*) 彼が通訳をした.

interrupt *vt.* **1** (break into) ... o ja˥ma suru ...をじゃまする ▯; bo˥ogai suru 妨害する ▯: He interrupted me while I was studying. (*Watashi ga beñkyoo shite iru toki kare wa watashi o jama shita.*) 私が勉強しているとき彼は私をじゃましました.

2 (stop) ... o chu˩udañ suru ...を中断する ▯; chu˩ushi suru 中止する ▯: He interrupted his work to eat his lunch. (*Kare wa chuushoku o ta-*

beru tame ni shigoto o chuudañ shita.) 彼は昼食を食べるために仕事を中断した.

— *vi.* ja˥ma suru じゃまする ▯: Excuse me for interrupting. (*O-jama shite sumimaseñ.*) おじゃましてすみません.

interruption *n.* (interrupting) bo˥ogai 妨害; (break) chu˩udañ 中断: work without interruption (*yasumi naku hataraku*) 休みなく働く.

intersection *n.* (crossroads) ko˥osa˩teñ 交差点.

interval *n.* **1** (of time) ka˩ñkaku 間隔; a˩ima 合間: Buses leave at fifteen-minute intervals. (*Basu wa juugo-fuñ-kañkaku de dete imasu.*) バスは 15 分間隔で出ています.

2 (of space) ka˩ñkaku 間隔; su˥ki-ma すき間: There is an interval of 2 meters between the houses. (*Ie to ie no aida ni wa ni-meetoru no sukima ga arimasu.*) 家と家の間には 2 メートルのすき間があります.

intervention *n.* (coming between) chu˥usai 仲裁; (interference) ka˥iñyuu 介入: military intervention (*guñji-kainyuu*) 軍事介入.

interview *n.* **1** (meeting) me˥ñsetsu 面接; me˥ñdañ 面談: a job interview (*shuushoku no meñsetsu*) 就職の面接.

2 (of a reporter) i˩ñtabyuu インタビュー.

— *vt.* ... to me˥ñsetsu suru ...と面接する ▯; ... ni i˩ñtabyuu suru ...にインタビューする ▯: The delegation was interviewed by reporters. (*Daihyoodañ wa kisha no iñtabyuu o uketa.*) 代表団は記者のインタビューを受けた.

intimacy *n.* shi˩ñmitsu 親密; shi˥tashi˩i a˩idagara 親しい間柄: I am on terms of intimacy with him. (*Watashi wa kare to shitashii aidagara desu.*) 私は彼と親しい間柄です.

intimate *adj.* **1** (familiar) shi˩ñmitsu na 親密な; shi˥tashi˩i 親しい: an intimate friend (*shitashii yuujiñ*)

親しい友人.

2 (private) ko⌐jiñ-teki na 個人的な; shi⌐teki na 私的な: one's intimate affairs (shiji) 私事.

3 (deep and thorough) ku⌐washi⌐i 詳しい; yo⌐ku shi⌐tte iru よく知っている: He has an intimate knowledge of the problem. (Kare wa sono moñdai o yoku shitte iru.) 彼はその問題をよく知っている.

into prep. **1** (to the inside of) … no na⌐ka e [ni] …の中へ[に]: go into the house (ie no naka e hairu) 家の中へ入る / look into the house (ie no naka o nozoku) 家の中をのぞく.

2 (to the condition of) … ni …に: The rain turned into snow. (Ame ga yuki ni natta.) 雨が雪になった. / put a sentence into Japanese (buñ o Nihoñgo ni yakusu) 文を日本語に訳す.

3 (against) … ni …に: His car ran into a tree. (Kare no kuruma wa ki ni butsukatta.) 彼の車は木にぶつかった.

intolerable adj. ta⌐erare⌐nai 耐えられない; ga⌐mañ de⌐ki⌐nai 我慢できない: intolerable working conditions (gamañ dekinai roodoo-jookeñ) 我慢できない労働条件.

intonation n. i⌐ñtone⌐eshoñ イントネーション; ko⌐e no yo⌐kuyoo 声の抑揚.

intricate adj. ko⌐mi-itta 込み入った; ko⌐mi-itte iru 込み入っている; fu⌐kuzatsu na 複雑な: an intricate story (komi-itta hanashi) 込み入った話.

introduce vt. **1** (acquaint) … o sho⌐okai suru …を紹介する ①: May I introduce Mr. Yamada to you? (Yamada-sañ o go-shookai itashimasu.) 山田さんをご紹介いたします.

2 (bring in) … o to⌐riireru …を取り入れる Ⓥ; tsu⌐taeru 伝える Ⓥ: Tea was introduced into Japan from China. (O-cha wa Chuugoku kara Nihoñ ni tsutaerareta.) お茶は中国から日本に伝えられた.

3 (make familiar) … ni te⌐ho⌐doki suru …に手ほどきする ①: He intro-

duced me to chess. (Kare wa watashi ni chesu o tehodoki shite kureta.) 彼は私にチェスを手ほどきしてくれた.

introduction n. **1** (of a person) sho⌐okai 紹介; hi⌐kiawase 引き合わせ: a letter of introduction (shookaijoo) 紹介状.

2 (of a book) jo⌐roñ 序論; jo⌐buñ 序文; (of music) jo⌐soo 序奏: write the introduction of a book (hoñ no joroñ o kaku) 本の序論を書く.

3 (elementary book) nyu⌐umoñsho 入門書.

intrude vi. … ni ta⌐chiiru …に立ち入る Ⓒ; … o ja⌐ma suru …をじゃまする ①: I don't want to intrude in his private affairs. (Watashi wa kare no shiteki na koto ni tachiiritaku nai.) 私は彼の私的なことに立ち入りたくない. / I hope I am not intruding. (O-jama de nakereba yoi no desu ga.) おじゃまでなければよいのですが.

— vt. … o (… ni) o⌐shitsuke⌐ru …を(…に)押しつける Ⓥ: intrude one's ideas on others (jibuñ no kañgae o hoka no hito ni oshitsukeru) 自分の考えをほかの人に押しつける.

intuition n. cho⌐kkañ 直感; cho⌐kkaku 直覚: woman's intuition (josee no chokkañ) 女性の直感.

invade vt. **1** (enter) … o shi⌐ñryaku suru …を侵略する ①; … ni shi⌐ñnyuu suru …に侵入する ①: invade other countries (takoku o shiñryaku suru) 他国を侵略する.

2 (violate) … o shi⌐ñgai suru …を侵害する ①: invade the privacy of others (taniñ no puraibashii o shiñgai suru) 他人のプライバシーを侵害する.

3 (rush into) … ni o⌐shiyose⌐ru …に押し寄せる Ⓥ: In summer, crowds of people invade this beach. (Natsu ni wa oozee no hito ga kono kaigañ ni oshiyosemasu.) 夏には大勢の人がこの海岸に押し寄せます.

invalid n. byo⌐oniñ 病人; byo⌐ojaku⌐sha 病弱者: a permanent invalid (fuji no byooniñ) 不治の病人.

— adj. byo⌐ojaku na 病弱な; byo⌐oniñ no 病人の: an invalid diet

(*byooniñshoku*) 病人食.

invasion *n.* **1** (entering) shiﾝryaku 侵略; shiﾝnyuu 侵入: repel invasion from another country (*takoku no shiñryaku o hanenokeru*) 他国の侵略をはねのける.
2 (violation) shiﾝgai 侵害: invasion of privacy (*puraibashii no shiñgai*) プライバシーの侵害.

invent *vt.* **1** (produce) ... o haﾝtsumee suru ...を発明する ①: Who invented the telephone? (*Deñwa o hatsumee shita no wa dare desu ka?*) 電話を発明したのはだれですか.
2 (make up) ... o deﾝtchiageﾞru ...をでっちあげる Ⓥ; koﾞshiraeru こしらえる Ⓥ: He invented the story. (*Kare wa sono hanashi o detchiageta.*) 彼はその話をでっちあげた.

invention *n.* **1** (inventing) haﾞtsumee 発明; soﾝoañ 創案: the invention of television (*terebi no hatsumee*) テレビの発明.
2 (something invented) haﾞtsumeehiñ 発明品: The computer is a marvelous invention. (*Koñpyuutaa wa subarashii hatsumeehiñ da.*) コンピューターはすばらしい発明品だ.
3 (false story) tsuﾞkurigoto 作り事.

inventor *n.* haﾞtsumeﾞesha 発明者; koﾞoaﾝnsha 考案者.

invert *vt.* ... o gyaﾞku ni suru ...を逆にする ①; haﾞñtai ni suru 反対にする ①: invert the order (*juñjo o gyaku ni suru*) 順序を逆にする.

invest *vt.* **1** (put money into business) ... o (... ni) toﾞoshi suru ...を(...に)投資する ①: He invested all his money in stocks. (*Kare wa okane o zeñbu kabu ni tooshi shita.*) 彼はお金を全部株に投資した.
2 (spend) ... o (... ni) tsuﾞiyaﾞsu ...を(...に)費やす Ⓒ; tsuﾞgikoﾞmu つぎ込む Ⓒ: He invested a lot of time in his study. (*Kare wa ooku no jikañ o keñkyuu ni tsuiyashita.*) 彼は多くの時間を研究に費やした.

investigate *vt.* ... o choﾞosa suru ...を調査する ①; shiﾞrabeﾞru 調べる Ⓥ: The police are investigating

the cause of the accident. (*Keesatsu wa sono jiko no geñiñ o shirabete imasu.*) 警察はその事故の原因を調べています.

investigation *n.* choﾞosa 調査; keﾞñkyuu 研究: It is under investigation. (*Sore wa choosa-chuu desu.*) それは調査中です.

investigator *n.* choﾞosaﾞsha 調査者; keﾞñkyuﾞusha 研究者.

investment *n.* **1** (investing) toﾞoshi 投資; shuﾞsshi 出資: make an investment in land (*tochi ni tooshi suru*) 土地に投資する.
2 (the amount invested) toﾞoshiﾞgaku 投資額; shuﾞsshiﾞgaku 出資額.

invisible *adj.* meﾞ ni mieﾞnai 目に見えない: Germs are invisible to the naked eye. (*Saikiñ wa nikugañ de wa mienai.*) 細菌は肉眼では見えない.

invitation *n.* **1** (inviting) shoﾞotai 招待; aﾞñnaﾞi 案内: accept [decline] an invitation to a party (*paatii e no shootai o ukeru [kotowaru]*) パーティーへの招待を受ける[断る].
2 (letter) shoﾞotaﾞijoo 招待状: send out invitations to a party (*paatii no shootaijoo o dasu*) パーティーの招待状を出す.

invite *vt.* **1** (ask to come) ... o shoﾞotai suru ...を招待する ①; maﾞneﾞku 招く Ⓒ: I invited her to dinner. (*Watashi wa kanojo o yuushoku ni shootai shita.*) 私は彼女を夕食に招待した.
2 (ask for) ... o moﾞtomeﾞru ...を求める Ⓥ; saﾞsou 誘う Ⓒ: Nobody invited his opinion. (*Dare mo kare no ikeñ o motomenakatta.*) だれも彼の意見を求めなかった.
3 (attract) ... o maﾞneﾞku ...を招く Ⓒ; moﾞtaraﾞsu もたらす Ⓒ: He invited danger by being careless. (*Kare wa fuchuui ni yori kikeñ o maneita.*) 彼は不注意により危険を招いた.

invoice *n.* iﾞñboﾞisu インボイス; seﾞekyuusho 請求書; oﾞkurijoo 送り状.

involve *vt.* **1** (mix up) ... o maﾞkiko¹mu ...を巻き込む C; ka¹kariai ni suru 掛かり合いにする I: I don't want to get involved with the police. (*Watashi wa keesatsu to kakariai ni naritaku nai.*) 私は警察と掛かり合いになりたくない.

2 (require) ... o hi¹tsuyoo to suru ...を必要とする I; to¹mona¹u 伴う C: This operation involves no risk. (*Kono shujutsu wa kiken o tomonawanai.*) この手術は危険を伴わない.

3 (absorb) ... ni mu¹chuu ni saseru ...に夢中にさせる V: He is involved in his book. (*Kare wa hon ni muchuu ni natte iru.*) 彼は本に夢中になっている.

inward *adj.* **1** (of the mind) ko¹koro no na¹ka no 心の中の; se¹eshin-teki na 精神的な: inward peace (*kokoro no heewa*) 心の平和.

2 (directed toward the inside) u¹chigawa e¹ no 内側への: an inward curve (*uchigawa e no kaabu*)内側へのカーブ.

— *adv.* na¹ka e 中へ; u¹chigawa e 内側へ: This door opens inward. (*Kono doa wa uchigawa e hirakimasu.*) このドアは内側へ開きます.

iron *n.* **1** (metal) te¹tsu 鉄.

2 (for clothes) a¹iron アイロン.

— *vt.* ... ni a¹iron o kake¹ru ...にアイロンをかける V: Won't you iron this shirt for me? (*Kono shatsu ni airon o kakete kuremasen ka?*) このシャツにアイロンをかけてくれませんか.

irony *n.* hi¹niku 皮肉: the irony of fate (*unmee no hiniku*) 運命の皮肉.

irregular *adj.* **1** (not regular) fu¹ki¹soku na 不規則な; he¹nsoku-teki na 変則的な: an irregular diet (*fukisoku na shokuji*) 不規則な食事.

2 (not straight) fu¹zo¹roi no ふぞろいの; de¹koboko shita [shite iru] でこぼこした[している]: an irregular shape (*fuzoroi no katachi*) ふぞろいの形.

irrelevant *adj.* mu¹ka¹nkee no 無関係の; fu¹te¹kisetsu na 不適切な: remarks irrelevant to the issues (*mondai to mukankee no iken*) 問題と無関係の意見.

irresistible *adj.* te¹ekoo deki¹nai 抵抗できない; o¹saerare¹nai 抑えられない: irresistible forces (*fukakooryoku*) 不可抗力.

irrespective *adj.* ka¹nkee no na¹i 関係のない.

irrespective of ... *perp.* ... ni ka¹nkee na¹ku ...に関係なく: Anyone can join the club, irrespective of sex. (*Seebetsu ni kankee naku dare de mo sono kurabu ni hairemasu.*) 性別に関係なくだれでもそのクラブに入れます.

irresponsible *adj.* mu¹se¹kinin na 無責任な; i¹ikagen na いいかげんな: an irresponsible mother (*musekinin na hahaoya*) 無責任な母親.

irritate *vt.* ... o i¹raira saseru ...をいらいらさせる V: He was irritated by the noise. (*Kare wa sono soo-on ni iraira shite ita.*) 彼はその騒音にいらいらしていた.

irritation *n.* i¹radachi いらだち; sho¹osoo 焦燥.

island *n.* shi¹ma¹ 島: What is that island called? (*Ano shima wa nan to iimasu ka?*) あの島は何と言いますか.

isolate *vt.* **1** ... o ko¹ritsu saseru ...を孤立させる V: The town was isolated because of the heavy snow. (*Sono machi wa ooyuki no tame ni koritsu shita.*) その町は大雪のために孤立した.

2 (of a patient) ... o ka¹kuri suru ...を隔離する I: A patient with an infectious disease must be isolated. (*Densenbyoo o motte iru kanja wa kakuri shinakereba naranai.*) 伝染病を持っている患者は隔離しなければならない.

isolation *n.* ko¹ritsu 孤立; (of a patient) ka¹kuri 隔離: an isolation ward (*kakuri-byootoo*) 隔離病棟.

issue *n.* **1** (problem) mo¹ndai 問題; ro¹nte¹n 論点: debate an issue (*mondai o ronjiru*) 問題を論じる.

2 (printed material) ha¹kko¹obutsu 発行物; ka¹nko¹obutsu 刊行物; -goo 号: the March issue of a magazine (*zasshi no sangatsu-goo*) 雑

誌の 3 月号.

3 (publication) haˈkkoo 発行; kaˈňkoo 刊行: the issue of a newspaper (shiňbuň no hakkoo) 新聞の発行.

— vt. **1** (publish) ... o haˈkkoo suru ...を発行する ⊺: issue a passport [magazine] (ryokeň [zasshi] o hakkoo suru) 旅券[雑誌]を発行する.

2 (give out) ... o daˈsu ...を出す ⊏; koˈofu suru 公布する ⊺: issue an order (meeree o dasu) 命令を出す.

— vi. deˈru 出る Ⅴ; naˈgaredeˈru 流れ出る Ⅴ: Blood issued from the wound. (Chi ga kizuguchi kara nagaredeta.) 血が傷口から流れ出た.

it pron. **1** (the thing that is understood) soˈre それ: How much is it? (Sore wa ikura desu ka?) それはいくらですか.

2 (the thing that is spoken of) soˈre それ: If you find my umbrella, please return it to me. (Moshi watashi no kasa o mitsuketara, (sore o) kaeshite kudasai.) もし私の傘を見つけたら(それを)返してください. ★ When self-explanatory, 'sore' is usually omitted.

3 (reference to a general condition) ★ No Japanese equivalent word: It's cold, isn't it? (Samui desu ne.) 寒いですね. / It is one o'clock now. (Ima ichi-ji desu.) 今 1 時です. / It is Monday today. (Kyoo wa getsuyoobi desu.) きょうは月曜日です. / How far is it from here to the station? (Koko kara eki made dono kurai arimasu ka?) ここから駅までどのくらいありますか.

Italian n. (people) Iˈtariaˈjiň イタリア人; (language) Iˈtariago イタリア語.

Italy n. Iˈtaria イタリア.

itch vi. **1** (have a tickling feeling) kaˈyuˈi かゆい: I itch all over. (Karada-juu ga kayui.) 体じゅうがかゆい.

2 (have a restless desire) muˈzumuzu suru むずむずする ⊺: He is itching to ask questions. (Kare wa shitsumoň o shitakute muzumuzu shite iru.) 彼は質問をしたくてむずむずしている.

item n. **1** (separate article) koˈomoku 項目; hiˈňmoku 品目: Please check each item on this list. (Kono risuto no kaku koomoku o shirabete kudasai.) このリストの各項目を調べてください.

2 (a piece of news) kiˈji 記事: I saw the item about the accident in the newspaper. (Watashi wa sono jiko no kiji o shiňbuň de mimashita.) 私はその事故の記事を新聞で見ました.

its pron. soˈre no その; soˈno その: I dropped the cup and broke its handle. (Watashi wa kappu o otoshite (sono) totte o kowashite shimatta.) 私はカップを落として(その)取っ手を壊してしまった. ★ When self-explanatory, 'sono' is usually omitted.

itself pron. **1** [reflexive use] soˈre jiˈshiň o [ni] それ自身を[に]: The dog scratched itself. (Inu wa jibuň no karada o kaita.) 犬は自分の体をかいた.

2 [emphatic use] soˈre jiˈshiň ga それ自身が; soˈno mono jiˈtai ga そのもの自体が: He is kindness itself. (Kare wa shiňsetsu sono mono da.) 彼は親切そのものだ.

ivory n. zoˈoge 象牙.

ivy n. tsuˈtaˈ つた.

J

jacket *n.* **1** (coat) uʳwagi 上着;
jaˈketto ジャケット: put on [take off]
a jacket (*uwagi o kiru* [*nugu*]) 上着
を着る[脱ぐ].
2 (of a book) kaˈbaa カバー; (of a
record) jaˈketto ジャケット.

jail *n.* (prison) keˈemuˈsho 刑務所;
(detention house) koˈochisho 拘置
所; ryuˈuchijoo 留置場.

jam¹ *n.* jaˈmu ジャム: spread jam on
bread (*pan ni jamu o nuru*) パンに
ジャムを塗る.

jam² *vt.* **1** (squeeze) ... o (... ni) tsu-
ˈmekoˈmu ...を(...に)詰め込む ⓒ:
jam clothes into a suitcase (*irui o
suutsukeesu ni tsumekomu*) 衣類
をスーツケースに詰め込む.
2 (push) ... o tsuˈyoku oˈsu ...を強く
押す ⓒ: jam one's foot on the
brakes (*bureeki o ashi de fumu*) ブ
レーキを足で踏む.
3 (block) ... o fuˈsagu ...をふさぐ ⓒ:
The road is jammed with cars.
(*Dooro wa kuruma de fusagatte
iru.*) 道路は車でふさがっている.
— *vi.* giˈsshiri iˈppai ni naˈru ぎっ
しりいっぱいになる ⓒ: We jammed
into the elevator. (*Watashi-tachi
wa erebeetaa ni gisshiri ippai
notta.*) 私たちはエレベーターにぎっしり
いっぱい乗った.

January *n.* iˈchi-gatsuˈ 1月.

Japan *n.* Niˈhoˈn 日本: Japan is an
island country. (*Nihon wa shima-
guni desu.*) 日本は島国です.

Japanese *n.* (people) Niˈhonjiˈn 日
本人; (language) Niˈhongo 日本語:
I cannot speak Japanese. (*Watashi
wa Nihongo o hanasemasen.*) 私は
日本語を話せません.
— *adj.* Niˈhoˈn no 日本の; Niˈhonjiˈn no 日本人の; Niˈhongo no 日本
語の: a Japanese doll (*Nihon-nin-
gyoo*) 日本人形 / Japanese grammar
(*Nihongo no bunpoo*) 日本語の文法

/ Japanese paper (*washi*) 和紙.

jar *n.* biˈn びん; tsuˈbo つぼ: put jam
into a jar (*jamu o bin ni ireru*) ジャ
ムをびんに入れる.

jaw *n.* aˈgoˈ あご: the lower jaw
(*shita-ago*) 下あご / the upper jaw
(*uwa-ago*) 上あご.

jealous *adj.* shiˈttobukaˈi しっと深
い; neˈtaˈnde (iru) ねたんで(いる): a
jealous husband (*shittobukai otto*)
しっと深い夫 / He is jealous of my
success. (*Kare wa watashi no seekoo o netande iru.*) 彼は私の成功をね
たんでいる.

jealousy *n.* shiˈtto しっと; neˈtamiˈ
ねたみ: burn with jealousy (*shitto ni
moeru*) しっとに燃える.

jeans *n.* jiˈinzu ジーンズ: He was in
jeans. (*Kare wa jiinzu o haite ita.*)
彼はジーンズをはいていた.

jelly *n.* zeˈrii ゼリー: apple jelly (*ringo no zerii jamu*) りんごのゼリージャム.

jerk *n.* guˈli to hiˈku koto くいと引くこ
と: give a rope a jerk (*roopu o gui
to hiku*) ロープをくいと引く.
— *vt.* ... o guˈli to hiˈku ...をくいと引
く ⓒ: He jerked the window open.
(*Kare wa mado o gui to hiraita.*)
彼は窓をくいと開いた.

jet *n.* **1** (airplane) jeˈttoˈki ジェット
機: get on board a jet (*jettoki ni
noru*) ジェット機に乗る.
2 (strong flow) fuˈnshutsu 噴出: a
jet of water (*mizu no funshutsu*)
水の噴出.

jet lag *n.* jiˈsa-boke 時差ぼけ.

Jew *n.* Yuˈdayaˈjin ユダヤ人.

jewel *n.* hoˈoseki 宝石: put on
jewels (*hooseki o mi ni tsukeru*)
宝石を身につける.

jewelry *n.* hoˈosekiˈrui 宝石類;
hoˈoseki sooshiˈngu 宝石装身具.

Jewish *adj.* Yuˈdayaˈjin no ユダヤ人
の: the Jewish people (*Yudaya min-
zoku*) ユダヤ民族.

job n. **1** (employment) tsuˈtomeˈ-guchi 勤め口; shoˈku 職: I am looking for a job. (*Watashi wa tsu-tomeguchi o sagashite imasu.*) 私は勤め口を探しています。 / He lost his job. (*Kare wa shoku o ushinatta.*) 彼は職を失った。
2 (work) shiˈgoto 仕事; (duty) tsuˈtomeˈ 務め: Now let's get on with the job. (*Saa shigoto ni torika-karoo.*) さあ仕事に取りかかろう。

jog vi. yuˈkkuˈri kakeˈru ゆっくり駆ける V; joˈgiňgu suru ジョギングする I: I jog every morning. (*Watashi wa maiasa jogiňgu o shimasu.*) 私は毎朝ジョギングをします。
— vt. ... o choˈtto tsuˈku ...をちょっと突く C: He jogged my elbow. (*Kare wa watashi no hiji o chotto tsuita.*) 彼は私のひじをちょっと突いた。

join vt. **1** (become a member) ni kuˈwawaˈru ...に加わる C; saˈňka suru 参加する I: She didn't join us in the game. (*Kanojo wa watashi-tachi no geemu ni saňka shina-katta.*) 彼女は私たちのゲームに参加しなかった。
2 (put together) ... o tsuˈnagu ...をつなぐ C; keˈtsugoo suru 結合する I: join two wires (*ni-hoň no hari-gane o tsunagu*) 2本の針金をつなぐ。
— vi. **1** (meet) aˈwasaˈru 合わさる C; maˈjiwaˈru 交わる C: Where do those two roads join? (*Kono futa-tsu no michi wa doko de majiwari-masu ka?*) この二つの道はどこで交わりますか。
2 (participate) iˈssho ni naˈru いっしょになる C; saˈňka suru 参加する I: I joined in the campaign. (*Watashi wa sono uňdoo ni saňka shita.*) 私はその運動に参加した。

joint n. **1** (of bones) kaˈňsetsu 関節: the joint of the arm (*ude no kaňsetsu*) 腕の関節。
2 (of a thing) tsuˈgime 継ぎ目: a joint in a water pipe (*suidookaň no tsugime*) 水道管の継ぎ目。
— adj. kyoˈodoo no 共同の: a joint statement (*kyoodoo seemee*) 共同声明。

joke n. joˈodaˈň 冗談; shaˈre しゃれ; joˈoku ジョーク: He often cracks jokes. (*Kare wa yoku joodaň o tobasu.*) 彼はよく冗談を飛ばす。

jolly adj. kaˈikatsu na 快活な; yoˈo-ki na 陽気な: a jolly old man (*yooki na roojiň*) 陽気な老人。

journal n. **1** (magazine) zaˈsshi 雑誌; (newspaper) niˈkkaň-shiˈňbuň 日刊新聞: a monthly journal (*gek-kaň-zasshi*) 月刊雑誌 / a business journal (*shoogyoo-shiňbuň*) 商業新聞。
2 (diary) niˈsshi 日誌; niˈkki 日記: keep a diary (*nikki o tsukeru*) 日記をつける。

journalism n. jaˈanariˈzumu ジャーナリズム。

journalist n. jaˈanariˈsuto ジャーナリスト; (of a newspaper) shiˈňbuň kiˈsha 新聞記者; (of a magazine) zaˈsshi kiˈsha 雑誌記者。

journey n. **1** (trip) ryoˈkoo 旅行; taˈbiˈ 旅: He made a journey to China. (*Kare wa Chuugoku e ryo-koo shita.*) 彼は中国へ旅行した。
★ 'Trip' and 'travel' are also called 'ryokoo.'
2 (distance) ryoˈtee 旅程; koˈotee 行程: a day's journey from here (*koko kara ichi-nichi no kootee*) ここから1日の行程。

joy n. **1** (feeling) yoˈrokobi 喜び; uˈreˈshisa うれしさ: She was filled with joy at the news. (*Kanojo wa sono shirase ni yorokoňda.*) 彼女はその知らせに喜んだ。
2 (source) yoˈrokobi no taˈne 喜びの種; uˈreshiˈi koˈtoˈ うれしいこと: He has tasted the joys and sorrows of life. (*Kare wa jiňsee no yorokobi ya kanashimi o ajiwatte kita.*) 彼は人生の喜びや悲しみを味わってきた。

joyful adj. yoˈrokobashiˈi 喜ばしい; uˈreshiˈi うれしい: joyful news (*ureshii shirase*) うれしい知らせ。

judge n. **1** (of a court) saˈibaňkaň 裁判官: The judge sentenced the man to two years in prison. (*Sai-*

bañkañ wa sono otoko ni kiñko ni-neñ no kee o iiwatashita.) 裁判官は
その男に禁固 2 年の刑を言い渡した.

2 (umpire) shiⁿpaⁿiñ 審判員: act
as judge in a speech contest (beñ-roñ-taikai no shiñpañiñ o tsu-tomeru) 弁論大会の審判員を務める.
★ 'Referee' and 'umpire' are also
called 'shiñpañ(iñ).'

— *vt.* **1** (decide) ... to haⁿdañ
suru ...と判断する ⦸: I cannot
judge which is better. (Watashi
wa dochira ga yoi ka handañ
dekinai.) 私はどちらがよいか判断できな
い.

2 (try) ... o saⁿbaⁿku ...を裁く ⦿;
... ni haⁿñketsu o kudasu ...に判決を
下す ⦿: The court judged him not
guilty. (Hootee wa kare ni muzai
no hañketsu o kudashita.) 法廷は彼
に無罪の判決を下した.

judgment *n.* **1** (decision) haⁿñdañ
判断; hyoⁿoka 評価: make a fair
judgment (koosee na hañdañ o
suru) 公正な判断をする.

2 (ability) haⁿñdaⁿñryoku 判断力;
fuⁿñbetsu 分別: a person of judgment (fuñbetsu no aru hito) 分別の
ある人.

3 (opinion) iⁿkeñ 意見; kaⁿñgaⁿe 考
え: In my judgment, she will make
a good president of our company.
(Watashi no kañgae de wa kanojo
wa waga-sha no ii shachoo ni
naru daroo.) 私の考えでは彼女は我が
社のいい社長になるだろう.

4 (sentence) haⁿñketsu 判決: pass
judgment on a person (hito ni hañketsu o kudasu) 人に判決を下す.

judicial *adj.* shiⁿhoo no 司法の;
saⁿibañ no 裁判の: a judicial decision (saibañ no hañketsu) 裁判の判
決.

juice *n.* juⁿusu ジュース; shiⁿru 汁:
fruit juice (kajuu) 果汁. ★ Japanese 'juusu' usually refers to soft
drinks.

July *n.* shiⁿchi-gatsu 7 月.

jump *vi.* **1** (spring) toⁿbu 跳ぶ ⦿;
toⁿbiagaⁿru 跳び上がる ⦿: He

jumped up to catch the ball. (Kare
wa booru o toru tame ni tobi-agatta.) 彼はボールをとるために跳び上
がった.

2 (start) biⁿkuⁿtto suru びくっとする
⦸: When the door banged shut, I
jumped. (Doa ga batañ to shimatta toki watashi wa bikkutto
shita.) ドアがばたんと閉まったとき私はび
くっとした.

3 (rise) kyuⁿu ni agaru 急に上がる
⦿: Prices have jumped. (Bukka
ga kyuu ni agatta.) 物価が急に上がっ
た.

— *vt.* ... o toⁿbikoeⁿru ...を跳び越え
る ⦶: The boy jumped the puddle
easily. (Sono otoko-no-ko wa mizutamari o yasuyasu to tobikoeta.) そ
の男の子は水たまりをやすやすと跳び越え
た.

— *n.* choⁿoyaku 跳躍; jaⁿñpu ジャン
プ: the broad [long] jump (haba-
tobi) 幅跳び / the high jump (ha-
shiri takatobi) 走り高跳び.

June *n.* roⁿku-gatsu 6 月.

junior *adj.* **1** (younger) toⁿshishita
no 年下の: She is three years ju-
nior to me. (Kanojo wa watashi
yori sañ-sai toshishita desu.) 彼女
は私より 3 歳年下です.

2 (lower) shiⁿta no 下の; koⁿohai
no 後輩の: He is junior to me at
the office. (Kare wa kaisha de
watashi no koohai desu.) 彼は会社
で私の後輩です.

— *n.* toⁿshishita no monoⁿ 年下の
者; koⁿohai 後輩: He is my junior
by two years. (Kare wa watashi
yori ni-sai toshishita desu.) 彼は私
より 2 歳年下です.

jury *n.* baⁿishiñ 陪審. ★ In Japan,
there is no jury system.

just[1] *adv.* **1** (exactly) choⁿodo ちょう
ど: It's just one o'clock. (Choodo
ichi-ji desu.) ちょうど 1 時です.

2 (very recently) taⁿtta iⁿma たった
今: She has just come back. (Kanojo wa tatta ima modotta tokoro
desu.) 彼女はたった今戻ったところです.

3 (only) choⁿtto ちょっと; hoⁿñ no ほ

んの: Wait just a moment. (*Chotto o-machi kudasai.*) ちょっとお待ちください.
4 (barely) yo「oyaku ようやく; ya「tto やっと: He was just in time. (*Kare wa yooyaku maniatta.*) 彼はようやく間に合った.

just² *adj.* **1** (fair) ko「osee na 公正な; ko「ohee na 公平な: The teacher was just to everyone. (*Señsee wa dare ni mo koohee datta.*) 先生はだれにも公平だった.
2 (reasonable) se「etoo na 正当な; to「ozeñ na 当然な: a just reward (*seetoo na hooshuu*) 正当な報酬.

justice *n.* **1** (fairness) ko「osee 公正; se「igi 正義: treat a person with justice (*hito o koosee ni atsukau*) 人を公正に扱う.
2 (judge) sa「ibañ 裁判: a court of justice (*saibañsho*) 裁判所.

justification *n.* se「etooka 正当化; be「ñmee 弁明.

justify *vt.* ... o se「etooka suru ...を正当化する ⓣ; be「ñmee suru 弁明する ⓣ: He justified his action. (*Kare wa jibuñ no koodoo o beñmee shita.*) 彼は自分の行動を弁明した.

K

keen *adj.* **1** (of the mind, senses) su「rudo「i 鋭い: have a keen intelligence (*surudoi atama o motte iru*) 鋭い頭を持っている / keen eyes 鋭い目.
2 (severe) ki「bishi「i 厳しい; ha「geshi「i 激しい: a keen, cold winter (*samusa no kibishii fuyu*) 寒さの厳しい冬 / keen competition (*hageshii kyoosoo*) 激しい競争.
3 (sharp) su「rudo「i 鋭い: a keen edge (*surudoi ha*) 鋭い刃.
4 (eager) ne「sshiñ na 熱心な: a keen golfer (*nesshiñ na gorufaa*) 熱心なゴルファー / Bill is keen on studying Japanese. (*Biru wa Nihoñgo no beñkyoo ni nesshiñ da.*) ビルは日本語の勉強に熱心だ.

keep *vt.* **1** (have; reserve) ... o mo「tte iru ...を持っている Ⓥ; to「tte oku 取っておく Ⓒ; a「zuka「ru 預かる Ⓒ: You can keep that book till next week. (*Sono hoñ wa raishuu made motte ite mo ii desu yo.*) その本は来週まで持っていてもいいですよ. / Please keep the change. (*Otsuri wa totte oite kudasai.*) おつりは取っておいてください. / Please keep this baggage until tomorrow. (*Kono nimotsu o ashita made azukatte kudasai.*) この荷物をあしたまで預かってください.

2 (cause to remain) zu「tto 〈verb〉-te [de] o「ku ずっと...て[で]おく Ⓒ: I kept the air-conditioner on all day. (*Kuuraa o ichi-nichi-juu zutto tsukete oita.*) クーラーを1日中ずっとつけておいた. / You mustn't keep your visitor waiting. (*O-kyaku o matasete oite wa ikemaseñ.*) お客を待たせておいてはいけません.
3 (fulfill; guard) ... o ma「mo「ru ...を守る Ⓒ: keep a promise [secret] (*yakusoku [himitsu] o mamoru*) 約束[秘密]を守る.
4 (own) ... o mo「tte iru ...を持っている Ⓥ; (of an animal) ka「tte iru 飼っている Ⓥ: He keeps three cars. (*Kare wa kuruma o sañdai motte iru.*) 彼は車を3台持っている. / I keep chickens. (*Watashi wa hiyoko o katte iru.*) 私はひよこを飼っている.
5 (delay) ... o hi「kitome「te oku ...を引き止めておく Ⓒ: I won't keep you long. (*Nagaku wa o-hikitome shimaseñ.*) 長くはお引き止めしません.
6 (write) ... o tsu「ke「ru ...をつける Ⓥ: keep a diary (*nikki o tsukeru*) 日記をつける / keep a record of the meeting (*kaigi no kiroku o tsukeru*) 会議の記録をつける.
— *vi.* **1** (remain) ... ma「ma「 de iru ...ままでいる Ⓥ: He kept awake.

(*Kare wa me o samashita mama de ita.*) 彼は目を覚ましたままでいた. / keep indoors all day (*ichi-nichi-juu ie ni tojikomotta mama de iru*) 1 日中家に閉じこもったままでいる.

2 (continue) 〈verb〉-tsu┌zukeru ...続ける ⓥ: keep crying (*naki-tsuzukeru*) 泣き続ける / It kept raining all day. (*Ichi-nichi-juu ame ga furi-tsuzuita.*) 1 日中雨が降り続いた.

3 (last) mo┌tsu もつ ⓒ: The weather will keep till Sunday. (*Kono teñki wa nichiyoobi made motsu deshoo.*) この天気は日曜日までもつでしょう.

kerosene *n.* to┌oyu 灯油.

kettle *n.* ya┌kañ やかん; yu┌wa┐kashi 湯沸かし: boil water in a kettle (*ya-kañ de o-yu o wakasu*) やかんでお湯を沸かす.

key *n.* **1** (to a lock) ka┌gi┐ 鍵: put a key in the lock (*kagi o joo ni sashi-komu*) 鍵を錠に差し込む. ★ 'Lock' is also called 'kagi.'

2 (vital ingredient) ka┌gi┐ 鍵; te┌ga┐kari 手がかり: This is the key to the problem. (*Kore ga sono moñ-dai o toku kagi da.*) これがその問題を解く鍵だ.

3 (of a piano, etc.) ki┌i キー: the keys of a typewriter (*taipuraitaa no kii*) タイプライターのキー.

— *adj.* (essential) ki┌hoñ-teki na 基本的な; ju┌uyoo na 重要な: a key color (*kihoñ-shoku*) 基本色 / a key issue (*juuyoo na moñdai*) 重要な問題.

kick *vt.* **1** (with a foot) ...o ke┌ru ...をける ⓒ: kick a ball (*booru o keru*) ボールをける.

2 (in sports) bo┌oru o ke┐tte i┌reru ボールをけって入れる ⓥ: kick a goal (*booru o ketto gooru ni ireru*) ボールをけってゴールに入れる.

— *vi.* (...o) ke┐ru (...を)ける ⓒ: The horse kicked me. (*Sono uma wa watashi o ketta.*) その馬は私をけった.

— *n.* ke┌ru ko┐to けること: give a kick at a door (*doa o keru*) ドアをけ

る.

kid *n.* **1** (child) ko┌domo 子ども; (young person) wa┌kamono 若者.

2 (young goat) ko┌ya┐gi 子やぎ.

— *vt.* (tease) ...o ka┌raka┐u ...をからかう ⓒ: He kidded me about my hat. (*Kare wa booshi no koto de watashi o karakatta.*) 彼は帽子のことで私をからかった.

— *vi.* jo┌oda┐ñ o i┐u 冗談を言う ⓒ: No kidding. (*Joodañ deshoo.*) 冗談でしょう.

kidnap *vt.* ...o yu┌ukai suru ...を誘拐する ⓘ: kidnap a child (*kodomo o yuukai suru*) 子どもを誘拐する.

kidnapper *n.* yu┌uka┐ihañ 誘拐犯.

kill *vt.* **1** (of an animal) ...o ko┌rosu ...を殺す ⓒ; (of a plant) ka┌rasu 枯らす ⓒ: Don't kill animals. (*Doobu-tsu o korosu na.*) 動物を殺すな. / The sudden frost killed the flowers. (*Totsuzeñ no shimo ga hana o karashita.*) 突然の霜が花を枯らした.

2 (in an accident, etc.) ...o shi┌boo saseru ...を死亡させる ⓥ: Many passengers were killed in the train crash. (*Ressha no shoototsu de oozee no jookyaku ga shiboo shita.*) 列車の衝突で大勢の乗客が死亡した.

3 (destroy) ...o da┌me ni suru ...をだめにする ⓘ; tsu┌busu つぶす ⓒ: His home run killed our hopes of victory. (*Kare no hoomurañ ga ware-ware no yuushoo no nozomi o tsu-bushita.*) 彼のホームランがわれわれの優勝の望みをつぶした.

kill time *vi.* ji┌kañ o tsubusu 時間をつぶす ⓒ.

killer *n.* sa┌tsujiñ┐sha 殺人者; ko┌ro-shiya 殺し屋.

kilogram *n.* ki┌rogu┐ramu キログラム ★ Often shortened to 'kiro': 250 kilograms of meat (*nihyaku gojuk-kiro no niku*) 250 キロの肉.

kilometer *n.* ki┌rome┐etoru キロメートル ★ Often shortened to 'kiro': walk two and a half kilometers (*ni-kiro hañ aruku*) 2 キロ半歩く.

kind[1] *n.* shu┌rui┐ 種類; bu┌rui 部類:

different kinds of apples (*chigatta shurui no riñgo*) 違った種類のりんご / What kind of tree is this? (*Kore wa nañ to iu shurui no ki desu ka?*) これは何という種類の木ですか.

kind[2] *adj.* shi¯ñsetsu na 親切な; ya¯sashii 優しい: Japanese policemen are generally very kind. (*Nihoñ no keesatsukañ wa ippañ ni hijoo ni shiñsetsu desu.*) 日本の警察官は一般に非常に親切です.

be kind enough to do shi¯ñsetsu ni mo ⟨verb⟩ 親切にも…: He was kind enough to lend me the money. (*Kare wa shiñsetsu ni mo watashi ni o-kane o kashite kureta.*) 彼は親切にも私にお金を貸してくれた.

kindergarten *n.* yo¯ochi¯eñ 幼稚園.

kindly *adv.* **1** (in a kind manner) shi¯ñsetsu ni (mo) 親切に(も); ya¯sashiku 優しく: He kindly helped me. (*Kare wa shiñsetsu ni mo watashi o tasukete kureta.*) 彼は親切にも私を助けてくれた.
2 (please) do¯ozo どうぞ; do¯o ka どうか: Would you kindly shut the window? (*Doo ka mado o shimete itadakemaseñ ka?*) どうか窓を閉めていただけませんか.
— *adj.* ya¯sashii 優しい; shi¯ñsetsu na 親切な: a kindly heart (*yasashii kokoro*) 優しい心.

kindness *n.* **1** (being kind) shi¯ñsetsu 親切; ya¯sa¯shisa 優しさ: show kindness to animals (*doobutsu ni yasashiku suru*) 動物に優しくする.
2 (kind action) shi¯ñsetsu na ko¯loi 親切な行為: I'll never forget your kindness. (*Anata no go-shiñsetsu wa wasuremaseñ.*) あなたのご親切は忘れません.

king *n.* **1** (ruler) o¯lo 王; ko¯lkuo¯lo 国王: the King of Sweden (*Suweedeñ kokuoo*) スウェーデン国王.
2 (most important one) … o¯lo … 王: the king of beasts (*hyakujuu no oo*) 百獣の王 / an oil king (*sekiyuoo*) 石油王.

3 (of cards) ki¯ñgu キング: the king of spades (*supeedo no kiñgu*) スペードのキング.

kingdom *n.* **1** (country) o¯lokoku 王国: the kingdom of Sweden (*Suweedeñ ookoku*) スウェーデン王国.
2 (of nature) … ¯kai …界: the animal [plant] kingdom (*doobutsu-kai [shokubutsu-kai]*) 動物界[植物界].

kiss *vt.* … ni ki¯lsu suru …にキスする ⊤; se¯lppuñ suru 接吻する ⊤: I kissed my mother on the cheek. (*Watashi wa haha no hoo ni kisu shita.*) 私は母のほおにキスした.
— *n.* ki¯lsu キス; ku¯lchizuke 口づけ; se¯lppuñ 接吻: She gave me a kiss. (*Kanojo wa watashi ni kisu shita.*) 彼女は私にキスした.

kit *n.* yo¯logu hi¯lto¯lsoroi 用具ひとそろい; yo¯loguba¯lko 用具箱: a first-aid kit (*kyuukyuubako*) 救急箱.

kitchen *n.* da¯idokoro 台所; ki¯ltchiñ キッチン: cook in the kitchen (*daidokoro de ryoori suru*) 台所で料理する.

kite *n.* ta¯lko たこ(凧): fly a kite (*tako o ageru*) たこを揚げる.

knee *n.* hi¯lza ひざ: My knees hurt. (*Hiza ga itai.*) ひざが痛い. / She got down on her knees. (*Kanojo wa hizamazuita.*) 彼女はひざまずいた.

kneel *vi.* hi¯lzamazu¯lku ひざまずく ⊙: kneel in prayer (*hizamazuite inoru*) ひざまずいて祈る / I knelt down to pull out a weed. (*Watashi wa zassoo o nuku tame ni hizamazuita.*) 私は雑草を抜くためにひざまずいた.

knife *n.* na¯lifu ナイフ; ko¯lgata¯lna 小刀: a kitchen knife (*hoochoo*) 包丁 / He cut the toast with his knife. (*Kare wa toosuto o naifu de kitta.*) 彼はトーストをナイフで切った.

knit *vt.* … o a¯lmu …を編む ⊙: knit a sweater (*seetaa o amu*) セーターを編む.

knob *n.* to¯ltte 取っ手; tsu¯lmami つまみ: turn the knob of a door (*doa no totte o mawasu*) ドアの取っ手を回す.

knock *vi.* **1** (tap) (… o) ta¯lta¯lku (…を)たたく ⊙; no¯lkku suru ノックする

①: The teacher knocked on her desk. (*Señsee wa tsukue no ue o tataita.*) 先生は机の上をたたいた. / You must knock before entering the room. (*Heya ni hairu mae ni wa nokku o shinakereba narimaseñ.*) 部屋に入る前にはノックをしなければなりません.

2 (collide) (... ni) tsu「kiata1ru (...に) 突き当たる ⓒ; bu「tsukaru ぶつかる ⓒ: Someone knocked into me. (*Dareka ga watashi ni butsukatta.*) だれかが私にぶつかった.

— *vt.* **1** (hit hard) ... o ta「ta1ku ... をたたく ⓒ; u「tsu 打つ ⓒ; na「gu1ru 殴る ⓒ: knock nails into a board (*ita ni kugi o uchikomu*) 板にくぎを打ち込む / He knocked me on the head. (*Kare wa watashi no atama o nagutta.*) 彼は私の頭を殴った.

2 (hit accidentally) ... ni a「taru ...に当たる ⓒ: He knocked the vase and it fell off the table. (*Kare ga atatte kabiñ ga teeburu kara ochita.*) 彼が当たって花瓶がテーブルから落ちた.

3 (hit intentionally) ... ni bu「tsukeru ...にぶつける Ⓥ: The child knocked his head against wall. (*Sono ko wa kabe ni atama o butsuketa.*) その子は壁に頭をぶつけた.

— *n.* ta「ta1ku ko「to1 たたくこと; u「tsu ko「to1 打つこと; no「kku ノック: There was a knock on the door. (*Doa o nokku suru oto ga shita.*) ドアをノックする音がした.

knot *n.* **1** (fastening) mu「subime 結び目: make a knot (*musubime o tsukuru*) 結び目を作る.

2 (group) mu「re1 群れ; a「tsumari 集まり: There were knots of people here and there. (*Achi kochi ni hito no mure ga dekite ita.*) あちこちに人の群れができていた.

3 (in a tree) ko「bu1 こぶ; fu「shi1 節.

4 (measure of speed) no「tto ノット: a ship going 30 knots (*sañjuu-notto no fune*) 30ノットの船.

— *vt.* ... o mu「subu ...を結ぶ ⓒ: knot one's tie (*nekutai o musubu*) ネクタイを結ぶ.

know *vt.* **1** (have knowledge of) ... o shi「tte iru ...を知っている Ⓥ: I know that he is honest. (*Kare ga shoojiki na koto wa shitte imasu.*) 彼が正直なことは知っています. / Do you know his name? (*Kare no namae o shitte imasu ka?*) 彼の名前を知っていますか.

2 (recognize) ... to wa「ka1ru ...とわかる ⓒ: I knew him at once. (*Sugu kare da to wakatta.*) すぐ彼だとわかった. / You will know my house by the red roof. (*Watashi no uchi wa yane ga akai no de wakarimasu.*) 私の家は屋根が赤いのでわかります.

3 (be acquainted with) ... to shi「riai da ...と知り合いだ: I have known him since he was a child. (*Kare to wa kodomo no toki kara no shiriai desu.*) 彼とは子どもの時からの知り合いです.

4 (experience) ... o ke「ekeñ suru ...を経験する ①: He has known both poverty and wealth. (*Kare wa biñboo mo kanemochi mo keekeñ shita.*) 彼は貧乏も金持ちも経験した.

— *vi.* shi「tte iru 知っている Ⓥ; wa「ka1tte iru わかっている Ⓥ: Most people know about the accident. (*Taitee no hito wa sono jiko no koto o shitte imasu.*) たいていの人はその事故のことを知っています.

let ... know *vt.* ... ni o「shieru ...に教える Ⓥ: Please let me know when we reach the station. (*Sono eki ni tsuitara oshiete kudasai.*) その駅に着いたら教えてください.

knowledge *n.* **1** (of facts, information, etc.) chi「shiki 知識; shi「tte iru koto1 知っていること: My knowledge of Japanese grammar is poor. (*Watashi no Nihoñgo no buñpoo no chishiki wa hiñjaku desu.*) 私の日本語の文法の知識は貧弱です.

2 (learning) ga「ku1moñ 学問: all branches of knowledge (*gakumoñ no arayuru buñya*) 学問のあらゆる分野.

known *adj.* shi「rarete iru 知られている: the oldest known church (*shi-*

rarete iru saiko no kyookai) 知られている最古の教会 / He is known to the public. (*Kare wa sekeñ ni na o shirarete iru.*) 彼は世間に名を知られている.

Korea *n.* Ka¹ñkoku 韓国; (historical name) Cho¹ose¹ñ 朝鮮: the Republic of Korea [South Korea] (*Dai-kañmiñkoku*) 大韓民国 / the Democratic People's Republic of Korea [North Korea] (*Chooseñ Miñshu-*

shugi Jiñmiñ Kyoowakoku) 朝鮮民主主義人民共和国.

Korean *adj.* Ka¹ñkoku no 韓国の; Cho¹ose¹ñ no 朝鮮の: Korean songs (*Kañkoku [Chooseñ] no uta*) 韓国[朝鮮]の歌.
— *n.* (people) Ka¹ñkoku¹jiñ 韓国人; Cho¹oseñji¹ñ 朝鮮人; (language) Cho¹oseñ¹go 朝鮮語; Ka¹ñkokugo 韓国語.

L

label *n.* ha¹rigami はり紙; ra¹beru ラベル: put a label on one's baggage (*nimotsu ni raberu o tsukeru*) 荷物にラベルをつける.
— *vt.* ... ni ha¹rigami o suru ...にはり紙をする Ⓣ; ra¹beru o ha¹ru ラベルをはる Ⓒ: label a box (*hako ni raberu o haru*) 箱にラベルをはる.

labor *n.* **1** (work) ro¹odoo 労働; shi¹goto 仕事; ho¹neori 骨折り: manual labor (*nikutai-roodoo*) 肉体労働 / a labor of love (*suki de suru shigoto*) 好きでする仕事.
2 (workers) ro¹odo¹osha 労働者; ro¹odooka¹ikyuu 労働階級: labor and management (*roodoosha to kee-eesha*) 労働者と経営者.
3 (giving birth) bu¹ñbeñ 分娩; shu¹ssañ 出産: go into labor (*jiñtsuu ga hajimaru*) 陣痛が始まる.
— *vi.* ha¹taraku 働く Ⓒ; ho¹neo¹ru 骨折る Ⓒ; do¹ryoku suru 努力する Ⓣ: He labored from dawn to dusk. (*Kare wa yoake kara kuraku naru made hataraita.*) 彼は夜明けから暗くなるまで働いた.

laboratory *n.* ji¹kke¹ñshitsu 実験室; ke¹ñkyuujo 研究所: a chemical laboratory (*kagaku jikkeñshitsu*) 化学実験室.

lace *n.* hi¹mo ひも; re¹esu レース: shoe laces (*kutsu himo*) 靴ひも / a lace curtain (*reesu no kaateñ*) レースのカーテン.

— *vt.* ... no hi¹mo o shime¹ru ...のひもを締める Ⓥ: lace up one's shoes (*kutsu no himo o shimeru*) 靴のひもを締める.

lack *n.* ke¹tsuboo 欠乏; fu¹soku 不足 ★ In a compound '*fusoku*' becomes '-*busoku*': lack of sleep (*suimiñ-busoku*) 睡眠不足 / The plants died for lack of water. (*Mizu-busoku de shokubutsu ga karete shimatta.*) 水不足で植物が枯れてしまった.
— *vt.* ... o ka¹ku ...を欠く Ⓒ; ... ga fu¹soku suru ...が不足する Ⓣ: He lacks courage. (*Kare wa yuuki o kaite iru.*) 彼は勇気を欠いている.

lacking *adj.* fu¹soku shite iru 不足している; ka¹kete iru 欠けている: Money is lacking for the trip. (*Ryokoo suru ni wa o-kane ga fusoku shite iru.*) 旅行するにはお金が不足している.

lacquer *n.* ra¹kkaa ラッカー; u¹rushi 漆: lacquer ware (*shikki*) 漆器.

ladder *n.* ha¹shigo はしご: climb up a ladder (*hashigo o noboru*) はしごを上る / set up a ladder against a tree (*ki ni hashigo o kakeru*) 木にはしごをかける.

lady *n.* **1** (woman of high social standing) ki¹fu¹jiñ 貴婦人.
2 (any woman) jo¹see 女性; fu¹jiñ 婦人: I want to buy something for a lady. (*Fujiñ no mono o kaitai no*

desu ga.) 婦人の物を買いたいのですが.
/ ladies' shoes (*fujiñgutsu*) 婦人靴.

lake *n.* mi⌐zuu⌐mi 湖: row a boat on the lake (*mizuumi de booto o kogu*) 湖でボートをこぐ / Lake Towada (*Towada-ko*) 十和田湖.

lamb *n.* (animal) ko⌐hi⌐tsuji 子羊; (meat) ko⌐hi⌐tsuji no ni⌐ku⌐ 子羊の肉.

lamp *n.* 1 (light) a⌐kari 明かり; de⌐ñ-ki-suta⌐ñdo 電気スタンド: turn on [off] a lamp (*akari o tsukeru [kesu]*) 明かりをつける[消す] / a desk lamp (*takujoo sutañdo*) 卓上スタンド.
2 (glass-covered light) ra⌐ñpu ラン⌐プ: an oil lamp (*sekiyu rañpu*) 石油ランプ.

land *n.* 1 (ground) to⌐chi 土地; ji⌐-meñ 地面: rich land (*koeta tochi*) 肥えた土地.
2 (earth's surface) ri⌐ku 陸; ri⌐ku-chi 陸地: We traveled over land and sea. (*Watashi-tachi wa riku ya umi o tabi shita.*) 私たちは陸や海を旅した.
3 (country) ku⌐ni 国; ko⌐kudo 国土: I visited many lands. (*Watashi wa ooku no kuni o tazuneta.*) 私は多くの国を訪ねた.
— *vi.* 1 (from the sea)(... ni) jo⌐o-riku suru (…に)上陸する ①: The party landed at Yokohama. (*Ikkoo wa Yokohama ni jooriku shita.*) 一行は横浜に上陸した.
2 (of an airplane) (... ni) cha⌐kuriku suru (…に)着陸する ①: The plane landed at Haneda. (*Hikooki wa Haneda ni chakuriku shita.*) 飛行機は羽田に着陸した.
— *vt.* 1 (of people) ... o jo⌐oriku saseru …を上陸させる ⑤.
2 (of an airplane) ... o cha⌐kuriku saseru …を着陸させる ⑤.

landing *n.* 1 (from the sea) jo⌐oriku 上陸; (of an airplane) cha⌐kuriku 着陸: landing procedures (*jooriku tetsuzuki*) 上陸手続 / a forced landing (*fujichaku*) 不時着.
2 (of stairs) o⌐doriba 踊り場.

landmark *n.* me⌐ji⌐rushi 目印: What landmarks are on the way?

(*Tochuu ni doñna mejirushi ga arimasu ka?*) 途中にどんな目印がありますか.

landscape *n.* 1 (scenery) ke⌐-shiki 景色; fu⌐ukee 風景: survey the landscape (*keshiki o miwatasu*) 景色を見渡す.
2 (painting) fu⌐ukeega 風景画.

lane *n.* 1 (narrow road) ko⌐michi 小道; ro⌐ji 路地: a blind lane (*fukurokooji*) 袋小路.
2 (division of a road) sha⌐señ 車線; re⌐eñ レーン: change lanes (*shseñ o heñkoo suru*) 車線を変更する.
3 (regular course) ko⌐oro 航路: an air lane (*kookuuro*) 航空路 / a sea lane (*kooro*) 航路.

language *n.* 1 (speech) ge⌐ñgo 言語; ko⌐toba⌐ 言葉: spoken language (*hanashi-kotoba*) 話し言葉 / written language (*kaki-kotoba*) 書き言葉.
2 (tongue) ko⌐kugo 国語; -go 語: the Japanese language (*Nihoñgo*) 日本語 / a foreign language (*gaikokugo*) 外国語.

lantern *n.* te⌐sage ra⌐ñpu 手提げランプ: a Japanese lantern (*choochiñ*) ちょうちん.

lap *n.* hi⌐za ひざ: The child sat on his mother's lap. (*Sono ko wa hahaoya no hiza no ue ni suwatta.*) その子は母親のひざの上に座った.

large *adj.* 1 (big) o⌐oki⌐i 大きい; o⌐oki-na 大きな: a large dog (*ookii inu*) 大きい犬 / He lives in a large house. (*Kare wa ooki-na ie ni suñde iru.*) 彼は大きな家に住んでいる.
2 (of quantity) ta⌐ryoo no 多量の; (of numbers) ta⌐su⌐u no 多数の: a large income (*tagaku no shuunyuu*) 多額の収入 / a large population (*tasuu no jiñkoo*) 多数の人口.

last[1] *adj.* 1 (final) sa⌐igo no 最後の: the last Sunday of June (*rokugatsu saigo no nichiyoobi*) 6月最後の日曜日 / This is his last painting. (*Kore wa kare no saigo no e desu.*) これは彼の最後の絵です.
2 (most recent) ko⌐no ma⌐e no この前の; señ- 先-; saku- 昨-: I met him

on Monday last. (*Kare to wa kono mae no getsuyoobi ni aimashita.*) 彼とはこの前の月曜日に会いました. / last week (*seňshuu*) 先週 / last month (*seňgetsu*) 先月 / last year (*sakuneň*) 昨年 / last night (*sakuya*) 昨夜.

— *adv.* sa˩igo ni 最後に: He spoke last at the meeting. (*Kare wa sono kai de saigo ni hatsugeň shita.*) 彼はその会で最後に発言した.

— *n.* (people) sa˩igo no hi˩to˩ 最後の人; (thing) sa˩igo no mo˩no˩ 最後のもの: I ate the last of the cake. (*Keeki no saigo wa watashi ga tabemashita.*) ケーキの最後は私が食べました.

last[2] *vi.* **1** (continue) tsu˩zuku 続く ©: The rain lasted for a week. (*Ame wa is-shuukaň tsuzuita.*) 雨は1週間続いた.
2 (remain) na˩gamo˩chi suru 長持ちする ⓤ; mo˩tsu もつ ©: Cheap shoes won't last long. (*Yasumono no kutsu wa nagaku motanai.*) 安物の靴は長くもたない.

lasting *adj.* e˩ezoku suru 永続する; e˩ekyuu no 永久の: a lasting peace (*eekyuu no heewa*) 永久の平和.

latch *n.* ka˩kegane 掛け金: set the latch (*kakegane o kakeru*) 掛け金をかける.

late *adj.* **1** (after the proper time) o˩kureta 遅れた; o˩kurete iru 遅れている: He was late for school. (*Kare wa gakkoo ni okureta.*) 彼は学校に遅れた. / I'm sorry I'm late. (*Okurete sumimaseň.*) 遅れてすみません.
2 (not early) o˩soi 遅い: It was late when I went to bed. (*Neta no wa osokatta.*) 寝たのは遅かった.
3 (toward the end) ma˩kki no 末期の; ko˩oki no 後期の: It happened in the late sixteenth century. (*Sore wa juuroku seeki no kooki ni okotta.*) それは16世紀の後期に起こった.
4 (recently dead) sa˩ikiň naku-natta 最近亡くなった; ko ... no ...: I knew his late father. (*Watashi wa*

kare no saikiň nakunatta chichi-oya o shitte imashita.*) 私は彼の最近亡くなった父親を知っていました. / the late Mr. Yamada (*ko Yamada-shi*) 故山田氏.

— *adv.* **1** (not in time) o˩kurete 遅れて: The train arrived one hour late. (*Ressha wa ichi-jikaň okurete toochaku shita.*) 列車は1時間遅れて到着した.
2 (not early) o˩soku 遅く: stay in bed late (*osoku made beddo ni iru*) 遅くまでベッドにいる.

lately *adv.* sa˩ikiň 最近; chi˩ka˩-goro 近ごろ: I haven't seen him lately. (*Watashi wa saikiň kare ni atte inai.*) 私は最近彼に会っていない. / What books have you read lately? (*Chikagoro doňna hoň o yomima-shita ka?*) 近ごろどんな本を読みましたか.

later *adv.* a˩to de 後で: I'll call again later. (*Mata ato de deňwa shimasu.*) また後で電話します. / See you later! (*De wa mata.*) ではまた.

— *adj.* mo˩tto o˩soi もっと遅い; mo˩tto ato no もっと後の: I'll take a later train. (*Motto ato no ressha ni norimasu.*) もっと後の列車に乗ります.

latest *adj.* sa˩ishiň no 最新の; sa˩i-kiň no 最近の: Have you heard the latest news? (*Saishiň no nyuusu o kikimashita ka?*) 最新のニュースを聞きましたか.

latter *adj.* **1** (nearer the end) a˩to no hoo no 後のほうの; ko˩ohaň no 後半の: the latter half of the year (*ichi-neň no koohaň*) 1年の後半.
2 (the second of two) ko˩osha no 後者の: I prefer the latter picture to the former. (*Watashi wa zeňsha no e yori koosha no hoo ga suki da.*) 私は前者の絵より後者のほうが好きだ.

laugh *vi.* **1** (express amusement) wa˩rau 笑う ©: Everyone laughed at his joke. (*Miňna wa kare no jooku ni waratta.*) みんなは彼のジョークに笑った.
2 (scorn) (... o) wa˩rau (...を)笑う

C: He laughed at my mistake. (*Kare wa watashi no machigai o waratta.*) 彼は私の間違いを笑った.
— *n.* wa¹rai 笑い: He answered with a laugh. (*Kare wa warai-nagara kotaeta.*) 彼は笑いながら答えた.

laughter *n.* wa¹rai 笑い; wa¹rai-go¹e 笑い声: burst into laughter (*fukidasu*) 吹き出す.

launch *vt.* **1** (send off) ... o ha¹ssha suru ...を発射する①: launch a rocket (*roketto o hassha suru*) ロケットを発射する.
2 (set afloat) ... o shi¹ñsui saseru ...を進水させる⑦: A new ship was launched. (*Atarashii fune ga shiñ-sui shita.*) 新しい船が進水した.
3 (begin) ... o ha¹jimeru ...を始める⑦: launch an election campaign (*señkyo-uñdoo o hajimeru*) 選挙運動を始める.

laundry *n.* **1** (clothes, etc.) se¹ñta-kumono 洗濯物: hang the laundry out to dry (*señtakumono o soto ni hosu*) 洗濯物を外に干す.
2 (place) se¹ñtakuya 洗濯屋; ku-¹riiniñgu¹teñ クリーニング店: send a shirt to the laundry (*waishatsu o kuriiniñguteñ ni dasu*) ワイシャツをクリーニング店に出す.

lavatory *n.* se¹ñmeñjo 洗面所; to¹i-re トイレ: I'd like to use the lavatory. (*Toire o o-kari shitai no desu ga.*) トイレをお借りしたいのですが.

lavish *adj.* mo¹no-o¹shimi shinai 物惜しみしない; ki¹mae no yo¹i 気前のよい: a lavish uncle (*kimae no yoi oji*) 気前のよいおじ.

law *n.* ho¹o 法; ho¹oritsu 法律: keep [break] the law (*hoo o mamoru [okasu]*) 法を守る[犯す] / It is against the law. (*Sore wa hooritsu ihañ desu.*) それは法律違反です.

lawful *adj.* go¹ohoo-teki na 合法的な; se¹etoo na 正当な: a lawful transaction (*goohoo-teki na tori-hiki*) 合法的な取り引き.

lawn *n.* shi¹bafu 芝生; shi¹ba 芝: mow the lawn (*shiba o karu*) 芝を刈る.

lawyer *n.* be¹ñgo¹shi 弁護士: consult a lawyer (*beñgoshi ni soodañ suru*) 弁護士に相談する.

lay *vt.* **1** (put down) ... o o¹ku ...を置く C: He laid his coat on the chair. (*Kare wa kooto o isu no ue ni oita.*) 彼はコートをいすの上に置いた.
2 (place in a lying position) ... o yo¹ko ni suru ...を横にする①; ne¹ka-seru 寝かせる⑦: She laid her baby on the bed. (*Kanojo wa akañboo o beddo ni nekaseta.*) 彼女は赤ん坊をベッドに寝かせた.
3 (set in place) ... o shi¹ku ...を敷く C: lay a carpet in the room (*heya ni juutañ o shiku*) 部屋にじゅうたんを敷く.
4 (prepare) ... o yo¹oi suru ...を用意する①: lay the table for dinner (*yuuhañ no shokutaku o yooi suru*) 夕飯の食卓を用意する.
5 (produce) ... o u¹mu ...を産む C: This hen lays an egg every day. (*Kono tori wa mainichi tamago o umu.*) この鶏は毎日卵を産む.

layer *n.* so¹o 層: a layer of clay (*neñdo no soo*) 粘土の層.

lazy *adj.* ta¹ida na 怠惰な; na¹ma¹-kete iru 怠けている: a lazy student (*taida na gakusee*) 怠惰な学生 / He is lazy. (*Kare wa namakemono da.*) 彼は怠け者だ.

lead¹ *vt.* **1** (guide) ... o mi¹chibi¹ku ...を導く C; a¹ñna¹i suru 案内する①: He led us to the hotel. (*Kare wa watashi-tachi o hoteru made añnai shite kureta.*) 彼は私たちをホテルまで案内してくれた.
2 (be first) ... no se¹ñtoo ni ta¹tsu ...の先頭に立つ C: A band led the parade. (*Gakutai ga kooshiñ no señtoo ni tatta.*) 楽隊が行進の先頭に立った.
3 (direct) ... o shi¹ki¹ suru ...を指揮する①; hi¹kii¹ru 率いる⑦: lead a party (*too o hikiiru*) 党を率いる.
— *vi.* **1** (act as a guide) a¹ñna¹i suru 案内する①: I'll lead. Please follow me. (*Watashi ga añnai shi-masu. Tsuite kite kudasai.*) 私が案

内します. ついて来てください.

2 (be ahead) seﾞñtoo ni taﾞtsu 先頭
に立つ C: My horse is leading.
(*Watashi no uma ga señtoo o hashitte iru.*) 私の馬が先頭を走っている.

3 (of a road) ... ni) tsuﾞujite iru (...
に)通じている V: This street leads to
the station. (*Kono michi wa eki ni
tsuujite imasu.*) この道は駅に通じてい
ます.

4 (direct) (... o) shiﾞdoo suru (...を)
指導する T: He led in the cam-
paign. (*Kare ga sono uñdoo o shidoo shita.*) 彼がその運動を指導した.

— *n.* **1** (front position) seﾞñtoo
先頭; shuﾞi 首位: He is in the lead.
(*Kare wa shui ni iru.*) 彼は首位にい
る.

2 (advance distance) yuﾞui 優位;
riﾞiido リード: Our team has a lead of
five points. (*Wareware no chiimu
wa go-teñ riido shite iru.*) われわれの
チームは5点リードしている.

3 (of a play) shuﾞyaku 主役: play
the lead in the play (*sono geki de
shuyaku o eñjiru*) その劇で主役を演
じる.

lead[2] *n.* (metal) naﾞmari 鉛.

leader *n.* **1** (guiding head) shi-
ﾞdoﾞosha 指導者; riﾞidaa リーダー:
He acted as our leader. (*Kare wa
watashi-tachi no riidaa o tsutometa.*) 彼は私たちのリーダーを務めた.

2 (in a race, competition, etc.)
seﾞñtoo ni taﾞtsu hiﾞto 先頭に立つ
人; shuﾞi no moﾞno¹ 首位の者.

3 (concertmaster) shiﾞkiﾞsha 指揮
者.

leadership *n.* shiﾞdoﾞokeñ 指導権;
shiﾞdoﾞoryoku 指導力: seize the
leadership (*shidookeñ o nigiru*) 指
導権を握る / exercise leadership (*shi-
dooryoku o hakki suru*) 指導力を発
揮する.

leading *adj.* **1** (chief) oﾞmo-na 主
な; shuﾞyoo na 主要な; iﾞchiryuu no
一流の: the leading countries of
Europe (*Yooroppa no ichiryuu-
koku*) ヨーロッパの一流国.

2 (important) shuﾞyoo na 主要な:

play the leading role (*shuyoo na
yakuwari o hatasu*) 主要な役割を果
たす.

leaf *n.* **1** (of a plant) ha 葉: sweep
up dead leaves (*kareha o hakiatsu-
meru*) 枯れ葉を掃き集める.

2 (of a book) iﾞchi¹-mai 1枚; iﾞchi¹-
yoo 1葉: tear a leaf out of a notebook (*nooto kara ichi-mai yabuku*)
ノートから1枚破る.

leaflet *n.* chiﾞrashi ちらし; riﾞifureﾞt-
to リーフレット: hand out leaflets
(*chirashi o kubaru*) ちらしを配る.

league *n.* doﾞomee 同盟; reﾞñmee
連盟; riﾞigu リーグ: join a league
(*reñmee ni kanyuu suru*) 連盟に加
入する / a league match (*riiguseñ*)
リーグ戦.

leak *n.* **1** (hole) moﾞreﾞguchi 漏れ
口; moﾞreana 漏れ穴: stop a leak
(*moreguchi o fusagu*) 漏れ口をふさぐ.

2 (leakage) moﾞreﾞ 漏れ: a gas leak
(*gasu-more*) ガス漏れ.

— *vi.* moﾞru 漏る C; moﾞreﾞru 漏れ
る V: This bucket leaks. (*Kono
baketsu wa moru.*) このバケツは漏る.
/ Gas is leaking from this pipe.
(*Kono kañ kara gasu ga morete
iru.*) この管からガスが漏れている.

— *vt.* ... o moﾞraﾞsu ...を漏らす C:
This boiler leaks water. (*Kono
boiraa wa mizu ga moreru.*) このボ
イラーは水が漏れる. / leak a secret
(*himitsu o morasu*) 秘密を漏らす.

lean[1] *vi.* **1** (bend) kaﾞtamuﾞku 傾く
C; mi o noﾞridaﾞsu 身を乗り出す C:
The fence leans so much it might
fall over. (*Hee ga katamuite taore-
soo da.*) 塀が傾いて倒れそうだ. / lean
out of the window (*mado kara mi
o noridasu*) 窓から身を乗り出す.

2 (rest) (... ni) yoﾞrikakaﾞru (...に)寄
りかかる C: lean against a tree (*ki ni
yorikakaru*) 木に寄りかかる.

— *vt.* **1** (bend) ... o kaﾞtamukeﾞru
...を傾ける V: lean one's head forward (*kubi o mae ni katamukeru*)
首を前に傾ける.

2 (rest) ... o (... ni) taﾞtekakeru ...を
(...に)立てかける V: I leaned my

umbrella against the wall. (*Watashi wa kasa o kabe ni tatekaketa.*) 私は傘を壁に立てかけた.

lean² *adj.* **1** (thin) yaˈseta やせた; yaˈseta iru やせている: a lean horse (*yaseta uma*) やせた馬.
2 (without fat) shiˈboo no naˈi 脂肪のない; aˈkami no 赤身の: lean meat (*akami no niku*) 赤身の肉.

leap *vi.* haˈneˈru 跳ねる Ⓥ; toˈbu 跳ぶ Ⓒ: leap up (*tobiagaru*) 跳び上がる / leap down (*tobioriru*) 跳び降りる / The dog leaped over the fence. (*Sono inu wa hee o tobikoeta.*) その犬は塀を跳び越えた.

learn *vt.* **1** (gain knowledge) ... o maˈnabu ...を学ぶ Ⓒ; shuˈutoku suru 習得する Ⓣ: She is learning flower arrangement. (*Kanojo wa ikebana o naratte imasu.*) 彼女は生け花を習っています.
2 (get to know) ... o shiˈru ...を知る Ⓒ; kiˈku 聞く Ⓒ: I've just learned that he is sick. (*Kare ga byooki da to tatta ima shitta.*) 彼が病気だとたった今知った.
3 (memorize) ... o oˈboeˈru ...を覚える Ⓥ: learn thirty words a day (*ichi-nichi ni sanjuu-go zutsu oboeru*) 1日に30語ずつ覚える.
— *vi.* maˈnabu 学ぶ Ⓒ; naˈraˈu 習う Ⓒ; oˈboeˈru 覚える Ⓥ: Children learn quickly. (*Kodomo wa oboeru no ga hayai.*) 子どもは覚えるのが早い.

learned *adj.* gaˈkuˈmoñ no aru 学問のある: a learned person (*gakusha*) 学者.

learner *n.* gaˈkushuˈusha 学習者; shoˈshiˈñsha 初心者: a learner's dictionary (*gakushuu-jiteñ*) 学習辞典.

learning *n.* **1** (getting knowledge) maˈnabu koto 学ぶこと; gaˈkushuu 学習: the learning of the Japanese language (*Nihoñgo no gakushuu*) 日本語の学習.
2 (knowledge) gaˈkuˈmoñ 学問; gaˈkushiki 学識: a person of learning (*gakumoñ no aru hito*) 学問のある人.

least *adj.* moˈttoˈmo suˈkunaˈi もっとも少ない: the least amount (*saishoo-ryoo*) 最少量.
not the least *adv.* suˈkoshi mo ... nai 少しも...ない: I haven't the least interest in the matter. (*Sono keñ ni tsuite wa sukoshi mo kañshiñ ga arimaseñ.*) その件については少しも関心がありません.
— *adv.* moˈttoˈmo suˈkuˈnaku もっとも少なく: the least expensive method (*mottomo hiyoo no kakaranai hoohoo*) もっとも費用のかからない方法.

leather *n.* kaˈwaˈi 革: leather gloves (*kawa no tebukuro*) 革の手袋.

leave¹ *vt.* **1** (go away) ... o saˈru ...を去る Ⓒ; deˈru 出る Ⓥ: He leaves the house at seven. (*Kare wa shichi-ji ni ie o demasu.*) 彼は7時に家を出ます.
2 (stop being in) ... o yaˈmeru ...をやめる Ⓥ: leave the tennis club (*tenisu kurabu o yameru*) テニスクラブをやめる.
3 (go without taking) ... o oˈkiwasureˈru ...を置き忘れる Ⓥ: I left my umbrella in a taxi. (*Watashi wa kasa o takushii ni okiwasureta.*) 私は傘をタクシーに置き忘れた.
4 (trust) ... o (... ni) maˈkaseˈru ...を(...に)任せる Ⓥ: I'll leave the decision with you. (*Kettee wa anata ni makasemasu.*) 決定はあなたに任せます.
— *vi.* taˈtsu 発つ Ⓒ; deˈru 出る Ⓥ: I am leaving tomorrow morning. (*Watashi wa ashita no asa tachimasu.*) 私はあしたの朝発ちます. / Will this flight leave on time? (*Kono biñ wa yotee doori demasu ka?*) この便は予定どおり出ますか.

leave² *n.* **1** (permission) kyoˈka 許可: May I have your leave to go? (*Itte mo yoroshii desu ka?*) 行ってもよろしいですか.
2 (holiday) kyuˈuka 休暇: take a month's leave (*ik-kagetsu no kyuuka o toru*) 1か月の休暇を取る.

lecture *n.* koˈogi 講義; koˈoeñ 講

演: give a lecture on literature (*buñgaku no koogi o suru*) 文学の講義をする.

— *vi.* ko˺ogi [ko˺oeñ] suru 講義[講演]する ①: He lectured on Japanese arts. (*Kare wa Nihoñ no bijutsu ni tsuite kooeñ shita.*) 彼は日本の美術について講演した.

left *adj.* hi˺dari no 左の: He writes with his left hand. (*Kare wa hidarite de kaku.*) 彼は左手で書く.

— *adv.* hi˺dari ni 左に: Turn left at the corner. (*Kado de hidari ni magari nasai.*) 角で左に曲がりなさい.

— *n.* 1 (left side) hi˺dari 左; hi˺darigawa 左側: He sat on her left. (*Kare wa kanojo no hidari ni suwatta.*) 彼は彼女の左に座った.

2 (political party) sa˺yoku 左翼; sa˺ha 左派.

left-handed *adj.* hi˺dari˺kiki no 左利きの: left-handed scissors (*hidarikiki-yoo no hasami*) 左利き用のはさみ.

leftist *n.* sa˺yoku [sa˺ha] no hi˺to˺ 左翼[左派]の人; kyu˺ushiñha no hito˺ 急進派の人.

— *adj.* sa˺yoku [sa˺ha] no 左翼[左派]の; kyu˺ushiñ-teki na 急進的な.

leg *n.* 1 (of an animal) a˺shi˺ 脚 [足]: She has nice legs. (*Kanojo wa kiree na ashi o shite iru.*) 彼女はきれいな脚をしている. ★ In Japanese, both 'leg' and 'foot' are called '*ashi*' あし, but written in different kanji: 'leg' 脚, and 'foot' 足.

2 (of a chair, etc.) a˺shi˺ 脚: One of the legs of the chair is broken. (*Isu no ashi ga ip-poñ orete iru.*) いすの脚が1本折れている.

legal *adj.* 1 (allowed by law) go˺ohoo-teki na 合法的な: a legal act (*goohoo-teki na kooi*) 合法的な行為.

2 (based on law) ho˺otee no 法定の: the legal interest (*hootee rishi*) 法定利子.

legend *n.* de˺ñsetsu 伝説: The story is based on a Japanese legend. (*Sono hanashi wa Nihoñ no deñsetsu ni motozuite imasu.*) その話は日本の伝説に基づいています.

legislation *n.* 1 (law) ho˺oritsu 法律; ho˺oree 法令.

2 (act) ho˺oritsu seetee 法律制定; ri˺ppoo 立法: the power of legislation (*rippokeñ*) 立法権.

legislative *adj.* ri˺ppoo no 立法の: legislative procedure (*rippoo tetsuzuki*) 立法手続き.

legislature *n.* ri˺ppo˺ofu 立法府; ri˺ppoo ki˺kañ 立法機関.

legitimate *adj.* go˺ohoo no 合法の; se˺etoo na 正当な: a legitimate claim (*seetoo na yookyuu*) 正当な要求.

leisure *n.* hi˺ma 暇; yo˺ka 余暇; re˺jaa レジャー: I have no leisure for reading. (*Watashi wa yukkuri hoñ o yomu hima ga nai.*) 私はゆっくり本を読む暇がない. ★ In Japanese, '*rejaa*' is usually associated with 'recreation.'

lemon *n.* re˺moñ レモン: squeeze a lemon (*remoñ o shiboru*) レモンを搾る / tea with lemon (*remoñ tii*) レモンティー.

lend *vt.* ... o ka˺su ...を貸す ©: Will you lend me your umbrella? (*Anata no kasa o kashite moraemasu ka?*) あなたの傘を貸してもらえますか. / I asked him to lend me some money. (*Watashi wa kare ni o-kane o sukoshi kashite kureru yoo ni tanoñda.*) 私は彼にお金を少し貸してくれるように頼んだ.

length *n.* 1 (of a thing) na˺gasa 長さ: measure the length of curtains (*kaateñ no nagasa o hakaru*) カーテンの長さを測る.

2 (of time) na˺gasa 長さ; ki˺ka˺ñ 期間: the length of a vacation (*kyuuka no nagasa*) 休暇の長さ / the intended length of stay (*yotee taizai kikañ*) 予定滞在期間.

lengthen *vt.* ... o na˺gaku suru ...を長くする ①: lengthen a dress (*doresu no take o nagaku suru*) ドレスの丈を長くする.

— *vi.* na˺gaku naru 長くなる ©: The days lengthen in spring.

(*Haru ni naru to hi ga nagaku naru.*) 春になると日が長くなる.

lens *n.* re^rñzu レンズ: a contact lens (*koñtakuto reñzu*) コンタクトレンズ.

leopard *n.* hyo^ro ひょう(豹).

less *adj.* yori su^rkuna^li より少ない: I made less money this year than last year. (*Kotoshi wa kyoneñ yori kasegi ga sukunakatta.*) ことしは去年よりかせぎが少なかった. / Please show me something less expensive. (*Moo sukoshi yasui no o misete kudasai.*) もう少し安いのを見せてください.

— *adv.* su^rku^lnaku 少なく: The less said the better. (*Kuchikazu wa sukunai hodo yoi.*) 口数は少ないほどよい.

— *pron.* su^rkuna^li ryoo 少ない量: You should eat less. (*Motto taberu ryoo o herasu beki da.*) もっと食べる量を減らすべきだ.

lessen *vi.* su^rku^lnaku naru 少なくなる ©; he^rru 減る ©: The pain has lessened a little. (*Itami ga sukoshi herimashita.*) 痛みが少し減りました.

— *vt.* o su^rku^lnaku suru …を少なくする Ⓣ; he^rrasu 減らす ©: lessen working hours (*roodoo-jikañ o herasu*) 労働時間を減らす.

lesson *n.* **1** (course of study) ga^rk-ka 学課; be^rñkyoo 勉強: neglect one's lessons (*beñkyoo o okotaru*) 勉強を怠る.
2 (period of teaching) ju^lgyoo 授業: a lesson in history (*rekishi no jugyoo*) 歴史の授業.
3 (of a textbook) ka 課: the Second Lesson (*dai ni-ka*) 第2課.
4 (wisdom) kyo^rokuñ 教訓: I learned my lesson from it. (*Ii kyookuñ ni narimashita.*) いい教訓になりました.

lest *conj.* ⟨verb⟩-nai yo^lo ni …ないように: We spoke quietly lest we disturb others. (*Watashi-tachi wa hoka no hito ni meewaku o kakenai yoo ni hikui koe de hanashita.*) 私たちはほかの人に迷惑をかけないように低い声で話した.

let *vt.* ⟨verb⟩-(sa)seru …(さ)せる Ⓥ; ya^rraseru やらせる Ⓥ: She let her children play in the park. (*Kanojo wa kodomo-tachi o kooeñ de asobaseta.*) 彼女は子どもたちを公園で遊ばせた. / Please let me do it again. (*Watashi ni moo ichi-do sore o yarasete kudasai.*) 私にもう一度それをやらせてください.

let … know *vt.* … ni shi^rraseru …に知らせる Ⓥ: Please let me know by telephone. (*Deñwa de watashi ni shirasete kudasai.*) 電話で私に知らせてください.

let's do ⟨verb⟩-(y)oo …(よ)う; ⟨verb⟩-mashoo …ましょう: Let's go together. (*Issho ni ikoo.*) いっしょに行こう. / Let's meet again. (*Mata o-ai shimashoo.*) またお会いしましょう.

letter *n.* **1** (written message) te-^rgami 手紙: I wrote a letter to my mother. (*Watashi wa haha ni tegami o kaita.*) 私は母に手紙を書いた. / Please send this letter by airmail. (*Kono tegami o kookuubiñ de dashite kudasai.*) この手紙を航空便で出してください. / letter paper (*biñseñ*) 便せん.
2 (sign in writing) mo^lji 文字: small letters (*komoji*) 小文字 / capital letters (*oomoji*) 大文字.

lettuce *n.* re^ltasu レタス: two heads of lettuce (*retasu ni-ko*) レタス2個.

level *adj.* **1** (flat and even) ta^rira na 平らな; su^rihee na 水平な: This floor is not level. (*Kono yuka wa suihee ja nai.*) この床は水平じゃない.
2 (of the same height) o^rnaji ta^lka-sa no 同じ高さの: The water was level with my knees. (*Mizu wa watashi no hiza to onaji takasa made atta.*) 水は私のひざと同じ高さまであった.
3 (even) go^rkaku no 互角の: a level race (*gokaku no kyoosoo*) 互角の競走.

— *n.* **1** (even line or surface) su^ri-hee 水平: bring the shelf to a level (*tana o suihee ni suru*) 棚を水平にする.

2 (height) ta⌐ka⌐sa 高さ: hang a picture at the level of one's eyes (*e o me no takasa ni kakeru*) 絵を目の高さに掛ける.

— *vt.* **1** (make flat) ... o ta⌐ira ni suru ...を平らにする 🔲; na⌐ra⌐su ならす 🄲: level ground with a bulldozer (*jimeñ o burudoozaa de narasu*) 地面をブルドーザーでならす.

2 (aim) (... ni) ... no ne⌐rai o tsu⌐ke⌐ru (...に)...のねらいをつける 🅅: level one's gun at a target (*mato ni juu no nerai o tsukeru*) 的に銃のねらいをつける.

liable *adj.* **1** (likely) ⟨verb⟩-gachi⌐ na ...がちな; ⟨verb⟩-yasu⌐i ...やすい: Difficulties are liable to occur. (*Meñdoo na koto wa okori-gachi da.*) 面倒なことは起こりがちだ. / I am liable to catch colds. (*Watashi wa kaze o hiki-yasui.*) 私はかぜをひきやすい.

2 (responsible) se⌐kiniñ ga a⌐ru 責任がある: We are liable for the damage. (*Wareware wa sono soñgai ni taishite sekiniñ ga aru.*) われわれはその損害に対して責任がある.

liar *n.* u⌐so⌐tsuki うそつき.

liberal *adj.* **1** (generous) ki⌐mae no yo⌐i 気前のよい; ka⌐ñdai na 寛大な: He gave the bellhop a liberal tip. (*Kare wa booi ni kimae no yoi chippu o ageta.*) 彼はボーイに気前のよいチップをあげた.

2 (in politics) ji⌐yuushu⌐gi no 自由主義の; sh⌐iñpo-teki na 進歩的な: liberal democracy (*jiyuu miñshushugi*) 自由民主主義.

— *n.* ji⌐yuushugi⌐sha 自由主義者; ri⌐berari⌐suto リベラリスト. ★ Japanese 'riberarisuto' comes from English 'liberalist'.

liberate *vt.* ... o ji⌐yu⌐u ni suru ...を自由にする 🔲; ka⌐ihoo suru 解放する 🔲: liberate hostages (*hitojichi o kaihoo suru*) 人質を解放する.

liberty *n.* **1** (freedom) ji⌐yu⌐u 自由: liberty of speech (*geñroñ no jiyuu*) 言論の自由.

2 (being free from control) ka⌐i-

hoo 解放.

library *n.* **1** (place) to⌐sho⌐kañ 図書館: a public library (*kookyoo toshokañ*) 公共図書館.

2 (collection of books) zo⌐osho 蔵書.

license *n.* **1** (permission) me⌐ñkyo 免許; ni⌐ñka 認可: get a license to hunt (*shuryoo no meñkyo o morau*) 狩猟の免許をもらう.

2 (written permission) me⌐ñkyo⌐shoo 免許証; kyo⌐ka⌐shoo 許可証: a driver's license (*uñteñ meñkyoshoo*) 運転免許証.

— *vt.* ... ni me⌐ñkyo [ni⌐ñka] o a⌐taeru ...に免許[認可]を与える 🅅: His shop is licensed to sell alcohol. (*Kare no mise wa arukooru iñryoo hañbai no niñka o ukete iru.*) 彼の店はアルコール飲料販売の認可を受けている.

lick *vt.* ... o na⌐me⌐ru ...をなめる 🅅: The dog licked my hand. (*Sono inu wa watashi no te o nameta.*) その犬は私の手をなめた.

lid *n.* fu⌐ta ふた: take off a lid (*futa o akeru*) ふたを開ける.

lie[1] *vi.* **1** (take a flat position) yo⌐ko ni na⌐ru 横になる 🄲; yo⌐kotawa⌐ru 横たわる 🄲: I lay on the bench. (*Watashi wa beñchi no ue ni yoko ni natta.*) 私はベンチの上に横になった.

2 (rest) a⌐ru ある 🄲; o⌐ite a⌐ru 置いてある 🄲: The book is lying on the desk. (*Hoñ wa tsukue no ue ni oite arimasu.*) 本は机の上に置いてあります.

3 (be situated) ... ni i⌐chi suru ...に位置する 🔲: The island lies to the south of Tokyo. (*Sono shima wa Tookyoo no minami ni ichi shite iru.*) その島は東京の南に位置している.

4 (exist) a⌐ru ある 🄲; so⌐ñzai suru 存在する 🔲: Happiness lies in health. (*Koofuku wa keñkoo ni aru.*) 幸福は健康にある.

lie[2] *n.* u⌐so うそ; i⌐tsuwari 偽り: tell a lie (*uso o tsuku*) うそをつく.

— *vi.* u⌐so o tsuku うそをつく 🄲; i⌐tsuwa⌐ru 偽る 🄲: He lied to me about it. (*Kare wa sono koto ni*

tsuite watashi ni uso o tsuita.) 彼は
そのことについて私にうそをついた.

life n. **1** (being alive) se˺emee 生
命; i˺nochi 命: He saved the
child's life. (*Kare wa sono ko no
inochi o sukutta.*) 彼はその子の命を
救った.
2 (living thing) i˹ki˺mono 生き物;
se˹ebutsu 生物: There is no life on
the moon. (*Tsuki ni wa seebutsu
wa inai.*) 月には生物はいない.
3 (the period between birth and
death) i˹sshoo 一生; sho˺ogai 生
涯: He remained single throughout his life. (*Kare wa isshoo dokushiñ de tooshita.*) 彼は一生独身で通
した.
4 (manner of living) se˹ekatsu 生
活; ku˹rashi 暮らし: She led a happy life. (*Kanojo wa shiawase na
seekatsu o okutta.*) 彼女は幸せな生
活を送った.

lift vt. (raise) ... o mo˹chiageru ...を
持ち上げる Ⓥ: I helped her lift the
box up. (*Watashi wa kanojo ga
sono hako o mochiageru no o tetsudatta.*) 私は彼女がその箱を持ち上げ
るのを手伝った.
— vi. **1** (go up) a˹garu 上がる Ⓒ:
This lid won't lift. (*Kono futa wa
agaranai.*) このふたは上がらない.
2 (disappear) ha˹re˺ru 晴れる Ⓥ:
The fog will soon lift. (*Kiri wa
sugu ni hareru deshoo.*) 霧はすぐに
晴れるでしょう.
— n. **1** (elevator) e˹rebe˺etaa エレ
ベーター.
2 (ride) ku˹ruma ni noseru koto˺ 車
に乗せること: I gave him a lift to the
station. (*Watashi wa kare o eki
made kuruma ni nosete yatta.*) 私
は彼を駅まで車に乗せてやった.

light[1] n. **1** (brightness) hi˹kari˺ 光;
a˹karusa 明るさ: the light of a can-
dle (*roosoku no hikari*) ろうそくの光
/ The light in this room is bad.
(*Kono heya no akarusa wa fujuubuñ da.*) この部屋の明るさは不十分だ.
2 (of a lamp) a˹kari 明かり; (electric light) de˹ñtoo 電灯: turn on

[off] a light (*akari o tsukeru [ke-
su]*) 明かりをつける[消す].
3 (traffic light) ko˹otsuushi˹ñgoo
交通信号: The lights changed to
green [red]. (*Shiñgoo ga ao [aka]
ni kawatta.*) 信号が青[赤]に変わった.
4 (flame) hi˹ 火: strike a light (*hi o
tsukeru*) 火をつける.
— adj. **1** (bright) a˹karui 明るい: a
light room (*akarui heya*) 明るい部屋.
2 (pale in color) u˹sui 薄い: light
green (*usumidori*) 薄緑.
— vt. **1** (set fire to) ... ni hi˹ o
tsu˹ke˺ru ...に火をつける Ⓥ: strike a
match and light a cigarette (*matchi
o sutte tabako ni hi o tsukeru*) マッ
チをすってたばこに火をつける.
2 (give light to) ... o te˹ra˺su ...を照
らす Ⓒ: light the way with a flashlight (*kaichuudeñtoo de michi o
terasu*) 懐中電灯で道を照らす.

light[2] adj. **1** (of little weight) ka˹-
rui 軽い: a light suitcase (*karui suutsukeesu*) 軽いスーツケース.
2 (not much) su˹kuna˹i 少ない:
Traffic is light today. (*Kyoo wa
kootsuuryoo ga sukunai.*) きょうは交
通量が少ない. / light rain (*kosame*)
小雨.
3 (easy) yo˹oi na 容易な; ra˹ku˹ na
楽な: light work (*raku na shigoto*)
楽な仕事.
4 (not serious) ka˹rui 軽い: light
reading (*karui yomimono*) 軽い読み
物.

lighten[1] vt. (make bright) ... o
a˹karuku suru ...を明るくする Ⓣ;
te˹rasu 照らす Ⓒ: The white wall
lightened the room. (*Shiroi kabe
ga heya o akaruku shita.*) 白い壁が
部屋を明るくした.
— vi. (become bright) a˹karuku
na˹ru 明るくなる Ⓒ: The sky lightened. (*Sora ga akaruku natta.*) 空が
明るくなった.

lighten[2] vt. (make less heavy) ... o
ka˹ruku suru ...を軽くする Ⓣ: I took
out some books to lighten my suitcase. (*Watashi wa suutsukeesu o
karuku suru tame ni nañ-satsu ka*

hoñ o dashita.) 私はスーツケースを軽くするために何冊か本を出した.

— *vi.* (become less heavy) kaʿruku naʾru 軽くなる Ⓒ: My heart lightened at the news. (*Sono shirase o kiite kokoro ga karuku natta.*) その知らせを聞いて心が軽くなった.

lighter *n.* raʿitaa ライター.

lighthouse *n.* toʿodai 灯台.

lighting *n.* shoʿomee 照明: direct [indirect] lighting (*chokusetsu [kañsetsu] shoomee*) 直接[間接]照明.

lightly *adv.* **1** (gently) kaʿruku 軽く; soʿtto そっと: press a bell lightly (*beru o sotto osu*) ベルをそっと押す.
2 (nimbly) keʿekai ni 軽快に: skip lightly along (*keekai ni tobihaneru*) 軽快に跳びはねる.
3 (cheerfully) yoʿoki ni 陽気に: dance lightly (*yooki ni odoru*) 陽気に踊る.

lightning *n.* iʿnabiʾkari 稲光; kaʿminaʾri 雷: be struck by lightning (*kaminari ni utareru*) 雷に打たれる.

like[1] *vt.* **1** (be fond of) ... ga suʿkiʾ da ...が好きだ; ... ga kiʿni iru ...が気に入る Ⓒ: I don't like this color. (*Watashi wa kono iro wa suki de wa arimaseñ.*) 私はこの色は好きではありません. / I like this very much. (*Kore ga taiheñ ki ni irimashita.*) これが大変気に入りました.
2 (wish) ⟨verb⟩-taʿi no desu ga ...たいのですが: I'd like to change my room. (*Heya o kaetai no desu ga.*) 部屋を替えたいのですが. / I'd like to reserve a hotel room in the city. (*Shinai no hoteru o yoyaku shitai no desu ga.*) 市内のホテルを予約したいのですが.
3 (want to have) ... ga hoʿshiʾi ...が欲しい: I'd like a sightseeing brochure for this town. (*Kono machi no kañkoo pañfuretto ga hoshii no desu ga.*) この町の観光パンフレットが欲しいのですが.

Would you like ... ? ... wa iʿkaʾga desu ka? ...はいかがですか: Would you like more coffee? (*Koohii o motto ikaga desu ka?*) コーヒーをもっ

といかがですか.

like[2] *adj.* (similar) niʿte iru 似ている: He is very like his older brother. (*Kare wa niisañ to yoku nite iru.*) 彼は兄さんとよく似ている.

— *prep.* **1** (the same as) ... no yoʿo na ...のような: a house like a castle (*shiro no yoo na ie*) 城のような家 / What is she like? (*Kanojo wa dono yoo na hito desu ka?*) 彼女はどのような人ですか.
2 (in the same way as) ... no yoʿo ni ...のように: He climbed the tree like a monkey. (*Kare wa saru no yoo ni sono ki ni nobotta.*) 彼は猿のようにその木に登った.

likely *adj.* **1** (about to happen) ⟨verb⟩-soʿo na ...そうな: It's likely to be fine this afternoon. (*Gogo wa hare-soo da.*) 午後は晴れそうだ.
2 (probable) aʿri-soʿo na ありそうな; moʿttomo-rashiʾi もっともらしい: a likely story (*ari-soo na hanashi*) ありそうな話 / a likely explanation (*mottomo-rashii setsumee*) もっともらしい説明.

likewise *adv.* oʿnaji yoʿo ni 同じように: He took off his shoes and I did likewise. (*Kare wa kutsu o nuida ga watashi mo onaji yoo ni shita.*) 彼は靴を脱いだが私も同じようにした.

liking *n.* koʿnomi 好み; shuʾmi 趣味: He has a particular liking for wine. (*Kare wa toku ni waiñ ga suki da.*) 彼は特にワインが好きだ.

lily *n.* (plant) yuʿri ゆり; (flower) yuʿri no hana[1] ゆりの花.

limb *n.* teʿashi 手足: He rested his tired limbs. (*Kare wa tsukareta teashi o yasumaseta.*) 彼は疲れた手足を休ませた.

limit *n.* **1** (boundary) geʿñkai 限界; geʿñdo 限度: There is a limit to everything. (*Nanigoto ni mo geñdo ga aru.*) 何事にも限度がある.
2 (restriction) seʿegeʾñ 制限: exceed the weight limit (*juuryoo seegeñ o koeru*) 重量制限を越える.

— *vt.* ... o seʿegeʾñ suru ...を制限す

る ①: You had better limit the number of cigarettes you smoke. (*Kimi wa suu tabako no hoñsuu o seegeñ shita hoo ga yoi.*) 君は吸うたばこの本数を制限したほうがいい.

limitation *n.* se「ege¬ñ 制限; ge「ñkai 限界: limitations on imports (*yunyuu seegeñ*) 輸入制限 / know one's limitations (*jibuñ no geñkai o shiru*) 自分の限界を知る.

limited *adj.* **1** (restricted) ka「gira¬reta 限られた; ka「gira¬rete iru 限られている: My experience is limited. (*Watashi no keekeñ wa kagirarete imasu.*) 私の経験は限られています.
2 (of a train or bus) to「kkyuu no 特急の: a limited express (*tokkyuu ressha*) 特急列車.

limp *vi.* a「shi o hi「kizuru 足を引きずる ©: He hurt his ankle and limped back home. (*Kare wa ashikubi o itame ashi o hikizutte ie e kaetta.*) 彼は足首を痛め足を引きずって家へ帰った.

line *n.* **1** (long, thin mark) se「ñ 線: draw a straight line (*chokuseñ o hiku*) 直線を引く.
2 (cord) hi「mo ひも, tsu「na¬ 綱: hang the washing on a line (*señtakumono o himo ni kakeru*) 洗濯物をひもにかける.
3 (row of people) re「tsu 列: stand in a line (*retsu ni narabu*) 列に並ぶ.
4 (row of words) gyo「o 行: the fifth line from the top (*ue kara go-gyoo-me*) 上から5行目.
5 (of a telephone) de「ñwaseñ 電話線: The line is busy. (*O-hanashichuu desu.*) お話し中です. / Please hold the line. (*Sono mama kirazu ni o-machi kudasai.*) そのまま切らずにお待ちください.
6 (business) sho「obai 商売; sho-「ku¬gyoo 職業: What is your line? (*Anata no go-shoobai wa nañ desu ka?*) あなたのご商売は何ですか.

linen *n.* a「sa¬ 麻.

liner *n.* (ship) te「ekiseñ 定期船; (airplane) te「eki ryoka¬kki 定期旅客機.

linger *vi.* gu「zuguzu suru ぐずぐずする

①: Don't linger on your way home. (*Uchi e kaeru tochuu guzuguzu shinai yoo ni.*) 家へ帰る途中ぐずぐずしないように.

link *vt.* ... o tsu「nagu ...をつなぐ ©; mu「subu 結ぶ ©: We linked arms. (*Watashi-tachi wa te o tsunaida.*) 私たちは手をつないだ. / a road linking the two towns (*futatsu no machi o musubu dooro*) 二つの町を結ぶ道路.
—— *n.* (ring) wa「 輪: a link in a chain (*kusari no wa*) 鎖の輪.
2 (anything connecting two things) ka「ñreñ 関連; tsu「nagari つながり: He has links with the political world. (*Kare wa seekai to tsunagari ga aru.*) 彼は政界とつながりがある.

lion *n.* ra「ioñ ライオン; shi「shi 獅子.

lip *n.* ku「chibiru 唇: the lower lip (*shita-kuchibiru*) 下唇 / the upper lip (*uwa-kuchibiru*) 上唇 / bite one's lips (*kuchibiru o kamu*) 唇をかむ. ★ Japanese '*kuchibiru*' refers only to either of the two edges of the mouth, and does not include the skin around them.

lipstick *n.* ku「chibeni 口紅: wear lipstick (*kuchibeni o tsukeru*) 口紅をつける.

liquid *n.* e「kitai 液体.
—— *adj.* e「kitai no 液体の; e「kijoo no 液状の: liquid fuel (*ekitai neñryoo*) 液体燃料 / liquid food (*ryuudooshoku*) 流動食.

liquor *n.* a「rukooru-i¬ñryoo アルコール飲料: a liquor store (*sakaya*) 酒屋.

list *n.* hyo「o 表; i「chirañhyoo 一覧表; ri「suto リスト; me「ebo 名簿: draw up a list (*ichirañhyoo o tsukuru*) 一覧表を作る / Show me a list of your rates, please. (*Ryookiñhyoo o misete kudasai.*) 料金表を見せてください.
—— *vt.* ... o hyo「o ni suru ...を表にする ①; hyo「o ni noseru 表に載せる ②: I listed the things I had to do. (*Watashi wa suru koto o hyoo ni shita.*) 私はすることを表にした.

listen *vi.* **1** (try to hear) (... o) ki-

「ku (...を)聞く C : listen to the radio (*rajio o kiku*) ラジオを聞く.
2 (follow the advice of) (... ni) mi-「mi」o ka「su (...に)耳を貸す C ; shi-「tagau 従う C : He didn't listen to my advice. (*Kare wa watashi no chuukoku ni mimi o kasanakatta.*) 彼は私の忠告に耳を貸さなかった.

listener *n.* ki「ku hito」 聴く人 ; ki-「kite 聞き手.

liter *n.* ri「ttoru リットル ; (of gasoline) ri「ttaa リッター : a liter of wine (*ichi-rittoru no waiñ*) 1 リットルのワイン / How much is gasoline per liter? (*Gasoriñ wa rittaa atari ikura desu ka?*) ガソリンはリッターあたりいくらですか. ★ Japanese use the metric system and 'quart' and 'pint' are not used.

literally *adv.* **1** (in the literal sense) mo「jido」ori ni 文字どおりに : I took what he said literally. (*Watashi wa kare ga itta koto o moji-doori ni uketotta.*) 私は彼が言ったことを文字どおりに受けとった.
2 [intensifier] mo「jido」ori 文字どおり ; ho「ñtoo ni 本当に : He was literally penniless. (*Kare wa moji-doori ichi-moñ nashi datta.*) 彼は文字どおり一文なしだった.

literary *adj.* **1** (of literature) bu「ñ-gaku no 文学の : literary works (*buñgaku-sakuhiñ*) 文学作品.
2 (of a written style) bu「ñgo no 文語の : literary style (*buñgotai*) 文語体.

literature *n.* **1** (written works) bu「ñgaku 文学 ; bu「ñgee 文芸 : Japanese literature (*Nihoñ buñ-gaku*) 日本文学.
2 (printed material) bu「ñkeñ 文献 : I am collecting the literature on Japan. (*Watashi wa Nihoñ ni kañ-suru buñkeñ o atsumete imasu.*) 私は日本に関する文献を集めています.

litter *n.* go「mi」 ごみ ; ku「zu くず : No litter, please. (*Gomi o sutenaide kudasai.*) ごみを捨てないでください.
— *vt.* ... o chi「rakasu ...を散らかす C : The children littered the room

with toys. (*Kodomo-tachi wa omo-cha de heya o chirakashita.*) 子どもたちはおもちゃで部屋を散らかした.

little[1] *adj.* **1** (small) chi「isa-na 小さな ; chi「isa」i 小さい : a little village (*chiisa-na mura*) 小さな村 / The boy is too little to ride a bicycle. (*Sono ko wa chiisakute jiteñsha ni norenai.*) その子は小さくて自転車に乗れない.
2 (young) ne「ñshoo no 年少の ; to-「shishita no 年下の : a little brother (*otooto*) 弟 / a little sister (*imooto*) 妹.

little[2] *adj.* **1** (small amount) su「ko」-shi no 少しの ; wa「zuka na わずかな : There is a little milk in the bottle. (*Biñ ni gyuunyuu ga sukoshi ari-masu.*) びんに牛乳が少しあります.
2 (not much) su「ko」shi shika nai 少ししかない ; ho「to」ñdo nai ほとんどない : I have little money with me. (*O-kane wa sukoshi shika motte imaseñ.*) お金は少ししか持っていません. / There is little hope of his recovery. (*Kare ga kaifuku suru mi-komi wa hotoñdo arimaseñ.*) 彼が回復する見込みはほとんどありません.
— *adv.* **1** (not much) su「ko」shi 少し : I feel a little better. (*Kibuñ wa sukoshi yoku narimashita.*) 気分は少し良くなりました. / I speak a little Japanese. (*Nihoñgo o sukoshi ha-nashimasu.*) 日本語を少し話します.
2 (not at all) su「koshi mo ‹verb›-nai 少しも...ない : I little knew that he was ill. (*Kare ga byooki to wa sukoshi mo shiranakatta.*) 彼が病気とは少しも知らなかった.
— *pron.* su「ko」shi 少し ; sho「oryoo 少量 : I'll give you a little of this cake. (*Kono keeki o sukoshi age-mashoo.*) このケーキを少しあげましょう.

live[1] *vi.* **1** (dwell) (... ni) su「mu (...に)住む C : He lives in Kanazawa. (*Kare wa Kanazawa ni suñde imasu.*) 彼は金沢に住んでいます.
2 (be alive) i「ki」ru 生きる V : She lived to the age of eighty. (*Kanojo wa hachijus-sai made ikita.*) 彼女

は 80 歳まで生きた.
— vt. ...no se「ekatsu o suru ...の
生活をする ①: live a simple life
(kañso na seekatsu o suru) 簡素な
生活をする.

live[2] adj. 1 (living) i「kite iru 生きて
いる: a live fish (ikite iru sakana)
生きている魚.
2 (of broadcasting) na「ma no 生の;
ji「kkyoo no 実況の: a live TV
broadcast (terebi no nama-hoosoo)
テレビの生放送.
3 (still burning) mo「ete iru 燃えてい
る: live coals (moete iru sekitañ) 燃
えている石炭.
4 (carrying electricity) de「ñryuu ga
tsuujite iru 電流が通じている: a live
battery (mada tsukaeru deñchi) ま
だ使える電池.

livelihood n. ku「rashi 暮らし; se「e-
kee 生計: earn one's livelihood
(seekee o tateru) 生計を立てる.

lively adj. 1 (full of life) ge「ñki no
yoi 元気のよい; ka「ppatsu na 活発
な: a lively boy (geñki no yoi shooneñ) 元気のよい少年.
2 (cheerful) yo「oki na 陽気な; ni-
「gi「yaka na にぎやかな: The street
was lively with shoppers. (Sono
toori wa kaimonokyaku de nigi-
yaka datta.) その通りは買い物客でにぎ
やかだった.

liver n. (organ) ka「ñzoo 肝臓;
(food) re「baa レバー.

living adj. 1 (alive) i「kite iru 生きて
いる: This fish is still living. (Kono
sakana wa mada ikite iru.) この魚は
まだ生きている.
2 (existing in use) ge「ñzoñ no 現存
の; ge「ñdai no 現代の: living language (geñdaigo) 現代語.
— n. se「ekatsu 生活; ku「rashi 暮ら
し: the standard of living (seekatsu-suijuñ) 生活水準 / make a
living (seekee o tateru) 生計を立て
る.

living room n. i「ma「 居間.

load n. 1 (something which is carried) tsu「mini 積み荷; ni「 荷: He
carried the heavy load on his back.

(Kare wa omoi ni o seotte hakoñ-
da.) 彼は重い荷を背負って運んだ.
2 (something which weighs on the
mind) fu「tañ 負担; o「moni 重荷: It
took a load off my mind. (Sore de
watashi no kokoro no omoni ga
toreta.) それで私の心の重荷が取れた.
— vt. 1 (put a load on) ... ni (...
o) tsu「mu ...に(...を)積む ⓒ: We
loaded the truck with vegetables.
(Watashi-tachi wa torakku ni
yasai o tsuñda.) 私たちはトラックに野
菜を積んだ.
2 (fill) ... o (... ni) i「reru ...を(...に)入
れる ⓥ: load film into a camera
(firumu o kamera ni ireru) フィルム
をカメラに入れる / This gun is not
loaded. (Kono juu ni wa tama ga
haitte imaseñ.) この銃には弾が入って
いません.

loaf n. hi「toka「tamari ひと塊: a loaf
of bread (pañ hitokatamari) パンひと
塊.

loan n. 1 (lending) ka「shitsuke 貸
し付け; ka「su koto「 貸すこと: ask for
the loan of money (o-kane no ka-
shitsuke o tanomu) お金の貸し付けを
頼む / Thanks for the loan of your
book. (Hoñ o kashite kurete arigatoo.) 本を貸してくれてありがとう.
2 (money) ka「shitsukekiñ 貸付金;
ro「oñ ローン: I got a loan from the
bank. (Watashi wa giñkoo kara
rooñ o karita.) 私は銀行からローンを
借りた.
— vt. ... ni (... o) ka「su ...に(...を)貸
す ⓒ; ka「shitsuke「ru 貸し付ける ⓥ:
I loaned him my car. (Watashi wa
kare ni kuruma o kashite yatta.)
私は彼に車を貸してやった.

lobby n. ro「bii ロビー; hi「roma 広間:
a hotel lobby (hoteru no robii) ホテ
ルのロビー.

lobster n. ro「busutaa ロブスター;
i「se「-ebi 伊勢えび. ★ In Japanese
'prawn' and 'shrimp' are also called
'ebi.'

local adj. 1 (of a certain place) to-
「chi no 土地の; chi「ho「o no 地方の:
I'd like some local sake. (Kono

tochi no sake o nomitai.) この土地の酒を飲みたい。/ a local newspaper (*Chihoo-shinbun*) 地方新聞。★ Japanese often use '*rookaru*' ローカル (from English 'local') in the sense of 'rural.'

2 (not limited) ka「kueki te」esha no 各駅停車の; fu「tsuu no 普通の: a local train (*futsuu-ressha*) 普通列車.

3 (of a particular part) kyo「kubu-teki na 局部的な: a local pain (*kyo-kubu-teki na itami*) 局部的な痛み.

local call *n.* shi「nai tsu」uwa 市内通話.

local time *n.* ge「nchi-ji」kan 現地時間.

locate *vt.* **1** (find the place) ... no ba「sho o sagashi ate」ru ...の場所を捜し当てる Ⓥ; sho「zai o tsukito-me」ru 所在を突き止める Ⓥ: The police located the missing girl. (*Kee-satsu wa yukue fumee no shoojo no shozai o tsukitometa.*) 警察は行方不明の少女の所在を突き止めた.

2 (situate) ... ni a「ru ...にある Ⓒ: Where is your hotel located? (*Anata no hoteru wa doko ni ari-masu ka?*) あなたのホテルはどこにありますか.

3 (settle) ... o (... ni) o「ku ...を(...に)置く Ⓒ: They located their office in Yokohama. (*Kare-ra wa jimu-sho o Yokohama ni oita.*) 彼らは事務所を横浜に置いた.

location *n.* ba「sho 場所; i「chi 位置; sho「za」ichi 所在地: The new school has a good location. (*Atara-shii gakkoo wa ii basho ni aru.*) 新しい学校はいい場所にある.

lock *vt.* **1** (fasten with a lock) ... ni ka「gi o ka「ke」ru ...に鍵をかける Ⓥ; jo「o o oro」su 錠を下ろす Ⓒ: Did you lock the gate? (*Mon ni kagi o kakemashita ka?*) 門に鍵をかけましたか.

2 (shut in) ... o (... ni) to「jikome」ru ...を(...に)閉じ込める Ⓥ; shi「maiko-mu しまい込む Ⓒ: She locked her jewels in the box. (*Kanojo wa hoo-seki o hako ni shimaikonda.*) 彼女

は宝石を箱にしまい込んだ.

— *vi.* ka「gi」 [jo「o」] ga ka「ka」ru 鍵 [錠]がかかる Ⓒ: This door doesn't lock. (*Kono to wa kagi ga kaka-ranai.*) この戸は鍵がかからない.

— *n.* jo「o 錠; jo「omae 錠前: open a lock with a key (*kagi de joo o akeru*) 鍵で錠を開ける.

locomotive *n.* ki「ka」nsha 機関車.

lodge *n.* sa「nsoo 山荘; ya「magoya 山小屋.

— *vt.* ... o to「meru ...を泊める Ⓥ: Can you lodge me overnight? (*Hito-ban tomete moraemasu ka?*) 一晩泊めてもらえますか.

— *vi.* (... ni) to「maru (...に)泊る Ⓒ: She lodged at her friend's house. (*Kanojo wa tomodachi no ie ni tomatta.*) 彼女は友だちの家に泊まった.

lodger *n.* ge「shukunin 下宿人.

lodging *n.* ka「shima 貸間; ge-「shukuya 下宿屋: live in lodgings (*magari suru*) 間借りする.

log *n.* ma「ruta 丸太: a log cabin (*marutagoya*) 丸太小屋.

logic *n.* **1** (way of reasoning) ro「nri 論理; ro「npoo 論法: I cannot fol-low your logic. (*Kimi no ronri ni wa tsuite ikenai.*) 君の論理にはついていけない.

2 (science) ro「nri」gaku 論理学.

logical *adj.* ro「nri-teki na 論理的な; su「ji no tootta [tootte iru] 筋の通った[通っている]: What you say is logi-cal. (*Anata no iu koto wa suji ga tootte iru.*) あなたの言うことは筋が通っている.

loneliness *n.* ko「doku 孤独; sa-「bi」shisa 寂しさ: endure loneliness (*kodoku ni taeru*) 孤独に耐える.

lonely *adj.* **1** (alone) ko「doku na 孤独な; hi「toribo」tchi no 独りぼっちの: lead a lonely life (*kodoku na seekatsu o okuru*) 孤独な生活を送る.

2 (unhappy) sa「bishi」i 寂しい: She felt lonely. (*Kanojo wa sabishi-katta.*) 彼女は寂しかった.

3 (away from other people) hi「to no sukuna」i 人の少ない; hi「tozato

hana┌reta 人里離れた: a lonely
street (*hitodoori no sukunai toori*)
人通りの少ない通り.

long[1] *adj.* **1** (of length, distance,
time, etc.) na┌ga┐i 長い: long hair
(*nagai kami*) 長い髪 / a long night
(*nagai yoru*) 長い夜 / a long vacation (*nagai kyuuka*) 長い休暇.

2 (measuring) na┌gasa no 長さの: a
rope five meters long (*go-meetoru
no nagasa no roopu*) 5メートルの長さ
のロープ.

— *adv.* **1** (for a long time) na┌ga-
ku 長く; na┌ga┐i aida 長い間: Have
you been waiting long? (*Nagaku
machi mashita ka?*) 長く待ちましたか.

2 (at a far distant time) zu┌tto ずっ
と: He died long ago. (*Kare wa
zutto mukashi ni nakunarimashita.*)
彼はずっと昔に亡くなりました.

how long *adv.* do┌no kurai どのく
らい: How long are you staying
here? (*Dono kurai koko ni taizai
shimasu ka?*) どのくらいここに滞在しま
すか.

So long. (*De wa mata.*) ではまた.

long[2] *vi.* se┌tsuboo suru 切望する 圓;
<verb>-tai …たい: I'm longing to go
home. (*Watashi wa kokyoo e
kaeritai.*) 私は故郷へ帰りたい.

long-distance *n.* cho┌okyori-
de┐nwa 長距離電話.

longing *n.* se┌tsuboo 切望; a┌ko-
gare あこがれ: a longing for fame
(*meesee e no akogare*) 名声へのあこ
がれ.

look *vi.* **1** (try to see) mi┌ru 見る Ⓥ:
I'm just looking. (*Chotto mite iru
dake desu.*) ちょっと見ているだけです.

2 (seem to be) … yoo ni mi┌e┐ru …
ように見える Ⓥ: He looked tired.
(*Kare wa tsukareta yoo ni mieta.*)
彼は疲れたように見えた.

— *vt.* **1** (give a look) … o ji┌tto
mi┐ru …をじっと見る Ⓥ: She looked
me in the face. (*Kanojo wa watashi no kao o jitto mita.*) 彼女は私の
顔をじっと見た.

2 (notice carefully) … o ta┌shi-
kame┐ru …を確かめる Ⓥ: Look to

see if he has come yet. (*Kare ga
kita ka doo ka tashikame nasai.*)
彼が来たかどうか確かめなさい.

— *n.* **1** (act) mi┌ru ko┌to┐ 見ること:
Please let me have a look at it.
(*Sore o misete kudasai.*) それを見せ
てください.

2 (expression) me┌tsuki 目つき;
ka┌otsuki 顔つき: an angry look
(*okotta metsuki*) 怒った目つき.

3 (appearance) ga┌ikañ 外観; yo┌o-
su 様子: I don't like the look of the
weather. (*Teñki no yoosu ga ki ni
iranai.*) 天気の様子が気に入らない.

4 (features) ki┌ryoo 器量: She has
good looks. (*Kanojo wa kiryoo ga
yoi.*) 彼女は器量がよい.

look after … *vt.* … ni ki ┌o tsu-
ke┐ru …に気をつける Ⓥ: look after
one's health (*keñkoo ni ki o tsukeru*) 健康に気をつける.

look at … *vt.* … o yo┌ku miru …を
よく見る Ⓥ: She looked at herself in
the mirror. (*Kanojo wa kagami no
naka no jibuñ no sugata o mita.*)
彼女は鏡の中の自分の姿を見た.

look down on … *vt.* … o mi┌ku-
dasu …を見下す Ⓒ: look down on a
person (*hito o mikudasu*) 人を見
下す.

look for … *vt.* … o sa┌gasu …を
捜す Ⓒ: He is looking for his glasses. (*Kare wa megane o sagashite
iru.*) 彼は眼鏡を捜している.

look forward to … *vt.* … o ta-
┌noshimi ni ma┐tsu …を楽しみに待つ
Ⓒ: I am looking forward to meeting you. (*O-ai suru no o tanoshimi
ni shite imasu.*) お会いするのを楽しみ
にしています.

look like … *vt.* … ni ni┌te iru …に
似ている Ⓥ: He looks like his father.
(*Kare wa o-toosañ ni nite iru.*) 彼は
お父さんに似ている.

look over … *vt.* … o shi┌rabe┐ru
…を調べる Ⓥ: look over the papers
(*shorui o shiraberu*) 書類を調べる.

look up *vi.*, *vt.* … o mi┌age┐ru …を
見上げる Ⓥ; shi┌rabe┐ru 調べる Ⓥ:
look up into the sky (*sora o mia-*

geru) 空を見上げる / look up a word in a dictionary (*jisho de tango o shiraberu*) 辞書で単語を調べる.

lookout *n.* mi⌐hari 見張り; ke⌐ekai 警戒: keep a careful lookout (*yudan naku miharu*) 油断なく見張る.

loop *n.* wa⌐ 輪: make a loop (*wa o tsukuru*) 輪を作る.
— *vt.* ... o wa⌐ ni suru …を輪にする: loop up a curtain (*kaaten o wa de tomeru*) カーテンを輪で留める.

loose *adj.* **1** (not tight) yu⌐rui 緩い: a loose knot (*yurui musubime*) 緩い結び目.
2 (not tied) shi⌐batte nai 縛ってない; (free) ji⌐yuu na 自由な: let a dog run loose (*inu o jiyuu ni shite yaru*) 犬を自由にしてやる.
3 (not put up) ta⌐banete nai 束ねてない; ba⌐ra no ばらの: buy cakes of soap loose (*sekken o bara de kau*) せっけんをばらで買う.
4 (not careful) fu⌐selekaku na 不正確な; zo⌐nzai na そんざいな: a loose translation (*zonzai na honyaku*) そんざいな翻訳.
5 (not moral) fu⌐shidara na ふしだらな: a loose life (*fushidara na seekatsu*) ふしだらな生活.

loosen *vt.* ... o yu⌐rumeru …を緩める V; to⌐ku 解く C: loosen one's tie (*nekutai o yurumeru*) ネクタイを緩める.
— *vi.* yu⌐rumu 緩む C; ta⌐rumu たるむ C.

lord *n.* **1** (God) ka⌐mi 神; (Christ) Ki⌐risuto キリスト.
2 (peer) ki⌐zoku 貴族.
3 (ruler) shi⌐haisha 支配者; ku⌐nshu 君主.

lose *vt.* **1** (fail to find) ... o na⌐kusu …をなくす C; o⌐kiwasureru 置き忘れる V: I lost my passport. (*Pasupooto o nakushimashita.*) パスポートをなくしました. / He lost his glasses somewhere. (*Kare wa megane o doko-ka ni okiwasureta.*) 彼は眼鏡をどこかに置き忘れた.
2 (have no longer) ... o u⌐shinau …を失う C: She lost her son in an

accident. (*Kanojo wa jiko de musuko o ushinatta.*) 彼女は事故で息子を失った.
3 (fail to win) ... ni ma⌐keru …に負ける V: lose the baseball game (*yakyuu no shiai ni makeru*) 野球の試合に負ける.
4 (fail to keep) ... o ta⌐motenai …を保てない; u⌐shinau 失う C: I have lost interest in politics. (*Watashi wa seeji ni kyoomi o ushinatta.*) 私は政治に興味を失った.
5 (fail to see) ... o mi⌐ushinau …を見失う C; ... ni ma⌐you …に迷う C: I lost him in the crowd. (*Watashi wa hitogomi de kare o miushinatta.*) 私は人込みで彼を見失った. / I'm lost. (*Michi ni mayotte shimaimashita.*) 道に迷ってしまいました.
6 (waste) ... o mu⌐da ni suru …を無駄にする I; ro⌐ohi suru 浪費する I: Don't lose any time. (*Jikan o muda ni shite wa ikenai.*) 時間を無駄にしてはいけない.
7 (of a clock) o⌐kureru 遅れる: This clock loses a minute a day. (*Kono tokee wa ichi-nichi ni ip-pun okureru.*) この時計は1日に1分遅れる.
— *vi.* **1** (be defeated) ma⌐keru 負ける V: They lost in the match. (*Kare-ra wa sono shiai de maketa.*) 彼らはその試合で負けた.
2 (suffer loss) so⌐n o suru 損をする I: He lost on the bet. (*Kare wa sono kake de son o shita.*) 彼はその賭で損をした.

loser *n.* ha⌐isha 敗者: a bad loser (*makeoshimi o iu hito*) 負け惜しみを言う人.

loss *n.* **1** (losing) na⌐kusu koto⌐ なくすこと; so⌐oshitsu 喪失: loss of memory (*kioku sooshitsu*) 記憶喪失.
2 (the amount lost) so⌐ngai 損害; so⌐nshitsu 損失: His losses were greater than his gains. (*Kare no sonshitsu wa rieki yori mo ookikatta.*) 彼の損失は利益よりも大きかった.
3 (failure to win) ma⌐ke 負け; ha⌐iboku 敗北: three wins and two

losses (sañ-shoo ni-hai) 3 勝 2 敗.

lost adj. **1** (missing) uˈshinatta 失った; fuˈñshitsu shita 紛失した: I looked for my lost watch. (Watashi wa nakushita tokee o sagashita.) 私はなくした時計を捜した. / lost articles (fuñshitsubutsu) 紛失物.

2 (wasted) muˈda ni naˈtta 無駄になった: make up lost time (muda ni natta jikañ o umeawaseru) 無駄になった時間を埋め合わせる.

3 (not won) maˈketa 負けた: a lost game (maketa shiai) 負けた試合.

4 (having lost one's way) miˈchi ni mayoˈtta 道に迷った: a lost child (maigo) 迷子.

lost-and-found (**office**) n. iˈshitsuˈbutsu toˈriatsukaijo˥ 遺失物取扱所: Where is the lost-and-found? (Ishitsubutsu toriatsukaijo wa doko desu ka?) 遺失物取扱所はどこですか.

lot[1] n. (great amount) taˈkusan たくさん: I want a lot more. (Motto takusañ hoshii.) もっとたくさん欲しい. / He has a lot of friends. (Kare wa takusañ tomodachi ga iru.) 彼はたくさん友だちがいる.

lot[2] n. **1** (objects used to decide something) kuˈji くじ: draw lots (kuji o hiku) くじを引く.

2 (section of land) jiˈsho 地所; shiˈkichi 敷地: an empty lot (akichi) 空き地 / a parking lot (chuushajoo) 駐車場.

3 (fate) uˈñmee 運命.

lotion n. keˈshoˈosui 化粧水; roˈoshoñ ローション.

lottery n. kuˈjibiki くじ引き; taˈkaraˈkuji 宝くじ.

loud adj. **1** (strong sound) oˈogoˈe no 大声の; koˈe ga taˈkaˈi 声が高い: We sang in loud voices. (Watashi-tachi wa oogoe de utatta.) 私たちは大声で歌った.

2 (noisy) yaˈkamashiˈi やかましい; soˈrozooshiˈi 騒々しい: a loud party (soozooshii paatii) 騒々しいパーティー.

3 (showy) haˈdeˈ na 派手な; keˈba-

kebashiˈi けばけばしい: This dress is too loud. (Kono doresu wa hade sugiru.) このドレスは派手すぎる.

loudly adv. oˈogoˈe de 大声で; yaˈkamaˈshiku やかましく: talk loudly (oogoe de shaberu) 大声でしゃべる.

loudspeaker n. kaˈkuseˈeki 拡声器; suˈpiˈikaa スピーカー.

lounge n. **1** (room) kyuˈukeˈeshitsu 休憩室; raˈuñji ラウンジ; (of an airport) maˈchiaˈishitsu 待合室; roˈbii ロビー.

2 (sofa) neˈisu 寝いす; aˈñrakuˈisu 安楽いす.

— vi. buˈrabura suru ぶらぶらする ①: We lounged on the beach all day. (Watashi-tachi wa kaigañ de ichi-nichi-juu burabura sugoshita.) 私たちは海岸で一日中ぶらぶら過ごした.

love vt. **1** (feel love) ... o aˈisuˈru ...を愛する ①: I love you. (Watashi wa anata o aishite imasu.) 私はあなたを愛しています. / She is loved by everybody. (Kanojo wa miñna ni aisarete iru.) 彼女はみんなに愛されている.

2 (be fond of) ... o koˈnoˈmu ...を好む ©; ... ga daˈisuki da ...が大好きだ: She loves to travel. (Kanojo wa ryokoo ga daisuki da.) 彼女は旅行が大好きだ.

— n. **1** (affection) aˈi 愛; aˈijoo 愛情: show a deep love for one's child (kodomo ni fukai aijoo o shimesu) 子どもに深い愛情を示す.

2 (sexual feeling) reˈñai 恋愛; koˈi 恋: one's first love (hatsukoi) 初恋.

3 (fondness) koˈnomiˈ 好み; shuˈmi 趣味: He has a love of books. (Kare wa hoñ ga suki da.) 彼は本が好きだ.

lovely adj. **1** (beautiful) uˈtsukushiˈi 美しい; kaˈwaiiˈi かわいい: a lovely dress (utsukushii doresu) 美しいドレス / a lovely girl (kawaii shoojo) かわいい少女.

2 (very pleasant) suˈbarashiˈi すばらしい; suˈteki na すてきな: lovely weather (subarashii teñki) すばらしい天気.

lover *n.* **1** (sweetheart) a⌐ijiñ 愛人; ko⌐ibito 恋人.

2 (person who likes something) a⌐iko⌐osha 愛好者: a music lover (*oñgaku no aikoosha*) 音楽の愛好者.

loving *adj.* a⌐isu⌐ru 愛する; a⌐ijoo no komo⌐tta [komo⌐tte iru] 愛情のこもった[こもっている]: a loving look (*aijoo no komotta manazashi*) 愛情のこもったまなざし.

low *adj.* **1** (not high) hi⌐ku⌐i 低い: a low building (*hikui tatemono*) 低い建物 / a low temperature (*hikui oñdo*) 低い温度 / a low voice (*hikui koe*) 低い声.

2 (not expensive) ya⌐su⌐i 安い: a low price (*yasui nedañ*) 安い値段.

3 (not strong) yo⌐wa⌐i 弱い: The fire is low. (*Hi ga yowai.*) 火が弱い.

4 (gloomy) ge⌐ñki no [ga] nai 元気の[が]ない: He is in very low spirits today. (*Kare wa kyoo wa geñki ga nai.*) 彼はきょうは元気がない.

— *adv.* hi⌐kuku 低く; ya⌐suku 安く: The plane flew low. (*Hikooki wa hikuku toñda.*) 飛行機は低く飛んだ. / buy low and sell high (*yasuku katte takaku uru*) 安く買って高く売る.

lower *adj.* **1** (below another) shi⌐ta no 下の: I'd like a room on a lower floor. (*Motto shita no kai no heya ni shitai.*) もっと下の階の部屋にしたい.

2 (of low rank) ka⌐kyuu no 下級の; ka⌐too no 下等の: a lower court of law (*kakyuu saibañsho*) 下級裁判所.

— *vt.* **1** (bring down) ... o o⌐ro⌐su ...を下ろす: lower a blind (*buraiñdo o orosu*) ブラインドを下ろす.

2 (reduce) ... o sa⌐ge⌐ru ...を下げる Ⅴ; o⌐tosu 落とす Ⅽ: lower the price (*nedañ o sageru*) 値段を下げる / lower one's voice (*koe o otosu*) 声を落とす.

loyal *adj.* chu⌐ujitsu na 忠実な; se⌐ejitsu na 誠実な: a loyal friend (*seejitsu na yuujiñ*) 誠実な友人.

loyalty *n.* chu⌐usee 忠誠; chu⌐ujitsu 忠実; se⌐ejitsu 誠実: swear one's loyalty (*chuusee o chikau*) 忠誠を誓う.

luck *n.* **1** (chance) u⌐ñ 運: Luck was with [against] me. (*Uñ ga yokatta [warukatta].*) 運がよかった[悪かった].

2 (fortune) ko⌐ouñ 幸運: I had the luck to win the prize. (*Watashi wa koouñ ni mo shoo o moratta.*) 私は幸運にも賞をもらった.

Good luck! (*Koouñ o inorimasu.*) 幸運を祈ります. ★ For encouragement, Japanese often say 'Gañbatte ne' 頑張ってね.

luckily *adv.* u⌐ñ yoku 運よく; ko⌐ouñ ni⌐ mo 幸運にも: Luckily I caught the train. (*Uñ yoku ressha ni maniatta.*) 運よく列車に間に合った.

lucky *adj.* u⌐ñ no yoi 運のよい; ko⌐ouñ na 幸運な: It was lucky that we met here. (*Wareware ga koko de aeta no wa koouñ datta.*) われわれがここで会えたのは幸運だった.

luggage *n.* te⌐ni⌐motsu 手荷物: I'll carry my luggage myself. (*Tenimotsu wa jibuñ de hakobimasu.*) 手荷物は自分で運びます.

lumber *n.* za⌐imoku 材木.

lump *n.* **1** (sugar) ka⌐kuza⌐too 角砂糖: I take one lump of sugar in my coffee. (*Watashi wa koohii ni kakuzatoo o ik-ko ireru.*) 私はコーヒーに角砂糖を1個入れる.

2 (solid mass) ka⌐tamari 塊: a lump of clay (*neñdo no katamari*) 粘土の塊.

3 (swelling) ko⌐bu こぶ: a lump on the head (*atama no kobu*) 頭のこぶ.

— *vt.* ... o hi⌐to⌐matome ni suru ...をひとまとめにする Ⅰ: lump items together (*koomoku o hitomatome ni suru*) 項目をひとまとめにする.

lunch *n.* chu⌐ushoku 昼食; hi⌐rugo⌐hañ 昼ご飯; be⌐ñtoo 弁当; ra⌐ñchi ランチ: What did you have for lunch? (*Chuushoku ni nani o tabemashita ka?*) 昼食に何を食べましたか. / take lunch with one (*beñtoo o motte iku*) 弁当を持って行く.

luncheon *n.* chu「ushoku「kai 昼食
会.

lung *n.* ha「i 肺: lung cancer (*hai-
gañ*) 肺癌.

luxurious *adj.* ze「eta「ku na ぜいたく
な; go「oka na 豪華な: a luxurious
hotel (*gooka na hoteru*) 豪華なホテル.

luxury *n.* **1** (great comfort) ze「eta「-
ku ぜいたく: live in luxury (*zeetaku
ni kurasu*) ぜいたくに暮らす.
2 (thing) ze「etakuhiñ ぜいたく品:
Jewels are luxuries. (*Hooseki wa
zeetakuhiñ da.*) 宝石はぜいたく品だ.

M

machine *n.* ki「ka「i 機械: Do you
know how to operate this machine? (*Kono kikai wa doo yatte
ugokasu no ka shitte imasu ka?*)
この機械はどうやって動かすのか知っていま
すか.

machinery *n.* ki「ka「irui 機械類;
ki「ka「i 機械: This factory has a
great deal of machinery. (*Kono
koojoo ni wa takusañ no kikai ga
aru.*) この工場にはたくさんの機械がある.

mad *adj.* **1** (insane) ki「ga kuru「tta
[kuru「tte iru] 気が狂った[狂っている]:
He must be mad to do such a
thing. (*Soñna koto o suru nañte
kare wa ki ga kurutta ni chigainai.*)
そんなことをするなんて彼は気が狂ったに違
いない.
2 (foolish) ba「ka「geta ばかげた; ba-
「ka「gete iru ばかげている; mu「boo na
無謀な: a mad plan (*muboo na keekaku*) 無謀な計画.
3 (angry) ha「ra o ta「teta [ta「tete
iru] 腹を立てた[立てている]: He was
mad at me for coming late. (*Kare
wa watashi ga okureta no de hara
o tateta.*) 彼は私が遅れたので腹を立て
た.
4 (enthusiastic) mu「chuu ni na「tte
(iru) 夢中になって(いる): He is mad
about horse racing. (*Kare wa keeba ni muchuu ni natte iru.*) 彼は競
馬に夢中になっている.

madam *n.* (older woman) o「ku-
sama 奥様.

madness *n.* (being insane) kyo「o-
ki 狂気; (being enthusiastic) ne「k-
kyoo 熱狂.

magazine *n.* za「sshi 雑誌: read a
magazine (*zasshi o yomu*) 雑誌を読
む / take a magazine (*zasshi o koo-
doku suru*) 雑誌を購読する / a weekly magazine (*shuukañshi*) 週刊誌 /
a monthly magazine (*gekkañshi*)
月刊誌.

magic *n.* **1** (strange powers) ma-
「hoo 魔法: believe in magic (*ma-
hoo o shiñjiru*) 魔法を信じる.
2 (tricks) te「jina 手品; ki「jutsu 奇
術: perform magic (*tejina o suru*)
手品をする.

magnet *n.* ji「shaku 磁石: A magnet attracts iron. (*Jishaku wa tetsu o hikitsukeru.*) 磁石は鉄を引きつ
ける.

magnificent *adj.* so「odai na 壮大
な; su「barashi「i すばらしい: The
views from the mountain were
magnificent. (*Yama kara no nagame wa subarashikatta.*) 山からの眺
めはすばらしかった.

magnify *vt.* ... o ka「kudai suru ...を
拡大する ①: magnify a thing with a
lens (*reñzu de mono o kakudai
suru*) レンズで物を拡大する.

maid *n.* o-「te「tsudai お手伝い.

mail *n.* yu「ubiñ 郵便: send by mail
(*yuubiñ de okuru*) 郵便で送る / deliver the mail (*yuubiñ o haitatsu
suru*) 郵便を配達する / Is there any
mail for me? (*Watashi ni yuubiñ
ga kite imasu ka?*) 私に郵便が来い
ますか. / air mail (*kookuubiñ*) 航空
便 / sea mail (*funabiñ*) 船便.
— *vt.* ... o yu「ubiñ de da「su ...を郵
便で出す ⓒ; yu「usoo suru 郵送する

□: I'd like to mail this letter to China. (*Kono tegami o Chuugoku e okuritai ñ desu ga.*) この手紙を中国へ送りたいんですが.

mailbox *n.* **1** (on a street) po˺suto ポスト: put a letter into the mailbox (*tegami o posuto ni ireru*) 手紙をポストに入れる.

2 (at a home) yu˹ubi˺ñuke 郵便受け: take a letter out of the mailbox (*yuubiñuke kara tegami o toridasu*) 郵便受けから手紙を取り出す.

mailman *n.* yu˹ubiñ-shuuhainiñ 郵便集配人; yu˹ubiñya 郵便屋.

main *adj.* o˺mo-na 主な; shu˹yoo na 主要な: the main characters in a play (*geki no omo-na toojoo jiñbutsu*) 劇の主な登場人物 / a main road (*shuyoo dooro*) 主要道路 / the main office (*hoñsha*) 本社.
— *n.* ho˹ñkañ 本管: a gas main (*gasu hoñkañ*) ガス本管.

mainland *n.* ho˹ñdo 本土: the Chinese mainland (*Chuugoku hoñdo*) 中国本土.

mainly *adv.* o˺mo ni 主に; shu˹ to shite 主として: I mainly drink coffee in the morning. (*Asa wa omo ni koohii o nomimasu.*) 朝は主にコーヒーを飲みます.

maintain *vt.* **1** (keep) ... o i˹ji suru ...を維持する □; ta˹mo˺tsu 保つ ©: Food is necessary to maintain life. (*Tabemono wa seemee o iji suru no ni hitsuyoo da.*) 食べ物は生命を維持するのに必要だ. / I tried to maintain a steady speed. (*Watashi wa ittee no sokudo o tamotsu yoo ni shita.*) 私は一定の速度を保つようにした.
2 (support) ... o ya˹shinau ...を養う ©: He maintains a large family on his income. (*Kare wa jibuñ no shuunyuu de dai-kazoku o yashinatte iru.*) 彼は自分の収入で大家族を養っている.
3 (declare) ... o shu˹choo suru ...を主張する □: He maintained that he was innocent. (*Kare wa mujitsu da to shuchoo shita.*) 彼は無実だと主張した.

maintenance *n.* i˹ji 維持; se˹ebi 整備; ka˹ñri 管理: the maintenance of peace (*heewa no iji*) 平和の維持 / car maintenance (*kuruma no seebi*) 車の整備 / the maintenance of a building (*biru no kañri*) ビルの管理.

majesty *n.* i˹geñ 威厳: the majesty of the king (*kokuoo no igeñ*) 国王の威厳 / His Imperial Majesty (*teñnoo heeka*) 天皇陛下 / Her Imperial Majesty (*koogoo heeka*) 皇后陛下.

major *adj.* (greater) o˹oki˺i hoo no 大きいほうの; (great) o˹oki-na 大きな; shu˹yoo na 主要な: The major part of my data was lost. (*Watashi no deeta no daibuñ ga kiete shimatta.*) 私のデータの大部分が消えてしまった. / I visited the major cities of Japan. (*Nihoñ no shuyoo na toshi wa tazunemashita.*) 日本の主要な都市は訪ねました.
— *n.* se˹ñkoo-ka˺moku 専攻科目: My major is Japanese literature. (*Watashi no señkoo wa Nihoñ buñgaku desu.*) 私の専攻は日本文学です.

major in *vt.* ... o se˹ñkoo suru ...を専攻する □: major in mathematics (*suugaku o señkoo suru*) 数学を専攻する.

majority *n.* **1** (most) da˹ita˺isuu 大多数; da˹ibu˺buñ 大部分: The majority of people agree with the plan. (*Daitasuu no hito wa sono añ ni sañsee desu.*) 大多数の人はその案に賛成です.
2 (party) ta˹suutoo 多数党; ta˹suuha 多数派.

make *vt.* **1** (create) ... o tsu˹ku˺ru ...を作る ©; se˹esaku suru 製作する □: She made a new dress. (*Kanojo wa atarashii doresu o tsukutta.*) 彼女は新しいドレスを作った. / This box is made of wood. (*Kono hako wa ki de dekite iru.*) この箱は木でできている.
2 (prepare) ... o yo˹oi suru ...を用意する □; to˹tonoe˺ru 整える Ⅴ: make a bed (*beddo o yooi suru*) ベッドを用意する / make coffee (*koohii o*

ireru) コーヒーを入れる.
3 (do) ... o su^ru ...をする ①; o^rkonau 行う ©: make a trip (*ryokoo o suru*) 旅行をする / make preparations (*junbi o suru*) 準備をする.
4 (compel; cause) ... o ⟨verb⟩-(sa)-「seru ...を...(さ)せる ▽: I made him go. (*Watashi wa kare o ikaseta.*) 私は彼を行かせた. / He made us laugh. (*Kare wa watashi-tachi o warawaseta.*) 彼は私たちを笑わせた. / The news made everyone glad. (*Sono shirase wa miñna o yorokobaseta.*) その知らせはみんなを喜ばせた.

make out *vt.* ... ga wa^rkaru ...がわかる ©: I cannot make out what you say. (*Anata no ossharu koto ga wakarimaseñ.*) あなたのおっしゃることがわかりません.

make up for ... *vt.* ... o to^rrikaesu ...を取り返す ©: I have to make up for lost time. (*Okureta buñ no jikañ o torikaesanakereba naranai.*) 遅れた分の時間を取り返さなければならない.

maker *n.* se^rezoomoto 製造元; me^rekaa メーカー: automakers (*jidoosha meekaa*) 自動車メーカー.

male *adj.* (of people) da^rñsee no 男性の; (of animals) o^rsu^l no 雄の: a male choir (*dañsee gasshoodañ*) 男性合唱団 / a male dog (*osu no inu*) 雄の犬.
— *n.* (of a person) da^rñsee 男性; (of an animal) o^rsu^l 雄.

malice *n.* a^lkui 悪意; te^rki-i 敵意: u^rrami^l 恨み: I bear him no malice. (*Watashi wa kare ni nañ no urami mo arimaseñ.*) 私は彼に何の恨みもありません.

man *n.* **1** (male person) o^rtoko 男; da^rñsee 男性: men and women (*otoko to oñna*) 男と女.
2 (human beings) ni^rñgeñ 人間; hi^rto 人: Man is mortal. (*Hito wa shinu.*) 人は死ぬ.
3 (manly person) o^rtokorashi^li o^rtoko 男らしい男: He acted like a man. (*Kare wa otokorashiku furumatta.*) 彼は男らしく振る舞った.

manage *vt.* **1** (direct) ... o ke^re-ee suru ...を経営する ①; ka^rñri suru 管理する ①: Who manages this store? (*Dare ga kono mise o kee-ee shite imasu ka?*) だれがこの店を経営していますか.
2 (do with difficulty) do^lo ni ka ⟨verb⟩ どうにか...: I managed to be in time for the train. (*Doo ni ka ressha ni maniatta.*) どうにか列車に間に合った.
3 (handle) ... o u^lmaku a^rtsukau ...をうまく扱う ©: He could not manage the horse well. (*Kare wa sono uma o umaku atsukaenakatta.*) 彼はその馬をうまく扱えなかった.
— *vi.* na^lñ toka ya^rtte iku なんとかやっていく ©: I can manage alone. (*Hitori de nañ to ka yatte ikemasu.*) 一人でなんとかやっていけます.

management *n.* **1** (managing) ke^re-ee 経営; ka^rñri 管理: Bad management caused the failure of the business. (*Kee-ee ga mazui tame ni jigyoo ga shippai shita.*) 経営がまずいために事業が失敗した.
2 (persons) ke^re-eesha-gawa 経営者側: The management refused to come to terms. (*Kee-eesha-gawa wa dakyoo o kyozetsu shita.*) 経営者側は妥協を拒絶した.

manager *n.* ke^re-e^lesha 経営者; shi^rha^liniñ 支配人: the manager of a shop (*mise no kee-eesha*) 店の経営者 / the manager of a hotel (*hoteru no shihainiñ*) ホテルの支配人.

managing director *n.* se^lñmu to^rrishimari^lyaku 専務取締役; (president) sha^rchoo 社長.

manhood *n.* se^rejiñ 成人; se^rene^l-ñki 成年期: come to manhood 成人する.

manifest *adj.* me^rehaku na 明白な; ha^rkki^lri shita [shite iru] はっきりした[している]: His innocence is manifest. (*Kare no mujitsu wa meehaku da.*) 彼の無実は明白だ.
— *vt.* (show) ... o ka^ro ni da^lsu ...を顔に出す ©: He manifested displeasure. (*Kare wa fukai o kao ni*

dashita.) 彼は不快を顔に出した.

mankind *n.* jiʼnrui 人類; niʼngen
人間: the history of mankind (*jin-
rui no rekishi*) 人類の歴史.

manly *adj.* oʼtokorashiʼi 男らしい;
daʼnsee-teki na 男性的な: a manly
bearing (*otokorashii taido*) 男らしい
態度 / a manly sport (*dansee-teki
na supootsu*) 男性的なスポーツ.

manner *n.* **1** (way) hoʼohoo 方法;
yaʼrikata やり方: He did it in his
own manner. (*Kare wa jibun no
yarikata de soo shita.*) 彼は自分のや
り方でそうした.
2 (behavior) taʼido 態度: I don't
like his arrogant manner. (*Kare no
oohee na taido ga ki ni iranai.*) 彼
の横柄な態度が気に入らない.
3 (manners) gyoʼogi 行儀; saʼhoo
作法: He has no manners. (*Kare
wa gyoogi ga warui.*) 彼は行儀が悪
い.
4 (habits) fuʼushuu 風習; fuʼuzoku
風俗: manners and customs (*fuu-
zoku shuukan*) 風俗習慣.

manual *adj.* **1** (of the hand) teʼ de
oʼkonau 手で行う; shuʼdoo no 手動
の: manual labor (*te-shigoto*) 手仕
事.
2 (of working) kiʼnniku no 筋肉の;
niʼkutai no 肉体の: a manual
worker (*nikutai roodoosha*) 肉体労
働者.
— *n.* (handbook) shoʼosaʼsshi 小
冊子; beʼnran 便覧: an instruction
manual (*setsumeesho*) 説明書.

manufacture *vt.* ... o seʼezoo
suru ... を製造する ①; seʼesaku suru
製作する ①: This factory manufac-
tures automobiles. (*Kono koojoo
wa jidoosha o seezoo shite iru.*) こ
の工場は自動車を製造している.
— *n.* seʼezoo 製造; seʼesaku 製
作: the date of manufacture (*seezoo nengappi*) 製造年月日.

manufacturer *n.* seʼezoo-gyoʼo-
sha 製造業者: an automobile manufacturer (*jidoosha seezoo-gyoo-
sha*) 自動車製造業者.

manuscript *n.* geʼnkoo 原稿:

proofread a manuscript (*genkoo o
koosee suru*) 原稿を校正する.

many *adj.* oʼoku no 多くの; taʼsuʼu
no 多数の; taʼkusaʼn no たくさんの:
Many people think so. (*Ooku no
hito ga soo kangaete imasu.*) 多く
の人がそう考えています. / How many
eggs are there in this box? (*Kono
hako ni tamago wa ikutsu arimasu ka?*) この箱に卵はいくつありま
すか.
— *pron.* (of people) oʼoku no hiʼto
多く人; (of things) oʼoku no moʼno
(多くの物); taʼsuʼu 多数: Many of
them were tired. (*Kare-ra no ooku
wa tsukarete ita.*) 彼らの多くは疲れて
いた. / How many came to the
party? (*Kai ni wa nan-nin kimashita ka?*) 会には何人来ましたか.

map *n.* chiʼzu 地図: Will you please
draw me a map to the station? (*Eki
made no chizu o kaite itadakemasu ka?*) 駅までの地図を書いていただ
けますか.

maple *n.* kaʼede かえで; moʼmiji もみ
じ.

marble *n.* daʼiriʼseki 大理石.

march *vi.* koʼoshin suru 行進する
①: We marched around the playground. (*Watashi-tachi wa undoojoo no mawari o kooshin shita.*) 私
たちは運動場の周りを行進した.
— *vt.* ... o koʼoshin saseru ...を行
進させる Ⅴ: The teacher marched
the children. (*Sensee wa kodomo-
tachi o kooshin saseta.*) 先生は子ど
もたちを行進させた.
— *n.* **1** (walk) koʼoshin 行進: a
march of five kilometers (*go-kiro
no kooshin*) 5 キロの行進.
2 (music) koʼoshiʼnkyoku 行進曲;
maʼachi マーチ: play a march (*koo-
shinkyoku o ensoo suru*) 行進曲を
演奏する.

March *n.* saʼn-gatsu 3 月.

margin *n.* **1** (space) yoʼhaku 余白;
raʼngai 欄外; maʼajin マージン: write
down in the margin (*rangai ni ka-
kikomu*) 欄外に書き込む.
2 (edge) fuʼchi 縁; heʼriʼ へり: the

margin of the swimming pool (*puuru no fuchi*) プールの縁.

3 (profit) riˈzaya 利ざや; maˈajiñ マージン: a large margin (*ooki-na rizaya*) 大きな利ざや.

marine *adj.* uˈmi no 海の; kaˈijoo no 海上の: marine products (*kaisañbutsu*) 海産物 / marine insurance (*kaijoo-hokeñ*) 海上保険.

mark *n.* **1** (spot) yoˈgore 汚れ; shiˈmi 染み; kiˈzu きず: What are those dirty marks on your trousers? (*Kono zuboñ no kitanai yogore wa nañ desu ka?*) このズボンの汚い汚れは何ですか.

2 (sign) shiˈrushi 印; kiˈgoo 記号: put a mark on paper (*kami ni shirushi o tsukeru*) 紙に印をつける.

3 (target) moˈkuhyoo 目標; maˈto 的: aim at the mark (*mato o nerau*) 的をねらう.

4 (grade) teˈñsuˈu 点数: I got 80 marks in mathematics. (*Watashi wa suugaku de hachijut-teñ o totta.*) 私は数学で 80 点を取った.

— *vt.* **1** (put a sign) ...ni shiˈrushi o tsukeˈru ...に印をつける Ⓥ: I marked his house on the map. (*Chizu ni kare no uchi no shirushi o tsuketa.*) 地図に彼の家の印をつけた.

2 (spoil) ...o yoˈgosu ...を汚す Ⓒ: His shoes marked the floor. (*Kare wa kutsu de yuka o yogoshita.*) 彼は靴で床を汚した.

3 (give marks) ...o saˈiteñ suru ...を採点する Ⓘ: mark exam-papers (*shikeñ no tooañ o saiteñ suru*) 試験の答案を採点する.

market *n.* **1** (shops) iˈchiba 市場: a vegetable market (*aomono ichiba*) 青物市場 / a fish market (*uo ichiba*) 魚市場.

2 (trade) shiˈjoo 市場. ★ '市場' is pronounced '*ichiba*' in meaning 1, and '*shijoo*' in 2: market research (*shijoo choosa*) 市場調査 / put a new product on the market (*shiñseehiñ o shijoo ni dasu*) 新製品を市場に出す.

3 (demand) juˈyoo 需要: There is

a good market for these kinds of goods. (*Kono shu no shoohiñ wa juyoo ga ookii.*) この種の商品は需要が大きい.

— *vt.* ...o shiˈjoo ni daˈsu ...を市場に出す Ⓒ: They market cars all over the world. (*Kare-ra wa kuruma o sekai-juu no shijoo ni dashite iru.*) 彼らは車を世界中の市場に出している.

marriage *n.* **1** (act) keˈkkoñ 結婚: a marriage partner (*kekkoñ aite*) 結婚相手 / an arranged marriage (*miai kekkoñ*) 見合い結婚.

2 (state) keˈkkoñ-seˈekatsu 結婚生活: Their marriage was not a happy one. (*Kare-ra no kekkoñ-seekatsu wa shiawase de nakatta.*) 彼らの結婚生活は幸せでなかった.

3 (ceremony) keˈkkoˈñshiki 結婚式: perform a marriage (*kekkoñshiki o ageru*) 結婚式を挙げる.

marry *vt.* ...to keˈkkoñ suru ...と結婚する Ⓘ: He married my sister. (*Kare wa watashi no imooto to kekkoñ shita.*) 彼は私の妹と結婚した. / Will you marry me? (*Watashi to kekkoñ shite kudasai.*) 私と結婚してください.

— *vi.* keˈkkoñ suru 結婚する Ⓘ: She married very young. (*Kanojo wa zuibuñ wakai toki ni kekkoñ shita.*) 彼女はずいぶん若いときに結婚した.

marvel *n.* kyoˈoi 驚異; fuˈshigi 不思議: the marvels of nature (*shizeñ no kyooi*) 自然の驚異.

— *vi.* (... ni) kyoˈotañ suru (...に) 驚嘆する Ⓘ; oˈdoroˈku 驚く Ⓒ: We marveled at his skill. (*Watashi-tachi wa kare no udemae ni kyootañ shita.*) 私たちは彼の腕前に驚嘆した.

marvelous *adj.* suˈbarashiˈi すばらしい; suˈteki na すてきな: He made a marvelous invention. (*Kare wa subarashii hatsumee o shita.*) 彼はすばらしい発明をした.

masculine *adj.* oˈtoko no 男の; daˈnsee no 男性の; (mannish) daˈñsee-teki na 男性的な: a masculine woman (*dañsee-teki na josee*) 男性的な女性.

mask *n.* ma˺suku マスク; m˺eñ 面; ka˺meñ 仮面: a gas mask (*boodoku masuku*) 防毒マスク / wear a face mask (*masuku o suru*) マスクをする / put on a mask (*kameñ o kaburu*) 仮面をかぶる.

mass *n.* **1** (lump) o˺oki-na ka˺tamari 大きな塊: a mass of clouds (*kumo no ooki-na katamari*) 雲の大きな塊.

2 (a large number) ta˺su˺u 多数: A mass of people gathered in the park. (*Tasuu no hito ga kooeñ ni atsumatta.*) 多数の人が公園に集まった.

3 (people) ta˺ishuu 大衆; sho˺miñ 庶民: protect the interests of the masses (*shomiñ no rieki o mamoru*) 庶民の利益を守る.

mass communication *n.* ma˺sukomi マスコミ; ta˺ishuu-de˺ñtatsu 大衆伝達. ★ Japanese '*masukomi*' usually refers to 'mass media.'

massive *adj.* do˺sshi˺ri shita [shite iru] どっしりした[している]; ju˺uryo˺okañ no aru 重量感のある: massive furniture (*dosshiri shita kagu*) どっしりした家具 / a massive building (*juuryookañ no aru tatemono*) 重量感のある建物.

mast *n.* ma˺suto マスト; ho˺ba˺shira 帆柱.

master *n.* **1** (head) shu˺jiñ 主人; (employer) ya˺toi˺nushi 雇い主; (of an animal) ka˺inushi 飼い主: He is the master of this house. (*Kare ga kono ie no shujiñ desu.*) 彼がこの家の主人です. / A dog knows his own master. (*Inu wa kainushi o shitte iru.*) 犬は飼い主を知っている.

2 (expert) me˺eji˺ñ 名人; ta˺ika 大家: a great master in painting (*e no taika*) 絵の大家.

3 (a person with an academic degree) shu˺ushi 修士: a Master of Arts (*buñgaku shuushi*) 文学修士.
— *vt.* ... o shu˺utoku suru ...を習得する C; ma˺sutaa suru マスターする

C: She mastered Japanese in a short period. (*Kanojo wa tañkikañ de Nihoñgo o shuutoku shita.*) 彼女は短期間で日本語を修得した.

masterpiece *n.* ke˺ssaku 傑作; me˺esaku 名作: This book is a masterpiece. (*Kono hoñ wa kessaku da.*) この本は傑作だ.

mat *n.* ma˺tto マット; (of straw) mu˺shiro˺ござ: place a mat (*matto o shiku*) マットを敷く.

match[1] *n.* **1** (game) shi˺ai 試合; kyo˺ogi 競技: have a football match (*futtobooru no shiai o suru*) フットボールの試合をする.

2 (counterpart) kyo˺osoo-a˺ite 競争相手; ko˺ote˺kishu 好敵手: meet one's match (*kootekishu o eru*) 好敵手を得る.

3 (marriage) ke˺kkoñ 結婚: arrange a match (*kekkoñ o matomeru*) 結婚をまとめる.
— *vt.* **1** (suit) ... ni a˺u ...に合う C; ... to cho˺owa suru ...と調和する I: A red tie will match your suit. (*Akai nekutai ga kimi no fuku ni au deshoo.*) 赤いネクタイが君の服に合うでしょう.

2 (be equal) ... to do˺otoo da ...と同等だ; ... ni ka˺na˺u ...にかなう C: Nobody can match him in golf. (*Gorufu de kare ni kanau mono wa inai.*) ゴルフで彼にかなう者はいない.

match[2] *n.* ma˺tchi マッチ: strike a match (*matchi o tsukeru*) マッチをつける.

mate *n.* (companion) na˺kama˺ 仲間; a˺ite˺ 相手: a teammate (*chiimu no nakama*) チームの仲間.

material *n.* **1** (substance) ge˺ñryo˺o 原料; za˺iryo˺o 材料: What are the raw materials for making beer? (*Biiru no geñryoo wa nañ desu ka?*) ビールの原料は何ですか.

2 (data) shi˺ryoo 資料; da˺izai 題材: collect material for a novel (*shoosetsu no shiryoo o atsumeru*) 小説の資料を集める.
— *adj.* **1** (of matter) bu˺sshitsu no 物質の: material civilization

(*busshitsu buñmee*) 物質文明.

2 (important) ju「uyoo na 重要な; ta「isetsu na 大切な: material evidence (*juuyoo na shooko*) 重要な証拠.

maternal *adj.* ha「ha no 母の; ha-「ha-rashi¹i 母らしい: maternal love (*boseeai*) 母性愛.

math *n.* su「ugaku 数学.

mathematics *n.* su「ugaku 数学: I am not good at mathematics. (*Suugaku wa nigate da.*) 数学は苦手だ.

matter *n.* **1** (trouble) ko「ma¹tta ko¹to¹ 困ったこと: What's the matter? (*Doo shita no desu ka?*) どうしたのですか. / Nothing is the matter. (*Nañ de mo arimaseñ.*) 何でもありません.

2 (affair) ko「togara 事柄; mo「ñdai 問題: I don't like to talk about private matters. (*Kojiñ-teki na mo ñdai ni tsuite wa hanashitaku arimaseñ.*) 個人的な問題については話したくありません.

3 (substance) bu「sshitsu 物質; bu「ttai 物体: solid matter (*kotai*) 固体. — *vi.* mo「ñdai to na¹ru 問題となる C; ju「uyoo da 重要だ: It matters much to me. (*Sore wa watashi ni totte juuyoo na koto desu.*) それは私にとって重要なことです. / It doesn't matter if you come late. (*Osoku kite mo kamaimaseñ.*) 遅く来てもまいません.

mattress *n.* ma「ttoresu マットレス.

mature *adj.* **1** (ripe) ju「ku¹shita 熟した; ju「kushite iru 熟している: mature fruit (*jukushita kudamono*) 熟した果物.

2 (fully grown) se「ejuku shita [shite iru] 成熟した[している]: mature girls (*seejuku shita musume-tachi*) 成熟した娘たち. — *vi.* **1** (grow fully) ju「kusu¹ru 熟する ①: Wine and wisdom mature with age. (*Sake to fuñbetsu wa toshi to tomo ni jukusuru.*) 酒と分別は年とともに熟する.

2 (become due) ma「ñki ni na¹ru 満

期になる C: When does this insurance policy mature? (*Kono hokeñ wa itsu mañki ni narimasu ka?*) この保険はいつ満期になりますか.

maximum *adj.* sa「idai no 最大の; sa「ikoo no 最高の: the maximum speed [temperature] (*saikoo sokudo [kioñ]*) 最高速度[気温]. — *n.* sa「ida¹igeñ 最大限; sa「iko¹oteñ 最高点: This luggage weighs more than the maximum. (*Kono nimotsu no omosa wa saidaigeñdo o koete imasu.*) この荷物の重さは最大限度を越えています.

may *aux.* **1** [possibility] ... ka mo shi「renai …かもしれない; o「so¹raku ... daroo おそらく…だろう: It may rain tomorrow. (*Ashita wa ame ga furu ka mo shirenai.*) あしたは雨が降るかもしれない. / It may be true. (*Sore wa osoraku hoñtoo daroo.*) それはおそらく本当だろう.

2 [permission] ⟨verb⟩-te[de] mo i¹i …て[で]もいい: You may go if you want to. (*Ikitakereba itte mo ii desu yo.*) 行きたければ行ってもいいですよ. / May I use this phone? (*Kono deñwa o tsukatte mo ii desu ka?*) この電話を使ってもいいですか.

3 [wish] ⟨verb⟩ yo¹o ni …ように: May you have a safe journey. (*Ryokoo ga buji de arimasu yoo ni.*) 旅行が無事でありますように.

May *n.* go¹-gatsu 5 月.

maybe *adv.* mo¹shi ka shitara もしかしたら; ko「to ni yoru to ことによると; ta「buñ たぶん: Maybe it will rain tomorrow. (*Moshi ka shitara ashita wa ame ka mo shirenai.*) もしかしたらあしたは雨かもしれない.

mayor *n.* (of a city) shi「choo 市長; (of a town) cho¹ochoo 町長: Mr. Tanaka was elected mayor. (*Tanaka-sañ ga shichoo ni erabareta.*) 田中さんが市長に選ばれた.

me *pron.* **1** [direct object] wa「tashi o 私を; [indirect object] wa「tashi ni 私に: He helped me. (*Kare wa watashi o tetsudatte kureta.*) 彼は私を手伝ってくれた. / She gave me the book. (*Kanojo wa watashi ni sono hoñ o kureta.*) 彼女は私にその本をくれた.

2 (I) wa「tashi 私: "Who is there?" "It's me." (*"Soko ni iru no wa dare desu ka?" "Watashi desu."*) 「そこにいるのはだれですか」「私です」

meadow *n.* bo「kuso]ochi 牧草地.

meal *n.* sho「kuji 食事: have three meals a day (*ichi-nichi sañ-kai shokuji o suru*) 1 日 3 回食事をする.

mean[1] *vt.* **1** (indicate) ... o i「mi suru ...を意味する ⃞: What does the Japanese word '*hana*' mean? (*Nihoñgo no 'hana' to iu go wa doo iu imi desu ka?*) 日本語の「はな」という語はどういう意味ですか.

2 (intend) ... tsu「mori da ...つもりだ: I meant it as a joke. (*Joodañ no tsumori de itta no desu.*) 冗談のつもりで言ったのです. / I didn't mean to surprise you. (*Anata o odorokasu tsumori wa arimaseñ deshita.*) あなたを驚かすつもりはありませんでした.

mean[2] *adj.* **1** (base) hi「retsu na 卑劣な: mean behavior (*hiretsu na furumai*) 卑劣な振る舞い.

2 (vicious) i「ji no waru]i 意地の悪い: a mean fellow (*iji no warui hito*) 意地の悪い人.

3 (stingy) ke「chi na けちな; ki「tana]i 汚い: He is mean about money. (*Kare wa o-kane ni kitanai.*) 彼はお金に汚い.

mean[3] *adj.* (middle) chu「ukañ no 中間の; (average) he「ekiñ no 平均の: the mean annual rainfall (*neñ-kañ no heekiñ koouryoo*) 年間の平均降雨量.
— *n.* chu「ukañ 中間; he「ekiñ 平均.

meaning *n.* i「mi 意味: look up the meaning of the word in a dictionary (*sono go no imi o jisho de sagasu*) その語の意味を辞書で探す.

means *n.* **1** (method) shu「dañ 手段; ho「ohoo 方法: a means to an end (*mokuteki no tame no shudañ*) 目的のための手段 / a means of transportation (*kootsuu kikañ*) 交

通機関.

2 (property) zai「sañ 財産; shu「u-nyuu 収入: live within one's means (*jibuñ no shuunyuu no hañi de kurasu*) 自分の収入の範囲内で暮らす.

meantime *n.* a「ima 合間: in the meantime (*sono kañ ni*) その間に.

meanwhile *adv.* sono ka「ñ ni その間に: He went shopping. Meanwhile she prepared the meal. (*Kare wa kaimono ni itta. Sono kañ ni kanojo wa shokuji no shitaku o shita.*) 彼は買い物に行った. その間に彼女は食事の支度をした.

measure *vt.* ... o ha「ka]ru ...を測る ⃞; so「kutee suru 測定する ⃞: She measured her waist. (*Kanojo wa jibuñ no uesuto o hakatta.*) 彼女は自分のウエストを測った.
— *vi.* ha「ka]ru 測る ⃞; a「ru ある ⃞: The width of this street measures 5 meters. (*Kono dooro no haba wa go-meetoru aru.*) この道路の幅は 5 メートルある.
— *n.* **1** (size) su「ñpoo 寸法.

2 (instrument) ke「eryoo]ki 計量器; mo「nosa]shi 物差し: a tape measure (*makijaku*) 巻尺.

3 (unit) ta「ñi 単位: The meter is a measure of length. (*Meetoru wa nagasa no tañi desu.*) メートルは長さの単位です.

4 (action) ta「isaku 対策; sho「chi 処置: We should take strong measures against drunken driving. (*Yopparai uñteñ ni wa kyookoo na taisaku o toru beki da.*) 酔っぱらい運転には強硬な対策をとるべきだ.

measurement *n.* **1** (size) o「o-kisa 大きさ; su「ñpoo 寸法: take the measurements for a suit (*yoofuku no suñpoo o toru*) 洋服の寸法を取る / What are the measurements of this room? (*Kono heya no ookisa wa dono kurai desu ka?*) この部屋の大きさはどのくらいですか.

2 (act of measuring) so「kutee 測定; so「kuryoo 測量: the measurement of time (*jikañ no sokutee*) 時間の測定.

meat n. ni⌐ku˩ 肉: cook meat (*niku o ryoori suru*) 肉を料理する.

mechanic n. ki⌐kai˩koo 機械工; shu⌐uri˩koo 修理工.

mechanical adj. ki⌐ka˩i no 機械の; ki⌐ka˩i de u⌐go˩ku 機械で動く: a mechanical toy (*kikai de ugoku omocha*) 機械で動くおもちゃ.

mechanical pencil n. sha⌐apu-pe˩ñshiru シャープペンシル.

mechanism n. ki⌐kaiso˩ochi 機械装置: The recording mechanism seems to be broken. (*Rokuoñ no kikaisoochi ga kowareta yoo da.*) 録音の機械装置が壊れたようだ.

medal n. me⌐daru メダル; ki⌐shoo 記章: win a gold medal (*kiñ-medaru o kakutoku suru*) 金メダルを獲得する.

meddle vi. (... ni) ka⌐ñshoo suru (…に)干渉する ⚟: Don't meddle in other people's affairs. (*Hoka no hito no koto ni kañshoo suru no wa yame nasai.*) ほかの人のことに干渉するのはやめなさい.

media n. ma⌐sume˩dia マスメディア; ma⌐sukomi マスコミ. ⇨ mass communication

mediate vi. (... o) cho⌐otee suru (…を)調停する ⚟; chu⌐usai suru 仲裁する ⚟: mediate between employers and their workers (*koyoosha to juugyooiñ no aida o chootee suru*) 雇用者と従業員の間を調停する.

medical adj. i⌐gaku no 医学の; i⌐ryoo no 医療の: a medical college (*ika-daigaku*) 医科大学 / a medical checkup (*keñkoo-shiñdañ*) 健康診断.

medicine n. 1 (substance) ku⌐suri 薬: take the medicine for a cold (*kaze no kusuri o nomu*) かぜの薬を飲む / The medicine proved very effective. (*Sono kusuri wa totemo yoku kiita.*) その薬はとてもよく効いた. 2 (science) i⌐gaku 医学; i⌐ryoo 医療: He is studying medicine. (*Kare wa igaku o beñkyoo shite iru.*) 彼は医学を勉強している.

medieval adj. chu⌐usee no 中世の: medieval architecture (*chuusee no*

keñchiku) 中世の建築.

meditate vi. fu⌐ka˩ku ka⌐ñga˩eru 深く考える ⚟; me⌐esoo suru 瞑想する ⚟: meditate on the meaning of life (*jiñsee no igi ni tsuite fukaku kañgaeru*) 人生の意義について深く考える.

meditation n. me⌐esoo 瞑想; ju⌐k-koo 熟考: He was deep in meditation. (*Kare wa meesoo ni fukette ita.*) 彼は瞑想にふけっていた.

medium adj. chu⌐ukurai no 中くらいの: a man of medium height (*chuu-kurai no se no dañsee*) 中くらいの背の男性.
— n. ba⌐itai 媒体; ki⌐kañ 機関: an advertising medium (*kookoku-baitai*) 広告媒体 / news media (*hoo-doo kikañ*) 報道機関.

meet vt. 1 (see) ... ni a⌐u …に会う ⚍: I met her in the library. (*Watashi wa toshokañ de kanojo ni atta.*) 私は図書館で彼女に会った. 2 (welcome) ... o de⌐mukaeru …を出迎える ⚟: He went to the station to meet her. (*Kare wa kanojo o demukaeru tame ni eki e itta.*) 彼は彼女を出迎えるために駅へ行った. 3 (join) ... to ma⌐jiwa˩ru …と交わる ⚍; go⌐oryuu suru 合流する ⚟: Where does this street meet the highway? (*Kono dooro wa doko de kañseñ dooro to gooryuu shimasu ka?*) この道路はどこで幹線道路と合流しますか. 4 (satisfy) ... ni o⌐jiru …に応じる ⚟; ko⌐tae˩ru こたえる ⚟: I'll do what I can to meet your wishes. (*Anata no kiboo ni kotaeru tame ni dekiru dake no koto wa shimasu.*) あなたの希望にこたえるためにできるだけのことはします.
— vi. 1 (see) a⌐u 会う ⚍: We met quite by chance. (*Watashi-tachi wa mattaku guuzeñ ni atta.*) 私たちはまったく偶然に会った. 2 (come together) a⌐tsuma˩ru 集まる ⚍; ka⌐igoo suru 会合する ⚟: We meet together once a week. (*Wata-shi-tachi wa shuu ni ichi-do atsu-*

marimasu.) 私たちは週に一度集まります.

meet with ... *vt.* ...ni a⌐u ...に遭う: meet with an accident (*jiko ni au*) 事故に遭う.

meeting *n.* ka⌐i 会; ka⌐igi 会議; shu⌐ukai 集会: hold a meeting (*kai o hiraku*) 会を開く / He was absent from the meeting. (*Kare wa kaigi o kesseki shita.*) 彼は会議を欠席した.

melody *n.* se⌐ñritsu 旋律; me⌐rodii メロディー: She played a beautiful melody on the piano. (*Kanojo wa utsukushii merodii o piano de hiita.*) 彼女は美しいメロディーをピアノで弾いた.

melt *vi.* to⌐ke⌐ru 溶ける Ⓥ: All the ice has melted. (*Koori ga zeñbu tokete shimatta.*) 氷が全部溶けてしまった.
— *vt.* ... o to⌐ka⌐su ...を溶かす Ⓒ: melt sugar in water (*satoo o mizu ni tokasu*) 砂糖を水に溶かす.

member *n.* ka⌐iiñ 会員; me⌐ñbaa メンバー: I am a member of this club. (*Watashi wa kono kurabu no kaiiñ desu.*) 私はこのクラブの会員です.

membership *n.* ka⌐iiñ no shikaku 会員の資格: He lost his membership. (*Kare wa kaiiñ no shikaku o ushinatta.*) 彼は会員の資格を失った.

memorial *n.* ki⌐ne⌐ñbutsu 記念物; ki⌐ne⌐ñhi 記念碑.
— *adj.* ki⌐neñ no 記念の: a memorial festival (*kineñsai*) 記念祭.

memorize *vt.* ... o ki⌐oku suru ...を記憶する Ⓘ; a⌐ñki suru 暗記する Ⓘ: memorize a poem (*shi o añki suru*) 詩を暗記する.

memory *n.* **1** (power of remembering) ki⌐oku⌐ryoku 記憶力: He has a good memory. (*Kare wa kio-kuryoku ga ii.*) 彼は記憶力がいい.
2 (something remembered) ki⌐oku 記憶; o⌐moide 思い出: I have no memory of my mother. (*Watashi wa haha no kioku ga nai.*) 私は母の記憶がない. / memories of one's childhood (*kodomo no koro no omoide*) 子どもの頃の思い出.

mend *vt.* **1** (repair) ... o na⌐osu ...を直す Ⓒ; shu⌐uzeñ suru 修繕する Ⓘ: mend a broken chair (*kowareta isu o naosu*) 壊れたいすを直す.
2 (correct) ... o a⌐ratame⌐ru ...を改める Ⓥ: mend one's ways (*okonai o aratameru*) 行いを改める.
— *vi.* yo⌐ku naru よくなる Ⓒ: The child will soon mend. (*Kodomo wa sugu yoku naru deshoo.*) 子どもはすぐよくなるでしょう.

mental *adj.* se⌐eshiñ no 精神の; chi⌐noo no 知能の: mental disorders (*seeshiñ shoogai*) 精神障害 / a mental test (*chinoo keñsa*) 知能検査.

mention *vt.* ... o ha⌐na⌐su ...を話す Ⓒ; ... to i⌐u ...と言う Ⓒ: He mentioned the plan, but gave no details. (*Kare wa sono keekaku no koto o hanashita ga kuwashii koto wa iwanakatta.*) 彼はその計画のことを話したが詳しいことは言わなかった.
Don't mention it. (*Doo itashimashite.*) どういたしまして.

menu *n.* ko⌐ñdatehyoo 献立表; me⌐ñyuu メニュー: Can I see the menu? (*Menyuu o misete kudasai.*) メニューを見せてください.

merchandise *n.* sho⌐ohiñ 商品: general merchandise (*zakka*) 雑貨.

merchant *n.* sho⌐oniñ 商人: a timber merchant (*zaimokushoo*) 材木商.

merciful *adj.* ji⌐hibuka⌐i 慈悲深い; na⌐sakebuka⌐i 情け深い: a merciful judge (*jihibukai saibañkañ*) 慈悲深い裁判官.

merciless *adj.* mu⌐ji⌐hi na 無慈悲な; na⌐sake yo⌐osha no nai 情け容赦のない: merciless criticism (*nasa-ke yoosha no nai hihyoo*) 情け容赦のない批評.

mercury *n.* su⌐igiñ 水銀.

mercy *n.* **1** (compassion) ji⌐hi 慈悲; a⌐waremi⌐ 哀れみ; na⌐sake 情け: show mercy toward one's enemy (*teki ni nasake o kakeru*) 敵に情けをかける.
2 (blessing) ko⌐ouñ 幸運: It was a

mercy that it did not rain. (*Ame ga furanakatta no wa koouñ datta.*) 雨が降らなかったのは幸運だった.

mere *adj.* ho⌐ñ no ほんの; ta⌐da no ただの: He is still a mere child. (*Kare wa mada hoñ no kodomo da.*) 彼はまだほんの子どもだ.

merely *adv.* ta⌐ñ ni ... dake 単に...だけ; ta⌐da ... dake ただ...だけ: I said so merely as a joke. (*Tañ ni joodañ to shite itta dake desu.*) 単に冗談として言っただけです.

merge *vi.* **1** (combine) ga⌐ppee suru 合併する ①; i⌐ssho ni na⌐ru いっしょになる ©: The roads merge two kilometers ahead. (*Sono michi wa ni-kiro saki de issho ni narimasu.*) その道は 2 キロ先でいっしょになります. **2** (blend gradually) shi⌐dai ni ... ni na⌐ru 次第に...になる ©: Twilight slowly merged into darkness. (*Tasogare ga shidai ni kurayami to natta.*) たそがれが次第に暗やみとなった.
— *vt.* ... o ga⌐ppee suru ...を合併する ①; he⌐egoo suru 併合する ①: The two companies were merged. (*Sono futatsu no kaisha ga gappee shita.*) その二つの会社は合併した.

merit *n.* **1** (worth) ka⌐chi 価値: This work has great merit. (*Kono shigoto wa hijoo ni kachi ga aru.*) この仕事は非常に価値がある. **2** (good quality) cho⌐osho 長所; to⌐rie⌐ とりえ: What are the merits of this plan? (*Kono keekaku no choosho wa nañ desu ka?*) この計画の長所は何ですか.
— *vt.* ... ni a⌐tai suru ...に値する ①: He merits the prize. (*Kare wa sono shoo ni atai suru.*) 彼はその賞に値する.

merry *adj.* yo⌐oki na 陽気な; yu⌐kai na 愉快な: a merry laugh (*yooki na warai*) 陽気な笑い / We had a merry time at the party. (*Watashi-tachi wa paatii de yukai na toki o sugoshita.*) 私たちはパーティーで愉快な時を過ごした.

mess *n.* (untidy condition) chi⌐rakatte iru koto⌐ 散らかっていること;

sa⌐ñrañ 散乱; me⌐chakucha めちゃくちゃ: The room was in a mess. (*Heya wa chirakatte ita.*) 部屋は散らかっていた.

message *n.* ko⌐tozuke⌐ 言づけ; de⌐ñgoñ 伝言: I left a message with him. (*Watashi wa kare ni deñgoñ o tanoñda.*) 私は彼に伝言を頼んだ.

messenger *n.* tsu⌐kai no mono⌐ 使いの者; shi⌐sha 使者: dispatch a messenger (*shisha o okuru*) 使者を送る.

metal *n.* ki⌐ñzoku 金属: precious metals (*kiñzoku*) 貴金属.

meter[1] *n.* me⌐etoru メートル: One meter is equal to about 40 inches. (*Ichi-meetoru wa yaku yoñjuu-iñchi ni hitoshii.*) 1 メートルは約 40 インチに等しい. ★ In Japan the metric system is used.

meter[2] *n.* ke⌐eryo⌐oki 計量器; me⌐etaa メーター: a gas meter (*gasu no meetaa*) ガスのメーター.

method *n.* ho⌐ohoo 方法; ho⌐oshi⌐ki 方式: the best method of learning Japanese (*Nihoñgo o manabu saizeñ no hoohoo*) 日本語を学ぶ最善の方法.

metropolis *n.* shu⌐to 首都; shu⌐yoo to⌐shi 主要都市.

metropolitan *adj.* shu⌐to no 首都の; da⌐ito⌐shi no 大都市の: the metropolitan area (*shutokeñ*) 首都圏.

microphone *n.* ma⌐ikuro⌐hoñ マイクロホン; ma⌐iku マイク: speak into a microphone (*maiku de hanasu*) マイクで話す.

microscope *n.* ke⌐ñbikyoo 顕微鏡: examine germs under a microscope (*keñbikyoo de saikiñ o shiraberu*) 顕微鏡で細菌を調べる.

midday *n.* sho⌐ogo 正午; ma⌐hiru 真昼.

middle *n.* **1** (of a place) ma⌐ñnaka 真ん中; chu⌐uo⌐o 中央: There is an island in the middle of the lake. (*Mizuumi no mañnaka ni shima ga aru.*) 湖の真ん中に島がある. **2** (of time) na⌐kagoro 中ごろ; na⌐ka⌐ba 半ば: The cherry blossoms

bloom in the middle of April. (*Sakura wa shi-gatsu nakaba ni sakimasu.*) 桜は4月半ばに咲きます.
— *adj.* maˈnnaka no 真ん中の; chuˈuneñ no 中央の: the middle seat in a row (*retsu no mañnaka no seki*) 列の真ん中の席.

middle age *n.* chuˈuneñ 中年; shoˈroo 初老: middle age spread (*chuuneñ-butori*) 中年太り.

midnight *n.* maˈyoˈnaka 真夜中; yoˈru no juˈuniˈ-ji 夜の12時: He returned home at midnight. (*Kare wa yoru no juuni-ji ni ie ni kaetta.*) 彼は夜の12時に家に帰った.

might *aux.* **1** [possibility] ... ka mo shiˈrenai ...かもしれない: He might be able to help you. (*Kare wa anata o tasukeru koto ga dekiru ka mo shirenai.*) 彼はあなたを助けることができるかもしれない. / It might rain tomorrow. (*Ashita wa ame ka mo shirenai.*) あしたは雨かもしれない.
2 [permission] ... <verb>-te[de] mo yoˈi ...て[で]もよい: I asked her if I might use the phone. (*Kanojo ni deñwa o tsukatte mo yoi ka to kiita.*) 彼女に電話を使ってもよいかと聞いた.

mighty *adj.* chiˈkarazuyoˈi 力強い; kyoˈoryoku na 強力な: a mighty blow (*kyooryoku na ichigeki*) 強力な一撃.

mild *adj.* **1** (of a person) oˈñkoo na 温厚な; oˈñwa na 穏和な; yaˈsashii 優しい: He is mild of manner. (*Kare wa taido ga oñkoo da.*) 彼は態度が温厚だ.
2 (of weather) oˈñdañ na 温暖な; oˈdaˈyaka na 穏やかな: We enjoyed a mild winter this year. (*Kotoshi no fuyu wa oñdañ datta.*) ことしの冬は温暖だった.
3 (of taste) tsuˈyoku nai 強くない; kaˈraku nai 辛くない: This curry is mild. (*Kono karee wa karaku nai.*) このカレーは辛くない.

mile *n.* maˈiru マイル: One mile equals about 1.6 kilometers. (*Ichi-mairu wa yaku it-teñ rok-kiro ni*

ataru.) 1マイルは約1.6キロにあたる.
★ In Japan the metric system is used.

military *adj.* guˈñ no 軍の: military forces (*guñtai*) 軍隊 / a military base (*guñji kichi*) 軍事基地.
— *n.* guˈñtai 軍隊.

milk *n.* gyuˈunyuu 牛乳; miˈruku ミルク: have a glass of milk (*koppu ippai no gyuunyuu o nomu*) コップ1杯の牛乳を飲む.
— *vt.* chiˈchi o shiˈboˈru 乳を搾る: milk a cow (*ushi no chichi o shiboru*) 牛の乳を搾る.

mill *n.* **1** (machine) seˈefuˈñki 製粉機: a coffee mill (*koohii-hiki*) コーヒーひき.
2 (factory) seˈefuñjo 製粉所: a water mill (*suishagoya*) 水車小屋.
— *vt.* ... o seˈefuñ suru ...を製粉する ⬚: mill grain (*kokurui o seefuñ suru*) 穀類を製粉する.

million *n.* hyaˈku-maˈñ 100万: ten million (*is-señ-mañ*) 1千万.

millionaire *n.* hyaˈkumañ-choˈoja 百万長者; oˈoganeˈmochi 大金持ち.

mind *n.* **1** (part of a person) koˈkoˈro 心; seˈeshiñ 精神: She is pure in mind. (*Kanojo wa kokoro ga kiree da.*) 彼女は心がきれいだ.
2 (intellect) chiˈsee 知性: improve one's mind (*chisee o migaku*) 知性を磨く.
3 (memory) kiˈoku 記憶: keep a person's name in mind (*hito no namae o kioku ni todomeru*) 人の名前を記憶にとどめる.
4 (opinion) iˈkeñ 意見; kaˈñgaˈe 考え: change one's mind (*kañgae o kaeru*) 考えを変える.
— *vt.* **1** (take care) ... ni chuˈui suru ...に注意する ⬚: Mind your step. (*Ashimoto ni chuui shi nasai.*) 足もとに注意しなさい.
2 [in the negative] ... o iˈyagaˈru ... をいやがる: I don't mind hard work. (*Tsurai shigoto de mo kamaimaseñ.*) つらい仕事でもかまいません.

do you mind if ... <verb>-te[de] mo iˈi desu ka? ...て[で]もいいですか:

Do you mind if I smoke here? (*Ko-ko de tabako o sutte mo ii desu ka?*) ここでたばこを吸ってもいいですか.

make up one's mind *vt.* ... to ke¹sshiñ suru ...と決心する ⬚: He made up his mind to be a doctor. (*Kare wa isha ni naroo to kesshiñ shita.*) 彼は医者になろうと決心した.

mine¹ *pron.* wa¹tashi no mono¹ 私のもの: This umbrella is mine. (*Kono kasa wa watashi no mono da.*) この傘は私のものだ. / Your shirt is white and mine is blue. (*Kimi no shatsu wa shiro de watashi no wa ao da.*) 君のシャツは白で私のは青だ.

mine² *n.* ko¹ozañ 鉱山: a diamond mine (*daiyamoñdo koozañ*) ダイヤモンド鉱山 / a coal mine (*tañkoo*) 炭鉱.
— *vt.* ... o ho¹rida¹su ...を掘り出す ⬚; sa¹ikutsu suru 採掘する ⬚: mine gold (*kiñ o horidasu*) 金を掘り出す.

miner *n.* ko¹oiñ 坑員; ta¹ñkoo roo-do¹osha 炭坑労働者.

mineral *n.* ko¹obutsu 鉱物.

mingle *vt.* ... o ma¹zeru ...を混ぜる ⬚: mingle two colors (*futatsu no iro o mazeru*) 二つの色を混ぜる.
— *vi.* (... to) i¹rimaji¹ru (...と)入り交じる ⬚; ma¹jiwa¹ru 交わる ⬚: She is too shy to mingle with others. (*Kanojo wa totemo uchiki de hoka no hito to majiwaranai.*) 彼女はとても内気でほかの人と交わらない.

minimum *adj.* sa¹ishoo no 最小の; sa¹itee no 最低の: the minimum temperature (*saitee oñdo*) 最低温度 / minimum wages (*saitee chiñ-giñ*) 最低賃金.
— *n.* sa¹isho¹ogeñ 最小限; sa¹i-te¹egeñ 最低限: have a minimum of eight hours of sleep (*saitee hachi-jikañ no suimiñ o toru*) 最低8時間の睡眠をとる.

minister *n.* da¹ijiñ 大臣; ko¹oshi 公使: the Prime Minister (*Soori daijiñ*) 総理大臣 / the United States Minister to Japan (*chuu-nichi Beekoku kooshi*) 駐日米国公使.

ministry *n.* sho¹o 省: the Ministry of Finance [Education] (*ookura [moñbu] shoo*) 大蔵[文部]省.

mink *n.* mi¹ñku ミンク.

minor *adj.* **1** (smaller) chi¹isa¹i hoo no 小さいほうの; chi¹isa-na 小さな: make a minor alteration to the plan (*sekkee ni chiisa-na heñkoo o kuwaeru*) 設計に小さな変更を加える. **2** (unimportant) ju¹uyoo de na¹i 重要でない; ta¹ishita ko¹to no na¹i たいしたことのない: a minor accident (*tai-shita koto no nai jiko*) たいしたことのない事故.
— *n.* **1** (person) mi¹seene¹ñsha 未成年者: No Minors. (*Miseeneñ-sha okotowari.*) 未成年者お断り. **2** (music) ta¹ñchoo 短調; ta¹ño¹ñ-kai 短音階.

minority *n.* sho¹osu¹u 少数; sho¹o-suuha 少数派: They were in the minority. (*Kare-ra wa shoosuuha datta.*) 彼らは少数派だった.

minus *adj.* **1** (negative) ma¹inasu no マイナスの; fu¹ no 負の: a minus quantity (*fusuu*) 負数. **2** (less than zero) hyo¹ote¹ñka ... 氷点下...; re¹eka ... 零下...: The temperature is minus ten degrees. (*Ki-oñ wa reeka juu-do desu.*) 気温は零下10度です.
— *prep.* (subtract) ... o hi¹ita ...を引いた: Seven minus three is four. (*Nana hiku sañ wa yoñ desu.*) 7引く3は4です.
— *n.* (sign) ma¹inasu-ki¹goo マイナス記号; fu¹su¹u 負数.

minute *n.* **1** (of time) fu¹ñ 分: It's five minutes to five. (*Go-ji go-fuñ mae desu.*) 5時5分前です. 《⇨ appendix》 **2** (moment) shu¹ñkañ 瞬間.

in a minute *adv.* su¹gu (ni) すぐ(に): I'll do it in a minute. (*Sugu yarimasu.*) すぐやります.

Just a minute. (*Chotto matte kudasai.*) ちょっと待ってください.

miracle *n.* **1** (supernatural event) ki¹seki 奇跡: perform a miracle (*kiseki o okonau*) 奇跡を行う.

2 (wonder) kyoˈoi 驚異; fuˈshigi na kotoˈ 不思議なこと: a miracle of science (*kagaku no kyooi*) 科学の驚異.

mirror *n.* kaˈgami¹ 鏡: look in a mirror (*kagami o nozoku*) 鏡をのぞく.

miscellaneous *adj.* iˈroiro na いろいろな; zaˈtta na 雑多な: miscellaneous goods (*zakka*) 雑貨.

mischief *n.* iˈtazura いたずら: get into mischief (*itazura o hajimeru*) いたずらを始める.

mischievous *adj.* iˈtazurazuki na いたずら好きな; waˈñpaku na わんぱくな: a mischievous child (*itazurak-ko*) いたずらっ子.

miser *n.* keˈchiñboo けちんぼう.

miserable *adj.* **1** (unhappy) miˈjime na 惨めな; fuˈkoˈo na 不幸な: I was miserable when I failed in the exam. (*Shikeñ ni shippai shita toki wa mijime datta.*) 試験に失敗したときは惨めだった.
2 (poor) soˈmatsu na 粗末な; miˈsuborashiˈi みすぼらしい: a miserable house (*misuborashii ie*) みすぼらしい家.
3 (unpleasant) fuˈyuˈkai na 不愉快な; iˈyaˈ na いやな: miserable weather (*iya na teñki*) いやな天気.

misery *n.* miˈjimeˈsa 惨めさ; kyuˈuboo 窮乏; kuˈnañ 苦難: live in misery (*mijime na seekatsu o suru*) 惨めな生活をする.

misfortune *n.* fuˈuñ 不運; fuˈkoˈo 不幸: He had the misfortune to have his wallet stolen. (*Kare wa fukoo ni mo saifu o nusumareta.*) 彼は不幸にも財布を盗まれた.

mishap *n.* fuˈkoˈo na deˈkiˈgoto 不幸な出来事; jiˈko 事故.

mislead *vt.* ... o maˈyowaseˈru ...を迷わせる Ⓥ; daˈmaˈsu だます Ⓒ: I was misled by his appearance. (*Watashi wa kare no mikake ni damasareta.*) 私は彼の見かけにだまされた.

misleading *adj.* hiˈto o ayamaraseˈru 人を誤らせる; goˈkai o maneˈku 誤解を招く: a misleading explanation (*gokai o maneku setsumee*) 誤解を招く説明.

misprint *n.* miˈsupuriˈñto ミスプリント; goˈshoku 誤植.

miss *vt.* **1** (fail to catch) ...o 〈verb〉-sokonaˈu ...を...そこなう Ⓒ: miss a catch (*booru o tori-sokonau*) ボールを捕りそこなう / I missed the last train. (*Watashi wa saishuu ressha ni nori-sokonatta.*) 私は最終列車に乗りそこなった.
2 (fail to obtain) ...o noˈgaˈsu ...を逃す Ⓒ: miss a good chance (*yoi kikai o nogasu*) よい機会を逃す.
3 (fail to keep) ...o nuˈkasu ...を抜かす Ⓒ: Don't miss my name off the list. (*Watashi no namae o mee-bo kara nukasanaide kudasai.*) 私の名前を名簿から抜かさないでください.
4 (feel sad) saˈbiˈshiku oˈmoˈu 寂しく思う Ⓒ: I will miss you when you move out. (*Anata ga hikkoshi suru to sabishiku narimasu.*) あなたが引っ越しすると寂しくなります.

Miss *n.* -sañ さん: Miss Brown (*Burauñ-sañ*) ブラウンさん.

missing *adj.* yuˈkuefuˈmee no 行方不明の; miˈataranai 見当たらない: a missing child (*yukuefumee no kodomo*) 行方不明の子ども / My glasses are missing. (*Megane ga miataranai.*) 眼鏡が見当たらない.

mission *n.* shiˈsetsu 使節; shiˈsetsuˈdañ 使節団: a trade mission (*booeki shisetsudañ*) 貿易使節団.

mist *n.* kiˈri 霧; kaˈsumi かすみ: The mist has cleared. (*Kiri ga hareta.*) 霧が晴れた.

mistake *n.* maˈchigaˈi 間違い; aˈyamari 誤り. ★ Japanese often say '*misu*' for English 'mistake': Everyone makes mistakes. (*Dare de mo machigai wa suru.*) だれでも間違いはする. / Someone took my umbrella by mistake. (*Dare-ka ga watashi no kasa o machigaete motte itta.*) だれかが私の傘を間違えて持って行った. / It was my mistake. (*Sore wa watashi no misu deshita.*) それは私のミス

でした.
— *vt.* ... o maˈchigaeˌru …を間違え
る Ⓥ; aˈyamaˌru 誤る Ⓒ: I mistook
the way. (*Watashi wa michi o machigaeta.*) 私は道を間違えた. / She is
often mistaken for her sister. (*Kanojo wa yoku imooto to machigae-
rareru.*) 彼女はよく妹と間違えられる.

mistaken *adj.* maˈchigaˌeta 間違え
た; maˈchigaˌete iru 間違っている:
He was mistaken about the date of
the meeting. (*Kare wa kaigi no hi
o machigaete ita.*) 彼は会議の日を間
違えていた.

mistress *n.* 1 (head of a household) oˈnnashuˌjiñ 女主人; shuˌfu
主婦.
2 (teacher) oˈnna no señseˌe 女の
先生.

mistrust *vt.* ... o shiˈñyoo shinai
…を信用しない; shiˈñrai shinai 信頼
しない: I mistrust what he says.
(*Watashi wa kare ga iu koto o
shiñyoo shimaseñ.*) 私は彼が言うこと
を信用しません.
— *n.* fuˈshiñ 不信; giˈwaku 疑惑.

misunderstand *vt.* ... o goˈkai
suru …を誤解する Ⓘ: I misunder-
stood his meaning. (*Watashi wa
kare no imi o gokai shite ita.*) 私は
彼の意味を誤解していた.
— *vi.* goˈkai suru 誤解する Ⓘ: He
often misunderstands. (*Kare wa
yoku gokai suru.*) 彼はよく誤解する.

misunderstanding *n.* goˈkai 誤
解; iˈkeñ no chiˈgai 意見の違い:
clear up a misunderstanding (*go-
kai o toku*) 誤解を解く.

misuse *vt.* ... o goˈyoo suru …を誤
用する Ⓘ; aˈkuyoo suru 悪用する Ⓘ:
misuse a tool (*doogu o goyoo
suru*) 道具を誤用する.
— *n.* goˈyoo 誤用; aˈkuyoo 悪用.

mix *vt.* 1 (blend) ... o maˈzeˌru …を
混ぜる Ⓥ: mix cement and sand
(*semeñto to suna o mazeru*) セメン
トと砂を混ぜる.
2 (prepare) ... o maˌzete tsuˌkuˌru
…を混ぜて作る Ⓒ: She is mixing a
cake. (*Kanojo wa keeki o tsukutte

iru tokoro desu.*) 彼女はケーキを作っ
ているところです.
— *vi.* 1 (blend) maˈzaˌru 混ざる
Ⓒ; koˈñgoo suru 混合する Ⓘ: Oil
and water will not mix. (*Abura to
mizu wa mazaranai.*) 油と水は混ざら
ない.
2 (go together) (... to) maˈjiwaˌru
(…と)交わる Ⓒ: I don't like to mix
with people. (*Watashi wa hito to
majiwaru no wa suki de wa nai.*)
私は人と交わるのは好きではない.

mixture *n.* 1 (act of mixing) koˈñgoo 混合: mixture of eggs and
milk (*tamago to gyuunyuu no koñ-
goo*) 卵と牛乳の混合.
2 (things mixed) koˈñgoˌobutsu 混
合物: Air is a mixture of gases.
(*Kuuki wa kitai no koñgoobutsu
desu.*) 空気は気体の混合物です.

mob *n.* boˈoto 暴徒; yaˈjiuma やじ馬.

mock *vt.* 1 (imitate) ... no maˌne o
suru …のまねをする Ⓘ: He mocked
his teacher. (*Kare wa señsee no
mane o shita.*) 彼は先生のまねをした.
2 (scorn) ... o aˈzakeˌru …をあざける
Ⓥ: He mocked my ideas. (*Kare
wa watashi no kañgae o azaketta.*)
彼は私の考えをあざけった.

mode *n.* 1 (manner) hoˈohoo 方
法; yoˈoshiki 様式: a mode of life
(*seekatsu yooshiki*) 生活様式.
2 (fashion) ryuˈukoo 流行; moˌodo
モード: She was dressed in the latest
mode. (*Kanojo wa saishiñ ryuukoo no fuku o kite ita.*) 彼女は最新
流行の服を着ていた.

model *n.* 1 (small copy) moˈkee 模
型: a model of a ship (*fune no mo-
kee*) 船の模型.
2 (version) kaˈtaˌ 型; deˈzaˌiñ デザイ
ン: My car is the latest model.
(*Watashi no kuruma wa saishiñ-
gata desu.*) 私の車は最新型です.
3 (example) moˈhañ 模範; teˈhoˌñ
手本: a model student (*mohañsee*)
模範生 / He made his father his
model. (*Kare wa chichioya o tehoñ to shita.*) 彼は父親を手本とした.
4 (person) moˌderu モデル: an art-

ist's model (*gaka no moderu*) 画家
のモデル.
— *vt.* **1** (shape) ... o tsu⌈ku⌉ru ...を
作る C: The children are modeling
animals in clay. (*Kodomo-tachi wa
neñdo de doobutsu o tsukutte iru.*)
子どもたちは粘土で動物を作っている.
2 (pose as a model) ... no mo⌈deru
o suru ...のモデルをする I: She mod-
eled swimming suits. (*Kanojo wa
mizugi no moderu o shita.*) 彼女は
水着のモデルをした.

moderate *adj.* **1** (not extreme)
te⌈kido no 適度の: moderate exercise (*tekido no uñdoo*) 適度の運動.
2 (temperate) o⌈ñkeñ na 穏健な:
He is moderate in his opinions.
(*Kare wa ikeñ ga oñkeñ da.*) 彼は
意見が穏健だ.
3 (reasonable) te⌈goro na 手ごろな:
The prices are moderate. (*Nedañ
wa tegoro desu.*) 値段は手ごろです.

modern *adj.* **1** (contemporary)
ge⌈ñdai no 現代の; ki⌈ñdai no 近代
の: modern times (*geñdai*) 現代 /
modern literature (*kiñdai buñgaku*) 近代文学.
2 (new) ge⌈ñdai-teki na 現代的な;
mo⌈dañ na モダンな: a modern hotel
(*geñdaifuu no hoteru*) 現代風のホテ
ル.

modest *adj.* **1** (humble) hi⌈kaeme⌉
na 控えめな; ke⌈ñsoñ shita けんそんし
た: a modest attitude (*hikaeme na
taido*) 控えめな態度.
2 (simple) sa⌈sa⌉yaka na ささやかな;
shi⌈sso na 質素な: He lives in a
modest house. (*Kare wa shisso na
ie ni suñde iru.*) 彼は質素な家に住ん
でいる.

modesty *n.* ke⌈ñsoñ けんそん;
ke⌈ñkyo 謙虚; (of a woman) shi-
⌈toya⌉kasa しとやかさ.

modification *n.* he⌈ñkoo 変更;
shu⌈usee 修正: The plan needs
slight modification. (*Keekaku wa
sukoshi shuusee ga hitsuyoo da.*)
計画は少し修正が必要だ.

modify *vt.* **1** (change) ... o he⌈ñ-
koo suru ...を変更する I: We modi-

fied our plans. (*Watashi-tachi wa
keekaku o heñkoo shita.*) 私たちは
計画を変更した.
2 (revise) ... o shu⌈usee suru ...を修
正する I: We slightly modified the
wording. (*Hyoogeñ o tashoo shuusee shita.*) 表現を多少修正した.
3 (moderate) ... o yu⌈rume⌉ru ...を
緩める V; ka⌈geñ suru 加減する I:
modify one's demand (*yookyuu o
yurumeru*) 要求を緩める.
4 (qualify) ... o shu⌈ushoku suru ...
を修飾する I: Adverbs modify
verbs. (*Fukushi wa dooshi o shuushoku suru.*) 副詞は動詞を修飾する.

moist *adj.* shi⌈metta 湿った; shi-
⌈mette iru 湿っている; nu⌈reta ぬれた;
nu⌈rete iru ぬれている: moist air (*shi-
metta kuuki*) 湿った空気.

moisten *vt.* ... o shi⌈merasu ...を湿
らす C; nu⌈rasu ぬらす C: moisten
one's lips (*kuchibiru o shimerasu*)
唇を湿らす.
— *vi.* shi⌈meru 湿る C; nu⌈reru ぬ
れる V.

moisture *n.* shi⌈kke 湿気; su⌈ibuñ
水分.

mold[1] *n.* ka⌈ta⌉ 型; na⌈gashigata 流
し型: a jelly mold (*zerii no nagashi-
gata*) ゼリーの流し型.
— *vt.* ... o ka⌈ta⌉ ni i⌈rete tsuku⌉ru
...を型に入れて作る C; ... de tsu⌈ku⌉-
ru ...で作る C: mold a vase out of
clay (*neñdo de kabiñ o tsukuru*) 粘
土で花びんを作る.

mold[2] *n.* ka⌈bi かび: This bread has
mold on it. (*Kono pañ wa kabi ga
haete iru.*) このパンはかびが生えている.

mole[1] *n.* (animal) mo⌈gura もぐら.

mole[2] *n.* (small spot on the skin)
ho⌈kuro ほくろ.

molecule *n.* bu⌈ñshi 分子.

moment *n.* **1** (a short period of
time) shu⌈ñkañ 瞬間; cho⌈tto no
aida ちょっとの間: Wait a moment,
please. (*Chotto matte kudasai.*) ちょ
っと待ってください. / He went out a
moment ago. (*Kare wa chotto mae
ni gaishutsu shimashita.*) 彼はちょっ
と前に外出しました.

2 (a particular time) to￼ki¹ 時;
ba￼ai 場合: Now is the moment to
decide. (*Ima ga ketsudañ suru
toki da.*) 今が決断する時だ. / He is
not here at the moment. (*Kare wa
ima koko ni imaseñ.*) 彼は今ここにい
ません.

monarch *n.* ku￼ñshu 君主.

monarchy *n.* ku￼ñshu-se￼eji 君主
政治; ku￼ñshu-se￼etai 君主政体.

monastery *n.* shu￼udo￼oiñ 修道院.

Monday *n.* ge￼tsuyo￼o(bi) 月曜(日).

money *n.* ka￼ne 金; o-￼kane お金;
(coin) ko￼oka 硬貨; (paper note) sa-
￼tsu 札; o-￼satsu お札; shi￼hee 紙幣:
I've spent all my money. (*O-kane
wa zeñbu tsukatte shimaimashita.*)
お金は全部使ってしまいました. / She is
saving money to buy a TV. (*Kanojo wa terebi o kau tame ni o-
kane o tamete iru.*) 彼女はテレビを買
うためにお金を貯めている.

monkey *n.* sa￼ru 猿.

monologue *n.* do￼kuhaku 独白.

monopolize *vt.* ... no do￼kuseñ-
keñ o e￼ru ...の独占権を得る Ⓥ; ... o
do￼kuseñ suru ...を独占する Ⓣ: This
company monopolizes the silk
market. (*Kono kaisha wa ki-ito
shijoo o dokuseñ shite iru.*) この会
社は生糸市場を独占している.

monopoly *n.* do￼kuseñ 独占; se￼ñ-
bai 専売: a government monopoly
(*seefu no señbai*) 政府の専売.

monotonous *adj.* ta￼ñchoo na 単
調な; ta￼ikutsu na 退屈な: My job
was very monotonous. (*Watashi
no shigoto wa hijoo ni taikutsu
datta.*) 私の仕事は非常に退屈だった.

monotony *n.* ta￼ñchoo 単調; ta-
￼ikutsu 退屈.

monster *n.* ka￼ibutsu 怪物; ba￼ke-
mono￼ 化け物.

monstrous *adj.* **1** (huge) kyo￼dai
na 巨大な; ka￼ibutsu no 怪物の: a
monstrous elephant (*kyozoo*) 巨象.
2 (horrible) o￼soru be￼ki 恐るべき;
to￼ñdemona￼i とんでもない: a monstrous lie (*toñdemonai uso*) とんでも
ないうそ.

month *n.* tsu￼ki¹ 月.

monthly *adj.* ma￼itsuki no 毎月の;
tsu￼ki¹￼k-ka￼i no 月1回の: a
monthly magazine (*gekkañ zasshi*)
月刊雑誌 / a monthly income (*ges-
shuu*) 月収.

monument *n.* **1** (structure) ki-
￼ne￼ñhi 記念碑: put up a monu-
ment (*kineñhi o tateru*) 記念碑を建
てる.
2 (remains) i￼seki 遺跡: an ancient
monument (*kodai no iseki*) 古代の
遺跡.

monumental *adj.* **1** (of memory) ki￼neñ no 記念の: a monumental statue (*kineñzoo*) 記念像.
2 (great) kyo￼dai na 巨大な; ta￼i-
heñ na 大変な: monumental efforts
(*taiheñ na doryoku*) 大変な努力.

mood *n.* ki￼buñ 気分; ki￼geñ 機嫌:
I'm in no mood for work. (*Shigoto
o suru kibuñ de wa nai.*) 仕事をする
気分ではない. / She was in a bad
mood. (*Kanojo wa kigeñ ga warukatta.*) 彼女は機嫌が悪かった.
⇨ atmosphere.

moon *n.* tsu￼ki¹ 月: a full moon
(*mañgetsu*) 満月 / a new moon
(*shiñgetsu*) 新月.

moonlight *n.* ge￼kkoo 月光; tsu-
￼kia￼kari 月明かり: walk in the
moonlight (*tsukiakari no naka o
aruku*) 月明かりの中を歩く.

mop *n.* mo￼ppu モップ: clean a floor
with a mop (*moppu de yuka o
fuku*) モップで床をふく.

moral *adj.* do￼otoku no 道徳の;
do￼otoku-teki na 道徳的な: the
moral sense (*dootoku kañneñ*) 道徳
観念 / moral education (*dootoku-
kyooiku*) 道徳教育.
— *n.* **1** (lesson) kyo￼okuñ 教訓:
There's a moral to this story.
(*Kono hanashi ni wa kyookuñ ga
aru.*) この話には教訓がある.
2 (principles) do￼otoku 道徳; mo￼-
raru モラル: public morals (*fuuki*) 風
紀.

morale *n.* shi￼ki 士気: lift morale
(*shiki o takameru*) 士気を高める /

Morale is high [low]. (*Shiki ga takai [hikui].*) 士気が高い[低い].

morality *n.* **1** (moral quality) do˥otoku 道徳; do˥ogi 道義: It is against public morality. (*Sore wa kooshuu dootoku ni hañsuru.*) それは公衆道徳に反する.

2 (virtue) hi˥ñkoo 品行; to˥kusee 徳性.

more *adj.* **1** (greater) mo˥tto ooi もっと多い; mo˥tto ta˥kusa˥ñ no もっとたくさんの: He has more money than me. (*Kare wa watashi yori mo takusañ o-kane o motte iru.*) 彼は私よりもたくさんお金を持っている.

2 (further) so˥re i˥joo no それ以上の; mo˥o もう: One more word. (*Moo hito-koto.*) もう一言. / Please give me two more apples. (*Riñgo o moo futatsu kudasai.*) りんごをもう二つ下さい.

— *pron.* mo˥tto ooku no hi˥to˥ [mo˥no˥; ko˥to˥] もっと多くの人[物; 事]; ... i˥joo no hi˥to˥ [mo˥no˥; ko˥to˥] ... 以上の人[物; 事]: I want to know more. (*Motto ooku no koto o shiritai.*) もっと多くの事を知りたい. / More than thirty people were present. (*Sañjuu-niñ ijoo no hito ga shusseki shita.*) 30人以上の人が出席した.

— *adv.* mo˥tto もっと; sa˥ra ni さらに: Be more careful. (*Motto chuui shi nasai.*) もっと注意しなさい. / Let's walk more slowly. (*Motto yukkuri arukimashoo.*) もっとゆっくり歩きましょう.

moreover *adv.* so˥no ue そのうえ; sa˥ra ni さらに: The price is too high, and moreover, the product is inferior in quality. (*Nedañ ga takasugi, sono ue hiñshitsu ga otorimasu.*) 値段が高すぎ, そのうえ品質が劣ります.

morning *n.* a˥sa 朝; go˥zeñ 午前. ★ '*Asa*' suggests early morning hours and '*gozeñ*' the forenoon: He worked from morning till night. (*Kare wa asa kara bañ made hataraita.*) 彼は朝から晩まで働いた. / I

will be free in the morning. (*Gozeñ-chuu wa hima desu.*) 午前中は暇です. / I got up at six this morning. (*Watashi wa kesa roku-ji ni okimashita.*) 私は今朝6時に起きました.

mortal *adj.* **1** (certain to die) shi˥nu koto ni na˥tte iru 死ぬことになっている: Man is mortal. (*Hito wa dare de mo shinu uñmee ni aru.*) 人はだれでも死ぬ運命にある.

2 (causing death) chi˥mee-teki na 致命的な: a mortal wound (*chimee-shoo*) 致命傷.

mortgage *n.* te˥etoo 抵当; ta˥ñpo 担保: lend money on mortgage (*teetoo o totte kane o kasu*) 抵当を取って金を貸す / He took out a mortgage on his house. (*Kare wa jibuñ no ie o teetoo ni ireta.*) 彼は自分の家を抵当に入れた.

mosquito *n.* ka 蚊: be bitten by a mosquito (*ka ni kuwareru*) 蚊に食われる.

most *adj.* **1** (greatest) mo˥tto˥mo ooi もっとも多い: He made the most mistakes. (*Kare ga mottomo ooku no machigai o shita.*) 彼がもっとも多くの間違いをした.

2 (almost all) ta˥itee no たいていの: Most people think so. (*Taitee no hito wa soo omotte imasu.*) たいていの人はそう思っています.

— *pron.* sa˥ida˥igeñ 最大限; da˥ibu˥buñ 大部分: This is the most I can do. (*Kore ga watashi no dekiru saidaigeñ desu.*) これが私のできる最大限です. / I did most of the work. (*Sono shigoto no daibubuñ wa watashi ga yarimashita.*) その仕事の大部分は私がやりました.

— *adv.* mo˥tto˥mo もっとも; i˥chibañ いちばん: the most beautiful flower (*mottomo utsukushii hana*) もっとも美しい花 / We can trust him most. (*Kare ga ichiban shiñyoo dekiru.*) 彼がいちばん信用できる.

mostly *adv.* da˥ibu˥buñ wa 大部分は; ta˥itee たいてい: I am out mostly on Sundays. (*Nichiyoo wa taitee* *gaishutsu shite imasu.*) 日曜はたいてい外出しています.

motel *n.* moˈoteru モーテル: stay overnight at a motel (*hito-ban mooteru ni tomaru*) ひと晩モーテルに泊まる.

moth *n.* ga が(蛾).

mother *n.* haˈha 母; haˈhaoya 母親; (someone else's) o-ˈkaˈasañ お母さん: My mother is a teacher. (*Haha wa señsee desu.*) 母は先生です. / How old is your mother? (*O-kaasañ wa o-ikutsu desu ka?*) お母さんはおいくつですか.

motion *n.* **1** (movement) uˈñdoo 運動; uˈgokiˈ 動き: observe the motion of the stars (*hoshi no ugoki o kañsatsu suru*) 星の動きを観察する.
2 (manner) doˈosa 動作; miˈburi 身ぶり: The policeman made a motion to me to stop. (*Keekañ wa watashi ni tomaru yoo ni miburi de aizu shita.*) 警官は私に止まるように身ぶりで合図した.
— *vt.* ... ni miˈburi de shiˈmeˈsu ...に身ぶりで示す C; aˈizu suru 合図する I: He motioned the child away. (*Kare wa sono ko ni mukoo e ike to miburi de shimeshita.*) 彼はその子に向こうへ行けと身ぶりで示した.

motion picture *n.* eˈega 映画.

motive *n.* doˈoki 動機: What was your motive for taking an interest in the Japanese language? (*Nihoñgo ni kyoomi o motsu yoo ni natta dooki wa nañ desu ka?*) 日本語に興味を持つようになった動機は何ですか.

motor *n.* moˈotaa モーター; haˈtsudoˈoki 発動機: an electric motor (*deñdooki*) 電動機 / start [cut off] a motor (*mootaa o ugokasu [tomeru]*) モーターを動かす[止める].
— *adj.* jiˈdoˈosha no 自動車の: a motor vehicle (*jidoosha*) 自動車 / a motor trip (*jidoosha ryokoo*) 自動車旅行.

motorcycle *n.* oˈotoˈbai オートバイ; taˈñsha 単車.

motto *n.* hyoˈogo 標語; moˈttoo モットー.

mound *n.* **1** (bank) tsuˈkaˈ 塚; tsuˈtsumi 堤.
2 (of baseball) maˈuñdo マウンド: take the mound (*mauñdo ni agaru*) マウンドに上がる.

mount *vt.* **1** (get up on) ... ni noˈru ...に乗る C: mount a bicycle [horse] (*jiteñsha [uma] ni noru*) 自転車[馬]に乗る.
2 (go up) ... ni noˈboru ...に登る C; ... o aˈgaru ...を上がる V: mount a hill (*koyama ni noboru*) 小山に登る / mount stairs (*kaidañ o agaru*) 階段を上がる.
3 (put in position) ... ni suˈeru ...に据える V; haˈru はる C: mount a photograph on cardboard (*daishi ni shashiñ o haru*) 台紙に写真をはる.
— *vi.* **1** (go up) (... ni) noˈru (...に)乗る C; noˈboru 上る C: mount to the top of a ladder (*hashigo no ue made noboru*) はしごの上まで上る.
2 (increase) zoˈodai suru 増大する I: The number of traffic accidents is mounting. (*Kootsuu jiko no kazu ga zoodai shite iru.*) 交通事故の数が増大している.

mountain *n.* yaˈmaˈ 山: go up a mountain (*yama ni noboru*) 山に登る / go down a mountain (*yama o kudaru*) 山を下る. ⇨ Mt.

mourn *vt.* ... o naˈgeki-kanashiˈmu ...を嘆き悲しむ C: She mourned the death of her father. (*Kanojo wa chichioya no shi o nageki-kanashiñda.*) 彼女は父親の死を嘆き悲しんだ.

mourning *n.* **1** (grief) hiˈtañ 悲嘆; aˈitoo 哀悼.
2 (period) mo 喪: go into mourning (*mo ni fukusu*) 喪に服す.

mouse *n.* neˈzumi ねずみ; haˈtsuka neˈzumi はつかねずみ. ★ Those that live in Japanese houses are rats.

mouth *n.* **1** (on the face) kuˈchi 口: open [close] one's mouth (*kuchi o hiraku [tojiru]*) 口を開く[閉じる].
2 (opening) kuˈchi 口: the mouth of a bottle (*biñ no kuchi*) びんの口.

move vt. **1** (change the position) … o uˬgokaˈ¹su …を動かす C; iˬdoo suru 移動する T: Please move your car. (Kuruma o idoo shite kudasai.) 車を移動してください.
2 (touch the heart) … o kaˈñdoo saseru …を感動させる V: I was moved by his speech. (Watashi wa kare no eñzetsu ni kañdoo shita.) 私は彼の演説に感動した.
3 (propose) … o teˈeañ suru …を提案する T: I move that we close the meeting. (Watashi wa heekai o teeañ shimasu.) 私は閉会を提案します.
— vi. **1** (be in motion) uˬgoˈku 動く C: Don't move while I take your picture. (Shashiñ o toru aida ugokanaide.) 写真を撮る間動かないで.
2 (to a new house) iˬteñ suru 移転する T; hiˬkkoˈsu 引っ越す C: He moved from Tokyo to Osaka. (Kare wa Tookyoo kara Oosaka e hikkoshita.) 彼は東京から大阪へ引っ越した.

movement n. **1** (moving) uˬñdoo 運動; uˬgokiˈ 動き: observe the movement of stars (hoshi no ugoki o kañsatsu suru) 星の動きを観察する.
2 (behavior) doˈosa 動作; miˈburi 身ぶり: Her movements are elegant. (Kanojo no doosa wa joohiñ da.) 彼女の動作は上品だ.
3 (activity) uˬñdoo 運動: a political movement (seeji uñdoo) 政治運動.

movie n. eˈega 映画: I want to see a movie. (Nani-ka eega ga [o] mitai.) 何か映画が[を]見たい. / a movie theater (eegakañ) 映画館.

Mr. n. -sañ さん; -shi 氏: There's a call for you, Mr. Yamada. (Yamada-sañ, o-deñwa desu.) 山田さん, お電話です. / Mr. Murakami was elected mayor. (Murakami-shi ga shichoo ni erabareta.) 村上氏が市長に選ばれた.

Mrs. n. -sañ さん; -fuˈjiñ 夫人: May I introduce Mrs. Yamamoto to you? (Yamamoto-sañ o go-shookai itashimasu.) 山本さんをご紹介いたしま

す. / This is Mrs. Ishikawa's picture. (Kore wa Ishikawa-fujiñ no e desu.) これは石川夫人の絵です.

Ms. n. -sañ さん; (teacher) seˈñseˈe 先生: Ms. Kimura (Kimura-sañ) 木村さん / Ms. White (Howaito señsee) ホワイト先生.

Mt. -sañ 山; -yama 山: Mt. Fuji (Fuji-sañ) 富士山 / Mt. Asama (Asama-yama) 浅間山. ★ '山' is pronounced either 'sañ' or 'yama.'

much adj. oˈoku no 多くの; taˈkusaˈñ no たくさんの: I don't have much time. (Jikañ wa taishite arimaseñ.) 時間はたいしてありません. / How much money do you need? (O-kane wa ikura hitsuyoo desu ka?) お金はいくら必要ですか.
— pron. taˈryoo 多量; taˈkusañ たくさん: I don't eat much for lunch. (Chuushoku wa amari tabemaseñ.) 昼食はあまり食べません. / I have too much to do. (Suru koto ga takusañ ari-sugiru.) することがたくさんありすぎる.
— adv. taˈiheñ (ni) 大変(に); oˈoi ni 大いに; hiˈjoo ni 非常に: Thank you very much. (Taiheñ arigatoo gozaimashita.) 大変ありがとうございました. / She is much like her mother. (Kanojo wa hahaoya ni hijoo ni yoku nite iru.) 彼女は母親に非常によく似ている.

mud n. doˈroˈ 泥; nuˈkarumi ぬかるみ: The car splashed me with mud. (Sono kuruma wa watashi ni doro o haneta.) その車は私に泥をはねた.

muddy adj. doˈro-daˈrake no 泥だらけの; nuˈkarumi no ぬかるみの: get muddy (doro-darake ni naru) 泥だらけになる / a muddy road (nukarumi no michi) ぬかるみの道.

multiple adj. taˈyoo na 多様な; fuˈkugoo no 複合の: multiple vitamin pills (soogoo bitamiñzai) 総合ビタミン剤.
— n. (of mathematics) baˈisuˈu 倍数.

multiplication n. kaˈkeˈzañ 掛け算.

multiply vt. ... o ka⌐ke⌐ru ...を掛ける ⟨V⟩: Multiply 5 by 3, and you get 15. (Go ni sañ o kakeru to juugo ni naru.) 5 に 3 を掛けると 15 になる.

multitude n. (number) ta⌐su⌐u 多数; (people) o⌐oze⌐e 大勢: a multitude of flowers (tasuu no hana) 多数の花 / a multitude of people (oozee no hito) 大勢の人.

mumble vt. mo⌐gumogu [bu⌐tsubustu] (to) i⌐u もぐもぐ[ぶつぶつ](と)言う ⟨C⟩: He mumbled something. (Kare wa nani-ka butsubutsu itta.) 彼は何かぶつぶつ言った.

municipal adj. to⌐shi no 都市の; shi⌐ [ma⌐chi⌐] no 市[町]の: a municipal office (shiyakusho [machiyakuba]) 市役所[町役場] / a municipal government (chihoo jichitai) 地方自治体.

murder n. sa⌐tsujiñ 殺人; sa⌐tsujiñ ji⌐keñ 殺人事件: commit murder (satsujiñ o okasu) 殺人を犯す / There were two murders in this town. (Kono machi ni satsujiñ jikeñ ga ni-keñ atta.) この町に殺人事件が 2 件あった.

murderer n. sa⌐tsuji⌐ñsha 殺人者; sa⌐tsuji⌐ñhañ 殺人犯.

murmur n. 1 (sound) ka⌐suka na o⌐to⌐ かすかな音: I heard the murmur of conversation from the next room. (Tonari no heya kara hisohiso hanasu koe ga kikoeta.) 隣の部屋からひそひそ話す声が聞こえた. / the murmur of a stream (ogawa no sarasara nagareru oto) 小川のさらさら流れる音.

2 (complaint) fu⌐hee no ko⌐e⌐ 不平の声: pay tax without a murmur (fuhee o iwazu ni zeekiñ o harau) 不平を言わずに税金を払う.

— vi. ka⌐suka na o⌐to⌐ o ta⌐te⌐ru かすかな音を立てる: a murmuring brook (sarasara nagareru ogawa) さらさら流れる小川.

muscle n. ki⌐ñniku 筋肉: I strained a muscle in my leg. (Watashi wa ashi no kiñniku o itameta.) 私は足の筋肉を痛めた.

museum n. ha⌐kubutsu⌐kañ 博物館; bi⌐jutsu⌐kañ 美術館: a science museum (kagaku hakubutsukañ) 科学博物館 / a museum of modern art (kiñdai bijutsukañ) 近代美術館.

mushroom n. ki⌐noko きのこ.

music n. 1 (art) o⌐ñgaku 音楽; kyo⌐ku 曲: compose music (sakkyoku suru) 作曲する.

2 (score) ga⌐kufu 楽譜: play without music (gakufu nashi de eñsoo suru) 楽譜なしで演奏する.

musical adj. o⌐ñgaku no 音楽の: a musical performance (eñsoo) 演奏.
— n. myu⌐ujikaru ミュージカル.

musician n. o⌐ñgakuka 音楽家; myu⌐uji⌐shañ ミュージシャン.

must aux. 1 [obligation] ⟨verb⟩-na⌐kereba na⌐ra⌐nai ...なければならない: I must go at once. (Watashi wa sugu ni ikanakereba naranai.) 私はすぐに行かなければならない.

2 [in the negative] ⟨verb⟩-te[de] wa i⌐kenai ...て[で]はいけない: You must not smoke in this room. (Kono heya de tabako o sutte wa ikenai.) この部屋でたばこを吸ってはいけない.

3 [certainty] ... ni chi⌐gainai ...に違いない: If he says so, it must be true. (Kare ga soo iu nara sore wa hoñtoo ni chigainai.) 彼がそういうならそれは本当に違いない.

mustache n. ku⌐chihige 口ひげ.

mustard n. ka⌐rashi からし; ma⌐suta⌐ado マスタード.

mute adj. da⌐ma⌐tte iru 黙っている; mu⌐goñ no 無言の: He remained mute. (Kare wa damatte ita.) 彼は黙っていた.

mutter vi. tsu⌐buya⌐ku つぶやく ⟨C⟩; bu⌐tsubutsu i⌐u ぶつぶつ言う ⟨C⟩: I heard him muttering. (Kare ga butsubutsu itte iru no o kiita.) 彼がぶつぶつ言っているのを聞いた.
— vt. ... o tsu⌐buya⌐ku ...をつぶやく ⟨C⟩; bu⌐tsubutsu i⌐u ぶつぶつ言う ⟨C⟩: He muttered a reply. (Kare wa butsubutsu to heñji o shita.) 彼はぶつぶつと返事をした.

mutton *n*. hiˈtsuji no niˈku˺ 羊の肉; yoˈoniku 羊肉; maˈtoñ マトン.

mutual *adj*. oˈtagai no お互いの; soˈogo 相互の: mutual understanding (*soogo rikai*) 相互理解.

my *pron*. waˈtashi no 私の: This is my umbrella. (*Kore wa watashi no kasa desu*.) これは私の傘です.

myself *pron*. **1** [reflexive use] waˈtashi jiˈshiñ o [ni] 私自身を[に]; jiˈbuñ o [ni] 自分を[に]: I poured myself a cup of tea. (*Watashi wa jibuñ de o-cha o ireta*.) 私は自分で お茶を入れた.
2 [emphatic use] jiˈbuñ de 自分で; waˈtashi jiˈshiñ de 私自身で: I did

it myself. (*Watashi ga jibuñ de sore o yarimashita*.) 私が自分でそれ をやりました.

mysterious *adj*. naˈzo no yoˈo na 謎のような; fuˈshigi na 不思議な: a mysterious event (*fushigi na ji-keñ*) 不思議な事件.

mystery *n*. fuˈkaˈkai na koˈto˺ 不可解なこと; shiˈñpiˈ 神秘; naˈzo 謎: The affair is still shrouded in mystery. (*Sono jikeñ wa ima mo nazo ni tsutsumarete iru*.) その事件 は今も謎に包まれている.

myth *n*. shiˈñwa 神話: Greek myths (*Girisha-shiñwa*) ギリシャ神 話.

N

nail *n*. **1** (fastener) kuˈgi くぎ: drive a nail into a board (*ita ni kugi o utsu*) 板にくぎを打つ.
2 (of a finger or toe) tsuˈme つめ: cut one's nails (*tsume o kiru*) つめを 切る.

naive *adj*. taˈñjuñ na 単純な; uˈbu na うぶな: It is naive of you to believe that. (*Soñna koto o shiñjiru nañte kimi mo tañjuñ da*.) そんなこと を信じるなんて君も単純だ.

naked *adj*. haˈdaka no 裸の: a naked body (*ratai*) 裸体.

name *n*. naˈmae 名前: May I have your name? (*O-namae wa?*) お名前 は. / Do you know the name of this flower? (*Kono hana no namae o shitte imasu ka?*) この花の名前を知 っていますか. ★ Japanese 'surname' is followed by 'given name.'
— *vt*. ... o (... to) naˈzukeˈru ...を (...と)名付ける Ⓥ: The parents named their child Akemi. (*Ryooshiñ wa kodomo o Akemi to nazuketa*.) 両親は子どもを明美と名付けた.

namely *adv*. suˈnaˈwachi すなわち; tsuˈmari つまり: Only one person was absent, namely, Mr. Tanaka. (*Hitori dake kesseki shimashita.*

Tsumari, Tanaka-sañ desu.) 一人だ け欠席しました. つまり, 田中さんです.

nap *n*. hiˈrune 昼寝: take a nap (*hirune o suru*) 昼寝をする.
— *vi*. uˈtatane suru うたた寝する Ⓘ; hiˈrune suru 昼寝する Ⓘ.

napkin *n*. naˈpukiñ ナプキン.

narrow *adj*. seˈmaˈi 狭い: a narrow road (*semai michi*) 狭い道. ★ Japanese '*semai*' also means 'small in area.'
— *vi*. seˈmaku naru 狭くなる Ⓒ: The road narrows ahead. (*Kono michi wa saki de semaku natte iru*.) この道は先で狭くなっている.

nasty *adj*. **1** (unkind) iˈjiˈwaru na 意地悪な: a nasty trick (*ijiwaru na itazura*) 意地悪ないたずら.
2 (unpleasant) iˈyaˈ na 嫌な: a nasty smell (*iya na nioi*) 嫌なにおい / nasty weather (*iya na teñki*) 嫌な天 気.

nation *n*. **1** (people) koˈkumiñ 国 民: the voice of the nation (*kokumiñ no koe*) 国民の声.
2 (state) koˈkka 国家: a democratic nation (*miñshu kokka*) 民主国家.

national *adj*. **1** (of the people) koˈkumiñ no 国民の: national sentiment (*kokumiñ kañjoo*) 国民感情.

2 (of the state) ko⌐kka no 国家の:
the national flower (*kokka*) 国花.

3 (run by the state) ko⌐kuritsu no
国立の: a national theater (*kokuritsu-gekijoo*) 国立劇場.

nationalism *n.* ko⌐kka-shuⁿgi 国家主義; mi⌐ñzoku-shuⁿgi 民族主義.

nationality *n.* ko⌐kuseki 国籍:
acquire Japanese nationality (*Nihoñ kokuseki o toru*) 日本国籍を取る.

nationalization *n.* ko⌐kuyuuka
国有化; ko⌐kuee 国営.

nationalize *vt.* ko⌐kuyuu ni suru
国有にする①; ko⌐kuee ni suru 国営にする①: nationalize the railroads
(*tetsudoo o kokuee ni suru*) 鉄道を
国営にする.

native *adj.* **1** (of one's homeland)
u⌐mare-ko⌐kyoo no 生まれ故郷の: a
native place (*umare kokyoo*) 生まれ
故郷 / one's native country (*boko-ku*) 母国 / native language (*bogo*)
母語.

2 (of that land) do⌐chaku no 土着
の: native plants (*dochaku no shokubutsu*) 土着の植物 / native craftwork (*miñgeehiñ*) 民芸品.

3 (innate) u⌐maretsuki no 生まれつき
の: native talent (*umaretsuki no sainoo*) 生まれつきの才能.

　　— *n.* ... u⌐mare no hi⌐to⌐ ...生まれの
人: a native of Tokyo (*Tookyoo umare no hito*) 東京生まれの人.

natural *adj.* **1** (of nature) shi⌐zeñ
no 自然の; te⌐ñneñ no 天然の: a
natural disaster (*shizeñ saigai*) 自
然災害 / natural resources (*teñneñ shigeñ*) 天然資源.

2 (to be expected) to⌐ozeñ no 当然
の: It is natural that he should get
angry. (*Kare ga okoru no wa toozeñ da.*) 彼が怒るのは当然だ.

naturally *adv.* **1** (not forced) shi⌐zeñ ni 自然に: He can speak Japanese naturally. (*Kare wa Nihoñgo o shizeñ ni hanaseru.*) 彼は日本語を
自然に話せる.

2 (of course) to⌐ozeñ 当然; mo-

⌐chi⌐roñ もちろん: Naturally, he got
angry. (*Toozeñ kare wa okotta.*) 当
然彼は怒った.

nature *n.* **1** (environment) shi⌐zeñ
自然: the beauty of nature (*shizeñ no bi*) 自然の美 / protect nature
(*shizeñ o mamoru*) 自然を守る.

2 (characteristic) se⌐eshitsu 性質:
a cheerful nature (*akarui seeshitsu*) 明るい性質.

by nature *adv.* u⌐maretsuki 生ま
れつき: He is smart by nature.
(*Kare wa umaretsuki atama ga yoi.*) 彼は生まれつき頭が良い.

naughty *adj.* i⌐tazura na いたずらな;
i⌐u koto⌐ o ki⌐kanai 言うことを聞かな
い: a naughty child (*itazura na kodomo*) いたずらな子ども.

naval *adj.* ka⌐iguñ no 海軍の: a naval base (*kaiguñ kichi*) 海軍基地.

navigation *n.* **1** (on sea) ko⌐okai
航海; (in air) ko⌐okuu 航空.

2 (science) ko⌐oka⌐ijutsu 航海術;
ko⌐oku⌐ujutsu 航空術.

navy *n.* ka⌐iguñ 海軍: join the navy
(*kaiguñ ni hairu*) 海軍に入る.

near *prep.* **1** (position) ... no chi⌐ka-ku ni [e] ...の近くに[へ]: He lives
near the station. (*Kare wa eki no chikaku ni suñde iru.*) 彼は駅の近く
に住んでいる.

2 (time) ... ni chi⌐ka⌐i ...に近い: It
was near noon. (*Shoogo ni chika-katta.*) 正午に近かった.

　　— *adj.* chi⌐ka⌐i 近い: Where is the
nearest post office? (*Ichibañ chikai yuubiñkyoku wa doko desu ka?*)
いちばん近い郵便局はどこですか. / I will
move to Hokkaido in the near
future. (*Watashi wa chikai shoorai Hokkaidoo e hikkoshimasu.*)
私は近い将来北海道へ引っ越します.

　　— *adv.* chi⌐kaku ni [e] 近くに[へ]:
Do you live near? (*Kono chikaku ni o-sumai desu ka?*) この近くにお住
まいですか.

nearly *adv.* **1** (almost) ho⌐to⌐ñdo
ほとんど; ho⌐bo ほぼ; mo⌐ sukoⁿshi
de もう少しで: It is nearly nine
o'clock. (*Moo sugu ku-ji da.*) もうす

く9時だ.

2 (closely) mo⌐fo suko⌐shi de ... もう少して...: I was nearly run over by a car. (*Moo sukoshi de kuruma ni hikareru tokoro datta.*) もう少して車にひかれるところだった.

neat *adj.* ki⌐fchi⌐nto shita [shite iru] きちんとした[している]; ki⌐free na きれいな: keep one's room neat (*heya o kichinto shite oku*) 部屋をきちんとしておく / neat handwriting (*kiree na ji*) きれいな字.

neatly *adv.* ki⌐fchi⌐nto きちんと: be neatly dressed (*kichinto shita minari o shite iru*) きちんとした身なりをしている.

necessarily *adv.* **1** ka⌐fnarazu 必ず: Important decisions are necessarily slow. (*Juuyoo na kettee wa kanarazu okureru.*) 重要な決定は必ず遅れる.

2 [with a negative] ... to wa ka⌐fgira⌐fnai ...とは限らない: Cheap goods are not necessarily poorly made. (*Yasui mono ga kanarazu shimo osomatsu da to wa kagiranai.*) 安い物が必ずしもお粗末だとは限らない.

necessary *adj.* hi⌐ftsuyoo na 必要な: Vitamins are necessary for health. (*Bitamiñ wa keñkoo ni hitsuyoo da.*) ビタミンは健康に必要だ.

necessity *n.* **1** (condition) hi⌐ftsuyoo 必要: There is no necessity for you to stay here. (*Anata ga koko ni nokotte iru hitsuyoo wa arimaseñ.*) あなたがここに残っている必要はありません.

2 (thing) hi⌐ftsujuhiñ 必需品: Cars are necessities in this town. (*Kuruma wa kono machi de wa hitsujuhiñ desu.*) 車はこの町では必需品です.

neck *n.* **1** (of a body) ku⌐fbi 首: I have a stiff neck. (*Kubi ga itakute mawaranai.*) 首が痛くて回らない.

2 (of a garment) e⌐fri⌐f 襟: the neck of a blouse (*burausu no eri*) ブラウスの襟.

3 (anything like a neck) ku⌐fbi 首: the neck of a bottle (*biñ no kubi*)

びんの首.

necklace *n.* ne⌐fkkuresu ネックレス; ku⌐fbika⌐fzari 首飾り.

necktie *n.* ne⌐fkutai ネクタイ.

need[1] *vt.* **1** (want) ... o hi⌐ftsuyoo to suru ...を必要とする □: I need your help. (*Watashi wa anata no eñjo o hitsuyoo to shite imasu.*) 私はあなたの援助を必要としています.

2 (have to do) 〈verb〉hi⌐ftsuyoo ga a⌐fru ...必要がある; 〈verb〉-na⌐fkereba na⌐fra⌐fnai ...なければならない: You need to do this at once. (*Anata wa sugu ni kore o shinakereba naranai.*) あなたはすぐにこれをしなければならない. / You don't need to come. (*Anata wa kuru hitsuyoo ga arimaseñ.*) あなたは来る必要がありません.

— *n.* hi⌐ftsuyoo 必要: There is no need for haste. (*Isogu hitsuyoo wa arimaseñ.*) 急ぐ必要はありません. / This car is in need of repairs. (*Kono kuruma wa shuuri ga hitsuyoo da.*) この車は修理が必要だ.

need[2] *aux.* 〈verb〉hi⌐ftsuyoo ga a⌐fru ...必要がある: "Need I go at once?" "No, you need not." (*"Sugu iku hitsuyoo ga arimasu ka?" "Iie, sono hitsuyoo wa arimaseñ."*) 「すぐ行く必要がありますか」「いいえ、その必要はありません」

needle *n.* ha⌐fri 針; a⌐fmi⌐fboo 編み棒: sew with a needle (*hari de nuu*) 針で縫う / knit with needles (*amiboo de amu*) 編み棒で編む.

needless *adj.* fu⌐fhi⌐ftsuyoo na 不必要な; mu⌐fda na むだな: one's needless worry (*muda na shiñpai*) むだな心配.

negative *adj.* **1** (refusing) hi⌐ftee no 否定の: He gave me a negative answer. (*Kare wa hitee no heñji o yokoshita.*) 彼は否定の返事をよこした.

2 (not positive) sho⌐fokyoku-teki na 消極的な; hi⌐fkaeme⌐f na 控えめな: take a negative attitude (*shookyoku-teki na taido o toru*) 消極的な態度をとる.

3 (of a disease) i⌐fñsee no 陰性の: The results of the test were nega-

tive. (*Keñsa no kekka wa iñsee datta.*) 検査の結果は陰性だった.
— *n.* (photography) ne¹ga ネガ; i¹ñga 陰画; (math) fu¹su¹u 負数.

neglect *vt.* ... o o¹kota¹ru ...を忘る C; o¹ro¹soka ni suru おろそかにする I: neglect one's work (*shigoto o orosoka ni suru*) 仕事をおろそかにする.
— *n.* ta¹imañ 怠慢; o¹kotaru koto¹ 忘ること: neglect of duty (*shokumu taimañ*) 職務怠慢.

negotiate *vi.* (... to) ko¹oshoo suru (...と)交渉する I: I have to negotiate with the landlord about the rent. (*Watashi wa yanushi to yachiñ ni tsuite kooshoo shina-kereba naranai.*) 私は家主と家賃について交渉しなければならない.
— *vt.* ... o to¹rikimeru ...を取り決める V: The two countries negoti-ated a treaty. (*Ryookoku wa joo-yaku o torikimeta.*) 両国は条約を取り決めた.

negotiation *n.* ko¹oshoo 交渉: enter into negotiations (*kooshoo o hajimeru*) 交渉を始める / The nego-tiations are now under way. (*Sono kooshoo wa ima shiñkoochuu desu.*) その交渉は今進行中です.

neighbor *n.* ki¹ñjo no hi¹to¹ 近所の人.

neighborhood *n.* ki¹ñjo 近所: There are many temples in my neighborhood. (*Uchi no kiñjo ni wa o-tera ga takusañ arimasu.*) うちの近所にはお寺がたくさんあります.

neither *adj.* do¹chira no ... mo ... na¹i どちらの...も...ない: I like neither flower. (*Watashi wa dochira no hana mo suki de wa nai.*) 私はどちらの花も好きではない.
— *pron.* do¹chira mo ... na¹i どちらも...ない: Neither of them was con-tent. (*Kare-ra wa dochira mo mañ-zoku shinakatta.*) 彼らはどちらも満足しなかった.
— *adv.* ... mo ma¹ta ... na¹i ...もまた...ない: "I don't want to go." "Nei-ther do I." (*"Watashi wa ikitaku arimaseñ." "Watashi mo ikitaku*

arimaseñ.")「私は行きたくありません」「私も行きたくありません」
neither ... nor ... *adv.* ... mo ... mo ... nai ...も...も...ない: Neither he nor I can swim. (*Kare mo wata-shi mo oyogenai.*) 彼も私も泳げない.

nephew *n.* (one's own) o¹i おい; (someone else's) o¹igo-sañ おいごさん.

nerve *n.* shi¹ñkee 神経: That noise gets on my nerves. (*Ano soo-oñ wa shiñkee ni sawaru.*) あの騒音は神経に障る.

nervous *adj.* shi¹ñke¹eshitsu na 神経質な; i¹raira shita [shite iru] いらいらした[している]; a¹gatta あがった; a¹gatte iru あがっている: nervous girl. (*shiñkeeshitsu na oñna-no-ko.*) 神経質な女の子. / I was nervous at the interview. (*Watashi wa meñsetsu no toki agatte ita.*) 私は面接のときあがっていた.

nest *n.* su¹ 巣: Birds have built a nest in our garden. (*Tori ga uchi no niwa ni su o tsukutta.*) 鳥がうちの庭に巣を作った.

net[1] *n.* a¹mi¹ 網; ne¹tto ネット: cast a net (*ami o utsu*) 網を打つ / set a net (*ami o haru*) 網を張る.

net[2] *adj.* sho¹omi no 正味の; ka¹ke¹-ne no nai 掛け値のない: net weight (*shoomi no omosa*) 正味の重さ / a net profit (*juñeki*) 純益.

network *n.* ho¹oso¹omoo 放送網; ne¹ttowa¹aku ネットワーク: a TV net-work (*terebi hoosoomoo*) テレビ放送網.

neutral *adj.* chu¹uritsu no 中立の: a neutral nation (*chuuritsu-koku*) 中立国 / a neutral zone (*chuuritsu chitai*) 中立地帯.

never *adv.* **1** (past experience) ... ko¹to¹ ga nai ...ことがない: I have never been abroad. (*Watashi wa gaikoku ni itta koto ga arimaseñ.*) 私は外国に行ったことがありません.
2 (strong negation) ke¹sshite ... na¹i 決して...ない: I'll never forget you. (*Kesshite anata no koto o wa-suremaseñ.*) 決してあなたのことを忘れません.

nevertheless *adv.* so｢re de｣mo それでも: He was very tired; nevertheless, he carried on walking. (*Kare wa totemo tsukarete ita ga sore de mo aruki-tsuzuketa.*) 彼はとても疲れていたが、それでも歩き続けた.

new *adj.* **1** (not old) a｢tarashi｣i 新しい: a new desk (*atarashii tsukue*) 新しい机 / a new car (*shinsha*) 新車.
2 (recent) shi｢ngata no 新型の: a new model of a word processor (*shingata no waapuro*) 新型のワープロ.
3 (just arrived) shi｢nnin no 新任の: a new teacher (*shinnin no sensee*) 新任の先生.
4 (unfamiliar) ha｢ji｣mete no 初めての: I'm new here. (*Koko wa hajimete desu.*) ここは初めてです.

news *n.* **1** (report) nyu｣usu ニュース: I heard the news on the radio this morning. (*Sono nyuusu wa kesa rajio de kikimashita.*) そのニュースは今朝ラジオで聞きました.
2 (recent events) ka｢watta koto｣ 変わったこと: Is there any news? (*Nani ka kawatta koto wa arimasu ka?*) 何か変わったことはありますか.

newspaper *n.* shi｢nbun 新聞: take a newspaper (*shinbun o toru*) 新聞をとる / I read the news in the newspaper. (*Sono kiji wa shinbun de yomimashita.*) その記事は新聞で読みました.

new year *n.* shi｢nnen 新年: A Happy New Year (*Shinnen omedetoo gozaimasu.*) 新年おめでとうございます. ★ At the New Year many Japanese send greeting cards, 'nengajoo' 年賀状.

New Year's Day *n.* ga｢njitsu 元日; ga｢ntan 元旦.

next *adj.* **1** (of place, order) tsu｢gi｣ no 次の: I get off at the next stop. (*Tsugi no teeryuujo de orimasu.*) 次の停留所で降ります.
2 (of time) tsu｢gi｣ no 次の; yo｢ku- 翌; rai- 来: next Monday (*tsugi no getsuyoobi*) 次の月曜日 / next day

(*yokujitsu*) 翌日 / next week (*raishuu*) 来週 / next month (*raigetsu*) 来月 / next year (*rainen*) 来年.
— *adv.* tsu｢gi｣ni 次に: What shall I do next? (*Tsugi ni nani o shimashoo ka?*) 次に何をしましょうか.

next to *adj.* ... no to｢nari ni [no] ... の隣に[の]: the seat next to mine (*watashi no tonari no seki*) 私の隣の席.
— *adv.* (almost) ho｢to｣ndo ほとんど: It is next to impossible to win first prize. (*It-too o toru nante hotondo fukanoo da.*) 一等をとるなんてほとんど不可能だ.

nice *adj.* **1** (good) su｢teki na すてきな; su｢barashi｣i すばらしい: a nice present (*suteki na purezento*) すてきなプレゼント / It's nice weather, isn't it? (*Ii o-tenki desu ne.*) いいお天気ですね. / It's nice to meet you. (*Hajimemashite.*) はじめまして.
2 (kind) shi｢nsetsu na 親切な: He was nice to me. (*Kare wa watashi ni shinsetsu ni shite kureta.*) 彼は私に親切にしてくれた.

nickname *n.* a｢dana あだな; ni｢k-kune｣emu ニックネーム: give a nickname to a person (*hito ni adana o tsukeru*) 人にあだ名をつける.

niece *n.* (one's own) me｢e めい; (someone else's) me｢ego-san めいごさん.

night *n.* yo｢ru 夜; ba｢n 晩: I studied till late at night. (*Watashi wa yoru osoku made benkyoo shita.*) 私は夜遅くまで勉強した. / I'll stay three nights. (*Konban kara sanpaku shimasu.*) 今晩から3泊します. / a night train (*yakoo ressha*) 夜行列車 / every night (*maiban*) 毎晩 / last night (*sakuya*) 昨夜.

nightclub *n.* na｢itoku｣rabu ナイトクラブ.

nightmare *n.* a｢kumu 悪夢: have a nightmare (*akumu o miru*) 悪夢を見る.

nine *pron.* ko｢ko｣notsu 九つ; (people) kyu｣u-nin 9人; (things) kyu｣u-ko 9個.

— n. (figure) ku⌐[kyu⌐u] 九; (hour) ku⌐-ji 9時; (minute) kyu⌐u-fuñ 9分; (age) kyu-u-sai 9歳.

— adj. ko⌐ko⌐notsu no 九つの; (people) kyu⌐u-niñ no 9人の; (things) kyu⌐u-ko no 9個の; (age) kyu⌐u-sai no 9歳の.

nineteen *pron.* ju⌐uku 19; (people) ju⌐ukyu⌐u-niñ 19人; (things) ju⌐-kyu⌐u-ko 19個.

— n. (figure) ju⌐uku 19; (hour) ju⌐uku-ji 19時; (minute) ju⌐ukyu⌐u-fuñ 19分; (age) ju⌐ukyu⌐u-sai 19歳.

— adj. ju⌐uku no 19の; (people) ju⌐ukyu⌐u-niñ no 19人の; (things) ju⌐ukyu⌐u-ko no 19個の; (age) ju⌐u-kyu⌐u-sai no 19歳の.

nineteenth *adj.* ju⌐ukyuu-bañme⌐ no 19番目の; da⌐i-juuku no 第19の.

— n. 1 (people) ju⌐ukyuu-bañme⌐ no hi⌐to⌐ 19番目の人; (things) ju⌐-kyuu-bañme⌐ no mo⌐no⌐ 19番目のもの.

2 (day) ju⌐uku-nichi 19日.

3 (fraction) ju⌐ukyuu-buñ no ichi⌐ 19分の1.

ninetieth *adj.* kyu⌐ujuu-bañme⌐ no 90番目の; da⌐i-kyuujuu no 第90の.

— n. 1 (people) kyu⌐ujuu-bañme⌐ no hi⌐to⌐ 90番目の人; (things) kyu⌐u-juu-bañme⌐ no mo⌐no⌐ 90番目のもの.

2 (fraction) kyu⌐ujuu-buñ no ichi⌐ 90分の1.

ninety *pron.* kyu⌐ujuu 90; (people) kyu⌐uju⌐u-niñ 90人; (things) kyu⌐u-ju⌐k-ko 90個.

— n. (figure) kyu⌐ujuu 90; (age) kyu⌐uju⌐u-sai 90歳.

— adj. kyu⌐ujuu no 90の; (people) kyu⌐uju⌐u-niñ no 90人の; (things) kyu⌐uju⌐k-ko no 90個の; (age) kyu⌐uju⌐u-sai no 90歳の.

ninth *adj.* kyu⌐u-bañme⌐ no 9番目の; da⌐i-kyuu [da⌐i-ku] no 第9の.

— n. 1 (people) kyu⌐u-bañme⌐ no hi⌐to⌐ 9番目の人; (things) kyu⌐u-bañme⌐ no mo⌐no⌐ 9番目のもの.

2 (day) ko⌐konoka 9日.

3 (fraction) kyu⌐u-buñ no ichi⌐ 9分の1.

nip *vt.* ... o tsu⌐ne⌐ru ...をつねる ⓒ; ha⌐sa⌐mu はさむ ⓒ: get one's finger nipped in the door (*doa ni yubi o hasamareru*) ドアに指をはさまれる.

no *adv.* **1** (not so) i⌐ie いいえ; ha⌐i は い. ★ *'lie'* means 'What you have said is wrong.' and *'hai'* means 'What you have said is right.': "Will you go?" "No, I won't." ("*Anata wa ikimasu ka?*" "*lie, iki-maseñ.*") 「あなたは行きますか」「いいえ, 行きません」 / "Won't you go?" "No, I won't." ("*Anata wa ikimaseñ ne?*" "*Hai, ikimaseñ.*") 「あなたは行きませんね」「はい, 行きません」 / No, thank you. (*Moo kekkoo desu.*) も う結構です.

2 [before an adjective] ke⌐sshite ... de na⌐i 決して...でない: The job was no easy one. (*Sono shigoto wa kesshite yasashii mono de nakatta.*) その仕事は決してやさしいものでなかった.

— adj. (of people) i⌐nai いない; i⌐maseñ いません; (of things) na⌐i な い; a⌐rimaseñ ありません: He has no children. (*Kare wa kodomo ga imaseñ.*) 彼は子どもがいません. / There is no swimming pool in this hotel. (*Kono hoteru ni wa puuru ga nai.*) このホテルにはプールがない. / No Smoking. (*Kiñeñ.*) 禁煙. / No Admittance. (*Tachiiri kiñshi.*) 立ち入り禁止. / No parking. (*Chuusha kiñshi.*) 駐車禁止.

No. da⌐i ... bañ 第...番; da⌐i ... goo 第...号: No. 5 (*dai-go-bañ*) 第5番 / Room No. 10 (*juu-goo-shitsu*) 10号室.

nobility *n.* **1** (quality) ke⌐daka⌐sa 気高さ; su⌐ukoo 崇高: a person of nobility (*jiñkaku no kedakai hito*) 人格の気高い人.

2 (people) ki⌐zoku 貴族; ki⌐zoku-ka⌐ikyuu 貴族階級.

noble *adj.* **1** (honorable) ke⌐daka⌐i 気高い; ko⌐oketsu na 高潔な: a no-ble deed (*kedakai kooi*) 気高い行為.

2 (of high birth) ko⌐oki na 高貴な: a noble family (*kooki na iegara*) 高貴な家柄.

nobody *pron.* da`re mo ... na`i だれ
も…ない: Nobody was in the room.
(*Heya ni wa dare mo inakatta.*) 部
屋にはだれもいなかった。

nod *vi.* **1** (show agreement) u`na-
zu`ku うなずく C: nod in agreement
(*dooi shite unazuku*) 同意してうなず
く。
2 (in greeting) e`shaku suru 会釈す
る T: I nodded to him. (*Watashi
wa kare ni eshaku shita.*) 私は彼に
会釈した。
3 (doze) u`touto suru うとうとする T.
— *vt.* **1** (move the head up and
down) o u`nazukase`ru …をうなず
かせる V: She nodded her head.
(*Kanojo wa unazuita.*) 彼女はうなず
いた。
2 (show agreement) u`nazu`ite ... o
shi`me`su うなずいて…を示す C: She
nodded her consent. (*Kanojo wa
unazuite shoodaku o shimeshita.*)
彼女はうなずいて承諾を示した。
— *n.* (nodding) u`nazuki うなずき;
(dozing) i`nemu`ri 居眠り。

noise *n.* o`to`i 音; so`o-oǹ 騒音:
Don't make any noise. (*Oto o
tatete wa ikemaseñ.*) 音を立ててはい
けません。

noisy *adj.* u`rusa`i うるさい; ya`kama-
shi`i やかましい: This room is noisy.
(*Kono heya wa urusai.*) この部屋はう
るさい。

nominate *vt.* ... o shi`mee suru 指
名する T; ni`ñmee suru 任命する T:
The committee nominated Mr.
Yamada for chairman. (*Iñkai wa
Yamada-sañ o gichoo ni shimee
shita.*) 委員会は山田さんを議長に指名
した。

nomination *n.* shi`mee 指名; ni`ñ-
mee 任命。

non- *pref.* hi- 非; fu- 不; mu- 無:
non-residents (*hi-kyojuusha*) 非居
住者 / Non-smoking section, please.
(*Kiñeñseki o onegai shimasu.*) 禁
煙席をお願いします。

none *pron.* **1** (no things) do`re mo
... na`i どれも…ない: None of the
stories is true. (*Sono hanashi wa

dore mo hoñtoo de wa nai.*) その話
はどれも本当ではない。
2 (no persons) da`re mo ... na`i だれ
も…ない: None have arrived. (*Dare
mo kite imaseñ.*) だれも来ていません。
3 (not any) su`koshi mo ... na`i 少
しも…ない; ze`ñzeñ ... na`i 全然…な
い: "How much milk do we have
left?" "None." (*"Gyuunyuu wa
dore kurai nokotte imasu ka?"
"Zeñzeñ arimaseñ."*) 「牛乳はどれく
らい残っていますか」「全然ありません」

nonsense *n.* mu`i`mi 無意味; ba-
`ka`geta ko`toba` ばかげた言葉; na`-
ñseñsu ナンセンス: talk nonsense
(*baka na koto o iu*) ばかなことを言う。
— *int.* Ba`ka na. ばかな。

noodle *n.* nu`udoru ヌードル: buck-
wheat noodles (*soba*) そば / wheat
noodles (*udoñ*) うどん / Chinese noodles (*raameñ*) ラーメン。

noon *n.* sho`ogo 正午; ma`hiru 真
昼: The bell rings at noon. (*Beru
wa shoogo ni narimasu.*) ベルは正午
に鳴ります。

no one *pron.* da`re mo ... na`i だれも
…ない。⇨ nobody

nor *conj.* ... mo ma`ta ...; `nai …もまた
…ない: I can't read French, nor
can I speak it. (*Watashi wa Furañ-
sugo ga yomenai shi, hanasu koto
mo dekinai.*) 私はフランス語が読めない
し、話すこともできない。

normal *adj.* **1** (standard) hyo`o-
juñ-teki na 標準的な; fu`tsuu no 普
通の: normal height (*hyoojuñ-teki
na shiñchoo*) 標準的な身長。
2 (usual) se`ejoo na 正常な: nor-
mal intelligence (*seejoo na chinoo*)
正常な知能。
— *n.* hyo`ojuñ 標準; fu`tsuu 普通;
se`ejoo 正常。

normally *adv.* **1** (as usual) se`e-
joo ni 正常に; i`tsu-mo do`ori ni い
つも通りに: There was an accident
an hour ago, but the Shinkansen is
running normally. (*Ichi-jikañ mae
ni jiko ga atta ga, Shiñkañseñ wa
seejoo ni uñkoo shite imasu.*) 1時
間前に事故があったが、新幹線は正常に

運行しています.
2 (ordinarily) fuˈtsuu 普通; fuˈdañ 普段: I normally get up at six. (*Watashi wa fudañ shichi-ji ni okimasu.*) 私は普段7時に起きます.

north *n.* kiˈta 北: Which way is north? (*Kita wa dochira desu ka?*) 北はどちらですか.
— *adj.* kiˈta no 北の: a north wind (*kita-kaze*) 北風.
— *adv.* kiˈta ni [e] 北に[へ]: My room faces north. (*Watashi no heya wa kitamuki desu.*) 私の部屋は北向きです.

northeast *n.* hoˈkutoo 北東.

northern *adj.* kiˈta no 北の: northern countries (*kitaguni*) 北国.

North Pole *n.* Hoˈkkyoku 北極.

northward *adv.* kiˈta ni mukatte 北に向かって; hoˈppoo e 北方へ: a northward journey (*hoppoo e no tabi*) 北方への旅.

northwest *n.* hoˈkusee 北西.

nose *n.* haˈna 鼻: a long [short] nose (*takai [hikui] hana*) 高い[低い]鼻 / blow one's nose (*hana o kamu*) 鼻をかむ.

nosebleed *n.* haˈnaji 鼻血.

nostril *n.* haˈna no anaˈ 鼻の穴; biˈkoo 鼻孔.

not *adv.* ... (de wa [ja]) naˈi ...(では[じゃ])ない; ⟨verb⟩-nai ...ない: This is not my umbrella. (*Kore wa watashi no kasa de wa arimaseñ.*) これは私の傘ではありません. / He will not succeed. (*Kare wa seekoo shinai deshoo.*) 彼は成功しないでしょう. / This window will not open. (*Kono mado wa dooshite mo akanai.*) この窓はどうしても開かない.
not at all *adv.* **1** zeˈñzeñ ... naˈi 全然...ない: I'm not at all tired. (*Watashi wa zeñzeñ tsukarete imaseñ.*) 私は全然疲れていません.
2 (answer to thanks) doˈo iˈtashimaˈshite どういたしまして.

notable *adj.* chuˈumoku ni atai suru 注目に値する: notable achievements (*chuumoku ni atai suru gyooseki*) 注目に値する業績.

note *n.* **1** (reminder) meˈmo メモ: take notes (*memo o toru*) メモを取る.
2 (short letter) miˈjikaˈi teˈgami 短い手紙.
3 (explanation) chuˈu 注: notes to a text (*tekisuto no chuu*) テキストの注.
4 (sound) oˈtoˈ 音; neˈiro 音色.
— *vt.* ... ni chuˈui suru ...に注意する ①: Note the underlined part. (*Kaseñbu ni chuui shi nasai.*) 下線部に注意しなさい.

notebook *n.* noˈoto ノート.

noted *adj.* yuˈumee na 有名な; choˈmee na 著名な: a noted writer (*yuumee na sakka*) 有名な作家.

nothing *pron.* naˈni mo ... naˈi 何も...ない: I have nothing to declare. (*Shiñkoku suru mono wa nani mo arimaseñ.*) 申告するものは何もありません. / Nothing at all. (*Nañ de mo arimaseñ.*) 何でもありません.
for nothing *adv.* taˈda de ただで: I got it for nothing. (*Watashi wa tada de sore o te ni ireta.*) 私はただでそれを手に入れた.
nothing but ... *adv.* taˈda ... shika ただ...しか: He thinks of nothing but money. (*Kare wa tada kane no koto shika kañgaenai.*) 彼はただ金のことしか考えない.
— *n.* muˈ 無: Nothing comes from nothing. (*Mu kara yuu wa shoojinai.*) 無から有は生じない. / come to nothing (*mu ni kisuru*) 無に帰する.

notice *n.* **1** (notification) tsuˈuchi 通知; shiˈrase 知らせ: give a notice of marriage (*kekkoñ no shirase o dasu*) 結婚の知らせを出す.
2 (bill) keˈeji 掲示: put up a notice of the game (*shiai no keeji o dasu*) 試合の掲示を出す.
3 (attention) chuˈui 注意: Her sudden laughter drew everyone's notice. (*Kanojo no totsuzeñ no warai wa miñna no chuui o hiita.*) 彼女の突然の笑いはみんなの注意を引いた.
4 (warning) yoˈkoku 予告: He quit his job without giving notice. (*Kare wa yokoku nashi ni shigoto o yameta.*) 彼は予告なしに仕事を辞めた.

— *vt.* (perceive) ... ni ki ｢ga tsu｣ku ...に気が付く Ｃ; ki｢zu｣ku 気付く Ｃ: She notices details. (*Kanojo wa komakai koto ni ki ga tsuku.*) 彼女は細かいことに気がつく.

take notice of ... *vt.* ... ni chuui o ha｢ra｣u ...に注意を払う Ｃ: He took no notice of what I said. (*Kare wa watashi ga itta koto ni chuui o harawanakatta.*) 彼は私が言ったことに注意を払わなかった.

notify *vt.* ... ni tsu｢uchi suru ...に通知する Ｉ; tsu｢uhoo suru 通報する Ｉ: notify the police (*keesatsu ni tsuuhoo suru*) 警察に通報する.

notion *n.* **1** (idea) ka｢nga｣e 考え; (concept) ga｢lineñ 概念: He has odd notions. (*Kare wa okashi-na kañgae o motte iru.*) 彼はおかしな考えを持っている.

2 (intention) i｢to 意図; tsu｢mori つもり: I had no notion of telling the truth. (*Watashi wa hoñtoo no koto o iu tsumori wa nakatta.*) 私は本当のことを言うつもりはなかった.

noun *n.* me｢eshi 名詞.

nourish *vt.* ... o i｢shina｣u ...を養う Ｃ; so｢date｣ru 育てる Ｖ: Milk nourishes a baby. (*Akañboo wa miruku de sodatsu.*) 赤ん坊はミルクで育つ.

nourishment *n.* e｢eyoo 栄養; (food) sho｢kulmotsu 食物: take nourishment (*eeyoo o toru*) 栄養をとる.

novel[1] *n.* sho｢osetsu 小説: write [read] a novel (*shoosetsu o kaku [yomu]*) 小説を書く[読む].

novel[2] *adj.* me｢atarashi｣i 目新しい; za｢ñshiñ na 斬新な: a dress of novel design (*zañshiñ na dezaiñ no doresu*) 斬新なデザインのドレス.

November *n.* ju｢u-ichi-gatsu｣ 11月.

now *adv.* **1** (at this moment) i｢ma 今; mo｢lo もう: What time is it now? (*Ima nañ-ji desu ka?*) 今何時ですか. / Where are we flying over now? (*Ima dono heñ o toñde ima-su ka?*) 今どの辺を飛んでいますか.

2 (at once) i｢ma sugu 今すぐ: Can I enter the room now? (*Ima sugu heya ni hairemasu ka?*) 今すぐ部屋に入れますか.

3 [as an interjection] sa｢te さて; sa｣la さあ: Now, let's begin. (*Saa, hajimeyoo.*) さあ, 始めよう. / Now it's finished. (*Saa owarimashita.*) さあ終わりました.

4 (at that time) i｢ma ya 今や; so｢no to｣ki そのとき: He was now a national hero. (*Kare wa ima ya koku-miñ no eeyuu datta.*) 彼は今や国民の英雄だった.

just now *adv.* **1** (at the moment) i｢ma wa 今は: I'm busy just now. (*Ima wa isogashii desu.*) 今は忙しいです.

2 (a moment ago) tsu｢i sakki ついさっき: She was here just now. (*Ka-nojo wa tsui sakki koko ni ima-shita.*) 彼女はついさっきここにいました.

— *conj.* ... da｣ kara ...だから: Now that you've grown up, you must be responsible for your own actions. (*Anata wa moo otona da kara, jibuñ no koodoo ni sekiniñ o mota-neba naranai.*) あなたはもう大人だから, 自分の行動に責任を持たねばならない.

— *n.* i｢ma 今: Now is the time to do what we promised. (*Ima koso yakusoku o hatasu toki da.*) 今こそ約束を果たすときだ.

by now *adv.* i｢ma goro wa mo｢lo 今ごろはもう: She will be in Tokyo by now. (*Kanojo wa ima goro wa moo Tookyoo ni tsuite iru daroo.*) 彼女は今ごろはもう東京に着いているだろう.

for now *adv.* i｢ma no tokoro｣ (wa) 今のところ(は): I am free for now. (*Ima no tokoro wa hima desu.*) 今のところは暇です.

nowadays *adv.* ko｢no-goro wa この ごろは; sa｢ikiñ wa 最近は: Everything is expensive nowadays. (*Kono-goro wa nañ de mo takai.*) このごろは何でも高い.

nowhere *adv.* do｢ko ni mo ... na｣i どこにも...ない: He was nowhere to be seen. (*Kare wa doko ni mo ina-*

katta.) 彼はどこにもいなかった.

nuclear adj. geｎshiｒryoku no 原子
力の; kaｌku no 核の: nuclear energy
(geｎshiryoku) 原子力 / a nuclear
weapon (kakuheeki) 核兵器.

nude adj. haｒdaka no 裸の; nuｌudo
no ヌードの: a nude photo (nuudo
shashiñ) ヌード写真.
— n. raｒtai 裸体.

nuisance n. uｒrusaｌi moｒnoｌ うるさ
いもの; yaｌkkai na moｒnoｌ 厄介なも
の: What a nuisance that child is!
(Ano ko wa nañte urusai ñ daroo.)
あの子は何てうるさいんだろう.

numb adj. kaｒñkaku no naｌi 感覚の
ない: My feet are numb with cold.
(Samusa de ashi no kañkaku ga
nakunatta.) 寒さで足の感覚がなくなっ
た.

number n. 1 (figure) kaｌzu 数: a
high [low] number (ookii [chiisai]
kazu) 大きい[小さい]数 / cardinal
[ordinal] numbers (ki [guu] suu)
奇[偶]数.
2 (No.) baｒñgoｌo 番号: Please tell
me how to call this number. (Kono
bañgoo ni deñwa suru hoohoo o
oshiete kudasai.) この番号に電話する
方法を教えてください. / a telephone
number (deñwa bañgoo) 電話番号
/ a passport number (ryokeñ bañgoo) 旅券番号 / a seat number
(zaseki bañgoo) 座席番号.

a great number of ... adj. taｒ
ｒkusaｌñ no たくさんの: There are a
great number of parks in this town.
(Kono machi ni wa takusañ no
kooeñ ga aru.) この町にはたくさんの公
園がある.

— vt. 1 (assign a number to) ...
ni baｒñgoｌo o tsuｒkeｌru ...に番号をつ
ける Ⓥ: number the pages (peeji ni
bañgoo o tsukeru) ページに番号をつけ
る.
2 (reach) ... ni taｒssuru ...に達する
Ⓘ: Those who attended numbered
thirty. (Shussekisha wa sañjuu-
niñ ni tasshita.) 出席者は 30 人に達
した.

numeral n. suｒuji 数字: Roman
numerals (rooma suuji) ローマ数字.

numerous adj. (of things) taｒsuｌu
no 多数の; (of people) oｒozeｌe no 大
勢の: There are numerous people
waiting in the room. (Heya de
matte iru hito ga oozee imasu.) 部
屋で待っている人が大勢います.

nun n. shuｒudoｌojo 修道女; niｒsoo
尼僧.

nurse n. 1 (female) kaｒñgoｌfu 看護
婦; (male) kaｒñgoｌshi 看護士.
2 (nanny) uｌba 乳母.
— vt. 1 (take care of) ... o kaｒñ-
byoo suru ...を看病する Ⓘ: She
nursed her sick mother. (Kanojo
wa byooki no hahaoya o kañbyoo
shita.) 彼女は病気の母親を看病した.
2 (give milk) ... ni chiｒchi o noｒma-
seｌru ...に乳を飲ませる Ⓥ: She is
nursing her baby. (Kanojo wa
akañboo ni chichi o nomasete iru.)
彼女は赤ん坊に乳を飲ませている.

nursery n. (for children) hoｒikuｌeñ
保育園; taｒkujisho 託児所.

nut n. 1 (edible seed) koｌ no mi 木
の実; naｌttsu ナッツ.
2 (for fastening) naｌtto ナット.

nylon n. naｌiroñ ナイロン.

O

oak n. (tree) oｌoku オーク; (material)
oｒokuｌzai オーク材.

oar n. kaｌi かい; oｒoru オール: pull on
the oars (ooru o kogu) オールをこぐ.

oath n. chiｒkai 誓い; seｒeyaku 誓約:
break [keep] one's oath (chikai o

yaburu [mamoru]) 誓いを破る[守る].

oatmeal n. oｒotomiｌiru オートミール.

obedience n. fuｒkujuu 服従; juｒujuñ 従順: obedience to an order
(meeree no fukujuu) 命令の服従.

obedient adj. juｒujuñ na 従順な;

su͡nao na 素直な: an obedient child (*sunao na kodomo*) 素直な子ども.

obey *vt.* ... ni shi͡tagau ...に従う ©; shi͡tagatte koodoo suru 従って行動する Ⓘ: We should obey the law. (*Watashi-tachi wa hooritsu ni shitagawanakereba naranai.*) 私たちは法律に従わなければならない.

object[1] *n.* **1** (material thing) mo͡no͡ 物; bu͡ttai 物体: I saw a strange object in the dark. (*Watashi wa kurayami no naka de heñ na mono o mita.*) 私は暗闇の中で変な物を見た.
2 (thing or person to which thought is directed) ta͡ishoo 対象; ta͡isho͡obutsu 対象物: an object of interest (*kyoomi no taishoo*) 興味の対象.
3 (aim) mo͡kuteki 目的; me͡ate 目当て: realize one's object (*mokuteki o tassee suru*) 目的を達成する.
4 (of grammar) mo͡kutekigo 目的語: the direct [indirect] object (*chokusetsu [kañsetsu] mokutekigo*) 直接[間接]目的語.

object[2] *vi.* (... ni) ha͡ñtai suru (...に)反対する Ⓘ: He objected to my plan. (*Kare wa watashi no keekaku ni hañtai shita.*) 彼は私の計画に反対した. / I object to smoking in the room. (*Watashi wa heya de tabako o suu no ni wa hañtai desu.*) 私は部屋でたばこを吸うのには反対です.

objection *n.* ha͡ñtai 反対; i͡gi 異議: He made no objection to my suggestion. (*Kare wa watashi no teeañ ni nani mo igi o tonaenakatta.*) 彼は私の提案に何も異議を唱えなかった.

objective *n.* mo͡kuteki 目的: achieve one's objective (*mokuteki o tassee suru*) 目的を達成する.
— *adj.* kya͡kkañ-teki na 客観的な: objective data (*kyakkañ-teki na deeta*) 客観的なデータ.

obligation *n.* **1** (duty) gi͡mu 義務; se͡kiniñ 責任: I have an obligation to support my family. (*Watashi wa kazoku o yashinau gimu ga aru.*) 私は家族を養う義務がある.
2 (debt) o͡ñgi 恩義; o͡ñ 恩: repay an obligation (*oñ ni mukuiru*) 恩に報いる.

obligatory *adj.* gi͡muzukera͡rete iru 義務づけられている; gi͡mu-teki na 義務的な: Attendance at the meeting is obligatory. (*Sono kai e no shusseki wa gimuzukerarete imasu.*) その会への出席は義務づけられています.

oblige *vt.* **1** (compel) ya͡mu o e͡zu ⟨verb⟩ やむを得ず...; kyo͡osee suru 強制する Ⓘ: He was obliged to sell his house to pay his debts. (*Kare wa shakkiñ heñsai no tame ni yamu o ezu ie o utta.*) 彼は借金返済のためにやむを得ず家を売った.
2 (do a favor) ... ni o͡ñkee o ho͡doko͡su ...に恩恵を施す ©: Will you oblige me with some money? (*Watashi ni o-kane o sukoshi kashite itadakemaseñ ka?*) 私にお金を少し貸していただけませんか.
be obliged *vi.* a͡rigata͡ku o͡mo͡u ありがたく思う ©: I am much obliged to you for your kindness. (*Go-shiñsetsu hoñtoo ni arigatoo gozaimasu.*) ご親切本当にありがとうございます.

oblique *adj.* (slanting) na͡na͡me no 斜めの; ha͡su no はすの: an oblique line (*shaseñ*) 斜線.

obscure *adj.* **1** (not clear) ha͡kki͡ri shinai はっきりしない; a͡imai na あいまいな: He gave an obscure explanation. (*Kare wa aimai na setsumee o shita.*) 彼はあいまいな説明をした.
2 (not well known) mu͡mee no 無名の: an obscure writer (*mumee no sakka*) 無名の作家.
— *vt.* ... o mi͡e͡naku suru ...を見えなくする Ⓘ; o͡oikaku͡su 覆い隠す ©: The moon was obscured by clouds. (*Tsuki ga kumo ni kakureta.*) 月が雲に隠れた.

obscurity *n.* ha͡kki͡ri shinai ko͡to͡ はっきりしないこと; fu͡me͡eryoo 不明瞭: His essay is full of obscurities. (*Kare no roñbun wa fumee-ryoo na teñ ga ooi.*) 彼の論文は不明瞭な点が多い.

observation *n.* **1** (watching) ka「ñsatsu 観察; ka「ñsoku 観測: the observation of the stars (*hoshi no kañsoku*) 星の観測.
2 (comment) i「keñ 意見; ka「ñga¹e 考え: He made some observations on the subject. (*Kare wa sono moñdai ni tsuite ikutsu-ka kañgae o nobeta.*) 彼はその問題についていくつか考えを述べた.

observatory *n.* ka「ñsokujo¹ 観測所; (astronomical) te「ñmoñdai 天文台; (meteorological) ki「shoodai 気象台.

observe *vt.* **1** (watch) ... o ka「ñsatsu suru ...を観察する ⓣ; ka「ñsoku suru 観測する ⓣ: observe the behavior of birds (*tori no koodoo o kañsatsu suru*) 鳥の行動を観察する.
2 (notice) ... ni ki 「ga tsu¹ku ...に気がつく ⓒ: I observed a letter on the desk. (*Watashi wa tsukue no ue no tegami ni ki ga tsuita.*) 私は机の上の手紙に気がついた.
3 (obey) ... o ma「mo¹ru ...を守る ⓒ; ju「ñshu suru 遵守する ⓣ: observe the traffic regulations (*kootsuu hooki o mamoru*) 交通法規を守る.
4 (celebrate) ... o i「wa¹u ...を祝う ⓒ: observe someone's birthday (*tañjoobi o iwau*) 誕生日を祝う.
5 (remark) ... to no「be¹ru ...と述べる ⓥ; i「u 言う ⓒ: "It's a lovely day," he observed. (*"Ii (o-)teñki desu ne." to kare wa itta.*) 「いい(お)天気ですね」と彼は言った.
— *vi.* **1** (watch) ka「ñsatsu [ka「ñsoku] suru 観察[観測]する ⓣ.
2 (remark) i「keñ [ka「ñga¹e] o no「be¹ru 意見[考え]を述べる ⓥ.

observer *n.* **1** (watcher) ka「ñsatsu¹sha 観察者; ka「ñsoku¹sha 観測者.
2 (of a meeting) o「buza¹abaa オブザーバー; ta「chiainiñ 立ち会い人.

obstacle *n.* sho「oga¹i 障害; ja「ma (mono) じゃま(物): clear an obstacle

from the road (*dooro kara shoogaibutsu o torinozoku*) 道路から障害物を取り除く.

obstinate *adj.* ga「ñko na 頑固な; go「ojoo na 強情な: an obstinate child (*goojoo na kodomo*) 強情な子ども.

obstruct *vt.* ... o ja「ma suru ...をじゃまする ⓣ; sa「matage¹ru 妨げる ⓥ; bo「ogai suru 妨害する ⓣ: Trees obstructed the view. (*Ki ga shikai o samatagete ita.*) 木が視界を妨げていた.

obtain *vt.* (get) ... o 「te¹ ni i「reru ...を手に入れる ⓥ; e「ru 得る ⓥ: Where did you obtain the perfume? (*Sono koosui wa doko de te ni iremashita ka?*) その香水はどこで手に入れましたか.

obvious *adj.* a「ki¹raka na 明らかな; me「ehaku na 明白な: It was obvious that the driver had been drinking. (*Uñteñsha ga sake o noñde ita no wa akiraka datta.*) 運転者が酒を飲んでいたのは明らかだった.

obviously *adv.* a「ki¹raka ni 明らかに; me「ehaku ni 明白に: he needs some help. (*Akiraka ni kare wa tasuke o hitsuyoo to shite iru.*) 明らかに彼は助けを必要としている.

occasion *n.* **1** (particular time) ba「ai 場合; to「ki¹ とき: I met her on the occasion of my first visit there. (*Watashi wa saisho ni soko o tazuneta toki kanojo to aimashita.*) 私は最初にそこを訪ねたとき彼女と会いました.
2 (special event) gyo「oji 行事: The party was a great occasion. (*Paatii wa seekai deshita.*) パーティーは盛会でした.
3 (opportunity) ki「ka¹i 機会; o「ri¹ 折: I want to change my job if the occasion arises. (*Kikai ga areba shoku o kaetai.*) 機会があれば職を替えたい.
— *vt.* ... o hi「kioko¹su ...を引き起こす ⓒ: His remarks occasioned the quarrel. (*Kare no kotoba ga kooroñ o hikiokoshita.*) 彼の言葉が口論

を引き起こした.

occasional *adj.* to̜ˈkiori no 時折の; to̜ˈkidoki no 時々の: Tokyo will be cloudy with occasional rain. (*Tookyoo wa kumori de tokidoki ame deshoo.*) 東京は曇りで時々雨でしょう.

occasionally *adv.* to̜ˈkiori 時折; to̜ˈkidoki 時々: My son occasionally writes to me. (*Musuko wa tokidoki tegami o yokoshimasu.*) 息子は時々手紙をよこします.

occupation *n.* **1** (job) sho̜ˈku˺-gyoo 職業; shi̜ˈgoto 仕事: What is his occupation? (*Kare no shoku-gyoo wa nañ desu ka?*) 彼の職業は何ですか. / He is a writer by occupation. (*Kare no shokugyoo wa sak-ka desu.*) 彼の職業は作家です.
2 (holding possession of) se̜ˈñryoo 占領; se̜ˈñyuu 占有: an occupation army (*señryooguñ*) 占領軍.

occupy *vt.* **1** (hold) ... o shi̜ˈme˺ru ...を占める Ⓥ: He occupies an important position in this firm. (*Kare wa kono kaisha de juuyoo na chii o shimete imasu.*) 彼はこの会社で重要な地位を占めています.
2 (fill) ... o fu̜ˈsagu ...をふさぐ Ⓒ: Is this seat occupied? (*Kono seki wa fusagatte imasu ka?*) この席はふさがっていますか. / The toilet is occupied. (*Toire wa shiyoo-chuu desu.*) トイレは使用中です.
3 (take possession of) ... o se̜ˈñryoo suru ...を占領する Ⓣ: They occupied the enemy's capital. (*Kare-ra wa teki no shuto o señryoo shita.*) 彼らは敵の首都を占領した.

occur *vi.* **1** (happen) o̜ˈko˺ru 起こる Ⓒ; sho̜ˈjiru 生じる Ⓥ: That accident occurred here. (*Sono jiko wa koko de okorimashita.*) その事故はここで起こりました.
2 (come to mind) o̜ˈmoitsu˺ku 思いつく Ⓒ; a̜ˈtama˺ ni u̜ˈkabu 頭に浮かぶ Ⓒ: A good idea occurred to me. (*Ii kañgae ga atama ni ukañda.*) いい考えが頭に浮かんだ.

occurrence *n.* **1** (event) de̜ˈki˺-goto 出来事: an unfortunate occurrence (*fukoo na dekigoto*) 不幸な出来事.
2 (happening) ha̜ˈssei 発生: the occurrence of a fire (*kaji no has-see*) 火事の発生.

ocean *n.* ta̜ˈiyoo 大洋; (sea) u̜ˈmi 海: the Pacific Ocean (*Taiheeyoo*) 太平洋 / the Atlantic Ocean (*Tai-seeyoo*) 大西洋 / go swimming in the ocean (*umi e oyogi ni iku*) 海へ泳ぎに行く.

o'clock *adv.* -ji 時: I get up at six o'clock. (*Watashi wa roku-ji ni oki-masu.*) 私は6時に起きます. / He came at exactly nine o'clock. (*Kare wa choodo ku-ji ni kimashita.*) 彼はちょうど9時に来ました.

October *n.* ju̜ˈu-gatsu˺ 10月.

oculist *n.* ga̜ˈñka˺-i 眼科医.

odd *adj.* **1** (of a number) ki̜ˈsu˺u no 奇数の: an odd number (*kisuu*) 奇数.
2 (strange) he̜ˈñ na 変な; myo̜ˈo na 妙な: His behavior is odd. (*Kare no taido wa heñ da.*) 彼の態度は変だ. / I smell an odd odor. (*Myoo na nioi ga suru.*) 妙なにおいがする.
3 (occasional) ri̜ˈñji no 臨時の: odd jobs (*riñji no shigoto*) 臨時の仕事.
4 (separated) ka̜ˈta˺hoo dake no 片方だけの: an odd glove (*katahoo dake no tebukuro*) 片方だけの手袋.

odds *n.* ka̜ˈchime˺ 勝ち目; mi̜ˈkomi 見込み: The odds are fifty-fifty. (*Kachime wa gobugobu desu.*) 勝ち目は五分五分です.

odor *n.* ni̜ˈo˺i におい; ka̜ˈori 香り: the odor of medicine (*kusuri no nioi*) 薬のにおい / the sweet odor of roses (*bara no yoi kaori*) バラのよい香り.

of *prep.* **1** (belonging) ... no ...の: the leg of a table (*teeburu no ashi*) テーブルの脚 / the teacher of our school (*watashi-tachi no gakkoo no señsee*) 私たちの学校の先生.
2 (containing) ... no ...の; ... no ryo̜ˈo no ...の量の: a cup of coffee (*ip-pai no koohii*) 1杯のコーヒー / a box of chocolates (*hito-hako no*

chokoreeto) 1 箱のチョコレート.

3 (forming) ... no ...の; ... no uˈchi de ...のうちで: He is one of my friends. (*Kare wa watashi no tomodachi no hitori desu.*) 彼は私の友だちの一人です. / Summer is the warmest season of the year. (*Natsu wa ichi-neñ no uchi de ichibañ atsui kisetsu desu.*) 夏は一年のうちでいちばん暑い季節です.

4 (made from) ... de deˈkite iru ...でできている: a plate of silver (*giñ de dekite iru sara*) 銀でできている皿.

5 (consisting) ... kara naˈru ...から成る: a committee of ten members (*juu-niñ kara naru iiñkai*) 10 人から成る委員会.

6 (origin) ... no ...の; ... kara ...から: the works of Shakespeare (*Sheekusupia no sakuhiñ*) シェークスピアの作品.

off *prep.* **1** (away from) ... kara (haˈnaˌrete) ...から(離れて): He fell off a ladder. (*Kare wa hashigo kara ochita.*) 彼ははしごから落ちた. / I took the book off the shelf. (*Watashi wa sono hoñ o tana kara totta.*) 私はその本を棚から取った.

2 (out of) ... kara ...から; ... o ...を: I got off the bus. (*Watashi wa basu o orita.*) 私はバスを降りた.

3 (not occupied) ... o haˈnaˌrete ...を離れて; maˈnugaˌrete 免れて: He is off duty. (*Kare wa hibañ desu.*) 彼は非番です.

— *adv.* **1** (away) haˈnaˌrete 離れて: The plane takes off at two. (*Hikooki wa ni-ji ni ririku shimasu.*) 飛行機は2時に離陸します.

2 (not being worn) nuˈide 脱いで: take off one's shoes (*kutsu o nugu*) 靴を脱ぐ.

3 (reduced) waˈribiki shite 割引して: take ten percent off (*ichi-wari waribiku*) 1 割引く.

4 (free from work) yaˈsuˌñde 休んで: He had a few days off. (*Kare wa ni-, sañ-nichi yasuñda.*) 彼は 2, 3 日休んだ.

— *adj.* **1** (far) haˈnaˌrete (iru) 離

れて(いる): The station is two kilometers off. (*Eki wa ni-kiro saki desu.*) 駅は 2 キロ先です.

2 (not connected) kiˈrete (iru) 切れている: The switch is off. (*Suitchi wa kirete imasu.*) スイッチは切れています.

3 (gone away) saˈtte (iru) 去って(いる): I must be off now. (*Moo oitoma shinakereba narimaseñ.*) もうおいとましなければなりません.

offend *vt.* **1** (make angry) ... o oˈkoraseˌru ...を怒らせる V: She was offended by his remarks. (*Kanojo wa kare no kotoba ni okotta.*) 彼女は彼の言葉に怒った.

2 (displease) ... ni fuˈkaˌikañ o aˈtaeru ...に不快感を与える V: That tall building offends the eye. (*Ano takai biru wa mezawari da.*) あの高いビルは目障りだ.

— *vi.* tsuˈmi o oˈkaˌsu 罪を犯す C; ... ni haˈñsuˌru ...に反する I: offend against custom (*shuukañ ni hañsuru*) 習慣に反する.

offense *n.* **1** (crime) tsuˈmi 罪; iˈhañ 違反: a traffic offense (*kootsuu-ihañ*) 交通違反.

2 (displeasure) ... ni ˈo waˈraku suru koˈtoˌ 気を悪くすること: She is quick to take offense. (*Kanojo wa sugu ki o waruku suru.*) 彼女はすぐ気を悪くする.

3 (attack) koˈogeki 攻撃: Offense is the best defense. (*Koogeki wa sairyoo no boogyo da.*) 攻撃は最良の防御だ.

offensive *adj.* **1** (unpleasant) iˈya na いやな; fuˈkai na 不快な: a noise offensive to the ear (*mimizawari na oto*) 耳障りな音.

2 (insulting) ki ˈni sawaru 気に障る; buˈree na 無礼な: offensive language (*hito no ki ni sawaru kotoba*) 人の気に障る言葉.

3 (used to attack) koˈogeki-yoo no 攻撃用の: offensive weapons (*koogeki-yoo no buki*) 攻撃用の武器.

offer *vt.* **1** (put forward) ... o teˈekyoo suru ...を提供する I; moˈoshideru 申し出る Ⓥ: I was offered a good post. (*Watashi wa yoi chii o teekyoo sareta.*) 私はよい地位を提供された.

2 (present for sale) ... o uri ni dasu ...を売りに出す Ⓒ: He offered his car for a million yen. (*Kare wa jibuñ no kuruma o hyakumañ-eñ de uri ni dashita.*) 彼は自分の車を100万円で売りに出した.

— *n.* teekyoo 提供; moshide 申し出: accept [decline] an offer (*mooshide o ukeireru [jitai suru]*) 申し出を受け入れる[辞退する].

office *n.* **1** (room) jimusho 事務所; jimushitsu 事務室: an information office (*añnaijo*) 案内所 / a doctor's office (*shiñryoo-shitsu*) 診療室.

2 (building) kaisha 会社; yakusho 役所: He works in an office. (*Kare wa kaisha ni tsutomete imasu.*) 彼は会社に勤めています. / a post office (*yuubiñkyoku*) 郵便局.

3 (department) choo 庁: the Patent Office (*Tokkyochoo*) 特許庁.

4 (position) kañshoku 官職; shoku 職: stay in office (*zaishoku suru*) 在職する / take office (*shuuniñ suru*) 就任する.

officer *n.* **1** (of armed forces) shikañ 士官: an army officer (*rikuguñ shikañ*) 陸軍士官.

2 (policeman) keesatsukañ 警察官; kekañ 警官. ★ Often called 'omawari-sañ' お巡りさん.

official *n.* koomuiñ 公務員; yakuniñ 役人: a government official (*kokka koomuiñ*) 国家公務員.

— *adj.* **1** (of a position) koomujoo no 公務上の; ooyake no 公の: official documents (*koobuñsho*) 公文書.

2 (authorized) kooniñ no 公認の; kooshiki no 公式の: an official record (*kooniñ-kiroku*) 公認記録.

officially *adv.* kooshiki ni 公式に; seeshiki ni 正式に: The hall was officially opened yesterday. (*Sono hooru wa kinoo seeshiki ni kaikañ shita.*) そのホールはきのう正式に開館した.

often *adv.* yoku よく; tabitabi たびたび; shibashiba しばしば: He is often absent. (*Kare wa shibashiba kesseki suru.*) 彼はしばしば欠席する.

how often *adv.* nañ kai 何回: How often do I take the medicine? (*Kusuri wa nañ-kai nomu no desu ka?*) 薬は何回飲むのですか.

oh *int.* oo おお; aa ああ; oya おや: Oh! I've forgotten again. (*Aa, mata wasurete shimatta.*) ああ, また忘れてしまった.

oil *n.* **1** (liquid) abura 油; oiru オイル: machine oil (*kikai-abura*) 機械油 / salad oil (*sarada-yu*) サラダ油.

2 (petroleum) sekiyu 石油: heavy oil (*juuyu*) 重油.

3 (paints) enogu 絵の具: paint in oils (*aburae o kaku*) 油絵をかく.

— *vt.* (put on) ...ni abura o nuru ...に油を塗る Ⓒ; (put into) abura o sasu 油を差す Ⓒ: oil a bicycle (*jiteñsha ni abura o sasu*) 自転車に油を差す.

OK *adv.* ookee オーケー; yoroshii よろしい: OK, I'll do it. (*Yoroshii, watashi ga yarimashoo.*) よろしい, 私がやりましょう.

— *adj.* ookee オーケー; yoroshii よろしい; kekkoo da 結構だ: Everything is OK. (*Subete ookee desu.*) すべてオーケーです.

— *vt.* ... o shooniñ suru ...を承認する Ⓣ: My boss OK'd my plan. (*Buchoo wa watashi no keekaku o shooniñ shita.*) 部長は私の計画を承認した.

old *adj.* **1** (advanced in age) toshi totta [totte iru] 年取った[取っている]; roojiñ no 老人の: He's far too old for the job. (*Kare wa sono shigoto ni wa toshi o torisugite iru.*) 彼はその仕事には年を取りすぎている. / a hospital for old people (*roojiñ no tame no byooiñ*) 老人のための病院.

2 (of age) -sai no 歳の; (of a building) -neñ[tsuki] ni naru 年[月]になる: He is sixty years old. (*Kare wa* rokujus-sai desu.) 彼は 60 歳です. / How old is your son? (Musuko-san wa nan-sai desu ka?) 息子さんは何歳ですか. / This building is fifty years old. (Kono biru wa tatte kara gojuu-nen ni naru.) このビルは建ってから 50 年になる.

3 (elder) to'shiue no 年上の: She is three years older than me. (Kanojo wa watashi yori mo mittsu toshi-ue desu.) 彼女は私よりも三つ年上です. / my oldest brother [sister] (watashi no ichiban ue no ani [ane]) 私のいちばん上の兄[姉].

4 (not new) fu'ru'i 古い; fu'ruku kara no 古くからの: an old building (furui tatemono) 古い建物 / an old friend (furuku kara no tomodachi) 古くからの友だち.

olive n. (tree) o'ri'ibu no ki' オリーブの木; (fruit) o'ri'ibu no mi オリーブの実.

omelet n. o'muretsu オムレツ.

omen n. ze'nchoo 前兆; ki'zashi きざし: a good omen (kitchoo) 吉兆 / a bad omen (kyoochoo) 凶兆.

omission n. sho'oryaku 省略; da-'tsuraku 脱落: I noticed several omissions in the list of names. (Watashi wa meebo ni namae ga ikutsu-ka datsuraku shite iru no ni ki ga tsuita.) 私は名簿に名前がいくつか脱落しているのに気がついた.

omit vt. (leave out) ... o nu'kasu ...を抜かす C; ha'bu'ku 省く C; sho'oryaku suru 省略する I: Let's omit this chapter. (Kono shoo wa shooryaku shimashoo.) この章は省略しましょう.

2 (fail to do) ... o wa'sureru ...を忘れる V: I omitted to sign the letter. (Tegami ni sain suru no o wasu-rete shimatta.) 手紙にサインするのを忘れてしまった.

on prep. **1** (touching) ... no u'e ni [o] ...の上に[を]; ... ni se'sshite ...に接して: The book is on the desk. (Sono hon wa tsukue no ue ni ari-masu.) その本は机の上にあります. / I hung her picture on the wall.

(Watashi wa kanojo no e o kabe ni kaketa.) 私は彼女の絵を壁にかけた. / Please sit on this chair. (Kono isu ni o-suwari kudasai.) このいすにお座りください.

2 (wearing) ... o mi 'ni 'tsu'kete ...を身につけて: put a hat on one's head (booshi o kaburu) 帽子をかぶる.

3 (of a day) ... ni ...に: She often goes to church on Sundays. (Ka-nojo wa nichiyoo ni yoku kyookai e ikimasu.) 彼女は日曜によく教会へ行きます.

4 (towards) ... ni mu'katte ...に向かって; ... no ho'o ni ...の方に: She turned her back on me. (Kanojo wa watashi no hoo ni se o muketa.) 彼女は私の方に背を向けた.

5 (concerning) ... ni tsu'ite ...について; ... ni ka'nsu'ru ...に関する: He lectured on democracy. (Kare wa min-shushugi ni tsuite kooen shita.) 彼は民主主義について講演した.

6 (by means of) ... de ...で: I talked with him on the phone. (Watashi wa kare to denwa de hanashita.) 私は彼と電話で話した.

7 (supported by) ... o mo'to' ni ...を基に: His story is based on experience. (Kare no hanashi wa kee-ken o moto ni shite iru.) 彼の話は経験を基にしている.

8 (as soon as) ⟨verb⟩ to su'gu ...とすぐ: On leaving school, she went to France. (Sotsugyoo suru to sugu kanojo wa Furansu e itta.) 卒業するとすぐ彼女はフランスへ行った.

— adv. **1** (forward) ma'e e 前へ; sa'ki e 先へ: go on (susumu) 進む / further on (sara ni saki no hoo e) さらに先の方へ.

2 (continuing) tsu'zuite 続いて: It went on raining. (Ame ga furi-tsuzuita.) 雨が降り続いた.

3 (worn) ... o mi 'ni 'tsu'kete ...を身につけて: I had nothing on. (Wata-shi wa nani mo mi ni tsukete ina-katta.) 私は何も身につけていなかった.

once adv. **1** (single time) i'chi-do 一度; i'k-kai 1 回: I go to the bookstore once a week. (*Watashi wa shuu ni ichi-do sono hoñya e ikimasu.*) 私は週に一度その本屋へ行きます.

2 (formerly) kaˈtsute かつて; iˈzeñ 以前: I once lived in Nagasaki. (*Watashi wa katsute Nagasaki ni suñde imashita.*) 私はかつて長崎に住んでいました.

— *conj.* iˈttañ ⟨verb⟩ to いったん…と: Once he begins, he never gives up. (*Ittañ hajimeru to kare wa akiramenai.*) いったん始めると彼はあきらめない.

at once *adv.* suˈgu ni すぐに: He came at once. (*Kare wa sugu ni kimashita.*) 彼はすぐに来ました.

once in a while *adv.* toˈkidoki 時々: I go to the movies once in a while. (*Watashi wa tokidoki eega ni ikimasu.*) 私は時々映画に行きます.

once more *adv.* moˈo ichi-do もう一度: Let me try once more. (*Moo ichi-do yarasete kudasai.*) もう一度やらせてください.

once upon a time *adv.* muˈkashi mukashi 昔々.

one[1] *pron.* hiˈtoˈtsu 一つ; (people) hiˈtoˈri 一人; (thing) iˈk-ko 1個: He is one of my friends. (*Kare wa watashi no tomodachi no hitori desu.*) 彼は私の友だちの一人です.

— *n.* (figure) iˈchiˈ 1; (hour) iˈchiˈji 1時; (minute) iˈp-puñ 1分; (age) iˈs-sai 1歳.

— *adj.* **1** (single) hiˈtotsu no 一つの; (people) hiˈtoˈri no 一人の; (thing) iˈk-ko no 1個の; (age) iˈs-sai no 1歳の.

2 (certain) aˈru ある: one fine day (*aru hareta hi*) ある晴れた日 / one night (*aru bañ*) ある晩.

one[2] *pron.* **1** (thing) moˈnoˈ もの: I want a cheaper one. (*Motto yasui mono ga hoshii.*) もっと安いものが欲しい. / Show me another one, please. (*Hoka no mono o misete kudasai.*) ほかのものを見せてください.

2 (person) hiˈto 人: One must do one's best. (*Hito wa saizeñ o tsu-*

kusu beki da.) 人は最善を尽くすべきだ.

oneself *pron.* jiˈbuñ jiˈshiñ 自分自身.

onion *n.* taˈmaneˈgi たまねぎ.

only *adj.* **1** (of people) taˈda hiˈtoˈri no ただ一人の; (of a thing) taˈda hiˈtoˈtsu no ただ一つの; taˈda … dake no ただ…だけの: He is the only friend that I have. (*Kare wa watashi no tada hitori no yuujiñ desu.*) 彼は私のただ一人の友人です. / They are the only people who know the truth. (*Sono shiñsoo o shitte iru no wa kare-ra dake da.*) その真相を知っているのは彼らだけだ.

2 (best) saˈiryoo no 最良の; saˈiteki no 最適の: He is the only man for the job. (*Kare wa sono shigoto ni saiteki no hito da.*) 彼はその仕事に最適の人だ.

— *adv.* **1** (merely) taˈtta … shika たった…しか: I had only two hundred yen. (*Watashi wa tatta ni-hyaku-eñ shika motte inakatta.*) 私はたった200円しか持っていなかった.

2 (solely) taˈda … dake ただ…だけ: Only he could solve the problem. (*Kare dake ga sono moñdai o toketa.*) 彼だけがその問題を解けた.

onto *prep.* … no uˈeˈ e [ni] …の上へ[に]: He jumped onto the stage. (*Kare wa butai no ue ni tobiagatta.*) 彼は舞台の上に飛び上がった.

opal *n.* oˈpaˈaru オパール.

open *vt.* **1** (move) … o aˈkeru …を開ける Ⓥ; (unfold) hiˈraˈku 開く Ⓒ: May I open the window? (*Mado o akete mo ii desu ka?*) 窓を開けてもいいですか. / Open your books to page five. (*Hoñ no go-peeji o hiraki nasai.*) 本の5ページを開きなさい.

2 (start) … o haˈjimeru …を始める Ⓥ; hiˈraˈku 開く Ⓒ: open a business (*jigyoo o hajimeru*) 事業を始める.

3 (make public) … o koˈokai suru …を公開する Ⓘ; hiˈraˈku 開く Ⓒ: open the gallery to the public (*biju-tsukañ o ippañ ni kookai suru*) 美

術館を一般に公開する.
— *vi.* **1** (become open) hiˈraˈku 開く ○: This door won't open. (*Kono to wa doo shite mo hirakanai.*) この戸はどうしても開かない.
2 (begin) haˈjimaru 始まる ○: In Japan school opens in April. (*Nihoñ de wa gakkoo wa shi-gatsu ni hajimarimasu.*) 日本では学校は4月に始まります.
— *adj.* **1** (not closed) aˈite iru 開いている: The doors are open. (*To wa aite imasu.*) 戸は開いています.
2 (operating) aˈite iru 開いている: Is the bank still open? (*Giñkoo wa mada aite imasu ka?*) 銀行はまだ開いていますか.
3 (free to all) daˈre de mo saˈñka dekiˈru だれでも参加できる: an open competition (*dare de mo sañka dekiru koñtesuto*) だれでも参加できるコンテスト.
4 (not hidden) kaˈkushidate no naˈi 隠しだてのない; koˈozeñ no 公然の: an open secret (*koozeñ no himitsu*) 公然の秘密.

opener *n.* aˈkeru monoˈ 開けるもの: a bottle opener (*señnuki*) 栓抜き / a can opener (*kañkiri*) 缶切り.

opening *n.* **1** (hole) aˈnaˈ 穴; suˈkima すき間: an opening in a wall (*kabe no ana*) 壁の穴.
2 (beginning) kaˈishi 開始; oˈopuniñgu オープニング: the opening of a new theater (*atarashii gekijoo no oopuniñgu*) 新しい劇場のオープニング.
3 (opportunity for work) shuˈushoku-guchi 就職口; aˈki 空き: Is there an opening in this firm? (*Kono kaisha ni shoku no aki wa arimasu ka?*) この会社に職の空きはありますか.

openly *adv.* koˈozeñ to 公然と; (frankly) soˈtchoku ni 率直に: criticize openly (*koozeñ to hinañ suru*) 公然と非難する / speak openly (*sotchoku ni hanasu*) 率直に話す.

opera *n.* oˈpera オペラ: stage an opera (*opera o jooeñ suru*) オペラを上演する.

operate *vt.* ... o uˈñteñ suru ...を運転する ○; uˈgokaˈsu 動かす ○: operate a truck (*torakku o uñteñ suru*) トラックを運転する.
— *vi.* **1** (perform an operation) (...ni) shuˈjutsu suru (...に)手術する ○: The surgeon operated on him for an appendicitis. (*Geka-i wa kare ni moochoo no shujutsu o shita.*) 外科医は彼に盲腸の手術をした.
2 (work) saˈdoo suru 作動する ○; uˈgoˈku 動く ○: The machine is operating properly. (*Kikai wa chooshi yoku ugoite imasu.*) 機械は調子よく動いています.

operation *n.* **1** (of surgery) shuˈjutsu 手術: He had an operation on his eye. (*Kare wa me no shujutsu o uketa.*) 彼は目の手術を受けた.
2 (action) saˈgyoo 作業; kaˈtsudoo 活動: a rescue operation (*kyuujo katsudoo*) 救助活動.
3 (working) uˈñteñ 運転; soˈosa 操作: The operation of this machine is simple. (*Kono kikai no soosa wa kañtañ desu.*) この機械の操作は簡単です.

operator *n.* **1** (of a machine) uˈñteˈñsha 運転者: an elevator operator (*erebeetaa uñteñgakari*) エレベーター運転係.
2 (of a telephone switchboard) koˈokaˈñshu 交換手.

opinion *n.* **1** (view) iˈkeñ 意見; kaˈñgaˈe 考え: express one's opinion (*jibuñ no ikeñ o noberu*) 自分の意見を述べる / public opinion (*yoroñ*) 世論.
2 (judgment) hyoˈoka 評価; haˈñdañ 判断: He has a good opinion of the method. (*Kare wa sono hoohoo o takaku hyooka shite iru.*) 彼はその方法を高く評価している.

opponent *n.* aˈiteˈ 相手; teˈki 敵: defeat one's opponent (*aite o yaburu*) 相手を破る.

opportune *adj.* tsuˈgoo no iˈi 都合のいい; teˈkisetsu na 適切な: He appeared at an opportune moment. (*Kare wa tsugoo no ii toki ni arawareta.*) 彼は都合のいいときに現れた.

opportunity *n.* ki¹kai 機会; ko¹o-ki 好機; cha¹ñsu チャンス: I have little opportunity for speaking Japanese. (*Watashi wa Nihoñgo o hanasu kikai ga hotoñdo arimaseñ.*) 私は日本語を話す機会がほとんどありません.

oppose *vt.* ... ni ha¹ñtai suru ...に反対する ⊡: We opposed his plan. (*Watashi-tachi wa kare no keekaku ni hañtai shita.*) 私たちは彼の計画に反対した.

opposite *adj.* **1** (contrary) ha¹ñtai no 反対の; gya¹ku no 逆の: go in the opposite direction (*hañtai no hookoo ni iku*) 反対の方向に行く / the opposite sex (*isee*) 異性.
2 (on the other side) ha¹ñtaigawa no 反対側の; mu¹koogawa no 向こう側の: The post office is on the opposite side of the street. (*Yuubiñ-kyoku wa toori no mukoogawa ni arimasu.*) 郵便局は通りの向こう側にあります.
— *n.* gya¹ku no koto¹ 逆のこと; se¹eha¹ñtai no mo¹no¹ 正反対のもの: I thought quite the opposite. (*Watashi wa mattaku gyaku no koto o kañgaeta.*) 私はまったく逆のことを考えた.
— *prep.* ...no mu¹kaigawa ni [no] ...の向かい側に[の]: the house opposite mine (*watashi no ie no mukai no ie*) 私の家の向かいの家 / We sat opposite each other. (*Watashi-tachi wa mukaiatte suwatta.*) 私たちは向かい合って座った.

opposition *n.* ha¹ñtai 反対: My plan met with opposition. (*Watashi no keekaku wa hañtai ni atta.*) 私の計画は反対にあった. / the opposition party (*yatoo*) 野党.

oppress *vt.* **1** (govern cruelly) ... o a¹ppaku suru ...を圧迫する ⊡; shi¹itage¹ru 虐げる ⊽: oppress the people (*kokumiñ o shiitageru*) 国民を虐げる.
2 (depress) ... o yu¹u-utsu ni suru ...を憂うつにする ⊡; me¹irase¹ru めいらせる ⊽: I felt oppressed by the heat. (*Atsusa de meitte shimatta.*) 暑さでめいってしまった.

oppression *n.* a¹ppaku 圧迫; a¹s-see 圧制: suffer under oppression (*assee no moto ni kurushimu*) 圧制の下に苦しむ.

optimism *n.* ra¹kkañ 楽観; ra¹ku-teñ-shu¹gi 楽天主義.

optimistic *adj.* ra¹kuteñ-teki na 楽天的な; ra¹kkañ-teki na 楽観的な: I am optimistic about the future. (*Watashi wa shoorai ni tsuite rak-kañ-teki desu.*) 私は将来について楽観的です.

option *n.* se¹ñtaku¹keñ 選択権; o¹pushoñ オプション: I have no option in the matter. (*Watashi wa sono keñ de wa señtakukeñ ga arimaseñ.*) 私はその件では選択権がありません.

or *conj.* **1** [show an alternative] ... ka so¹re to¹mo ...ka ...かそれとも...か; ... ka ... ka ...か...か: Which would you like, tea or coffee? (*Koo-cha ni shimasu ka, sore tomo koo-hii ni shimasu ka?*) 紅茶にしますか, それともコーヒーにしますか. / Are your shoes brown or black? (*Anata no kutsu wa chairo desu ka kuro desu ka?*) あなたの靴は茶色ですか黒ですか. / Are you coming or not? (*Anata wa kuru no desu ka konai no desu ka?*) あなたは来るのですか来ないのですか.
2 (otherwise) sa¹mo nai to さもないと: Hurry up or you'll be late. (*Isogi nasai. Samo nai to okure-masu yo.*) 急ぎなさい. さもないと遅れますよ.

oral *adj.* ko¹otoo no 口頭の; (spoken) ko¹ojutsu no 口述の: an oral examination (*koojutsu shikeñ*) 口述試験.

orange *n.* o¹re¹ñji オレンジ: orange juice (*oreñji juusu*) オレンジジュース.
— *adj.* o¹reñji iro no オレンジ色の: an orange dress (*oreñji iro no do-resu*) オレンジ色のドレス.

orator *n.* e¹ñzetsu¹sha 演説者; (eloquent) yu¹ubeñka 雄弁家.

orbit n. **1** ki˥doo 軌道: put a satellite in orbit (eesee o kidoo ni noseru) 衛星を軌道に乗せる.

orchard n. ka˥jueñ 果樹園: an apple orchard (riñgoeñ) りんご園.

orchestra n. o˥oke˥sutora オーケストラ; ka˥ñgeñga˥kudañ 管弦楽団: a symphony orchestra (kookyooga-kudañ) 交響楽団.

order n. **1** (arrangement) ju˥ñ 順; ju˥ñjo 順序; ju˥ñbañ 順番: put names in alphabetical order (namae o arufabetto-juñ ni naraberu) 名前をアルファベット順に並べる.
2 (command) me˥eree 命令; sa˥shizu 指図: I obeyed the doctor's orders. (Watashi wa isha no sashizu ni shitagatta.) 私は医者の指図に従った.
3 (request) chu˥umoñ 注文: give out [cancel] an order (chuumoñ o dasu [torikesu]) 注文を出す[取り消す] / My order hasn't come yet. (Chuumoñ shita mono ga mada kimaseñ.) 注文したものがまだ来ません.
4 (condition properly arranged) se˥etoñ 整頓; se˥eri 整理: set a room in order (heya o seetoñ suru) 部屋を整頓する.
5 (peaceful condition) chi˥tsujo 秩序: keep order (chitsujo o tamotsu) 秩序を保つ.

out of order adj. ko˥shoo shite (iru) 故障して(いる): The elevator is out of order. (Erebeetaa wa koshoo desu.) エレベーターは故障です.
— vt. **1** (give a command) 〈verb〉 yo˥o ni me˥ejiru …ように命じる Ⓥ; shi˥ji suru 指示する Ⓘ: He was ordered not to smoke. (Kare wa tabako o suwanai yoo ni meejirareta.) 彼はたばこを吸わないように命じられた.
2 (request) … o chu˥umoñ suru …を注文する Ⓘ: I ordered the book from the publisher. (Watashi wa sono hoñ o shuppañsha ni chuumoñ shita.) 私はその本を出版社に注文した.

orderly adj. se˥etoñ sareta [sarete iru] 整頓された[されている]; ki˥chi˥ñto shita [shite iru] きちんとした[している]: keep one's room orderly (heya o kichiñto shite oku) 部屋をきちんとしておく.

ordinary adj. **1** (usual) fu˥tsuu no 普通の; tsu˥ujoo no 通常の: ordinary clothes (futsuu no fuku) 普通の服 / an ordinary meeting (reekai) 例会.
2 (common) he˥eboñ na 平凡な; (average) na˥mi no 並の: an ordinary person (heeboñ na hito) 平凡な人.

organ n. **1** (of a body) ki˥kañ 器官; zo˥oki 臓器: the digestive organs (shooka kikañ) 消化器官 / an organ transplant (zooki-ishoku) 臓器移植.
2 (means) ki˥kañ 機関; so˥shiki 組織: organs of government (seeji kikañ) 政治機関.
3 (musical instrument) o˥rugañ オルガン: play the organ (orugañ o hiku) オルガンを弾く.

organic adj. **1** (of a chemical compound) yu˥uki˥butsu no 有機物の: organic fertilizer (yuuki hiryoo) 有機肥料.
2 (of a bodily organ) ki˥kañ no 器官の; zo˥oki no 臓器の: organic disease (naizoo no byooki) 内臓の病気.

organization n. **1** (organized group) so˥shiki 組織; da˥ñtai 団体: a religious organization (shuukyoo-dañtai) 宗教団体.
2 (organizing) so˥shiki-ka 組織化; he˥ñsee 編成: the organization of working people (hataraku hitotachi no soshiki-ka) 働く人たちの組織化.

organize vt. **1** (form into a group) … o so˥shiki suru …を組織する Ⓘ; he˥ñsee suru 編成する Ⓘ: organize a political party (seetoo o soshiki suru) 政党を組織する / organize a baseball team (yakyuu no chiimu o heñsee suru) 野球のチームを編成する.
2 (arrange) … o ju˥ñbi suru …を準

備する Ⅰ: organize a conference (*kaigi o juñbi suru*) 会議を準備する. **3** (put into working order) keʳetoo-date¬ru 系統だてる Ⅴ; maʳtomeru まとめる② organize one's thoughts (*kañgae o matomeru*) 考えをまとめる.

Orient *n.* Toʳoyoo 東洋.

oriental *adj.* toʳoyoo no 東洋の: oriental art (*tooyoo bijutsu*) 東洋美術.

origin *n.* **1** (beginning) kiʳgeñ 起源; haʳjimari 始まり: the origins of civilization (*buñmee no kigeñ*) 文明の起源.
2 (birth) uʳmare 生まれ; suʳjoo 素性: an American of Japanese origin (*nikkee Amerikajiñ*) 日系アメリカ人.

original *adj.* **1** (first) saʳisho no 最初の; moʳto no 元の: the original plan (*saisho no keekaku*) 最初の計画.
2 (creative) doʳkusoo-teki na 独創的な: an original design (*dokusoo-teki na dezaiñ*) 独創的なデザイン.
3 (new) kiʳbatsu na 奇抜な: an original idea (*kibatsu na aidea*) 奇抜なアイデア.
— *n.* (of art) geʳñga 原画; (of literature) geʳñsho 原書: read a book in the original (*hoñ o geñsho de yomu*) 本を原書で読む.

originality *n.* doʳkusoo¬ryoku 独創力; doʳkusoosee 独創性.

originally *adv.* moʳto wa 元は; haʳjime wa 初めは: Originally the firm was a small factory. (*Sono kaisha wa moto wa chiisa-na koojoo datta.*) その会社は元は小さな工場だった.

originate *vi.* (come into being) haʳssee suru 発生する Ⅰ; oʳko¬ru 起こる Ⓒ: The accident originated from carelessness. (*Sono jiko wa fuchuui kara okotta.*) その事故は不注意から起こった.
— *vt.* (bring into being) ... o oʳko¬su ...を起こす Ⓒ; haʳjimeru 始める Ⅴ: originate a new movement (*atarashii uñdoo o okosu*) 新しい運動を起こす.

ornament *n.* soʳoshokuhiñ 装飾品; kaʳzari 飾り: ornaments for a Christmas tree (*Kurisumasu tsurii no kazari*) クリスマスツリーの飾り.
— *vt.* ... o kaʳzaru ...を飾る Ⓒ: ornament a room with flowers (*heya o hana de kazaru*) 部屋を花で飾る.

orphan *n.* koʳji 孤児; miʳnashi¬go みなしご.

orthodox *adj.* seʳetoo-teki na 正統的な; oʳosodo¬kkusu na オーソドックスな: the orthodox way of singing (*seetoo-teki na utaikata*) 正統的な歌い方.

ostrich *n.* daʳchoo だちょう.

other *adj.* **1** (different) hoʳka no ほかの; taʳ¬ no 他の; beʳtsu no 別の: Please check other airlines' flights. (*Hoka no kookuugaisha no biñ o shirabete kudasai.*) ほかの航空会社の便を調べてください.
2 (being the one left of two) moʳo ippo¬o no もう一方の; taʳho¬o no 他方の: Show me your other hand. (*Moo ippoo no te o mise nasai.*) もう一方の手を見せなさい.
3 (being the ones left of several) noʳkori no 残りの: The other children returned home. (*Nokori no kodomo-tachi wa ie ni kaerima-shita.*) 残りの子どもたちは家に帰りました.
4 (opposite) muʳkoogawa no 向こう側の: the other side of the road (*dooro no mukoogawa*) 道路の向こう側.
5 (recently past) koʳno aida no この間の: the other night (*kono aida no yoru*) この間の夜 / the other day (*señjitsu*) 先日.
— *pron.* **1** (different thing) hoʳka no mono¬ ほかの物; (different people) hoʳka no hito¬ ほかの人: Show me some others. (*Hoka no mono o misete kudasai.*) ほかの物を見せてください. / She is always kind to others. (*Kanojo wa itsu-mo hoka no hito-tachi ni yasashii.*) 彼女はいつもほかの人たちに優しい.
2 (the remaining ones) moʳo ippo¬o no mono¬ [hi¬to¬] もう一方の物[人];

soᵗnoˡ hoka no moᵗnoˡ [hiˡtoˡ] そのほ
かの物[人]: Two of them went out
and the others stayed behind. (*Futari ga dekake sono hoka no hito
wa ato ni nokorimashita.*) 二人が出
かけそのほかの人は後に残りました.

otherwise *adv.* **1** (in different
way) beᵗtsu no hoohoo de 別の方法
で: He seems to think otherwise.
(*Kare wa betsu no kañgaekata no
yoo da.*) 彼は別の考え方のようだ.
2 (in other respects) soᵗnoˡ ta no
teᵗñ deˡ wa その他の点では: The rent
is high, but is otherwise satisfactory. (*Yachiñ ga takai ga sono ta
no teñ de wa mooshibuñ arimaseñ.*)
家賃が高いがその他の点では申し分ありま
せん.
— *conj.* saˡmo nai to さもないと:
Start at once, otherwise you will be
late. (*Sugu shuppatsu shi nasai.
Samo nai to okuremasu yo.*) すぐ出
発しなさい. さもないと遅れますよ.

ouch *int.* iˡtaiˡ 痛い: Ouch! Stop
that! (*Itai. Yamete.*) 痛い. やめて.

ought *aux. v.* **1** [obligation] ⟨verb⟩
beˡki de aru …べきである; ⟨verb⟩-naˡ-
kereba iˡkenai …なければいけない:
We ought to follow rules. (*Wareware wa kisoku ni shitagau beki
de aru.*) われわれは規則に従うべきである.
/ You ought to be more careful.
(*Motto ki o tsukenakereba ikenai.*)
もっと気をつけなければいけない.
2 [indicates what is advisable]
⟨verb⟩-ta hoˡo ga iˡi …したほうがいい:
You ought to see a doctor. (*Isha ni
mite moratta hoo ga ii yo.*) 医者に
診てもらったほうがいいよ.
3 [likelihood] …ha zu da …はずだ:
The weather ought to be fine
tomorrow. (*Ashita wa teñki ni
naru hazu da.*) あしたは天気になるはず
だ.

ounce *n.* oˡñsu オンス: This parcel
weighs 20 ounces. (*Kono tsutsumi
wa omosa ga nijuu-oñsu aru.*) この
包みは重さが 20 オンスある. ★ In Japan
the metric system is used.

our *pron.* waˡtashiˡ-tachi no 私たち

の; [formal] waˡreware no われわれ
の: This is our house. (*Kore ga
watashi-tachi no ie desu.*) これが私
たちの家です.

ours *pron.* waˡtashiˡ-tachi no
(moˡnoˡ) 私たちの(もの); [formal]
waˡreware no monoˡ われわれの(も
の): This car is ours. (*Kono
kuruma wa watashi-tachi no
(mono) desu.*) この車は私たちの(もの)
です.

ourselves *pron.* **1** [reflexive use]
jiˡbun jiˡshiñ o [ni] 自分自身を[に].
★ Usually not translated: We were
careful not to hurt ourselves.
(*Watashitachi wa kega o shinai-
yoo ni ki o tsuketa.*) 私たちはけがをし
ないように気をつけた.
2 [emphatic use] jiˡbuˡñ-tachi de
自分たちで; waˡtashi-tachi jiˡshiñ
de わたしたち自身で: We went to see
him ourselves. (*Watashi-tachi wa
watashi-tachi jishiñ de kare ni ai
ni itta.*) 私たちは私たち自身で彼に会い
に行った.

out *adv.* **1** (away from inside) soˡto
e [ni] 外へ[に]: He has gone out to
lunch. (*Kare wa chuushoku ni
soto e ikimashita.*) 彼は昼食に外へ
行きました.
2 (from inside) ⟨verb⟩-dasu …出す:
take out a pen (*peñ o toridasu*) ペン
を取り出す.
3 (far away) toˡoku no 遠くの: He
lives out in the country. (*Kare wa
tooku no inaka ni suñde imasu.*)
彼は遠くの田舎に住んでいます.
4 (completely) suˡkkaˡri すっかり: I
am tired out. (*Watashi wa sukkari
tsukarete shimatta.*) 私はすっかり疲れ
てしまった.
5 (clearly) haˡkkiˡri to はっきりと:
speak out (*hakkiri to noberu*) はっき
りと述べる.
— *adj.* **1** (absent) fuˡzai de 不在
で; gaˡishutsu shite (iru) 外出して(い
る): My father is out. (*Chichi wa
gaishutsu-chuu desu.*) 父は外出中で
す.
2 (being outside) soˡto ni dete

(iru) 外に出て(いる): He is out in the garden. (*Kare wa niwa ni dete imasu.*) 彼は庭に出ています.

3 (in the open) de]te (iru) 出て(いる): The stars are out. (*Hoshi ga dete iru.*) 星が出ている.

out of ... *prep.* **1** (from inside of) ... kara ...から: He went out of the room. (*Kare wa heya kara dete itta.*) 彼は部屋から出て行った.

2 (from) ... kara ...から: drink out of a cup (*kappu kara nomu*) カップから飲む.

3 (without) ... ga ki]rete ...が切れて: My car is out of gas. (*Watashi no kuruma wa gasorin ga kireta.*) 私の車はガソリンが切れた.

outbreak *n.* ha]ssee 発生; bo]ppatsu 勃発: an outbreak of dysentery (*sekiri no hassee*) 赤痢の発生 / an outbreak of war (*sensoo no boppatsu*) 戦争の勃発.

outcome *n.* ke]kka 結果; se]eka 成果: the outcome of an election (*senkyo no kekka*) 選挙の結果.

outdoor *adj.* ko]gai no 戸外の; o]kugai no 屋外の / an outdoor swimming pool (*okugai puuru*) 屋外プール.

outdoors *adv.* ko]gai de [e] 戸外で[へ]; o]kugai de [e] 屋外で[へ]; u]chi no so]to de [e] 家の外で[へ]: It is cold outdoors. (*Soto wa samui.*) 外は寒い.

— *n.* ko]gai 戸外; o]kugai 屋外.

outer *adj.* so]togawa no 外側の; ga]ibu no 外部の: the outer walls (*soto-kabe*) 外壁 / the outer world (*gaikai*) 外界.

outfit *n.* so]obi i]sshiki 装備一式: a traveling outfit (*ryokoo yoogu isshiki*) 旅行用具一式.

outlet *n.* **1** (passage) de]guchi 出口; ha]keguchi はけ口: an outlet for water (*mizu no hakeguchi*) 水のはけ口.

2 (means of releasing) ha]keguchi はけ口: an outlet for emotion (*kanjoo no hakeguchi*) 感情のはけ口.

3 (wall socket) ko]nsento コンセン

ト: put a plug in the outlet (*puragu o konsento ni sashikomu*) プラグをコンセントに差し込む.

outline *n.* **1** (line) ri]nkaku 輪郭; ga]ikee 外形: draw an outline (*rinkaku o egaku*) 輪郭を描く.

2 (summary) ga]iryaku 概略; ta]iyoo 大要; a]ramashi あらまし: give an outline of a story (*hanashi no taiyoo o noberu*) 話の大要を述べる.

— *vt.* **1** (draw) ... no ri]nkaku o ega]ku ...の輪郭を描く ⃝C; rya]kuzu o ka]ku 略図を書く ⃝C: He outlined the map of his town. (*Kare wa machi no ryakuzu o kaita.*) 彼は町の略図を書いた.

2 (give the main features of) ... no a]ramashi [ga]iryaku] o nobe]ru ...のあらまし[概略]を述べる ⃝V: I outlined my plans to my friends. (*Watashi wa keekaku no gairyaku o tomodachi ni hanashita.*) 私は計画の概略を友だちに話した.

outlook *n.* **1** (view) na]game] 眺め; mi]harashi 見晴らし: His house has a splendid outlook. (*Kare no uchi wa nagame ga subarashii.*) 彼の家は眺めがすばらしい.

2 (prospect) mi]tooshi 見通し; mi]komi 見込み: The business outlook for this year is bright. (*Kotoshi no keeki no mitooshi wa akarui.*) ことしの景気の見通しは明るい.

output *n.* **1** (quantity) se]esa]ndaka 生産高: The output of this factory is increasing. (*Kono koojoo no seesandaka wa fuete imasu.*) この工場の生産高は増えています.

2 (of a computer) a]utopu]tto アウトプット.

3 (power) shu]tsu]ryoku 出力.

outrage *n.* ra]nboo 乱暴; bo]okoo 暴行: acts of outrage (*booryoku kooi*) 暴力行為.

— *vt.* ... o fu]ngai saseru ...を憤慨させる ⃝V: I was outraged by his behavior. (*Watashi wa kare no taido ni fungai shita.*) 私は彼の態度に憤慨した.

outrageous *adj.* bu]sa]hoo na 無

作法な; ho̍ogai na 法外な: outrageous behavior (*busahoo na furumai*) 無作法な振る舞い / an outrageous price (*hoogai na nedañ*) 法外な値段.

outside *adv.* so̍to ni [de, e, wa] 外に[で, へ, は]: play outside (*soto de asobu*) 外で遊ぶ / take one's dog outside (*inu o soto e tsuredasu*) 犬を外へ連れ出す.

— *adj.* so̍togawa no 外側の; ga̍ibu no 外部の: the outside door (*sotogawa no to*) 外側の戸 / outside interference (*gaibu kara no kañshoo*) 外部からの干渉.

— *n.* so̍togawa no 外側; ga̍ibu 外部: I painted the outside of the house white. (*Watashi wa ie no sotogawa o peñki de shiroku nutta.*) 私は家の外側をペンキで白く塗った.

outsider *n.* bu̍gali̍sha 部外者; yo̍somono よそ者: They did not welcome outsiders. (*Kare-ra wa yosomono o kañgee shinakatta.*) 彼らはよそ者を歓迎しなかった.

outskirts *n.* ko̍ogai 郊外: He lives on the outskirts of Tokyo. (*Kare wa Tookyoo no koogai ni suñde imasu.*) 彼は東京の郊外に住んでいます.

outstanding *adj.* **1** (prominent) me̍da̍tsu 目立つ; ke̍sshutsu shita [shite iru] 傑出した[している]: He is outstanding as a statesman. (*Kare wa seejika to shite kesshutsu shite iru.*) 彼は政治家として傑出している.
2 (unpaid) mi̍ha̍rai no 未払いの; (unsettled) mi̍ka̍liketsu no 未解決の: That problem is still outstanding. (*Sono moñdai wa mada mikaiketsu da.*) その問題はまだ未解決だ.

outward *adj.* **1** (of the outside) ga̍imeñ-teki na 外面的な; u̍wabe no うわべの: You should not judge by the outward appearance of things. (*Monogoto no gaikeñ dake de hañdañ shite wa ikenai.*) 物事の外見だけで判断してはいけない.
2 (going out) so̍to e mu̍kau 外へ

向かう: an outward voyage (*yuki no kooro*) 行きの航路.

— *adv.* **1** (toward the outside) so̍to e [ni] 外へ[に]: This door opens outward. (*Kono to wa soto ni hirakimasu.*) この戸は外に開きます.
2 (away from home) ko̍ku̍gai e [ni] 国外へ[に]: a ship bound outward (*gaikoku yuki no fune*) 外国行きの船.

oven *n.* o̍obuñ オーブン; te̍ñpi 天火: a microwave oven (*deñshi-reñji*) 電子レンジ.

over *prep.* **1** (above) ... no u̍e ni [o] ...の上に[を]: Our plane flew over the mountains. (*Watashi-tachi no hikooki wa yama no ue o toñda.*) 私たちの飛行機は山の上を飛んだ.
2 (covering) ... o o̍otte ...をおおって: She put her hands over her face. (*Kanojo wa ryoote de kao o ootta.*) 彼女は両手で顔をおおった.
3 (across) ... o ko̍ete ...を越えて: My house is over the hill. (*Watashi no ie wa ano oka o koeta tokoro ni arimasu.*) 私の家はあの丘を越えた所にあります.
4 (more than) ... i̍joo no ...以上の; ... o ko̍ete ...を越えて: He is over eighty. (*Kare wa hachijuu o koete imasu.*) 彼は80を越えています.
5 (while doing) ⟨verb⟩-nagara ...ながら: We talked over a glass of beer. (*Watashi-tachi wa biiru o nominagara hanashita.*) 私たちはビールを飲みながら話した.
6 (during) ... ni wa̍tatte ...にわたって; ... no a̍ida ...の間: I read the book over the weekend. (*Watashi wa shuumatsu no aida-juu sono hoñ o yoñda.*) 私は週末の間じゅうその本を読んだ.
7 (concerning) ... no ko̍to̍ de ...のことで: They quarreled over money. (*Kare-ra wa o-kane no koto de iiarasotta.*) 彼らはお金のことで言い争った.

— *adv.* **1** (above) jo̍ohoo ni 上方に; zu̍joo ni 頭上に: A helicopter flew over. (*Herikoputaa ga zujoo o toñde itta.*) ヘリコプターが頭上を飛んで行った.

2 (to another side) mu「koo e 向こうへ; so「chira [ko「chira] e そちら[こちら]へ: go over to France (*Furañsu e wataru*) フランスへ渡る / I'll be right over. (*Sugu ni sochira e ikimasu.*) すぐにそちらへ行きます.

3 (again) mo「o ichido もう一度: I had to do it over. (*Watashi wa sore o moo ichido yaranakereba naranakatta.*) 私はそれをもう一度やらなければならなかった.

over there *adv.* a「soko ni [de] あそこに[で]: The ticket machine is over there. (*Keñbaiki wa asoko desu.*) 券売機はあそこです.

— *adj.* (finished) o「watte (iru) 終わって(いる): The rainy season is over. (*Tsuyu ga owatta.*) 梅雨が終わった.

over- *pref.* **1** ka「do ni 過度に; a「mari ni o「oku あまりに多く: overestimate (*kadai-hyooka suru*) 過大評価する / overproduction (*seesañ-kajoo*) 生産過剰.

2 u「e ni [kara] 上に[から]: overhang (*... no ue ni sashikakaru*) …の上にさしかかる.

overall *adj.* ze「ñtai no 全体の; ze「ñbu no 全部の: the overall length of a bridge (*hashi no zeñchoo*) 橋の全長.

— *adv.* ze「ñbu de 全部で: How much will it cost overall? (*Zeñbu de ikura kakarimasu ka?*) 全部でいくらかかりますか.

overcoat *n.* o「obaa オーバー; ga「too 外套: put on [take off] an overcoat (*oobaa o kiru [nugu]*) オーバーを着る[脱ぐ].

overcome *vt.* **1** (defeat) ... ni u「chikatsu …に打ち勝つ C; ... o ma「kasu …を負かす C: overcome all difficulties (*arayuru koñnañ ni uchikatsu*) あらゆる困難に打ち勝つ / overcome the enemy (*teki o makasu*) 敵を負かす.

2 (exhaust) ... o ma「irase「ru …を参

らせる V: I was overcome by the heat. (*Atsusa de maitta.*) 暑さで参った.

overdo *vt.* **1** (carry too far) ... o ya「ri-sugi「ru …をやりすぎる V; do 「o kosu 度を越す C: Don't overdo exercise. (*Uñdoo o yari-suginai yoo ni.*) 運動をやりすぎないように.

2 (cook too long) ... o ni-「sugi「ru …を煮すぎる V; ya「ki-sugi「ru 焼きすぎる V: overdo a piece of meat (*niku o yaki-sugiru*) 肉を焼きすぎる.

overflow *vi.* **1** (flow over the edge) a「fure「ru あふれる V; (of a river) ha「ñrañ suru はんらんする I: This river overflows every year. (*Kono kawa wa maitoshi hañrañ suru.*) この川は毎年はんらんする.

2 (be filled) i「ppai de a「ru いっぱいである C; a「riama「ru あり余る C: My heart is overflowing with joy. (*Watashi no kokoro wa yorokobi de ippai desu.*) 私の心は喜びでいっぱいです.

— *vt.* ... kara a「furede「ru …からあふれ出る V: The crowd overflowed the hall into the street. (*Guñshuu wa hooru kara toori ni afuredeta.*) 群衆はホールから通りにあふれ出た.

overhead *adv.* zu「joo ni 頭上に; ta「kaku 高く: The moon was shining overhead. (*Tsuki ga zujoo ni kagayaite ita.*) 月が頭上に輝いていた.

overlap *vi.* ka「sanaru 重なる C: overlapping tiles (*kasanatte iru tairu*) 重なっているタイル / His vacation overlapped with mine. (*Kare no kyuuka ga watashi no kyuuka to kasanatta.*) 彼の休暇が私の休暇と重なった.

overlook *vt.* **1** (look down on) ... o mi「orosu …を見下ろす C; mi「watasu 見渡す C: We overlook the lake from the room. (*Heya kara mizuumi ga miwatasemasu.*) 部屋から湖が見渡せます.

2 (fail to see) ... o mi「otosu …を見落とす C: overlook a typographical error (*goshoku o miotosu*) 誤植を見落とす.

3 (ignore) ... o oｒome ni miｒru ...を大目に見る Ⓥ; miｒnogasu 見逃す Ⓒ: overlook bad conduct (*warui okonai o oome ni miru*) 悪い行いを大目に見る.

overnight *adv.* **1** (during the night) yoｒdooshi 夜通し; hiｒtobañjuu 一晩中: stay overnight (*hitobañ tomaru*) ひと晩泊まる.

2 (suddenly) iｒchiｒya ni shite 一夜にして; toｒtsuzeñ 突然: become rich overnight (*ichiya ni shite kanemochi ni naru*) 一夜にして金持ちになる.

— *adj.* iｒppaku no 一泊の: an overnight trip (*ippaku-ryokoo*) 一泊旅行.

overseas *adv.* kaｒigai e 海外へ; gaｒikoku e 外国へ: go overseas (*gaikoku e iku*) 外国へ行く.

— *adj.* kaｒigai no 海外の; kaｒigaimuke no 海外向けの: make an overseas trip (*kaigai-ryokoo o suru*) 海外旅行をする / an overseas broadcast (*kaigaimuke no hoosoo*) 海外向けの放送.

overtake *vt.* **1** (catch up with) ... ni oｒitsuｒku ...に追いつく Ⓒ: I overtook him at the entrance. (*Watashi wa iriguchi no tokoro de kare ni oitsuita.*) 私は入り口の所で彼に追いついた.

2 (pass) ... o oｒikoｒsu ...を追い越す Ⓒ: He overtook several cars. (*Kare wa nañ-dai mo kuruma o oikoshita.*) 彼は何台も車を追い越した.

overthrow *vt.* **1** (overturn) ... o hiｒkkurikaｒesu ...をひっくり返す Ⓒ; taｒoｒsu 倒す Ⓒ: The tree was overthrown by the storm. (*Sono ki wa arashi de taosareta.*) その木は嵐で倒された.

2 (defeat) ... o taｒoｒsu ...を倒す: overthrow the government (*seefu o taosu*) 政府を倒す.

— *n.* daｒtoo 打倒; teｒñpuku 転覆.

overtime *n.* choｒoka kiｒñmu 超過勤務; zaｒñgyoo 残業: do overtime (*zañgyoo o suru*) 残業をする.

— *adj.* jiｒkaｒñgai no 時間外の; choｒoka kiｒñmu no 超過勤務の:

overtime pay (*chooka kiｒñmu teate*) 超過勤務手当.

— *adv.* jiｒkaｒñgai de 時間外で; choｒoka kiｒñmu de 超過勤務で: work overtime (*jikañgai kiñmu o suru*) 時間外勤務をする.

overturn *vi.* hiｒkkurikaｒeru ひっくり返る Ⓒ; teｒñpuku suru 転覆する Ⓘ: The boat was hit by a wave and it overturned. (*Booto wa oonami o ukete teñpuku shita.*) ボートは大波を受けて転覆した.

— *vt.* ... o hiｒkkurikaｒesu ...をひっくり返す Ⓒ; taｒoｒsu 倒す Ⓒ: The rebels overturned the government. (*Hañrañguñ ga seefu o taoshita.*) 反乱軍が政府を倒した.

overwhelm *vt.* **1** (defeat) ... o aｒttoo suru ...を圧倒する Ⓘ: be overwhelmed by the enemy (*teki ni attoo sareru*) 敵に圧倒される.

2 (overcome) ... o maｒiraseｒru ...を参らせる Ⓥ; uｒchihishiｒgu 打ちひしぐ Ⓒ: She was overwhelmed with grief. (*Kanojo wa kanashimi ni uchihishigareta.*) 彼女は悲しみに打ちひしがれた.

overwhelming *adj.* aｒttoo-teki na 圧倒的な: an overwhelming majority (*attoo-teki na tasuu*) 圧倒的な多数.

overwork *vt.* ... o haｒtarakasesugiｒru ...を働かせすぎる Ⓥ; koｒkushi suru 酷使する Ⓒ: overwork a horse (*uma o kokushi suru*) 馬を酷使する.

— *vi.* haｒtaraki-sugiｒru 働きすぎる Ⓥ: He always overworks. (*Kare wa itsu-mo hataraki-sugiru.*) 彼はいつも働きすぎる.

— *n.* kaｒroo 過労; haｒtaraki-sugi 働きすぎ: fall ill from overwork (*karoo de byooki ni naru*) 過労で病気になる.

owe *vt.* **1** (be in debt) ... ni kaｒri ga aｒru ...に借りがある Ⓒ: I owe her five thousand yen. (*Watashi wa kanojo ni go-señ-eñ kari ga aru.*) 私は彼女に5千円借りがある.

2 (be obliged) ... no oｒkage da ...のおかげだ: I owe my success to you.

(*Watashi no seekoo wa anata no okage desu.*) 私の成功はあなたのおかげです.

3 (be under an obligation) ... no gi⌐mu ga aru ...の義務がある C; 〈verb〉-ba na⌐ra¬nai ...ばならない: I owe him my thanks. (*Kare ni o-ree o iwanakereba naranai.*) 彼にお礼を言わなければならない.
— *vi.* sha⌐kki¬ñ shite iru 借金している V.

owl *n.* fu⌐kuro¬o ふくろう; mi⌐mi¬zuku みみずく.

own *adj.* ji⌐buñ ji¬shiñ no 自分自身の: I saw it with my own eyes. (*Watashi wa sore o jibuñ jishiñ no me de mimashita.*) 私はそれを自分自身の目で見ました.
— *pron.* ji⌐buñ ji¬shiñ no mo¬no¬ 自分自身のもの: This house is my own. (*Kono ie wa watashi jishiñ no mono desu.*) この家は私自身のものです.
— *vt.* (possess) ... o mo⌐tte iru ...を持っている C; sho⌐yuu suru 所有する I: I own a car. (*Watashi wa kuruma o motte imasu.*) 私は車を持っています.

owner *n.* mo⌐chi¬nushi 持ち主; sho⌐yu¬usha 所有者: Who is the owner of this land? (*Kono tochi no shoyuusha wa dare desu ka?*) この土地の所有者はだれですか. / a store owner (*shooteñ kee-eisha*) 商店経営者.

ox *n.* o⌐ushi 雄牛. ★ '*Ushi*' is the generic term for ox, bull, cow, etc.

oxygen *n.* sa⌐ñso 酸素: an oxygen mask (*sañso masuku*) 酸素マスク.

oyster *n.* ka⌐ki かき(牡蠣).

P

pace *n.* **1** (step) ho⌐choo 歩調: walk at a slow pace (*yukkuri shita hochoo de aruku*) ゆっくりした歩調で歩く.
2 (stride) i⌐p-po 1歩; ho⌐haba 歩幅: step backward two steps (*ni-ho ushiro e sagaru*) 2歩後へ下がる.
3 (rate of speed) ha⌐yasa 速さ; pe⌐esu ペース: He worked at his own pace. (*Kare wa jibuñ no peesu de hataraita.*) 彼は自分のペースで働いた.
— *vi.* yu⌐kku¬ri a⌐ru¬ku ゆっくり歩く C: pace up and down (*ittari kitari suru*) 行ったり来たりする.
— *vt.* ... o a⌐rukima¬waru ...を歩き回る C: pace the floor (*yuka no ue o arukimawaru*) 床の上を歩き回る.

Pacific *adj.* Ta⌐ihe¬eyoo no 太平洋の: the Pacific Ocean (*Taiheeyoo*) 太平洋.
— *n.* Ta⌐ihe¬eyoo 太平洋.

pack *vt.* **1** (wrap together) ... o ni⌐zu¬kuri suru ...を荷造りする I; ko⌐ñpoo suru 梱包する I: pack goods (*shinamono o koñpoo suru*) 品物を梱包する.
2 (put together) ... o tsu⌐me¬ru ...を詰める V: pack one's clothes into a suitcase (*irui o suutsukeesu ni tsumeru*) 衣類をスーツケースに詰める.
3 (fill) ... o tsu⌐mekomu ...を詰め込む C: pack passengers into a bus (*jookyaku o basu ni tsumekomu*) 乗客をバスに詰め込む.
— *vi.* ni⌐zu¬kuri o suru 荷造りをする I: Please help me pack. (*Nizukuri o suru no o tetsudatte kudasai.*) 荷造りをするのを手伝ってください.
— *n.* **1** (bundle) tsu⌐tsumi 包み; ni⌐motsu 荷物: carry a pack on one's back (*nimotsu o seotte hakobu*) 荷物を背負って運ぶ.
2 (packet) hi⌐to¬-hako ひと箱: I smoke two packs of cigarettes a day. (*Watashi wa ichi-nichi ni tabako o futa-hako suimasu.*) 私は1日にたばこを二箱吸います.

package *n.* tsu⌐tsumi 包み; ko⌐zu¬tsumi 小包: open a package (*kozu-*

tsumi o akeru) 小包を開ける.

— *vt.* ... o ni「zu」kuri suru ...を荷造
りする ⟦: package books (*hoñ o nizukuri suru*) 本を荷造りする.

packet *n.* chi「isa-na tsu「tsumi」 小さ
な包み; ta「ba 束: a packet of letters
(*tegami no taba*) 手紙の束.

pad *n.* **1** (cushion) tsu「me」mono 詰
め物; a「temono 当て物; pa「ddo パッ
ド.

2 (sheets of paper) tsu「zuri つづり: a
writing pad (*biñseñ no tsuzuri*) 便
箋のつづり.

— *vt.* ... ni tsu「me」mono o suru ...
に詰め物をする ⟦: pad a cushion
with cotton (*kusshoñ ni wata o tsumeru*) クッションに綿を詰める.

page *n.* pe「eji ページ: turn pages
(*peeji o mekuru*) ページをめくる.

pail *n.* ba「ketsu バケツ; te「oke 手おけ:
carry water in a pail (*mizu o teoke
de hakobu*) 水を手おけで運ぶ.

pain *n.* **1** (hurting) i「tami」 痛み: I
have a dull pain in my back. (*Watashi wa senaka ni nibui itami ga
aru.*) 私は背中に鈍い痛みがある.

2 (suffering) ku「tsuu 苦痛; ku「noo
苦悩: She is in pain. (*Kanojo wa
kunoo shite iru.*) 彼女は苦悩している.

take pains *vi.* ho「ne」o o「ru 骨を
折る ⟦: He took pains to complete
the work. (*Kare wa sono shigoto o
kañsee suru no ni hone o otta.*) 彼
はその仕事を完成するのに骨を折った.

painful *adj.* **1** (sore) i「ta」i 痛い: a
painful wound (*itai kizu*) 痛い傷.

2 (unpleasant) tsu「rai つらい; ku-
「rushi」i 苦しい: That job was painful to me. (*Sono shigoto wa watashi ni wa tsurakatta.*) その仕事は私
にはつらかった.

painkiller *n.* chi「ñtsu」uzai 鎮痛剤;
i「tamidome 痛み止め.

paint *vt.* **1** (decorate) ... o pe「ñki
de nuru ...をペンキで塗る ⟦: I
painted the chair white. (*Watashi
wa isu o peñki de shiroku nutta.*)
私はいすをペンキで白く塗った.

2 (make a picture) e「l o kaku 絵をか
く ⟦: She painted flowers. (*Kanojo

wa hana no e o kaita.*) 彼女は花の絵
をかいた.

— *vi.* e「l o kaku 絵をかく ⟦: paint
in oils (*aburae o kaku*) 油絵をかく.

— *n.* **1** (of decoration) pe「ñki ペン
キ; to「ryoo 塗料: put bright paint
on the walls (*kabe ni akarui peñki
o nuru*) 壁に明るいペンキを塗る / Wet
[Fresh] Paint. (*Peñki nuritate.*) ペン
キ塗り立て.

2 (of a picture) e「nogu 絵の具:
water paints (*suisai enogu*) 水彩絵
の具.

painter *n.* **1** (artist) e「kaki」絵かき;
ga「ka 画家: a painter in the Japanese style (*Nihoñ gaka*) 日本画家.

2 (person whose work is painting)
pe「ñkiya ペンキ屋.

painting *n.* **1** (picture) e「l 絵:
make a painting (*e o kaku*) 絵をかく.

2 (work) e「l o kaku ko「to」絵をかくこ
と: I like painting. (*Watashi wa e o
kaku koto ga suki desu.*) 私は絵をか
くことが好きです.

pair *n.* **1** (two things) hi「to」-kumi ひ
と組; i「t-tsui 一対: a pair of gloves
(*tebukuro hito-kumi*) 手袋ひと組 / a
pair of shoes (*kutsu is-soku*) 靴1
足.

2 (single thing) i「k-ko 1個; i「t-
chaku 1着: a pair of glasses (*megane ik-ko*) 眼鏡1個 / a pair of
trousers (*zuboñ it-chaku*) ズボン1
着 / a pair of scissors (*hasami it-
choo*) はさみ1丁.

3 (man and woman) hi「to」-kumi no
dañjo 1組の男女; ka「ppuru カップル:
a nice pair (*niai no kappuru*) 似合い
のカップル.

4 (male and female animals) tsu-
「gai つがい: two pairs of doves (*hato
futa-tsugai*) はと二つがい.

— *vt.* ... o ku「miawase」ru ...を組み
合わせる Ⓥ; tsu「i ni suru 対にする ⟦:
The two of them were paired at
the party. (*Sono futari ga paatii de
tsui ni natta.*) その二人がパーティーで
対になった.

pajamas *n.* pa「jama パジャマ; ne-
「maki 寝巻き: a pair of pajamas

(*pajama it-chaku*) パジャマ 1 着.

pal *n.* to「modachi 友だち; na「kama」仲間; na「ka」yoshi 仲良し: a drinking pal (*nomi tomodachi*) 飲み友だち.

palace *n.* (royal residence) kyu「u-deñ 宮殿; (large house) da「i-te」e-taku 大邸宅.

pale *adj.* **1** (wan) ka「oiro ga waru」i 顔色が悪い; a「ojiro」i 青白い: You look pale. (*Kaoiro ga warui desu ne.*) 顔色が悪いですね.
2 (faint) u「sui 薄い; a「wa」i 淡い: pale blue (*usui aoiro*) 薄い青色.
—— *vi.* **1** (turn pale) a「ozame」ru 青ざめる ▽: She paled at the news. (*Kanojo wa sono shirase o kiite aozameta.*) 彼女はその知らせを聞いて青ざめた.
2 (seem less important) i「roa」sete mi「e」ru 色あせて見える ▽: My work pales beside yours. (*Watashi no sakuhiñ wa kimi no to narabu to iroasete mieru.*) 私の作品は君のと並ぶと色あせて見える.

palm *n.* te-「no」-hira 手のひら: read a person's palm (*hito no tesoo o miru*) 人の手相を見る.

pamphlet *n.* pa「ñfuretto パンフレット; sho「osa」sshi 小冊子.

pan *n.* hi「ranabe 平なべ: a frying-pan (*furaipañ*) フライパン.

pancake *n.* pa「ñke」eki パンケーキ.

panel *n.* **1** (flat piece of wood) pa「neru パネル.
2 (group of people) -da「ñ 団; i「ñ 委員: a panel of judges (*shiñsaiñ-dañ*) 審査委員団 / a panel of experts (*señmoñka no iiñ-tachi*) 専門家の委員たち.
3 (section containing dials) ke「eki-bañ 計器盤.

panic *n.* kyo「okoo 恐慌; pa「nikku パニック: They were in a panic. (*Ka-re-ra wa kyookoo jootai ni atta.*) 彼らは恐慌状態にあった.

panorama *n.* pa「norama パノラマ; ze「ñkee 全景.

pant *vi.* a「e」gu あえぐ ⓒ; ha「a haa i」u はあはあ言う ⓒ: He panted as he

ran. (*Kare wa hashiri-nagara haa haa itta.*) 彼は走りながらはあはあ言った.
—— *vt.* ... o a「egi-na」gara i「u ...をあえぎながら言う ⓒ: He panted out the news. (*Kare wa aegi-nagara sono shirase o tsutaeta.*) 彼はあえぎながらその知らせを伝えた.

panties *n.* pa「ñtii パンティー.

pants *n.* (trousers) zu「bo」ñ ズボン; (short undergarment) pa「ñtsu パンツ.

paper *n.* **1** (thin sheet) ka「mi」紙: two sheets of paper (*ni-mai no kami*) 2 枚の紙 / a paper bag (*kami-bukuro*) 紙袋 / a paper cup (*kami-koppu*) 紙コップ.
2 (newspaper) shi「ñbuñ 新聞: subscribe to a paper (*shiñbuñ o koo-doku suru*) 新聞を購読する.
3 (exam paper) to「oañ(yo」oshi) 答案(用紙): mark papers (*tooañ o sai-teñ suru*) 答案を採点する.
4 (document) sho「rui 書類; bu「ñ-sho 文書: look through papers (*shorui ni me o toosu*) 書類に目を通す.
5 (report) ro「ñbuñ 論文; re「po」oto レポート: a paper on the population problem (*jiñkoo-moñdai ni kañ-suru roñbuñ*) 人口問題に関する論文.
—— *vt.* ... ni ka「mi」o ha「ru ...に紙をはる ⓒ: paper a wall green (*kabe ni guriiñ no kabegami o haru*) 壁にグリーンの壁紙をはる.

parachute *n.* pa「rashu」uto パラシュート; ra「kka」sañ 落下傘.

parade *n.* ko「oshiñ 行進; gyo「ore-tsu 行列; pa「re」edo パレード.
—— *vi.* ko「oshiñ suru 行進する Ⅰ: They paraded through the streets. (*Kare-ra wa gairo o kooshiñ shita.*) 彼らは街路を行進した.

paradise *n.* te「ñgoku 天国; ra「ku-eñ 楽園: This amusement park is a paradise for children. (*Kono yuueñ-chi wa kodomo no teñgoku da.*) この遊園地は子どもの天国だ.

paradox *n.* gya「kusetsu 逆説; pa-「rado」kkusu パラドックス.

paragraph *n.* da「ñraku 段落; pa」-ragurafu パラグラフ.

parallel adj. 1 (running side by side) he「ekoo no 平行の; he「ekoo shita [shite iru] 平行した[している]: parallel lines (heekoosen) 平行線 / The highway runs parallel to the railroad. (Kansendooro wa senro to heekoo shite hashitte iru.) 幹線道路は線路と平行して走っている.
2 (similar) ni「te iru 似ている; ru「iji shita [shite iru] 類似した[している]: Our case is parallel to yours. (Wareware no jijoo wa anata no baai to nite iru.) われわれの事情はあなたの場合と似ている.
— n. 1 (line) he「ekoosen 平行線: draw a parallel (heekoosen o hiku) 平行線を引く.
2 (likeness) ru「iji (suru mono) 類似(するもの); hi「tteki (suru mono) 匹敵(するもの): There is no parallel to it. (Sore ni hitteki suru mono wa nai.) それに匹敵するものはない.
3 (of latitude) i「dosen 緯度線.
— vt. ... to he「ekoo shite iru ...と平行している Ⅴ: The road parallels the river. (Dooro wa kawa to heekoo shite iru.) 道路は川と平行している.

paralysis n. ma「hi まひ: infantile paralysis (shooni mahi) 小児まひ.

paralyze vt. ... o ma「hi saseru ...をまひさせる Ⅴ; fu「zui ni suru 不随にする Ⅰ: My right arm was paralyzed. (Migi ude ga mahi shita.) 右腕がまひした.

parcel n. tsu「tsumi 包み; ko「zu「tsumi 小包: wrap up a parcel (kozutsumi o hoosoo suru) 小包を包装する.

pardon n. yu「rushi 許し: ask for a person's pardon (hito no yurushi o kou) 人の許しを乞う.
— vt. yu「ru「su 許す Ⅽ: Please pardon me my rudeness. (Busahoo o o-yurushi kudasai.) 無作法をお許しください. / Pardon me for interrupting. (Ojama shite sumimasen.) おじゃましてすみません.

I beg your pardon. [apologizing]

(Gomen nasai.) ごめんなさい. / [disturbing someone] (Shitsuree shimasu.) 失礼します. / I beg your pardon for being late. (Okurete sumimasen.) 遅れてすみません. / I beg your pardon? [asking for repetition] (Osoreirimasu ga moo ichido osshatte kudasai.) 恐れ入りますがもう一度おっしゃってください.

----

parent n. o「ya」 親: one's parents (ryooshin) 両親 / a parent bird (oya-dori) 親鳥.

parenthesis n. (ma「ru)ka「kko (丸)かっこ; pa「aren パーレン.

park n. 1 (public piece of ground) ko「oen 公園: play in the park (kooen de asobu) 公園で遊ぶ.
2 (car park) chu「ushajoo 駐車場.
— vt. ... o chu「usha suru ...を駐車する Ⅰ: Can I park my car on this street? (Kono dooro ni kuruma o chuusha suru no i desu ka?) この道路に車を駐車してもいいです か.

parking n. chu「usha 駐車: No Parking. (Chuusha kinshi.) 駐車禁止.

parliament n. (of the United Kingdom) gi「kai 議会; ko「kkai 国会. ★ In Japan, 'the Diet' is called 'kokkai,' and in the United States 'the Congress' is called 'gikai.'

part n. 1 (section) bu「bun 部分: parts of the body (karada no bubun) 体の部分.
2 (piece) bu「hin 部品: automobile parts (jidoosha no buhin) 自動車の部品.
3 (region) chi「ho」o 地方; chi「iki 地域: What part of Japan are you from? (Nihon no dono chihoo no shusshin desu ka?) 日本のどの地方の出身ですか.
4 (of a book) -bu 部; he「n 編: a novel in three parts (san-bu-saku no shoosetsu) 3部作の小説.
5 (duty) ya「kuwa」ri 役割; ya「kume」役目: play a part (yakume o hatasu) 役目を果たす.

take part vi. ... ni sa「nka suru ...に参加する Ⅰ: I took part in the

demonstration. (*Watashi wa sono demo ni sañka shita.*) 私はそのデモに参加した.
— *vt.* **1** (divide) ... o waˈkeˈru ...分ける Ⅴ; buˈñkatsu suru 分割する Ⅰ: part an apple in two (*riñgo o futatsu ni wakeru*) りんごを二つに分ける.
2 (separate) ... o hiˈkihanaˈsu ...を引き離す Ⓒ: part the fighting children (*keñka shite iru kodomo-tachi o hikihanasu*) けんかしている子どもたちを引き離す.
— *vi.* waˈkareˈru 別れる Ⅴ: We parted at the station. (*Watashi-tachi wa eki de wakareta.*) 私たちは駅で別れた.

partial *adj.* **1** (of a part) iˈchibuˈ-buñ no 一部分の; buˈbuñ-teki na 部分的な: partial damage (*bubuñ-teki na soñgai*) 部分的な損害.
2 (biased) fuˈkoˈohee na 不公平な: A referee should not be partial. (*Shiñpañ wa fukoohee de atte wa naranai.*) 審判は不公平であってはならない.

partially *adv.* buˈbuñ-teki ni 部分的に: The bridge is partially completed. (*Hashi wa bubuñ-teki ni kañsee shite iru.*) 橋は部分的に完成している.

participate *vt.* ... ni saˈñka suru ...に参加する Ⅰ; kaˈnyuu suru 加入する Ⅰ: I participated in the discussion. (*Watashi wa sono tooroñ ni sañka shita.*) 私はその討論に参加した.

participation *n.* saˈñka 参加; kaˈnyuu 加入: participation in a demonstration (*demo ni sañka suru koto*) デモに参加すること.

particle *n.* **1** chiˈisa-na tsubu 小さな粒: A particle of dirt was in my eye. (*Gomi no tsubu ga me ni haitta.*) ごみの粒が目に入った.
2 (of grammar) fuˈheñkaˈshi 不変化詞.

particular *adj.* **1** (specific) toˈku-tee no 特定の: Do you have a particular color in mind? (*Tokutee no iro o o-kañgae desu ka?*) 特定の色

をお考えですか.
2 (special) toˈkubetsu no 特別の: pay particular attention (*tokubetsu no chuui o harau*) 特別の注意を払う / I have nothing particular to do today. (*Kyoo wa toku ni suru koto wa arimaseñ.*) きょうは特にすることはありません.
3 (hard to please) yaˈkamashiˈi やかましい; kiˈmuzukashiˈi 気難しい: He is particular about his food. (*Kare wa taberu mono ni yakamashii.*) 彼は食べるものにやかましい.
— *n.* (details) shoˈosai 詳細: go into particulars (*shoosai ni wataru*) 詳細にわたる.

particularly *adv.* toˈku ni 特に; toˈriwake とりわけ: I am particularly interested in Japanese history. (*Watashi wa toku ni Nihoñ no rekishi ni kyoomi o motte imasu.*) 私は特に日本の歴史に興味を持っています.

partly *adv.* **1** (not wholly) iˈchi-buˈbuñ wa 一部分は; buˈbuñ-teki ni 部分的に: The bridge was partly damaged. (*Hashi wa ichibu ga kowareta.*) 橋は一部が壊れた.
2 (to some extent) aˈru teˈedo ある程度: His success is due partly to luck. (*Kare no seekoo wa aru teedo uñ ni yoru.*) 彼の成功はある程度運による.

partner *n.* **1** (one of two people) aˈiˈte 相手; paˈatonaa パートナー: a tennis partner (*tenisu no paatonaa*) テニスのパートナー / a dancing partner (*dañsu no aite*) ダンスの相手.
2 (person who shares in the same activity) naˈkamaˈ 仲間; kyoˈo-ryokuˈsha 協力者: a partner in business (*jigyoo no nakama*) 事業の仲間.

partnership *n.* kyoˈoryoku 協力; teˈekee 提携: I entered into partnership with him. (*Watashi wa kare to teekee shita.*) 私は彼と提携した.

part-time *adj.* paˈato-taˈimu no パートタイムの; aˈrubaˈito no アルバイト

の; hi「jo」okiñ no 非常勤の: a part-time job (*paato-taimu no shigoto*) パートタイムの仕事 / a part-time teacher (*hijookiñ kooshi*) 非常勤講師.

party *n.* 1 (gathering) a「tsumari」集まり; pa「atii パーティー; ka「i 会: give a party (*paatii o hiraku*) パーティーを開く / a welcome party (*kañgeekai*) 歓迎会.

2 (political group) se「etoo 政党; to「o 党: the Liberal Democratic Party (*Jimiñ-too*) 自民党.

3 (group of people) i「chidañ 一団; i「kkoo 一行: The party left for London. (*Ikkoo wa Roñdoñ e mukatte tachimashita.*) 一行はロンドンへ向かって立ちました. / a party of tourists (*kañkoodañ*) 観光団.

pass *vi.* 1 (of time) ta「tsu たつ C; ke「eka suru 経過する I: Two weeks have passed since I came to Tokyo. (*Tookyoo e kite kara ni-shuukañ tachimashita.*) 東京へ来てから2週間たちました.

2 (go) to「oru 通る C; su「sumu 進む C: Where are we passing now? (*Ima doko o tootte iru no desu ka?*) 今どこを通っているのですか.

3 (go away) ki「esa」ru 消え去る C; na「kunaru なくなる C: The pain has passed. (*Itami ga nakunarimashita.*) 痛みがなくなりました.

4 (of a test) (… ni) u「ka」ru (…に)受かる C; go「okaku suru 合格する I: pass in an examination (*shikeñ ni gookaku suru*) 試験に合格する.

— *vt.* 1 (go through) … o to「oru …を通る C: No one is allowed to pass this gate. (*Dare mo kono moñ o tooru koto wa dekimaseñ.*) だれもこの門を通ることはできません.

2 (overtake) … o o「iko」su …を追い越す C: He passed my car on the road. (*Kare wa michi de watashi no kuruma o oikoshita.*) 彼は道で私の車を追い越した.

3 (hand) … o wa「tasu …を渡す C; ma「wasu 回す C: Please pass this note to him. (*Kono memo o kare

ni watashite kudasai.*) このメモを彼に渡してください.

4 (of a test) … ni u「ka」ru 受かる C; go「okaku suru 合格する I: She passed her driving test. (*Kanojo wa uñteñmeñkyo shikeñ ni ukatta.*) 彼女は運転免許試験に受かった.

5 (enact) … o ka「ketsu suru …を可決する I: The Diet passed the bill. (*Kokkai wa sono giañ o kaketsu shita.*) 国会はその議案を可決した.

6 (give a judgment) … o ku「dasu …を下す C; no「be」ru 述べる V: The judge passed sentence on him. (*Saibañkañ wa kare ni hañketsu o kudashita.*) 裁判官は彼に判決を下した.

7 (spend) … o su「go」su …を過ごす C: I passed the summer in the country. (*Watashi wa inaka de natsu o sugoshita.*) 私は田舎で夏を過ごした.

8 (of a ball) … o pa「su suru …をパスする I: pass a ball to a person (*hito ni booru o pasu suru*) 人にボールをパスする.

— *n.* 1 (free ticket) mu「ryoo-nyuujo」okeñ 無料入場券: a boarding pass (*toojoo-keñ*) 搭乗券.

2 (narrow path) to「oge」峠; ya「ma」-michi 山道: cross a pass (*tooge o kosu*) 峠を越す.

3 (successful result in an examination) go「okaku 合格; kyu「udai 及第.

passage *n.* 1 (way) tsu「uro 通路: Don't leave your bicycle in the passage. (*Tsuuro ni jiteñsha o oite wa ikemaseñ.*) 通路に自転車を置いてはいけません.

2 (act of passing) tsu「ukoo 通行; tsu「uka 通過: block a person's passage (*hito no tsuukoo o jama suru*) 人の通行をじゃまする.

3 (journey) ryo「koo 旅行; (by sea) fu「ne no ta「bi」船の旅; (by air) so「ra no ta「bi」空の旅.

4 (of time) na「gare 流れ; ke「eka 経過: the passage of time (*toki no nagare*) 時の流れ.

5 (part of writing) i「ssetsu 一節: a passage from the Bible (*seesho

kara no issetsu) 聖書からの一節.

passenger *n.* joﾞokyaku 乗客; ryoﾞkaku 旅客: passengers on a bus (*basu no jyookyaku*) バスの乗客 / a passenger ship (*kyakuseñ*) 客船.

passing *adj.* **1** (going by) tsuﾞuka suru 通過する; toﾞorigakari no 通りがかりの: catch a passing taxi (*toorigakari no takushii o tsukamaeru*) 通りがかりのタクシーを捕まえる.
2 (lasting only a short time) iﾞchiﾞi no 一時の; tsuﾞkanoma no つかの間の: passing joys (*tsukanoma no yorokobi*) つかの間の喜び.
— *n.* tsuﾞuka 通過; tsuﾞukoo 通行: No passing. (*Oikoshi kiñshi.*) 追い越し禁止.

passion *n.* **1** (strong feeling) geﾞkijoo 激情; joﾞonetsu 情熱: a person of passion (*joonetsu-teki na hito*) 情熱的な人.
2 (strong liking) neﾞtchuu 熱中; neﾞtsuai 熱愛: He has a passion for golf. (*Kare wa gorufu ni netchuu shite iru.*) 彼はゴルフに熱中している.
3 (strong anger) geﾞkido 激怒: fly into a passion (*katto natte okoru*) かっとなって怒る.

passionate *adj.* joﾞonetsu-teki na 情熱的な; neﾞtsuretsu na 熱烈な: a passionate woman (*joonetsu-teki na josee*) 情熱的な女性 / a passionate speech (*netsuretsu na eñzetsu*) 熱烈な演説.

passive *adj.* **1** (not active) juﾞdoo-teki na 受動的な; shoﾞokyoku-teki na 消極的な: He is passive in everything. (*Kare wa nani o suru ni mo shookyoku-teki da.*) 彼は何をするにも消極的だ.
2 (of grammar) uﾞkemi no 受身の; juﾞdootai no 受動態の: a passive sentence (*judoo buñ*) 受動文.
— *n.* (passive voice) juﾞdootai 受動態.

passport *n.* paﾞsupoﾞoto パスポート; ryoﾞkeñ 旅券: I lost my passport. (*Pasupooto o nakushimashita.*) パスポートをなくしました. / a passport number (*ryokeñ-bañgoo*) 旅券番号.

past *adj.* **1** (gone by) suﾞgisatta 過ぎ去った; kaﾞko no 過去の: The danger is past now. (*Kikeñ wa moo sugisatta.*) 危険はもう過ぎ去った. / He spoke about his past life. (*Kare wa jibuñ no kako no seekatsu ni tsuite katatta.*) 彼は自分の過去の生活について語った.
2 (recent) koﾞno この; señ- 先-: She has been ill for the past three days. (*Kono mikka-kañ kanojo wa byooki deshita.*) この三日間彼女は病気でした. / the past week (*señshuu*) 先週.
3 (former) moﾞto no 元の: the past president (*moto no shachoo*) 元の社長.
4 (of grammar) kaﾞko no 過去の: the past form of a verb (*dooshi no kakokee*) 動詞の過去形.
— *n.* **1** (the time gone by) kaﾞko 過去; suﾞgisatta kotoﾞ 過ぎ去ったこと: Let's forget the past. (*Kako no koto wa wasuremashoo.*) 過去のことは忘れましょう.
2 (one's earlier life) kaﾞko no reﾞkishi 過去の歴史: Nobody knows his past. (*Kare no kako wa dare mo shiranai.*) 彼の過去はだれも知らない.
— *prep.* **1** (beyond) ... o toﾞorisuﾞgite ...を通り過ぎて: A taxi went past me. (*Takushii ga watashi no yoko o toorisugite itta.*) タクシーが私の横を通り過ぎて行った. / I rode past my stop. (*Norikoshite shimaimashita.*) 乗り越してしまいました.
2 (after) ... o suﾞgite ...を過ぎて: It's a quarter past eight. (*Hachi-ji juugo-fuñ sugi desu.*) 8時15分過ぎです. / I got up at half past six. (*Watashi wa roku-ji hañ ni okimashita.*) 私は6時半に起きました.
— *adv.* toﾞorisuﾞgite 通り過ぎて: He ran past. (*Kare wa hashitte toorisugita.*) 彼は走って通り過ぎた.

paste *n.* **1** (mixture of flour and water) noﾞri のり: seal an envelope with paste (*fuutoo o nori de haru*) 封筒をのりではる.
2 (any mixture) neﾞriﾞmono 練り物;

pe˺esuto ペースト: tooth paste (neri hamigaki) 練り歯磨き.

— vt. ... o no˹ri˺ de ha˹ru ...をのりではる C: paste pictures in an album (shashiñ o arubamu ni haru) 写真をアルバムにはる.

pasture n. bo˹kujoo 牧場.

pat vt. ... o ka˹ruku tata˺ku ...を軽くたたく C: He patted me on the shoulder. (Kare wa watashi no kata o karuku tataita.) 彼は私の肩を軽くたたいた.

— n. ka˹ruku tata˺ku ko˹to˺ 軽くたたくこと.

patch n. 1 (piece of material) tsu˹gikire 継ぎきれ; a˹tenuno 当て布: a jacket with patches on the elbows (hiji ni atenuno o shita uwagi) ひじに当て布をした上着.

2 (bandage put on an eye) ga˹ñtai 眼帯.

3 (small section of land) ha˹take 畑: a patch of cabbages (kyabetsu-batake) キャベツ畑.

— vt. ... ni tsu˹gi o ateru ...に継ぎを当てる V: patch trousers (zuboñ ni tsugi o ateru) ズボンに継ぎを当てる.

patent n. to˹kkyo 特許; to˹kkyo˺-keñ 特許権: take out a patent on an invention (hatsumee no tokkyo o toru) 発明の特許を取る.

— adj. to˹kkyo no aru 特許のある: a patent lock (tokkyo no aru joo) 特許のある錠.

— vt. ... no to˹kkyo o toru ...の特許を取る C.

path n. 1 (narrow way) ko˹michi 小道; ho˹soˈmichi 細道: a mountain path (yama no komichi) 山の小道.

2 (course) to˹ori˺michi 通り道; ki˹doo 軌道: the path of a satellite (eesee no kidoo) 衛星の軌道.

pathetic adj. (causing pity) a˹ware na 哀れな; i˹tamashi˺i 痛ましい: a pathetic sight (itamashii kookee) 痛ましい光景.

patience n. ni˹ñtai 忍耐; shi˹ñboo 辛抱: She waited for the delayed bus with patience. (Kanojo wa okureta basu o shiñboo-zuyoku matta.) 彼女は遅れたバスを辛抱強く待った.

patient n. ka˹ñja 患者; byo˹oniñ 病人: The doctor examined the patient carefully. (Isha wa kañja o teenee ni shiñsatsu shita.) 医者は患者を丁寧に診察した.

— adj. ga˹mañ-zuyo˺i 我慢強い; shi˹ñboo-zuyo˺i 辛抱強い: He is a very patient man. (Kare wa totemo gamañ-zuyoi otoko da.) 彼はとても我慢強い男だ.

patriot n. a˹iko˺kusha 愛国者.

patriotism n. a˹iko˺kushiñ 愛国心.

patrol vt. ... o ju˹ñkai suru ...を巡回する I; pa˹toro˺oru suru パトロールする I: Policemen patrol this street. (Keekañ ga kono toori o patorooru shite imasu.) 警官がこの通りをパトロールしています.

— n. ju˹ñkai 巡回; pa˹toro˺oru パトロール: a patrol car (patokaa) パトカー.

patron n. (supporter) ko˹oe˺ñsha 後援者; (customer) o˹tokui お得意; hi˹iki˺kyaku ひいき客.

pattern n. 1 (design) mo˹yoo 模様; ga˹ra 柄: What does this pattern represent? (Kono moyoo wa nani o arawashimasu ka?) この模様は何を表しますか.

2 (model) ge˹ñkee 原型; ka˹ta-gami 型紙: make a dress from a pattern (katagami ni shitagatte doresu o tsukuru) 型紙に従ってドレスを作る.

3 (way of acting) ka˹ta˺ 型; yo˹o-shiki 様式; pa˹ta˺añ パターン: new patterns of life (atarashii seekatsu yooshiki) 新しい生活様式.

— vt. (copy) ... o ma˹neru ...をまねる V; te˹ho˺ñ to suru 手本とする I: He patterned himself after his father. (Kare wa chichioya o tehoñ to shita.) 彼は父親を手本とした.

pause n. sho˹okyu˺ushi 小休止; chu˹udañ 中断: a pause in the conversation (kaiwa no chuudañ) 会話の中断.

— vi. 1 (make a brief stop) cho˹tto ya⌐su¬mu ちょっと休む Ⓒ; to⌐gire¬-ru 途切れる Ⓥ: He paused to light a cigarette. (*Kare wa chotto te o yasumete tabako ni hi o tsuketa.*) 彼はちょっと手を休めてたばこに火をつけた. **2** (hesitate) ta⌐mera¬u ためらう Ⓒ: pause to find the right word (*tekitoo na kotoba o motomete tamerau*) 適当な言葉を求めてためらう.

pave *vt.* ... o ho⌐soo suru ...を舗装する ▯: pave a road with asphalt (*dooro o asufaruto de hosoo suru*) 道路をアスファルトで舗装する.

pavement *n.* **1** (surface) ho⌐soo 舗装: a crack in the pavement (*hosoo no hibiware*) 舗装のひび割れ. **2** (sidewalk) ho⌐doo 歩道: walk on the pavement (*hodoo o aruku*) 歩道を歩く.

paw *n.* a⌐shi¬ 足: a dog's paw (*inu no ashi*) 犬の足.
— *vt.* ... o a⌐shi¬ de kaku ...を足でかく Ⓒ: The bull pawed the ground. (*Ushi wa ashi de jimeñ o kaita.*) 牛は足で地面をかいた.

pay *vt.* **1** (give money) ... o ha⌐ra¬u ...を払う Ⓒ; shi⌐hara¬u 支払う Ⓒ: I paid two thousand yen for the book. (*Watashi wa sono hoñ ni niseñ-eñ haratta.*) 私はその本に 2 千円払った. **2** (settle) ... o shi⌐hara¬u ...を支払う Ⓥ: I haven't paid taxes yet. (*Zeekiñ o mada shiharatte imaseñ.*) 税金をまだ支払っていません. **3** (give) ... o ha⌐ra¬u ...を払う Ⓒ: pay attention to the matter (*sono moñdai ni chuui o harau*) その問題に注意を払う. **4** (make) su⌐ru する ▯: pay a call on a person (*hito o hoomoñ suru*) 人を訪問する.
— *vi.* **1** (give money) shi⌐harai o suru 支払いをする ▯; da⌐ikiñ o ha⌐ra¬u 代金を払う Ⓒ: Can I pay with a traveler's check? (*Ryokoo kogitte de shiharai dekimasu ka?*) 旅行小切手で支払いできますか. **2** (be profitable) hi⌐kia¬u 引き合う Ⓒ; mo⌐oka¬ru もうかる Ⓒ: This

business doesn't pay. (*Kono shoobai wa hikiawanai.*) この商売は引き合わない.
— *n.* kyu⌐uryoo 給料; ho⌐oshuu 報酬: We get our pay at the end of the month. (*Watashi-tachi wa kyuuryoo o getsumatsu ni moraimasu.*) 私たちは給料を月末にもらいます.

payment *n.* **1** (paying) shi⌐harai 支払い: What are the terms of payment? (*Shiharai jookeñ wa doo natte imasu ka?*) 支払い条件はどうなっていますか. **2** (amount) shi⌐haraikiñ 支払い金.

pea *n.* e⌐ñdo¬omame えんどう豆.

peace *n.* **1** (freedom from war) he⌐ewa 平和: The country is now at peace. (*Sono kuni wa ima heewa desu.*) その国はいま平和です. **2** (freedom from disturbance) chi⌐añ 治安; chi⌐tsujo 秩序: keep the peace (*chiañ o mamoru*) 治安を守る. **3** (freedom from anxiety) he⌐eoñ 平穏; ya⌐suragi 安らぎ: peace of mind (*kokoro no yasuragi*) 心のやすらぎ.

peaceful *adj.* **1** (be fond of peace) he⌐ewa o kono¬mu 平和を好む; he⌐ewa-teki na 平和的な: solve a dispute by peaceful means (*fuñsoo o heewa-teki na shudañ de kaiketsu suru*) 紛争を平和的な手段で解決する. **2** (quiet) shi⌐zuka na 静かな; he⌐ewa na 平和な: spend a peaceful day (*shizuka na ichi-nichi o sugosu*) 静かな一日を過ごす.

peach *n.* mo⌐mo 桃; (fruit) mo⌐mo no mi 桃の実; (tree) mo⌐mo no ki¬ 桃の木. ★ Japanese peaches are larger than those of Europe and North America.

peak *n.* **1** (top of a mountain) sa⌐ñchoo 山頂; mi⌐ne¬ 峰: The mountain peak was covered with snow. (*Yama no mine wa yuki ni oowarete ita.*) 山の峰は雪におおわれていた. **2** (highest point) sa⌐ikoo¬teñ 最高点; ze⌐tchoo 絶頂: She was at the peak of her popularity. (*Kanojo wa* niŋki no zetchoo ni atta.) 彼女は人気の絶頂にあった.

— vi. cho｢oteŋ [pi'iku] ni ta｢ssuru 頂点[ピーク]に達する ①: The sales peaked in June. (*Uriage wa rokugatsu ni piiku ni tasshita.*) 売り上げは6月にピークに達した.

peanut n. pi'inattsu ピーナッツ; ra'kka'see 落花生.

pear n. se'eyo'o-nashi 西洋なし.
★ Japanese pears (simply '*nashi*') are round.

pearl n. shi'ŋju 真珠: an imitation pearl (*jiŋzoo shiŋju*) 人造真珠.
— adj. shi'ŋju no 真珠の; shi'ŋjuiro no 真珠色の: pearl earrings (*shiŋju no mimikazari*) 真珠の耳飾り.

peasant n. no'ofu 農夫; no'omiŋ 農民.

pebble n. ko'ishi 小石.

peck vi. (of a bird) ku'chibashi de tsutsu'ku くちばしでつつく ②: The bird pecked at my finger. (*Sono tori wa watashi no yubi o kuchibashi de tsutsuita.*) その鳥は私の指をくちばしでつついた.
— vt. ... o tsu'tsu'ku ...をつつく ②; tsu'iba'mu ついばむ ②: The birds pecked the corn. (*Tori-tachi wa toomorokoshi o tsuibaŋda.*) 鳥たちはとうもろこしをついばんだ.

peculiar adj. 1 (strange) myo'o na 妙な; he'ŋ na 変な: This meat has a peculiar taste. (*Kono niku wa heŋ na aji ga suru.*) この肉は変な味がする.
2 (special) to'kubetsu no 特別の; to'kushu no 特殊の: a matter of peculiar interest (*toku ni kyoomibukai moŋdai*) 特に興味深い問題.
3 (distinctive) to'kuyuu no 特有の; do'kutoku no 独特の: a custom peculiar to Japan (*Nihoŋ tokuyuu no shuukaŋ*) 日本特有の習慣.

pedal n. pe'daru ペダル.
— vt. pe'daru o fuŋde hashirase'ru ペダルを踏んで走らせる Ⓥ: pedal a bicycle (*jiteŋsha o hashiraseru*) 自転車を走らせる.

pedestrian n. ho'ko'osha 歩行者.
— adj. to'ho no 徒歩の; ho'ko'osha no 歩行者の: a pedestrian crossing (*oodaŋhodoo*) 横断歩道.

pediatrician n. sho'onika'i-i 小児科医.

peel vt. 1 (of fruit and vegetables) ... no ka'wa' o mu'ku ...の皮をむく ②: peel a banana (*banana no kawa o muku*) バナナの皮をむく.
2 (of a tree) ... no ka'wa' o hagu ...の皮をはぐ ②: peel the bark off a tree (*ki no kawa o hagu*) 木の皮をはぐ.
— n. ka'wa' 皮: the peel of an apple (*riŋgo no kawa*) りんごの皮.

peep vi. no'zokimi suru のぞき見する ①: He peeped through the keyhole. (*Kare wa kagiana kara nozokimi shita.*) 彼は鍵穴からのぞき見した.
— n. no'zokimi のぞき見; chi'ra'ri to miru ko'to' ちらりと見ること: She took a peep at him. (*Kanojo wa kare o chirari to mita.*) 彼女は彼をちらりと見た.

peer n. 1 (nobleman) ki'zoku 貴族.
2 (equal in rank) do'ootoo no mono' 同等の者; do'oryoo 同僚; na'kama' 仲間: He asked for the opinion of his peers. (*Kare wa dooryoo no ikeŋ o motometa.*) 彼は同僚の意見を求めた.

peg n. to'mekugi 止めくぎ; ka'kekugi 掛けくぎ: hang one's coat on a peg (*uwagi o kakekugi ni kakeru*) 上着を掛けくぎにかける / a hat peg (*booshikake*) 帽子掛け.
— vt. ... o ku'gi de tomeru ...をくぎで留める Ⓥ: peg a notice to the wall (*keeji o kugi de kabe ni tomeru*) 掲示をくぎで壁に留める.

pen[1] n. (instrument for writing) pe'ŋ ペン: write with a pen (*peŋ de kaku*) ペンで書く / a ballpoint pen (*boorupeŋ*) ボールペン / a fountain pen (*maŋneŋhitsu*) 万年筆.

pen[2] n. (small enclosure) ka'koi 囲い; o'ri' おり.
— vt. ... o ka'koi [o'ri'] ni i'reru ...を囲い[おり]に入れる Ⓥ.

penalty *n.* **1** (punishment) keʼebatsu 刑罰; baʼtsu 罰: The penalty for drunken driving is heavy. (*Yopparai uñteñ no batsu wa omoi.*) 酔っぱらい運転の罰は重い.

2 (fine) baʼkkiñ 罰金: pay a penalty for violating the rules (*kisoku ihañ no bakkiñ o harau*) 規則違反の罰金を払う.

pencil *n.* eʼñpitsu 鉛筆: sharpen a pencil (*eñpitsu o kezuru*) 鉛筆を削る / the lead of a pencil (*eñpitsu no shiñ*) 鉛筆のしん / a mechanical pencil (*shaapu peñshiru*) シャープペンシル.

pendant *n.* peʼñdañto ペンダント.

penetrate *vt.* **1** (enter) ... o tsuʼranuʼku ...を貫く C; kaʼñtsuu suru 貫通する I: The bullet penetrated the wall. (*Dañgañ wa kabe o kañtsuu shita.*) 弾丸は壁を貫通した.

2 (spread) ... ni hiʼrogaru ...に広がる C: The smell penetrated the room. (*Sono nioi ga heya ni hirogatta.*) そのにおいが部屋に広がった.

— *vi.* tsuʼranuʼku 貫く C; shiʼmitoʼoru しみ通る C: The rain penetrated through my coat. (*Ame ga uwagi ni shimitootta.*) 雨が上着にしみ通った.

peninsula *n.* haʼñtoo 半島.

pension *n.* neʼñkiñ 年金; oʼñkyuu 恩給: He lives on a pension. (*Kare wa neñkiñ de kurashite iru.*) 彼は年金で暮らしている.

people *n.* **1** (persons) hiʼtoʼbito 人人; hiʼto 人: The street was crowded with people. (*Toori wa hito de koñzatsu shite ita.*) 通りは人で混雑していた. / There were thirty people present at the meeting. (*Kai ni wa sañjuu-niñ ga shusseki shita.*) 会には 30 人が出席した.

2 (nation) koʼkumiñ 国民: the Japanese people (*Nihoñ kokumiñ*) 日本国民.

3 (race) miʼñzoku 民族: There are many English-speaking peoples. (*Eego o hanasu miñzoku wa ooi.*) 英語を話す民族は多い.

pepper *n.* koʼshoʼo こしょう: put

pepper on meat (*niku ni koshoo o furikakeru*) 肉にこしょうを振りかける.

— *vt.* ... ni koʼshoʼo o fuʼrikakeʼru ...にこしょうを振りかける V.

per *prep.* ... ni tsuʼki ...につき: What is the fee per day? (*Ryookiñ wa ichi-nichi ni tsuki ikura desu ka?*) 料金は一日につきいくらですか. / 60 kilometers per hour (*jisoku rokujuk-kiro*) 時速 60 キロ.

perceive *vt.* **1** (become aware of) ... ni kiʼzuʼku ...に気づく C: I perceived the difference between them. (*Watashi wa ryoosha no chigai ni kizuita.*) 私は両者の違いに気づいた.

2 (understand) ... ga waʼkaʼru ...がわかる C: I quickly perceived his joke. (*Watashi wa kare no jooku ga sugu ni wakatta.*) 私は彼のジョークがすぐにわかった.

percent *n.* paʼaseʼñto パーセント: Ten percent equals one 'wari'. (*Jup-paaseñto wa ichi-wari desu.*) 10 パーセントは 1 割です. / an interest of three percent (*sañ-paaseñto no risoku*) 3 パーセントの利息.

percentage *n.* **1** (rate) hyaʼkubuʼñritsu 百分率; buʼai 歩合: on a percentage basis (*buaisee de*) 歩合制で.

2 (part) waʼriai 割合; buʼbuñ 部分: The greater percentage of students go to university. (*Seeto no daibubuñ wa daigaku e ikimasu.*) 生徒の大部分は大学へ行きます.

perception *n.* chiʼkaku 知覚: a person of keen perception (*chikaku no surudoi hito*) 知覚の鋭い人.

perfect *adj.* **1** (complete) kaʼñzeñ na 完全な; kaʼñpeki na 完ぺきな: a perfect crime (*kañzeñ-hañzai*) 完全犯罪 / Nobody is perfect. (*Kañpeki na hito wa inai.*) 完ぺきな人はいない.

2 (exact) seʼekaku na 正確な: draw a perfect circle (*seekaku na eñ o egaku*) 正確な円を描く.

3 (excellent) saʼiteki no 最適の: moʼoshibuñ no naʼi 申し分のない: He is perfect for this job. (*Kare*

wa kono shigoto ni saiteki da.) 彼
はこの仕事に最適だ.

4 (thorough) ma⌐ttaku˺ no まったく
の: He is a perfect stranger. (*Ano
hito wa mattaku shiranai hito desu.*) あの人はまったく知らない人です.

— *vt.* ... o ka⌐ñsee suru ...を完成す
る ①: perfect one's theory (*jibuñ
no riroñ o kañsee suru*) 自分の理論
を完成する.

perfection *n.* ka⌐ñzeñ 完全; ka⌐ñ-
peki 完ぺき; ka⌐ñsee 完成: Perfection is difficult to achieve. (*Kañpeki o kisuru no wa muzukashii.*)
完ぺきを期するのは難しい.

perfectly *adv.* ka⌐ñzeñ ni 完全に;
ka⌐ñpeki ni 完ぺきに: He speaks
Japanese perfectly. (*Kare wa
Nihoñgo o kañpeki ni hanashimasu.*) 彼は日本語を完ぺきに話します.

perform *vt.* **1** (carry out) ... o ji⌐k-
koo suru ...を実行する ①; ha⌐ta˺su
果たす ©: I performed the task faith-
fully. (*Watashi wa sono shigoto
o chuujitsu ni hatashita.*) 私はその
仕事を忠実に果たした.

2 (of a play) ... o jo⌐oeñ suru ...を上
演する ①; (of music) e⌐ñsoo suru 演
奏する ①: perform a musical (*myuu-
jikaru o jooeñ suru*) ミュージカルを上
演する.

— *vi.* (of a play) (... o) e⌐ñjiru (...
を)演じる Ⓥ; (of music) e⌐ñsoo suru
演奏する ①: perform on the violin
(*baioriñ o eñsoo suru*) バイオリンを演
奏する.

performance *n.* **1** (of a play)
ko⌐oeñ 公演; jo⌐oeñ 上演; (of music) e⌐ñsoo 演奏: What time does
the performance begin? (*Kaieñ wa
nañ-ji desu ka?*) 開演は何時ですか.

2 (doing) ji⌐kkoo 実行; su⌐ikoo 遂
行: the performance of one's duty
(*shokumu no jikkoo*) 職務の実行.

3 (ability) se⌐enoo 性能; no⌐o-
ryoku 能力: engine performance
(*eñjiñ no seenoo*) エンジンの性能.

performer *n.* (of a play) e⌐ñgi˺sha
演技者; (of music) e⌐ñso˺osha 演奏
者.

perfume *n.* **1** (liquid) ko⌐osui 香
水: put on perfume (*koosui o tsukeru*) 香水をつける.

2 (smell) ka⌐ori 香り; ni⌐o˺i におい:
the perfume of roses (*bara no kaori*) ばらの香り.

perhaps *adv.* ko⌐to ni yoru to こと
によると; ta⌐buñ 多分; o⌐so˺raku 恐ら
く: Perhaps he will come. (*Tabuñ
kare wa kuru deshoo.*) 多分彼は来
るでしょう.

peril *n.* ki⌐keñ 危険: He faced
many perils. (*Kare wa ooku no
kikeñ ni chokumeñ shita.*) 彼は多く
の危険に直面した.

period *n.* **1** (length of time) ki⌐kañ
期間; ji⌐ki 時期: He stayed here for
a short period of time. (*Kare wa
tañkikañ koko ni taizai shita.*) 彼は
短期間ここに滞在した.

2 (punctuation mark) pi⌐riodo ピリ
オド; shu⌐ushi˺fu 終止符: put a period at the end of a sentence (*buñ
no saigo ni shuushifu o utsu*) 文の
最後に終止符を打つ.

3 (division of a school day) ji⌐geñ
時限; ji⌐kañ 時間: the third period
(*dai sañ-jigeñ*) 第3時限 / a study
period (*jishuu-jikañ*) 自習時間.

4 (era) ji⌐dai 時代: the Kamakura
period (*Kamakura jidai*) 鎌倉時代.

5 (menstrual period) se⌐eri 生理;
ge⌐kkee 月経.

periodical *n.* te⌐eki kañko˺obutsu
定期刊行物; za⌐sshi 雑誌.

perish *vi.* (die) shi⌐nu 死ぬ ©; (be
destroyed) ho⌐robi˺ru 滅びる Ⓥ:
Hundreds of people perished in
the earthquake. (*Nañ-byaku-niñ
mo no hito ga sono jishiñ de shiñda.*) 何百人もの人がその地震で死んだ.

permanent *adj.* e⌐ekyuu no 永久
の; fu⌐heñ no 不変の: permanent
peace (*eekyuu no heewa*) 永久の平
和 / a permanent domicile (*hoñ-
seki*) 本籍.

— *n.* (permanent wave) pa⌐ama-
ne˺ñto パーマネント; pa⌐ama パーマ: A
soft [tight] permanent, please. (*Karuku [Kitsuku] paama shitekuda-*

sai.) 軽く[きつく]パーマしてください.

permission *n.* kyo「ka 許可; yu-「rushi」 許し; ni「ñka 認可: The teacher gave me permission to leave early. (*Señsee wa watashi ni sootai no kyoka o kureta.*) 先生は私に早退の許可をくれた.

permit *vt.* ... o kyo「ka suru ...を許可する 1; yu「ru」su 許す C: My father permitted me to go abroad. (*Chichi wa watashi ga gaikoku e iku no o yurushite kureta.*) 父は私が外国へ行くのを許してくれた. / Smoking is not permitted here. (*Koko wa kiñeñ desu.*) ここは禁煙です.
— *vi.* yu「ru」su 許す C: We will depart tomorrow if the weather permits. (*Teñkoo ga yuruseba asu shuppatsu shimasu.*) 天候が許せば明日出発します.
— *n.* kyo「ka」shoo 許可証; meñ-kyo「shoo 免許証: an International Driving Permit (*Kokusai uñteñ meñkyoshoo*) 国際運転免許証.

perpetual *adj.* **1** (continuing) ta-「ema no na」i 絶え間のない: perpetual noise (*taema no nai soo-oñ*) 絶え間のない騒音.
2 (lasting) e「ekyuu no 永久の; fu-「kyuu no 不朽の: perpetual fame (*fukyuu no meesee*) 不朽の名声.

perplex *vt.* ... o na「yamase」ru ...を悩ませる V; to「owaku saseru 当惑させる V: The problem perplexed me. (*Sono moñdai wa watashi o nayamaseta.*) その問題は私を悩ませた.

persecute *vt.* ... o ha「kugai suru ...を迫害する 1: They were persecuted for their religion. (*Kare-ra wa shiñkoo no tame ni hakugai sareta.*) 彼らは信仰のために迫害された.

persevere *vi.* (... o) shi「ñboo suru (...を)辛抱する 1; ga「ñba」ru がんばる C: He persevered in his work. (*Kare wa shigoto o gañbatta.*) 彼は仕事をがんばった.

persist *vt.* **1** (continue firmly) ko-「shitsu suru 固執する 1; a「ku」made to「osu あくまで通す C: persist in one's opinion (*jibuñ no ikeñ o aku-*

made mo toosu*) 自分の意見をあくまでも通す.
2 (last) tsu「zuku 続く C: The rain persisted for three days. (*Ame wa mikka tsuzuita.*) 雨は三日続いた.

persistent *adj.* **1** (continuing) ko「shitsu suru 固執する; shi「tsuko」i しつこい: a persistent salesman (*shitsukoi seerusumañ*) しつこいセールスマン.
2 (lasting) na「gaku tsu「zuku 長く続く: a persistent rain (*nagaku tsu-zuku ame*) 長く続く雨.

person *n.* hi「to 人; (human being) ni「ñgeñ 人間: He is a very nice person. (*Kare wa totemo yoi hito desu.*) 彼はとてもよい人です. / How many persons are there in the room? (*Heya ni wa nañ-niñ imasu ka?*) 部屋には何人いますか.

personal *adj.* **1** (private) ko「jiñ no 個人の; ko「jiñ-teki na 個人的な: This is my personal affair. (*Kore wa watashi no kojiñ-teki na moñ-dai desu.*) これは私の個人的な問題です.
2 (one's own) ji「buñ no 自分の: This camera is for my personal use. (*Kono kamera wa watashi ga ji-buñ de tsukatte iru mono desu.*) このカメラは私が自分で使っているものです.
3 (done by oneself) ho「ñniñ no 本人の; ji「shiñ no 自身の: The mayor made a personal visit to him. (*Shi-choo jishiñ ga kare o hoomoñ shi-ta.*) 市長自身が彼を訪問した.

personal effects *n.* mi-「no-mawari-hiñ 身の回り品.

personality *n.* **1** (character) ji「ñ-kaku 人格; ko「see 個性: He has a very strong personality. (*Kare wa kosee ga tsuyoi.*) 彼は個性が強い.
2 (well-known person) yu「ume」ejiñ 有名人; ta「reñto タレント: a TV personality (*terebi tareñto*) テレビタレント.

personally *adv.* **1** (in person) cho「kusetsu jibuñ de 直接自分で: He wrote the answer personally. (*Kare wa chokusetsu jibuñ de sono heñji o kaita.*) 彼は直接自分で

その返事を書いた.

2 (as a person) ni｢ ngeñ [ko｢ jiñ] to shite¹ (wa) 人間[個人]として(は): I don't like him personally, but I respect his talent. (*Kojiñ-teki ni wa suki de wa nai ga, kare no sainoo wa soñkee shite imasu.*) 個人的には好きではないが, 彼の才能は尊敬しています.

3 (as far as oneself is concerned) ji｢ buñ to shite¹ wa 自分としては: Personally, I am against the plan. (*Watashi to shite wa sono keekaku ni hañtai desu.*) 私としてはその計画に反対です.

personnel *n.* ji｢ ñiñ 人員; sho｢ ku¹-iñ 職員: a personnel department (*jiñji-ka*) 人事課.

perspective *n.* **1** (the way of drawing) e｢ ñkiñ-ga¹ hoo 遠近画法. **2** (view) mi｢ tooshi 見通し: get a clear perspective on a problem (*moñdai ni tsuite hakkiri shita mitooshi o motsu*) 問題についてはっきりした見通しを持つ.

persuade *vt.* **1** (make someone do by talking) ... o to｢ kifuse¹ ru ...を説き伏せる ⓥ; se｢ ttoku shite 〈verb〉-(sa)seru 説得して...(さ)せる ⓥ: I persuaded him to go. (*Watashi wa kare o tokifusete ikaseta.*) 私は彼を説き伏せて行かせた.

2 (convince) ... o na｢ ttoku saseru ...を納得させる ⓥ; ka｢ kushiñ saseru 確信させる ⓥ: I persuaded him that I was right. (*Watashi wa kare ni watashi ga tadashii koto o nattoku saseta.*) 私は彼に私が正しいことを納得させた.

persuasion *n.* **1** (persuading) se｢ ttoku 説得: I gave in to his persuasion. (*Watashi wa kare no settoku ni shitagatta.*) 私は彼の説得に従った.

2 (belief) ka｢ kushiñ 確信: I have a strong persuasion that this is true. (*Watashi wa kore wa tadashii to tsuyoi kakushiñ o motte iru.*) 私はこれは正しいと強い確信を持っている.

pertinent *adj.* (relevant) ka｢ ñkee ga a｢ ru 関係がある; te｢ kisetsu na 適切な: His remarks are not pertinent to this issue. (*Kare ga nobeta koto wa kono moñdai to kañkee ga nai.*) 彼が述べたことはこの問題と関係がない.

pet *n.* pe｢ tto ペット; a｢ igañ-do¹ obu-tsu 愛玩動物: I have a rabbit as a pet. (*Watashi wa usagi o petto ni katte imasu.*) 私はうさぎをペットに飼っています.

— *adj.* **1** (kept as a pet) pe｢ tto no ペットの: a pet turtle (*petto no kame*) ペットのかめ.

2 (favorite) o-｢ ki ni iri no お気に入りの; to｢ kui no 得意の: It is his pet theme. (*Sore wa kare no tokui no teema da.*) それは彼の得意のテーマだ.

petrol *n.* ga｢ soriñ ガソリン.

petty *adj.* to｢ ru ni ta｢ ranai 取るに足らない; sa｢ sai na ささいな: petty faults (*sasai na ketteñ*) ささいな欠点.

pharmacist *n.* ya｢ kuza¹ ishi 薬剤師.

pharmacy *n.* ya｢ kkyoku 薬局; ku｢ suriya 薬屋.

phase *n.* **1** (aspect) me｢ ñ 面; so｢ ku-meñ 側面: a problem with many phases (*ooku no sokumeñ o motsu moñdai*) 多くの側面を持つ問題.

2 (stage) da｢ ñkai 段階: We entered a new phase in the negotiations. (*Wareware wa kooshoo no atarashii dañkai ni haitta.*) われわれは交渉の新しい段階に入った.

phenomenon *n.* ge｢ ñshoo 現象: a natural phenomenon (*shizeñ-geñshoo*) 自然現象.

philosopher *n.* te｢ tsugaku¹ sha 哲学者.

philosophy *n.* te｢ tsu¹ gaku 哲学.

phone *n.* de｢ ñwa 電話: talk on the phone (*deñwa de hanasu*) 電話で話す / make a phone call (*deñwa o kakeru*) 電話をかける / May I use your phone? (*Deñwa o o-kari deki-masu ka?*) 電話をお借りできますか. / a phone book (*deñwachoo*) 電話帳 / a phone booth (*deñwa bokkusu*) 電話ボックス / a phone number (*deñwa-bañgoo*) 電話番号.

photo *n.* sha「shiñ 写真.

photograph *n.* sha「shiñ 写真:
Can I take photographs here?
(*Koko de shashiñ o totte mo ii
desu ka?*) ここで写真を撮ってもいい
ですか. / No Photographs. (*Satsuee
kiñshi.*) 撮影禁止.

photographer *n.* ka「mera」mañ カ
メラマン; sha「shiñ-ka 写真家: a
press photographer (*shiñbuñsha no
kameramañ*) 新聞社のカメラマン.
★ In Japan, professional photo-
graphers are called '*kameramañ*'
(cameraman).

photography *n.* sha「shiñ」jutsu 写
真術; sha「shiñ-sa」tsuee 写真撮影.

phrase *n.* **1** (group of words) ku「
句; fu「re」ezu フレーズ: a noun phrase
(*meeshi-ku*) 名詞句 / a set phrase
(*seeku*) 成句.
2 (expression) ko「tobazu」kai 言葉
遣い; i「imawashi 言い回し: a happy
turn of phrase (*umai iimawashi*) う
まい言い回し.

physical *adj.* **1** (of the body)
shi「ñtai no 身体の; ni「kutai no 肉体
の: a physical examination (*shiñtai
keñsa*) 身体検査.
2 (material) bu「sshitsu no 物質の;
shi「ze」ñ no 自然の: the physical
world (*shizeñkai*) 自然界.
3 (of the natural science) bu「tsuri-
teki na 物理的な: a physical change
(*butsuri-teki heñka*) 物理的変化.

physician *n.* na「ika-」i 内科医;
(doctor) i「shi 医師; i「sha 医者:
You'd better see a physician. (*Isha
e itta hoo ga ii desu yo.*) 医者へ行っ
たほうがいいですよ.

physics *n.* bu「tsuri」gaku 物理学:
nuclear physics (*geñshi butsurigaku*) 原子物理学.

pianist *n.* pi「ani」suto ピアニスト; pi-
「ano eñsooka ピアノ演奏家.

piano *n.* pi「ano ピアノ: She played
Chopin on the piano. (*Kanojo wa
piano de Shopañ o hiita.*) 彼女はピ
アノでショパンを弾いた.

pick *vt.* **1** (select) ... o e「ra」bu ...を
選ぶ ⓒ: He picked a nice tie. (*Kare

wa suteki na nekutai o erañda.*) 彼
はすてきなネクタイを選んだ.
2 (of a flower) ... o tsu「mu ...を摘む
ⓒ; (of a fruit) ... o mo「gu ...をもぐ
ⓒ: pick flowers (*hana o tsumu*) 花
を摘む / pick apples (*riñgo o mogu*)
りんごをもぐ.
3 (take off) ... o ho「ji」ru ...をほじる
ⓒ: pick one's nose (*hana o hojiru*)
鼻をほじる.
4 (dig into) ... o tsu「tsu」ku ...をつつ
く ⓒ: pick a little hole (*tsutsuite
chiisa-na ana o akeru*) つついて小さな
穴を開ける.

pick up *vt.* ... o te「 ni toru ...を手
に取る ⓒ: May I pick it up? (*Te ni
totte mo ii desu ka?*) 手に取っても
いですか.

pickle *n.* pi「kurusu ピクルス; tsu「ke-
mono 漬物.

picnic *n.* (pleasure trip) pi「kuni」kku
ピクニック: go on a picnic to the lake
(*mizuumi e pikunikku ni iku*) 湖へ
ピクニックに行く.

picture *n.* **1** (painting) e「 絵:
draw a picture (*e o kaku*) 絵をかく /
a picture frame (*gakubuchi*) 額縁.
2 (photograph) sha「shiñ 写真:
May I take your picture? (*Anata
no shashiñ o totte mo yoroshii
desu ka?*) あなたの写真を撮ってもよろ
しいですか.
3 (movie) e「ega 映画: go to the
pictures (*eega o mi ni iku*) 映画を
見に行く.
— *vt.* (imagine) ... o ko「ko」ro ni
e「ga」ku ...を心に描く ⓒ: I pictured
the scene. (*Watashi wa sono ba-
meñ o kokoro ni egaita.*) 私はその場
面を心に描いた.

picture postcard *n.* e「ha」gaki
絵はがき.

picturesque *adj.* e「 no yoo ni
u「tsukushi」i 絵のように美しい: a picturesque view (*e no yoo ni utsukushii nagame*) 絵のように美しい眺め.

pie *n.* pa「i パイ: bake a pie (*pai o
yaku*) パイを焼く.

piece *n.* **1** (single thing) hi「to」tsu
一つ; i「k-ko 1個: I have 3 pieces of

baggage in all. (*Nimotsu wa zeñbu de sañ-ko desu.*) 荷物は全部で3個です. ★ Japanese use different counters, depending on the type of thing being counted: a piece of paper (*kami ichi-mai*) 紙1枚 / a piece of chalk (*chooku ip-poñ*) チョーク1本 / a piece of furniture (*kagu it-teñ*) 家具1点 / a piece of information (*joohoo hitotsu*) 情報一つ.
2 (part) bu'buñ 部分; ku'kaku 区画: cut a pie into six equal pieces (*pai o roku-toobuñ suru*) パイを6等分する.
3 (work) sa'kuhiñ 作品: write a piece for the piano (*piano no tame no sakuhiñ o kaku*) ピアノのための作品を書く.

pier *n.* sa'ñbashi 桟橋; fu'too 埠頭.

pierce *vt.* **1** (pass through) ... o tsu'kisa'su ...を突き刺す C; tsu'ra-nu'ku 貫く C: A nail pierced the tire. (*Kugi ga taiya o tsukisashita.*) くぎがタイヤを突き刺した.
2 (make a hole) ... ni a'na' o a'keru ...に穴を開ける V: pierce a hole in the wall (*kabe ni ana o akeru*) 壁に穴を開ける.

pig *n.* bu'ta 豚.

pigeon *n.* ha'to はと(鳩).

pile *n.* tsu'mikasane 積み重ね; ya-'ma' 山: a pile of newspapers (*shiñ-buñ no yama*) 新聞の山.
— *vt.* ... o tsu'mikasane'ru ...を積み重ねる V: I piled old newspapers in the corner. (*Watashi wa furu-shiñbuñ o sumi ni tsumikasaneta.*) 私は古新聞を隅に積み重ねた.

pill *n.* ga'ñyaku 丸薬; jo'ozai 錠剤; ku'suri 薬: take a pill (*gañyaku [joozai] o nomu*) 丸薬[錠剤]を飲む / a sleeping pill (*suimiñyaku*) 睡眠薬.

pillar *n.* ha'shira 柱; shi'chuu 支柱: set up a pillar (*hashira o tateru*) 柱を立てる.

pillow *n.* ma'kura 枕: pillowcase (*makura kabaa*) 枕カバー.

pilot *n.* **1** (of an airplane) so'oju'u-shi 操縦士; pa'iro'tto パイロット: a

jet pilot (*jettoki no pairotto*) ジェット機のパイロット.
2 (of a ship) mi'zusaki añnainiñ 水先案内人.
— *adj.* (experimental) shi'keñ no 試験の; ji'kkeñ no 実験の: a pilot farm (*shikeñ-noojoo*) 試験農場.
— *vt.* **1** (act as a pilot) ... o so'o-juu suru ...を操縦する T: pilot a plane (*hikooki o soojuu suru*) 飛行機を操縦する.
2 (guide) ... o a'ñna'i suru ...を案内する T: He piloted me through Tokyo. (*Kare ga Tookyoo o añnai shi-te kureta.*) 彼が東京を案内してくれた.

pin *n.* pi'ñ ピン; to'meba'ri 留め針.
— *vt.* ... o pi'ñ de to'meru ...をピンで留める V: pin a flower to a coat (*hana o piñ de uwagi ni tomeru*) 花をピンで上着に留める.

pinch *vt.* **1** (squeeze) ... o tsu'ne'ru ...をつねる C: She pinched my arm. (*Kanojo wa watashi no ude o tsu-netta.*) 彼女は私の腕をつねった.
2 (press tightly) ... o ha'sa'mu ...を挟む C: I pinched my finger in the door. (*Watashi wa yubi o doa ni hasañda.*) 私は指をドアに挟んだ.
— *n.* tsu'ne'ru ko'to' つねること; ha-'sa'mu ko'to' 挟むこと: give a child a pinch on the cheek (*kodomo no hoo o tsuneru*) 子どもの頬をつねる.

pine *n.* ma'tsu 松; (tree) ma'tsu no ki 松の木.

pink *adj.* mo'moiro no 桃色の; pi'ñ-ku no ピンクの: a pink rose (*momo-iro no bara*) 桃色のばら.
— *n.* mo'moiro 桃色; pi'ñku ピンク.

pint *n.* pa'iñto パイント. ★ In Japan the metric system is used.

pioneer *n.* **1** (early settler) ka'i-ta'kusha 開拓者.
2 (person who is the first) se'ñku'-sha 先駆者; so'oshi'sha 創始者: He is a pioneer in this field. (*Kare wa kono buñya no señkusha da.*) 彼はこの分野の先駆者だ.

pious *adj.* ke'ekeñ na 敬虔な; shi'ñ-jiñbuka'i 信心深い: a pious Christian (*keekeñ na kurisuchañ*) 敬虔な

クリスチャン.

pipe *n.* **1** (tube) ka⌐ĭ 管; pa⌐ipu パ
イプ: a gas pipe (*gasu-kaĩ*) ガス管.

2 (of tobacco) pa⌐ipu パイプ: smoke
a pipe (*paipu de ippuku suu*) パイプ
で一服吸う.

— *vt.* ... o ka⌐ĭ [pa⌐ipu] de o⌐kuru
...を管[パイプ]で送る C: The oil is
piped into the tank. (*Sekiyu wa
paipu de tañku ni okuraremasu.*)
石油はパイプでタンクに送られます.

pit *n.* **1** (hole) a⌐na⌐ 穴: dig a pit for
rubbish (*gomi o ireru ana o horu*)
ごみを入れる穴を掘る.

2 (coal-mine) ta⌐ĭkoo 炭坑.

pitch *n.* **1** (of a sound) ta⌐kasa 高
さ; cho⌐oshi 調子: the pitch of a
voice (*koe no takasa*) 声の高さ.

2 (throwing) to⌐okyuu 投球: a wild
pitch (*bootoo*) 暴投.

3 (slope) ko⌐obai 勾配: the pitch
of a roof (*yane no koobai*) 屋根の勾
配.

— *vt.* **1** (throw) ... o na⌐ge⌐ru ...を
投げる V: pitch a fast ball (*sok-
kyuu o nageru*) 速球を投げる.

2 (set up) ... o ha⌐ru ...を張る C;
ta⌐te⌐ru 立てる V: pitch a tent (*teñto o haru*) テントを張る.

— *vi.* (rise and fall) jo⌐oge ni yu-
⌐reru 上下に揺れる V: The ship
pitched violently in the storm.
(*Fune wa arashi de jooge ni hageshiku yureta.*) 船は嵐で上下に激しく
揺れた.

pitcher[1] *n.* (container) mi⌐zusashi⌐
水差し: pour water into a pitcher
(*mizusashi ni mizu o sosogu*) 水差
しに水を注ぐ.

pitcher[2] *n.* (baseball player) to⌐o-
shu 投手; pi⌐tchaa ピッチャー.

pitiful *adj.* ka⌐waiso⌐o na かわいそう
な; a⌐ware na 哀れな: a pitiful sight
(*aware na kookee*) 哀れな光景.

pity *n.* **1** (feeling of sorrow) a⌐wa-
remi 哀れみ; do⌐ojoo 同情: I feel
pity for him. (*Kare o ki no doku ni
omou.*) 彼を気の毒に思う.

2 (regret) za⌐ĭne⌐ĭ na ko⌐to⌐ 残念な
こと: It's a pity that he cannot

come. (*Kare ga korarenai no wa
zañneñ da.*) 彼が来られないのは残念だ.

— *vt.* ... o ki⌐no doku⌐ ni o⌐mo⌐u
...を気の毒に思う C: I pity the sick
old man. (*Watashi wa sono byooki no roojiñ o ki no doku ni omou.*)
私はその病気の老人を気の毒に思う.

place *n.* **1** (location) ba⌐sho 場所;
to⌐koro⌐ 所: Is there a place to
change money near here? (*Kono
chikaku ni ryoogae o suru tokoro
wa arimasu ka?*) この近くに両替をす
る所はありますか.

2 (spot) ka⌐sho 箇所; to⌐koro⌐ 所:
He rubbed the sore place on his
arm. (*Kare wa ude no itamu ka-
sho o sasutta.*) 彼は腕の痛む箇所をさ
すった.

3 (house) ju⌐utaku 住宅; i⌐e⌐ 家:
He has a nice place in the suburbs.
(*Kare wa koogai ni ii ie ga aru.*)
彼は郊外にいい家がある.

4 (position) ju⌐ĭi 順位: I took
second place in the race. (*Watashi
wa kyoosoo de ni-i datta.*) 私は競走
で2位だった.

5 (job) sho⌐ku 職; shi⌐goto 仕事:
He found a new place in the firm.
(*Kare wa sono kaisha de atarashii
shoku o mitsuketa.*) 彼はその会社で
新しい職を見つけた.

— *vt.* **1** (put) ... o o⌐ku ...を置く
C: She placed a vase on the table.
(*Kanojo wa kabiñ o teeburu no ue
ni oita.*) 彼女は花びんをテーブルの上に
置いた.

2 (of an order) ... o da⌐su ...を出す
C; su⌐ru する I: I placed an order
for the book with the bookstore.
(*Watashi wa sono hoñ o shoteñ ni
chuumoñ shita.*) 私はその本を書店に
注文した.

3 (entrust) ... o o⌐ku ...を置く C: I
place my confidence in him. (*Watashi wa kare ni shiñrai o oite imasu.*) 私は彼に信頼を置いています.

plain *adj.* **1** (not decorated) mu⌐ji
no 無地の: a plain blouse (*muji no
burausu*) 無地のブラウス.

2 (clear) me⌐ehaku na 明白な; ha⌐k-

ki⌐ri shita [shite iru] はっきりした[して
いる]: It is quite plain that he wants
to quit his job. (*Kare ga shigoto o
yametagatte iru no wa hakkiri
shite iru.*) 彼が仕事を辞めたがっている
のははっきりしている.

3 (easy to understand) wa⌐kari-
yasu⌐i わかりやすい: explain in plain
language (*wakariyasui kotoba de
setsumee suru*) わかりやすい言葉で説
明する.

4 (simple) ka⌐nso na 簡素な; shi⌐s-
so na 質素な: a plain way of life
(*shisso na kurashikata*) 質素な暮ら
し方.

5 (not pretty) na⌐mi no 並の; bu-
⌐ki⌐ryoo na 不器量な.

— *adv.* ha⌐kki⌐ri to はっきりと:
speak plain (*hakkiri to hanasu*) はっ
きりと話す.

— *n.* he⌐echi 平地; he⌐eya 平野.

plainly *adv.* **1** (clearly) wa⌐kari-
ya⌐suku わかりやすく; ha⌐kki⌐ri to はっ
きりと: explain one's ideas plainly
(*jibun no kangae o hakkiri to setsumee suru*) 自分の考えをはっきりと
説明する.

2 (obviously) a⌐ki⌐raka ni 明らかに;
me⌐ehaku ni 明白に: Plainly, he is
wrong. (*Akiraka ni kare wa machigatte iru.*) 明らかに彼は間違っている.

3 (simply) ka⌐nso ni 簡素に; shi⌐s-
so ni 質素に: She was dressed
plainly. (*Kanojo wa shisso na fukusoo o shite ita.*) 彼女は質素な服装を
していた.

plan *n.* **1** (idea) ke⌐ekaku 計画; a⌐n
案; pu⌐ran プラン: carry out a plan
(*keekaku o jikkoo suru*) 計画を実
行する.

2 (line drawing) zu⌐men 図面:
plans for a new library (*atarashii
toshokan no zumen*) 新しい図書館の
図面.

— *vt.* **1** (think out) ... o ke⌐ekaku
suru ...を計画する 🄸; yo⌐tee suru 予
定する 🄸: He is planning a tour of
Hokkaido this summer. (*Kare wa
kono natsu Hokkaidoo-ryokoo o
keekaku shite iru.*) 彼はこの夏北海

道旅行を計画している.

2 (make a drawing) ... o se⌐kkee
suru ...を設計する 🄸; ... no zu⌐men
o ka⌐ku ...の図面をかく 🄲: plan a
garden (*niwa o sekkee suru*) 庭を設
計する.

plane[1] *n.* hi⌐ko⌐oki 飛行機: get on a
plane (*hikooki ni noru*) 飛行機に乗
る / get off a plane (*hikooki kara
oriru*) 飛行機から降りる / take a
plane to Hawaii (*hikooki de Hawai e iku*) 飛行機でハワイへ行く.

plane[2] *n.* he⌐emen 平面; me⌐n 面: a
horizontal plane (*suiheemen*) 水平
面.

— *adj.* ta⌐ira na 平らな: a plane
surface (*taira na hyoomen*) 平らな表
面.

— *vt.* ... ni ka⌐nna o ka⌐keru ...に
かんなをかける 🄅: plane a board
smooth (*ita ni kanna o kakete nameraka ni suru*) 板にかんなをかけて滑
らかにする.

planet *n.* wa⌐kusee 惑星.

plant *n.* **1** (living thing) sho⌐ku⌐bu-
tsu 植物; (grass) ku⌐sa⌐ 草: grow a
plant (*shokubutsu o saibai suru*)
植物を栽培する.

2 (factory) ko⌐ojo⌐o 工場: a chemical plant (*kagaku-koojoo*) 化学工場.

— *vt.* **1** (put into the ground) ...
o u⌐eru ...を植える 🄅: plant roses in
a garden (*niwa ni bara o ueru*) 庭に
ばらを植える.

2 (instill) ... o u⌐etsuke⌐ru ...を植え
付ける 🄅; fu⌐kiko⌐mu 吹き込む 🄲:
plant an idea (*kangae o fukikomu*)
考えを吹き込む.

plaster *n.* shi⌐kkui しっくい.

— *vt.* ... ni shi⌐kkui o nuru ...にしっ
くいを塗る 🄲: plaster walls (*kabe ni
shikkui o nuru*) 壁にしっくいを塗る.

plastic *adj.* pu⌐rasuchikkusee no プ
ラスチック製の; go⌐oseeju⌐shi no 合成
樹脂の; bi⌐niirusee no ビニール製の:
a plastic dish (*purasuchikku no
sara*) プラスチックの皿 / a plastic bag
(*biniiru-bukuro*) ビニール袋. ★ Japanese '*purasuchikku*' refers only to
a hard material.

— *n.* pu「rasuchi」kku プラスチック; go「oseeju」shi 合成樹脂; bi「ni」iru ビニール.

plate *n.* **1** (flat dish) sa「ra 皿; hi「razara 平皿: a soup plate (*suupuzara*) スープ皿.

2 (plateful) hi「tosara」buñ 一皿分: a plate of vegetables (*yasai hitosara*) 野菜一皿.

3 (sheet of metal) ki「ñzokubañ 金属板; i「tagane 板金: a steel plate (*koobañ*) 鋼板.

4 (license plate) na「ñbaa-pure」eto ナンバープレート.

platform *n.* **1** (of a station) pu「rattoho」omu プラットホーム; ho「omu ホーム: Which platform does the train leave from? (*Sono ressha wa dono hoomu kara demasu ka?*) その列車はどのホームから出ますか.

2 (raised part) da「ñ 壇; e「ñdañ 演壇: stand on a platform (*eñdañ ni tatsu*) 演壇に立つ.

platinum *n.* pu「rachina プラチナ; ha「kkiñ 白金.

platter *n.* o「ozara 大皿.

play *vi.* **1** (have fun) a「sobu 遊ぶ ©: The children are playing with their toys. (*Kodomo-tachi wa omocha de asoñde imasu.*) 子どもたちはおもちゃで遊んでいます.

2 (take part in a game) kyo「ogi ni sa「ñka suru 競技に参加する Ⓘ; shi「ai o suru 試合をする Ⓘ: We played against their team. (*Watashi-tachi wa kare-ra to shiai o shita.*) 私たちは彼らと試合をした.

3 (perform music) e「ñsoo suru 演奏する Ⓘ: play in an orchestra (*ookesutora de eñsoo suru*) オーケストラで演奏する.

4 (act in a play) shu「tsueñ suru 出演する Ⓘ: She played in the movie. (*Kanojo wa sono eega ni shutsueñ shita.*) 彼女はその映画に出演した.

— *vt.* **1** (take part in) ... o su「ru ...をする Ⓘ: play baseball (*yakyuu o suru*) 野球をする / play a game (*shiai o suru*) 試合をする / play chess (*chesu o suru*) チェスをする.

2 (of a musical instrument) ... o hi「ku ...を弾く ©; e「ñsoo suru 演奏する Ⓘ: play the piano (*piano o hiku*) ピアノを弾く.

3 (of a drama) ... o e「ñjiru ...を演じる Ⓥ: play the part of Hamlet (*Hamuretto no yaku o eñjiru*) ハムレットの役を演じる.

4 (perform) ... o ha「ta」su ...を果たす ©: play an important role (*juuyoo na yakuwari o hatasu*) 重要な役割を果たす.

— *n.* **1** (recreation) a「sobi 遊び; ki「barashi 気晴らし.

2 (drama) ge「ki 劇; e「ñgeki 演劇; shi「bai 芝居: go to a play (*shibai o mi ni iku*) 芝居を見に行く.

3 (playing of the game) shi「aiburi 試合ぶり; pu「re」e プレー: fair play (*fea-puree*) フェアプレー.

player *n.* **1** (of a game) kyo「ogi」-sha 競技者; se「ñshu 選手: a tennis player (*tenisu no señshu*) テニスの選手.

2 (of a musical instrument) e「ñso」osha 演奏者.

3 (of a drama) ya「kusha 役者; ha「iyuu 俳優.

4 (record player) pu「re」eyaa プレーヤー; e「ñsoo so」ochi 演奏装置.

playground *n.* (of a school) u「ñdoojoo 運動場; (of a park) a「sobi-ba 遊び場.

plea *n.* ta「ñgañ 嘆願: make a plea for help (*eñjo o tañgañ suru*) 援助を嘆願する.

plead *vi.* **1** (ask earnestly) (... ni) ta「ñgañ suru (...に)嘆願する Ⓘ: She pleaded with him not to go. (*Kanojo wa kare ni ikanai yoo ni tañgañ shita.*) 彼女は彼に行かないように嘆願した.

2 (speak in support of) (... o) be「ñgo suru (...を)弁護する Ⓘ: plead for the defendant (*hikoku no beñgo o suru*) 被告の弁護をする.

— *vt.* (give as an excuse) ... o be「ñkai suru ...を弁解する Ⓘ; i「iwake o suru 言い訳をする Ⓘ: He pleaded ignorance of the rule. (*Kare wa sono kisoku wa shiranakatta to beñkai shita.*) 彼はその規則は知らなかったと弁解した.

pleasant *adj.* **1** (enjoyable) taˈnoshiˈi 楽しい; kaˈriteki na 快適な: We had a pleasant time. (*Watashi-tachi wa tanoshii toki o sugoshita.*) 私たちは楽しい時を過ごした.
2 (nice) iˈi いい; kiˈmochi ga yoˈi 気持ちがよい: It is pleasant this morning. (*Kesa wa kimochi ga yoi.*) けさは気持ちがよい.
3 (agreeable) kaˈñji no iˈi 感じのいい: a pleasant person (*kañji no ii hito*) 感じのいい人.

please[1] *adv.* **1** [asking politely] doˈozo どうぞ; 〈verb〉-te[de] kuˈdasaˈi ... て[で]ください; o-ˈnegai shimasu お願いします: Please sit down. (*Doozo o-kake kudasai.*) どうぞお掛けください. / Let me off here, please. (*Koko de oroshite kudasai.*) ここで降ろしてください. / Speak slowly, please. (*Yukkuri hanashite kudasai.*) ゆっくり話してください. / The check, please. (*O-kañjoo o o-negai shimasu.*) お勘定をお願いします.
2 [calling attention] suˈmimaseˈñ ga すみませんが; doˈoka どうか: Will you pass the salt, please? (*Sumimaseñ ga shio o totte itadakemasu ka?*) すみませんが塩を取っていただけますか. / Will you please come with me? (*Dooka watashi to issho ni kite kudasai.*) どうか私といっしょに来てください.

please[2] *vt.* **1** (give pleasure) ... o yoˈrokobaseˈru ...を喜ばせる Ⓥ; (satisfy) maˈñzoku saseru 満足させる Ⓥ: You cannot please everybody. (*Subete no hito o mañzoku saseru koto wa dekinai.*) すべての人を満足させることはできない.
2 (like) ... o koˈnoˈmu ...を好む Ⓒ: Do what you please. (*Suki na yoo ni shi nasai.*) 好きなようにしなさい.

pleased *adj.* yoˈrokoˈñde 喜んで; maˈñzoku shite (iru) 満足して(いる); ki ˈni itte (iru) 気に入って(いる): She is pleased with her new dress.

(*Kanojo wa atarashii doresu ga ki ni itte imasu.*) 彼女は新しいドレスが気に入っています.
be pleased to do yoˈrokoˈñde 〈verb〉喜んで...: I am pleased to help you. (*Yorokoñde o-tetsudai shimasu.*) 喜んでお手伝いします.

pleasure *n.* **1** (feeling of happiness) taˈnoshiˈmi 楽しみ; yoˈrokobi 喜び: I find pleasure in listening to music. (*Watashi wa oñgaku o kiku no ga tanoshimi desu.*) 私は音楽を聴くのが楽しみです.
2 (cause of happiness) taˈnoshiˈi koˈtoˈ 楽しいこと; (satisfaction) kaˈiraku 快楽: It is a pleasure to watch TV. (*Terebi o miru no wa tanoshii koto desu.*) テレビを見るのは楽しいことです.

pledge *n.* chiˈkai 誓い; seˈeyaku 誓約: He gave me a ring as a pledge of his love. (*Kare wa ai no chikai to shite yubiwa o watashi ni kureta.*) 彼は愛の誓いとして指輪を私にくれた.
— *vt.* ... o chiˈkaˈu ...を誓う Ⓒ; yaˈkusoku suru 約束する Ⓘ: He pledged to do his best. (*Kare wa saizeñ o tsukusu koto o chikatta.*) 彼は最善を尽くすことを誓った.

plentiful *adj.* taˈkusañ aˈru たくさんある; juˈubuˈñ na 十分な; hoˈofu na 豊富な: Fish are plentiful in this lake. (*Kono mizuumi ni wa sakana ga takusañ imasu.*) この湖には魚がたくさんいます.

plenty *n.* taˈppuˈri たっぷり; juˈubuˈñ 十分; hoˈofu 豊富: We have plenty of time to go there. (*Soko e iku jikañ wa tappuri arimasu.*) そこへ行く時間はたっぷりあります. / I have plenty of money for my trip. (*Ryokoo no o-kane wa juubuñ arimasu.*) 旅行のお金は十分あります.

plot *n.* **1** (secret plan) iˈñboo 陰謀; taˈkurami たくらみ: hatch a plot to overthrow the government (*seefu o taosu iñboo o kuwadateru*) 政府を倒す陰謀を企てる.
2 (of a novel, play) suˈji 筋; koˈo-

soo 構想: The novel has a complicated plot. (*Sono shoosetsu wa suji ga komiitte iru.*) その小説は筋が込み入っている.

3 (small piece of land) to「chi 土地; ji「sho 地所: a vegetable plot (*saien*) 菜園.

—— *vt.* **1** (plan) ... o ta「kura¹mu ...をたくらむ ©; ke「ekaku suru 計画する ①: They plotted to kidnap the girl. (*Kare-ra wa sono shoojo o yuukai suru koto o takuranda.*) 彼らはその少女を誘拐することをたくらんだ.

2 (outline) ... o chi「zu ni ki「nyuu suru ...を地図に記入する ①: plot a ship's course (*fune no koosu o chizu ni kinyuu suru*) 船のコースを地図に記入する.

—— *vi.* i「nboo o ta「kura¹mu 陰謀をたくらむ ©.

plow *n.* su「ki すき: turn over the earth with a plow (*suki de tochi o tagayasu*) すきで土地を耕す.

—— *vt.* ... o ta「gaya¹su ...を耕す ©: plow a field (*hatake o tagayasu*) 畑を耕す.

pluck *vt.* **1** (pull) ... o hi「ppa¹ru ...を引っ張る ©: pluck a person's sleeve (*hito no sode o hipparu*) 人のそでを引っ張る.

2 (pull out feathers) ... o mu「shiru ...をむしる ©: pluck feathers from a chicken (*niwatori no hane o mushiru*) 鶏の羽をむしる.

3 (pick) ... o mo¹gu ...をもぐ ©; to「ru 取る ©: pluck an apple from a tree (*ringo o ki kara mogu*) りんごを木からもぐ.

plug *n.* **1** (object used to block a hole) se「n 栓: pull out a plug (*sen o nuku*) 栓を抜く.

2 (of electricity) sa「shikomi 差し込み; pu「ragu プラグ: insert a plug in an outlet (*puragu o konsento ni sashikomu*) プラグをコンセントに差し込む.

—— *vt.* ... ni se「n o tsu「me¹ru ...に栓を詰める Ⓥ: plug up a hole (*ana ni sen o tsumeru*) 穴に栓を詰める.

plum *n.* pu「ramu プラム; su「momo す

もも.

plunder *vt.* ... o rya「kudatsu suru ...を略奪する ①; go「odatsu suru 強奪する ①: plunder a village (*mura o ryakudatsu suru*) 村を略奪する.

plunge *vt.* (thrust) ... o tsu「kko¹mu ...を突っ込む ©: plunge one's hand into the water (*te o mizu ni tsukkomu*) 手を水に突っ込む.

—— *vi.* (throw oneself) (... ni) to「biko¹mu (...に) 飛び込む ©: plunge into the river (*kawa ni tobikomu*) 川に飛び込む.

—— *n.* to「biko¹mu ko「to¹ 飛び込むこと: take a plunge into a pool (*puuru ni tobikomu*) プールに飛び込む.

plural *adj.* fu「kusu¹u no 複数の; fu「tatsu i¹joo no 二つ以上の: a plural noun (*fukusuu-meeshi*) 複数名詞.

—— *n.* fu「kusuukee 複数形.

plus **1** *adj.* (above zero) pu「rasu no プラスの; se「e no 正の: a plus quantity (*seesuu*) 正数.

2 (more than) ... i「joo ...以上: It will cost ¥10,000 plus. (*Sore wa ichi-man-en ijoo kakaru deshoo.*) それは1万円以上かかるでしょう.

—— *prep.* ... o ku「waete ...を加えて; ta「shite 足して: Three plus four equals seven. (*San tasu yon wa nana desu.*) 3足す4は7です.

—— *n.* (sign) pu「rasu-ki¹goo プラス記号; se「esu¹u 正数.

p.m. *adv., adj.* go「go 午後: 11 p.m. (*gogo juuichi-ji*) 午後11時 / I'd like to make an appointment for 5 p.m. today. (*Kyoo no gogo go-ji ni o-ai shitai no desu ga.*) きょうの午後5時にお会いしたいのですが.

pneumonia *n.* ha「i-en 肺炎.

pocket *n.* po「ke¹tto ポケット: He put the money in his pocket. (*Kare wa sono o-kane o poketto ni ireta.*) 彼はそのお金をポケットに入れた. / a pocket calculator (*dentaku*) 電卓.

poem *n.* shi 詩: write a poem (*shi o kaku*) 詩を書く. ★ 'Poetry' is also called 'shi.'

poet *n.* shi「jin 詩人.

poetic *adj.* shi no 詩の; shi-「teki

na 詩的な: a poetic drama (shigeki) 詩劇.

poetry n. shi 詩; shiˈika 詩歌: a collection of poetry (shishuu) 詩集. ★ 'Poem' is also called 'shi.'

point n. **1** (sharp tip) saˈki 先; seˈñtañ 先端: the point of a needle (hari no saki) 針の先. **2** (exact spot) teˈñ 点; chiˈteñ 地点: a starting point (shuppatsu-teñ) 出発点. **3** (dot) teˈñ 点: a decimal point (shoosuu-teñ) 小数点. **4** (special quality) toˈkuchoo 特徴; toˈkushitsu 特質: a strong point (choosho) 長所 / a weak point (tañ-sho) 短所. **5** (mark in scoring) teˈñsuˈu 点数; toˈkuteñ 得点: win by three points (sañ-teñ-sa de katsu) 3 点差で勝つ. **6** (important part) yoˈoteˈñ 要点; poˈiñto ポイント: the point of one's speech (eñzetsu no yòoteñ) 演説の要点. **7** (place on a scale) teˈñ 点; do 度: the boiling point of water (mizu no futteñ) 水の沸点.
— vi. (hold out a finger) (... o) yuˈbisaˈsu (...を)指さす C: He pointed to the picture. (Kare wa sono e o yubisashita.) 彼はその絵を指さした.
— vt. (direct) ... o muˈkeru ...を向ける V: point a gun toward a bird (juu o tori ni mukeru) 銃を鳥に向ける.

point out vt. ... o shiˈteki suru ...を指摘する T: Please point out where I am on this map. (Kono chizu de geñzai iru tokoro o sa-shite kudasai.) この地図で現在いる所を指してください.

pointed adj. toˈgaˈtta とがった; toˈgaˈtte iru とがっている; suˈrudoˈi 鋭い: a pointed tower (togatta too) と がった塔 / a pointed beak (surudoi kuchibashi) 鋭いくちばし.

poison n. doˈkuˈ 毒; doˈkuyaku 毒薬: She tried to kill herself by taking poison. (Kanojo wa doku o noñde jisatsu shiyoo to shita.) 彼

女は毒を飲んで自殺しようとした.
— vt. ... o doˈkusatsu suru ...を毒殺する T; doˈkuˈ de koˈrosu 毒で殺す C: poison rats (nezumi o doku de korosu) ねずみを毒で殺す.

poisoning n. chuˈudoku 中毒: food poisoning (shoku-chuudoku) 食中毒.

poisonous adj. yuˈudoku na 有毒な; yuˈugai na 有害な: a poisonous snake (dokuhebi) 毒へび.

poke vt. **1** (prod) ... o tsuˈku ...を突く C; tsuˈtsuˈku つつく C: He poked me in the ribs. (Kare wa watashi no wakibara o tsuita.) 彼は私のわき腹を突いた. **2** (protrude) ... o tsuˈkidaˈsu ...を突き出す C: poke one's head out of the window (mado kara atama o tsukidasu) 窓から頭を突き出す.
— vi. (... o) tsuˈtsuˈku (...を)つつく C: poke at a frog with a stick (boo de kaeru o tsutsuku) 棒でかえるをつつく.

pole[1] n. boˈo 棒; saˈoˈ さお: support with a pole (boo de sasaeru) 棒で支える.

pole[2] n. kyoˈku 極: the North Pole (hokkyoku) 北極 / the South Pole (nañkyoku) 南極.

police n. **1** (department) keˈesa-tsu 警察: Get me the police. (Kee-satsu ni tsunaide kudasai.) 警察につないでください. / a police box (koo-bañ) 交番. **2** (members) keˈesatsuˈkañ 警察官; keˈesatsu 警察: The police are looking for the criminal. (Keesatsu wa sono hañniñ o sagashite iru.) 警察はその犯人を捜している.

policeman n. keˈekañ 警官; o-ˈmaˈwari-sañ お巡りさん: ask a policeman the way to the station (keekañ ni eki e iku michi o kiku) 警官に駅へ行く道を聞く / Call a policeman. (Keekañ o yoñde kudasai.) 警官を呼んでください.

policewoman n. fuˈjiñ-keˈekañ 婦人警官; fuˈkee 婦警.

policy n. **1** (of a government) se-

「esaku 政策; (of a company) hoˈo-shiñ 方針: a foreign policy (*gai-koo-seesaku*) 外交政策.

2 (method) hoˈosaku 方策; shuˈ-dañ 手段: A strike is not the best policy. (*Sutoraiki wa saizeñ no shudañ de wa nai.*) ストライキは最善の手段ではない.

polish *vt.* **1** (make shiny) ... o miˈgaku ...を磨く Ⓒ; ... no tsuˈya o daˈsu ...のつやを出す Ⓒ: polish one's shoes (*kutsu o migaku*) 靴を磨く.

2 (improve) ... ni miˈgaki o kakeˈ-ru ...に磨きをかける Ⓥ: polish one's performance (*eñgi ni migaki o kakeru*) 演技に磨きをかける.

polite *adj.* **1** (courteous) reˈegi tadashiˈi 礼儀正しい; teˈenee na 丁寧な: He has a polite way of speaking. (*Kare wa kotobazukai ga teenee da.*) 彼は言葉遣いが丁寧だ.

2 (cultured) seˈñreñ sareta 洗練された; joˈoryuu no 上流の: polite society (*jooryuu shakai*) 上流社会.

politeness *n.* reˈegi tadaˈshisa 礼儀正しさ; teˈenee 丁寧.

political *adj.* seˈeji(joo) no 政治(上)の; seˈeji-teki na 政治的な: a political party (*seetoo*) 政党 / a political problem (*seeji-teki na moñdai*) 政治的な問題.

politician *n.* seˈejika 政治家.

politics *n.* **1** (management of political affairs) seˈeji 政治: I have no interest in politics. (*Watashi wa seeji ni wa kyoomi ga arimaseñ.*) 私は政治には興味がありません.

2 (science) seˈejiˈgaku 政治学: major in politics (*seejigaku o señkoo suru*) 政治学を専攻する.

3 (political principles) seˈesaku 政策; (political opinions) seˈekeñ 政見.

poll *n.* **1** (voting) toˈohyoo 投票: The poll will be held tomorrow. (*Toohyoo wa ashita okonawaremasu.*) 投票はあした行われます.

2 (the number of votes) toˈohyooˈo-suu 投票数; toˈohyoo-keˈkka 投票結果: declare the poll (*toohyoo-*

kekka o happyoo suru) 投票結果を発表する.

3 (opinion poll) yoˈroñ-choˈosa 世論調査.

pollute *vt.* ... o yoˈgosu ...を汚す Ⓒ; osˈeñ suru 汚染する Ⓘ: Smoke from factories is polluting the air. (*Koojoo kara no kemuri ga taiki o yogoshite iru.*) 工場からの煙が大気を汚している.

pollution *n.* yoˈgosu kotoˈ 汚すこと; osˈeñ 汚染: air pollution (*taiki-oseñ*) 大気汚染.

polo shirt *n.* poˈroshatsu ポロシャツ.

polyester *n.* poˈrieˈsuteru ポリエステル.

pond *n.* iˈke 池: row a boat on a pond (*ike de booto o kogu*) 池でボートをこぐ.

pool *n.* **1** (swimming pool) puˈuru プール: He went swimming in the pool. (*Kare wa puuru e oyogi ni itta.*) 彼はプールへ泳ぎに行った.

2 (small area of still water) miˈzu-tamari 水たまり: The rain left pools on the road. (*Ame de dooro ni mizutamari ga dekita.*) 雨で道路に水たまりができた.

poor *adj.* **1** (having little money) maˈzushiˈi 貧しい; biˈñboo na 貧乏な: She was too poor to buy a coat. (*Kanojo wa mazushikute kooto ga kaenakatta.*) 彼女は貧しくてコートが買えなかった.

2 (of bad quality) shiˈtsu no waruˈi 質の悪い; soˈmatsu na 粗末な: goods of poor quality (*shitsu no warui shinamono*) 質の悪い品物.

3 (not good) heˈtaˈi na へたな; oˈtoˈtta 劣った; oˈtoˈtte iru 劣っている: I am poor at Japanese. (*Watashi wa Nihoñgo ga heta desu.*) 私は日本語がへたです.

4 (deserving pity) aˈware na 哀れな; kaˈwaisoˈo na かわいそうな: The poor bird had broken its wing. (*Kawaisoo na tori ga hane o otte ita.*) かわいそうな鳥は羽を折っていた.

pop[1] *adj.* taˈishuu muki no 大衆向きの; poˈpyuraa na ポピュラーな: pop

music (*popyuraa oñgaku*) ポピュラー
音楽.

pop[2] *vi.* **1** (make a short sound)
poˈñ to oˈtoˡ o taˈteˡru ポンと音を立
てる Ⓥ: The balloon popped. (*Fuuseñ ga poñ to wareta.*) 風船がポンと
割れた.

2 (move in a sudden way) kyuˈu ni
ugoˡku 急に動く Ⓒ: pop out of bed
(*beddo kara kyuu ni okidasu*) ベッ
ドから急に起き出す.

— *vt.* ... o poˈñ to nuˈku ...をポンと
抜く Ⓒ: pop a cork (*koruku no señ
o poñ to nuku*) コルクの栓をポンと抜く.

— *n.* poˈñ to iu oˈtoˡ ポンという音.

popular *adj.* **1** (well-liked) niˈñki
no aˈru 人気のある; haˈyaˡtte iru はや
っている: The circus is popular with
children. (*Saakasu wa kodomo-
tachi ni niñki ga aru.*) サーカスは子ど
もたちに人気がある. / What is popular
now? (*Ima nani ga hayatte imasu
ka?*) 今何がはやっていますか.

2 (favored among the public) taˈi-
shuumuki no 大衆向きの; poˡpyuraa
na ポピュラーな: a popular magazine
(*taishuu-zasshi*) 大衆雑誌 / a popular song (*ryuukooka*) 流行歌.

popularity *n.* niˈñki 人気; ryuˈukoo 流行: win popularity (*niñki o
hakusu*) 人気を博す.

population *n.* jiˈñkoo 人口: What
is the population of this country?
(*Kono kuni no jiñkoo wa dono
kurai desu ka?*) この国の人口はどのく
らいですか.

porch *n.* **1** (roofed entrance) geˈñ-
kañ 玄関; poˡochi ポーチ.

2 (veranda) beˈrañda ベランダ.

pork *n.* buˈtaniku 豚肉; poˡoku ポー
ク: roast some pork (*butaniku o yaku*) 豚肉を焼く.

port *n.* (harbor) miˈnato 港; (city)
miˈnatoˡmachi 港町: clear port
(*shukkoo suru*) 出港する / come
into port (*nyuukoo suru*) 入港する.

portable *adj.* moˈchihakobi de-
kiˡru 持ち運びできる; keˈetaiyoo no
携帯用の; poˡotaburu no ポータブル
の: a portable radio (*pootaburu*

rajio) ポータブルラジオ.

— *n.* keˈetaiyoo kiˡgu 携帯用器具;
poˡotaburu ポータブル.

porter *n.* poˡotaa ポーター; aˈkaboo
赤帽: Please get me a porter. (*Pootaa o yoñde kudasai.*) ポーターを呼ん
でください.

portion *n.* **1** (part) buˈbuñ 部分;
iˈchiˡbu 一部: He sold a portion of
his land. (*Kare wa tochi no ichibu
o utta.*) 彼は土地の一部を売った.

2 (share) waˈkemaˡe 分け前: He
asked for his portion of the money.
(*Kare wa o-kane no wakemae o
yookyuu shita.*) 彼はお金の分け前を
要求した.

3 (one serving of food) iˈchi-niñ
mae 一人前: order three portions
of steak (*suteeki o sañ-niñ mae
chuumoñ suru*) ステーキを 3 人前注文
する.

portrait *n.* shoˈozooga 肖像画; ji-
ˈñbutsuga 人物画.

pose *n.* **1** (position) shiˈsee 姿勢;
poˡozu ポーズ: assume a relaxed
pose (*kutsuroida shisee o toru*) くつ
ろいだ姿勢をとる.

2 (false manner) miˈsekake 見せか
け; kiˈdori 気取り: What he says is
a mere pose. (*Kare ga iu koto wa
tañnaru misekake da.*) 彼が言うこと
は単なる見せかけだ.

— *vi.* **1** (hold a position) poˡozu
o toru ポーズをとる Ⓒ: She posed for
her portrait. (*Kanojo wa shoo-
zooga o kaite morau tame ni poozu o totta.*) 彼女は肖像画をかいてもら
うためにポーズをとった.

2 (pretend to be) ... no fuˈriˡ o suru
...のふりをする Ⓘ: He posed as a doc-
tor. (*Kare wa isha no furi o shita.*)
彼は医者のふりをした.

position *n.* **1** (location) iˈchi 位
置; baˈsho 場所: I found the position of the village on the map.
(*Watashi wa sono mura no basho
o chizu de mitsuketa.*) 私はその村の
場所を地図で見つけた.

2 (the way of holding the body)
shiˈsee 姿勢: sit in a comfortable

position (*raku na shisee de suwaru*) 楽な姿勢で座る.

3 (job) tsu｢tome¹guchi 勤め口; sho-｢ku 職: He got a position as a lecturer. (*Kare wa kooshi no tsutomeguchi o mitsuketa.*) 彼は講師の勤め口を見つけた.

4 (stand) ta｢chiba¹ 立場; kyo｢oguu 境遇: Put yourself in my position. (*Watashi no tachiba ni mo natte mite kudasai.*) 私の立場にもなってみてください.

5 (rank) chi｢i 地位; mi¹buñ 身分: a high position in society (*takai shakai-teki chii*) 高い社会的地位.

positive *adj.* **1** (not negative) se｢kkyoku-teki na 積極的な: take a positive attitude (*sekkyoku-teki na taido o toru*) 積極的な態度をとる.

2 (certain) ka｢kushiñ shita [shite iru] 確信した[している]: I am positive of his innocence. (*Watashi wa kare no muzai o kakushiñ shite imasu.*) 私は彼の無罪を確信しています.

3 (of a disease) yo｢osee no 陽性の: The results of the test were positive. (*Keñsa no kekka wa yoosee datta.*) 検査の結果は陽性だった.

4 (affirmative) ko｢otee-teki na 肯定的な: a positive answer (*kootee-teki na heñji*) 肯定的な返事.

— *n.* (photography) po¹ji ポジ; yo-｢oga 陽画; (math) se｢esu¹u 正数.

possess *vt.* **1** (own) ... o sho｢yuu suru ...を所有する ①; mo｢tte iru 持っている Ⅴ: He possesses a villa in the country. (*Kare wa inaka ni bessoo o motte iru.*) 彼は田舎に別荘を持っている.

2 (have) ... ga a¹ru ...がある ⓒ: He possesses the ability to do it. (*Kare ni wa sore o suru nooryoku ga aru.*) 彼にはそれをする能力がある.

possession *n.* **1** (ownership) sho｢yuu 所有; mo｢tte iru ko｢to¹ 持っていること: the possession of land (*tochi no shoyuu*) 土地の所有.

2 (thing possessed) sho｢yu¹ubutsu 所有物; za｢isañ 財産: He lost all his possessions in the fire. (*Kare*

wa kaji de zeñ zaisañ o ushinatta.) 彼は火事で全財産を失った.

possibility *n.* **1** (state of being possible) ka｢noosee 可能性: There is no possibility of war. (*Señsoo no kanoosee wa nai.*) 戦争の可能性はない.

2 (likelihood) o｢koriu¹ru ko｢to¹ 起こりうること; a｢riu¹ru ko｢to¹ ありうること: Failure is a possibility. (*Shippai wa ariuru koto da.*) 失敗はありうることだ.

possible *adj.* **1** (able to be done) ka｢noo na 可能な; <verb> ko｢to¹ ga de｢ki¹ru ...ことができる: It is possible to prevent disease. (*Byooki no yoboo wa kanoo desu.*) 病気の予防は可能です. / Is it possible to look around your factory? (*Anata no koojoo o keñgaku suru koto wa dekimasu ka?*) あなたの工場を見学することはできますか.

2 (likely to happen) o｢koriu¹ru ko｢to¹ 起こりうる; <verb>-soo na ...そうな: Rain is possible tomorrow. (*Ashita wa ame ga furi-soo da.*) あしたは雨が降りそうだ.

if possible *adv.* de｢ki¹reba できれば: If possible, I'll come tomorrow. (*Dekireba ashita ikimasu.*) できればあした行きます.

possibly *adv.* **1** (perhaps) ko｢to ni yoru to ことによると; mo¹shi ka suru to もしかすると: Possibly it will be true. (*Moshi ka suru to sore wa hoñtoo ka mo shirenai.*) もしかするとそれは本当かもしれない.

2 (in any possible way) na¹ñ to ka shite 何とかして; de｢kiru ka¹giri できる限り: I will do everything I possibly can. (*Dekiru kagiri no koto wa yarimasu.*) できる限りのことはやります.

post¹ *n.* **1** (mail) yu｢ubiñ 郵便: send a book by post (*hoñ o yuubiñ de okuru*) 本を郵便で送る.

2 (letters, parcels, etc.) yu｢ubi¹ñbutsu 郵便物.

— *vt.* ... o yu｢ubiñ de da¹su ...を郵便で出す ⓒ; yu｢usoo suru 郵送する ①: I posted the letter yesterday.

(*Sono tegami wa kinoo dashima-shita.*) その手紙はきのう出しました.

post² *n.* 1 (upright pole) ha⌐shira 柱; ku⌐i くい: set fence posts (*saku no hashira o tateru*) 柵の柱を立てる.
— *vt.* ... o ha⌐ru ...をはる C; ke⌐eji suru 掲示する I: post a notice on a door (*doa no ue ni keeji o haru*) ドアの上に掲示をはる.

post³ *n.* 1 (position) chi⌐i 地位; sho⌐ku 職: get a post as professor (*kyooju no chii ni tsuku*) 教授の地位に就く.
2 (place of duty) mo⌐chiba 持ち場; bu⌐sho 部署: leave one's post (*mochiba o hanareru*) 持ち場を離れる.

postage *n.* yu⌐ubiñ-ryo⌐okiñ 郵便料金: How much did the postage cost? (*Yuubiñ-ryookiñ wa ikura kakarimashita ka?*) 郵便料金はいくらかかりましたか.

postage stamp *n.* yu⌐ubiñ-ki⌐tte 郵便切手; ki⌐tte 切手.

postcard *n.* yu⌐ubiñ-ha⌐gaki 郵便はがき; ha⌐gaki はがき: I'd like to send this postcard by air mail. (*Kono hagaki o kookuubiñ de o-negai shimasu.*) このはがきを航空便でお願いします. / a picture postcard (*e-hagaki*) 絵はがき.

poster *n.* po⌐sutaa ポスター: put up a poster (*posutaa o haru*) ポスターをはる.

postman *n.* yu⌐ubiñ shuuhainiñ 郵便集配人.

post office *n.* yu⌐ubi⌐ñkyoku 郵便局: Where is the post office? (*Yuubiñkyoku wa doko desu ka?*) 郵便局はどこですか.

postpone *vt.* ... o e⌐ñki suru ...を延期する I; o⌐kuraseru 遅らせる V: I postponed my trip because of illness. (*Watashi wa byooki no tame ni ryokoo o eñki shita.*) 私は病気のために旅行を延期した.

postponement *n.* e⌐ñki 延期; a⌐toma⌐washi 後回し.

postposition *n.* ko⌐ochi⌐shi 後置詞.

pot *n.* 1 (used for cooking) na⌐be なべ; fu⌐kanabe 深なべ: I cooked the soup in a pot. (*Watashi wa nabe de suupu o tsukutta.*) 私はなべでスープを作った.
2 (round container) tsu⌐bo つぼ; ha⌐chi⌐ 鉢; bi⌐ñ びん; po⌐tto ポット.
— *vt.* ... o ha⌐chi⌐ ni u⌐eru ...を鉢に植える: pot a plant (*kusabana o hachi ni ueru*) 草花を鉢に植える.

potage *n.* po⌐ta⌐aju ポタージュ.

potato *n.* ja⌐gaimo じゃがいも: boil [bake] potatoes (*jagaimo o yuderu [yaku]*) じゃがいもをゆでる[焼く].

potential *adj.* ka⌐noosee no a⌐ru 可能性のある; se⌐ñzai suru 潜在する: potential ability (*señzai nooryoku*) 潜在能力.
— *n.* ka⌐noosee 可能性; se⌐ñza⌐i-ryoku 潜在力.

pound¹ *n.* 1 (unit of weight) po⌐ñdo ポンド. ★ In Japan the metric system is used.
2 (unit of money) po⌐ñdo ポンド.

pound² *vt.* 1 (hit) ... o do⌐ñdoñ ta⌐ta⌐ku ...をどんどんたたく C; re⌐ñda suru 連打する I: pound a door (*doa o doñdoñ tataku*) ドアをどんどんたたく.
2 (crush) ... o u⌐chikuda⌐ku ...を打ち砕く C; tsu⌐ite ko⌐na⌐ ni suru ついて粉にする I: pound corn into meal (*toomorokoshi o tsuite kona ni suru*) とうもろこしをついて粉にする.
— *vi.* do⌐ñdoñ ta⌐ta⌐ku どんどんたたく C; tsu⌐yoku utsu 強く打つ C: I feel my heart pound. (*Shiñzoo ga dokidoki suru no ga wakaru.*) 心臓がどきどきするのがわかる.

pour *vt.* ... o so⌐sogu ...を注ぐ C; tsu⌐gu つぐ C: She poured wine into my glass. (*Kanojo wa waiñ o watashi no gurasu ni sosoida.*) 彼女はワインを私のグラスに注いだ.
— *vi.* 1 (flow) na⌐garede⌐ru 流れ出る V: Water is pouring from the pipe. (*Mizu ga paipu kara nagaredete iru.*) 水がパイプから流れ出ている.
2 (of people) do⌐tto de⌐ru どっと出る V: The crowd poured out of the stadium. (*Guñshuu ga kyoogijoo*

kara dotto dete kita.) 群衆が競技場からどっと出てきた.

3 (of rain) ha「ge]shiku fu「ru 激しく降る Ⓒ: The rain poured down last night. (*Yuube wa ame ga hageshiku futta.*) ゆうべは雨が激しく降った.

poverty *n.* bi「ñboo 貧乏; hi「ñkoñ 貧困: live in poverty (*mazushii kurashi o suru*) 貧しい暮らしをする.

powder *n.* ko「na]粉; fu「ñmatsu 粉末: grind into powder (*hiite kona ni suru*) ひいて粉にする.

—— *vt.* (apply powder) ... ni o「shiroi o tsu「ke]ru ...におしろいをつける Ⓥ: She powdered her face. (*Kanojo wa kao ni oshiroi o tsuketa.*) 彼女は顔におしろいをつけた.

power *n.* **1** (ability) no「oryoku 能力; chi「kara 力: He has the power to tell the future. (*Kare ni wa mirai o yogeñ suru nooryoku ga aru.*) 彼には未来を予言する能力がある. I will do all in my power. (*Dekiru kagiri no koto wa yarimasu.*) できる限りのことはやります.

2 (force) chi「kara 力; do「oryoku 動力; (electric power) de「ñryoku 電力: atomic power (*geñshi-ryoku*) 原子力 / The power went out in the hotel. (*Hoteru ga teedeñ ni natta.*) ホテルが停電になった.

3 (authority) ke「ñryoku 権力; chi「kara 力: the power of the law (*hooritsu no chikara*) 法律の力.

4 (right) ke「ñge]ñ 権限: The police have the power of arrest. (*Keesatsu wa taiho no keñgeñ o motte iru.*) 警察は逮捕の権限を持っている.

5 (strong country) kyo「okoku 強国; ta「ikoku 大国: an economic power (*keezai taikoku*) 経済大国.

powerful *adj.* **1** (strong) kyo「oryoku na 強力な; tsu「yo]i 強い: a powerful engine (*kyooryoku na eñjiñ*) 強力なエンジン.

2 (influential) se「eryoku no aru 勢力のある; yu「uryoku na 有力な: a powerful politician (*yuuryoku na seejika*) 有力な政治家.

practical *adj.* **1** (learned through practice) ji「ssai no 実際の; ji「tchi no 実地の: practical experience (*jissai no keekeñ*) 実際の経験.

2 (useful) ji「tsuyoo-teki na 実用的な; ya「ku]ni tatsu 役に立つ: Your invention is practical. (*Kimi no hatsumee wa jitsuyoo-teki da.*) 君の発明は実用的だ.

3 (concerned with actual conditions) ge「ñjitsu-teki na 現実的な; ji「ssai-teki na 実際的な: His ideas are hardly practical. (*Kare no kañgae wa jissai-teki to wa ienai.*) 彼の考えは実際的とは言えない.

practically *adv.* **1** (almost) ho「to]ñdo ... mo do「ozeñ de ほとんど...も同然で: The work is practically finished. (*Shigoto wa hotoñdo owatta mo doozeñ da.*) 仕事はほとんど終わったも同然だ.

2 (in a practical way) ji「ssai-joo wa 実際上は; ji「sshitsu-teki ni]wa 実質的には: Practically, the plan didn't work well. (*Jissai ni wa sono keekaku wa umaku ikanakatta.*) 実際にはその計画はうまくいかなかった.

practice *n.* **1** (repeated exercise) re「ñshuu 練習; ke「eko けいこ: You need more practice to play the piano. (*Kimi wa piano o hiku no ni motto reñshuu ga hitsuyoo da.*) 君はピアノを弾くのにもっと練習が必要だ.

2 (habit) shu「ukañ 習慣; ka「ñree 慣例: It is my practice to get up early. (*Hayaoki ga watashi no shuukañ desu.*) 早起きが私の習慣です.

3 (actual doing) ji「kkoo 実行; ji「sshi 実施: He put his plan into practice. (*Kare wa jibuñ no keekaku o jikkoo ni utsushita.*) 彼は自分の計画を実行に移した.

4 (work) gyo「omu 業務: He has a practice in Tokyo. (*Kare wa Tookyoo de kaigyoo shite iru.*) 彼は東京で開業している.

—— *vt.* **1** (do exercises) ... o re「ñshuu [ke「eko] suru ...を練習[けいこ]する Ⓣ: practice speaking Japanese (*Nihoñgo o hanasu reñshuu o*

suru) 日本語を話す練習をする.
2 (follow) ... o kaˈigyoo suru ...を
開業する ①: Ten years have passed
since he started practicing medicine. (*Kare wa isha o kaigyoo
shite kara juu-neñ ni naru.*) 彼は医
者を開業してから 10 年になる.
3 (carry out) ... o reˈekoo suru ...を
励行する ①: practice economy (*keñyaku o reekoo suru*) 倹約を励行する.
— *vi.* **1** (do exercises) (... o) reˈn-
shuu suru (...を)練習する ①: prac-
tice on the violin (*baioriñ o reñshuu suru*) バイオリンを練習する.
2 (follow) (... o) kaˈigyoo suru (...
を)開業する ①: practice as a lawyer
(*beñgoshi o kaigyoo suru*) 弁護士
を開業する.

praise *vt.* ... o hoˈmeˈru ...をほめる
Ⓥ; shoˈosañ suru 賞賛する ①: Everybody praised his courage. (*Dare
mo ga kare no yuuki o hometa.*) だ
れもが彼の勇気をほめた.
— *n.* hoˈmeˈru koˈtoˈ ほめること;
shoˈosañ 賞賛: His deeds are worthy of praise. (*Kare no kooi wa
shoosañ ni atai suru.*) 彼の行為は賞
賛に値する.

prawn *n.* kuˈruma ebi 車海老. ★ In
Japanese, 'lobster,' 'prawn,' and
'shrimp' are all called 'ebi.'

pray *vi.* iˈnoˈru 祈る Ⓒ; kiˈgañ suru
祈願する ①: She knelt down and
prayed. (*Kanojo wa hizamazuite
inotta.*) 彼女はひざまづいて祈った.
— *vt.* ... ni iˈnoˈru ...に祈る Ⓒ:
pray God (*kami ni inoru*) 神に祈る.

prayer *n.* **1** (act of praying) iˈnoriˈ
祈り; kiˈgañ 祈願: a prayer for
peace (*heewa no inori*) 平和の祈り.
2 (words) iˈnori no kotobaˈ 祈りの
言葉: say one's prayers (*o-inori o
iu*) お祈りを言う.

preach *vt.* (give a sermon) ... o
seˈkkyoˈo suru ...を説教する ①;
toˈku 説く Ⓒ: preach the Gospel
(*fukuiñ o toku*) 福音を説く.
— *vi.* (advise) (... ni) seˈkkyoˈo
suru (...に)説教する ①: He preached
to his son. (*Kare wa musuko ni

sekkyoo shita.) 彼は息子に説教した.

precaution *n.* yoˈojiñ 用心; keˈe-
kai 警戒: take an umbrella as a precaution (*yoojiñ no tame ni kasa o
motte iku*) 用心のために傘を持って行
く.

precede *vt.* (come before) ... yoˈri
mo saˈki ni kuˈru ...よりも先に来る
①; (go before) ... yoˈri mo saˈki ni
iku ...よりも先に行く Ⓒ: She preceded me into the room. (*Kanojo
wa watashi yori mo saki ni heya
ni haitta.*) 彼女は私よりも先に部屋に
入った.

preceding *adj.* maˈe no 前の; sa-
ˈki no 先の: the preceding page
(*mae no peeji*) 前のページ.

precious *adj.* kiˈchoo na 貴重な;
koˈoka na 高価な; taˈisetsu na 大切
な: waste one's precious time (*ki-
choo na jikañ o muda ni suru*) 貴
重な時間を無駄にする / precious
metals (*kikiñzoku*) 貴金属.

precise *adj.* (exact) seˈekaku na 正
確な; teˈkikaku na 的確な: a precise
translation (*seekaku na hoñyaku*)
正確な翻訳 / a precise explanation
(*tekikaku na setsumee*) 的確な説明.

precisely *adv.* seˈekaku ni 正確に;
choˈodo ちょうど: The plane took
off at twelve precisely. (*Hikooki
wa juuni-ji choodo ni ririku shita.*)
飛行機は 12 時ちょうどに離陸した.

precision *n.* seˈekaku 正確; seˈemitsu 精密: speak with precision
(*seekaku ni hanasu*) 正確に話す /
precision instruments (*seemitsu
kikai*) 精密機械.

predecessor *n.* zeˈñniˈñsha 前任
者; seˈñpai 先輩.

predict *vt.* ... to yoˈgeñ suru ...と予
言する ①; yoˈsoku suru 予測する ①:
Scientists predicted that there
would be an earthquake. (*Kagaku-
sha-tachi wa jishiñ ga okoru daroo to yogeñ shita.*) 科学者たちは地
震が起こるだろうと予言した.

preface *n.* joˈbuñ 序文.

prefecture *n.* keˈñ 県; fuˈ 府:
Chiba Prefecture (*Chiba-keñ*) 千葉

県 / Osaka-fu (*Oosaka-fu*) 大阪府.
★ '*Fu*' is only used with reference to Osaka and Kyoto.

prefer *vt.* ... no ho˺o ga su˺ki˺ da ...のほうが好きだ; ... no ho˺o ga ii ... のほうがいい: Which do you prefer, tea or coffee? (*Koocha to koohii to dochira ga o-suki desu ka?*) 紅茶とコーヒーとどちらがお好きですか. / I prefer going by train to flying. (*Watashi wa hikooki yori mo ressha de iku hoo ga ii.*) 私は飛行機よりも列車で行くほうがいい.

preferable *adj.* ko˺nomashi˺i 好ましい; no˺zomashi˺i 望ましい: It is preferable that you have knowledge of Japanese. (*Nihoñgo no chishiki o motte iru koto ga nozomashii.*) 日本語の知識を持っていることが望ましい.

preference *n.* ko˺nomi 好み: Her preference in reading is mysteries. (*Kanojo no dokusho no konomi wa misuterii desu.*) 彼女の読書の好みはミステリーです.

pregnant *adj.* ni˺ñshiñ shite iru 妊娠している: She is six months pregnant. (*Kanojo wa niñshiñ rok-kagetsu desu.*) 彼女は妊娠6か月です.

prejudice *n.* he˺ñkeñ 偏見; se˺ñnyu˺ukañ 先入観: He has a prejudice against modern art. (*Kare wa geñdai geejutsu ni heñkeñ o motte iru.*) 彼は現代芸術に偏見を持っている.
— *vt.* ... ni he˺ñkeñ o mo˺tase˺ru ...に偏見を持たせる Ⓥ; ha˺ñkañ o motase˺ru 反感を持たせる Ⓥ: He is prejudiced against the police. (*Kare wa keesatsu ni taishite hañkañ o motte iru.*) 彼は警察に対して反感を持っている.

preliminary *adj.* yo˺bi no 予備の; ju˺ñbi no 準備の: a preliminary examination (*yobi shikeñ*) 予備試験.

preparation *n.* ju˺ñbi 準備: The meal is in preparation. (*Shokuji wa juñbi-chuu desu.*) 食事は準備中です.

prepare *vt.* 1 (make ready) ... no ju˺ñbi o suru ...の準備をする Ⓣ; yo˺oi o suru 用意をする Ⓣ: He is

preparing his speech for tomorrow. (*Kare wa ashita no kooeñ no juñbi o shite imasu.*) 彼はあしたの講演の準備をしています.
2 (put together) ... no shi˺taku o suru ...のしたくをする Ⓣ: I'll prepare the table. (*Watashi ga shokuji no shitaku o shimasu.*) 私が食事のしたくをします.
— *vi.* ju˺ñbi suru 準備する Ⓘ; yo˺oi suru 用意する Ⓘ: prepare for an examination (*shikeñ no juñbi o suru*) 試験の準備をする.

preposition *n.* ze˺ñchi˺shi 前置詞.

prescribe *vt.* 1 (of a medicine) ... o sho˺hoo suru ...を処方する Ⓣ: The doctor prescribed a medicine for my stomach pains. (*Isha wa watashi no fukutsuu ni kusuri o shohoo shite kureta.*) 医者は私の腹痛に薬を処方してくれた.
2 (state) ... o ki˺tee suru ...を規定する Ⓣ; shi˺ji suru 指示する Ⓣ: The rules prescribe what we should do. (*Kisoku wa wareware ga nani o nasu beki ka kitee shite iru.*) 規則はわれわれが何をなすべきか規定している.

prescription *n.* sho˺hoo 処方; sho˺hooseñ 処方せん: Please fill this prescription. (*Kono shohooseñ de kusuri o kudasai.*) この処方せんで薬を下さい.

presence *n.* 1 (attendance) shu˺sseki 出席: Your presence is requested. (*Go-shusseki o o-negai itashimasu.*) ご出席をお願いいたします.
2 (the fact of being present) so˺ñzai 存在; i˺ru koto˺ いること: No one noticed his presence. (*Kare ga iru koto ni dare mo kizukanakatta.*) 彼がいることにだれも気づかなかった.

present[1] *adj.* 1 (being at the place) shu˺sseki shite iru 出席している: Were you present at the party? (*Anata wa sono kai ni shusseki shimashita ka?*) あなたはその会に出席しましたか.
2 (existing now) ge˺ñzai no 現在の: the present government (*geñzai no seefu*) 現在の政府.

3 (of grammar) geʰnzai no 現在の: the present form of a verb (dooshi no geñzai-kee) 動詞の現在形.
—— n. geʰnzai 現在; iˈma 今: He is not here at present. (Kare wa ima koko ni imaseñ.) 彼は今ここにいません.

present[2] n. (gift) oˈkurimono 贈り物; puˈreˈzeñto プレゼント: This is a present for you. (Kore wa anata e no okurimono desu.) これはあなたへの贈り物です.

present[3] vt. **1** (give) ... o oˈkuru ...を贈る ⓒ; zoˈotee suru 贈呈する ⓘ: I presented a book to her. (Watashi wa hoñ o kanojo ni okutta.) 私は本を彼女に贈った.
2 (offer) ... o teˈeshutsu suru ...を提出する ⓘ: He presented his plan at the meeting. (Kare wa kaigi ni jibuñ no keekaku o teeshutsu shita.) 彼は会議に自分の計画を提出した.
3 (introduce) ... o shoˈokai suru ...を紹介する ⓘ: May I present Mr. Ogawa to you? (Ogawa-shi o go-shookai itashimasu.) 小川氏をご紹介いたします.
4 (of a play) ... o joˈoeñ suru ...を上演する ⓘ: present a drama (geki o jooeñ suru) 劇を上演する.

presently adv. **1** (soon) ma-ˈmoˈ-naku まもなく; yaˈgate やがて: He will be here presently. (Kare wa ma-mo-naku koko e yatte kuru deshoo.) 彼はまもなくここへやって来るでしょう.
2 (now) geˈnzai wa 現在は; moˈk-ka 目下: She is presently abroad. (Kanojo wa geñzai gaikoku ni imasu.) 彼女は現在外国にいます.

preservation n. **1** (keeping) hoˈzoñ 保存; choˈzoo 貯蔵: preservation of food (shokuryoo no hozoñ) 食糧の保存.
2 (protection) hoˈgo 保護: preservation of nature (shizeñ hogo) 自然保護.

preserve vt. **1** (keep) ... o hoˈzoñ suru ...を保存する ⓘ; hoˈkañ suru 保管する ⓘ: preserve old documents (furui shorui o hozoñ suru) 古い書類を保存する.
2 (protect) ... o hoˈgo suru ...を保護する ⓘ: preserve the environment (kañkyoo o hogo suru) 環境を保護する.
3 (maintain) ... o taˈmoˈtsu ...を保つ ⓒ; iˈji suru 維持する ⓘ: preserve one's health (keñkoo o tamotsu) 健康を保つ.
4 (of food) ... o hoˈzoñ suru ...を保存する ⓘ; tsuˈkeru 漬ける ⓥ: preserve fruit in sugar (kudamono o satoo-zuke ni suru) 果物を砂糖漬けにする.

preside vi. (act as chairman) giˈ-choo o suru 議長をする ⓘ; (of a meeting) shiˈkai o suru 司会をする ⓘ: preside over a meeting (kaigi no shikai o suru) 会議の司会をする.

president n. (of a republic) daˈi-toˈoryoo 大統領; (of a company) shaˈchoo 社長; (of a university) gaˈkuchoo 学長.

press vt. **1** (push) ... o oˈsu ...を押す ⓒ: press a doorbell (doa no beru o osu) ドアのベルを押す.
2 (squeeze out) ... o shiˈboˈru ...を搾る ⓒ: press the juice out of grapes (budoo kara juusu o shiboru) ぶどうからジュースを搾る.
3 (iron) aˈiroñ o kakeˈru アイロンをかける ⓥ: This is to be pressed. (Kore wa airoñ o kakeru mono desu.) これはアイロンをかけるものです.
4 (hold close) ... o niˈgirishimeˈru ...を握り締める ⓥ; daˈkishimeˈru 抱き締める ⓥ: He pressed my hand firmly. (Kare wa watashi no te o shikkari to nigirishimeta.) 彼は私の手をしっかりと握り締めた.
5 (urge) ... o seˈkitateru ...をせきたてる ⓥ; seˈmaˈru 迫る ⓒ: He pressed me for an answer. (Kare wa watashi ni kaitoo o sematta.) 彼は私に回答を迫った.
—— vi. **1** (weigh down) (... o) oˈshi-tsukeˈru (...を)押しつける ⓥ; (with a foot) (... o) fuˈmitsukeˈru (...を)踏みつける ⓥ: He pressed down on the brake pedal. (Kare wa bureeki o

funda.) 彼はブレーキを踏んだ.

2 (crowd) (... ni) o⌐shiyose⌐ru (...に)
押し寄せる Ⅴ: They pressed around
her. (*Kare-ra wa kanojo no mawari
ni oshiyoseta*.) 彼らは彼女の周りに押
し寄せた.

3 (urge) (... o) se⌐gamu (...を)せがむ
Ⓒ; sa⌐isoku suru 催促する Ⓘ: He
pressed for payment. (*Kare wa
shiharai o saisoku shita*.) 彼は支払
いを催促した.

── *n.* **1** (newspapers) shi⌐ñbuñ 新
聞; (magazines) za⌐sshi 雑誌; (publishing) shu⌐ppañ 出版: freedom of
the press (*shuppañ no jiyuu*) 出版の
自由.

2 (people) ho⌐odo⌐ojiñ 報道陣; ki⌐
⌐sha⌐dañ 記者団: The Premier
meets the press on Monday. (*Shushoo wa getsuyoo ni kishadañ to
au*.) 首相は月曜に記者団と会う.

3 (printing press) i⌐ñsatsu⌐ki 印刷
機.

pressing *adj.* kyu⌐u o yoosu⌐ru 急を
要する; ki⌐ñkyuu no 緊急の: pressing
business (*kyuu o yoosuru shigoto*)
急を要する仕事.

pressure *n.* **1** (force) a⌐tsu⌐ryoku
圧力: the air pressure in a tire (*taiya no kuuki no atsuryoku*) タイヤの
空気の圧力 / blood pressure (*ketsuatsu*) 血圧.

2 (strain) a⌐ppaku 圧迫; ju⌐uatsu 重
圧; mental pressure (*seeshiñ-teki
na juuatsu*) 精神的な重圧.

prestige *n.* me⌐esee 名声; i⌐shiñ 威
信: The doctor enjoys great prestige. (*Sono isha wa meesee ga takai*.) その医者は名声が高い.

presume *vt.* (suppose) ... to su⌐i-
tee suru ...と推定する Ⓘ; ... da to o-
⌐mo⌐u ...だと思う Ⓒ: I presume him
innocence. (*Watashi wa kare wa
muzai da to omou*.) 私は彼は無罪だと
思う.

pretend *vt.* **1** (give a false appearance) ... no fu⌐ri⌐ o suru ...のふりをする
Ⓘ: She pretended not to know me.
(*Kanojo wa watashi o shiranai furi
o shita*.) 彼女は私を知らないふりをした.

2 (imagine) ... go⌐kko o suru ...ごっ
こをする Ⓘ: Let's pretend that we
are pirates. (*Kaizoku-gokko o shiyoo*.) 海賊ごっこをしよう.

pretext *n.* ko⌐ojitsu 口実; be⌐ñkai
弁解: He was absent on the pretext
of illness. (*Kare wa byooki o kooji-
tsu ni yasuñda*.) 彼は病気を口実に休
んだ.

pretty *adv.* ka⌐nari かなり; so⌐otoo
相当: I'm pretty tired. (*Watashi
wa kanari tsukaremashita*.) 私はかな
り疲れました.

── *adj.* **1** (of a child) ka⌐wairashi-
i⌐ かわいらしい; ki⌐ree na きれいな: a
pretty girl (*kawairashii oñna-no-
ko*) かわいらしい女の子.

2 (of a thing) ki⌐ree na きれいな: a
pretty garden (*kiree na niwa*) きれい
な庭.

prevail *vi.* **1** (be widespread) fu⌐
⌐kyuu shite iru 普及している Ⅴ;
ryu⌐ukoo suru 流行する Ⓘ: This
style will prevail this summer. (*Kono sutairu ga kono natsu ryuukoo
suru deshoo*.) このスタイルがこの夏流
行するでしょう.

2 (win out) (... ni) u⌐chika⌐tsu (...に)
打ち勝つ Ⓒ: prevail over an enemy
(*teki ni uchikatsu*) 敵に打ち勝つ.

prevalent *adj.* ryu⌐ukoo shite iru
流行している; ha⌐ya⌐tte iru はやってい
る: Colds are prevalent now. (*Kaze
ga ima hayatte iru*.) かぜが今はやって
いる.

prevent *vt.* **1** (stop) ... o fu⌐se⌐gu
...を防ぐ Ⓒ; bo⌐oshi suru 防止する
Ⓘ: prevent accidents (*jiko o fusegu*) 事故を防ぐ.

2 (hinder) ... o sa⌐ftmatage⌐ru ...を妨
げる Ⅴ; ja⌐ma suru じゃまする Ⓘ: He
prevented us from getting married.
(*Kare wa watashi-tachi no kekkoñ
o jama shita*.) 彼は私たちの結婚をじゃ
ました.

prevention *n.* bo⌐oshi 防止; yo⌐
⌐boo 予防: Prevention is better
than cure. (*Yoboo wa chiryoo ni
masaru*.) 予防は治療に勝る.

preventive *adj.* yo⌐boo no 予防の:

preventive measures (*yoboosaku*) 予防策.
— *n.* yo「bo」oyaku 予防薬.

previous *adj.* sa「ki no 先の; ma「e no 前の: The figure is on the previous page. (*Zu wa mae no peeji ni arimasu.*) 図は前のページにあります. / I have a previous engagement. (*Watashi wa señyaku ga arimasu.*) 私は先約があります.

previously *adv.* i「zeñ ni 以前に; ma「e ni 前に: He had arrived three days previously. (*Kare wa mikka mae ni tsuite ita.*) 彼は三日前に着いていた.

prey *n.* e「jiki えじき: The lion leaped upon its prey. (*Raioñ wa ejiki ni tobikakatta.*) ライオンはえじきに飛びかかった.
— *vi.* (... o) e「jiki ni suru (...を)えじきにする I: Large animals prey upon smaller ones. (*Ookii doobutsu wa chiisai doobutsu o ejiki ni suru.*) 大きい動物は小さい動物をえじきにする.

price *n.* 1 (amount of money) ne「dañ 値段; ka「kaku 価格: What is the price of this bag? (*Kono kabañ no nedañ wa ikura desu ka?*) このかばんの値段はいくらですか. / a fixed price (*teeka*) 定価.
2 (what one must suffer) da「ishoo 代償; gi「see 犠牲: He succeeded at the price of his health. (*Kare wa keñkoo o gisee ni shite seekoo shita.*) 彼は健康を犠牲にして成功した.
— *vt.* ... ni ne「dañ o tsu「ke」ru ...に値段をつける V: The watch was priced at 10,000 yen. (*Sono tokee wa ichi-mañ-eñ no nedañ ga tsuite ita.*) その時計は1万円の値段がついていた.

prick *vt.* ... o chi「ku」ri to sa「su ...をちくりと刺す C: I pricked my finger with a pin. (*Watashi wa piñ de yubi o chikuri to sashita.*) 私はピンで指をちくりと刺した.

pride *n.* 1 (pleasant feeling of satisfaction) ji「mañ 自慢; to「ku」i 得意: He takes pride in his son. (*Kare wa jibuñ no musuko o jimañ shite iru.*) 彼は自分の息子を自慢している.
2 (self-respect) ji「so」ñshiñ 自尊心; ho「kori 誇り: His pride was hurt by her words. (*Kanojo no kotoba de kare no jisoñshiñ wa kizutsukerareta.*) 彼女の言葉で彼の自尊心は傷つけられた.
3 (conceit) u「nubore うぬぼれ.

priest *n.* shi「sai 司祭: a Buddhist priest (*boosañ*) 坊さん.

primarily *adv.* o「mo ni 主に; shu「to shite 主として: This idea is primarily his. (*Kono aidea wa omo ni kare no mono desu.*) このアイデアは主に彼のものです.

primary *adj.* 1 (first in order) sho「kyuu no 初級の; sho「too no 初等の: primary education (*shotoo kyooiku*) 初等教育.
2 (first) da「i-ichi no 第一の; (most important) mo「tto」mo ju「uyoo na 最も重要な: The primary cause of the accident is his carelessness. (*Sono jiko no dai-ichi no geñiñ wa kare no fuchuui desu.*) その事故の第一の原因は彼の不注意です.
3 (chief) shu「yoo na 主要な; o「mo-na 主な: a primary road (*shuyoo dooro*) 主要道路.

primary school *n.* sho「oga」kkoo 小学校.

prime *adj.* 1 (most important) mo「tto」mo ju「uyoo na 最も重要な: Safety is a matter of prime importance. (*Añzeñ ga mottomo juuyoo na kotogara desu.*) 安全が最も重要な事柄です.
2 (best) sa「iryoo no 最良の; go「kujoo no 極上の: prime beef (*gokujoo no gyuuniku*) 極上の牛肉.
— *n.* ze「ñsee 全盛; sa「kari 盛り: He is already past his prime. (*Kare wa sude ni sakari o sugita.*) 彼はすでに盛りを過ぎた.

prime minister *n.* so「ori-da」ijiñ 総理大臣; shu「shoo 首相.

primitive *adj.* 1 (of the earliest times) ge「ñshi no 原始の: primitive man (*geñshijiñ*) 原始人.

2 (simple) ge⌐ñshi-teki na 原始的
な: primitive weapons (*geñshi-teki
na buki*) 原始的な武器.

prince *n.* **1** (son of a king or
queen) o⌐oji 王子; a: a crown prince
(*kootaishi*) 皇太子.
2 (ruler) ku⌐ñshu 君主.

princess *n.* **1** (daughter of a king
or queen) o⌐ojo 王女.
2 (wife of a prince) hi⌐ 妃: a crown
princess (*kootaishi-hi*) 皇太子妃.

principal *adj.* (most important)
mo⌐tto⌐mo ju⌐uyoo na 最も重要な;
(chief) o⌐mo na 主な: the principal
cities of Japan (*Nihoñ no omo na
toshi*) 日本の主な都市.
— *n.* **1** (head of a school) ko⌐o-
choo 校長.
2 (amount of money) ga⌐ñkiñ 元金.

principally *adv.* shu⌐ to shite 主と
して; o⌐mo ni 主に: Accidents occur
principally on rainy days. (*Jiko wa
omo ni ame no hi ni okorimasu.*) 事
故は主に雨の日に起こります.

principle *n.* **1** (general truth)
ge⌐ñri 原理; (rule) ge⌐ñsoku 原則:
the principles of economics (*keezaigaku no geñri*) 経済学の原理.
2 (guide to behavior) shu⌐gi 主義;
shi⌐ñjoo 信条: That is against my
principles. (*Sore wa watashi no
shiñjoo ni hañsuru.*) それは私の信条に
反する.
3 (scientific law) ge⌐ñri 原理: the
principle of the lever (*teko no
geñri*) てこの原理.
in principle *adv.* geñsoku to
shite 原則として.
on principle *adv.* shu⌐gi to shite
主義として.

print *vt.* **1** (on paper) ... o i⌐ñsatsu
suru ...を印刷する ☐; su⌐ru 刷る ☐:
The publisher printed 7,000 copies
of his book. (*Shuppañsha wa kare
no hoñ o nana-señ-bu iñsatsu shita.*)
出版社は彼の本を7千部印刷した.
2 (write) ... o ka⌐tsujitai de ka⌐ku
...を活字体で書く ☐: Please print
your name. (*Namae o katsujitai de
kaite kudasai.*) 名前を活字体で書い

てください.
3 (of a photograph) ... o ya⌐kitsu-
ke⌐ru ...を焼き付ける ☑: print out a
negative (*nega o yakitsukeru*) ネガを
焼き付ける.
— *n.* **1** (act of printing) i⌐ñsatsu
印刷.
2 (printed lettering) i⌐ñsatsu shita
mo⌐ji 印刷した文字; ka⌐tsuji 活字: a
book in large print (*ooki-na katsuji
no hoñ*) 大きな活字の本.
3 (printed reproduction) ha⌐ñga 版
画: a woodblock print (*mokuhañga*) 木版画.
4 (photography) i⌐ñga 印画; pu⌐riñ-
to プリント: a film for color prints
(*karaa puriñto-yoo firumu*) カラープ
リント用フィルム.
5 (mark) a⌐to 跡: the print of a foot
(*ashiato*) 足跡.

printed matter *n.* i⌐ñsatsu⌐butsu
印刷物.

printer *n.* **1** (people) i⌐ñsatsu⌐koo
印刷工; i⌐ñsatsu gyo⌐osha 印刷業者.
2 (machine) i⌐ñsatsu⌐ki 印刷機;
pu⌐riñtaa プリンター.

printing *n.* **1** (work of printer)
i⌐ñsatsu 印刷; i⌐ñsatsu⌐gyoo 印刷業.
2 (printed copies) i⌐ñsatsu busu⌐u
印刷部数; ha⌐ñ 版; su⌐ri⌐ 刷り: a first
printing of 5,000 copies (*shohañ go-
señ-bu*) 初版5千部.

prior *adj.* ma⌐e no 前の; sa⌐ki no 先
の: I have a prior engagement. (*Watashi wa señyaku ga arimasu.*) 私は
先約があります.

priority *n.* yu⌐useñ 優先; (right)
yu⌐useñ⌐keñ 優先権: This plan has
priority over others. (*Kono keekaku wa ta ni yuuseñ shimasu.*) こ
の計画は他に優先します. / give priori-
ty to elderly people (*o-toshiyori o
yuuseñ suru*) お年寄りを優先する.

prison *n.* ke⌐emu⌐sho 刑務所; ko⌐o-
chisho 拘置所: He is in prison. (*Kare wa keemusho ni haitte iru.*) 彼は
刑務所に入っている.

prisoner *n.* shu⌐ujiñ 囚人: release a
prisoner (*shuujiñ o shakuhoo suru*)
囚人を釈放する / a prisoner of war

(*horyo*) 捕虜.

privacy *n.* pu⌐rai⌐bashii プライバシー; shi⌐ji 私事: an invasion of privacy (*puraibashii no shiñgai*) プライバシーの侵害.

private *adj.* **1** (personal) ko⌐jiñ no 個人の; ko⌐jiñ-teki na 個人的な: These are my private affairs. (*Kore wa watashi no kojiñ-teki na moñdai desu.*) これは私の個人的な問題です. **2** (secret) na⌐imitsu no 内密の; hi⌐mitsu no 秘密の: Please keep this private. (*Kore wa naimitsu ni shite oite kudasai.*) これは内密にしておいてください. **3** (not public) shi⌐ritsu no 私立の: a private university (*shiritsu-daigaku*) 私立大学.

privately *adv.* na⌐isho⌐ de ないしょで; ko⌐jiñ-teki ni 個人的に: I'd like to speak to you privately. (*Naisho de o-hanashi o shitai no desu ga.*) ないしょでお話をしたいのですが.

privilege *n.* (special advantage) to⌐kuteñ 特典; (right) to⌐kkeñ 特権: They were given the privilege of using the room. (*Kare-ra wa sono heya o tsukau tokkeñ o ataerareta.*) 彼らはその部屋を使う特権を与えられた.

prize *n.* sho⌐o 賞; sho⌐ohiñ 賞品: She received a prize for her painting. (*Kanojo wa e de shoo o totta.*) 彼女は絵で賞を取った. / win first prize (*it-too-shoo o toru*) 1 等賞を取る.

probability *n.* **1** (likelihood) mi⌐komi 見込み; ko⌐osañ 公算: Is there any probability that he will win? (*Kare wa katsu mikomi wa arimasu ka?*) 彼は勝つ見込みはありますか. **2** (something that is probable) o⌐kori-so⌐o na ko⌐to⌐ 起こりそうなこと: It is a probability. (*Sore wa okori-soo na koto da.*) それは起こりそうなことだ.

probable *adj.* a⌐ri-so⌐o na ありそうな; ta⌐buñ ... daroo たぶん...だろう: It is probable that he will succeed. (*Kare wa tabuñ seekoo suru daroo.*)

彼はたぶん成功するだろう.

probably *adv.* ta⌐buñ たぶん; o⌐so⌐raku 恐らく: I'll probably be a little late. (*Tabuñ sukoshi okureru deshoo.*) たぶん少し遅れるでしょう.

problem *n.* **1** (question) mo⌐ñdai 問題: the problem of housing (*juutaku-moñdai*) 住宅問題 / solve a problem in mathematics (*suugaku no moñdai o toku*) 数学の問題を解く. **2** (difficulty) mo⌐ñdai 問題: There is little problem about it. (*Sore wa taishita moñdai de wa nai.*) それはたいした問題ではない. / a problem child (*moñdaiji*) 問題児.

No problem. (*Ii desu tomo.*) いいですとも; (*Doo itashimashite.*) どういたしまして.

procedure *n.* te⌐tsu⌐zuki 手続き; te⌐juñ 手順: an embarkation procedure (*shukkoku tetsuzuki*) 出国手続き / a landing procedure (*jooriku tetsuzuki*) 上陸手続き.

proceed *vi.* **1** (go on) (... ni) su⌐sumu (...に)進む C: After lunch we proceeded to the next destination. (*Chuushoku-go watashi-tachi wa tsugi no mokutekichi ni susuñda.*) 昼食後私たちは次の目的地に進んだ. **2** (continue) (... o) tsu⌐zukeru (...を)続ける V: Please proceed with your story. (*Doozo o-hanashi o tsuzukete kudasai.*) どうぞお話を続けてください.

process *n.* **1** (series of changes) ka⌐tee 課程: the process of learning (*gakushuu no katee*) 学習の課程. **2** (method) se⌐ehoo 製法; ko⌐otee 工程: make glass by a new process (*atarashii seehoo de garasu o tsukuru*) 新しい製法でガラスを作る. — *vt.* (of a material) ... o ka⌐koo suru ...を加工する I; (of information) ... o sho⌐ri suru ...を処理する I: process the data by computer (*deeta o koñpyuutaa de shori suru*) データをコンピューターで処理する.

procession *n.* gyo⌐oretsu 行列: a funeral procession (*soogi no* *gyooretsu* 葬儀の行列.

proclaim *vt.* ... o se⌐nge¬n suru ...を宣言する⌐]; ko⌐ohyoo suru 公表する⌐]: The colony proclaimed its independence. (*Sono shokuminchi wa dokuritsu o sengen shita.*) その植民地は独立を宣言した.

proclamation *n.* se⌐nge¬n 宣言; fu⌐koku 布告: a proclamation of war (*sensen fukoku*) 宣戦布告.

produce *vt.* 1 (manufacture) ... o tsu⌐ku¬ru ...を作る⌐C]; se⌐esan suru 生産する⌐]: This factory produces motorcycles. (*Kono koojoo wa ootobai o tsukutte imasu.*) この工場はオートバイを作っています.

2 (bring forth) ... o u⌐mu ...を産む⌐C]; sa⌐nshutsu suru 産出する⌐]: Hens produce an egg a day. (*Mendori wa ichi-nichi ni ik-ko tamago o umu.*) めんどりは1日に1個卵を産む.

3 (cause) ... o hi⌐kioko¬su ...を引き起こす⌐C]; mo⌐tara¬su もたらす⌐C]: Hard work produces good results. (*Isshookenmee yareba yoi kekka o motarashimasu.*) 一生懸命やればよい結果をもたらします.

4 (show) ... o da⌐shite mi¬se¬ru ...を出して見せる⌐V]: He produced his driver's license. (*Kare wa unten menkyoshoo o dashite miseta.*) 彼は運転免許証を出して見せた.

5 (bring to the public) ... o se⌐esaku suru ...を製作する⌐]; (of a play) jo⌐oen suru 上演する⌐]: produce a new play (*shinsaku no shibai o jooen suru*) 新作の芝居を上演する.

producer *n.* 1 (of a play, movie, etc.) pu⌐rodyu¬usaa プロデューサー; se⌐esa¬kusha 制作者.

2 (of goods) se⌐esa¬nsha 生産者.

product *n.* 1 (something produced) sa⌐nbutsu 産物; se⌐ehin 製品: a new product (*shin-seehin*) 新製品.

2 (result) ke⌐kka 結果; se⌐eka 成果: products of endeavor (*doryoku no kekka*) 努力の結果.

production *n.* 1 (act of making) se⌐esan 生産; se⌐ezoo 製造: mass production (*tairyoo-seesan*) 大量生産 / the production of arms (*buki no seezoo*) 武器の製造.

2 (the amount produced) se⌐esa¬ndaka 生産高: the production of automobiles (*jidoosha no seesandaka*) 自動車の生産高.

3 (of a play, movie, etc.) se⌐esaku 制作; e⌐nshutsu 演出.

productive *adj.* (producing much) se⌐esa¬nryoku no aru 生産力のある; (fertile) hi⌐yoku na 肥沃な; (fruitful) mi⌐nori no o¬oi 実りの多い: The discussion was productive. (*Sono tooron wa minori ga ookatta.*) その討論は実りが多かった.

productivity *n.* se⌐esa¬nryoku 生産力; se⌐esansee 生産性: low costs and high productivity (*hikui kosuto to takai seesansee*) 低いコストと高い生産性.

profess *vt.* (state) ... to ko⌐ogen suru ...と公言する⌐]; ha⌐kki¬ri i¬u はっきり言う⌐C]: He professed to know nothing about the matter. (*Kare wa sono koto ni tsuite nani mo shiranai to hakkiri itta.*) 彼はそのことについて何も知らないとはっきり言った.

profession *n.* 1 (occupation) sho⌐ku¬gyoo 職業; se⌐nmo¬nshoku 専門職: He is a lawyer by profession. (*Kare no shokugyoo wa bengoshi desu.*) 彼の職業は弁護士です.

2 (open declaration) ko⌐ogen 公言; ko⌐kuhaku 告白: professions of faith (*shinkoo no kokuhaku*) 信仰の告白.

professional *adj.* 1 (of a profession) sho⌐ku¬gyoo no 職業の; se⌐nmon-teki na 専門的な: professional skill (*senmon-teki na gijutsu*) 専門的な技術.

2 (not amateur) ho⌐nshoku no 本職の; pu⌐ro プロの: a professional golfer (*puro gorufaa*) プロゴルファー.
— *n.* ho⌐nshoku no hito¬ 本職の人; pu⌐ro プロ.

professor *n.* kyo⌐oju 教授: a professor of Japanese literature (*Ko-*

kubuñgaku kyooju) 国文学教授.

profile *n.* yoˈkogao 横顔; puˈrofiˈiru プロフィール.

profit *n.* **1** (money) riˈeki 利益; moˈoke¹ もうけ: make a profit (*rieki o ageru*) 利益をあげる / a net profit (*juñeki*) 純益.

2 (benefit) toˈku 得; eˈki 益: There is no profit in complaining. (*Fuhee o itte mo nañ no toku ni mo naranai.*) 不平を言っても何の得にもならない.
— *vi.* riˈeki o eˈru 利益を得る Ⓥ: He profited from the sale of his land. (*Kare wa tochi o utte rieki o eta.*) 彼は土地を売って利益を得た.

profitable *adj.* **1** (producing profit) moˈoke¹ ni naru もうけになる; yuˈuri na 有利な: a profitable business (*yuuri na jigyoo*) 有利な事業.

2 (benefit) taˈmeˈ ni naru ためになる; yuˈueki na 有益な: profitable advice (*yuueki na jogeñ*) 有益な助言.

profound *adj.* **1** (deep understanding) shiˈñeñ na 深遠な; fuˈkaˈi 深い: a man of profound learning (*gakushiki no fukai hito*) 学識の深い人.

2 (very deep) koˈkoˈro no soˈko kara¹ no 心の底からの; fuˈkaˈi 深い: profound sorrow (*fukai kanashimi*) 深い悲しみ.

program *n.* **1** (details of events) puˈroguˈramu プログラム; (of a TV and radio) baˈñgumi 番組: the program of a concert (*oñgakukai no puroguramu*) 音楽会のプログラム.

2 (plan) keˈekaku 計画: draw up a business program (*jigyoo-keekaku o tateru*) 事業計画を立てる.

3 (of a computer) puˈroguˈramu プログラム.

progress *n.* **1** (development) shiˈñpo 進歩; haˈttatsu 発達: the progress of civilization (*buñmee no hattatsu*) 文明の発達.

2 (forward movement) zeˈñshiñ 前進; shiˈñkoo 進行: We made slow progress through the crowd. (*Watashi-tachi wa guñshuu no aida o yukkuri zeñshiñ shita.*) 私たちは群衆の間をゆっくり前進した.

— *vi.* **1** (advance) zeˈñshiñ suru 前進する Ⓘ; shiˈñkoo suru 進行する Ⓘ: How is the work progressing? (*Shigoto wa ikaga shiñkoo shite imasu ka?*) 仕事はいかが進行していますか.

2 (develop) shiˈñpo suru 進歩する Ⓘ; joˈotatsu suru 上達する Ⓘ: He progressed in Japanese little by little. (*Kare no Nihoñgo wa sukoshi zutsu jootatsu shita.*) 彼の日本語は少しずつ上達した.

progressive *adj.* **1** (going ahead) zeˈñshiñ suru 前進する; shiˈñkoo shite iru 進行している: progressive movement (*zeñshiñ-uñdoo*) 前進運動.

2 (using new ideas) shiˈñpo-teki na 進歩的な: a progressive policy (*shiñpo-teki na seesaku*) 進歩的な政策.

prohibit *vt.* **1** (forbit) ... o kiˈñshi suru ...を禁止する Ⓘ; kiˈñjiru 禁じる Ⓥ: Parking is prohibited in this area. (*Kono chiiki wa chuusha ga kiñshi sarete imasu.*) この地域は駐車が禁止されています. / prohibited articles (*mochikomi kiñshihiñ*) 持込み禁止品.

2 (prevent) ... o saˈmatageˈru ...を妨げる Ⓥ; haˈbaˈmu 阻む Ⓒ: The rain prohibited us from going out. (*Ame ga watashi-tachi no gaishutsu o habañda.*) 雨が私たちの外出を阻んだ.

prohibition *n.* kiˈñshi 禁止; (order) kiˈñshi-meˈeree 禁止命令: a prohibition against swimming (*yuuee kiñshi*) 遊泳禁止.

project[1] *n.* keˈekaku 計画; kiˈkaku 企画: carry out one's project (*keekaku o jikkoo suru*) 計画を実行する.

project[2] *vt.* **1** (throw an image) ... o eˈesha suru ...を映写する Ⓘ; toˈo-ee suru 投影する Ⓘ: project a slide on a screen (*suraido o sukuriiñ ni eesha suru*) スライドをスクリーンに映写する.

2 (plan) ... o keˈekaku suru ...を計画する Ⓘ: A new dam is projected

for this area. (*Atarashii damu ga kono chiiki ni keekaku sarete imasu.*) 新しいダムがこの地域に計画されています.
— *vi.* (stick out) tsu「kide¹ru 突き出る: The rock projected from the sea. (*Sono iwa wa umi kara tsukidete ita.*) その岩は海から突き出ていた.

prolong *vt.* ... o e「nchoo suru ...を延長する ①; hi「kinoba¹su 引き延ばす ②: He prolonged his visit. (*Kare wa taizai o enchoo shita.*) 彼は滞在を延長した.

prominent *adj.* 1 (standing out) tsu「kide¹ta 突き出た; tsu「kide¹te iru 突き出ている: His front teeth are prominent. (*Kare no maeba wa tsukidete iru.*) 彼の前歯は突き出ている.
2 (famous) su「gu¹reta 優れた; su「gu¹rete iru 優れている; cho「mee na 著名な: a prominent politician (*chomee na seejika*) 著名な政治家.

promise *vt.* 1 (give one's word) ... ni (... to) ya「kusoku suru ...に(...と)約束する ①: He promised me to come at three. (*Kare wa watashi ni san-ji ni kuru to yakusoku shita.*) 彼は私に3時に来ると約束した.
2 (give a reason to expect) ... no mi「komi ga a¹ru ...の見込みがある ②; ... ni na「ri-so¹o da ...になりそうだ: It promises to be fine tomorrow. (*Ashita wa tenki ni nari-soo da.*) あしたは天気になりそうだ.
— *n.* 1 (agreement) ya「kusoku 約束: keep [carry out] one's promise (*yakusoku o mamoru [jikkoo suru]*) 約束を守る[実行する].
2 (expectation) mi「komi 見込み; yu「uboo 有望: a young writer of promise (*zento yuuboo na wakai sakka*) 前途有望な若い作家.

promising *adj.* mi「komi no a¹ru 見込みのある; ze「nto yu¹uboo no 前途有望の: She is a promising pianist. (*Kanojo wa zento yuuboo na pianisuto desu.*) 彼女は前途有望なピアニストです.

promote *vt.* 1 (advance in rank) ... o sho「oshin saseru ...を昇進させる ⑤; (of a student) ... o shi「nkyuu saseru ...を進級させる ⑤: He was promoted to manager. (*Kare wa kachoo ni shooshin shita.*) 彼は課長に昇進した.
2 (encourage) ... o so「kushin suru ...を促進する ①; zo「oshin suru 増進する ①: promote the sale of new products (*shin-seehin no hanbai o sokushin suru*) 新製品の販売を促進する.

promotion *n.* 1 (raising to a higher rank) sho「oshin 昇進; sho「okaku 昇格: He got a promotion last month. (*Kare wa sengetsu shooshin shita.*) 彼は先月昇進した.
2 (encouragement) so「kushin 促進; zo「oshin 増進: the promotion of world peace (*sekai-heewa no sokushin*) 世界平和の促進.

prompt *adj.* bi「nsoku na 敏速な; ha「ya¹i 速い: prompt action (*binsoku na koodoo*) 敏速な行動 / He is prompt in his payments. (*Kare wa shiharai ga hayai.*) 彼は支払いが速い.
— *vt.* ... o u「naga¹su ...を促す ⑤; shi「geki suru 刺激する ①: What prompted this hasty action? (*Nani ga kono yoo na hayamatta koodoo o unagashita no daroo ka?*) 何がこのような早まった行動を促したのだろうか.

promptly *adv.* bi「nsoku ni 敏速に; so「kuza ni 即座に: He promptly answered my letter. (*Kare wa sokuza ni henji o kureta.*) 彼は即座に返事をくれた.

pronoun *n.* da「ime¹eshi 代名詞.

pronounce *vt.* 1 (speak sounds) ... o ha「tsuon suru ...を発音する ①: How do you pronounce this word? (*Kono go wa doo hatsuon shimasu ka?*) この語はどう発音しますか.
2 (declare officially) ... o se「nge¹n suru ...を宣言する ①; se「nkoku suru 宣告する ①; da「nge¹n suru 断言する ①: pronounce sentence on a prisoner (*hikoku ni hanketsu o kudasu*) 被告に判決を下す / The doctor pronounced the patient cured. (*Isha wa kanja wa naotta to dan-*

geñ shita.) 医者は患者は治ったと断言
した.

pronunciation n. ha⌐tsuoñ 発音：
Her pronunciation is clear. (*Kanojo
no hatsuoñ wa hakkiri shite iru.*)
彼女の発音ははっきりしている.

proof n. **1** (evidence) sho⌐oko 証
拠; sho⌐omee 証明: We have no
proof that he is guilty. (*Kare ga
yuuzai da to iu shooko wa nai.*) 彼
が有罪だという証拠はない.
2 (trial print) ko⌐oseezuri 校正刷
り): correct the proofs of a textbook
(*tekisuto no kooseezuri o naosu*) テ
キストの校正刷りを直す.

proper adj. **1** (suitable) te⌐kisetsu
na 適切な; te⌐kitoo na 適当な: I am
looking for a proper place for the
meeting. (*Kaigi ni tekitoo na basho o sagashite iru tokoro desu.*)
会議に適当な場所を探しているところです.
2 (well-mannered) re⌐egi tadashi⌐i
礼儀正しい; sa⌐hoo ni ka⌐na⌐tta [ka-
⌐na⌐tte iru] 作法にかなった[かなってい
る]: His behavior is not proper.
(*Kare no taido wa sahoo ni kanatte
inai.*) 彼の態度は作法にかなっていない.

properly adv. **1** (correctly) ta⌐da⌐-
shiku 正しく: speak Japanese prop-
erly (*Nihoñgo o tadashiku hanasu*)
日本語を正しく話す.
2 (suitably) te⌐kitoo ni 適当に; ki-
⌐chi⌐ñto きちんと: He did his work
properly. (*Kare wa shigoto o kichiñto yatta.*) 彼は仕事をきちんとやった.

property n. **1** (something owned)
za⌐isañ 財産; shi⌐sañ 資産: real
property (*fudoosañ*) 不動産.
2 (land) sho⌐yu⌐uchi 所有地; ji⌐sho
地所: He has a large property in
Tokyo. (*Kare wa Tookyoo ni ooki-
na tochi o motte iru.*) 彼は東京に大き
な土地を持っている.
3 (characteristic) to⌐kusee 特性:
the properties of metal (*kiñzoku no
tokusee*) 金属の特性.

proportion n. **1** (ratio) wa⌐riai 割
合; hi⌐ritsu 比率: The proportion of
boys to girls in this class is three to
two. (*Kono kurasu no dañshi to

joshi no hiritsu wa sañ tai ni desu.*)
このクラスの男子と女子の比率は3対2
です.
2 (part) bu⌐buñ 部分: The larger
proportion of the earth is covered
with water. (*Chikyuu no daibubuñ
wa mizu de oowarete iru.*) 地球の大
部分は水で覆われている.
3 (balance) tsu⌐riai つり合い; ki⌐ñ-
koo 均衡: The desk and the chair
are not in proportion. (*Tsukue to
isu ga tsuriatte inai.*) 机といすがつり
合っていない.
4 (of mathematics) hi⌐ree 比例:
direct proportion (*seehiree*) 正比例
/ inverse proportion (*hañpiree*) 反
比例.

proposal n. **1** (something proposed) te⌐eañ 提案; mo⌐oshikomi
申し込み: My proposal was not accepted. (*Watashi no teeañ wa uke-
irerarenakatta.*) 私の提案は受け入れ
られなかった.
2 (offer of marriage) ke⌐kkoñ no
mooshikomi 結婚の申し込み;
pu⌐ropo⌐ozu プロポーズ: make a proposal to a woman (*josei ni puro-
poozu suru*) 女性にプロポーズする.

propose vt. **1** (suggest) ... o te⌐e-
añ suru ...を提案する ⊤; mo⌐oshi-
de⌐ru 申し出る Ⓥ: I proposed another meeting. (*Watashi wa moo
ichi-do kaigi o hiraku koto o teeañ
shita.*) 私はもう一度会議を開くことを
提案した.
2 (plan) ... o ke⌐ekaku suru ...を計
画する ⊤; (intend) tsu⌐mori da つもり
だ: He proposed to buy a car. (*Kare
wa kuruma o kau tsumori datta.*)
彼は車を買うつもりだった.
— vi. (make an offer of marriage)
ke⌐kkoñ o mooshiko⌐mu 結婚を申し
込む Ⓒ; pu⌐ropo⌐ozu suru プロポーズす
る ⊤: He proposed to her. (*Kare
wa kanojo ni kekkoñ o mooshi-
koñda.*) 彼は彼女に結婚を申し込んだ.

proposition n. **1** (proposal) te⌐e-
añ 提案; ke⌐ekaku 計画: I accepted
his proposition to share expenses.
(*Watashi wa hiyoo o wakeau to iu

kare no teeañ o ukeireta.) 私は費用を分け合うという彼の提案を受け入れた.
2 (statement) shu「choo 主張; chi「ñjutsu 陳述.

prose *n*. sa「ñbuñ 散文: write in prose (sañbuñ de kaku) 散文で書く.

prosecute *vt*. **1** (put on trial) ... o ki「so suru ...を起訴する ⊡: The man was prosecuted for theft. (*Sono otoko wa nusumi no kado de kiso sareta*.) その男は盗みのかどで起訴された.
2 (carry on) ... o o「konau ...を行う ⓒ; su「ikoo suru 遂行する ⊡: prosecute an inquiry (*choosa o okonau*) 調査を行う.

prospect *n*. **1** (outlook) mi「komi 見込み; ki「tai 期待: There is little prospect of his success. (*Kare no seekoo no mikomi wa amari nai*.) 彼の成功の見込みはあまりない.
2 (view) na「game」眺め; mi「harashi 見晴らし: The hotel commands a fine prospect. (*Sono hoteru wa nagame ga subarashii*.) そのホテルは眺めがすばらしい.

prospectus *n*. a「ññaisho 案内書; (of books) shi「ñkañ-a「ññai 新刊案内.

prosper *vi*. ha「ñee suru 繁栄する ⊡; ha「ñjoo suru 繁盛する ⊡: His business is prospering. (*Kare no shoobai wa hañjoo shite iru*.) 彼の商売は繁盛している.

prosperity *n*. ha「ñee 繁栄; ha「ñjoo 繁盛; se「ekoo 成功: I wish you happiness and prosperity. (*Go-takoo to go-seekoo o o-inori itashimasu*.) ご多幸とご成功をお祈りいたします.

prosperous *adj*. ha「ñee shite iru 繁栄している; ha「ñjoo shite iru 繁盛している: a prosperous business (*hañjoo shite iru shoobai*) 繁盛している商売.

protect *vt*. ... o ho「go suru ...を保護する ⊡; ma「moru 守る ⓒ: protect wild animals (*yasee no doobutsu o hogo suru*) 野生の動物を保護する / protect children from danger (*kodomo-tachi o kikeñ kara mamoru*)

子どもたちを危険から守る.

protection *n*. **1** (act of protecting) ho「go 保護: I asked for police protection. (*Watashi wa keesatsu no hogo o motometa*.) 私は警察の保護を求めた.
2 (something that protects) ho「go suru mo「no」保護する物: a protection from the sun (*hiyoke*) 日よけ.

protectionism *n*. ho「gobooekishu「gi 保護貿易主義; ho「gose」saku 保護政策.

protective *adj*. ho「go suru 保護する: protective trade (*hogo booeki*) 保護貿易.

protest *vi*. (... ni) ko「ogi suru (...に)抗議する ⊡; i「gi o mo「oshitateru 異議を申し立てる ⓥ: We protested against the new tax. (*Watashi-tachi wa atarashii zee ni koogi shita*.) 私たちは新しい税に抗議した.
— *vt*. **1** (object) ... ni ko「ogi suru ...に抗議する ⊡: He protested the umpire's decision. (*Kare wa shiñpañ no hañtee ni koogi shita*.) 彼は審判の判定に抗議した.
2 (insist) ... o shu「choo suru ...を主張する ⊡: I protested my innocence. (*Watashi wa keppaku o shuchoo shita*.) 私は潔白を主張した.
— *n*. ko「ogi 抗議; i「gi no mo「oshitate 異議の申し立て: a protest march (*koogi-demo*) 抗議デモ.

Protestant *n*. shi「ñkyo」oto 新教徒; pu「rote」sutañto プロテスタント.
— *adj*. shi「ñkyoo no 新教の.

proud *adj*. **1** (feeling satisfaction) ho「kori ni omo「u 誇りに思う; to「ku」i na 得意な: I am proud of my profession. (*Watashi wa jibuñ no shigoto o hokori ni omotte iru*.) 私は自分の仕事を誇りに思っている.
2 (conceited) u「nuboreta うぬぼれた; u「nuborete iru うぬぼれている; ko「omañ na 高慢な: I don't like his proud manner. (*Kare no koomañ na taido ga ki ni iranai*.) 彼の高慢な態度が気に入らない.
3 (having self-respect) ji「so」ñshiñ no aru 自尊心のある; ho「kori no ta-

「ka¹i 誇りの高い: He was too proud to accept the money. (*Kare wa ji-soñshiñ ga aru kara sono o-kane o uketoranakatta.*) 彼は自尊心があるからそのお金を受け取らなかった.

proudly *adv.* ho「korashi¹ge ni 誇らしげに; ji「mañ shite 自慢して: He talked about his experience proudly. (*Kare wa jibuñ no keekeñ o hokorashige ni katatta.*) 彼は自分の経験を誇らしげに語った.

prove *vt.* **1** (show to be true) ... o sho「omee suru ...を証明する ①; ri「sshoo suru 立証する ①: I proved him to be innocent. (*Watashi wa kare ga keppaku de aru koto o shoomee shita.*) 私は彼が潔白であることを証明した.

2 (test) ... o ta「me¹su ...を試す ⓒ: prove a new engine (*atarashii eñjiñ o tamesu*) 新しいエンジンを試す.

— *vi.* (turn out) ... de a「ru koto ga wa「ka¹ru ...であることがわかる ⓒ: The rumor proved to be false. (*Sono uwasa wa uso de aru koto ga wakatta.*) そのうわさはうそであることがわかった.

proverb *n.* ko「towaza ことわざ; ka「kugeñ 格言.

provide *vt.* **1** (supply) ... o kyo「okyuu suru ...を供給する ①; a「taeru 与える Ⓥ; yo「oi suru 用意する ①: We provided the victims with food. (*Watashi-tachi wa hisaisha ni tabemono o ataeta.*) 私たちは被災者に食べ物を与えた.

2 (set forth) ... to ki「tee suru ...と規定する ①: It is provided that the rent should be paid monthly. (*Yachiñ wa tsuki goto ni shiharau yoo ni kitee sarete iru.*) 家賃は月ごとに支払うように規定されている.

— *vi.* **1** (prepare) (... ni) so「nae¹ru (...に)備える Ⓥ; ju「ñbi suru 準備する ①: provide against typhoon (*taifuu ni sonaeru*) 台風に備える.

2 (support) (... o) ya「shina¹u (...を)養う ⓒ: provide for one's family (*kazoku o yashinau*) 家族を養う.

provided *conj.* mo「shi ⟨verb⟩-ba も

し...ば: I can buy it provided I have enough money. (*Moshi o-kane ga juubuñ ni areba sore o kau koto ga dekimasu.*) もしお金が十分にあればそれを買うことができます.

province *n.* **1** (region) chi「hoo 地方; i「naka いなか: He is from the provinces. (*Kare wa chihoo shusshiñ desu.*) 彼は地方出身です.

2 (field of knowledge) bu「ñya 分野; ha「ñi 範囲: It does not come within my province. (*Sore wa watashi no buñya de wa arimaseñ.*) それは私の分野ではありません.

3 (division of a country) shu「u 州.

provision *n.* **1** (preparation) yo「oi 用意; ju「ñbi 準備: I have to make provision for old age. (*Roogo no juñbi o shinakereba narimaseñ.*) 老後の準備をしなければなりません.

2 (food) sho「ku¹ryoo 食糧: Provisions have run out. (*Shokuryoo ga nakunatta.*) 食糧がなくなった.

3 (rule) ki「tee 規定; jo「okoo 条項.

provoke *vt.* **1** (make angry) ... o o「korase¹ru ...を怒らせる Ⓥ: Don't provoke the animals. (*Doobutsu o okorasete wa ikemaseñ.*) 動物を怒らせてはいけません.

2 (rouse) ... o hi「kioko¹su ...を引き起こす ⓒ: His words provoked laughter. (*Kare no kotoba wa warai o hikikoshita.*) 彼の言葉は笑いを引き起こした.

prudent *adj.* shi「ñchoo na 慎重な; fu「ñbetsu no a¹ru 分別のある: a prudent attitude (*shiñchoo na taido*) 慎重な態度.

prune¹ *n.* pu「ru¹uñ プルーン; ho「shisu¹momo 干しすもも.

prune² *vt.* ... o ka「riko¹mu ...を刈り込む ⓒ; ki「ritoru 切り取る ⓒ: prune hedges (*ikegaki o karikomu*) 生け垣を刈り込む / prune off dead branches (*kare-eda o kiritoru*) 枯れ枝を切り取る.

psychological *adj.* shi「ñri-teki na 心理的な: a psychological effect (*shiñri-teki kooka*) 心理的の効果.

psychology *n.* shi「ñri¹gaku 心理

学: child psychology (*jidoo shiñri-gaku*) 児童心理学.

public *adj.* **1** (of the people as a whole) ko「okyoo no 公共の: a public library (*kookyoo toshokañ*) 公共図書館.

2 (for the use of everyone) ko「o-shuu no 公衆の: a public telephone (*kooshuu-deñwa*) 公衆電話 / Is there a public restroom near here? (*Kono chikaku ni kooshuu toire wa arimasu ka?*) この近くに公衆トイレはありますか.

3 (acting for the people) ko「omu no 公務の: a public official (*koomuiñ*) 公務員.

4 (known by all) shu「uchi no 周知の: a matter of public knowledge (*shuuchi no kotogara*) 周知の事柄.

— *n.* (people in general) ji「ñmi¬ñ 人民; ko「kumiñ 国民; ko「oshuu 公衆: (*Kokumiñ wa shiru keñri ga aru.*) 国民は知る権利がある.

publication *n.* **1** (something published) shu「ppa¬ñbutsu 出版物; ka「ñ-ko¬obutsu 刊行物: new publications (*shiñkañshoo*) 新刊書.

2 (publishing) shu「ppañ 出版; ha「k-koo 発行; ka「ñkoo 刊行: the date of publication (*hakkoo neñgappi*) 発行年月日.

publicity *n.* **1** (being widely known) yo「ku shi「rewata¬ru ko「to¬ よく知れ渡ること; hyo「obañ 評判: His novel gained wide publicity. (*Kare no shoosetsu wa hiroku hyoobañ ni natta.*) 彼の小説は広く評判になった.

2 (advertising) ko「okoku 広告; se「ñdeñ 宣伝: publicity for a movie (*eega no señdeñ*) 映画の宣伝.

publish *vt.* **1** (bring out) ... o shu「ppañ suru ...を出版する①; ha「k-koo suru 発行する①; ka「ñkoo suru 刊行する①: His new novel will be published in September. (*Kare no atarashii shoosetsu wa ku-gatsu ni shuppañ saremasu.*) 彼の新しい小説は9月に出版されます.

2 (make known) ... o ha「ppyoo suru ...を発表する①; ko「ohyoo suru 公表する①: publish a secret (*himitsu o koohyoo suru*) 秘密を公表する.

publisher *n.* shu「ppa¬ñsha 出版社; shu「ppañ gyo「osha 出版業者.

puff *n.* **1** (small blast) hi「to¬fuki ひと吹き; pu「tto fuku ko「to¬ ぷっと吹くこと: blow out a candle in one puff (*roosoku o hito-fuki de kesu*) ろうそくをひと吹きで消す.

2 (soft round object) fu「wa¬tto shita mo「no¬ ふわっとした物: puffs of cloud (*fuwatto shita kumo*) ふわっとした雲 / a cream puff (*shuukuriimu*) シュークリーム.

— *vi.* **1** (blow out) pu「tto fu「ki-da¬su ぷっと吹き出す©: puff at one's pipe (*paipu o fukasu*) パイプを吹かす.

2 (breathe hard) i「ki o ki「ra¬su 息を切らす©; a「e¬gu あえぐ©: He puffed up the stairs. (*Kare wa aegi-nagara kaidañ o nobotta.*) 彼はあえぎながら階段を上った.

— *vt.* pa「ppato haku ぱっぱと吐く©: puff cigarette smoke (*tabako no kemuri o haku*) たばこの煙を吐く.

pull *vt.* **1** (draw) ... o hi「ppa¬ru ...を引っ張る©; hi「ku 引く©: pull a rope (*tsuna o hipparu*) 綱を引っ張る / He pulled my sleeve. (*Kare wa watashi no sode o hiita.*) 彼は私のそでを引いた.

2 (pluck out) ... o nu「ku ...を抜く©; mu「shiru むしる©: I need to pull a tooth. (*Ha o ip-poñ nukanakereba naranai.*) 歯を1本抜かなければならない. / pull up weeds in the garden (*niwa no zassoo o mushiru*) 庭の雑草をむしる.

— *vi.* **1** (draw) (... o) hi「ppa¬ru (...を)引っ張る©; hi「ku 引く©: A fish is pulling on the line. (*Sakana ga ito o hiite iru.*) 魚が糸を引いている.

2 (row) ko「gu 漕ぐ©: He pulled toward the shore. (*Kare wa kishi e mukatte koida.*) 彼は岸へ向かって漕いだ.

3 (steer) (... ni) yo「ru (...に)寄る©: The car pulled into the side of the road. (*Kuruma wa dooro waki ni*

yotta.) 車は道路わきに寄った.
— *n.* **1** (act of pulling) hi「ppa¹ru
ko「to」引っ張ること; hi「ku koto¹ 引く
こと: give the handle a pull (*haṅdo-
ru o gui to hiku*) ハンドルをぐいと引く.
2 (pulling force) hi「ku chikara¹ 引く
力; i¹ṅryoku 引力: the pull of the
moon (*tsuki no iṅryoku*) 月の引力.

pulse *n.* mya「kuhaku 脈拍; mya「ku¹
脈: feel a person's pulse (*hito no
myaku o miru*) 人の脈を診る.

pump *n.* po「ṅpu ポンプ: a bicycle
pump (*kuuki-ire*) 空気入れ.
— *vt.* ... o po「ṅpu de su「ida¹su ...を
ポンプで吸い出す C; ku「mida¹su くみ
出す C: pump water from a well
(*ido kara mizu o poṅpu de kumidasu*) 井戸から水をポンプでくみ出す.

pumpkin *n.* ka「bocha かぼちゃ.

punch *vt.* ... o ge「ṅkotsu de u¹tsu ...
をげんこつで打つ C; ... ni pa¹ṅchi o
ku「rawasu ...にパンチをくらわす C: He
punched me on the chin. (*Kare wa
watashi no ago ni paṅchi o kurawa-
seta.*) 彼は私のあごにパンチをくらわせた.
— *n.* pa¹ṅchi パンチ; ge「ṅkotsu de
u¹tsu ko「to」げんこつで打つこと: give a
person a punch in the face (*hito no
kao o naguru*) 人の顔を殴る.

punctual *adj.* (on time) ji「kaṅ o
mamo¹ru 時間を守る; (of a date)
ki¹jitsu o ma「mo¹ru 期日を守る: He
is always punctual for appoint-
ments. (*Kare wa itsu-mo yakusoku
no jikaṅ o mamoru.*) 彼はいつも約束
の時間を守る.

punish *vt.* ... o ba「ssuru ...を罰する
I; ko「rashime¹ru 懲らしめる V: He
was punished for cheating in the
exam. (*Kare wa shikeṅ de kaṅni-
ṅgu o shite basserareta.*) 彼は試験で
カンニングをして罰せられた.

punishment *n.* sho「batsu 処罰;
ke「ebatsu 刑罰: inflict punishment
on a person (*hito o shobatsu suru*)
人を処罰する.

pupil[1] *n.* (child) se「eto 生徒: This
school has 500 pupils. (*Kono gakkoo ni wa seeto ga go-hyaku-niṅ
iru.*) この学校には生徒が500人いる.

pupil[2] *n.* (of the eye) hi「tomi ひとみ;
do「okoo どう孔.

purchase *vt.* ... o k「au ...を買う C;
ko「onyuu suru 購入する I: He pur-
chased a new car. (*Kare wa shiṅsha
o katta.*) 彼は新車を買った.
— *n.* **1** (buying) ko「onyuu 購入;
ka「iire 買い入れ: save money for the
purchase of a house (*ie o koonyuu
suru tame ni o-kane o tameru*) 家を
購入するためにお金をためる.
2 (article) ko「onyuuhiṅ 購入品;
ka「imono 買い物: make a good purchase (*toku na kaimono o suru*) 得
な買い物をする.

pure *adj.* **1** (not mixed) ju「ṅsui na
純粋な; ma「jirike no na¹i 混じり気の
ない: pure gold (*juṅkiṅ*) 純金.
2 (clean) se「eketsu na 清潔な; ki¹-
ree na きれいな: pure water (*kiree na
mizu*) きれいな水.

purity *n.* (being pure) ju「ṅsui 純粋;
(cleanness) se「eketsu 清潔.

purple *adj.* mu「rasaki iro no 紫色
の: a purple flower (*murasaki iro no
hana*) 紫色の花.
— *n.* mu「rasaki-iro 紫色.

purpose *n.* **1** (aim) mo「kuteki 目
的; mo「kuhyoo 目標: What is the
purpose of your trip? (*Anata no ryokoo no mokuteki wa naṅ desu ka?*)
あなたの旅行の目的は何ですか. / He
attained his purpose. (*Kare wa
mokuteki o tasshita.*) 彼は目的を達
した.
2 (use) yo「oto 用途: This tool has
various purposes. (*Kono doogu wa
iroiro na yooto o motte imasu.*) この
道具はいろいろな用途を持っています.

purse *n.* **1** (handbag) ha「ṅdoba¹g-
gu ハンドバッグ.
2 (small bag for carrying money)
ko「zeni¹-ire 小銭入れ; ga「maguchi
がま口.

purser *n.* (of an airplane, ship)
pa¹asaa パーサー.

pursue *vt.* **1** (chase) ... o o「ikake¹-
ru ...を追いかける V; tsu「iseki suru
追跡する I: He pursued the thief.
(*Kare wa doroboo o oikaketa.*) 彼は

どろぼうを追いかけた.

2 (continue) ... o tsuˈzukeru ...を続ける Ⓥ: I want to pursue my research at the university. (*Watashi wa daigaku de keñkyuu o tsuzuketai.*) 私は大学で研究を続けたい.

pursuit *n.* **1** (pursuing) tsuˈiseki 追跡; tsuˈikyuu 追求: the pursuit of happiness (*koofuku no tsuikyuu*) 幸福の追求.

2 (occupation) shiˈgoto 仕事; shoˈkuˈgyoo 職業: daily pursuits (*nichijoo no shigoto*) 日常の仕事.

3 (hobby) shuˈmi 趣味: Fishing is my favorite pursuit. (*Tsuri ga watashi no shumi desu.*) 釣りが私の趣味です.

push *vt.* **1** (press) ... o oˈsu ...を押す Ⓒ: push a button (*botañ o osu*) ボタンを押す / He pushed the door open. (*Kare wa doa o oshite aketa.*) 彼はドアを押して開けた.

2 (urge on) ... ni (... o) kaˈritateˈru ...に(...を)駆り立てる Ⓥ; seˈkitateru せきたてる Ⓥ: He pushed me for payment. (*Kare wa watashi ni shiharai o sekitateta.*) 彼は私に支払いをせきたてた.

3 (promote) ... o oˈshisusumeˈru ...を押し進める Ⓥ; gaˈñbaˈru がんばる Ⓒ: push one's plans (*keekaku o oshisusumeru*) 計画を押し進める.

— *vi.* 1 (press) oˈsu 押す Ⓒ: You push while I pull. (*Watashi ga hikimasu kara oshite kudasai.*) 私が引きますから押してください.

2 (advance with effort) oˈshisusuˈmu 押し進む Ⓒ: I pushed through the crowd. (*Watashi wa hitogomi no naka o oshisusuñda.*) 私は人込みの中を押し進んだ.

— *n.* 1 (pushing) oˈsu kotoˈ 押すこと; oˈshi 押し: give a door a hard push (*doa o tsuyoku osu*) ドアを強く押す.

2 (vigorous effort) gaˈñbariˈ がんばり; doˈryoku 努力: make a push (*gañbaru*) がんばる.

put *vt.* **1** (place) ... o oˈku ...を置く Ⓒ; suˈeru 据える Ⓥ: She put the vase by the window. (*Kanojo wa kabiñ o mado no soba ni oita.*) 彼女は花びんを窓のそばに置いた.

2 (cause to be in a condition) ... o ... suˈru ...を...する Ⓘ: I put my room in order. (*Watashi wa heya o seetoñ shita.*) 私は部屋を整頓した.

3 (submit) ... o daˈsu ...を出す Ⓒ; teˈeshutsu suru 提出する Ⓘ: He put several questions to me. (*Kare wa watashi ni ikutsu-ka shitsumoñ o shita.*) 彼は私にいくつか質問をした.

4 (express) ... o iˈiarawaˈsu ...を言い表す Ⓒ: put one's thoughts into words (*kañgae o kotoba ni iiarawasu*) 考えを言葉に言い表す.

5 (attach) ... o tsuˈkeˈru ...を付ける Ⓥ: put a knob on a door (*doa ni totte o tsukeru*) ドアに取っ手を付ける.

6 (write down) ... o kaˈkikomu ...を書き込む Ⓒ; kiˈñnyuu suru 記入する Ⓘ: He put something in his notebook. (*Kare wa nooto ni nani-ka o kakikoñda.*) 彼はノートに何かを書き込んだ.

put away *vt.* ... o kaˈtazukeˈru ...を片づける Ⓥ: put toys away (*omocha o katazukeru*) おもちゃを片づける.

put down *vt.* ... o shiˈta ni oku ...を下に置く Ⓒ: put a glass down (*koppu o shita ni oku*) コップを下に置く.

put in *vt.* ... ni iˈreru ...に入れる Ⓥ: Put the garbage in here. (*Gomi wa koko ni ire nasai.*) ごみはここに入れなさい.

put on *vt.* ... o mi ˈni tsukeˈru ...を身につける Ⓥ: put on a coat (*kooto o kiru*) コートを着る / put on shoes (*kutsu o haku*) 靴をはく / put on a hat (*booshi o kaburu*) 帽子をかぶる / put on glasses (*megane o kakeru*) 眼鏡をかける / put on a ring (*yubiwa o hameru*) 指輪をはめる.

put out *vt.* ... o keˈsu ...を消す Ⓒ: put out a light (*akari o kesu*) 明かりを消す.

puzzle *vt.* (perplex) ... o koˈmaraseˈru ...を困らせる Ⓥ; naˈyamaˈsu 悩ます Ⓒ: I am puzzled about what to do. (*Watashi wa doo shite yoi ka* *nayañde iru.*) 私はどうしてよいか悩んでいる.

— *vi.* (think hard) aˈtamaˈo shiˈboˈru 頭を絞る C: He puzzled over the question. (*Kare wa sono moñdai ni atama o shibotta.*) 彼はその問題に頭を絞った.

— *n.* 1 (problem) naˈñmoñ 難問;

naˈzo なぞ: His behavior is a puzzle to us. (*Kare no koodoo wa watashi-tachi ni totte nazo da.*) 彼の行動は私たちにとってなぞだ.

2 (game) paˈzuru パズル: a jigsaw puzzle (*jigusoo pazuru*) ジグソーパズル.

Q

quaint *adj.* fuˈugaˈwari na 風変わりな: quaint customs (*fuugawari na shuukañ*) 風変わりな習慣.

qualification *n.* 1 (diploma) shiˈkaku 資格: She has a nurse's qualifications. (*Kanojo wa kañgofu no shikaku o motte imasu.*) 彼女は看護婦の資格を持っています.

2 (restriction) joˈokeˈñ 条件: The committee accepted my suggestion without any qualification. (*Iñkai wa nañ no jookeñ mo nashi de watashi no teeañ o mitometa.*) 委員会は何の条件もなしで私の提案を認めた.

qualified *adj.* shiˈkaku no aˈru 資格のある: a qualified architect (*shikaku no aru keñchikushi*) 資格のある建築士.

qualify *vt.* 1 (make fit) ... ni shiˈkaku o ataeru ...に資格を与える V: She is qualified to teach Japanese. (*Kanojo wa Nihoñgo o oshieru shikaku ga arimasu.*) 彼女は日本語を教える資格があります.

2 (make less strict) ... o yaˈwarageˈru ...を和らげる V: qualify one's anger (*ikari o yawarageru*) 怒りを和らげる.

3 (modify) ... o shuˈushoku suru ...を修飾する I: Adjectives qualify nouns. (*Keeyooshi wa meeshi o shuushoku suru.*) 形容詞は名詞を修飾する.

— *vi.* shiˈkaku o eˈru 資格を得る V: He qualified to receive a scholarship. (*Kare wa shoogakukiñ o*

morau shikaku o eta.) 彼は奨学金をもらう資格を得た.

quality *n.* 1 (nature) shiˈtsu 質; hiˈñshitsu 品質: goods of good [poor] quality (*shitsu no yoi [warui] shinamono*) 質のよい[悪い]品物.

2 (characteristic) toˈkushitsu 特質; toˈkusee 特性: Hardness is one quality of iron. (*Katai no ga tetsu no hitotsu no tokusee desu.*) 硬いのが鉄の一つの特性です.

3 (excellence) ryoˈoshitsu 良質; koˈokyuu 高級: quality goods (*kookyuuhiñ*) 高級品.

quantity *n.* ryoˈo 量; suˈuryoˈo 数量; buˈñryoˈo 分量: I prefer quality to quantity. (*Watashi wa ryoo yori mo shitsu o erabimasu.*) 私は量よりも質を選びます. / a large [small] quantity of cement (*tairyoo [shooryoo] no semeñto*) 大量[少量]のセメント.

quarantine *n.* kaˈkuri 隔離; keˈñeki 検疫: put a person in quarantine (*hito o kakuri suru*) 人を隔離する.

— *vt.* ... o kaˈkuri suru ...を隔離する I; keˈñeki suru 検疫する I: All the passengers were quarantined. (*Jookyaku wa zeñiñ keñeki o uketa.*) 乗客は全員検疫を受けた.

quarrel *vi.* koˈoroñ suru 口論する I; keˈñka suru けんかする I: He quarreled with his wife over trifles. (*Kare wa tsumaranai koto de okusañ to kooroñ shita.*) 彼はつまらないことで奥さんと口論した. / They are always quarreling with each other.

(*Kare-ra wa o-tagai ni keñka bakari shite iru.*) 彼らはお互いにけんかばかりしている.

— *n.* ko¹oroñ 口論; ku¹chige¹ñka 口げんか: He had a quarrel with her. (*Kare wa kanojo to kuchigeñka o shita.*) 彼は彼女と口げんかをした.

quart *n.* ku¹o¹oto クォート. ★ In Japan the metric system is used.

quarter *n.* **1** (fourth part) yo¹ñbuñ no ichi¹ 4 分の 1: a quarter of a kilometer (*yoñbuñ no ichi-kiro*) 4 分の 1 キロ / three quarters (*yoñbuñ no sañ*) 4 分の 3.

2 (15 minutes) ju¹ugo-fuñ 15 分: It's quarter past seven. (*Shichi-ji juugo-fuñ sugi desu.*) 7 時 15 分過ぎです.

3 (three months) shi¹ha¹ñki 4 半期: the profits for the first quarter (*dai-ichi shihañki no rieki*) 第一 4 半期の利益.

4 (region) chi¹iki 地域; chi¹ku 地区: the residential quarter (*juukyo chiku*) 住居地区.

— *vt.* ... o yo¹ttsu¹ ni wa¹ke¹ru ... を 4 つに分ける ▽; yo¹ñtoobuñ suru 4 等分する ▯: quarter an apple (*riñgo o yottsu ni kiru*) りんごを 4 つに切る.

queen *n.* **1** (ruler) jo-¹o¹o 女王: the Queen of England (*Eekoku jo-oo*) 英国女王.

2 (excellent woman) jo-¹o¹o 女王; ha¹nagata 花形: a beauty queen (*bijiñ koñtesuto no jo-oo*) 美人コンテストの女王.

queer *adj.* **1** (strange) ki¹myoo na 奇妙な; he¹ñ na 変な: It is queer that he didn't show up. (*Kare ga sugata o misenakatta no wa heñ da.*) 彼が姿を見せなかったのは変だ.

2 (causing suspicion) a¹yashii 怪しい; u¹tagawashii 疑わしい: There was a queer noise in the attic. (*Ya-neura de ayashii mono-oto ga shita.*) 屋根裏で怪しい物音がした.

3 (sick) ki¹buñ ga wa¹ru¹i 気分が悪い: I do feel a bit queer. (*Watashi wa sukoshi kibuñ ga warui.*) 私は少し気分が悪い.

quench *vt.* ... o i¹ya¹su ...をいやす ▢: quench one's thirst (*nodo no kawaki o iyasu*) のどの渇きをいやす.

question *n.* **1** (expression) shi¹tsumoñ 質問; to¹i 問い: May I ask you a question? (*Shitsumoñ shite mo yoroshii desu ka?*) 質問してもよろしいですか.

2 (problem) mo¹ñdai 問題: the housing question (*juutaku-moñdai*) 住宅問題.

3 (doubt) gi¹moñ 疑問; u¹tagai 疑い: There is no question that he is telling the truth. (*Kare ga hoñtoo no koto o itte iru no wa utagai nai.*) 彼が本当のことを言っているのは疑いない.

— *vt.* **1** (ask a question) ... ni shi¹tsumoñ suru ...に質問する ▯: I was questioned by a policeman. (*Watashi wa keekañ ni shitsumoñ sareta.*) 私は警官に質問された.

2 (doubt) ... o u¹tagau ...を疑う ▢: I question his honesty. (*Watashi wa kare no shoojikisa o utagau.*) 私は彼の正直さを疑う.

question mark *n.* gi¹mo¹ñfu 疑問符.

queue *n.* re¹tsu 列: form a queue (*retsu o tsukuru*) 列を作る.

— *vi.* re¹tsu o tsu¹ku¹ru 列を作る ▢; na¹rañde ma¹tsu 並んで待つ ▢: We queued up for a taxi. (*Watashi-tachi wa ichi-retsu ni narañde takushii o matta.*) 私たちは一列に並んでタクシーを待った.

quick *adj.* **1** (fast) ha¹ya¹i 速[早]い: He is a quick walker. (*Kare wa aruku no ga hayai.*) 彼は歩くのが速い.

2 (alert) bi¹ñkañ na 敏感な; ha¹ya¹i 早い: She is quick at learning Japanese. (*Kanojo wa Nihoñgo o oboeru no ga hayai.*) 彼女は日本語を覚えるのが早い.

3 (easily aroused) o¹korippo¹i 怒りっぽい: Mr. Tanaka has a quick temper. (*Tanaka-sañ wa okorippoi.*) 田中さんは怒りっぽい.

— *adv.* ha¹yaku 速[早]く; i¹so¹ide 急いで: Can't you run quicker? (*Motto hayaku hashirenai no?*) もっ

と速く走れないの. / Come quick. (*Isoide ki nasai.*) 急いで来なさい.

quickly *adv.* ha⌐ya⌐ku 速く[早]; i⌐so⌐ide 急いで; su⌐gu ni すぐに: Quickly, please. (*Hayaku o-negai shimasu.*) 早くお願いします. / He walked quickly. (*Kare wa isoide aruita.*) 彼は急いで歩いた. / The doctor came quickly. (*Isha wa sugu ni kita.*) 医者はすぐに来た.

quiet *adj.* **1** (not noisy) shi⌐zuka na 静かな: I'd like a quiet room. (*Shizuka na heya o tanomimasu.*) 静かな部屋を頼みます.
2 (peaceful) he⌐eoñ na 平穏な; he⌐e-wa na 平和な: live a quiet life (*heeoñ na kurashi o suru*) 平穏な暮らしをする.
3 (still) shi⌐zuka na 静かな; u⌐goka⌐-nai 動かない: The lake is quiet. (*Mizuumi wa shizuka da.*) 湖は静かだ.
4 (gentle) o⌐tonashi⌐i おとなしい; shi⌐to⌐yaka na しとやかな: a quiet woman (*shitoyaka na josee*) しとやかな女性.
5 (not showy) ji⌐mi⌐ na 地味な: a quiet color (*jimi na iro*) 地味な色.
— *n.* shi⌐zuke⌐sa 静けさ; se⌐ejaku 静寂: the quiet after a storm (*arashi no ato no shizukesa*) 嵐の後の静けさ.
2 (peace) he⌐eoñ 平穏; he⌐ewa 平和.
— *vt.* ... o shi⌐zume⌐ru ...を静める Ⓥ; na⌐dame⌐ru なだめる Ⓥ: quiet a

crying baby (*naite iru akañboo o nadameru*) 泣いている赤ん坊をなだめる.
— *vi.* shi⌐zuma⌐ru 静まる Ⓒ: The storm quieted down. (*Arashi wa shizumatta.*) 嵐は静まった.

quietly *adv.* shi⌐zuka ni 静かに: walk quietly (*shizuka ni aruku*) 静かに歩く.

quit *vt.* ... o ya⌐meru ...を辞める Ⓥ: He quit his job last month. (*Kare wa señgetsu tsutome o yamemashita.*) 彼は先月勤めを辞めました.

quite *adv.* **1** (completely) ma⌐ttaku まったく; ka⌐ñzeñ ni 完全に: I quite agree with you. (*Watashi mo anata to mattaku onaji ikeñ desu.*) 私もあなたとまったく同じ意見です. / He is not quite well yet. (*Kare wa mada kañzeñ ni yoku natte imaseñ.*) 彼はまだ完全によくなっていません.
2 (rather) na⌐kanaka なかなか; ka⌐-nari かなり: It is quite cold this morning. (*Kesa wa kanari samui.*) けさはかなり寒い.

quiz *n.* **1** (short test) sho⌐o-shike⌐ñ 小試験; sho⌐o-te⌐suto 小テスト.
2 (game) ku⌐izu クイズ.

quotation *n.* i⌐ñyoo 引用; i⌐ñyoo-buñ 引用文.

quote *vt.* ... o i⌐ñyoo suru ...を引用する Ⓘ: He quoted the phrase from the Bible. (*Kare wa sono ku o seesho kara iñyoo shita.*) 彼はその句を聖書から引用した.

R

race[1] *n.* **1** (competition in speed) kyo⌐osoo 競走; re⌐esu レース: run a race (*kyoosoo suru*) 競走する / the races (*keeba*) 競馬.
2 (contest) kyo⌐osoo 競争: an arms race (*guñbi-kyoosoo*) 軍備競争.
— *vi.* (... to) kyo⌐osoo suru (...と) 競走する Ⓘ: I raced with him. (*Watashi wa kare to kyoosoo*

shita.*) 私は彼と競走した.
— *vt.* ... to kyo⌐osoo suru ...と競走する Ⓘ: I'll race you to the station. (*Eki made kimi to kyoosoo shiyoo.*) 駅まで君と競走しよう.

race[2] *n.* ji⌐ñshu 人種; mi⌐ñzoku 民族: the race problem (*jiñshu-moñdai*) 人種問題.

rack *n.* **1** (shelf) o⌐kidana 置き棚: a baggage rack (*amidana*) 網棚.

2 (framework) -¹kake 掛け: a hat rack (booshi-kake) 帽子掛け / a towel rack (taoru-kake) タオル掛け.

racket n. ra⸢ke⸣tto ラケット.

radar n. re⸢edaa レーダー: a radar system (reedaa soochi) レーダー装置.

radiate vt. ... o ho⸢osha suru ...を放射する ①: A fire radiates heat. (Hi wa netsu o hoosha suru.) 火は熱を放射する.
— vi. ho⸢osha suru 放射する ①.

radiation n. ho⸢osha 放射; ho⸢onetsu 放熱: radiation of heat (netsu no hoosha) 熱の放射.

radical adj. **1** (extreme) ka⸢geki na 過激な; kyu⸢ushiñ-teki na 急進的な: radical students (kageki na gakusee-tachi) 過激な学生たち / a radical politician (kyuushiñ-teki na seejika) 急進的な政治家.
2 (basic) ko⸢ñpoñ-teki na 根本的な; (thorough) te⸢ttei-teki na 徹底的な: make radical improvements to the tax system (zeesee o koñpoñ-teki ni kaizen suru) 税制を根本的に改善する.

radio n. ra⸢jio ラジオ: turn the radio on [off] (rajio o tsukeru [kesu]) ラジオをつける[消す] / listen to the radio (rajio o kiku) ラジオを聞く.

rag n. bo⸢ro ぼろ; bo⸢ro⸣kire ぼろきれ.

rage n. **1** (great anger) i⸢kari 怒り; ge⸢kido 激怒: fly into a rage (katto naru) かっとなる.
2 (violence) ha⸢ge⸣shisa 激しさ; mo⸢oi 猛威: the rage of the wind (kaze no mooi) 風の猛威.
— vi. **1** (show great anger) ge⸢kido suru 激怒する ①; ha⸢ra⸣ o ta⸢te⸣ru 腹を立てる ⑤: He raged when he heard the news. (Kare wa sono shirase o kiite gekido shita.) 彼はその知らせを聞いて激怒した.
2 (be violent) mo⸢oi o fu⸢ruu 猛威をふるう ⓒ; a⸢rekuru⸣u 荒れ狂う ⓒ: The storm raged all night. (Arashi wa hito-bañ-juu arekurutta.) 嵐は一晩中荒れ狂った.

ragged adj. **1** (torn) bo⸢roboro no ぼろぼろの: a ragged coat (boroboro no uwagi) ぼろぼろの上着.
2 (uneven) gi⸢zagiza no ぎざぎざの: a ragged coastline (gizagiza no kaigañseñ) ぎざぎざの海岸線.

raid n. **1** (sudden attack) shu⸢ugeki 襲撃; kyu⸢ushuu 急襲: make a raid on the enemy (teki o kyuushuu suru) 敵を急襲する.
2 (sudden entry by the police) te⸢ire⸣ 手入れ: make a raid on a nightclub (naitokurabu no teire o okonau) ナイトクラブの手入れを行う.
— vt. ... o o⸢sou ...を襲う ⓒ; te⸢ire⸣ o suru 手入れをする ①: The thieves raided the bank. (Doroboo ga giñkoo o osotta.) どろぼうが銀行を襲った.

rail n. **1** (track) re⸢eru レール; se⸢ñro 線路: run on rails (reeru no ue o hashiru) レールの上を走る.
2 (railroad) te⸢tsudoo 鉄道: lay rails (tetsudoo o shiku) 鉄道を敷く.
3 (bar of wood or metal) yo⸢koboo 横棒; te⸢suri 手すり: lean on a rail (tesuri ni yorikakaru) 手すりに寄り掛かる.

railroad n. te⸢tsudoo 鉄道: a railroad crossing (tetsudoo no fumikiri) 鉄道の踏切 / a railroad bridge (tekkyoo) 鉄橋.
— vt. ... o te⸢tsudoo de yusoo suru ...を鉄道で輸送する ①.

railway n. = railroad.

rain n. a⸢me 雨: It looks like rain. (Ame ni nari-soo da.) 雨になりそうだ. / The rain stopped suddenly. (Ame ga kyuu ni yañda.) 雨が急にやんだ.
— vi. a⸢me ga furu 雨が降る ⓒ: It has begun raining. (Ame ga furi-hajimeta.) 雨が降り始めた.

rainbow n. ni⸢ji にじ: After the rain, a rainbow formed in the sky. (Ame no ato de sora ni niji ga deta.) 雨の後で空ににじが出た.

rain check n. (ticket) u⸢teñ hi⸢kika⸣keñ 雨天引換券; (promise) go⸢jitsu no sho⸣otai 後日の招待: Give me a rain check. (Mata no kikai ni yoroshiku.) またの機会によろしく.

raincoat *n.* re「eñko˥oto レーンコート.

rainfall *n.* ko「ou˥ryoo 降雨量: the annual average rainfall (*neñkañ heekiñ koouryoo*) 年間平均降雨量.

rainy *adj.* a˥me no 雨の; a「me˥furi no 雨ふりの: a rainy day (*ame no hi*) 雨の日 / the rainy season (*tsuyu*) 梅雨.

raise *vt.* **1** (lift) ... o a「geru ...を上げる Ⅴ: She raised her hand and waved. (*Kanojo wa te o agete futta.*) 彼女は手を上げて振った.
2 (make higher) ... o a「geru ...を上げる Ⅴ: raise the rent (*yachiñ o ageru*) 家賃を上げる.
3 (bring up) ... o so「date˥ru ...を育てる Ⅴ: I was born and raised in Tokyo. (*Watashi wa Tookyoo de umare sodatta.*) 私は東京で生まれ育った.
4 (grow) ... o sa「ibai suru ...を栽培する Ⅰ: raise vegetables in a field (*hatake de yasai o saibai suru*) 畑で野菜を栽培する.
5 (gather) ... o a「tsume˥ru ...を集める Ⅴ: raise money for charity (*jizeñ no tame ni o-kane o atsumeru*) 慈善のためにお金を集める.
6 (bring forward) ... o te「eki suru ...を提起する Ⅰ: raise an important question (*juuyoo na moñdai o teeki suru*) 重要な問題を提起する.
— *n.* (of pay) sho「okyuu 昇給; chi「ñage 賃上げ: demand a raise (*chiñage o yookyuu suru*) 賃上げを要求する.

raisin *n.* ho「shibu˥doo 干しぶどう.

rake *n.* ku「made くま手; re「eki レーキ.
— *vt.* ... o ka「kiatsume˥ru ...をかき集める Ⅴ; ka「kinara˥su かきならす Ⅽ: rake fallen leaves (*ochiba o kakiatsumeru*) 落ち葉をかき集める / rake the flower beds (*kadañ o kakinarasu*) 花壇をかきならす.

rally *vi.* **1** (come together) a「tsuma˥ru 集まる Ⅽ: rally around the leader (*shidoosha no moto ni atsumaru*) 指導者のもとに集まる.
2 (recover strength) ka「ifuku suru 回復する Ⅰ: As the fever left him, he began to rally. (*Netsu ga tore, kare wa kaifuku shi-hajimeta.*) 熱が取れ, 彼は回復し始めた.
— *vt.* ... o fu「tatabi atsume˥ru ...を再び集める Ⅴ: rally the scattered soldiers (*barabara ni natta heetai-tachi o futatabi atsumeru*) ばらばらになった兵隊たちを再び集める.
— *n.* da「i-shu˥ukai 大集会; ta「ikai 大会: a peace rally (*heewa-uñdoo shuukai*) 平和運動集会.

random *adj.* **1** (without method) te「atarishi˥dai no 手当たり次第の; de「tarame na でたらめな: a random guess (*detarame na suisoku*) でたらめな推測.
2 (statistics) mu「sa˥kui no 無作為の; ni「ñi no 任意の.
at random *adv.* de「tarame ni でたらめに: select at random (*detarame ni erabu*) でたらめに選ぶ.

range *n.* **1** (extent) ha「ñi 範囲; ha˥「ba 幅: a wide range of knowledge (*hiroi hañi no chishiki*) 広い範囲の知識 / a range of prices (*nedañ no haba*) 値段の幅.
2 (row or line) na「rabi 並び; tsu˥「zuki 続き: a mountain range (*sañmyaku*) 山脈.
3 (distance) kyo「ori 距離: fire a gun at close range (*shikiñ kyori kara happoo suru*) 至近距離から発砲する.
— *vi.* o「yobu 及ぶ Ⅽ: The children's ages range from 5 to 10. (*Kodomo-tachi no neñree wa go-sai kara jus-sai ni oyoñde iru.*) 子どもたちの年齢は5歳から10歳に及んでいる.
— *vt.* ... o na「raberu ...を並べる Ⅴ: range the pupils in a line (*seeto o ichi-retsu ni naraberu*) 生徒を一列に並べる.

rank *n.* **1** (grade) ka「ikyuu 階級; to「okyuu 等級: people of all ranks (*arayuru kaikyuu no hito-tachi*) あらゆる階級の人たち / a painter of the first rank (*ichi-ryuu no gaka*) 一流の画家.
2 (row) re「tsu 列: stand in a rank (*retsu ni narabu*) 列に並ぶ.

— *vt.* **1** (arrange) ... o na͡raberu ...を並べる V: rank books on a shelf (*tana ni ho͡n o naraberu*) 棚に本を並べる.

2 (make much of) ... o hyo͡oka suru ...を評価する T: I rank his abilities high. (*Watashi wa kare no sainoo o takaku hyooka shite iru.*) 私は彼の才能を高く評価している.

— *vi.* (hold a position) shi͡me͡ru 占める V: He ranks first in his class. (*Kare wa kurasu de ichiba͡n o shimete iru.*) 彼はクラスで一番を占めている.

rank and file *n.* (company workers) i͡ppa͡n sha͡i͡n 一般社員; (soldiers) he͡eshi-tachi 兵士たち.

ransom *n.* mi͡noshiroki͡n 身代金: They held the child for ransom. (*Kare-ra wa sono ko o hitojichi ni shite minoshiroki͡n o yookyuu shita.*) 彼らはその子を人質にして身代金を要求した.

rap *vi.* (... o) ko͡tsukotsu [to͡nto͡n] to ta͡ta͡ku (...を)こつこつ[とんとん]とたたく C: rap at a door (*doa o to͡nto͡n to tataku*) ドアをとんとんとたたく.

— *n.* ko͡tsukotsu [to͡nto͡n] to ta͡ta͡ku o͡to͡ こつこつ[とんとん]とたたく音.

rape *vt.* ... o go͡oka͡n suru ...を強姦する T; re͡epu suru レイプする T.

rapid *adj.* ha͡ya͡i 速い; kyu͡usoku na 急速な: a rapid river (*nagare no hayai kawa*) 流れの速い川 / make rapid progress (*kyuusoku na shi͡npo o togeru*) 急速な進歩を遂げる.

rapidly *adv.* ha͡yaku 速く; su͡ba͡yaku すばやく: Don't speak so rapidly. (*So͡nna ni hayaku shabera-naide kudasai.*) そんなに速くしゃべらないでください.

rapture *n.* u͡cho͡ote͡n 有頂天; kyo͡oki 狂喜: He was in raptures about the news. (*Kare wa sono shirase ni uchoote͡n datta.*) 彼はその知らせに有頂天だった.

rare[1] *adj.* **1** (unusual) ma͡re͡i na まれな; me͡zurashi͡i 珍しい: It is rare for him to be absent. (*Kare ga yasumu no wa mezurashii.*) 彼が休むのは珍しい.

2 (thin) u͡sui 薄い; ki͡haku na 希薄な: The air is rare in the high mountains. (*Takai yama wa kuuki ga kihaku desu.*) 高い山は空気が希薄です.

rare[2] *adj.* (partly cooked) na͡maya-ke no 生焼けの; re͡a no レアの: I like rare beef. (*Watashi wa namayake no gyuuniku ga suki desu.*) 私は生焼けの牛肉が好きです.

rarely *adv.* ma͡re͡i ni まれに; me͡tta ni ⟨verb⟩-nai めったに...ない: I'm rarely ill. (*Watashi wa metta ni byooki o shinai.*) 私はめったに病気をしない.

rash[1] *adj.* ke͡esotsu na 軽率な; mu͡fu͡nbetsu na 無分別な: It was rash of you to say so. (*Kimi ga soo itta no wa keesotsu datta.*) 君がそう言ったのは軽率だった.

rash[2] *n.* ha͡sshi͡n 発疹; fu͡kidemono 吹き出物.

rat *n.* ne͡zumi ねずみ. ★ In Japanese 'mouse' is also called 'nezumi.'

rate *n.* **1** (amount) ri͡tsu 率; wa͡ri-ai 割合: interest rates (*ri-ritsu*) 利率 / an exchange rate (*kookan-ritsu*) 交換率 / the rate of discount (*waribiki-ritsu*) 割引率.

2 (speed) so͡kudo 速度; ha͡yasa 速さ: drive at the rate of 50 kilometers an hour (*jisoku gojuk-kiro no hayasa de kuruma o u͡nte͡n suru*) 時速50キロの速さで車を運転する.

3 (price) ryo͡oki͡n 料金; ne͡da͡n 値段: a telephone rate (*de͡nwa-ryoo-ki͡n*) 電話料金 / What's the rate? (*Ryooki͡n wa ikura desu ka?*) 料金はいくらですか.

— *vi.* (set a value) ... to mi͡tsu-moru ...と見積もる C: I rated the diamond at 50,000 yen. (*Watashi wa sono daiyamo͡ndo o go-ma͡n-e͡n to mitsumotta.*) 私はそのダイヤモンドを5万円と見積もった.

rather *adv.* **1** (more willing) mu͡-shiro むしろ: I would rather stay home than go out. (*Watashi wa dekakeru yori mo mushiro uchi ni*

itai.) 私は出かけるよりもむしろ家にいたい.
2 (somewhat) ka̶nari かなり; da̶ibu だいぶ: I am rather tired. (*Watashi wa kanari tsukareta.*) 私はかなり疲れた. / It's rather hot, isn't it? (*Daibu atsui desu ne.*) だいぶ暑いですね.

ratio *n*. hi̶ 比; hi̶ritsu 比率; wa̶ri-ai 割合: The ratio of boys and girls is two to one. (*Otoko-no-ko to oñna-no-ko no hiritsu wa ni tai ichi desu.*) 男の子と女の子の比率は2対1です.

rational *adj*. **1** (able to reason) ri̶see no aru 理性のある; ri̶see-teki na 理性的な: Man is a rational animal. (*Niñgeñ wa risee-teki na doobutsu desu.*) 人間は理性的な動物です.
2 (reasonable) go̶ori-teki na 合理的な: a rational explanation (*goori-teki na setsumee*) 合理的な説明.

rattle *vi*. **1** (cause sounds) ga̶ragara o̶to̶ ga suru がらがら音がする ①; ga̶tagata na̶ru がたがた鳴る ©: The windows rattled in the wind. (*Mado ga kaze de gatagata natta.*) 窓が風でがたがた鳴った.
2 (move with sounds) ga̶tagata to ha̶shi̶ru がたがたと走る ©: The old car rattled by. (*Furui kuruma ga gatagata to hashitte itta.*) 古い車ががたがたと走って行った.
— *n*. ga̶tagata iu o̶to̶ がたがたいう音.

raw *adj*. **1** (uncooked) na̶ma no 生の: a raw egg (*nama-tamago*) 生卵 / sliced raw fish (*sashimi*) 刺身.
2 (not prepared) ge̶ñryo̶o no ma̶ma no 原料のままの: raw petroleum (*geñyu*) 原油 / raw silk (*ki-ito*) 生糸.
3 (sore) a̶kamuke no 赤むけの; hi̶rihiri suru ひりひりする: a raw wound (*akamuke no kizu*) 赤むけの傷.
4 (inexperienced) mi̶ke̶ekeñ no 未経験の; mi̶juku na 未熟な: a raw recruit (*shiñpee*) 新兵.

ray *n*. **1** (beam) ko̶oseñ 光線: the sun's rays (*taiyoo-kooseñ*) 太陽光線 / ultraviolet rays (*shigaiseñ*) 紫外線.
2 (tiny amount) wa̶zuka わずか: a

ray of hope (*wazuka na nozomi*) わずかな望み.

razor *n*. ka̶miso̶ri かみそり: shave one's face with a razor (*kamisori de kao o soru*) かみそりで顔をそる.

reach *vt*. **1** (arrive at) ... ni tsu̶ku ...に着く ©; to̶ochaku suru 到着する ①: Telephone me when you reach Narita. (*Narita ni tsuitara deñwa o kudasai.*) 成田に着いたら電話をください. / They reached their destination safely. (*Kare-ra wa buji ni mokutekichi ni toochaku shita.*) 彼らは無事に目的地に到着した.
2 (touch) ... ni te̶ ga to̶do̶ku ...に手が届く ©: Can you reach the top shelf? (*Ichibañ ue no tana ni te ga todokimasu ka?*) いちばん上の棚に手が届きますか.
3 (get to) ... ni to̶do̶ku ...に届く ©; ta̶ssuru 達する ①: The letter reached me this morning. (*Sono tegami wa kesa todokimashita.*) その手紙は今朝届きました.
— *vi*. (extend a hand) te̶ o no̶-̶ba̶su 手を伸ばす ©: He reached out for a cigarette. (*Kare wa tabako o toroo to te o nobashita.*) 彼はたばこを取ろうと手を伸ばした.

react *vi*. **1** (act in response) ha̶ñnoo suru 反応する ①: Our eyes react to light. (*Me wa hikari ni hañnoo suru.*) 目は光に反応する.
2 (act opposing) ha̶ñpatsu suru 反発する ①: react against despotism (*señsee-seeji ni hañpatsu suru*) 専制政治に反発する.

reaction *n*. **1** (response) ha̶ñnoo 反応: What was his reaction to your proposal? (*Anata no teeañ ni taisuru kare no hañnoo wa doo deshita?*) あなたの提案に対する彼の反応はどうでした.
2 (opposing action) ha̶ñpatsu 反発; ha̶ñkoo 反抗: reaction against the tax increase (*zoozee ni taisuru hañpatsu*) 増税に対する反発.

read *vt*. **1** (get the meaning) ... o yo̶mu ...を読む ©: Have you read this book? (*Kono hoñ wa yomima-*

shita ka?) この本は読みましたか.

2 (speak printed words) koʰe o dashite yomu 声を出して読む ⓒ; roʰodoku suru 朗読する Ⓣ: read a textbook aloud *(kyookasho o roodoku suru)* 教科書を朗読する.
— *vi.* doʰkusho suru 読書する Ⓣ: I want more time to read. *(Motto dokusho suru jikañ ga hoshii.)* もっと読書する時間が欲しい.

reader *n.* **1** (person) doʰkusha 読者; doʰkushoka 読書家: I am a slow reader. *(Watashi wa hoñ o yomu no ga osoi.)* 私は本を読むのが遅い.
2 (textbook) kyoʰokaʰsho 教科書; toʰkuhoñ 読本.

readily *adv.* **1** (willingly) koʰkoroyoʰku 快く: He lent me the money readily. *(Kare wa kokoroyoku sono o-kane o kashite kureta.)* 彼は快くそのお金を貸してくれた.
2 (easily) taʰyaʰsuku たやすく: I cannot readily answer the question. *(Sono moñdai wa tayasuku heñtoo dekimaseñ.)* その問題はたやすく返答できません.

reading *n.* **1** (act of reading) doʰkusho 読書: She is fond of reading. *(Kanojo wa dokusho ga suki da.)* 彼女は読書が好きだ.
2 (something to be read) yoʰmimoʰno 読み物: suitable reading for children *(kodomo-tachi ni fusawashii yomimono)* 子どもたちにふさわしい読み物.
3 (of a gauge) hyoʰoji 表示; shiʰdo 示度: the reading on a thermometer *(oñdokee no shido)* 温度計の示度.

ready *adj.* **1** (prepared) yoʰoi no dekita [dekite iru] 用意のできた[できている]: Dinner is ready. *(Yuuhañ no yooi ga dekimashita.)* 夕飯の用意ができました. / Are you ready to go out? *(Dekakeru yooi wa dekimashita ka?)* 出かける用意はできましたか.
2 (willing) yoʰrokoʰñde 喜んで...: I am always ready to help. *(Itsu de mo yorokoñde o-tetsudai*

shimasu.) いつでも喜んでお手伝いします.
3 (about to) iʰma ni mo 〈verb〉-soo da いまにも...そうだ: She was ready to cry. *(Kanojo wa ima ni mo nakidashi-soo datta.)* 彼女はいまにも泣きだしそうだった.

ready-made *adj.* deʰkiai no 出来合いの; kiʰsee-hiñ no 既製品の: ready-made clothes *(kisee-fuku)* 既製服.

real *adj.* **1** (actually existing) jiʰtsuzai no 実在の; jiʰssai no 実際の: a real person in history *(rekishi-joo jitsuzai no jiñbutsu)* 歴史上実在の人物 / real events *(jissai no dekigoto)* 実際の出来事.
2 (true) hoʰñtoo no 本当の; shiʰñ no 真の: What is the real reason for his absence? *(Kare no kesseki no hoñtoo no riyuu wa nañ desu ka?)* 彼の欠席の本当の理由は何ですか.
3 (genuine) hoʰñmono no 本物の: a real pearl *(honmono no shiñju)* 本物の真珠.

reality *n.* geʰñjitsu 現実: His dream became a reality. *(Kare no yume wa geñjitsu to natta.)* 彼の夢は現実となった.

realization *n.* **1** (understanding) riʰkai 理解; niʰñshiki 認識: I have a full realization of the situation. *(Jookyoo o juubuñ niñshiki shite imasu.)* 状況は十分認識しています.
2 (making real) jiʰtsugeñ 実現; taʰssee 達成: the realization of one's hopes *(kiboo no jitsugeñ)* 希望の実現.

realize *vt.* **1** (understand) ... o riʰkai suru ...を理解する Ⓣ; saʰtoru 悟るⓒ: He realized that he was mistaken. *(Kare wa jibuñ ga machigatte iru koto o satotta.)* 彼は自分が間違っていることを悟った.
2 (make real) ... o jiʰtsugeñ suru ...を実現する Ⓣ: She realized her dream of becoming an actress. *(Kanojo wa joyuu ni naru to iu yume o jitsugeñ shita.)* 彼女は女優になるという夢を実現した.

really *adv.* **1** (truly) hoʰñtoo ni 本

当に; jiˈssai ni 実際に: I really
don't know. (*Watashi wa hoñtoo
ni shirimaseñ.*) 私は本当に知りません.
2 (indeed) maˈttaku まったく: It is
really a pity. (*Mattaku zañneñ da.*)
まったく残念だ.

realm *n.* **1** (area) ryoˈoiki 領域;
haˈñi 範囲: the realm of science
(*kagaku no ryooiki*) 科学の領域.
2 (kingdom) oˈokoku 王国; (national territory) koˈkudo 国土.

reap *vt.* ... o kaˈri-ireˈru ...を刈り入れ
る Ⓥ; shuˈukaku suru 収穫する Ⓘ:
reap crops (*sakumotsu o kari-ireru*) 作物を刈り入れる.
— *vi.* kaˈritoˈru 刈り取る Ⓒ: reap
as one has sown (*jibuñ no maita
tane o karitoru*) 自分のまいた種を刈り
取る.

rear[1] *adj.* uˈshiro no 後ろの; uˈra no
裏の: a rear entrance (*uraguchi*) 裏
口.
— *n.* uˈshiro 後ろ; koˈobu 後部:
the rear of a house (*ie no ushiro*)
家の後ろ.

rear[2] *vt.* **1** (bring up) ... o soˈdateˈ-
ru ...を育てる Ⓥ: rear one's children
(*kodomo o sodateru*) 子どもを育てる.
2 (lift up) ... o moˈchiageru ...を持
ち上げる Ⓥ: The snake reared its
head. (*Hebi wa atama o mochi-
ageta.*) へびは頭を持ち上げた.

reason *n.* **1** (cause) riˈyuu 理由;
waˈke 訳: What is the reason for
your absence? (*Anata ga kesseki
shita riyuu wa nañ desu ka?*) あなた
が欠席した理由は何ですか. / He re-
signed for some reason. (*Kare wa
doo iu wake ka jishoku shita.*) 彼
はどういう訳か辞職した.
2 (the power to think) riˈsee 理性;
haˈñdaˈñ-ryoku 判断力: Animals
have no reason. (*Doobutsu ni wa
risee ga nai.*) 動物には理性がない.
3 (good judgment) fuˈñbetsu 分別;
shoˈoki 正気: lose one's reason
(*fuñbetsu o nakusu*) 分別をなくす.
— *vt.* ... o seˈttoku shite ⟨verb⟩-
(sa)seru ...を説得して...(さ)せる Ⓥ: I
reasoned him into giving up the

plan. (*Watashi wa kare o settoku
shite sono keekaku o akiramesa-
seta.*) 私は彼を説得してその計画をあき
らめさせた.
— *vi.* suˈiri suru 推理する Ⓘ: the
ability to reason (*suiriryoku*) 推理
力.

reasonable *adj.* **1** (sensible)
moˈttoˈmo na もっともな; riˈkutsu ni
aˈtta 理屈に合った: reasonable demands (*mottomo na yookyuu*) もっ
ともな要求.
2 (fair) teˈgoro na 手ごろな; hoˈdo
yoˈi ほどよい: a reasonable price
(*tegoro na nedañ*) 手ごろな値段.

reasoning *n.* suˈiri 推理; suˈiroñ
推論: Your reasoning is correct.
(*Kimi no suiri wa tadashii.*) 君の推
理は正しい.

reassure *vt.* ... o añshiñ saseru
...を安心させる Ⓥ: The doctor reas-
sured him that he would soon get
well. (*Isha wa sugu yoku narimasu to itte kare o añshiñ saseta.*)
医者はすぐよくなりますと言って彼を安心
させた.

rebel *vi.* (... ni) haˈñkoo suru (...に)
反抗する Ⓘ; soˈmuˈku 背く Ⓒ: rebel
against a ruler (*shihaisha ni hañkoo suru*) 支配者に反抗する.
— *n.* haˈñgyakuˈsha 反逆者; haˈñ-
koˈosha 反抗者.

rebellion *n.* haˈñrañ 反乱; muˈhoñ
謀反: rise in rebellion (*hañrañ o
okosu*) 反乱を起こす.

rebuild *vt.* ... o taˈtenaoˈsu ...を建て
直す Ⓒ; kaˈichiku suru 改築する Ⓘ:
rebuild an old house (*furui ie o
tatenaosu*) 古い家を建て直す.

recall *vt.* **1** (remember) ... o oˈmoidaˈsu ...を思い出す Ⓒ: I can't recall
his name. (*Watashi wa kare no
namae o omoidasenai.*) 私は彼の名
前を思い出せない.
2 (call back) ... o yoˈbimodoˈsu ...
を呼び戻す Ⓒ; shoˈokañ suru 召還す
る Ⓘ: He was recalled to the head
office. (*Kare wa hoñsha e yobi-
modosareta.*) 彼は本社へ呼び戻された.
3 (take back) ... o toˈrimodoˈsu ...

を取り戻す Ⓒ; kaｲishuu suru 回収する Ⓘ: recall defective cars (*kekkañsha o kaishuu suru*) 欠陥車を回収する.

— *n.* **1** (order to return) shoｲokañ 召還: the recall of an ambassador (*taishi no shookañ*) 大使の召還.

2 (remembrance) kiｲokuｲryoku 記憶力: He has total recall. (*Kare wa subarashii kiokuryoku o motte iru.*) 彼はすばらしい記憶力を持っている.

3 (by a vote) riｲkoｲoru リコール.

receipt *n.* **1** (written statement) ryoｲoshuusho 領収書; reｲshiｲito レシート: May I have a receipt? (*Reshiito o kudasai.*) レシートを下さい.

2 (receiving) uｲketoru koto 受け取ること; juｲryoo 受領: On receipt of your payment, we will send you the goods. (*O-shiharai o uketori shidai shinamono o hassoo itashimasu.*) お支払いを受け取り次第品物を発送いたします.

receive *vt.* **1** (get) ... o uｲketoru ...を受け取る Ⓒ; uｲkeｲru 受ける Ⓥ: I received your letter yesterday. (*Kinoo o-tegami o uketorimashita.*) きのうお手紙を受け取りました. / She received her education abroad. (*Kanojo wa gaikoku de kyooiku o uketa.*) 彼女は外国で教育を受けた.

2 (welcome) ... o muｲkaeru ...を迎える Ⓥ; moｲtenaｲsu もてなす Ⓒ: He received his guests warmly. (*Kare wa o-kyaku o atatakaku mukaeta.*) 彼はお客を温かく迎えた.

receiver *n.* **1** (of a telephone) juｲwaｲki 受話器; (of a radio) juｲshiｲiñki 受信機: pick up [hang up] the receiver (*juwaki o toru [oku]*) 受話器を取る[置く].

2 (person) uｲketoriniñ 受け取り人.

recent *adj.* saｲikiñ no 最近の; chiｲkaｲgoro no 近ごろの: Have you read his recent work? (*Kare no saikiñ saku o yomimashita ka?*) 彼の最近作を読みましたか.

recently *adv.* saｲikiñ 最近; chiｲkaｲgoro 近ごろ: I have put on weight recently. (*Watashi wa saikiñ futotta.*) 私は最近太った.

reception *n.* **1** (party) kaｲñgeｲekai 歓迎会; reｲseｲpushoñ レセプション: give a reception (*kañgeekai o hiraku*) 歓迎会を開く / a wedding reception (*kekkoñ hirooeñ*) 結婚披露宴.

2 (welcome) kaｲñgee 歓迎; seｲttai 接待: They got a cordial reception. (*Kare-ra wa kokoro kara no kañgee o uketa.*) 彼らは心からの歓迎を受けた.

3 (receiving) juｲryoo 受領; (of a radio) juｲshiñ 受信.

recess *n.* **1** (pause) kyuｲukee 休憩; yaｲsumi 休み: take a ten-minute recess (*jup-puñ-kañ kyuukee suru*) 10分間休憩する.

2 (hidden place) oｲkumaｲtta toｲkoroｲ 奥まった所.

recipe *n.* choｲorihoo 調理法; tsuｲkurikata 作り方: a recipe for stew (*shichuu no tsukurikata*) シチューの作り方.

reciprocal *adj.* soｲogo no 相互の; oｲtagai no お互いの: reciprocal help (*soogo fujo*) 相互扶助.

recite *vt.* **1** (repeat aloud from memory) ... o aｲñshoo suru ...を暗唱する Ⓘ: recite a poem (*shi o añshoo suru*) 詩を暗唱する.

2 (tell in detail) kuｲwaｲshiku noｲbeｲru 詳しく述べる Ⓥ: He recited his adventures. (*Kare wa jibuñ no bookeñdañ o kuwashiku nobeta.*) 彼は自分の冒険談を詳しく述べた.

reckless *adj.* muｲkoｲomizu na 向こう見ずな; muｲboo na 無謀な: a reckless boy (*mukoomizu na otoko-no-ko*) 向こう見ずな男の子 / reckless driving (*muboo-uñteñ*) 無謀運転.

recline *vt.* (of a seat) taｲoｲsu 倒す Ⓒ; yoｲkotaeｲru 横たえる Ⓥ: May I recline my seat? (*Shiito o taoshite mo ii desu ka?*) シートを倒してもいいですか.

— *vi.* moｲtareｲru もたれる Ⓥ; yoｲko ni naｲru 横になる Ⓒ.

recognition *n.* (recognizing) miｲtomeru koto 認めること; shoｲoniñ

承認: recognition of defeat (*hai-boku o mitomeru koto*) 敗北を認めること / recognition of a new state (*shiñkokka no shooniñ*) 新国家の承認.

recognize *vt.* **1** (know) ... to waˈkaˈru ...とわかる C; (recall) ... o oˈmoidaˈsu ...を思い出す C: I recognized him as one of my old friends. (*Watashi wa kare ga kyuuyuu no hitori da to wakatta.*) 私は彼が旧友の一人だとわかった.
2 (admit) ... o miˈtomeru ...を認める V: He did not recognize his mistake. (*Kare wa jibuñ no machigai o mitomenakatta.*) 彼は自分の間違いを認めなかった.
3 (accept) ... o miˈtomeru ...を認める V; shoˈoniñ suru 承認する I: recognize a new government (*shiñseefu o shooniñ suru*) 新政府を承認する.

recollect *vt.* ... o oˈmoidaˈsu ...を思い出す C: I cannot recollect his name. (*Watashi wa kare no namae ga omoidasenai.*) 私は彼の名前が思い出せない.

recollection *n.* **1** (memory) kiˈoku 記憶; oˈmoidaˈsu koˈtoˈ 思い出すこと: I have no recollection of it. (*Watashi ni wa sono kioku wa nai.*) 私にはその記憶はない.
2 (something in one's memory) oˈmoide 思い出; tsuˈioku 追憶: happy recollections (*tanoshii omoide*) 楽しい思い出.

recommend *vt.* **1** (praise) ... o suˈsumeru ...を勧める V; oˈshieru 教える V; suˈiseñ suru 推薦する I: The teacher recommended the dictionary to us. (*Señsee wa sono jisho o watashi-tachi ni susumeta.*) 先生はその辞書を私たちに勧めた. / Can you recommend a good restaurant near here? (*Kono chikaku no yoi resutorañ o oshiete kudasai.*) この近くのよいレストランを教えてください. / I recommended him for the job. (*Watashi wa kare o sono shigoto ni suiseñ shita.*) 私は彼をその仕事に

推薦した.
2 (advise) 〈verb〉 yoˈo ni suˈsumeru ...ように勧める V; chuˈukoku suru 忠告する I: The doctor recommended that he should give up smoking. (*Isha wa kare ni tabako o yameru yoo ni susumeta.*) 医者は彼にたばこをやめるように勧めた.

recommendation *n.* **1** (advice) suˈiseñ 推薦; suˈsume 勧め: a letter of recommendation (*suiseñjoo*) 推薦状 / I bought this car on his recommendation. (*Watashi wa kare no susume de kono kuruma o katta.*) 私は彼の勧めでこの車を買った.
2 (written statement) suˈiseñjoo 推薦状: write a recommendation (*suiseñjoo o kaku*) 推薦状を書く.

reconcile *vt.* **1** (make friendly) naˈkanaˈori saseru 仲直りさせる V: The couple are completely reconciled. (*Futari wa kañzeñ ni nakanaori shita.*) 二人は完全に仲直りした.
2 (harmonize) ... o choˈowa saseru ...を調和させる V; iˈtchi saseru 一致させる V: reconcile one's ideal with reality (*risoo to geñjitsu o itchi saseru*) 理想と現実を一致させる.

reconfirm *vt.* ... o saˈikakuniñ suru ...を再確認する I: I'd like to reconfirm a reservation. (*Yoyaku o saikakuniñ shitai no desu ga.*) 予約を再確認したいのですが.

reconstruct *vt.* ... o saˈikeñ suru ...を再建する I: reconstruct an old temple (*furui tera o saikeñ suru*) 古い寺を再建する.

reconstruction *n.* saˈikeñ 再建: reconstruction of a bridge (*hashi no saikeñ*) 橋の再建 / reconstruction of the economy (*keezai no saikeñ*) 経済の再建.

record *vt.* **1** (write down) ... o kiˈroku suru ...を記録する I; kaˈkitomeru 書き留める V: record an event in a diary (*dekigoto o nikki ni kiroku suru*) 出来事を日記に記録する.
2 (set down on a disk or tape) ... o roˈkuoñ suru ...を録音する I: I re-

corded his speech on tape. (*Watashi wa kare no eñzetsu o teepu ni rokuoñ shita.*) 私は彼の演説をテープに録音した.
— *n.* **1** (written report) ki⌐roku 記録: I kept a record of everything discussed. (*Tooroñ sareta koto wa subete kiroku ni totta.*) 討論されたことはすべて記録に取った.
2 (best performance) ki⌐roku 記録: break the world record (*sekai-kiroku o yaburu*) 世界記録を破る.
3 (collected facts) ke⌐reki 経歴; se⌐seki 成績: The child has a good school record. (*Sono ko wa gakkoo no seeseki ga yoi.*) その子は学校の成績がよい.
4 (disk) re⌐koodo レコード: play a record (*rekoodo o kakeru*) レコードをかける.

recording *n.* (radio) ro⌐kuoñ 録音; (TV) ro⌐kuga 録画: make a recording of music on tape (*oñgaku o teepu ni rokuoñ suru*) 音楽をテープに録音する.

recover *vt.* (get back) ... o to⌐rimodo⌐su ...を取り戻す C: The police recovered the stolen jewelry. (*Keesatsu wa nusumareta hooseki o torimodoshita.*) 警察は盗まれた宝石を取り戻した.
— *vi.* (return to a normal condition) ka⌐ifuku suru 回復する I: The patient recovered quickly. (*Kañja wa sugu ni kaifuku shita.*) 患者はすぐに回復した.

recovery *n.* ka⌐ifuku 回復; ka⌐ishuu 回収: an economic recovery (*keezai no kaifuku*) 経済の回復 / the recovery of stolen jewels (*nusumareta hooseki no kaishuu*) 盗まれた宝石の回収.

recreation *n.* ki⌐barashi 気晴らし; go⌐raku 娯楽; re⌐kurie⌐eshoñ レクリエーション: My favorite recreation is fishing. (*Watashi no ichibañ no kibarashi wa tsuri desu.*) 私のいちばんの気晴らしは釣りです. / a recreation ground (*yuueñchi*) 遊園地

recruit *n.* **1** (new member) shi⌐ñ-

ka⌐iiñ 新会員; shi⌐ñjiñ 新人.
2 (soldier) shi⌐ñpee 新兵.
— *vt.* ... o bo⌐shuu suru ...を募集する I: recruit new employees (*shiñnyuu shaiñ o boshuu suru*) 新入社員を募集する.

rectangle *n.* ku⌐kee 矩形; cho⌐oho⌐okee 長方形.

red *adj.* a⌐kai 赤い; a⌐kairo no 赤色の: a red rose (*akai bara*) 赤いばら / a red traffic light (*akashiñgoo*) 赤信号 / He turned red with anger. (*Kare wa okotte akaku natta.*) 彼は怒って赤くなった.
— *n.* a⌐ka 赤.
be in the red *vi.* a⌐kaji o da⌐shite iru 赤字を出している V.

redeem *vt.* ... o to⌐rimodo⌐su ...を取り戻す C; ka⌐ifuku suru 回復する I: redeem a mortgage (*teetoo o torimodosu*) 抵当を取り戻す.

reduce *vt.* ... o he⌐rasu ...を減らす C; su⌐ku⌐naku suru 少なくする I: reduce one's weight (*taijuu o herasu*) 体重を減らす / reduce a price (*nedañ o sageru*) 値段を下げる / reduce speed (*supiido o otosu*) スピードを落とす.

reduction *n.* **1** (making less) ge⌐ñshoo 減少: tax reduction (*geñ-zee*) 減税.
2 (discount) wa⌐ribiki 割引: I bought this sweater at a reduction of 10 percent. (*Watashi wa kono seetaa o ichi-waribiki de katta.*) 私はこのセーターを1割引きで買った.

refer *vi.* **1** (look for information) (... o) sa⌐ñshoo suru (...を)参照する I: refer to a book (*hoñ o sañshoo suru*) 本を参照する.
2 (mention) (... o) ku⌐chi ni da⌐su (...を)口に出す C: He often refers to his mother. (*Kare wa yoku haha-oya no koto o kuchi ni dasu.*) 彼はよく母親のことを口に出す.
3 (concern) (... ni) te⌐kiyoo sareru (...に)適用される V: This rule refers only to students. (*Kono kisoku wa gakusee dake ni tekiyoo sareru.*) この規則は学生だけに適用される.

— *vt.* 1 (send) ... o iˈkaseru ...を
行かせる ⱽ: I referred him to a doctor. (*Watashi wa kare o isha ni
ikaseta.*) 私は彼を医者に行かせた.

2 (assign) ... o maˈkaseˈru ...を任せ
る ⱽ: They referred the problem
to the committee. (*Kare-ra wa
sono moñdai o iiñkai ni makaseta.*)
彼らはその問題を委員会に任せた.

referee *n.* reˈferii レフェリー; shiˈñ-
pañ 審判; shiˈñpaˈñiñ 審判員.
★ 'Judge' and 'umpire' are also
called '*shiñpañ(iñ)*.'

reference *n.* 1 (mentioning) fu-
ˈreru kotoˈ 触れること: He made no
reference to the accident. (*Kare wa
sono jiko ni furenakatta.*) 彼はその
事故に触れなかった.

2 (consulting) saˈñshoo 参照; saˈñ-
koo 参考: He keeps a dictionary on
his desk for easy reference. (*Kare
wa sugu sañshoo dekiru yoo ni
jisho o tsukue no ue ni oite iru.*)
彼はすぐ参照できるように辞書を机の上に
置いている.

3 (note about one's character) jiˈñ-
butsu shoˈomeesho 人物証明書;
suˈiseñjoo 推薦状: an excellent
reference from a former employer
(*mae no yatoinushi kara no rippa
na suiseñjoo*) 前の雇い主からのりっぱ
な推薦状.

refine *vt.* 1 (make pure) ... o seˈesee suru ...を精製する I: refine
sugar (*satoo o seesee suru*) 砂糖を
精製する.

2 (polish) ... o joˈohiˈñ ni suru ...を
上品にする I: refine one's language
(*kotobazukai o joohiñ ni suru*) 言
葉遣いを上品にする.

refined *adj.* 1 (polished) seˈñreñ
sareta 洗練された; joˈohiˈñ na 上品
な: refined manners (*joohiñ na
monogoshi*) 上品な物腰.

2 (purified) seˈesee shita 精製した:
refined sugar (*seeseetoo*) 精製糖.

refinement *n.* 1 (good manners)
joˈohiˈñ 上品; seˈñreñ 洗練: a lady
of refinement (*joohiñ na fujiñ*) 上
品な婦人.

2 (refining) seˈesee 精製: the refinement of oil (*sekiyu no seesee*)
石油の精製.

reflect *vt.* 1 (throw back) ... o
haˈñsha suru ...を反射する I: The
white sand reflects heat. (*Shiroi
suna wa netsu o hañsha suru.*) 白い
砂は熱を反射する.

2 (give back an image) ... o uˈtsuˈsu
...を映す ⱽ: White clouds are reflected on the lake. (*Shiroi kumo
ga mizuumi ni utsutte iru.*) 白い雲
が湖に映っている.

3 (express) ... o aˈrawaˈsu ...を表す
⑨: His clothes reflect his good
taste. (*Kare no fuku wa kare no
yoi shumi o arawashite iru.*) 彼の
服は彼のよい趣味を表している.

4 (think carefully) ... o haˈñsee
suru ...を反省する I: reflect one's
past errors (*kako no ayamachi o
hañsee suru*) 過去の過ちを反省する.
— *vi.* 1 (give back) haˈñsha suru
反射する I; uˈtsuˈsu 映す ⑨: Light
reflected on the roof. (*Hikari ga
yane de hañsha shite ita.*) 光が屋根
で反射していた.

2 (consider) yoˈku kaˈñgaˈeru よく
考える ⱽ: reflect on what to do
(*nani o suru ka yoku kañgaeru*) 何
をするかよく考える.

reflection *n.* 1 (image) eˈezoo 映
像; uˈtsuˈtta sugata 映った姿: look
at one's reflection in the mirror
(*kagami ni utsutta jibuñ no sugata o miru*) 鏡に映った自分の姿を見
る.

2 (reflecting) haˈñsha 反射: the reflection of light (*hikari no hañsha*)
光の反射.

3 (consideration) yoˈku kaˈñgaˈeru
koˈtoˈ よく考えること; haˈñsee 反省:
He has bought it without much
reflection. (*Kare wa yoku kañgaenai de sore o katte shimatta.*)
彼はよく考えないでそれを買ってしまった.

reform *vt.* 1 (improve) ... o kaˈi-
kaku suru ...を改革する I; kaˈisee
suru 改正する I: reform the tax
system (*zeesee o kaisee suru*) 税制

を改正する.
2 (make better) ... o ka⌉ishiñ saseru …を改心させる [V]; kyo⌈osee suru 矯正する [I]: reform a criminal (*hañzaisha o kaishiñ saseru*) 犯罪者を改心させる.
— *vi.* (become better) ka⌉ishiñ suru 改心する [I].
— *n.* ka⌈ikaku 改革; ka⌈izeñ 改善: social reforms (*shakai-kaikaku*) 社会改革.

refrain *vi.* (... o) tsu⌈tsushi⌉mu (…を)慎む [C]; e⌈ñryo suru 遠慮する [I]: Please refrain from smoking. (*Tabako wa go-eñryo kudasai.*) たばこはご遠慮ください.

refresh *vt.* **1** (give energy) ... o sa⌈wa⌉yaka ni suru …をさわやかにする [I]; ge⌈ñki-zuke⌉ru 元気づける [V]: I felt refreshed after a short nap. (*Sukoshi netara kibuñ ga sawayaka ni natta.*) 少し寝たら気分がさわやかになった.
2 (make fresh) ... o a⌉rata ni suru …を新たにする [I]: refresh one's memory (*kioku o arata ni suru*) 記憶を新たにする.

refreshment *n.* **1** (food and drink) ka⌈rui shokuji 軽い食事; cha⌈ga⌉shi 茶菓子: serve refreshments at a party (*paatii de karui shokuji o dasu*) パーティーで軽い食事を出す.
2 (time to recover) kyu⌈uyoo 休養; ge⌉ñki ka⌈ifuku 元気回復: You need some refreshment. (*Anata wa sukoshi kyuuyoo o toru hitsuyoo ga arimasu.*) あなたは少し休養をとる必要があります.

refrigerator *n.* re⌈ezo⌉oko 冷蔵庫: Meat should be kept in the refrigerator. (*Niku wa reezooko ni irete okanakereba narimaseñ.*) 肉は冷蔵庫に入れておかなければなりません.

refugee *n.* na⌈ñmiñ 難民; hi⌈na⌉ñsha 避難者.

refund *vt.* ... o ha⌈raimodo⌉su …を払い戻す [C]; ka⌉esu 返す [C]: He refunded the money to me. (*Kare wa watashi ni sono o-kane o kaeshite kureta.*) 彼は私にそのお金を返してくれた.

refusal *n.* kyo⌈zetsu 拒絶; kyo⌉hi 拒否: He gave me a flat refusal. (*Kare wa watashi ni kippari to kotowatta.*) 彼は私にきっぱりと断った.

refuse *vt.* ... o ko⌈towa⌉ru …を断る [C]; kyo⌈zetsu suru 拒絶する [I]; kyo⌉hi suru 拒否する [I]: He refused our offer. (*Kare wa wareware no mooshide o kotowatta.*) 彼はわれわれの申し出を断った. / refuse a request (*yookyuu o kyozetsu suru*) 要求を拒絶する.
— *vi.* ko⌈towa⌉ru 断る [C].

regard *vt.* **1** (consider) ... to ka⌈ñga⌉eru …と考える [V]: I regard the situation as serious. (*Watashi wa jitai wa juudai da to kañgaete iru.*) 私は事態は重大だと考えている.
2 (pay attention) ... ni chu⌉ui o ha⌈ra⌉u …に注意を払う [C]: He did not regard our warning. (*Kare wa watashi-tachi no keekoku ni chuui o harawanakatta.*) 彼は私たちの警告に注意を払わなかった.
3 (respect) ... o so⌈ñchoo suru …を尊重する [I]: regard the rights of others (*hoka no hito no keñri o soñchoo suru*) ほかの人の権利を尊重する.
— *n.* **1** (attention) chu⌉ui 注意; ka⌈ñshiñ 関心: He pays no regard to his safety. (*Kare wa añzeñ ni chuui o harawanai.*) 彼は安全に注意を払わない.
2 (respect) so⌈ñkee 尊敬; ke⌉ei 敬意: I have high regard for my teacher. (*Watashi wa señsee o taiheñ soñkee shite imasu.*) 私は先生を大変尊敬しています.

regarding *prep.* ... ni ka⌉ñshite (wa) …に関して(は): Have you any suggestions regarding this problem? (*Kono moñdai ni kañshite nani ka teeañ wa arimasu ka?*) この問題に関して何か提案はありますか.

regime *n.* se⌈ekeñ 政権: a military regime (*guñji-seekeñ*) 軍事政権.

region *n.* **1** (area) chi⌈ho⌉o 地方; (district) chi⌉iki 地域; chi⌉tai 地帯:

tropical regions (*nettai chihoo*) 熱帯地方 / an industrial region (*koogyoo chitai*) 工業地帯.

2 (part of the body) bu˹i 部位; a˹tari あたり: I have a pain in the region of my stomach. (*I no atari ga itai.*) 胃のあたりが痛い.

register *vt.* **1** (enter) ... o to˹roku suru ...を登録する Ⓘ; to˹doke˺ru 届ける Ⓥ: register the names of members (*kaiiñ no namae o tooroku suru*) 会員の名前を登録する / register a birth (*shusshoo [shussee] o todokeru*) 出生を届ける.

2 (record) ... o ki˹roku suru ...を記録する Ⓘ; sa˹su 指す Ⓒ: The thermometer registered minus 5 degrees. (*Oñdokee wa mainasu godo o sashite ita.*) 温度計はマイナス 5 度を指していた.

3 (of mail) ... o ka˹kitome ni suru ...を書留にする Ⓘ: Please register this letter. (*Kono tegami o kakitome ni shite kudasai.*) この手紙を書留にしてください.

— *vi.* (... ni) to˹oroku suru (...に)登録する Ⓘ; ki˹mee suru 記名する Ⓘ: register at a hotel (*hoteru no shukuhakusha-meebo ni kimee suru*) ホテルの宿泊者名簿に記名する.

— *n.* **1** (list) to˹orokubo 登録簿; me˹ebo 名簿: the register of voters (*señkyoniñ meebo*) 選挙人名簿.

2 (device) ji˹doo-kiroku˺ki 自動記録器: a cash register (*kiñseñ tooro-kuki*) 金銭登録器.

registration *n.* to˹oroku 登録: a registration number (*toorokubañgoo*) 登録番号 / a registration card (*shukuhakusha kaado*) 宿泊者カード.

regret *vt.* **1** (feel sorry) ... o za˹ñne˺ñ ni o˺mo˺u ...を残念に思う Ⓒ: I regret that you have to resign. (*Anata ga taishoku shinakereba naranai no o zañneñ ni omoimasu.*) あなたが退職しなければならないのを残念に思います.

2 (remember with remorse) ... o ko˹okai suru ...を後悔する Ⓘ: You

will regret what you have done. (*Anata wa shita koto o kookai suru deshoo.*) あなたはしたことを後悔するでしょう.

— *n.* za˹ñne˺ñ 残念; ko˹okai 後悔: a matter for regret (*zañneñ na koto*) 残念なこと / I feel regret for having been unkind to her. (*Kanojo ni taishite fushiñsetsu datta koto o kookai shite imasu.*) 彼女に対して不親切だったことを後悔しています.

regular *adj.* **1** (usual) te˹eki-teki na 定期的な: a regular meeting (*teeki-teki na atsumari*) 定期的な集まり / a regular holiday (*teekyuubi*) 定休日 / a regular flight (*teekibiñ*) 定期便.

2 (steady) ki˹soku-teki na 規則的な: lead a regular life (*kisoku tadashii seekatsu o suru*) 規則正しい生活をする.

3 (balanced) to˹tono˺tta 整った: have regular features (*totonotta kao o shite iru*) 整った顔をしている.

4 (formal) se˹eshiki no 正式の: a regular player (*see-señshu*) 正選手.

— *n.* se˹ekai˺iñ 正会員; re˹gyuraa レギュラー.

regularly *adv.* te˹eki-teki ni 定期的に; ki˹soku-teki ni 規則的に: We meet regularly once a month. (*Watashi-tachi wa tsuki ni ichi-do kimatte kaigoo o hirakimasu.*) 私たちは月に一度きまって会合を開きます.

regulate *vt.* **1** (control) ... o ki˹see suru ...を規制する Ⓘ; to˹rishima˺ru 取り締まる Ⓒ: regulate air pollution (*taiki oseñ o kisee suru*) 大気汚染を規制する.

2 (adjust) ... o cho˹osetsu suru ...を調節する Ⓘ: regulate the room temperature (*shitsuoñ o choosetsu suru*) 室温を調節する.

regulation *n.* **1** (rule) ki˹soku 規則; ki˹tee 規定: traffic regulations (*kootsuu kisoku*) 交通規則.

2 (regulating) ki˹see 規制: the regulation of prices (*bukka no kisee*) 物価の規制.

3 (adjustment) cho˹osetsu 調節:

the regulation of temperature (*oñdo no choosetsu*) 温度の調節.

rehearsal *n*. ke¹eko けいこ; re¹ñ-shuu 練習; ri¹ha¹asaru リハーサル: hold a rehearsal (*rihaasaru o suru*) リハーサルをする.

reign *n*. chi¹see 治世; ku¹riñ 君臨: The king's reign lasted a long time. (*Sono oo no chisee wa nagaku tsuzuita.*) その王の治世は長く続いた.
— *vi.* ku¹ñriñ suru 君臨する ⒤; to¹ochi suru 統治する ⒤.

reinforce *vt.* ... o ho¹kyoo suru ...を補強する ⒤; zo¹okyoo suru 増強する ⒤: reinforce a bridge (*hashi o hokyoo suru*) 橋を補強する / reinforce staff members (*staffu o zookyoo suru*) スタッフを増強する.

reissue *vt.* ... o sa¹iha¹kkoo suru ...を再発行する ⒤: Can I have the certificate reissued? (*Shoomeesho o saihakkoo shite moraemasu ka?*) 証明書を再発行してもらえますか.
— *n.* sa¹iha¹kkoo 再発行.

reject *vt.* ... o kyo¹zetsu suru ...を拒絶する ⒤; ko¹towa¹ru 断る Ⓒ: He rejected my proposal. (*Kare wa watashi no teeañ o kotowatta.*) 彼は私の提案を断った.

rejoice *vi.* (... o) yo¹roko¹bu (...を)喜ぶ Ⓒ; u¹reshiga¹ru うれしがる Ⓒ: She rejoiced at the news. (*Kanojo wa sono shirase o yorokoñda.*) 彼女はその知らせを喜んだ.

relate *vt.* **1** (tell) ... o ha¹na¹su ...を話す Ⓒ: We listened as he related his experiences. (*Watashi-tachi wa kare ga taikeñ o hanasu no o kiita.*) 私たちは彼が体験を話すのを聞いた.
2 (connect) ... o ka¹ñreñzuke¹ru ...を関連づける Ⓥ: relate the two events (*sono futatsu no jikeñ o kañreñzukeru*) その二つの事件を関連づける.
— *vi.* (... ni) ka¹ñkee ga a¹ru (...に)関係がある Ⓒ: The letter relates to him. (*Sono tegami wa kare ni kañkee suru mono desu.*) その手紙は彼に関係するものです.

related *adj.* **1** (of the same fami-

ly) shi¹ñrui no 親類の; ke¹tsueñ no 血縁の: She is not related to me. (*Kanojo wa watashi no shiñrui de wa arimaseñ.*) 彼女は私の親類ではありません.
2 (connected) ka¹ñkee no a¹ru 関係のある; ka¹ñreñ shita 関連した: a related question (*kañreñ-shitsumoñ*) 関連質問.

relation *n.* **1** (connection) ka¹ñkee 関係; ka¹ñreñ 関連: Weight has a close relation to health. (*Taijuu wa keñkoo to missetsu na kañkee ga arimasu.*) 体重は健康と密接な関係があります. / business relations (*torihiki-kañkee*) 取引関係.
2 (relative) shi¹ñrui 親類; shi¹ñseki 親戚: Is he a relation of yours? (*Ano kata wa anata no go-shiñseki desu ka?*) あの方はあなたのご親戚ですか.

relationship *n.* ka¹ñkee 関係; ka¹ñreñ 関連: We have a good relationship with our neighbors. (*Watashi-tachi wa tonari no hito-tachi to yoi kañkee ni arimasu.*) 私たちは隣の人たちとよい関係にあります.

relative *adj.* hi¹kaku-teki 比較的: live in relative luxury (*hikaku-teki zeetaku na seekatsu o suru*) 比較的ぜいたくな生活をする.
— *n.* (relation) ni¹kushiñ 肉親; mi¹uchi 身内; shi¹ñseki 親戚: All his relatives attended the wedding. (*Kare no nikushiñ wa miñna kekkoñshiki ni shusseki shita.*) 彼の肉親はみんな結婚式に出席した. / She is a relative on my father's side. (*Kanojo wa watashi no chichi-kata no shiñseki desu.*) 彼女は私の父方の親戚です.

relatively *adv.* hi¹kaku-teki 比較的; wa¹riai 割合: It is relatively warm today. (*Kyoo wa wariai ataka desu.*) きょうはわりあい暖かです.

relax *vt.* **1** (make less tight) ... o ku¹tsurogase¹ru ...をくつろがせる Ⓥ; ri¹ra¹kkusu saseru リラックスさせる Ⓥ: I felt relaxed after a bath. (*O-furo ni haittara kutsuroida kibuñ*

ni natta.) おふろに入ったらくつろいだ気
分になった.

2 (loosen) ... o yuˈrumeˈru ...を緩め
る V: I relaxed my grip on the
rope. (*Watashi wa roopu o nigiru
te o yurumeta.*) 私はローブを握る手を
緩めた.

3 (make less strict) ... o kaˈñwa
suru ...を緩和する I: relax import
regulations (*yunyuu kisee o kañ-
wa suru*) 輸入規制を緩和する.

— *vi.* **1** (rest from work) kuˈtsu-
roˈgu くつろぐ C: relax by going
fishing (*sakanatsuri ni itte kutsu-
rogu*) 魚釣りに行ってくつろぐ.

2 (become less severe) yuˈruˈmu 緩
む C: The cold has been relaxing.
(*Samusa ga yuruñde kita.*) 寒さが緩
んできた.

relaxation *n.* kyuˈuyoo 休養;
hoˈneyaˈsume 骨休め.

release *vt.* **1** (set free) ... o haˈnaˈ-
su ...を放す C; kaˈihoo suru 解放す
る I: I released the bird from the
cage. (*Watashi wa tori o kago
kara hanashite yatta.*) 私は鳥をかごか
ら放してやった.

2 (offer to public) ... o koˈrokai
suru ...を公開する I; (of a movie)
fuˈukiˈru 封切る C; (of a record) ha-
ˈtsubai suru 発売する I: The new
film will be released next week.
(*Sono eega wa raishuu fuukirare-
masu.*) その映画は来週封切られます.

— *n.* **1** (setting free) shaˈkuhoo
釈放; kaˈihoo 解放: a release from
prison (*keemusho kara no shakuhoo*) 刑務所からの釈放.

2 (of news) haˈppyoo 発表; (of a
movie) fuˈukiri 封切り; (of a record)
haˈtsubai 発売.

relevant *adj.* (related) kaˈñreñ
shita [shite iru] 関連した[している];
(pertinent) teˈkisetsu na 適切な:
the relevant data (*kañreñ shita
shiryoo*) 関連した資料 / a relevant
remark (*tekisetsu na kotoba*) 適切
なことば.

reliable *adj.* (dependable) shiˈñrai
dekiˈru 信頼できる; taˈshika na 確か

な: a reliable person (*shiñrai dekiru hito*) 信頼できる人 / reliable information (*tashika na joohoo*) 確か
な情報.

reliance *n.* shiˈñrai 信頼; shiˈñyoo
信用: put reliance on a person (*hito
o shiñyoo suru*) 人を信用する.

relic *n.* iˈbutsu 遺物; iˈseki 遺跡:
relics of an ancient civilization
(*kodai buñmee no iseki*) 古代文明
の遺跡.

relief[1] *n.* **1** (feeling of comfort)
hoˈtto suru kotoˈ ほっとすること; aˈñ-
shiñ 安心: It was a great relief to
find nothing had been stolen.
(*Nani mo nusumarenakatta to
wakari hotto shita.*) 何も盗まれなかっ
たとわかりほっとした.

2 (lessening of pain) keˈegeñ 軽減;
joˈkyo 除去: a drug for the relief of
pain (*kutsuu o keegeñ suru kusuri*) 苦痛を軽減する薬.

3 (help) kyuˈusai 救済; kyuˈujo 救
助: The money was used for the
relief of the poor. (*Sono o-kane wa
mazushii hito-tachi no kyuusai no
tame ni tsukawareta.*) そのお金は貧
しい人たちの救済のために使われた.

relief[2] *n.* (sculpture) uˈkibori 浮き彫
り; reˈriˈifu レリーフ.

relieve *vt.* **1** (lessen) ... o yaˈwarageˈru ...を和らげる V; raˈkuˈ ni
suru 楽にする I: This medicine
will relieve your pain. (*Kono kusuri wa anata no itami o yawa-
ragemasu.*) この薬はあなたの痛みを和ら
げます.

2 (free from worry) ... o hoˈtto
saseru ...をほっとさせる V; aˈñshiñ
saseru 安心させる V: I was relieved
to be back home. (*Uchi ni kaette
hotto shita.*) 家に帰ってほっとした.

3 (replace) ... o koˈotai saseru ...を
交替させる V: I will be relieved at
five. (*Watashi wa go-ji ni kootai
shimasu.*) 私は5時に交替します.

religion *n.* shuˈukyoo 宗教; shiˈñkoo 信仰: What is your religion?
(*Anata no shuukyoo wa nañ desu
ka?*) あなたの宗教は何ですか.

religious adj. shuˈukyoo no 宗教
の; shiˈnkoo no 信仰の: religious
freedom (shiñkoo no jiyuu) 信仰の
自由.

relish n. (of food) aˈjiwai 味わい;
(liking) koˈnomi 好み: She drank
the wine with relish. (Kanojo wa
sono waiñ o oishisoo ni noñda.) 彼
女はそのワインをおいしそうに飲んだ.

reluctance n. ki ˈga susumanai
kotoˈ 気が進まないこと; iˈyagaˈru
koˈtoˈ 嫌がること: He accepted the
offer with reluctance. (Kare wa
iyaiya nagara sono mooshide ni
oojita.) 彼はいやいやながらその申し出に
応じた.

reluctant adj. ki ˈga susumanai
気が進まない; iˈyagaˈru 嫌がる: I am
reluctant to ask for his help. (Kare
no eñjo o motomeru no wa ki ga
susumanai.) 彼の援助を求めるのは気
が進まない.

rely vi. taˈnomi ni suˈru 頼みにする
①; shiˈñrai suru 信頼する ①: You
can rely on him. (Kare wa shiñrai
dekimasu.) 彼は信頼できます.

remain vi. 1 (stay) toˈdomaˈru とど
まる ©: He went out but I remained. (Kare wa dekaketa ga
watashi wa todomatta.) 彼は出かけ
たが私はとどまった.
   2 (continue to be) ... no maˈmaˈ de
iˈru …のままでいる Ⓥ: She remained
silent for a long time. (Kanojo wa
nagai aida damatta mama de ita.)
彼女は長い間黙ったままでいた.
   3 (be left) noˈkoˈru 残る ©: The
snow still remains. (Yuki wa mada
nokotte iru.) 雪はまだ残っている.

remainder n. noˈkoriˈ 残り; noˈko-
rimono 残り物: give the remainder
of the meal to a dog (shokuji no
nokori o inu ni yaru) 食事の残りを
犬にやる.

remark n. 1 (comment) iˈkeñ 意
見; kaˈñsoo 感想: He made some
remarks on the work. (Kare wa
sono sakuhiñ ni tsuite ikura ka
kañsoo o nobeta.) 彼はその作品につ
いていくらか感想を述べた.

   2 (notice) chuˈumoku 注目; chuˈui
注意: a novel worthy of remark
(chuumoku ni atai suru shoosetsu)
注目に値する小説.
   — vt. (say) ... to noˈbeˈru …と述べ
る Ⓥ; iˈu 言う ©: He remarked that
she was beautiful. (Kanojo wa
bijiñ da to kare wa itta.) 彼女は美
人だと彼は言った.

remarkable adj. chuˈumoku su
beˈki 注目すべき; iˈchijirushiˈi 著し
い: a remarkable event (chuumoku
su beki jikeñ) 注目すべき事件 /
make remarkable progress (ichijiru-
shii shiñpo o suru) 著しい進歩をする.

remedy n. 1 (cure) chiˈryoohoo
治療法; ryoˈohoo 療法: Is there
any good remedy for colds? (Kaze
ni yoi chiryoohoo wa arimasu
ka?) かぜによい治療法はありますか.
   2 (means of correcting) kaˈizeñ-
saku 改善策; kyoˈoseehoo 矯正法:
a remedy for unemployment (shitsugyoo no kaizeñsaku) 失業の改善
策.
   — vt. (put to right) ... o kyoˈosee
suru …を矯正する ①; kaˈizeñ suru
改善する ①: remedy a deficiency
(kekkañ o kyoosee suru) 欠陥を矯
正する.

remember vt. 1 (keep in the
mind) ... o oˈboˈete iru …を覚えてい
る Ⓥ; kiˈoku shite iru 記憶している
Ⓥ: I don't remember his name.
(Watashi wa kare no namae o
oboete imaseñ.) 私は彼の名前を覚え
ていません.
   2 (recall) ... o oˈmoidaˈsu …を思い
出す ©: I cannot remember where
I met him. (Doko de kare ni atta
ka omoidasenai.) どこで彼に会ったか
思い出せない.
   3 (take care not to forget) waˈsu-
renaˈide ⟨verb⟩ 忘れないで…: I'll
remember to mail this letter. (Kono tegami o wasurenaide dashi-
masu.) この手紙を忘れないで出します.
   — vi. oˈmoidaˈsu 思い出す ©; kiˈ-
ˈoku suru 記憶する ①: If I remember rightly, he is a graduate of this

school. (*Watashi no kioku ni ma-chigai nakereba, kare wa koko no gakkoo no sotsugyoosee da.*) 私の記憶に間違いなければ、彼はここの学校の卒業生だ。

remembrance *n.* kiˈoku 記憶; oˈmoide 思い出: I have no remembrance of the accident. (*Sono jiko wa kioku ga nai.*) その事故は記憶がない。/ I have many good remembrances of my schooldays. (*Watashi wa gakusee-jidai no yoi omoide ga takusañ aru.*) 私は学生時代のよい思い出がたくさんある。

remind *vt.* **1** (make remember) ... ni (... o) oˈmoidasaseˈru ...に(...を) 思い出させる Ⓥ: This picture reminds me of my home town. (*Kono e wa watashi ni furusato o omoidasaseru.*) この絵は私にふるさとを思い出させる。
2 (make think of) ... ni (... o) kiˈzukaseˈru ...に(...を)気づかせる Ⓥ; chuˈui suru 注意する Ⓘ: Please remind me to take my medicine. (*Kusuri o nomu yoo ni watashi ni chuui shite kudasai.*) 薬を飲むように私に注意してください。

remorse *n.* koˈokai 後悔; ryoˈo-shiñ no kaˈshaku 良心のかしゃく: I feel remorse for what I have done. (*Watashi wa shita koto o kookai shite iru.*) 私はしたことを後悔している。

remote *adj.* **1** (of a place) toˈoku hanaˈreta 遠く離れた; heˈñpi na へんぴな: a remote village (*heñpi na mura*) へんぴな村。
2 (of time) toˈoi 遠い: the remote past (*tooi mukashi*) 遠い昔。
3 (not closely related) kaˈñkee no usui 関係の薄い; toˈoi 遠い: remote relatives (*tooi shiñrui*) 遠い親類。
4 (slight) kaˈsuka na かすかな: a remote chance (*kasuka na chañsu*) かすかなチャンス。

removal *n.* **1** (moving) iˈdoo 移動; iˈteñ 移転: removal to a new office (*atarashii jimusho e no iteñ*) 新しい事務所への移転。
2 (taking away) joˈkyo 除去。

remove *vt.* **1** (get rid of) ... o toˈrinozoku ...を取り除く Ⓒ: remove the snow on a street (*toori no yuki o torinozoku*) 通りの雪を取り除く。
2 (take off) ... o nuˈgu ...を脱ぐ Ⓒ: remove one's hat and coat (*booshi to kooto o nugu*) 帽子とコートを脱ぐ。
3 (dismiss) ... o meˈñshoku suru ...を免職する Ⓘ: He was removed from office. (*Kare wa meñshoku sareta.*) 彼は免職された。/ be removed from school (*taigaku sase-rareru*) 退学させられる。
— *vi.* (move house) hiˈkkoˈsu 引っ越す Ⓒ: remove from Tokyo to Yokohama (*Tookyoo kara Yoko-hama e hikkosu*) 東京から横浜へ引っ越す。

render *vt.* **1** (give) ... o aˈtaeru ...を与える Ⓥ: Nobody rendered him help. (*Dare mo kare ni eñjo o ataenakatta.*) だれも彼に援助を与えなかった。
2 (make) ... o ... ni suˈru ...を...にする Ⓘ: render a contract invalid (*keeyaku o mukoo ni suru*) 契約を無効にする。
3 (perform) ... o eˈñjiru ...を演じる Ⓥ: render the part of Hamlet (*Hamuretto no yaku o eñjiru*) ハムレットの役を演じる。

renew *vt.* **1** (begin again) ... o saˈikai suru ...を再開する Ⓘ: renew negotiations (*kooshoo o saikai suru*) 交渉を再開する。
2 (make new) ... o aˈtarashiˈku suru ...を新しくする Ⓘ: I renewed the door by painting it. (*Watashi wa doa ni peñki o nutte atara-shiku shita.*) 私はドアにペンキを塗って新しくした。
3 (replace) ... o koˈoshiñ suru ...を更新する Ⓘ: renew a driver's license (*uñteñ meñkyoshoo o kooshiñ suru*) 運転免許証を更新する。

rent *n.* chiˈñtaˈiryoo 賃貸料; (of a house) yaˈchiñ 家賃; (of a room) heˈyadai 部屋代; (of land) chiˈjiˈdai 地代: How much is the rent for this house? (*Koko no yachiñ* *wa ikura desu ka?*) ここの家賃はいくらですか.

— *vt.* 1 (pay) ... o chi⌐ŋgari suru ...を賃借りする ①; ka⌐riru 借りる Ⅴ: I'd like to rent a car. (*Kuruma o ichi-dai karitai no desu ga.*) 車を一台借りたいのですが.

2 (receive) ... o chi⌐ŋgashi suru ...を賃貸しする ①; ka⌐su 貸す Ⓒ: She rents a room to a student. (*Kanojo wa gakusee ni heya o kashite iru.*) 彼女は学生に部屋を貸している.

rent-a-car *n.* re⌐ñta¹kaa レンタカー: Can I reserve a rent-a-car here? (*Koko de reñtakaa o yoyaku dekimasu ka?*) ここでレンタカーを予約できますか.

repair *vt.* 1 (mend) ... o shu¹uri suru ...を修理する ①; (of a part) shu⌐uzeñ suru 修繕する ①: Can you repair this camera? (*Kono kamera o shuuri dekimasu ka?*) このカメラを修理できますか. / I repaired the roof. (*Watashi wa yane o shuuzeñ shita.*) 私は屋根を修繕した.

2 (correct) ... o ta⌐da¹su ...を正す Ⓒ: repair a mistake (*ayamari o tadasu*) 誤りを正す.

— *n.* 1 (repairing) shu¹uri 修理; shu⌐uzeñ 修繕: The bridge is under repair. (*Hashi wa shuurichuu desu.*) 橋は修理中です. / make repairs on a house (*ie o shuuzeñ suru*) 家を修繕する.

2 (condition) te⌐ire¹ no jo⌐otai 手入れの状態: The car is in good repair. (*Kuruma wa teire ga yukitodoite iru.*) 車は手入れが行き届いている.

repay *vt.* 1 (pay back) ... o he⌐ñsai suru ...を返済する ①; ka⌐esu 返す Ⓒ: I repaid him the money. (*Watashi wa kare ni sono o-kane o kaeshita.*) 私は彼にそのお金を返した.

2 (reward) ... ni mu⌐kui¹ru ...に報いる Ⅴ; o⌐ñga¹eshi suru 恩返しする ①: repay a person's kindness (*hito no shiñsetsu ni mukuiru*) 人の親切に報いる / How can I ever repay you? (*Anata ni doo yatte oñgaeshi o shite ii ka wakarimaseñ.*) あなたにど

うやって恩返しをしていいかわかりません.

repeat *vt.* 1 (say again) ... o ku⌐rika¹eshite i⌐u ...を繰り返して言う Ⓒ; mo⌐o ichido iu もう一度言う Ⓒ: Could you repeat that? (*Moo ichido itte itadakemaseñ ka?*) もう一度言っていただけませんか.

2 (do again) ... o ku⌐rika¹esu ...を繰り返す Ⓒ: Don't repeat the same error. (*Onaji machigai o kurikaeshite wa ikenai.*) 同じ間違いを繰り返してはいけない.

3 (recite) ... o a⌐ñshoo suru ...を暗唱する ①: repeat a poem (*shi o añshoo suru*) 詩を暗唱する.

— *vi.* (say again) ku⌐rika¹eshite i⌐u 繰り返して言う Ⓒ; ku⌐rika¹esu 繰り返す Ⓒ: Please repeat after me. (*Ato ni tsuite kurikaeshite itte kudasai.*) 後について繰り返して言ってください.

repent *vi.* ko⌐okai suru 後悔する ①: He repented and changed his ways. (*Kare wa kookai shite okonai o aratameta.*) 彼は後悔して行いを改めた.

— *vt.* ... o ko⌐okai suru ...を後悔する ①; ku⌐ya¹mu 悔やむ Ⓒ: He repented having said no. (*Kare wa kotowatta koto o kookai shita.*) 彼は断ったことを後悔した.

repetition *n.* ku⌐rikaeshi 繰り返し; ha⌐ñpuku 反復: Repetition is important in learning a language. (*Kotoba o narau ni wa hañpuku ga juuyoo desu.*) 言葉を習うには反復が重要です.

replace *vt.* 1 (put back) mo⌐to no to⌐koro¹ ni o⌐ku 元の所に置く Ⓒ; mo⌐do¹su 戻す Ⓒ: replace a book on the shelf (*hoñ o tana ni modosu*) 本を棚に戻す.

2 (change) ... o to⌐rikaeru ...を取り替える Ⅴ; ko⌐okañ suru 交換する ①: replace a worn tire (*hetta taiya o torikaeru*) 減ったタイヤを取り替える.

3 (take the place of) ... ni to⌐tteka-waru ...に取って代わる Ⓒ; ... no a⌐to o tsu⌐gu ...の後を継ぐ Ⓒ: Mr. Aoki replaced Mr. Yamada as our company president. (*Aoki-shi ga Ya-*

mada-shi no ato o tsuide warewa-re no shachoo ni natta.) 青木氏が山田氏の後を継いでわれわれの社長になった.

reply vi. (... ni) he⌐nji⌐ o suru (…に) 返事をする Ⅰ; ko⌐tae⌐ru 答える Ⅴ: I replied to his letter at once. (Watashi wa kare no tegami ni sugu ni heñji o shita.) 私は彼の手紙にすぐに返事をした.
— vt. ... to ko⌐tae⌐ru …と答える Ⅴ: He replied that he knew nothing about it. (Kare wa sore ni tsuite nani mo shiranai to kotaeta.) 彼はそれについて何も知らないと答えた.
— n. he⌐nji⌐ 返事; ko⌐tae⌐ 答え: I have received no reply from him yet. (Kare kara mada nani mo heñji o moratte imaseñ.) 彼からまだ何も返事をもらっていません.

report n. 1 (statement) ho⌐okoku 報告; (written form) ho⌐okokusho 報告書; sho⌐omeesho 証明書: a police report on the accident (kee-satsu no jiko hookokusho) 警察の事故報告書 / Please make out a theft report. (Toonañ shoomeesho o tsukutte kudasai.) 盗難証明書を作ってください.
2 (piece of news) ho⌐odoo 報道; ki⌐ji 記事: a newspaper report (shi⌐ñbuñ kiji) 新聞記事.
3 (school report) se⌐esekihyoo 成績表; tsu⌐uchihyoo 通知表.
4 (of an explosion) ba⌐kuhatsu⌐oñ 爆発音; (of a shot) ju⌐usee 銃声.
— vt. 1 (give a statement) ... o ho⌐okoku suru …を報告する Ⅰ: He reported the results of the election at the meeting. (Kare wa señkyo no kekka o kai de hookoku shita.) 彼は選挙の結果を会で報告した.
2 (give an account) ... o ho⌐odoo suru …を報道する Ⅰ; ho⌐ojiru 報じる Ⅴ: It is reported that a ship is missing. (Fune ga is-seki yukue-fumee da to hoojirarete iru.) 船が1隻行方不明だと報じられている.
3 (notify) ... o to⌐dokede⌐ru …を届け出る Ⅴ; shi⌐ñkoku suru 申告する Ⅰ: I reported the accident to the

police. (Watashi wa sono jiko o keesatsu ni todoketa.) 私はその事故を警察に届けた.
— vi. 1 (make a statement) ho⌐okoku suru 報告する Ⅰ: He reported on the conference. (Kare wa sono kaigi ni tsuite hookoku shita.) 彼はその会議について報告した.
2 (appear) shu⌐ttoo suru 出頭する Ⅰ: He was told to report to the police. (Kare wa keesatsu ni shut-too suru yoo ni iwareta.) 彼は警察に出頭するように言われた.

reporter n. shu⌐zai ki⌐sha 取材記者; (of a newspaper) shi⌐ñbuñ ki⌐-sha 新聞記者; re⌐po⌐otaa レポーター.

represent vt. 1 (act for) ... o da⌐i-hyoo suru …を代表する Ⅰ: We chose committee members to represent us. (Watashi-tachi wa watashi-tachi o daihyoo suru iiñ o erañda.) 私たちは私たちを代表する委員を選んだ.
2 (stand for) ... o a⌐rawa⌐su …を表す Ⅽ: The blue lines on the map represent rivers. (Chizu no aoi señ wa kawa o arawashimasu.) 地図の青い線は川を表します.
3 (show) ... o e⌐ga⌐ku …を描く Ⅽ: This painting represents a storm at sea. (Kono e wa umi no arashi o egaite imasu.) この絵は海の嵐を描いています.
4 (be an example of) ... no te⌐ñkee o shime⌐su …の典型を示す Ⅽ: He represents the Japanese business-man. (Kare wa Nihoñjiñ no jitsu-gyooka no teñkee o shimeshite iru.) 彼は日本人の実業家の典型を示している.

representation n. hyo⌐oge⌐ñ 表現; byo⌐osha 描写: This novel pro-vides a vivid representation of ru-ral life. (Kono shoosetsu wa inaka no seekatsu o iki-iki to byoosha shite iru.) この小説は田舎の生活を生き生きと描写している.

representative n. 1 (person acting for others) da⌐ihyoo 代表: We sent a representative to the meeting. (Wareware wa sono

shuukai ni daihyoo o okutta.) われ
われはその集会に代表を送った.
2 (member of the House of Repre-
sentatives) da「igi¹shi 代議士: a representative from Tokyo (*Tookyoo
señshutsu no daigishi*) 東京選出の
代議士.
— *adj.* **1** (representing) da「ihyoo
suru 代表する: a representative
body (*daihyoodañ*) 代表団.
2 (typical) da「ihyoo-teki na 代表的
な; te「ñkee-teki na 典型的な: This
is one of the buildings representative of modern architecture. (*Kore
wa kiñdai keñchiku no daihyoo-
teki na tatemono no hitotsu desu.*)
これは近代建築の代表的な建物のひとつ
です.

reprimand *vt.* ... o shi「sseki suru
...を叱責する ①; shi「karu しかる ©:
He was reprimanded for his negligence in his job. (*Kare wa shokumu taimañ o shisseki sareta.*)
彼は職務怠慢を叱責された.
— *n.* shi「sseki 叱責; cho「okai 懲
戒.

reproach *vt.* (scold) ... o shi「karu
...をしかる ©; (blame) hi「nañ suru
非難する ①: I reproached him for
carelessness. (*Watashi wa kare no
fuchuui o shikatta.*) 私は彼の不注意
をしかった.
— *n.* (scolding) shi「sseki 叱責;
(blaming) hi「nañ 非難: a look of
reproach (*hinañ no kaotsuki*) 非難
の顔つき.

reproduce *vt.* **1** (produce again)
... o sa「isee suru ...を再生する ①;
sa「igeñ suru 再現する ①: Tape re-
corders reproduce sound. (*Teepurekoodaa wa oto o saisee suru.*) テ
ープレコーダーは音を再生する.
2 (copy) ... o fu「kusee suru ...を複
製する ①; fu「kusha suru 複写する ①:
This picture was reproduced from
the original. (*Kono e wa geñga o
fukusei shita mono desu.*) この絵は
原画を複製したものです.
— *vi.* (have offspring) ha「ñshoku
suru 繁殖する ①: Insects reproduce

by laying eggs. (*Koñchuu wa tamago o uñde hañshoku suru.*) 昆虫
は卵を生んで繁殖する.

reproduction *n.* **1** (reproduc-
ing) sa「isee 再生; sa「igeñ 再現:
the reproduction of sound (*oto no
saisee*) 音の再生.
2 (copy) fu「kusha 複写; fu「kusee
複製: This picture is a reproduction. (*Kono e wa fukusee desu.*) こ
の絵は複製です.

republic *n.* kyo「owa¹koku 共和国:
the People's Republic of China
(*Chuuka jiñmiñ kyoowakoku*) 中
華人民共和国.

republican *adj.* (of a country)
kyo「owa¹koku no 共和国の; (of a
party) kyo「owatoo no 共和党の.
— *n.* kyo「owashugi¹sha 共和主義
者; kyo「owato¹iñ 共和党員.

reputation *n.* **1** (opinion) hyo「o-
bañ 評判: He has a good [bad]
reputation. (*Kare wa hyoobañ ga
ii [warui].*) 彼は評判がいい[悪い].
2 (good name) me「esee 名声;
ko「ohyoo 好評: The scandal damaged his reputation. (*Sono sukyañdaru wa kare no meesee o
kizu tsuketa.*) そのスキャンダルは彼の
名声を傷つけた.

request *n.* **1** (demand) ne「ga¹i 願
い; ta「nomi¹ 頼み; yo「osee 要請: I
have a request to make of you. (*O-
negai ga aru no desu ga.*) お願いがあ
るのですが. / I bought this at her request. (*Kanojo no tanomi de kore
o katta.*) 彼女の頼みでこれを買った.
2 (something asked for) ne「gai-
goto¹ 願い事; ri「kue¹suto リクエスト:
grant a request (*negaigoto o ka-
naeru*) 願い事をかなえる / play requests from listeners (*chooshusha
kara no rikuesuto-kyoku o eñsoo
suru*) 聴取者からのリクエスト曲を演奏
する.
— *vt.* ... o ta「no¹mu ...を頼む ©;
yo「okyuu suru 要求する ①: I requested his help. (*Watashi wa
kare no eñjo o tanoñda.*) 私は彼の援
助を頼んだ.

require *vt.* **1** (need) ... o hiʳtsuyoo to suru ...を必要とする ①: Is there anything else you require? (*Hoka ni nani ka hitsuyoo to suru mono wa arimasu ka?*) ほかに何か必要とするものはありますか. / The roof requires repairing. (*Yane wa shuuri ga hitsuyoo da.*) 屋根は修理が必要だ.
2 (demand) ... o yoʳokyuu suru ...を要求する ①; meʳejiru 命じる Ⓥ: We have done all that is required of us. (*Yookyuu sareta koto wa subete yarimashita.*) 要求されたことはすべてやりました.

requirement *n.* hiʳtsuyoo na mono ① 必要な物; hiʳtsuyoojoʳokeñ 必要条件: This store can supply all your requirements. (*Kono mise ni wa anata ga hitsuyoo to suru mono wa subete arimasu.*) この店にはあなたが必要とする物はすべてあります.

rescue *vt.* ... o sukuu 救う Ⓒ; kyuʳujo suru 救助する ①: He rescued a drowning child. (*Kare wa oborekakete iru kodomo o sukutta.*) 彼はおぼれかけている子どもを救った.
— *n.* kyuʳushutsu 救出; kyuʳujo 救助: go to the rescue of a person (*hito no kyuujo ni iku*) 人の救助に行く.

research *n.* choʳosa 調査; keʳñkyuu 研究: carry out market research (*shijoo choosa o okonau*) 市場調査を行う / He is engaged in cancer research. (*Kare wa gañ no keñkyuu ni juuji shite iru.*) 彼はがんの研究に従事している.
— *vi.* (... o) choʳosa suru (...を)調査する ①; keʳñkyuu suru 研究する ①: We are researching into the problem. (*Watashi-tachi wa sono moñdai no choosa o shite imasu.*) 私たちはその問題の調査をしています.

resemblance *n.* ruʳiji 類似; niʳte iru tokoro 似ているところ: There is little resemblance between them. (*Kare-ra ni wa nite iru tokoro ga hotoñdo nai.*) 彼らには似ているところがほとんどない.

resemble *vt.* ... ni niʳte iru ...に似ている Ⓥ: She resembles her mother. (*Kanojo wa hahaoya ni nite iru.*) 彼女は母親に似ている.

resent *vt.* ... ni haʳraʳ o taʳteʳru ...に腹を立てる Ⓥ; fuʳñgai suru 憤慨する ①: He resented my remarks. (*Kare wa watashi no kotoba ni hara o tateta.*) 彼は私の言葉に腹を立てた.

resentment *n.* fuʳñgai 憤慨; iʳkidoori 憤り: I felt resentment at the way I had been treated. (*Watashi wa uketa taiguu ni fuñgai shita.*) 私は受けた待遇に憤慨した.

reservation *n.* yoʳyaku 予約: I'd like to make a reservation for 7:00. (*Shichi-ji ni yoyaku shite kudasai.*) 7時に予約してください. / Cancel this reservation, please. (*Kono yoyaku o torikeshite kudasai.*) この予約を取り消してください.

reserve *vt.* **1** (book) ... o yoʳyaku suru ...を予約する ①: I reserved a table at the restaurant for seven. (*Watashi wa sono resutorañ ni shichi-ji ni teeburu o yoyaku shita.*) 私はそのレストランに7時にテーブルを予約した.
2 (set apart) ... o toʳtte oku ...をとっておく Ⓒ: reserve Sunday for fishing (*tsuri ni nichiyoo o totte oku*) 釣りに日曜をとっておく.
— *n.* **1** (store) taʳkuwae 蓄え: a reserve of food (*shokuryoo no takuwae*) 食糧の蓄え.
2 (troops) yoʳbiʳguñ 予備軍.

reservoir *n.* choʳsuʳichi 貯水池.

reside *vi.* suʳmu 住む Ⓒ; kyoʳjuu suru 居住する ①: He resides in the suburbs. (*Kare wa koogai ni suñde iru.*) 彼は郊外に住んでいる.

residence *n.* juʳukyo 住居; juʳutaku 住宅: take up residence in the country (*inaka ni kyo o sadameru*) 田舎に居を定める.

resident *n.* kyoʳjuusha 居住者: foreign residents (*kyoryuu gaikokujiñ*) 居留外国人.
— *adj.* kyoʳjuu suru 居住する; suʳmikomi no 住み込みの: a resident

tutor (*sumikomi no katee kyooshi*) 住み込みの家庭教師.

resign *vi.* ji⌐shoku suru 辞職する Ⅰ; ya⌐meru 辞める Ⅴ: He decided to resign from his job. (*Kare wa shigoto o yameru koto ni kimeta.*) 彼は仕事を辞めることに決めた.

— *vt.* ... o ji⌐shoku suru ...を辞職する Ⅰ; ji⌐niñ suru 辞任する Ⅰ: He resigned his post as headmaster. (*Kare wa koochoo no shoku o jiniñ shita.*) 彼は校長の職を辞任した.

resignation *n.* **1** (the act of resigning) ji⌐shoku 辞職; ji⌐niñ 辞任. **2** (written statement) ji⌐hyoo 辞表: send in one's resignation (*jihyoo o dasu*) 辞表を出す.

resist *vt.* **1** (oppose) ... ni te⌐ekoo suru ...に抵抗する Ⅰ: The crowd resisted the police. (*Guñshuu wa keekañtai ni teekoo shita.*) 群衆は警官隊に抵抗した. **2** (withstand) ... ni ta⌐eru ...に耐える Ⅴ; ... o ga⌐mañ suru ...を我慢する Ⅰ: resist temptation (*yuuwaku ni taeru*) 誘惑に耐える / I can't resist sweets. (*Watashi wa amai mono o gamañ dekinai.*) 私は甘いものを我慢できない.

resistance *n.* te⌐ekoo 抵抗; ha⌐ñtai 反対: They put up a strong resistance to our plan. (*Kare-ra wa watashi-tachi no keekaku ni tsuyoi hañtai o shimeshita.*) 彼らは私たちの計画に強い反対を示した. / resistance to disease (*byooki ni taisuru teekooryoku*) 病気に対する抵抗力.

resolute *adj.* da⌐ñko to shita 断固とした; ke⌐tsuzeñ to shita 決然とした: I am resolute against war. (*Watashi wa dañko to shite señsoo ni hañtai da.*) 私は断固として戦争に反対だ.

resolution *n.* **1** (formal agreement) ke⌐tsugi 決議: adopt a resolution for building a new city hall (*shiñ-shichoosha keñsetsu no ketsugi o saitaku suru*) 新市庁舎建設の決議を採択する. **2** (firm decision) ke⌐tsui 決意; ke⌐s-

shiñ 決心: I made a resolution to get up early. (*Watashi wa hayaoki no ketsui o shita.*) 私は早起きの決意をした. **3** (determination) ke⌐tsuda⌐ñ-ryoku 決断力: a man of great resolution (*ketsudañ-ryoku no aru hito*) 決断力のある人. **4** (solution) ka⌐iketsu 解決: the resolution of the problem (*moñdai no kaiketsu*) 問題の解決.

resolve *vt.* **1** (decide) ... to ke⌐s-shiñ suru ...と決心する Ⅰ: I resolved to quit smoking. (*Watashi wa tabako o yameyoo to kesshiñ shita.*) 私はたばこをやめようと決心した. **2** (pass a resolution) ... o ke⌐tsugi suru ...を決議する Ⅰ: It was resolved to raise the membership fee. (*Kaihi o neage suru koto ga ketsugi sareta.*) 会費を値上げすることが決議された. **3** (settle) ... o ka⌐iketsu suru ...を解決する Ⅰ: resolve a conflict (*arasoi o kaiketsu suru*) 争いを解決する.

— *vi.* (... o) ke⌐sshiñ suru (...を)決心する Ⅰ; ki⌐meru 決める Ⅴ: She resolved on marrying him. (*Kanojo wa kare to kekkoñ suru koto o kimeta.*) 彼女は彼と結婚することを決めた.

resort *vi.* (turn for help) ta⌐yo⌐ru 頼る Ⅽ; u⌐ttae⌐ru 訴える Ⅴ: resort to violence (*booryoku ni uttaeru*) 暴力に訴える.

— *n.* **1** (vacation place) ko⌐oraku⌐-chi 行楽地; ri⌐zo⌐oto リゾート: a summer resort (*natsu no koorakuchi*) 夏の行楽地. **2** (turning for help) ta⌐yori 頼り: You are my only resort. (*Anata dake ga tayori desu.*) あなただけが頼りです.

resource *n.* **1** (reserve) shi⌐geñ 資源; za⌐igeñ 財源: natural resources (*teñneñ shigeñ*) 天然資源 / We have limited financial resources. (*Wareware no zaigeñ wa kagirarete iru.*) われわれの財源は限られている.

2 (means) shu'dañ 手段; ho'ohoo 方法: We had no other resource but to apologize. (*Watashi-tachi wa ayamaru yori hoka ni hoohoo ga nakatta.*) 私たちは謝るよりほかに方法がなかった。

respect *n.* **1** (polite regard) so'ñkee 尊敬; ke'lei 敬意: I have respect for my teacher. (*Watashi wa señsee o soñkee shite imasu.*) 私は先生を尊敬しています。

2 (concern) so'ñchoo 尊重; chu'ui 注意: have respect for the law (*hooritsu o soñchoo suru*) 法律を尊重する。

3 (point) te'ñ 点: I cannot agree with you in some respects. (*Watashi wa aru teñ de anata ni dooi dekinai.*) 私はある点であなたに同意できない。

4 (regards) yo'roshiku よろしく: Give my respects to your mother. (*O-kaasañ ni yoroshiku.*) お母さんによろしく。

— *vt.* **1** (look up to) ... o u'ya-ma'u ...を敬う C; so'ñkee suru 尊敬する I: He is respected by everyone. (*Kare wa miñna ni soñkee sarete iru.*) 彼はみんなに尊敬されている。

2 (show consideration for) ... o so'ñchoo suru ...を尊重する I: respect another's rights (*hoka no hito no keñri o soñchoo suru*) ほかの人の権利を尊重する。

respectable *adj.* **1** (proper) ma'tomo na まともな: get a respectable job (*matomo na shoku ni tsuku*) まともな職に就く。

2 (decent) ki'chi'ñto shita [shite iru] きちんとした[している]: He looked respectable. (*Kare wa kichiñto shita kakkoo o shite ita.*) 彼はきちんとした格好をしていた。

3 (fairly large) ka'nari no かなりの: a respectable income (*kanari no shuunyuu*) かなりの収入。

respectful *adj.* ke'lei o hyo'osu'ru 敬意を表する; te'lenee na 丁寧な: be respectful to one's superiors (*ue no hito ni keei o hyoosuru*) 上の人に敬

意を表する / make a respectful bow (*teenee na ojigi o suru*) 丁寧なおじぎをする。

respective *adj.* so're'zore no それぞれの; me'eme'e no めいめいの: They went their respective ways. (*Kare-ra wa meemee no michi o itta.*) 彼らはめいめいの道を行った。

respectively *adv.* so're'zore それぞれ; me'eme'e ni めいめいに: Taro and Jiro were first and second, respectively. (*Taroo to Jiroo wa sorezore ichi-bañ to ni-bañ ni natta.*) 太郎と次郎はそれぞれ一番と二番になった。

respond *vi.* **1** (answer) (... ni) ko'tae'ru (...に)答える V: respond to a question (*shitsumoñ ni kotaeru*) 質問に答える / respond to a letter (*tegami ni heñji o dasu*) 手紙に返事を出す。

2 (react) (... ni) ha'ñnoo suru (...に)反応する I; o'ojiru 応じる V: He didn't respond to our demands. (*Kare wa wareware no yookyuu ni oojinakatta.*) 彼はわれわれの要求に応じなかった。

response *n.* **1** (answer) he'ñtoo 返答: I made a quick response to his inquiry. (*Kare no toiawase ni sugu ni heñtoo shita.*) 彼の問い合わせにすぐに返答した。

2 (reaction) ha'ñnoo 反応: response to a stimulus (*shigeki ni taisuru hañnoo*) 刺激に対する反応。

responsibility *n.* se'kiniñ 責任: I will take responsibility for the consequences. (*Kekka ni taishite wa watashi ga sekiniñ o torimasu.*) 結果に対しては私が責任を取ります。

responsible *adj.* **1** (having duty) se'kiniñ ga a'ru 責任がある: Drivers are responsible for their passengers' safety. (*Uñteñshu wa jookyaku no añzeñ ni sekiniñ ga aru.*) 運転手は乗客の安全に責任がある。

2 (reliable) shi'ñrai deki'ru 信頼できる: He is a responsible person. (*Kare wa shiñrai dekiru hito desu.*) 彼は信頼できる人です。

3 (being the cause) geʾñiñ no 原因
の: What is responsible for the accident? (*Jiko no geñin wa nañ desu
ka?*) 事故の原因は何ですか。

rest[1] *n.* **1** (taking one's ease) yaʾsu-
miʾ 休み; kyuʾusoku 休息: We
stopped for a rest. (*Watashi-tachi
wa yasumu tame ni tomatta.*) 私た
ちは休むために止まった。/ take a rest
(*hitoyasumi suru*) ひと休みする。
2 (sleep) suʾimiñ 睡眠: have a
good night's rest (*hito-bañ juubuñ
ni suimiñ o toru*) 一晩十分に睡眠を
とる。
3 (being still) teʾeshi 停止: The
machine is now at rest. (*Kikai wa
ima teeshi shite imasu.*) 機械は今
停止しています。
— *vi.* **1** (take one's ease) yaʾsuʾ-
mu 休む C; kyuʾusoku suru 休息する
I: You must rest for a time after
a meal. (*Shokugo wa shibaraku
yasumanakereba ikemaseñ.*) 食後
はしばらく休まなければいけません。
2 (be at ease) aʾñshiñ shite iru 安
心している V: He couldn't rest until
he found his wallet. (*Kare wa saifu o mitsukeru made añshiñ dekinakatta.*) 彼は財布を見つけるまで安心
できなかった。
3 (lie) (... ni) noʾtte iru (…)のってい
る I: The statue rested on a pedes-
tal. (*Zoo wa dai no ue ni notte ita.*)
像は台の上にのっていた。
4 (rely) (... ni) kaʾkaʾtte iru (…)に)か
かっている V: Our hopes rest on you.
(*Watashi-tachi no kiboo wa anata
ni kakatte imasu.*) 私たちの希望はあ
なたにかかっています。
— *vt.* **1** (give rest) ... o yaʾsuma-
seʾru …を休ませる V; kyuʾusoku
saseru 休息させる V: I stopped
reading and rested my eyes. (*Watashi wa dokusho o yamete me o
yasumaseta.*) 私は読書をやめて目を休
ませた。
2 (set) ... o oʾku …を置く C; (lean)
taʾitekakeʾru 立てかける V: rest a
pair of skis against the wall (*kabe
ni sukii o tatekakeru*) 壁にスキーを

立てかける。

rest[2] *n.* **1** (remainder) noʾkori 残り:
I saved the rest of the money. (*Nokori no o-kane wa chokiñ shimashita.*) 残りのお金は貯金しました。
2 (people) noʾkori no hiʾtoʾ-tachi
残りの人たち: The rest stayed be-
hind. (*Nokori no hito-tachi wa ato
ni nokorimashita.*) 残りの人たちは後
に残りました。

restaurant *n.* reʾsutorañ レストラ
ン; ryoʾriʾya 料理屋; shoʾkudoo 食
堂: Is there a Japanese restaurant
near here? (*Kono chikaku ni
Nihoñ ryooriya wa arimasu ka?*)
この近くに日本料理屋はありますか。

restless *adj.* oʾchitsukanai 落ち着
かない; soʾwasowa shita [shite iru]
そわそわした[している]: a restless child
(*ochitsukanai kodomo*) 落ち着かない
子ども。

restoration *n.* kaʾifuku 回復;
shuʾufuku 修復: the restoration of
order (*chitsujo no kaifuku*) 秩序の
回復 / the restoration of a building
(*tatemono no shuufuku*) 建物の修復。

restore *vt.* **1** (repair) ... o fuʾk-
kyuu suru …を復旧する C: restore
an old temple (*furui tera o fuk-
kyuu suru*) 古い寺を復旧する。
2 (of health) ... o kaʾifuku saseru
…を回復させる V: He has been re-
stored to health. (*Kare wa keñkoo
o kaifuku shita.*) 彼は健康を回復した。
3 (bring back) ... o moʾto ni mo-
ʾdoʾsu …を元に戻す C; kaʾesu 返す
C: I restored the book to its rightful owner. (*Watashi wa sono hoñ
o tadashii mochinushi ni kaeshita.*)
私はその本を正しい持ち主に返した。

restrain *vt.* ... o oʾsaeʾru …を抑える
V; seʾeshi suru 制止する I: He
could not restrain his anger. (*Kare
wa ikari o osaeru koto ga dekinakatta.*) 彼は怒りを抑えることができなかっ
た。

restraint *n.* yoʾkusee 抑制; koʾo-
soku 拘束: put restraints on prices
(*bukka o yokusee suru*) 物価を抑制
する / He is kept under restraint.

(*Kare wa koosoku sarete iru.*) 彼は
拘束されている.

restrict *vt.* ... o se⸍ege⸍ñ suru ...を
制限する①; ge⸍ñtee suru 限定する
①: The speed is restricted to 40
kilometers an hour here. (*Koko de
wa sokudo wa jisoku yoñjuk-kiro
ni seegeñ sarete imasu.*) ここでは速
度は時速40キロに制限されています.

restriction *n.* 1 se⸍ege⸍ñ 制限;
ge⸍ñtee 限定: place restrictions on
the import of oranges (*oreñji no
yunyuu ni seegeñ o kuwaeru*) オレ
ンジの輸入に制限を加える.

rest room *n.* te⸍a⸍rai 手洗い; to⸍-
ire トイレ: Where is the rest room?
(*Toire wa doko desu ka?*) トイレはど
こですか.

result *n.* 1 (outcome) ke⸍kka 結
果: the results of an election (*señkyo no kekka*) 選挙の結果.
2 (final score) ke⸍kka 結果; se⸍e-
seki 成績: baseball results (*yakyuu
no shiai no kekka*) 野球の試合の結
果 / the results of an examination
(*shikeñ no seeseki*) 試験の成績.
3 (answer) ko⸍ta⸍e 答え: What is
the result of the calculation? (*Keesañ no kotae wa ikura desu ka?*)
計算の答えはいくらですか.
— *vi.* (... ni) ki⸍iñ suru (...に)起因す
る①: His illness resulted from
overwork. (*Kare no byooki wa
karoo ni kiiñ suru.*) 彼の病気は過労
に起因する.

resume *vt.* ... o fu⸍tatabi hajimeru
...を再び始める Ⓥ; sa⸍ikai suru 再開
する①: He resumed working after
lunch. (*Kare wa chuushoku-go
futatabi shigoto o hajimeta.*) 彼は
昼食後再び仕事を始めた.
— *vi.* fu⸍tatabi hajimaru 再び始まる
Ⓒ; sa⸍ikai suru 再開する①: After
tea, the meeting resumed. (*O-cha o
noñde kara kaigi wa saikai shita.*)
お茶を飲んでから会議は再開した.

retail *n.* ko⸍uri 小売り: a retail price
(*kouri kakaku*) 小売り価格.
— *vi.* ko⸍uri sareru 小売りされる Ⓥ;
u⸍rareru 売られる Ⓥ: This article

retails at 100 yen. (*Kono shina wa
hyaku-eñ de urarete imasu.*) この品
は100円で売られています.

retain *vt.* 1 (keep) ... o ta⸍mo⸍tsu
...を保つ①: This china dish retains
heat well. (*Kono tooki no sara wa
netsu o yoku tamochimasu.*) この陶
器の皿は熱をよく保ちます.
2 (remember) ... o o⸍bo⸍ete iru ...を
覚えている Ⓥ: I cannot retain everything I learned. (*Naratta koto o
subete oboete iru koto wa dekimaseñ.*) 習ったことをすべて覚えていることは
できません.

retaliate *vi.* shi⸍kaeshi suru 仕返し
する①; ho⸍ofuku suru 報復する①: I
will retaliate if kicked. (*Moshi ke-
raretara shikaeshi shite yaru.*) もし
蹴られたら仕返ししてやる.

retire *vi.* 1 (stop working) ta⸍ishoku
suru 退職する①: He retired at
the age of sixty. (*Kare wa rokujus-
sai de taishoku shimashita.*) 彼は
60歳で退職しました.
2 (withdraw) hi⸍kisaga⸍ru 引き下が
る Ⓒ: He retired to the study after
dinner. (*Kare wa yuushoku-go sho-
sai ni hikisagatta.*) 彼は夕食後書斎
に引き下がった.
— *vt.* ... o ta⸍ishoku saseru ...を退
職させる Ⓥ; i⸍ñtai saseru 引退させる
Ⓥ: He was compulsorily retired.
(*Kare wa muri ni taishoku saserareta.*) 彼は無理に退職させられた.

retirement *n.* ta⸍ishoku 退職;
i⸍ñtai 引退: give written notice of
one's retirement (*taishoku negai o
dasu*) 退職願いを出す.

retreat *vi.* 1 (get back) ... o to⸍ri-
modo⸍su ...を取り戻す Ⓒ; ka⸍ishuu
suru 回収する①: I retrieved my
lost bag. (*Watashi wa nakushita
kabañ o torimodoshita.*) 私はなくした
かばんを取り戻した.

2 (computing) ... o ke¯nsaku suru …を検索する Ⅰ; hiˈkiˈdasu 引き出す Ⅽ: retrieve data (deeta o kensaku suru) データを検索する.

return vi. kaˈeru 帰る Ⅽ; moˈdoˈru 戻る Ⅽ: He returned to his hometown. (Kare wa kokyoo e kaerimashita.) 彼は故郷へ帰りました. / What time will he return? (Kare wa nanji ni modorimasu ka?) 彼は何時に戻りますか.
— vt. ... o kaˈesu …を返す Ⅽ: Please return this umbrella to her. (Kono kasa o kanojo ni kaeshite kudasai.) この傘を彼女に返してください.
— n. **1** (coming back) kaˈeri 帰り: I am looking forward to your return from China. (Anata no Chuugoku kara no o-kaeri o o-machi shite imasu.) あなたの中国からのお帰りをお待ちしています.
2 (paying back) heˈnkyaku 返却: He is demanding the return of the money. (Kare wa sono o-kane no henkyaku o yookyuu shite iru.) 彼はそのお金の返却を要求している.

reunion n. **1** (meeting) saˈikai no atsumari 再会の集まり: a class reunion (doosookai) 同窓会.
2 (coming together again) saˈikai 再会: a family reunion (kazoku no saikai) 家族の再会.

reveal vt. **1** (disclose) ... o aˈkiˈraka ni suru …を明らかにする Ⅰ: He did not reveal his identity. (Kare wa jibun no mimoto o akiraka ni shinakatta.) 彼は自分の身元を明らかにしなかった.
2 (show) ... o shiˈmeˈsu …を示す Ⅽ; miˈseˈru 見せる Ⅴ: I opened the door and revealed the garden. (Watashi wa doa o hiraite niwa o miseta.) 私はドアを開いて庭を見せた.

revenge vt. ... ni fuˈkushuu suru …に復讐する Ⅰ; shiˈkaeshi o suru 仕返しをする Ⅰ: He revenged himself on his enemies. (Kare wa teki ni fukushuu shita.) 彼は敵に復讐した.
— n. fuˈkushuu 復讐; shiˈkaeshi 仕返し: take revenge on a person

(hito ni shikaeshi o suru) 人に仕返しをする.

revenue n. (of a government) saˈinyuu 歳入; (income) shuˈunyuu 収入.

revenue stamp n. shuˈunyuu-iˈnshi 収入印紙.

reverence n. soˈnkee 尊敬; keˈeai 敬愛: He is held in reverence by many people. (Kare wa ooku no hito ni keeai sarete imasu.) 彼は多くの人に敬愛されています.

reverse n. **1** (opposite) gyaˈku 逆; haˈntai 反対: He did the reverse of what I expected. (Kare wa watashi no yosoo to hantai no koto o shita.) 彼は私の予想と反対のことをした.
2 (back side) uˈraˈ 裏; riˈmen 裏面: the reverse of a painting (e no ura) 絵の裏.
3 (misfortune) fuˈun 不運; shiˈppai 失敗: suffer a reverse (fuun ni mimawareru) 不運に見舞われる.
4 (reverse gear) baˈkku バック: shift into reverse (giya o bakku ni ireru) ギヤをバックに入れる.
— adj. **1** (contrary) gyaˈku no 逆の; aˈbekobe no あべこべの: read the numbers in reverse order (suuji o gyaku no jun ni yomu) 数字を逆の順に読む.
2 (back) uˈraˈ no 裏の: the reverse side of a dress (doresu no uragawa) ドレスの裏側.
— vt. **1** (change to the opposite) ... o gyaˈku ni suru …を逆にする Ⅰ: reverse the order (junjo o gyaku ni suru) 順序を逆にする.
2 (turn backward) ... o baˈkku saseru …をバックさせる Ⅴ: reverse one's car (kuruma o bakku saseru) 車をバックさせる.
— vi. (go backward) gyaˈkushin suru 逆進する Ⅰ.

review n. **1** (criticism) hiˈhyoo 批評; hyoˈoron 評論: a book review (shohyoo) 書評.
2 (studying again) fuˈkushuu 復習: a review of today's lesson (kyoo no jugyoo no fukushuu) きょうの授業の

復習.

— *vt.* **1** (criticize) ... o hiｒhyoo suru ...を批評する ①: The play was favorably reviewed. (*Sono shibai wa koohyoo datta.*) その芝居は好評だった.

2 (study again) ... o fuｒkushuu suru ...を復習する ①: review the main subjects (*omo-na kamoku o fukushuu suru*) 主な科目を復習する.

3 (investigate again) ... o saｒichoｒosa suru ...を再調査する ①; saｒikeｒntoo suru 再検討する ①: review the cause of an accident (*jiko geﾟniﾟn o saichoosa suru*) 事故原因を再調査する.

— *vi.* hiｒhyoo [hyoｒoroﾟn] o kaｒku 批評[評論]を書く ⓒ: He reviews for that magazine. (*Kare wa sono zasshi ni hyooroﾟn o kaite iru.*) 彼はその雑誌に評論を書いている.

revise *vt.* **1** (bring up-to-date) ... o kaｒitee suru ...を改訂する ①: revise a dictionary (*jisho o kaitee suru*) 辞書を改訂する.

2 (amend) ... o shuｒusee suru ...を修正する ①: He revised his opinion. (*Kare wa jibuﾟn no ikeﾟn o shuusee shita.*) 彼は自分の意見を修正した.

revision *n.* kaｒitee 改訂; shuｒusee 修正.

revival *n.* fuｒkkatsu 復活; fuｒkkoo 復興: the revival of an old custom (*furui shuukaﾟn no fukkatsu*) 古い習慣の復活 / the Revival of Learning (*Buﾟngee fukkoo*) 文芸復興.

revive *vi.* **1** (come back to life) iｒkikaｒeru 生き返る ⓒ; kaｒifuku suru 回復する ①: The flower will revive if you water it. (*Mizu o yareba sono hana wa ikikaeru deshoo.*) 水をやればその花は生き返るでしょう.

2 (become popular again) fuｒkkatsu suru 復活する ①: The old custom is reviving. (*Sono furui shuukaﾟn wa fukkatsu shite kite iru.*) その古い習慣は復活してきている.

— *vt.* **1** (bring to life) ... o iｒkikaeraseｒru ...を生き返らせる Ⓥ; iｒshiki o kaｒifuku saseru 意識を回復させる

Ⓥ: He revived her with cold water. (*Kare wa tsumetai mizu de kanojo no ishiki o kaifuku saseta.*) 彼は冷たい水で彼女の意識を回復させた.

2 (make popular again) ... o fuｒkkatsu saseru ...を復活させる Ⓥ; saｒijooeﾟn suru 再上演する ①: revive an old play (*furui geki o saijooeﾟn suru*) 古い劇を再上演する.

revolt *vt.* haｒnraﾟn o okoｒsu 反乱を起こす ①: revolt against a ruler (*shihaisha ni taishite haﾟnraﾟn o okosu*) 支配者に対して反乱を起こす.

— *n.* haｒnraﾟn 反乱; haｒnkoo 反抗.

revolution *n.* **1** (great social change) kaｒkumee 革命: the French Revolution (*Furaﾟnsu-kakumee*) フランス革命 / the Industrial Revolution (*Saﾟngyoo-kakumee*) 産業革命.

2 (circular movement) kaｒiteﾟn 回転: the revolution of the moon around the earth (*tsuki no chikyuu o meguru kaiteﾟn*) 月の地球をめぐる回転.

revolutionary *adj.* kaｒkumee no 革命の; kaｒkumee-teki na 革命的な: a revolutionary invention (*kakumee-teki na hatsumee*) 革命的な発明.

revolve *vi.* kaｒiteﾟn suru 回転する ①; maｒwaru 回る ⓒ: The earth revolves around the sun. (*Chikyuu wa taiyoo no mawari o mawaru.*) 地球は太陽の周りを回る.

revue *n.* reｒbyuu レビュー.

reward *n.* **1** (something given in return) hoｒoshuu 報酬; hoｒobi ほうび: He was given a watch as a reward for his services. (*Kare wa kare no jiﾟnryoku no hoobi to shite tokee o moratta.*) 彼は彼の尽力のほうびとして時計をもらった.

2 (money) hoｒoshookiﾟn 報奨金; shaｒreekiﾟn 謝礼金: A reward of a million yen is offered for useful information. (*Yuueki na joohoo ni hyakumaﾟn-eﾟn no sharee-kiﾟn ga teekyoo sarete iru.*) 有益な情報に100

万円の謝礼金が提供されている.

— *vt.* ... ni muʳkuiˈru ...に報いる Ⅴ; shaˈree [hoˈobi] o ataeru 謝礼[ほうび]を与える Ⅴ: I'll reward the person who brings back the lost dog. (*Inaku natta inu o tsurete kite kureta hito ni sharee o itashimasu.*) いなくなった犬を連れてきてくれた人に謝礼をいたします.

rhythm *n.* riˈizumu リズム; riˈtsudoo 律動.

rib *n.* **1** (bone) roˈkkotsu 肋骨: He broke a rib in his fall. (*Kare wa koroɴde rokkotsu o ip-poɴ otta.*) 彼は転んで肋骨を1本折った.
2 (of an umbrella) hoˈneˈ 骨: the ribs of an umbrella (*kasa no hone*) 傘の骨.

ribbon *n.* riˈboɴ リボン: put on a ribbon (*riboɴ o tsukeru*) リボンをつける.

rice *n.* koˈme 米; goˈhaɴ ごはん.
★ Japanese refer to 'rice' in various ways depending on the stage of production: rice plant (*ine*) 稲, rough rice (*momi*) もみ, grains (*kome*) 米, brown rice (*geɴmai*) 玄米, polished rice (*hakumai*) 白米, cooked rice (*gohaɴ, raisu*) ごはん, ライス.

rice cake *n.* moˈchi 餅: make [grill] rice cake (*mochi o tsuku [yaku]*) 餅をつく[焼く].

rich *adj.* **1** (wealthy) kaˈnemochi no 金持ちの: He is a rich man. (*Kare wa kanemochi da.*) 彼は金持ちだ.
2 (having much) hoˈofu na 豊富な; yuˈtaka na 豊かな: Oranges are rich in vitamin C. (*Oreɴji wa bitamiɴ shii ga hoofu desu.*) オレンジはビタミンCが豊富です.
3 (producing much) koˈeta 肥えた; koˈete iru 肥えている: rich land (*koeta tochi*) 肥えた土地.
4 (full of fats, sugar, etc.) shiˈtsukoˈi しつこい: a rich diet (*shitsukoi shokuji*) しつこい食事.

rid *vt.* ... o toˈrinozoku ...を取り除く Ⅽ; joˈkyo suru 除去する Ⅰ: rid a garden of weeds (*niwa kara kusaˈ o torinozoku*) 庭から草を取り除く.

get rid of ... *vt.* ... o noˈzoku ...を除く Ⅽ; kaˈtazukeˈru 片づける Ⅴ: I have finally got rid of my debt. (*Watashi wa yatto shakkiɴ o katazuketa.*) 私はやっと借金を片づけた.

riddle *n.* naˈzo なぞ; naˈzonazo なぞなぞ: solve a riddle (*nazo o toku*) なぞを解く.

ride *vi.* (... ni) noˈru (...に)乗る Ⅽ: ride in a train (*ressha ni noru*) 列車に乗る / He was riding on a horse. (*Kare wa uma ni notte ita.*) 彼は馬に乗っていた.
— *vt.* ... ni noˈtte iku ...に乗って行く Ⅽ: I ride my bicycle to school. (*Watashi wa jiteɴsha ni notte gakkoo e ikimasu.*) 私は自転車に乗って学校へ行きます.
— *n.* noˈru [noˈseru] koto 乗る[乗せる]こと: give a person a ride (*hito o nosete yaru*) 人を乗せてやる.

rider *n.* noˈru hito 乗る人; (of a horse) kiˈshu 騎手.

ridge *n.* oˈne 尾根; yaˈma no se 山の背: walk along mountain ridges (*one-zutai ni aruku*) 尾根伝いに歩く.

ridiculous *adj.* baˈkaˈgeta ばかげた; baˈkaˈgete iru [baˈkaˈgete iru] ばかげている; oˈkashiˈi おかしい: a ridiculous idea (*bakageta kaɴgae*) ばかげた考え.

rifle *n.* raˈifuruˈjuu ライフル銃: shoot a rifle (*raifurujuu de utsu*) ライフル銃で撃つ.

right[1] *adj.* **1** (correct) taˈdashiˈi 正しい; seˈekaku na 正確な: You are right. (*Anata wa tadashii.*) あなたは正しい. / Will you tell me the right time? (*Seekaku na jikaɴ o oshiete kudasai.*) 正確な時間を教えてください. / That's right. (*Soo desu.*) そうです.
2 (proper) teˈkitoo na 適当な; fuˈsawashiˈi ふさわしい: the right dress for the occasion (*sono ba ni fusawashii doresu*) その場にふさわしいドレス.
3 (morally good) taˈdashiˈi 正しい; yoˈi よい: Telling lies is not right. (*Uso o tsuku no wa yoku nai.*) うそをつくのはよくない.
4 (satisfactory) moˈoshibuɴ no naˈi

申し分のない: Everything is just right. (*Subete mooshibuñ arimaseñ.*) すべて申し分ありません.

5 (healthy) keʰñkoo na 健康な; choʰoshi no yoʰi 調子のよい: I feel perfectly all right now. (*Ima wa karada no chooshi wa totemo yoi.*) 今は体の調子はとてもよい.

— *adv.* **1** (correctly) taʰdaʰshiku 正しく; seʰekaku ni 正確に: He answered right. (*Kare wa tadashiku kotaeta.*) 彼は正しく答えた.

2 (directly) maʰssuʰgu ni 真っすぐに: Go right on to the end of this street. (*Kono michi no tsukiatari made massugu ni iki nasai.*) この道の突き当たりまで真っすぐに行きなさい.

3 (exactly) choʰodo ちょうど; maʰttaku まったく: The ball hit me right on the head. (*Booru wa choodo watashi no atama ni atatta.*) ボールはちょうど私の頭に当たった.

right away *adv.* suʰgu ni すぐに: I'll come back right away. (*Sugu ni modorimasu.*) すぐに戻ります.

— *n.* **1** (lawful claim) keʰñri 権利: rights and duties (*keñri to gimu*) 権利と義務 / stand on one's rights (*jibuñ no keñri o shuchoo suru*) 自分の権利を主張する.

2 (what is right) taʰdashiʰi koʰtoʰ 正しいこと: I always did right. (*Watashi wa itsu-mo tadashii koto o shimashita.*) 私はいつも正しいことをしました.

right[2] *adj.* miʰgi no 右の: write with one's right hand (*migite de kaku*) 右手で書く.

— *adv.* miʰgi ni 右に: turn right (*migi ni magaru*) 右に曲がる.

— *n.* **1** (right side) miʰgi 右; miʰgigawa 右側: keep to the right (*migigawa o tsuukoo suru*) 右側を通行する.

2 (political party) uʰyoku 右翼; uʰha 右派.

right-handed *adj.* miʰgikiki no 右利きの: a right-handed person (*migikiki no hito*) 右利きの人.

rightist *n.* uʰyoku [uʰha] no hiʰtoʰ 右翼[右派]の人; hoʰshuha no hitoʰ 保守派の人.

rigid *adj.* **1** (stiff) kaʰtai 堅い; koʰwabaʰtta こわばった; koʰwabaʰtte iru こわばっている: a rigid bar (*katai boo*) 堅い棒 / a rigid face (*kowabatta kao*) こわばった顔.

2 (severe) geʰñkaku na 厳格な; kiʰbishiʰi 厳しい: The rules are rigid. (*Kisoku ga kibishii.*) 規則が厳しい.

rigor *n.* kiʰbiʰshisa 厳しさ; geʰñkaku 厳格: enforce the law with rigor (*hooritsu o geñkaku ni shikoo suru*) 法律を厳格に施行する.

rigorous *adj.* kiʰbishiʰi 厳しい; geʰñkaku na 厳格な: a rigorous training (*kibishii kuñreñ*) 厳しい訓練 / a rigorous climate (*kibishii kikoo*) 厳しい気候.

ring[1] *n.* **1** (circle) waʰ 輪: We sat in a ring. (*Watashi-tachi wa wa ni natte suwatta.*) 私たちは輪になって座った.

2 (round band) yuʰbiwa 指輪: She wears a diamond ring. (*Kanojo wa daiyamoñdo no yubiwa o shite iru.*) 彼女はダイヤモンドの指輪をしている.

ring[2] *vi.* **1** (sound) naʰru 鳴る [C]: The telephone is ringing. (*Deñwa ga natte imasu.*) 電話が鳴っています.

2 (summon) beʰru o naʰrashite yobu ベルを鳴らして呼ぶ [C]: ring for a bellboy (*beru o narashite booi o yobu*) ベルを鳴らしてボーイを呼ぶ.

— *vt.* **1** (cause to sound) ... o naʰrasu ...を鳴らす [C]: ring the bell (*beru o narasu*) ベルを鳴らす.

2 (summon) ... o naʰrashite yobu ...を鳴らして呼ぶ [C]: He rang the bell for the nurse. (*Kare wa beru o narashite kañgofu o yoñda.*) 彼はベルを鳴らして看護婦を呼んだ.

ring up *vt.* ... ni deʰñwa suru ...に電話する [I]: I'll ring you up tonight. (*Koñya deñwa shimasu.*) 今夜電話します.

rinse *vt.* ... o yuʰsugu ...をゆすぐ [C]; suʰsugu すすぐ [C]: rinse one's mouth (*kuchi o yusugu*) 口をゆすぐ / rinse out socks (*kutsushita o* *susugu*) 靴下をすすぐ.

riot *n.* boˈodoo 暴動: raise [put down] a riot (*boodoo o okosu* [*chiˈnatsu suru*]) 暴動を起こす[鎮圧する].

ripe *adj.* juˈkuˈshita 熟した; juˈkuˈ-shite iru 熟している; taˈbegoro no 食べごろの: Apples are not ripe yet. (*Riˈngo wa mada jukushite imaseˈn.*) りんごはまだ熟していません. / ripe cheese (*tabegoro no chiizu*) 食べごろのチーズ.

ripen *vi.* juˈkuˈsu 熟す C; uˈreˈ-ru うれる V: The corn has ripened. (*Toomorokoshi ga jukushita.*) とうもろこしが熟した.

rise *vi.* **1** (increase) maˈsu 増す C; aˈgaru 上がる C: The river is rising after a heavy rain. (*Ooame no ato de kawa no mizu ga mashite iru.*) 大雨の後で川の水が増している. / Prices will rise again. (*Bukka wa mata agaru deshoo.*) 物価はまた上がるでしょう.

2 (move upward) noˈboru 昇る C: The sun rises in the east. (*Taiyoo wa higashi kara noboru.*) 太陽は東から昇る.

3 (stand up) taˈchiagaru 立ち上がる C: She rose from her chair. (*Kanojo wa isu kara tachiagatta.*) 彼女はいすから立ち上がった.

4 (get up) oˈkiˈru 起きる V: I have to rise early tomorrow morning. (*Ashita no asa wa hayaku okinakereba naranai.*) あしたの朝は早く起きなければならない.

5 (slope upwards) soˈbieˈru そびえる V: The mountain rose above the clouds. (*Yama wa kumo no ue ni sobiete ita.*) 山は雲の上にそびえていた.

— *n.* **1** (increase) joˈoshoo 上昇: a rise in wages (*chiˈngiˈn no jooshoo*) 賃金の上昇.

2 (slope) noˈborizaka 昇り坂; (hill) taˈkadai 高台: His villa was built on a rise. (*Kare no bessoo wa takadai ni taterareta.*) 彼の別荘は高台に建てられた.

risk *n.* kiˈkeˈn 危険: run a risk (*ki-*

keˈn o okasu) 危険を冒す / There is no risk of your drowning in this stream. (*Kono nagare de wa oboreru kikeˈn wa arimaseˈn.*) この流れでは溺れる危険はありません.

at one's own risk *adv.* jiˈbuˈn no sekiniˈn de 自分の責任で: Do it at your own risk. (*Anata no sekiniˈn de yari nasai.*) あなたの責任でやりなさい.

— *vt.* ... o kaˈkeˈru …を賭ける V: He risked his life to save the child. (*Kare wa sono ko o sukuu tame ni inochi o kaketa.*) 彼はその子を救うために命を賭けた.

ritual *n.* giˈshiki 儀式; saˈishiki 祭式: a religious ritual (*shuukyoo-teki na gishiki*) 宗教的な儀式.

rival *n.* kyoˈosoo aˈite 競争相手; raˈibaru ライバル: He and I are rivals for the job. (*Kare to watashi wa shigoto-joo no raibaru dooshi da.*) 彼と私は仕事上のライバル同士だ.

— *vt.* ... to kyoˈosoo suru …と競争する I; ... ni taˈikoo suru …に対抗する I: The two of them rivaled each other for first place. (*Futari wa o-tagai ni taikoo shite ichi-i o arasotta.*) 二人はお互いに対抗して1位を争った.

river *n.* kaˈwaˈ 川: fish in the river (*kawa de tsuri o suru*) 川で釣りをする / the Tone river (*Tonegawa*) 利根川.

road *n.* **1** (way) doˈoro 道路; miˈchi 道: Be careful when you cross the road. (*Michi o wataru toki wa ki o tsuke nasai.*) 道を渡るときは気をつけなさい. / Does this road go to Nikko? (*Kono michi wa Nikkoo e ikimasu kaˀ*) この道は日光へ行きますか.

2 (course) miˈchi 道; hoˈohoo 方法: the road to success (*seekoo e no michi*) 成功への道.

road map *n.* doˈoro chiˈzu 道路地図.

roar *vi.* **1** (of an animal) hoˈeˈru ほえる V: The lion roared in anger. (*Raioˈn wa okotte hoeta.*) ライオンは

怒ってほえた.

2 (make a deep sound) goˈo-oñ o taˈteˈru ごう音を立てる Ⓥ: A truck roared down the road. (*Torakku ga goo-oñ o tatete hashiri-satta.*) トラックがごう音を立てて走り去った.

3 (shout) doˈnaˈru どなる Ⓒ; (laugh) oˈowaˈrai suru 大笑いする Ⓘ: He roared with laughter. (*Kare wa oowarai shita.*) 彼は大笑いした.

— *n.* hoˈeˈru koˈe ほえる声; doˈyomekiˈ どよめき: the roars of a tiger (*tora no hoeru koe*) とらのほえる声.

roast *vt.* **1** (of meat) ... o yaˈku ...を焼く Ⓒ; aˈbuˈru あぶる Ⓒ: roast meat in an oven (*teñpi de niku o yaku*) 天火で肉を焼く.

2 (of beans) ... o iˈru 炒る Ⓒ: roast coffee beans (*koohii mame o iru*) コーヒー豆を炒る.

rob *vt.* ... kara (... o) uˈbaˈu ...から(...を)奪う Ⓒ; ... o oˈsoˈu ...を襲う Ⓒ: The man robbed her of her money. (*Sono otoko wa kanojo kara o-kane o ubatta.*) その男は彼女からお金を奪った. ★ The object of English 'rob' is a person or an office, etc., but the object of the Japanese equivalent is a 'thing.' / The jewelry store was robbed last night. (*Sono hoosekiteñ wa sakuya osowareta.*) その宝石店は昨夜襲われた.

robber *n.* goˈotoo 強盗; doˈroboo どろぼう: catch a robber (*doroboo o tsukamaeru*) どろぼうを捕まえる.

robbery *n.* goˈotoo 強盗; goˈodatsu 強奪: commit a bank robbery (*giñkoo gootoo o hataraku*) 銀行強盗を働く.

robe *n.* reˈefuku 礼服; roˈobu ローブ.

robin *n.* koˈmaˈdori こまどり; roˈbiñ ロビン.

robot *n.* roˈboˈtto ロボット: industrial robots (*sañgyooyoo robotto*) 産業用ロボット.

robust *adj.* taˈkumashiˈi たくましい; kyoˈokeñ na 強健な: a robust young man (*takumashii seeneñ*) たくましい青年.

rock[1] *n.* **1** (mass) iˈwaˈ 岩; gaˈñ-seki 岩石: a house built on a rock (*iwa no ue ni taterareta ie*) 岩の上に建てられた家.

2 (pieces) iˈshi 石: They threw rocks at the police. (*Kare-ra wa keekañ ni ishi o nageta.*) 彼らは警官に石を投げた.

rock[2] *vt.* ... o yuˈriugokaˈsu ...を揺り動かす Ⓒ: rock a cradle (*yurikago o yuriugokasu*) 揺りかごを揺り動かす.

— *vi.* yuˈreru 揺れる Ⓥ: The boat rocked to and fro. (*Booto wa zeñgo ni yureta.*) ボートは前後に揺れた.

rocket *n.* roˈkeˈtto ロケット: launch a rocket (*roketto o uchiageru*) ロケットを打ち上げる.

rocky *adj.* iˈwa no oˈoi 岩の多い; iˈwadaˈrake no 岩だらけの: a rocky coastline (*iwadarake no kaigañ*) 岩だらけの海岸.

rod *n.* boˈo 棒; saˈoˈ さお: hang curtains on a rod (*kaateñ o boo ni tsurusu*) カーテンを棒につるす / a fishing rod (*tsurizao*) 釣りざお.

roe *n.* saˈkana no tamaˈgo 魚の卵.

role *n.* **1** (of an actor) yaˈkuˈ 役: play the leading role (*shuyaku o eñjiru*) 主役を演じる.

2 (part) yaˈkuwari 役割; yaˈkumeˈ 役目: play an important role in the convention (*taikai de juuyoo na yakuwari o hatasu*) 大会で重要な役割を果たす.

roll *vi.* **1** (turn over) koˈrogaru 転がる Ⓒ: The ball rolled into the hole. (*Booru wa korogatte ana ni haitta.*) ボールは転がって穴に入った.

2 (move on) suˈsumu 進む Ⓒ: The car rolled down the street. (*Kuruma wa michi o susuñde itta.*) 車は道を進んで行った.

3 (rock) yoˈko ni yureru 横に揺れる Ⓥ: The ship rolled in the storm. (*Fune wa arashi no naka de yoko ni yureta.*) 船は嵐の中で横に揺れた.

4 (move gently) uˈneˈru うねる Ⓒ: The waves are rolling. (*Nami ga unette iru.*) 波がうねっている.

— *vt.* **1** (cause to turn over) ... o koˈrogasu ...を転がす Ⓒ: roll a bar-

rel over (*taru o korogasu*) たるを転が
す.
2 (wind round) ... o maˈrumeru ...
を丸める Ⓥ; maˈku 巻く Ⓒ: roll an
umbrella (*kasa o maku*) 傘を巻く.
3 (make flat) ... o naˈrasu ...をなら
す Ⓒ: roll a road (*michi o narasu*)
道をならす.
— *n.* **1** (anything rolled) maˈita
monoˈ 巻いた物; hiˈtoˈmaki ひと巻き:
a roll of toilet paper (*toiretto peepaa hitomaki*) トイレットペーパーひと巻
き / a 36-exposure roll of film (*sanjuu-roku-mai-dori no firumu*) 36
枚撮りのフィルム.
2 (list) meˈebo 名簿: Is my name
on the rolls? (*Watashi no namae
wa meebo ni notte imasu ka?*) 私の
名前は名簿に載っていますか.
3 (bread) roˈoruˈpaň ロールパン.

romance *n.* **1** (love affair) roˈmaˈ-
ňsu ロマンス; reˈňai jiˈkeň 恋愛事件.
2 (story) deˈňki shoˈosetsu 伝奇小
説; reˈňai shoˈosetsu 恋愛小説.

romantic *adj.* **1** (fanciful) kuˈu-
soo-teki na 空想的な; roˈmaňchiˈk-
ku na ロマンチックな: a romantic
poem (*romaňchikku na shi*) ロマンチ
ックな詩.
2 (of art) roˈmaňshuˈgi no ロマン主
義の; roˈmaňha no ロマン派の: the
Romantic Movement (*Romaň-
shugi uňdoo*) ロマン主義運動.

romanticism *n.* roˈmaňshuˈgi ロ
マン主義.

roof *n.* yaˈne 屋根.
— *vt.* ... ni yaˈne o tsuˈkeˈru ...に
屋根をつける Ⓥ; yaˈne o fuˈku 屋根を
ふく Ⓒ: roof a house with tiles
(*kawara de yane o fuku*) かわらで屋
根をふく.

room *n.* **1** (of a house) heˈyaˈ 部屋;
-shitsu 室; -ma 間; -doo 堂: enter
a room (*heya ni hairu*) 部屋に入る /
leave a room (*heya kara deru*) 部屋
から出る / a bathroom (*yokushitsu*)
浴室 / a living room (*ima*) 居間 / a
dining room (*shokudoo*) 食堂.
2 (space) kuˈukaň 空間; baˈsho 場
所: A piano takes up room. (*Piano

wa basho o toru.*) ピアノは場所を取る.
/ Make room, please. (*Basho o
akete kudasai.*) 場所を空けてください.
3 (chance) yoˈchi 余地; kiˈkaˈi 機
会: There is room for improvement. (*Kaizeň no yochi ga arimasu.*) 改善の余地があります.

root *n.* **1** (of a plant) neˈ 根: the
root of a tree (*ki no ne*) 木の根.
2 (of a hair, tooth, etc.) tsuˈkene
付け根: the root of a hair (*mookoň*)
毛根.
3 (origin) koˈňgeˈň 根源; (cause)
geˈňiň 原因: Love of money is the
root of all evil. (*Kiňseňyoku ga
shoaku no koňgeň da.*) 金銭欲が諸
悪の根源だ. / What is the root of
the trouble? (*Momegoto no geňiň
wa naň desu ka?*) もめごとの原因は何
ですか.

rope *n.* naˈwaˈ 縄; tsuˈnaˈ 綱; roˈo-
pu ロープ: tie with a rope (*nawa de
shibaru*) 縄で縛る.
— *vt.* ... o naˈwaˈ [roˈopu] de shiˈ-
ˈbaˈru ...を縄[ロープ]で縛る Ⓒ: rope
a box to the roof of a car (*hako o
kuruma no yane ni roopu de shibaru*) 箱を車の屋根にロープで縛る.

rose *n.* **1** (flower) baˈra ばら: a wild
rose (*nobara*) 野ばら.
2 (color) baˈrairo ばら色: Her dress
was rose colored. (*Kanojo no doresu wa barairo datta.*) 彼女のドレス
はばら色だった.

rosy *adj.* **1** (rose-colored) baˈrairo
no ばら色の; keˈsshoku no yoˈi 血色
のよい: rosy cheeks (*kesshoku no
yoi hoo*) 血色のよいほお.
2 (bright) aˈkarui 明るい; yuˈuboo
na 有望な: a rosy future (*akarui
mirai*) 明るい未来.

rot *vi.* kuˈsaˈru 腐る Ⓒ: The toma-
toes are rotting in the basket. (*Tomato ga kago no naka de kusatte
iru.*) トマトがかごの中で腐っている.
— *vt.* ... o kuˈsaraseˈru ...を腐らせる
Ⓥ: Too much water rotted the
roots. (*Mizu o yarisugite ne ga
kusatte shimatta.*) 水をやりすぎて根が
腐ってしまった.

— *n*. fuʰhai 腐敗.

rotate *vi*. kaʰiteñ suru 回転する ①:
The earth rotates once in twenty-
four hours. (*Chikyuu wa nijuuyo-
jikañ de ichi-do kaiteñ suru*.) 地球
は 24 時間で一度回転する.

rotation *n*. kaʰiteñ 回転: the rotation of an engine (*eñjiñ no kaiteñ*)
エンジンの回転.

rough *adj*. **1** (not smooth) aʰrai 粗
い; zaʰrazara shita [shite iru] ざらざ
らした[している]; (uneven) deʰkoboko
no でこぼこの: rough paper (*zarazara
shita kami*) ざらざらした紙 / a rough
road (*dekoboko no michi*) でこぼこの
道.
2 (not complete) oʰomaka na 大ま
かな; oʰozaʰppa na 大ざっぱな: a
rough estimate of repair costs
(*shuurihi no oozappa na mitsumori*) 修理費の大ざっぱな見積もり.
3 (not gentle) soʰya na 粗野な; bu-
ʰsaʰhoo na 無作法な: He is a man
with rough manners. (*Kare wa
busahoo na otoko da*.) 彼は無作法な
男だ.
4 (not finished) miʰkaʰñsee no 未
完成の; fuʰkaʰñzeñ na 不完全な: a
rough copy (*shitagaki*) 下書き.

roughly *adv*. **1** (about) oʰyoso およ
そ; daʰitai 大体; yaʰku 約: It will
cost roughly ten thousand yen.
(*Oyoso ichi-mañ-eñ kakarimasu*.)
およそ 1 万円かかります.
2 (in a rough manner) raʰñboo ni
乱暴に; teʰaraku 手荒く: treat a person roughly (*hito o tearaku atsukau*) 人を手荒く扱う.

round¹ *prep*. **1** (in a circle) ... no
maʰwari o ...の周りを: The earth
goes round the sun. (*Chikyuu wa
taiyoo no mawari o mawaru*.) 地球
は太陽の周りを回る.
2 (on all sides of) ... no maʰwari ni
...の周りに: We sat round the table.
(*Watashi-tachi wa teeburu no mawari ni suwatta*.) 私たちはテーブルの
周りに座った.
3 (here and there) ... o aʰchiʰkochi
...をあちこち: He looked round the

room. (*Kare wa heya no naka o
achikochi mimawashita*.) 彼は部屋
の中をあちこち見回した.
— *adv*. **1** (in a circle) guʰruʰri to
ぐるりと; kaʰiteñ shite 回転して: turn
a chair round (*isu o gururi to mawasu*) いすをぐるりと回す.
2 (in circumference) shuʰui ga 周
囲が: His waist measures 82 centimeters round. (*Kare wa koshi no
shuui ga hachijuu-ni-señchi aru*.)
彼は腰の周囲が 82 センチある.
3 (from one to another) tsuʰgiʰ
kara tsuʰgiʰ e to 次から次へと:
Drinks were passed round. (*Nomimono ga tsugi kara tsugi e to
mawasareta*.) 飲物が次から次へと回さ
れた.

round² *adj*. **1** (shaped like a ball)
maʰrui 丸い; kyuʰukee no 球形の:
The earth is round. (*Chikyuu wa
marui*.) 地球は丸い.
2 (circular) maʰrui 丸い; eʰñkee no
円形の: a round plate (*marui sara*)
丸い皿.
3 (plump) maʰrumaʰru to shita
[shite iru] 丸々とした[している]: a
round face (*marumaru to shita
kao*) 丸々とした顔.
4 (complete) kaʰñzeñ na 完全な;
haʰsuʰu no naʰi 端数のない: a round
number (*hasuu no nai kazu*) 端数の
ない数.
— *n*. **1** (beat) juʰñkai 巡回: make
one's rounds (*juñkai suru*) 巡回する.
2 (one complete game) hiʰtoʰ-
shoobu ひと勝負; hiʰtoʰshiai ひと試
合: play a round (*hitoshoobu suru*)
ひと勝負する.
— *vt*. ... o maʰwaru ...を回る ⓒ;
maʰgaru 曲がる ⓒ: round a corner
(*kado o magaru*) 角を曲がる.

round-trip ticket *n*. oʰofuku-
kiʰppu 往復切符.

rouse *vt*. ... no meʰ o saʰmaseʰru
...の目を覚まさせる ⓥ; ... o oʰkoʰsu ...
を起こす ⓒ: Please rouse me at six.
(*Roku-ji ni okoshite kudasai*.) 6 時
に起こしてください.

route *n*. miʰchi 道; ruʰuto ルート:

That restaurant is on our route. (*Sono resutorañ wa watashi-tachi ga iku michi no tochuu ni arimasu.*) そのレストランは私たちが行く道の途中にあります。 / an air route (*kookuuro*) 航空路.

routine *n.* kiˈmarikiˈtta shiˈgoto 決まりきった仕事: one's daily routine (*mainichi no kimatta shigoto*) 毎日の決まった仕事.

— *adj.* kiˈmarikiˈtta 決まりきった; teˈeki-teki na 定期的な: a routine physical exam (*teeki-teki na keñkoo shiñdañ*) 定期的な健康診断.

row[1] *n.* reˈtsu 列: a row of trees (*namiki*) 並木 / sit in the front row (*ichibañ mae no retsu ni suwaru*) いちばん前の列に座る.

row[2] *vt.* **1** (move) ... o koˈgu ...をこぐ ⓒ: row a boat (*booto o kogu*) ボートをこぐ.

2 (carry) ... o koˈide haˈkobu ...をこいで運ぶ ⓒ: He rowed me across the river. (*Kare wa fune o koide watashi o kawa mukoo made hakoñde kureta.*) 彼は舟をこいで私を川向こうまで運んでくれた.

— *vi.* fuˈne o koˈgu 舟をこぐ ⓒ.

row[3] *n.* oˈogeˈñka 大げんか; saˈwagi 騒ぎ: He had a row with his wife. (*Kare wa okusañ to oogeñka o shita.*) 彼は奥さんと大げんかをした.

royal *adj.* oˈo no 王の: a royal family (*oozoku*) 王族 / a royal palace (*ookyuu*) 王宮.

rub *vt.* ... o koˈsuˈru ...をこする ⓒ; suˈrikoˈmu すり込む ⓒ: rub one's eyes (*me o kosuru*) 目をこする / rub oil on one's skin (*hada ni abura o surikomu*) 肌にオイルをすり込む.

— *vi.* suˈreˈru すれる Ⓥ; koˈsuˈru こする ⓒ: The wheel is rubbing against something. (*Shariñ ga nani-ka kosutte iru.*) 車輪が何かこすっている.

rubber *n.* **1** (elastic substance) goˈmu ゴム: a rubber band (*wagomu*) 輪ゴム / a rubber stamp (*gomuiñ*) ゴム印.

2 (eraser) keˈshigomu 消しゴム.

3 (condom) koˈñdoˈomu コンドーム.

rubbish *n.* goˈmiˈ ごみ; kuˈzu くず: throw rubbish away (*gomi o suteru*) ごみを捨てる.

ruby *n.* ruˈbii ルビー.

rude *adj.* **1** (not polite) shiˈtsuˈree na 失礼な; buˈree na 無礼な; buˈsaˈhoo na 無作法な: It is rude of you not to thank him. (*Kare ni o-ree o iwanai no wa shitsuree desu.*) 彼にお礼を言わないのは失礼です. / say rude things (*buree na koto o iu*) 無礼なことを言う.

2 (rough) raˈñboo na 乱暴な: rude treatment (*rañboo na toriatsukai*) 乱暴な取り扱い.

rug *n.* shiˈkimono 敷物; juˈutañ じゅうたん.

rugby *n.* raˈgubii ラグビー.

rugged *adj.* **1** (uneven) deˈkoboko no でこぼこの: a rugged road (*dekoboko no michi*) でこぼこの道.

2 (strong-looking) iˈkatsui いかつい: rugged features (*ikatsui kaodachi*) いかつい顔立ち.

3 (not refined) seˈñreñ sarete inai 洗練されていない: rugged manners (*señreñ sarete inai furumai*) 洗練されていない振る舞い.

ruin *vt.* ... o haˈmetsu saseru ...を破滅させる Ⓥ; daˈinashi ni suru 台なしにする Ⓘ: Drink ruined his career. (*Sake ga kare no isshoo o dainashi ni shita.*) 酒が彼の一生を台なしにした.

— *n.* **1** (destruction) haˈmetsu 破滅; koˈohai 荒廃: The castle fell into ruin. (*Sono shiro wa koohai shite shimatta.*) その城は荒廃してしまった.

2 (building) haˈikyo 廃墟; iˈseki 遺跡: ancient Greek ruins (*kodai Girisha no iseki*) 古代ギリシャの遺跡.

rule *n.* **1** (regulation) kiˈsoku 規則; kiˈtee 規定: obey [break] a rule (*kisoku o mamoru* [*yaburu*]) 規則を守る[破る] / It's against the rules. (*Kisoku ihañ da.*) 規則違反だ.

2 (reign) shiˈhai 支配; toˈochi 統治: The country was under military rule. (*Sono kuni wa guñ no shihaika ni atta.*) その国は軍の支配下にあった.

3 (custom) shu⌐ukañ 習慣; na⌐rawashi 習わし: It is my rule to rise early. (*Hayaku okiru no ga watashi no shuukañ desu.*) 早く起きるのが私の習慣です.

— *vt.* **1** (govern) ... o shi⌐hai suru ...を支配する ⊡; to⌐ochi suru 統治する ⊡: The queen ruled her country for a long period. (*Jo-oo wa kuni o nagai aida toochi shita.*) 女王は国を長い間統治した.

2 (decide) ... o sa⌐iketsu suru ...を裁決する; ha⌐ñtee suru 判定する ⊡: The court ruled him innocent. (*Hootee wa kare o muzai to saiketsu shita.*) 法廷は彼を無罪と裁決した.

3 (draw) se⌐ñ o hi⌐ku 線を引く ⊡: rule straight lines on paper (*kami ni massugu na señ o hiku*) 紙に真っすぐな線を引く.

— *vi.* **1** (govern) shi⌐hai suru 支配する ⊡.

2 (decide) ha⌐ñketsu suru 判決する ⊡; ki⌐tee suru 規定する ⊡.

ruler *n.* **1** (person) shi⌐ha⌐isha 支配者; to⌐ochisha 統治者.

2 (material) jo⌐ogi 定規; mo⌐nosa⌐shi 物差し: draw a line with a ruler (*joogi de señ o hiku*) 定規で線を引く.

ruling *n.* **1** (decision) ha⌐ñketsu 判決; sa⌐itee 裁定: a ruling of the Supreme Court (*Saikoo-saibañsho no hañketsu*) 最高裁判所の判決.

2 (governing) shi⌐hai 支配; to⌐ochi 統治.

— *adj.* shi⌐hai shite iru 支配している: the ruling class (*shihai-kaikyuu*) 支配階級 / the ruling party (*yotoo*) 与党.

rumor *n.* u⌐wasa うわさ: There is a rumor that they are getting married. (*Kare-ra wa kekkoñ suru to iu uwasa da.*) 彼らは結婚するといううわさだ.

run *vi.* **1** (move rapidly) ha⌐shi⌐ru 走る ⊡; ka⌐ke⌐ru 駆ける Ⓥ: I ran to the station. (*Watashi wa eki made hashitta.*) 私は駅まで走った.

2 (escape) ni⌐ge⌐ru 逃げる Ⓥ: I ran for my life. (*Watashi wa inochi karagara nigeta.*) 私は命からがら逃げた.

3 (take part in a race) kyo⌐osoo ni de⌐ru 競走に出る Ⓥ; ri⌐kko⌐oho suru 立候補する ⊡: He ran in the 100-meter race. (*Kare wa hyaku-meetoru kyoosoo ni deta.*) 彼は100メートル競走に出た. / run for mayor (*shichoo ni rikkooho suru*) 市長に立候補する.

4 (work) u⌐go⌐ku 動く Ⓒ: This car runs by electricity. (*Kono kuruma wa deñki de ugokimasu.*) この車は電気で動きます.

5 (travel regularly) u⌐ñkoo suru 運行する ⊡; ha⌐shi⌐ru 走る Ⓒ: The buses run every fifteen minutes. (*Basu wa juugo-fuñ oki ni hashitte imasu.*) バスは15分おきに走っています.

6 (flow) na⌐gare⌐ru 流れる Ⓥ: Sweat was running from his forehead. (*Ase ga kare no hitai kara nagarete ita.*) 汗が彼の額から流れていた.

7 (extend) to⌐otte iru 通っている Ⓥ: The path runs through the woods. (*Sono komichi wa mori no naka o tootte imasu.*) その小道は森の中を通っています.

8 (continue) tsu⌐zuku 続く Ⓒ: The play ran for three months. (*Sono shibai wa sañ-kagetsu tsuzuita.*) その芝居は3か月続いた.

— *vt.* **1** (cause to run) ... o ha⌐shirase⌐ru ...を走らせる: run a dog (*inu o hashiraseru*) 犬を走らせる.

2 (cause to work) ... o u⌐goka⌐su ...を動かす Ⓒ: run a machine (*kikai o ugokasu*) 機械を動かす.

3 (manage) ... o ke⌐e-ee suru ...を経営する ⊡: run a hotel (*hoteru o kee-ee suru*) ホテルを経営する.

4 (publish) ... o da⌐su ...を出す Ⓒ: run an advertisement in a newspaper (*shiñbuñ ni kookoku o dasu*)

新聞に広告を出す.

— *n.* 1 (running) ha⌐shi⌐ru ko⌐to⌐ 走ること: I was tired after my run. (*Hashitta no de tsukareta.*) 走ったので疲れた.

2 (series) re⌐nzoku 連続; tsu⌐zuki 続き: a run of fine weather (*kooten tsuzuki*) 好天続き.

3 (score) to⌐kuten 得点: score three runs (*san-ten ageru*) 3 点あげる / a home run (*hoomuran*) ホームラン.

4 (ladder) de⌐nsen 伝線: get a run in one's tights (*taitsu ni densen ga dekiru*) タイツに伝線ができる.

runner *n.* ha⌐shi⌐ru hi⌐to⌐ 走る人; so⌐osha 走者; ra⌐nnaa ランナー: a long-distance runner (*chookyori rannaa*) 長距離ランナー.

rural *adj.* i⌐naka no 田舎の: a rural town (*inaka no machi*) 田舎の町 / rural life (*deňen-seekatsu*) 田園生活.

rush *vi.* 1 (hurry) to⌐sshin suru 突進する □; i⌐sogu 急ぐ ⓒ: The police rushed to the scene. (*Keekantai wa genba e isoida.*) 警官隊は現場へ急いだ.

2 (act in haste) ke⌐esotsu ni koodoo suru 軽率に行動する □: She rushed into marriage. (*Kanojo wa keesotsu ni kekkon shita.*) 彼女は軽率に結婚した.

— *vt.* (casue to rush) ... o to⌐sshin saseru ...を突進させる Ⓥ; i⌐sogase⌐ru 急がせる Ⓥ: Don't rush me. (*Isogasenaide kudasai.*) 急がせないでください.

— *n.* to⌐sshin 突進; sa⌐ttoo 殺到: make a rush for the door (*doa ni mukatte sattoo suru*) ドアに向かって殺到する.

rust *n.* sa⌐bi⌐ さび: a knife covered with rust (*sabitsuita naifu*) さびついたナイフ.

— *vi.* sa⌐bi⌐ru さびる Ⓥ: This bicycle does not rust. (*Kono jitensha wa sabimasen.*) この自転車はさびません.

rustic *adj.* i⌐naka no いなかの: rustic life (*denen seekatsu*) 田園生活.

rusty *adj.* sa⌐bita さびた; sa⌐bite iru さびている: a rusty nail (*sabita kugi*) さびた釘.

rye *n.* ra⌐imugi ライ麦; ha⌐dakamu⌐gi 裸麦.

S

sack *n.* o⌐obu⌐kuro 大袋: a potato sack (*jagaimo no fukuro*) じゃがいもの袋 / a sack of coal (*sekitan hitofukuro*) 石炭ひと袋.

sacred *adj.* shi⌐nsee na 神聖な: a sacred book (*seeten*) 聖典.

sacrifice *n.* gi⌐see 犠牲: I made great sacrifices to educate my children. (*Watashi wa kodomo o kyooiku suru no ni tadai no gisee o haratta.*) 私は子どもを教育するのに多大の犠牲を払った.

— *vt.* 1 (give up) ... o gi⌐see ni suru ...を犠牲にする □: I cannot sacrifice business for pleasure. (*Watashi wa asobi no tame ni shigoto o gisee ni suru koto wa dekinai.*) 私は遊びのために仕事を犠牲にすることはできない.

2 (offer to a deity) ... o i⌐kenie to shite sasageru ...をいけにえとしてささげる Ⓥ: sacrifice sheep to gods (*hitsuji o kami ni ikenie to shite sasageru*) 羊を神にいけにえとしてささげる.

sad *adj.* ka⌐nashii 悲しい; a⌐ware na 哀れな: the sad news (*kanashii shirase*) 悲しい知らせ / We all felt sad about his death. (*Watashi-tachi wa minna kare no shi o kanashinda.*) 私たちはみんな彼の死を悲しんだ.

saddle *n.* (of a horse) ku⌐ra⌐ くら; (of a bicycle) sa⌐doru サドル: put a saddle on a horse (*uma ni kura o oku*) 馬にくらを置く.

sadly *adv.* ka⌐nashi⌐nde 悲しんで; ka⌐nashi-so⌐o ni 悲しそうに: The girl was weeping sadly. (*Sono onna-no-ko wa kanashi-soo ni naite ita.*) その女の子は悲しそうに泣いていた.

sadness *n.* ka⌐nashimi 悲しみ; hi⌐ai 悲哀.

safe¹ *adj.* **1** (out of danger) a⌐ñzeñ na 安全な: We are safe here. (*Koko ni ireba añzeñ desu.*) ここにいれば安全です.
2 (not injured) bu⌐ji na 無事な: I hope that you have a safe trip. (*Tabi no go-buji o inorimasu.*) 旅のご無事を祈ります.

safe² *n.* ki⌐ñko 金庫: put the money in the safe (*kiñko ni o-kane o shimau*) 金庫にお金をしまう.

safely *adv.* a⌐ñzeñ ni 安全に; bu⌐ji ni 無事に: He reached home safely. (*Kare wa buji ni kitaku shimashita.*) 彼は無事に帰宅しました.

safety *n.* a⌐ñzeñ 安全; bu⌐ji 無事: Safety First. (*Añzeñ dai-ichi.*) 安全第一.

sail *n.* ho⌐ 帆: raise [lower] a sail (*ho o ageru [orosu]*) 帆を揚げる[下ろす].
— *vi.* ha⌐ñsoo suru 帆走する ①; ko⌐okai suru 航海する ①: They sailed across the Pacific. (*Kare-ra wa Taiheeyoo o watatte kookai shita.*) 彼らは太平洋を渡って航海した.

sailor *n.* **1** (crew) se⌐ñiñ 船員; fu⌐na⌐nori 船乗り: a good [poor] sailor (*fune ni tsuyoi [yowai] hito*) 船に強い[弱い]人.
2 (not officer) su⌐ihee 水兵.

saint *n.* se⌐ñjiñ 聖人; se⌐ja 聖者.

sake *n.* (...no) ta⌐me⌐ (...の)ため; mo⌐kuteki 目的: They fought for their country's sake. (*Kare-ra wa sokoku no tame ni tatakatta.*) 彼らは祖国のために戦った.

for the sake of ... *adv.* ...no ta⌐me⌐ ni ...のために: He would do anything for the sake of money. (*Kane no tame nara kare wa nañ de mo yaru.*) 金のためなら彼は何でもやる.

salad *n.* sa⌐rada サラダ: make a vegetable salad (*yasai sarada o tsukuru*) 野菜サラダを作る.

salary *n.* kyu⌐uryoo 給料; sa⌐rarii サラリー: a high [low] salary (*takai [hikui] kyuuryoo*) 高い[低い]給料 / I can't live on my salary now. (*Ima no kyuuryoo de wa seekatsu dekinai.*) 今の給料では生活できない.

sale *n.* **1** (act of selling) ha⌐ñbai 販売: make a sale (*hañbai o suru*) 販売をする.
2 (at lower prices) ya⌐suuri 安売り; to⌐kubai 特売: I bought this coat at a sale. (*Watashi wa kono kooto o tokubai de katta.*) 私はこのコートを特売で買った.
3 (the amount sold) u⌐riage 売り上げ: The sales of cars are up [down] this month. (*Kuruma no uriage ga koñgetsu wa agatta [sagatta].*) 車の売り上げが今月は上がった[下がった].

salesman *n.* te⌐ñiñ 店員; se⌐erusu⌐mañ セールスマン: The salesmen in this store are all very kind. (*Koko no mise no teñiñ wa miñna shiñsetsu da.*) ここの店の店員はみんな親切だ. / a car salesman (*kuruma no seerusumañ*) 車のセールスマン.
★ Japanese 'seerusumañ' refers only to 'commercial traveler.'

saleswoman *n.* jo⌐see-te⌐ñiñ 女性店員.

salmon *n.* sa⌐ke 鮭.

salt *n.* shi⌐o⌐ 塩: This soup needs a little more salt. (*Kono suupu wa moo sukoshi shio o kikaseta hoo ga ii.*) このスープはもう少し塩を利かせたほうがいい. / Please pass the salt. (*Shio o mawashite kudasai.*) 塩を回してください.

salute *vt.* **1** (show respect) ... ni ke⌐eree suru ...に敬礼する ①: salute the flag (*kokki ni keeree suru*) 国旗に敬礼する.
2 (greet) ... ni a⌐isatsu suru ...にあいさつする ①: She saluted me with a smile. (*Kanojo wa egao de watashi ni aisatsu shita.*) 彼女は笑顔で私にあいさつした.

salvation *n.* kyuˈusai 救済; kyuˈu-jo 救助.

same *adj.* oˈnaji 同じ; doˈoitsu no 同一の: He and I are the same age. (*Kare to watashi wa onaji toshi desu.*) 彼と私は同じ年です。
— *pron.* oˈnaji mono [koto] 同じ物[事]: She ordered coffee and I ordered the same. (*Kanojo wa koo-hii o chuumoñ shita ga watashi mo onaji mono o chuumoñ shita.*) 彼女はコーヒーを注文したが私も同じ物を注文した。

sample *n.* miˈhoñ 見本; saˈñpuru サンプル: This is different from the sample. (*Kore wa mihoñ to chigau.*) これは見本と違う。
— *vt.* ... no aˈji o miˈru ...の味をみる ⓥ: sample wine (*waiñ no aji o miru*) ワインの味をみる。

sand *n.* suˈna 砂.

sandal *n.* saˈñdaru サンダル.

sandwich *n.* saˈñdoiˈtchi サンドイッチ: make a ham sandwich (*hamu sañdoitchi o tsukuru*) ハムサンドイッチを作る。

sandy *adj.* suˈna no 砂の; suˈnachi no 砂地の: a sandy beach (*suna-hama*) 砂浜。

sane *adj.* shoˈoki no 正気の; keˈñ-zeñ na 健全な: He doesn't seem sane at all. (*Kare wa totemo shoo-ki ni wa omoenai.*) 彼はとても正気とは思えない。 / make a sane decision (*keñzeñ na ketsudañ o suru*) 健全な決断をする。

sanitary *adj.* eˈesee-teki na 衛生的な; seˈeketsu na 清潔な: The public lavatory in the park was not sanitary. (*Kooeñ no kooshuu beñjo wa seeketsu de nakatta.*) 公園の公衆便所は清潔でなかった。

sarcasm *n.* hiˈniku 皮肉; iˈyami 嫌み: bitter sarcasm (*tsuuretsu na hiniku*) 痛烈な皮肉。

sarcastic *adj.* hiˈniku na 皮肉な; iˈyami o iˈu 嫌みをいう: a sarcastic person (*hinikuya*) 皮肉屋。

sardine *n.* iˈwashi いわし; saˈadiñ サーディン.

sash *n.* oˈbi 帯; kaˈzarioˈbi 飾り帯.

satellite *n.* **1** (natural body) eˈesee 衛星: The moon is a satellite of the earth. (*Tsuki wa chikyuu no eesee desu.*) 月は地球の衛星です。 **2** (man-made body) jiˈñkoo-eˈesee 人工衛星: launch a satellite (*jiñ-koo-eesee o uchiageru*) 人工衛星を打ち上げる / satellite broadcasting (*eesee hoosoo*) 衛星放送。

satin *n.* shuˈsu しゅす; saˈteñ サテン.

satisfaction *n.* maˈñzoku 満足; naˈttoku 納得: The matter was settled to the satisfaction of all. (*Sono koto wa miñna ga mañzoku suru yoo ni kaiketsu shita.*) そのことはみんなが満足するように解決した。

satisfactory *adj.* maˈñzoku no iˈku 満足のいく; naˈttoku no iku 納得のいく: He gave a satisfactory explanation. (*Kare wa nattoku no iku setsumee o shita.*) 彼は納得のいく説明をした。

satisfied *adj.* maˈñzoku shita [shite iru] 満足した[している]; naˈt-toku shita [shite iru] 納得した[している]: She was satisfied with her new house. (*Kanojo wa atarashii ie ni mañzoku shite ita.*) 彼女は新しい家に満足していた。

satisfy *vt.* ... o maˈñzoku saseru 満足させる ⓥ; naˈttoku saseru 納得させる ⓥ: His explanation failed to satisfy her. (*Kare no setsumee wa kanojo o nattoku saseru koto ga dekinakatta.*) 彼の説明は彼女を納得させることができなかった。

saturate *vt.* ... ni shiˈmikomaˈsu ...にしみ込ます; ... o zuˈbunure ni suru ...をずぶぬれにする ⓣ: a cloth saturated with oil (*abura no shi-mikoñda kire*) 油のしみ込んだ布。

Saturday *n.* doˈyoˈo(bi) 土曜(日).

sauce *n.* soˈosu ソース。 ★ In Japan, it usually refers to a thick brown sauce.

saucer *n.* uˈkeˈzara 受け皿: a cup and saucer (*ukezara tsuki no cha-wañ*) 受け皿付きの茶わん。

sausage *n.* soˈoseˈeji ソーセージ:

Vienna sausage (*Uiínna sooseeji*) ウ
インナソーセージ.

savage *adj.* **1** (cruel) do「omoo na
どうもうな; za「ñkoku na 残酷な: a
savage beast (*doomoo na kemono*)
どうもうな獣.

2 (uncivilized) ya「bañ na 野蛮な:
savage customs (*yabañ na fuushuu*) 野蛮な風習.

save *vt.* **1** (rescue) ... o su「kuu ...を
救う C; ta「suke」ru 助ける V: He
saved the child's life. (*Kare wa
sono ko no inochi o sukutta.*) 彼は
その子の命を救った.

2 (store up) ... o ta「kuwae」ru ...を
蓄える V; cho「kiñ suru 貯金する I:
I save some money out of my
salary every month. (*Watashi wa
maitsuki kyuuryoo kara ikura ka
chokiñ shite imasu.*) 私は毎月給料
からいくらか貯金しています.

3 (avoid wasting) ... o se「tsuyaku
suru ...を節約する I; ha「bu」ku 省く
C: He saved his bus fares and
walked. (*Kare wa basu-dai o setsuyaku shite aruita.*) 彼はバス代を節約
して歩いた.

savings *n.* yo「kiñ 預金; cho「kiñ 貯
金: savings account (*futsuuyokiñ
kooza*) 普通預金口座.

savior *n.* kyu「usa」isha 救済者; su-
「kui」nushi 救い主.

saw *n.* no「kogi」ri のこぎり: cut wood
with a saw (*nokogiri de ki o kiru*)
のこぎりで木を切る.
— *vt.* ... o no「kogi」ri de ki「ru ...を
のこぎりで切る C: saw a tree down
(*ki o nokogiri de kitte taosu*) 木を
のこぎりで切って倒す.

say *vt.* **1** (speak) ... to i「u ...と言う
C; ha「na」su 話す C: They say that
you are wrong. (*Miñna wa kimi ga
machigatte iru to itte iru.*) みんなは
君が間違っていると言っている. / What
did he say about the problem?
(*Sono moñdai ni tsuite kare wa
nañ to itte imashita ka?*) その問題に
ついて彼は何と言っていましたか.

2 (state) ... to ka「ite aru ...と書いて
ある C: The sign says "Danger."

(*Sono hyooshiki ni wa "Kikeñ" to
kaite aru.*) その標識には「危険」と書
いてある.

3 (indicate) ... o shi「me」su ...を示す
C; sa「su 指す C: My watch says
ten o'clock. (*Watashi no tokee wa
juu-ji o sashite iru.*) 私の時計は10
時を指している.

4 (order) ... to shi「ji suru ...と指示す
る I; i「u 言う C: We must do
whatever the teacher says. (*Señsee
no iu koto wa nañ de mo shinakereba naranai.*) 先生の言うことは何でも
しなければならない.

scale[1] *n.* **1** (of a measure) me「mori
目盛り: read the scale on a ther-
mometer (*oñdokee no memori o
yomu*) 温度計の目盛りを読む.

2 (of a map) shu「ukushaku 縮尺: a
map with a scale of one centimeter
to one kilometer (*ichi-kiro o is-
señchi ni shukushaku shita chizu*)
1キロを1センチに縮尺した地図.

3 (size) ki「bo 規模: a business on a
large scale (*dai-kibo na jigyoo*) 大
規模な事業.

4 (of music) o「ñkai 音階.

scale[2] *n.* te「ñbiñ てんびん; ta「ijuukee
体重計: weigh oneself on the bathroom scales (*yokushitsu no taijuu-
kee de taijuu o hakaru*) 浴室の体重
計で体重を量る.

scan *vt.* **1** (look at attentively) ... o
ji「tto mitsumeru ...をじっと見つめる
V: scan the horizon for a ship
(*fune o motomete suiheeseñ o
jitto mitsumeru*) 船を求めて水平線を
じっと見つめる.

2 (glance) ... ni za「tto me」o toosu
...にざっと目を通す C: scan a newspa-
per (*shiñbuñ ni zatto me o toosu*)
新聞にざっと目を通す.

scandal *n.* su「kya」ñdaru スキャンダ
ル; o「shoku ji」keñ 汚職事件: cause
a scandal (*sukyañdaru o okosu*) ス
キャンダルを起こす.

scanty *adj.* to「boshi」i 乏しい; wa「-
zuka na わずかな: scanty information (*toboshii joohoo*) 乏しい情報.

scar *n.* ki「zuato 傷跡: He has a scar

on his face. (*Kare wa kao ni kizu-ato ga aru.*) 彼は顔に傷跡がある。

scarce *adj.* fuˈsoku shite (iru) 不足して(いる); suˈkunaˈi 少ない: Vegetables are scarce and dear. (*Yasai ga fusoku shite nedañ ga takai.*) 野菜が不足して値段が高い。

scarcely *adv.* **1** (hardly) hoˈtoˈñ-do ... naˈi ほとんど...ない: He was so tired that he could scarcely walk. (*Kare wa hijoo ni tsukarete ite hotoñdo aruku koto ga dekina-katta.*) 彼は非常に疲れていてほとんど歩くことができなかった。

2 (barely) yaˈtto やっと; karoˈojite かろうじて: Scarcely 10 people were present. (*Yatto juu-niñ ga shusseki shita.*) やっと 10 人が出席した。

scare *vt.* ... o biˈkkuˈri saseru ...をびっくりさせる Ⅴ; oˈdokaˈsu 脅かす Ⅽ: I was scared by the sudden barking. (*Totsuzeñ inu ga hoete bik-kuri shita.*) 突然犬がほえてびっくりした。

scarf *n.* suˈkaˈafu スカーフ; eˈriˈmaki えり巻き: wear a scarf (*sukaafu o kakeru*) スカーフをかける。

scarlet *adj.* hiˈiro ... no 緋色の; shiˈñ-kuiro no 深紅色の: He turned scarlet. (*Kare wa kao ga makka ni natta.*) 彼は顔が真っ赤になった。
— *n.* hiˈiro 緋色; shiˈñkuiro 深紅色。

scatter *vt.* **1** (sprinkle) ... o baˈramaˈku ...をばらまく Ⅽ; maˈkichi-rasu まき散らす Ⅽ: scatter seed over the fields (*hatake ni tane o maku*) 畑に種をまく。

2 (drive) ... o oˈichiraˈsu ...を追い散らす Ⅽ: The police scattered the crowd. (*Keekañ-tachi wa guñshuu o oichirashita.*) 警官たちは群集を追い散らした。
— *vi.* chiˈrijiri ni naˈru ちりぢりになる Ⅽ: The children scattered when it began to rain. (*Ame ga furi-dasu to kodomo-tachi wa chirijiri ni natta.*) 雨が降り出すと子どもたちはちりぢりになった。

scene *n.* **1** (the place of occurrence) geˈñba 現場: We rushed to the scene of the accident. (*Wata-shi-tachi wa jiko no geñba ni isoida.*) 私たちは事故の現場に急いだ。

2 (view) keˈshiki 景色; fuˈukee 風景: I like to paint rural scenes. (*Watashi wa inaka no fuukee o egaku no ga suki da.*) 私は田舎の風景を描くのが好きだ。

3 (part of a play) ba 場; baˈmeñ 場面: She appears in Act I, Scene 2. (*Kanojo wa dai ichi-maku dai ni-ba ni toojoo suru.*) 彼女は第 1 幕第 2 場に登場する。

scenery *n.* **1** (view) fuˈukee 風景; keˈshiki 景色: The mountain scenery was beautiful. (*Yama no ke-shiki wa utsukushikatta.*) 山の景色は美しかった。

2 (of a stage) haˈikee 背景; buˈtai-soˈochi 舞台装置。

scent *n.* niˈoˈi におい; kaˈori 香り: the scent of flowers (*hana no kao-ri*) 花の香り。
— *vt.* ... o kaˈgitsukeˈru ...をかぎつける Ⅴ: The dog scented a fox. (*Inu ga kitsune no nioi o kagitsu-keta.*) 犬がきつねのにおいをかぎつけた。

schedule *n.* **1** (plan) yoˈtee 予定; yoˈteehyoo 予定表; suˈkeˈjuuru スケジュール: My schedule for tomorrow is very tight. (*Ashita no yotee wa gisshiri tsumatte iru.*) あしたの予定はぎっしり詰まっている。

2 (timetable) jiˈkokuhyoo 時刻表: a train schedule (*ressha no jikoku-hyoo*) 列車の時刻表。
— *vt.* ... o yoˈtee suru ...を予定する Ⅰ: The next meeting is scheduled for Monday. (*Tsugi no kaigi wa getsuyoobi ni yotee sarete iru.*) 次の会議は月曜日に予定されている。

scheme *n.* **1** (plan) keˈekaku 計画: carry out a scheme (*keekaku o jikkoo suru*) 計画を実行する。

2 (plot) iˈñboo 陰謀; taˈkurami たくらみ: He had a scheme to rob the bank. (*Kare wa giñkoo o osou koto o takurañde ita.*) 彼は銀行を襲うことをたくらんでいた。
— *vt.* ... o keˈekaku suru ...を計画

する ①: He schemed to escape from the prison. (*Kare wa datsugoku o keekaku shita.*) 彼は脱獄を計画した.

scholar *n.* ga⌐kusha 学者: a famous scholar of Japanese literature (*Nihoñ buñgaku no yuumee na gakusha*) 日本文学の有名な学者.

scholarship *n.* **1** (financial aid) sho⌐gakukiñ 奨学金: receive a scholarship to university (*daigaku shiñgaku no shoogakukiñ o ukeru*) 大学進学の奨学金を受ける.
2 (learning) ga⌐ku¹moñ 学問; ga⌐kushiki 学識: a person of great scholarship (*hijoo-ni gakushiki no aru hito*) 非常に学識のある人.

school *n.* **1** (building) ga⌐kkoo 学校: He goes to school by bus. (*Kare wa basu de gakkoo ni kayotte iru.*) 彼はバスで学校に通っている.
2 (class) ju¹gyoo 授業: We have no school today. (*Kyoo wa jugyoo wa arimaseñ.*) きょうは授業はありません.
3 (department) ga⌐kubu 学部: medical school (*igakubu*) 医学部.
4 (group) ryu⌐uha 流派: a school of flower arrangement (*ikebana no ryuuha*) いけばなの流派.

schoolboy *n.* da⌐ñshi-se¹eto 男子生徒.

school building *n.* ko⌐osha 校舎.

schoolchild *n.* ga⌐kudoo 学童.

schoolgirl *n.* jo⌐shi-se¹eto 女子生徒.

schoolteacher *n.* se⌐ñse¹e 先生; kyo¹oshi 教師.

science *n.* ka¹gaku 科学: natural science (*shizeñ kagaku*) 自然科学.

scientific *adj.* ka¹gaku no 科学の; ka⌐gaku-teki na 科学的な: His methods are scientific. (*Kare no hoohoo wa kagaku-teki da.*) 彼の方法は科学的だ.

scientist *n.* ka⌐ga¹kusha 科学者: a social scientist (*shakai kagakusha*) 社会科学者.

scissors *n.* ha⌐sami¹ はさみ: use scissors (*hasami o tsukau*) はさみを使う.

scold *vt.* ... o shi⌐karu ...をしかる ⓒ: She scolded her son for being lazy. (*Kanojo wa musuko ga namakete iru no de shikatta.*) 彼女は息子が怠けているのでしかった.

scope *n.* ha¹ñi 範囲; shi¹ya 視野: broaden the scope of an investigation (*choosa no hañi o hirogeru*) 調査の範囲を広げる.

score *n.* **1** (points in a game) to⌐kuteñ 得点; (in a test) te⌐ñsu¹u 点数: win by a score of three to two (*sañ tai ni de katsu*) 3対2で勝つ / I got a score of eighty on the math test. (*Watashi wa suugaku no shikeñ de hachijut-teñ o totta.*) 私は数学の試験で80点を取った.
2 (of music) ga⌐kufu 楽譜; su⌐ko¹a スコア.
— *vt.* ... te¹ñ o to¹ru ...点を取る ⓒ: We scored five points late in the game. (*Wareware wa shiai no koohañ de go-teñ ireta.*) われわれは試合の後半で5点入れた.

scorn *n.* ke⌐ebetsu 軽蔑: She looked at me with scorn. (*Kanojo wa watashi o keebetsu shita me de mita.*) 彼女は私を軽蔑した目で見た.
— *vt.* ... o ke⌐ebetsu suru ...を軽蔑する ①: I scorn people who tell lies. (*Watashi wa uso o tsuku hito o keebetsu suru.*) 私はうそをつく人を軽蔑する.

scornful *adj.* ke⌐ebetsu shita [shite iru] 軽蔑した[している]: a scornful look (*keebetsu shita kaotsuki*) 軽蔑した顔つき / He was scornful of us. (*Kare wa watashi-tachi o keebetsu shite ita.*) 彼は私たちを軽蔑していた.

scout *n.* **1** (soldier) se⌐kkoo 斥候: send out scouts (*sekkoo o dasu*) 斥候を出す.
2 (Boy Scouts) bo⌐oisuka¹uto ボーイスカウト.
— *vi.* (... o) sa⌐gashimawa¹ru (...を)探し回る ⓒ: scout about for a good restaurant (*yoi shokudoo o sagashimawaru*) よい食堂を探し回る.

scramble *vi.* **1** (climb) (... ni) yo-

「jinobo「ru (…に…)よじ登る C: scramble up into a tree (*ki ni yojinoboru*) 木によじ登る.

2 (struggle) (… o) u「baia「u (…を)奪い合う C: scramble for good seats (*yoi seki o toriau*) よい席を取り合う.

scrambled eggs *n.* i「rita「mago いり卵.

scrap *n.* **1** (fragment) ki「rehashi 切れ端; sho「ohen 小片: a scrap of paper (*kamikire*) 紙切れ.

2 (refuse) su「kura「ppu スクラップ; ha「ibutsu 廃物: This old car will soon go for scrap. (*Kono furui kuruma wa moo sugu sukurappu da.*) この古い車はもうすぐスクラップだ.

scrape *vt.* **1** (rub) … o ko「suri-oto「su …をこすり落とす C: scrape the mud off one's shoes (*kutsu no doro o kosuriotosu*) 靴の泥をこすり落とす.

2 (injure) … o su「rimu「ku …をすりむく C: I fell and scraped my knee. (*Watashi wa koronde hiza o surimuita.*) 私は転んでひざをすりむいた.

scratch *vt.* **1** (tear) … o hi「kka「ku …をひっかく C: The cat scratched me with its claws. (*Neko ga watashi o tsume de hikkaita.*) 猫が私を爪でひっかいた.

2 (rub) … o ka「ku …をかく C; ko「su「ru こする C: scratch one's head (*atama o kaku*) 頭をかく.

— *n.* ka「ki「kizu かき傷: He got a scratch on his hand. (*Kare wa te ni kakikizu o koshiraeta.*) 彼は手にかき傷をこしらえた.

scream *vi.* ka「nakirigo「e o a「geru 金切り声を上げる V: She screamed for help. (*Kanojo wa sukui o motomete kanakirigoe o ageta.*) 彼女は救いを求めて金切り声を上げた.

— *n.* ka「nakirigo「e 金切り声: give a scream (*kanakirigoe o dasu*) 金切り声を出す.

screen *n.* **1** (partition) tsu「itate ついたて; shi「kiri しきり: a sliding screen (*shooji*) 障子.

2 (display surface) ga「men 画面; su「kuri「in スクリーン: a TV screen

(*terebi no gamen*) テレビの画面.

3 (net) a「mi「do 網戸: put up screens to keep out insects (*mushi ga hairanai yoo ni amido o tsukeru*) 虫が入らないように網戸をつける.

— *vt.* **1** (hide) … o (… kara) sa「egi「ru …を(…から)さえぎる C: The tall trees screened us from view. (*Takai ki ga shikai o saegitte ita.*) 高い木が視界をさえぎっていた.

2 (separate) … o shi「ki「ru …を仕切る C: Part of the room was screened off. (*Heya no ichibu wa shikirarete ita.*) 部屋の一部は仕切られていた.

screw *n.* **1** (metal nail) ne「ji ねじ: tighten a screw (*neji o shimeru*) ねじを締める.

2 (propeller) (of a ship) su「ku「ryuu スクリュー; (of a plane) pu「ropera プロペラ.

— *vt.* **1** (fasten) … o ne「ji de shi「me「ru …をねじで締める V: screw a box shut (*hako o neji de shimeru*) 箱をねじで締める.

2 (twist) … o hi「ne「ru …をひねる C; ne「ji「ru ねじる C: screw the lid onto a jar (*bin no futa o hinette shimeru*) びんのふたをひねって締める.

scribble *vt.* … o zo「nza「i ni ka「ku …をぞんざいに書く C; ha「shirigaki suru 走り書きする I: scribble a message (*messeeji o hashirigaki suru*) メッセージを走り書きする.

script *n.* **1** (the text of a play) da「ihon 台本: read from a script (*daihon o yomu*) 台本を読む.

2 (handwriting) te「gaki 手書き.

scroll *n.* ma「kimono 巻物; ka「kejiku 掛け軸.

scrub *vt.* … o go「shigoshi a「rau …をごしごし洗う C: scrub the floor with a brush (*burashi de yuka o goshigoshi arau*) ブラシで床をごしごし洗う.

scrutiny *n.* se「emitsu na ke「nsa 精密な検査; gi「nmi 吟味: undergo careful scrutiny (*shinchoo na kensa o ukeru*) 慎重な検査を受ける.

sculpture *n.* cho「okoku 彫刻.

sea 414

sea *n.* uˈmi 海: swim in the sea (*umi de oyogu*) 海で泳ぐ / I like traveling by sea. (*Watashi wa funatabi ga suki da.*) 私は船旅が好きだ.

seal¹ *n.* **1** (impression) haˈñ 判; iˈñ 印: attach one's seal to a document (*shorui ni iñ o osu*) 書類に印を押す. ★ In Japan the seal has legal force and is used instead of a signature. **2** (enclosure) shiˈiru シール.
— *vt.* **1** (mark with a seal) haˈñ o oˈsu 判を押す [C]; choˈoiñ suru 調印する [I]: sign and seal a treaty (*jooyaku ni shomee chooiñ suru*) 条約に署名調印する. **2** (close) ... ni fuˈu o suru ...に封をする [I]: seal an envelope (*fuutoo ni fuu o suru*) 封筒に封をする.

seal² *n.* (animal) aˈzaˈrashi あざらし; oˈttoˈsee おっとせい.

seam *n.* nuˈimeˈ 縫い目: The sleeve has come apart at the seam. (*Sode no nuime ga hokoronita.*) そでの縫い目がほころびた.

seaman *n.* seˈñiñ 船員; fuˈnaˈnori 船乗り.

search *vt.* **1** (look for) ... o saˈgasu ...を捜す [C]: I searched the room for the lost pen. (*Watashi wa nakushita peñ o heyajuu sagashita.*) 私はなくしたペンを部屋中捜した. **2** (examine) ... o shiˈraberu ...を調べる [V]; keˈñsa suru 検査する [I]: My bag was searched at customs. (*Watashi no kabañ wa zeekañ de shiraberareta.*) 私のかばんは税関で調べられた.
— *n.* soˈosaku 捜索; tsuˈikyuu 追求: He came to Tokyo in his search for work. (*Kare wa shoku o motomete Tookyoo e kita.*) 彼は職を求めて東京へ来た.

seashore *n.* kaˈigañ 海岸; uˈmibe 海辺.

seasick *adj.* fuˈne ni yotta [yotte iru] 船に酔った[酔っている]: get seasick (*fune ni you*) 船に酔う.

seaside *n.* kaˈigañ 海岸; uˈmibe 海辺: a seaside hotel (*umibe no hoteru*) 海辺のホテル.

season *n.* **1** (of the year) kiˈsetsu 季節: Autumn is the best season for traveling. (*Aki wa ryokoo ni ichibañ ii kisetsu desu.*) 秋は旅行にいちばんいい季節です. **2** (period) jiˈki 時期; shiˈizuñ シーズン: the harvest season (*toriire no jiki*) 取り入れの時期 / the rainy season (*uki*) 雨季.
— *vt.* ... ni aˈji o tsukeˈru ...に味をつける [V]; choˈomi suru 調味する [I]: season meat with salt and pepper (*niku ni shio to koshoo de aji o tsukeru*) 肉に塩とこしょうで味をつける.

seat *n.* zaˈseki 座席; seˈki 席: Is this seat occupied? (*Kono seki wa fusagatte imasu ka?*) この席はふさがっていますか / Please have a seat. (*Doozo o-kake kudasai.*) どうぞおかけください.
— *vt.* ... o seˈki ni tsuˈkaseˈru ...を席に着かせる [V]: I seated myself beside her. (*Watashi wa kanojo no soba ni suwatta.*) 私は彼女のそばに座った.

second¹ *adj.* **1** (after the first) niˈbañme no 2番目の; daiˈ-ni no 第2の: He was second in the race. (*Kare wa kyoosoo de ni-bañ datta.*) 彼は競争で2番だった. / the Second World War (*dai-niji sekai taiseñ*) 第2次世界大戦. **2** (another) moˈo hitoˈtsu no もう一つの: have a second helping (*okawari o suru*) お代わりをする.
— *n.* **1** (people) daiˈ-ni no hiˈtoˈ 第2の人; (things) daiˈ-ni no moˈnoˈ 第2のもの: You are the second to ask that question. (*Kimi wa sono shitsumoñ o suru futari-me da.*) 君はその質問をする二人目だ. **2** (day) fuˈtsuka 2日.

second² *n.* **1** (one sixtieth of a minute) byoˈo 秒: three minutes and fifty seconds (*sañ-pun gojuubyoo*) 3分50秒. **2** (moment) choˈtto no ma ちょっとの間: Wait a second. (*Chotto matte kudasai.*) ちょっと待ってください.

secondary *adj.* daiˈ-ni no 第2の;

ni-ˈji-teki na 2 次的な: a secondary product (*fukusañbutsu*) 副産物.

secondary school *n.* chuˈutoo-gaˈkkoo 中等学校.

secret *n.* hiˈmitsu 秘密; kiˈmitsu 機密: keep [reveal] a secret (*himitsu o mamoru [uchiakeru]*) 秘密を守る[打ち明ける] / The secret has leaked out. (*Sono himitsu wa moreta.*) その秘密は漏れた. / the secret of success (*seekoo no himitsu*) 成功の秘密.
— *adj.* hiˈmitsu no 秘密の: We have to keep this secret from him. (*Kore wa kare ni himitsu ni shite okanakereba naranai.*) これは彼に秘密にしておかなければならない.

secretary *n.* **1** (of an office) hiˈsho 秘書: She is the president's secretary. (*Kanojo wa shachoo no hisho desu.*) 彼女は社長の秘書です.
2 (of an organization) shoˈki 書記: a chief secretary (*shokichoo*) 書記長.
3 (of a government) choˈokañ 長官: the Secretary of State (U. S.) (*Kokumu-chookañ*) 国務長官.

secretly *adv.* hiˈmitsu ni 秘密に; koˈssoˈri to こっそりと: He secretly copied the document. (*Kare wa kossori sono shorui o kopii shita.*) 彼はこっそりその書類をコピーした.

sect *n.* (religion) shuˈuha 宗派; (group) buˈñpa 分派; (party) toˈoha 党派.

section *n.* **1** (part) buˈbuñ 部分: cut a cake into six sections (*o-kashi o muttsu ni kiru*) お菓子を六つに切る.
2 (department) buˈmoñ 部門; kaˈ課: the personnel section (*jiñjika*) 人事課.
3 (area) chiˈku 地区; kuˈiki 区域: a city's business section (*toshi no shoogyoo chiku*) 都市の商業地区.
4 (division) seˈtsu 節; raˈñ 欄: Section 2 of Chapter 1 (*dai is-shoo dai ni-setsu*) 第1章第2節 / the sports section of a newspaper (*shiñbuñ no supootsu-rañ*) 新聞のスポーツ欄.

secure *adj.* **1** (safe) aˈñzeñ na 安

全な: This house is secure in an earthquake. (*Kono uchi wa jishiñ ga kite mo añzeñ desu.*) この家は地震がきても安全です.
2 (firm) shiˈkkaˈri shita [shite iru] しっかりした[している]: Is the door secure? (*Doa wa shikkari shimatte imasu ka?*) ドアはしっかり閉まっていますか.
— *vt.* **1** (obtain) ... o kaˈkuho suru ...を確保する ⟨Ⅰ⟩: I secured my seat early. (*Watashi wa seki o hayame ni kakuho shita.*) 私は席を早めに確保した.
2 (fasten tightly) ... o shiˈkkaˈri shiˈmeˈru ...をしっかり閉める ⟨Ⅴ⟩: secure a window (*mado o shikkari shimeru*) 窓をしっかり閉める.
3 (make safe) ... o aˈñzeñ ni suru ...を安全にする ⟨Ⅰ⟩: secure one's house against robbery (*uchi ni gootoo ga hairanai yoo ni suru*) 家に強盗が入らないようにする.

security *n.* **1** (protection) boˈoee 防衛; hoˈshoo 保障: social security (*shakai-hoshoo*) 社会保障.
2 (safety) aˈñzeñ 安全: peace and security (*heewa to añzeñ*) 平和と安全.
3 (pledge) hoˈshoo 保証: security against loss (*soñgai ni taisuru hoshoo*) 損害に対する保証.

see *vt.* **1** (perceive with eyes) ... ga miˈeˈru ...が見える ⟨Ⅴ⟩: Can you see the bird over there? (*Asoko no tori ga miemasu ka?*) あそこの鳥が見えますか. / I saw her enter the room. (*Kanojo ga heya ni hairu no ga mieta.*) 彼女が部屋に入るのが見えた.
2 (look at) ... o miˈru ...を見る ⟨Ⅴ⟩: I saw the game on TV. (*Sono shiai wa terebi de mimashita.*) その試合はテレビで見ました. / See page 12. (*Juu-ni-peeji o mi nasai.*) 12ページを見なさい.
3 (understand) ... ga waˈkaˈru ...がわかる ⟨Ｃ⟩: I don't see why he failed. (*Kare ga doo shite shippai shita no ka wakaranai.*) 彼がどうして失敗したのかわからない.

seed 416

4 (meet) ... ni a｢u ...に会う C: I'm seeing her today. (*Kyoo kanojo ni au koto ni natte iru.*) きょう彼女に会うことになっている. / It's nice to see you. (*O-ai dekite ureshii desu.*) お会いできてうれしいです.
— *vi.* **1** (have the power of sight) mi｢e｣ru 見える V: Cats can see in the dark. (*Neko wa kurayami de mo me ga mieru.*) ねこは暗闇でも目が見える.
2 (understand) wa｢ka｣ru わかる C: I see. (*Wakarimashita.*) わかりました.
see off *vt.* ... o mi｢okuru ...を見送る C: I saw him off at the station. (*Watashi wa kare o eki de miokutta.*) 私は彼を駅で見送った.
seed *n.* **1** (of a plant) ta｢ne 種: sow seeds (*tane o maku*) 種をまく.
2 (source) ta｢ne 種: the seeds of doubt (*utagai no tane*) 疑いの種.
seek *vt.* **1** (look for) ... o sa｢gasu ...を捜す C: seek shelter from the rain (*amayadori no basho o sagasu*) 雨宿りの場所を捜す.
2 (try to obtain) ... o mo｢tome｣ru ...を求める V: She sought help from a lawyer. (*Kanojo wa bengoshi ni sukui o motometa.*) 彼女は弁護士に救いを求めた.
seem *vi.* ... no yo｢o ni mi｢e｣ru ...のように見える V; ... no yo｢o da ...のようだ: He seems tired. (*Kanojo wa tsukarete iru yoo ni mieru.*) 彼女は疲れているように見える. / It seems that the weather is improving. (*Tenki wa kaifuku suru yoo da.*) 天気は回復するようだ.
seize *vt.* **1** (grasp) ... o tsu｢ka｣mu ...をつかむ C: He seized me by the arm. (*Kare wa watashi no ude o tsukañda.*) 彼は私の腕をつかんだ.
2 (take possession of) ... o o｢oshuu suru ...を押収する I: The police seized a lot of drugs. (*Keesatsu wa tairyoo no mayaku o ooshuu shita.*) 警察は大量の麻薬を押収した.
— *vi.* (... o) tsu｢ka｣mu (...を)つかむ C; to｢rae｣ru とらえる V: seize on a chance (*kikai o toraeru*) 機会をとら

える.
seldom *adv.* me｢tta ni ‹verb›-nai めったに...ない: My father is seldom ill. (*Chichi wa metta ni byooki o shinai.*) 父はめったに病気をしない / He is seldom at home. (*Kare wa metta ni uchi ni inai.*) 彼はめったに家にいない.
select *vt.* ... o e｢ra｣bu ...を選ぶ C; se｢ñtaku suru 選択する I: I selected the present carefully. (*Watashi wa okurimono o shiñchoo ni erañda.*) 私は贈り物を慎重に選んだ.
selection *n.* se｢ñtaku 選択; e｢ra｣bu ko｢to｣ 選ぶこと: His selection of a computer took a long time. (*Kare wa koñpyuutaa o erabu no ni nagai jikañ ga kakatta.*) 彼はコンピューターを選ぶのに長い時間がかかった. / That store has a good selection of wines. (*Sono mise wa yoi waiñ o soroete iru.*) その店はよいワインをそろえている.
self *n.* ji｢buñ 自分; ji｢shiñ 自身: reveal one's true self (*hoñshoo o arawasu*) 本性を現わす.
selfish *adj.* ji｢buñ ho｢ñi no 自分本位の; wa｢gamama na わがままな: That's too selfish. (*Sore wa añmari jibuñ katte sugiru.*) それはあんまり自分勝手すぎる. / a selfish child (*wagamama na kodomo*) わがままな子ども.
sell *vt.* **1** (give something for money) ... o u｢ru ...を売る C: He sold his motorbike for ¥100,000. (*Kare wa baiku o juu-mañ-eñ de utta.*) 彼はバイクを10万円で売った.
2 (deal in) ... o u｢tte iru ...を売っている V: That store sells fruits. (*Ano mise wa kudamono o utte iru.*) あの店は果物を売っている.
— *vi.* u｢ru 売る C; u｢reru 売れる V: This book is selling well. (*Kono hoñ wa yoku urete iru.*) この本はよく売れている.
seller *n.* **1** (people) u｢rite 売り手; ha｢ñbainiñ 販売人.
2 (things) u｢reru mono｣ 売れるもの: a good seller (*yoku ureru mono*) よ

く売れるもの.

senate n. joˈoiñ 上院. ★ The Japanese equivalent is the House of Councilors (Saˈngiiñ) 参議院) of the Japanese Diet.

senator n. joˈoiñ giˈiñ 上院議員. ★ The Japanese equivalent is a member of the House of Councilors of the Japanese Diet.

send vt. **1** (of things) ... o oˈkuru ...を送る Ⓒ: I sent her a picture postcard. (Watashi wa kanojo ni ehagaki o okutta.) 私は彼女に絵はがきを送った.
2 (of people) ... o iˈkaseru ...を行かせる Ⓥ: He is going to send his son to college. (Kare wa musuko o daigaku e ikaseru tsumori de iru.) 彼は息子を大学へ行かせるつもりでいる.
send for ... vt. ... o yoˈbiˈ ni yaˈru ...を呼びにやる Ⓒ: send for a doctor (isha o yobi ni yaru) 医者を呼びにやる.

senior adj. **1** (older) toˈshiue no 年上の: He is senior to me by three years. (Kare wa watashi yori sañsai toshiue da.) 彼は私より3歳年上だ.
2 (higher in rank) uˈwayaku no 上役の; (in length of service) seˈñpai no 先輩の: Mr. Yamada is senior to me in our firm. (Yamada-sañ wa kaisha de watashi no señpai desu.) 山田さんは会社で私の先輩です.
3 (of a student) saˈijoˈokyuu no 最上級の.
— n. neˈñchoˈosha 年長者; seˈñpai 先輩; saˈijookyuusee 最上級生.

sensation n. **1** (feeling) kaˈñkaku 感覚; kaˈñji 感じ: have a sensation of fear (osoroshii kañji ga suru) 恐ろしい感じがする.
2 (excitement) daˈihyoˈobañ 大評判; seˈñseˈeshoñ センセーション: His novel caused a sensation. (Kare no shoosetsu wa daihyoobañ ni natta.) 彼の小説は大評判になった.

sense n. **1** (power to feel) kaˈñkaku 感覚: the sense of hearing (chookaku) 聴覚.

2 (feeling) kaˈñji 感じ: a sense of fatigue (hirookañ) 疲労感.
3 (wisdom) shiˈryo 思慮; fuˈñbetsu 分別; joˈoshiki 常識: a person of sense (fuñbetsu no aru hito) 分別のある人.
4 (ability to appreciate) ... o kaˈisuˈru koˈkoˈro ...を解する心; kaˈñneñ 観念: a sense of humor (yuumoa o kaisuru kokoro) ユーモアを解する心 / a sense of time (jikañ no kañneñ) 時間の観念.
5 (meaning) iˈmi 意味: the sense of a word (gogi) 語義 / This sentence does not make sense. (Kono buñ wa imi o nasanai.) この文は意味をなさない. / What he says is right in a sense. (Kare no itte iru koto wa aru imi de wa tadashii.) 彼の言っていることはある意味では正しい.
— vt. ... o kaˈñjiru ...を感じる Ⓥ: sense danger (kikeñ o kañjiru) 危険を感じる.

senseless adj. **1** (unconcious) kiˈo ushinatta [ushinatte iru] 気を失った[失っている]; muˈiˈshiki no 無意識の: He was knocked senseless. (Kare wa nagurarete ki o ushinatta.) 彼は殴られて気を失った.
2 (foolish) oˈroka na 愚かな; muˈfuˈñbetsu na 無分別な: senseless behavior (oroka na koodoo) 愚かな行動.

sensibility n. kaˈñkaku 感覚; (delicate feeling) kaˈñjusee 感受性: the sensibility of the skin to heat and cold (kandañ ni taisuru hifu no kañkaku) 寒暖に対する皮膚の感覚 / a writer of great sensibility (kañjusee no yutaka na sakka) 感受性の豊かな作家.

sensible adj. fuˈñbetsu no aˈru 分別のある; keˈñmee na 賢明な: It was sensible of you to follow his advice. (Kare no chuukoku ni shitagatta no wa keñmee datta.) 彼の忠告に従ったのは賢明だった.

sensitive adj. **1** (easily affected) biˈñkañ na 敏感な: a sensitive ear (biñkañ na mimi) 敏感な耳.

2 (easily hurt) su⌐gu ki ni suru すぐ気にする: She is sensitive to gossip. (*Kanojo wa uwasa o sugu ki ni suru.*) 彼女はうわさをすぐ気にする.

sentence *n.* **1** (group of words) bu⌐ń 文; bu⌐ńshoo 文章: write a sentence (*buń o kaku*) 文を書く.
2 (judgment) ha⌐ńketsu 判決; ke⌐ie 刑: a sentence of death (*shikee no hańketsu*) 死刑の判決 / serve one's sentence (*kee ni fukusu*) 刑に服す.

sentiment *n.* **1** (feeling) ka⌐ńjoo 感情: appeal to sentiment (*kańjoo ni uttaeru*) 感情に訴える.
2 (emotion) ka⌐ńshoo 感傷: There is no room for sentiment in competition. (*Shoobu ni kańshoo ga hairu yochi wa nai.*) 勝負に感傷が入る余地はない.
3 (thought) i⌐keń 意見; ka⌐ńsoo 感想: What are your sentiments about this problem? (*Kono mońdai ni tsuite no anata no kańsoo wa doo desu ka?*) この問題についてのあなたの感想はどうですか.

sentimental *adj.* ka⌐ńshoo-teki na 感傷的な; na⌐midamoro⌐i 涙もろい: a sentimental movie (*kańshoo-teki na eega*) 感傷的な映画 / a sentimental girl (*namidamoroi ońna-no-ko*) 涙もろい女の子.

separate *vt.* **1** (divide) ... o wa⌐ke⌐ru …分ける Ⓥ; ku⌐ǵiru 区切る Ⓒ: The two prefectures are separated by the river. (*Sono futatsu no keń wa kawa de wakerarete iru.*) その二つの県は川で分けられている.
2 (keep apart) ... o ki⌐rihana⌐su …を切り離す Ⓒ; bu⌐ńri suru 分離する ①: separate cream from milk (*kuriimu o gyuunyuu kara buńri suru*) クリームを牛乳から分離する.
— *vi.* wa⌐kare⌐ru 別れる Ⓥ; ha⌐nare⌐ru 離れる Ⓥ: We separated at the station. (*Watashi-tachi wa eki de wakareta.*) 私たちは駅で別れた.
— *adj.* **1** (not together) wa⌐ka⌐reta 分かれた; wa⌐ka⌐rete iru 分かれている: two separate gardens (*futatsu ni wakareta niwa*) 二つに分かれ

た庭.
2 (different) be⌐tsubetsu no 別々の: sit at separate tables (*betsubetsu no teeburu ni suwaru*) 別々のテーブルに座る.

separately *adv.* wa⌐ka⌐rete 分かれて; be⌐tsubetsu ni 別々に: We paid separately. (*Watashi-tachi wa betsubetsu ni okane o haratta.*) 私たちは別々にお金を払った.

separation *n.* **1** (being apart) bu⌐ńri 分離; be⌐tsuri 別離: I met him after a long separation. (*Kare to wa hisashiburi ni atta.*) 彼とは久しぶりに会った.
2 (living apart) be⌐kkyo 別居.

September *n.* ku⌐-gatsu 9 月.

sequence *n.* **1** (order) ju⌐ńjo 順序: arrange the names in alphabetical sequence (*namae o arufabetto juń ni naraberu*) 名前をアルファベット順に並べる.
2 (series) re⌐ńzoku 連続: a sequence of lectures (*ichireń no koogi*) 一連の講義.

serene *adj.* no⌐doka na のどかな; (peaceful) he⌐ewa na 平和な: serene weather (*nodoka na teńki*) のどかな天気 / lead a serene life (*heewa na seekatsu o okuru*) 平和な生活を送る.

series *n.* hi⌐to⌐tsuzuki ひと続き; re⌐ńzoku 連続: A series of rainy days followed. (*Amefuri no hi ga tsuzuita.*) 雨降りの日が続いた. / a television series (*reńzoku terebi bańgumi*) 連続テレビ番組.

serious *adj.* **1** (grave) ju⌐udai na 重大な: a serious mistake (*juudai na ayamari*) 重大な誤り.
2 (in earnest) ma⌐jime na まじめな; shi⌐ńkeń na 真剣な: He looked serious. (*Kare wa shińkeń na kao o shite ita.*) 彼は真剣な顔をしていた.

seriously *adv.* o⌐moku 重く; ma⌐jime ni まじめに: He is seriously ill. (*Kare wa juubyoo desu.*) 彼は重病です. / Don't take it seriously. (*Majime ni toranaide kudasai.*) まじめにとらないでください.

sermon *n.* se˥kkyoo 説教: preach a sermon (*sekkyoo suru*) 説教する.

serpent *n.* he˥bi 蛇.

servant *n.* shi˥yoonin 使用人; me-˥shitsu˥kai 召し使い: engage [dismiss] a servant (*shiyoonin o yatou [kaiko suru]*) 使用人を雇う[解雇する].

serve *vt.* **1** (wait at table) ... o da˥-su ...を出す ⓒ: She served us sushi. (*Kanojo wa watashi-tachi ni sushi o dashite kureta.*) 彼女は私たちにすしを出してくれた. / What time is dinner served? (*Yuushoku wa nan-ji desu ka?*) 夕食は何時ですか.

2 (work) ... ni tsu˥kaeru ...に仕える ⓥ; ha˥taraku 働く ⓒ: Mr. Suzuki served this company for thirty years. (*Suzuki-san wa kono kaisha ni sanjuu-nen-kan hataraita.*) 鈴木さんはこの会社に30年間働いた.

3 (be useful) ... no ya˥ku˥ ni tatsu ...の役に立つ ⓒ: I am glad if I can serve you. (*O-yaku ni tateba ure-shiku omoimasu.*) お役に立てばうれしく思います.

4 (supply) ... ni kyo˥okyuu suru ...に供給する Ⓣ: serve a town with water (*machi ni mizu o kyookyuu suru*) 町に水を供給する.

— *vi.* **1** (work) tsu˥tome˥ru 勤める ⓥ: She serves as secretary. (*Kanojo wa hisho to shite tsutomete iru.*) 彼女は秘書として勤めている.

2 (be useful) ya˥ku˥ ni tatsu 役に立つ ⓒ: This box serves for a seat. (*Kono hako wa isu to shite yaku ni tatsu.*) この箱はいすとして役に立つ.

service *n.* **1** (attention) sa˥abisu サービス: The service at this store is poor. (*Kono mise no saabisu wa yoku nai.*) この店のサービスはよくない. / Does this bill include the service charge? (*Kono kanjoo ni saabisu-ryoo wa fukumarete imasu ka?*) この勘定にサービス料は含まれていますか.

★ The Japanese 'saabisu' is often used in the sense of 'discount' or 'a free gift.'

2 (business) ji˥gyoo 事業; gyo˥omu 業務: the telephone service (*denwa*

jigyoo) 電話事業 / domestic [international] airline service (*kokunai-sen [kokusaisen]*) 国内[国際]線.

3 (duty) tsu˥tome˥ 勤め: public service (*koomu*) 公務.

4 (helpful act) ji˥nryoku 尽力; ho-˥neori˥ 骨折り: do a person a service (*hito no yaku ni tatsu*) 人の役に立つ.

session *n.* **1** (meeting) ka˥igi 会議: go into session (*kaikai suru*) 開会する.

2 (period) ka˥iki 会期: a session of the Diet (*kokkai no kaiki*) 国会の会期.

set *vt.* **1** (put) ... o o˥ku ...を置く ⓒ: set a book on the desk (*tsukue no ue ni hon o oku*) 机の上に本を置く.

2 (arrange) ... o to˥tonoe˥ru ...を整える ⓥ; se˥tto suru セットする Ⓣ: I want my hair washed and set. (*Kami o aratte setto shite kudasai.*) 髪を洗ってセットしてください.

3 (fix) ... o ki˥meru ...を決める ⓥ: set the date for a meeting (*kaigi no hidori o kimeru*) 会議の日取りを決める.

4 (record) ... o ta˥te˥ru ...を立てる ⓥ: set a new record (*shin kiroku o tateru*) 新記録を立てる.

— *vi.* **1** (sink) shi˥zumu 沈む ⓒ: The sun sets in the west. (*Taiyoo wa nishi ni shizumu.*) 太陽は西に沈む.

2 (become solid) ka˥tamaru 固まる ⓒ: The jelly has set. (*Zerii ga katamatta.*) ゼリーが固まった.

— *n.* **1** (group) hi˥to˥soroi ひとそろい; se˥tto セット: a set of tools (*doo-gu hitosoroi*) 道具ひとそろい / a coffee set (*koohii setto*) コーヒーセット.

2 (apparatus) ju˥shi˥nki 受信機; ju˥zo˥oki 受像機: a television set (*terebi juzooki*) テレビ受像機.

— *adj.* **1** (fixed) ki˥merareta 決められた: a set phrase (*kimari monku*) 決まり文句.

2 (ready) 〈verb〉-(y)oo to suru ...(よ)うとする: I was set to leave when he came. (*Dekakeyoo to shita toki* *kare ga kita.*) 出かけようとしたとき彼が来た.

set about ... *vt.* ... o ha⌐jimeru ...を始める V: set about a job (*shigoto o haˈjimeru*) 仕事を始める.

set off *vi.* shu⌐ppatsu suru 出発する I: set off on a trip (*tabi ni shuppatsu suru*) 旅に出発する.

set up *vt.* ... o su⌐etsuke⌐ru ...を据え付ける V: set up a tent (*teñto o haru*) テントを張る.

setting *n.* bu⌐tai so⌐ochi 舞台装置; haˈikee 背景: Kyoto is the setting of this play. (*Kyooto ga kono geki no butai desu.*) 京都がこの劇の舞台です.

settle *vt.* **1** (put in order) ... o ka⌐iketsu suru ...を解決する I: The lawyer settled the matter. (*Beñgoshi wa sono moñdai o kaiketsu shita.*) 弁護士はその問題を解決した.
2 (place) ... o o⌐ku ...を置く C: She gently settled the vase on the table. (*Kanojo wa sono kabiñ o sotto teeburu no ue ni oita.*) 彼女はその花びんをそっとテーブルの上に置いた.
3 (pay) ... o shi⌐hara⌐u ...を支払う C; se⌐esañ suru 清算する I: settle a bill (*kañjoo o harau*) 勘定を払う.
— *vi.* **1** (make a home) (... ni) te⌐ejuu suru (...に)定住する I; sho⌐kumiñ suru 植民する I: They decided to settle in Hokkaido. (*Karera wa Hokkaidoo ni teejuu suru koto ni kimeta.*) 彼らは北海道に定住することに決めた.
2 (be decided) ki⌐maru 決まる C: Have you settled on a date for your departure? (*Shuppatsu no hi wa kimarimashita ka?*) 出発の日は決まりましたか.
3 (come to rest) (... ni) to⌐maru (...に)止まる C: The birds settled on the branches. (*Tori ga eda ni tomatta.*) 鳥が枝に止まった.

settlement *n.* **1** (agreement) ka⌐iketsu 解決: the settlement of a dispute (*fuñsoo no kaiketsu*) 紛争の解決.
2 (payment) se⌐esañ 清算: the set-

tlement of debts (*shakkiñ no seesañ*) 借金の清算.
3 (colony) sho⌐kumiñ⌐chi 植民地.

seven *pron.* na⌐na⌐tsu 七つ; (things) na⌐na-ko 7個; (people) shi⌐chi⌐-niñ 7人.
— *n.* (figure) na⌐na [shi⌐chi⌐] 7; (hour) shi⌐chi⌐-ji 7時; (minute) shi⌐chi[na⌐na]-fuñ 7分; (age) na⌐na-sai 7歳.
— *adj.* na⌐na⌐tsu no 七つの; (people) shi⌐chi⌐-niñ no 7人の; (things) na⌐na-ko no 7個の; (age) na⌐na-sai no 7歳の.

seventeen *pron.* ju⌐ushichi⌐ [ju⌐una⌐na] 17; (people) ju⌐ushichi⌐-niñ 17人; (things) ju⌐unana-ko 17個.
— *n.* (figure) ju⌐ushichi⌐ [ju⌐una⌐na] 17; (hour) ju⌐ushichi⌐-ji 17時; (minute) ju⌐unana⌐-fuñ 17分; (age) ju⌐unana⌐-sai 17歳.
— *adj.* ju⌐ushichi⌐ [ju⌐una⌐na] no 17の; (people) ju⌐ushichi⌐-niñ no 17人の; (things) ju⌐unana-ko no 17個の; (age) ju⌐unana⌐-sai no 17歳の.

seventeeth *adj.* ju⌐unana-bañme⌐ no 17番目の; da⌐i-ju⌐una⌐na no 第17の.
— *n.* **1** (people) ju⌐unana-bañme⌐ no hiˈto⌐ 17番目の人; (things) ju⌐unana-bañme⌐ no mo⌐no⌐ 17番目のもの.
2 (day) ju⌐ushichi-nichi⌐ 17日.
3 (fraction) ju⌐ushichi-buñ no ichi⌐ 17分の1.

seventh *adj.* na⌐na-bañme⌐ no 7番目の; da⌐i-⌐na⌐na no 第7の.
— *n.* **1** (people) na⌐na-bañme⌐ no hiˈto⌐ 7番目の人; (things) na⌐na-bañme⌐ no mo⌐no⌐ 7番目のもの.
2 (day) na⌐noka 7日.
3 (fraction) na⌐na-buñ no ichi⌐ 7分の1.

seventieth *adj.* na⌐najuu-bañme⌐ no 70番目の; da⌐i-na⌐na⌐juu no 第70の.
— *n.* **1** (people) na⌐najuu-bañme⌐ no hiˈto⌐ 70番目の人; (things) na⌐na-juu-bañme⌐ no mo⌐no⌐ 70番目のもの.

seventy pron. shiｒchijuｌu [naｒnaｌjuu] 70; (people) shiｒchijuｌu-niñ 70 人; (things) shiｒchijuｌk-ko [naｒnajuｌk-ko] 70 個.
— n. (figure) shiｒchijuｌu [naｒnaｌjuu] 70; (age) shiｒchijuｌs-sai [naｒnajuｌs-sai] 70 歳.
— adj. shiｒchijuｌu no 70 の; (people) shiｒchijuｌu-niñ no 70 人の; (things) shiｒchijuｌk-ko [naｒnajuｌk-ko] no 70 個の; (age) shiｒchijuｌs-sai [naｒnajuｌs-sai] 70 歳の.

several adj. iｒkutsu-ka no いくつかの; (people) suｒu-niñ no 数人の; (things) suｒu-ko no 数個の: I stayed at the hotel for several days. (Watashi wa sono hoteru ni suu-jitsu taizai shita.) 私はそのホテルに数日滞在した.

severe adj. 1 (strict, rigorous) kiｒbishiｌi 厳しい: a severe teacher (kibishii señsee) 厳しい先生 / a severe winter (kibishii fuyu) 厳しい冬.
2 (keen) haｒgeshiｌi 激しい: severe competition (hageshii kyoosoo) 激しい競争.

sew vt. ... o nuｌu ...を縫う Ⓒ: sew a dress (doresu o nuu) ドレスを縫う.

sewer n. (underground pipe) geｒsuｌidoo 下水道; geｒsuikañ 下水管.

sex n. seｌe 性; seｒebetsu 性別; seｌkkusu セックス: Anybody can apply, regardless of sex. (Seebetsu ni kañkee naku dare de mo oobo dekimasu.) 性別に関係なくだれでも応募できます. ★ The Japanese 'sekkusu' is used only in the sense of 'sexual behavior.'

sexual adj. seｌe no 性の; seｒe-teki na 性的な: sexual harassment (seku-hara) セクハラ / sexual intercourse (see-kooshoo) 性交渉.

sexy adj. seｒe-teki miryoku no aｒru 性的魅力のある; seｌkushii na セクシーな: a sexy woman (sekushii na josee) セクシーな女性.

shabby adj. boｒroboro no ぼろぼろの; kiｒfuruｌshita 着古した: a shabby coat (boroboro no uwagi) ぼろぼろの上着.

shade n. 1 (shelter) kaｌge 陰; hiｒkage 日陰: Please dry it in the shade. (Sore wa hikage ni hoshite kudasai.) それは日陰に干してください.
2 (color) iｒroai 色合い: a lighter shade of green (usui iroai no midori) 薄い色合いの緑.
3 (of a lamp) kaｌsa かさ; (of a window) hiｒyoke 日除け; buｒraiñdo ブラインド: pull down [up] the shades (buraiñdo o sageru [ageru]) ブラインドを下げる[上げる].
— vt. ... o saｒegiｌru ...を遮る Ⓒ: I shaded my eyes from the sun with my hand. (Watashi wa te de hizashi o saegitta.) 私は手で日差しを遮った.

shadow n. 1 (dark image) kaｌge 影: a man's shadow on the wall (kabe ni utsutta hito no kage) 壁に映った人の影.
2 (darkness) kaｌge 陰: The north side of the house is in shadow. (Ie no kitagawa wa kage ni natte iru.) 家の北側は陰になっている.

shady adj. kaｌge no ooi 陰の多い; hiｒkage no 日陰の: a shady path (hikage no komichi) 日陰の小道.

shaft n. e 柄; jiｒku 軸: the shaft of an ax (ono no e) 斧の柄 / the shaft of an arrow (ya no jiku) 矢の軸.

shake vt. 1 (move quickly) ... o fuｒru ...を振る Ⓒ; yuｒsuru 揺する Ⓒ: He shook his head. (Kare wa kubi o yoko ni futta.) 彼は首を横に振った. / An earthquake shook the building. (Jishiñ ga biru o yusutta.) 地震がビルを揺すった.
2 (disturb) ... o doｒoyoo saseru ...を動揺させる Ⓥ: We were shaken by the news. (Watashi-tachi wa sono shirase ni dooyoo shita.) 私たちはその知らせに動揺した.
— vi. fuｒrueru 震える Ⓥ; yuｒreru 揺れる Ⓥ: The children were shaking with cold. (Kodomo-tachi wa samukute furuete ita.) 子どもたちは寒くて震えていた.
— n. shiｒñdoo 振動[震動]: give a pole a shake (sao o yusuru) さおを揺

する.

shall *aux.* **1** [show the future] ... deˈshoˈo ...でしょう; daˈroˈo だろう: I shall succeed this time. (*Koñdo wa seekoo suru deshoo.*) 今度は成功するでしょう.

2 [request] ⟨verb⟩-mashoˈo ...ましょう: Shall I open the window? (*Mado o akemashoo ka?*) 窓を開けましょうか. / Shall we dance? (*Odori-mashoo ka?*) 踊りましょうか.

shallow *adj.* **1** (not deep) aˈsai 浅い: a shallow lake (*asai mizuumi*) 浅い湖.

2 (not serious) aˈsaˈhaka na あさはかな: a shallow mind (*asahaka na kokoro*) あさはかな心.

sham *n.* miˈsekake 見せかけ; goˈma-kashi ごまかし: His bravery is a mere sham. (*Kare no yuuki wa tañ-naru misekake da.*) 彼の勇気は単なる見せかけだ.
— *adj.* niˈse no 偽の: a sham pearl (*nise no shiñju*) 偽の真珠.

shame *n.* **1** (feeling) haˈzukashiˈi oˈmoˈi 恥ずかしい思い: The child blushed with shame. (*Sono ko wa hazukashikute akaku natta.*) その子は恥ずかしくて赤くなった.

2 (disgrace) haˈji 恥: His behavior brought shame on his school. (*Kare no koodoo wa gakkoo ni haji o kakaseta.*) 彼の行動は学校に恥をかかせた.

3 (pity) zaˈñneˈñ na koˈtoˈ 残念なこと: It's a shame that you missed the party. (*Kimi ga paatii ni de-rarenakatta no wa zañneñ da.*) 君がパーティーに出られなかったのは残念だ.
— *vt.* ... ni haˈjiˈ o kaˈkaseˈru ...に恥をかかせる ⟨V⟩: He has shamed his parents. (*Kare wa oya ni haji o kakaseta.*) 彼は親に恥をかかせた.

shameful *adj.* haˈzubeˈki 恥ずべき: shameful conduct (*hazubeki kooi*) 恥ずべき行為.

shameless *adj.* haˈjishiˈrazu no 恥知らずの; zuˈuzuushiˈi ずうずうしい: a shameless liar (*hajishirazu no usotsuki*) 恥知らずのうそつき.

shampoo *n.* shaˈñpuu シャンプー; seˈñpatsu 洗髪.
— *vt.* kaˈmiˈ o aˈrau 髪を洗う ⟨C⟩: Shampoo and set, please. (*Kami o aratte setto shite kudasai.*) 髪を洗ってセットしてください.

shape *n.* **1** (figure) kaˈtachi 形; suˈgata 姿: What shape is it? (*Sore wa doñna katachi o shite imasu ka?*) それはどんな形をしていますか.

2 (condition) joˈotai 状態; choˈo-shi 調子: He is in good shape. (*Kare wa karada no chooshi ga yoi.*) 彼は体の調子がよい.
— *vt.* ... no kaˈtachi ni tsukuˈru ...の形に作る ⟨C⟩: shape clay into a cup (*neñdo de chawañ o tsukuru*) 粘土で茶碗を作る.

shapeless *adj.* kaˈtachi ga kuzu-zuˈreta [kuzuˈrete iru] 形が崩れた[崩れている]; buˈkaˈkkoo na 不格好な: a shapeless hat (*bukakkoo na boo-shi*) 不格好な帽子.

share *vt.* ... o waˈkeˈru ...を分ける ⟨V⟩: We shared the profits equally. (*Watashi-tachi wa rieki o hito-shiku waketa.*) 私たちは利益を等しく分けた.
— *vi.* (... o) buˈñtañ suru (...を)分担する ⟨I⟩: share in the expense (*hi-yoo o buñtañ suru*) 費用を分担する.
— *n.* **1** (part) waˈkemaˈe 分け前: He asked for a share of the prop-erty. (*Kare wa zaisañ no wakemae o yookyuu shita.*) 彼は財産の分け前を要求した.

2 (stock) kaˈbu 株: I have shares in that company. (*Watashi wa ano kaisha no kabu o motte imasu.*) 私はあの会社の株を持っています.

shareholder *n.* kaˈbuˈnushi 株主.

sharp *adj.* **1** (of an edge) suˈrudoˈi 鋭い: a sharp knife (*surudoi naifu*) 鋭いナイフ.

2 (abrupt; steep) kyuˈu na 急な: make a sharp turn (*kyuu-kaabu o kiru*) 急カーブを切る / a sharp slope (*kyuu na sakamichi*) 急な坂道.

3 (clear) haˈkkiˈri shita [shite iru] はっきりした[している]: a sharp contrast (*hakkiri shita taishoo*) はっきりした対照.

4 (shrewd) a⌐tama no kire¬ru 頭の切れる: a sharp businessman (*atama no kireru jitsugyooka*) 頭の切れる実業家.
— *n.* (musical note) sha⌐apu シャープ.

shapen *vt.* ... o to⌐garaseru ...をとがらせる Ⓥ; ke⌐zuru 削る Ⓒ: sharpen a pencil (*eñpitsu o kezuru*) 鉛筆を削る.

shatter *vt.* ... o ko⌐nagona ni kowa¬su ...を粉々に壊す Ⓒ: The ball shattered the window. (*Sono booru wa mado o konagona ni kowashita.*) そのボールは窓を粉々に壊した.

shave *vi.* hi⌐ge o so¬ru ひげをそる Ⓒ: I shave every day. (*Watashi wa mainichi hige o soru.*) 私は毎日ひげをそる.
— *vt.* ... o so¬ru ...をそる Ⓒ: shave one's beard (*hige o soru*) ひげをそる.
— *n.* hi⌐gesori¬ ひげそり: Haircut and shave, please. (*Sañpatsu to higesori o o-negai shimasu.*) 散髪とひげそりをお願いします.

she *pron.* ka⌐nojo 彼女; a⌐no oñna no hito¬ あの女の人; [polite] a⌐no kata¬ あの方: She wanted to know my name. (*Kanojo wa watashi no namae o kikitagatta.*) 彼女は私の名前を聞きたがった. / She is my teacher. (*Ano oñna no hito wa watashi no señsee desu.*) あの女の人は私の先生です. / Who is she? (*Ano kata wa dare desu ka?*) あの方はだれですか.

shed[1] *n.* ko⌐ya 小屋; mo⌐nookigoya 物置小屋.

shed[2] *vt.* **1** (make flow) ... o na⌐ga¬su ...を流す Ⓒ: shed tears (*namida o nagasu*) 涙を流す.
2 (drop off) ... o o⌐to¬su ...を落とす Ⓒ: Those trees shed their leaves in autumn. (*Kono ki wa aki ni ha o otoshimasu.*) この木は秋に葉を落とします.

sheep *n.* hi⌐tsuji 羊.

sheer *adj.* **1** (complete) ma⌐ttaku no まったくの: It's sheer nonsense to try that. (*Soñna koto o suru no wa mattaku no nañseñsu da.*) そんなことをするのはまったくのナンセンスだ.
2 (very thin) go⌐ku u¬sui ごく薄い: sheer stockings (*goku usui sutokkiñgu*) ごく薄いストッキング.

sheet *n.* **1** (cloth) shi⌐itsu シーツ; shi⌐kifu 敷布: put clean sheets on the bed (*kiree na shiitsu o beddo ni shiku*) きれいなシーツをベッドに敷く.
2 (single piece) i⌐chi¬-mai 1 枚: a sheet of paper (*kami ichi-mai*) 紙 1 枚.

sheet music *n.* ga⌐kufu 楽譜.

shelf *n.* ta⌐na 棚: fix a shelf (*tana o tsukeru*) 棚をつける / put a book on the shelf (*hoñ o tana no ue ni oku*) 本を棚の上に置く.

shell *n.* **1** (seashell) ka⌐igara 貝殻: gather shells (*kaigara o hirou*) 貝殻を拾う.
2 (nutshell) ka⌐ra¬ 殻: peanut shells (*piinattsu no kara*) ピーナッツの殻.
3 (pod) sa⌐ya さや.
— *vt.* ... o ka⌐ra¬ kara to⌐rida¬su ...を殻から取り出す Ⓒ; ... no sa⌐ya o mu⌐ku ...のさやをむく Ⓒ: shell peas (*mame no saya o muku*) 豆のさやをむく.

shellfish *n.* ka⌐i 貝.

shelter *n.* **1** (protection) hi⌐nañ 避難; ho⌐go 保護: take shelter from the rain (*amayadori o suru*) 雨宿りをする.
2 (place) hi⌐nañjo 避難所: a bus shelter (*basu no machiaijo*) バスの待合所.
— *vt.* ... o ho⌐go suru ...を保護する Ⓣ: The trees sheltered the house from a storm. (*Ki ga arashi kara ie o mamotta.*) 木が嵐から家を守った.
— *vi.* hi⌐nañ suru 避難する Ⓣ: shelter under a tree (*ki no shita ni hinañ suru*) 木の下に避難する.

shepherd *n.* hi⌐tsuji¬kai 羊飼い.

sherbet *n.* sha⌐abetto シャーベット.

shield *n.* (protection against weapons) ta⌐te 楯; (protective cover) ho⌐go¬butsu 保護物.

— *vt.* ...o ho⌐go¬ suru ...を保護する ①; ka⌐ba¬u かばう ©: He shielded me from danger. (*Kare wa kikeñ kara watashi o kabatte kureta.*) 彼は危険から私をかばってくれた.

shift *vt.* (change) ...o ka⌐e¬ru ...を変える ⓥ; (move) u⌐tsu¬su 移す ©: I shifted the bed from the room. (*Watashi wa beddo o heya kara utsushita.*) 私はベッドを部屋から移した.

— *vi.* ka⌐wa¬ru 変わる ©: The wind shifted to the south. (*Kaze ga minami muki ni kawatta.*) 風が南向きに変わった.

— *n.* **1** (change) he⌐ñka¬ 変化; te⌐ñkañ 転換: a shift in policy (*seesaku no teñkañ*) 政策の転換.

2 (a period of work) ko⌐otai 交替: They work in eight-hour shifts. (*Kare-ra wa hachi-jikañ kootai de hataraku.*) 彼らは8時間交替で働く.

shine *vi.* ka⌐gaya¬ku 輝く; hi⌐¬ka¬ru 光る ©: The moon is shining brightly. (*Tsuki ga akaruku kagayaite iru.*) 月が明るく輝いている.

— *vt.* **1** (give out light) ...o te⌐¬ra¬su ...を照らす ©: He shone a flashlight on me. (*Kare wa watashi ni kaichuu-deñtoo o terashita.*) 彼は私に懐中電灯を照らした.

2 (polish) ...o mi⌐gaku ...を磨く ©: shine one's shoes (*kutsu o migaku*) 靴を磨く.

ship *n.* fu⌐ne 船: When does the ship sail? (*Fune wa nañ-ji ni demasu ka?*) 船は何時に出ますか. / a passenger ship (*kyakuseñ*) 客船.
★ 'Boat' is also called '*fune.*'

— *vt.* **1** (send) ...o o⌐kuru ...を送る ©: We will ship the goods to you immediately. (*Shinamono wa sugu ni o-okuri shimasu.*) 品物はすぐにお送りします.

2 (carry by ship) ...o fu⌐ne de ha⌐¬kobu ...を船で運ぶ ©: The cars were shipped to Hokkaido. (*Kuruma wa fune de Hokkaidoo e hakobareta.*) 車は船で北海道へ運ばれた.

shipment *n.* ha⌐ssoo 発送; (goods) tsu⌐mini 積み荷: The goods are ready for shipment. (*Shinamono wa hassoo no juñbi ga dekite imasu.*) 品物は発送の準備ができています. / When can we expect the shipment to arrive? (*Tsumini wa itsu tsukimasu ka?*) 積み荷はいつ着きますか.

shirt *n.* **1** (garment) wa⌐ishatsu ワイシャツ: put on [take off] a shirt (*waishatsu o kiru [nugu]*) ワイシャツを着る[脱ぐ].

2 (undershirt) sha⌐tsu シャツ.
★ Japanese '*shatsu*' is used only in this sense.

shiver *vi.* fu⌐rueru 震える ⓥ: He was shivering with cold. (*Kare wa samukute furuete ita.*) 彼は寒くて震えていた.

— *n.* fu⌐rue 震え; mi⌐bu¬rui 身震い.

shock *n.* **1** (blow) da⌐geki 打撃; sho⌐kku ショック: My father's death was a great shock to me. (*Chichi no shi wa watashi ni totte ooki-na dageki datta.*) 父の死は私にとって大きな打撃だった.

2 (violent shake) sho⌐ogeki 衝撃; shi⌐ñdoo 震動: the shock of an explosion (*bakuhatsu no shoogeki*) 爆発の衝撃 / the shock of an earthquake (*jishiñ no shiñdoo*) 地震の震動.

— *vt.* ...ni sho⌐ogeki [sho¬kku] o a⌐taeru ...に衝撃[ショック]を与える ⓥ: We were shocked by the accident. (*Watashi-tachi ni wa sono jiko wa shokku datta.*) 私たちにはその事故はショックだった.

shoe *n.* ku⌐tsu 靴: put on [take off] one's shoes (*kutsu o haku [nugu]*) 靴をはく[脱ぐ] / shoe store (*kutsuya*) 靴屋.

shoemaker *n.* ku⌐tsu¬ya 靴屋; ku⌐tsuna¬oshi 靴直し.

shoot *vt.* **1** (fire) ...o u⌐tsu ...を撃つ ©: shoot a gun (*teppoo o utsu*) 鉄砲を撃つ.

2 (make a film) ...o sa⌐tsuee suru ...を撮影する ①: The film was shot in New York. (*Sono eega wa Nyuu Yooku de satsuee sareta.*) そ

の映画はニューヨークで撮影された.
— **vi. 1** (fire) (... o) uｌtsu (...を)撃
つ C: He shot at the target. (*Kare
wa mato o megakete utta.*) 彼は的
をめがけて撃った.
2 (move quickly) iｌkioi yoｌku to-
ｌbidaｌsu 勢いよく飛び出す C: A cat
shot out of the room. (*Neko ga
heya kara ikioi yoku tobidashita.*)
猫が部屋から勢いよく飛び出した.
— **n.** (bud) shiｌﾑme 新芽: a bamboo shoot (*take no ko*) 筍.

shop *n.* miｌse 店; shoｌoteﾑ 商店:
open [close] a shop (*mise o hiraku
[shimeru]*) 店を開く[閉める] / an antique shop (*kottoohiﾑ-teﾑ*) 骨董品
店 / a duty-free shop (*meﾑzee-teﾑ*)
免税店.
— **vi.** kaｌimono o suru 買い物をする
I: I always shop at this supermarket. (*Watashi wa itsu-mo koko no
suupaa de kaimono o shimasu.*) 私
はいつもここのスーパーで買い物をします.

shopping *n.* kaｌimono 買い物:
Can we do some shopping at the
airport? (*Kono kuukoo de kaimono wa dekimasu ka?*) この空港で買
い物はできますか. / a shopping street
(*shooteﾑgai*) 商店街.

shore *n.* kiｌshiｌ 岸; (seashore) kaｌri-
gaﾑ 海岸.

short *adj.* **1** (not long) miｌjikaｌi 短
い: I had my hair cut short. (*Kami
o mijikaku katte moratta.*) 髪を短く
刈ってもらった. / a short vacation
(*mijikai kyuuka*) 短い休暇.
2 (not tall) seｌ no hiｌkuｌi 背の低い:
He is shorter than you. (*Kare wa
kimi yori se ga hikui.*) 彼は君より背
が低い.
3 (not enough) fuｌsoku shite iru 不
足している: We are short of hands.
(*Hitode ga fusoku shite iru.*) 人手
が不足している.

shortage *n.* fuｌsoku 不足; keｌtsu-
boo 欠乏: a shortage of food (*shokuryoo no fusoku*) 食料の不足.

shorten *vt.* ... o miｌjiｌkaku suru ...
を短くする I: shorten trousers by
three centimeters (*zuboﾑ o saﾑ-

seﾑchi mijikaku suru*) ズボンを3セン
チ短くする.

shorthand *n.* soｌkki 速記: write
in shorthand (*sokki de kaku*) 速記
で書く.

shortly *adv.* maｌmoｌnaku まもなく;
suｌgu ni すぐに: He will arrive shortly. (*Kare wa mamonaku toochaku
suru deshoo.*) 彼はまもなく到着するで
しょう.

shorts *n.* shoｌotopaｌﾑtsu ショートパ
ンツ; haｌﾑzuｌboﾑ 半ズボン.

shot *n.* **1** (firing) haｌssha 発射;
haｌppoo 発砲: take a shot at a bird
(*tori o neratte utsu*) 鳥をねらって撃つ.
2 (sound) juｌusee 銃声: I heard
two shots. (*Watashi wa juusee o
ni-hatsu kiita.*) 私は銃声を2発聞い
た.
3 (bullet) taｌmaｌ 弾: fire a shot
(*tama o utsu*) 弾を撃つ.
4 (photograph) saｌtsuee 撮影;
shaｌshiﾑ 写真: take a shot of a
shrine (*jiﾑja no shashiﾑ o toru*) 神
社の写真を撮る.
5 (golf) shoｌtto ショット.

should *aux.* **1** [obligation] ⟨verb⟩
beｌki da ...べきだ: You should go as
soon as possible. (*Kimi wa dekiru
dake hayaku iku beki da.*) 君はでき
るだけ早く行くべきだ. / What should I
do? (*Doo sureba yoi deshoo?*) どう
すればよいでしょう.
2 [expectation] ... haｌzu da ...はずだ:
The bus should be coming soon.
(*Basu wa sugu kuru hazu da.*) バス
はすぐ来るはずだ.
3 [concessive conditional] maｌﾑ-
ichi ⟨verb⟩-te[de] mo 万一...て[で]
も: If I should fail, I will try again.
(*Maﾑichi shippai shite mo moo
ichido yarimasu.*) 万一失敗してもも
う一度やります.

shoulder *n.* kaｌta 肩: carry a bag
over one's shoulder (*kabaﾑ o kata
ni kakeru*) かばんを肩にかける.

shout *vi.* oｌogoｌe de saｌkeｌbu 大声
で叫ぶ C: He shouted for help.
(*Kare wa tasuke o motomete oogoe de sakeﾑda.*) 彼は助けを求めて大

声で叫んだ.

shove vt. ... o oʰshinokeʰru ...を押しのける V: He shoved me aside. (Kare wa watashi o waki ni oshinoketa.) 彼は私を脇に押しのけた.
— n. hiʰtoʰoshi ひと押し; tsuʰki 突き: give a shove (gutto osu [tsuku]) ぐっと押す[突く].

shovel n. shaʰberu シャベル: remove snow with a shovel (shaberu de yuki o kaku) シャベルで雪をかく.
— vt. ... o shaʰberu de suʰkuu ...をシャベルですくう C: shovel sand into a bucket (suna o shaberu de sukutte baketsu ni ireru) 砂をシャベルですくってバケツに入れる.

show vt. (let be seen) ... o miʰseʰru ...を見せる V: Please show me some rings. (Yubiwa o misete kudasai.) 指輪を見せてください. / Please show me another. (Hoka no o misete kudasai.) ほかのを見せてください.
2 (point out) ... o oʰshieru ...を教える V: Please show me how to fill in this form. (Kono shorui no kakikata o oshiete kudasai.) この書類の書き方を教えてください. / Show me the way, please. (Michi o oshiete kudasai.) 道を教えてください.
3 (prove) ... o shiʰmeʰsu ...を示す C: He showed that he was right. (Kare wa jibuñ ga tadashii koto o shimeshita.) 彼は自分が正しいことを示した.
4 (guide) ... o aʰñnaʰi suru ...を案内する I: Please show me to my seat. (Watashi no seki o añnai shite kudasai.) 私の席に案内してください.
— vi. (appear) aʰrawareʰru 現れる V; miʰeʰru 見える V: Light was showing under the door. (Doa no shita kara akari ga miete ita.) ドアの下から明かりが見えていた.
— n. 1 (performance) shoʰo ショー; miʰsemonoʰ 見せ物: I would like to see a show while in town. (Machi ni iru aida ni shoo o mitai.) 町にいる間にショーを見たい.
2 (exhibition) teʰñjiʰkai 展示会;

teʰñraʰñkai 展覧会.

shower n. 1 (bath) shaʰwaa シャワー: take a shower (shawaa o abiru) シャワーを浴びる / I'd like a room with shower. (Shawaa tsuki no heya ni shitai.) シャワーつきの部屋にしたい. ★ Japanese 'shawaa' is used only in this sense.
2 (rain) niʰwaka-aʰme にわか雨: I was caught in a shower. (Watashi wa niwaka-ame ni atta.) 私はにわか雨に遭った.
— vi. 1 (wash) shaʰwaa o aʰbiru シャワーを浴びる V: I shower every morning. (Watashi wa maiasa shawaa o abiru.) 私は毎朝シャワーを浴びる.
2 (rain) niʰwaka-aʰme ga furu にわか雨が降る C: Suddenly it began to shower. (Totsuzeñ niwaka-ame ga furi-dashita.) 突然にわか雨が降り出した.

shriek vi. kaʰnakirigoʰe o dasu 金切り声を出す C; kyaʰtto saʰkeʰbu きゃっと叫ぶ C: She shrieked in horror. (Kanojo wa osoroshikute kyatto sakeñda.) 彼女は恐ろしくてきゃっと叫んだ.

shrill adj. suʰrudoʰi 鋭い; kaʰñdakaʰi かん高い: a shrill whistle (surudoi keeteki) 鋭い警笛.
— n. kaʰnakirigoʰe 金切り声; hiʰmee 悲鳴.

shrimp n. koʰebi 小えび. ★ In Japanese, 'lobster,' 'prawn,' and 'shrimp' are all called 'ebi.'

shrine n. jiʰñja 神社: Meiji Shrine (Meeji jiñguu) 明治神宮.

shrink vi. 1 (become smaller) chiʰjimu 縮む C: The shirt shrank when it was washed. (Arattara shatsu ga chijiñda.) 洗ったらシャツが縮んだ.
2 (draw back) hiʰruʰmu ひるむ C; shiʰrigoʰmi suru しりごみする I: He didn't shrink from danger. (Kare wa kikeñ ni hirumanakatta.) 彼は危険にひるまなかった.

shrub n. teʰeboku 低木; kaʰñboku 灌木.

shun *vt.* ... o sa𝄐ke𝄐ru ...を避ける Ⓥ: shun temptation (*yuuwaku o sakeru*) 誘惑を避ける.

shut *vt.* **1** (close) ... o shi𝄐me𝄐ru ...を閉める Ⓥ: Please shut the window. (*Mado o shimete kudasai.*) 窓を閉めてください.
2 (fold) ... o to𝄐ji𝄐ru ...を閉じる Ⓥ: shut a book (*hoñ o tojiru*) 本を閉じる.
— *vi.* shi𝄐ma𝄐ru 閉まる Ⓒ: This door won't shut. (*Kono doa wa shimaranai.*) このドアは閉まらない.

shutter *n.* **1** (of a camera) sha𝄐t-taa シャッター: press the shutter (*shattaa o osu*) シャッターを押す.
2 (of a house) a𝄐ma𝄐do 雨戸; sha𝄐t-taa シャッター: The shutter doesn't work well. (*Shattaa no guai ga warui.*) シャッターのくあいが悪い.

shy *adj.* ha𝄐zukashigari no 恥ずかしがりの; u𝄐chiki na 内気な: She is shy and dislikes parties. (*Kanojo wa hazukashigari de paatii ga kirai da.*) 彼女は恥ずかしがりでパーティーが嫌いだ.

sick *adj.* **1** (ill) byo𝄐oki no 病気の: He is sick in bed. (*Kare wa byooki de nete imasu.*) 彼は病気で寝ています.
2 (ready to vomit) ha𝄐kike𝄐 ga suru 吐き気がする; mu𝄐kamuka suru むかむかする: I am going to be sick. (*Haki-soo da.*) 吐きそうだ. / I feel sick. (*Kibuñ ga warui.*) 気分が悪い.
3 (tired of) u𝄐ñza𝄐ri shite (iru) うんざりして(いる): I am sick of the rain. (*Kono ame ni wa uñzari da.*) この雨にはうんざりだ.

sickness *n.* byo𝄐oki 病気: absence due to sickness (*byooki no tame no kesseki*) 病気のための欠席.

side *n.* **1** (edge) ga𝄐wa𝄐 側: the right [left] side of a road (*michi no migi[hidari]gawa*) 道の右[左]側.
2 (outside) so𝄐kume𝄐ñ 側面; yo𝄐ko 横: the side of a building (*biru no sokumeñ*) ビルの側面.
3 (surface) me𝄐ñ 面: the right [wrong] side of the paper (*kami no omote [ura] meñ*) 紙の表[裏]面.

4 (of a body) wa𝄐kibara わき腹: I feel a pain in my side. (*Wakibara ga itai.*) わき腹が痛い.
5 (next to something) so𝄐ba そば; wa𝄐ki𝄐 わき: Come and sit by my side. (*Soba e kite suwari nasai.*) そばへ来て座りなさい.
— *adj.* yo𝄐ko no 横の; so𝄐kume𝄐ñ no 側面の: a side gate (*yoko no moñ*) 横の門.

sideboard *n.* sho𝄐kki𝄐dana 食器棚: put the dishes in a sideboard (*shokkidana ni sara o ireru*) 食器棚に皿を入れる.

sidewalk *n.* ho𝄐doo 歩道: walk on the sidewalk (*hodoo o aruku*) 歩道を歩く.

siege *n.* ho𝄐oikolo𝄐geki 包囲攻撃: break a siege (*hooi o yaburu*) 包囲を破る.

sigh *vi.* ta𝄐mei𝄐ki o tsuku ため息をつく Ⓒ: He sighed with relief. (*Kare wa hotto shite tameiki o tsuita.*) 彼はほっとしてため息をついた.
— *n.* ta𝄐mei𝄐ki ため息: breathe a deep sigh (*fukai tameiki o tsuku*) 深いため息をつく.

sight *n.* **1** (power) shi𝄐ryoku 視力: have weak sight (*shiryoku ga yowai*) 視力が弱い.
2 (act) mi𝄐ru ko𝄐to 見ること: I caught sight of him in the crowd. (*Watashi wa hitogomi no naka de kare o mitsuketa.*) 私は人込みの中で彼を見つけた.
3 (view) ko𝄐okee 光景; na𝄐game𝄐 眺め: The sight of the lake was wonderful. (*Mizuumi no nagame wa subarashikatta.*) 湖の眺めはすばらしかった.
4 (something worth seeing) me𝄐e-sho𝄐 名所: the sights of Kyoto (*Kyooto no meesho*) 京都の名所.

sightseeing *n.* ka𝄐ñkoo 観光: I'd like a sightseeing brochure for this town. (*Kono machi no kañkoo pañfuretto ga hoshii no desu ga.*) この町の観光パンフレットが欲しいのですが. / a sightseeing bus (*kañkoo basu*) 観光バス / a sightseeing boat (*yuurañ-*

señ) 遊覧船.

sign *n*. **1** (notice) ke⌐eji 掲示; hyo⌐oshiki 標識: a road sign (*dooro hyooshiki*) 道路標識.

2 (signal) shi⌐ñgoo 信号: a stop sign (*teeshi shiñgoo*) 停止信号.

3 (indication) cho⌐okoo 兆候; ki⌐zashi 兆し: a sign of spring (*haru no kizashi*) 春の兆し.

4 (gesture) a⌐izu 合図: He gave me a sign to go. (*Kare wa ike to watashi ni aizu shita.*) 彼は行けと私に合図した.

— *vt*. ... ni sho⌐mee suru ...に署名する □; sa⌐iñ suru サインする □: He signed the check. (*Kare wa kogitte ni shomee shita.*) 彼は小切手に署名した. ★ Japanese use '*saiñ*' in the sense of 'signature.'

— *vi*. sho⌐mee suru 署名する □; sa⌐iñ suru サインする □: Please sign here. (*Koko ni saiñ shite kudasai.*) ここにサインしてください.

signal *n*. shi⌐ñgoo 信号; a⌐izu 合図: a signal of danger (*kikeñ shiñgoo*) 危険信号 / the signal for the start (*sutaato no aizu*) スタートの合図.

— *vt*. ... ni a⌐izu suru ...に合図する □: signal a taxi (*takushii ni aizu suru*) タクシーに合図する.

— *vi*. (... ni) a⌐izu suru (...に)合図する □: The policeman signaled to me to stop. (*Sono keekañ wa watashi ni tomare to aizu shita.*) その警官は私に止まれと合図した.

signature *n*. sho⌐mee 署名; sa⌐iñ サイン: put one's signature on a document (*shorui ni shomee suru*) 書類に署名する.

significance *n*. **1** (importance) ju⌐uyoosee 重要性; ju⌐udaisa 重大さ: a matter of great significance (*juuyoo na moñdai*) 重要な問題.

2 (meaning) i⌐gi 意義; i⌐mi 意味: the significance of a symbol (*kigoo no imi*) 記号の意味.

significant *adj*. **1** (important) ju⌐uyoo na 重要な: a significant promise (*juuyoo na yakusoku*) 重要な約束.

2 (having a meaning) i⌐miarige na 意味ありげな: a significant gesture (*imiarige na miburi*) 意味ありげな身ぶり.

signify *vt*. **1** (mean) ... o i⌐mi suru ...を意味する □: What does this road sign signify? (*Kono dooro hyooshiki wa nani o imi shimasu ka?*) この道路標識は何を意味しますか.

2 (show) ... o shi⌐me⌐su ...を示す ©; shi⌐raseru 知らせる Ⓥ: He signified his agreement by raising his right hand. (*Kare wa migite o agete sañi o shimeshita.*) 彼は右手を挙げて賛意を示した.

silence *n*. **1** (stillness) shi⌐zuke⌐sa 静けさ: the silence of the night (*yoru no shizukesa*) 夜の静けさ.

2 (no talking) chi⌐ñmoku 沈黙: break [keep] the silence (*chiñmoku o yaburu* [*mamoru*]) 沈黙を破る[守る].

silent *adj*. **1** (quiet) shi⌐zuka na 静かな: a silent forest (*shizuka na mori*) 静かな森.

2 (not speaking) da⌐ma⌐tte iru 黙っている; mu⌐goñ no 無言の: He remained silent. (*Kare wa damatte ita.*) 彼は黙っていた. / a silent protest (*mugoñ no koogi*) 無言の抗議.

silently *adv*. shi⌐zuka ni 静かに; da⌐ma⌐tte 黙って: The child nodded silently. (*Sono ko wa damatte unazuita.*) その子は黙ってうなずいた.

silk *n*. ki⌐nu 絹: raw silk (*ki-ito*) 生糸.

silkworm *n*. ka⌐iko かいこ.

silly *adj*. ba⌐ka na ばかな; ba⌐ka⌐geta ばかげた; ba⌐ka⌐gete iru ばかげている: Stop being silly. (*Baka na koto wa yoshi nasai.*) ばかなことはよしなさい. / a silly question (*bakageta shitsumoñ*) ばかげた質問.

silver *n*. gi⌐ñ 銀: This ring is made of silver. (*Kono yubiwa wa giñ de dekite iru.*) この指輪は銀でできている.

— *adj*. gi⌐ñ no 銀の; gi⌐ñsee no 銀製の: a silver spoon (*giñ no supuuñ*) 銀のスプーン.

similar *adj*. ru⌐iji shita [shite iru]

類似した[している]; ni￢te iru 似ている: Our tastes are similar. (*Watashi-tachi no shumi wa nite iru.*) 私たちの趣味は似ている.

similarity *n.* ru￢iji 類似; ni￢te iru koto¹ 似ていること: There are some similarities between their opinions. (*Kare-ra no iken ni wa nita tokoro ga aru.*) 彼らの意見には似たところがある.

similarly *adv.* do￢oyoo ni 同様に; o￢na¹jiku 同じく: I am to blame. But similarly, you are wrong. (*Watashi wa warui. Shikashi kimi mo dooyoo ni yoku nai.*) 私は悪い. しかし君も同様によくない.

simple *adj.* 1 (easy) ka￢ntan na 簡単な; ya￢sashii やさしい: a simple task (*kantan na shigoto*) 簡単な仕事 / The question was simple. (*Sono mondai wa yasashikatta.*) その問題はやさしかった.
2 (plain) shi￢sso na 質素な: lead a simple life (*shisso na seekatsu o okuru*) 質素な生活を送る.
3 (natural) ju￢nshin na 純真な: He is as simple as a child. (*Kare wa kodomo no yoo ni junshin da.*) 彼は子どものように純真だ.

simplicity *n.* 1 (easiness) ka￢ntan 簡単; yo￢oi 容易: The problem is simplicity itself. (*Sono mondai wa mattaku kantan da.*) その問題はまったく簡単だ.
2 (plainness) shi￢sso 質素: I like the simplicity of her dress. (*Kanojo no fukusoo no shisso na tokoro ga suki da.*) 彼女の服装の質素なところが好きだ.
3 (naturalness) ju￢nshinsa 純真さ; mu￢jaki¹sa 無邪気さ: a look of simplicity (*mujaki na hyoojoo*) 無邪気な表情.

simplify *vt.* ... o ka￢ntan ni suru ...を簡単にする □; ka￢nketsu ni suru 簡潔にする □: simplify sentences (*bunshoo o kanketsu ni suru*) 文章を簡潔にする.

simply *adv.* 1 (easily) ka￢ntan ni 簡単に; wa￢kariya¹suku わかりやすく:

explain simply (*wakariyasuku setsumee suru*) わかりやすく説明する.
2 (merely) ta￢n ni ... dake 単に...だけ; ta￢da ただ: He did it simply for the money. (*Kare wa tada o-kane no tame ni dake sore o yatta.*) 彼はただお金のためにだけそれをやった.
3 (really) ma￢ttaku まったく; ji￢tsu¹ ni 実に: That's simply ridiculous. (*Sore wa mattaku bakagete iru.*) それはまったくばかげている.

simultaneous *adj.* do￢oji no 同時の: simultaneous interpretation (*dooji tsuuyaku*) 同時通訳.

sin *n.* tsu￢mi 罪: commit a sin (*tsumi o okasu*) 罪を犯す.

since *prep.* ... i￢rai ...以来; i￢go 以後: I haven't seen her since last year. (*Kyonen irai kanojo ni atte imasen.*) 去年以来彼女に会っていません.
— *conj.* 1 (after that time) <verb>-te[de] i￢rai ...て[で]以来; <verb>-te [de] kara ...て[で]から: Two years have passed since I came to Japan. (*Nihon ni kite kara ni-nen tachimashita.*) 日本に来てから2年たちました.
2 (because) ... kara ...から: Since I have a meeting, I must go. (*Kaigi ga arimasu kara, ikanakereba narimasen.*) 会議がありますから, 行かなければなりません.

sincere *adj.* ko￢ko¹ro kara no 心からの; se￢ejitsu na 誠実な: sincere thanks (*kokoro kara no kansha*) 心からの感謝 / a sincere politician (*seejitsu na seejika*) 誠実な政治家.

sincerely *adv.* ko￢ko¹ro kara 心から; ho￢ntoo ni 本当に: I sincerely hope you will get well soon. (*Hayaku yoku narareru koto o kokoro kara o-inori shimasu.*) 早く良くなられることを心からお祈りします.
Sincerely yours, (at the end of a letter) ke￢egu 敬具.

sincerity *n.* se￢ejitsu 誠実; se￢ei 誠意: He spoke with sincerity. (*Kare wa seei o motte hanashita.*) 彼は誠意をもって話した.

sing *vi.* 1 (with the voice) u￢ta¹ o

uꞌtau 歌を歌う Ⓒ: I like to sing.
(Watashi wa uta o utau no ga suki
da.) 私は歌を歌うのが好きだ.
2 (of birds, etc.) naꞌku 鳴く Ⓒ; sa-
ꞌezuꞌru さえずる Ⓒ: The crickets are
singing. (Koorogi ga naite iru.) こお
ろぎが鳴いている. / The birds are
singing. (Tori ga saezutte iru.) 鳥
がさえずっている.
— vt. ... o uꞌtau ...を歌う Ⓒ: She
sang a sad song. (Kanojo wa kanashii uta o utatta.) 彼女は悲しい歌を
歌った.

singer n. kaꞌshu 歌手; uꞌtau hitoꞌ
歌う人: an opera singer (opera
kashu) オペラ歌手.

single adj. **1** (only one) taꞌtta hiꞌtoꞌtsu no たった一つの: I missed my
single chance. (Watashi wa tatta
hitotsu no chañsu o nogashita.) 私
はたった一つのチャンスを逃した.
2 (unmarried) doꞌkushiñ no 独身
の: He remained single. (Kare wa
dokushiñ de tooshita.) 彼は独身で
通した.
3 (for one person) hiꞌtori-yoo no
一人用の: reserve a single room (hi-
tori-beya o yoyaku suru) 一人部屋
を予約する.
— n. **1** (one thing) hiꞌtoꞌtsu no
moꞌnoꞌ 一つのもの.
2 (ticket) kaꞌtamichi-kiꞌppu 片道切
符.
3 (baseball) taꞌñda 単打; shiꞌñguru
hiꞌtto シングルヒット.

singles n. (of tennis) shiꞌñgurusu
シングルス: the men's singles (dañshi
shiñgurusu no shiai) 男子シングルス
の試合.

singular adj. **1** (remarkable) na-
ꞌmihazureta 並外れた; naꞌmiha-
zurete iru 並外れている; maꞌre ni
miꞌru まれに見る: a woman of singular beauty (mare ni miru bijiñ) まれ
に見る美人.
2 (strange) kiꞌmyoo na 奇妙な; fuꞌu-
gaꞌwari na 風変わりな: a person of
singular habits (fuugawari na kuse
no hito) 風変わりな癖の人.
3 (in grammar) taꞌñsuꞌu no 単数の:

a singular form (tañsuu-kee) 単数
形.

sink vi. **1** (go down) shiꞌzumu 沈む
Ⓒ: The ship hit a rock and sank.
(Sono fune wa iwa ni atatte shi-
zuñda.) その船は岩に当たって沈んだ.
2 (go lower) saꞌgaꞌru 下がる Ⓒ:
Prices are sinking. (Bukka ga sa-
gatte iru.) 物価が下がっている.
— vt. ... o shiꞌzumeru ...を沈める
Ⓥ: sink a ship (fune o shizumeru)
船を沈める.
— n. naꞌgashiꞌ 流し: wash the
dishes in the sink (nagashi de sara
o arau) 流して皿を洗う.

sip vt. ... o suꞌkoshi zutsu noꞌmu ...
を少しずつ飲む Ⓒ; suꞌsuru する Ⓒ:
sip hot coffee (atsui koohii o su-
suru) 熱いコーヒーをすする.

sir n. [used in polite expressions]:
Good morning, sir. (Ohayoo gozaimasu.) お早うございます. / May I help
you, sir? (Irasshaimase.) いらっしゃい
ませ. ★ There is no direct Japanese
equivalent. Various polite expressions are used instead.

sister n. (older) aꞌne 姉; (someone
else's older sister) (o-)ꞌneꞌesañ (お)
姉さん; (younger) iꞌmootoꞌ 妹;
(someone else's younger sister)
iꞌmooto-sañ 妹さん: sisters (shimai)
姉妹. ★ There is no direct Japanese equivalent to 'sister.'

sister-in-law n. (older) giꞌri no
ane 義理の姉; (younger) giꞌri no
imootoꞌ 義理の妹.

sit vi. **1** (rest) (... ni) suꞌwaru (...に)
座る Ⓒ; kaꞌkeꞌru かける Ⓥ: May I
sit here? (Koko ni suwatte mo ii
desu ka?) ここに座ってもいいです. /
He sat on the stool. (Kare wa sono
maruisu ni kaketa.) 彼はその丸いすに
かけた.
2 (perch) (... ni) toꞌmaru (...に)止ま
る Ⓒ: A strange bird is sitting in
the tree. (Minarenai tori ga ki ni
tomatte iru.) 見慣れない鳥が木に止ま
っている.

sit down vi. suꞌwaru 座る Ⓒ:
Please sit down. (Doozo o-suwari

kudasai.) どうぞお座りください.

site *n.* **1** (land) yo﹁ochi 用地; shi-﹁kichi 敷地: a site for a factory (*koo-joo no yoochi*) 工場の用地.

2 (place) ba﹁sho 場所; ge﹁ñba 現場: the site of an accident (*jiko-geñba*) 事故現場.

situation *n.* **1** (state of affairs) jo﹁osee 情勢; jo﹁okyoo 状況: The political situation has changed. (*Seeji-joosee ga kawatta*.) 政治情勢が変わった.

2 (position) ta﹁chiba﹂ 立場; kyo﹁o-guu 境遇: I am now in an awkward situation. (*Watashi wa ima mazui tachiba ni aru*.) 私はいままずい立場にある.

3 (job) tsu﹁tome﹂guchi 勤め口; sho-﹁ku 職: He's looking for a situation. (*Kare wa shoku o sagashite iru*.) 彼は職を探している.

six *pron.* mu﹁ttsu﹂ 六つ; (people) ro-﹁ku-niñ 6 人; (things) ro﹁k-ko 6 個.
　— *n.* (figure) ro﹁ku 6; (hour) ro-﹁ku﹂-ji 6 時; (minute) ro﹁p-puñ 6 分; (age) ro﹁ku﹂-sai 6 歳.
　— *adj.* mu﹁ttsu﹂ no 六つの; (people) ro﹁ku﹂-niñ no 6 人の; (things) ro﹁k-ko no 6 個の; (age) ro﹁ku﹂-sai no 6 歳の.

sixteen *pron.* ju﹁uroku﹂ 16; (people) ju﹁uroku﹂-niñ 16 人; (things) ju-﹁ro﹂k-ko 16 個.
　— *n.* (figure) ju﹁uroku﹂ 16; (hour) ju﹁uroku﹂-ji 16 時; (minute) ju﹁uro﹂p-puñ 16 分; (age) ju﹁uroku﹂-sai 16 歳.
　— *adj.* ju﹁uroku﹂ no 16 の; (people) ju﹁uroku﹂-niñ no 16 人の; (things) ju﹁uro﹂k-ko no 16 個の; (age) ju﹁uroku﹂-sai no 16 歳の.

sixteenth *adj.* ju﹁uroku-bañme﹂ no 16 番目の; da﹁i-ju﹁uroku﹂ no 第 16 の.
　— *n.* **1** (people) ju﹁uroku-bañme﹂ no hi﹁to﹂ 16 番目の人; (things) ju﹁uroku-bañme﹂ no mo﹁no﹂ 16 番目のもの.
　2 (day) ju﹁uroku-nichi 16 日.
　3 (fraction) ju﹁uroku-buñ no ichi﹂ 16 分の 1.

sixth *adj.* ro﹁ku-bañme﹂ no 6 番目の; da﹁i-ro﹁ku﹂ no 第 6 の.
　— *n.* **1** (things) ro﹁ku-bañme﹂ no mo﹁no﹂ 6 番目の; (people) ro﹁ku-bañme﹂ no hi﹁to﹂ 6 番目の人.
　2 (day) mu﹁ika 6 日.
　3 (fraction) ro﹁ku-buñ no ichi﹂ 6 分の 1.

sixtieth *adj.* ro﹁kujuu-bañme﹂ no 60 番目の; da﹁i-ro﹁kujuu﹂ no 第 60 の.
　— *n.* **1** (things) ro﹁kujuu-bañme﹂ no mo﹁no﹂ 60 番目のもの; (people) ro﹁kujuu-bañme﹂ no hi﹁to﹂ 60 番目の人.
　2 (fraction) ro﹁kujuu-buñ no ichi﹂ 60 分の 1.

sixty *pron.* ro﹁kuju﹂u 60; (people) ro﹁kuju﹂u-niñ 60 人; (things) ro﹁ku-ju﹂k-ko 60 個.
　— *n.* (figure) ro﹁kuju﹂u 60; (minute) ro﹁kujuu﹂p-puñ 60 分; (age) ro﹁ku-ju﹂s-sai 60 歳.
　— *adj.* ro﹁kuju﹂u no 60 の; (people) ro﹁kuju﹂u-niñ no 60 人の; (things) ro﹁kuju﹂k-ko no 60 個の; (age) ro﹁kuju﹂s-sai no 60 歳の.

size *n.* **1** (bigness) o﹁okisa 大きさ: The two rooms are the same size. (*Sono futatsu no heya wa onaji ookisa desu*.) その二つの部屋は同じ大きさです. / Show me something in this size, please. (*Kono ookisa no mono o misete kudasai*.) この大きさの物を見せてください.

2 (measurement) sa﹁izu サイズ; su﹁ñpoo 寸法: What is your shoe size? (*Anata no kutsu no saizu wa dono kurai desu ka?*) あなたの靴のサイズはどのくらいですか.

skate *n.* su﹁keeto﹂-gutsu スケート靴: a pair of skates (*sukeeto-gutsu is-soku*) スケート靴 1 足. ★ Japanese '*sukeeto*' is used in the sense of 'skating.'
　— *vi.* su﹁keeto o suru スケートをする 〔: skate on a pond (*ike de sukee-to o suru*) 池でスケートをする / go skating (*sukeeto ni iku*) スケートに行く.

skeleton *n.* **1** (bones) ko﹁kkaku 骨格; ga﹁ikotsu がい骨.

2 (building) ho｢negumi｣ 骨組み: the steel skeleton of a building (*biru no tekkotsu no honegumi*) ビルの鉄骨の骨組み.

sketch *n.* **1** (drawing) su｢ke｣tchi スケッチ; rya｢kuzu 略図: make a sketch of a tree (*ki no suketchi o suru*) 木のスケッチをする.

2 (outline) a｢rasuji あら筋; ga｢iryaku 概略: I gave them a rough sketch of my plan. (*Watashi wa kare-ra ni keekaku no gairyaku o shimeshita.*) 私は彼らに計画の概略を示した.

— *vt.* ... no su｢ke｣tchi o kaku ...のスケッチをかく ⓒ; ... o sha｢see suru ...を写生する ⓣ: sketch a cat (*neko o shasee suru*) ねこを写生する.

ski *n.* su｢ki｣i スキー: glide on skis (*sukii de suberu*) スキーで滑る.

★ Japanese '*sukii*' is used in the sense of 'skiing.'

— *vi.* su｢ki｣i o suru スキーをする ⓣ: ski down a slope (*shameñ o sukii de suberioriru*) 斜面をスキーで滑り下りる.

skill *n.* **1** (ability) shu｢wañ 手腕; jo｢ozu じょうず: play the violin with skill (*baioriñ o joozu ni hiku*) バイオリンをじょうずに弾く.

2 (craft) gi｢noo 技能; gi｢jutsu 技術: Reading and writing are different skills. (*Yomu no to kaku no wa chigau ginoo da.*) 読むのと書くのは違う技能だ.

skilled *adj.* u｢de no i｣i 腕のいい; ju｢kureñ shita [shite iru] 熟練した[している]: a skilled carpenter (*ude no ii daiku*) 腕のいい大工 / skilled hands (*jukureñkoo*) 熟練工.

skillfull *adj.* ju｢kureñ shita [shite iru] 熟練した[している]; jo｢ozu na じょうずな: a skillful surgeon (*jukureñ shita geka-i*) 熟練した外科医 / He is skillful at teaching. (*Kare wa oshieru no ga joozu da.*) 彼は教えるのがじょうずだ.

skim *vt.* **1** (remove) ... o su｢kuito｣ru ...をすくい取る ⓒ: skim the cream off the milk (*gyuunyuu kara ku-*

riimu o sukuitoru) 牛乳からクリームをすくい取る.

2 (read quickly) ... o za｢tto yo｣mu ...をざっと読む ⓒ: skim the headlines of a newspaper (*shiñbuñ no midashi o zatto yomu*) 新聞の見出しをざっと読む.

3 (move swiftly) ... o su｢resure ni tobu ...をすれすれに飛ぶ ⓒ: A bird skimmed the water. (*Tori ga suimeñ o suresure ni toñda.*) 鳥が水面をすれすれに飛んだ.

— *vi.* **1** (look through) za｢tto me｣ o toosu ざっと目を通す ⓒ: skim through a catalog (*katarogu ni zatto me o toosu*) カタログにざっと目を通す.

2 (glide lightly) su｢be｣ru yoo ni su｢sumu 滑るように進む ⓒ: The motorboat seemed to skim over the surface of the water. (*Mootaabooto ga suijoo o suberu yoo ni susuñda.*) モーターボートが水上を滑るように進んだ.

skin *n.* **1** (of a human) hi｢fu 皮膚; ha｣da 肌: She has fair skin. (*Kanojo wa hada ga shiroi.*) 彼女は肌が白い.

2 (of an animal) ka｢wa｣ 皮; ke｢gawa 毛皮: a coat made from a fox skin (*kitsune no kegawa no kooto*) きつねの毛皮のコート.

3 (peel) ka｢wa｣ 皮: an apple skin (*riñgo no kawa*) りんごの皮.

— *vt.* **1** (hide) ... no ka｢wa o ha｣gu ...の皮をはぐ ⓒ; (peel) ... no ka｢wa｣ o mu｢ku ...の皮をむく ⓒ: skin a deer (*shika no kawa o hagu*) 鹿の皮をはぐ.

skip *vi.* **1** (hop) to｢bihane｣ru 飛び跳ねる Ⓥ; su｢ki｣ppu suru スキップする ⓣ: skip about (*hanemawaru*) 跳ね回る.

2 (pass over) sho｢oryaku suru 省略する ⓣ; to｢bashite yo｣mu 飛ばして読む ⓒ: I skipped chapter two of the book. (*Watashi wa sono hoñ no dai-ni-shoo o tobashite yoñda.*) 私はその本の第2章を飛ばして読んだ.

— *vt.* **1** (jump) ... o to｢biko｣su ...を飛び越す ⓒ: skip a stream (*ogawa* *o tobikosu*) 小川を飛び越す.

2 (miss out) ... o sho'oryaku suru ...を省略する Ⅰ; nu'ku 抜く Ⓒ: skip breakfast (*chooshoku o nuku* 朝食を抜く.

skirt *n.* su'kaʌato スカート: put on [wear] a skirt (*sukaato o haku [haite iru]*) スカートをはく[はいている].

skull *n.* zu'gaʌikotsu 頭蓋骨; do'kuro どくろ.

sky *n.* so'ra 空: a blue sky (*aozora*) 青空 / a cloudy sky (*kumorizora*) 曇り空 / There was not a cloud in the sky. (*Sora ni wa kumo hitotsu nakatta.*) 空には雲一つなかった.

slacks *n.* su'raʌkkusu スラックス: put on slacks (*surakkusu o haku*) スラックスをはく. ★ Japanese 'surakkusu' usually refers to casual trousers.

slam *vt.* **1** (shut violently) ba'taʌn to shi'meʌru ばたんと閉める Ⓥ: slam the door shut (*to o batan to shimeru*) 戸をばたんと閉める.

2 (place violently) do'suʌn to o'ku どすんと置く Ⓒ: slam a parcel on the floor (*nimotsu o yuka ni dosun to oku*) 荷物を床にどすんと置く.

slander *n.* wa'ruʌkuchi 悪口; chu'ushoo 中傷.

slang *n.* zo'kugo 俗語; su'raʌngu スラング.

slant *vi.* ka'tamuʌku 傾く Ⓒ: His handwriting slants to the left. (*Kare no ji wa hidari ni katamuite iru.*) 彼の字は左に傾いている.
 — *vt.* ... o ka'tamukeʌru ...を傾ける Ⓥ: The picture is a little slanted. (*Sono e wa sukoshi katamuite iru.*) その絵は少し傾いている.
 — *n.* ke'esha 傾斜; sha'meʌn 斜面: The slant of this roof is steep. (*Kono yane no keesha wa kyuu da.*) この屋根の傾斜は急だ.

slap *vt.* ... o hi'rate de pisha'riʌto ta'taʌku ...を平手でぴしゃりとたたく Ⓒ: slap someone on the face (*hito no kao o pishari to tataku*) 人の顔をぴしゃりとたたく.
 — *n.* hi'rateuchi 平手打ち: She gave him a slap on the cheek. (*Ka-*

nojo wa kare no hoo ni hirateuchi o kurawashita.) 彼女は彼のほおに平手打ちをくらわした.

slash *vt.* **1** (cut) ... o ki'ru ...を切る Ⓒ: The knife slipped and I slashed my finger. (*Naifu ga subette yubi o kitte shimatta.*) ナイフが滑って指を切ってしまった.

2 (reduce) ... o ki'risageru ...を切り下げる Ⓥ: slash prices (*nedaʌn o kirisageru*) 値段を切り下げる.
 — *vi.* ta'takitsukeʌru たたきつける Ⓥ: slash the bushes with a stick (*boo de yabu o tatakitsukeru*) 棒でやぶをたたきつける.
 — *n.* ki'riʌkizu 切り傷: a slash on one's cheek (*hoo no kirikizu*) ほおの切り傷.

slate *n.* su'reeto スレート; se'kibaʌn 石板.

slaughter *n.* (people) gya'kusatsu 虐殺; (animals) chi'kusatsu 畜殺.
 — *vt.* ... o gya'kusatsu suru ...を虐殺する Ⓘ; chi'kusatsu suru 畜殺する Ⓘ: slaughter hogs for food (*shokuryoo no tame ni buta o chikusatsu suru*) 食料のために豚を畜殺する.

slave *n.* do'ree 奴隷: work like a slave (*doree no yoo ni hataraku*) 奴隷のように働く.

slavery *n.* (condition) do'ree no mi'buʌn 奴隷の身分; (system) do'ree se'edo 奴隷制度.

sled *n.* so'ri そり.

sleep *vi.* ne'muru 眠る Ⓒ; ne'mureru 眠れる Ⓥ: The baby is sleeping. (*Akaʌnboo wa nemutte iru.*) 赤ん坊は眠っている. / I slept well last night. (*Sakuya wa yoku nemureta.*) 昨夜はよく眠れた.
 — *n.* ne'muri 眠り; su'imiʌn 睡眠: get some sleep (*sukoshi suimiʌn o toru*) 少し睡眠をとる.

sleeping pill *n.* su'imiʌnyaku 睡眠薬: take a sleeping pill (*suimiʌnyaku o nomu*) 睡眠薬を飲む.

sleepy *adj.* ne'mui 眠い: I feel sleepy. (*Nemuku natta.*) 眠くなった. / I was sleepy all day today. (*Kyoo wa ichinichi-juu nemukatta.*) きょう

は一日中眠かった.

sleeve *n.* so'de そで: a dress with long sleeves (*nagasode no doresu*) 長そでのドレス.

slender *adj.* ho'sso'ri shita [shite iru] ほっそりした[している]; su'ra'ri to shita [shite iru] すらりとした[している]: slender fingers (*hossori shita yubi*) ほっそりした指 / a slender girl (*surari to shita shoojo*) すらりとした少女.

slice *n.* hi'to'l-kire 一切れ: a slice of bread (*pan hito-kire*) パン一切れ.
—— *vt.* ... o u'suku ki'ru ...を薄く切る ©; ki'ritoru 切り取る ©: slice a cake (*keeki o usuku kiru*) ケーキを薄く切る / slice off a piece of ham (*hamu o hito-kire kiritoru*) ハムを一切れ切り取る.

slide *vi.* su'be'ru 滑る ©: Let's slide on the ice. (*Koori no ue o suberoo.*) 氷の上を滑ろう.
—— *vt.* ... o su'berase'ru ...を滑らせる V: slide a glass across a table (*koppu o teeburu no ue de suberaseru*) コップをテーブルの上で滑らせる.
—— *n.* **1** (sliding) su'be'ru ko'to'l 滑ること; ka'ssoo 滑走.
2 (apparatus) su'beri'dai 滑り台: play on a slide (*suberidai de asobu*) 滑り台で遊ぶ.
3 (film) su'raido スライド: a film for color slides (*suraido-yoo firumu*) スライド用フィルム.

slight *adj.* wa'zuka na わずかな; su'ko'shi no 少しの: There is a slight difference between the two. (*Sono futatsu ni wa wazuka na chigai ga aru.*) その二つにはわずかな違いがある.

slightly *adv.* wa'zuka ni わずかに; su'koshi ba'kari 少しばかり: It was raining slightly. (*Ame ga sukoshi futte ita.*) 雨が少し降っていた.

slim *adj.* ho'sso'ri shita [shite iru] ほっそりした[している]; su'ra'ri to shita [shite iru] すらりとした[している]: She has a slim figure. (*Kanojo wa surari to shita karada o shite iru.*) 彼女はすらりとした体をしている.
—— *vi.* ta'ijuu o herasu 体重を減らす ©: I'm slimming down now. (*Wa-*

tashi wa ima taijuu o herashite imasu.*) 私はいま体重を減らしています.

slip[1] *vi.* **1** (slide) su'be'ru 滑る ©: I slipped on the ice and hurt my hand. (*Watashi wa koori de subette te ni kega o shita.*) 私は氷で滑って手にけがをした.
2 (escape) so'tto nige'ru そっと逃げる V: He slipped out of the room. (*Kare wa sotto heya kara dete itta.*) 彼はそっと部屋から出て行った.
3 (move smoothly) su'be'ru yoo ni u'go'ku 滑るように動く ©: The ship slipped through the waves. (*Fune wa nami no aida o suberu yoo ni hashitta.*) 船は波の間を滑るように走った.
—— *vt.* ... o su'berase'ru ...を滑らせる V; so'tto ⟨verb⟩ そっと...: He slipped his wallet out of his pocket. (*Kare wa poketto kara saifu o sotto dashita.*) 彼はポケットから財布をそっと出した.
—— *n.* **1** (slipping) su'be'ru ko'to'l 滑ること.
2 (mistake) ma'chiga'i 間違い: a slip of the pen (*kakichigai*) 書き違い.
3 (undergarment) su'ri'ppu スリップ; shi'mi'izu シミーズ.

slip[2] *n.* ho'sonaga'i ka'mikire'l 細長い紙切れ; de'npyoo 伝票: a sales slip (*uriage-denpyoo*) 売上伝票.

slipper *n.* shi'tsunaibaki 室内ばき.
★ In Japan 'mules' or 'scuffs' are called 'surippa' スリッパ.

slippery *adj.* su'beriyasu'i 滑りやすい; tsu'rutsuru shita [shite iru] つるつるした[している]: a slippery floor (*suberiyasui yuka*) 滑りやすい床.

slogan *n.* su'ro'ogan スローガン; hyo'ogo 標語.

slope *n.* sa'ka'l 坂; sa'ka'michi 坂道: a steep [gentle] slope (*kyuu [yuruyaka] na saka*) 急[緩やか]な坂.

slot *n.* su'ro'tto スロット; mi'zo 溝.

slow *adj.* **1** (not fast) o'soi 遅い; no'ro'i のろい: a slow worker (*shigoto ga osoi hito*) 仕事が遅い人.
2 (of clocks) o'kurete iru 遅れている:

This clock is three minutes slow. (*Kono tokee wa sañ-puñ okurete iru.*) この時計は 3 分遅れている.

3 (dull) o˺soi 遅い; ni˺bu˺i 鈍い: He is slow in his movements. (*Kare wa doosa ga nibui.*) 彼は動作が鈍い.

4 (not busy) fu˺keˌeki na 不景気な: Business is slow now. (*Ima wa fukeeki da.*) いまは不景気だ.

— *adv.* yu˺kku˺ri to ゆっくりと; o˺soku 遅く: Drive slower, please. (*Motto yukkuri uñteñ shite kudasai.*) もっとゆっくり運転してください.

— *vt.* ... o o˺soku suru ...を遅くする ⊡.

slow down *vi.* su˺piido o oto˺su スピードを落とす ⓒ.

slowly *adv.* yu˺kku˺ri to ゆっくりと; o˺soku 遅く: Please speak a little more slowly. (*Moo sukoshi yukkuri hanashite kudasai.*) もう少しゆっくり話してください.

slum *n.* su˺ramu˺gai スラム街.

slumber *n.* u˺tatane うたた寝; ma˺doromi まどろみ: fall into a slumber (*utatane suru*) うたた寝する.

— *vi.* ne˺muru 眠る ⓒ; ma˺doro˺mu まどろむ ⓒ.

sly *adj.* zu˺ru˺i ずるい; wa˺rugashiko˺i 悪賢い: He is as sly as a fox. (*Kare wa kitsune no yoo ni zurui.*) 彼はきつねのようにずるい.

smack *vt.* **1** (slap) ... o pi˺sha˺ri to utsu ...をぴしゃりと打つ ⓒ: smack a naughty child (*itazura na ko o pishari to utsu*) いたずらな子をぴしゃりと打つ.

2 (kiss) ... ni chu˺tto kisu o suru ...にちゅっとキスをする ⊡: She smacked a kiss on my cheek. (*Kanojo wa watashi no hoo ni chutto kisu o shita.*) 彼女は私のほおにちゅっとキスをした.

— *n.* (sound) pi˺shatto iu oto˺ ぴしゃっという音; (blow) hi˺rateuchi 平手打ち.

small *adj.* **1** (little in size) chi˺isa˺i 小さい; chi˺isa-na 小さな: Do you have a smaller one? (*Motto chiisai no wa arimasu ka?*) もっと小さいのは

ありますか. / a small car (*chiisa-na kuruma*) 小さな車.

2 (little in amount) su˺kuna˺i 少ない: a small number (*shoosuu*) 少数 / a small sum (*shoogaku*) 少額.

3 (not important) tsu˺mara˺nai つまらない; ku˺daranai くだらない: a small problem (*tsumaranai moñdai*) つまらない問題.

smart *adj.* **1** (clever) ri˺koo na 利口な; a˺tama no yo˺i 頭のよい: a smart student (*atama no yoi gakusee*) 頭のよい学生.

2 (stylish) su˺ma˺ato na スマートな: a smart uniform (*sumaato na seefuku*) スマートな制服.

3 (painful) ha˺geshi˺i 激しい; hi˺hiri suru ひりひりする: a smart pain in the side (*wakibara no hageshii itami*) わき腹の激しい痛み.

— *vi.* hi˺rihiri i˺ta˺mu ひりひり痛む ⓒ: The cut smarts. (*Kirikizu ga itamu.*) 切り傷が痛む.

smash *vt.* **1** (crush) ... o ko˺nagona ni waru 粉々に割る ⓒ: She dropped the plate and smashed it. (*Kanojo wa sara o otoshite konagona ni watte shimatta.*) 彼女は皿を落として粉々に割ってしまった.

2 (hit) ... o na˺gu˺ru ...を殴る ⓒ: He smashed me with his fist. (*Kare wa watashi o geñkotsu de nagutta.*) 彼は私をげんこつで殴った.

— *vi.* ge˺kitotsu suru 激突する ⊡: The car smashed into a tree. (*Sono kuruma wa ki ni gekitotsu shita.*) その車は木に激突した.

smear *vt.* **1** (spread) ... ni (... o) nu˺ru ...に(...を)塗る ⓒ: smear one's face with cream (*kao ni kuriimu o nuru*) 顔にクリームを塗る.

2 (smudge) ... o yo˺gosu ...を汚す ⓒ: The boy smeared the table with jam. (*Sono ko wa jamu de teeburu o yogoshita.*) その子はジャムでテーブルを汚した.

3 (spoil) ... o ki˺zutsuke˺ru ...を傷つける Ⓥ: smear a person's reputation (*hito no meesee o kizutsukeru*) 人の名声を傷つける.

smell n. **1** (odor) niˈoˈi におい; (aroma) kaˈori 香り: There is a smell of something burning. (*Nani-ka ga kogete iru nioi ga suru.*) 何かが焦げているにおいがする. / the smell of coffee (*koohii no kaori*) コーヒーの香り.
2 (sense) shuˈukaku 臭覚: Dogs have a keen sense of smell. (*Inu wa surudoi shuukaku o motte iru.*) 犬は鋭い臭覚を持っている.
— vi. niˈoˈi ga suru においがする Ⓘ: This flower smells sweet. (*Kono hana wa ii nioi ga suru.*) この花はいいにおいがする.
— vt. ... no niˈoˈi o kaˈgu ...のにおいをかぐ Ⓒ: He smelled the fish. (*Kare wa sono sakana no nioi o kaida.*) 彼はその魚のにおいをかいだ.

smile vi. biˈshoo suru 微笑する Ⓘ; niˈkkoˈri suru にっこりする Ⓘ; hoˈhoeˈmu ほほ笑む Ⓘ: She smiled when she saw me. (*Kanojo wa watashi o mite nikkori shita.*) 彼女は私を見てにっこりした.
— vt. biˈshoo shite 〈verb〉 微笑して ...: He smiled his thanks. (*Kare wa bishoo shite kañsha shita.*) 彼は微笑して感謝した.
— n. biˈshoo 微笑; hoˈhoemi ほほ笑み: a cheerful smile (*tanoshi-soo na bishoo*) 楽しそうな微笑 / with a smile (*nikoniko shite*) にこにこして.

smog n. suˈmoˈggu スモッグ; eˈñmu 煙霧.

smoke n. **1** (from burning) keˈmuri 煙: I see black smoke coming out of the chimney. (*Eñtotsu kara kuroi kemuri ga dete iru no ga mieru.*) 煙突から黒い煙が出ているのが見える.
2 (smoking) kiˈtsueñ 喫煙; iˈppuku 一服: have a smoke (*ippuku suru*) 一服する.
— vi. **1** (of a cigarette) taˈbako o suu たばこを吸う Ⓒ: Do you mind if I smoke here? (*Koko de tabako o sutte mo ii desu ka?*) ここでたばこを吸ってもいいですか.
2 (give off smoke) keˈmuri o daˈsu 煙を出す Ⓒ: The volcano is smoking. (*Kazañ ga kemuri o dashite iru.*) 火山が煙を出している.
— vt. **1** (inhale) ... o suˈu ...を吸う Ⓒ: smoke a cigar (*hamaki o suu*) 葉巻を吸う.
2 (treat) ... o kuˈñsee ni suru ...を薫製にする Ⓘ: smoke salmon (*sake o kuñsee ni suru*) さけを薫製にする.

smoking n. kiˈtsueñ 喫煙: No smoking. (*Kiñeñ.*) 禁煙 / a smoking car (*kitsueñsha*) 喫煙車.

smooth adj. **1** (not rough) naˈmeˈraka na 滑らかな; suˈbesube no すべすべの: smooth skin (*subesube no hada*) すべすべの肌.
2 (even surface) heˈetaˈñ na 平坦な: a smooth road (*heetañ na michi*) 平坦な道.
3 (calm) shiˈzuka na 静かな: smooth water on the lake (*mizuumi no shizuka na suimeñ*) 湖の静かな水面.
4 (steady in motion) naˈmeˈraka na 滑らかな; eˈñkatsu na 円滑な: smooth driving (*nameraka na uñteñ*) 滑らかな運転.
— vt. ... o naˈmeˈraka ni suru ...を滑らかにする Ⓘ; taˈira ni suru 平らにする Ⓘ: smooth a board with sandpaper (*kamiyasuri de ita o nameraka ni suru*) 紙やすりで板を滑らかにする.

smoothly adv. naˈmeˈraka ni 滑らかに; juˈñchoo ni 順調に: Everything went smoothly. (*Subete juñchoo ni itta.*) すべて順調にいった.

smuggle vt. ... o miˈtsuyu suru ...を密輸する Ⓘ: smuggle in [out] drugs (*mayaku o mitsuyunyuu [mitsuyushutsu] suru*) 麻薬を密輸入[密輸出]する.

snack bar n. keˈeshoˈkudoo 軽食堂; suˈnaˈkku スナック.

snake n. heˈbi 蛇.

snap vi. **1** (break) puˈtsuˈri to kiˈreˈru ぷつりと切れる Ⓥ; poˈkiˈñ to oˈreˈru ぽきんと折れる Ⓥ: The rope snapped when I pulled it tight. (*Sono tsuna wa gyuutto hippattara* *putsuri to kireta.*) その綱はぎゅーっと引っぱったらぷつりと切れた. / The branch snapped off. (*Eda ga pokiñ to oreta.*) 枝がぽきんと折れた.

2 (close) pa⌐chi⌐ñ to shi⌐ma⌐ru ぱちんと閉まる ©: The lock snapped shut. (*Kagi wa pachiñ to shimatta.*) 鍵はぱちんと閉まった.

3 (try to bite) (... ni) ka⌐mitsuko⌐o to suru (...に)かみつこうとする ①: The dog snapped at me. (*Sono inu wa watashi ni kamitsukoo to shita.*) その犬は私にかみつこうとした.

4 (speak) (... ni) ga⌐migami i⌐u (...に)がみがみ言う ©: She snapped at the child. (*Kanojo wa sono ko ni gamigami itta.*) 彼女はその子にがみがみ言った.

— *vt.* ... o pa⌐chi⌐ñ to na⌐rasu ...をぱちんと鳴らす ©: snap a whip (*pachiñ to muchi o narasu*) ぱちんとむちを鳴らす / snap down a lid (*pachiñ to futa o shimeru*) ぱちんとふたを閉める.

— *n.* **1** (sound) pa⌐chi⌐ñ [po⌐ki⌐ri] to i⌐u oto⌐ ぱちん[ぽきり]という音.
2 (fastening device) to⌐megane 留め金; su⌐na⌐ppu スナップ.

snapshot *n.* su⌐nappu-sha⌐shiñ スナップ写真: take a snapshot of a child (*kodomo no sunappu-sha-shiñ o toru*) 子どものスナップ写真を撮る.

snatch *vt.* ... o hi⌐ttaku⌐ru ...をひったくる ©; u⌐baito⌐ru 奪い取る ©: The thief snatched the money and ran away. (*Doroboo wa kane o ubaitotte nigeta.*) どろぼうは金を奪い取って逃げた.

— *n.* hi⌐ttakuri ひったくり: make a snatch at a bag (*baggu o hittakuroo to suru*) バッグをひったくろうとする.

sneer *vi.* re⌐eshoo suru 冷笑する ①; a⌐zawara⌐u あざ笑う ©: He sneered at my idea. (*Kare wa watashi no aidea o azawaratta.*) 彼は私のアイデアをあざ笑った.

sneeze *vi.* ku⌐sha⌐mi o suru くしゃみをする ①: She had a cold and was sneezing. (*Kanojo wa kaze o hiite*

kushami o shite ita.) 彼女はかぜを引いてくしゃみをしていた.

— *n.* ku⌐sha⌐mi くしゃみ: give a sneeze (*kushami o suru*) くしゃみをする.

snore *vi.* i⌐biki o kaku いびきをかく ©: He snores loudly. (*Kare wa ooki-na ibiki o kaku.*) 彼は大きないびきをかく.

snow *n.* yu⌐ki⌐ 雪: Ten centimeters of snow covered the ground. (*Yuki ga jus-señchi tsumotta.*) 雪が10センチ積もった.

— *vi.* yu⌐ki⌐ ga furu 雪が降る ©: It snowed all night. (*Yuki ga hito-bañ-juu futta.*) 雪がひと晩中降った.

snowman *n.* yu⌐kida⌐ruma 雪だるま: make a snowman (*yukidaruma o tsukuru*) 雪だるまを作る.

snowstorm *n.* fu⌐buki 吹雪.

snowy *adj.* yu⌐ki⌐ ni o⌐owareta [o⌐owarete iru] 雪に覆われた[覆われている]: snowy mountains (*yuki ni oowareta yama*) 雪に覆われた山.

so *adv.* **1** (to such a degree) so⌐re hodo それほど; so⌐ñna ni そんなに: This problem is not so difficult. (*Kono moñdai wa sore hodo muzukashiku nai.*) この問題はそれほど難しくない.

2 (in such a way) so⌐o そう; so⌐no yo⌐o ni そのように: Is that really so? (*Hoñtoo ni soo desu ka?*) 本当にそうですか.

3 (as a result) so⌐ko de そこで; so⌐re de それで: He caught a cold and so he stayed away from school. (*Kare wa kaze o hiita. Sore de gakoo o yasuñda.*) 彼はかぜを引いた. それで学校を休んだ.

4 (very) hi⌐joo ni 非常に; ta⌐iheñ 大変: I was so tired. (*Watashi wa hijoo ni tsukareta.*) 私は非常に疲れた.

5 (also) ... mo ma⌐ta ...もまた: He's left-handed and so am I. (*Kare wa hidari-kiki da ga watashi mo mata soo desu.*) 彼は左利きだが私もまたそうです.

So long. Sa⌐yoona⌐ra. さようなら.

so ... that ... hi⌐joo ni ... na no

de 非常に…なので: It was raining so hard that I didn't go out. (*Ame ga hidoku futte ita no de gaishutsu shinakatta.*) 雨がひどく降っていたので外出しなかった.

so that ... can do ... de˺ki˺ru yoo ni ...できるように: I worked hard so that I could pass the examination. (*Shiken ni ukaru yoo ni isshookeñmee ni beñkyoo shita.*) 試験に受かるように一生懸命に勉強した.

soak *vt.* **1** (place in liquid) ... o hi-˺tasu ...を浸す ⓒ: soak beans in water (*mame o mizu ni hitasu*) 豆を水に浸す.

2 (make wet) ... o zu˺bunure ni suru ...をずぶぬれにする Ⓣ: I got soaked in a shower. (*Watashi wa yuudachi de zubunure ni natta.*) 私は夕立でずぶぬれになった.

3 (suck up) ... o su˺ito˺ru ...を吸い取る ⓒ: use a sponge to soak up the spilled water (*koboreta mizu o suitoru no ni supoñji o tsukau*) こぼれた水を吸い取るのにスポンジを使う.

— *vi.* **1** (remain in liquid) (... ni) tsu˺keru (...に)つける Ⓥ: let the clothes soak in water (*fuku o mizu ni tsukeru*) 服を水につける.

2 (penetrate) (... ni) shi˺mito˺oru (...に)しみ通る ⓒ: The rain soaked through my coat. (*Ame ga kooto ni shimitootta.*) 雨がコートにしみ通った.

soap *n.* se˺kkeñ せっけん: wash with soap and water (*sekkeñ to mizu de arau*) せっけんと水で洗う.

soar *vi.* **1** (fly up) ma˺iaga˺ru 舞い上がる ⓒ; ta˺kaku a˺garu 高く上がる ⓒ: The skylark soared into the sky. (*Hibari wa sora ni maiagatta.*) ひばりは空へ舞い上がった.

2 (rise) ko˺otoo suru 高騰する Ⓣ: Prices have soared. (*Bukka ga kootoo shita.*) 物価が高騰した.

sob *vi.* su˺surina˺ku すすり泣く ⓒ; shi˺kushiku na˺ku しくしく泣く ⓒ: She sobbed at the news. (*Kanojo wa sono shirase o kiite susurinaita.*) 彼女はその知らせを聞いてすすり泣いた.

sober *adj.* yo˺tte inai 酔っていない; shi˺rafu no しらふの: He was the only sober man at the party. (*Sono paatii de yotte inai no wa kare dake datta.*) そのパーティーで酔っていないのは彼だけだった. / become sober (*yoi ga sameru*) 酔いが覚める.

so-called *adj.* i˺wayu˺ru いわゆる: so-called high society (*iwayuru jooryuu shakai*) いわゆる上流社会.

soccer *n.* sa˺kkaa サッカー: play soccer (*sakkaa o suru*) サッカーをする.

sociable *adj.* sha˺koo-teki na 社交的な; sha˺koozuki na 社交好きな: He is a sociable man. (*Kare wa shakoo-teki na otoko da.*) 彼は社交的な男だ.

social *adj.* **1** (of human society) sha˺kai no 社会の: a social problem (*shakai-moñdai*) 社会問題.

2 (of companionship) sha˺koojoo no 社交上の; sha˺koo-teki na 社交的な: a social club (*shakoo kurabu*) 社交クラブ / a social gathering (*koñshiñkai*) 懇親会.

society *n.* **1** (community) sha˺kai 社会: a civilized society (*buñmee shakai*) 文明社会.

2 (organization) kyo˺okai 協会; ka˺i 会: set up a society (*kyookai o setsuritsu suru*) 協会を設立する.

3 (upper class) jo˺oryuu sha˺kai 上流社会.

sock *n.* ku˺tsu˺shita 靴下: a pair of socks (*kutsushita is-soku*) 靴下1足. ★ Japanese '*kutsushita*' refers to 'socks' and 'stockings.'

socket *n.* so˺ke˺tto ソケット; sa˺shi-komi 差し込み.

soda *n.* so˺oda ソーダ; ta˺ñsa˺ñsui 炭酸水: a whisky and soda (*haibooru*) ハイボール.

sofa *n.* so˺faa ソファー: sit on a sofa (*sofaa ni suwaru*) ソファーに座る.

soft *adj.* **1** (not hard) ya˺waraka˺i 柔らかい: a soft bed (*yawarakai beddo*) 柔らかいベッド / a soft-boiled egg (*hañjuku-tamago*) 半熟卵.

2 (smooth) na˺me˺raka na 滑らかな:

Silk is soft to the touch. (*Kinu wa tezawari ga nameraka da.*) 絹は手触りが滑らかだ.

3 (gentle) ya﹂sashii 優しい: She has a soft heart. (*Kanojo wa yasashii kokoro o motte iru.*) 彼女は優しい心を持っている.

4 (quiet) shi﹂zuka na 静かな: soft music (*shizuka na oñgaku*) 静かな音楽.

soften *vt.* ... o ya﹁wara﹂kaku suru ...を柔らかくする ⊤: soften leather (*kawa o yawarakaku suru*) 革を柔らかくする
— *vi.* ya﹁wara﹂kaku naru 柔らかくなる ⊂: Wax softens when heated. (*Roo wa nessuru to yawarakaku naru.*) ろうは熱すると柔らかくなる.

software *n.* so﹁futouea﹂ ソフトウェア.

soil *n.* tsu﹁chi﹂ 土: cultivate the soil (*tsuchi o tagayasu*) 土を耕す.

solar *adj.* ta﹂iyoo no 太陽の: solar heat (*taiyoo-netsu*) 太陽熱 / a solar battery (*taiyoo deñchi*) 太陽電池.

soldier *n.* he﹁eshi 兵士; he﹁etai 兵隊; ri﹁ku﹂guñ no gu﹁ñjiñ 陸軍の軍人.

sole *adj.* ta﹂da hi﹁to﹂tsu no ただ一つの; yu﹂i-itsu no 唯一の: He is the sole survivor. (*Kare wa yui-itsu no seezoñsha da.*) 彼は唯一の生存者だ.

solemn *adj.* **1** (serious) ma﹂jime na まじめな: a solemn face (*majime na kao*) まじめな顔.

2 (sacred) o﹁go﹂soka na 厳かな: a solemn ceremony (*ogosoka na gishiki*) 厳かな儀式.

solicit *vt.* ... o se﹁ga﹂mu ...をせがむ ⊂; mo﹁tome﹂ru 求める Ⓥ: He solicited my help. (*Kare wa watashi no eñjo o motometa.*) 彼は私の援助を求めた.

solid *adj.* **1** (hard) ko﹁tai no 固体の; ko﹁kee no 固形の: Water is liquid and ice is solid. (*Mizu wa ekitai de koori wa kotai desu.*) 水は液体で氷は固体です. / solid fuel (*kokee-neñryoo*) 固形燃料.

2 (strong) ga﹁ñjoo na がんじょうな: This desk is solid. (*Kono tsukue*

wa gañjoo da.) この机はがんじょうだ.

3 (not hollow) chu﹁ukuu de na﹂i 中空でない: a solid bar of iron (*chuukuu de nai tetsu no boo*) 中空でない鉄の棒.
— *n.* ko﹁tai 固体.

solitary *adj.* ko﹁doku na 孤独な; sa﹁bishi﹂i 寂しい: a solitary traveler (*kodoku na tabibito*) 孤独な旅人.

solitude *n.* ko﹁doku 孤独; hi﹁tori-kiri ひとりきり: enjoy solitude (*kodoku o tanoshimu*) 孤独を楽しむ.

soluble *adj.* to﹁ke﹂ru 溶ける; to﹁keyasu﹂i 溶けやすい: Vitamin B is soluble in water. (*Bitamiñ bii wa mizu ni tokeyasui.*) ビタミン B は水に溶けやすい.

solution *n.* **1** (answer) ko﹁ta﹂e 答え; ka﹁iketsu 解決: I found the solution to the question. (*Sono moñdai no kotae ga wakatta.*) その問題の答えがわかった.

2 (dissolving) yo﹁okai 溶解; yo﹂o-eki 溶液: a solution of salt in water (*shio no yooeki*) 塩の溶液.

solve *vt.* ... o to﹁ku ...を解く ⊂; ka﹁iketsu suru 解決する ⊤: I have solved all the problems. (*Moñdai wa zeñbu toita.*) 問題は全部解いた. / solve a difficult case (*muzukashii jikeñ o kaiketsu suru*) 難しい事件を解決する.

some *adj.* ★ There is no Japanese equivalent to 'some' and it is often not translated: I need some bread and milk. (*Pañ to miruku ga hoshii.*) パンとミルクが欲しい. / Would you like some tea? (*O-cha wa ikaga desu ka?*) お茶はいかがですか.

1 (of a number) i﹂kutsu ka no いくつかの: I bought some apples. (*Watashi wa riñgo o ikutsu ka katta.*) 私はりんごをいくつか買った.

2 (of an amount) i﹂kura ka no いくらかの: I'd like some coins in the change. (*Kozeni mo ikura ka mazete kudasai.*) 小銭もいくらか混ぜてください. / Can we do some shopping in this airport? (*Kono kuukoo de ikura ka kaimono ga dekimasu*

*ka?) この空港でいくらか買物ができます
か.

3 (of people) naˈññiñ ka no 何人か
の: Some people were injured in
the accident. (*Sono jiko de naññiñ
ka no hito ga kega o shita.*) その事
故で何人かの人がけがをした.

4 (certain) aˈru ... ある...; naˈni-ka
no 何かの: For some reason, the
train was delayed. (*Nani-ka no
riyuu de ressha ga okureta.*) 何かの
理由で列車が遅れた.

— *pron.* **1** (of a number) iˈkutsu
ka いくつか: I have read some of
these books. (*Kono hoñ no naka no
ikutsu ka wa yomimashita.*) この本
の中のいくつかは読みました.

2 (of an amount) iˈkura ka いくらか:
Some of the milk was spilled on
the table. (*Gyuunyuu no ikura ka
ga teeburu no ue ni koboreta.*) 牛
乳のいくらかがテーブルの上にこぼれた.

3 (of people) aˈru hiˈtoˈ-tachi ある人
たち: Some agreed with me. (*Aru
hito-tachi wa watashi ni sañsee
shita.*) ある人たちは私に賛成した.

— *adv.* yaˈku 約; oˈyoso およそ: It
is some five kilometers. (*Yaku go-
kiro desu.*) 約 5 キロです.

somebody *pron.* aˈru hiˈtoˈ ある人;
daˈre-ka だれか: There's somebody
at the door. (*Geñkañ ni dare-ka
kite imasu.*) 玄関にだれか来ています.

someday *adv.* iˈtsu-ka いつか; ya-
ˈgate やがて: Someday you'll understand. (*Itsu-ka kimi mo wakaru
daroo.*) いつか君もわかるだろう.

somehow *adv.* naˈñ to ka 何とか;
toˈmokaku (mo) ともかく(も): I'll
finish the work somehow. (*Nañ to
ka sono shigoto o kañsee shimasu.*)
何とかその仕事を完成します.

someone *pron.* aˈru hiˈtoˈ ある人;
daˈre-ka だれか: Can someone here
speak English? (*Dare-ka koko de
Eego ga hanasemasu ka?*) だれかこ
こで英語が話せますか. / Please send
someone for my baggage. (*Nimotsu o tori ni dare-ka o yokoshite kudasai.*) 荷物を取りにだれかを

yokoshite kudasai.

something *pron.* aˈru moˈnoˈ ある
もの; nani-ka 何か: I want to buy
something for a man. (*Otoko mono
o kaitai no desu ga.*) 男ものを買い
たいのですが. / Can you give me something to read? (*Nani-ka yomu
mono o kudasai.*) 何か読むものをくだ
さい.

sometime *adv.* iˈtsu-ka いつか: I
think I can meet him sometime
next week. (*Raishuu no itsu-ka
kare ni aeru to omoimasu.*) 来週の
いつか彼に会えると思います.

sometimes *adv.* toˈkidoki 時々;
toˈkiˈ ni wa 時には: I sometimes
play tennis with him. (*Watashi wa
tokidoki kare to tenisu o shimasu.*)
私は時々彼とテニスをします. / Some-
times I do the washing by myself.
(*Toki ni wa jibuñ de señtaku o
shimasu.*) 時には自分で洗濯をします.

somewhat *adv.* suˈkoˈshi 少し;
iˈkubuñ いくぶん; yaˈya やや: The
train arrived somewhat late. (*Ressha wa sukoshi okurete toochaku
shita.*) 列車は少し遅れて到着した. / I
am somewhat tired. (*Watashi wa
yaya tsukareta.*) 私はやや疲れた.

somewhere *adv.* doˈko-ka ni どこ
かに; doˈko-ka e どこかへ: I left my
gloves somewhere. (*Watashi wa
tebukuro o doko-ka ni okiwasureta.*) 私は手袋をどこかに置き忘れた. /
Let's go somewhere quiet. (*Doko-
ka shizuka na tokoro e ikoo.*) どこか
静かな所へ行こう.

son *n.* muˈsukoˈ 息子; (someone
else's) muˈsuko-sañ 息子さん: I
have two sons. (*Watashi ni wa
musuko ga futari iru.*) 私には息子が
二人いる.

song *n.* **1** (of music) uˈtaˈ 歌: sing
a song (*uta o utau*) 歌を歌う / a
popular song (*ryuukooka*) 流行歌.
2 (of birds) saˈezuri さえずり; (of
insects) naˈkigoˈe 鳴き声: the song
of birds (*tori no saezuri*) 鳥のさえず
り / the song of insects (*mushi no
nakigoe*) 虫の鳴き声.

soon *adv.* **1** (in a short time) ma「mo」naku まもなく: The train is leaving soon. (*Ressha wa mamonaku demasu.*) 列車はまもなく出ます.

2 (quickly) ha「yaku 早く: Please come as soon as possible. (*Dekiru dake hayaku kite kudasai.*) できるだけ早く来てください.

3 (early) ha「yame」ni 早めに: The sooner, the better. (*Hayakereba hayai hodo yoi.*) 早ければ早いほどよい. / Come again soon! (*Mata kite kudasai.*) また来てください.

soot *n.* su「su すす; ba「ieñ 煤煙.

soothe *vt.* ... o na「dame」ru ...をなだめる Ⅴ; na「gusame」ru 慰める Ⅴ: soothe an angry person (*okotte iru hito o nadameru*) 怒っている人をなだめる.

sophisticated *adj.* **1** (of taste) se「ñreñ sareta [sarete iru] 洗練された[されている]: sophisticated tastes (*señreñ sareta shumi*) 洗練された趣味.

2 (well-developed) se「ekoo na 精巧な: a sophisticated machine (*seekoo na kikai*) 精巧な機械.

sore *adj.* i「ta」i 痛い: I have a sore throat. (*Nodo ga itai.*) のどが痛い.

sorrow *n.* **1** (sadness) ka「nashimi 悲しみ: We felt deep sorrow at his death. (*Watashi-tachi wa kare no shi o fukaku kanashiñda.*) 私たちは彼の死を深く悲しんだ.

2 (regret) i「kañ 遺憾: He expressed sorrow for what he had done. (*Kare wa jibuñ no shita koto ni taishite ikañ no i o arawashita.*) 彼は自分のしたことに対して遺憾の意を表した.

sorry *adj.* **1** (full of sorrow) ki「nodoku」na 気の毒な: I'm sorry that you're sick. (*Go-byooki de kinodoku desu.*) ご病気で気の毒です.

2 (regretful) za「ññ」eñ na 残念な: I'm sorry I can't come to the party. (*Zañneñ desu ga paatii ni wa deraremaseñ.*) 残念ですがパーティーには出られません.

Sorry. Go「meñ nasa」i. ごめんなさい;

Su「mimase」ñ. すみません.

sort *n.* **1** (kind) shu「rui 種類: What sort of music do you like best? (*Doo iuu shurui no oñgaku ga ichibañ suki desu ka?*) どういう種類の音楽がいちばん好きですか.

2 (type) ... no hi「to」 ...の人: He is a good sort. (*Kare wa ii hito da.*) 彼はいい人だ.

— *vt.* ... o bu「ñrui suru ...を分類する Ⅰ: sort business cards (*meeshi o buñrui suru*) 名刺を分類する.

soul *n.* **1** (spirit) ta「mashii 魂; re「koñ 霊魂: Christians believe that at death their soul goes to heaven. (*Kurisuchañ wa shinu to tamashii wa teñgoku e iku to shiñjite iru.*) クリスチャンは死ぬと魂は天国へ行くと信じている.

2 (mind) se「eshiñ 精神; ko「koro 心: body and soul (*nikutai to seeshiñ*) 肉体と精神.

3 (deep feeling) ne「tsujoo 熱情; ki「haku 気迫: His painting has no soul. (*Kare no e ni wa kihaku ga nai.*) 彼の絵には気迫がない.

4 (person) ni「ñgeñ 人間; hi「to」 人: Not a soul left the room. (*Dare hitori heya kara dete ikanakatta.*) だれ一人部屋から出て行かなかった.

sound[1] *n.* o「to」音; mo「no-oto」物音: make a sound (*oto o tateru*) 音を立てる / There was no sound. (*Mono-oto hitotsu shinakatta.*) 物音一つしなかった.

— *vi.* **1** (make a sound) na「ru 鳴る Ⓒ: The doorbell sounded. (*Doa no beru ga natta.*) ドアのベルが鳴った.

2 (seem) ... no yo「o ni o「moware」ru ...のように思われる Ⅴ; ... mi「tai da ...みたいだ: The plan sounds all right. (*Sono keekaku wa ii yoo ni omowareru.*) その計画はいいように思われる.

— *vt.* ... o na「rasu ...を鳴らす Ⓒ: sound a horn (*keeteki o narasu*) 警笛を鳴らす.

sound[2] *adj.* **1** (healthy) ke「ñzeñ na 健全な: He is sound in mind and body. (*Kare wa shiñshiñ tomo ni* *keñzeñ da.*) 彼は心身ともに健全だ.

2 (secure) shi「kka」ri shita [shite iru] しっかりした[している]; ke「ñjitsu na 堅実な: a sound investment (*keñjitsu na tooshi*) 堅実な投資.

3 (sensible) ta「dashi」i 正しい; da-「too na 妥当な: a sound judgment (*datoo na hañdañ*) 妥当な判断.

4 (complete) ju「ubu」ñ na 十分な: have a sound sleep (*jukusui suru*) 熟睡する.

soup *n.* su「upu スープ: eat soup (*suupu o nomu*) スープを飲む. ★ Don't say '*suupu o taberu*' スープを食べる. / miso soup (*misoshiru*) みそ汁.

sour *adj.* **1** (acid taste) su「ppa」i 酸っぱい: Those grapes taste sour. (*Kono budoo wa suppai.*) このぶどうは酸っぱい.

2 (unpleasant) fu「ki」geñ na 不きげんな: He was in a sour mood. (*Kare wa fukigeñ datta.*) 彼は不きげんだった.

source *n.* **1** (origin) mi「namoto [ge」ñ] 源: a source of income (*shuunyuu-geñ*) 収入源.

2 (the beginning of a river) mi-「namoto 源; su「igeñ 水源: This river has its source in Lake Suwa. (*Kono kawa wa Suwako ni minamoto o hassuru.*) この川は諏訪湖に源を発する.

3 (of information) de「do」koro 出所; su「ji 筋: information from a reliable source (*tashika na suji kara no joohoo*) 確かな筋からの情報.

south *n.* mi「nami 南; na「ñbu 南部: The birds flew to the south. (*Tori wa minami e toñde itta.*) 鳥は南へ飛んで行った.

— *adj.* mi「nami no 南の: a south wind (*minami-kaze*) 南風.

— *adv.* mi「nami e [ni] 南へ[に]: go south (*minami e iku*) 南へ行く.

southeast *n.* na「ñtoo 南東.

southern *adj.* mi「nami no 南の: Southern Europe (*Minami Yoo-roppa*) 南ヨーロッパ.

southwest *n.* na「ñsee 南西.

souvenir *n.* ki「neñhiñ 記念品; o-「miyage おみやげ; mi「yage みやげ: I

bought a doll as a souvenir. (*Watashi wa o-miyage ni niñgyoo o katta.*) 私はおみやげに人形を買った. ★ Japanese '*miyage*' refers to something that is given to others.

sovereign *n.* ku「ñshu 君主; ge「ñshu 元首; shu「ke」ñsha 主権者.

— *adj.* **1** (ruling) shu「keñ no a」ru 主権のある: sovereign authority (*shukeñ*) 主権.

2 (independent) do「kuritsu no 独立の: a sovereign state (*dokuritsu-koku*) 独立国.

sow *vt.* ... o ma「ku ...をまく C: He sowed wheat in the field. (*Kare wa hatake ni mugi o maita.*) 彼は畑に麦をまいた.

— *vi.* ta「ne o maku 種をまく C: As you sow, so shall you reap. (*Maita tane wa karanakereba naranai.*) まいた種は刈らなければならない.

soybean *n.* da「izu 大豆: fermented soybean paste (*miso*) みそ / soybean paste soup (*misoshiru*) みそ汁.

soy sauce *n.* sho「oyu しょうゆ.

space *n.* **1** (universe) u「chuu 宇宙: travel in space (*uchuu o ryokoo suru*) 宇宙を旅行する. ★ 'Universe' is also called '*uchuu.*'

2 (empty part) ku「ukañ 空間: time and space (*jikañ to kuukañ*) 時間と空間.

3 (distance) ka「ñkaku 間隔; su「kima すきま: Leave a space between the cars. (*Kuruma no aida ni kañkaku o ake nasai.*) 車の間に間隔を空けなさい.

4 (room) ku「usho 空所; yo「chi 余地; su「pe」esu スペース: There is no space for another bed. (*Moo hitotsu beddo o ireru yochi wa arimaseñ.*) もう一つベッドを入れる余地はありません.

spacious *adj.* hi「robi」ro to shita [shite iru] 広々とした[している]; ko「odai na 広大な: a spacious living-room (*hirobiro to shita ima*) 広々とした居間.

spade *n.* (tool) su「ki すき(鋤).

span *n.* **1** (stretch) na「gasa 長さ;

zeⁿchoo 全長; zeⁿpuku 全幅: the span of one's arms (*ryoo-ude o hirogeta nagasa*) 両腕を広げた長さ / the span of a bridge (*hashi no zeⁿchoo*) 橋の全長.

2 (space of time) kiˈkaⁿ 期間: the average span of life (*heekiⁿ jumyoo*) 平均寿命.

— *vt.* ... ni kaˈkaru ...に架かる C: The bridge spans the river. (*Hashi wa sono kawa ni kakatte iru.*) 橋はその川に架かっている.

spare *vt.* **1** (afford) ... o saˈku ...を割く C: Can you spare me five minutes? (*Jikaⁿ o go-fuⁿ saite itadakemasu ka?*) 時間を5分割いていただけますか.

2 (keep from using) ... o oˈshiˈmu ...を惜しむ C: He spared no efforts. (*Kare wa doryoku o oshimanakatta.*) 彼は努力を惜しまなかった.

3 (save) ... o haˈbuˈku ...を省く C: This will save me trouble. (*Kore de tema ga habukeru.*) これで手間が省ける.

spark *n.* hiˈbana 火花: produce sparks (*hibana o dasu*) 火花を出す.

sparkle *vi.* kaˈgayaˈku 輝く C; kiˈrameˈku きらめく C: The diamond sparkled in the sunlight. (*Daiyamoⁿdo ga hi no hikari o ukete kirameita.*) ダイヤモンドが日の光を受けてきらめいた.

— *n.* kaˈgayaki 輝き; kiˈrameki きらめき.

sparrow *n.* suˈzume すずめ.

speak *vi.* **1** (say words) haˈnaˈsu 話す C: May I speak in English? (*Eego de hanashite mo ii desu ka?*) 英語で話してもいいですか. / Please speak more slowly. (*Motto yukkuri hanashite kudasai.*) もっとゆっくり話してください.

2 (give a speech) eˈⁿzetsu suru 演説する I: The lecturer spoke for about an hour. (*Kooshi wa yaku ichi-jikaⁿ eⁿzetsu shita.*) 講師は約1時間演説した.

— *vt.* **1** (say words) ... o haˈnaˈsu ...を話す C; shaˈbeˈru しゃべる C: I

speak only a little Japanese. (*Watashi wa Nihoⁿgo o sukoshi dake hanashimasu.*) 私は日本語を少しだけ話します.

2 (tell) ... o kaˈtaru ...を語る C: speak the truth (*shiⁿjitsu o kataru*) 真実を語る.

speaker *n.* **1** (person) haˈnaˈsu hiˈtoˈ 話す人; eˈⁿzetsuˈsha 演説者: a native speaker (*bokokugo o hanasu hito*) 母国語を話す人 / a fine speaker (*eⁿzetsu no umai hito*) 演説のうまい人.

2 (chairperson) giˈchoo 議長.

3 (loudspeaker) suˈpiˈikaˈ スピーカー; kaˈkuseˈeki 拡声器.

special *adj.* **1** (not ordinary) toˈkubetsu no 特別の: This is a special present for you. (*Kore wa anata e no tokubetsu no okurimono desu.*) これはあなたへの特別の贈り物です.

2 (particular) toˈkuyuu no 特有の: a custom special to Japan (*Nihoⁿ tokuyuu no shuukaⁿ*) 日本特有の習慣.

3 (not general) seˈⁿmon no 専門の; toˈkushu na 特殊な: What is your special field of study? (*Anata no seⁿmoⁿ buⁿya wa naⁿ desu ka?*) あなたの専門分野は何ですか.

4 (exceptional) riˈⁿji no 臨時の: a special issue of a magazine (*zasshi no riⁿji zookaⁿ-goo*) 雑誌の臨時増刊号.

specialist *n.* seˈⁿmoⁿka 専門家; (doctor) seˈⁿmoⁿˈi 専門医: a specialist in heart diseases (*shiⁿzoobyoo no seⁿmoⁿˈi*) 心臓病の専門医.

specialize *vi.* (... o) seˈⁿmoⁿ ni suru (...を)専門にする I; seˈⁿkoo suru 専攻する I: She specializes in Japanese literature. (*Kanojo wa Nihoⁿ buⁿgaku o senkoo shite iru.*) 彼女は日本文学を専攻している.

specially *adv.* toˈkubetsu ni 特別に; waˈzawaza わざわざ: I came here specially to see you. (*Kimi ni wazawaza ai ni kita ⁿ da.*) 君にわざわざ会いに来たんだ.

specialty *n.* **1** (special study) seⁿmoñ 専門; seⁿkoo 専攻.
2 (special product) toꞋkuseehiñ 特製品; (food) meꞋebutsu ryoꞋori 名物料理.

species *n.* shuꞋ 種: butterflies of many species (*kakushu no choo*) 各種のちょう.

specific *adj.* **1** (definite) meꞋekaku na 明確な; guꞋtaiteki na 具体的な: make specific plans for a trip (*ryokoo no gutai-teki na keekaku o suru*) 旅行の具体的な計画をする.
2 (particular) toꞋkushu no 特殊の: a specific remedy (*tokushu ryoohoo*) 特殊療法.

specifically *adv.* toꞋku ni 特に; toꞋriwake とりわけ: a book written specifically for children (*toku ni kodomo no tame ni kakareta hoñ*) 特に子どものために書かれた本.

specify *vt.* ... o shiꞋtee suru ...を指定する []; meꞋegeñ suru 明言する []: Please specify the time and place. (*Jikañ to basho o shitee shite kudasai.*) 時間と場所を指定してください.

specimen *n.* miꞋhoñ 見本; hyoꞋohoñ 標本: specimens of a new product (*shiñ-seehiñ no mihoñ*) 新製品の見本 / butterfly specimens (*choo no hyoohoñ*) ちょうの標本.

speck *n.* chiꞋisaꞋi shiꞋmi [kiꞋzu] 小さい染み[きず]: a speck of ink (*iñku no chiisai shimi*) インクの小さい染み.

spectacle *n.* (unusual sight) koꞋokee 光景; soꞋokañ 壮観: The sunrise was a splendid spectacle. (*Hinode wa subarashii kookee datta.*) 日の出はすばらしい光景だった.

spectacles *n.* meꞋgane 眼鏡.

spectacular *adj.* suꞋbarashiꞋi すばらしい; soꞋokañ na 壮観な: a spectacular view of the Alps (*Arupusu no subarashii nagame*) アルプスのすばらしい眺め.

spectator *n.* kaꞋñkyaku 観客; keꞋñbutsuniñ 見物人: spectators at a game (*shiai no kañkyaku*) 試合の観客.

speculate *vi.* **1** (guess) suiꞋsoku suru 推測する []; aꞋreꞋkore kaꞋñgaeꞋru あれこれ考える [V]: speculate about one's future life (*shoorai no seekatsu ni tsuite are-kore kañgaeru*) 将来の生活についてあれこれ考える.
2 (engage in risky business) toꞋoki suru 投機する []: speculate in land (*tochi ni tooki suru*) 土地に投機する.

speculation *n.* **1** (guess) suꞋisoku 推測: Your speculations are close to the truth. (*Anata no suisoku wa shiñjitsu ni chikai.*) あなたの推測は真実に近い.
2 (investment) toꞋoki 投機: speculation in stocks (*kabu no tooki*) 株の投機.

speech *n.* **1** (public talk) eꞋñzetsu 演説; koꞋoeñ 講演; supꞋiꞋichi スピーチ: He made an impromptu speech. (*Kare wa sokuseki de eñzetsu o shita.*) 彼は即席で演説をした. / an opening [closing] speech (*kaikai [heekai] no ji*) 開会[閉会]の辞.
2 (the act of speaking) haꞋnaꞋsu koꞋtoꞋ 話すこと; geꞋñroñ 言論: freedom of speech (*geñroñ no jiyuu*) 言論の自由.
3 (the manner of speaking) haꞋnashikaꞋta 話し方; haꞋnashiburi 話しぶり: His speech is not clear. (*Kare no hanashikata wa hakkiri shinai.*) 彼の話し方ははっきりしない.

speed *n.* **1** (swiftness) haꞋyasa 速さ; soꞋkuꞋryoku 速力: the speed of light (*hikari no hayasa*) 光の速さ / The train gradually gathered speed. (*Ressha wa jojo ni sokuryoku o mashita.*) 列車は徐々に速力を増した.
2 (velocity) soꞋkudo 速度; suꞋpiido スピード: He drove at a speed of 50 kilometers an hour. (*Kare wa jisoku gojuk-kiro no sokudo de uñteñ shita.*) 彼は時速50キロの速度で運転した.

speedy *adj.* biꞋñsoku na 敏速な; haꞋyaꞋi 速い: a speedy worker (*shigoto no hayai hito*) 仕事の速い人.

spell¹ *vt.* ... o tsuꞋzuru ...をつづる [C]:

How do you spell your name?
(*Anata no namae wa doo tsuzuri-masu ka?*) あなたの名前はどうつづりますか.

spell[2] *n.* **1** (period) hiˈtoˈtsuzuki ひと続き; shiˈbaˈraku no aida しばらくの間: a long spell of rainy weather (*nagai uteñ no tsuzuki*) 長い雨天の続き.

2 (work) hiˈtoˈshigoto ひと仕事; koˈotai 交替: take a spell at the oars (*kootai de ooru o kogu*) 交替でオールをこぐ.

spelling *n.* tsuˈzuri つづり; suˈpeˈriñgu スペリング.

spend *vt.* **1** (pay out) ... o tsuˈkau ...を使う C; tsuˈiyaˈsu 費やす C: He spends a lot of money on books. (*Kare wa hoñ ni o-kane o takusañ tsukau.*) 彼は本にお金をたくさん使う.

2 (pass) ... o suˈgoˈsu ...を過ごす C: Where do you spend the summer vacation? (*Natsuyasumi wa doko de sugoshimasu ka?*) 夏休みはどこで過ごしますか.

sphere *n.* **1** (round object) kyuˈu 球; kyuˈukee 球形.

2 (range) haˈñi 範囲; ryoˈoiki 領域: a sphere of activity (*katsudoo hañi*) 活動範囲.

spice *n.* yaˈkumi 薬味; koˈoshiˈñryoo 香辛料: use spices in cooking (*ryoori ni kooshiñryoo o tsukau*) 料理に香辛料を使う.

spider *n.* kuˈmo くも(蜘蛛).

spill *vt.* ... o koˈboˈsu ...をこぼす C: Who is it that spilled water on the floor? (*Yuka ni mizu o koboshita no wa dare desu ka?*) 床に水をこぼしたのはだれですか.

— *vi.* koˈboreˈru こぼれる V: Milk spilled from the glass. (*Gyuunyuu ga koppu kara koboreta.*) 牛乳がコップからこぼれた.

spin *vt.* **1** (turn) ... o maˈwasu ...を回す C: spin a top (*koma o mawasu*) こまを回す.

2 (twist) ... o tsuˈmuˈgu ...を紡ぐ C: spin wool into thread (*yoomoo o tsumuide ito ni suru*) 羊毛を紡いで糸にする.

3 (form a thread) ... o kaˈkeˈru ...をかける V: Spiders spin webs. (*Kumo wa su o kakeru.*) くもは巣をかける.

— *vi.* kuˈrukuru maˈwaru くるく回る C: The wheel began to spin around. (*Shariñ ga mawari-hajimeta.*) 車輪が回り始めた.

— *n.* kaˈiteñ 回転.

spinach *n.* hoˈoreˈñsoo ほうれん草.

spirit *n.* **1** (mind) koˈkoˈro 心: the poor in spirit (*kokoro no mazushii hito-tachi*) 心の貧しい人たち.

2 (mood) kiˈbuñ 気分; kiˈgeñ きげん: He is in good spirits. (*Kare wa kigeñ ga ii.*) 彼はきげんがいい.

3 (principle) seˈeshiñ 精神: fighting spirit (*tooshi*) 闘志.

4 (vigor) kaˈkki 活気; geˈñki 元気: a team with lots of spirit (*kakki no aru chiimu*) 活気のあるチーム.

5 (soul) reˈekoñ 霊魂; yuˈuree 幽霊: believe in spirits (*yuuree o shiñjiru*) 幽霊を信じる.

6 (alcohol) aˈrukooru アルコール; tsuˈyoˈi sake 強い酒.

spiritual *adj.* seˈeshiñ-teki na 精神的な: spiritual love (*seeshiñ-teki na ai*) 精神的な愛.

spit *vt.* ... o haˈkidaˈsu ...を吐き出す C: He spat out the grape seeds. (*Kare wa budoo no tane o hakidashita.*) 彼はぶどうの種を吐き出した.

— *vi.* tsuˈba o haku つばを吐く C: Don't spit on the road. (*Dooro ni tsuba o haite wa ikemaseñ.*) 道路につばを吐いてはいけません.

spite *n.* aˈkui 悪意; iˈjiˈwaru 意地悪: do something out of spite (*akui kara nani-ka o suru*) 悪意から何かをする.

in spite of ... *prep.* ... ni mo kaˈkawaˈrazu ...にもかかわらず: In spite of his efforts, he failed. (*Doryoku ni mo kakawarazu kare wa shippai shita.*) 努力にもかかわらず彼は失敗した.

splash *vt.* ... o haˈnekaˈsu ...をはねかす C; haˈnekakeˈru はねかける V: The car splashed mud on me. (*So-

no kuruma wa watashi ni doro o hanekaketa.) その車は私に泥をはねかけた.

— *vi.* baˈshabasha haˈnekaˈsu ばしゃばしゃはねかす ⓒ: We splashed through the river. (*Watashi-tachi wa mizu o bashabasha hanekashite kawa o watatta.*) 私たちは水をばしゃばしゃはねかして川を渡った.

splendid *adj.* **1** (magnificent) soˈoree na 壮麗な; goˈoka na 豪華な: He lives in a splendid house. (*Kare wa gooka na uchi ni sunde iru.*) 彼は豪華な家に住んでいる.

2 (brilliant) suˈbarashiˈi すばらしい; suˈteki na すてきな: I hit on a splendid idea. (*Watashi wa subarashii kangae o omoitsuita.*) 私はすばらしい考えを思いついた.

3 (glorious) kaˈgayakashiˈi 輝かしい: splendid achievements (*kagayakashii gyooseki*) 輝かしい業績.

splendor *n.* (brightness) kaˈgayakiˈ 輝き; (magnificence) soˈoreesa 壮麗さ: the splendor of a palace (*ookyuu no sooreesa*) 王宮の壮麗さ.

split *vt.* **1** (break) ... o waˈru ...を割る ⓒ: split logs (*maki o waru*) まきを割る.

2 (divide) ... o buˈnkatsu suru ...を分割する ⓣ; waˈkeˈru 分ける Ⓥ: I split the profits with him. (*Watashi wa rieki o kare to waketa.*) 私は利益を彼と分けた.

— *vi.* **1** (break) waˈreru 割れる Ⓥ: The ship split on a rock. (*Fune wa iwa ni atatte futatsu ni wareta.*) 船は岩に当たって二つに割れた.

2 (separate) buˈnretsu suru 分裂する ⓣ: The party split up into two factions. (*Too wa futa-ha ni bunretsu shita.*) 党は二派に分裂した.

spoil *vt.* **1** (damage) ... o daˈmeˈ ni suru ...をだめにする ⓣ: She spoiled the soup by putting too much salt in it. (*Kanojo wa suupu ni shio o iresugite dame ni shita.*) 彼女はスープに塩を入れすぎてだめにした.

2 (overindulge) ... o aˈmayakashite dameˈ ni suru ...を甘やかしてだめに

する ⓣ: spoil a child (*kodomo o amayakashite dame ni suru*) 子どもを甘やかしてだめにする.

— *vi.* daˈmeˈ ni naru だめになる ⓒ; waˈruku naru 悪くなる ⓒ: Food spoils quickly in summer. (*Natsu wa tabemono ga sugu ni waruku naru.*) 夏は食べ物がすぐに悪くなる.

sponge *n.* suˈponji スポンジ; kaˈimeñ 海綿: wash a car with a sponge (*suponji de kuruma o arau*) スポンジで車を洗う.

— *vt.* ... o suˈponji de nuguˈu ...をスポンジでぬぐう ⓒ: sponge out a stain (*yogore o suponji de nugutte toru*) 汚れをスポンジでぬぐって取る.

sponsor *n.* **1** (of advertising) suˈpoˈnsaa スポンサー.

2 (responsible person) hoˈshooniñ 保証人: stand sponsor for a person (*hito no hoshooniñ to naru*) 人の保証人となる.

— *vt.* ... no suˈpoˈnsaa to naru ...のスポンサーとなる ⓒ: sponsor a TV program (*terebi bañgumi no suponsaa to naru*) テレビ番組のスポンサーとなる.

spontaneous *adj.* jiˈhatsu-teki na 自発的な; shiˈzeñ ni okoˈru 自然に起こる: a spontaneous action (*jihatsuteki na koodoo*) 自発的な行動 / break into spontaneous song (*shizeñ ni utaidasu*) 自然に歌い出す.

spoon *n.* suˈpuˈuñ スプーン; saˈji さじ: eat soup with a spoon (*supuuñ de suupu o nomu*) スプーンでスープを飲む.

sport *n.* suˈpoˈotsu スポーツ; uˈñdoo 運動: play sports (*supootsu o suru*) スポーツをする / sports equipment (*supootsu yoohiñ*) スポーツ用品.

sportsman *n.* suˈpootsuˈmañ スポーツマン; uˈñdoozuki no hito運動好きの人. ★ Japanese 'spootsumañ' usually refers to 'athlete.'

spot *n.* **1** (mark) shiˈmi 染み; yoˈgore 汚れ: You have a spot on your dress. (*Doresu ni shimi ga tsuite imasu yo.*) ドレスに染みがついていますよ.

2 (place) chi「teñ 地点; ba「sho 場所: a good fishing spot (*yoi tsuri-ba*) よい釣り場 / famous spots (*mee-sho*) 名所.
—— *vt.* **1** (see) ... o mi「tsukeru ...を見つける: I spotted his car in the parking lot. (*Watashi wa chuusha-joo de kare no kuruma o mitsu-keta.*) 私は駐車場で彼の車を見つけた.
2 (mark) ... ni shi「mi o tsuke「ru ...に染みをつける Ⓥ; ... o yo「gosu ...を汚す Ⓒ: I spotted my tie with sauce. (*Watashi wa soosu de neku-tai o yogoshita.*) 私はソースでネクタイを汚した.

sprain *vt.* ... o ku「ji「ku ...をくじく Ⓒ: I think I have sprained my ankle. (*Ashi o kujiita rashii.*) 足をくじいたらしい.

sprawl *vi.* te「ashi o no「ba「su 手足を伸ばす Ⓒ; ne「sobe「ru 寝そべる Ⓒ: sprawl on the lawn (*shibafu ni ne-soberu*) 芝生に寝そべる.

spray *n.* **1** (mist) shi「buki「 しぶき: Spray from the waterfall hit our faces. (*Taki no shibuki ga wata-shi-tachi no kao ni kakatta.*) 滝のしぶきが私たちの顔にかかった.
2 (instrument) fu「ñmu「ki 噴霧器; su「pu「ree スプレー: use a spray to kill insects (*mushi o korosu no ni su-puree o tsukau*) 虫を殺すのにスプレーを使う.
—— *vt.* ... o sa「ñpu suru ...を散布する Ⓘ; fu「kikake「ru 吹きかける Ⓥ: She sprayed perfume on herself. (*Ka-nojo wa jibuñ ni koosui o fukika-keta.*) 彼女は自分に香水を吹きかけた.

spread *vt.* **1** (open out) ... o hi「ro-geru ...を広げる Ⓥ: He spread a newspaper on the table. (*Kare wa teeburu no ue ni shiñbuñ o hiro-geta.*) 彼はテーブルの上に新聞を広げた.
2 (cover) ... o nu「ru ...を塗る Ⓒ: spread butter on bread (*pañ ni bataa o nuru*) パンにバターを塗る.
3 (scatter) ... o ma「kichira「su ...をまき散らす Ⓒ: Flies spread disease. (*Hae wa byooki o makichirasu.*) はえは病気をまき散らす.

—— *vi.* **1** (be extended) hi「rogaru 広がる Ⓒ: The fire spread to the house next door. (*Kaji wa tonari no uchi ni hirogatta.*) 火事は隣の家に広がった.
2 (be scattered) hi「roma「ru 広まる Ⓒ: The news spread fast. (*Sono shirase wa sugu ni hiromatta.*) その知らせはすぐに広まった.
—— *n.* hi「rogari 広がり; fu「kyuu 普及: the spread of education (*kyooiku no fukyuu*) 教育の普及.

spring[1] *n.* ha「ru 春: Plants start to grow in spring. (*Shokubutsu wa haru ni seechoo shi-hajimeru.*) 植物は春に生長し始める.

spring[2] *vi.* **1** (leap) ha「ne「ru 跳ねる Ⓥ; to「biaga「ru 跳び上がる Ⓒ: He sprang into the boat. (*Kare wa booto ni tobinotta.*) 彼はボートに跳び乗った.
2 (come into being) a「raware「ru 現れる Ⓥ; u「mareru 生まれる Ⓥ: A new town sprang up at that site. (*Sono basho ni atarashii machi ga uma-reta.*) その場所に新しい町が生まれた.
3 (flow forth) wa「kide「ru 湧き出る Ⓥ: Hot water sprang out of the earth. (*Jimeñ kara oñseñ ga waki-deta.*) 地面から温泉が湧き出た.
—— *n.* **1** (flow of water) i「zumi 泉; su「igeñ 水源: a hot spring (*oñseñ*) 温泉.
2 (coil) ba「ne ばね; su「puriñgu スプリング.
3 (jump) cho「oyaku 跳躍.

sprinkle *vt.* ... o ma「ku ...をまく Ⓒ: sprinkle water on the lawn (*shiba-fu ni mizu o maku*) 芝生に水をまく.

sprout *vi.* me「 o dasu 芽を出す Ⓒ: The seeds began to sprout. (*Tane ga me o dashi-hajimeta.*) 種が芽を出し始めた.
—— *n.* me「 芽; shi「ñme 新芽: bean sprouts (*moyashi*) もやし.

spur *n.* **1** (metal device) ha「kusha 拍車: put spurs to a horse (*uma ni hakusha o kakeru*) 馬に拍車をかける.
2 (stimulus) shi「geki 刺激: put spurs to a person (*hito ni shigeki o*

ataeru) 人に刺激を与える。
— *vt.* **1** (apply spurs) ... ni haʅkusha o ateru ...に拍車を当てる Ⓥ: spur a horse on (*uma ni hakusha o atete hashiraseru*) 馬に拍車を当てて走らせる。

2 (urge) ... o kaʅritateʅru ...を駆り立てる Ⓥ; shiʅgeki suru 刺激する Ⓣ: The prize money spurred him on. (*Shookiñ ga kare o karitateta.*) 賞金が彼を駆り立てた。

spy *n.* suʅpai スパイ: an industrial spy (*sañgyoo supai*) 産業スパイ。
— *vi.* (... o) suʅpai suru (...を)スパイする Ⓘ; koʅssoʅri shiʅrabeʅru こっそり調べる Ⓥ: His job is to spy on the enemy. (*Kare no shigoto wa teki o supai suru koto da.*) 彼の仕事は敵をスパイすることだ。
— *vt.* ... o saʅguridaʅsu ...を探り出す Ⓒ: spy out a secret (*himitsu o saguridasu*) 秘密を探り出す。

square *n.* **1** (flat figure) seʅehoʅokee 正方形; shiʅkaʅkukee 四角形。
2 (open area) hiʅroba 広場: a town square (*machi no hiroba*) 町の広場。
3 (mathematics) heʅehoo 平方; niʅjoo 2乗: Nine is the square of three. (*Kyuu wa sañ no heehoo da.*) 9は3の平方だ。
— *adj.* **1** (shape) seʅehoʅokee no 正方形の; shiʅkakuʅi 四角い: a square table (*shikakui teeburu*) 四角いテーブル。
2 (mathematics) heʅehoo no 平方の: A table 2 meters square has an area of 4 square meters. (*Ni-meetoru heehoo no teeburu no meñseki wa yoñ heehoo meetoru aru.*) 2メートル平方のテーブルの面積は4平方メートルある。
— *vt.* ... o heʅehoo suru ...を平方する Ⓘ; niʅjoo suru 2乗する Ⓘ: 3 squared is 9. (*Sañ no ni-joo wa kyuu.*) 3の2乗は9。

squash *n.* (vegetable) kaʅbocha かぼちゃ。

squeak *vi.* kiʅshiʅru きしる Ⓒ: This door squeaks. (*Kono doa wa kishiru.*) このドアはきしる。

— *n.* chuʅu-chuu naʅku koʅe ちゅうちゅう鳴く声; kiʅi-kii to iu oʅtoʅ きーきーという音: the squeak of a mouse (*nezumi no chuu-chuu naku koe*) ねずみのちゅうちゅう鳴く声。

squeeze *vt.* **1** (press hard) ... o tsuʅyoku oʅsu ...を強く押す Ⓒ; tsuʅyoku niʅgiru 強く握る Ⓒ: I took his hand and squeezed it. (*Watashi wa kare no te o totte tsuyoku nigitta.*) 私は彼の手をとって強く握った。
2 (extract) ... o shiʅboʅru ...を搾る Ⓒ; shiʅboridaʅsu 搾り出す Ⓒ: squeeze the juice from a lemon (*remoñ kara juusu o shiboridasu*) レモンからジュースを搾り出す。★ Japanese '*shiboru*' also means 'wring.'
3 (cram) ... o tsuʅmekomu ...を詰め込む Ⓒ: squeeze things into a suitcase (*suutsukeesu ni mono o tsumekomu*) スーツケースにものを詰め込む。
— *vi.* waʅrikoʅmu 割り込む Ⓒ: squeeze between two cars (*ni-dai no kuruma no aida ni warikomu*) 2台の車の間に割り込む。
— *n.* shiʅboʅru koʅtoʅ 搾ること; daʅkishimeʅru koʅtoʅ 抱き締めること。

squirrel *n.* riʅsu りす。

stab *vt.* ... o tsuʅkisaʅsu ...を突き刺す Ⓒ: The man stabbed him with a knife. (*Sono otoko wa naifu de kare o sashita.*) その男はナイフで彼を刺した。
— *vi.* (... ni) tsuʅkikakaʅru (...に)突きかかる Ⓒ: He stabbed at me. (*Kare wa watashi ni tsukikakatta.*) 彼は私に突きかかった。
— *n.* (thrust) saʅsu koʅtoʅ 刺すこと; (wound) saʅshiʅkizu 刺し傷。

stability *n.* aʅñtee 安定; aʅñteesee 安定性: political stability (*seejiteki na añtee*) 政治的な安定。

stable[1] *adj.* **1** (unchanging) aʅñtee shita [shite iru] 安定した[している]: Prices are stable now. (*Bukka wa ima añtee shite iru.*) 物価はいま安定している。
2 (firm) shiʅkkaʅri shita [shite iru] しっかりした[している]: stable foundations (*shikkari shita kiso*) しっかりし

た基礎.

stable[2] *n.* **1** (of a horse) uˈmagoya 馬小屋; uˈmaya 馬屋.
2 (club) kuˈrabu クラブ: a stable of sumo wrestlers (*sumoo-beya*) 相撲部屋.

stack *n.* **1** (pile) tsuˈmikasane 積み重ね; yaˈma 山: a stack of old newspapers (*furushiñbuñ no yama*) 古新聞の山.
2 (haystack) hoˈshikusa no yamaˈ 干し草の山.
—— *vt.* ... o tsuˈmikasaneˈru ...を積み重ねる Ⓥ: He stacked the books on the desk. (*Kare wa tsukue no ue ni hoñ o tsumikasaneta.*) 彼は机の上に本を積み重ねた.

stadium *n.* suˈtaˈjiamu スタジアム; kyoˈogijoo 競技場.

staff *n.* shoˈkuˈiñ 職員; buˈiñ 部員; suˈtaˈffu スタッフ: the teaching staff of a school (*gakkoo no kyooshokuiñ*) 学校の教職員 / the editorial staff (*heñshuu buiñ*) 編集部員.
★ Japanese 'sutaffu' usually refers to a staff member.

stage *n.* **1** (of a theater) buˈtai 舞台; suˈteˈeji ステージ: appear on the stage (*butai ni tatsu*) 舞台に立つ.
2 (period) daˈñkai 段階; jiˈki 時期: The research is still in the testing stage. (*Keñkyuu wa mada jikkeñ dañkai da.*) 研究はまだ実験段階だ.
—— *vt.* ... o joˈoeñ suru ...を上演する Ⓣ: They staged the play for the first time. (*Kare-ra wa sono geki o hajimete jooeñ shita.*) 彼らはその劇を初めて上演した.

stagger *vi.* **1** (sway) yoˈromeˈku よろめく Ⓒ; yoˈroyoro aˈruˈku よろろ歩く Ⓒ: The drunk man staggered along the road. (*Yopparai wa yoroyoro michi o aruite itta.*) 酔っぱらいはよろよろ道を歩いて行った.
2 (be shocked) guˈratsuku ぐらつく Ⓒ; taˈjiroˈgu たじろぐ Ⓒ: He was staggered by the price. (*Kare wa sono nedañ ni tajiroida.*) 彼はその値段にたじろいだ.
—— *vt.* **1** (make stagger) ... o yoˈromekaˈsu ...をよろめかす Ⓒ: The blow staggered him. (*Sono ichigeki ga kare o yoromekashita.*) その一撃が彼をよろめかした.
2 (shock) ... o guˈratsukaseru ...をぐらつかせる Ⓥ: The news staggered his determination. (*Sono shirase wa kare no kesshiñ o guratsukaseta.*) その知らせは彼の決心をぐらつかせた.

stain *vt.* ... o yoˈgosu ...を汚す Ⓒ: The coffee he spilt stained his trousers. (*Kare wa koohii o koboshite zuboñ o yogoshita.*) 彼はコーヒーをこぼしてズボンを汚した.
—— *vi.* yoˈgoreru 汚れる Ⓥ: White cloth stains easily. (*Shiroi nuno wa sugu yogoreru.*) 白い布はすぐ汚れる.
—— *n.* yoˈgore 汚れ; shiˈmi 染み: remove a stain (*shimi o toru*) 染みをとる.

stair *n.* kaˈidañ 階段: go up [down] the stairs (*kaidañ o agaru [oriru]*) 階段を上がる[下りる].

staircase *n.* kaˈidañ 階段: a spiral staircase (*raseñ-kaidañ*) らせん階段.

stake *n.* kuˈi くい; boˈo 棒: drive a stake into the ground (*kui o jimeñ ni uchikomu*) くいを地面に打ち込む.

stale *adj.* fuˈruku natta 古くなった; shiˈñseñ de naˈi 新鮮でない: stale bread (*furuku natta pañ*) 古くなったパン.

stalk *n.* (stem of a plant) kuˈkiˈ 茎.

stall *n.* baˈiteñ 売店; yaˈtai 屋台.

stammer *vi.* kuˈchigomoˈru 口ごもる Ⓒ; doˈmoˈru どもる Ⓒ: He stammers when he is angry. (*Kare wa okotte iru toki domoru.*) 彼は怒っているときどもる.
—— *vt.* ... o kuˈchigomori-naˈgara iˈu ...を口ごもりながら言う Ⓒ; doˈmori-naˈgara iˈu どもりながら言う Ⓒ: He stammered an apology. (*Kare wa domori-nagara ayamatta.*) 彼はどもりながら謝った.

stamp *n.* **1** (of a letter) kiˈtte 切手; (of tax) iˈñshi 印紙: a postage stamp (*yuubiñ-kitte*) 郵便切手 / a commemorative stamp (*kineñ-*

kitte) 記念切手 / a revenue stamp (*shuunyuu-inshi*) 収入印紙.
2 (seal) su「tañpu スタンプ; ha¹ñ 判; i¹ñ 印: a rubber stamp (*gomu-iñ*) ゴム印.

— *vt.* **1** (bring one's foot down) ... o fu「mitsuke¹ru ...を踏みつける Ⓥ; fu「minara¹su 踏み鳴らす Ⓒ: He stamped his foot in anger. (*Kare wa okotte ashi o fuminarashita.*) 彼は怒って足を踏み鳴らした.
2 (print) ... ni ha¹ñ o o「su ...に判を押す Ⓒ: stamp a passport (*pasupooto ni hañ o osu*) パスポートに判を押す.
3 (paste) ... ni ki「tte [i「ñshi] o haru ...に切手[印紙]をはる Ⓒ: stamp a letter (*tegami ni kitte o haru*) 手紙に切手をはる.

— *vi.* (... o) fu「mitsuke¹ru (...を)踏みつける Ⓥ: He stamped on the insect. (*Kare wa sono mushi o fumitsuketa.*) 彼はその虫を踏みつけた.

stand *vi.* **1** (be in an upright position) ta¹tte iru 立っている Ⓥ: He was standing by the window. (*Kare wa mado no soba ni tatte ita.*) 彼は窓のそばに立っていた.
2 (rise to one's feet) ta「chiagaru 立ち上がる Ⓒ: Everybody stood when the teacher came in. (*Señsee ga haitte kita toki zeñiñ ga tachiagatta.*) 先生が入って来たとき全員が立ち上がった.
3 (be situated) a¹ru ある Ⓒ: The castle stands on a hill. (*Sono shiro wa oka no ue ni arimasu.*) その城は丘の上にあります.
4 (be stopped) to「matte iru 止まっている Ⓥ: A taxi was standing in front of the station. (*Takushii ga eki no mae ni tomatte ita.*) タクシーが駅の前に止まっていた.

— *vt.* **1** (place in an upright position) ... o ta「te¹ru ...を立てる Ⓥ: stand a candle on the table (*roosoku o teeburu no ue ni tateru*) ろうそくをテーブルの上に立てる.
2 (bear) ... o ga「mañ suru ...を我慢する Ⓘ: I cannot stand her smoking.

(*Watashi wa kanojo ga tabako o suu no o gamañ dekinai.*) 私は彼女がたばこを吸うのを我慢できない.

stand for ... *vt.* ... o a「rawa¹su ...を表す Ⓒ: What does this mark stand for? (*Kono shirushi wa nani o arawashimasu ka?*) この印は何を表しますか.

stand out *vi.* me「da¹tsu 目立つ Ⓒ: The tall man stood out from the rest. (*Sono se no takai hito wa hoka no hito yori mo medatta.*) その背の高い人はほかの人よりも目立った.

— *n.* **1** (position) ta「chiba¹ 立場: He made his stand on the question clear. (*Kare wa sono moñdai ni tsuite no tachiba o akiraka ni shita.*) 彼はその問題についての立場を明らかにした.
2 (for spectators) ka「ñkyaku¹seki 観客席; su「tañdo スタンド.

standard *n.* hyo「ojuñ 標準; sui「juñ 水準: the living standard (*seekatsu-suijuñ*) 生活水準.

— *adj.* hyo「ojuñ no 標準の; fu「tsuu no 普通の: standard size (*hyoojuñ saizu*) 標準サイズ.

standing *n.* mi「buñ 身分; chi¹i 地位: people of high standing (*mibuñ no takai hito-tachi*) 身分の高い人たち / the social standing of women (*josee no shakai-teki chii*) 女性の社会的地位.

standpoint *n.* ta「chiba¹ 立場; ke「ñchi 見地: consider the problem from various standpoints (*iroiro na keñchi kara moñdai o kañgaeru*) いろいろな見地から問題を考える.

star *n.* **1** (heavenly body) ho「shi 星; (figure) ho「shiji¹rushi 星印.
2 (famous performer) su「ta¹a スター: a movie star (*eega sutaa*) 映画スター.

— *vi.* shu「eñ suru 主演する Ⓘ: She starred in the movie. (*Kanojo wa sono eega de shueñ shita.*) 彼女はその映画で主演した.

stare *vi.* (... o) ji「tto mitsumeru (...を)じっと見つめる Ⓥ: She was staring out of the window. (*Kanojo wa* *mado kara soto o jitto mitsumete ita.*) 彼女は窓から外をじっと見つめていた.

— *vt.* ... *o ji*「*tto mitsumeru* …をじっと見つめる Ⅴ; *ji*「*rojiro na*「*game*「*ru* じろじろ眺める Ⅴ: She stared me in the face. (*Kanojo wa watashi no kao o jitto mitsumeta.*) 彼女は私の顔をじっと見つめた.

start *vi.* **1** (begin) ha「*jimaru* 始まる Ⓒ: The concert starts at seven. (*Koñsaato wa shichi-ji ni hajimarimasu.*) コンサートは7時に始まります.
2 (leave) shu「*ppatsu suru* 出発する Ⅰ; de「*kakeru* 出かける Ⅴ: He started on his trip yesterday. (*Kare wa kinoo ryokoo ni shuppatsu shimashita.*) 彼はきのう旅行に出発しました.

— *vt.* **1** (casue to begin) ... *o* ha「*jimeru* …を始める Ⅴ: He started working at six in the morning. (*Kare wa asa roku-ji ni shigoto o hajimeta.*) 彼は朝6時に仕事を始めた.
2 (set in motion) ... *o* shi「*doo saseru* …を始動させる Ⅴ: start the engine (*eñjiñ o shidoo saseru*) エンジンを始動させる.

— *n.* **1** (beginning) ka「*ishi* 開始; ha「*jime* 始め: The play was boring at the start. (*Sono geki wa hajime wa tsumaranakatta.*) その劇は始めはつまらなかった.
2 (leaving) shu「*ppatsu* 出発; su「*ta*「*ato* スタート: make an early start (*hayame ni shuppatsu suru*) 早めに出発する.

startle *vt.* ... *o* bi「*kku*「*ri saseru* びっくりさせる Ⅴ; to「*biagarase*「*ru* 跳び上がらせる Ⅴ: I was startled to hear the news. (*Watashi wa sono shirase o kiite bikkuri shita.*) 私はその知らせを聞いてびっくりした.

starve *vi.* **1** (suffer from hunger) u「*e*「*ru* 飢える Ⅴ; ga「*shi suru* 餓死する Ⅰ: There was no food and many people starved to death. (*Taberu mono ga nakute ooku no hito ga gashi shita.*) 食べる物がなくて多くの人が餓死した.
2 (be very hungry) o-「*naka ga pe*-

kopeko da お腹がぺこぺこだ: I'm starving. (*O-naka ga pekopeko da.*) お腹がぺこぺこだ.

— *vt.* ... *o* u「*esase*「*ru* …を飢えさせる Ⅴ; ga「*shi saseru* 餓死させる Ⅴ: starve animals (*doobutsu o gashi saseru*) 動物を餓死させる.

state *n.* **1** (country) ko「*kka* 国家; (administrative unit) shu「*u* 州: an independent state (*dokuritsu kokka*) 独立国家 / There are fifty states in the U.S. (*Gasshuukoku ni wa gojuu no shuu ga aru.*) 合衆国には50の州がある.
2 (condition) jo「*otai* 状態: I inquired about her state of health. (*Watashi wa kanojo no keñkoo-jootai ni tsuite tazuneta.*) 私は彼女の健康状態について尋ねた.

— *vt.* ... *o* no「*beru* …を述べる Ⅴ: state one's opinion (*jibuñ no ikeñ o noberu*) 自分の意見を述べる.

stately *adj.* do「*odo*「*o to shita* [shite iru] 堂々とした[している]; i「*geñ no a*「*ru* 威厳のある: a stately building (*doodoo to shita tatemono*) 堂々とした建物.

statement *n.* **1** (the act of stating) chi「*ñjutsu* 陳述; mo「*oshitate* 申し立て: make a false statement (*uso no chiñjutsu o suru*) うその陳述をする.
2 (formal declaration) se「*emee* 声明; su「*te*「*etomeñto* ステートメント: a joint statement (*kyoodoo-seemee*) 共同声明.

statesman *n.* se「*ejika* 政治家.

station *n.* **1** (stopping place) e「*ki* 駅: I get off at the next station. (*Tsugi no eki de orimasu.*) 次の駅で降ります. / Where is the nearest subway station? (*Ichibañ chikai chikatetsu no eki wa doko desu ka?*) いちばん近い地下鉄の駅はどこですか.
2 (building) sho「*sho* 署; kyo「*ku* 局: a police station (*keesatsu-sho*) 警察署 / a fire station (*shooboo-sho*) 消防署 / a broadcasting station (*hoosoo-kyoku*) 放送局.

stationery *n.* (materials for writing) buˈnboˈlogu 文房具; (letter paper) biˈñseñ 便せん.

statistics n. toˈokee 統計: Statistics show that the population is increasing. (*Tookee ni yoreba jiñkoo wa fuete iru.*) 統計によれば人口は増えている.

statue n. zoˈlo 像; choˈrozoo 彫像: a bronze statue (*doozoo*) 銅像 / a wooden statue (*mokuzoo*) 木像.

status n. **1** (position) chiˈli 地位; miˈlbuñ 身分: the social status of women (*josee no shakai-teki chii*) 女性の社会的地位.
2 (condition) joˈotai 状態: the current status of the negotiations (*geñzai no kooshoo no jootai*) 現在の交渉の状態.

stay vi. **1** (remain) (... ni) toˈdomaˈ-ru (...に)とどまる Ⓒ; iˈru いる Ⓥ: I stayed in the house all day. (*Watashi wa ichi-nichi-juu ie ni ima-shita.*) 私は一日中家にいました.
2 (live for a time) (... ni) taˈizai suru (...に)滞在する Ⓘ; toˈmaru 泊まる Ⓒ: How long are you staying here? (*Dono kurai koko ni taizai shimasu ka?*) どのくらいここに滞在しますか. / I'll stay at the Tokyo Hotel. (*Watashi wa Tookyoo Hoteru ni tomarimasu.*) 私は東京ホテルに泊まります.
3 (continue to be) maˈmaˈ de iˈru ままでいる Ⓥ: Please stay seated. (*Doozo suwatta mama de ite kuda-sai.*) どうぞ座ったままでいてください.
— n. taˈizai 滞在: I hope you enjoy your stay in Kyoto. (*Kyooto ni go-taizai-chuu wa tanoshiku o-sugoshi kudasai.*) 京都にご滞在中は楽しくお過ごしください.

steadily adv. chaˈkujitsu ni 着実に; shiˈkkaˈri to しっかりと: His Japanese is improving steadily. (*Kare no Nihoñgo wa chakujitsu ni jootatsu shite imasu.*) 彼の日本語は着実に上達しています.

steady adj. **1** (not changing) kaˈwa-ranai 変わらない; iˈchiyoo na 一様な: walk at a steady pace (*kawa-*

ranai hochoo de aruku) 変わらない歩調で歩く.
2 (firm) shiˈkkaˈri shita [shite iru] しっかりした[している]; aˈñtee shita [shite iru] 安定した[している]: This table is steady. (*Kono teeburu wa shikkari shite iru.*) このテーブルはしっかりしている.
3 (serious) keˈñjitsu na 堅実な; maˈjime na まじめな: a steady young man (*majime na seeneñ*) まじめな青年.
— vt. ... o aˈñtee saseru ...を安定させる Ⓥ; oˈchitsukaseru 落ち着かせる Ⓥ: These pills will steady your nerves. (*Kono kusuri wa anata no shiñkee o ochitsukaseru deshoo.*) この薬はあなたの神経を落ち着かせるでしょう.

steak n. suˈteˈleki ステーキ; biˈfuteki ビフテキ.

steal vt. ... o nuˈsuˈlmu ...を盗む Ⓒ: Somebody has stolen my bag. (*Dare-ka ga watashi no kabañ o nusuñda.*) だれかが私のかばんを盗んだ. / I had my wallet stolen. (*Watashi wa saifu o nusumareta.*) 私は財布を盗まれた.
— vi. nuˈsumiˈ o suru 盗みをする Ⓘ: It is wrong to steal. (*Nusumi o suru koto wa warui koto da.*) 盗みをすることは悪いことだ.

steam n. suˈijoˈloki 水蒸気; yuˈlge 湯気: Steam is rising from the kettle. (*Yakañ kara yuge ga agatte iru.*) やかんから湯気が上がっている.
— vt. ... o muˈlsu ...を蒸す Ⓒ; fuˈlkaˈsu ふかす Ⓒ: steam potatoes (*jagaimo o fukasu*) じゃがいもをふかす.
— vi. yuˈlge o taˈteˈlru 湯気を立てる Ⓥ; kuˈmoˈru 曇る Ⓒ: My glasses steamed up. (*Megane ga kumotta.*) 眼鏡が曇った.

steamer n. (steamship) kiˈlseñ 汽船; (container) muˈshiˈlki 蒸し器.

steamship n. kiˈlseñ 汽船.

steel n. koˈotetsu 鋼鉄; haˈgane 鋼: This tool is made of steel. (*Kono doogu wa kootetsu de de-kite iru.*) この道具は鋼鉄でできている.

steep adj. kyu⌐u na 急な; ke⌐washi⌐i 険しい: a steep slope (kyuu na saka) 急な坂 / a steep hill (kewashii oka) 険しい丘.

steer vt. (direct the movement) (... ni) ... o mu⌐keru (…に)…を向ける Ⓥ: The ship steered a course for the island. (Fune wa shima no hoo ni koosu o muketa.) 船は島の方にコースを向けた.
— vi. (of a car) u⌐ñteñ suru 運転する Ⓘ; (of a ship) ka⌐ji o toru 舵を取る Ⓒ: This car steers easily. (Kono kuruma wa uñteñ shi-yasui.) この車は運転しやすい.

steering wheel n. (of a car) ha⌐ñdoru ハンドル.

stem n. (trunk) mi⌐ki 幹; (stalk) ku⌐ki⌐i 茎.

stenographer n. so⌐kki⌐sha 速記者.

stenography n. so⌐kki 速記; so⌐kki⌐jutsu 速記術.

step n. **1** (one motion of the leg) a⌐yumi 歩み; i⌐p-po 一歩: He took a step back. (Kare wa ip-po ushiro e sagatta.) 彼は一歩後ろへ下がった. **2** (gait) a⌐rukiburi 歩きぶり; a⌐shidori 足どり: walk with a light step (karui ashidori de aruku) 軽い足りで歩く. **3** (sound) a⌐shioto 足音: I heard steps outside. (Soto de ashioto ga kikoeta.) 外で足音が聞こえた. **4** (of a stair) ka⌐idañ 階段; su⌐te⌐p-pu ステップ.
— vi. (walk) a⌐ru⌐ku 歩く Ⓒ; su⌐sumu 進む Ⓒ: step forward (mae e susumu) 前へ進む.

stereo n. su⌐tereo ステレオ; su⌐tereo so⌐ochi ステレオ装置: record in stereo (sutereo de rokuoñ suru) ステレオで録音する.

sterile adj. (of land) fu⌐moo no 不毛の; (of animals) fu⌐niñ no 不妊の; (of germs) mu⌐kiñ no 無菌の.

stern adj. ge⌐ñkaku na 厳格な; ki⌐bishi⌐i 厳しい: a stern teacher (geñkaku na señsee) 厳格な先生 / He is stern to his pupils. (Kare wa seeto ni kibishii.) 彼は生徒に厳しい.

stew n. shi⌐chu⌐u シチュー.
— vt. ... o to⌐robi de niru …をとろ火で煮る Ⓥ; shi⌐chu⌐u ni suru シチューにする Ⓥ: stewed beef (biifu shichuu) ビーフシチュー.

steward n. su⌐chuwa⌐ado スチュワード; kyu⌐uji 給仕.

stewardess n. su⌐chuwa⌐adesu スチュワーデス.

stick[1] vt. **1** (pierce) ... o tsu⌐kisa⌐su …を突き刺す Ⓒ: I stuck my hand with a pin. (Watashi wa piñ de te o tsukisashita.) 私はピンで手を突き刺した. **2** (thrust) ... ni tsu⌐kko⌐mu …に突っ込む Ⓒ: He stuck his hands in his pockets. (Kare wa ryoote o poketto ni tsukkoñda.) 彼は両手をポケットに突っ込んだ. **3** (fasten) ... o ku⌐ttsuke⌐ru …をくっつける Ⓥ; ha⌐ru はる Ⓒ; to⌐meru 留める Ⓥ: stick a stamp on an envelope (fuutoo ni kitte o haru) 封筒に切手をはる / stick a notice on the wall with tacks (bira o kabe ni byoo de tomeru) ビラを壁にびょうで留める.
— vi. **1** (be pierced) sa⌐sa⌐ru 刺さる Ⓒ: A nail stuck in the tire. (Kugi ga taiya ni sasatta.) くぎがタイヤに刺さった. **2** (be fastened) ku⌐ttsu⌐ku くっつく Ⓒ: This glue sticks well. (Kono nori wa yoku kuttsuku.) このりはよくくっつく.

stick[2] n. **1** (twig) bo⌐okire 棒切れ; ki⌐gire⌐i 木切れ: collect sticks for firewood (takigi ni suru tame ni kigire o atsumeru) 薪にするために木切れを集める. **2** (slender piece) bo⌐ojoo no mono⌐i 棒状のもの: a stick of candy (boojoo no kyañdee) 棒状のキャンデー. **3** (cane) tsu⌐e つえ; su⌐te⌐kki ステッキ: walk with a stick (tsue o tsuite aruku) つえをついて歩く.

sticky adj. ne⌐baneba suru ねばねばする; be⌐tobeto na べとべとな: His fingers are sticky with jam. (Kare no yubi wa jamu de betobeto da.)

彼の指はジャムでべとべとだ.

stiff *adj.* **1** (rigid) ka⌐tai 堅い; ko-⌐waba¬tta こわばった; ko⌐waba¬tte iru こわばっている: stiff cardboard (*katai boorugami*) 堅いボール紙.

2 (formal) ka⌐takurushi¬i 堅苦しい; (awkward) gi⌐kochina¬i ぎこちない: make a stiff bow (*katakurushii ojigi o suru*) 堅苦しいおじぎをする / a stiff style of writing (*gikochinai buntai*) ぎこちない文体.

stiffen *vt.* ... o ka⌐taku suru ...を硬くする Ⅰ; ko⌐wabarase¬ru こわばらせる Ⅴ: stiffen a collar with starch (*karaa o nori de kataku suru*) カラーをのりで硬くする.
— *vi.* ka⌐taku na¬ru 硬くなる Ⅽ: The body stiffens with age. (*Karada wa toshi o toru to kataku naru.*) 体は年をとると硬くなる.

still[1] *adv.* **1** (up to now) ma⌐¬da まだ; i¬ma mo 今も: He is still in bed. (*Kare wa mada nete iru.*) 彼はまだ寝ている. / I still don't feel well. (*Mada kibuñ wa yoku arimaseñ.*) まだ気分は良くありません.

2 (nevertheless) so⌐re de¬ mo nao それでもなお: He failed, but still he wants to try again. (*Kare wa shippai shita ga sore de mo nao moo ichi-do yatte mitai to omotte iru.*) 彼は失敗したがそれでもなおもう一度やってみたいと思っている.

3 (even) na⌐o i¬ssoo なおいっそう; sa⌐ra ni さらに: It became still colder. (*Nao issoo samuku natta.*) なおいっそう寒くなった.

still[2] *adj.* **1** (quiet) shi⌐zuka na 静かな; shi¬ñ to shita [shite iru] しんとした[している]: a still night (*shizuka na yoru*) 静かな夜 / The empty house was still. (*Akiya wa shiñ to shite ita.*) 空き家はしんとしていた.

2 (motionless) se⌐eshi shita [shite iru] 静止した[している]; jit⌐to shita [shite iru] じっとした[している]: sit still (*jitto suwatte iru*) じっと座っている.

stimulate *vt.* **1** (excite) ... o shi-⌐geki suru ...を刺激する Ⅰ; ko⌐ofuñ saseru 興奮させる Ⅴ: The smells of cooking stimulated his appetite. (*Ryoori no nioi ga kare no shoku-yoku o shigeki shita.*) 料理のにおいが彼の食欲を刺激した.

2 (encourage) ... no ha⌐gemi to na⌐ru ...の励みとなる Ⅽ: Praise stimulated him to further efforts. (*Homerareta koto ga hagemi to natte kare wa issoo doryoku shita.*) ほめられたことが励みとなって彼はいっそう努力した.

stimulus *n.* shi⌐geki 刺激; shi⌐ge-ki¬butsu 刺激物: a stimulus to industrial development (*sañgyoo no hattatsu o unagasu shigeki*) 産業の発達を促す刺激.

sting *vt.* **1** (prick) ... o sa⌐su ...を刺す Ⅽ: An insect stung me. (*Mushi ga watashi o sashita.*) 虫が私を刺した.

2 (cause pain) ... o hi⌐rihiri saseru ...をひりひりさせる Ⅴ: The salt water made my cut sting. (*Shiomizu de kizuguchi ga hirihiri shita.*) 塩水で傷口がひりひりした.
— *vi.* sa⌐su 刺す Ⅽ: This bee does not sting. (*Kono hachi wa sashimaseñ.*) この蜂は刺しません.

stingy *adj.* ke⌐chi na けちな; ke⌐chi-kusa¬i けちくさい: a stingy person (*kechi na hito*) けちな人.

stir *vt.* **1** (mix) ... o ka⌐kimawasu ...をかき回す Ⅰ; ka⌐kimazeru かき混ぜる Ⅴ: stir some sugar into one's coffee (*koohii ni satoo o irete kakimazeru*) コーヒーに砂糖を入れてかき混ぜる.

2 (excite) ... o ka⌐kitateru ...をかき立てる Ⅴ: His story stirred my curiosity. (*Kare no hanashi wa watashi no kookishiñ o kakitateta.*) 彼の話は私の好奇心をかき立てた.
— *vi.* (move) u⌐goku 動く Ⅽ: Something stirred in the darkness. (*Nani-ka ga kurayami de ugoita.*) 何かが暗やみで動いた.

stitch *n.* hi⌐to¬-hari ひと針; hi⌐to¬-nui ひと縫い: take up a stitch (*hito-hari nuu*) ひと針縫う.

stock *n.* **1** (shares) ka⌐bu 株; ka-

「bu˥shiki 株式: Stocks are going up. (*Kabu ga agatte iru.*) 株が上がっている.

2 (supply) ta˥kuwae 蓄え; cho˥zoo 貯蔵: The stock of food is getting low. (*Shokuryoo no takuwae ga geñshoo shite iru.*) 食糧の蓄えが減少している.

3 (store of goods) za˥iko 在庫: The book is in stock. (*Sono hoñ wa zaiko ga arimasu.*) その本は在庫があります.

4 (livestock) ka˥chiku 家畜.

stocking *n.* ku˥tsu˥shita 靴下; su-˥to˥kkiñgu ストッキング: put on [take off] one's stockings (*kutsushita o haku [nugu]*) 靴下をはく[脱ぐ].

★ 'Socks' are also called '*kutsu-shita.*'

stomach *n.* **1** (organ) i˥ 胃: I have a pain in my stomach. (*Watashi wa i ga itai.*) 私は胃が痛い. / stomach medicine (*i no kusuri*) 胃の薬.

2 (abdomen) ha˥ra˥] 腹; o˥naka お腹.

stomachache *n.* i˥tsuu 胃痛; fu-˥kutsuu 腹痛: I have a stomachache. (*I [Onaka] ga itai.*) 胃[お腹]が痛い.

stone *n.* i˥shi˥] 石; ko˥ishi 小石: a monument built of stone (*ishi de dekite iru kineñhi*) 石でできている記念碑 / The stone hit the window. (*Koishi ga mado ni atatta.*) 小石が窓に当たった.

stool *n.* ma˥ruisu 丸いす; ko˥shika-ke˥] 腰掛け.

stoop *vi.* ma˥eka˥gami ni naru 前かがみになる Ⓒ; ka˥gamu かがむ Ⓒ: I stooped down and picked up a pencil. (*Watashi wa kagañde eñpitsu o hiroiageta.*) 私はかがんで鉛筆を拾い上げた.

stop *vt.* **1** (halt) ... o to˥meru ...を止める Ⓥ: I stopped my car at the traffic lights. (*Watashi wa shiñgoo de kuruma o tometa.*) 私は信号で車を止めた.

2 (discontinue) ... o chu˥ushi suru ...を中止する Ⓘ; ya˥meru やめる Ⓥ: He stopped smoking. (*Kare wa tabako o suu no o yameta.*) 彼はたば

こを吸うのをやめた.

— *vi.* **1** (cease moving) to˥maru 止まる Ⓒ: Does this train stop at Nara? (*Kono ressha wa Nara ni tomarimasu ka?*) この列車は奈良に止まりますか.

2 (come to an end) chu˥udañ suru 中断する Ⓘ; ya˥mu やむ Ⓒ: The rain has stopped. (*Ame ga yañda.*) 雨がやんだ.

3 (stay) (... ni) ta˥izai suru (...に)滞在する Ⓘ; to˥maru 泊まる Ⓒ: I'm going to stop at a hotel. (*Watashi wa hoteru ni tomarimasu.*) 私はホテルに泊まります.

— *n.* **1** (halting) to˥maru koto˥] 止まること: come to a stop (*tomaru*) 止まる / This train goes to Ueno without a stop. (*Kono ressha wa Ueno made tomarazu ni ikimasu.*) この列車は上野まで止まらずに行きます.

2 (place where a bus stops) te˥e-ryuujo 停留所; (of a train) te˥e-shaba 停車場: I get off at the next stop. (*Tsugi no teeryuujo de orimasu.*) 次の停留所で降ります.

3 (stay) ta˥izai 滞在; shu˥kuhaku 宿泊: I want to make a week's stop in Kyoto. (*Watashi wa Kyooto ni is-shuukañ taizai shitai.*) 私は京都に1週間滞在したい.

store *n.* **1** (shop) mi˥se˥] 店; sho˥o-teñ 商店: The store opens at ten o'clock. (*Mise wa juu-ji ni hirakimasu.*) 店は10時に開きます.

2 (stock) ta˥kuwae 蓄え; cho˥zoo 貯蔵: have a good store of food (*tabemono o juubuñ ni takuwaete aru*) 食べ物を十分に蓄えてある.

— *vt.* **1** (put aside) ... o ta˥ku-wae˥ru ...を蓄える Ⓥ: store up fuel for the winter (*fuyu ni sonaete neñ-ryoo o takuwaeru*) 冬に備えて燃料を蓄える.

2 (put in a storehouse) ... o (... ni) ho˥kañ suru ...を(...に)保管する Ⓘ: store the furniture in a warehouse (*kagu o sooko ni hokañ suru*) 家具を倉庫に保管する.

stork *n.* ko˥ono˥tori こうのとり.

storm *n.* aˈrashi 嵐; boˈofuˈu-u 暴
風雨: The antenna was damaged
by the storm. (*Añtena ga arashi
de kowareta.*) アンテナが嵐で壊れた.
— *vi.* aˈrashi ga fuku 嵐が吹く C:
It stormed all night long. (*Arashi
ga hito-bañ-juu fuita.*) 嵐が一晩中
吹いた.

story[1] *n.* **1** (imaginary account)
moˈnogaˈtari 物語; (novel) shoˈosetsu 小説: a love story (*koi monogatari*) 恋物語 / a detective story (*sui-
ri-shoosetsu*) 推理小説.
2 (true account) haˈnashiˈ 話;
(news) kiˈji 記事: It is the same old
story. (*Sore wa yoku aru hanashi
da.*) それはよくある話だ.

story[2] *n.* (level of building) kaˈi 階:
the upper [lower] story (*ue* [*shita*]
no kai) 上[下]の階.

stove *n.* (cooking device) reˈñji レン
ジ; (heater) suˈtoˈobu ストーブ.
★ Japanese '*sutoobu*' is used only
for 'heater.'

straight *adj.* **1** (without a bend)
maˈssuˈgu na 真っすぐな; iˈtchoˈku-
señ no 一直線の: a straight path
(*massugu na michi*) 真っすぐな道.
2 (upright) choˈkuritsu shita [shite
iru] 直立した[している]; maˈssuˈgu na
真っすぐな: drive a stake straight
into the ground (*kui o jimeñ ni
massugu ni uchikomu*) くいを地面に
真っすぐに打ち込む.
3 (in good order) kiˈchiˈñto shita
[shite iru] きちんとした[している]: keep
one's room straight (*heya o kichiñto shite oku*) 部屋をきちんとしておく.
— *adv.* **1** (directly) choˈkusetsu
ni 直接に; maˈssuˈgu 真っすぐ: I
went straight home. (*Watashi wa
massugu uchi e kaerimashita.*) 私
は真っすぐ家へ帰りました.
2 (in a straight line) maˈssuˈgu ni
真っすぐに; iˈtchoˈkuseñ ni 一直線に:
Keep straight on. (*Massugu ni iki
nasai.*) 真っすぐに行きなさい.

straighten *vt.* **1** (make straight)
... o maˈssuˈgu ni suru ...を真っすぐに
する □: straighten one's tie (*neku-*

tai o massugu ni naosu) ネクタイを
真っすぐに直す.
2 (put in order) ... o seˈetoñ suru
...を整頓する □: straighten one's
room (*heya o seetoñ suru*) 部屋を
整頓する.

strain *vt.* **1** (hurt) ... o iˈtameˈru ...
を痛める V: I strained my eyes by
reading too much. (*Hoñ o yomi-
sugite me o itameta.*) 本を読みすぎて
目を痛めた.
2 (stretch tight) piˈñ to haru ぴんと
張る C: strain a wire (*harigane o
piñ to haru*) 針金をぴんと張る.
3 (separate a liquid) ... o koˈsu ...を
こす C; miˈzu o kiˈru 水を切る C:
strain the coffee (*koohii o kosu*) コ
ーヒーをこす / strain the vegetables
(*yasai no mizu o kiru*) 野菜の水を切
る.
— *vi.* **1** (pull) (... o) hiˈppaˈru (...
を)引っぱる C: We strained at the
rope. (*Watashi-tachi wa sono
roopu o hippatta.*) 私たちはそのロープ
を引っ張った.
2 (try very hard) keˈñmee ni doˈ-
ryoku suru 懸命に努力する □: strain
for victory (*shoori o mezashite
keñmee ni doryoku suru*) 勝利を目
指して懸命に努力する.
— *n.* **1** (force exerted) hiˈppaˈru
chiˈkaraˈ 引っ張る力: The strain
broke under the strain. (*Hipparu
chikara ga tsuyokute tsuna ga
kireta.*) 引っ張る力が強くて綱が切れた.
2 (overwork) kaˈroo 過労: The
strain made him ill. (*Karoo de
kare wa byooki ni natta.*) 過労で彼
は病気になった.

strange *adj.* **1** (odd) kiˈmyoo na
奇妙な; heˈñ na 変な: There is something strange about him. (*Kare wa
doko-ka heñ da.*) 彼はどこか変だ.
2 (unfamiliar) miˈshiranu 見知らぬ;
shiˈranai 知らない: visit a strange
land (*shiranai kuni o tazuneru*) 知
らない国を訪ねる.

stranger *n.* **1** (unknown person)
shiˈranai hito 知らない人: The dog
barked at a stranger. (*Inu ga shi-*

ranai hito ni hoeta.) 犬が知らない人
にほえた.

2 (outsider) ha｢ji｣mete no hi｢to｣ 初
めての人: I am a stranger here.
(*Watashi wa koko wa hajimete
desu.*) 私はここは初めてです.

strap *n.* (narrow strip) ka｢wahimo
革ひも; (of a train) tsu｢rikawa つり
革: hold on to a strap (*tsurikawa
ni tsukamaru*) つり革につかまる.
— *vt.* ... o ka｢wahimo de shiba｣ru
...を革ひもで縛る Ⓒ: strap up a
trunk (*toranku o kawahimo de shibaru*) トランクを革ひもで縛る.

strategy *n.* **1** (military opera-
tions) se｢ñryaku 戦略: nuclear
strategy (*kaku señryaku*) 核戦略.
2 (skill) se｢ñryaku 戦略; shu｢dañ
手段: marketing strategy (*maake-
tiñgu señryaku*) マーケティング戦略.

straw *n.* **1** (stalk) wa｢ra わら: a
straw hat (*mugiwara-booshi*) 麦わ
ら帽子.
2 (for drinking) su｢to｣roo ストロー:
drink orange juice through a straw
(*oreñji juusu o sutoroo de nomu*)
オレンジュースをストローで飲む.

strawberry *n.* i｢chigo いちご(苺).

streak *n.* su｢ji 筋; shi｢ma｣ しま: He
has streaks of gray in his hair.
(*Kare wa kami no ke ni shiraga
ga majitte iru.*) 彼は髪の毛に白髪が
混じっている. / streaks of lightning
(*inazuma*) 稲妻.

stream *n.* **1** (brook) o｢gawa 小川:
cross a stream (*ogawa o wataru*)
小川を渡る.
2 (current) na｢gare｣ 流れ: go with
[against] the stream (*nagare ni shitagau* [*sakarau*]) 流れに従う[逆らう].
— *vi.* na｢gare｣ru 流れる Ⓥ: Tears
streamed down her cheeks. (*Namida ga kanojo no hoo o nagare-
ochita.*) 涙が彼女のほおを流れ落ちた.

street *n.* to｢ori｣ 通り; ga｢iro 街路:
His house is on this street. (*Kare
no uchi wa kono toori ni arimasu.*)
彼の家はこの通りにあります. / Follow
this street. (*Kono toori o iki nasai.*)
この通りを行きなさい. / a street map

(*gairo chizu*) 街路地図.

streetcar *n.* ro｢meñde｣ñsha 路面
電車.

strength *n.* **1** (power) chi｢kara｣
力; ta｢iryoku 体力: I don't have
the strength to lift the box. (*Watashi ni wa sono hako o mochiageru
chikara ga nai.*) 私にはその箱を持ち上
げる力がない. / He regained his
strength. (*Kare wa tairyoku o kaifuku shita.*) 彼は体力を回復した.
2 (mental power) chi｢ryoku 知力:
strength of mind (*seeshiñryoku*)
精神力.

strengthen *vt.* ... o tsu｢yoku suru
...を強くする Ⓣ; jo｢obu ni suru 丈夫
にする Ⓣ: strengthen one's body
(*karada o joobu ni suru*) 体を丈夫
にする.

stress *n.* **1** (pressure) a｢tsu｣ryoku
圧力: the stress of a roof on a
beam (*hari ni kakaru yane no
atsuryoku*) はりにかかる屋根の圧力.
2 (worry) su｢to｣resu ストレス: diseases caused by stress (*sutoresu de
okoru byooki*) ストレスで起こる病気.
3 (emphasis) kyo｢ochoo 強調; ju｢-
shi 重視: Our school places stress
on foreign languages. (*Watashi-
tachi no gakkoo wa gaikokugo o
juushi shite iru.*) 私たちの学校は外
国語を重視している.
— *vt.* ... o kyo｢ochoo suru ...を強
調する Ⓣ: He stressed the importance of health. (*Kare wa keñkoo
no juuyoosa o kyoochoo shita.*) 彼
は健康の重要さを強調した.

stretch *vt.* ... o no｢ba｣su ...を伸ばす
Ⓒ; hi｢rogeru 広げる Ⓥ: stretch
one's arms and yawn (*ude o noba-
shite akubi o suru*) 腕を伸ばしてあく
びをする / I stretched the carpet on
the floor. (*Watashi wa sono juutañ o yuka ni hirogeta.*) 私はそのじゅ
うたんを床に広げた.
— *vi.* no｢bi｣ru 伸びる Ⓥ; hi｢rogaru
広がる Ⓒ: My sweater stretched in
the wash. (*Arattara seetaa ga
nobite shimatta.*) 洗ったらセーターが
伸びてしまった. / The lake stretched

away into the distance. (*Mizuumi wa eñpoo made hirogatte ita.*) 湖は遠方まで広がっていた.

strict *adj.* **1** (rigid) ki⸢bishi⸣i 厳しい; ge⸢ñkaku na 厳格な: a strict teacher (*kibishii señsee*) 厳しい先生. **2** (exact) se⸢ñmitsu na 厳密な; se⸢ekaku na 正確な: a strict translation (*seekaku na hoñyaku*) 正確な翻訳.

strictly *adv.* ki⸢bi⸣shiku 厳しく; ge⸢ñmitsu ni 厳密に: Strictly speaking, this is illegal. (*Geñmitsu ni iu to kore wa ihoo da.*) 厳密に言うところれは違法だ.

stride *vi.* o⸢omata ni aru⸣ku 大またに歩く ©: He strode along the street. (*Kare wa toori o oomata ni aruita.*) 彼は通りを大またに歩いた. — *n.* o⸢omata no i⸣ppo 大またの一歩; hi⸢to⸣matagi ひとまたぎ: in one stride (*hitomatagi de*) ひとまたぎで.

strife *n.* a⸢raso⸣i 争い; to⸢osoo 闘争: factional strife (*habatsu no arasoi*) 派閥の争い.

strike *vt.* **1** (hit) ... o u⸢tsu ...を打つ ©; ... ni bu⸢tsukaru ...にぶつかる ©: strike a ball (*booru o utsu*) ボールを打つ / The car struck the guardrail. (*Kuruma wa gaadoreeru ni butsukatta.*) 車はガードレールにぶつかった. **2** (give a blow) ... o na⸢gu⸣ru ...を殴る ©: He hit me in the face. (*Kare wa watashi no kao o nagutta.*) 彼は私の顔を殴った. **3** (make a sound) ... o u⸢tsu ...を打つ ©; na⸢rasu 鳴らす ©: The clock struck seven. (*Tokee ga shichi-ji o utta.*) 時計が7時を打った. **4** (set on fire) ... o su⸢ru ...をする ©; tsu⸢ke⸣ru つける Ⓥ: He struck a match and lit a cigarette. (*Kare wa matchi o sutte tabako ni hi o tsuketa.*) 彼はマッチを擦ってたばこに火をつけた. **5** (enter the mind) ko⸢koro⸣ni u⸢kabu 心に浮かぶ ©: A good idea struck me. (*Yoi kañgae ga atama ni ukañda.*) よい考えが頭に浮かんだ. — *vi.* **1** (hit) (... ni) na⸢guri-ka-

ka⸣ru (...に)殴りかかる ©: He struck at the dog with a stick. (*Kare wa boo de inu ni naguri-kakatta.*) 彼は棒で犬に殴りかかった. **2** (quit work) su⸢tora⸣iki o suru ストライキをする Ⓘ: They are striking for higher wages. (*Kare-ra wa chiñage no tame ni sutoraiki o shite iru.*) 彼らは賃上げのためにストライキをしている. **3** (attack) (... o) ko⸢ogeki suru (...を)攻撃する Ⓘ: strike at the enemy (*teki o koogeki suru*) 敵を攻撃する. — *n.* **1** (the act of hitting) u⸢tsu ko⸣to⸣ 打つこと; ko⸢ogeki 攻撃. **2** (the act of quitting work) su⸢tora⸣iki ストライキ; su⸣to⸣ スト: go on strike (*suto ni hairu*) ストに入る. **3** (in baseball) su⸢tora⸣iku ストライク.

striking *adj.* me⸢da⸣tsu 目立つ: a striking dress (*medatsu doresu*) 目立つドレス.

string *n.* **1** (thin cord) hi⸢mo ひも; (thread) i⸢to 糸: tie up a parcel with string (*tsutsumi o himo de shibaru*) 包みをひもで縛る. **2** (connected series) re⸢ñzoku 連続; re⸣tsu 列: a string of cars (*kuruma no retsu*) 車の列.

strip¹ *vt.* **1** (take off) ... o ha⸢ga⸣su ...をはがす ©; mu⸢ku むく ©: strip the wallpaper off (*kabegami o hagasu*) 壁紙をはがす / strip the bark from a tree (*ki no kawa o muku*) 木の皮をむく. **2** (make bare) ... o ha⸢daka ni suru ...を裸にする Ⓘ: strip oneself (*hadaka ni naru*) 裸になる. **3** (remove) ... o to⸢rihara⸣u ...を取り払う ©: strip a room of furniture (*heya kara kagu o toriharau*) 部屋から家具を取り払う.

strip² *n.* ho⸢sonaga⸣i ki⸣re⸣ 細長い切れ: a strip of paper (*hosonagai kami kire*) 細長い紙切れ.

stripe *n.* su⸢ji 筋; shi⸢ma⸣ しま: a tie with stripes (*shima no nekutai*) しまのネクタイ.

strive *vi.* do⸢ryoku suru 努力する Ⓘ; tsu⸢tome⸣ru 努める Ⓥ: strive to win (*yuushoo shiyoo to tsutomeru*)

優勝しようと努める.

stroke[1] *n.* **1** (blow) iˈchigeki 一撃; daˈgeki 打撃: fell a tree with one stroke of the ax (*ono no ichigeki de ki o taosu*) おのの一撃で木を倒す.
2 (sudden attack of illness) hoˈssa 発作; soˈtchuu 卒中: have a stroke (*sotchuu ni kakaru*) 卒中にかかる.
3 (mark made in writing) hiˈtoˈfude 一筆; fuˈdezuˈkai 筆づかい: the final stroke (*shiage no hitofude*) 仕上げの一筆.
4 (movement) doˈosa 動作; suˈtoˈroˈoku ストローク: He swam with strong strokes. (*Kare wa chikara-zuyoi sutorooku de oyoida.*) 彼は力強いストロークで泳いだ.

stroke[2] *vt.* ... o naˈderu ...をなでる Ⓥ; saˈsuru さする Ⓒ: stroke a cat (*neko o naderu*) 猫をなでる.

stroll *vi.* buˈrabura aˈruˈku ぶらぶら歩く Ⓒ; saˈnpo suru 散歩する Ⓘ: I strolled along the beach. (*Watashi wa umibe o burabura sanpo shita.*) 私は海辺をぶらぶら散歩した.

strong *adj.* **1** (powerful) tsuˈyoˈi 強い: a strong man (*tsuyoi otoko*) 強い男 / strong winds (*tsuyoi kaze*) 強い風.
2 (durable) joˈobu na 丈夫な: strong cloth (*joobu na kiji*) 丈夫な生地.
3 (of drinks) koˈi 濃い: strong black coffee (*koi burakku koohii*) 濃いブラックコーヒー.

strongly *adv.* kyoˈokoo ni 強硬に; neˈsshiñ ni 熱心に: protest strongly (*kyookoo ni koogi suru*) 強硬に抗議する.

structure *n.* **1** (construction) koˈozoo 構造; soˈshiki 組織: the structure of a machine (*kikai no koozoo*) 機械の構造.
2 (building) keˈnzoˈobutsu 建造物; taˈteˈmono 建物: a marble structure (*dairiseki no tatemono*) 大理石の建物.

struggle *n.* **1** (great effort) doˈryoku 努力; fuˈntoo 奮闘: a desperate struggle (*hisshi no doryoku*

2 (fight) kyoˈosoo 競争; toˈosoo 闘争: the struggle for existence (*seezoñ-kyoosoo*) 生存競争.
— *vi.* fuˈntoo suru 奮闘する Ⓘ; doˈryoku suru 努力する Ⓘ: struggle for a living (*seekatsu no tame ni funtoo suru*) 生活のために奮闘する.

stubborn *adj.* gaˈnko na がんこな; goˈojoo na 強情な: a stubborn child (*goojoo na kodomo*) 強情な子ども.

student *n.* gaˈkusee 学生; seˈeto 生徒. ★ Junior and senior high school students are called 'seeto' and college and university students 'gakusee': a foreign student (*ryuugakusee*) 留学生.

studio *n.* **1** (of an artist) shiˈgotoba 仕事場; aˈtorie アトリエ.
2 (of a broadcasting station) hoˈosoˈoshitsu 放送室; suˈtajio スタジオ.

study *vt.* **1** (learn) ... o beˈnkyoo suru ...を勉強する Ⓘ; keˈnkyuu suru 研究する Ⓘ: I am studying law. (*Watashi wa hooritsu o benkyoo shite imasu.*) 私は法律を勉強しています.
2 (examine) ... o shiˈraberu ...を調べる Ⓥ; choˈosa suru 調査する Ⓘ: study a timetable (*jikokuhyoo o shiraberu*) 時刻表を調べる.
— *vi.* beˈnkyoo suru 勉強する Ⓘ: He is studying to be a lawyer. (*Kare wa bengoshi ni naru tame ni benkyoo shite iru.*) 彼は弁護士になるために勉強している.
— *n.* **1** (learning) beˈnkyoo 勉強; gaˈkushuu 学習: I like study better than sports. (*Watashi wa undoo yori benkyoo no hoo ga suki da.*) 私は運動より勉強のほうが好きだ.
2 (research) keˈnkyuu 研究: the study of physics (*butsurigaku no kenkyuu*) 物理学の研究.
3 (room) shoˈsai 書斎; keˈnkyuˈushitsu 研究室.

stuff *n.* **1** (substance) moˈnoˈ もの; (material) geˈnryoˈo 原料: What is this black stuff? (*Kono kuroi mono*

wa nañ desu ka?) この黒いものは何で
すか.

2 (belongings) mo「chi」mono 持ち
物: empty all the stuff from one's
pockets (*poketto no naka no mochimono o zeñbu kara ni suru*) ポケット
の中の持ち物を全部空にする.

— *vt.* … ni (… o) tsu「mekomu …に
(…を)詰め込む C: I stuffed the bag
with old clothes. (*Watashi wa
kabañ ni furugi o tsumekoñda.*) 私
はかばんに古着を詰め込んだ.

stumble *vi.* **1** (trip) tsu「mazuku つ
まずく C; yo「rome」ku よろめく C:
She stumbled on a stone and fell.
(*Kanojo wa ishi ni tsumazuite
koroñda.*) 彼女は石につまずいて転んだ.
2 (hesitate in speaking) tsu「kae」ru
つかえる V; do「mo」ru どもる C: stum-
ble over one's words (*kotoba ga
tsukaeru*) 言葉がつかえる.

stump *n.* ki「ri」kabu 切り株: sit on a
stump (*kirikabu ni suwaru*) 切り株
に座る.

stun *vt.* **1** (make unconcious) … o
ki「zetsu saseru …を気絶させる V:
The blow stunned him. (*Sono ichi
geki de kare wa kizetsu shita.*) そ
の一撃で彼は気絶した.
2 (surprise) … o gyo「oteñ saseru
…を仰天させる V: We were stunned
by the news. (*Watashi-tachi wa
sono shirase ni gyooteñ shita.*) 私
たちはその知らせに仰天した.

stunt *n.* myo「ogi 妙技; ha「nare-
waza」離れ技: perform a stunt
(*myoogi o okonau*) 妙技を行う.

stupid *adj.* ba「ka na ばかな; o「roka
na 愚かな: a stupid mistake (*baka
na ayamari*) ばかな誤り / It was stupid of me to believe that. (*Sore o
shiñjiru to wa watashi mo oroka
datta.*) それを信じるとは私も愚かだった.

stupidity *n.* o「roka」sa 愚かさ; ba「-
ka sa 愚かさ.

sturdy *adj.* (strong) ta「kumashi」i た
くましい; (firm) ga「ñjoo na 頑丈な:
He is small but sturdy. (*Kare wa
chiisai ga takumashii.*) 彼は小さいが
たくましい. / a sturdy chair (*gañjoo*

na isu) 頑丈ないす.

stutter *vi.* do「mo」ru どもる C; ku-
「chigomo」ru 口ごもる C: He stutters
a little. (*Kare wa sukoshi domoru.*)
彼は少しどもる.

style *n.* **1** (manner) ya「rikata やり
方; yo「oshiki 様式: change one's
style of living (*seekatsu-yooshiki o
kaeru*) 生活様式を変える.
2 (fashion) ryu「ukoo(gata) 流行
(型); su「ta」iru スタイル: the latest
style in shoes (*kutsu no saishiñ
ryuukoogata*) 靴の最新流行型.
3 (original way of writing) bu「ñtai
文体: write in an easy style (*wakariyasui buñtai de kaku*) わかりや
すい文体で書く.

subdue *vt.* … o se「efuku suru …を
征服する I; chi「ñatsu suru 鎮圧する
I: subdue a revolt (*boodoo o
chiñatsu suru*) 暴動を鎮圧する.

subject¹ *n.* **1** (theme) shu「dai 主
題; wa「dai 話題: change the sub-
ject (*wadai o kaeru*) 話題を変える.
2 (course of study) ka「moku 科目:
What is your favorite subject?
(*Anata no suki na kamoku wa nañ
desu ka?*) あなたの好きな科目は何です
か.
3 (of grammar) shu「bu 主部;
(word) shu「go 主語.
4 (person) ko「kumiñ 国民.
— *adj.* **1** (likely to receive) (… ni)
ka「kariyasu」i (…に)かかりやすい: I am
subject to colds. (*Watashi wa kaze
o hiki-yasui.*) 私はかぜを引きやすい.
2 (depending on) (… o) u「keru hi-
「tsuyoo ga a」ru (…を)受ける必要があ
る: The plan is subject to his approval. (*Sono keekaku wa kare no
shooniñ o ukeru hitsuyoo ga aru.*)
その計画は彼の承認を受ける必要がある.
3 (under the power of) shi「hai o
u「ke」ru 支配を受ける: We are subject to the laws. (*Wareware wa
hoo no shihai o ukete iru.*) われわれ
は法の支配を受けている.

subject² *vt.* **1** (bring under control) … o fu「kujuu saseru …を服従さ
せる V; … no shi「ha」ika ni o「ku …の

支配下に置く C: The country was subjected to foreign rule. (*Sono kuni wa gaikoku no shihaika ni okareta.*) その国は外国の支配下に置かれた.
2 (cause to suffer) ... o u「ke¹ru ...を受ける V: He was subjected to cruel treatment. (*Kare wa zankoku na atsukai o uketa.*) 彼は残酷な扱いを受けた.

subjective *adj.* shu「kañ-teki na 主観的な: a subjective judgment (*shukañ-teki na hañdañ*) 主観的な判断.

submarine *n.* se「ñsuikañ 潜水艦: a nuclear submarine (*geñshiryoku señsuikañ*) 原子力潜水艦.

submission *n.* (obedience) fu「kujuu 服従; ko「ofuku 降伏.

submit *vt.* ... o te「eshutsu suru ...を提出する I: I submitted the application form to the office. (*Watashi wa mooshikomi-yooshi o yakusho ni teeshutsu shita.*) 私は申込用紙を役所に提出した.
— *vi.* (... ni) fu「kujuu suru (...に)服従する: They submitted without a fight. (*Kare-ra wa tatakawazu ni fukujuu shita.*) 彼らは戦わずに服従した.

subordinate *adj.* ka「i no 下位の; ju「uzoku shita 従属した: a subordinate rank (*kai no kurai*) 下位の位.

subscribe *vi.* **1** (of a magazine, etc.) (... o) te「eki-ko¹odoku suru (...を)定期購読する I: I subscribe to two newspapers. (*Watashi wa shiñbuñ o ni-shi teeki koodoku shite iru.*) 私は新聞を2紙定期購読している.
2 (contribute) (... ni) ki「fu suru (...に)寄付する I: subscribe to a relief fund (*eñjo kikiñ ni kifu suru*) 援助基金に寄付する.

subscription *n.* te「eki-ko¹odoku 定期購読: cancel [renew] one's subscription (*teeki-koodoku o yameru [kooshiñ suru]*) 定期購読をやめる[更新する].

subside *vi.* (of land) chi「ñka suru 沈下する I; (of floods) hi「ku 引く

C; (of a storm) o「sama¹ru 収まる C.

subsidy *n.* jo「oseekiñ 助成金; ho「jo-kiñ 補助金.

substance *n.* **1** (matter) bu「sshitsu 物質; -tai 体: a chemical substance (*kagaku-busshitsu*) 化学物質 / a liquid [gaseous] substance (*eki[ki]tai*) 液[気]体.
2 (essential part) na「ka¹mi 中身; na「iyoo 内容: an argument of little substance (*nakami no nai giroñ*) 中身のない議論.

substantial *adj.* **1** (large) ka「nari no かなりの; so「otoo na 相当な: a substantial sum of money (*kanari no gaku no kane*) かなりの額の金.
2 (strong) ga「ñjoo na がんじょうな: The house doesn't look very substantial. (*Sono uchi wa amari gañjoo ni mienai.*) その家はあまりがんじょうに見えない.
3 (rich) na「ka¹mi no aru 中身のある; ta「ppu¹ri shita [shite iru] たっぷりした[している]: have a substantial meal (*tappuri shita shokuji o toru*) たっぷりした食事をとる.
4 (essential) ho「ñshitsu-teki na 本質的な; ji「jitsujoo no 事実上の: We are in substantial agreement. (*Wareware wa hoñshitsu-teki ni ikeñ ga itchi shite iru.*) われわれは本質的に意見が一致している.

substitute *vt.* ... o ka「wari ni tsukau ...を代わりに使う C: substitute margarine for butter (*bataa no kawari ni maagariñ o tsukau*) バターの代わりにマーガリンを使う.
— *vi.* (... no) ka「wari ni na¹ru (...の)代わりになる C: I'm looking for someone who will substitute for me. (*Watashi wa watashi no kawari ni naru hito o sagashite iru.*) 私は私の代わりになる人を探している.
— *n.* (people) da「iriniñ 代理人; (things) da「iyoohiñ 代用品.

subtle *adj.* **1** (delicate) bi「myoo na 微妙な: There is a subtle difference between them. (*Ryoosha no aida ni wa bimyoo na chigai ga*

aru.) 両者の間には微妙な違いがある.
2 (faint) ka⌐suka na かすかな: a subtle perfume (*kasuka na kaori*) かすかな香り.

3 (sensitive) bi⌐ŋkaŋ na 敏感な; su⌐rudoɿi 鋭い: a subtle observer (*surudoi kaŋsatsusha*) 鋭い観察者.

subtract *vt.* ... o hi⌐ku ...を引く C; ge⌐ŋjiru 減じる V: Subtract 2 from 5 and you get 3. (*Go kara ni o hiku to saŋ ni naru.*) 5から2を引くと3になる.

subtraction *n.* hi⌐ki↓zaŋ 引き算: do subtraction (*hikizaŋ o suru*) 引き算をする.

suburb *n.* ko⌐ogai 郊外: He lives in the suburbs. (*Kare wa koogai ni suŋde iru.*) 彼は郊外に住んでいる.

subway *n.* chi⌐katetsu 地下鉄: Where is the nearest subway station? (*Ichibaŋ chikai chikatetsu no eki wa doko desu ka?*) いちばん近い地下鉄の駅はどこですか.

succeed[1] *vi.* (... ni) se⌐ekoo suru (...に)成功する I; go⌐okaku suru 合格する I: He succeeded in his business. (*Kare wa shoobai ni seekoo shita.*) 彼は商売に成功した. / succeed in an examination (*shikeŋ ni gookaku suru*) 試験に合格する.

succeed[2] *vt.* ... no a↓to o tsu⌐gu ...の跡を継ぐ C: elect a person who succeeds the mayor (*shichoo no ato o tsugu hito o seŋkyo suru*) 市長の跡を継ぐ人を選挙する.
— *vi.* (... o) tsu⌐gu (...を)継ぐ C: He succeeded to his father's business. (*Kare wa chichioya no shoobai o tsuida.*) 彼は父親の商売を継いだ.

success *n.* se⌐ekoo 成功: She achieved great success as a singer. (*Kanojo wa kashu to shite hijoo na seekoo o osameta.*) 彼女は歌手として非常な成功を収めた. / I wish you success. (*Go-seekoo o inorimasu.*) ご成功を祈ります.

successful *adj.* se⌐ekoo shita [shite iru] 成功した[している]; go⌐okaku shita [shite iru] 合格した[している]: a successful plan (*seekoo shita keekaku*) 成功した計画 / He was successful in the entrance examination. (*Kare wa nyuugaku shikeŋ ni gookaku shita.*) 彼は入学試験に合格した.

successfully *adv.* shu⌐bi↓-yoku 首尾よく; u↓maku うまく: Everything turned out successfully. (*Subete umaku ikimashita.*) すべてうまくいきました.

succession *n.* **1** (series) re⌐ŋ-zoku 連続; -tsu⌐zuki 続き: a succession of misfortunes (*fukoo no reŋzoku*) 不幸の連続 / a succession of fine days (*seeteŋ-tsuzuki*) 晴天続き. **2** (the right to succeed) ke⌐eshoo 継承; ke⌐eshoɿokeŋ 継承権: the succession to the throne (*ooi keeshoo*) 王位継承.

successive *adj.* tsu⌐zuite↓ no 続いての; re⌐ŋzoku no 連続の: It rained three successive days. (*Mikka-kaŋ tsuzuite ame ga futta.*) 3日間続いて雨が降った.

successor *n.* ko⌐okeɿesha 後継者; ko⌐oniŋ 後任; ke⌐eshoɿosha 継承者: the president's successor (*shachoo no kooniŋ*) 社長の後任 / the successor to the throne (*ooi kee-shoosha*) 王位継承者.

such *adj.* so⌐no yo↓o na そのような; so⌐ŋna そんな: Can you recommend such a place? (*Sono yoo na tokoro o hitotsu oshiete moraemasu ka?*) そのような所を一つ教えてもらえますか. / I don't know such a person. (*Soŋna hito wa shirimaseŋ.*) そんな人は知りません.

such as ... ... no yo↓o na ...のような: I like a painting such as this. (*Watashi wa kono yoo na e ga suki desu.*) 私はこのような絵が好きです.
— *adv.* so⌐ŋna ni そんなに: Is he such a good golf player? (*Kare wa soŋna ni gorufu no joozu na hito desu ka?*) 彼はそんなにゴルフのじょうずな人ですか.

suck *vt.* **1** (draw in) ... o su⌐u ...を吸う C; su⌐ikoɿmu 吸い込む C: suck

the juice from an orange (*oreñji no shiru o suu*) オレンジの汁を吸う.
2 (lick) ... o sha「buru ...をしゃぶる C; na「me」ru なめる V: suck a candy (*kyañdee o shaburu*) キャンデーをしゃぶる.

sudden *adj*. to「tsuzeñ no 突然の; kyu「u na 急な: His sudden death was a shock. (*Kare no totsuzeñ no shi wa shokku datta.*) 彼の突然の死はショックだった. / There was a sudden change in the weather. (*Teñkoo ga kyuu ni kawatta.*) 天候が急に変わった.

suddenly *adv*. to「tsuzeñ 突然; fu「i ni 不意に: Suddenly the light went out. (*Totsuzeñ akari ga kieta.*) 突然明かりが消えた.

sue *vt*. ... o ko「kuso suru ...を告訴する ①: I sued him for libel. (*Watashi wa meeyo-kisoñ de kare o kokuso shita.*) 私は名誉毀損で彼を告訴した.
— *vi*. so「shoo ni oko」su 訴訟を起こす C: sue for damages (*soñgai-baishoo no soshoo o okosu*) 損害賠償の訴訟を起こす.

suffer *vt*. **1** (experience) ... o ko「muru ...を被る C; o「u 負う C: The company suffered great losses. (*Sono kaisha wa dai-soñgai o koomutta.*) その会社は大損害を被った. / suffer serious wounds (*juushoo o ou*) 重傷を負う.
2 (endure) ... ni ta「e」ru ...に耐える V: I cannot suffer such insults. (*Watashi wa sono yoo na bujoku ni taerarenai.*) 私はそのような侮辱に耐えられない.
— *vi*. **1** (feel pain) (... ni) ku「rushi」mu (...に)苦しむ C: They are suffering from hunger. (*Kare-ra wa ue ni kurushiñde iru.*) 彼らは飢えに苦しんでいる.
2 (of illness) (... o) ya「mu (...を)病む C; wa「zurau 患う C: suffer from gout (*tsuufuu o yamu*) 痛風を病む / suffer from rheumatism (*ryuumachi o wazurau*) リューマチを患う.
3 (receive ill treatment) i「tade o

uke「ru 痛手を受ける V: It is always the consumers who suffer. (*Itade o ukeru no wa itsu-mo shoohisha da.*) 痛手を受けるのはいつも消費者だ.

suffering *n*. ku「rushimi 苦しみ, C; ku「roo 苦労: endure suffering (*kurushimi ni taeru*) 苦しみに耐える.

sufficient *adj*. ju「ubuñ na 十分な; ta「riru 足りる: There is sufficient food for us all. (*Shokuryoo wa watashi-tachi miñna ni juubuñ arimasu.*) 食糧は私たちみんなに十分あります. / The pension is not sufficient for living expenses. (*Neñkiñ wa seekatsuhi ni tarinai.*) 年金は生活費に足りない.

sufficiently *adv*. ju「ubuñ ni 十分に; ta「riru dake 足りるだけ: The water was sufficiently warm to swim in. (*Mizu wa oyogeru hodo juubuñ ni atatakakatta.*) 水は泳げるほど十分に温かかった.

sugar *n*. sa「to」o 砂糖: Do you take sugar in your coffee? (*Koohii ni satoo o iremasu ka?*) コーヒーに砂糖を入れますか.

suggest *vt*. **1** (propose) ... o te「eañ suru ...を提案する ①: He suggested a new plan to the committee. (*Kare wa atarashii keekaku o iiñkai ni teeañ shita.*) 彼は新しい計画を委員会に提案した.
2 (hint) ... o a「ñ ni shi「me」su ...を暗に示す C: Clouds suggest rain. (*Kumo wa ame ga furu koto o añ ni shimeshite iru.*) 雲は雨が降ることを暗に示している.
3 (bring to mind) ... o o「moidasaseru ...を思い出させる V: This music suggests the ocean. (*Kono oñgaku wa umi o omoidasaseru.*) この音楽は海を思い出させる.

suggestion *n*. (proposal) te「eañ 提案; (hint) shi「sa 示唆: make a new suggestion (*atarashii teeañ o suru*) 新しい提案をする / a newspaper article full of suggestions (*shisa ni tomu shiñbuñ kiji*) 示唆に富む新聞記事.

suicide *n*. ji「satsu 自殺: commit

suicide (*jisatsu suru*) 自殺する.

suit *n.* **1** (clothes) su「utsu スーツ; se「biro jo「oge 背広上下: put on a suit (*suutsu o kiru*) スーツを着る.
2 (lawsuit) so「shoo 訴訟; ko「kuso 告訴: a civil [criminal] suit (*miñji [keeji] soshoo*) 民事[刑事]訴訟.
— *vt.* **1** (be convenient) ... ni tsu-「goo ga yo「i 都合がよい: Would ten o'clock suit you? (*Juu-ji de go-tsugoo wa yoroshii desu ka?*) 10時でご都合はよろしいですか.
2 (satisfy) ... ni te「kisuru ...に適する C: The climate suits me very well. (*Ima no kikoo wa watashi ni hi-joo-ni tekishite iru.*) 今の気候は私に非常に適している.
3 (be becoming) ... ni ni「a「u ...に似合う C: Long hair doesn't suit her. (*Nagai kami wa kanojo ni niawa-nai.*) 長い髪は彼女に似合わない.

suitable *adj.* te「kitoo na 適当な; ... ni mu「ita [mu「ite iru] ...に向いた[向いている]: I found a suitable present for her. (*Kanojo ni tekitoo na okurimono o mitsuketa.*) 彼女に適当な贈り物を見つけた. / Those shoes are not suitable for mountain climbing. (*Kono kutsu wa yama-nobori ni wa muite inai.*) この靴は山登りには向いていない.

suitcase *n.* su「utsuke「esu スーツケース.

sullen *adj.* fu「ki「geñ na 不機嫌な; mu「ttsu「ri shita [shite iru] むっつりした[している]: a sullen look (*fukigeñ na kao*) 不機嫌な顔.

sum *n.* **1** (of money) ga「ku 額: a large [small] sum of money (*ta-gaku [shoogaku] no o-kane*) 多額[少額]のお金.
2 (total) go「okee 合計; so「okee 総計; wa「 和: find the sum (*gookee o motomeru*) 合計を求める.
3 (of arithmetic) ke「esañ 計算: do sums (*keesañ suru*) 計算する.
— *vt.* ... o ma「tomeru ...をまとめる V; yo「oyaku suru 要約する I: sum up the main points of the story (*hanashi no yooteñ o matomeru*)

話の要点をまとめる.

summary *n.* ga「iyoo 概要; yo「o-yaku 要約: a summary of a speech (*eñzetsu no gaiyoo*) 演説の概要.
— *adj.* te「mijika na 手短な: a sum-mary account (*temijika na setsu-mee*) 手短な説明.

summer *n.* na「tsu「 夏: summer clothes (*natsu fuku*) 夏服.

summit *n.* **1** (top) cho「ojo「o 頂上: the summit of a hill (*oka no choo-joo*) 丘の頂上.
2 (meeting) shu「noo ka「idañ 首脳会談.

summon *vt.* ... o yo「bida「su ...を呼び出す C; sho「okañ suru 召喚する I: He was summoned to appear in court. (*Kare wa saibañsho ni shuttoo suru yoo yobidasareta.*) 彼は裁判所に出頭するよう呼び出された.

summons *n.* sho「okañ 召喚; yo-「bidashi 呼び出し: receive a sum-mons (*yobidashi o ukeru*) 呼び出しを受ける.

sun *n.* **1** (heavenly body) ta「iyoo 太陽: The sun rises in the east and sets in the west. (*Taiyoo wa higa-shi kara nobori nishi ni shizumu.*) 太陽は東から上り西に沈む.
2 (heat and light) ni「kkoo 日光; hi 日: My room gets a lot of sun. (*Watashi no heya wa yoku hi ga ataru.*) 私の部屋はよく日が当たる.

sunbeam *n.* ni「kkoo 日光; ta「i-yoo-ko「oseñ 太陽光線.

sunburn *n.* hi「yake 日焼け: suffer from sunburn (*hiyake suru*) 日焼けする.

Sunday *n.* ni「chiyo「o(bi) 日曜(日).

sunglasses *n.* sa「ñgu「rasu サングラス: He was wearing sunglasses. (*Kare wa sañgurasu o kakete ita.*) 彼はサングラスをかけていた.

sunlight *n.* ni「kkoo 日光: the right to sunlight (*nisshookeñ*) 日照権.

sunny *adj.* hi「atari no yo「i 日当たりのよい: a sunny room (*hiatari no yoi heya*) 日当たりのよい部屋.

sunrise *n.* hi-「no-de 日の出: get up before sunrise (*hi-no-de mae ni*) *okiru*) 日の出前に起きる.

sunset *n.* hiˈno-iri 日の入り; niˈchibotsu 日没; hiˈgure 日暮れ: go home at sunset (*higure ni ie ni kaeru*) 日暮れに家に帰る.

sunshine *n.* niˈkkoo 日光; hiˈnata ひなた: play in the sunshine (*hinata de asobu*) ひなたで遊ぶ.

superb *adj.* suˈbarashiˈi すばらしい; miˈgoto na 見事な: a superb performance (*migoto na engi*) 見事な演技.

superficial *adj.* **1** (of the surface) hyoˈomeˈn no 表面の; aˈsai 浅い: a superficial wound (*gaishoo*) 外傷. **2** (not thorough) hyoˈomen-teki na 表面的な; hiˈsoo-teki na 皮相的な: superficial observation (*hyoomen-teki na kansatsu*) 表面的な観察.

superfluous *adj.* yoˈbun no 余分の; yoˈkee na よけいな: a superfluous remark (*yokee na hitokoto*) よけいなひと言.

superintendent *n.* (of work) kaˈntoku 監督; (of a building) kaˈninin 管理人; (police officer) keˈesatsu-shoˈchoo 警察署長.

superior *adj.* **1** (better) suˈguˈreta 優れた; suˈguˈrete iru 優れている; joˈtoo no 上等の: His computer is superior to this one. (*Kare no konpyuutaa wa kore yori mo sugurete iru.*) 彼のコンピューターはこれよりも優れている. **2** (higher) joˈokyuu no 上級の; joˈoi no 上位の: a superior court (*jookyuu saibansho*) 上級裁判所. — *n.* (person) uˈwayaku 上役; joˈoshi 上司: He is my superior. (*Kare wa watashi no jooshi desu.*) 彼は私の上司です.

superiority *n.* yuˈuetsu 優越; taˈkuetsu 卓越: a sense of superiority (*yuuetsukan*) 優越感.

supermarket *n.* suˈupaamaˈaketto スーパーマーケット; suˈupaa スーパー: go shopping at a supermarket (*suupaa e kaimono ni iku*) スーパーへ買い物に行く.

superstition *n.* meˈeshin 迷信: believe in superstitions (*meeshin o shinjiru*) 迷信を信じる.

supervise *vt.* ... o kaˈntoku suru ...を監督する Ⓣ; kaˈnri suru 管理する Ⓣ: supervise work (*shigoto o kantoku suru*) 仕事を監督する.

supervision *n.* kaˈntoku 監督; kaˈnri 管理: The research was carried out under his supervision. (*Choosa wa kare no kantoku no moto de okonawareta.*) 調査は彼の監督のもとで行われた.

supervisor *n.* kaˈntokuˈsha 監督者; kaˈninin 管理人.

supper *n.* yuˈushoku 夕食; yuˈugoˈhan 夕ご飯: have a steak for supper (*yuushoku ni suteeki o taberu*) 夕食にステーキを食べる.

supplement *n.* fuˈroku 付録; hoˈsoku 補足: a supplement to a magazine (*zasshi no furoku*) 雑誌の付録.

supply *vt.* ... ni (... o) kyoˈokyuu suru ...に(...を)供給する Ⓣ; aˈtaeru 与える Ⓥ: We supplied them with food. (*Watashi-tachi wa kare-ra ni taberu mono o ataeta.*) 私たちは彼らに食べる物を与えた. — *n.* **1** (the act of supplying) kyoˈokyuu 供給: supply and demand (*kyookyuu to juyoo*) 供給と需要. **2** (store) taˈkuwae 蓄え; soˈnae 備え: We have a good supply of food. (*Tabemono no sonae wa juubun ni aru.*) 食べ物の備えは十分にある. **3** (things needed) seˈekatsu hitsujuhin 生活必需品.

support *vt.* **1** (hold up) ... o saˈsaeru ...を支える Ⓥ: The walls support the roof. (*Kabe ga yane o sasaete iru.*) 壁が屋根を支えている. **2** (provide for) ... o yaˈshinaˈu ...を養う Ⓒ; fuˈyoo suru 扶養する Ⓣ: He supports a large family. (*Kare wa dai-kazoku o yashinatte iru.*) 彼は大家族を養っている. **3** (help prove) ... o uˈrazukeˈru ...を裏づける Ⓥ: The theory was supported by facts. (*Sono riron wa jijitsu ni yotte urazukerareta.*) その

理論は事実によって裏づけられた.
— *n.* **1** (the act of supporting) sa「sae 支え; shi「ji 支持: The baby stood without support. (*Akañboo wa sasae nashi de tatta.*) 赤ん坊は支えなしで立った. / win public support (*taishuu no shiji o eru*) 大衆の支持を得る.
2 (person) se「ekatsu o sasaeru hito¹ 生活を支える人: He is the sole support of his family. (*Kare wa hitori de ikka o sasaete iru.*) 彼は一人で一家を支えている.

suppose *vt.* **1** (think) ... to o「mo¹u ...と思う C: What do you suppose he will do? (*Kare wa doo suru to omoimasu ka?*) 彼はどうすると思いますか.
2 (assume) ... to ka「tee suru ...と仮定する ①: Let's suppose you are right. (*Kimi ga tadashii to katee shite miyoo.*) 君が正しいと仮定してみよう.
be supposed to do ⟨verb⟩ ko-「to¹ ni na¹tte iru ...ことになっている V: I am supposed to meet him at five. (*Kare to go-ji ni au koto ni natte iru.*) 彼と5時に会うことになっている.

suppress *vt.* **1** (subdue) ... o yo-「kuatsu suru ...を抑圧する ①; chi「ñ-atsu suru 鎮圧する ①: The rebellion was suppressed. (*Hañrañ wa chiñatsu sareta.*) 反乱は鎮圧された.
2 (keep back) ... o o「sae¹ru ...を抑える V: suppress one's anger (*ikari o osaeru*) 怒りを抑える.
3 (hide) ... o ka「ku¹su ...を隠す C: suppress the truth (*shiñsoo o kakusu*) 真相を隠す.

supreme *adj.* sa「ikoo no 最高の: the supreme commander (*saikoo shireekañ*) 最高司令官 / the Supreme Court (*Saikoo-saibañsho*) 最高裁判所.

sure *adj.* **1** (confident) ka「kushiñ shite (iru) 確信して(いる): I am sure of his innocence. (*Watashi wa kare no muzai o kakushiñ shite imasu.*) 私は彼の無罪を確信しています.

2 (unlikely to fail) ki「tto ⟨verb⟩ きっと...: He is sure to succeed. (*Kare wa kitto seekoo suru.*) 彼はきっと成功する. / When you visit Tokyo, please be sure to come to see us. (*Tookyoo e kita toki wa kitto yotte kudasai.*) 東京へ来たときはきっと寄ってください.
3 (reliable) shi「ñrai de「ki¹ru 信頼できる; ta「shika na 確かな: a sure friend (*shiñrai dekiru yuujiñ*) 信頼できる友人 / sure proof (*tashika na shooko*) 確かな証拠.
make sure *vt.* ... o ta「shikame¹ru ...を確かめる V: I telephoned to make sure that she was coming. (*Kanojo ga kuru koto o tashika-meru tame ni deñwa o shita.*) 彼女が来ることを確かめるために電話をした.
— *adv.* **1** (certainly) ke「kkoo desu けっこうです; do¹ozo どうぞ: "May I smoke here?" "Sure." ("*Koko de tabako o sutte mo ii desu ka?*" "*Ee, doozo.*") 「ここでたばこを吸ってもいいですか」「ええ, どうぞ」
2 (surely) ta「shika ni 確かに; ma「t-taku まったく: It sure is hot. (*Iya mattaku atsui.*) いやまったく暑い.

surely *adv.* **1** (without doubt) ta-「shika ni 確かに; ki「tto きっと: He will surely succeed. (*Kare wa kitto seekoo suru deshoo.*) 彼はきっと成功するでしょう.
2 [with a negative] ma「saka まさか: Surely you are not going alone? (*Masaka hitori de iku no de wa nai deshoo ne?*) まさか一人で行くのではないでしょうね.
3 (certainly) i「i desu tomo いいですとも; mo「chi¹roñ もちろん: "May I come with you?" "Surely." ("*Issho ni itte mo ii desu ka?*" "*Ii desu tomo.*") 「いっしょに行ってもいいですか」「いいですとも」

surf *n.* yo「seru nami¹ 寄せる波.
— *vi.* na「minori¹ o suru 波乗りをする ①; sa「afiñ o suru サーフィンをする ①: go surfing (*saafiñ ni iku*) サーフィンに行く.

surface *n.* **1** (outer side) hyo「o-

me｢ñ 表面: the surface of the earth (*chikyuu no hyoomeñ*) 地球の表面 / the surface of water (*suimeñ*) 水面.
2 (outer appearance) u｢wabe うわべ; ga｢ikañ 外観: look only at the surface of things (*monogoto no uwabe dake o miru*) 物事のうわべだけを見る.
— *adj.* hyo｢ome｢ñ no 表面の; u｢wabe dake no うわべだけの: surface friendship (*uwabe dake no yuujoo*) うわべだけの友情.

surface mail *n.* fu｢tsuu-yu｢ubiñ 普通郵便.

surgeon *n.* ge｢ka｢-i 外科医.

surgery *n.* **1** (science) ge｢ka 外科: plastic surgery (*keesee-geka*) 形成外科.
2 (operation) shu｢jutsu 手術.
3 (operating room) shu｢jutsu｢-shitsu 手術室.

surmount *vt.* ... o no｢rikoe｢ru ...を乗り越える Ⓥ; ... ni u｢chika｢tsu ...に打ち勝つ Ⓒ: surmount difficulties (*koññañ o norikoeru*) 困難を乗り越える.

surname *n.* se｢e 姓; myo｢oji 名字.
★ Japanese 'surname' is followed by 'given name.'

surpass *vt.* ... o u｢wamawa｢ru ...を上回る Ⓒ; ko｢eru 越える Ⓥ: The result surpasses our expectations. (*Kekka wa watashi-tachi no yosoo o uwamawatta.*) 結果は私たちの予想を上回った.

surplus *n.* a｢mari 余り; yo｢joo 余剰: have a surplus of rice (*kome ga amaru*) 米が余る.
— *adj.* yo｢buñ na 余分な; ka｢joo no 過剰の: a surplus population (*kajoo-jiñkoo*) 過剰人口.

surprise *vt.* **1** (cause a feeling of wonder) ... o o｢doroka｢su ...を驚かす Ⓒ; bi｢kku｢ri saseru びっくりさせる Ⓥ: The news surprised us. (*Sono shirase wa watashi-tachi o odorokashita.*) その知らせは私たちを驚かした. / I was surprised to hear the news. (*Watashi wa sono shirase o kiite bikkuri shita.*) 私はその知らせを聞いて

びっくりした.
2 (attack unexpectedly) ... o fu｢iuchi suru ...を不意打ちする Ⓘ; ki｢shuu suru 奇襲する Ⓘ: surprise the enemy (*teki o fuiuchi suru*) 敵を不意打ちする.
— *n.* **1** (astonishment) o｢doroki｢ 驚き: jump with surprise (*odoroite tobiagaru*) 驚いて跳び上がる.
2 (something unexpected) i｢gai na koto｢ 意外なこと: His visit was a surprise. (*Kare no hoomoñ wa igai datta.*) 彼の訪問は意外だった.

surprised *adj.* o｢doro｢ita 驚いた; o｢doro｢ite iru 驚いている; bi｢kku｢ri shita [shite iru] びっくりした[している]: He looked surprised. (*Kare wa bikkuri shita kao o shite ita.*) 彼はびっくりした顔をしていた.

surprising *adj.* o｢doroku be｢ki 驚くべき; i｢gai na 意外な: It is not surprising that he failed. (*Kare ga shippai shita no wa igai de wa nai.*) 彼が失敗したのは意外ではない.

surrender *vi.* (... ni) ko｢ofuku suru (...に)降伏する Ⓘ: surrender to the enemy (*teki ni koofuku suru*) 敵に降伏する.
— *vt.* ... o ho｢oki suru ...を放棄する Ⓘ; su｢teru 捨てる Ⓥ: surrender hope (*kiboo o suteru*) 希望を捨てる.
— *n.* ko｢ofuku 降伏: an unconditional surrender (*mujookeñ koofuku*) 無条件降伏.

surround *vt.* ... o ka｢komu ...を囲む Ⓒ; to｢rimaku 取り巻く Ⓒ: The house is surrounded by trees. (*Sono uchi wa ki ni kakomarete iru.*) その家は木に囲まれている. / The girls surrounded the singer. (*Oñna-no-ko-tachi wa sono kashu o torimaita.*) 女の子たちはその歌手を取り巻いた.

surroundings *n.* ka｢ñkyoo 環境: social surroundings (*shakai-kañkyoo*) 社会環境.

survey *vt.* **1** (measure) ... o so｢kuryoo suru ...を測量する Ⓘ: survey the land (*tochi o sokuryoo suru*) 土地を測量する.

2 (look over) ... o miˈwatasu ...を
見渡す C: He stood on the hill and
surveyed the scenery. (*Kare wa
oka no ue ni tatte keshiki o miwa-
tashita.*) 彼は丘の上に立って景色を見
渡した.
— *n.* **1** (examination) choˈosa 調
査; soˈkuryoo 測量: a market survey (*shijoo choosa*) 市場調査.
2 (general study) gaˈikañ 概観;
gaˈisetsu 概説: a survey of Japanese history (*Nihoñshi no gaise-
tsu*) 日本史の概説.

survival *n.* seˈezoñ 生存; iˈkinokoˈru koˈto¹ 生き残ること: The climb-
er's survival is doubtful. (*Sono to-
zañka no seezoñ wa utagawashii.*)
その登山家の生存は疑わしい.

survive *vt.* **1** (remain alive) ...
yori naˈgaikiˈ suru ...より長生きする
I: She suvived her husband by
ten years. (*Kanojo wa otto yori
juu-neñ nagaiki shita.*) 彼女は夫よ
り 10 年長生きした.
2 (continue to live) ... o iˈkinobiˈru
...を生き延びる V: Only one person
survived the plane crash. (*Sono hikooki jiko de wa tatta hitori ga
seezoñ shite ita.*) その飛行機事故で
はたった一人が生存していた.
— *vi.* iˈkinokoˈru 生き残る C;
zaˈñzoñ suru 残存する I: That custom still survives. (*Sono shuukañ
wa mada zañzoñ shite iru.*) その習
慣はまだ残存している.

susceptible *adj.* (easily influ-
enced) kaˈñji-yasuˈi 感じやすい; (easily affected) kaˈkari-yasuˈi かかりやす
い: She is susceptible to colds.
(*Kanojo wa kaze o hiki-yasui.*) 彼
女はかぜをひきやすい.

suspect *vt.* **1** (believe a person to
be guilty) ... ni uˈtagai o kaˈkeˈru
...に疑いをかける V: The police suspects him of murder. (*Keesatsu
wa kare ni satsujiñ no utagai o
kakete iru.*) 警察は彼に殺人の疑いを
かけている.
2 (believe to be probable) ... de wa
nai ka to oˈmoˈu ...ではないかと思う

C: I suspect that he is ill. (*Kare
wa byooki de wa nai ka to omou.*)
彼は病気ではないかと思う.
3 (have doubts) ... o uˈtagau ...を疑
う C: I suspect his honesty. (*Watashi wa kare no shoojikisa o utagau.*) 私は彼の正直さを疑う. ★ Jap-
anese '*utagau*' is also used in the
sense of 'doubt.'
— *n.* yoˈogiˈsha 容疑者: The
police arrested two suspects. (*Keesatsu wa yoogisha o futari taiho
shita.*) 警察は容疑者を二人逮捕した.

suspend *vt.* **1** (hang) ... o tsuˈrusu
...をつるす C: suspend a lamp from
the ceiling (*teñjoo kara rañpu o
tsurusu*) 天井からランプをつるす.
2 (stop temporarily) ... o iˈchiˈji
chuˈushi suru ...を一時中止する I:
The project was suspended. (*Sono
keekaku o ichiji chuushi sareta.*)
その計画は一時中止された.
3 (keep out of a job) ... o teˈeshoku
saseru ...を停職させる V; (of a
school) teˈegaku saseru 停学させる
V: He was suspended from school.
(*Kare wa teegaku ni natta.*) 彼は停
学になった.

suspense *n.* **1** (uncertainty) fu-
ˈañ 不安; kiˈgaˈkari 気がかり: wait
in suspense for the result (*hara-
hara shite kekka o matsu*) はらは
らして結果を待つ.
2 (of a novel) saˈsupeˈñsu サスペンス.

suspicion *n.* uˈtagai 疑い; giˈwaku
疑惑: He looked at me with suspicion. (*Kare wa utagai no me de
watashi o mita.*) 彼は疑いの目で私を
見た; arouse suspicion (*giwaku o
umu*) 疑惑を生む.

suspicious *adj.* uˈtagawashiˈi 疑
わしい; aˈyashiˈi 怪しい: I am suspicious of his story. (*Watashi wa
kare no hanashi wa ayashii to
omotte iru.*) 私は彼の話は怪しいと思っ
ている.

sustain *vt.* **1** (maintain) ... o iˈji
suru ...を維持する I; tsuˈzukeru 続
ける V: sustain one's efforts (*doryoku o tsuzukeru*) 努力を続ける.

2 (undergo) ... o u⌐ke⌐ru ...を受ける Ⓥ; o⌐u 負う Ⓒ: sustain a serious injury (*juushoo o ou*) 重傷を負う.

swallow *vt.* **1** (take into the stomach) ... o no⌐mikomu ...を飲み込む Ⓒ: swallow food without chewing (*tabemono o kamazu ni nomikomu*) 食べ物をかまずに飲み込む.

2 (take in) ... o no⌐mikomu ...を飲み込む Ⓒ: The boat was swallowed by the waves. (*Booto wa nami ni nomikomarete shimatta.*) ボートは波に飲み込まれてしまった.

3 (accept) ... o u⌐nomi⌐ ni suru ...をうのみにする Ⓘ: He swallows everything that he is told. (*Kare wa iwareta koto wa nañ de mo unomi ni suru.*) 彼は言われたことは何でもうのみにする.

swamp *n.* nu⌐machi 沼地; shi⌐tchi 湿地.

swan *n.* ha⌐kuchoo 白鳥.

swarm *n.* mu⌐re⌐ 群れ: a swarm of bees (*hachi no mure*) はちの群れ / swarms of tourists (*kañkookyaku no mure*) 観光客の群れ.
— *vi.* mu⌐raga⌐ru 群がる Ⓒ; mu⌐re⌐ o nasu 群れをなす Ⓒ: Shoppers swarmed into the store. (*Kaimonok-yaku ga mure o nashite mise ni haitta.*) 買い物客が群れをなして店に入った.

sway *vi.* **1** (move back and forth) yu⌐reru 揺れる Ⓥ: The flowers are swaying in the breeze. (*Hana ga kaze ni yurete iru.*) 花が風に揺れている.

2 (lean) ka⌐tamu⌐ku 傾く Ⓒ: The car swayed to the left on the curve. (*Kuruma wa kaabu de hidari ni katamuita.*) 車はカーブで左に傾いた.
— *vt.* **1** (move) ... o yu⌐riugoka⌐su ...を揺り動かす Ⓒ: The wind swayed the branches of the trees. (*Kaze ga ki no eda o yuriugoka-shita.*) 風が木の枝を揺り動かした.

2 (influence) ... o u⌐goka⌐su ...を動かす Ⓒ: His speech swayed the audience. (*Kare no eñzetsu wa chooshuu no kokoro o ugokashita.*)

彼の演説は聴衆の心を動かした.

swear *vi.* **1** (curse) (... o) no⌐no-shi⌐ru (...を)ののしる Ⓒ: The drunk swore at the policeman. (*Yopparai wa keekañ o nonoshitta.*) 酔っぱらいは警官をののしった.

2 (state with an oath) chi⌐ka⌐u 誓う Ⓒ; da⌐ñge⌐ñ suru 断言する Ⓘ: swear on the Bible (*seesho ni te o oite chikau*) 聖書に手を置いて誓う.
— *vt.* ... o chi⌐ka⌐u ...を誓う Ⓒ: swear eternal love (*ee-eñ no ai o chikau*) 永遠の愛を誓う.

sweat *n.* a⌐se 汗: wipe the sweat off one's brow (*hitai no ase o nu-guu*) 額の汗をぬぐう.
— *vi.* a⌐se o kaku 汗をかく: Running fast made me sweat. (*Isoide hashittara ase o kaita.*) 急いで走ったら汗をかいた.

sweater *n.* se⌐etaa セーター: put on [take off] a sweater (*seetaa o kiru [nugu]*) セーターを着る[脱ぐ] / She was wearing a red sweater. (*Kanojo wa akai seetaa o kite ita.*) 彼女は赤いセーターを着ていた.

sweep *vt.* **1** (clean) ... o ha⌐ku ...を掃く; so⌐oji suru 掃除する Ⓘ: sweep a floor (*yuka o haku*) 床を掃く / I swept the room clean. (*Watashi wa heya o kiree ni sooji shita.*) 私は部屋をきれいに掃除した.

2 (push away) ... o o⌐shinaga⌐su ...を押し流す Ⓒ; (blow away) fu⌐ki-toba⌐su 吹き飛ばす Ⓒ: The flood swept away the bridge. (*Koozui ga sono hashi o oshinagashita.*) 洪水がその橋を押し流した.
— *vi.* ha⌐ku 掃く Ⓒ; so⌐oji suru 掃除する Ⓘ: She is busy sweeping. (*Kanojo wa sooji ni isogashii.*) 彼女は掃除に忙しい.

sweet *adj.* **1** (having the taste of sugar) a⌐mai 甘い: I like sweet things. (*Watashi wa amai mono ga suki desu.*) 私は甘いものが好きです.

2 (pleasant) ko⌐koroyo⌐i 快い; u⌐tsu-kushi⌐i 美しい: a sweet sleep (*ko-koroyoi nemuri*) 快い眠り / a sweet voice (*utsukushii koe*) 美しい声.

— n. aˈmai monoˈ 甘い物; kyaˈn-dee キャンデー.

sweeten vt. ... o aˈmaku suru ...を甘くする ①: sweeten coffee (koohii o amaku suru) コーヒーを甘くする.

swell vi. 1 (become larger) fuˈkuramu 膨らむ ⓒ: The buds are swelling. (Tsubomi ga fukurande kite iru.) つぼみが膨らんできている. 2 (of limbs) haˈreru はれる ⓥ: My injured arm began to swell. (Kega shita ude ga hare-dashita.) けがした腕がはれだした.
— vt. ... o fuˈkuramaseru ...を膨らませる ⓥ: The wind swelled the sails. (Kaze ga ho o fukuramaseta.) 風が帆を膨らませた.

swift adj. 1 (very fast) haˈyaˈi 速い: a swift horse (ashi no hayai uma) 足の速い馬. 2 (prompt) suˈgu ni ⟨verb⟩ すぐに...: He was swift to act. (Kare wa sugu ni koodoo shita.) 彼はすぐに行動した.

swim vi. oˈyoˈgu 泳ぐ ⓒ: The children swam in the pond. (Kodomotachi wa ike de oyoida.) 子どもたちは池で泳いだ.
— vt. ... o oˈyoˈgu ...を泳ぐ ⓒ; oˈyoˈide waˈtaru 泳いで渡る ⓒ: He swam the river. (Kare wa sono kawa o oyoide watatta.) 彼はその川を泳いで渡った.

swimming n. oˈyogi 泳ぎ; suˈiee 水泳: a swimming pool (puuru) プール.

swindler n. saˈgiˈshi 詐欺師; peˈteˈnshi ぺてん師.

swing vi. 1 (move back and forth) yuˈreru 揺れる ⓥ; buˈrabura suru ぶらぶらする ①: The lamp is swinging in the wind. (Ranpu ga kaze ni yurete iru.) ランプが風に揺れている. 2 (turn) guˈruˈri to maˈwaru くるりと回る ⓒ: He swung around and stared at me. (Kare wa gururi to mawatte watashi o mitsumeta.) 彼はくるりと回って私を見つめた.
— vt. ... o fuˈru ...を振る ⓒ; guˈruˈri to maˈwasu くるりと回す ⓒ:

swing a bat (batto o furu) バットを振る.
— n. buˈranko ぶらんこ: get on a swing (buranko ni noru) ぶらんこに乗る.

switch n. 1 (device) suˈiˈtchi スイッチ: turn on [off] a switch (suitchi o ireru [kiru]) スイッチを入れる[切る]. 2 (change) teˈnkan 転換; heˈnkoo 変更: a switch of plans (keekaku no henkoo) 計画の変更.
— vt. ... o kaˈeru ...を替える ⓥ: switch seats (seki o kaeru) 席を替える.
— vi. suˈiˈtchi o hiˈneˈru スイッチをひねる ⓒ: switch on [off] the radio (suitchi o hinette rajio o tsukeru [kesu]) スイッチをひねってラジオをつける[消す].

sword n. kaˈtanaˈ 刀; keˈn 剣: draw [sheath] a sword (katana o nuku [osameru]) 刀を抜く[納める].

symbol n. 1 (something that stands for) shoˈochoo 象徴: The dove is a symbol of peace. (Hato wa heewa no shoochoo desu.) はとは平和の象徴です. 2 (sign) kiˈgoo 記号: a chemical symbol (kagaku-kigoo) 化学記号.

symbolic adj. shoˈochoo-teki na 象徴的な: a symbolic meaning (shoochoo-teki na imi) 象徴的な意味.

symbolize vt. ... o shoˈochoo suru ...を象徴する ①: This picture symbolizes the sun. (Kono e wa taiyoo o shoochoo shite iru.) この絵は太陽を象徴している.

symmetry n. (saˈyuu)taˈiˈshoo (左右)対称; tsuˈriai つり合い.

sympathetic adj. doˈojoo-teki na 同情的な; oˈmoiyari no aˈru 思いやりのある: a sympathetic person (omoiyari no aru hito) 思いやりのある人.

sympathize vi. (... ni) doˈojoo suru (...に)同情する ①: He sympathized with me when I was in trouble. (Kare wa watashi ga komatte iru toki doojoo shite kureta.) 彼は

私が困っているとき同情してくれた.

sympathy *n.* **1** (feeling for another) do「ojoo 同情; o「moiyari 思いやり: feel sympathy for the poor (*mazushii hito-tachi ni doojoo suru*) 貧しい人たちに同情する / a letter of sympathy (*o-kuyami no tegami*) お悔やみの手紙.
2 (agreement) do「okañ 同感; sa「ñ-see 賛成: I have no sympathy with their plans. (*Watashi wa kare-ra no keekaku ni sañsee dekinai.*) 私は彼らの計画に賛成できない.

symphony *n.* ko「okyo」okyoku 交響曲; shi「ñfonii シンフォニー.

symptom *n.* cho「okoo 徴候; ki-「zashi 兆し: A cough is a symptom of the common cold. (*Seki wa kaze no chookoo desu.*) せきはかぜの徴候です.

syrup *n.* shi「roppu シロップ.

system *n.* **1** (organization) so「-shiki 組織: a system of government (*seeji soshiki*) 政治組織.
2 (a set of things) ta「ikee 体系; ke「etoo 系統: the solar system (*tai-yoo-kee*) 太陽系 / the nervous system (*shiñkee-keetoo*) 神経系統.
3 (plan) ho「oshiki 方式; (method) ho「ohoo 方法: a sales system (*hañ-bai-hoohoo*) 販売方法.

systematic *adj.* so「shiki-teki na 組織的な; ke「etoo-teki na 系統的な: a systematic method (*keetoo-teki na hoohoo*) 系統的な方法.

T

table *n.* **1** (furniture) te「eburu テーブル; sho「kutaku 食卓; da「i 台: set [clear] the table (*shokutaku o yooi-suru [katazukeru]*) 食卓を用意する [片づける] / sit at the negotiating table (*kooshoo no teeburu ni tsuku*) 交渉のテーブルにつく.
2 (list) hyo「o 表: a table of contents (in a book) (*mokuji*) 目次 / a multiplication table (*kuku no hyoo*) 九九の表. ★ The Japanese system covers as far as 9×9.

tablecloth *n.* te「eburu ku」rosu テーブルクロス; te「eburu」kake テーブル掛け.

table d'hôte *n.* te「eshoku 定食: I'll have the table d'hôte. (*Watashi wa teeshoku ni shimasu.*) 私は定食にします.

tablespoon *n.* o「osaji 大さじ.

tablet *n.* jo「ozai 錠剤: Take two tablets after each meal. (*Mai-shokugo ni ni-joo nomi nasai.*) 毎食後に2錠飲みなさい.

tacit *adj.* a「ñmoku no 暗黙の; mu-「goñ no 無言の: tacit consent (*añ-moku no shoodaku*) 暗黙の承諾.

taciturn *adj.* mu「kuchi na 無口な; ku「chikazu no sukuna」i 口数の少ない: a taciturn child (*mukuchi na kodomo*) 無口な子ども.

tack *n.* byo「o びょう; to「megane 留め金.
— *vt.* ... o byo「o de to「meru ...をびょうで留める Ⅴ: tack down a carpet (*juutañ o byoo de tomeru*) じゅうたんをびょうで留める.

tact *n.* ki「teñ 機転; jo「saina」sa 如才なさ: He has great tact. (*Kare wa hijoo ni kiteñ ga kiku.*) 彼は非常に機転がきく.

tactics *n.* se「ñjutsu 戦術; se「ñpoo 戦法; ka「ke」hiki 駆け引き: use clever tactics (*koomyoo na señjutsu o toru*) 巧妙な戦術をとる / surprise [delaying] tactics (*kishuu [hikino-bashi] señpoo*) 奇襲[引き延ばし]戦法.

tag *n.* fu「da 札: a name tag (*nafuda*) 名札 / a price tag (*nefuda*) 値札.

tail *n.* **1** (part of an animal's body) o「o 尾; shi「ppo」 しっぽ: wag a tail (*shippo o furu*) しっぽを振る.
2 (end) bi「bu 尾部; ko「obu 後部; sa「igo 最後: I joined the tail of the line. (*Watashi wa retsu no saigo*

ni tsuita.) 私は列の最後についた.
3 (coin) u'ra' 裏: Heads or tails?
(*Ura desu ka omote desu ka?*) 裏で
すか表ですか.
— *vt.* ... o bi'koo suru ...を尾行する
①: tail a suspect (*yoogisha o bikoo suru*) 容疑者を尾行する.

tailor *n.* yo'ofuku-ya 洋服屋; te'e-
raa テーラー: a tailor's shop (*shiñshi-
fuku-teñ*) 紳士服店.
— *vt.* ... o shi'tate'ru ...を仕立てる
Ⓥ: His suit is well tailored. (*Kare
no fuku wa shitate ga ii.*) 彼の服は
仕立てがいい.

tailor-made *adj.* chu'umoñ ni
yoru 注文による; a'tsurae no あつらえ
の: a tailor-made suit (*atsurae no
suutsu*) あつらえのスーツ.

take *vt.* **1** (carry) ... o mo'tte iku ...
を持って行く Ⓒ; tsu'rete iku 連れてい
く Ⓒ: Please take this baggage to
the taxi stand. (*Kono nimotsu o
takushii noriba made motte itte
kudasai.*) この荷物をタクシー乗り場まで
持って行ってください. / Please take me
to the hospital. (*Byooiñ e tsurete
itte kudasai.*) 病院へ連れて行ってくだ
さい.
2 (hold) ... o mo'tsu ...を持つ Ⓒ;
to'ru 取る Ⓒ: She took his hand
and helped him across the road.
(*Kanojo wa kare no te o totte
dooro o wataraseta.*) 彼女は彼の手を
取って道路を渡らせた.
3 (need) ... o hi'tsuyoo to suru ...を
必要とする Ⓣ; (of time) ... ga ka'ka'-
ru ...がかかる Ⓒ: This task took two
hours. (*Kono shigoto wa ni-jikañ
kakatta.*) この仕事は2時間かかった. /
How long does it take to go to the
airport by taxi? (*Kuukoo made
takushii de dono kurai kakarimasu ka?*) 空港までタクシーでどのくら
いかかりますか.
4 (use) ... o ri'yoo suru ...を利用する
Ⓣ: I take a bus to school. (*Gakkoo
e wa basu o riyoo shite imasu.*) 学
校へはバスを利用しています.
5 (do) ... o su'ru ...をする Ⓣ: take a
bath (*nyuuyoku suru*) 入浴する /

take a walk (*sañpo o suru*) 散歩をす
る / take good care of a pet (*petto
no sewa o yoku suru*) ペットの世話を
よくする.
6 (record) ... o to'ru ...をとる Ⓒ:
take notes (*memo o toru*) メモをとる
/ May I take your picture? (*Anata
no shashiñ o totte mo ii desu ka?*)
あなたの写真を撮ってもいいですか.
7 (occupy) ... o to'ru ...をとる Ⓒ;
shi'me'ru 占める Ⓥ: This desk takes
too much space. (*Kono tsukue wa
basho o tori-sugiru.*) この机は場所を
とりすぎる. / Is this seat taken?
(*Kono seki wa fusagatte imasu
ka?*) この席はふさがっていますか.
8 (choose; buy) ... o e'ra'bu ...を選
ぶ; ... ni su'ru ...にする Ⓣ: OK. I'll
take this. (*Wakarimashita. Kore ni
shimasu.*) わかりました. これにします.
9 (consume) ... o ta'be'ru ...を食べる
Ⓥ; no'mu 飲む Ⓒ: How many
times a day should I take this medicine? (*Kono kusuri o ichi-nichi
ni nañ-kai nomu no desu ka?*) この
薬は一日に何回飲むのですか. / Do you
take sugar in your tea? (*Koocha ni
satoo o iremasu ka?*) 紅茶に砂糖を
入れますか.
10 (consider) ... o (... to) to'ru ...を
(...と)とる Ⓒ; u'ketomeru 受け止める
Ⓥ: Don't take my joke as for an
insult. (*Joodañ o waruguchi to
toranaide kudasai.*) 冗談を悪口とと
らないでください. / He doesn't take
what I say seriously. (*Kare wa
watashi no iu koto o shiñkeñ ni
uketomenai.*) 彼は私の言うことを真剣
に受け止めない.
11 (assume) ... o hi'kiuke'ru ...を引
き受ける Ⓥ; to'ru とる Ⓒ: take a job
of baby-sitting (*komori o hikiukeru*) 子守を引き受ける / take responsibility (*sekiniñ o toru*) 責任をとる.
12 (accept) ... o u'keireru ...を受け
入れる Ⓥ; o'u 負う Ⓒ: take advice
(*chuukoku o ukeireru*) 忠告を受け
入れる / take the blame (*seme o ou*)
責めを負う.
13 (measure) ... o ha'ka'ru ...を測る

Ⓒ: A nurse took my temperature. (*Kaⁿgofu ga watashi no taioⁿ o hakatta.*) 看護婦が私の体温を測った。
14 (feel) ... o moˈtsu ...を持つ Ⓒ; iˈdaˈku 抱く Ⓒ: She takes no interest in my offer. (*Kanojo wa watashi no mooshide ni mattaku kyoomi o motte inai.*) 彼女は私の申し出に全く興味を持っていない。

take off *vt.* **1** (remove) ... o nuˈgu ...を脱ぐ Ⓒ: take off one's shoes (*kutsu o nugu*) 靴を脱ぐ.
2 (have holidays) yaˈsumi o toru 休みをとる Ⓒ: I took yesterday off. (*Kinoo wa yasumi o totta.*) きのうは休みをとった。
— *vi.* (of an aircraft) riˈriku suru 離陸する Ⓘ.

take out *vt.* **1** (go out with) ... o tsuˈredaˈsu ...を連れ出す Ⓒ: I took her out for a meal. (*Kanojo o shokuji ni tsurete itta.*) 彼女を食事に連れて行った。
2 (remove) ... o toˈridasu ...を取り出す Ⓒ: take a book out of a bag (*hoⁿ o kabaⁿ kara toridasu*) 本をカバンから取り出す.

take up *vt.* (start doing) ... o haˈjimeru ...を始める Ⓥ: take up golf (*gorufu o hajimeru*) ゴルフを始める.

takeoff *n.* riˈriku 離陸.

tale *n.* **1** (story) haˈnashiˈ 話; moˈnogaˈtari 物語: a fairy tale (*otogibanashi*) おとぎ話.
2 (lie) tsuˈkuri-baˈnashi 作り話.

talent *n.* saˈinoo 才能: She has a talent for music [drawing]. (*Kanojo ni wa oⁿgaku [e] no sainoo ga aru.*) 彼女には音楽[絵]の才能がある。★ In Japan, a 'TV personality' is called '(*terebi*) tareⁿto' (テレビ)タレント, literally '(TV) talent.'

talk *vi.* haˈnaˈsu 話す Ⓒ; haˈnashiˈ o suru 話をする Ⓘ: He is going to talk about the political reform tonight. (*Koⁿbaⁿ kare wa seeji-kaikaku ni tsuite hanashimasu.*) 今晩彼は政治改革について話します。
— *vt.* ... no koˈtoˈ o haˈnaˈsu ...のことを話す Ⓒ: talk music (*oⁿgaku no koto o hanasu*) 音楽のことを話す.
— *n.* **1** (conversation) haˈnashiˈ 話; haˈnashiai 話し合い: I had a long talk about the matter with him. (*Sono koto ni tsuite kare to nagaku hanashiatta.*) そのことについて彼と長く話し合った。
2 (conference) kaˈidaⁿ 会談; kyoˈogi 協議: high-level talks (*kookaⁿ ni yoru kyoogi*) 高官による協議.

talkative *adj.* haˈnashizuki na 話好きな; oˈshaˈberi na おしゃべりな: a talkative person (*oshaberi na hito*) おしゃべりな人.

tall *adj.* **1** (high) taˈkaˈi 高い; (of a person) seˈ ga taˈkaˈi 背が高い: a tall building (*takai biru*) 高いビル / a tall man (*se no takai hito*) 背の高い人 / "How tall are you?" "I'm 170 centimeters tall." ("*Shiⁿchoo wa dono kurai desu ka?*" "*Hyaku nanajus-seⁿchi desu.*") 「身長はどのくらいですか」「170センチです」
2 (unreasonable) shiˈⁿjirareˈnai 信じられない: a tall story (*shiⁿjirarenai hanashi*) 信じられない話.

tame *adj.* **1** (not wild) kaˈinarasaˈreta 飼いならされた; kaˈinarasaˈrete iru 飼いならされている: a tame animal (*kainarasareta doobutsu*) 飼いならされた動物.
2 (unexciting) tsuˈmaraˈnai つまらない; taˈⁿchoo na 単調な: a tame job (*taⁿchoo na shigoto*) 単調な仕事.
— *vt.* (train) ... o kaˈinaraˈsu ...を飼いならす Ⓒ; (control) oˈmoidoˈori ni suru 思い通りにする Ⓘ: tame a bear (*kuma o narasu*) 熊をならす.

tan *n.* hiˈyake 日焼け: get a tan (*hiyake suru*) 日焼けする.
— *vt.* (expose to the sun) ... o hiˈyake saseru ...を日焼けさせる Ⓥ: He is deeply tanned. (*Kare wa hidoku hiyake shite iru.*) 彼はひどく日焼けしている。
— *vi.* hiˈni yakeru 日に焼ける Ⓥ: I tan easily. (*Watashi wa sugu hi ni yakeru.*) 私はすぐ日に焼ける。

tangle *vt.* ... o moˈtsure saseru ...をもつれさせる Ⓥ; kaˈramaseˈru 絡ませる Ⓥ: Your hair is tangled. (*Kami* *no ke ga motsurete imasu yo.*) 髪の毛がもつれていますよ.

tank *n.* **1** (container) ta⌐nku タンク: a water [fish] tank (*suisoo*) 水槽.
2 (military vehicle) se⌐nsha 戦車.

tanker *n.* (ship) ta⌐nkaa タンカー; (truck) ta⌐nku ro⌐orii タンクローリー.

tap *vt.* (hit gently) ... o ka⌐ruku ta-ta⌐ku ...を軽くたたく ⃝; (beat repeatedly) ko⌐tsukotsu to ta⌐ta⌐ku こつこつとたたく ⃝: He tapped me on the shoulder. (*Kare wa watashi no kata o poñ to tataita.*) 彼は私の肩をポンとたたいた.
— *n.* (water-controlling handle) ja⌐guchi 蛇口; (for gas, etc.) se⌐ñ 栓: turn the tap on [off] (*jaguchi o akeru [shimeru]*) 蛇口を開ける[締める].

tape *n.* **1** (strip) te⌐epu テープ; hi⌐mo ひも: bind a parcel with tape (*tsutsumi o teepu de shibaru*) 包みをテープで縛る.
2 (of a cassette) ka⌐setto te⌐epu カセットテープ; (of a video) bi⌐deo te⌐epu ビデオテープ: play a tape (*teepu o kakeru*) テープをかける / rewind [fast-forward] a tape (*teepu o maki-modosu [hayaokuri suru]*) テープを巻き戻す[早送りする].
3 (sticky tape) ne⌐ñchaku te⌐epu 粘着テープ: insulating tape (*zetsueñ teepu*) 絶縁テープ.
— *vt.* (record on cassette) ... o ro⌐kuoñ suru ...を録音する ⃝; (on video) ro⌐kuga suru 録画する ⃝: record TV programs (*terebi-bañgumi o rokuga suru*) テレビ番組を録画する.

tape recorder *n.* te⌐epu reko⌐odaa テープレコーダー.

tar *n.* ta⌐aru タール.

target *n.* **1** (mark) ma⌐to 的; hyo⌐oteki 標的: The missile hit the target. (*Misairu wa hyooteki ni meechuu shita.*) ミサイルは標的に命中した.
2 (objective) mo⌐kuhyoo 目標; (numerical) mo⌐kuhyo⌐ochi 目標値; (monetary) mo⌐kuhyo⌐ogaku 目標

額: set a target (*mokuhyoochi o settee suru*) 目標値を設定する.

task *n.* shi⌐goto 仕事: I was assigned a difficult task. (*Watashi wa yakkai na shigoto o waria-terareta.*) 私は厄介な仕事を割り当てられた.

taste *n.* **1** (flavor) a⌐ji 味: This orange has a sweet taste. (*Kono ore-ñji wa amai.*) このオレンジは甘い.
2 (sense) mi⌐kaku 味覚: This herb is bitter to the taste. (*Kono haabu wa aji ga nigai.*) このハーブは味が苦い.
3 (appreciation) se⌐ñsu センス: She has excellent taste in clothes. (*Kanojo wa fuku no señsu ga totemo ii.*) 彼女は服のセンスがとてもいい.
4 (liking) ko⌐nomi 好み; shu⌐mi 趣味: It's a matter of taste. (*Sore wa konomi no moñdai desu.*) それは好みの問題です. / This music isn't to my taste. (*Kono oñgaku wa watashi no shumi ni awanai.*) この音楽は私の趣味に合わない.
— *vi.* (have a flavor) ... no a⌐ji ga suru ...の味がする ⃝: This soup tastes of garlic. (*Kono suupu wa niñniku no aji ga suru.*) このスープはにんにくの味がする.
— *vt.* **1** (test) ... no a⌐ji o mi⌐ru ...の味を見る ⃝: She tasted the soup. (*Kanojo wa sono suupu no aji o mita.*) 彼女はそのスープの味を見た.
2 (experience) ... o a⌐jiwa⌐u ...を味わう ⃝: taste the bitterness of defeat (*haiboku no kurushimi o aji-wau*) 敗北の苦しみを味わう.

tax *n.* ze⌐e 税; ze⌐ekiñ 税金: an income tax (*shotoku-zee*) 所得税 / collect taxes (*zeekiñ o chooshuu suru*) 税金を徴収する / Does this include tax and service? (*Kore wa zee to saabisuryoo komi desu ka?*) これは税とサービス料込みですか.
— *vt.* ... ni ze⌐ekiñ o ka⌐ke⌐ru ...に税金をかける ⃝; ka⌐zee suru 課税する ⃝: Alcohol is heavily taxed. (*Sake ni wa omoi zeekiñ ga kakerarete iru.*) 酒には重い税金がかけられている.

tax-free *adj.* me⌐ñzee no 免税の;

mu˥zee no 無税の: Do they sell tax-free goods on board? (*Meñzee-hiñ wa kinai de hañbai shite imasu ka?*) 免税品は機内で販売していますか. — *adv.* me˥ñzee de 免税で: Can I buy it tax-free? (*Sore wa meñzee de kaemasu ka?*) それは免税で買えますか.

taxi *n.* ta˥kushii タクシー: Please call a taxi for me. (*Takushii o yoñde kudasai.*) タクシーを呼んでください. / Where can I catch a taxi? (*Takushii ni wa doko de noremasu ka?*) タクシーにはどこで乗れますか.

taxi stand *n.* ta˥kushii no˥riba タクシー乗り場: Where is the taxi stand? (*Takushii noriba wa doko ni arimasu ka?*) タクシー乗り場はどこにありますか.

taxpayer *n.* no˥oze˥esha 納税者.

tea *n.* o-˥cha お茶; ti˥i ティー: black tea (*koocha*) 紅茶 / green tea (*ryokucha*) 緑茶 / strong [weak] tea (*koi [usui] o-cha*) 濃い[薄い]お茶 / make tea (*o-cha o ireru*) お茶を入れる.

teach *vt.* ... o o˥shieru ...を教える Ⓥ: He teaches English to junior high school students. (*Kare wa chuugakusee ni Eego o oshiete imasu.*) 彼は中学生に英語を教えています. / She taught me how to swim. (*Kanojo ga watashi ni oyogikata o oshiete kureta.*) 彼女が私に泳ぎ方を教えてくれた. — *vi.* o˥shieru 教える Ⓥ: He teaches at senior high school. (*Kare wa kookoo de oshiete imasu.*) 彼は高校で教えています.

teacher *n.* se˥ñse˥e 先生; [formal] kyo˥oshi 教師: a teacher of mathematics (*suugaku no señsee*) 数学の先生.

teaching *n.* **1** (art or job) o˥shieru koto˥ 教えること: go into teaching (*kyooshoku ni tsuku*) 教職に就く.
2 (beliefs) o˥shie 教え: the teachings of Gandhi (*Gañjii no oshie*) ガンジーの教え.

team *n.* **1** (of sports) chi˥imu チーム; -bu 部: What is your favorite professional baseball team? (*Anata no suki na puro yakyuu no chiimu wa doko desu ka?*) あなたの好きなプロ野球のチームはどこですか. / He is on the tennis team. (*Kare wa tenisubu no ichiiñ desu.*) 彼はテニス部の一員です.
2 (group) -dañ 団; -hañ 班: a team of medical doctors (*ishi-dañ*) 医師団.

tear[1] *vt.* **1** (pull apart) ... o ya˥bu˥ru ...を破る Ⓒ: I have torn my shirt on a nail. (*Watashi wa shatsu o kugi ni hikkakete yabuite shimatta.*) 私はシャツをくぎに引っ掛けて破いてしまった.
2 (remove) ... o ha˥gito˥ru ...をはぎ取る Ⓒ; ya˥burito˥ru 破り取る Ⓒ: tear a poster off a wall (*kabe kara posutaa o hagitoru*) 壁からポスターをはぎ取る / He tore the page out of the book. (*Kare wa hoñ kara sono peeji o yaburitotta.*) 彼は本からそのページを破り取った. — *vi.* ya˥bure˥ru 破れる Ⓥ: This fabric does not tear easily. (*Kono kiji wa kañtañ ni yaburenai.*) この生地は簡単に破れない.

tear down *vt.* ... o to˥rikowa˥su ...を取り壊す Ⓒ: tear down an old house (*furui ie o torikowasu*) 古い家を取り壊す. — *n.* ya˥bureme 破れ目; (of clothes) ka˥gizaki かぎ裂き: mend a tear (*kagizaki o tsukurou*) かぎ裂きを繕う.

tear[2] *n.* na˥mida 涙: wipe one's tears (*namida o nuguu*) 涙をぬぐう / hold back one's tears (*namida o koraeru*) 涙をこらえる / Tears streamed down his cheeks. (*Namida ga kare no hoo o tsutatta.*) 涙が彼のほおを伝った.

tease *vt.* ... o ka˥raka˥u ...をからかう Ⓒ: They teased him about his new hairdo. (*Kare-ra wa kare no atarashii kamigata o karakatta.*) 彼らは彼の新しい髪型をからかった.

teaspoon n. ko「saji 小さじ; cha-「saji 茶さじ.

technical adj. **1** (of technique) gi「jutsujoo no 技術上の; gijutsu-teki na 技術的な: technical cooperation (gijutsu teekee) 技術提携.
2 (special) se「nmon-teki na 専門的な: technical knowledge (senmon chishiki) 専門知識 / technical terms (senmon yoogo) 専門用語.

technician n. (skilled worker) gi「jutsu「sha 技術者; gi「shi 技師; (specialist) se「nmonka 専門家: an electrical technician (denki gishi) 電気技師.

technique n. **1** (skill) gi「jutsu 技術; te「kunikku テクニック: improve one's technique (gijutsu o taka-meru) 技術を高める / That pianist has an excellent technique. (Ano pianisuto wa tekunikku ga subara-shii.) あのピアニストはテクニックがすばらしい.
2 (method) ho「ohoo 方法: teaching techniques (kyoojuhoo) 教授法.

technological adj. ka「gakugi「jutsu no 科学技術の; gi「jutsu-teki na 技術的な: technological advances (kagakugijutsu no hat-tatsu) 科学技術の発達 / a highly technological problem (kiwamete gijutsu-teki na mondai) きわめて技術的な問題.

technology n. ka「gakugi「jutsu 科学技術; te「kuno「rojii テクノロジー: high technology (sentan gijutsu) 先端技術 / an institute of technology (kooka [koogyoo] daigaku) 工科[工業]大学.

tedious adj. ta「ikutsu na 退屈な; tsu「mara「nai つまらない: a tedious lecture (taikutsu na koogi) 退屈な講義.

teenager n. ti「ine「ejaa ティーンエージャー; ju「udai no wa「kamono 十代の若者.

teens n. ju「udai 十代: He is in his early [late] teens. (Kare wa juudai zenhan [koohan] desu.) 彼は十代前半[後半]です.

telegram n. de「npoo 電報: Send this telegram, please. (Kono den-poo o utte kudasai.) この電報を打ってください. / an urgent telegram (shi-kyuu denpoo) 至急電報 / a tele-gram of congratulations [condo-lence] (shukuden [chooden]) 祝電[弔電].

telegraph n. de「nshin 電信; de「n-poo 電報: a telegraph office (den-pookyoku) 電報局.
— vt. ... ni de「npoo o u「tsu ...に電報を打つ ©: His parents tele-graphed him to come home imme-diately. (Kare no ryooshin wa kare ni sugu kaeru yoo ni denpoo o utta.) 彼の両親は彼にすぐ帰るように電報を打った.

telephone n. de「nwa 電話; (ma-chine) de「nwa「ki 電話機: a public telephone (kooshuu denwa) 公衆電話 / make a telephone call (denwa o kakeru) 電話をかける / answer the telephone (denwa ni deru) 電話に出る / install a telephone (denwa o hiku) 電話を引く / Can I use your telephone? (Denwa o karite mo ii desu ka?) 電話を借りてもいいですか.
— vt. ... ni de「nwa o kake「ru ...に電話をかける Ⓥ: I telephoned her that I couldn't make it. (Watashi wa kanojo ni ikenaku natta to denwa shita.) 私は彼女に行けなくなったと電話した.
— vi. de「nwa o kake「ru 電話をかける Ⓥ: I telephoned for a taxi. (Wa-tashi wa denwa o kakete takushii o yonda.) 私は電話をかけてタクシーを呼んだ.

telephone directory n. de「n-wachoo 電話帳.

telephone number n. de「nwa-ba「ngoo 電話番号: What is your telephone number? (Denwa-ban-goo wa nan-ban desu ka?) 電話番号は何番ですか. / Give me your tele-phone number. (Denwa-bangoo o oshiete kudasai.) 電話番号を教えてください.

telescope n. bo「oenkyoo 望遠鏡:

look at stars through a telescope (*booeñkyoo de hoshi o miru*) 望遠鏡で星を見る / an astronomical telescope (*teñtai-booeñkyoo*) 天体望遠鏡.

television *n.* te¹rebi テレビ: turn on [off] the television (*terebi o tsukeru* [*kesu*]) テレビをつける[消す] / I watched the game on television. (*Watashi wa sono shiai o terebi de mimashita.*) 私はその試合をテレビで見ました.

tell *vt.* **1** (say) ... o i¹u ...を言う C; (talk) ha¹na¹su 話す C: tell a lie (*uso o tsuku*) うそをつく / Tell me about your experiences in Africa. (*Afurika de no keekeñ ni tsuite hanashite kudasai.*) アフリカでの経験について話してください.
2 (inform) ... ni (... o) o¹shieru ...に(...を)教える V; tsu¹taeru 伝える V: Please tell me the way to the station. (*Eki e iku michi o oshiete kudasai.*) 駅へ行く道を教えてください. / Please tell him to call me. (*Kare ni deñwa suru yoo tsutaete kudasai.*) 彼に電話するよう伝えてください.
3 (order) ... ni (...) o me¹ejiru ...に(...)命じる V; i¹u 言う C: I told him not to be late again. (*Kare ni nido to chikoku suru na to itta.*) 彼に二度と遅刻するなと言った.
4 (know) ... ga [wa] wa¹ka¹ru ...が[は]わかる C: Nobody can tell the truth. (*Dare ni mo sono shiñsoo wa wakaranai.*) だれにもその真相はわからない.
— *vi.* ha¹na¹su 話す C; i¹u 言う C: He told about his strange experience. (*Kare wa jibuñ no fushigi na taikeñ ni tsuite hanashita.*) 彼は自分の不思議な体験について話した.

temper *n.* **1** (mood) ki¹geñ 機嫌; (nature) ki¹shoo 気性: He is in a good [bad] temper. (*Kare wa ki-geñ ga ii* [*warui*].) きげんがいい[悪い]. / He has a quick temper. (*Kare wa kishoo ga hageshii.*) 彼は気性が激しい.
2 (rage) ka¹ñshaku かんしゃく: He is

in a temper. (*Kare wa kañshaku o okoshite iru.*) 彼はかんしゃくを起こしている.

temperance *n.* **1** (self-control) se¹ssee 節制; ji¹see 自制: temperance in eating and drinking (*iñshoku no sessee*) 飲食の節制.
2 (the taking of no alcohol) ki¹ñshu 禁酒.

temperate *adj.* **1** (of climate) o¹ñdañ na 温暖な: a temperate climate (*oñdañ na kikoo*) 温暖な気候.
2 (of a person) o¹da¹yaka na 穏やかな: a temperate disposition (*odayaka na seekaku*) 穏やかな性格.

temperature *n.* **1** (of atmosphere) ki¹oñ 気温: The average temperature of Tokyo is about 15℃. (*Tookyoo no heekiñ kioñ wa sesshi juugo-do gurai desu.*) 東京の平均気温は摂氏15度ぐらいです.
2 (of a person) ta¹ioñ 体温: My temperature went up [came down]. (*Taioñ ga agatta* [*sagatta*].) 体温が上がった[下がった].

tempest *n.* o¹oa¹rashi 大嵐; bo¹fofu¹u-u 暴風雨.

temple[1] *n.* (of a god) shi¹ñdeñ 神殿; (in Buddhism) ji¹iñ 寺院; te¹ra 寺; -ji 寺. ★ Used at the end of the name of a temple: Horyuji Temple (*Hooryuuji*) 法隆寺.

temple[2] *n.* (parts of a head) ko¹mekami こめかみ.

temporarily *adv.* i¹chiji-teki ni 一時的に; ka¹ri ni 仮に: The shop is temporarily closed. (*Sono mise wa ichiji-teki ni shimatte imasu.*) その店は一時的に閉まっています.

temporary *adj.* i¹chiji-teki na 一時的な; ka¹ri no 仮の; ri¹ñji no 臨時の: a temporary place of refuge (*riñji no hinañjo*) 臨時の避難所 / The economic recovery was only temporary. (*Keezai no kaifuku wa hoñno ichiji-teki na mono datta.*) 経済の回復はほんの一時的なものだった.

tempt *vt.* **1** (try to persuade) ... o yu¹uwaku shiyo¹o to suru ...を誘惑しようとする T: He tempted me with money. (*Kare wa watashi o o-kane de yuuwaku shiyoo to shita.*) 彼は私をお金で誘惑しようとした.

2 (attract) ... o saˈsou ...を誘う ⓒ; suˈru ki ni saseru する気にさせる Ⓥ: The beautiful weather tempted me to go out. (*Seeteñ ni sasowarete watashi wa soto ni deta.*) 晴天に誘われて私は外に出た.

temptation *n.* **1** (tempting) yuˈuwaku 誘惑: resist [succumb to] temptation (*yuuwaku ni makenai [kussuru]*) 誘惑に負けない[屈する].
2 (thing that tempts) yuˈuwakuˈ-butsu 誘惑物: Big cities provide many temptations. (*Dai-tokai wa yuuwakubutsu ga ooi.*) 大都会は誘惑物が多い.

ten *pron.* toˈo [juˈu] 十; (people) juˈu-niñ 10人; (things) juˈk-ko 10個.
— *n.* (figure) juˈu 10; (hour) juˈu-ji 10時; (minute) juˈp-puñ 10分; (age) juˈs-sai 10歳.
— *adj.* juˈu no 10の; (people) juˈu-niñ no 10人の; (things) juˈk-ko no 10個の; (age) juˈs-sai no 10歳の.

ten thousand *n.* maˈñ 万.

tenacious *adj.* koˈshitsu suru 固執する; neˈbarizuyoˈi 粘り強い: He was tenacious of his rights. (*Kare wa jibuñ no keñri ni koshitsu shita.*) 彼は自分の権利に固執した.

tenant *n.* (of a house) shaˈkuyaniñ 借家人; (of land) shaˈkuchiniñ 借地人; (of a building) teˈnañto テナント.

tend *vi.* ... keˈekoo ni aˈru ...傾向にある ⓒ; ⟨verb⟩-gachi da ...がちだ: Prices are tending to go up. (*Bukka wa agaru keekoo ni aru.*) 物価は上がる傾向にある. / He tends to be late. (*Kare wa okure-gachi da.*) 彼は遅れがちだ.

tendency *n.* keˈekoo 傾向: Unemployment is showing a tendency to increase. (*Shitsugyooritsu wa zooka no keekoo o shimeshite iru.*) 失業率は増加の傾向を示している.

tender[1] *adj.* **1** (soft) yaˈwarakaˈi 柔らかい: a tender steak (*yawarakai suteeki*) 柔らかいステーキ.
2 (kind) yaˈsashii 優しい; oˈmoi-yari no aˈru 思いやりのある: He was tender to me. (*Kare wa watashi ni yasashikatta.*) 彼は私に優しかった. / She has a tender heart. (*Kanojo wa omoiyari ga aru.*) 彼女は思いやりがある.
3 (sore) saˈwaru to itaˈi 触ると痛い: The bruise is still tender. (*Uchimi wa sawaru to mada itai.*) 打ち身は触るとまだ痛い.

tender[2] *vt.* ... o teˈeshutsu suru ...を提出する ⓣ: tender a resignation (*jihyoo o teeshutsu suru*) 辞表を提出する.

tennis *n.* teˈnisu テニス: play tennis (*tenisu o suru*) テニスをする.

tense *adj.* **1** (tightly stretched) piˈñ to haˈtta [haˈtte iru] ぴんと張った[張っている]: a tense rope (*piñ to hatta roopu*) ぴんと張ったロープ.
2 (nervous) kiˈñchoo shita [shite iru] 緊張した[している]; haˈritsuˈmeta 張りつめた; haˈritsumete iru 張りつめている: a tense situation (*haritsu-meta joosee*) 張りつめた情勢.

tension *n.* **1** (being tense) haˈri 張り; haˈritsumeˈru koˈto 張りつめること: lessen the tension of a net (*net-to no hari o yurumeru*) ネットの張りを緩める.
2 (mental strain) kiˈñchoo 緊張: She was under extreme tension. (*Kanojo wa kyokudo ni kiñchoo shite ita.*) 彼女は極度に緊張していた.

tent *n.* teˈñto テント: put up [take down] a tent (*teñto o haru [tata-mu]*) テントを張る[畳む].

tentative *adj.* (not definite) kaˈri no 仮の; zaˈñtee-teki na 暫定的な: a tentative agreement (*kari no gooi*) 仮の合意.

tenth *adj.* juˈubañmeˈ no 10番目の; daˈi-juu no 第10の.
— *n.* **1** (people) juˈubañmeˈ no hiˈto 10番目の人; (things) juˈubañ-meˈ no moˈno 10番目のもの.
2 (day) toˈoka 10日.
3 (fraction) juˈu-buñ no ichiˈ 10分

の 1.

tepid adj. na¯manuru¯i なまぬるい: tepid water (nurumayu) ぬるま湯.

term n. **1** (period) ki¯kañ 期間; (of an office) ni¯ñki 任期: a prison term (keeki) 刑期 / His term expires next year. (Kare no niñki wa raineñ de kireru.) 彼の任期は来年で切れる.

2 (of a school) ga¯kki 学期: the spring term (haru no gakki) 春の学期.

3 (words) se¯ñmoñ yo¯ogo 専門用語; (wording) ko¯tobazu¯kai 言葉づかい: technical [legal] terms (señmoñ [hooritsu] yoogo) 専門[法律]用語.

4 (conditions) jo¯okeñ 条件: the terms of employment (koyoo jookeñ) 雇用条件 / I sold my apartment on favorable terms. (Watashi wa yuuri na jookeñ de mañshoñ o utta.) 私は有利な条件でマンションを売った.

5 (relationship) a¯idagara 間柄; ka¯ñkee 関係: I am on good terms with him. (Watashi to kare wa naka no yoi aidagara desu.) 私と彼は仲のよい間柄です.

in terms of ... prep. ...no te¯ñ de ...の点で: In terms of rent this room is much better. (Yachiñ no teñ de wa kono heya no hoo ga zutto ii.) 家賃の点ではこの部屋の方がずっといい.

terminal n. **1** (of a station) shu¯uteñ 終点; ta¯laminaru ターミナル(駅); (of an airport) (e¯a)ta¯laminaru (エア)ターミナル.

2 (of an electric circuit) de¯ñkyoku 電極; (of a computer) ta¯ñmatsu 端末: the positive [negative] terminal (purasu [mainasu] kyoku) プラス[マイナス]極.

— adj. **1** (of a station) shu¯uteñ no 終点の; ta¯laminaru no ターミナルの.

2 (of disease) ma¯kki no 末期の: terminal cancer (makki gañ) 末期癌.

terminate vt. ... o o¯warase¯ru ...

を終わらせる Ⓥ; ya¯meru やめる Ⓥ: terminate a discussion (hanashiai o yameru) 話し合いをやめる.

— vi. o¯waru 終わる Ⓒ; to¯maru 止まる Ⓒ: The meeting terminated at three. (Kaigi wa sañ-ji ni owatta.) 会議は3時に終わった.

terrace n. (of a house) te¯rasu テラス; (of land) da¯ñkyuu 段丘.

terrible adj. **1** (bad) hi¯do¯i ひどい; hi¯doku he¯ta¯ na ひどくへたな: The weather was terrible. (Hidoi teñki datta.) ひどい天気だった. / He is a terrible golfer. (Kare wa gorufu ga heta da.) 彼はゴルフがへただ.

2 (fearful) o¯soroshi¯i 恐ろしい: a terrible disaster (osoroshii saigai) 恐ろしい災害.

terribly adv. hi¯doku ひどく; (very) hi¯joo ni 非常に: I'm terribly busy today. (Kyoo wa hidoku isogashii.) 今日はひどく忙しい. / I'm terribly sorry. (Hontoo ni mooshiwake arimaseñ.) 本当に申し訳ありません.

terrific adj. **1** (wonderful) su¯barashi¯i すばらしい: terrific weather (subarashii teñki) すばらしい天気.

2 (extreme) mo¯nosugo¯i ものすごい: a terrific noise (monosugoi soo-oñ) ものすごい騒音.

terrify vt. ... o ko¯wagarase¯ru ...を怖がらせる Ⓥ; zo¯tto saseru ぞっとさせる Ⓥ: The passengers were terrified by the turbulence. (Jookyaku wa rañkiryuu ni zotto shita.) 乗客は乱気流にぞっとした.

territory n. **1** (region) chi¯iki 地域: an uninhabited territory (hito no suñde inai chiiki) 人の住んでいない地域.

2 (the land ruled by a government) ryo¯odo 領土: This island is Japanese territory. (Kono shima wa Nihoñ no ryoodo desu.) この島は日本の領土です.

3 (of knowledge) (se¯ñmoñ)bu¯ñya (専門)分野: Accounting is outside my territory. (Kaikeegaku wa watashi no señmoñgai desu.) 会計学は私の専門外です.

terror n. kyo¹ofu 恐怖: I couldn't even speak because of terror. (*Kyoofu no amari koe mo denakatta.*) 恐怖のあまり声も出なかった.

test n. te¹suto テスト; shi¹ke¹ñ 試験; ke¹ñsa 検査: take [give] a test (*shikeñ o ukeru [suru]*) 試験を受ける[する] / pass [fail] a test (*shikeñ ni ukaru [ochiru]*) 試験に受かる[落ちる] / a blood [vision] test (*ketsueki [shiryoku] keñsa*) 血液[視力]検査.
— vt. ... o te¹suto suru ...をテストする Ⅰ; ke¹ñsa suru 検査する Ⅰ; shi¹rabe¹ru 調べる Ⅴ: I had my eyes tested. (*Watashi wa me o keñsa shite moratta.*) 私は目を検査してもらった.

testify vi. (in a court) sho¹ogeñ suru 証言する Ⅰ: The witness testified for the plaintiff. (*Shooniñ wa geñkoku ni yuuri na shoogeñ o shita.*) 証人は原告に有利な証言をした.
— vt. (give evidence) ... to sho¹ogeñ suru ...と証言する Ⅰ; ... no sho¹oko to na¹ru ...の証拠となる Ⅽ: He testified that he had seen nobody. (*Kare wa dare mo minakatta to shoogeñ shita.*) 彼はだれも見なかったと証言した.

testimony n. (statement) sho¹ogeñ 証言; (evidence) sho¹oko 証拠: She gave testimony against the accused. (*Kanojo wa hikoku ni furi na shoogeñ o shita.*) 彼女は被告に不利な証言をした.

text n. 1 (main part) ho¹ñbuñ 本文: The text of this book exceeds 200 pages. (*Kono hoñ no hoñbuñ wa nihyaku-peeji o koeru.*) この本の本文は200ページを超える. ★ Japanese '*tekisuto*' (text) often means 'textbook.'
2 (original) ge¹ñbuñ 原文: consult the original text (*geñteñ ni ataru*) 原典に当たる.

textbook n. kyo¹oka¹sho 教科書; te¹kisuto テキスト: a Japanese textbook (*Nihoñgo no kyookasho*) 日本語の教科書. ★ 'Textbook' is usually called '*tekisuto*' in Japa-

nese.

textile n. o¹rimono 織物.

than conj. ... yo¹ri mo ...よりも; ... no ho¹ka ni ...のほかに: It was hotter than I had expected. (*Omotta yori mo atsukatta.*) 思ったよりも暑かった. / Don't you have any other colors than this? (*Kono hoka ni ta no iro wa nai ñ desu ka?*) このほかに他の色はないんですか.
— prep. ... yo¹ri mo ...よりも: He is five years older than me. (*Kare wa watashi yori mo go-sai toshiue desu.*) 彼は私よりも5歳年上です.

thank vt. ... ni o-¹ree [re¹e] o iu ...にお礼[礼]を言う Ⅽ; ka¹ñsha suru 感謝する Ⅰ: I thanked him for the present. (*Watashi wa kare ni okurimono no o-ree o itta.*) 私は彼に贈り物のお礼を言った. / She thanked you for your help. (*Kanojo wa anata no eñjo o kañsha shite imashita.*) 彼女はあなたの援助を感謝していました.

thankful adj. ka¹ñsha shite iru 感謝している; a¹riga¹taku o¹mo¹u ありがたく思う: I am thankful for my good fortune. (*Watashi wa koouñ o kañsha shite imasu.*) 私は好運を感謝しています.

thanks int. a¹ri¹gatoo ありがとう; do¹omo どうも: Thanks a lot. (*Doomo arigatoo.*) どうもありがとう. / Many thanks for a wonderful dinner. (*Oishii yuuhañ o arigatoo gozaimashita.*) おいしい夕飯をありがとうございました. / No, thanks. (*Iya, kekkoo desu.*) いや, 結構です.
— n. ka¹ñsha (no ki¹mochi) 感謝 (の気持ち); o-¹ree [re¹e] お礼[礼]: I wrote her a letter of thanks. (*Watashi wa kanojo ni o-ree no tegami o kaita.*) 私は彼女にお礼の手紙を書いた.

thanks to ... prep. ... no ta¹me¹ ni ...のために: Thanks to the bad weather, the match was canceled. (*Akuteñkoo no tame ni shiai wa chuushi ni natta.*) 悪天候のために試合は中止になった.

thank you int. 1 [expressing gratitude] a⌐ri⌐gatoo ありがとう; ka⌐nsha shimasu 感謝します: Thank you very much for everything. (*Iroiro doomo arigatoo gozaimashita.*) いろいろどうもありがとうございました。/ Thank you very much for your attention. (*Go-seechoo o kañsha shimasu.*) ご清聴を感謝します。/ No, thank you. (*Iie, kekkoo desu.*) いいえ、結構です。

2 [at the conclusion of a speech] ko⌐re de owarima⌐su これで終わります; i⌐joo desu 以上です。

that[1] *pron.* **1** [something located at some distance from both the speaker and the listener] a⌐re あれ: Give me the same thing as that. (*Are to onaji mono o kudasai.*) あれと同じものを下さい。/ Who's that? (*Are wa dare desu ka?*) あれはだれですか。

2 [something located away from the speaker and close to the listener] so⌐re それ: Where can I buy that? (*Sore wa doko de kaemasu ka?*) それはどこで買えますか。

3 (substitute) (... no) so⌐re (...の)それ: The climate here is that of California. (*Koko no kikoo wa Kariforunia no sore to nite iru.*) この気候はカリフォルニアのそれと似ている。

— *adj.* a⌐no あの; so⌐no その: That car is mine. (*Ano [Sono] kuruma wa watashi no desu.*) あの[その]車は私のです。/ What is that building? (*Ano tatemono wa nañ desu ka?*) あの建物は何ですか。

— *adv.* so⌐nna ni そんなに; so⌐re hodo それほど: It's not that bad. (*Sore wa soñna ni waruku arimaseñ.*) それはそんなに悪くありません。/ Playing tennis is not that easy. (*Tenisu o suru no wa sore hodo kañtañ ja nai.*) テニスをするのはそれほど簡単じゃない。

that[2] *conj.* ... to i⌐u (koto⌐) ...という(こと); to と: The problem is that we are short of money. (*Moñdai wa o-kane ga tarinai to iu koto da.*) 問題はお金が足りないということだ。/ I think that you are right. (*Watashi wa anata wa tadashii to omou.*) 私はあなたは正しいと思う。

so that *conj.* ... yo⌐o ni ...ように: She got up early so that she could catch the first train. (*Kanojo wa shihatsu ni maniau yoo ni hayaku okita.*) 彼女は始発に間に合うように早く起きた。

so ... that a⌐mari ... no de あまり...ので: I was so tired that I went to bed early. (*Amari tsukareta no de hayaku nemashita.*) あまり疲れたので早く寝ました。

that[3] *rel. pron.* ... (to⌐koro no) ...(ところの): This is the picture that I painted. (*Kore ga watashi ga kaita (tokoro no) e desu.*) これが私がかいた(ところの)絵です。★ The insertion of 'tokoro no' sounds unnatural, so it is usually omitted.

thaw *vi.* (melt) to⌐ke⌐ru 解ける Ⅴ; (of frozen food) ka⌐itoo suru 解凍する Ⅰ: The snow began to thaw. (*Yuki ga toke-hajimeta.*) 雪が解け始めた。/ The frozen meat took one hour to thaw. (*Sono reetoo niku wa kaitoo suru no ni ichi-jikañ kakatta.*) その冷凍肉は解凍するのに1時間かかった。

— *vt.* (melt) ... o to⌐ka⌐su ...を解かす Ⅽ; (of frozen food) ka⌐itoo suru 解凍する Ⅰ: thaw out frozen food (*reetoo shokuhiñ o kaitoo suru*) 冷凍食品を解凍する。

— *n.* (of snow) yu⌐kidoke 雪解け。

the[1] *def. art.* **1** [before a noun mentioned previously] so⌐no その: Once there lived a queen. The queen had two daughters. (*Muka-shi joo-oo ga suñde ita. (Sono) jo-oo ni wa futari no musume ga ita.*) 昔女王が住んでいた。(その)女王には二人の娘がいた。

2 [before a noun understood] re⌐e no 例の; i⌐tsu-mo no いつもの: Come and meet me at the station. ((*Itsu-mo no) eki e mukae ni kite kuda-sai.*) (いつもの)駅へ迎えに来てください。

3 [before an adjective] (of people) hi⌐to⌐-tachi 人たち; (of a thing) mo-

「no」もの: the poor (*mazushii hito-
tachi*) 貧しい人たち / the beautiful
(*utsukushii mono*) 美しいもの.
4 [before a unit] ... ta「ni de ...単位
で: It's cheaper to buy by the doz-
en. (*Daasu tani de katta hoo ga
yasui.*) ダース単位で買った方が安い.

the[2] *adv.* [used in comparisons] so-
「re dake それだけ: With one of us
away, the task is all the tougher.
(*Hitori inai no de sore dake shigoto ga taiheñ da.*) 一人いないのでそ
れだけ仕事が大変だ.
　the ..., the ... ⟨adjective⟩ -ba ...
ho「do ...は...ほど: The sooner, the
better. (*Hayakereba hayai hodo
yoi.*) 早ければ早いほどよい.
theater *n.* ge「kijoo 劇場: a movie
theater (*eegakañ*) 映画館.
theatrical *adj.* ge「kijoo no 劇場の;
e「ñgeki no 演劇の: a theatrical company (*gekidañ*) 劇団.
theft *n.* nu「sumi」盗み; [formal] se「t-
to」o 窃盗: commit theft (*nusumi o
hataraku*) 盗みを働く.
their *pron.* (people) a「no hito」-tachi
no あの人たちの; ka「re-ra no 彼らの;
(females) ka「nojo-ra no 彼女らの;
(things) so「re(」-ra) no それ(ら)の:
They helped their father's business. (*Kare-ra wa chichioya no shigoto o tetsudatta.*) 彼らは父親の仕事
を手伝った.
theirs *pron.* (people) a「no hito」-
tachi no mo「no」あの人たちのもの;
ka「re-ra no mo「no」彼らのもの; (females) ka「nojo-ra[-tachi] no mo-
「no」彼女ら[たち]のもの: These books
are theirs. (*Kono hoñ wa kare-ra
no mono desu.*) この本は彼らのものです.
them *pron.* **1** [direct object] (people) a「no hito」-tachi o あの人たちを;
ka「re-ra[-tachi] o 彼らを; (females)
ka「nojo-ra[-tachi] o 彼女[たち]を;
(things) so「re(」-ra) o それ(ら)を: I
visited them yesterday. (*Watashi
wa kinoo kare-ra o tazuneta.*) 私は
きのう彼らを訪ねた. / We ate them
with salt. (*Watashi-tachi wa sore
o shio de tabeta.*) 私たちはそれを塩で

食べた.
　2 [indirect object] (people) a「no
hito」-tachi ni あの人たちに; ka「re-ra
ni 彼らに; (females) ka「nojo-ra ni 彼
女らに; (things) so「re(」-ra) ni それ(ら)
に: Give them the rest. (*Nokori wa
kare-ra ni age nasai.*) 残りは彼らにあ
げなさい.
theme *n.* **1** (subject) da「imoku 題
目; te「ema テーマ; (topic) wa「dai 話
題: the theme of an essay (*roñbuñ
no teema*) 論文のテーマ.
　2 (of music) shu「dai 主題: a theme
song (*shudaika*) 主題歌.
themselves *pron.* **1** [reflexive
use] ji「buñ-tachi ji「shiñ o [ni] 自分
たち自身を[に]; so「re-ra ji「tai o [ni]
それら自体を[に]: They had to take
care of themselves. (*Kare-ra wa
jibuñ-tachi jishiñ no sewa o shinakereba naranakatta.*) 彼らは自分
たち自身の世話をしなければならなかった.
　2 [emphatic use] ka「re-ra ji「shiñ
de 彼ら自身で; ji「buñ-tachi ji「shiñ
de 自分たち自身で: They did the
job themselves. (*Kare-ra wa jibuñ-
tachi de sono shigoto o shita.*) 彼ら
は自分たちでその仕事をした.
then *adv.* **1** (at that time) so「no
to「ki その時; to「oji 当時: I have not
seen her since then. (*Kanojo ni wa
sono toki irai atte imaseñ.*) 彼女に
はその時以来会っていません. / I was
still a student then. (*Watashi wa
tooji wa mada gakusee deshita.*)
私は当時はまだ学生でした.
　2 (after that) so「re kara それから: I
stayed in Kyoto and then went to
Nara. (*Watashi wa Kyooto ni
tomari sore kara Nara e itta.*) 私は
京都に泊まりそれから奈良へ行った.
　3 (in that case) so「re na「ra それなら:
"I don't quite agree." "What do
you think we should do, then?"
(*"Watashi wa sañsee to iu wake
de wa arimaseñ." "Sore nara doo
sureba ii to omoimasu ka?"*) 「私
は賛成というわけではありません」「それな
らどうすればいいと思いますか」
theoretical *adj.* ri「roñ-teki na 理

論的な; riˈroñjoo no 理論上の: theoretical linguistics (*riroñ geñgo-gaku*) 理論言語学.

theory *n.* **1** (general principles) riˈroñ 理論: In theory it is possible but in practice I don't know. (*Riroñ-teki ni wa kanoo desu ga, jissai wa wakarimaseñ.*) 理論的には可能ですが, 実際はわかりません.
2 (idea offered) gaˈkusetsu 学説; -roñ 論: the theory of relativity (*sootaisee riroñ*) 相対性理論.

there[1] *adv.* **1** (that place) soˈko ni [e, de] そこに[へ, で]; aˈsoko ni [e, de] あそこに[へ, で]: Sit there. (*Soko ni suwari nasai.*) そこに座りなさい. / The accident took place there. (*Jiko wa asoko de okotta.*) 事故はあそこで起こった. ★ '*Soko*' refers to a place near the listener and slightly distant from the speaker, and '*asoko*' refers to a place which is some distance away from both the speaker and the listener.
2 (in that respect) soˈno teñ de その点で: There I cannot agree with you. (*Sono teñ de watashi wa anata ni dooi dekimaseñ.*) その点で私はあなたに同意できません.
— *int.* hoˈra ほら; soˈre それ: There, I told you so. (*Hora, watashi ga itta toori deshoo.*) ほら, 私が言ったとおりでしょう.

there[2] **is [are]** *vi.* **1** [with an inanimate subject] ... ga aˈru ...がある Ⓒ: Is there a bookstore near here? (*Kono chikaku ni hoñya wa arimasu ka?*) この近くに本屋はありますか. **2** [with an animate subject] ... ga iˈru ...がいる Ⓥ: How many students are there in your school? (*Anata no gakkoo wa gakusee ga nañ-niñ imasu ka?*) あなたの学校は学生が何人いますか.

thereafter *adv.* soˈno go その後: Thereafter we got out of touch. (*Sono go watashi-tachi wa reñraku o toriatte imaseñ.*) その後私たちは連絡を取り合っていません.

thereby *adv.* soˈre ni yotte それによ

って: I went on a diet and thereby lost five kilos. (*Daietto o yari, sore ni yotte go-kiro yasemashita.*) ダイエットをやり, それによって5キロやせました.

therefore *adv.* soˈre yueˈ ni それゆえに; soˈko de そこで; shiˈtagatte 従って: It was a rainy day; therefore I didn't go out. (*Sono hi wa amefuri deshita. Soko de watashi wa gaishutsu shimaseñ deshita.*) その日は雨降りでした. そこで私は外出しませんでした.

thermometer *n.* oˈñdokee 温度計; kaˈñdañkee 寒暖計; (clinical) taˈioñkee 体温計: The thermometer stands at 10ºC. (*Oñdokee wa sesshi juu-do o sashite iru.*) 温度計は摂氏10度を指している. ★ In Japan the Celsius scale is used.

these *pron.* koˈreˈ-ra これら; koˈre こ れ: These are all my books. (*Kore wa miñna watashi no hoñ desu.*) これはみんな私の本です.
— *adj.* koˈreˈ-ra no これらの; koˈno この: These people are all nice. (*Kono hito-tachi wa mina shiñsetsu desu.*) この人たちは皆親切です.

thesis *n.* roˈñbuñ 論文: a doctoral thesis (*hakase-roñbuñ*) 博士論文.

they *pron.* **1** (people) aˈno hitoˈ-tachi あの人たち; kaˈre-ra 彼ら; (females) kaˈnojo-raˈ[-tachi] 彼女ら[たち]; (things) soˈre(ˈ-ra) それ(ら); aˈre あれ: They are tourist. (*Karera wa kañkookyaku desu.*) 彼らは観光客です. / What are they? (*Sore wa nañ desu ka?*) それは何ですか. **2** (generic) ★ In Japanese, it is omitted: Do they carry cigarettes at that store? (*Asoko no mise de wa tabako o utte imasu ka?*) あその店ではたばこを売っていますか. / They say there will be a wet spell. (*Ame no hi ga tsuzuku to iu koto desu.*) 雨の日が続くということです.

thick *adj.* **1** (not thin) aˈtsui 厚い; aˈtsusa ga ... aˈru 厚さが...ある: a thick book (*atsui hoñ*) 厚い本 / The ice was two centimeters thick. (*Koori wa atsusa ga ni-señchi atta.*)

氷は厚さが 2 センチあった.

2 (great in diameter) fuˈtoˈi 太い: thick neck [tree-trunk] (*futoi kubi [miki]*) 太い首[幹].

3 (dense) miˈtsu na 密な; (of liquid) koˈi 濃い: a thick forest (*mitsuriñ*) 密林 / thick soup [fog] (*koi suupu [kiri]*) 濃いスープ[霧].

thicken *vt.* **1** (make thick) ... o aˈtsuku suru ...を厚くする ⊤: thicken a wall (*kabe o atsuku suru*) 壁を厚くする.

2 (of liquid) ... o koˈku suru ...を濃くする ⊤: thicken soup (*suupu o koku suru*) スープを濃くする.

— *vi.* aˈtsuku naˈru 厚くなる ⊂; koˈku naru 濃くなる ⊂: The clouds are thickening. (*Kumo ga atsuku natte kite iru.*) 雲が厚くなってきている. / The fog is thickening. (*Kiri ga koku natte kite iru.*) 霧が濃くなってきている.

thicket *n.* shiˈgemiˈ 茂み; yaˈbu やぶ: hide in a thicket (*shigemi no naka ni kakureru*) 茂みの中に隠れる.

thickness *n.* aˈtsusa 厚さ; (of a diameter) fuˈtosa 太さ: a board with a thickness of two centimeters (*atsusa ni-señchi no ita*) 厚さ 2 センチの板 / The tree is two meters in thickness. (*Sono ki wa futosa ga ni-meetoru aru.*) その木は太さが 2 メートルある.

thief *n.* doˈroboo どろぼう: catch a thief (*doroboo o tsukamaeru*) どろぼうを捕まえる.

thigh *n.* fuˈtomomo 太もも.

thimble *n.* yuˈbinuki 指ぬき.

thin *adj.* **1** (not thick) uˈsui 薄い: a thin blanket (*usui moofu*) 薄い毛布.

2 (small in diameter) hoˈsoˈi 細い: a thin wire (*hosoi harigane*) 細い針金.

3 (not fat) yaˈseta やせた; yaˈsete iru やせている: She is thin. (*Kanojo wa yasete iru.*) 彼女はやせている.

4 (not dense) maˈbara na まばらな: a thin audience (*mabara na chooshuu*) まばらな聴衆.

5 (watery) uˈsui 薄い; miˈzuppoˈi 水っぽい: thin soup (*mizuppoi suupu*) 水っぽいスープ.

— *vt.* ... o uˈsumeru ...を薄める Ⅴ: thin soup (*suupu o usumeru*) スープを薄める.

— *vi.* uˈsuku naˈru 薄くなる ⊂: I'm thinning on top. (*Kami ga usuku natte kite iru.*) 髪が薄くなってきている.

thing *n.* **1** (object) moˈnoˈ 物: There are a lot of things on the desk. (*Tsukue no ue ni wa iroiro na mono ga aru.*) 机の上にはいろいろな物がある.

2 (matter) koˈto こと: I have a lot of things to do. (*Shinakereba naranai koto ga takusañ aru.*) しなければならないことがたくさんある.

3 (belongings) moˈchiˈmono 持ち物; shoˈjihiñ 所持品: pack one's things (*shojihiñ o matomeru*) 所持品をまとめる.

4 (circumstances) joˈokyoo 状況; jiˈjoo 事情: Things are getting better. (*Jookyoo wa yoku natte kite imasu.*) 状況はよくなってきています.

5 (event) moˈnoˈgoto 物事; koˈtoˈ 事: A strange thing happened. (*Fushigi na koto ga okotta.*) 不思議な事が起こった.

think *vt.* **1** (form in the mind) ... to oˈmoˈu ...と思う ⊂: What do you think of Tokyo? (*Tookyoo o doo omoimasu ka?*) 東京をどう思いますか. / I don't think she will come. (*Kanojo ga kuru to wa omoimaseñ.*) 彼女が来るとは思いません.

2 (consider) ... to kaˈñgaˈeru ...と考える Ⅴ: I am thinking what to do next. (*Tsugi ni nani o shiyoo ka to kañgaete iru tokoro desu.*) 次に何をしようかと考えているところです.

— *vi.* **1** (have in the mind) kaˈñgaˈeru 考える Ⅴ: I'm still thinking. (*Mada kañgae-chuu desu.*) まだ考え中です.

2 (consider) yoˈku kaˈñgaˈeru よく考える Ⅴ: We have to think hard about the problem. (*Wareware wa sono moñdai ni tsuite yoku kañgaenakereba naranai.*) われわれはその

問題についてよく考えなければならない.

think of ... *vt.* ... o o⌐moitsu⌐ku
...を思いつく Ⓒ: I can't think of any
good ideas. (*Ii kañgae ga omoi tsukanai.*) いい考えが思いつかない.

third *adj.* sa⌐ñ-bañme⌐ no 3 番目の;
da⌐i-⌐sañ no 第 3 の.
 — *n.* **1** (people) sa⌐ñ-bañme⌐ no
hi⌐to⌐ 3 番目の人; (things) sa⌐ñ-
bañme⌐ no mo⌐no⌐ 3 番目のもの.
 2 (day) mi⌐kka 三日.
 3 (of a fraction) sa⌐ñ-buñ no ichi⌐
3 分の 1.
 — *adv.* sa⌐ñbañme⌐ ni 3 番目に:
Nagoya is the third largest city in
Japan. (*Nagoya wa Nihoñ de sañ-
bañme ni ooki-na toshi desu.*) 名古
屋は日本で 3 番目に大きな都市です.

thirst *n.* **1** (feeling of dryness)
no⌐do no ka⌐waki⌐ のどの渇き:
quench one's thirst (*nodo no kawaki o iyasu*) のどの渇きをいやす.
 2 (desire) ka⌐tsuboo 渇望; yo⌐ku-
boo 欲望: a thirst for knowledge
(*chishikiyoku*) 知識欲.

thirsty *adj.* **1** (suffering from
thirst) no⌐do ga ka⌐wa⌐ita [ka⌐wa⌐-
ite iru] のどが渇いた[渇いている]: I'm
thirsty. (*Nodo ga kawaita.*) のどが渇
いた.
 2 (eager) tsu⌐yoku mo⌐to⌐mete iru
強く求めている: He is thirsty for
information. (*Kare wa joohoo o
tsuyoku motomete iru.*) 彼は情報を
強く求めている.

thirteen *pron.* ju⌐usañ 13; (people)
ju⌐usa⌐ñ-niñ 13 人; (things) ju⌐u-
sa⌐ñ-ko 13 個.
 — *n.* (figure) ju⌐usañ 13; (hour)
ju⌐usa⌐ñ-ji 13 時; (minute) ju⌐usa⌐ñ-
puñ 13 分; (age) ju⌐usa⌐ñ-sai 13 歳.
 — *adj.* ju⌐usañ no 13 の; (people)
ju⌐usa⌐ñ-niñ no 13 人の; (things)
ju⌐usa⌐ñ-ko no 13 個の; (age) ju⌐u-
sa⌐ñ-sai no 13 歳の.

thirteenth *adj.* ju⌐usañ-bañme⌐
no 13 番目の; da⌐i-⌐ju⌐usañ no 第 13
の.
 — *n.* **1** (people) ju⌐usañ-bañme⌐
no hi⌐to⌐ 13 番目の人; (things) ju⌐u-

sa⌐ñ-bañme⌐ no mo⌐no⌐ 13 番目のも
の.
 2 (day) ju⌐usa⌐ñ-nichi 13 日.
 3 (fraction) ju⌐usañ-buñ no ichi⌐ 13
分の 1.

thirtieth *adj.* sa⌐ñjuu-bañme⌐ no
30 番目の; da⌐i-⌐sañjuu no 第 30 の.
 — *n.* **1** (people) sañjuu-bañme⌐
no hi⌐to⌐ 30 番目の人; (things) sa⌐ñ-
juu-bañme⌐ no mo⌐no⌐ 30 番目のもの.
 2 (day) sa⌐ñju⌐u-nichi 30 日.
 3 (fraction) sa⌐ñjuu-buñ no ichi⌐ 30
分の 1.

thirty *pron.* sa⌐ñjuu 30; (people)
sa⌐ñju⌐u-niñ 30 人; (things) sa⌐ñ-
ju⌐k-ko 30 個.
 — *n.* (figure) sa⌐ñjuu 30; (minute)
sa⌐ñju⌐p-puñ 30 分; (age) sa⌐ñju⌐s-
sai 30 歳.
 — *adj.* sa⌐ñjuu no 30 の; (people)
sa⌐ñju⌐u-niñ 30 人の; (things)
sa⌐ñju⌐k-ko no 30 個の; (age) sa⌐ñ-
jus-sai no 30 歳の.

this *pron.* **1** [something that is
closer to the speaker] ko⌐re これ:
What's this? (*Kore wa nañ desu
ka?*) これは何ですか. / Do you have
one like this? (*Kore to onaji mono
wa arimasu ka?*) これと同じものはあり
ますか. / I'll take this. (*Kore o kudasai.*) これを下さい.
 2 [someone that is closer to the
speaker] ko⌐chira こちら: This is my
teacher. (*Kochira wa watashi no
sensee desu.*) こちらは私の先生です.
 3 [something a person is about to
describe] ko⌐re これ: This is my
first visit to Japan. (*Nihoñ e kita
no wa kore ga hajimete desu.*) 日
本へ来たのはこれが初めてです.
 4 (here) ko⌐ko ここ: This is where
I was born. (*Koko ga watashi no
umareta tokoro desu.*) ここが私の生
まれたところです.
 — *adj.* **1** (being the one near)
ko⌐no この: This room is 303. (*Kono heya wa sañ maru sañ desu.*) こ
の部屋は 303 です. / This apple is
delicious. (*Kono riñgo wa oishii.*)
このリンゴはおいしい.

2 (present) ge⌐ňzai no 現在の；
ko⌐ň- 今：this week (*koň-shuu*) 今
週 / (*koň-getsu*) 今月 / this year
(*kotoshi*) ことし / this morning
(*kesa*) けさ / this evening (*koň-bań*)
今晩.
— *adv.* ko⌐ňna ni こんなに：I didn't
expect this many people. (*Koňna ni
ooku no hito ga kuru to wa omo-
wanakatta.*) こんなに多くの人が来ると
は思わなかった.

thorn *n.* to⌐ge⌐ とげ：get a thorn in
one's finger (*yubi ni toge ga
sasaru*) 指にとげが刺さる / remove a
thorn (*toge o nuku*) とげを抜く.

thorough *adj.* **1** (complete) ka⌐ň-
zeň na 完全な；te⌐ttee shita [shite
iru] 徹底した[している]：a thorough
investigation (*tettee shita choosa*)
徹底した調査.
2 (of a person) ki⌐choome⌐ň na きち
ょうめんな：He is thorough in his
work. (*Kare wa shigoto ga ki-
choomeň da.*) 彼は仕事がきちょうめん
だ.

thoroughly *adv.* ka⌐ňzeň ni 完全
に；te⌐tteeteki ni 徹底的に：He
searched his room thoroughly for
the papers. (*Kare wa sono shorui o
motomete heya-juu o tetteeteki ni
sagashita.*) 彼はその書類を求めて部屋
中を徹底的に捜した.

those *pron.* **1** ko⌐re⌐(¬-ra) これ(ら)；
a⌐re⌐(¬-ra) あれ(ら)：Those are all my
books. (*Kore wa miňna watashi no
hoň desu.*) これはみんな私の本です. /
Those are my children. (*Are wa
watashi no kodomo-tachi desu.*) あ
れは私の子どもたちです.
2 (of people) hi⌐to⌐(¬-tachi) 人(たち)：
Those who are interested, raise
your hands. (*Kyoomi no aru hito
wa te o agete kudasai.*) 興味のある
人は手を挙げてください.
— *adj.* so⌐re⌐-ra no それらの；so⌐no
その；a⌐re⌐-ra no あれらの；a⌐no あの：
Who are those people? (*Ano hito-
tachi wa dare desu ka?*) あの人たち
はだれですか.

though *conj.* **1** (despite) ke⌐re-

domo けれども；… ni mo ka⌐kawa⌐-
razu にもかかわらず：He went out,
though it was raining. (*Ame ga
futte ita keredomo kare wa gaishutsu shita.*) 雨が降っていたけれども
彼は外出した. / Though she had a
high fever, she went to work.
(*Kanojo wa koonetsu ga atta ni
mo kakawarazu, shigoto ni itta.*)
彼女は高熱があったにもかかわらず, 仕事
に行った.
2 (even if) ta⌐toe … -te[de] mo たと
え…て[で]も：Though you don't feel
like it, you have to go. (*Tatoe ki ga
susumanakute mo, anata wa ikanakereba narimaseň.*) たとえ気が進まな
くても, あなたは行かなければなりません.
— *adv.* (however) de⌐ mo でも；
ya⌐ha⌐ri やはり：The work was hard.
I enjoyed it, though. (*Shigoto wa
kitsukatta. De mo tanoshikatta.*)
仕事はきつかった. でも楽しかった.

thought *n.* **1** (idea) ka⌐ňga⌐e 考え；
(opinion) i⌐keň 意見：Tell me your
thoughts on this matter. (*Kono
moňdai ni tsuite anata no ikeň o
kikasete kudasai.*) この問題についてあ
なたの意見を聞かせてください.
2 (thinking) ka⌐ňgae⌐ru ko⌐to⌐ 考え
ること；mo⌐noo⌐moi もの思い：I
haven't given it enough thought
yet. (*Sore ni tsuite wa mada juu-
buň ni kaňgaete imaseň.*) それについ
てはまだ十分に考えていません. / He was
deep in thought. (*Kare wa mono-
omoi ni fukette ita.*) 彼はもの思いにふ
けっていた.

thoughtful *adj.* **1** (considerate)
o⌐moiyari no a⌐ru 思いやりのある；
(kind) shi⌐ňsetsu na 親切な：a
thoughtful person (*omoiyari no
aru hito*) 思いやりのある人 / It is
thoughtful of you to do that. (*Soo
shite kudasaru no wa go-shiňse-
tsu na koto desu.*) そうしてくださるのは
ご親切なことです.
2 (thinking deeply) ka⌐ňgaeko⌐ňde
iru 考え込んでいる：She looks
thoughtful. (*Kanojo wa kaňgae-
koňde iru yoo da.*) 彼女は考え込んで

いるようだ.

thoughtless *adj.* keˈesotsu na 軽率な; fuˈchuˈui na 不注意な: thoughtless behavior (keesotsu na furumai) 軽率な振る舞い.

thousand *n.* seˈñ 千: ten thousand (ichi-mañ) 1万 / fourteen thousand (ichi-mañ yoñ-señ) 1万4千 / a hundred thousand (juu-mañ) 10万 / Thousands of people were killed in the earthquake. (Sono jishiñ de nañ-zeñ to iu hito ga shiñda.) その地震で何千という人が死んだ.
— *adj.* seˈñ no 千の: There are a thousand meters in a kilometer. (Ichi-kiro wa señ-meetoru desu.) 1キロは千メートルだ.

thread *n.* 1 (string) iˈto 糸: sew with silk thread (kinu-ito de nuu) 絹糸で縫う.
2 (plot) suˈji 筋; (course) suˈjiˈ-michi 筋道: I cannot follow the thread of his story. (Watashi wa kare no hanashi no suji ni tsuite ikenai.) 私は彼の話の筋についていけない.
— *vt.* ... ni iˈto o toosu …に糸を通す ⓒ: thread a needle (hari ni ito o toosu) 針に糸を通す.

threat *n.* 1 (warning) oˈdoshi 脅し: They carried out their threat to go on strike. (Kare-ra wa sutoraiki o suru to odoshi o kaketa.) 彼らはストライキをすると脅しをかけた.
2 (source of danger) kyoˈoi 脅威: The excessive appreciation of the yen is a threat to the Japanese economy. (Eñdaka no ikisugi wa Nihoñ keezai ni totte kyooi da.) 円高の行き過ぎは日本経済にとって脅威だ.

threaten *vt.* 1 (make a threat) ... o oˈdosu …を脅す ⓒ; [formal] kyoˈohaku suru 脅迫する Ⓘ: The man threatened me with a knife. (Sono otoko wa watashi o naifu de odoshita.) その男は私をナイフで脅した.
2 (give a sign) ⟨verb⟩-soˈo da …そうだ: It is threatening to rain. (Ame ga furi-soo da.) 雨が降りそうだ.

three *pron.* miˈttsu 三つ; (people) saˈñ-niˈñ 3人; (things) saˈñ-ko 3個.
— *n.* (figure) saˈñ 3; (hour) saˈñ-ji 3時; (minute) saˈñ-puñ 3分; (age) saˈñ-sai 3歳.
— *adj.* miˈttsu no 三つの; saˈñ no 3の; (people) saˈñ-niˈñ no 3人の; (things) saˈñ-ko no 3個の; (age) saˈñ-sai no 3歳の.

threshold *n.* 1 (of a doorway) shiˈkii 敷居: cross the threshold (shikii o matagu) 敷居をまたぐ.
2 (beginning) haˈjime 始め: He is on the threshold of a new career. (Kare wa atarashii shigoto o hajimeyoo to shite iru.) 彼は新しい仕事を始めようとしている.

thrifty *adj.* keˈñyaku suru 倹約する; tsuˈmashiˈi つましい: a thrifty meal (tsumashii shokuji) つましい食事.

thrill *n.* (feeling) zoˈkuzoku [waˈkuwaku] suru kaˈñji ぞくぞく[わくわく]する感じ; suˈriru スリル: It is a real thrill to meet the star in person. (Ano sutaa ni jika ni aeru nañte wakuwaku suru.) あのスターにじかに会えるなんてわくわくする.
— *vt.* ... o zoˈkuzoku [waˈkuwaku] saseru …をぞくぞく[わくわく]させる Ⓥ: She was thrilled by the invitation. (Kanojo wa sono shootai ni wakuwaku shita.) 彼女はその招待にわくわくした.

thrive *vi.* 1 (prosper) saˈkaeˈru 栄える Ⓥ; haˈñee suru 繁栄する Ⓘ: His business is thriving. (Kare no shoobai wa sakaete iru.) 彼の商売は栄えている.
2 (grow) soˈdaˈtsu 育つ ⓒ: This plant thrives in a warm climate. (Kono shokubutsu wa atatakai tokoro de sodachimasu.) この植物は暖かい所で育ちます.

throat *n.* noˈdo のど: I have a sore throat. (Nodo ga itai.) のどが痛い. / clear one's throat (sekibarai o suru) せき払いをする.

throb *vi.* (of a heart) doˈkidoki suru どきどきする Ⓘ; (of a wound) zuˈkizuki suru ずきずきする Ⓘ: The cut was throbbing with pain. (Kirikizu ga itami de zukizuki shite ita.) 切

り傷が痛んでずきずきしていた.
— *n.* do「oki 動悸; ko「doo 鼓動: a throb of the heart (*shinzoo no dooki*) 心臓の動悸.

throne *n.* o「oza 王座; o「oi 王位: come to the throne (*ooi ni tsuku*) 王位につく.

throng *n.* gu「nshuu 群集; mu「re」群れ: a throng of people (*hito no mure*) 人の群れ.
— *vi.* ... mu「raga」ru 群がる C; sa「ttoo suru 殺到する I: The returning spectators thronged toward the exit. (*Kaeri no kankyaku ga deguchi ni sattoo shita.*) 帰りの観客が出口に殺到した.
— *vt.* ... ni mu「raga」ru ...に群がる C; ... de go「ttaga」esu ...でごった返す C: The street was thronged with shoppers. (*Sono toori wa kaimonokyaku de gottagaeshite ita.*) その通りは買物客でごった返していた.

through *prep.* **1** (from side to side) ... o to「otte ...を通って: The river runs through the city. (*Sono kawa wa shichuu o tootte nagarete iru.*) その川は市中を通って流れている.
2 (from beginning to end) sa「isho kara sa「igo made 最初から最後まで; -juu 中: I read through the book. (*Watashi wa sono hon o saigo made yonda.*) 私はその本を最後まで読んだ. / The rain lasted all through the night. (*Ame wa hitoban-juu futta.*) 雨は一晩中降った.
3 (up to) ... ma「de ...まで: I work from Monday through Friday. (*Watashi wa getsuyoo kara kinyoo made hatarakimasu.*) 私は月曜から金曜まで働きます.
4 (by means of) ... ni yo「tte ...によって; ... o to「oshite ...を通して: He reserved a hotel room through a travel agency. (*Kare wa ryokoo-dairiten o tooshite hoteru no heya o yoyaku shita.*) 彼は旅行代理店を通してホテルの部屋を予約した.
— *adv.* **1** to「oshite 通して: I have a permit; let me through. (*Kyoka-shoo ga aru no de tooshite kudasai.*) 許可証があるので通してください.
2 (from beginning to end) sa「igo made 最後まで: Please hear me through. (*Doo ka saigo made kiite kudasai.*) どうか最後まで聞いてください.
— *adj.* **1** (finished) o「watte 終わって; su「n de 済んで: Are you through? (*Moo sumimashita ka?*) もう済みましたか.
2 (direct) cho「kutsuu no 直通の: a through train (*chokutsuu ressha*) 直通列車.

throughout *prep.* **1** (in every part) ... no su「mi kara sumi made ...の隅から隅まで; -juu 中: search throughout the house (*ie-juu sagasu*) 家中捜す.
2 (from beginning to end) -juu (zu「tto) 中(ずっと): He was asleep throughout the lecture. (*Kare wa koogi no aida-juu zutto nete ita.*) 彼は講義の間じゅうずっと寝ていた.

throw *vt.* **1** (hurl) ... o na「ge」ru ...を投げる V: I threw the ball to him. (*Watashi wa sono booru o kare ni nageta.*) 私はそのボールを彼に投げた.
2 (make fall down) ... o na「geto-ba」su ...を投げ飛ばす C: He threw his wrestling opponent. (*Kare wa resuringu no aite o nagetobashita.*) 彼はレスリングの相手を投げ飛ばした
3 (put on hastily) ... o sa「tto ki「ru ...をさっと着る V; (take off) nu「gu 脱ぐ C: throw one's jacket on [off] (*uwagi o satto kiru [nugu]*) 上着をさっと着る[脱ぐ].
4 (cast) ... o mu「keru ...を向ける V: He threw me a threatening look. (*Kare wa watashi ni odosu yoo na shisen o muketa.*) 彼は私に脅すような視線を向けた.

thrust *vt.* **1** (push) ... o tsu「yoku o「su ...を強く押す C; tsu「kko」mu 突っ込む C: He thrust me aside. (*Kare wa watashi o waki ni tsuyoku oshita.*) 彼は私をわきに強く押した. / He thrust his wallet into his pocket. (*Kare wa saifu o poketto no naka ni tsukkonda.*) 彼は財布をポケットの

中に突っ込んだ.

2 (stab) ... o tsu「kisa¬su ...を突き刺
す ©: thrust a knife into a person's
back (*hito no senaka ni naifu o tsu-
kisasu*) 人の背中にナイフを突き刺す.
— *vi.* ka「mina¬ri o osu 押す ©; (stab)
sa¬su 刺す ©: thrust through a
crowd (*hitogomi o oshiwakete
susumu*) 人込みを押し分けて進む.

thumb *n.* o「yayubi 親指: raise
one's thumb (*oyayubi o tateru*) 親
指を立てる.

thunder *n.* ka「mina¬ri 雷; ra「imee
雷鳴: the rolling sound of thunder
(*kaminari no gorogoro iu oto*) 雷の
ごろごろいう音.
— *vi.* ka「mina¬ri ga na¬ru 雷が鳴る
©; (make a loud noise) go「o-oñ o
tate¬ru 轟音を立てる Ⓥ: It's thun-
dering in the distance. (*Tooku de
kaminari ga natte iru.*) 遠くで雷が鳴
っている.

Thursday *n.* mo「kuyo¬o(bi) 木曜
(日).

thus *adv.* **1** (in this way) ko「no
yo¬o ni このように: Do it thus. (*Kono
yoo ni yari nasai.*) このようにやりなさ
い.
2 (for this reason) da「kara だから;
shi「tagatte 従って: He is ill and
thus absent. (*Kare wa byooki desu.
Shitagatte yasuñde imasu.*) 彼は病
気です.従って休んでいます.

ticket *n.* ki「ppu 切符; ke¬ñ 券; chi-
「ke¬tto チケット: Where can I buy a
ticket for a sightseeing bus? (*Kañkoo basu no kippu wa doko de
kaemasu ka?*) 観光バスの切符はどこで
買えますか. / Can I cancel this ticket? (*Kono kippu wa torikesemasu
ka?*) この切符は取り消せますか.

tickle *vt.* ... o ku「suguru ...をくすぐる
©: The mother tickled her baby's
feet. (*Hahaoya wa akañboo no
ashi o kusugutta.*) 母親は赤ん坊の足
をくすぐった.

tide *n.* **1** (of the sea) shi「o¬ 潮: The
tide is coming in [going out]. (*Shio
ga michi-hajimete [hiki-hajimete]
iru.*) 潮が満ち始めて[引き始めて]いる.

2 (trend) fu「uchoo 風潮; jo「osee 情
勢; ke「esee 形勢: the tide of international affairs (*kokusai-joosee*) 国
際情勢 / The tide turned against
me. (*Keesee wa watashi ni furi ni
natta.*) 形勢は私に不利になった.

tidy *adj.* ki「chi¬ñto shita [shite iru]
きちんとした[している]: keep a kitchen
tidy (*daidokoro o kichiñto shite
oku*) 台所をきちんとしておく / She
always looks tidy. (*Kanojo wa itsu-
mo minari ga kichiñto shite iru.*)
彼女はいつも身なりがきちんとしている.

tie *n.* **1** (necktie) ne「kutai ネクタイ:
put on [take off] a tie (*nekutai o
shimeru [hazusu]*) ネクタイを締める[は
ずす] / a tie pin (*taipiñ*) タイピン.
2 (something that joins) tsu「nagari
つながり; ki「zuna きずな: business ties
(*shoobai-joo no tsunagari*) 商売上
のつながり / family ties (*kazoku no
kizuna*) 家族のきずな.
3 (draw) do「oteñ 同点; hi「kiwake
引き分け: The game ended in a tie.
(*Shiai wa hikiwake ni owatta.*) 試
合は引き分けに終わった.
— *vt.* **1** (fasten) ... o mu「subu ...を
結ぶ ©; shi「ba¬ru 縛る ©: tie one's
shoelaces (*kutsu no himo o musubu*) 靴のひもを結ぶ / tie a parcel with
string (*kozutsumi o himo de shibaru*) 小包をひもで縛る.
2 (bind) ... o so「kubaku suru ...を束
縛する ①; shi「baritsuke¬ru 縛りつける
Ⓥ: I work all day tied to my desk.
(*Watashi wa ichinichi-juu tsukue
ni shibaritsukerarete shigoto o
shite iru.*) 私は一日中机に縛りつけられ
て仕事をしている.
3 (equal) ... to do「oteñ ni na¬ru ...
と同点になる ©: The Giants tied
the Tigers in the ninth inning.
(*Jaiañtsu wa kyuukai ni Taigaasu
to dooteñ ni natta.*) ジャイアンツは9
回にタイガースと同点になった.

tiger *n.* to「ra とら(虎).

tight *adj.* **1** (fitting closely) shi-
「ma¬tta 締まった; shi「ma¬tte iru 締っ
ている; ki「tchi¬ri shita [shite iru] きっ
ちりした[している]; ki「tsui きつい: shut

a door tight (*to o kitchiri shimeru*) 戸をきっちり閉める / My trousers are too tight. (*Watashi no zuboñ wa kitsu-sugiru.*) 私のズボンはきつすぎる.

2 (stretched) pi´ñ to hatta [hatte iru] ぴんと張った[張っている]: a tight rope (*piñ to hatta roopu*) ぴんと張ったロープ.

3 (strict) yoyu´u no na´i 余裕のない; ki´tsui きつい: a tight schedule (*yoyuu no nai yotee*) 余裕のない予定.

tighten *vt.* ... o shi´kka´ri to shi´ me´ru …をしっかりと締める Ⅴ: tighten up a screw (*neji o shikkari to shimeru*) ねじをしっかりと締める.

tightly *adv.* shi´kka´ri to しっかりと; ki´tsuku きつく.

tile *n.* ta´iru タイル; (of a Japanese roof) ka´wara かわら.

till *prep.* ... ma´de …まで: He worked from nine till five. (*Kare wa kuji kara goji made hataraita.*) 彼は9時から5時まで働いた. / I haven't heard of it till now. (*Watashi wa sore ni tsuite ima made kiita koto ga nakatta.*) 私はそれについて今まで聞いたことがなかった.

— *conj.* ... ma´de …まで: I waited there till the rain let up. (*Watashi wa ame ga yamu made soko de matte ita.*) 私は雨がやむまでそこで待っていた.

tilt *vt.* ... o ka´tamuke´ru …を傾ける Ⅴ: He tilted the chair backward. (*Kare wa isu o ushiro ni katamuketa.*) 彼はいすを後ろに傾けた.

— *vi.* ka´tamu´ku 傾く Ⓒ: The pillar tilted and fell. (*Sono hashira wa katamuite taoreta.*) その柱は傾いて倒れた.

timber *n.* za´imoku 材木; mo´ku´ zai 木材.

time *n.* **1** (passing hours) to´ki´ 時; ji´kañ 時間: Time is money. (*Toki wa kane nari.*) 時は金なり. / waste time (*jikañ o muda ni suru*) 時間を無駄にする / kill time (*jikañ o tsubusu*) 時間をつぶす.

2 (the hour of the day) ji´koku 時刻; ji´kañ 時間; -ji 時: What time

is it? (*Ima nañ-ji desu ka?*) 今何時ですか. / What time does the dining room open? (*Shokudoo wa nañ-ji ni akimasu ka?*) 食堂は何時に開きますか.

3 (particular moment) ji´kañ 時間: It's time for bed. (*Neru jikañ desu.*) 寝る時間です. / Do you have time? (*O-jikañ wa arimasu ka?*) お時間はありますか.

4 (experience) to´ki´ 時: We had a good time this evening. (*Koñya wa tanoshii toki o sugoshita.*) 今夜は楽しい時を過ごした.

5 (period) ki´kañ 期間; a´ida 間: for a long time (*nagai aida*) 長い間 / for some time (*shibaraku no aida*) しばらくの間 / for the time being (*toobuñ no aida*) 当分の間.

6 (age) ji´dai 時代: the good old times (*furuki yoki jidai*) 古きよき時代.

7 (number of times) -ka´i 回; -do 度: We meet three times a week for practice. (*Watashi-tachi wa reñshuu no tame ni shuu sañ-kai aimasu.*) 私たちは練習のために週3回会います. / How many times have you come to Tokyo? (*Tookyoo ni wa nañ-do koraremashita ka?*) 東京には何度来られましたか.

8 (multiplication) -bai 倍: China is 26 times larger than Japan. (*Chuugoku no hirosa wa Nihoñ no nijuuroku-bai desu.*) 中国の広さは日本の26倍です.

at a time *adv.* i´chi-do´ ni 一度に: Can you eat that much at a time? (*Ichi-do ni soñna ni taberaremasu ka?*) 一度にそんなに食べられますか.

in time *adv., adj.* ma´nia´tte 間に合って: We arrived just in time for the concert. (*Koñsaato ni nañ to ka maniatta.*) コンサートに何とか間に合った.

on time *adv., adj.* ji´kañ do´ori ni 時間どおりに: The train arrived on time. (*Deñsha wa jikañ doori ni toochaku shita.*) 電車は時間どおり

に到着した.

time difference n. ji￢sa 時差: The time difference between Tokyo and New York is 14 hours. (*Tookyoo to Nyuu Yooku no jisa wa juuyo-jikañ desu.*) 東京とニューヨークの時差は14時間です.

timetable n. (of transportation) ji￢kokuhyoo 時刻表; (of school) ji￢kañwari 時間割.

timid adj. o￢kubyoo￢na 臆病な; u￢chiki na 内気な: a timid person (*okubyoo na hito*) 臆病な人.

tin n. **1** (can) ka￢ñ 缶; (canned food) ka￢ñzu￢me 缶詰.
2 (metal) su￢zu すず(錫); (tinplate) bu￢riki ブリキ.
— vt. ... o ka￢ñzu￢me ni suru ...を缶詰にする ⃞: tin fruit (*kudamono o kañzume ni suru*) 果物を缶詰にする.

tiny adj. chi￢tcha￢na ちっちゃな: a tiny little boy (*chitcha na otoko-no-ko*) ちっちゃな男の子.

tip[1] n. chi￢ppu チップ: I gave the taxi driver a good tip. (*Watashi wa sono takushii no uñteñshu ni tappuri chippu o hazuñda.*) 私はそのタクシーの運転手にたっぷりチップを弾んだ.
— vt. ... ni chi￢ppu o ya￢ru ...にチップをやる ⃝: I tipped the bellboy. (*Watashi wa booi ni chippu o yatta.*) 私はボーイにチップをやった.

tip[2] n. sa￢ki 先; se￢ñtañ 先端: the tip of the finger (*yubi no saki*) 指の先.

tire[1] vt. **1** (exhaust) ... o tsu￢kare sase￢ru ...を疲れさせる ⃡: Walking tired the patient. (*Hokoo wa byooniñ o tsukare saseta.*) 歩行は病人を疲れさせた.
2 (make weary) a￢kia￢ki saseru あきあきさせる ⃡; u￢ñza￢ri saseru うんざりさせる ⃡: His same old story tired her. (*Kare no onaji hanashi wa kanojo o uñzari saseta.*) 彼の同じ話は彼女をうんざりさせた.

tire[2] n. ta￢iya タイヤ: pump up a tire (*taiya ni kuuki o ireru*) タイヤに空気を入れる / I got a flat tire. (*Taiya ga*

pañku shita.*) タイヤがパンクした.

tired adj. **1** (exhausted) tsu￢ka￢reta 疲れた; tsu￢ka￢rete iru 疲れている: I'm tired from swimming. (*Watashi wa suiee de tsukareta.*) 私は水泳で疲れた.
2 (wearied) a￢kita 飽きた; a￢kite iru 飽きている: I'm tired of your conversation. (*Kimi no hanashi ni wa moo akita.*) 君の話にはもう飽きた.

tireless adj. tsu￢kare￢o shi￢ranai 疲れを知らない; se￢eryoku-teki na 精力的な: a tireless worker (*tsukare o shiranai hatarakimono*) 疲れを知らない働き者.

tiresome adj. ya￢kkai na やっかいな; ta￢ikutsu na 退屈な: a tiresome child (*yakkai na kodomo*) やっかいな子ども / a tiresome game (*taikutsu na shiai*) 退屈な試合.

tissue n. **1** (of organs) so￢shiki 組織: nervous tissue (*shiñkee soshiki*) 神経組織.
2 (paper) ti￢sshu ティッシュ; chi￢rigami ちり紙: toilet tissue (*toiretto peepaa*) トイレットペーパー. ★ 'Tissue' is often called 'tisshu peepaa' (tissue paper).

title n. **1** (name) da￢imee 題名: the title of a book (*hoñ no daimee*) 本の題名.
2 (of a rank) ka￢tagaki 肩書: a person with a title (*katagaki no aru hito*) 肩書のある人.
3 (championship) se￢ñshu￢keñ 選手権: She holds the world title. (*Kanojo wa sekai chañpioñ da.*) 彼女は世界チャンピオンだ.

to[1] prep. **1** (toward) ... e [ni] ...へ[に]: Is this the bus to Shibuya? (*Kore wa Shibuya e iku basu desu ka?*) これは渋谷へ行くバスですか. / I wrote a letter to her. (*Watashi wa kanojo ni tegami o kaita.*) 私は彼女に手紙を書いた.
2 (as far as) ... ma￢de ...まで: It is two kilometers from my house to the station. (*Watashi no uchi kara eki made ni-kiro desu.*) 私の家から駅まで2キロです.

3 (till) ... ma¹de まで: He worked from morning to night. (*Kare wa asa kara baň made hataraita.*) 彼は朝から晩まで働いた.

4 (concerning) ... ni (to¹tte) ...に(とって): His resignation is a great loss to our company. (*Kare ga yameta no wa kaisha ni totte ooki-na soñshitsu da.*) 彼が辞めたのは会社にとって大きな損失だ.

5 (connection) ... no ...の: an assistant to Dr. Kimura (*Kimura hakase no joshu*) 木村博士の助手 / the key to a laboratory (*keñkyuushitsu no kagi*) 研究室の鍵.

6 (comparison) ... ni ta¹ishite ...に対して: We won the game by a score of three to two. (*Watashi-tachi wa sañ tai ni de shiai ni katta.*) 私たちは 3 対 2 で試合に勝った.

7 (agreement) ... ni a¹wa¹sete ...に合わせて: We danced to the music. (*Watashi-tachi wa sono oñgaku ni awasete odotta.*) 私たちはその音楽に合わせて踊った.

to² [marking the infinitive] **1** [noun use] ... ko¹to¹ ...こと; ... no ga [wa] ...のが[は]: I decided to work there. (*Watashi wa soko de hataraku koto ni shita.*) 私はそこで働くことにした. / I like to play tennis. (*Watashi wa tenisu o suru no ga suki desu.*) 私はテニスをするのが好きです. / It's good to keep early hours. (*Hayane hayaoki o suru no wa ii koto desu.*) 早寝早起きをするのはいいことです.

2 [adjective use] ... ta¹me¹ no ...ための; ... be¹ki ...べき: a house to live in (*sumu tame no ie*) 住むための家 / I want to eat. (*Nani-ka taberu mono ga hoshii.*) 何か食べる物が欲しい. / I have no friends to talk with. (*Watashi ni wa tomo ni kataru beki tomo wa inai.*) 私には共に語るべき友はいない.

3 [adverb use] ... ta¹me¹ ni ...ために; <verb>-te[de] ...て[で]: We eat to live. (*Watashi-tachi wa ikiru tame ni taberu.*) 私たちは生きるために食べる. / I'm very glad to see you again.

(*Anata to mata o-ai dekite ureshii desu.*) あなたとまたお会いできてうれしいです.

toast *n.* to¹osuto トースト: a slice of toast (*toosuto ichi-mai*) トースト 1 枚 / make toast (*pañ o yaku*) パンを焼く.

tobacco *n.* ki¹zami-ta¹bako 刻みたばこ: chewing tobacco (*kami tabako*) かみたばこ.

today *adv.* **1** (this day) kyo¹o (wa) きょう(は): I'm busy today. (*Kyoo wa isogashii.*) きょうは忙しい.
2 (the present time) ge¹ñzai de wa 現在では; ko¹ñnichi de wa 今日では: Studying abroad is not unusual today. (*Ryuugaku wa koňnichi de wa mezurashiku arimaseñ.*) 留学は今日では珍しくありません.
— *n.* kyo¹o きょう: today's newspaper (*kyoo no shiñbuñ*) きょうの新聞.

toe *n.* (of a foot) a¹shi no yubi¹ 足の指; (of a shoe, sock) tsu¹masaki つま先: the big [little] toe (*ashi no oyayubi [koyubi]*) 足の親指[小指] / a hole in the toe of a sock (*kutsushita no tsumasaki no ana*) 靴下のつま先の穴.

together *adv.* **1** (in company) i¹ssho ni いっしょに; to¹mo ni 共に: Let's go together. (*Issho ni ikimashoo.*) いっしょに行きましょう. / How about having dinner together? (*Yuuhañ o go-issho ni ikaga desu ka?*) 夕飯をごいっしょにいかがですか.
2 (joined) a¹wa¹sete 合わせて: How much is it all together? (*Awasete zeñbu de ikura desu ka?*) 合わせて全部でいくらですか.
3 (at the same time) do¹oji ni 同時に: They got a promotion together. (*Kare-ra wa dooji ni shookaku shita.*) 彼らは同時に昇格した.

toil *vi.* (... ni) ho¹ne¹ o oru (...に)骨を折る C; se¹e o dasu 精を出す C: toil at the task (*shigoto ni see o dasu*) 仕事に精を出す.
— *n.* ho¹neori 骨折り; ku¹roo 苦労.

toilet *n.* se¹ñmeñjo 洗面所; to¹ire トイレ; be¹ñjo¹ 便所: flush a toilet (*toire no mizu o nagasu*) トイレの水

を流す / a public toilet (*kooshuu-benjo*) 公衆便所.

token *n.* **1** (sign) shi⌐rushi 印: This is just a token of my gratitude. (*Kore wa watashi no hoñ no kañsha no shirushi desu.*) これは私のほんの感謝の印です.
2 (keepsake) ki⌐neñ no shina 記念の品: He gave me a necklace as a token of our first date. (*Kare wa saisho no deeto no kineñ ni nek-kuresu o kureta.*) 彼は最初のデートの記念にネックレスをくれた.

tolerable *adj.* ga⌐mañ de⌐ki⌐ru 我慢できる: This heat is not tolerable. (*Kono atsusa wa gamañ dekinai.*) この暑さは我慢できない.

tolerant *adj.* ka⌐ñdai na 寛大な; ka⌐ñyoo na 寛容な: He is tolerant of other's errors. (*Kare wa hoka no hito no machigai ni taishite kañdai da.*) 彼はほかの人の間違いに対して寛大だ.

tolerate *vt.* **1** (allow) ... o yu⌐ru⌐su ...を許す Ⓒ: We should not tolerate any violence. (*Doñna booryoku mo yurusu wake ni wa ikanai.*) どんな暴力も許す訳にはいかない.
2 (endure) ... o ga⌐mañ suru ...を我慢する Ⓘ: I cannot tolerate this noise. (*Kono soo-oñ wa gamañ dekinai.*) この騒音は我慢できない.

toll *n.* **1** (charge) ryo⌐okiñ 料金: pay a toll to cross a bridge (*hashi o wataru no ni ryookiñ o harau*) 橋を渡るのに料金を払う / a toll road (*yuuryoo dooro*) 有料道路.
2 (casualty) shi⌐shoosha 死傷者; gi⌐se⌐esha 犠牲者; (damage) so⌐ñ-gai 損害: the death toll in the accident (*sono jiko no giseesha*) その事故の犠牲者.

tomato *n.* to⌐mato トマト: tomato juice (*tomato juusu*) トマトジュース.

tomb *n.* ha⌐ka⌐ 墓: a tombstone (*hakaishi*) 墓石.

tomorrow *adv.* a⌐shita⌐ (wa) あした(は); a⌐su⌐ (wa) あす(は); [formal] myo⌐onichi 明日: It'll be fine tomorrow. (*Ashita wa hareru de-*

shoo.) あしたは晴れるでしょう.
— *n.* a⌐shita⌐ あした; a⌐su⌐ あす: Tomorrow is a holiday. (*Ashita wa kyuujitsu desu.*) あしたは休日です. / I am leaving tomorrow morning. (*Watashi wa asu no asa tachimasu.*) 私はあすの朝立ちます. / the day after tomorrow (*asatte* [*myoo-gonichi*]) あさって[明後日].

ton *n.* to⌐ñ トン: One cubic meter of water weighs a ton. (*Ichi-rippoo-meetoru no mizu no omosa wa it-toñ desu.*) 1立方メートルの水の重さは1トンです.

tone *n.* **1** (sound) cho⌐oshi 調子; ne⌐ɾiro 音色: the clear tone of a flute (*furuuto no suñda neiro*) フルートの澄んだ音色.
2 (of a voice) ku⌐choo 口調: He spoke in a gentle tone. (*Kare wa yasashii kuchoo de hanashita.*) 彼はやさしい口調で話した.
3 (shade of color) i⌐ɾoai 色合い; shi⌐kichoo 色調: a picture in warm tones (*atatakai shikichoo no e*) 暖かい色調の絵.

tongs *n.* -ba⌐sami ばさみ: ice tongs (*koori-basami*) 氷ばさみ / coal tongs (*sekitañ-basami*) 石炭ばさみ.

tongue *n.* **1** (organ) shi⌐ta⌐ 舌: stick out one's tongue (*shita o dasu*) 舌を出す.
2 (food) ta⌐ñ タン: ox-tongue (*gyuu tañ*) 牛タン.
3 (language) ko⌐ɾtoba⌐ 言葉: Watch your tongue. (*Kotoba ni ki o tsuke nasai.*) 言葉に気をつけなさい.

tonight *adv.* ko⌐ñya (wa) 今夜(は): I'm free tonight. (*Koñya wa hima desu.*) 今夜は暇です.
— *n.* ko⌐ñya 今夜; ko⌐ñbañ 今晩: Can I get a room for tonight? (*Koñ-bañ tomaremasu ka?*) 今晩泊まれますか.

too[1] *adv.* (also) ... mo ...も; ma⌐ta ま た: I'm tired, too. (*Watashi mo tsu-karemashita.*) 私も疲れました. / He can speak Chinese, and Korean, too. (*Kare wa Chuugokugo o hana-semasu shi, mata Kañkokugo mo* *hanasemasu.*) 彼は中国語を話せますし、また韓国語も話せます。

too[2] *adv.* **1** (to a great extent) -sugi-ru すぎる: This room is too small. (*Kono heya wa sema-sugiru.*) この部屋は狭すぎる。 / It's too expensive for me. (*Watashi ni wa taka-sugimasu.*) 私には高すぎます。 / Don't eat too much. (*Tabe-suginai yoo ni.*) 食べすぎないように。

2 (very) hiˈjoo ni 非常に; [in the negative] aˈmari ... -naˈi あまり...ない: I'm not feeling too well. (*Watashi wa amari kibuñ ga yokunai.*) 私はあまり気分がよくない。

tool *n.* doˈogu 道具: the tools of one's trade (*shoobai-doogu*) 商売道具。

tooth *n.* haˈ 歯: brush one's teeth (*ha o migaku*) 歯を磨く / pull a tooth (*ha o nuku*) 歯を抜く / a bad tooth (*mushiba*) 虫歯 / a false tooth (*ireba*) 入れ歯。

toothache *n.* haˈ no iˈtamiˈ 歯の痛み; shiˈtsuu 歯痛: I have a toothache. (*Ha ga itai.*) 歯が痛い。

toothbrush *n.* haˈbuˈrashi 歯ブラシ。

toothpaste *n.* neˈrihamiˈgaki 練り歯磨き。

toothpick *n.* tsuˈmayoˈoji つまようじ; yoˈoji ようじ。

top *n.* **1** (upper part) uˈe 上; joˈobu 上部: the fifth line from the top (*ue kara go-gyoo-me*) 上から5行目。 **2** (surface) uˈe 上; hyoˈomeˈñ 表面: clear a table top (*teeburu no ue o katazukeru*) テーブルの上を片付ける。 **3** (of a mountain) choˈojoˈo 頂上: We finally reached the top of the mountain. (*Watashi-tachi wa yatto choojoo ni tsuita.*) 私たちはやっと頂上に着いた。 **4** (highest rank) iˈchi¹bañ 一番; toˈppu トップ: He is at the top of our class. (*Kare wa kurasu de ichi-bañ desu.*) 彼はクラスで一番です。 ★ In Japan 'leading runner' is often called '*toppu rañnaa*' (top runner). **5** (covering) fuˈta ふた; seˈñ 栓: a

box top (*hako no futa*) 箱のふた。
— *vt.* **1** (crown) ... no iˈtadaki o ooˈu ...の頂を覆う C: Snow topped the mountain. (*Yuki ga yama no itadaki o ootta.*) 雪が山の頂を覆った。 **2** (surpass) ... yori suˈgureˈru ...より優れる V: He topped all the others at golf. (*Kare wa gorufu de wa hoka no dare yori mo sugurete ita.*) 彼はゴルフではほかのだれよりも優れていた。

topic *n.* waˈdai 話題: bring up a topic (*wadai o kiridasu*) 話題を切り出す / the topic for a discussion (*kaigi no gidai*) 会議の議題。

torch *n.* (flaming light) taˈimatsu たいまつ; (flashlight) kaˈichuudeˈñtoo 懐中電灯: turn on a torch (*kaichuu-deñtoo o tsukeru*) 懐中電灯をつける。

torment *n.* kuˈtsuu 苦痛; kuˈnoo 苦悩: He is in torment. (*Kare wa kunoo shite iru.*) 彼は苦悩している。
— *vt.* ... o kuˈrushimeˈru ...を苦しめる V: She is tormented with a headache. (*Kanojo wa zutsuu de kurushiñde iru.*) 彼女は頭痛で苦しんでいる。

torture *n.* **1** (of punishment) goˈomoñ 拷問: He was put to torture. (*Kare wa goomoñ ni kakerareta.*) 彼は拷問にかけられた。 **2** (suffering) kuˈtsuu 苦痛: It was torture doing it over again. (*Sore o mata yarinaosu no wa tsurai datta.*) それをまたやり直すのは苦痛だった。
— *vt.* (punish) ... o goˈomoñ ni kakeˈru ...を拷問にかける V; (make suffer) kuˈrushimeˈru 苦しめる V: He was tortured into making a confession. (*Kare wa goomoñ ni kake-rarete jihaku shita.*) 彼は拷問にかけられて自白した。

toss *vt.* **1** (throw) ... o naˈgeˈru ...を投げる V: Toss that bag to me. (*Sono kabañ o nagete kudasai.*) そのかばんを投げてください。 **2** (in cooking) ... o kaˈkimazeru ...をかき混ぜる V: toss a salad (*sarada o kakimazeru*) サラダをかき混ぜる。
— *vi.* **1** (move up and down) yuˈreru 揺れる V: The ship tossed on

the waves. (*Fune wa nami no ue de yurete ita.*) 船は波の上で揺れていた.
2 (flip a coin) to¹su de ki¹meru トスで決める Ⓥ: Let's toss up. (*Tosu de kimeyoo.*) トスで決めよう.
— *n.* na¹geru koto¹ 投げること: decide by the toss of a coin (*koiñ o nagete kimeru*) コインを投げて決める.

total *n.* so¹okee 総計; go¹okee 合計: The total comes to 5,000 yen. (*Sookee wa gosen-eñ ni narimasu.*) 総計は5千円になります.
— *adj.* **1** (whole) ze¹ñtai no 全体の; so¹o- 総: What will be the total amount? (*Soo-gaku wa ikura desu ka?*) 総額はいくらですか.
2 (complete) ma¹ttaku¹ no まったくの; ka¹ñzeñ na 完全な: a total failure (*kanzeñ na shippai*) 完全な失敗.
— *vt.* ... o go¹okee suru …を合計する Ⓣ: total the expenditures (*hiyoo o gookee suru*) 費用を合計する.

totally *adv.* ma¹ttaku まったく; ka¹ñzeñ ni 完全に: I was totally unaware of his illness. (*Watashi wa kare no byooki no koto o mattaku shiranakatta.*) 私は彼の病気のことをまったく知らなかった.

touch *vt.* **1** (contact) ... ni sa¹waru …に触る Ⓒ; fu¹reru 触れる Ⓥ: Do not touch the exhibits. (*Teñjihiñ ni sawaranaide kudasai.*) 展示品に触らないでください. / The branch almost touches the electric wire. (*Sono eda wa deñseñ ni fure-soo da.*) その枝は電線に触れそうだ.
2 (move) ... o ka¹ñdoo saseru …を感動させる Ⓥ: I was touched by his words. (*Watashi wa kare no kotoba ni kañdoo shita.*) 私は彼の言葉に感動した.
3 (eat, drink) ... ni te¹ o tsu¹ke¹ru …に手をつける Ⓥ: She didn't touch the supper. (*Kanojo wa yuushoku ni te o tsukenakatta.*) 彼女は夕食に手をつけなかった.
— *n.* **1** (sensation) ka¹ñshoku 感触; (of a hand) te¹za¹wari 手触り: the soft touch of fur (*kegawa no*

yawarakai tezawari*) 毛皮の柔らかい手触り.
2 (act of touching) sa¹waru koto¹ 触ること; se¹sshoku 接触: I felt a touch on my arm. (*Watashi wa dare-ka ga ude ni sawaru no o kañjita.*) 私はだれかが腕に触るのを感じた.
3 (communication) re¹ñraku 連絡: It has been a long time since he went out of touch. (*Kare kara reñraku ga todaete moo kanari tatsu.*) 彼から連絡が途絶えてもうかなりたつ.
4 (bit) su¹ko¹shi 少し: This salad needs a touch of salt. (*Kono sarada wa sukoshi shio ga tarinai.*) このサラダは少し塩が足りない.

tough *adj.* **1** (difficult) ko¹ñnañ na 困難な; mu¹zukashii 難しい: He is in a tough position now. (*Kare wa ima muzukashii tachiba ni aru.*) 彼は今難しい立場にある.
2 (not tender) ka¹tai 堅い: This steak is rather tough. (*Kono suteeki wa sukoshi katai.*) このステーキは少し堅い.
3 (strong) tsu¹yo¹i 強い; jo¹obu na 丈夫な; ta¹fu na タフな: tough shoes (*joobu na kutsu*) 丈夫な靴 / He's tough. (*Kare wa tafu da.*) 彼はタフだ.

tour *n.* **1** (journey) ryo¹koo 旅行: She went on a tour of China. (*Kanojo wa Chuugoku ryokoo ni itta.*) 彼女は中国旅行に行った.
2 (visit) ke¹ñbutsu 見物; tsu¹aa ツアー: Is there an all-day tour? (*Ichinichi no tsuaa wa arimasu ka?*) 一日のツアーはありますか.

tourist *n.* (traveler) ryo¹ko¹osha 旅行者; (sightseeing) ka¹ñko¹okyaku 観光客: I'm a tourist. (*Watashi wa kañkookyaku desu.*) 私は観光客です. / a tourist information office (*kañkoo añnaijo*) 観光案内所.

tournament *n.* to¹ornameñto トーナメント: a tennis tournament (*tenisu no toonameñto*) テニスのトーナメント.

toward *prep.* **1** (in the direction of) ... no ho¹o e [ni] …の方へ[に]; ...

e mu「katte ...へ向かって: He went toward the door. (*Kare wa doa no hoo e itta.*) 彼はドアの方へ行った. / The plane is flying toward the south. (*Hikooki wa minami e mukatte toñde imasu.*) 飛行機は南へ向かって飛んでいます.

2 (in relation to) ... ni ta「ishite ...に対して: He was friendly toward me. (*Kare wa watashi ni taishite kooi-teki datta.*) 彼は私に対して好意的だった.

3 (of time) ... ni chi「kaku ...に近く; ko「ro ころ: He returned toward midnight. (*Kare wa mayonaka chi-kaku ni kaette kita.*) 彼は真夜中近くに帰ってきた.

4 (leading to) ... ni mu「katte ...に向かって: the first step toward peace (*heewa ni mukatte no dai-ip-po*) 平和に向かっての第一歩.

towel *n.* ta「oru タオル: a bath towel (*basu taoru*) バスタオル / He dried his hands with a towel. (*Kare wa taoru de te o fuita.*) 彼はタオルで手をふいた.

tower *n.* to「o 塔; ta「waa タワー: a church tower (*kyookai no too*) 教会の塔.
— *vi.* (rise high) ta「kaku so「bie-ta「tsu 高くそびえ立つ ⓒ: The build-ing towers over this town. (*Sono biru wa kono machi ni takaku sobietate iru.*) そのビルはこの街に高くそびえ立っている.

town *n.* ma「chi 町; (city) to「shi 都市; to「kai 都会. ★ Large towns are often called 'shi' 市: Where is the shopping district in this town? (*Kono machi no shooteñgai wa doko ni arimasu ka?*) この町の商店街はどこにありますか. / an industrial town (*sañgyoo toshi*) 産業都市.

toy *n.* o「mo「cha おもちゃ: a toy gun (*omocha no pisutoru*) おもちゃのピストル / a toy shop (*omocha-ya*) おもちゃ屋.
— *vi.* ... o mo「teasobu ...をもてあそぶ ⓒ: The boy was toying with his food. (*Sono ko wa tabemono o

moteasoñde ita.*) その子は食べ物をもてあそんでいた.

trace *n.* **1** (mark) a「to 跡; (foot-print) a「shia「to 足跡: The police followed the trace of the man. (*Keesatsu wa sono otoko no ato o otta.*) 警察はその男の跡を追った.

2 (small amount) ho「ñno wa「zuka ほんのわずか: Traces of poison were found in the food. (*Tabemono ni hoñno wazuka no doku ga mitsu-katta.*) 食べ物にほんのわずかの毒が見つかった.
— *vt.* ... o ta「do「ru ...をたどる ⓒ: trace the history of a race (*miñ-zoku no rekishi o tadoru*) 民族の歴史をたどる.

track *n.* **1** (trace) to「otta ato 通った跡; (footprint) a「shia「to 足跡: fol-low tire tracks in the sand (*suna ni tsuita taiya no ato o tadoru*) 砂につ いたタイヤの跡をたどる.

2 (railroad line) se「ñro 線路; -señ 線: The train for Osaka leaves from track 2. (*Oosaka yuki no deñ-sha wa ni-bañ-señ kara hassha shi-masu.*) 大阪行きの電車は2番線から発車します.

3 (path) ko「michi 小道: A track runs through the woods. (*Komichi ga mori no naka o tootte iru.*) 小道が森の中を通っている.

4 (racetrack) kyo「oso「oro 競走路; to「ra「kku トラック: a cycling track (*jiteñsha kyosooro*) 自転車競走路 / track events (*torakku kyoogi*) トラック競技.

tract *n.* **1** (land) hi「rogari 広がり; chi「tai 地帯: large tracts of forest (*koodai na shiñriñ chitai*) 広大な森林地帯.

2 (organ) ka「ñ 管: the digestive tract (*shooka-kañ*) 消化管.

tractor *n.* to「ra「kutaa トラクター.

trade *n.* **1** (business transaction) to「ri「hiki 取り引き; bo「oeki 貿易: foreign trade (*gaikoku-booeki*) 外国貿易 / promote trade with Asian nations (*Ajia shokoku to no boo-eki o sokushiñ suru*) アジア諸国との

貿易を促進する.

2 (occupation) sho⌐ku⌐gyoo 職業;
sho⌐obai 商売: He is a shoemaker
by trade. (*Kare no shokugyoo wa
kutsu-ya desu.*) 彼の職業は靴屋です.
　— *vi.* (buy and sell) (... o) ba⌐ibai
suru ...を売買する ①; a⌐tsukau 扱う
Ⓒ: His firm trades in groceries.
(*Kare no kaisha wa shokuryoohiñ
o atsukatte iru.*) 彼の会社は食料品を
扱っている.
　— *vt.* (exchange) ... o ko⌐okañ
suru ...を交換する ①: trade stamps
with a friend (*kitte o tomodachi to
kookañ suru*) 切手を友達と交換する.

trader *n.* bo⌐oeki gyo⌐osha 貿易業
者; sho⌐oniñ 商人.

tradition *n.* **1** (customs) de⌐ñtoo
伝統; ka⌐ñree 慣例: maintain an
old tradition (*furuku kara no deñtoo o mamoru*) 古くからの伝統を守る.
2 (story) de⌐ñsetsu 伝説; i⌐itsutae
言い伝え.

traditional *adj.* de⌐ñtoo-teki na
伝統的な: a traditional costume
(*deñtoo-teki na ishoo*) 伝統的な衣
装.

traditionally *adv.* de⌐ñtoo-teki ni
伝統的に: Traditionally, the students of this school wear a uniform. (*Deñtoo-teki ni kono gakkoo
no seeto wa seefuku o kite iru.*) 伝
統的にこの学校の生徒は制服を着ている.

traffic *n.* ko⌐otsuu 交通: a traffic
accident (*kootsuu jiko*) 交通事故 /
Traffic is heavy around here. (*Kono heñ wa kootsuu ga hageshii.*) こ
の辺は交通が激しい.
　— *vi.* (... o) ba⌐ibai suru (...を)売買
する ①: traffic in drugs (*mayaku o
baibai suru*) 麻薬を売買する.

tragedy *n.* **1** (drama) hi⌐geki 悲
劇: Shakespeare's tragedies (*Sheekusupia no higeki*) シェークスピアの悲
劇.
2 (unfortunate event) hi⌐sañ na
[ka⌐nashii] de⌐ki⌐goto 悲惨な[悲しい]
出来事: His death was a great tragedy for his family. (*Kare no shi wa
kazoku ni totte hijoo ni kanashii*

dekigoto datta.) 彼の死は家族にとっ
て非常に悲しい出来事だった.

tragic *adj.* hi⌐geki no 悲劇の; (disastrous) hi⌐sañ na 悲惨な: a tragic air
accident (*hisañ na kookuuki jiko*)
悲惨な航空機事故.

trail *n.* **1** (track) a⌐to 跡: follow the
trail of a bear (*kuma no ato o tadoru*) 熊の跡をたどる.
2 (path) ko⌐michi 小道: a mountain trail (*yama no komichi*) 山の小
道.
　— *vt.* **1** (drag) ... o hi⌐kizuru ...を
引きずる Ⓒ: She trailed her long
skirt along the floor. (*Kanojo wa
nagai sukaato o yuka ni hikizutte
aruita.*) 彼女は長いスカートを床に引き
ずって歩いた.
2 (follow) ... no a⌐to ni tsuite i⌐ku
...の後について行く Ⓒ; ... o bi⌐koo
suru ...を尾行する ①: A detective
trailed the suspect. (*Keeji wa yoogisha o bikoo shita.*) 刑事は容疑者
を尾行した.

train[1] *n.* **1** (of a railroad) re⌐ssha
列車; de⌐ñsha 電車. ★ 'Ressha'
usually refers to a long-distance
train: Does this train stop at Sendai? (*Kono ressha wa Señdai ni
tomarimasu ka?*) この列車は仙台に
止まりますか. / get on a train (*deñsha
ni noru*) 電車に乗る / get off a train
(*deñsha o oriru*) 電車を降りる /
change trains (*deñsha o norikaeru*)
電車を乗り換える.
2 (line) re⌐tsu 列: a funeral train
(*sooshiki no retsu*) 葬式の列.

train[2] *vt.* ... o ku⌐ñreñ suru ...を訓練
する ①: train employees for an
emergency (*hijoojitai ni sonaete
juugyooiñ o kuñreñ suru*) 非常事
態に備えて従業員を訓練する / He was
trained as an interpreter. (*Kare wa
tsuuyaku to shite no kuñreñ o
uketa.*) 彼は通訳としての訓練を受けた.

training *n.* ku⌐ñreñ 訓練; (of
sports) re⌐ñshuu 練習; to⌐re⌐eniñgu
トレーニング: vocational training (*shokugyoo kuñreñ*) 職業訓練 / baseball training (*yakyuu no reñshuu*)

野球の練習.

traitor n. ha⌐ngyaku⌐sha 反逆者;
u⌐ragirimono 裏切り者.

tram n. ro⌐men-de⌐nsha 路面電車.

tramp vi. **1** (walk with heavy
steps) do⌐shi⌐ndoshin to a⌐ru⌐ku どし
んどしんと歩く ⌐C⌐: He tramped along
the corridor. (*Kare wa rooka o
doshiñdoshiñ to aruita.*) 彼は廊下を
どしんどしんと歩いた.
2 (walk over) te⌐kuteku a⌐ru⌐ku てく
てく歩く ⌐C⌐: I tramped five kilometers in the heat. (*Watashi wa atsui
naka o go-kiro tekuteku aruita.*) 私
は暑い中を 5 キロてくてく歩いた.
— n. **1** (long walk) to⌐horyo⌐koo
徒歩旅行: go for a tramp (*tohoryo-
koo ni dekakeru*) 徒歩旅行に出かけ
る.
2 (homeless person) fu⌐ro⌐osha 浮
浪者.

trample vt. ... o fu⌐mitsuke⌐ru ...を
踏みつける ⌐V⌐: The children tram-
pled the flower bed. (*Kodomo-
tachi wa kadañ o fumitsuketa.*) 子
どもたちは花壇を踏みつけた.
— vi. (... o) fu⌐miniji⌐ru (...を)踏みに
じる ⌐C⌐: trample on a person's feelings (*hito no kañjoo o fuminijiru*)
人の感情を踏みにじる.

tranquil adj. shi⌐zuka na 静かな;
o⌐da⌐yaka na 穏やかな: a tranquil
lake (*shizuka na mizuumi*) 静かな湖.

transaction n. to⌐ri⌐hiki 取り引き;
gyo⌐omu 業務: business transac-
tions (*shootorihiki*) 商取引.

transfer vt. ... o u⌐tsu⌐tsu ...を移す
⌐C⌐: transfer a document from the
drawer to the shelf (*shorui o hikidashi kara tana e utsusu*) 書類を引
き出しから棚へ移す / He was trans-
ferred to the personnel department.
(*Kare wa jiñjibu ni utsusareta.*) 彼
は人事部に移された.
— vi. (move) u⌐tsu⌐ru 移る ⌐C⌐;
(change) no⌐rika⌐eru 乗り換える ⌐V⌐:
transfer to another school (*teñkoo
suru*) 転校する / At what station do
I transfer? (*Dono eki de norikaeru
no desu ka?*) どの駅で乗り換えるのです

か.
— n. i⌐doo 移動; (of transportation) no⌐rikae 乗り換え.

transform vt. ... o tsu⌐kurika⌐eru
...を造り変える ⌐V⌐; su⌐kka⌐ri ka⌐eru
すっかり変える ⌐V⌐: transform a storehouse to a disco (*sooko o disuko
ni tsukurikaeru*) 倉庫をディスコに造
り変える.

transistor n. to⌐ranji⌐sutaa トランジ
スター.

transit n. **1** (carrying) yu⌐soo 輸
送; u⌐ñsoo 運送: My baggage was
lost in transit. (*Watashi no nimotsu wa yusoo-chuu ni fuñshitsu
shita.*) 私の荷物は輸送中に紛失した.
2 (at an airport) no⌐ritsugi 乗り継
ぎ: I'm in transit to Hong Kong.
(*Watashi wa Hoñkoñ e iku nori-
tsugi-kyaku desu.*) 私は香港へ行く
乗り継ぎ客です.

transition n. u⌐tsurikawari 移り変
わり; i⌐koo 移行: a transition from
communism to liberalism (*kyoo-
sañshugi kara jiyuushugi e no
ikoo*) 共産主義から自由主義への移行.

translate vt. **1** (put into another
language) ... o ya⌐ku⌐su ...を訳する ⌐C⌐;
ho⌐ñyaku suru 翻訳する ⌐I⌐: translate a book from Japanese into English (*hoñ o Nihoñgo kara Eego ni
yakusu*) 本を日本語から英語に訳す.
2 (interpret) ... o ka⌐ishaku suru ...
を解釈する ⌐I⌐: How would you
translate his silence? (*Kare no chiñmoku o doo kaishaku shimasu
ka?*) 彼の沈黙をどう解釈しますか.

translation n. ho⌐ñyaku 翻訳;
-yaku 訳: This translation is full of
errors. (*Kono hoñyaku wa machigai darake da.*) この翻訳は間違い
だらけだ. / literal translation (*choku-
yaku*) 直訳 / free translation (*iya-
ku*) 意訳.

translator n. ya⌐kusha 訳者; ho⌐ñ-
yakuka 翻訳家.

transmission n. **1** (of a message) de⌐ñtatsu 伝達; (of a disease)
de⌐ñseñ 伝染: the transmission of
information (*joohoo no deñtatsu*)

情報の伝達 / the transmission of a disease (*byooki no deñseñ*) 病気の伝染.

2 (broadcast) hoˈosoo 放送: the transmission of a TV program (*terebi-bañgumi no hoosoo*) テレビ番組の放送.

transmit *vt.* **1** (send) ... o oˈkuru ...を送る C: transmit a message by radio (*tsuushiñ o mudeñ de okuru*) 通信を無電で送る.
2 (pass on) ... o tsuˈtaeru ...を伝える V; (of a disease) deˈñseñ saseru 伝染させる V: transmit a tradition to the younger generation (*deñtoo o wakai sedai ni tsutaeru*) 伝統を若い世代に伝える / Rats transmit diseases. (*Nezumi wa byooki o deñseñ saseru.*) ねずみは病気を伝染させる.
3 (of a TV station, etc.) ... o hoˈosoo suru ...を放送する C: The accident was transmitted live from the site. (*Sono jiko wa geñba kara nama de hoosoo sareta.*) その事故は現場から生で放送された.

transparent *adj.* toˈomee na 透明な; suˈkitoˈotte iru 透き通っている: a transparent plastic case (*toomee na purasuchikku no keesu*) 透明なプラスチックのケース.

transplant *vt.* ... o iˈshoku suru ...を移植する I: transplant a heart (*shiñzoo o ishoku suru*) 心臓を移植する.
— *n.* iˈshoku 移植.

transport *n.* yuˈsoo 輸送; uˈñsoo 運送: a transport ship (*yusoo-señ*) 輸送船.
— *vt.* ... o yuˈsoo suru ...を輸送する I; uˈñsoo suru 運送する I: transport goods by truck (*nimotsu o torakku de yusoo suru*) 荷物をトラックで輸送する.

transportation *n.* yuˈsoo 輸送; uˈñsoo 運送: a transportation company (*uñsoo-gaisha*) 運送会社.

trap *n.* **1** (device) waˈna わな; oˈtoshiˈana 落とし穴: set a trap for a fox (*kitsune ni wana o shikakeru*) きつねにわなをしかける.

2 (trick) keˈryaku 計略; waˈna わな: fall into a trap (*wana ni hamaru*) わなにはまる.
— *vt.* ... o waˈna de toˈraeˈru ...をわなで捕らえる V: trap an animal (*doobutsu o wana de toraeru*) 動物をわなで捕らえる.

trash *n.* goˈmiˈ ごみ; kuˈzu くず: sweep up trash (*gomi o haku*) ごみを掃く.

travel *vi.* **1** (journey) ryoˈkoo suru 旅行する I; taˈbiˈ o suru 旅をする I: He traveled around the world. (*Kare wa sekai-is-shuu-ryokoo o shita.*) 彼は世界一周旅行をした.
2 (move) suˈsumu 進む C; tsuˈtawaru 伝わる C: Sound travels through the air. (*Oto wa kuuchuu o tsutawaru.*) 音は空中を伝わる.
3 (go as a salesperson) seˈerusu shite maˈwaru セールスして回る C: She travels selling insurance. (*Kanojo wa hokeñ o seerusu shite mawatte iru.*) 彼女は保険をセールスして回っている.
— *n.* ryoˈkoo 旅行; taˈbiˈ 旅: I've just returned from my travels. (*Watashi wa ryokoo kara kaette kita tokoro desu.*) 私は旅行から帰って来たところです. ★ 'Journey,' 'trip' and 'tour' are also called 'ryokoo.'

traveler *n.* ryoˈkoˈosha 旅行者; taˈbibito 旅人: a fellow traveler (*tabi no michizure*) 旅の道連れ.

traveler's check *n.* ryoˈkoosha kogiˈtte 旅行者小切手; toˈraberaazu cheˈkku トラベラーズチェック: Can I pay with a traveler's check? (*Ryokoosha kogitte de shiharai dekimasu ka?*) 旅行者小切手で支払いできますか. / I'd like to cash this traveler's check. (*Kono toraberaazu chekku o geñkiñ ni shite kudasai.*) このトラベラーズチェックを現金にしてください.

tray *n.* boˈñ 盆: carry glasses on a tray (*gurasu o boñ ni nosete hakobu*) グラスを盆に乗せて運ぶ.

treacherous *adj.* uˈragiri no 裏切りの; fuˈjitsu na 不実な: a treacherous act (*uragiri kooi*) 裏切り行為.

tread *vi.* (... o) fuʼmu (...を)踏む ⓒ;
fuʼmitsukeʼru 踏みつける Ⓥ: He trod
on my foot. (*Kare wa watashi no
ashi o funda.*) 彼は私の足を踏んだ.

—— *vt.* ... o fuʼmu ...を踏む ⓒ; fuʼmi-
tsubuʼsu 踏みつぶす ⓒ: tread out
one's cigarette (*tabako no hi o
funde kesu*) たばこの火を踏んで消す.

treason *n.* haʼn̄gyaku 反逆; muʼ-
hon̄ 謀反: plot treason (*muhon̄ o
takuramu*) 謀反をたくらむ.

treasure *n.* **1** (gold, jewels, etc.)
taʼkara(mono¹) 宝(物); zaʼihoo 財
宝: hidden treasure (*kakusareta
takara*) 隠された宝.

2 (valued object) kiʼchoohin̄ 貴重
品: national treasures (*kokuhoo*) 国
宝.

—— *vt.* ... o taʼisetsu ni suru ...を大
切にする Ⓘ: I treasure the watch he
gave me. (*Watashi wa kare ga
kureta tokee o taisetsu ni shite
imasu.*) 私は彼がくれた時計を大切にし
ています.

treasurer *n.* kaʼikeegaʼkari 会計
係.

treasury *n.* (of a government)
koʼoko 公庫; (funds) shiʼkin̄ 資金;
(of a book) hoʼoten̄ 宝典.

treat *vt.* **1** (behave toward) ... o
aʼtsukau ...を扱う ⓒ: He treated
me as one of the family. (*Kare wa
watashi o kazoku no ichiin̄ no yoo
ni atsukatte kureta.*) 彼は私を家族の
一員のように扱ってくれた.

2 (consider) ... o (... to) miʼnaʼsu ...
を(...と)みなす ⓒ: They treated the
rumor as a fact. (*Kare-ra wa sono
uwasa o jijitsu to minashita.*) 彼ら
はそのうわさを事実とみなした.

3 (give medical care) ... o chiʼryoo
suru ...を治療する Ⓘ; teʼate suru 手
当てする Ⓘ: treat a patient with a
new drug (*atarashii kusuri de
kan̄ja o chiryoo suru*) 新しい薬で患
者を治療する.

4 (discuss) ... o roʼn̄jiru ...を論じる
Ⓥ; noʼbeʼru 述べる Ⓥ: treat a subject thoroughly (*mon̄dai o tettee-

teki ni ron̄jiru*) 問題を徹底的に論じ
る.

5 (of a meal) ... ni (... o) oʼgoru ...に
(...を)おごる ⓒ: I'll treat you.
(*Ogotte yaru yo.*) おごってやるよ.

treatment *n.* **1** (treating) toʼria-
tsukai 取り扱い; aʼtsukaikata 扱い
方: receive kind treatment (*shin̄se-
tsu na toriatsukai o ukeru*) 親切な
取り扱いを受ける.

2 (of a disease) chiʼryoo(hoo) 治療
(法): She is under treatment in the
hospital. (*Kanojo wa byooin̄ de
chiryoo o ukete imasu.*) 彼女は病院
で治療を受けています. / a new treatment for cancer (*gan̄ no atarashii
chiryoohoo*) がんの新しい治療法.

treaty *n.* joʼoyaku 条約: conclude
a peace treaty (*heewa-jooyaku o
musubu*) 平和条約を結ぶ.

tree *n.* ki¹ 木: cut down a tree (*ki o
kiritaosu*) 木を切り倒す.

tremble *vi.* **1** (of a body) fuʼrueru
震える Ⓥ: His hands were trem-
bling with cold. (*Kare no te wa
samusa de furuete ita.*) 彼の手は寒
さで震えていた.

2 (of a thing) yuʼreru 揺れる Ⓥ;
shiʼn̄doo suru 震動する Ⓘ: This
bridge trembles as cars cross it.
(*Kono hashi wa kuruma ga tooru
to yureru.*) この橋は車が通ると揺れる.

tremendous *adj.* **1** (enormous)
kyoʼdai na 巨大な: a tremendous
pumpkin (*kyodai na kabocha*) 巨
大なかぼちゃ.

2 (extraordinary) moʼnosugoʼi ものす
ごい; oʼsoroshiʼi 恐ろしい: a tremendous explosion (*monosugoi bakuhatsu*) ものすごい爆発.

trench *n.* miʼzo 溝; hoʼriʼ 堀: dig a
trench (*mizo o horu*) 溝を掘る.

trend *n.* keʼekoo 傾向; naʼriyuki 成
り行き: Prices are on an upward
trend. (*Bukka wa jooshoo no keekoo ni aru.*) 物価は上昇の傾向にある.

trespass *vi.* (... ni) shiʼn̄nyuu suru
(...に)侵入する Ⓘ; (... o) shiʼn̄gai
suru (...を)侵害する Ⓘ: trespass on a
person's privacy (*hito no puraiba-

shii o shiñgai suru) 人のプライバシーを侵害する / No Trespassing. (*Tachiiri kiñshi.*) 立ち入り禁止.

trial *n.* **1** (legal process) saˈibañ 裁判; shiˈñri 審理: a criminal trial (*keeji saibañ*) 刑事裁判 / stand trial (*saibañ o ukeru*) 裁判を受ける.
2 (test) shiˈkeˈñ 試験; koˈkoromi 試み: put a machine to trial (*kikai o tameshi ni tsukatte miru*) 機械を試しに使ってみる / He succeeded on his second trial. (*Kare wa ni-dome no kokoromi de seekoo shita.*) 彼は2度目の試みで成功した.
3 (trouble) shiˈreñ 試練; saiˈnaˈñ 災難: a time of trial (*shireñ no toki*) 試練の時.

triangle *n.* saˈñkaku 三角; (shape) saˈñkakukee 三角形; (set triangle) saˈñkaku joˈogi (三角定規).

tribe *n.* shuˈzoku 種族; buˈzoku 部族.

tribute *n.* **1** (expression of praise) saˈñji 賛辞; (something given to show respect) oˈkurimono 贈り物: a floral tribute (*keñka*) 献花.
2 (payment to a ruler) miˈtsugimono 貢ぎ物: pay tribute to a ruler (*shihaisha ni mitsugimono o suru*) 支配者に貢ぎ物をする.

trick *n.* **1** (joke) joˈodaˈñ 冗談; iˈtazura いたずら: play a trick on a person (*hito ni itazura o suru*) 人にいたずらをする.
2 (artifice) taˈkurami たくらみ; saˈkuryaku 策略: He got the license by a trick. (*Kare wa sakuryaku o tsukatte sono meñkyo o eta.*) 彼は策略を使ってその免許を得た.
3 (magic) teˈjina 手品; kiˈjutsu 奇術: card tricks (*torañpu no tejina*) トランプの手品.
— *vt.* ... o daˈmaˈsu ...をだます C: He tricked the old woman out of her money. (*Kare wa sono rooba o damashite kane o totta.*) 彼はその老婆をだまして金を取った.

trifle *n.* **1** (anything of little value) tsuˈmaraˈnai moˈnoˈ つまらない物; kuˈdaranai mono くだらない物: quar-

rel over trifles (*tsumarani koto de keñka o suru*) つまらないことでけんかをする.
2 (small amount of money) waˈzuka na oˈkane わずかなお金: It cost me just a trifle. (*Hoñno wazuka na o-kane shika kakarimaseñ deshita.*) ほんのわずかなお金しかかかりませんでした.

trifling *adj.* kuˈdaranai くだらない; saˈsai na ささいな: a trifling error (*sasai na ayamari*) ささいな誤り.

trim *vt.* **1** (clip) ... o kaˈrikoˈmu ...を刈り込む C; (of hair) aˈtamaˈ o kaˈru 頭を刈る C: trim a hedge (*ikegaki o karikomu*) 生け垣を刈り込む / I got my hair trimmed. (*Watashi wa atama o katte moratta.*) 私は頭を刈ってもらった.
2 (decorate) ... o kaˈzaru ...を飾る C: trim a dress with lace (*fuku o reesu de kazaru*) 服をレースで飾る.
— *adj.* kiˈchiˈñto shita [している] きちんとした; teˈire no yoˈi 手入れのよい: a trim garden (*teire no yoi niwa*) 手入れのよい庭.

trip *n.* ryoˈkoo 旅行; taˈbiˈ 旅: go on a trip (*ryokoo ni dekakeru*) 旅行に出かける / make a business trip to China (*shigoto de Chuugoku e ryokoo suru*) 仕事で中国へ旅行する / Have a good trip! (*Yoi go-ryokoo o.*) よいご旅行を. ★ 'Journey,' 'tour' and 'travel' are also called '*ryokoo*.'
— *vi.* (catch one's foot) (... ni) tsuˈmazuku (...に)つまずく C: trip on the root of a tree (*ki no ne ni tsumazuku*) 木の根につまずく.

triple *adj.* saˈñ-juu no 3 重の; saˈñbai no 3 倍の: a triple mirror (*sañmeñkyoo*) 三面鏡.

tripod *n.* saˈñkyaku 三脚.

triumph *n.* shoˈori 勝利; daˈiseˈekoo 大成功: win a triumph (*shoori o kachitoru*) 勝利を勝ち取る.

trivial *adj.* (of little importance) saˈsai na ささいな; (of a person) kuˈdaranai くだらない: trivial mistakes (*sasai na ayamari*) ささいな誤り / a trivial man (*kudaranai otoko*) くだらない男.

troop n. 1 (crowd) muˈreˈ 群れ; iˈchiguň 一群; iˈchidaň 一団: a troop of demonstrators (demotai no ichiguň) デモ隊の一群.
2 (of soldiers) guˈňtai 軍隊.

trophy n. toˈrofiiˈ トロフィー; shoˈo-hiň 賞品: win a trophy (torofii o kakutoku suru) トロフィーを獲得する.

tropical adj. neˈttai no 熱帯の; neˈttai chiˈhoo no 熱帯地方の: a tropical fish (nettaigyo) 熱帯魚 / a tropical climate (nettai-see kikoo) 熱帯性気候.

trot vi. (horse) haˈyaˈ-ashi de kaˈˈkeˈru 速足で駆ける Ⓥ; (people) iˈsoˈide aˈruˈku 急いで歩く Ⓒ: The horse trotted down the road. (Uma ga haya-ashi de michi o kakete itta.) 馬が速足で道を駆けて行った.
— n. haˈyaˈ-ashi 速足; iˈsogiˈ-ashi 急ぎ足.

trouble n. 1 (inconvenience) meˈewaku 迷惑; yaˈkkai やっかい: I'm sorry I've given you so much trouble. (Taiheň go-meewaku o o-kake shite sumimaseň.) 大変ご迷惑をおかけしてすみません.
2 (difficulty) koˈňnaň 困難; kuˈroo 苦労; hoˈneoriˈ 骨折り: I had a lot of trouble finding the book. (Sono hoň o mitsukeru no ni taiheň kuroo shita.) その本を見つけるのに大変苦労した.
3 (worry) shiˈňpai(gotoˈ) 心配(事); naˈyamiˈ 悩み: Tell me your troubles if you have any. (Shiňpaigoto ga areba watashi ni hanashi nasai.) 心配事があれば私に話しなさい.
4 (illness) byoˈoki 病気: heart trouble (shiňzoobyoo) 心臓病.
5 (disturbance) goˈtagotaˈ ごたごた; fuˈňsoo 紛争: labor troubles (roo-doo soogi) 労働争議.
— vt. 1 (cause worry) ... o shiˈň-pai saseru ...を心配させる Ⓥ; naˈˈyamaˈsu 悩ます Ⓒ: He is troubled about family matters. (Kare wa katee no koto de nayaňde iru.) 彼は家庭のことで悩んでいる.
2 (cause inconvenience) ... ni

meˈewaku o kaˈkeˈru ...に迷惑をかける Ⓥ; yaˈkkai o kaˈkeˈru やっかいをかける Ⓥ: I don't like to trouble you about a thing like this. (Koňna koto de go-meewaku o kaketaku arimaseň.) こんなことでご迷惑をかけたくありません.

troublesome adj. yaˈkkai na やっかいな; meˈňdoˈo na 面倒な: a troublesome problem (meňdoo na moň-dai) 面倒な問題.

trousers n. zuˈboˈň ズボン: put on [take off] trousers (zuboň o haku [nugu]) ズボンをはく[脱ぐ].

truck n. (car) toˈraˈkku トラック: transport goods by truck (shina-mono o torakku de yusoo suru) 品物をトラックで輸送する.

true adj. 1 (of a story) hoˈňtoo no 本当の; jiˈjitsu no 事実の: Do you think his story is true? (Kare no hanashi wa hoňtoo da to omoi-masu ka?) 彼の話は本当だと思いますか.
2 (genuine) hoˈňmono no 本物の; shiˈň no 真の: a true friend (shiň no tomo) 真の友.
3 (faithful) seˈejitsu na 誠実な; chuˈujitsu na 忠実な: He was true to his word. (Kare wa yakusoku ni seejitsu datta.) 彼は約束に誠実だった.

truly adj. 1 (truthfully) shiˈňjitsu ni 真実に; iˈtsuwari naˈku 偽りなく: speak truly (shiňjitsu o kataru) 真実を語る.
2 (sincerely) seˈejitsu ni 誠実に; koˈˈkoˈro kara 心から: I feel truly grateful. (Kokoro kara kaňsha shimasu.) 心から感謝します.
3 (really) hoˈňtoo ni 本当に; maˈt-taku まったく: I am truly happy. (Watashi wa hoňtoo ni shiawase desu.) 私は本当に幸せです.

trumpet n. toˈraňpeˈtto トランペット: blow a trumpet (toraňpetto o fuku) トランペットを吹く.

trunk n. 1 (of a tree) miˈki 幹.
2 (of an elephant) zoˈo no haˈna 象の鼻.
3 (box) toˈraˈňku トランク.

4 (body) do¹otai 胴体.

trust vt. **1** (have confidence) ... o shi¹ñrai suru …を信頼する ⊥; shi¹ñyoo suru 信用する ⊥: We can trust what he says. (Kare no iu koto wa shiñyoo dekimasu.) 彼の言うことは信用できます.

2 (entrust) ... o a¹zuke¹ru …を預ける ⊻; ma¹kase¹ru 任せる ⊻: I trusted the details to him. (Komakai koto wa kare ni makasemashita.) 細かいことは彼に任せました.

3 (expect) ... o ki¹tai suru …を期待する ⊥; ka¹kushiñ suru 確信する ⊥: I trust you will have a good journey. (Yoi tabi o kitai shite imasu.) よい旅を期待しています.

— n. **1** (confidence) shi¹ñrai 信頼; shi¹ñyoo 信用: have trust in a person (hito o shiñyoo suru) 人を信用する.

2 (charge) i¹taku 委託; ho¹kañ 保管; (care) ho¹go 保護: I left my valuables in trust with him. (Watashi wa kichoohiñ o kare ni hokañ shite moratta.) 私は貴重品を彼に保管してもらった.

3 (responsibility) se¹kiniñ 責任: a position of great trust (omoi sekiniñ no aru chii) 重い責任のある地位.

trustworthy adj. shi¹ñrai deki¹ru 信頼できる; a¹te ni na¹ru 当てになる: a trustworthy driver (shiñrai dekiru uñteñshu) 信頼できる運転手.

truth n. **1** (true fact) ho¹ñtoo no koto¹ 本当のこと; ji¹jitsu 事実; shi¹ñsoo 真相: tell the truth (hoñtoo no koto o hanasu) 本当のことを話す

2 (trueness) shi¹ñri 真理: seek truth (shiñri o tañkyuu suru) 真理を探究する.

truthful adj. se¹ejitsu na 誠実な; sho¹ojiki na 正直な: a truthful child (shoojiki na kodomo) 正直な子ども.

try vt. **1** (attempt) ... to tsu¹tome¹ru …と努める ⊻; do¹ryoku suru 努力する ⊥: I tried to do my best. (Watashi wa zeñryoku o tsukusoo to tsu-tometa.) 私は全力を尽くそうと努めた.

2 (test) ... o ta¹me¹su …を試す C; ko¹koromi¹ru 試みる ⊻: He tried a different method. (Kare wa chigau hoohoo o tameshite mita.) 彼は違う方法を試してみた.

3 (conduct the trial) ... o shi¹ñri suru …を審理する ⊥; sa¹ba¹ku 裁く C: try the case (jikeñ o shiñri suru) 事件を審理する.

— vi. ya¹tte mi¹ru やってみる ⊻: I tried again and again. (Watashi wa nañ-do mo yatte mita.) 私は何度もやってみた.

try on vt. ... o ki¹te mi¹ru …を着てみる ⊻: May I try this on? (Kore o kite mite mo ii desu ka?) これを着てみてもいいですか.

tub n. **1** (container) o¹ke おけ: wash clothes in a tub (oke de kimono o arau) おけで着物を洗う.

2 (of a bath) yo¹kusoo 浴槽; yu¹-bune 湯ぶね.

tube n. **1** (pipe) ka¹ñ 管; tsu¹tsu 筒: a rubber tube (gomu-kañ) ゴム管.

2 (container) chu¹ubu チューブ: a tube of paint (enogu no chuubu) 絵の具のチューブ.

tuck vt. **1** (gather up) ... o ma¹ku-riage¹ru …をまくり上げる ⊻: tuck up one's sleeves (sode o makuriageru) そでをまくり上げる.

2 (push) ... o o¹shiko¹mu …を押し込む C: tuck a handkerchief in one's pocket (hañkachi o poketto ni oshikomu) ハンカチをポケットに押し込む.

3 (fold) ... o ku¹rumiko¹mu …をくるみ込む C: tuck a baby in a bed (akañboo o beddo ni kurumikoñde nekaseru) 赤ん坊をベッドにくるみ込んで寝かせる.

Tuesday n. ka¹yo¹o(bi) 火曜(日).

tug vt. ... o hi¹ku …を引く C; hi¹ppa¹ru 引っ張る: I tugged the door but it wouldn't open. (Watashi wa doa o hippatta ga akanakatta.) 私はドアを引っ張ったが開かなかった.

— *n.* tsu'yoku hi'ku koto¹ 強く引くこと: He gave me a tug at my hair. (*Kare wa watashi no kami no ke o tsuyoku hippatta.*) 彼は私の髪の毛を強く引っ張った.

tumble *vi.* **1** (fall) ta'ore'ru 倒れる V; ko'robu 転ぶ C: I tumbled over the roots of a tree. (*Watashi wa ki no ne ni tsumazuite koroñda.*) 私は木の根につまずいて転んだ.
2 (roll over) ko'rogemawa'ru 転げ回る C: The children tumbled about on the grass. (*Kodomo-tachi wa kusa no ue o korogemawatta.*) 子どもたちは草の上を転げ回った.

tune *n.* **1** (musical tones) kyo'ku 曲; (melody) me'rodii メロディー: play a tune on the piano (*piano de kyoku o hiku*) ピアノで曲を弾く.
2 (correct pitch) cho'oshi 調子: Your violin is out of tune. (*Kimi no baioriñ wa chooshi ga kurutte iru.*) 君のバイオリンは調子が狂っている.
— *vt.* **1** (of a radio, TV) ... o a'wase'ru ...を合わせる V: tune the television to Channel 1 (*terebi o dai-ichi chañneru ni awaseru*) テレビを第1チャンネルに合わせる.
2 (of an instrument) ... no cho'oshi o awase'ru ...の調子を合わせる V; ... o cho'oritsu suru ...を調律する I: tune a piano (*piano o chooritsu suru*) ピアノを調律する.

tunnel *n.* to'ñneru トンネル: build a tunnel (*toñneru o horu*) トンネルを掘る.

turf *n.* shi'ba 芝: artificial turf (*jiñkoo-shiba*) 人口芝.

turkey *n.* shi'chimeñchoo 七面鳥.

turmoil *n.* sa'wagi 騒ぎ; ko'ñrañ 混乱: The town was in a turmoil during the election. (*Señkyo no aida machi wa oosawagi datta.*) 選挙の間町は大騒ぎだった.

turn *vt.* **1** (revolve) ... o ma'wasu ...を回す C; ka'iteñ saseru 回転させる V: turn the knob of a door (*doa no totte o mawasu*) ドアの取っ手を回す / turn the wheel to the right (*handoru o migi e mawasu*) ハンド

ルを右へ回す.
2 (move around) ... o hi'kkurika'-esu ...をひっくり返す C; u'raga'esu 裏返す C; (of a page) me'kuru めくる C: turn the steak over (*suteeki o uragaesu*) ステーキを裏返す / turn the pages of a book (*hoñ no peeji o mekuru*) 本のページをめくる.
3 (go around) ... o ma'garu ...を曲がる C; ma'waru 回る C: The car turned the corner. (*Sono kuruma wa kado o magatta.*) その車は角を曲がった.
4 (change direction) ... o ka'eru ...を変える V; mu'keru 向ける V: She turned her back to me. (*Kanojo wa senaka o watashi no hoo e muketa.*) 彼女は背中を私の方へ向けた.
5 (change) ... o ka'eru ...を変える V: Heat turns water into vapor. (*Netsu wa mizu o jooki ni kaeru.*) 熱は水を蒸気に変える.
— *vi.* **1** (rotate) ma'waru 回る C; ka'iteñ suru 回転する I: The faucet turned easily. (*Señ wa kañtañ ni mawatta.*) 栓は簡単に回った.
2 (change direction) mu'ki o ka'-eru 向きを変える V; ma'garu 曲がる C: Turn to the left at the next corner. (*Tsugi no kado o hidari e magari nasai.*) 次の角を左へ曲がりなさい.
3 (change) ka'waru 変わる C: The traffic light turned from red to green. (*Shiñgoo ga aka kara ao ni kawatta.*) 信号が赤から青に変わった.

turn off *vt.* ... o to'meru ...を止める V; ke'su 消す C: turn off the gas (*gasu o tomeru*) ガスを止める / turn off the radio (*rajio o kesu*) ラジオを消す.

turn on *vt.* ... o da'su ...を出す C; tsu'ke'ru つける V: turn on the water (*mizu o dasu*) 水を出す / turn on the television (*terebi o tsukeru*) テレビをつける.

turn out *vt.* ... o ke'su ...を消す C: turn out the light (*akari o kesu*) 明かりを消す.
— *n.* **1** (turning) ma'wasu koto¹

回すこと; maʨwaru koto¹ 回ること; kaʨiteñ 回転: I gave the handle a turn to the right. (*Watashi wa hañdoru o migi e mawashita.*) 私はハンドルを右へ回した.
2 (change of direction) maʨgaru koto¹ 曲がること; teʨñkai 転回: make a turn to the left (*hidari e magaru*) 左へ曲がる.
3 (rightful duty) juʨñbañ 順番; baʨñ 番: Now it's your turn to sing. (*Koñdo wa kimi ga utau bañ da.*) 今度は君が歌う番だ.
4 (change) heʨñka 変化; teʨñkai 展開: an unexpected turn of events (*yoki shinai koto no teñkai*) 予期しない事の展開.
5 (turning point) kaʨwarime 変わり目: the turn of the century (*seeki no kawarime*) 世紀の変わり目.

turnip *n.* kaʨbu かぶ(蕪).

turnpike *n.* koʨosoku yuuryoo doʨoro 高速有料道路.

TV *n.* teʨrebi テレビ: I watched the baseball game on TV. (*Watashi wa sono yakyuu no shiai o terebi de mita.*) 私はその野球の試合をテレビで見た. / a TV set (*terebi juzooki*) テレビ受像機.

twelfth *adj.* juʨuni-bañme¹ no 12 番目の; daʨi-juʨuni¹ no 第 12 の.
— *n.* **1** (person) juʨuni-bañme¹ no hiʨto¹ 12 番目の人; (things) juʨuni-bañme¹ no moʨno¹ 12 番目のもの.
2 (day) juʨuni-nichi¹ 12 日.
3 (fraction) juʨunibuñ no ichi¹ 12 分の 1.

twelve *pron.* juʨuni¹ 12; (people) juʨuni¹-niñ 12 人; (things) juʨuni¹-ko 12 個.
— *n.* (figure) juʨuni¹ 12; (hour) juʨuni¹-ji 12 時; (minute) juʨuni¹-fuñ 12 分; (age) juʨuni¹-sai 12 歳.
— *adj.* juʨuni¹ no 12 の; (people) juʨuni¹-niñ no 12 人の; (things) juʨuni¹-ko no 12 個の; (age) juʨuni¹-sai no 12 歳の.

twentieth *adj.* niʨjuu-bañme¹ no 20 番目の; daʨi-nijuu no 第 20 の.
— *n.* **1** (person) niʨjuu-bañme¹ no

hiʨto¹ 20 番目の人; (thing) niʨjuu-bañme¹ no moʨno¹ 20 番目のもの.
2 (day) haʨtsuka 20 日.
3 (fraction) niʨjuubuñ no ichi¹ 20 分の 1.

twenty *pron.* niʨjuu 20; (people) niʨju¹u-niñ 20 人; (things) niʨju¹k-ko 20 個.
— *n.* (figure) niʨjuu 20; (hour) niʨju¹u-ji 20 時; (minute) niʨju¹p-puñ 20 分; (age) niʨju¹s-sai [haʨtachi] 20 歳.
— *adj.* niʨjuu 20 の; (people) niʨju¹u-niñ no 20 人の; (of things) niʨju¹k-ko no 20 個の; (age) niʨju¹s-sai [haʨtachi] no 20 歳の.

twice *adv.* **1** (two times) niʨdo 2 度; niʨka¹i 2 回: I have visited Kyoto twice. (*Watashi wa Kyooto e ni-kai ikimashita.*) 私は京都へ 2 回行きました.
2 (two times as much) niʨbai 2 倍: I worked twice as hard as you. (*Watashi wa anata no ni-bai hataraita.*) 私はあなたの 2 倍働いた.

twilight *n.* taʨsogare たそがれ; uʨsua¹kari 薄明かり: stroll in the twilight (*tasogare no naka o sañpo suru*) たそがれの中を散歩する.

twin *n.* soʨose¹eji 双生児; fuʨtago 双子.
— *adj.* fuʨtago no 双子の: twin brothers (*futago no kyoodai*) 双子の兄弟 / twin sisters (*futago no shimai*) 双子の姉妹.

twin bed *n.* tsuʨiñ be¹ddo ツインベッド.

twist *vt.* **1** (turn) ... o neʨji¹ru ...をねじる [C]; hiʨne¹ru ひねる [C]: twist a knob (*totte o hineru*) 取っ手をひねる.
2 (wind) ... o maʨku ...を巻く [C]: twist a cord around a package (*tsutsumi ni himo o maku*) 包みにひもを巻く.
3 (wind together) ... o yoʨru ...をよる [C]; aʨmu 編む [C]: twist wires to make a rope (*harigane o yotte roopu o tsukuru*) 針金をよってロープを作る.
— *vi.* **1** (of a path) maʨgarikune¹-

ru 曲がりくねる ©: The road twists through the mountains. (*Michi wa yama no aida o magarikunette iru.*) 道は山の間を曲がりくねっている.

2 (of a body) mi o mo「ga」ku 身をもがく ©: She twisted with pain. (*Kanojo wa kutsuu de mi o mogaita.*) 彼女は苦痛で身をもがいた.

— *n.* **1** (twisting) ne「jiri ねじり; yo「ri より: give a twist to a person's arm (*hito no ude o nejiru*) 人の腕をねじる.

2 (bend) ma「gari 曲がり; ka「abu カーブ: The road has a lot of twists. (*Sono michi wa kaabu ga ooi.*) その道はカーブが多い.

two *pron.* fu「tatsu」 二つ; (people) fu「tari」 二人; (things) ni」-ko 2個.

— *n.* (figure) ni」 2; (hour) ni」-ji 2時; (minute) ni」-fuñ 2分; (age) ni」-sai 2歳.

— *adj.* fu「tatsu」 no 二つの; (people) fu「tari」 no 二人の; (things) ni」-ko no 2個の; (age) ni」-sai no 2歳の.

type *n.* **1** (kind) ka「ta」 型; ta「ipu タイプ: cars of the same type (*onaji kata no kuruma*) 同じ型の車 / My blood type is B. (*Watashi no ketsueki-gata wa B desu.*) 私の血液型は B です.

2 (letter used in printing) ka「tsuji 活字: set up type (*katsuji o kumu*) 活字を組む / italic type (*itarikku-tai*) イタリック体.

— *vt.* ... o ta「ipu suru ...をタイプする

□: type a letter (*tegami o taipu suru*) 手紙をタイプする.

typewriter *n.* ta「ipura」itaa タイプライター: write a letter on a typewriter (*taipuraitaa de tegami o kaku*) タイプライターで手紙を書く.

typical *adj.* **1** (representative) te「ñ-kee-teki na 典型的な; da「ihyoo-teki na 代表的な: a typical Japanese dish (*daihyoo-teki na Nihoñ ryoori*) 代表的な日本料理.

2 (characteristic) do「kutoku na 独特な; to「kuyuu no 特有の: his typical way of speaking (*kare tokuyuu no hanashikata*) 彼特有の話し方.

typically *adv.* i「ppañ ni 一般に; ga「ishite 概して: Typically, winter in Japan is mild. (*Gaishite Nihoñ no fuyu wa oñdañ desu.*) 概して日本の冬は温暖です.

typist *n.* ta「ipi」suto タイピスト.

tyranny *n.* se「ñsee-se」eji 専制政治; a「ssee 圧制.

tyrant *n.* se「ñsee ku「ñshu 専制君主; bo「okuñ 暴君.

U

ugly *adj.* **1** (unpleasing) mi「niku」i 醜い; mi「gurushi」i 見苦しい: an ugly duckling (*minikui ahiru no ko*) 醜いあひるの子.

2 (disgusting) fu「kai na 不快な; i「ya」 na いやな: an ugly rumor (*iya na uwasa*) いやなうわさ.

ulcer *n.* ka「iyoo 潰瘍: stomach ulcers (*ikaiyoo*) 胃潰瘍.

ultimate *adj.* **1** (final) sa「igo no 最後の; sa「ishuu no 最終の: an ultimate decision (*saishuu kettee*) 最終決定.

2 (greatest) sa「ikoo no 最高の: the ultimate speed (*saikoo sokudo*) 最

高速度.

ultimately *adv.* sa「igo ni 最後に; ke「kkyoku 結局: Ultimately, he decided not to go. (*Kekkyoku kare wa ikanai koto ni kimeta.*) 結局彼は行かないことに決めた.

umbrella *n.* ka「sa 傘: put up an umbrella (*kasa o sasu*) 傘をさす / open [close] an umbrella (*kasa o hirogeru* [*tatamu*]) 傘を広げる[畳む] / a collapsible umbrella (*oritatami no kasa*) 折り畳みの傘.

umpire *n.* shi「ñpañ 審判; shi「ñpa」ñ-iñ 審判員; a「ñpa」ia アンパイア.

★ 'Judge' and 'referee' are also

called 'shiˈñpañ(iñ).'

unable adj. ... ga deˈkiˈnai ...できない: I was unable to attend the party. (Watashi wa sono paatii ni shusseki suru koto ga dekinakatta.) 私はそのパーティーに出席することができなかった.

unaccompanied adj. (of a person) tsuˈre no naˈi 連れのない; (of baggage) beˈssoo no 別送の: Please send this as unaccompanied baggage. (Kore o bessoo tenimotsu ni shite okutte kudasai.) これを別送手荷物にして送ってください.

unanimous adj. maˈñjoo itchi no 満場一致の: a unanimous decision (mañjoo itchi no kettee) 満場一致の決定.

unanimously adv. maˈñjoo itchi de 満場一致で: He was elected chairperson unanimously. (Kare wa mañjoo itchi de gichoo ni erabareta.) 彼は満場一致で議長に選ばれた.

unaware adj. ... o shiˈranaˈi de ...を知らないで; ... ni ki ˈga tsukaˈnai de ...に気がつかないで: I was unaware that she was there. (Watashi wa kanojo ga soko ni iru no ni ki ga tsukanakatta.) 私は彼女がそこにいるのに気がつかなかった.

unbearable adj. taˈerareˈnai 耐えられない; gaˈmañ deˈkiˈnai 我慢できない: This heat is unbearable. (Kono atsusa wa gamañ dekinai.) この暑さは我慢できない.

unbelievable adj. shiˈñjirareˈnai 信じられない: His good luck is unbelievable. (Kare no koouñ wa shiñjirarenai.) 彼の幸運は信じられない.

unbutton vt. ... no boˈtañ o haˈzusu ...のボタンをはずす ⒸC: unbutton one's coat (uwagi no botañ o hazusu) 上着のボタンをはずす.

uncertain adj. 1 (not sure) kaˈkushiñ ga naˈi 確信がない: I am uncertain of success. (Seekoo no kakushiñ wa arimaseñ.) 成功の確信はありません.
2 (not definite) fuˈkaˈkujitsu na 不

確実な; haˈkkiˈri shinai はっきりしない: The date of their arrival is uncertain. (Kare-ra no toochaku suru hi wa hakkiri shimaseñ.) 彼らの到着する日ははっきりしません.
3 (not steady) fuˈaˈntee na 不安定な; kaˈwariyasuˈi 変わりやすい: uncertain weather (kawariyasui teñki) 変わりやすい天気.

uncertainty n. fuˈkaˈkujitsu 不確実; fuˈaˈntee 不安定.

unchangeable adj. kaˈwaranai 変わらない; fuˈheñ no 不変の: unchangeable facts (fuheñ no jijitsu) 不変の事実.

uncle n. oˈji おじ: I stayed at my uncle's. (Watashi wa oji no ie ni tomatta.) 私はおじの家に泊まった.

uncomfortable adj. 1 (not comfortable) ⟨verb⟩-gokochi no yoˈku nai ...心地のよくない: an uncomfortable chair (suwari-gokochi no yoku nai isu) 座り心地のよくないいす / an uncomfortable uniform (ki-gokochi no yoku nai seefuku) 着心地のよくない制服.
2 (uneasy) oˈchitsukanai 落ち着かない; fuˈañ na 不安な: I feel uncomfortable with strangers. (Shiranai hito to iru to ochitsukanai.) 知らない人といると落ち着かない.

uncommon adj. 1 (rare) meˈzurashiˈi 珍しい; maˈre na まれな: an uncommon bird (mezurashii tori) 珍しい鳥.
2 (remarkable) iˈjoo na 異常な; hiˈboñ na 非凡な: uncommon ability (hiboñ na sainoo) 非凡な才能.

unconscious adj. 1 (not conscious) iˈshiki o uˈshinatta [uˈshinatte iru] 意識を失った[失っている]: become unconscious (ishiki o ushinau) 意識を失う.
2 (not aware) (... ni) kiˈzukaˈnai (...に)気づかない: He was unconscious of his mistake. (Kare wa jibuñ no ayamari ni kizukanakatta.) 彼は自分の誤りに気づかなかった.
3 (not intended) muˈiˈshiki no 無意識の: an unconscious habit (mu-

ishiki ni deru kuse) 無意識に出る癖.

uncover *vt.* **1** (remove) ... no fuˈta o toˈru ...のふたを取る C: uncover a box (*hako no futa o toru*) 箱のふたを取る.

2 (make known) ... o baˈkuro suru ...を暴露する I; aˈbaˈku 暴く C: uncover a conspiracy (*iñboo o abaku*) 陰謀を暴く.

undecided *adj.* keˈsshiñ ga tsuˈite nai 決心がついてない; (of a matter) kiˈmatte naˈi 決まってない; miˈtee no 未定の: The date of the meeting is still undecided. (*Kaigi no hi wa mada mitee desu.*) 会議の日はまだ未定です.

undeniable *adj.* hiˈtee dekiˈnai 否定できない; meˈehaku na 明白な: undeniable facts (*meehaku na jijitsu*) 明白な事実.

under *prep.* **1** (below) ... no shiˈta ni [de] ...の下に[で]: The cat is under the table. (*Neko wa teeburu no shita ni imasu.*) 猫はテーブルの下にいます. / We took a rest under a tree. (*Watashi-tachi wa ki no shita de yasuñda.*) 私たちは木の下で休んだ.

2 (less than) ... miˈmañ no [de] ...未満の[で]: children under 13 years of age (*juusañ-sai mimañ no kodomo-tachi*) 13 歳未満の子どもたち.

3 (directed by) ... no moˈtoˈ de ...のもとで: I studied law under Professor Tanaka. (*Watashi wa Tanaka kyooju no moto de hooritsu o manañda.*) 私は田中教授のもとで法律を学んだ.

4 (in course of) ... chuu no ...中の: a road under repair (*shuuri-chuu no dooro*) 修理中の道路.

undergo *vt.* ... o uˈkeˈru ...を受ける V; keˈekeñ suru 経験する I: undergo an operation (*shujutsu o ukeru*) 手術を受ける / undergo many hardships (*ooku no koñnañ o keekeñ suru*) 多くの困難を経験する.

underground *adj.* **1** (beneath the surface of the earth) chiˈka no 地下の: an underground passage

(*chika no tsuuro*) 地下の通路.

2 (secret) hiˈmitsu no 秘密の: an underground organization (*himitsu soshiki*) 秘密組織.

— *n.* (subway) chiˈkatetsu 地下鉄.

underline *vt.* ... no shiˈta ni seˈñ o hiˈku ...の下に線を引く C: underline a word (*go no shita ni señ o hiku*) 語の下に線を引く.

— *n.* kaˈseñ 下線; uˈñdaaraˈiñ アンダーライン.

underneath *prep.* ... no shiˈta ni [o] ...の下に[を]: I have nothing on beneath my sweater. (*Watashi wa seetaa no shita ni nani mo kite imaseñ.*) 私はセーターの下に何も着ていません. / look beneath a bed (*beddo no shita o miru*) ベッドの下を見る.

undershirt *n.* shiˈtagi 下着; shaˈtsu シャツ.

undershorts *n.* paˈñtsu パンツ.

understand *vt.* **1** (get the meaning of) ... o riˈkai suru ...を理解する I; ... ga waˈkaˈru ...がわかる C: Do you understand what I say? (*Watashi no iu koto ga wakarimasu ka?*) 私の言うことがわかりますか.

2 (interpret) ... to oˈmoˈu ...と思う C; kaˈishaku suru 解釈する I: I understood his silence to be a refusal. (*Watashi wa kare ga damatte iru no wa iya na no da to omotta.*) 私は彼が黙っているのはいやなのだと思った.

3 (know the feelings) ... o riˈkai suru ...を理解する I: No one understood her. (*Dare mo kanojo o rikai shinakatta.*) だれも彼女を理解しなかった.

— *vi.* riˈkai suru 理解する I; waˈkaˈru わかる C: Do you understand? (*Wakarimashita ka?*) わかりましたか.

understanding *n.* riˈkai 理解; riˈkaˈiryoku 理解力: I have a full understanding of the situation. (*Jookyoo wa yoku rikai shite imasu.*) 状況はよく理解しています.

undertake *vt.* **1** (accept) ... o hi-

「kiukeｒru …を引き受ける Ⓥ: undertake a task (*shigoto o hikiukeru*) 仕事を引き受ける.
2 (enter on) … ni chaｒkushu suru …に着手する Ⓘ; … o haｒjimeru …を始める Ⓥ: undertake an enterprise (*jigyoo o hajimeru*) 事業を始める.

undertaking *n.* jiｒgyoo 事業; shiｒgoto 仕事: a social undertaking (*shakai jigyoo*) 社会事業 / a difficult undertaking (*muzukashii shigoto*) 難しい仕事.

undesirable *adj.* noｒzomashiku naｒi 望ましくない; koｒnomashiku naｒi 好ましくない: an undesirable friend (*konomashiku nai tomodachi*) 好ましくない友だち.

undo *vt.* **1** (unfasten) … o hoｒdoｒku …をほどく Ⓒ; hiｒraｒku 開く Ⓒ; haｒzusu 外す Ⓒ: undo a knot (*musubime o hodoku*) 結び目をほどく / undo a package (*tsutsumi o hiraku*) 包みを開く / undo a button (*botañ o hazusu*) ボタンをはずす.
2 (reverse) … o moｒto ni moｒdoｒsu …を元に戻す Ⓒ: What is done cannot be undone. (*Shite shimatta koto wa moto ni modoranai.*) してしまったことは元に戻らない.

undress *vt.* … no fuｒku o nuｒgaseｒru …の服を脱がせる Ⓥ: undress a child (*kodomo no fuku o nugaseru*) 子どもの服を脱がせる.

uneasiness *n.* fuｒañ 不安; shiｒñpai 心配: give a person uneasiness (*hito o fuañ ni suru*) 人を不安にする.

uneasy *adj.* fuｒañ na 不安な; shiｒñpai na 心配な: I feel uneasy about my son's future. (*Watashi wa musuko no shoorai ga fuañ da.*) 私は息子の将来が不安だ.

unemployed *adj.* shiｒgoto no naｒi 仕事のない; shiｒtsugyoo shita [shite iru] 失業した[している]: He was unemployed for three months. (*Kare wa sañ-kagetsu shigoto ga nakatta.*) 彼は3か月仕事がなかった. / the unemployed (*shitsugyoosha*) 失業者.

unemployment *n.* shiｒtsugyoo

失業: unemployment benefit (*shitsugyoo teate*) 失業手当.

unequal *adj.* hiｒtoｒshiku naｒi 等しくない; doｒotoo de naｒi 同等でない: rooms of unequal size (*ookisa ga hitoshiku nai heya*) 大きさが等しくない部屋.

uneven *adj.* taｒira de naｒi 平らでない; deｒkoboko no でこぼこの: an uneven road (*dekoboko no michi*) でこぼこの道.

unexpected *adj.* yoｒki shiｒnai 予期しない; iｒgai na 意外な: an unexpected accident (*yoki shinai jiko*) 予期しない事故 / That's unexpected. (*Sore wa igai da.*) それは意外だ.

unexpectedly *adv.* oｒmoigakenaｒku 思いがけなく; iｒgai ni 意外に: I unexpectedly met him at the station. (*Watashi wa omoigakenaku kare to eki de deatta.*) 私は思いがけなく彼と駅で出会った.

unfair *adj.* fuｒkoｒohee na 不公平な; fuｒtoo na 不当な: receive unfair treatment (*fukoohee na atsukai o ukeru*) 不公平な扱いを受ける.

unfamiliar *adj.* yoｒku shiｒranai よく知らない; miｒnarenai 見慣れない; naｒjimi no naｒi なじみのない: The subject is unfamiliar to me. (*Sono moñdai wa yoku shirimaseñ.*) その問題はよく知りません.

unfavorable *adj.* tsuｒgoo no waｒruｒi 都合の悪い; fuｒri na 不利な: unfavorable conditions (*furi na jookeñ*) 不利な条件.

unfit *adj.* fuｒteｒkitoo na 不適当な; fuｒmuki no 不向きの: This water is unfit for drinking. (*Kono mizu wa iñyoo ni tekisanai.*) この水は飲用に適さない.

unfold *vt.* … o hiｒrogeru …を広げる Ⓥ; hiｒraｒku 開く Ⓒ: unfold a map (*chizu o hirogeru*) 地図を広げる.

unforgettable *adj.* waｒsurerarenai 忘れられない: an unforgettable experience (*wasurerarenai keekeñ*) 忘れられない経験.

unfortunate *adj.* fuｒuñ na 不運な; fuｒkoｒo na 不幸な: He was unfortunate to meet with the accident. (*Kare ga sono jiko ni atta no wa fuuñ datta.*) 彼がその事故に遭ったのは不運だった.

unfortunately *adv.* uˈñ warukuˈ 運悪く; aˈiniku あいにく: Unfortunately it began to rain. (*Uñ waruku ame ga furi-dashita.*) 運悪く雨が降りだした. / Unfortunately I have a previous engagement. (*Ainiku señyaku ga arimasu.*) あいにく先約があります.

ungrateful *adj.* oˈñshiˈrazu no 恩知らずの: an ungrateful person (*oñshirazu no hito*) 恩知らずの人.

unhappy *adj.* **1** (not happy) fuˈkoˈo na 不幸な; miˈjime na 惨めな: lead an unhappy life (*fukoo na seekatsu o okuru*) 不幸な生活を送る. **2** (not satisfactory) fuˈmañ na 不満な; oˈmoshiroˈkunai おもしろくない: We were unhappy about the result. (*Watashi-tachi wa sono kekka ni fumañ datta.*) 私たちはその結果に不満だった.

unhealthy *adj.* fuˈkeˈñkoo na 不健康な; keˈñkoo ni waruˈi 健康に悪い: unhealthy habits (*keñkoo ni warui shuukañ*) 健康に悪い習慣.

uniform *n.* seˈefuku 制服; yuˈniˈfoˈomu ユニフォーム.
— *adj.* **1** (not changing) iˈchiyoo na 一様な; iˈttee no 一定の: drive at a uniform speed (*ittee no sokudo de kuruma o uñteñ suru*) 一定の速度で車を運転する. **2** (not different) doˈoitsu no 同一の; oˈnaji katachi no 同じ形の: a row of uniform houses (*onaji katachi no ie no narabi*) 同じ形の家の並び.

unify *vt.* ... o toˈoitsu suru ...を統一する Ⅰ; toˈogoo suru 統合する Ⅰ: unify factions (*tooha o tooitsu suru*) 党派を統一する.

unimportant *adj.* juˈuyoo de naˈi 重要でない; saˈsai na ささいな: an unimportant problem (*juuyoo de nai moñdai*) 重要でない問題.

union *n.* **1** (organization) kuˈmiai

組合: join a union (*kumiai ni kanyuu suru*) 組合に加入する / a labor union (*roodoo-kumiai*) 労働組合. **2** (act of uniting) keˈtsugoo 結合; gaˈppee 合併: the union of two companies (*futatsu no kaisha no gappee*) 二つの会社の合併. **3** (of states) reˈñpoo 連邦; reˈñgoo koˈkka 連合国家.

unique *adj.* ruˈi no nai 類のない; doˈkutoku no 独特の: a unique building (*rui no nai tatemono*) 類のない建物 / This custom is one that is unique to Japan. (*Kono fuushuu wa Nihoñ dokutoku no mono desu.*) この風習は日本独特のものです.

unit *n.* **1** (single group) taˈñi 単位: The family is a unit of society. (*Kazoku wa shakai no tañi desu.*) 家族は社会の単位です. **2** (measurement) taˈñi 単位: A meter is a unit of length. (*Meetoru wa nagasa no tañi desu.*) メートルは長さの単位です.

unite *vt.* **1** (join together) ... o keˈtsugoo suru ...を結合する Ⅰ; muˈsubitsukeˈru 結びつける Ⅴ: unite theory and practice (*riroñ to jisseñ o musubitsukeru*) 理論と実践を結びつける. **2** (act together) ... o daˈñketsu saseru ...を団結させる Ⅴ: We were united in our efforts. (*Wareware wa dañketsu shite doryoku shita.*) われわれは団結して努力した.
— *vi.* **1** (join together) gaˈppee suru 合併する Ⅰ: The two companies united to form a new company. (*Sono futatsu no kaisha wa gappee shite hitotsu no atarashii kaisha ni natta.*) その二つ会社は合併して一つの新しい会社になった. **2** (act together) daˈñketsu suru 団結する Ⅰ: unite in fighting (*dañketsu shite tatakau*) 団結して戦う.

united *adj.* daˈñketsu shita [shite iru] 団結した[している]; iˈtchi shita [shite iru] 一致した[している]: make a united effort (*itchi kyooryoku suru*) 一致協力する.

United States of America *n.*
Aˈmerika (gasshuˈukoku) アメリカ(合
衆国); Beˈekoku 米国.

unity *n.* taˈnitsu 単一; toˈoitsu 統
一: the unity of a race (*miñzoku
no tooitsu*) 民族の統一.

universal *adj.* **1** (of the whole
world) zeˈñ seˈkai no 全世界の: universal peace (*sekai-heewa*) 世界平
和.
2 (general) fuˈheñ-teki na 普遍的
な; iˈppañ-teki na 一般的な: a universal rule (*ippañ hoosoku*) 一般法
則.

universe *n.* uˈchuu 宇宙; zeˈñ seˈ-
kai 全世界. ★ 'Space' is also called
'*uchuu.*'

university *n.* daˈigaku 大学; soˈo-
goo-daˈigaku 総合大学: a university student (*daigakusee*) 大学生 /
go to university (*daigaku e iku*) 大
学へ行く. ★ 'College' is also called
'*daigaku.*'

unjust *adj.* fuˈkoˈohee na 不公平な;
fuˈsee na 不正な: an unjust judge
(*fukoohee na saibañkañ*) 不公平な
裁判官.

unkind *adj.* fuˈshiˈñsetsu na 不親切
な; haˈkujoo na 薄情な: He was
very unkind to me. (*Kare wa watashi ni hijoo ni fushiñsetsu datta.*)
彼は私に非常に不親切だった.

unknown *adj.* shiˈrarete inai 知ら
れていない; miˈchi no 未知の; mu-
ˈmee no 無名の: an unknown place
(*michi no basho*) 未知の場所 / an
unknown actress (*mumee no joyuu*) 無名の女優.

unlawful *adj.* fuˈhoo na 不法な;
hiˈgoohoo-teki na 非合法的な: unlawful entry (*fuhoo shiñnyuu*) 不法
侵入.

unless *conj.* moshi ... (-)naˈkereba
もし…なければ: Don't go unless you
want to. (*Ikitaku nakereba iku no
wa yoshi nasai.*) 行きたくなければ行く
のはよしなさい. / I will go unless it
rains. (*Ame ga furanakereba ikimasu.*) 雨が降らなければ行きます.

unlike *adj.* niˈte inai 似ていない;

oˈnaji de naˈi 同じでない: The two
sisters are quite unlike. (*Futari no
shimai wa mattaku nite inai.*) 二人
の姉妹はまったく似ていない.
— *prep.* ... ni niˈte inai de …に似て
いないで; ... to chiˈgatte …と違って:
The picture is quite unlike him.
(*Sono shashiñ wa kare ni marude
nite inai.*) その写真は彼にまるで似てい
ない.

unlikely *adj.* ⟨verb⟩-soo mo naˈi
…そうもない: an unlikely story (*ari-
soo mo nai hanashi*) ありそうもない話
/ He is unlikely to come. (*Kare wa
ki-soo mo nai.*) 彼は来そうもない.

unlimited *adj.* kaˈgiri naˈi 限りな
い; muˈgeñ no 無限の: unlimited
liability (*mugeñ sekiniñ*) 無限責
任.

unload *vt.* (... kara) niˈ o oˈroˈsu
(…から)荷を降ろす ⓒ: unload the
cargo from a ship (*fune kara ni o
orosu*) 船から荷を降ろす.

unlock *vt.* ... no joˈo [kaˈgi] o
aˈkeru …の錠[鍵]を開ける Ⓥ: unlock
a door (*doa no joo o akeru*) ドアの
錠を開ける.

unlucky *adj.* uˈñ no waˈruˈi 運の悪
い; fuˈuñ na 不運な: an unlucky person (*uñ no warui hito*) 運の悪い人.

unnatural *adj.* **1** (not natural) fu-
ˈshiˈzeñ na 不自然な; iˈjoo na 異常
な: an unnatural silence (*fushizeñ
na shizukesa*) 不自然な静けさ.
2 (artificial) waˈza-to-rashiˈi わざと
らしい: an unnatural smile (*tsukuri
warai*) 作り笑い.

unnecessary *adj.* hiˈtsuyoo ga
naˈi 必要がない; fuˈhitsuˈyoo na 不
必要な: It is unnecessary for you to
go there. (*Anata wa soko e iku hitsuyoo wa arimaseñ.*) あなたはそこへ
行く必要はありません.

unofficial *adj.* hiˈkoˈoshiki no 非公
式の; shiˈteki na 私的な: an unofficial meeting (*hikooshiki no kaigoo*) 非公式の会合.

unpaid *adj.* miˈhaˈrai no 未払いの:
an unpaid bill (*miharai no see-
kyuusho*) 未払いの請求書.

unpleasant *adj.* fuˈyuˈkai na 不愉快な; iˈyaˈna いやな: unpleasant noises (*fuyukai na soo-oñ*) 不愉快な騒音 / have an unpleasant experience (*iya na keekeñ o suru*) いやな経験をする.

unreasonable *adj.* **1** (not sensible) suˈji ga toˈoraˈnai 筋が通らない; muˈfuˈñbetsu na 無分別な: What he says is unreasonable. (*Kare no iu koto wa suji ga tooranai.*) 彼の言うことは筋が通らない.
2 (too great) fuˈtoo na 不当な; hoˈogai na 法外な: unreasonable prices (*hoogai na nedañ*) 法外な値段.

unrest *n.* fuˈañ 不安; shiˈñpai 心配: social unrest (*shakai fuañ*) 社会不安.

unsatisfactory *adj.* fuˈmaˈñzoku na 不満足な; fuˈjuˈubuñ na 不十分な: His answer was unsatisfactory. (*Kare no kotae wa fumañzoku datta.*) 彼の答えは不満足だった.

unspeakable *adj.* koˈtobaˈ de aˈrawaseˈnai 言葉で表せない; iˈiyoo no naˈi 言いようない: unspeakable suffering (*iiyoo no nai kurushimi*) 言いようのない苦しみ.

unsteady *adj.* fuˈaˈñtee na 不安定な; guˈragura suru ぐらぐらする: an unsteady table (*guragura suru teeburu*) ぐらぐらするテーブル.

unthinkable *adj.* kaˈñgaerareˈnai 考えられない; oˈmoˈi mo yoˈranai 思いもよらない: Cancellation at this stage is unthinkable. (*Kono dañkai de chuushi nañte kañgaerarenai.*) この段階で中止なんて考えられない.

untidy *adj.* daˈrashi naˈi だらしない; chiˈrakatta 散らかった; chiˈrakatte iru 散らかっている: an untidy appearance (*darashi nai kakkoo*) だらしない格好 / an untidy room (*chirakatta heya*) 散らかった部屋.

untie *vt.* ... o toˈku ...を解く Ⓒ; hoˈdoˈku ほどく Ⓒ: untie a knot (*musubime o hodoku*) 結び目をほどく.

until *prep.* ... maˈde ...まで: I was waiting for you until three o'clock.

(*Watashi wa sañ-ji made anata o matte imashita.*) 私は3時まであなたを待っていました. / He will not come home until Monday. (*Kare wa getsuyoo made uchi ni kaette kimaseñ.*) 彼は月曜まで家に帰って来ません.
— *conj.* ... maˈde ...まで: Please keep this baggage until I come back. (*Kono nimotsu o watashi ga modoru made azukatte kudasai.*) この荷物を私が戻るまで預かってください.

unusual *adj.* fuˈtsuu de naˈi 普通でない; meˈzurashiˈi 珍しい: It is unusual for him to be absent. (*Kare ga yasumu no wa mezurashii.*) 彼が休むのは珍しい.

unwilling *adj.* iˈyaiya-naˈgara no いやいやながらの; kiˈ ga susumanai 気が進まない: He was unwilling to go. (*Kare wa iku no wa ki ga susumanakatta.*) 彼は行くのは気が進まなかった.

unworthy *adj.* aˈtaishinai 値しない; kaˈchi no nai 価値のない: conduct unworthy of praise (*shoosañ ni ataishinai kooi*) 賞賛に値しない行為.

up *adv.* **1** (to or in a higher place) uˈe e [ni] 上へ[に]; taˈkaˈi toˈkoroˈ ni [de] 高い所に[で]: pull one's socks up (*kutsushita o ue e hipparu*) 靴下を上へ引っ張る / He lives five floors up. (*Kare wa go-kai ue ni suñde imasu.*) 彼は5階上に住んでいます.
2 (totally) suˈkkaˈri すっかり: We ate up the cake. (*Watashi-tachi wa keeki o sukkari tabete shimatta.*) 私たちはケーキをすっかり食べてしまった.
— *prep.* **1** (to a higher place) ... no uˈe ni ...の上に: We climbed up the hill. (*Watashi-tachi wa oka no ue ni nobotta.*) 私たちは丘の上に登った.
2 (along) ... ni soˈtte ...に沿って: walk up the street (*michi ni sotte aruku*) 道に沿って歩く.
— *adj.* noˈbori no 上りの: an up elevator (*nobori no erebeetaa*) 上りのエレベーター / an up train (*nobori-*

ressha) 上り列車.

up to ... *prep.* ... ma˺de ...まで: I was up to my knees in water. (*Watashi wa hiza made mizu ni tsukatta.*) 私はひざまで水につかった.

uphold *vt.* ... o shi˺ji suru ...を支持する ⊥: He upheld my opinions. (*Kare wa watashi no ikeñ o shiji shite kureta.*) 彼は私の意見を支持してくれた.

upper *adj.* **1** (higher) u˺e no 上の: an upper room (*ue no heya*) 上の部屋 / the upper lip (*uwa-kuchibiru*) 上唇.
2 (superior) jo˺oi no 上位の; jo˺o-kyuu no 上級の: the upper class (*jooryuu kaikyuu*) 上流階級.

upright *adj.* **1** (erect) ma˺ssu˺gu na 真っすぐな; cho˺kuritsu no 直立の: an upright tree (*massugu na ki*) 真っすぐな木 / an upright posture (*chokuritsu no shisee*) 直立の姿勢.
2 (honest) sho˺oji˺ki na 正直な; ko˺osee na 公正な: upright dealings (*koosee na torihiki*) 公正な取り引き.
— *adv.* ma˺ssu˺gu ni 真っすぐに: stand upright (*massugu ni tatsu*) 真っすぐに立つ.

uproar *n.* o˺osa˺wagi 大騒ぎ; so˺odoo 騒動.

upset *vt.* **1** (turn over) ... o hi˺k-kurika˺esu ...をひっくり返す ⊂: upset a cup (*chawañ o hikkurikaesu*) 茶碗をひっくり返す.
2 (disturb) ... o da˺me˺ ni suru ...をだめにする ⊥: The rain upset our plans. (*Ame ga watashi-tachi no keekaku o dame ni shita.*) 雨が私たちの計画をだめにした.
3 (cause to worry) ... o ro˺obai saseru ...をろうばいさせる Ⓥ: The bad news upset him. (*Sono warui shirase wa kare o roobai saseta.*) その悪い知らせは彼をろうばいさせた.
— *n.* **1** (upsetting) te˺ñpuku 転覆: the upset of a boat (*booto no teñpuku*) ボートの転覆.
2 (confusion) ko˺ñrañ 混乱: an upset of one's plans (*keekaku no*

koñrañ) 計画の混乱.
3 (slight illness) fu˺choo 不調: a stomach upset (*i no fuchoo*) 胃の不調.

upside down *adv.* sa˺kasama ni 逆さまに; hi˺kkurika˺ette ひっくり返って: turn a glass upside down (*koppu o hikkurikaesu*) コップをひっくり返す.

upstairs *adv.* u˺e no ka˺i e [ni] 上の階へ[に]: go upstairs (*ue no kai e iku*) 上の階へ行く.
— *adj.* ka˺ijoo no 階上の: the upstairs rooms (*kaijoo no heya*) 階上の部屋.

up-to-date *adj.* sa˺ishiñ no 最新の: an up-to-date catalog (*saishiñ no katarogu*) 最新のカタログ.

upward *adv.* u˺e no ho˺o 上の方: look upward (*ue no hoo o miru*) 上の方を見る.
— *adj.* u˺wamuki no 上向きの: an upward slope (*noborizaka*) 上り坂.

uranium *n.* u˺rañ ウラン; u˺rani˺umu ウラニウム.

urban *adj.* to˺shi no 都市の; to˺kai no 都会の: urban life (*toshi-see-katsu*) 都市生活.

urge *vt.* **1** (force onward) ... o ka˺ritate˺ru ...を駆り立てる Ⓥ; se˺kita-teru せきたてる Ⓥ: urge a horse on (*uma o karitateru*) 馬を駆り立てる.
2 (ask earnestly) ... ni shi˺kiri ni susumeru ...にしきりに勧める Ⓥ: I urged him to stay overnight. (*Watashi wa kare ni ip-paku suru yoo ni shikiri ni susumeta.*) 私は彼に1泊するようにしきりに勧めた.
3 (press upon) ... o shu˺choo suru ...を主張する ⊥; ri˺kisetsu suru 力説する ⊥: He urged restraint. (*Kare wa jisee o shuchoo shita.*) 彼は自制を主張した.

urgent *adj.* ki˺ñkyuu no 緊急の: He went to Osaka on urgent business. (*Kare wa kiñkyuu no yooji de Oosaka e ikimashita.*) 彼は緊急の用事で大阪へ行きました. / an urgent telegram (*shikyuu-deñpoo*) 至急電報.

urinate *vi.* sho˺obe˺ñ o suru 小便を

する □; ho「onyoo suru 放尿する □.

us *pron.* **1** [direct object] wa「re-ware o われわれを; wa「tashi」-tachi o 私たちを: She showed us into the room. (*Kanojo wa wareware o heya ni tooshita.*) 彼女はわれわれを部屋に通した.

2 [indirect object] wa「reware ni わ れわれに; wa「tashi」-tachi ni 私たちに: She showed us her picture. (*Kanojo wa watashi-tachi ni kanojo no shashiñ o miseta.*) 彼女は私たちに彼女の写真を見せた.

U.S.A. *n.* A「merika (gasshu「ukoku) アメリカ(合衆国); Be「ekoku 米国.

use[1] *vt.* **1** (employ) ... o tsu「kau ... を使う ○; ri「yoo suru 利用する □: May I use this telephone? (*Kono deñwa o tsukatte mo ii desu ka?*) この電話を使ってもいいですか. / He used a taxi to go there. (*Kare wa soko e iku no ni takushii o riyoo shita.*) 彼はそこへ行くのにタクシーを利用した.

2 (consume) ... o sho「ohi suru ...を消費する □; tsu「kau 使う ○: She used up all the soap. (*Kanojo wa sekkeñ o zeñbu tsukatte shimatta.*) 彼女はせっけんを全部使ってしまった.

use[2] *n.* **1** (using) shi「yoo 使用; ri-「yoo 利用: This park is for the use of children. (*Kono kooeñ wa ko-domo-tachi no riyoo no tame ni arimasu.*) この公園は子どもたちの利用のためにあります.

2 (purpose) yo「oto 用途; mo「ku-teki 目的: This tool has several uses. (*Kono doogu wa iroiro na yooto ga aru.*) この道具はいろいろな用途がある.

3 (value) ko「oyoo 効用; ya「ku」 ni tatsu ko「to」 役に立つこと: These shoes are of no use. (*Kono kutsu wa yaku ni tatanai.*) この靴は役に立たない.

make use of ... *vt.* ... o ri「yoo suru ...を利用する □.

used *adj.* tsu「katta 使った; chu「uko no 中古の: a used car (*chuukosha*) 中古車 / used nuclear fuel (*shiyoo-zumi no kakuneñryoo*) 使用済みの核燃料.

used to[1] *vi.* i「zeñ [mu「kashi] wa 〈verb〉-ta 以前[昔]は...た: He used to work hard but does not now. (*Izeñ wa kare wa yoku hataraita ga ima wa soo de nai.*) 以前は彼はよく働いたが今はそうでない.

used to[2] *adj.* ... ni na「rete iru ...に慣れている: He is used to driving a car. (*Kare wa kuruma no uñteñ ni narete iru.*) 彼は車の運転に慣れている.

useful *adj.* ya「ku」 ni ta「tsu 役に立つ; yu「ueki na 有益な: This guide-book was very useful to me. (*Kono aññaisho wa totemo yaku ni tatta.*) この案内書はとても役に立った. / useful information (*yuueki na joohoo*) 有益な情報.

useless *adj.* ya「ku」 ni ta「ta」nai 役に立たない; mu「da na 無駄な: This tool is useless. (*Kono doogu wa yaku ni tatanai.*) この道具は役に立たない. / a useless attempt (*muda na kokoromi*) 無駄な試み.

usher *vt.* ... o a「ñna」i suru ...を案内する □; se「ñdoo suru 先導する □: She ushered me into the room. (*Kanojo wa watashi o heya ni añ-nai shite kureta.*) 彼女は私を部屋に案内してくれた.

— *n.* a「ñnaiga」kari 案内係.

usual *adj.* i「tsu-mo no いつもの; fu-「tsuu no 普通の: He took his usual seat at the table. (*Kare wa teeburu no itsu-mo no seki ni tsuita.*) 彼はテーブルのいつもの席に着いた. / It is usual for him to sit up late at night. (*Kare ga yoru osoku made okite iru no wa futsuu desu.*) 彼が夜遅くまで起きているのは普通です.

as usual *adv.* i「tsu-mo no to」ori いつものとおり.

usually *adv.* fu「tsuu wa 普通は; i「tsu-mo wa いつもは: I usually get up at six. (*Watashi wa futsuu wa roku-ji ni okimasu.*) 私は普通は6時に起きます.

utility *n.* yu「uyoosee 有用性; ko「o-yoo 効用: the utility of cars (*ku-*

ruma no kooyoo) 車の効用.
— *adj.* ji「tsuyoo-teki na 実用的な:
utility furniture (*jitsuyoo-teki na kagu*) 実用的な家具.

utilize *vt.* ... o ri「yoo suru ...を利用する ⊡; ka「tsuyoo suru 活用する ⊡:
utilize atomic power for peaceful purposes (*geñshiryoku o heewa mokuteki ni riyoo suru*) 原子力を平和目的に利用する.

utmost *adj.* sa「idai no 最大の; sa「ikoo no 最高の: with one's utmost effort (*saidai no doryoku o shite*) 最大の努力をして.

　do one's utmost *vi.* ze「ñryoku o tsu「ku」su 全力を尽くす ⓒ.

utter[1] *adj.* ma「ttaku」 no まったくの; ka「ñzeñ na 完全な: He is an utter stranger to me. (*Kare wa watashi ga mattaku shiranai hito desu.*) 彼は私がまったく知らない人です.

utter[2] *vt.* (of a word) ... o ha「ssuru ...を発する ⊡; (of a cry) a「geru 上げる Ⅴ: He did not utter a word. (*Kare wa hitokoto mo hasshinakatta.*) 彼はひと言も発しなかった. /
utter a cry (*sakebigoe o ageru*) 叫び声を上げる.

utterly *adv.* ma「ttaku まったく; su「kka」ri すっかり: He was utterly exhausted. (*Kare wa sukkari tsukarete ita.*) 彼はすっかり疲れていた.

V

vacant *adj.* **1** (empty) a「ite iru 空いている; ka「ra」 no 空の: a vacant seat (*aite iru seki*) 空いている席 /
Are there any vacant rooms in this hotel? (*Kono hoteru ni akishitsu wa arimasu ka?*) このホテルに空室はありますか.
2 (free from work) hi「ma na 暇な; yo「oji no na」i 用事のない: vacant hours (*hima na jikañ*) 暇な時間.

vacation *n.* kyu「uka 休暇; kyu「ujitsu 休日 / ya「sumi」 休み: take a vacation of a week (*is-shuukañ no kyuuka o toru*) 1週間の休暇を取る /
a summer vacation (*natsu-yasumi*) 夏休み.

vacuum *n.* **1** (space) shi「ñkuu 真空: Sound does not travel in a vacuum. (*Oto wa shiñkuu-chuu de wa tsutawaranai.*) 音は真空中では伝わらない.
2 (cleaner) de「ñki-sooji」ki 電気掃除機.

vacuum bottle *n.* ma「ho」obiñ 魔法びん.

vacuum cleaner *n.* de「ñki-sooji」ki 電気掃除機.

vague *adj.* ha「kki」ri shinai はっきりしない; a「imai na あいまいな; ba「kuzeñ to shita [shite iru] 漠然とした[している]: give a vague answer (*aimai na heñji o suru*) あいまいな返事をする.

vain *adj.* **1** (useless) mu「da na 無駄な; mu「eki na 無益な: make a vain effort (*muda na doryoku o suru*) 無駄な努力をする.
2 (too proud) u「nubore no tsuyo」i うぬぼれの強い; kyo「e」eshiñ no tsu「yo」i 虚栄心の強い: She is vain about her beauty. (*Kanojo wa jibuñ no biboo o unuborete iru.*) 彼女は自分の美貌をうぬぼれている.

　in vain *adv.*, *adj.* mu「da ni 無駄に; mu「na」shiku むなしく: I tried, but in vain. (*Yatte mita ga muda datta.*) やってみたが無駄だった.

valid *adj.* **1** (reasonable) da「too na 妥当な; se「etoo na 正当な: He didn't have a valid reason for his absence. (*Kare wa kesseki shita koto no seetoo na riyuu o motte inakatta.*) 彼は欠席したことの正当な理由を持っていなかった.
2 (legally effective) yu「ukoo na 有効な; go「ohoo-teki na 合法的な: This passport is valid for five years. (*Kono pasupooto wa go-neñkañ yuukoo desu.*) このパスポートは5年間

有効です.

validity *n.* se「etoosa 正当さ; da-「toosee 妥当性; yu「ukoo 有効: the term of validity (*yuukoo kikañ*) 有効期間.

valley *n.* ta「ni¹ 谷; ta「nima¹ 谷間: The river flows through the valley. (*Sono kawa wa tanima o nagarete iru.*) その川は谷間を流れている.

valuable *adj.* **1** (worth much) ka「chi no aru 価値のある; ki「choo na 貴重な: a valuable experience (*ki-choo na keekeñ*) 貴重な経験.
2 (costly) ko「oka na 高価な: a valuable jewel (*kooka na hooseki*) 高価な宝石.
— *n.* ki「choohiñ 貴重品: Please leave your valuables at the reception desk. (*Kichoohiñ wa furoñto ni azukete kudasai.*) 貴重品はフロントに預けてください.

value *n.* **1** (worth) ka「chi 価値; ne「uchi 値打ち: the value of education (*kyooiku no kachi*) 教育の価値.
2 (price) ka「kaku 価格; ne「dañ 値段: What is the value of this house? (*Kono ie no kakaku wa ikura desu ka?*) この家の価格はいくらですか.
— *vt.* **1** (place a value) ... o hyo¹o-ka suru ...を評価する ⊡: He valued the land at five million yen. (*Kare wa sono tochi o gohyakumañ-eñ to hyooka shita.*) 彼はその土地を500万円と評価した.
2 (think highly of) ... o so「ñchoo suru ...を尊重する ⊡; ta「isetsu ni suru 大切にする ⊡: I value his friendship. (*Watashi wa kare no yuujoo o taisetsu ni shite iru.*) 私は彼の友情を大切にしている.

valve *n.* be「ñ 弁; ba「rubu バルブ: a safety valve (*añzeñ-beñ*) 安全弁.

van *n.* ba「ñ バン; yu「ugai-tora¹kku 有蓋トラック.

vanilla *n.* ba「nira バニラ: vanilla ice cream (*banira no aisu kuriimu*) バニラのアイスクリーム.

vanish *vi.* **1** (disappear) ki「eru 消える Ⓥ; mi「e¹naku naru 見えなくなる

Ⓒ: The man vanished in the crowd. (*Sono otoko wa hitogomi no naka de mienakunatta.*) その男は人込みの中で見えなくなった.
2 (cease to exist) sho「ometsu suru 消滅する ⊡; na「kunaru なくなる Ⓒ: Many species of animal have vanished from the earth. (*Ooku no shu no doobutsu ga chijoo kara shoo-metsu shita.*) 多くの種の動物が地上から消滅した.

vanity *n.* kyo「e¹eshiñ 虚栄心; u「nubore うぬぼれ: Miss Takahashi is full of vanity. (*Takahashi-sañ wa kyooeeshiñ ga tsuyoi.*) 高橋さんは虚栄心が強い.

vapor *n.* jo「oki 蒸気: water vapor (*suijooki*) 水蒸気.

variable *adj.* **1** (changeable) ka-「wariyasu¹i 変わりやすい: variable weather (*kawariyasui teñki*) 変わりやすい天気.
2 (that can be changed) ka「erareru 変えられる: The temperature in this room is variable. (*Kono heya no oñdo wa kaeraremasu.*) この部屋の温度は変えられます.

variation *n.* he「ñka 変化; he「ñdoo 変動: variations in air pressure (*kia-tsu no heñka*) 気圧の変化.

varied *adj.* sa「ma¹zama na さまざまな; ta「sai na 多彩な: He has had varied careers. (*Kare wa sama-zama na shoku ni tsuita.*) 彼はさまざまな職に就いた.

variety *n.* **1** (change) he「ñka 変化; ta「ryoosee 多様性: a life full of variety (*heñka ni toñda jiñsee*) 変化に富んだ人生.
2 (kind) shu「rui 種類: a new variety of tulip (*chuurippu no shiñshu*) チューリップの新種.
a variety of ... *adj.* i「roiro na いろいろな: a variety of magazines (*iroiro no zasshi*) いろいろな雑誌.

various *adj.* **1** (different) i「roiro na いろいろな; sa「ma¹zama na さまざまな: I planted various seeds. (*Watashi wa iroiro na tane o maita.*) 私はいろいろな種をまいた.

2 (several) iˈkutsu ka no いくつかの; oˈoku no 多くの: Various people asked me about you. (*Ooku no hito ga watashi ni anata no koto o kiita.*) 多くの人が私にあなたのことを聞いた.

varnish *n.* niˈsu ニス: put varnish on the floor (*yuka ni nisu o nuru*) 床にニスを塗る.

vary *vi.* **1** (change) kaˈwaru 変わる Ⓒ: The weather varies from day to day. (*Tenkoo wa hi goto ni kawaru.*) 天候は日ごとに変わる.
2 (differ) koˈtonaru 異なる Ⓒ; chiˈgau 違う Ⓒ: Customs vary from country to country. (*Shuukan wa kuni ni yotte kotonaru.*) 習慣は国によって異なる.
— *vt.* ... o kaˈeru ...を変える Ⓥ: She varied her hair style. (*Kanojo wa kamigata o kaeta.*) 彼女は髪型を変えた.

vase *n.* kaˈbin 花びん: put flowers in a vase (*kabin ni hana o sasu*) 花びんに花を挿す.

vast *adj.* **1** (very great in extent) koˈodai na 広大な: a vast desert (*koodai na sabaku*) 広大な砂漠.
2 (very great in amount) baˈkudai na 莫大な: a vast sum of money (*bakudai na kingaku no o-kane*) 莫大な金額のお金.

vault *n.* (roof) aˈachigata no tenjoo アーチ形の天井; (cellar) chiˈkaˈshitsu 地下室.

veal *n.* koˈushi no nikuˈ 子牛の肉.

vegetable *n.* yaˈsai 野菜: grow vegetables (*yasai o saibai suru*) 野菜を栽培する / fresh vegetables (*shinsen na yasai*) 新鮮な野菜.

vehement *adj.* haˈgeshiˈi 激しい; geˈkiretsu na 激烈な: a vehement argument (*gekiron*) 激論.

vehicle *n.* noˈrimono 乗り物; kuˈruma 車: The road was crowded with vehicles. (*Dooro wa kuruma de konde ita.*) 道路は車で込んでいた.

veil *n.* beˈeru ベール; kaˈburimono かぶり物: wear a veil (*beeru o kaburu*) ベールをかぶる.

vein *n.* **1** (blood vessel) joˈomyaku 静脈.
2 (in a leaf) yoˈomyaku 葉脈; (in rock) koˈomyaku 鉱脈.
3 (mood) kiˈbun 気分: in a light-hearted vein (*karui kibun de*) 軽い気分で.

velocity *n.* soˈkudo 速度; haˈyasa 速さ.

velvet *n.* biˈroodo ビロード.

venerable *adj.* soˈnkee subeˈki 尊敬すべき; riˈppa na 立派な: a venerable scholar (*rippa na gakusha*) 立派な学者.

vengeance *n.* fuˈkushuu 復讐: take vengeance on a person (*hito ni fukushuu suru*) 人に復讐する.

ventilation *n.* kaˈzetooshi 風通し; kaˈnki 換気.

venture *n.* boˈoken 冒険; toˈoki 投機: a venture business (*tooki-teki jigyoo*) 投機的な事業.
— *vt.* oˈmoˈikitte 〈verb〉思い切って...: We ventured a protest. (*Watashi-tachi wa omoikitte koogi shita.*) 私たちは思い切って抗議した.

verb *n.* doˈoshi 動詞: a transitive verb (*tadooshi*) 他動詞 / an intransitive verb (*jidooshi*) 自動詞.

verge *n.* fuˈchiˈ 縁; kyoˈokai 境界: the verge of a cliff (*gake no fuchi*) がけの縁.

verify *vt.* ... o taˈshikameˈru ...を確かめる Ⓥ: verify a fact (*jijitsu o tashikameru*) 事実を確かめる.

verse *n.* iˈnbun 韻文; shi 詩: a story written in verse (*inbun de kakareta monogatari*) 韻文で書かれた物語 / epic [lyrical] verse (*joji [jojoo]-shi*) 叙事[叙情]詩.

version *n.* **1** (translation) -yaˈku 訳: I have the French version of the book. (*Watashi wa sono hon no Furansugo-yaku o motte iru.*) 私はその本のフランス語訳を持っている.
2 (particular form) -ban 版: an abridged version of a dictionary (*jisho no kanyaku-ban*) 辞書の簡約版.
3 (description) seˈtsumee 説明:

He gave a different version of the accident. (*Kare wa sono jiko ni tsuite chigatta setsumee o shita.*) 彼はその事故について違った説明をした.

versus *prep.* ... ta¹i ...対: Waseda versus Keio (*Waseda tai Keeoo*) 早稲田対慶応.

vertical *adj.* su⌐ichoku no 垂直の; ta¹te no 縦の: The cliff is almost vertical. (*Gake wa hotoñdo suichoku da.*) がけはほとんど垂直だ. / a vertical line (*tate no señ*) 縦の線.
— *n.* su⌐ichokuseñ 垂直線.

very *adv.* 1 (extremely) hi¹joo ni 非常に; to¹temo とても; ta¹iheñ 大変: I'm very tired. (*Watashi wa hijoo ni tsukaremashita.*) 私は非常に疲れました. / Your story is very interesting. (*Kimi no hanashi wa taiheñ omoshiroi.*) 君の話は大変おもしろい.
2 (really) ma¹ttaku まったく; ho¹ñtoo ni 本当に: It was the very first time that I met him. (*Kare ni atta no wa mattaku hajimete deshita.*) 彼に会ったのはまったく初めてでした.
— *adj.* ma¹sa ni so¹no まさにその: This is the very book I was looking for. (*Kore wa masa ni watashi ga sagashite ita sono hoñ desu.*) これはまさに私が捜していたその本です.

vessel *n.* 1 (ship) fu¹ne 船.
2 (container) yo¹oki 容器; i¹remono 入れ物.

vest *n.* (waistcoat) cho¹kki チョッキ: a life vest (*kyumee dooi*) 救命胴衣.

veteran *n.* ro¹oreñ na hito¹ 老練な人; be¹terañ ベテラン. ★ Japanese '*beterañ*' is usually used in the sense of an 'experienced person.'

via *prep.* ... ke¹eyu de ...経由で; ... o he¹te ...を経て: I went to Japan via Hawaii. (*Watashi wa Hawai keeyu de Nihoñ e ikimashita.*) 私はハワイ経由で日本へ行きました.

vibrate *vi.* 1 (quiver) shi¹ñdoo suru 振動する ①: The house vibrates whenever a heavy truck passes. (*Omoi torakku ga tooru tabi ni ie ga shiñdoo suru.*) 重いトラックが通るたびに家が振動する.
2 (resound) na¹rihibi¹ku 鳴り響く Ⓒ: The hall vibrated with cheers. (*Hooru ni hakushu ga narihibiita.*) ホールに拍手が鳴り響いた.
— *vt.* ... o shi¹ñdoo saseru ...を振動させる Ⓥ; yu¹riugoka¹su 揺り動かす Ⓒ.

vice *n.* 1 (bad habit) a¹kushuu 悪習: the vice of smoking (*kitsueñ no akushuu*) 喫煙の悪習.
2 (evil) a¹ku 悪; a¹kutoku 悪徳: virtue and vice (*bitoku to akutoku*) 美徳と悪徳.

vice president *n.* fu¹ku-daito¹oryoo 副大統領; (of a company) fu¹ku-sha¹choo 副社長.

vicinity *n.* ki¹ñjo 近所; fu¹kiñ 付近: There is no hospital in my vicinity. (*Kiñjo ni byooiñ wa arimaseñ.*) 近所に病院はありません.

vicious *adj.* a¹kui no aru 悪意のある; i¹ji no waru¹i 意地の悪い: vicious remarks (*akui no aru kotoba*) 悪意のある言葉.

victim *n.* gi¹se¹esha 犠牲者; hi¹ga¹isha 被害者: victims of war (*señsoo no giseesha*) 戦争の犠牲者 / the victim of an accident (*jiko no higaisha*) 事故の被害者.

victor *n.* sho¹ori¹sha 勝利者; (winner) yu¹usho¹osha 優勝者.

victory *n.* sho¹ori 勝利: lead a team to victory (*chiimu o shoori ni michibiku*) チームを勝利に導く / win a victory in an election (*señkyo ni katsu*) 選挙に勝つ.

video *n.* bi¹deo ビデオ: record a movie on video (*eega o bideo ni rokuga suru*) 映画をビデオに録画する.

vie *vi.* ki¹soia¹u 競い合う Ⓒ; ha¹ria¹u 張り合う Ⓒ: vie with one another for a prize (*shoo o mezashite otagai ni kisoiau*) 賞を目指してお互いに競い合う.

view *n.* 1 (scene) na¹game¹ 眺め; mi¹harashi 見晴らし: We reserved a room with a good view. (*Watashitachi wa nagame no yoi heya o yoyaku shita.*) 私たちは眺めのよい部

屋を予約した.
2 (act of seeing) miˈru ˈkotoˈ 見ること: It was our first view of Mt. Fuji. (*Watashi-tachi wa Fuji-san o hajimete mita.*) 私たちは富士山を初めて見た.
3 (opinion) kaˈngaeˈ 考え; iˈkeñ 意見: Tell me your views on the matter. (*Sono mondai ni tsuite anata no kangae o kikasete kudasai.*) その問題についてあなたの考えを聞かせてください.
— *vt.* ... o naˈgameˈru ...を眺める Ⓥ: view a lake from an airplane (*hikooki kara mizuumi o nagameru*) 飛行機から湖を眺める.

viewpoint *n.* kaˈñteñ 観点; keˈnchi 見地: Look at the problem from a different viewpoint. (*Sono mondai o chigatta kañteñ kara mite gorañ nasai.*) その問題を違った観点から見てご覧なさい.

vigor *n.* kaˈtsuˈryoku 活力; kiˈryoku 気力: I don't have the vigor to begin a new job. (*Watashi wa atarashii shigoto o hajimeru kiryoku ga nai.*) 私は新しい仕事を始める気力がない.

vigorous *adj.* seˈeryoku oˈosee na 精力旺盛な; kaˈkki ni miˈchita [miˈchite iru] 活気に満ちた[満ちている]: a vigorous young man (*kakki ni michita wakamono*) 活気に満ちた若者.

vile *adj.* (mean) geˈretsu na 下劣な; (disgusting) iˈya na いやな: a vile smell (*iya na nioi*) いやなにおい.

village *n.* muˈraˈ 村: live in a village (*mura ni sumu*) 村に住む.

villain *n.* waˈrumono 悪者; aˈkutoˈo 悪党.

vine *n.* **1** (grapevine) buˈdoo no kiˈ [tsuruˈ] ぶどうの木[つる].
2 (climbing plant) tsuˈruˈ つる; tsuˈrukusa つる草: Pumpkins grow on vines. (*Kabocha wa tsuru ni naru.*) かぼちゃはつるになる.

vinegar *n.* suˈ 酢.

violate *vt.* **1** (break) ... o yaˈbuˈru ...を破る Ⓒ; oˈkaˈsu 犯す Ⓒ: violate

an agreement (*kyootee o yaburu*) 協定を破る / violate the law (*hooritsu o okasu*) 法律を犯す.
2 (disturb) ... o shiˈñgai suru ...を侵害する Ⓘ; saˈmatageˈru 妨げる Ⓥ: violate a person's privacy (*hito no puraibashii o shiñgai suru*) 人のプライバシーを侵害する.

violation *n.* iˈhañ 違反; shiˈñgai 侵害: violation of the law (*hooritsu-ihañ*) 法律違反 / violation of human rights (*jiñkeñ shiñgai*) 人権侵害.

violence *n.* **1** (conduct) boˈoryoku 暴力; raˈñboo 乱暴: use violence (*booryoku o mochiiru*) 暴力を用いる.
2 (great strength) haˈgeˈshisa 激しさ; moˈoi 猛威: the violence of a typhoon (*taifuu no mooi*) 台風の猛威.

violent *adj.* **1** (showing great force) haˈgeshiˈi 激しい; moˈoretsu na 猛烈な: a violent earthquake (*hageshii jishiñ*) 激しい地震.
2 (showing strong feelings) haˈgeshiˈi 激しい: a person of violent temper (*hageshii kishoo no hito*) 激しい気性の人.
3 (wild) raˈñboo na 乱暴な; boˈoryoku-teki na 暴力的な: resort to violent means (*booryoku ni uttaeru*) 暴力に訴える.

violently *adv.* haˈgeˈshiku 激しく; moˈoretsu ni 猛烈に: The wind is blowing violently. (*Kaze ga hageshiku fuite iru.*) 風が激しく吹いている.

violet *n.* (flower) suˈmire すみれ; (color) suˈmireiro すみれ色; muˈrasaki-iro 紫色.

violin *n.* baˈioriñ バイオリン: play the violin (*baioriñ o hiku*) バイオリンを弾く.

virgin *n.* shoˈjo 処女.
— *adj.* shoˈjo no 処女の; juˈñketsu na 純潔な: virgin snow (*shojo yuki*) 処女雪.

virtue *n.* **1** (morality) toˈku 徳; biˈtoku 美徳: a person of virtue (*toku no aru hito*) 徳のある人.

2 (merit) cho⌐osho 長所; ri⌐teṇ 利点: This house has the virtue of being easy to clean. (*Kono uchi wa sooji shi-yasui to iu riteṇ ga aru.*) この家は掃除しやすいという利点がある.

visa *n*. bi⌐za ビザ; sa⌐shoo 査証: I applied for a visa to China. (*Watashi wa Chuugoku e no biza o shiṇsee shita.*) 私は中国へのビザを申請した. — *vt*. ... ni sa⌐shoo suru ...に査証する Ⓣ; bi⌐za o a⌐taeru ビザを与える Ⓥ: get one's passport visaed (*pasupooto ni biza o morau*) パスポートにビザをもらう.

visible *adj*. **1** (able to be seen) me⌐ ni mi⌐e⌐ru 目に見える: That star is visible to the naked eye. (*Sono hoshi wa nikugaṇ de miemasu.*) その星は肉眼で見えます.
2 (evident) a⌐ki⌐raka na 明らかな; me⌐ehaku na 明白な: a visible increase in crime (*haṇzai no meehaku na zooka*) 犯罪の明白な増加.

vision *n*. **1** (sight) shi⌐ryoku 視力; shi⌐kaku 視覚: I am slowly losing my vision. (*Watashi wa sukoshi zutsu shiryoku ga ochite iru.*) 私は少しずつ視力が落ちている.
2 (imagination) so⌐ozo⌐oryoku 想像力; do⌐osatsu⌐ryoku 洞察力: a statesman of vision (*doosatsuryoku no aru seejika*) 洞察力のある政治家.

visit *vt*. **1** (call on) ... o ta⌐zune⌐ru ...を訪ねる Ⓥ; ho⌐omoṇ suru 訪問する Ⓣ: I visited him at his office. (*Watashi wa kare o kaisha ni tazuneta.*) 私は彼を会社に訪ねた.
2 (go to see) ... o o⌐tozure⌐ru 訪れる Ⓥ; ke⌐ṇbutsu ni iku 見物に行く Ⓒ: Many people visit Kyoto. (*Oozee no hito ga Kyooto o otozuremasu.*) 大勢の人が京都を訪れます.
3 (stay) ... ni ta⌐maru ...に泊まる Ⓒ; ta⌐izai suru 滞在する Ⓣ: They visited us for a week. (*Kare-ra wa watashi-tachi no tokoro ni isshuukaṇ tomatta.*) 彼らは私たちのところに1週間泊まった. — *n*. ho⌐omoṇ 訪問; ke⌐ṇbutsu 見

物; ta⌐izai 滞在: This is my second visit. (*Kore ga ni-kaime no hoomoṇ desu.*) これが2回目の訪問です. / a visit to Nikko (*Nikkoo keṇbutsu*) 日光見物.

visitor *n*. **1** (caller) ho⌐omoṇ-kyaku 訪問客; ra⌐ikyaku 来客: We had two visitors today. (*Kyoo wa raikyaku ga futari atta.*) きょうは来客が二人あった.
2 (sightseer) ka⌐ṇko⌐okyaku 観光客: visitors to Tokyo from Hawaii (*Hawai kara Tookyoo e yatte kuru kaṇkookyaku*) ハワイから東京へやって来る観光客.

visual *adj*. shi⌐kaku no 視覚の; shi⌐ryoku no 視力の: visual effects (*shikaku kooka*) 視覚効果 / a visual test (*shiryoku keṇsa*) 視力検査.

vital *adj*. **1** (important) ki⌐wa⌐mete ju⌐udai na きわめて重大な; (essential) ze⌐ttai ni hitsuyoo na 絶対に必要な: make a vital decision (*kiwamete juudai na kesshiṇ o suru*) きわめて重大な決心をする / Your help is vital for our success. (*Wareware ga seekoo suru tame ni wa anata no eṇjo ga zettai ni hitsuyoo desu.*) われわれが成功するためにはあなたの援助が絶対に必要です.
2 (of life) se⌐emee no 生命の: vital energy (*katsuryoku*) 活力.

vitality *n*. ka⌐kki 活気; ka⌐tsu⌐ryoku 活力: a person full of vitality (*kakki ni michita hito*) 活気に満ちた人.

vitamin *n*. bi⌐ta⌐miṇ ビタミン: vitamin pills (*bitamiṇzai*) ビタミン剤.

vivid *adj*. **1** (full of life) i⌐ki-i⌐ki to shita [shite iru] 生き生きとした[している]: a vivid performance (*iki-iki to shita eṇgi*) 生き生きとした演技.
2 (bright) a⌐za⌐yaka na 鮮やかな: vivid colors (*azayaka na iro*) 鮮やかな色.

vocabulary *n*. go⌐i 語い: He has a large vocabulary. (*Kare wa goi ga hoofu da.*) 彼は語いが豊富だ.

vocal *adj*. **1** (of the voice) ko⌐e no 声の: vocal sounds (*oṇsee*) 音声 /

vocal music (*seegaku*) 声楽.
2 (oral) ko⌐otoo no 口頭の: a vocal communication (*kootoo no deñtatsu*) 口頭の伝達.

vogue *n.* ryu⌐ukoo 流行; ha⌐yari⌝ はやり: Long hair is no longer in vogue. (*Choohatsu wa moo hayari de wa arimaseñ.*) 長髪はもうはやりではありません.

voice *n.* **1** (sound) ko⌝e 声: She spoke in a quiet voice. (*Kanojo wa shizuka na koe de hanashita.*) 彼女は静かな声で話した.
2 (expressed opinion) i⌝keñ 意見; ko⌝e 声: the voice for peace (*heewa o motomeru koe*) 平和を求める声.

volcano *n.* ka⌝zañ 火山: When is it that this volcano last erupted? (*Kono kazañ ga saigo ni fuñka shita no wa itsu desu ka?*) この火山が最後に噴火したのはいつですか.

volleyball *n.* ba⌐reebo⌝oru バレーボール: play volleyball (*bareebooru o suru*) バレーボールをする.

volume *n.* **1** (book) ho⌝ñ 本; -kañ 巻; -satsu 冊: a dictionary in two volumes (*ni-kañ kara naru jisho*) 2巻からなる辞書 / You can borrow three volumes at a time. (*Ichi-do ni sañ-satsu kariraremasu.*) 一度に3冊借りられます.
2 (loudness) o⌐ñryoo 音量; bo⌐ryuumu ボリューム: turn up [down] the volume on the TV (*terebi no oñryoo o ookiku* [*chiisaku*] *suru*) テレビの音量を大きく[小さく]する.
3 (solid content) ta⌝iseki 体積; (the amount of space inside) yo⌝oseki 容積: The volume of this box is 10 cubic centimeters. (*Kono hako no yooseki wa juu-rippoo-señchi-meetoru desu.*) この箱の容積は10立方センチメートルです.
4 (amount) ryo⌝o 量: a large volume of sales (*ooku no hañbai-ryoo*) 多くの販売量.

voluntary *adj.* ji⌐hatsu-teki na 自発的な; ji⌐yu⌝u na ishi ni yo⌐ru 自由な意志による: a voluntary helper (*jihatsu-teki na eñjosha*) 自発的な援助者.

volunteer *n.* shi⌐ga⌝ñsha 志願者; yu⌝ushi 有志; bo⌐ra⌝ñtia ボランティア.
— *vt.* ... o su⌐suñde mooshide⌝ru ...を進んで申し出る [V]: I volunteered to do the job. (*Watashi wa susuñde sono shigoto o suru koto o mooshideta.*) 私は進んでその仕事をすることを申し出た.
— *vi.* ji⌐hatsu-teki ni mooshide⌝ru 自発的に申し出る [V].

vomit *vt.* ... o ha⌝ku ...を吐く [C]; mo⌐do⌝su もどす [C]: The boy vomited up what he had eaten. (*Sono otoko-no-ko wa tabeta mono o haita.*) その男の子は食べたものを吐いた.

vote *n.* **1** (choice) to⌐ohyoo 投票: We took a vote on the matter. (*Watashi-tachi wa sono moñdai ni tsuite toohyoo o okonatta.*) 私たちはその問題について投票を行った.
2 (ballot) to⌐ohyo⌝osuu 投票数; hyo⌐osu⌝u 票数: count the votes (*hyoosuu o kazoeru*) 票数を数える.
— *vi.* to⌐ohyoo o suru 投票をする [I]: I voted for [against] the project. (*Watashi wa sono keekaku ni sañsee* [*hañtai*] *no toohyoo o shita.*) 私はその計画に賛成[反対]の投票をした.
— *vt.* ... o to⌐ohyoo de kimeru ...を投票で決める [V]: We voted to go on a hike next Sunday. (*Tsugi no nichiyoobi ni haikiñgu ni iku koto o toohyoo de kimeta.*) 次の日曜日にハイキングに行くことを投票で決めた.

voter *n.* to⌐ohyooniñ 投票人; to⌐ohyo⌝osha 投票者.

vow *n.* chi⌐kai 誓い; se⌐eyaku 誓約: make a vow (*chikai o tateru*) 誓いを立てる.
— *vt.* ... o chi⌐ka⌝u ...を誓う [C]: He vowed never to smoke. (*Kare wa kesshite tabako o suwanai to chikatta.*) 彼は決してたばこを吸わないと誓った.

vowel *n.* bo⌐iñ 母音.

voyage *n.* ko⌝okai 航海; fu⌐natabi 船旅: go on a long voyage (*nagai kookai ni deru*) 長い航海に出る.

vulgar *adj.* zo⌐kuaku na 俗悪な; ge-

「hiˈñ na 下品な: a vulgar TV program (*zokuaku na terebi bañgumi*) 俗悪なテレビ番組 / vulgar language (*gehiñ na kotoba*) 下品な言葉.

vulnerable *adj.* kiˈzutsuki-yasuˈi 傷つきやすい; yoˈwaˈi 弱い: a vulnerable girl (*kizutsuki-yasui shoojo*) 傷つきやすい少女.

W

wade *vi.* aˈruˈite suˈsumu 歩いて進む ⓒ: wade across a stream (*nagare o aruite wataru*) 流れを歩いて渡る.

waffle *n.* waˈffuru ワッフル.

wage *n.* chiˈñgiñ 賃金; kyuˈuryoo 給料: He works for low wages. (*Kare wa hikui chiñgiñ de hataraite iru.*) 彼は低い賃金で働いている.

wagon *n.* 1 (used to carry food) waˈgoñ ワゴン.
2 (four-wheeled vehicle pulled by horses) niˈbaˈsha 荷馬車.

waist *n.* 1 (of a person) uˈeˈsuto ウエスト; koˈshi 腰: She has a slender waist. (*Kanojo wa hossori shita uesuto o shite iru.*) 彼女はほっそりしたウエストをしている. ★ Japanese 'koshi' refers to 'waist,' 'hips,' and 'lower back.'
2 (of a garment) uˈeˈsuto ウエスト.

wait *vi.* (... o) maˈtsu (...を)待つ ⓒ: Wait a moment, please. (*Chotto matte kudasai.*) ちょっと待ってください. / Are you waiting for someone? (*Dare-ka o matte iru no desu ka?*) だれかを待っているのですか.

waiter *n.* uˈeˈetaa ウエーター; boˈoi ボーイ; kyuˈuji 給仕: Waiter, please. (*Booi-sañ.*) ボーイさん.

waiting room *n.* maˈchiaˈishitsu 待合室.

waitress *n.* uˈeˈetoresu ウエートレス.

wake *vi.* meˈ ga saˈmeˈru 目が覚める ⓥ; oˈkiˈru 起きる ⓥ: I woke up early this morning. (*Watashi wa kesa hayaku me ga sameta.*) 私はけさ早く目が覚めた.
— *vt.* ... o oˈkoˈsu ...を起こす ⓒ; ... no meˈ o saˈmaˈsu ...の目を覚ます ⓒ: Please wake me up at six.

(*Roku-ji ni okoshite kudasai.*) 6時に起こしてください.

walk *vi.* 1 aˈruˈku 歩く ⓒ; aˈruˈite iku 歩いて行く ⓒ: He walked two kilometers. (*Kare wa ni-kiro aruita.*) 彼は2キロ歩いた. / I walk to school. (*Watashi wa aruite gakkoo e ikimasu.*) 私は歩いて学校へ行きます.
2 (take a walk) saˈñpo suru 散歩する ⓘ.
— *vt.* 1 (travel on foot) ... o aˈruˈku ...を歩く ⓒ; aˈruki-mawaˈru 歩き回る ⓒ: I walked the beach for hours. (*Watashi wa nañ-jikañ mo umibe o aruita.*) 私は何時間も海辺を歩いた.
2 (accompany) ... o oˈkuru ...を送る ⓒ: He walked her home. (*Kare wa kanojo o ie made okutta.*) 彼は彼女を家まで送った.
— *n.* 1 (stroll) saˈñpo 散歩: My grandfather usually goes out for a walk in the afternoon. (*Sofu wa taitee gogo sañpo ni dekakeru.*) 祖父はたいてい午後散歩に出かける.
2 (distance to walk) miˈchinori 道のり: It's a ten-minute walk from here to the station. (*Koko kara eki made wa aruite jup-puñ desu.*) ここから駅までは歩いて10分です.
3 (path) hoˈdoo 歩道; saˈñpoˈ-michi 散歩道; yuˈuhoˈdoo 遊歩道.
4 (manner of walking) aˈruki-kaˈta 歩き方; aˈruki-buri 歩き振り: I recognized him by his walk. (*Watashi wa aruki-kata de kare da to wakatta.*) 私は歩き方で彼だとわかった.

wall *n.* 1 (of a room) kaˈbe 壁: hang a calendar on the wall (*kabe ni kareñdaa oˈkakeru*) 壁にカレンダ-

をかける.

2 (outside) he⌐e 塀: The house has a brick wall around it. (*Sono ie wa mawari ni reṅga no hee ga aru.*) その家は周りにれんがの塀がある.

—— *vt.* (surround) ... o he⌐e de kakomu ...を塀で囲む ⓒ; ... ni he⌐e o megurasu ...に塀を巡らす ⓒ: The garden is walled in. (*Sono niwa wa hee de kakomarete iru.*) その庭は塀で囲まれている.

wallet *n.* sa⌐ifu 財布: My wallet was lifted in the train. (*Saifu o deṅsha no naka de surareta.*) 財布を電車の中ですられた.

walnut *n.* (nut) ku⌐rumi くるみ; (tree) ku⌐rumi no ki⌐ くるみの木.

waltz *n.* wa⌐rutsu ワルツ: dance a waltz (*warutsu o odoru*) ワルツを踊る.

wander *vi.* **1** (walk aimlessly) a⌐ruki-mawa⌐ru 歩き回る ⓒ; bu⌐ratsuku ぶらつく ⓒ: She wandered about the town to kill time. (*Kanojo wa jikaṅ o tsubusu tame ni machi o buratsuita.*) 彼女は時間をつぶすために町をぶらついた.

2 (go astray) ha⌐gure⌐ru はぐれる Ⓥ: He wandered away from his companions. (*Kare wa nakama kara hagurete shimatta.*) 彼は仲間からはぐれてしまった.

3 (move away) yo⌐komichi e sore⌐ru 横道へそれる Ⓥ: The speaker often wandered from the subject. (*Kooeṅsha wa shibashiba wadai kara yokomichi e soreta.*) 講演者はしばしば話題から横道へそれた.

want *vt.* **1** (want something) [with 1st and 2nd persons] ... ga ho⌐shi⌐i ...が欲しい; [with 1st person] ... o ku⌐dasa⌐i ...を下さい; [with 3rd person] ... o ho⌐shiga⌐ru ...を欲しがる ⓒ: I want a better seat. (*Motto yoi seki ga hoshii.*) もっと良い席が欲しい. / Do you want this book? (*Anata wa kono hoṅ ga hoshii desu ka?*) あなたはこの本が欲しいですか. / Please, I want five of these. (*Kore o itsutsu kudasai.*) これを五つ下さい. / The girl wants a doll for her birthday.

(*Sono oṅna-no-ko wa taṅjoobi ni niṅgyoo o hoshigatte iru.*) その女の子は誕生日に人形を欲しがっている.

2 (want to do) [with 1st and 2nd persons] ⟨verb⟩-tai ...たい; [with 3rd person] ⟨verb⟩-tagaru ...たがる ⓒ: I want to read a detective story. (*Suiri shoosetsu ga yomitai.*) 推理小説が読みたい. / Where do you want to go? (*Doko e ikitai desu ka?*) どこへ行きたいですか. / These days, many young people want to go abroad. (*Chikagoro wa oozee no wakamono ga gaikoku e ikitagaru.*) 近頃は大勢の若者が外国へ行きたがる.

3 (want someone to do) (... ni) ⟨verb⟩-te[de] ho⌐shi⌐i (...に)...て[で]欲しい, ⟨verb⟩-te[de] mo⌐raitai ...て[で]もらいたい: I want you to go shopping for me. (*Kimi ni kawari ni kaimono ni itte moraitai.*) 君に代わりに買い物に行ってもらいたい.

4 (want something done) ⟨verb⟩-te[de] ku⌐dasa⌐i ...て[で]ください: I want my hair washed and set. (*Kami o aratte setto shite kudasai.*) 髪を洗ってセットしてください.

5 (call) ... o yo⌐bu ...を呼ぶ ⓒ: "Mom, Dad wants you." (*"O-kaa-saṅ, O-toosaṅ ga yoṅde iru yo."*) 「お母さん, お父さんが呼んでいるよ」/ Somebody wants you on the phone. (*Anata ni deṅwa desu.*) あなたに電話です.

—— *n.* **1** (lack) fu⌐soku 不足; ke⌐tsuboo 欠乏: The tree is dying from want of water. (*Ki wa mizu ga fusoku shite karekakete iru.*) 木は水が不足して枯れかけている.

2 (need) hi⌐tsuyoo 必要; nyu⌐uyoo 入用: I am in want of money. (*Watashi wa o-kane o hitsuyoo to shite imasu.*) 私はお金を必要としています.

wanting *adj.* ... ni ta⌐rinai ...に足りない; ka⌐kete iru 欠けている: She is wanting in courtesy. (*Kanojo wa reegi ni kakete iru.*) 彼女は礼儀に欠けている.

war *n.* se⌐ńsoo 戦争: A war broke
out. (*Seńsoo ga hajimatta.*) 戦争が
始まった. / At that time Japan was
at war with China. (*Tooji Nippoń
wa Chuugoku to seńsoo chuu
datta.*) 当時日本は中国と戦争中だった.
/ World War II (*dai ni-ji sekai tai-
seń*) 第二次世界大戦.

warble *vi.* sa⌐ezu⌐ru さえずる Ⓒ: A
bird is warbling in a tree. (*Tori ga
ki de saezutte iru.*) 鳥が木でさえずっ
ている.

ward *n.* **1** (of a hospital) byo⌐otoo
病棟: a children's ward (*shooni
byootoo*) 小児病棟.
2 (division in an area) ku⌐ 区: Chi-
yoda Ward (*Chiyoda-ku*) 千代田区.
3 (person) hi-ho⌐go⌐sha 被保護者.

wardrobe *n.* **1** (closet) yo⌐ofuku-
da⌐ńsu 洋服だんす; i⌐shoo-da⌐ńsu 衣
装だんす.
2 (clothes) fu⌐ku⌐ 服; i⌐rui 衣類:
She has a large wardrobe. (*Kanojo
wa ishoo o takusań motte iru.*) 彼
女は衣装をたくさん持っている.

warehouse *n.* so⌐oko 倉庫; cho-
⌐zoojo 貯蔵所.

warfare *n.* se⌐ńsoo 戦争: nuclear
warfare (*kaku seńsoo*) 核戦争 /
guerilla warfare (*gerira-seń*) ゲリラ
戦.

warm *adj.* **1** (comfortably warm)
a⌐tataka⌐i 暖かい: It's getting warmer day by day. (*Hi ni hi ni atatakaku natte kite iru.*) 日に日に暖かく
なってきている.
2 (uncomfortably warm) a⌐tsu⌐i 暑
い: This room is too warm. (*Kono
heya wa atsui.*) この部屋は暑い.
3 (kind) a⌐tataka⌐i 温かい: He has a
warm heart. (*Kare wa atatakai kokoro o motte iru.*) 彼は温かい心を持
っている. / They gave her a warm
welcome. (*Kare-ra wa kanojo o
atatakaku mukaeta.*) 彼らは彼女を温
かく迎えた.
— *vt.* **1** (of things) ... o a⌐tata-
me⌐ru ...を暖[温]める Ⓥ; a⌐tata⌐kaku
suru 暖かくする Ⓣ: warm up a room
(*heya o atatameru*) 部屋を暖める /

I'll warm the soup. (*Watashi ga
suupu o atatamemashoo.*) 私がスープ
を温めましょう.
2 (of heart) ... o a⌐tatame⌐ru ...を温
める Ⓥ; a⌐tataka⌐i ki⌐mochi ni
saseru 温かい気持ちにさせる Ⓥ: It
warms my heart to hear her story.
(*Kanojo no hanashi o kiku to kokoro ga atatamaru.*) 彼女の話を聞く
と心が温まる.
— *vi.* a⌐tatama⌐ru 暖[温]まる Ⓒ;
a⌐tataka⌐ku naru 暖[温]かくなる Ⓒ:
The soup on the stove is warming.
(*Reńji ni kaketa suupu ga atata-
matte kita.*) レンジにかけたスープが温ま
ってきた

warmth *n.* **1** (of things) a⌐tatai⌐-
kasa 暖かさ: The warmth of the
room felt good. (*Heya no atata-
kasa ga kokochi yokatta.*) 部屋の暖
かさが心地よかった.
2 (of heart) o⌐moiyari 思いやり;
shi⌐ńsetsu 親切: He has no
warmth. (*Kare wa omoiyari ga nai.*)
彼は思いやりがない.

warn *vt.* **1** (caution) ... ni ke⌐ekoku
suru ...に警告する Ⓣ; chu⌐ui suru 注
意する Ⓣ: The police warned reckless drivers. (*Keesatsu wa muboo
na uńteńsha ni keekoku shita.*) 警
察は無謀な運転者に警告した.
2 (tell in advance) ... ni (... to) yo-
⌐koku suru ...に(...と)予告する Ⓣ:
The boss warned him that he
would be fired in a month. (*Jooshi
wa kare ni ikkagetsu-go ni kaiko
suru to yokoku shita.*) 上司は彼に1
か月後に解雇すると予告した.

warning *n.* ke⌐ekoku 警告; chu⌐ui
注意: I gave him a warning not to
go there. (*Watashi wa kare ni
soko e iku na to keekoku shita.*)
私は彼にそこへ行くなと警告した.

warrior *n.* bu⌐shi 武士; gu⌐ńjiń 軍
人.

wash *vt.* **1** (clean) ... o a⌐rau ...を
洗う Ⓒ: I washed my car clean.
(*Watashi wa kuruma o kiree ni
aratta.*) 私は車をきれいに洗った.
2 (of clothes) ... o se⌐ńtaku suru ...

を洗濯する ⚟; aˈrau 洗う ⚞: wash trousers (*zuboñ o señtaku suru*) ズボンを洗濯する.

3 (sweep) … o oˈshinagaˈsu …を押し流す ⚞: The bridge was washed away by the flood. (*Hashi ga koozui de oshinagasareta.*) 橋が洪水で押し流された.

4 (flow) … ni uˈchiyoseru …に打ち寄せる Ⓥ: Waves are washing the beach. (*Nami ga kishi ni uchiyosete iru.*) 波が岸に打ち寄せている.

— *vi.* **1** (clean) aˈrau 洗う ⚞: wash before meals (*shokuji no mae ni te o arau.*) 食事の前に手を洗う.

2 (can be washed) seˈñtaku ga kiku 洗濯がきく ⚞: This curtain washes well. (*Kono kaateñ wa señtaku ga kiku.*) このカーテンは洗濯がきく.

3 (of detergents) yoˈgore o otoˈsu 汚れを落とす ⚞: This detergent doesn't wash well. (*Kono señzai wa amari ochinai.*) この洗剤はあまり落ちない.

4 (do the laundry) seˈñtaku suru 洗濯する ⚟: Mr. Tanaka washes on Mondays. (*Tanaka-sañ wa getsuyoobi ni señtaku suru.*) 田中さんは月曜日に洗濯する.

— *n.* **1** (act of washing) aˈrau kotoˈ 洗うこと; (of clothes) seˈñtaku 洗濯: I gave my car a good wash. (*Watashi wa kuruma o yoku aratta.*) 私は車をよく洗った.

2 (laundry) seˈñtakumono 洗濯物: I have a big wash today. (*Kyoo wa señtakumono ga takusañ aru.*) 今日は洗濯物がたくさんある.

washing machine *n.* seˈñtakuˈki 洗濯機: wash in a washing machine (*señtakuki de arau*) 洗濯機で洗う.

washroom *n.* seˈñmeñjo 洗面所; teˈaˈrai 手洗い.

waste *vt.* … o muˈda ni suru …を無駄にする ⚟; roˈohi suru 浪費する ⚟: Don't waste money. (*O-kane o muda ni shite wa ikemaseñ.*) お金を無駄にしてはいけません.

— *vi.* **1** (spend carelessly) muˈda ni suru 無駄にする ⚟.

2 (lose strength) suˈijaku suru 衰弱する ⚟: He wasted away through an illness. (*Kare wa byooki no tame ni suijaku shita.*) 彼は病気のために衰弱した.

— *n.* **1** (meaningless use) muˈda 無駄; roˈohi 浪費: It's a waste of time. (*Sore wa jikañ no muda da.*) それは時間の無駄だ.

2 (refuse) haˈikiˈbutsu 廃棄物; (liquid) haˈieki 廃液: industrial waste (*sañgyoo haikibutsu*) 産業廃棄物.

wasteful *adj.* muˈda na 無駄な; fuˈkeˈezai na 不経済な: This method is wasteful. (*Kono hoohoo wa fukeezai da.*) この方法は不経済だ.

watch[1] *n.* (wristwatch) uˈdedoˈkee 腕時計; (pocket watch) kaˈichuudoˈkee 懐中時計: a watch shop (*tokee-teñ*) 時計店. ★ 'Clock' is also called '*tokee*.'

watch[2] *vt.* **1** (look at) … o miˈru …を見る Ⓥ: watch TV (*terebi o miru*) テレビを見る.

2 (keep watch) … o miˈharu …を見張る ⚞: Will you watch my bags while I go to make a phone call? (*Deñwa o kakete kuru aida, nimotsu o mihatte ite kuremaseñ ka?*) 電話をかけてくる間, 荷物を見張っていてくれませんか.

— *vi.* **1** (watch carefully) yoˈku miru よく見る Ⓥ: Watch while I write this kanji. (*Watashi ga kono kañji o kaku aida yoku mite i nasai.*) 私がこの漢字を書く間よく見ていなさい.

2 (be careful) ki ˈo tsukeˈru 気をつける Ⓥ; chuˈui suru 注意する ⚟: Watch when you cross the street. (*Michi o wataru toki wa ki ni tsuke nasai.*) 道を渡るときは気をつけなさい.

3 (await) (… o) maˈchikamaeˈru (…を)待ち構える Ⓥ: We were watching for an opportunity. (*Watashi-tachi wa chañsu o machikamaete ita.*) 私たちはチャンスを待ち構えていた.

watchful *adj.* yo「ojiñbuka」i 用心深い; yu「dañ no [ga] na」i 油断の[が]ない: watchful eyes (*yoojinbukai me*) 用心深い目.

water *n.* **1** (cold) mi「zu 水; (hot) (o)「yu」 (お)湯: Please give me a glass of water. (*Mizu o ip-pai kudasai.*) 水を1杯下さい. / The water is boiling. (*O-yu ga waite imasu.*) お湯が沸いています.

2 (in water) su「ichuu 水中: jump into the water (*suichuu ni tobikomu*) 水中に飛び込む.

3 (sea) u「mi 海; (lake) mi「zu」umi 湖; (river) ka「wa」 川.

4 (territorial waters) ryo「okai 領海: A ship of unknown nationality violated Japanese waters. (*Kokuseki fumee no fune ga Nihoñ no ryookai o shiñpañ shita.*) 国籍不明の船が日本の領海を侵犯した.

5 [compound words] -sui 水: soda water (*tañsañ-sui*) 炭酸水 / toilet water (*keshoo-sui*) 化粧水.

— *vt.* ... ni mi「zu o yaru ...に水をやる ⓒ: water the flowers (*hana ni mizu o yaru*) 花に水をやる.

waterfall *n.* ta「ki 滝.

waterproof *adj.* bo「osui no 防水の: This watch is waterproof. (*Kono udedokee wa boosui desu.*) この腕時計は防水です.

watt *n.* wa「tto ワット.

wave *n.* **1** (of water) na「mi」 波: The waves are high. (*Nami ga takai.*) 波が高い.

2 (of a hand) te「 o fu「ru koto」 手を振ること: She gave me a cheerful wave when she recognized me. (*Kanojo wa watashi ni ki ga tsuku to ureshi-soo ni te o futta.*) 彼女は私に気がつくとうれしそうに手を振った.

— *vi.* **1** (move a hand) te「 o fu「ru 手を振る ⓒ: When she saw me, she waved at me. (*Kanojo wa watashi o mite te o futta.*) 彼女は私を見て手を振った.

2 (move to and fro) yu「reru 揺れる Ⓥ; (of cloth) hi「ruga」eru 翻る ⓒ: The sheet on the washline waved in the wind. (*Monohoshi no shiitsu ga kaze ni hirugaette ita.*) 物干しのシーツが風に翻っていた.

— *vt.* **1** (hold, flag, etc.) ... o fu「ru ...を振る ⓒ: Children waved small flags as the procession went by. (*Kodomo-tachi wa gyooretsu ga toorisugiru toki kobata o futta.*) 子どもたちは行列が通り過ぎるとき小旗を振った.

2 (of greeting) ... ni te「 o fu「ru ...に手を振る ⓒ: He waved her good-bye. (*Kare wa kanojo ni te o futte wakare o tsugeta.*) 彼は彼女に手を振って別れを告げた.

waver *vi.* (be uncertain) ma「yo」u 迷う ⓒ; ta「mera」u ためらう ⓒ: He wavered in his judgment. (*Kare wa hañdañ ni mayotta.*) 彼は判断に迷った.

wax *n.* (beeswax) ro「o ろう; (polish) wa「kkusu ワックス.

way *n.* **1** (method) ho「ohoo 方法; ya「rikata やり方: Please tell me the best way to do this. (*Kore o yaru ichibañ yoi hoohoo o oshiete kudasai.*) これをやるいちばんよい方法を教えてください.

2 (direction) ho「okoo 方向: This way, please. (*Kochira e doozo.*) こちらへどうぞ. / He didn't know which way to go. (*Kare wa dotchi no hookoo e ikeba ii no ka wakaranakatta.*) 彼はどっちの方向へ行けばいいのかわからなかった.

3 (road) mi「chi 道: Will you tell me the way to the station? (*Eki e iku michi o oshiete kudasai.*) 駅へ行く道を教えてください.

4 (distance) mi「chinori 道のり; kyo「ri 距離: We still have quite a way to walk. (*Watashi-tachi wa mada kanari no michinori o arukanakereba naranai.*) 私たちはまだかなりの道のりを歩かなければならない.

5 (respect) te「ñ 点; me「ñ 面: His advice was helpful in many ways. (*Kare no adobaisu wa ooku no meñ de yaku ni tatta.*) 彼のアドバイスは多くの面で役に立った.

all the way *adv.* (from beginning to end) zu「tto ずっと: The train was crowded and I stood all the way to Tokyo. (*Ressha ga koňde ite, watashi wa Tookyoo made zutto tatte ita.*) 列車が込んでいて, 私は東京までずっと立っていた.

by the way *adv.* to「koro¹ de とこ ろで.

in the way *adv., adj.* ja「ma ni na¹tte (iru) じゃまになって(いる): You'll be in the way if you stand there. (*Soko ni tatsu to jama ni narimasu.*) そこに立つとじゃまになります.

on the way *adv., adj.* to「chuu (de) 途中(で): What landmarks are on the way? (*Tochuu no mejirushi wa naň desu ka?*) 途中の目印は何ですか.

we *pron.* wa「tashi¹-tachi 私たち; [formal] wa「reware われわれ. ★ Used mainly by men. Women use '*watashi-tachi*.'

weak *adj.* **1** (of a body, character, etc.) yo「wa¹i 弱い: My mother is physically weak. (*Haha wa karada ga yowai.*) 母は体が弱い / He is weak-willed so he gives up easily. (*Kare wa ishi ga yowai no de sugu akirameru.*) 彼は意志が弱いのですぐあきらめる.
2 (of knowledge, ability, etc.) (... ga) ni「gate na (…が)苦手な; (... ni) yo「wa¹i 弱い: He is weak in math. (*Kare wa suugaku ga nigate da.*) 彼は数学が苦手だ. / weak point (*jakuteň*) 弱点.

weaken *vt.* ... o yo「wame¹ru ...を 弱める Ⓥ; yo「waku suru 弱くする Ⓘ: The illness weakened him. (*Kare wa byooki de yowatta.*) 彼は病気で 弱った.
— *vi.* yo「waku naru 弱くなる Ⓒ.

weakness *n.* **1** (frailty) yo「wasa¹ 弱さ; yo「wa¹i ko「to¹ 弱いこと: His physical weakness was his parents' constant worry. (*Kare no karada ga yowai koto wa ryooshiň no shiňpai no tane datta.*) 彼の体が弱い ことは両親の心配の種だった.

2 (shortcoming) ja「kute¹ň 弱点; ta¹ňsho 短所; ke「tte¹ň 欠点: Everyone has weaknesses. (*Dare de mo jakuteň wa aru.*) だれでも弱点は ある.

wealth *n.* to「mi 富; za「isaň 財産: He aquired great wealth through land speculation. (*Kare wa tochi-tooki de ooki-na zaisaň o kizuita.*) 彼は土地投機で大きな財産を築いた.

wealthy *adj.* yu「ufuku na 裕福な; ka「nemochi no 金持ちの: He comes from a wealthy family. (*Kare wa yuufuku na iegara no de su.*) 彼 は裕福な家柄の出です.

weapon *n.* bu「ki 武器; he¹eki 兵 器: nuclear weapons (*kaku-heeki*) 核兵器 / conventional weapons (*tsuujoo-heeki*) 通常兵器.

wear *vt.* **1** (of clothes) ... o ki「te iru ...を着ている Ⓥ; (of shoes, trousers, skirt) ha「ite iru はいている Ⓥ; (of a hat) ka「bu¹tte iru かぶっている Ⓥ; (of glasses) ka「kete iru かけている Ⓥ; (of a necktie) shi「mete iru 締め ている Ⓥ; (of gloves, ring) ha「mete iru はめている Ⓥ; (of a scarf, watch) shi「te iru している Ⓥ; (of a ribbon, perfume) tsu「kete iru つけている Ⓥ: Miss Yamada was wearing a kimono. (*Yamada-saň wa kimono o kite ita.*) 山田さんは着物を着ていた.
2 (of a mustache) ... o ha「ya¹shite iru ...を生やしている Ⓥ; (of hair) yu「tte iru 結っている Ⓥ: Mr. Tanaka wears a mustache. (*Tanaka-saň wa kuchi hige o hayashite iru.*) 田中さ んは口ひげを生やしている. / My wife wears her hair short. (*Kanai wa kami o mijikaku shite iru.*) 家内は 髪を短くしている.
3 (of an expression) ... o shi「te iru ...をしている Ⓥ: His face wore a troubled look. (*Kare wa shiňpai-soo na kao o shite ita.*) 彼は心配そうな顔をし ていた
4 (make thin) ... o su「riherasu をす り減らす Ⓒ: The carpet is worn thin. (*Juutaň ga surihette usuku natte iru.*) じゅうたんがすり減って薄くな

っている.

— *vi.* **1** (last) moˈtsu もつ C: This cloth will wear for years. (*Kono kiji wa nañ-neñ mo motsu deshoo*.) この生地は何年ももつでしょう.
2 (become worn) suˈriheru すり減る C; (of cloth) suˈrikireru すり切れる V: The heels of these shoes are worn down. (*Kono kutsu wa kakato ga surihette iru*.) この靴はかかとがすり減っている.
— *n.* **1** (use of clothing) chaˈkuyoo 着用: clothes for everyday wear (*fudañ-gi*) ふだん着.
2 (clothes) iˈrui 衣類; iˈfuku 衣服: men's [ladies'] wear (*shiñshi [fujiñ] fuku*) 紳士[婦人]服.
3 (damage) suˈrikire すり切れ; (clothes) kiˈfurushi 着古し: The coat showed signs of wear. (*Sono kooto wa kifurushita ato ga atta*.) そのコートは着古した跡があった.

weary *adj.* **1** (tired) tsuˈkaˈreta 疲れた; tsuˈkaˈrete iru 疲れている: I was weary from the long walk. (*Nagai aida aruita no de tsukaremashita*.) 長い間歩いたので疲れました.
2 (bored) aˈkiaˈki shite (iru) 飽き飽きして(いる); uˈñzaˈri shite (iru) うんざりして(いる): I'm weary of sitting at home. (*Watashi wa ie ni iru no wa uñzari da*.) 私は家にいるのはうんざりだ.

weather *n.* teˈñki 天気; teˈñkoo 天候: How is the weather? (*O-teñki wa doo desu ka?*) お天気はどうですか. / It's nice weather, isn't it? (*Ii o-teñki desu ne*.) いいお天気ですね.

weatherman *n.* teˈñkiyohoˈokañ 天気予報官; kiˈshoo yohoˈoshi 気象予報士.

weave *vt.* ... o oˈru ...を織る C: She is weaving a rug. (*Kanojo wa juutañ o otte iru*.) 彼女はじゅうたんを織っている.

wedding *n.* keˈkkoˈñshiki 結婚式: I was invited to my cousin's wedding. (*Watashi wa itoko no kekkoñshiki ni shootai sareta*.) 私はいとこの結婚式に招待された.

wedge *n.* kuˈsabi くさび: drive a wedge into a log (*maruta ni kusabi o uchikomu*) 丸太にくさびを打ち込む.

Wednesday *n.* suˈiyoˈo(bi) 水曜(日).

weed *n.* zaˈssoo 雑草: pull weeds (*zassoo o nuku*) 雑草を抜く.

week *n.* **1** shuˈu 週: last week (*señshuu*) 先週 / this week (*koñshuu*) 今週 / next week (*raishuu*) 来週/ the week after next (*saraishuu*) 再来週 / every week (*maishuu*) 毎週 / How many Japanese lessons do you take a week? (*Shuu ni nañ-do Nihoñgo no ressuñ o ukemasu ka?*) 週に何度日本語のレッスンを受けますか.
2 iˈs-shuukañ 1週間: two weeks (*ni-shuukañ*) 2週間 / I haven't seen him for weeks. (*Watashi wa nañ-shuukañ mo kare ni atte imaseñ*.) 私は何週間も彼に会っていません.

weekday *n.* heˈejitsu 平日; uˈiˈikudee ウイークデー: I am very busy on weekdays. (*Watashi wa heejitsu wa hijoo ni isogashii*.) 私は平日は非常に忙しい.

weekend *n.* shuˈumatsu 週末: We went skiing over the weekend. (*Watashi-tachi wa shuumatsu ni sukii ni ikimashita*.) 私たちは週末にスキーに行きました.

weekly *adj.* (every week) maˈishuu no 毎週の; (once a week) shuˈu iˈkkaˈi no 週1回の; (published once a week) shuˈukañ no 週刊の: weekly wages (*shuukyuu*) 週給 / a weekly magazine (*shuukañshi*) 週刊誌.
— *n.* (magazine) shuˈukaˈñshi 週刊誌; (newspaper) shuˈukaˈñshi 週刊紙.

weep *vi.* naˈku 泣く C: She wept at the news. (*Kanojo wa sono shirase o kiite naita*.) 彼女はその知らせを聞いて泣いた.

weigh *vt.* ... no oˈmosa o hakaˈru ...の重さを量る C: weigh a parcel (*kozutsumi no omosa o hakaru*) 小包の重さを量る / I weighed myself. (*Jibuñ no taijuu o hakatta*.) 自分の

体重を量った.

— *vi.* oˈmosa ga ... aˈru 重さが…ある C: "How much do you weigh?" "About 50 kilograms." (*Taijuu wa dono kurai arimasu ka?* "*Gojuk-kiro kurai desu.*") 「体重はどのくらいありますか」「50 キロくらいです」

weight *n.* 1 (things) oˈmosa 重さ; (people) taˈijuu 体重: gain [lose] weight (*taijuu ga fueru* [*heru*]) 体重が増える[減る].

2 (burden) oˈmoni 重荷; juˈuatsu 重圧: That's a real weight off my mind. (*Sore de watashi no kokoro no omoni mo toreta.*) それで私の心の重荷もとれた.

welcome *int.* yoˈokoso ようこそ: Welcome to Japan! (*Nihoñ e yookoso.*) 日本へようこそ.

— *vt.* ... o kaˈñgee suru …を歓迎する ①: They welcomed the guest. (*Kare-wa kyaku o kañgee shita.*) 彼らは客を歓迎した.

— *adj.* kaˈñgee sareru 歓迎される; yoˈrokobashiˈi 喜ばしい: a welcome guest (*kañgee sareru o-kyaku*) 歓迎されるお客 / welcome news (*yorokobashii nyuusu*) 喜ばしいニュース.

— *n.* kaˈñgee 歓迎: They gave their guest a warm welcome. (*Kare-wa o-kyaku o atatakaku mukaeta.*) 彼らはお客を温かく迎えた.

You are welcome. Doˈo iˈtashimaˈshite. どういたしまして: "Thank you very much." "You're welcome." (*"Arigatoo gozaimasu." "Doo itashimashite."*) 「ありがとうございます」「どういたしまして」

welfare *n.* fuˈkuˈshi 福祉: promote welfare (*fukushi o zooshiñ suru*) 福祉を増進する / welfare work (*fukushi-jigyoo*) 福祉事業 / social welfare (*shakai-fukushi*) 社会福祉.

well[1] *adv.* 1 (skillfully) uˈmaˈku うまく; joˈozuˈni 上手に: sing a song well (*uta o umaku utau*) 歌をうまく歌う.

2 (satisfactorily) yoˈku よく; uˈmaku うまく: Well done! (*Yoku yatta.*) よくやった. / The shutter of my cam-

era doesn't work well. (*Kamera no shattaa ga umaku ugokanai.*) カメラのシャッターがうまく動かない.

3 (thoroughly) yoˈku よく; juˈubuˈin ni 十分に: I know her well. (*Watashi wa kanojo o yoku shitte imasu.*) 私は彼女をよく知っています.

4 (much) kaˈnari かなり; juˈubuˈin ni 十分に: He is well over sixty. (*Kare wa rokujus-sai o kanari koete iru.*) 彼は 60 歳をかなり越えている.

... as well *adv.* soˈno ue ... mo その上…も: He speaks Japanese, and Chinese as well. (*Kare wa Nihoñgo o hanasemasu shi, Chuugokugo mo hanasemasu.*) 彼は日本語を話せますし, 中国語も話せます.

may as well do ⟨verb⟩-te[de] mo iˈi daroo …て[で]もいいだろう: You may as well know the truth. (*Shiñjitsu o shitte oite mo ii daroo.*) 真実を知っておいてもいいだろう.

may well do ... no mo moˈttoˈmo da …のももっともだ: He may well think so. (*Kare ga soo omou no mo mottomo da.*) 彼がそう思うのももっともだ.

— *adj.* 1 (healthy) keˈñkoo na 健康な; geˈñki na 元気な: My family are well. (*Kazoku wa miñna geñki desu.*) 家族はみんな元気です. / I don't feel well. (*Kibuñ ga yoku arimaseñ.*) 気分がよくありません.

2 (good) moˈoshibuñ naˈi 申し分ない; uˈmaku iˈtte iru うまくいっている: All's well. (*Bañji mooshibuñ nai.*) 万事申し分ない.

— *int.* 1 (used in reply) soˈo desu ne. そうですね.; Eˈe maa. ええま.

2 (to change the subject) toˈkoroˈde ところで; saˈte さて.

well[2] *n.* iˈdo 井戸: draw water from a well (*ido kara mizu o kumu*) 井戸から水をくむ.

well-known *adj.* yuˈumee na 有名な; yoˈku shiˈrarete iru よく知られている: This restaurant is best-known for its good wine. (*Kono resutorañ wa waiñ ga yoi no de*

ichibañ yoku shirarete imasu.) この
レストランはワインがよいのでいちばんよく知
られています.

west *n.* **1** (direction) ni⌐shi 西:
The wind is blowing from the
west. (*Kaze wa nishi kara fuite
imasu.*) 風は西から吹いています.
2 (Occident) se⌐eyoo 西洋.
— *adj.* ni⌐shi no 西の: a west wind
(*nishi kaze*) 西風.
— *adv.* ni⌐shi ni [e] 西に[へ]: This
room faces west. (*Kono heya wa
nishi-muki desu.*) この部屋は西向き
です.

western *adj.* ni⌐shi no 西の; (Occi-
dental) se⌐eyoo no 西洋の: the
western sky (*nishi no sora*) 西の空 /
Western countries (*seeyoo shokoku*) 西洋諸国.

westward *adv.* ni⌐shi no ho⌐o e
西の方へ: The ship turned westward. (*Fune wa nishi no hoo e
mukatta.*) 船は西の方へ向かった.
— *adj.* ni⌐shi ni mukau 西に向かう:
a westward voyage (*nishi ni mukau kookai*) 西に向かう航海.

wet *adj.* **1** (covered with liquid)
nu⌐reta ぬれた; nu⌐rete iru ぬれている;
shi⌐metta 湿った; shi⌐mette iru 湿っ
ている: a wet towel (*nureta taoru*) ぬ
れたタオル / I got wet in the rain.
(*Ame de nureta.*) 雨でぬれた. / Wet
Paint. (*Peñki nuritate.*) ペンキ塗り立
て.
2 (rainy) a⌐me⌐furi no 雨降りの;
a⌐me no [ga] ooi 雨の[が]多い: wet
weather (*ame moyoo no teñki*) 雨
模様の天気 / the wet season (*uki*)
雨季.
— *vt.* ... o nu⌐rasu ...をぬらす ⓒ;
shi⌐meraseru 湿らせる Ⓥ: He wet
the towel with water. (*Kare wa
taoru o mizu de shimeraseta.*) 彼は
タオルを水で湿らせた.

whale *n.* ku⌐jira 鯨.

what¹ *pron.* **1** (inquiry) na⌐ni 何;
(things) do⌐ñna mo⌐no⌐ どんなもの;
(state) do⌐ñna ko⌐to⌐ どんなこと:
What is this? (*Kore wa nañ desu
ka?*) これは何ですか. / What is

'goboo'? (*'Goboo' to wa doñna
mono desu ka?*) 「ごぼう」とはどんな
ものですか. / What did he talk
about? (*Kare wa doñna koto o
hanashimashita ka?*) 彼はどんなこと
を話しましたか. / What does this
mean? (*Kore wa doo iu imi desu
ka?*) これはどういう意味ですか.
2 (of money) i⌐kura いくら: What is
the fee per day? (*Ichi-nichi no ryookiñ wa ikura desu ka?*) 一日の料金
はいくらですか. / What is the dollar
rate? (*Doru no reeto wa ikura
desu ka?*) ドルのレートはいくらですか.

What about ...? ... wa do⌐o
desu ka? ...はどうですか: What about
a drink? (*Ippai doo desu ka?*) 一杯
どうですか. / What about going to a
movie? (*Eega ni iku no wa doo
desu ka?*) 映画に行くのはどうですか.
— *adj.* **1** [question] na⌐ñ no 何の;
na⌐ñ to iu という; do⌐ñna どんな;
na⌐ni [na⌐ñ]- 何: What time is it?
(*Nañ-ji desu ka?*) 何時ですか. /
What day of the week is it today?
(*Kyoo wa nañ-yoobi desu ka?*) 今
日は何曜日ですか. / What flowers do
you like? (*Anata wa doñna hana
ga suki desu ka?*) あなたはどんな花が
好きですか.
2 [exclamation] na⌐ñte 何て; na⌐ñ-
to 何と: What a cute baby! (*Nañte
kawaii aka-chañ deshoo!*) 何てかわ
いい赤ちゃんでしょう!
— *adv.* do⌐re hodo どれほど; do⌐no
te⌐edo どの程度: What does it matter? (*Sore ga dore hodo moñdai ni
naru no ka?*) それがどれほど問題になる
のか.
— *int.* **1** [used when a person
could not catch what another said]
e⌐ えっ; na⌐ni 何.
2 [shows surprise] na⌐ñ datte 何だ
って; na⌐ni 何.

what² *rel. pron.* ... ko⌐to⌐ ...こと; ...
mo⌐no⌐ ...もの: What he said is not
true. (*Kare ga itta koto wa hoñtoo
de wa arimaseñ.*) 彼が言ったことは本
当ではありません. / The girl showed
her mother what her grandmother

gave her. (*Sono oñna-no-ko wa sobo ga kureta mono o hahaoya ni miseta.*) その女の子は祖母がくれたものを母親に見せた.

whatever *rel. pron.* **1** ... mo¯no [ko¯to] wa na¯ñ de mo ...もの[こと]は何でも: You may do whatever you like. (*Anata wa nañ de mo suki na koto o shite kamaimaseñ.*) あなたは何でも好きなことをしてかまいません.

2 (no matter what) na¯ni ga ⟨verb⟩-te[de] mo 何が...て[で]も: Whatever happens, don't give up. (*Nani ga atte mo, akiramete wa ikenai.*) 何があってもあきらめてはいけない.

— *rel. adj.* **1** do¯ñna ... de mo どんな...でも: You may read whatever book you like. (*Kimi ga suki na hoñ nara doñna hoñ de mo yoñde yoi.*) 君が好きな本ならどんな本でも読んでよい.

2 (no matter what) do¯ñna ⟨verb⟩-(y)oo to mo どんな...(よ)うとも: Whatever results follow, I will go. (*Doñna kekka ni naroo to mo, watashi wa ikimasu.*) どんな結果になろうとも, 私は行きます.

wheat *n.* ko¯mu¯gi 小麦: Bread is made from wheat. (*Pañ wa ko-mugi kara tsukurareru.*) パンは小麦から作られる.

wheel *n.* **1** sha¯riñ 車輪; ku¯ruma 車: The wheel of my bicycle came off. (*Watashi no jiteñsha no sha-riñ ga hazurete shimatta.*) 私の自転車の車輪がはずれてしまった.

2 (steering wheel) ha¯ñdoru ハンドル: take the wheel of a car (*kuruma no hañdoru o nigiru*) 車のハンドルを握る.

— *vi.* **1** (turn around) ku¯ruri to mu¯ki o ka¯eru くるりと向きを変える V: He wheeled around and looked at me. 彼はくるりと向きを変えて私を見た.

2 (move in circles) se¯ñkai suru 旋回する ①: Gulls are wheeling around over the sea. (*Kamome ga umi no ue o señkai shite iru.*) カモメが海の上を旋回している.

— *vt.* (push) ... o o¯su ...を押す C; (pull) hi¯ku 引く C: She wheeled the baby carriage around the park. (*Kanojo wa kooeñ de ubaguruma o oshite aruita.*) 彼女は公園で乳母車を押して歩いた.

when[1] *adv.* i¯tsu いつ: When did you come to Japan? (*Anata wa itsu Nihoñ e koraremashita ka?*) あなたはいつ日本へ来られたのですか. / I don't know when she will get back. (*Kanojo ga itsu kaette kuru ka wakarimaseñ.*) 彼女がいつ帰ってくるかわかりません.

— *pron.* i¯tsu いつ: Untill when are you going to stay here? (*Itsu made koko ni irasshaimasu ka?*) いつまでここにいらっしゃいますか.

when[2] *conj.* **1** ... to¯ki ...とき: When it rains, I usually stay at home. (*Ame no toki wa taitei uchi ni imasu.*) 雨のときはたいてい家にいます. / I was reading a book when he came in. (*Kare ga haitte kita toki, watashi wa hoñ o yoñde ita.*) 彼が入ってきたとき, 私は本を読んでいた.

2 (whenever) ... toki wa i¯tsu-mo ...ときはいつも: He calls on me when he comes to Osaka. (*Kare wa Oo-saka ni kuru toki wa itsu-mo wata-shi o tazunete kimasu.*) 彼は大阪に来るときはいつも私を訪ねて来ます.

when[3] *rel. adv.* ... to¯ki ...時: Monday is when I'm busiest. (*Getsu-yoobi wa watashi ga ichibañ iso-gashii toki desu.*) 月曜日は私がいちばん忙しい時です.

whenever *conj.* **1** ... toki wa i¯tsu-mo ...ときはいつも: Whenever he goes for a walk he takes his dog with him. (*Kare wa sañpo ni deka-keru toki wa itsu-mo inu o tsurete ikimasu.*) 彼は散歩に出かけるときはいつも犬を連れて行きます.

2 (no matter when) i¯tsu ⟨verb⟩-te [de] mo いつ ...て[で]も: Whenever I phone him, he is out. (*Watashi ga itsu deñwa o shite mo, kare wa dekakete iru.*) 私がいつ電話をしても, 彼は出かけている.

where[1] *adv.* do⌐ko どこ; [polite] do⌐chira どちら: Where is the post office? (*Yuubiñkyoku wa doko desu ka?*) 郵便局はどこですか。/ Where do you live? (*Dochira ni o-sumai desu ka?*) どちらにお住まいですか。/ Where can I change money? (*O-kane wa doko de kaeraremasu ka?*) お金はどこで換えられますか。/ I don't know where she went. (*Watashi wa kanojo ga doko e itta no ka shirimaseñ.*) 私は彼女がどこへ行ったのか知りません。

— *pron.* do⌐ko どこ; [polite] do⌐chira どちら: Where are you from? (*Shusshiñchi wa dochira desu ka?*) 出身地はどちらですか。

where[2] *rel. adv.* ... to⌐koro⌐ …ところ: This is where we keep towels. (*Koko ga taoru o shimatte oku tokoro desu.*) ここがタオルをしまっておくところです。/ This is the town where I was born. (*Koko ga watashi no umareta machi desu.*) ここが私の生まれた町です。

— *conj.* ... to⌐koro⌐ ni [e, o] …所に[へ, を]: Please stay where you are. (*Ima iru tokoro ni ite kudasai.*) 今いる所にいてください。/ I will go where you go. (*Watashi wa anata no iku tokoro e ikimasu.*) 私はあなたの行く所へ行きます。

wherever *conj.* **1** ... to⌐koro⌐ wa do⌐ko de mo …所はどこでも: Please sit wherever you like. (*Doko de mo o-suki na tokoro ni o-suwari kudasai.*) どこでもお好きな所にお座りください。

2 (no matter where) ta⌐toe do⌐ko ni [e] <verb>-te[de] mo たとえどこに[へ]…て[で]も: Wherever you go, please write to us. (*Tatoe doko e itte mo, tegami o kudasai.*) たとえどこへ行っても、手紙を下さい。

whether *conj.* **1** [expressing doubt] ... ka do⌐o ka …かどうか: I don't know whether that is true or not. (*Watashi wa sore ga hoñtoo ka doo ka shirimaseñ.*) 私はそれが本当かどうか知りません。

2 (no matter) <verb>-te[de] mo …て[で]も: Whether he comes or not, the result will be the same. (*Kare ga kite mo konakute mo, kekka wa onaji deshoo.*) 彼が来ても来なくても、結果は同じでしょう。

which *pron.* **1** [selection from two things] do⌐chira どちら: Which way shall we go? (*Dochira no michi o ikimasu ka?*) どちらの道を行きますか。/ Which do you like better, coffee or tea? (*Koohii to koocha to dochira ga suki desu ka?*) コーヒーと紅茶とどちらが好きですか。

2 [selection of one out of three or more things] do⌐re どれ: Which of these flowers do you like best? (*Kore-ra no hana no uchi dore ga ichibañ suki desu ka?*) これらの花のうちどれがいちばん好きですか。

— *adj.* do⌐chira no どちらの; do⌐no どの: Which umbrella is yours? (*Dono kasa ga anata no desu ka?*) どの傘があなたのですか。

whichever *pron.* **1** (of things) do⌐chira de mo どちらでも; do⌐re de mo どれでも: Take whichever you like. (*Dochira de mo suki na hoo o tori nasai.*) どちらでも好きな方を取りなさい。

2 (of people) da⌐re de mo だれでも: Whichever of you finishes first will receive a prize. (*Dare de mo it-too ni natta hito wa shoohiñ ga moraemasu.*) だれでも1等になった人は賞品がもらえます。

3 (no matter which) do⌐chira ga [o, ni] <verb>-te[de] mo どちらが[を, に]…て[で]も: Whichever you choose, there won't be much difference. (*Dochira o erañde mo amari chigai wa nai deshoo.*) どちらを選んでもあまり違いはないでしょう。

— *adj.* **1** do⌐chira no ... de mo どちらの…でも; do⌐no ... de mo どの…でも: Take whichever book you like. (*Dochira de mo anata no suki na hoñ o tori nasai.*) どちらでもあなたの好きな本を取りなさい。

2 (no matter which) do⌐chira ga

〈verb〉-te[de] mo どちらが…て[で]も : Whichever side wins, I don't care. (*Dochira no gawa ga katte mo, watashi wa kamaimaseñ.*) どちらの側が勝っても私はかまいません.

while *conj.* **1** (during the time) … a⌐ida …間 : Did anyone call while I was away? (*Watashi ga inai aida ni dare-ka kara deñwa ga arimashita ka?*) 私がいない間にだれかから電話がありましたか.
2 (on the other hand) i⌐ppo˥o de wa 一方では : The book was scorned by critics, while it was applauded by the public. (*Sono hoñ wa hihyooka ni keebetsu sareta ga, ippoo de wa taishuu ni kañgee sareta.*) その本は批評家に軽蔑されたが、一方では大衆に歓迎された.
3 (although) … ga …が : While I understand what you say, I can't agree with your plan. (*Anata no ossharu koto wa mitomemasu ga, anata no keekaku ni wa sañsee dekimaseñ.*) あなたのおっしゃることは認めますが、あなたの計画には賛成できません.

whim *n.* ki⌐magure 気まぐれ; mu⌐raki むら気 : full of whims (*kimagure na*) 気まぐれな.

whip *n.* mu˥chi むち : beat a person with a whip (*hito o muchi de utsu*) 人をむちで打つ.
— *vt.* … o mu˥chi de utsu …をむちで打つ C : He whipped the horse to make it run faster. (*Kare wa uma ga motto hayaku hashiru yoo ni muchi de utta.*) 彼は馬がもっと早く走るようにむちで打った.

whirl *vi.* gu⌐ruguru ma˥waru ぐるぐる回る C ; u⌐zuma˥ku 渦巻く C : Scraps of paper whirled in the wind. (*Kamikire ga kaze de guruguru mawatte ita.*) 紙切れが風でぐるぐる回っていた.
— *vt.* … o gu⌐ruguru ma˥wasu …をぐるぐる回す C ; u⌐zu o ma˥kaseru 渦を巻かせる V : The wind whirled the fallen leaves about. (*Kaze ga ochiba o fuite uzu o makaseta.*) 風が落ち葉を吹いて渦を巻かせた.

— *n.* (spin) ka⌐iteñ 回転, señkai 旋回.

whisk(e)y *n.* u⌐iskii ウイスキー : whiskey and water (*uisukii no mizuwari*) ウイスキーの水割り / whiskey and soda (*haibooru*) ハイボール.

whisper *vi.* sa⌐saya˥ku ささやく C : She whispered in his ear. (*Kanojo wa kare no mimi ni sasayaita.*) 彼女は彼の耳にささやいた.
— *vt.* … o sa⌐saya˥ku …をささやく C : She whispered a word or two to me. (*Kanojo wa watashi ni hitokoto futakoto sasayaita.*) 彼女は私に一言二言ささやいた.
— *n.* sa⌐sayaki ささやき; ko⌐goe 小声.

whistle *vi.* **1** (make a sound using the lips) ku⌐chibue o fu˥ku 口笛を吹く C : The boy whistled to his dog. (*Sono otoko-no-ko wa inu ni mukatte kuchibue o fuita.*) その男の子は犬に向かって口笛を吹いた.
2 (blow a whistle) fu⌐e o narasu 笛を鳴らす C : The policeman whistled for the car to stop. (*Keekañ wa fue o narashite sono kuruma ni tomare to meejita.*) 警官は笛を鳴らしてその車に止まれと命じた.
— *vt.* … o ku⌐chibue de fu˥ku …を口笛で吹く C : He was whistling a march. (*Kare wa kuchibue de maachi o fuite ita.*) 彼は口笛でマーチを吹いていた.
— *n.* **1** (musical instrument) fu⌐e 笛; (used for warning) ke⌐feteki 警笛; (of a steam train, ship, etc.) ki⌐teki 汽笛.
2 (the sound made by the lips) ku⌐chibue 口笛.

white *adj.* **1** (as opposed to black) shi⌐ro˥i 白い; (of hair) shi⌐raga no 白髪の: white clouds (*shiroi kumo*) 白い雲 / His hair turned white. (*Kare no kami wa shiroku natta.*) 彼の髪は白くなった.
2 (pale) a⌐ojiro˥i 青白い; (bloodless) chi⌐no ke no na˥i 血の気のない: Her face turned white at the news. (*Kanojo wa sono shirase o kiite*

massao ni natta.) 彼女はその知らせを
聞いて真っ青になった.
3 (race) ha「kujiñ 白 白人の; shi「ro」i
白い.
— *n.* **1** (color) shi「ro 白; ha「ku-
shoku 白色.
2 (race) ha「kujiñ 白人.
whiteness *n.* shi「rosa 白さ.
who *pron.* da「re だれ; [polite] do」-
nata どなた: Who is it? (*Donata
desu ka?*) どなたですか. / Who said
so? (*Dare ga soo iimashita ka?*) だ
れがそう言いましたか. / Who is it you
wish to see? (*Dare ni aitai no desu
ka?*) だれに会いたいのですか.
whoever *pron.* **1** (anyone who)
da「re de mo だれでも: Whoever
comes will be welcome. (*Dare de
mo kuru hito wa kañgee shimasu.*)
だれでも来る人は歓迎します.
2 (no matter who) da「re ga 〈verb〉-
te[de] mo だれが…て[で]も: Whoever
says so, I won't change my mind.
(*Dare ga soo itte mo watashi wa
kañgae o kaeru tsumori wa arimaseñ.*) だれがそう言っても私は考えを変え
るつもりはありません.
whole *adj.* **1** (entire) ze「ñtai no 全
体の; (everything) ze「ñbu no 全部
の; ze「ñ- 全: the whole world (*zeñ-
sekai*) 全世界 / the whole class
(*kurasu zeñ-iñ*) クラス全員 / He
devoted his whole life to education.
(*Kare wa isshoo o kyooiku ni sasageta.*) 彼は一生を教育に捧げた.
2 (as much as) ma「ru ... 丸…: a
whole year (*maru ichi-ñeñ*) 丸1年
/ three whole days (*maru mikka-
kañ*) 丸3日間.
— *n.* ze「ñtai 全体; ze「ñbu 全部:
the whole of Japan (*Nihoñ zeñtai*)
日本全体.
on the whole *adv.* ze「ñtai to
shite 全体として: Everything went
well on the whole. (*Zeñtai to shite
subete umaku itta.*) 全体としてすべて
うまくいった.
wholesale *adj.* o「roshiuri no 卸し
売りの: a wholesale dealer (*oroshi-
uri gyoosha*) 卸売業者.

— *n.* o「roshi」uri 卸し売り.
wholesome *adj.* ke「ñkoo ni yo」i
健康によい: wholesome exercise
(*keñkoo ni yoi uñdoo*) 健康によい運
動.
wholly *adv.* su「kka」ri すっかり; ma「t-
taku まったく; ka「ñzeñ ni 完全に:
His suggestion was wholly unac-
ceptable. (*Kare no teeañ wa mattaku ukeirerarenai mono datta.*) 彼
の提案はまったく受け入れられないものだっ
た.
whom *pron.* da「re o [ni] だれを[に];
[polite] do」nata o [ni] どなたを[に]:
Whom did you choose captain?
(*Anata-tachi wa dare o kyaputeñ
ni erabimashita ka?*) あなたたちはだれ
をキャプテンに選びましたか. / Whom
did you meet? (*Anata wa dare ni
aimashita ka?*) あなたはだれに会いまし
たか.
whose *pron.* da「re no だれの;
[polite] do」nata no どなたの: Whose
bag is this? (*Kore wa dare no
kabañ desu ka?*) これはだれのかばんで
すか. / Whose is this? (*Kore wa
dare no desu ka?*) これはだれのですか.
why *adv.* na「ze なぜ; do」o-shite どう
して: Why aren't the subways running? (*Naze chikatetsu wa ugoite
inai no desu ka?*) なぜ地下鉄は動いて
いないのですか. / Tell me why he did
such a thing. (*Kare ga doo-shite
añna koto o shita no ka oshiete
kudasai.*) 彼がどうしてあんなことをしたの
か教えてください.
Why don't ...? 〈verb〉-maseñ
ka? ませんか: Why don't we go for a
walk? (*Sañpo ni ikimaseñ ka?*) 散
歩に行きませんか. / Why don't you
come and see me next Sunday?
(*Koñdo no nichiyoobi ni asobi ni
kimaseñ ka?*) 今度の日曜日に遊びに
来ませんか.
Why not? do」o shite 〈verb〉-nai
no ka? どうして…ないのか: " I am not
going to the pary." "Why not?"
(*"Watashi wa paatii e ikimaseñ."
"Doo shite ikanai no?"*)「私はパーテ
ィーへ行きません」「どうして行かないの」

— *rel. adv.* ri¹yuu 理由; wa¹ke 訳: This is why he came. (*Kore ga kare ga kita riyuu desu.*) これが彼が来た理由です.

— *int.* o¹ya おや; ma¹a まあ.

why ever *adv.* i¹ttai na¹ze [do¹o-shite] いったいなぜ[どうして]: Why ever did she say such a thing? (*Ittai naze kanojo wa soñna koto o itta no desu ka?*) いったいなぜ彼女はそんなことを言ったのですか.

wicked *adj.* wa¹ru¹i 悪い; ja¹aku na 邪悪な: a wicked man (*akuniñ*) 悪人 / a wicked deed (*akuji*) 悪事.

wicket *n.* (of a station) ka¹isatsu¹-guchi 改札口; (of a ticket office) ma¹do¹guchi 窓口.

wide *adj.* **1** (broad) hi¹ro¹i 広い: a wide road (*hiroi michi*) 広い道 / wide knowledge (*hiroi chishiki*) 広い知識. ★ Japanese '*hiroi*' also means 'large in area.'

2 [used with measurements] ha¹ba ga ... (a¹ru) 幅が...(ある): "How wide is the doorway?" "It's 70 cm wide." (*"Toguchi no haba wa dono kurai arimasu ka?" "Haba wa nanajus-señchi arimasu."*) 「戸口の幅はどのくらいありますか」「幅は70センチあります」

3 (of eyes, doors, etc.) o¹okiku hi¹ra¹ita [hi¹ra¹ite iru] 大きく開いた[開いている]: The child stared with wide eyes. (*Sono kodomo wa me o maruku shite mitsumeta.*) その子どもは目を丸くして見つめた. / He opened the window wide. (*Kare wa mado o ookiku aketa.*) 彼は窓を大きく開けた.

— *adv.* hi¹roku 広く; o¹okiku hi¹ra¹ite (iru) 大きく開いて(いる): The door was wide open. (*Doa wa ookiku hiraite ita.*) ドアは大きく開いていた.

widely *adv.* **1** (to a wide extent) hi¹roku 広く; ko¹oha¹ñi ni 広範囲に: He has traveled widely. (*Kare wa hiroku achikochi ryokoo shita.*) 彼は広くあちこち旅行した.

2 (greatly) o¹okiku 大きく; o¹oi ni

大いに; hi¹joo ni 非常に: differ widely (*ooi ni kotonaru*) 大いに異なる.

widen *vt.* ... o hi¹roku suru 広くする □: The city is planning to widen the road. (*Shi wa sono michi o hiroku suru keekaku o shite iru.*) 市はその道を広くする計画をしている.

— *vi.* hi¹roku naru 広くなる ©: The river widens up ahead. (*Kawa wa kono saki de hiroku natte imasu.*) 川はこの先で広くなっています.

widespread *adj.* hi¹roma¹tta 広まった; hi¹roma¹tte iru 広まっている; fu¹kyuu shita [shite iru] 普及した[している]: Fear of the disease is widespread among the people. (*Sono byooki ni taisuru kyoofu wa hitobito no aida ni hiromatte iru.*) その病気に対する恐怖は人々の間に広まっている.

widow *n.* mi¹bo¹ojiñ 未亡人; ya¹mome やもめ.

widower *n.* o¹tokoya¹mome 男やもめ.

width *n.* ha¹ba 幅; hi¹rosa 広さ: What is the width of this road? (*Kono michi no haba wa dore kurai desu ka?*) この道の幅はどれくらいですか. / The width of the fabric is 90 cm. (*Sono kiji no haba wa kyuujus-señchi arimasu.*) その生地の幅は90センチあります.

wife *n.* (one's own and generic) tsu¹ma 妻; (one's own) ka¹nai 家内; (someone else's) o¹kusañ 奥さん: This is my wife. (*Kore ga kanai desu.*) これが家内です.

wig *n.* ka¹tsura かつら: wear a wig (*katsura o tsukeru*) かつらをつける.

wild *adj.* **1** (of plants and animals) ya¹see no 野生の: wild plants (*yasee shokubutsu*) 野生植物 / wild dogs (*yakeñ*) 野犬.

2 (of land) shi¹zeñ no mama no 自然のままの; a¹reha¹teta 荒れ果てた; a¹rehatete iru 荒れ果てている: a wild land (*arechi*) 荒れ地.

3 (of the weather, sea, etc.) a¹reta 荒れた; a¹rete iru 荒れている: a wild sea (*araumi*) 荒海.

4 (violent) raｒñboo na 乱暴な; kyoｒoboo na 凶暴な: He was wild in his youth. (*Kare wa wakai koro wa rañboo datta.*) 彼は若い頃は乱暴だった.

5 (crazy) kyoｒoki jiｒmita [jiｒmite iru] 狂気じみた[じみている]; (excited) koｒofuñ shita [shite iru] 興奮した[している]: He was wild with anger. (*Kare wa gekido shite ita.*) 彼は激怒していた.

wilderness *n.* aｒreno 荒れ野; aｒrechi 荒れ地; miｒkaｒichi 未開地.

wildly *adv.* (violently) raｒñboo ni 乱暴に; kyoｒoboo ni 凶暴に; (crazily) ki ｒga kuruｒtta yoo ni 気が狂ったように: They were beating on the door wildly. (*Kare-ra wa ki ga kurutta yoo ni doa o tataite ita.*) 彼らは気が狂ったようにドアをたたいていた.

will *aux.* **1** [future] 〈verb〉daｒroｒo …だろう; [polite] 〈verb〉deｒshoｒo …でしょう: It will be fine tomorrow. (*Ashita wa hareru daroo.*) あしたは晴れるだろう. / He will graduate next year. (*Kare wa raineñ sotsugyoo suru deshoo.*) 彼は来年卒業するでしょう.

2 [probability] 〈verb〉daｒroｒo …だろう; [polite] 〈verb〉deｒshoｒo …でしょう: He will become a good teacher. (*Kare wa yoi señsee ni naru deshoo.*) 彼はよい先生になるでしょう. / How long will it take? (*Jikañ wa dono kurai kakaru deshoo ka?*) 時間はどのくらいかかるでしょうか.

3 [intention] 〈verb〉tsuｒmori da …つもりだ; 〈verb〉-(y)oo to oｒmoｒu …(よ)うと思う: I will ask him for advice. (*Watashi wa kare ni jogeñ o motomeru tsumori da.*) 私は彼に助言を求めるつもりだ.

4 [asking for a favor] 〈verb〉-te[de] kuｒremaseｒñ ka …て[で]くれませんか: Will you help me move this table? (*Kono teeburu o ugokasu no o tetsudatte kuremaseñ ka?*) このテーブルを動かすのを手伝ってくれませんか.

5 [insist] doｒoshite mo 〈verb〉-(y)oｒo to suru どうしても…(よ)うとする: He will have his own way. (*Kare wa dooshite mo jibuñ no suki na yoo ni shiyoo to suru.*) 彼はどうしても自分の好きなようにしようとする.

will *n.* **1** (wish) iｒshi 意志; iｒto 意図: free will (*jiyuu ishi*) 自由意志 / He has a strong will. (*Kare wa ishi ga tsuyoi.*) 彼は意志が強い.

2 (document) yuｒigoñ 遺言; yuｒigoñshoｒ 遺言書: make a will (*yuigoñsho o tsukuru*) 遺言書を作る.

willful *adj.* waｒgamaｒma na わがまま な; goｒojoo na 強情な: a willful child (*wagamama na kodomo*) わがままな子ども.

willing *adj.* **1** (don't mind) 〈verb〉-te[de] mo kaｒmawaｒnai …て[で]もかまわない; … no o iｒtowaｒnai …のをいとわない: The old couple was willing to take care of their grandchildren. (*Sono roo-fuufu wa mago no sewa o shite mo kamawanai to omotte ita.*) その老夫婦は孫の世話をしてもかまわないと思っていた.

2 (eager) suｒsuñde suru 進んでする; koｒkoｒro kara no 心からの: willing help (*kokoro kara no eñjo*) 心からの援助.

willingly *adv.* yoｒrokoｒñde 喜んで; koｒkoroyoｒku 快く; suｒsuñde 進んで: He willingly helped me move into this house. (*Kare wa watashi ga kono ie ni hikkosu no o yorokoñde tetsudatte kureta.*) 彼は私がこの家に引っ越すのを喜んで手伝ってくれた.

win *vt.* **1** (of a game, battle, etc.) … ni kaｒtsu …に勝つ ○: Our team won the game 5–3. (*Watashi-tachi no chiimu wa go tai sañ de shiai ni katta.*) 私たちのチームは5対3で試合に勝った. / Who will win the election? (*Dare ga señkyo ni katsu daroo?*) だれが選挙に勝つだろう.

2 (of a victory, prize, etc.) … o kaｒchitoru …を勝ち取る ○; kaｒkutoku suru 獲得する □: He won first prize in the contest. (*Kare wa koñtesuto de it-too-shoo o kachitotta.*) 彼はコンテストで一等賞を勝ち取った.

3 (of a fame, trust, etc.) … o eｒru

...を得る V; te¹ ni i⁻reru 手に入れる V: He won the confidence of those around him. (*Kare wa mawari no hito no shiñrai o eta.*) 彼は周りの人の信頼を得た.
— *vi.* ka¹tsu 勝つ C.
— *n.* sho¹ori 勝利; ka¹chi¹ 勝ち: The team has had three wins and two losses. (*Chiimu wa sañ-shoo ni-hai da.*) チームは3勝2敗だ.

wind¹ *n.* ka¹ze 風: a strong wind (*tsuyoi kaze*) 強い風 / The wind is blowing from the north. (*Kaze wa kita kara fuite iru.*) 風は北から吹いている.

wind² *vt.* ... o ma⁻ku ...を巻く C: wind a watch (*tokee no neji o maku*) 時計のねじを巻く / wind thread onto a spool (*ito o itomaki ni maku*) 糸を糸巻きに巻く.
— *vi.* **1** (curve) ma⁻garikune¹ru 曲がりくねる C: The road winds around the hills. (*Michi wa oka no aida o magarikunette iru.*) 道は丘の間を曲がりくねっている.
2 (wrap around) ma⁻kitsu¹ku 巻きつく C; ka⁻ramitsu¹ku 絡みつく C: The morning glories wind around the pole. (*Asagao wa sao ni karamitsuku.*) 朝顔はさおに絡みつく.

window *n.* **1** ma¹do 窓: open [close] the window (*mado o akeru [shimeru]*) 窓を開ける[閉める] / look out the window (*mado kara soto o miru*) 窓から外を見る.
2 (windowpane) ma¹do-ga¹rasu 窓ガラス.
3 (of a ticket office) ma¹do¹guchi 窓口: Tickets are sold at window No. 2. (*Kippu wa ni-bañ no madoguchi de utte imasu.*) 切符は2番の窓口で売っています.

windy *adj.* ka¹ze no tsuyo¹i 風の強い; ka¹ze no [ga] a¹ru 風の[が]ある: a windy night (*kaze no tsuyoi yoru*) 風の強い夜.

wine *n.* **1** (from grapes) wa¹iñ ワイン; bu⁻do¹oshu ぶどう酒: red [white] wine (*aka [shiro] waiñ*) 赤[白]ワイン.
2 (from other fruits) ka⁻jitsu¹shu

果実酒: apple wine (*riñgoshu*) りんご酒.

wing *n.* **1** (of birds) tsu¹basa 翼; (of insects) ha¹ne 羽.
2 (of planes, etc.) tsu¹basa 翼.
3 (of buildings) yo¹ku 翼; so⁻de そで: the south wing of a building (*tatemono no minami no yoku*) 建物の南の翼.

wink *vi.* (... ni) u⁻i¹ñku suru (...に)ウインクする I; me⁻ku¹base suru I: She winked at me. (*Kanojo wa watashi ni uiñku shita.*) 彼女は私にウインクした.
— *n.* (intentional) me⁻ku¹base 目くばせ; u⁻i¹ñku ウインク; (unintentional) ma⁻ba¹taki まばたき.

winner *n.* **1** (victor) sho¹osha 勝者: the winner of the race (*reesu no shoosha*) レースの勝者.
2 (person who wins a prize) ju⁻ˈsho¹osha 受賞者; nyu⁻ˈyu¹osha 入賞者: a Nobel prize winner (*Nooberu-shoo jushoosha*) ノーベル賞受賞者.

winter *n.* fu⁻ˈyu¹ 冬: We had a cold winter this year. (*Kotoshi no fuyu wa samukatta.*) 今年の冬は寒かった.

wipe *vt.* ... o fu⁻ku ...をふく C; fu⁻ˈkito¹ru ふき取る C: He wiped the spilled soup off the table. (*Kare wa teeburu ni koboreta suupu o fukitotta.*) 彼はテーブルにこぼれたスープをふき取った.
— *n.* fu⁻ku koto¹ ふくこと; nu⁻ˈgu¹u koto¹ ぬぐうこと; nu⁻ˈguito¹ru ko¹to¹ ぬぐい取ること.

wire *n.* **1** ha⁻rigane 針金; (of electricity) de⁻ˈñseñ 電線: telephone wires (*deñwa señ*) 電話線 / barbed wire (*yuushi tesseñ*) 有刺鉄線.
2 (telegram) de⁻ˈñpoo 電報: Send him a wire. (*Kare ni deñpoo o utte kudasai.*) 彼に電報を打ってください.
— *vt.* ... ni de⁻ñpoo o u¹tsu ...に電報を打つ C: She wired her friend to congratulate her on her marriage. (*Kanojo wa tomodachi ni kekkoñ o iwau deñpoo o utta.*) 彼女は友達に結婚を祝う電報を打った.

— *vi.* de⌐ñpoo o u⌐tsu 電報を打つ
C.

wisdom *n.* ka⌐shiko⌐i ko⌐to⌐ 賢いこ
と; ke⌐ñmee 賢明; chi⌐e⌐ 知恵; fu⌐ñ-
betsu 分別: He had enough wisdom to refuse the offer. (*Kare ni
wa sono mooshide o kotowaru
dake no fuñbetsu ga atta.*) 彼にはそ
の申し出を断わるだけの分別があった.

wise *adj.* ka⌐shiko⌐i 賢い; ke⌐ñmee
na 賢明な; fu⌐ñbetsu no [ga] a⌐ru 分
別の[が]ある: a wise judgment (*keñmee na hañdañ*) 賢明な判断 / You
were wise to have withheld any
comment. (*Anata ga komeñto o
saketa no wa keñmee datta.*) あなた
がコメントを避けたのは賢明だった.

wisely *adv.* **1** ke⌐ñmee ni 賢明に;
shi⌐ryobu⌐kaku 思慮深く: You have
chosen wisely. (*Anata wa keñmee
na señtaku o shita.*) あなたは賢明な選
択をした.
2 [sentence qualifier] ke⌐ñmee ni⌐
mo 賢明にも: He wisely kept his secret. (*Kare wa keñmee ni mo himitsu o mamotta.*) 彼は賢明にも秘密を
守った.

wish *vt.* **1** (have a desire) ⟨verb⟩-
ba[tara] yo⌐i [i⌐i] no ni (to o⌐mo⌐u)
…ば[たら]よい[いい]のに(と思う) C: I
wish I could go with you. (*Anata
to issho ni iketara ii no ni.*) あなたと
いっしょに行けたらいいのに. / I wished I
hadn't said such a thing. (*Watashi
wa añna koto o iwanakereba
yokatta to omotta.*) 私はあんなことを
言わなければよかったと思った.
2 (want to do) [1st and 2nd per-
sons] ⟨verb⟩-tai (to o⌐mo⌐u) …たい(と
思う) C; [3rd person] ⟨verb⟩-tagaru
…たがる C: I wish to become a doctor. (*Watashi wa isha ni naritai to
omotte imasu.*) 私は医者になりたいと
思っています. / The boss wishes to
see you. (*Jooshi ga kimi ni aitai
to itte imasu.*) 上司が君に会いたいと
言っています.
3 (hope for) … o i⌐no⌐ru …を祈る
C; ne⌐ga⌐u 願う C: I wish you
luck. (*Koouñ o inorimasu.*) 幸運を

祈ります. / I wish you a happy new
year. (*Yoi shiñneñ o omukae kudasai.*) よい新年をお迎えください.

wish for … *vt.* … o no⌐zomu …
を望む C: We wish for world peace.
(*Watashi-tachi wa sekai heewa o
nozomimasu.*) 私たちは世界平和を望
みます.

— *n.* no⌐zomi 望み; ne⌐ga⌐i 願い;
ga⌐ñboo 願望: Her wish to go
abroad has finally come true. (*Gaikoku e ikitai to iu kanojo no negai
wa tsui ni jitsugeñ shita.*) 外国へ行
きたいという彼女の願いはついに実現した.

send one's best wishes to
… *vt.* … ni yo⌐roshiku⌐ to tsu⌐taeru
…によろしくと伝える V: Please send
my best wishes to your mother.
(*Doozo o-kaasañ ni yoroshiku otsu-
tae kudasai.*) どうぞお母さんによろしく
お伝えください.

wit *n.* **1** (humor) ki⌐chi 機知; u⌐i⌐t-
to ウイット: a person of wit (*kichi ni
toñda hito*) 機知に富んだ人.
2 (intelligence) ri⌐kai⌐ryoku 理解力,
chi⌐e⌐ 知恵: have quick [slow] wits
(*rikai ga hayai [osoi]*) 理解が早い
[遅い].

witch *n.* ma⌐jo 魔女; o⌐ñnamahoo-
tsu⌐kai 女魔法使い.

with *prep.* **1** (together) … to i⌐ssho
ni といっしょに; to⌐mo ni ともに: She
lives with her aunt. (*Kanojo wa
oba to issho ni kurashite imasu.*)
彼女はおばといっしょに暮らしています. /
Please come with me. (*Issho ni
kite kudasai.*) いっしょに来てください.
2 (having) … no [ga] a⌐ru …の[が]あ
る; -tsu⌐ku no tsuku …の付いた: a box with a
lid (*futa ga aru hako*) ふたがある箱 /
I'd like a room with bath. (*Furo-
tsuki no heya ni shitai.*) 風呂つきの
部屋にしたい.
3 (carrying) … o mo⌐tte …を持って:
Take an umbrella with you. (*Kasa
o motte iki nasai.*) 傘を持って行きな
さい.
4 (using) … de …で; … o tsu⌐katte
…を使って: write with a pen (*peñ
de kaku*) ペンで書く.

5 (cause) ... de ...で; ... no seｒde ...のせいで: tremble with rage (*ikari de furueru*) 怒りで震える.

6 (concerning) ... ni kaｒnshite ...に関して; ... ni に: He was angry with me. (*Kare wa watashi ni hara o tatete ita.*) 彼は私に腹を立てていた.

7 (against) ... to ...と; ... o aｒiteｒ ni ...を相手に: I discussed the matter with him. (*Watashi wa sono koto o kare to hanashiatta.*) 私はそのことを彼と話し合った.

8 (at the same time) ... to doｒoji ni ...と同時に; ... to toｒmo ni ...とともに: rise with the sun (*taiyoo to tomo ni okiru*) 太陽とともに起きる.

9 (corresponding to) ... ni tsuｒrete ...につれて; ... to toｒmo ni ...とともに: His memory faded with time. (*Kare no omoide wa toki to tomo ni usureta.*) 彼の思い出は時とともに薄れた.

withdraw *vt.* **1** (of money) ... o hiｒkidaｒsu ...を引き出す Ⓒ; oｒroｒsu 下ろす Ⓒ: I withdrew 30,000 yen from my account. (*Watashi wa kooza kara sanmañ-eñ oro-shita.*) 私は口座から3万円を下ろした.

2 (of troops) ... o teｒttai saseru ...を撤退させる Ⓥ; (from school) taｒigaku saseru 退学させる Ⓥ: The country withdrew its troops. (*Sono kuni wa guñtai o tettai saseta.*) その国は軍隊を撤退させた. / His parents withdrew him from school. (*Ryooshiñ wa kare o taigaku saseta.*) 両親は彼を退学させた.

3 (of an offer) ... o teｒkkai suru ...を撤回する Ⓘ: withdraw an offer (*mooshide o tekkai suru*) 申し出を撤回する.

— *vi.* hiｒkisagaｒru 引き下がる Ⓒ; taｒishutsu suru 退出する Ⓘ: The children withdrew to their own rooms at bedtime. (*Neru jikañ ni naru to kodomo-tachi wa jibuñ no heya ni hikisagatta.*) 寝る時間になると子どもたちは自分の部屋に引き下がった.

wither *vi.* shiｒoreru しおれる Ⓥ; kaｒreru 枯れる Ⓥ: The flowers withered because they had no water. (*Mizu ga nai no de hana ga karete shimatta.*) 水がないので花が枯れてしまった.

withhold *vt.* ... o saｒshihikaeｒru 差し控える Ⓥ; hoｒryuu suru 保留する Ⓘ: withhold a question (*shitsu-moñ o sashihikaeru*) 質問を差し控える.

within *prep.* ... iｒnai ni [de] ...以内に[で]; ... no haｒｒniｒnai ni [de] ...の範囲内に[で]: I'll be back within five minutes. (*Go-fuñ inai ni modotte kimasu.*) 5分以内に戻ってきます. / live within one's income (*shuunyuu no hañinai de kurasu*) 収入の範囲内で暮らす.

without *prep.* **1** (not having) ... no naｒi ...のない; ... naｒshi de ...なしで: a room without a window (*mado no nai heya*) 窓のない部屋 / I usually drink coffee without cream. (*Watashi wa futsuu kuriimu nashi de koohii o nomimasu.*) 私は普通クリームなしでコーヒーを飲みます.

2 (without ~ing) 〈verb〉-nai de ...ないで; 〈verb〉-zu ni ...ずに: He went out without saying good-by. (*Kare wa sayonara o iwanai de dete itta.*) 彼はさよならを言わないで出て行った.

3 (if it wasn't for) ... ga naｒkattara ...がなかったら: Without water, we couldn't live. (*Mizu ga nakattara watashi-tachi wa ikite ikenai.*) 水がなかったら私たちは生きていけない.

witness *n.* **1** (eyewitness) moｒgekiｒsha 目撃者; shoｒoniñ 証人: a witness of the accident (*jiko no mokugekisha*) 事故の目撃者.

2 (someone who testifies in court) shoｒoniñ 証人: a witness for the defense (*hikoku-gawa no shooniñ*) 被告側の証人.

3 (evidence) shoｒoko 証拠; (testimony) shoｒogeñ 証言: bear witness (*shoogeñ suru*) 証言する.

— *vt.* ... o moｒkugeki suru ...を目撃する Ⓘ: Did you witness the accident? (*Anata wa sono jiko o mokugeki shita no desu ka?*) あなたはその

事故を目撃したのですか.

witty *adj.* ki「chi ni toǹda [toǹde iru] 機知に富んだ[富んでいる]; sa「iki no [ga] aru 才気の[が]ある: witty remarks (*kichi ni toǹda hatsugeǹ*) 機知に富んだ発言.

wolf *n.* o「okami 狼.

woman *n.* o「ǹna-no-hito¹ 女の人; jo「sei 女性; fu「jiǹ 婦人; o「ǹna¹ 女.
★ '*Oǹna*' often has a derogatory connotation, especially when referring to a young woman.

wonder *vt.* **1** (want to know) ... da「ro¹o ...だろう: I wonder where he went. (*Kare wa doko e itta no daroo.*) 彼はどこへ行ったのだろう. / I wonder what happened. (*Nani ga okotta no daroo*) 何が起こったのだろう.
2 (think) ... to ka「ǹga¹eru ...と考える V̄: I'm now wondering what to do next Sunday. (*Tsugi no nichiyoo wa nani o shiyoo ka to kaǹgaete iru tokoro desu.*) 次の日曜は何をしようかと考えているところです.
— *vi.* **1** (doubt) u「tagau 疑う C̄; i「buka¹ru いぶかる C̄: I wonder about its innocence. (*Watashi wa kare no keppaku o utagau.*) 私は彼の潔白を疑う.
2 (be surprised) fu「shigi ni omo¹u 不思議に思う C̄; o「doro¹ku 驚く C̄: Everybody wondered at the boy's talent. (*Miǹna ga sono shooneǹ no sainoo ni odoroita.*) みんながその少年の才能に驚いた.
— *n.* o「doroki¹ 驚き: It's a wonder you came back safe. (*Anata ga buji ni kaette kita no wa odoroki da.*) あなたが無事に帰ってきたのは驚きだ.

wonderful *adj.* **1** (good) su「barashi¹i すばらしい; su「teki na すてきな: The view from the top of the mountain was wonderful. (*Yama no choojoo kara no nagame wa subarashikatta.*) 山の頂上からの眺めはすばらしかった. / Many thanks for a wonderful dinner. (*Suteki na yuushoku o arigatoo gozaimashita.*) すてきな夕食をありがとうございました.
2 (strange) fu「shigi na 不思議な; (surprising) o「doroku be¹ki 驚くべき: a wonderful story (*fushigi na monogatari*) 不思議の物語.

wood *n.* **1** (lumber) mo「ku¹zai 木材; za「imoku 材木; (material) ki¹ 木: This table is made of wood. (*Kono teeburu wa ki de dekite imasu.*) このテーブルは木でできています.
2 (forest) mo「ri 森; ha「yashi 林.
★ '*Mori*' refers to a large area of land more thickly covered with trees than '*hayashi*.'

wooden *adj.* mo「kusee no 木製の; ki¹ de dekita [dekite iru] 木でできた[できている]: a wooden chair (*mokusee no isu*) 木製のいす / wooden Japanese-style clogs (*geta*) げた.

wool *n.* **1** (hair) yo「omoo 羊毛.
2 (yarn) ke「ito 毛糸: wind up knitting wool (*keito o maku*) 毛糸を巻く.
3 (fabric) u「uru ウール; ke「orimono 毛織物: I wear wool in winter. (*Fuyu wa uuru o kimasu.*) 冬はウールを着ます.

woolen *adj.* yo「omoo no 羊毛の; ke「ori no 毛織りの: a woolen blanket (*yoomoo no moofu*) 羊毛の毛布.

word *n.* **1** (unit of language) ta「ǹgo 単語; go¹ 語; ko「toba¹ 言葉: What does this word mean? (*Kono taǹgo wa doo iu imi desu ka?*) この単語はどういう意味ですか.
2 (talk) ha「nashi¹ 話: I'd like to have a word with you. (*O-hanashi ga shitai no desu ga.*) お話がしたいのですが.
3 (news) shi「rase 知らせ; ta「yori 便り; sho「osoku 消息: Word came that it was snowing in Tokyo. (*Tookyoo de wa yuki ga futte iru to iu shirase ga todoita.*) 東京では雪が降っているという知らせが届いた.
4 (promise) ya「kusoku 約束: keep one's word (*yakusoku o mamoru*) 約束を守る.

in other words *adv.* i「ika¹reba 言いかえれば.

work *n.* **1** (task) shi「goto 仕事;

sa⌐gyoo 作業; ro⌐odoo 労働;
(study) be⌐ñkyoo 勉強: hard [easy]
work (tsurai [raku na] shigoto) つら
い[楽な]仕事 / I have a lot of work
to do today. (Kyoo wa shinakereba naranai shigoto ga takusañ aru.)
今日はしなければならない仕事がたくさんあ
る.
2 (job) shi⌐goto 仕事; tsu⌐tome⌐-
guchi 勤め口: He is looking for
work. (Kare wa tsutomeguchi o
sagashite iru.) 彼は勤め口を探してい
る.
3 (workplace) tsu⌐tomesaki 勤め先;
sho⌐kuba 職場; ka⌐isha 会社: He
goes to work by train. (Kare wa
deñsha de kaisha ni ikimasu.) 彼は
電車で会社に行きます.
4 (handiwork) sa⌐iku⌐ 細工; (of
one's making) se⌐esaku 製作:
Making this brooch required careful work. (Kono buroochi o tsukuru ni wa neñiri na saiku ga hitsuyoo datta.) このブローチを作るには
念入りな細工が必要だった.
5 (work of art) sa⌐kuhiñ 作品:
This sculpture is Rodin's work.
(Kono chookoku wa Rodañ no
sakuhiñ desu.) この彫刻はロダンの作
品です.
6 (factory) ko⌐ojo⌐o 工場.
— vi. **1** (do work) ha⌐taraku 働く
Ⓒ; shi⌐goto o suru 仕事をする Ⓘ:
He works at a bank. (Kare wa giñkoo de hataraite imasu.) 彼は銀行で
働いています. / I work for a trading
company. (Watashi wa booekigai-
sha ni tsutomete imasu.) 私は貿易
会社に勤めています.
2 (study) be⌐ñkyoo suru 勉強する
Ⓘ: I'm working at my Japanese.
(Watashi wa Nihoñgo o beñkyoo
shite imasu.) 私は日本語を勉強してい
ます.
3 (operate) u⌐go⌐ku 動く Ⓒ: Is the
elevator working? (Erebeetaa wa
ugoite imasu ka?) エレベーターは動い
ていますか. / This shutter doesn't
work well. (Kono shattaa wa guai
ga warui.) このシャッターは具合が悪い.

4 (of plans) u⌐maku i⌐ku うまくいく
Ⓒ; (of medicine, etc.) ki⌐ku 効く
Ⓒ: The plan worked well. (Sono
keekaku wa umaku itta.) その計画
はうまくいった. / This medicine
works for headaches. (Kono kusuri
wa zutsuu ni kiku.) この薬は頭痛に
効く.
— vt. **1** (operate) ... o u⌐goka⌐su
...を動かす Ⓒ; u⌐ñteñ suru 運転する
Ⓘ: How do you work this machine? (Kono kikai wa doo yatte
ugokasu ñ desu ka?) この機械はどう
やって動かすんですか.
2 (make work) ... o ha⌐tarakaseru
...を働かせる Ⓥ; ko⌐kitsukau こき使う
Ⓒ: You must not work your employees too hard. (Juugyooiñ o
hatarakase-sugite wa ikenai.) 従業
員を働かせ過ぎてはいけない.
work on ... vt. ... ni to⌐rikumu ...
に取り組む Ⓒ: They are working on
a new project. (Kare-ra wa atarashii purojekuto ni torikuñde iru.)
彼らは新しいプロジェクトに取り組んでいる.
work out vt. (think of) ka⌐ñgae-
da⌐su 考え出す Ⓒ: work out a solution to a problem (mondai no kaiketsuhoo o kañgaedasu) 問題の解
決法を考え出す.
— vi. (turn out) na⌐ru なる Ⓒ:
How did your plan work out?
(Anata no keekaku wa doo narimashita ka?) あなたの計画はどうなりました
か.

worker n. ha⌐taraku hito⌐ 働く人;
ro⌐odo⌐osha 労働者: factory workers (koojoo roodoosha) 工場労働者.

working adj. **1** (having a job) ha⌐-
taraku 働く: working people (ha⌐-
taraku hitobito) 働く人々.
2 (useful) ji⌐ssai ni yakuda⌐tsu 実
際に役立つ; ji⌐tsuyoo-teki na 実用
的な: a working knowledge of
Japanese (Nihoñgo no jitsuyoo-
teki na chishiki) 日本語の実用的な
知識.

workshop n. **1** (place) sa⌐gyoo⌐-
ba 作業場; shi⌐gotoba 仕事場.
2 (study group) wa⌐akusho⌐ppu ワ

ークショップ; keｒñkyuushuｌukai 研究
集会; keｒñkyuu guruｌupu 研究グルー
プ.

world *n.* **1** (the earth) seｒkai 世界：
travel around the world (*sekai
isshuu no tabi o suru*) 世界一周の
旅をする / That is the highest building in the world. (*Are ga sekai de
ichibañ takai biru desu.*) あれが世界
でいちばん高いビルです。/ a world
record (*sekai kiroku*) 世界記録.

2 (people) seｒkaijuu no hitoｌbito 世
界中の人々：The news shocked the
world. (*Sono nyuusu wa sekaijuu
no hitobito ni shoogeki o ataeta.*)
そのニュースは世界中の人々に衝撃を与
えた。

3 (society) yoｰｒnoｌｰnaka 世の中；
seｒkeñ 世間：It's a small world.
(*Sekeñ wa semai.*) 世間は狭い.

worldwide *adj.* seｒkai-teki na 世
界的な; seｒkai-juu ni shirewataｌtta
[shirewattaｌte iru] 世界中に知れわた
った[知れわたっている]: His fame is
worldwide. (*Kare no meesee wa
sekai-juu ni shirewattatte iru.*) 彼
の名声は世界中に知れわたっている。
—— *adv.* seｒkai-juu ni [de] 世界中に
[で]; seｒkai-teki ni 世界的に: spread
worldwide (*sekai-juu ni hiromaru*)
世界中に広まる.

worm *n.* muｒshi 虫; (earthworm)
miｒmizu みみず; (caterpillar) keｒmu-
shiｌ 毛虫. ★ 'Insects' is also called
'*mushi*'.

worn *adj.* **1** (being used) suｒriki-
reta すり切れた; suｒrikirete iru すり切
れている: worn clothes (*surikireta
fuku*) すり切れた服.

2 (being tired) tsuｒkarekiｌtta 疲れき
った; tsuｒkarekiｌtte iru 疲れきっている;
yaｒtsuｌreta やつれた; yaｒtsuｌrete iru
やつれている: a worn face (*yatsureta
kao*) やつれた顔.

worried *adj.* shiｒñpai-soo na 心配
そうな; shiｒñpai shite iru 心配してい
る: a worried look (*shiñpai-soo na
kao*) 心配そうな顔 / I am worried
about his health. (*Watashi wa
kare no keñkoo o shiñpai shite iru.*)

私は彼の健康を心配している.

worry *vi.* shiｒñpai suru 心配する □;
naｒyaｌmu 悩む ©: You worry too
much. (*Anata wa shiñpai shi-
sugiru.*) あなたは心配しすぎる。/ Don't
worry. (*Shiñpai wa irimaseñ.*) 心
配はいりません。
—— *vt.* **1** (annoy) ... o naｒyamaｌsu
悩ます ©; iｒraira saｒseru いらいらさせ
る Ⓥ: The child worried its mother by asking difficult questions.
(*Sono kodomo wa muzukashii
shitsumoñ o shite hahaoya o naya-
mashita.*) その子どもは難しい質問をし
て母親を悩ました。

2 (make anxious) ... no ki ｒo moma-
seru ...の気をもませる Ⓥ; ... o shiｒñpai saseru ...を心配させる Ⓥ: Her
long absence from school worried
her classmates. (*Kanojo no chooki
kesseki wa kurasumeeto o shiñpai
saseta.*) 彼女の長期欠席はクラスメート
を心配させた。
—— *n.* **1** (anxiety) shiｒñpai 心配;
kiｒguｌroo 気苦労: Worry kept me
awake. (*Shiñpai de watashi wa
nemurenakatta.*) 心配で私は眠れなか
った。

2 (cause for anxiety) shiｒñpaigoto
心配事; shiｒñpai no taｌne 心配の種:
Life is full of worries. (*Jiñsee ni
wa shiñpaigoto ga ooi.*) 人生には心
配事が多い.

worse *adj.* moｒtto waｒruｌi もっと悪
い; ... yori waｒruｌi ...より悪い: The
weather is getting worse. (*Teñki
ga dañdañ waruku natte kite iru.*)
天気がだんだん悪くなってきている。/ The
patient is worse than yesterday.
(*Byooniñ wa kinoo yori guai ga
warui.*) 病人はきのうより具合が悪い.
—— *adv.* moｒtto waruku もっと悪く;
moｒtto hidoku もっとひどく: It's
raining worse than before. (*Mae
yori hidoku ame ga futte iru.*) 前よ
りひどく雨が降っている.

worship *n.* **1** (reverence) suｒuhai
崇拝; soｒñkee 尊敬: hero worship
(*eeyuu suuhai*) 英雄崇拝.

2 (of a church) reｒehai 礼拝; (of a

shrine, temple) saⁿpai 参拝.

— *vt.* (give worship) ... o suʻuhai suru 崇拝する Ⓣ; soⁿkee suru 尊敬する Ⓣ: He worships his father. (*Kare wa chichioya o soñkee shite iru.*) 彼は父親を尊敬している.

— *vi.* (take part in worship) reʻehai suru 礼拝する Ⓣ: I worship at that church. (*Watashi wa ano kyookai de reehai shite imasu.*) 私はあの教会で礼拝しています.

worst *adj.* moʻttomo [iʻchibañ] waʻruʻi もっとも[いちばん]悪い; saʻiaku no 最悪の: This is the worst time for young people to look for work. (*Ima wa wakai hito ga shoku o sagasu no ni saiaku no toki da.*) 今は若い人が職を探すのに最悪の時だ.

— *adv.* moʻttoʻmo [iʻchibañ] waʻruku もっとも[いちばん]悪く; moʻttoʻmo [iʻchibañ] hiʻdoku もっとも[いちばん]ひどく: That child behaves the worst in this class. (*Sono ko wa kono kurasu de ichibañ taido ga warui.*) その子はこのクラスでいちばん態度が悪い.

worth *adj.* 1 (equal in value) kaʻchi ga aru 価値がある; neʻuchi ga aʻru 値打ちがある: This old car is worth 200,000 yen. (*Kono chuuko-sha wa nijuumañ-eñ no neuchi ga aru.*) この中古車は 20 万円の値打ちがある.

2 (good enough) kaʻchi ga aru 価値がある; neʻuchi ga aʻru 値打ちがある; ... ni aʻtai suru ...に値する: That is worth trying. (*Sore wa yatte miru kachi ga aru.*) それはやってみる価値がある.

— *n.* (value) kaʻchi 価値: a painting of great worth (*hijoo ni kachi no aru e*) 非常に価値のある絵.

worthless *adj.* kaʻchi no [ga] nai 価値の[が]ない; yaʻkuʻi ni taʻtaʻnai 役に立たない: a worthless book (*kachi no nai hoñ*) 価値のない本.

worthwhile *adj.* kaʻchi no [ga] aru 価値の[が]ある; yaʻrigai no [ga] aʻru やりがいの[が]ある: a worthwhile job (*yarigai no aru shigoto*) やりが

いのある仕事.

worthy *adj.* ... ni aʻtai suru ...に値する; fuʻsawashiʻi ふさわしい: His action is worthy of praise. (*Kare no kooi wa shoosañ ni atai suru.*) 彼の行為は賞賛に値する.

would *aux.* 1 [future] ⟨verb⟩ daʻroʻo ...だろう; [polite] ⟨verb⟩ deʻshoʻo ...でしょう: I thought you would come. (*Watashi wa anata ga kuru daroo to omoimashita.*) 私はあなたが来るだろうと思いました.

2 [intention] ⟨verb⟩ tsuʻmori da ...つもりだ: He said he would go on a trip next month. (*Kare wa raigetsu ryokoo ni iku tsumori da to itta.*) 彼は来月旅行に行くつもりだと言った.

3 [determination] doʻo shite mo ⟨verb⟩-(y)oʻo to suru どうしても ...(よ)うとする: He would do everything his way. (*Kare wa nañ de moo shite mo jibuñ no yarikata de shi-yoo to suru.*) 彼は何でもどうしても自分のやり方でしようとする.

4 [possibility] ⟨verb⟩ daʻroʻo ...だろう; [polite] ⟨verb⟩ deʻshoʻo ...でしょう: If I were you, I would accept the offer. (*Moshi watashi ga anata dattara sono mooshide o ukeireta deshoo.*) もし私があなただったらその申し出を受け入れたでしょう.

I would like ... o kuʻdasaʻi ...を下さい: I would like a roll of film. (*Firumu o ip-poñ kudasai.*) フィルムを 1 本下さい.

I would like to do ⟨verb⟩-tai ...たい: I would like to see the room. (*Watashi wa sono heya o mitai no desu ga.*) 私はその部屋を見たいのですが.

Would you ...? ⟨verb⟩-te[de] iʻtadakemaseⁿñ ka? ...て[で]いただけませんか: Would you please open the window? (*Mado o akete itadakemaseñ ka?*) 窓を開けていただけませんか.

wound *vt.* 1 (injure physically) ... o fuʻshoo saseru ...を負傷させる Ⓥ; ... ni keʻgaʻ o saʻseru ...にけがをさせる Ⓥ: Fifty people were wounded in the railway accident. (*Sono ressha*

jiko de gojuu-niñ ga fushoo shita.)
その列車事故で 50 人が負傷した.

2 (hurt feelings) ... o ki⌐zutsuke⌐ru
...を傷つける Ⓥ: His words wound-
ed her. (Kare no kotoba wa kanojo o kizutsuketa.) 彼の言葉は彼女を
傷つけた.
— n. ke⌐ga⌐ けが; ki⌐zu 傷; fu⌐shoo
負傷: a slight wound (keeshoo) 軽
傷 / He suffered a fatal wound.
(Kare wa chimeeshoo o otta.) 彼は
致命傷を負った.

wrap vt. ... o tsu⌐tsu⌐mu ...を包む
Ⓒ; ku⌐ru⌐mu くるむ Ⓒ: She wrapped
the present in paper. (Kanojo wa
purezeñto o kami ni tsutsuñda.) 彼
女はプレゼントを紙に包んだ.

wrapper n. tsu⌐tsumi⌐gami 包み紙;
ho⌐oso⌐oshi 包装紙.

wreath n. ha⌐nawa 花輪: a funeral
wreath (soogi no hanawa) 葬儀の花
輪.

wreck n. **1** (ruin of a ship) na⌐ñpa
難破; so⌐onañ 遭難; (damaged
ship) na⌐ñpaseñ 難破船: The
storm caused many wrecks. (Sono
arashi de soonañ jiko ga ooku
deta.) その嵐で遭難事故が多く出た.
2 (what is left of anything destroyed) za⌐ñgai 残骸: clear away
the wreck of the plane that crashed
(tsuiraku shita hikooki no zañgai
o katazukeru) 墜落した飛行機の残骸
を片づける.
— vt. (of a ship) ... o na⌐ñpa saseru ...を難破させる Ⓥ; (of a vehicle) ... o ko⌐wa⌐su ...を壊す Ⓒ; ta⌐l-
iha saseru 大破させる Ⓥ: The ship
was wrecked in a storm. (Sono
fune wa arashi de nañpa shita.) そ
の船は嵐で難破した.

wrestle vi. **1** (with a person) to⌐r-
kumiai o suru 取っ組み合いをする Ⓘ;
re⌐suriñgu o suru レスリングをする Ⓘ:
The boys are wrestling. (Sono
otoko-no-ko-tachi wa tokkumiai o
shite iru.) その男の子たちは取っ組み合
いをしている.
2 (with a difficulty) (... to) to⌐ri-
kumu (...と)取り組む Ⓒ: We must

wrestle with the problem. (Watashi-tachi wa sono moñdai ni tori-
kumanakereba naranai.) 私たちはそ
の問題に取り組まなければならない.

wrestler n. re⌐suriñgu no señshu
レスリングの選手; a sumo wrestler
(sumootori) 相撲取り.

wrestling n. re⌐suriñgu レスリング.

wretched adj. (miserable) mi⌐l-
jime na 惨めな; a⌐lware na 哀れな:
lead a wretched life (mijime na seekatsu o okuru) 惨めな生活を送る.

wring vt. **1** (squeeze) ... o shi⌐bo⌐l-
ru ...を絞る Ⓒ: Wring the towels
before you hang them out to dry.
(Hosu mae ni taoru o shibori nasai.)
干す前にタオルを絞りなさい. ★ Japa-
nese 'shiboru' also means
'squeeze.'
2 (twist) ... o hi⌐ne⌐ru ...をひねる Ⓒ:
I'll wring your neck if you say that
again! (Moo ichido ittara kubi o
hineru zo!) もう一度言ったら首をひね
るぞ.
3 (clasp) ... o ka⌐taku nigiru ...を固
く握る Ⓒ: He wrung his friend's
hand. (Kare wa yuujiñ no te o
kataku nigitta.) 彼は友人の手を固く
握った.

wrinkle n. shi⌐lwa しわ: smooth out
the wrinkles of one's jacket (uwagi
no shiwa o nobasu) 上着のしわを伸ば
す / She has wrinkles about her
mouth. (Kanojo wa kuchi no mawari ni shiwa ga aru.) 彼女は口の回
りにしわがある
— vt. ... ni shi⌐lwa o yoseru ...にし
わを寄せる Ⓥ: He wrinkled his forehead. (Kare wa hitai ni shiwa o
yoseta.) 彼は額にしわを寄せた.
— vi. shi⌐lwa ga yoru しわが寄る
Ⓒ; shi⌐lwa ni na⌐ru しわになる Ⓒ:
This cloth wrinkles easily. (Kono
kire wa shiwa ni nari-yasui.) この
きれはしわになりやすい.

wrist n. te⌐lkubi 手首: He seized
me by the wrist. (Kare wa watashi
no tekubi o tsukañda.) 彼は私の手
首をつかんだ.

wristwatch n. u⌐dedo⌐lkee 腕時計.

write vt. ... o ka˥ku ...を書く C:
Please write your name here.
(*Koko ni namae o kaite kudasai.*)
ここに名前を書いてください。/ He is
writing a book. (*Kare wa hoñ o
kaite iru.*) 彼は本を書いている。
— vi. ka˥ku 書く C; (of a letter)
te˥gami o ka˥ku 手紙を書く C:
write in pencil (*eñpitsu de kaku*)
鉛筆で書く / I write to my parents
every month. (*Watashi wa maitsuki ryooshiñ ni tegami o kaki-
masu.*) 私は毎月両親に手紙を書きます。
write down vt. ... o ka˥kitomeru
...を書き留める V: write down a
phone number (*deñwa bañgoo o
kakitomeru*) 電話番号を書き留める。

writer n. 1 (one who wrote) ka˥i-
ta hi˥to˩ 書いた人; hi˥ssha 筆者; (of
fiction) sa˥kusha 作者: the writer
of this letter (*kono tegami o kaita
hito*) この手紙を書いた人 / the writer
of a novel (*shoosetsu no sakusha*)
小説の作者。
2 (author) sa˥kka 作家; (reporter)
ki˥sha 記者。

writing n. 1 (act of writing) ka˥ku
ko˥to˩ 書くこと; shi˥ppitsu 執筆。
2 (handwriting) ji˥ 字; hi˥sseki 筆
跡: His writing is neat. (*Kare no ji
wa kiree da.*) 彼の字はきれいだ。
3 (something that is written) ka˥i-
ta mo˥no˩ 書いたもの; sho˥meñ 書面:
Please submit complaints in writing. (*Kujoo wa shomeñ de teeshutsu shite kudasai.*) 苦情は書面で提
出してください。
4 (work) cho˥saku 著作; sa˥kuhiñ
作品; the writings of Yukio Mishima (*Mishima Yukio no sakuhiñ*)
三島由紀夫の作品。

writing paper n. bi˥ñseñ 便せん。

written adj. 1 (not oral) ka˥ita 書
いた; hi˥kki no 筆記の: a written test
(*hikki shikeñ*) 筆記試験。
2 (of language) ka˥kiko˥toba no 書
き言葉の: written language (*kakiko-
toba*) 書き言葉。

wrong adj. 1 (bad) wa˥ru˩i 悪い;
fu˥see na 不正な: It is wrong to tell
a lie. (*Uso o tsuku koto wa warui.*)
うそをつくことは悪い。
2 (incorrect) ma˥chiga˥tta 間違っ
た; ma˥chiga˥tte iru 間違っている;
a˥yama˥tta 誤った; a˥yama˥tte iru
誤っている: a wrong answer (*machi-
gatta kotae*) 間違った答え / You got
the wrong number. (*Bañgoo ga
chigaimasu.*) 番号が違います。
3 (of a condition) gu˥ai no [ga]
waru˥i 具合の[が]悪い; cho˥oshi ga
kuru˥tte iru 調子が狂っている: This
clock is wrong. (*Kono tokee wa
kurutte iru.*) この時計は狂っている。/
What's wrong with him? (*Kare wa
doo shita no desu ka?*) 彼はどうした
のですか。
4 (inappropriate) fu˥te˥kitoo na 不
適当な; ma˥zu˩i まずい: He came at
the wrong time. (*Kare wa mazui
toki ni yatte kita.*) 彼はまずい時にやっ
て来た。
— adv. 1 (badly) wa˥ruku 悪く;
fu˥see ni 不正に。
2 (incorrectly) ma˥chiga˥tte 間違っ
て; a˥yama˥tte 誤って: answer
wrong (*machigatta kotae o suru*)
間違った答えをする。
3 (not properly) gu˥ai ga wa˥ruku
具合が悪く; cho˥oshi ga kuru˥tte 調
子が狂って。

go wrong vi. shi˥ppai suru 失敗
する I: Our plans went wrong.
(*Watashi-tachi no keekaku wa
shippai shita.*) 私たちの計画は失敗し
た。
— n. a˥ku 悪; fu˥see 不正; wa˥ru˩i
ko˥to˩ 悪いこと: do wrong (*warui
koto o suru*) 悪いことをする / know
right from wrong (*zeñaku no kubetsu ga tsuku*) 善悪の区別がつく。

be in the wrong vi. ma˥chi-
ga˥tte iru 間違っている V: I admit I
was in the wrong. (*Watashi ga
machigatte ita koto o mitomemasu.*) 私が間違っていたことを認めます。

X

Xerox *n.* [trademark] Ze⌐ro⌐kkusu ゼロックス.

X-rated *adj.* (for adults) se⌐ejiñ-muki no 成人向きの: an X-rated movie (*seejiñ-muki eega*) 成人向き映画.

X-ray *n.* **1** (ray) re⌐ñtogeñ-señ レントゲン線; e⌐kkusu-señ エックス線.
2 (photograph) re⌐ñtogeñ-sha⌐shiñ レントゲン写真.

— *vt.* ... no re⌐ñtogeñ-sha⌐shiñ o toru ...のレントゲン写真を撮る ©: I was X-rayed. (*Watashi wa reñto-geñ-shashiñ o totte moratta.*) 私はレントゲン写真を撮ってもらった.

xylophone *n.* shi⌐rohoñ シロホン; mo⌐kkiñ 木琴: play the xylophone (*mokkiñ o eñsoo suru*) 木琴を演奏する.

Y

yacht *n.* yo⌐tto ヨット; ka⌐isooseñ 快走船. ★ Japanese '*yotto*' usually refers to a dinghy or sailboat.

yard¹ *n.* (ground) ni⌐wa 庭: The children are playing in the yard. (*Kodomo-tachi ga niwa de asoñde iru.*) 子どもたちが庭で遊んでいる.
★ Japanese '*niwa*' also refers to a 'garden.'

yard² *n.* (measure) ya⌐ado ヤード; ya⌐aru ヤール: 1 yard (*ichi-yaado*) 1 ヤード (= about 91.4 centimeters).
★ In Japan the metric system is used.

yarn *n.* i⌐to 糸; ke⌐ito 毛糸: spin a yarn (*ito o tsumugu*) 糸を紡ぐ.

yawn *vi.* a⌐kubi o suru あくびをする ①: He yawned and fell asleep. (*Kare wa akubi o shite nete shi-matta.*) 彼はあくびをして寝てしまった.
— *n.* a⌐kubi あくび: give [stifle] a yawn (*akubi o suru [koraeru]*) あくびをする[こらえる].

year *n.* **1** (time period) ne⌐ñ 年: I came to Japan three years ago. (*Watashi wa sañ-neñ mae ni Ni-hoñ e kimashita.*) 私は 3 年前に日本へ来ました. / this year (*kotoshi*) ことし / last year (*kyoneñ [sakuneñ]*) 去年[昨年] / next year (*raineñ*) 来年.

2 (age) -sai 歳: My son will be 18 years old next month. (*Watashi no musuko wa raigetsu juuhas-sai ni narimasu.*) 私の息子は来月 18 歳になります.
3 (school year) ga⌐kuneñ 学年: We were in the same year in high school. (*Watashi-tachi wa kookoo de onaji gakuneñ deshita.*) 私たちは高校で同じ学年でした.

yearly *adj.* **1** (every year) ma⌐ito-shi no 毎年の: a yearly event (*mai-toshi no gyooji*) 毎年の行事.
2 (for a year) i⌐chi-ne⌐ñkañ no 1 年間の: a yearly income (*neñshuu*) 年収.

yearn *vi.* (... ni) a⌐kogareru (...に)あこがれる Ⓥ; (... o) ne⌐tsuboo suru (...を)熱望する ①: yearn for fame (*mee-see ni akogareru*) 名声にあこがれる / He yearns to go to Greece. (*Kare wa Girisha e iku koto o netsuboo shite iru.*) 彼はギリシャへ行くことを熱望している.

yeast *n.* ko⌐obokiñ 酵母菌; i⌐isuto イースト.

yell *vi.* o⌐ogo⌐e o a⌐geru 大声を上げる Ⓥ; sa⌐ke⌐bu 叫ぶ ©: He yelled for help. (*Kare wa oogoe o agete ta-suke o motometa.*) 彼は大声を上げて

助けを求めた.

— n. sa⌐kebigo⌐e 叫び声: give a yell (*sakebigoe o ageru*) 叫び声を上げる.

yellow adj. ki⌐iroi 黄色い: a yellow flower (*kiiroi hana*) 黄色い花.

— n. ki⌐iro 黄色: deep [light] yellow (*koi* [*usui*] *kiiro*) 濃い[薄い]黄色.

yen n. e⌐ñ 円: The yen has gone up [down]. (*Eñ ga agatta* [*sagatta*].) 円が上がった[下がった]. / What is the current exchange rate of the yen against the dollar? (*Geñzai no doru ni taisuru eñ no kawase-sooba wa ikura desu ka?*) 現在のドルに対する円の為替相場はいくらですか. / I'd like to change some dollars into yen. (*Doru o eñ ni kaetai no desu ga.*) ドルを円に換えたいのですが.

yes adv. 1 [in answer to an affirmative question] ha⌐i はい; so⌐o desu そうです: "Is this your car?" "Yes, it is." ("*Kore wa anata no kuruma desu ka?*" "*Hai, soo desu.*") 「これはあなたの車ですか」「はい, そうです」 ★ '*Hai*' literally means 'That's right' and is used to confirm a statement, whether affirmative or negative. Note that this use is different from that of 'yes' and 'no' in English.
2 [in answer to a negative question] i⌐ie いいえ; chi⌐gaima⌐su 違います: "Isn't it raining?" "Yes, it is." ("*Ame wa futte inai no desu ka?*" "*Iie, futte imasu.*") 「雨は降っていないのですか」「いいえ, 降っています」
3 [in answer to a call] ha⌐i はい: "Mr. Yamada." "Yes." ("*Yamada-kuñ.*" "*Hai.*") 「山田君」「はい」

yesterday adv. ki⌐no⌐o (wa) きのう(は); sa⌐ku⌐jitsu (wa) 昨日(は): I was at home yesterday. (*Kinoo wa ie ni imashita.*) きのうは家にいました.

— n. ki⌐no⌐o きのう; sa⌐ku⌐jitsu 昨日: Yesterday was my birthday. (*Kinoo wa watashi no tañjoobi deshita.*) きのうは私の誕生日でした. / the day before yesterday (*ototoi*) お

とい.

yet adv. 1 [with a negative] ma⌐da まだ: My order hasn't come yet. (*Chuumoñ shita mono ga mada kimaseñ.*) 注文したものがまだ来ません.
2 [in questions] mo⌐o もう; su⌐de ni すでに: Has he come yet? (*Kare wa moo kimashita ka?*) 彼はもう来ましたか.
3 [in the affirmative] ma⌐da まだ; i⌐ma nao 今なお: I have yet much to say. (*Watashi wa mada iu koto ga takusañ arimasu.*) 私はまだ言うことがたくさんあります.

yield vt. 1 (produce) ... o mo⌐tara⌐su ...をもたらす Ⓒ; u⌐mu 生む Ⓒ: The land yielded a good crop. (*Sono tochi wa yoi shuukaku o motarashita.*) その土地はよい収穫をもたらした. / His business yielded large profits. (*Kare no shoobai wa ooki-na rieki o uñda.*) 彼の商売は大きな利益を生んだ.
2 (give up) ... o yu⌐zuru ...を譲る Ⓒ: He yielded his property to his son. (*Kare wa musuko ni zaisañ o yuzutta.*) 彼は息子に財産を譲った.
— vi. (submit) (... ni) ma⌐keru (... に)負ける Ⓥ; ku⌐ssuru 屈する Ⓘ: They never yielded to violence. (*Kare-ra wa kesshite booryoku ni kusshinakatta.*) 彼らは決して暴力に屈しなかった.

yolk n. ta⌐ma⌐go no ki⌐mi 卵の黄身; ra⌐ñoo 卵黄.

you pron. 1 [the person spoken to] a⌐na⌐ta あなた; ki⌐mi 君; [plural] a⌐nata gata あなたがた; ki⌐mi⌐-tachi 君たち: May I take a picture of you? (*Anata no shashiñ o totte mo ii desu ka?*) あなたの写真を撮ってもいいですか. / You are right. (*Kimi no iu toori da.*) 君の言うとおりだ. ★ '*Anata*' is used toward those of the same or lower status. Those who are higher in status are referred to by their occupation or position. '*Kimi*' is used among males of the same status or toward subordinates..

2 [any person] hiʈto wa (daʈre de mo) 人は(だれでも). ★ Often omitted in Japanese: You have to be careful in crossing the street. (*Michi o oodañ suru toki wa ki o tsukenakereba ikemaseñ.*) 道を横断するときは気をつけなければいけません.

young *adj.* **1** (not old) waʈkaʈi 若い: He looks young for his age. (*Kare wa toshi no wari ni wakaku mieru.*) 彼は年の割に若く見える.

2 (of age) toʈshi shita no 年下の: I am three years younger than Mr. Yamakawa. (*Watashi wa Yamakawa-sañ yori sañ-sai toshi shita desu.*) 私は山川さんより3歳年下です.

your *pron.* aʈnaʈta no あなたの; kiʈmi no 君の; [plural] aʈnata gata no あなたがたの; kiʈmiʈ-tachi no 君たちの: Where is your company? (*Anata no kaisha wa doko ni arimasu ka?*) あなたの会社はどこにありますか. / Is this your school? (*Kore wa kimi-tachi no gakkoo desu ka?*) これは君たちの学校ですか. ★ Often omitted in Japanese: May I have your name? (*O-namae o kikasete kudasai.*) お名前を聞かせてください. ⇨ you 1 ★

yours *pron.* aʈnaʈta no moʈnoʈ あなたのもの; kiʈmi no monoʈ 君のもの; [plural] aʈnata-gata no monoʈ あなたがたのもの; kiʈmiʈ-tachi no moʈnoʈ 君たちのもの: Are these shoes yours? (*Kono kutsu wa anata no mono desu ka?*) この靴はあなたのものですか. / Yours is better than mine. (*Kimi no mono no hoo ga watashi no yori mo yoi.*) 君のものの方が私のよりもよい. ⇨ you 1 ★

Yours sincerely [**truly**], keʈegu 敬具.

yourself *pron.* **1** [reflexive use] jiʈbuñ jiʈshiñ o [ni] 自分自身を[に]. ★ Usually not translated: How did you hurt yourself?. (*Doo shite kega o shita no desu ka?*) どうしてけがをしたのですか. / Please take good care of yourself. (*O-karada o taisetsu ni.*) お体を大切に.

2 [emphatic use] jiʈbuñ de 自分で; aʈnata jiʈshiñ de あなた自身で: Do it yourself. (*Anata ga jibuñ de sore o yari nasai.*) あなたが自分でそれをやりなさい.

yourselves *pron.* **1** [reflexive use] jiʈbuñ jiʈshiñ o [ni] 自分自身を[に]. ★ Usually not translated: You should be ashamed of yourselves. (*Kimi-tachi wa haji to omou beki da.*) 君たちは恥と思うべきだ.

2 [emphatic use] jiʈbuʈñ-tachi de 自分たちで; aʈnatagata jiʈshiñ de あなたがた自身で: You said so yourselves. (*Anatagata jishiñ ga soo itta de wa nai ka.*) あなたがた自身がそう言ったではないか.

youth *n.* **1** (period) seʈeneñ [seʈeshuñ] jiʈdai 青年[青春]時代; waʈkaʈi koro 若いころ: the friends of my youth (*watashi no seeshuñ jidai no yuujiñ-tachi*) 私の青春時代の友人たち.

2 (young man) waʈkamono 若者; seʈeneñ 青年: a group of youths (*wakamono no ichidañ*) 若者の一団.

3 (being young) waʈkasa 若さ: keep one's youth (*wakasa o tamotsu*) 若さを保つ.

youthful *adj.* waʈkawakashiʈi 若々しい; geʈñki na 元気な: He has a very youthful face. (*Kare wa totemo wakawakashii kao o shite iru.*) 彼はとても若々しい顔をしている.

Z

zeal *n.* neˈtsui 熱意; neˈsshiñ 熱心: work with great zeal (*hijoo ni nesshiñ ni hataraku*) 非常に熱心に働く.

zealous *adj.* neˈsshiñ na 熱心な; neˈkkyoo-teki na 熱狂的な: zealous efforts (*nesshiñ na doryoku*) 熱心な努力.

zero *n.* **1** (number) zeˈro ゼロ; reˈe 零.
2 (on a thermometer) reˈedo 零度; (no score) reˈeteˈñ 零点: The temperature dropped to zero. (*Oñdo ga reedo ni sagatta.*) 温度が零度に下がった.

zigzag *n.* jiˈguzagu ジグザグ.
— *adj.* jiˈguzagu no ジグザグの: a zigzag path (*jiguzagu no michi*) ジグザグの道.
— *vi.* jiˈguzagu ni susumu ジグザグに進む Ⓒ.

zip code *n.* yuˈubiñ-baˈñgoo 郵便番号.

zipper *n.* (fastener) jiˈppaa ジッパー; faˈsunaa ファスナー; chaˈkku チャック: do up one's zipper (*jippaa o shimeru*) ジッパーを締める.

zone *n.* **1** (area) chiˈtai 地帯; chiˈiki 地域; chiˈku 地区: a safety [danger] zone (*añzeñ [kikeñ] chitai*) 安全[危険]地帯 / a residential zone (*juutaku chiku*) 住宅地区.
2 (earth's surface) -tai 帯: the frigid zone (*kañtai*) 寒帯 / the temperate zone (*oñtai*) 温帯 / the torrid zone (*nettai*) 熱帯.
— *vt.* ... o chiˈku ni waˈkeˈru ...を地区に分ける Ⓥ: This area is zoned for industry. (*Kono chiiki wa sañgyoo chiku ni natte iru.*) この地域は産業地区になっている.

zoo *n.* doˈobutsuˈeñ 動物園: I took my children to the zoo. (*Watashi wa kodomo-tachi o doobutsueñ ni tsurete itta.*) 私は子どもたちを動物園に連れて行った.

APPENDIX 1

Guide to Japanese Pronunciation

1. Standard pronunciation of the Japanese language

The variety of Japanese of greatest practical importance for foreign learners is that called **Standard Japanese**. This is understood throughout Japan. The pronunciation of Standard Japanese is based on that of educated people who were born and brought up in Tokyo, or its vicinity.

2. Vowels

2.1 Short and Long Vowels

The vowel system of Japanese (hereafter abbreviated to J) is much simpler than that of English (abbreviated to E). It consists of five short vowels **i**, **e**, **a**, **o**, **u**, and the corresponding long vowels. Long vowels may also be interpreted as double vowels, and in this dictionary they are written **ii**, **ee**, **aa**, **oo**, **uu**. It should be noted that the distinction between short and long vowels is significant in Japanese in that it affects the meanings of words. For example, *i* (stomach) vs. *ii* (good), *tesee* (handmade) vs. *teesee* (correction), *kado* (corner) vs. *kaado* (card), *toru* (take) vs. *tooru* (pass), *kuki* (stem) vs. *kuuki* (air).

In pronouncing a long vowel, foreign learners should nearly double the length of the corresponding short vowel. E speakers are especially advised not to lengthen J short vowels, but to cut them short.

2.2 i and ii (い, イ and いー, イー)

J **i** is phonetically [i] and [i:]. It is close to the French vowel in *qui*, *ici*, etc. E short *i*-vowel in words like *sit*, *miss* is halfway between J **i** and **e**, and, if used, sometimes sounds like **e** to Japanese listeners. It would be better for E-speaking learners to make their *i*-vowel more like long *e*, though they must cut it short. On the other hand, E long *e*-vowel in *be*, *seat*, etc. can safely be used for J **ii**.

2.3 e and ee (え, エ and えー, エー)

J **e** is phonetically halfway between [e] and [ε], and is close to the short *e*-vowel in *get*, *less*, etc. The *a*-vowel in *day*, *late*, etc. can safely be used for J **ee**, though the latter is less diphthongal than the former.

2. 4   a and aa (あ, ア and あー, アー)

Phonetically between [a] and [ɑ], J **a** has rather a wide range. The nearest vowel to this is British (abbreviated to B hereafter) E short *u*-vowel in *cut*, *fun*, etc. J **a** is halfway between American (abbreviated to A) E short *u*-vowel (*hut*, *luck*, etc.) and short *o*-vowel (*not*, *lock*, etc.) The initial part of the long *i*-vowel in *ice*, *fine*, etc. will also do for J **a**.

Learners are warned against using E short *a*-vowel in *back*, *man*, etc., since this sometimes sounds a little like **e** to Japanese listeners. E *a*-vowel in words like *father*, *Chicago* can be used for J **aa**.

2. 5   o and oo (お, オ and おー, オー)

J **o** is phonetically halfway between [o] and [ɔ]. The nearest approach to this vowel is the initial part of A E long *o*-vowel in *go*, *most*, etc., or the B E *au*-vowel in *cause*, *law*, etc., but these should be cut short. B E short *o*-vowel in *hot*, *lock*, etc. is too open for J **o**, and A E short *o*-vowel in *hot*, *lock*, etc. is more like J **a** than J **o**. The nearest vowel to J **oo** is B E *au*-vowel, A E *au*-vowel being too open. It is also like A E long *o*-vowel in *go*, *road*, etc., though less diphthongal. British learners (especially those from southern England) should never use their long *o*-vowel in *go*, *road*, etc., because it sometimes sounds like **au** to Japanese listeners.

2. 6   u and uu (う, ウ and うー, ウー)

J **u** is phonetically [ɯ], that is, it lacks the lip-rounding which accompanies the *u*-vowel of most European languages. Therefore learners are advised not to round the corners of their mouths, but to draw them back when making this vowel. This also holds true in the pronunciation of long **uu**.

2. 7   Devoicing of vowels

J vowels, especially **i** and **u** are often devoiced (i.e. become voiceless) when they do not carry the accent nucleus (see 5.) and occur between voiceless consonants, or occur at the end of a word or an utterance, preceded by a voiceless consonant. The devoicing is represented by a small circle under the phonetic symbols thus [i̥] and [ɯ̥]. For example, *chikara* [tʃi̥kara] (strength), *pittari* [pi̥ttari] (closely), *ashi* [aʃi̥] (reed); *suppai* [sɯ̥ppai] (sour), *futoi* [ɸɯ̥toi] (thick), *karasu* [karasɯ̥], etc. In the final **su** in ...*masu*. or ...*desu*., **u** is very often devoiced or dropped completely, and the preceding **s** is compensatorily lengthened. However, failure to devoice these **i**'s and **u**'s does not impair intelligibility.

3. Consonants

3.1   k (**ka** か, カ, **ki** き, キ, **ku** く, ク, **ke** け, ケ, **ko** こ, コ; **kya** きゃ, キャ, **kyu** きゅ, キュ, **kyo** きょ, キョ)

Phoetically [k].   It is like E *k* in *keep*, *cold*, etc., but the aspiration, or *h*-like sound, after J **k** is weaker than in E.

3.2   g (**ga** が, ガ, **gi** ぎ, ギ, **gu** ぐ, グ, **ge** げ, ゲ, **go** ご, ゴ; **gya** ぎゃ, ギャ, **gyu** ぎゅ, ギュ, **gyo** ぎょ, ギョ)

Phonetically [g].   It is like E *g* in *get*, *good*, etc. In the middle of words like *kago* (basket), *agaru* (rise) and in the particle *ga* (が), **g** is often pronounced [ŋ] (as in E *sing*) in traditional standard J, but [ŋ] is currently being replaced by [g].   Foreign learners can safely use [g] in these positions.

3.3   s (**sa** さ, サ, **su** す, ス, **se** せ, セ, **so** そ, ソ)

Phonetically [s], the sound in E *set*, *soon*, etc.

3.4   sh (**shi** し, シ, **sha** しゃ, シャ, **shu** しゅ, シュ, **sho** しょ, ショ)

Phonetically [ʃ]. It is like E *sh* in *shine*, *short*, etc., but lacks the lip-protrusion which often accompanies E *sh*.

3.5   z (**za** ざ, ザ, **zu** ず, ズ, **ze** ぜ, ゼ, **zo** ぞ, ゾ)

At the beginning of words, J **z** is phonetically [dz], like E *ds* in *cards*, *leads*, etc. In the middle of words it is usually [z], like E *z* in *zone*, *lazy*, etc. However, *z* is always intelligible in all positions.

3.6   j (**ji** じ, ジ; **ja** じゃ, ジャ, **ju** じゅ, ジュ, **jo** じょ, ジョ)

Phonetically [dʒ], the sound in E *judge*, *George*, etc.

3.7   t (**ta** た, タ, **te** て, テ, **to** と, ト)

Phonetically dental [t] with the tip of the tongue against the front upper teeth, rather than against the teethridge as in the E *t* in *time*, *talk*, etc., which, however, can safely be used. The aspiration after J **t** is weaker than in E. American learners are warned against using their *t* before a weak vowel as in words like *city*, *matter*, because it sometimes sounds like **r** to Japanese listeners.

3.8   d (**da** だ, ダ, **de** で, デ, **do** ど, ド)

Phonetically [d] pronounced in the same way as J **t** but with voice.   However, the E *d* as in in *dark*, *date*, etc., can safely be used for J **d**. Again, Americans should avoid using their *d* before a weak vowel as in *ladder*, *pudding*, etc., since it sometimes sounds like **r** to Japanese listeners.

3.9   ch (**chi** ち, チ; **cha** ちゃ, チャ, **chu** ちゅ, チュ, **cho** ちょ, チョ)

Phonetically [tʃ], the sound in E *church*, *nature*, etc.

3.10   ts (tsu つ, ツ)

Phonetically [ʦ], the sound in E *cats*, *roots*, etc. English speakers often find it difficult to say [ʦ] initially as in *tsuzuku* (continue), *tsuru* (crane). You can practice this sound by saying it in words like *cat's-eye* and then omitting the first part of that word (*ca*).

3.11   n (na な, ナ, ni に, ニ, nu ぬ, ヌ, ne ね, ネ, no の, ノ; nya にゃ, ニャ, nyu にゅ, ニュ, nyo にょ, ニョ)

Phonetically dental [n], not alveolar as the E *n* in *night*, *none*, etc., but this causes no practical problems. It is more important that foreign learners should distinguish this sound from ñ treated in 3.20.

3.12   h (ha は, ハ, hi ひ, ヒ, he へ, ヘ, ho ほ, ホ; hya ひゃ, ヒャ, hyu ひゅ, ヒュ, hyo ひょ, ヒョ)

Phonetically [h], the sound in E *house*, *hold*, etc. To be more exact, the **h** before **i** and **y** is phonetically [ç], the sound heard in German *ich*. [ç] is accompanied by more friction in the mouth than E *h*.

3.13   f (fu ふ, フ)

Phonetically [ɸ]. Though spelled with **f**, it is slightly different from the *f* in European languages. While European *f* is formed with the lower lip against the upper teeth, the J **f** is produced with the upper and the lower lips close together. The friction sound of J **f** is weaker than European *f*.

3.14   b (ba ば, バ, bi び, ビ, bu ぶ, ブ, be べ, ベ, bo ぼ, ボ; bya びゃ, ビャ, byu びゅ, ビュ, byo びょ, ビョ)

Phonetically [b]. Like E *b* in *be*, *ball*, etc.

3.15   p (pa ぱ, パ, pi ぴ, ピ, pu ぷ, プ, pe ぺ, ペ, po ぽ, ポ; pya ぴゃ, ピャ, pyu ぴゅ, ピュ, pyo ぴょ, ピョ)

Phonetically [p]. It is like E *p* in *pay*, *post*, etc., but the aspiration after J **p** is weaker than in E.

3.16   m (ma ま, マ, mi み, ミ, mu む, ム, me め, メ, mo も, モ; mya みゃ, ミャ, myu みゅ, ミュ, myo みょ, ミョ)

Phonetically [m], the sound in E *meet*, *most*, etc.

3.17   y (ya や, ヤ, yu ゆ, ユ, yo よ, ヨ)

Phonetically [j], the semivowel corresponding to the vowel **i** [i]. It is like the sound in E *yes*, *you*, etc. **ya, yu, yo** can follow consonants such as **p, b, k, g, h, m, n** and form one syllable. In that case the resulting combinations are called yoo-oñ.

3.18   r (ra ら, ラ, ri り, リ, ru る, ル, re れ, レ, ro ろ, ロ; rya りゃ, リャ, ryu りゅ, リュ, ryo りょ, リョ)

Phonetically, J **r** is often a retroflex stop [ɖ] initially and flap [ɾ] between vowels. Unlike E and other European *r*, it is made with a single tap of the tip of the tongue against the front upper teeth. It sometimes sounds like *d* to a European ear.

3. 19   w (wa わ, ワ**)**

Phonetically [ɥ], the semivowel corresponding to the vowel **u** [ɯ]. Like J **u**, it lacks lip-rounding which usually accompanies European *w*-sound.

3. 20   ñ (ん, ン)

ñ is peculiar to J. Learners should never confuse this sound with **n** treated in 3.11. Though usually spelled with the same letter **n** in the Roman alphabet, **n** and **ñ** are quite different in J. While **n** is a pure consonant and is always followed by a vowel or **y**, **ñ** appears word-finally, before a consonant, a vowel, and **y**, but never at the beginning of a word. **ñ** is called hatsuoñ. It is always long enough to make a syllable by itself (see 4). Besides, **ñ** has the following varieties according to the position in which it appears. The phonetic property common to all the following variants is that they are syllabic nasals. Thus,

(1) in word-final position: Phonetically syllabic [N], a rather difficult sound for foreign learners. It is made further back than E *ng* [ŋ] (between the backmost part of the tongue and uvula). Examples *eñ* (yen), *hoñ* (book).

(2) before **z**, **j**, **t**, **d**, **ch**, **ts**, **n**, and **r**: Phonetically syllabic [n], nearly the same as E *n*, but longer. Examples *bañzai* (hurrah), *heñji* (answer), *kañtoku* (manager), *koñdo* (this time), *deñchi* (cell), *kañtsuu* (penetration), *oñna* (woman), *señro* (rail).

(3) before **f**, **b**, **p**, and **m**: Phonetically syllabic [m], the same as E *m*, but longer. Examples *iñfure* (inflation), *biñboo* (poverty), *kiñpatsu* (blonde), *koñmori* (thickly).

(4) before **k** and **g**: Phonetically syllabic [ŋ], the same as E *ng*, but longer. Examples *keñka* (quarrel), *sañgo* (coral).

(5) before **s** and **sh**: To be phonetically exact, a nasalized vowel [ĩ], but learners may use [N] in this position. Examples *keñsa* (inspection), *deñsha* (electric train). English-speaking people are advised not to use their *n* here, because they often insert a *t*-sound between *n* and the following *s* or *sh*. The result is *nts* or *nch*, which may sometimes be unintelligible to a Japanese listener.

(6) before **h**, **y**, **w**, and a vowel: Phonetically nasalized vowels like [ĩ], [ẽ], [ũ], etc. Learners, however, may use [N] in these positions. Examples *hañhañ* (fifty-fifty), *pañya* (bakery), *deñwa* (telephone), *heñi* (variation), *dañatsu* (oppression). They should

never use *n* in these positions, since the resulting pronunciation would often be unintelligible. Note the following distinctions: *hiñi* (dignity) vs. *hi ni* (by a day), *kiñeñ* (no smoking) vs. *kineñ* (commemoration), *fuñeñ* (smoke of a volcano) vs. *funeñ* (non-flammable).

3. 21 Double consonants (っ, ッ)

In J, double consonants appear in the combination of **kk**, **ss**, **ssh** (**s**+**sh**), **tt**, **tch** (**t**+**ch**), **tts** (**t**+**ts**), and **pp** as in *sekkeñ* (soap), *bessoo* (villa), *issho* (together), *kitto* (certainly), *itchi* (agreement), *mittsu* (three), *suppai* (sour). English-speaking learners are warned against regarding them as single consonants as in *lesson*, *butter*, *catcher*, etc. They should pronounce them twice as the *c*'s in *thick cloud*, *sh*'s in *reddish shoes*, *t*'s in *hot tea*, *tch* in *hit children*, *p*'s in *hope peace*, etc. To Japanese ears, the first part of a double consonant is considered an independent sound and is counted as consituting another syllable (see 4.). For example, while the second **t** in *kitto* (certainly) is the "normal" **t**, the first **t** is regarded as an independent sound referred to as sokuoñ and is written with a smaller *kana* letter っ, ッ (the Roman letter **q** is used by some linguists to represent it, as in *kiqto*), and the word is counted as making three syllables (not two). Likewise, *sekkeñ* (i.e. *seqkeñ*) constitutes four syllables. Note the following distinctions between single and double consonants: *sekeñ* (world) vs. *sekkeñ* (soap), *sasoo to* (in order to stab) vs. *sassoo to* (smartly), *hato* (pigeon) vs. *hatto* (surprisedly), *ichi* (location) vs. *itchi* (agreement), *mitsu* (honey) vs. *mittsu* (three), *supai* (spy) vs. *suppai* (sour).

4. Syllables

J syllables (to be more exact, beats, or technically, morae) are normally composed of a consonant and a vowel in that order, the exceptions being **ñ** ん, ン (see 3.20) and **q** っ, ッ (see 3.21). See the table of the J syllabary on the front endpaper. J syllables tend to be of nearly equal length, though **ñ** and **q** are usually pronounced slightly shorter. Thus, *teashi* (limbs) (three syllables) is said nearly three times longer than *te* (hand) (one syllable).

5. Accent

J does not have an accent system of strong and weak stress like E, and each syllable is said with nearly equal strength. Instead, J has a pitch accent system. The degrees of the pitch of voice depend on the rate of vibration of the vocal cords. When the vibration is fast the pitch is high, and when the rate is slow the pitch is low. The accent patterns of standard J are most clearly explained in terms of two significant levels of pitch: **high** and **low**, and the **accent nucleus**. Words are divided into two classes: words with and without an accent nucleus. In all words which have an accent nucleus, the syllable where the nucleus falls and the preceding syllables (except the first one which is automatically low) are pronounced high, and every syllable that follows the nucleus is said low. In this dictionary accent nucleus is marked with ˺, and the automatic rise on the second syllable is marked with ˹. Thus,

(1) Words with an accent nucleus on the first syllable are: *hi˺* (fire), *ne˺ko* (cat), *i˺nochi* (life), *so˺rosoro* (slowly).

(2) Words with a nucleus on the second syllable are: *i˹nu˺* (dog), *ko˹ko˺ro* (mind), *i˹ke˺bana* (flower arrangement).

(3) Words with a nucleus on the third syllable are: *o˹toko˺* (man), *a˹maga˺sa* (umbrella), *ka˹rai˺bari* (bravado).

(4) Words with a nucleus on the fourth syllable are: *o˹tooto˺* (younger brother), *wa˹tashibu˺ne* (ferry boat), *shi˹dareya˺nagi* (weeping willow).

(5) Words without an accent nucleus are automatically pronounced with the first syllable low and all the succeeding syllables are kept high (though actually with a slight gradual descent). They are: *hi* (day), *u˹shi* (cattle), *ka˹tachi* (shape), *to˹modachi* (friend). Compare the following pair of phrases: *hi˺ ga* (the fire is...) and *hi˹ ga* (the day is...), the former *hi* having a nucleus on it, the latter *hi* without a nucleus.

A word may lose its original accent pattern when it becomes a part of a compound word which then has its own accent pattern as a single word. Thus, *ga˹ikoku* (foreign country) and *yu˹ubiñ* (mail) but *ga˹ikoku-yu˺ubiñ* (foreign mail), *o˹ñgaku* (music) and *ga˹kkoo* (school), but *o˹ñgaku-ga˺kkoo* (music school), and so on. In this dictionary, only those compounds given as main entries are marked with accent.

APPENDIX 2

Numbers

Native Japanese counting system

1	hi⌐to¹tsu	6	mu⌐ttsu¹
2	fu⌐tatsu¹	7	na⌐na¹tsu
3	mi⌐ttsu¹	8	ya⌐ttsu¹
4	yo⌐ttsu¹	9	ko⌐ko¹notsu
5	i⌐tsu¹tsu	10	to⌐o
		?	i¹kutsu

Chinese-derived system

1	i⌐chi¹ (一)	100	hya⌐ku¹ (百)
2	ni¹ (二)	200	ni-⌐hyaku
3	sa⌐ñ (三)	300	sañ¹-byaku
4	shi¹, yo⌐ñ (四)	400	yoñ¹-hyaku
5	go¹ (五)	500	go-⌐hyaku
6	ro⌐ku¹ (六)	600	rop-⌐pyaku
7	na⌐na, shi⌐chi¹ (七)	700	na⌐na¹-hyaku
8	ha⌐chi¹ (八)	800	hap-⌐pyaku
9	ku¹, kyu⌐u (九)	900	kyu⌐u-hyaku
10	ju⌐u (十)	1,000	se¹ñ (千)
11	ju⌐u-ichi¹	2,000	ni-⌐se¹ñ
12	ju⌐u-ni¹	3,000	sa⌐ñ-ze¹ñ
13	ju⌐u-sañ	4,000	yo⌐ñ-se¹ñ
14	ju⌐u-shi¹, ju⌐u-yoñ¹	5,000	go-⌐se¹ñ
15	ju⌐u-go	6,000	ro⌐ku-se¹ñ
16	ju⌐u-roku¹	7,000	na⌐na-se¹ñ
17	ju⌐u-shichi¹, ju⌐u-na¹na	8,000	ha⌐s-se¹ñ
18	ju⌐u-hachi¹	9,000	kyu⌐u-se¹ñ
19	ju⌐u-ku, ju⌐u-kyu¹u	10,000	i⌐chi-ma¹ñ (1万)
20	ni¹-juu	100,000	ju⌐u-ma¹ñ
30	sa⌐ñ-juu	1,000,000	hya⌐ku-ma¹ñ
40	yo⌐ñ-juu	10,000,000	se⌐ñ-ma¹ñ
50	go-⌐ju¹u	100,000,000	i⌐chi¹-oku (1億)
60	ro⌐ku-ju¹u	1,000,000,000	ju⌐u-oku
70	shi⌐chi-ju¹u, na⌐na¹-juu	10,000,000,000	hya⌐ku¹-oku
80	ha⌐chi-ju¹u	100,000,000,000	se¹ñ-oku
90	kyu¹u-juu	1,000,000,000,000	i¹t-choo (1兆)

APPENDIX 3

Days, Weeks and Months

1st	tsuᒥitachi˥	11th	juᒥu-ichi-nichi˥	21st	ni˥juu-ichi-nichi
2nd	fuᒥtsuka	12th	juᒥu-ni-nichi˥	22nd	ni˥juu-ni-nichi
3rd	miᒥkka	13th	juᒥu-saˀñ-nichi	23rd	ni˥juu-sañ-nichi
4th	yoᒥkka	14th	juᒥu-yokka	24th	ni˥juu-yokka
5th	iᒥtsuka	15th	juᒥu-go-nichi	25th	ni˥juu-go-nichi
6th	muᒥika	16th	juᒥu-roku-nichi˥	26th	ni˥juu-roku-nichi
7th	naᒥnu[o]ka	17th	juᒥu-shichi-nichi˥	27th	ni˥juu-shichi-nichi
8th	yoᒥoka	18th	juᒥu-hachi-nichi˥	28th	ni˥juu-hachi-nichi
9th	koᒥkonoka˥	19th	juᒥu-ku-nichi	29th	ni˥juu-ku-nichi
10th	toᒥoka	20th	haᒥtsuka	30th	saˀñjuᒥu-nichi
				31st	saˀñjuᒥu-ichi-nichi

niᒥchiyoᒥo(bi)	日曜(日)	Sunday
geᒥtsuyoᒥo(bi)	月曜(日)	Monday
kaᒥyoᒥo(bi)	火曜(日)	Tuesday
suᒥiyoᒥo(bi)	水曜(日)	Wednes- day
moᒥkuyoᒥo(bi)	木曜(日)	Thursday
kiᒥñyoᒥo(bi)	金曜(日)	Friday
doᒥyoᒥo(bi)	土曜(日)	Saturday

January	iᒥchi-gatsu˥
February	ni-ᒥgatsu˥
March	saᒥñ-gatsu
April	shi-ᒥgatsu˥
May	goᒥ-gatsu
June	roᒥku-gatsu˥
July	shiᒥchi-gatsu˥
August	haᒥchi-gatsu˥
September	kuᒥ-gatsu
October	juᒥu-gatsu˥
November	juᒥu-ichi-gatsu˥
December	juᒥu-ni-gatsu˥

APPENDIX 4

National Holidays

January	1	Gañjitsu	New Year's Day
2nd Mon. in Jan.		Seejiñ-no-hi	Coming-of-Age Day
February	11	Keñkoku-kineñ-no-hi	National Foundation Day
ca. March	21	Shuñbuñ-no-hi	Vernal Equinox Day
April	29	Midori-no-hi	Greenery Day
May	3	Keñpoo-kineñbi	Constitution Day
May	5	Kodomo-no-hi	Children's Day
July	20	Umi-no-hi	Marine Day
September	15	Keeroo-no-hi	Respect-for-the-Aged Day
ca. Sept.	23	Shuubuñ-no-hi	Autumnal Equinox Day
2nd Mon. in Oct.		Taiiku-no-hi	Health-Sports Day
November	3	Buñka-no-hi	Culture Day
November	23	Kiñroo-kañsha-no-hi	Labor Thanksgiving Day
December	23	Teñnoo-tañjoobi	The Emperor's Birthday

APPENDIX 5 Counters

	-fuñ (分) minutes	-hai (杯) cups	-haku (泊) stays	-hatsu (発) shots	-heñ (遍) times	-hiki (匹) fish	-ho (歩) steps	-hoñ (本) bottles	-kai (階) floors	-keñ (軒) houses	-soku (足) shoes	-wa (羽) birds
1	iˈp-puñ	iˈp-pai	iˈp-paku	iˈp-patsuˈ	iˈp-peñ	iˈp-pikiˈ	iˈp-po	iˈp-poñ	iˈk-kai	iˈk-keñ	iˈs-sokuˈ	iˈchiˈ-wa
2	niˈ-fuñ	niˈ-hai	niˈ-haku	niˈ-hatsu	niˈ-heñ	niˈ-hiki	niˈ-ho	niˈ-hoñ	niˈ-kai	niˈ-keñ	niˈ-soku	niˈ-wa
3	saˈñ-puñ	saˈñ-bai	saˈñ-paku	saˈñ-patsu	saˈñ-beˈñ	saˈñ-biki	saˈñ-po	saˈñ-boñ	saˈñ-gai	saˈñ-geñ	saˈñ-zoku	saˈñ-ba
4	yoˈñ-puñ	yoˈñ-hai	yoˈñ-haku	yoˈñ-hatsu	yoˈñ-heñ	yoˈñ-hiki	yoˈñ-ho	yoˈñ-hoñ	yoˈñ-kai	yoˈñ-keñ	yoˈñ-soku	yoˈñ-wa
5	goˈ-fuñ	goˈ-hai	goˈ-haku	goˈ-hatsu	goˈ-heˈñ	goˈ-hiki	goˈ-ho	goˈ-hoñ	goˈ-kai	goˈ-keñ	goˈ-soku	goˈ-wa
6	roˈp-puñ	roˈp-pai	roˈp-paku	roˈp-patsuˈ	roˈp-peˈñ	roˈp-pikiˈ	roˈp-po	roˈp-poñ	roˈk-kai	roˈk-keñ	roˈku-sokuˈ	roˈkuˈ-wa
7	naˈnaˈ-fuñ	naˈnaˈ-hai	naˈnaˈ-haku	naˈnaˈ-hatsu	naˈnaˈ-heñ	naˈnaˈ-hiki	naˈnaˈ-ho	naˈnaˈ-hoñ	naˈnaˈ-kai	naˈnaˈ-keñ	naˈnaˈ-soku	naˈnaˈ-wa
8	haˈp-puñ	haˈp-pai	haˈp-paku	haˈp-patsuˈ	haˈp-peˈñ	haˈp-pikiˈ	haˈp-po	haˈp-poñ	haˈk-kai	haˈk-keñ	haˈs-sokuˈ	haˈchiˈ-wa
9	kyuˈu-fuñ	kyuˈu-hai	kyuˈu-haku	kyuˈu-hatsu	kyuˈu-heñ	kyuˈu-hiki	kyuˈu-ho	kyuˈu-hoñ	kyuˈu-kai	kyuˈu-keñ	kyuˈu-soku	kyuˈu-wa
10	jiˈp-puñ	jiˈp-pai	jiˈp-paku	jiˈp-patsuˈ	jiˈp-peˈñ	jiˈp-pikiˈ	jiˈp-po	jiˈp-poñ	jiˈk-kai	jiˈk-keñ	jiˈs-sokuˈ	jiˈp-pa
	juˈp-puñ	juˈp-pai	juˈp-paku	juˈp-patsuˈ	juˈp-peˈñ	juˈp-pikiˈ	juˈp-po	juˈp-poñ	juˈk-kai	juˈk-keñ	juˈs-sokuˈ	juˈp-pa
How many	naˈñ-puñ	naˈñ-bai	naˈñ-paku	naˈñ-patsu	naˈñ-beñ	naˈñ-biki	naˈñ-po	naˈñ-boñ	naˈñ-gai	naˈñ-geñ	naˈñ-zoku	naˈñ-ba

APPENDIX 6

Conjugations of Verbs

Basic Verb Forms

	Ending	Consonant-stem verbs		Vowel-stem verb	Irregular verb	Irregular verb
Dictionary form	-u	kak·u (write)	yob·u (call)	tabe·ru (eat)	s·uru (do)	k·uru (come)
masu-form	-masu	kaki-masu	yobi-masu	tabe-masu	shi-masu	ki-masu
Negative	-nai	kaka-nai	yoba-nai	tabe-nai	shi-nai	ko-nai
te-form	-t[d]e	kai-te	yoñ-de	tabe-te	shi-te	ki-te
ta-form	-t[d]a	kai-ta	yoñ-da	tabe-ta	shi-ta	ki-ta
tara-form	-t[d]ara	kai-tara	yoñ-dara	tabe-tara	shi-tara	ki-tara
tari-form	-t[d]ari	kai-tari	yoñ-dari	tabe-tari	shi-tari	ki-tari
Desiderative	-tai	kaki-tai	yobi-tai	tabe-tai	shi-tai	ki-tai
Provisional	-ba	kake-ba	yobe-ba	tabere-ba	sure-ba	kure-ba
Tentative	-oo -yoo	kak-oo	yob-oo	tabe-yoo	shi-yoo	ko-yoo
Imperative	-e -ro	kak-e	yob-e	tabe-ro	shi-ro	ko-i
Potential	-eru -rareru	kak-eru	yob-eru	tabe-rareru	(dekiru)	ko-rareru
Passive	-reru -rareru	kaka-reru	yoba-reru	tabe-rareru	sa-reru	ko-rareru
Causative	-seru -saseru	kaka-seru	yoba-seru	tabe-saseru	sa-seru	ko-saseru
Causative-passive	-serareru -saserareru	kaka-serareru	yoba-serareru	tabe-saserareru	saserareru	ko-saserareru